Inside

Windows® 2000

Server

New
Riders

Other Books by New Riders Publishing

Planning for Windows 2000
Eric Cone, Jon Boggs, & Sergio Perez
ISBN: 0-7357-0048-6

Windows NT DNS
Michael Masterson, Herman Knief,
Scott Vinick, & Eric Roul
ISBN: 1-56205-943-2

Windows NT Network Management:
Reducing Total Cost of Ownership
Anil Desai
ISBN: 1-56205-946-7

Windows NT Performance Monitoring,
Benchmarking & Tuning
Mark Edmead & Paul Hinsburg
ISBN: 1-56205-942-4

Windows NT Power Toolkit
Stu Sjouwerman & Ed Tittel
ISBN: 0-7357-0922-x

Windows NT Registry
Sandra Osborne
ISBN: 1-56205-941-6

Windows NT TCP/IP
Karanjit Siyan
ISBN 1-56205-887-8

Windows NT Terminal Server
& Citrix MetaFrame
Ted Harwood
ISBN: 1-56205-944-0

Exchange System Administration
Janice Rice Howd
ISBN: 0-7357-0081-8

Implementing Exchange Server
Doug Hauger, Marywynne Leon
& William C. Wade III
ISBN: 1-56205-931-9

SQL Server Administration
Sean Baird, Chris Miller, et al.
ISBN: 1-56205-955-6

Domino System Administration
Rob Kirkland
ISBN: 1-56205-948-3

Cisco Router Configuration &
Troubleshooting
Mark Tripod
ISBN: 0-7357-0024-9

Network Intrusion Detection:
An Analyst's Handbook
Stephen Northcutt
ISBN: 0-7357-0868-1

Understanding Data Communications,
Sixth Edition
Gilbert Held
ISBN: 0-7357-0036-2

Understanding Directory Services
Doug & Beth Sheresh
ISBN: 0-7357-0910-6

Understanding the Network
Michael Martin
ISBN: 0-7357-0977-7

Inside Windows® 2000 Server

201 West 103rd Street,
Indianapolis, Indiana 46290

William Boswell

Inside Windows® 2000 Server

Trademarks

Warning and Disclaimer

Publisher
David Dwyer

Executive Editor
Al Valvano

Development Editor
Katherine Pendergast

Product Marketing Manager
Stephanie Layton

Managing Editor
Gina Brown

Project Editor
Elise Walter

Copy Editors
Keith Cline
Audrey Doyle

Indexer
Brad Herriman

Technical Reviewers
Desmond Banks
Jim Kelly
David Shackelford

Book Designer
Louisa Klucznik

Cover Designer
Aren Howell

Proofreader
Erich Richter

Compositor
Amy Parker

Contents

About the Author

William Boswell, MCSE, is a Senior Consultant for ASA Solutions, a telecommunications and network services firm based in Scottsdale, Arizona. He has extensive experience in the design and management of NT-based information systems. In addition to his project management responsibilities, Mr. Boswell is also an accomplished instructor with a unique sense of humor and a flair for analogy that that earns him enthusiastic commendations from his students. He can be reached at `boswell@primenet.com`.

About the Technical Reviewers

Desmond Banks is an MCSE and Novell Master CNE who has been working in the computer industry for over 13 years. He has an extensive background in designing Windows NT and Novell Networks for large enterprises.

Jim Kelly is a Systems Engineer at Technology Partners International in Houston, TX. TPI assists clients with the evaluation, negotiation, and management of outsourcing transactions. He received his B.A. in English in 1994 from the University of West Florida in Pensacola, FL, and his B.S. in industrial engineering in 1996 from Florida State University in Tallahassee, FL. He is currently an MCSE and an MCT.

David Shackelford holds a master's degree from California State University at Fullerton. His background includes working as a beekeeper, screening submissions for a popular poetry journal, and teaching NT operating system and networking courses at Hewlett Packard and Intel. He currently works for a firm in southern California as an overseer of network operations.

This book is dedicated to Christine, who never complained about the long hours, the snarl of equipment and cables, the piles of paper and disks everywhere, and the coffee stains in the sink.

–Bill Boswell

Acknowledgments

The book you hold in your hands represents the end result of a project that started back before the initial beta of Windows 2000. I consider myself incredibly fortunate to have worked with a great team during that time. Many thanks to Al Valvano, the Executive Editor, and David Dwyer, the Publisher, who supported this effort over the long months and never doubted that it would produce the right book at the right time.

Thanks to Katie Pendergast, the Development Editor, whose experience, professionalism, and devotion to craftsmanship made all the difference. Katie, you're a star.

Thanks to Elise Walter, the Project Editor, for her cheerfulness when finding goofs. Thanks, too, to Keith Cline, the Copy Editor, and Brad Herriman, the Indexer, who pored over every single solitary word. I appreciate their patience.

I want to give a special thanks to my technical reviewers, David Shackelford, Jim Kelly, and Desmond Banks. Their diligent pursuit of quality and their first-rate systems knowledge set a high standard. I hope the book measures up. These poor guys also suffered through some really appalling puns. Be grateful they made me take most of them out.

A big, big thank you to the good people at ASA Solutions who gave me the time and equipment I needed to do this project. Without their help, the book never would have been finished successfully.

Finally, thanks to everyone on the Microsoft beta team who went out of their way to help me with questions. I consider it an honor and a privilege to have worked with professionals of such high caliber.

Your Feedback Is Valuable

As the reader of this book, you are our most important critic and commentator. We value your opinion and want to know what we're doing right, what we could do better, what areas you'd like to see us publish in, and any other words of wisdom you're willing to pass our way.

As the Executive Editor for the Networking team at New Riders Publishing, I welcome your comments. You can fax, email, or write me directly to let me know what you did or didn't like about this book—as well as what we can do to make our books stronger.

Please note that I cannot help you with technical problems related to the topic of this book, and that due to the high volume of mail I receive, I might not be able to reply to every message.

When you write, please be sure to include this book's title and author, as well as your name and phone or fax number. I will carefully review your comments and share them with the author and editors who worked on the book.

Fax: 317-581-4663
Email: newriders@mcp.com
Mail: Al Valvano
            Executive Editor
            New Riders Publishing
            201 West 103rd Street
            Indianapolis, IN 46290 USA

Introduction

After one the longest and most extensive beta trials in the history of the software industry, Windows 2000 (née Windows NT) has finally arrived. There are lots of goodies in those legendary 30 million lines of code: a new Directory Service, a standards-based security system, a network operating system that fully embraces TCP/IP and DNS, Plug-and-Play hardware support, a new disk storage system, an improved file system, policy-based user and security management, a fully integrated remote access and router subsystem, an improved backup system, terminal services in the shrink-wrap, and many improved troubleshooting and diagnostic tools. The list goes on and on.

In spite of the size and scope of the beta testing, many of those new features have yet to face comprehensive trials in production systems where uncomprehending users, malevolent hackers, and frustrated executives conspire against an operating system and its administrators in a thousand unforeseen ways. Nagging little difficulties could become enormous bottlenecks or security holes or compatibility failures. This book is designed to help you get the most out of the new features while coping with the problems.

What Is *Inside?*

This book contains practical strategies and procedures for installing, configuring, deploying, and managing Windows 2000 servers and desktops. In every subject area, it gives comprehensive answers to the four questions most often asked by systems administrators:

- **How does it work?** Each chapter contains a detailed functional description of the services it covers. This overview explains how the services and features interact with hardware, other services, other systems, and the user.

- **How do I run it?** Each chapter contains specific instructions for putting a service into production including steps to verify that the service is working properly. There are over 300 "Procedures" detailing specific operations, accompanied by over 500 illustrations and screen shots.

- **How does it break?** Something always goes wrong. Each chapter includes common errors along with diagnostic hints, troubleshooting techniques and workarounds.
- **How do I fix it?** In addition to including typical failure modes, each chapter contains steps and references to correct the failures or put the system in a stable condition while you continue troubleshooting. The final chapter contains strategies for recovering from full system failures.

The chapters are laid out roughly in a deployment sequence, starting with installing the operating system, deploying DNS, and upgrading to Active Directory-based domains, then continuing through setting up storage, configuring file systems, implementing security, publishing shared resources, managing user environments, and configuring dial-up and routing services. Each chapter stands on its own so that you can use them in any sequence.

This book does not cover services that are fundamentally unchanged from NT4. This includes Services for NetWare, Services for Macintosh, DHCP (except for dynamic DNS support), using and managing the Registry, and navigating the Explorer shell. IIS and Internet Explorer are covered in another New Riders book, *Internet Information Services Administration*, by Kelli Adam.

Who Is This Book For?

Inside Windows 2000 Server is primarily addressed to systems administrators. You might be wondering if it applies to you. Here are a few characteristics shared by systems administrators regardless of their actual job titles.

- If your job involves keeping end users happy and productive in an infuriatingly complex computing environment, you're a systems administrator.
- If you carry a beeper that interrupts your personal life whenever a server hiccups or a backup tape jams or a dial-up connection stops responding, you're a systems administrator.
- If you get an angry lecture from an executive wearing a $2000 Armani suit when he can't figure out how to open his email, you're a systems administrator.

- If you're a department computer guru who gets panicky calls whenever something goes wrong and "those guys in IS aren't getting it fixed fast enough," you're a systems administrator.

- If you own a business and you're working on a Sunday afternoon to fix your computers because you can't afford to pay $100+ an hour to a consultant, you're a systems administrator.

- If you're a technology professional who uses Windows 2000 as a platform for just about any kind of development, you probably also act as a systems administrator whether you like it or not.

Essentially, what sets systems administrators apart is an attitude. We are problem solvers. We have to be. We are tasked with building an information system using parts that never seem to fit quite right. We don't welcome complexity, but we darned well want to be prepared to handle complexity when it's unavoidable.

At What Level Is This Book Written?

If there were a thermometer on the cover, it would hover somewhere between *intermediate* and *advanced*. You do not have to be an experienced NT systems administrator, but you should have experience managing Windows along with some form of network operating system, such as NetWare, VMX, UNIX, Banyan, or the like.

For administrators with no NT experience, each chapter contains a summary of classic NT features and limitations and puts them in context for comparison with Windows 2000. These summaries are compartmentalized so that more seasoned NT administrators can skip them.

If you are just getting started with computers and networking, you might get frustrated with the number of technical terms that go unexplained in this book. If terms like *transport protocol* and *virtual memory* and *ISO model* and *admin privileges* don't conjure up fairly clear images and processes in your mind, you might want to do some additional background reading. The LAN Times *Encyclopedia of Networking* is an excellent resource.

Conventions Used

There are several typographical conventions that are used in *Inside Windows 2000 Server*.

Element	Style	Example
Code, window titles, key names, radio buttons, screen dumps, and Web sites	Monotype font	`LocalNTP - 0`
Menu names	Small capital letters	START | PROGRAMS | ADMINISTRATIVE TOOLS
Screen errors	Italics	There are no more endpoints available from the *RPC Endpoint Mapper*.

The non-typographical conventions that are used in Inside Windows 2000 Server include Figures, Sidebars, Tables, Registry Tips, and Procedures. Registry Tips and Procedures are unique to this book.

Registry Tips, like the following, are designed to help you make the most of your Registry settings.

Registry Tip: Enabling a Modem for RAS or Routing

Enabling a modem for RAS or Routing is controlled by values in HKLM | `System` | `CurrentControlSet` | `{Modem CLSID}` | `0000` | `Clients` | `Ras`. You will also find these values for each WAN interface under the CLSID for Network Adapters.

Procedures are the numbered, titled lists that are common throughout *Inside Windows 2000 Server.* These are designed to help you perform step-by-step technical operations without wordy explanations of basic functions. The appendix in the back of this book lists all the Procedures and where they are located for easy reference. Here is a snippet of one from Chapter 17, "Managing Remote Access and Internet Routing":

Procedure 17.1   **Manually Initiating a PnP Bus Scan**

1. Connect the serial cable between the modem and a COM port on the computer and energize the modem.

2. Open the `Computer Management` console by right-clicking the `My Computer` icon on the desktop and selecting MANAGE from the fly-out menu.

1

Installing and Configuring Windows 2000

INSTALLING WINDOWS 2000 IS A LITTLE LIKE FILING an income tax return. The most difficult part isn't so much knowing what to do, but knowing what you can safely avoid doing.

The Windows 2000 installation has been streamlined considerably compared with NT4, partly thanks to *Plug and Play* (PnP) and partly because Microsoft has listened to the thousands and thousands of administrators and their CIOs who have demanded easier deployment methods. The simplicity of the installation is deceptive, however. You make decisions at each stage that can affect performance and reliability for the life of the machine. Even if you're a seasoned NT administrator, it's worth walking through an entire Windows 2000 installation step-by-step before beginning production rollouts.

The installation picture is complicated somewhat by the new family of Windows 2000 products. You now have four flavors of high-end Windows to choose from:

- **Windows 2000 Professional.** Intended for business desktops. Supports up to two processors and 4GB of RAM. Intended for individual users, but permits up to 10 network connections for basic file, print, and FTP sharing with unlimited anonymous browsing for Web sharing.

- **Windows 2000 Server.** Intended for file-and-print services and general-purpose applications. Supports four-way *symmetrical multiprocessor* (SMP) and 4GB of RAM.

- **Windows 2000 Advanced Server.** Intended as a specialty application server. Supports eight-way SMP and 64GB of RAM. Has options for clustering, network load balancing, application load balancing, and high-performance database sorting.

- **Windows 2000 Datacenter Server.** Intended for high-end, memory- and CPU-intensive applications, such as data warehouses, graphic and econometric modeling, and *online analytical processing* (OLAP). Supports 16-way SMP out of the box and 32-way SMP and *Non-Uniform Memory Architecture* (NUMA) through OEM channels. Supports 64GB of RAM, 64-bit data channels, and has advanced clustering features. Datacenter Server will ship mid-2000.

The installation steps for Windows 2000 Server and Advanced Server are the same. The differences in memory handling, clustering, and transaction support are implemented after installation. It is too early in the Datacenter Server beta cycle to present installation or configuration details.

This chapter covers the following topics:

- Hardware recommendations for Windows 2000 Server, Advanced Server, and Professional
- Installation checklist
- Installation overview covering operations that occur during setup and critical decision points
- Detailed installation steps
- Analysis of boot sequence to use for troubleshooting
- Tips for correcting common setup problems

Chapter 2, "Performing Upgrades and Automated Installations," finishes up by covering upgrades, automated deployments, a detailed analysis of the Windows 2000 boot sequence, and installation of Terminal Services for remote administration.

Chapter 3, "Adding Additional Hardware," contains information about installing additional hardware after setup is complete and how to isolate and correct PnP problems. Chapter 9, "Deploying Windows 2000 Domains," covers upgrading NT4 domain controllers and deploying Windows 2000 domains.

Before installing or upgrading production servers, you should familiarize yourself with the IP-based services in Windows 2000, especially name resolution and DNS, covered in Chapter 4, "Understanding NetBIOS Name

Resolution," and Chapter 5, "Managing Domain Name System (DNS) Services and Dynamic Host Configuration (DHCP) Services," and Kerberos authentication, covered in Chapter 6, "Understanding Network Access Security and Kerberos." If this is your first operational taste of deploying TCP/IP services, you might want to read *Windows NT TCP/IP* from New Riders Publishing. It was written by the Socrates of TCP/IP himself, Dr. Karanjit S. Siyan.

Hardware Recommendations

Nothing is more likely to incite an argument among a group of system administrators than making unequivocal statements about hardware superiority. Fortunately, Windows 2000 is remarkably adaptable. The same Windows 2000 Server code can run on a Pentium 166 clone and an SMP multimegahertz powerhouse.

The number of supported systems drops somewhat if you install Windows 2000 Advanced Server. The list gets even shorter if you plan on installing Datacenter Server (when it is released), because of its requirement to have 64-bit addressing throughout the main data paths. The fact remains, however, that you face a wide variety of hardware when you decide to do a Windows 2000 deployment. Even if there were not one single bug in the product—and no one is foolish enough to believe that—the number of potential problems that could arise when trying to install Windows 2000 on all the machines that could possibly run it, with all the possible combinations of devices and applications that might be present in those machines, is staggering.

There is an old story that the inventor of chess was offered any gift he desired by a delighted Chinese emperor who had just learned the game. The inventor asked for a simple gift, to have a single grain of rice placed on the first square of a chessboard, then two grains on the second, four on the third, and so on. Using this progression, the emperor would need to put 18,446,744,073,709,551,616 grains of rice on the 64th square to fulfill the request, not to mention filling all the other squares first. As the story goes, the emperor decided it was simpler and cheaper just to execute the inventor. You may make a similar decision concerning your hardware vendor, depending on your Windows 2000 installation experiences.

No book could begin to cover all the myriad combinations of hardware and software problems that might come up when deploying Windows 2000. This chapter contains advice on making basic configuration decisions that can cut down on the number of potential problems, or at last reduce the number to something less than 18,446,744,073,709,551, 616.

General Hardware Decisions

The newest, hottest machines might sell lots of magazines, but as a general rule, it's fair to say that system administrators value reliability, interoperability, and high-quality technical support over performance and slick features.

No matter what hardware you choose, make certain that the computer and all peripherals are on Microsoft's *Hardware Compatibility List* (HCL). Microsoft takes the following position on the use of supported hardware, as quoted from "Windows NT Hardware Compatibility," John Jacobs, Microsoft BackOffice Technical Notes, September 1999 TechNet:

> Many unsupported systems and devices work correctly with Windows NT. However, the Windows NT support staff at Microsoft will not offer a full range of support services for problems that are specific to unsupported hardware or drivers.

A component or system is considered "supported" under the following conditions:

- It is specifically listed, by make and model, on the HCL.
- A Microsoft-designated driver is used to control the hardware.
- The hardware is used in the configuration under which it was tested.

Microsoft KnowledgeBase article Q142865 describes the technical support options available if you do not use equipment listed on the HCL. Essentially, these support options consist of a Microsoft support representative putting forth a good-faith effort to resolve a problem with the understanding that a satisfactory conclusion is not guaranteed. Ultimately, the support representative decides how far the troubleshooting will proceed before referring you to the hardware vendor. In my experience, the technicians lean way over the line to help resolve problems involving unsupported hardware. You are not likely to be denied help with a DNS query failure because you are using an unsupported network card. On the other hand, you are not likely to get the full range of support for an ongoing database corruption problem if you use an unsupported RAID adapter.

The HCL is maintained on Microsoft's Web site at www.microsoft.com\hcl. The site divides components into product types and lists their compatibility with all current Windows products. Microsoft also has a logo program for compatible hardware that is operated by their *Windows Hardware Quality Lab* (WHQL). Details of the logo program are available at the HCL Web page or at www.microsoft.com\hwtest. If you really want to get into the nuts and bolts of the development and testing requirements, take a look at www.microsoft. com\hwdev. For the last word on driver development, go to the Open System Resources Web site at www.osr.com. This is where you find the engineers who teach the engineers.

From the perspective of a systems administrator, the most compelling reason to buy logo-branded hardware is the unstinting commitment to support that accompanies it. To get that logo on the box, a hardware vendor must successfully run a suite of acceptance tests designed by Microsoft. The vendor then delivers the test results to the WHQL for validation along with sample hardware and drivers with source code. If you have a support issue that gets escalated to a certain level, Microsoft support engineers will attempt to replicate your problem using the sample hardware from the vendor. You should also stay current with firmware updates, because your problem will not be escalated until you get to the most current firmware revision.

Don't Rely Exclusively on the HCL

Use care when mixing and matching components. Even if every component in a system is on the HCL, the mixture might expose timing or other compatibility problems. Vendors typically submit entire systems for compatibility testing, and you will get best results by using these systems.

That being said, millions of copies of NT4 and soon-to-be millions of copies of Windows 2000 are running just fine on hardware that is not on the HCL. The key is getting the vendor's support. If you are upgrading an existing system or buying a new one, make sure your vendor supports that system running Windows 2000. This is especially true for laptops and older machines that might be unstable or lack their full range of power-management features under Windows 2000.

First-tier vendors often take a long time getting up to speed on a major OS upgrade. The Dells and Compaqs and IBMs of the world spend a lot of money advertising their support for Windows 2000, but only when running it on their new equipment. They may completely refuse to talk to you if you are trying to install Windows 2000 on older gear. Second-tier vendors often react more quickly because of competitive pressures, but the quality of the support might not be as good. Watch out for vendors who cobble together machines and peddle them as blazing Windows 2000 systems.

No matter where you buy a system, check the vendor's Web site to make sure that you have the most current Windows 2000 drivers for every component. Look for configuration tips in Microsoft's KnowledgeBase and the Microsoft public newsgroups. A quick search of all newsgroups, via

Dejanews, www.dejanews.com, is always a good idea. Buggy drivers are common and word of them gets out fast. Why go through the same grief as hundreds of other administrators? Better to find new and unique sources of grief.

Processor Speed and SMP

The hardware evolution for Windows 2000/NT reads like an Agatha Christie novel. And then there was...one. Previous versions of NT ran on various RISC platforms, such as MIPS and R4000 and Power PC as well as DEC/Compaq Alpha. The field has dwindled to just the Intel x86 platform, Pentium or better. Compaq announced cancellation of support for Windows 2000 on the Alpha chip in August 1999. It remains to be seen whether future versions of Windows 2000 will retain the odd assortment of loaders and ARC paths that NT used for RISC support.

Processor Model

Just because there is now only one choice of microprocessor architecture for Windows 2000, that doesn't mean there is any shortage of choices for processor models. The minimum processor requirement (and I mean absolute minimum) to run Windows 2000, either Professional or Server, is a P5 processor, Pentium 166 or AMD K5, with a 128KB L2 cache. This includes the current crop of Celeron processors, but don't even think about using an older Celeron with no L2 cache. In theory, the Cyrix 6X86 chip should be able to run Windows 2000, but it has a spotty history and is now in transition to its new owners, Via Technologies. Via may improve the Cyrix track record; but for now, approach any Cyrix system with care if you plan on running Windows 2000 without undue problems.

Processor Speed

In practical terms, if you are satisfied with the performance of a machine running NT4, you'll be satisfied with performance under Windows 2000. Increasing memory is much more crucial than getting more raw processor power when upgrading.

Processors tuned to run a 32-bit instruction set are preferable. This includes Pentium Pro, Pentium II and III, AMD K6, and AMD Athlon. Pentium III gives little performance improvement over PII for servers beyond the extra processor speed. Xeon is especially attractive for servers because the L2 cache runs at bus speeds.

SMP Support

Windows 2000 Professional supports 2x SMP processors and Windows 2000 Server supports 4x SMP. Windows 2000 Advanced Server supports 8x SMP and Datacenter Server supports 16x SMP out of the box and up to 32x SMP and NUMA in OEM configurations. If you are upgrading an SMP machine currently running NT4, be aware that many vendors supply an OEM version of the *Hardware Abstraction Layer* (HAL) driver, HAL.DLL, tailored for their machine. This is especially true if you have an SMP machine with more than four CPUs and is certainly true for NUMA machines. Don't upgrade without first checking with the vendor to get their reengineered HAL, if one is required.

L2 Cache

If you are upgrading your hardware in preparation for running Windows 2000, keep a close eye on the processor's L2 cache specifications. The newer processors have made significant improvements in onboard cache (L1) and bus-attached cache (L2) architecture. The Windows 2000 Memory Manager uses L2 cache extensively, so it is a significant contributor to overall system performance.

A common mistake made by some administrators is to put more main memory in a machine than the Windows 2000 Virtual Memory Manager can comfortably handle given the processor's L2 cache size. Adding too much memory can cause performance to drop or make the system unstable. Older Pentium 333 and slower servers often refuse to work when loaded with more than 512MB of RAM.

A rough rule of thumb is to have 256KB of L2 cache for every 256MB of RAM. This means a server with 2GB of RAM needs a processor with 2MB of L2 cache. Only Xeon has an L2 cache that big, and you'll pay a premium to get it.

Advanced Configurations

If you are buying a server that you plan on clustering with Windows 2000 Advanced Server, or if you plan on loading Datacenter Server with or without clustering, be sure to check the HCL very carefully. Only a limited number of platforms meet all the requirements. This is especially true for Datacenter Server. Here are the minimum requirements that Microsoft has proposed to run Datacenter Server (for more details, see `msdn.microsoft.com/library/backgrnd/html/awewindata.htm`):

- All host bus adapters and drivers must be Dual Address Cycle or 64-bit capable.

- All network and *Storage Attached Network* (SAN) adapters drivers must be Dual Address Cycle or 64-bit capable.
- Every device and its 64-bit driver must be tested in 8GB Intel Architecture systems configured for *Physical Address Extensions* (PAEs).
- 32-bit PCI adapters are supported on Datacenter Server only if they are not on the primary data path. This means you could use a 32-bit PCI network adapter for your tape backup network, but not for the main network path for an OLAP application.

Chipsets, Motherboards, and BIOS

The trade magazines often have bubble charts that show price/performance ratios between many different machines of comparable processor speed. The chipset plays a considerable role in determining a system's place on that bubble chart. Intel is the leading chipset manufacturer, with SiS and Via being the only real competition.

The ultimate source for motherboard and chipset comparisons is Tom's Hardware, www.tomshardware.com. You can be sure of getting impartial data from Tom and his colleagues without wondering, as I often do, whether a four-page ad for a particular brand of server in a trade magazine had any bearing on its being chosen as a top-rated box. After you decide on a motherboard vendor, stick with their products for a while. You'll get to know their idiosyncrasies and be better able to diagnose any problems that come up.

Memory and Memory Architecture

The absolute minimum memory requirement for Windows 2000 Server is 64MB. Setup will refuse to upgrade or install on a machine with anything less. From my experience, Windows 2000 file and print servers should have a bare minimum of 96MB. Application servers should have at least 128MB, and be prepared to double or quadruple that number for a big Oracle or SQL database or an ERP solutions, such as SAP or PeopleSoft. If you are building a dedicated domain controller, start with 128MB for an average domain with 100–500 users and 512MB–1GB for a Global Catalog server in a big enterprise with 100,000 users in a forest.

Windows 2000 Professional does not enforce a memory floor, but you won't be happy with anything less than 32MB. The sweet spot for running a standard mix of business automation applications without constantly hitting the paging file is about 64MB depending on the applications. Power users and graphics folks will want at least 128MB, and make sure it's fast.

Windows 2000 Professional and Server use the same basic memory management as classic NT. They have a 32-bit addressing scheme that supports 4GB of flat memory. Standard Windows 2000 memory management divvies this virtual address space into two 2GB portions, one for the OS and one for applications. The maximum physical memory supported by Professional and Server is 4GB.

Windows 2000 Advanced Server has the same *4GB Tuning option* (4GT) introduced in NT4 Advanced Server. This option gives 3GB of virtual memory to applications and reserves 1GB for the OS. This gives a little extra boost to applications that need extra memory.

Pentium II and higher processors, paired with the right chipsets, have a feature called Physical Address Extension (PAE). This feature extends the addressing to 36 bit from 32 bit, making it possible to directly address 64GB of main memory.

NT4 Advanced Server made use of PAE by relying on Intel's *Page Size Extension* (PSE36) driver, which essentially used PAE to configure physical memory above 4GB as a big RAM disk that the operating system could use as a fast paging file. Think of PSE36 as EMM386 on steroids.

Windows 2000 leaves PSE36 behind. Instead, it uses a new API, called *Address Windowing Extension* (AWE), that can access the extended memory directly. You can download a white paper that describes the AWE API from `www.microsoft.com/hwdev/ntdrivers/awe.htm`. Using the AWE API, applications can directly access the additional memory pages made available by PAE. This permits applications to use up to 64GB of memory, providing you can stuff that into your server. The capability to support AWE is highly hardware dependent, so watch the HCL closely and arrange for specific application testing before committing to a purchase.

Video and Executive Architecture

It's worth taking a couple of minutes to look at a few aspects of Windows 2000 architecture to see why video plays such an important role in system operation and stability.

Windows 2000 makes use of the ring protection scheme in the Intel family of processors that is designed to protect system memory and resources. The innermost ring, Ring 0, is the most privileged. Only code running in Ring 0 can directly access system resources, such as memory, hard drive interfaces, network interfaces, and video. Code running in the outer ring, Ring 3, is the least privileged. Code running in Ring 3 cannot directly access system memory or system resources. Rings 1 and 2 have special functions which are not implemented in Windows.

All operating system functions are collected into a set of modules under an umbrella called the *Windows 2000 Executive*. The Executive includes the Hardware Abstraction Layer (HAL.DLL), the microkernel driver (NTOSKRNL.EXE or NTKRNLMP.EXE), and several so-called managers, such as the Virtual Memory Manager, the I/O Manager, the Security Reference Manager, and so forth.

All these Executive processes run in Ring 0. User processes running in Ring 3 are hosted by the 32-bit Windows subsystem, Win32. All applications run in the context of Win32 regardless of whether they use native 32-bit code. This includes Win16 apps, DOS apps, OS/2 version 1.1 apps, and POSIX apps.

User applications running in Ring 3 can get access to system services running in Ring 0, but only indirectly. They do so through Win32, which lives in both worlds. The client-side services of Win32 run in user space in the form of a set of DLLs, such as the USER32.DLL, GDI32.DLL, CONSOLE.DLL, and so forth. The server-side part of Win32 comes in the form of a system driver, WIN32K.SYS, which incorporates a set of graphics drivers and a Windows manager.

The bridge between user space and executive space inside Win32 is the *Client/Server Runtime Subsystem* (CSRSS). If you've ever seen a Mozart opera, you have a pretty good idea of how CSRSS works. Opera plays games with social privileges in the same way that CSRSS plays games with system privileges.

Under normal circumstances, application code can sing in the Ring 3 chorus, while Kernel-mode code takes center stage in Ring 0. But every character acts on behalf of another character that, in turn, has sworn allegiance to still another character. Client applications running under Win32 get the machine to do their bidding by sending messages to server processes running in Ring 0. The server processes take advantage of their privileged place in the Executive to manipulate hardware, and then report the results back to the user process.

All this activity to and fro across the imaginary line between user space and kernel space involves lots of overhead. Starting with NT4 and continuing on into Windows 2000, Microsoft incorporated graphics handling into the Executive to avoid the messaging inside CSRSS and to improve performance.

For a period during the transition to Executive-based graphics handling, many instabilities could be traced to video. During the past two years, as vendors have gotten better and better at writing NT video drivers and Microsoft has become more diligent about quality assurance, the number of failures directly attributable to video problems has dwindled to an odd trickle. The *Windows Driver Model* (WDM) drivers used by Windows 2000 do an even better job of protecting the operating system by keeping the drivers coded by vendors away from the core graphics functions, which are coded by Microsoft.

Still, you should make your video choices with care when putting together specifications for Windows 2000 machines. Servers do not need high-end video cards that might introduce instabilities. A cheap VGA adapter is sufficient, if you can still find one nowadays. And don't slap the latest video accelerator into a desktop running Windows 2000 Professional until you've verified that the hardware is on the HCL and that other administrators have not had problems with it in production.

Storage

The drives and drive controllers you use can make as much or more difference in performance and reliability as processor and memory. If a budget battle forces you to pare down your wish list for a server, lean toward improving I/O before upping processor speed.

Interfaces

The Windows 2000 CD comes with a large number of SCSI interface drivers along with standard interface drivers for IDE. SCSI has long been the choice for high-speed storage on servers, with IDE and EIDE being the low-cost alternative for desktops. That story is changing a little, and Windows 2000 is trying to keep up.

If you have money and don't mind doing a little lab work to check stability and compatibility, look at the new Fibre Channel controllers and drives and SAN devices. Not only do you get 100MBps (that's mega*bytes* per second) of full-duplex data transfer out of Fibre Channel—which blows ultraSCSI and SSA into a crumpled garbage pail—but a high-end Fibre Channel controller also supports dynamic LUN changes, enabling you to add gigabytes onto a volume just by slipping in a disk and making a couple of configuration changes.

The Fibre Channel story has its downside. Interoperability is virtually impossible to obtain, so after you get married to a vendor, expect that marriage to last for a while. And device interconnections can achieve levels of complexity that were once only the province of Token Ring.

On the desktop and for small department servers, you may want to take a look at the newest crop of ATA66 controllers and drives. The performance gains using the higher sustained bus speeds and very high burst rates in the ATA66 spec can give you significant performance gains. You might have difficulty finding the controllers and drives on the HCL because of the rapidly developing technology. Beta ATA66 drivers for Windows 2000 are available from most major vendors. It's worth keeping your eye on this technology and experimenting with it as it matures.

RAID

Windows 2000 introduces a new Logical Disk Manager from Veritas that improves the reliability and speed of software-based RAID. Under most circumstances, however, you're better off with hardware RAID. A good RAID controller gives you hot-swap capabilities, hot spares, and dynamic expansion, none of which is provided by Windows 2000 software RAID. Also, hardware RAID controllers do a much better job of detecting cascading sector failures. Bottom line: Use hardware RAID if you can afford it; software RAID if money is tight.

If you opt for software RAID, you'll get better performance with SCSI compared to IDE, and better performance still by using multiple channels instead of putting all devices on the same SCSI bus.

Windows 2000 Professional does not support RAID 5 or mirroring. For high-end graphics and scientific uses, however, you can get a performance advantage by striping at RAID 0. This is not a fault-tolerant option, so the files should be uploaded to a server or backed up locally.

CD-ROM, CD-R, CD-RW, and DVD

Windows 2000 has drivers for the most popular CD-based drives, but CD-RW is a rapidly changing technology and the vendors focus their attention on Windows 9x and NT4 because that is where the current revenues come from. Adaptec has a patch for their ASPI driver so that you can use EZ CD Creator, and the new version is fully Windows 2000 compatible (see www.adaptec.com). The CD writer from Golden Hawk Technology, www.goldenhawk.com, is also very good and was compatible with Windows 2000 throughout the beta cycle.

DVD support comes in the form of a new file system driver, UDFS.SYS, along with the usual WDM drivers for communicating with the hardware. You might encounter erratic video when viewing movies if the driver is still being tuned. Check the vendor's Web site for the latest driver.

If a machine supports the El Torito bootable CD-ROM specification, you can boot directly from the Windows 2000 CD to run Setup or do an emergency repair. This may seem like a small convenience, but it sure speeds up diagnostic work in the event of a problem. Most current systems support bootable CDs, but sometimes you may find that an administrator has disabled it because it can be a little irritating to have the system boot to a CD if you forget to take it out of the caddy. Check the CMOS settings to see whether `CD-ROM Booting` is an option and enable it.

Installation Checklist

The vast majority of Windows 2000 installations and upgrades proceed without a hitch. Before you start, however, you should be aware of some common sources of problems. A few precautions taken early can forestall nasty problems later on.

Backup

It goes without saying that you should get a reliable backup of any server prior to performing an upgrade. Any number of scenarios can lead to data loss. If you back up religiously but have not attempted a full restore lately, do so before you upgrade. At the very least, you should recover a file or folder from the latest tape, just as a test. You don't want to discover, too late, that the backup tapes you've been using for a while have become so old that you can see daylight through the Mylar.

While on the subject of backups, the Registry changes in Windows 2000 are fairly extensive. You cannot recover from a Registry problem after upgrading just by overwriting a hive file. Your current Registry can be corrupted with no overt symptoms, and that can cause problems during and after the upgrade. You may want to run a Registry cleanup tool to clear out all the unused entries and compact the hives prior to upgrading.

Component Configurations

One of the most significant changes in Windows 2000 is the use of Plug and Play. It's very nearly a certainty that you'll encounter a situation where PnP is not your friend. In addition, certain configurations are known to cause problems regardless of PnP. Here are a few preparations you might want to make before installing or upgrading to Windows 2000:

- **Firmware.** Make absolutely, positively, completely certain that you are running with the most current firmware versions for your BIOS and all peripherals. This is especially true for laptops.

- **ACPI.** If you have an ACPI motherboard that is more than a year or so old, you might need to disable ACPI or turn off PnP support to get Windows 2000 to install. This should be your first troubleshooting step if Setup hangs.

- **Enable Plug and Play.** If you routinely disable PnP features to get NT4 to run correctly, you should enable them again just prior to upgrading. Windows 2000 Setup does an extensive hardware scan during installation and it might make an appropriate resource allocation if you do not have all PnP components enabled.

- **Disable shadowing.** Turn off ROM Shadowing and Video Shadowing. Windows 2000 does not use them, doesn't like them, and may slap you for using them.

- **Disable disk caching.** Only enable hardware disk caching if you have a system specifically designed to support caching under Windows 2000. Many incidents involving massive data corruption on classic NT have been traced to hardware disk caching. Windows 2000 uses essentially the same subsystem, so you face the same potential for damage. Windows 2000 file caching is extremely efficient. You should not see much performance degradation.

- **Preconfigure legacy adapters.** If you have legacy (non-PnP) devices in your system, reserve their IRQs in CMOS before upgrading or installing Windows 2000. This avoids conflicts when the PnP enumerator assigns resources. Symptoms of incorrect resource assignments are an *Inaccessible Boot Device* stop error (caused by IRQ conflict with the host bus adapter) or failure of the legacy device to function.

- **Prepare for multimedia devices.** Configuring multimedia devices can be infuriatingly time-consuming. Make sure all multimedia hardware in the system has Windows 2000 drivers, and verify that the makes and models match the HCL listing precisely. Double-check the vendor's Web site to get the most current drivers. And after all that, you can still count on losing at least one afternoon sweating over a seemingly trivial glitch.

- **Prepare for dual monitors.** Windows 2000 supports using dual monitors, similar to Windows 98. PnP can detect both video cards, but if something goes wrong with the initialization routines, you may find yourself unable to see what's going on. A typical problem occurs when you have two models of the same card, one for AGP and one for PCI. The drivers may have the same name, but differ slightly and cannot be loaded simultaneously.

- **Use bus-mastering NICs.** Use only top-quality, bus-mastering PCI NICs for Windows 2000 servers and, if at all possible, on the desktop. These cards cost only slightly more than their Programmed I/O (PIO) counterparts and perform much, much better. Heavy network users will benefit more from a bus-mastering NIC than from a faster processor, all other things being equal.

Configuring Storage

Perform the following checks to make sure the system is ready to store the Windows 2000 system files:

- **Do a fresh install, if possible.** If you have a classic NT server with a history of file system instabilities, consider deleting all partitions on all drives and doing a fresh installation of Windows 2000 instead of upgrading. This eliminates any possibility that unsupported applications, buggy device drivers, or invalid Registry entries will carry the instabilities over to Windows 2000. Reformatting also refreshes the disks on systems that are a couple of years old.

- **Check SCSI cables.** If you use SCSI drives, Windows 2000 demands tighter timing tolerances than classic NT. If you have a SCSI cable that's right on the edge of length spec, you might run into data corruption problems after upgrading.

- **Enable bootable CD-ROM drive.** If you have a relatively new system, especially one designed to be a server, it should have a bootable CD-ROM drive. If the drive meets the El Torito specifications with no emulation, it should boot the Windows 2000 CD. If the CD does not boot, check whether the feature is available but disabled in CMOS. If you enable CD-ROM booting and the machine attempts to boot from the Windows 2000 CD but you get the error message *Unable to find NTLDR*, you're probably out of luck. Either the CD-ROM device or the system BIOS does not support the full El Torito specification.

- **Break software mirrors.** If you are installing over an existing copy of NT running on mirrored drives, you must break the mirror prior to performing the installation. Remirror the drives after the upgrade. This limitation does not apply to hardware RAID.

Mirroring Unsupported in NT4 Workstation and Windows 2000 Professional

Windows 2000 Professional, like its NT4 Workstation predecessor, does not support software mirroring. If you have hacked an NT4 workstation to enable mirroring, you'll need to give up the hack before upgrading. The *Logical Disk Manager* (LDM) in Windows 2000 handles fault-tolerant disks differently from classic NT.

There will probably be ways to hack LDM to get mirroring on a Professional desktop; but frankly, with the low cost of hardware nowadays, you may want to spend a couple of hundred dollars extra to get a RAID card and avoid risking your data on an unsupported configuration.

- **Use standard disk access.** For EIDE drives, verify that file I/O and disk access is set to "Standard" and not "32-bit" or "Enhanced" in CMOS. Windows 2000 does not support the direct INT13 calls used by enhanced interfaces.

- **Removable media drives.** You can install Windows 2000 to a removable media drive, such as an Iomega Jaz or Castlewood Orb drive. You would not want to do this on a production system, of course, but it makes for a flexible lab environment. If for some reason you cannot make the removable media bootable, you can boot from a fixed drive and put the system files on the removable media drive.

- **Make room for the system files.** Leave lots of room in the Windows 2000 partition, at least 1GB, with 2GB being preferable. Classic NT would fit comfortably in a 400MB partition, but Windows 2000 has grown appreciably tubbier. If you make the partition too small, you will fragment the NTFS *Master File Table* (MFT), which has a severe impact on performance. The MFT cannot be defragmented, so give the partition lots of room.

- **Watch out for application file locations.** Applications often insist on putting their DLLs and support files into the System and System32 directories. Newer 32-bit applications are getting flabbier, as well, so watch carefully when you install them to see whether you can redirect the files to another partition. For Professional desktops, the new IntelliMirror suite of services may help reduce the number of applications that need to be installed locally.

- **Upgrading requires free space.** You should have at least 850MB of free space in the NT4 partition to upgrade. Add another 250MB to store temporary files if you are installing across the network or directly from CD. Setup determines the necessary free space using entries in a *Setup Information File* (SIF) called TXTSETUP.SIF, located on the first Setup disk or the \I386 directory on the CD. The entries are under the

[DiskSpaceRequirements] section. The space requirements differ depending on the cluster size in use on the disk. To install Windows 2000 from CD into an empty partition, for example, you need 686736 bytes, about 671MB to install onto a disk with 512-byte clusters, and 829MB if you have 32KB clusters.

Large System Files

Windows 2000 has two files that can take up a lot of space. These are the paging file, PAGEFILE.SYS, and the Active Directory information store, NTDS.DIT. You need to make special allowances for storing these files.

Paging File

Setup puts the paging file, PAGEFILE.SYS, into the root of the boot partition. You can change this location after initial setup, but until then you'll need enough room in the boot partition to accommodate the file. Setup sizes the paging file to be 11MB larger than main memory. This is often inadequate for heavily used servers and desktops that do lots of graphics. Paging files of 400MB–600MB on CAD or graphics workstations are not unusual.

- **Move the paging file to another disk.** You can reduce the size of the Windows 2000 partition by moving the paging file to another drive or drives. You can have up to 16 paging files as long as each one is on a separate logical drive. You will not get a performance improvement unless the paging files are on separate physical drives, as well. If there is no paging file in the system partition, you cannot dump the contents of memory to disk following a Kernel-mode stop error (Blue Screen of Death). This feature is really only required if you are troubleshooting an unstable system. You can configure a paging file in the system partition when one becomes necessary.

Paging File Alternatives for Systems with Large Amounts of Memory

The option to dump system memory to disk in the event of a stop error can force you to set aside very large chunks of disk real estate if you have lots of memory. Instead, you can configure the system to dump only the contents of kernel memory, not application memory. Do this as follows:

Procedure 1.1   **Configuring the System to Dump Only the Contents of the Kernel Memory**

1. Open the System applet in Control Panel.

2. Select the Advanced tab.

3. Click Startup and Recovery.

4. Uncheck the Write Debugging Information option.

This saves considerable disk space and gives Microsoft technical support a more compact file to examine in the event of a crash.

Microsoft recommends a paging file of 1GB for a system with 2GB of RAM and a paging file of 2GB for a system with 4GB of RAM. Putting this amount of memory on a standard Windows 2000 server is not very common, but Advanced Server and Datacenter Server are likely to ship on some very big iron. The Data General AViiON 25000, for example, supports 64 Xeon processors and 64GB of system memory.

- **Avoid paging file fragmentation.** The paging file can become fragmented, which hurts performance in two ways. First, finding pages in a fragmented paging file requires more work from the file system. Second, the paging file is locked, so the disk defragmenter must work around it to defrag the remaining files. One technique that administrators have used with good success is to create a second partition (or use a second hard drive, which also improves performance) for the sole purpose of holding the paging file. This keeps it from becoming fragmented. You can also set NTFS permissions to block the user from seeing this partition, reducing the likelihood that they will accidentally do something to the file.

Active Directory Information Store

If you are installing a server that will eventually become a domain controller, or upgrading an existing domain controller, provide drives for the Active Directory information store. There are two major sets of files: the main store, NTDS.DIT; and the transaction logs and checkfile.

- **Put NTDS.DIT on its own drive.** For best performance, give the main information store its own drive, preferably on its own controller. This is not so critical for average user populations (50–1,000) but can improve performance for large populations of 1,000–10,000, and is essential for populations of more than 10,000. Chapter 7, "Understanding Active Directory Services," has information correlating user populations and directory sizes.

- **Put the AD transaction logs on their own drive.** If the drive holding the main information store should crash, you can recover a previous copy from tape, and then fully recover from the log files. However, you can't do the full recovery if the same disk crash that took NTDS.DIT also took its log files.

- **Consider a separate drive for Sysvol.** In addition to the AD information store, a Windows 2000 domain controller holds group policies and distributed software. These files are downloaded by client computers during morning logon and periodically throughout the working day. To get the best performance, consider putting Sysvol on its own drive and controller. Small organizations with a few hundred users that do not make extensive use of policies can put the Sysvol directory and the Active Directory information store on the same disk.

Drive Formats

You can install Windows 2000 onto a partition that is preformatted with FAT, FAT32, or NTFS 4. You cannot install Windows 2000 onto an HPFS, NetWare, or UNIX partition. You can choose to convert a FAT or FAT32 boot partition to NTFS during setup, but do not do so if you plan on dual-booting the machine. See the "Dual-Boot Considerations" section later in this chapter for details.

- **Remove Windows 9x compressed volumes.** You cannot install Windows 2000 onto a drive that has been compressed with DoubleSpace or DriveSpace. Also, Windows 2000 does not recognize DoubleSpace or DriveSpace volumes in other partitions. Some administrators use this to protect Windows 9x files from being changed in dual-boot configurations with Windows 2000/NT as the second operating system.

- **Consider decompressing NTFS volumes.** You can install Windows 2000 onto a compressed NTFS 4 partition, but watch out for free space. All system files are decompressed as they are replaced, so you may run out of room, which would cause Setup to freeze in the middle of the file transfers and force you to recover from tape. I advise turning off compression prior to upgrading. If you don't have enough room, you can use Partition Magic, System Commander, or some other partition manager to increase the size of the system partition. You'll need the extra space, anyway.

Configuring Network Adapters

Unless you install Windows 2000 on a home machine, you probably will connect it to a network. Networking is much easier to configure in Windows 2000 compared to NT4 and even Windows 9x, but there's still a lot that can go wrong.

- **Check the HCL.** The network adapter is a critical component, so make sure it is on the HCL. Microsoft has officially retired several adapters, most notably legacy Token Ring and PCMCIA adapters. Still others might not have Windows 2000 drivers. Do not install Windows 2000 on a machine with 8-bit adapters, such as Novell NE1000, Artisoft AE-1, and 8-bit offerings from SMC and 3Com.

- **Resolve resource conflicts first.** Windows 2000 uses PnP to discover and enumerate network adapters. It will attempt to identify legacy adapters and load the correct drivers. If you have a legacy adapter, make sure that you know the resources it uses. These include the following:

  - IRQ
  - I/O base address
  - RAM address (necessary only if the adapter uses memory addressing). All PC Card network adapters use memory addressing. Windows 2000 accommodates 16-bit memory addressing by remapping the onboard RAM to its 32-bit memory space. You should encounter conflicts only if you have multiple network adapters with the same RAM addresses.
  - DMA channels for bus-mastering adapters

  If Setup hangs, try changing the settings. If you experience connection problems using PnP adapters that have PnP disabled, enable PnP and try again.

- **Avoid shared interrupts.** Shared interrupts may pose a problem depending on your motherboard and chipset. Some machines have no problem at all sharing six or seven devices on the same IRQ. Others are plagued by Kernel-mode stop errors and unstable network connections when sharing just two. If Setup hangs during network driver enumeration (give it a couple of hours), this is a sign of possible problems sharing interrupts.

Dual-Boot Considerations

You need to take several issues into account when attempting to run several operating systems along with Windows 2000.

- **Bootstrap loader limitations.** The Windows 2000 bootstrap loader, NTLDR, can load any version of NT or Windows 2000 from any drive or partition on the local system (except for some flavors of removable media drive), but it can load only *one* alternate operating system. It does so by storing the boot sector for the alternate OS in a file called BOOTSECT.DOS at the root of the boot partition. If the alternate OS is selected from the Windows 2000 BOOT menu, NTLDR shifts the processor back to Real mode, loads the image from BOOTSECT.DOS into memory at 0x700h just as if it had been loaded by a standard INT13 call, and then turns control over to the executable code in the image.

Booting Two Alternate Operating Systems with NTLDR

If you need to boot more than two operating systems and one of them is not a Windows OS, use a partition manager, such as Partition Magic, System Commander, or Linux Loader (LILO).

If you want to configure a triple-boot machine to load DOS/Windows, Windows 9x, and Windows 2000, you can create a triple-boot menu with two alternate BOOTSECT files by layering your installations. This process is described in detail in Microsoft's KnowledgeBase article Q157992. The basic steps are as follows:

Procedure 1.2   Booting Two or More Alternate Operating Systems

1. Install DOS.

2. Install Windows 2000. This saves the DOS boot sector to BOOTSECT.DOS.

3. Toggle the read-only, hidden, and system attributes on BOOTSECT.DOS.

4. Rename BOOTSECT.DOS to BOOTSECT.622, for DOS version 6.22.

5. Install Windows 9x. This overwrites the Windows 2000 boot sector with its own boot sector.

6. Run the Windows 2000 Repair Console (see Chapter 18, "Recovering from System Failures"). Use it to restore a Windows 2000 boot sector, and save the existing boot sector as BOOTSECT.DOS.

7. Toggle the read-only attribute on BOOT.INI.

8. Edit BOOT.INI to add the following lines:

```
[Operating Systems]
    c:\bootsect.622="DOS" /win95dos
    c:\bootsect.dos="Win9x" /win95
```

The switches enable multiple boot features in Windows 9x.

- **NTFS version Incompatibilities.** When Windows 2000 installs, it converts the existing NTFS 4 volumes to NTFS version 5. If you dual-boot between Windows 2000 and NT4, the NT4 side will crash with Kernel-mode stop error *0x00000007d, Inaccessible Boot Device.* You must be running NT4 Service Pack 4 or higher to get the NTFS.SYS driver that supports NTFS 5. If you forget to install the service pack prior to installing Windows 2000, you can replace the NT4 NTFS.SYS driver from Windows 2000, and then dual-boot back to NT4.

- **Dynamic disks.** Windows 2000 includes a new Logical Disk Manager (LDM) service that permits dynamically configuring fault-tolerant volumes, such as mirroring, RAID 5, volume extensions, and RAID 0 striping. When a *basic disk* (standard Intel disk configuration) is converted to *dynamic disk* (LDM configuration), the partition table in the Master Boot Record is changed to point at the LDM database at the end of the drive. Only LDM can read this database, so only Windows 2000 can boot to a dynamic disk. There are no service pack updates and no workarounds.

- **Separate windows partitions.** Microsoft *strongly* recommends using separate system partitions for each version of 32-bit Windows on a multiple-boot system. The various flavors of Windows have become too similar to keep them on the same partition. There are too many shared folders outside of the main \WINNT system folder that can affect dual-boot operation. Many field testers can attest to the problems they encountered when they did not use separate partitions.

- **NT4 service packs overwrite key system files.** If you install an NT4 service pack on a dual-boot machine, it overwrites the Windows 2000 version of NTLDR in the root of the boot drive. This prevents Windows 2000 from booting because the NT4 version of NTLDR will not boot Windows 2000. Before applying an NT4 service pack, make a copy of NTLDR at the root of the boot partition. Copy it back when the service pack has been applied. NT4 service packs also overwrite key IE5 and IIS files, so be careful about applying them to dual-boot systems if you have not been scrupulous in keeping the operating systems in separate partitions.

- **Disk defragmentation.** You can defrag an NTFS 5 volume when running NT4 if the defragmentation tool uses *standard File System Control* (FSCTL) calls. Executive Software's Diskkeeper is an example. Norton's Speedisk for NT is another. If you dual-boot to Windows 98, you can defrag a FAT or FAT32 volume containing Windows 2000. Do not use a DOS defragger on a FAT volume containing Windows 2000. It may delete the directory entries containing long filenames.

Virus Scanning

Always disable and de-install virus scanning before upgrading to Windows 2000. Special features in the new version of NTFS may cause virus scanning to become unstable and could result in data loss. All antivirus software packages require upgrading to work with Windows 2000 and NTFS 5.

Even if you are using a newly released virus scanner that has a "Ready for Windows 2000" logo, be careful. Any administrator who lived through the Norton Antivirus debacle during the release of NT4 will tell you to be especially cautious when running virus scans after major OS upgrades. Watch diligently for file corruption until you've verified after several weeks that the virus scans are not damaging files, either on servers or at client desktops.

MAPI Support

Some applications use MAPI calls or special features that may not be exposed in exactly the same way in Windows 2000. Be sure to test both your email client and server software in the lab, along with any applications that make use of MAPI before deploying Windows 2000 in production.

Functional Overview of Windows 2000 Setup

This section covers the details of what happens during an installation of Windows 2000 and the major milestones that come up between the time you start the installation and the time you do the initial logon. This gives you an idea of what to expect and gives you a basis for making configuration decisions. The step-by-step instructions for performing an installation are in the "Installing Windows 2000 Using Setup Disks" section.

Windows 2000 Setup works like an able seaman docking a ship to a pier. The seaman tosses a light line to shore and uses it to pull over a heavier line. He wraps the heavier line around a winch and uses it to pull across a much heavier line, and then he uses the heavier line to the secure the ship to the pier.

Setup docks Windows 2000 to a computer with three separate rounds of file copies performed in two phases, with a third phase for final user and manual system configuration:

- **Character phase.** The first set of files are loaded from a set of four floppy disks or from the bootable Windows 2000 CD. These files are used to build a miniature version of Windows 2000 sufficient for partitioning and formatting the hard drive and mounting the CD. Setup then does a second round of file copies to bring over files from the CD that can support a graphical phase of installation. The system restarts after this phase.

- **Graphical phase.** In this phase, Setup discovers and enumerates the system hardware, queries the administrator for system settings, such as the computer name, its TCP/IP settings, any additional services to load, and so forth. It then performs a final set of file copies to bring over the drivers it needs based on the configuration choices made by the administrator. The system restarts again.

- **Configuration phase.** This phase starts when a user logs on to the machine for the first time. If it is a server, the system launches a server configuration wizard. In addition, a final round of PnP discovery commences to look for any devices that were not discovered during setup. The user may be prompted to provide drivers if they are not present on the local drive or CD. Depending on the nature of the components and the resource allocations necessary accommodate them, the system may need to be restarted one final time.

After the third stage, the system is ready for production. The following sections look at each of these phases in detail and explain what happens and what kind of configuration choices need to be made.

Character Setup Phase

This phase begins by booting from the Setup disks or, if the hardware supports it, from the Windows 2000 CD. Booting from CD makes the text-based portion of setup go much faster.

Bootable CDs and ARC Paths

If you boot from the Setup disks on a system with a bootable CD-ROM drive, you should not put the Windows 2000 CD in the CD-ROM drive until you are prompted to do so by Setup. You may encounter a problem if you have the Windows 2000 CD in the drive during the initial floppy boot sequence.

Windows 2000 specifies the location of the boot partition by means of an advanced RISC computing (ARC) path. An example of an ARC path is `multi(0)disk(0)rdisk(0)partition(1)\WINNT`.

The `rdisk()` component of the ARC path specifies the relative location of the boot disk with respect to the other SCSI devices on the bus. If the boot partition were on the third SCSI disk, for example, the `rdisk()` value would be `rdisk(2)`. See Chapter 2 for a complete discussion of BOOT.INI and ARC paths.

Ordinarily, Setup ignores passive devices, such as tape devices, scanners, and CD-ROM/DVD devices when calculating an `rdisk()` value. If the SCSI controller identifies the Windows 2000 CD as bootable, however, the drive will be included in the `rdisk()` calculations. This leads to an incorrect ARC path because the relative disk location of the boot partition will be wrong when the Windows 2000 CD is not in the drive. If this happens, you will get an *Unable to Find NTOSKRNL* error on the first restart following the character phase of Setup.

You can change an improper ARC path in BOOT.INI by booting from a DOS floppy disk (or a Windows 9x floppy disk if the boot partition is larger than 2GB) and editing the file. It is flagged as read-only, so you must toggle the attribute before saving the file.

Initial Setup File Loads

The Setup boot disk (Disk 1) has executable code in its boot sector that is designed to look for SETUPLDR.BIN, the Windows 2000 Setup loader. SETUPLDR.BIN is actually just a copy of the standard Windows 2000 bootstrap loader, NTLDR, with a few changes that support installation. SETUPLDR.BIN orchestrates the character portion of Setup using a script called TXTSETUP.SIF. This script tells Setup the following:

- Where to find the boot files
- What directories to put on the boot partition
- What files to copy to the system and boot partitions
- What drivers to load initially
- What to do with existing files
- What keys to put in a skeleton Registry built to support the graphical phase of Setup

You can add entries to the list of files and Registry entries in TXTSETUP.SIF if you want to include additional drivers in Setup. For example, you might have a special NIC driver that needs to be included in a desktop deployment. See the "Automating Windows 2000 Deployments" section in the next chapter for details on simplifying this process.

Initial Hardware Recognition

Intel machines do not have a hardware recognizer in firmware like a RISC machine, so the first thing SETUPLDR.BIN does is load a software-based hardware recognizer called NTDETECT.COM. At this point, you see the message *Setup is inspecting your computer's hardware configuration.*

NTDETECT.COM finds hardware information needed by the Windows 2000 kernel driver, NTKRNLMP.EXE, and the Hardware Abstraction Layer driver, HAL.DLL. NTDETECT does not perform comprehensive hardware checks like those performed by PnP. The PnP checks occur during the graphical phase of Setup.

Multipurpose Hardware Drivers

NTDETECT.COM, HAL.DLL, and the Windows 2000 kernel driver work together as a set. There are different sets of these hardware drivers for uniprocessor machines, multiprocessor machines, and a few specific machines that require tailored drivers. Many vendors also supply OEM hardware drivers, especially for multiprocessor machines.

The default hardware drivers loaded by SETUPLDR.BIN support general-purpose, single or multiprocessor computers. During the graphical phase, after the rest of the system setup files have been copied from CD, Setup takes another look at the system configuration. If appropriate, it selects a different set of hardware drivers.

The new class of hardware drivers in Windows 2000 supports the *Advanced Configuration and Power Interface* (ACPI) standard. This ACPI "standard" has been evolving rapidly lately, so the drivers selected by Setup may not be correct for your machine. This can cause Setup to hang. This is especially prevalent on laptops. Some laptop manufacturers ship OEM hardware drivers, so check their Web site if the system does not respond properly.

If you need to install OEM hardware drivers, press F5 when you see the message *Setup is inspecting your computer's hardware configuration.* This displays a list of the hardware driver sets on the setup disks and gives you the opportunity to load an alternative set. The list does not display until the kernel driver loads, so give the system a few minutes to respond after you press F5.

NTDETECT uses the hardware information it finds to fill out a data structure that the kernel driver uses to build a volatile Registry hive called Hardware. You can view the contents of the Hardware hive using Regedt32 or Regedit. This identical process is repeated each time Windows 2000 boots. The Hardware hive is never committed to disk.

SETUPLDR.BIN compares the hardware results from NTLDR to a list of systems in the BIOSINFO.INF file on the first setup disk. This file contains the ACPI and the *Advanced Power Management* (APM) settings for a long list of machines. If your system is unstable or fails to boot, look at the BIOSINFO.INF file to see whether your equipment is listed. If not, make sure it is on the HCL and contact the vendor for possible workarounds.

Remaining Setup Disk Files Load

At this point, SETUPLDR.BIN loads the kernel driver, NTKRNLMP.EXE, along with HAL.DLL and BOOTVID.DLL, the driver used to communicate in Text mode to the console. The *MP* in the kernel driver name stands for *multiprocessor.* Setup always uses multiprocessor hardware drivers to simplify initial installation. If a machine has only one processor, the uniprocessor drivers are loaded later, in the graphical phase. If a machine is SMP capable but has only one processor, Setup loads uniprocessor drivers. See Chapter 3 for instructions on adding a second processor and installing the multiprocessor hardware drivers.

SETUPLDR.BIN now loads the remaining files from the setup floppy disks or the CD. The files are compressed on the floppy disk. SETUPLDR.BIN expands them and loads them into memory. It does not have access to the hard disk yet.

The files on the setup disks contain the video drivers, keyboard drivers, disk drivers, and file system drivers needed by Setup to proceed to the graphical phase. Here are the most important drivers and their functions:

- **Hardware Abstraction Layer (HAL).** There are three HAL drivers on the setup disks and a lot more on the CD. You can see the full list by searching for HAL*.DL_ in the \I386 directory on the CD. When Setup eventually decides which hardware drivers to use, it selects the driver and then renames it as HAL.DLL and copies it to the \WINNT\System32 directory.

- **SETUPREG.HIV.** This is a small Registry file with the keys necessary to initialize the Windows 2000 Kernel-mode driver, SETUPDD.SYS. SETUPDD.SYS is the mother driver that loads all the other device drivers. You can view the contents of SETUPREG.HIV after the installation is complete by loading the file into the Registry Editor.

- **National Language Support (NLS).** These files contain locale information for character sets, punctuation, and so forth. Two files are Code Pages, C_1252.NLS and C_437.NLS; and one is for the primary language, L_INTL.NLS.

- **VGA.SYS, VIDEOPRT.SYS,** and **VGAOEM.FON.** These are the standard VGA video drivers and one display font.

- **I/O extenders.** These include PCMCIA.SYS, PCIIDE.SYS, INTELIDE.SYS, and FDC.SYS (floppy disk controller). These are WDM bus drivers that work with PnP Manager to define data paths.

- **FLOPPY.SYS.** The floppy disk minidriver.

- **MOUNTMGR.SYS, FTDISK.SYS,** and **PARTMGR.SYS.** This set of drivers supports basic disk configurations and classic fault-tolerant disk sets.

- **DMBOOT.SYS, DMIO.SYS,** and **DMLOAD.SYS.** This set of drivers supports the new Logical Disk Manager (LDM).

- **SCSIPORT.SYS.** This is the SCSI bus driver. It is accompanied by a slew of SCSI miniport drivers, such as AHA154X.SYS, and so forth.

Loading Alternative SCSI Adapter Driver

If you are unlucky enough to have a SCSI adapter without a driver on the setup disks, you can load it manually during setup. Obtain the Windows 2000 driver from the vendor's Web site along with the associated INF file. This INF tells the Windows 2000 class loader how to install the driver, where to put the files, and what Registry entries to make.

The standard INF format changed in Windows 2000; therefore, even if the vendor says that Windows 2000 supports an older driver, you might not be able to load it because the INF script is incorrectly formatted.

- **I8042PRT.SYS. The keyboard driver.** This driver virtualizes the 8042 controller BIOS and also controls PS/2 bus mice. If you get garbage onscreen when you type, or experience odd results when using your mouse, this driver might not be compatible with your keyboard, mouse, or PS/2 motherboard interface.

- **KBDCLASS.SYS** and **KBDUS.DLL.** These are the keyboard class driver and the keyboard mapping driver. These two drivers can sometimes cause trouble with cheap components. If you keep having problems with the Caps Lock key not working properly or the repeat rate being unstable, you may need to upgrade your equipment.

- **DISK.SYS, CLASS2.SYS,** and **CLASSPNP.SYS.** These are mass storage interface drivers and their PnP enumerator.

- **ATAPI.SYS.** This is the IDE/EIDE driver. The older ATDISK.SYS driver is no longer used. Support for ESDI/WD1003 drives has been dropped.

- **ISAPNP.SYS.** The PnP enumerator for the ISA bus. You may recognize this driver from NT4. It came in the \Support directory on the NT4 CD. Multimedia vendors, such as Creative Labs used this driver to provide a simpler way to install their ISA sound cards and game boards.

- **SERIAL.SYS** and **SERENUM.SYS.** The serial bus controller and PnP enumerator. These two drivers work together to find PnP and legacy devices connected to RS232 ports. This search can be a tedious process because the RS232 interface is so slow. For this reason, the standard BOOT.INI entry includes a /fastdetect switch that delays the serial bus enumeration until after the system has loaded.

- **OPENHCI.SYS, UHCD.SYS, USBD.SYS, USBHUB.SYS,** and **HIDUSB.SYS.** The *Universal Serial Bus* (USB) drivers. These work with a set of *Human Interface Device* (HID) drivers to support USB components.

- **NTDLL.DLL.** The Windows 2000 API function library. This file is located in the \SYSTEM32 directory on the first setup disk.

- **SMSS.EXE.** The Session Manager Subsystem driver. The Session Manager is responsible for loading and initializing system drivers. Also located in the \SYSTEM32 directory on the first setup disk.
- **NTFS.SYS, FASTFAT.SYS,** and **CDFS.SYS.** The NT file system driver, FAT file system driver, and CD file system driver. FASTFAT.SYS includes both FAT16 and FAT32 support. The Windows 2000 CD contains other file system drivers, but Setup does not need them at this point.

Choosing a Disk Format

After SETUPLDR.BIN has loaded the drivers from the Setup disks or the CD disk images, it initializes NTKRLMP.EXE, which works with the Session Manager driver to start the operating system. At this point, Setup walks you through creating and formatting a boot partition for the operating system.

Setup prompts you to decide between NTFS and FAT when formatting the boot partition. I recommend using NTFS for all partitions, including the system partition. See Chapter 13, "Managing File Systems," for details on the various file system options.

The only real advantage of FAT or FAT32 over NTFS is the capability to boot with a DOS floppy disk to access the system partition. Windows 2000 incorporates a Recovery Console that permits booting to a command prompt and accessing an NTFS drive. This is similar to the NTFSDOS utility created by the legendary Mark Russinovich and Bryce Cogswell at www.sysinternals.com. Armed with the Recovery Console to simplify individual file replacements on an NTFS partition, you can join Oprah and say goodbye to FAT forever.

Even if you specify NTFS, the system first formats the partition as FAT (<=2GB) or FAT32 (>2GB) then converts it to NTFS after the system restarts. This is because the small NTFS driver in SETUPLDR cannot format an NTFS partition. Only the full NTFS.SYS driver can do that.

If you specify NTFS or FAT on a partition that is larger than 2GB (the limit for DOS partitions with 32KB clusters), SETUPLDR.BIN automatically formats the partition as FAT32. The maximum size for a FAT32 partition under Windows 2000 is 32GB.

If you specify an NTFS boot partition larger than 2GB, Setup automatically uses FAT32 to do the initial formatting. This avoids the problem in classic NT where a boot partition could not be larger than 2GB (7.8GB if you were willing to do some fancy footwork).

After the boot partition is formatted, the files necessary to support the graphical phase of startup are copied from the CD. The system restarts automatically after the file copy has completed and commences the graphical phase of Setup.

Definition of Boot Partition and System Partition

When I use the terms *boot partition* and *system partition*, I try to stay faithful to the Microsoft documentation. You may find their definitions to be a little cross-eyed.

- **System partition.** This is the partition that contains the files required to boot the system. For an Intel platform, these are NTLDR, BOOT.INI, NTDETECT.COM, BOOTSECT.DOS, and NTBOOTDD.SYS (if the SCSI device has no onboard BIOS). The system partition must be flagged as Active (or bootable) in the Master Boot Record and it must be at the root of the boot drive. Setup assumes that the first IDE drive on the primary IDE controller or the first SCSI drive on the primary SCSI controller is the boot drive.

- **Boot partition.** This is the partition that contains the Windows 2000 system files. By default, Setup puts these files in a directory called \WINNT. The boot partition can be on any drive, but it cannot be in an Extended DOS partition. If you put the boot partition somewhere other than the boot drive, Setup prompts you to create a small system partition on the boot drive. This partition can be less than 1MB, just big enough for the boot files.

In a nutshell, the boot files in the system partition load the system files from the boot partition. Confusing? You bet it is. These terms are rooted in RISC and don't translate well to Intel platforms. Now that Windows 2000 runs only on Intel, maybe Microsoft will change the way it uses these terms. It's doubtful, but hope springs eternal.

Graphical Setup Phase

Setup reloads when the machine restarts, but like Dorothy leaving drab old Kansas for colorful Oz, the character-based screens are left behind and the system shifts to graphics mode.

Quite a bit more happens during this phase of Setup than the character phase, but you get a lot more information onscreen, so it requires less explanation. There are several critical decision points. These concern licensing, naming servers, setting the Administrator password, configuring workgroups and domains, and setting the system time.

Licensing

When you purchase a license for a Windows 2000 server, you do not necessarily purchase the license to connect any clients to that server. For this, you need a *Client Access License* (CAL). A CAL is a piece of paper costing between $15 and $40, depending on volume and reseller markup, that gives you legal authorization to connect a client to a Windows 2000 server.

The purchase price of a Windows 2000 server typically includes a pack of 5 or 10 CALs, but there are *Stock Keeping Units* (SKUs) that do not include any CALs at all, so you need to read the catalog carefully when you order. Keep those CAL certificates in a safe place. You'll need them if you ever get audited by the *Software Publishers Association* (SPA) or by your corporate auditors.

When you upgrade from NT4 to Windows 2000, you must buy CAL upgrades as well. This is the real expense of the upgrade. You pay only $400 or $500 for the server upgrade disk itself, but the CAL upgrade might cost you $10 to $20 per license. If you have purchased 500 CALs for a particular NT4 server, you'll owe Microsoft a few thousand dollars when you upgrade it to Windows 2000.

Windows 2000, like is predecessors, has two forms of licensing: *Per Seat* and *Per Client*. Both forms require purchasing a CAL, but the number of CALs you need to buy and how you track them differs dramatically.

CALs and Application Servers

It is not necessary to purchase a Windows 2000 CAL if you are using a server as a platform for a client/server application. If you have a Lotus Notes service running on Windows 2000, for example, you do not need a CAL to connect a Notes client to that Notes service. If the user maps a drive to the Windows 2000 server to run the Notes client executable across the network, however, you do need a CAL.

If you purchase the BackOffice suite of server products, you get a big discount in the cost of the CALs as compared to purchasing the licenses separately. If you use alternative SQL database or mail products, however, the BackOffice package price is not quite so attractive.

Per Server Licensing

This licensing method resembles traditional licensing that you might recognize from NetWare or Banyan. Per Server licensing is a "concurrent connection" license. If you buy a copy of Windows 2000 Server with 25 CALs, for example, you set the `Per Server` license value to 25 during Setup. The 26th concurrent user will be denied access. If the time comes when you have more than 25 users who need to access the server simultaneously, you purchase additional CALs and push up the allowable number of licensed connections in the License Manager utility available from the START menu via START | PROGRAMS | ADMINISTRATIVE TOOLS | LICENSE MANAGER.

Recovering from a License Lockout

Sometimes users stay connected to a server even though they are no longer using any resources on it. This chews up licensed connections and could cause a "license lockout" where no further connections are accepted. A user with administrative privileges is permitted to log on during a license lockout to reset the license value or to disconnect users.

Per Server licensing can be expensive if you have more than one server. If you install a second Windows 2000 server with Per Server licensing, for example, you must purchase another 25 CALs to legally permit the users to connect to the second server.

For the most part, Per Server licensing makes sense only when a server has separate user populations, or at least there is very little overlap. Otherwise, it is much cheaper to use Per Seat licensing.

Per Seat Licensing

Per Seat licensing permits a user with a CAL to connect to any Windows 2000 computer in a domain. Using this licensing method, you purchase CALs based on the number of users who access Windows 2000 servers.

The catch to Per Seat licensing is that you must purchase a CAL for *every* client machine that accesses *any* Windows 2000 server in your network *at any time*. There is no "concurrent use" umbrella. If you have 1000 assembly-line workers who only log on to a Windows 2000 domain once a week to file their time cards electronically, each of those users must have a CAL.

When you configure a server for Per Seat licensing, the Licensing Manager keeps track of everyone who accesses the server in a licensable manner. This includes file services, print services, network authentication, and so forth. If the Licensing Manager on a server says that 5,000 different users have connected to the machine at one time or another, you need to be able to show an auditor 5,000 CALs.

The logistics of keeping track of CALs for Per Seat users in a big network is enormous. If you elect to use Per Seat licensing, you might as well plan on buying a CAL for every user who sits at a computer with a Microsoft client redirector. Also, if you run third-party products that provide file-and-print services, such as an NFS server or File and Print Services for NetWare or FTP services, you must purchase a CAL for each user who accesses the service. This is true even if you also have to pay license fees to the third-party vendor, as well.

Here's another catch to Per Seat licensing. When you purchase a CAL, it is for a specific version of NT or Windows 2000. When you upgrade, you owe money for the new CALs. Say, for example, that you have a 1,000-user NT4 network configured in a master domain model with a few resource domains. You are using Per Seat licensing. When you upgrade the master account domain to Windows 2000, you owe the tab for 1,000 CAL upgrades because all users authenticate in the account domain.

One final caveat to keep in mind for licensing: You can change from Per Server to Per Seat licensing after you install Windows 2000, but you cannot go back.

Server Naming

One of the decisions you have to make during setup is what to name the server or desktop. A few naming rules are based on NetBIOS standards that go back to the dark ages of the middle 1980s when Microsoft and IBM worked together with other companies to develop PC networking standards and OS/2 LAN Manager. Here they are:

- The computer name must be no more than 15 characters long. The actual limit is 16, but the operating system inserts a final character, not ordinarily visible from the user interface, that identifies the NetBIOS service using the name. For example, the Workstation service running on a computer named RUMPLESTILTSKIN would have a full NetBIOS name of RUMPLESTILTSKIN[03], where [03] is the hex ID for the Workstation service.

- The NetBIOS name cannot match any other computer name or domain name on the network. Forget about structured naming hierarchies. If two Windows machines are in the same broadcast domain and subnet or they are registered with the same WINS server, they cannot use the same name. Make sure your naming convention ensures unique computer name throughout your enterprise.

- NetBIOS permits a few special characters in names that you should avoid. Spaces are permitted, but they are not supported by DNS and they create problems when mapping drives. Don't use them. You may also want to avoid underscores if you are concerned about full DNS compatibility. Until recently, underscores were not on of the official list of supported special characters in DNS. Windows 2000 DNS supports them and so do current BIND implementations, so it should be safe to use them.

The computer names in this book use a role-based naming convention. The name of the first domain controller in the Phoenix office would be PHX-DC-01, for example, and the tenth Windows 2000 Professional desktop in the Houston office would be HOU-W2KP-010.

Identifying servers by work role helps users to locate resources on the network. It's easy to remember that the Notes servers are PHX-NOTES-## and the mail servers are PHX-SMTP-## and so on. Role-based naming has its problems, however. You may decide to change the role of a server but do not want to change its name because it has other functions that are name sensitive.

Changing the name of a desktop is fairly painless, but changing a server name requires users to remap their network drives and printers and may disturb applications running on the server. Windows 2000 has a *Link Tracking Service* (LTS) that helps repair links to files that have moved, but LTS is not effective for computer name changes.

You can avoid some of the pain of renaming a server by putting an alias in WINS and DNS. See Chapter 4 for details on these name resolution methods. You can also use the *Distributed File System* (Dfs) to represent your server-based resources as elements in a virtual directory tree. This enables you to rename servers and shares without disturbing the users. Building a reliable Dfs system is a complex task, but it has other benefits, such as fault tolerance and directory integration that make it attractive. See Chapter 15, "Managing Shared Resources," for more information.

If you want to rename a Windows 2000 domain controller, you must demote it to a regular server, rename it, and then promote it back to a domain controller. See Chapter 9 for details.

Managing Administrator Passwords

All Windows 2000 servers and desktops have a default account called Administrator. The Administrator account has full privileges on the machine. During setup, you assign a password to the Administrator account. The password is saved in the local *Security Account Manager* (SAM) database.

Admin Account In Professional

In addition to the default Administrator account, Windows 2000 Professional also has an Admin account with the same privileges. It exists for compatibility with the Windows 9x Admin account. It is also used in two special contexts:

- **Autologon.** Users of standalone Professional desktops are not required to log on to access the computer from the console. The system logs the user on automatically using the default Admin account. This was also an option in classic NT, but it required setting up the AUTOLOGON feature manually or using TweakUI.

- **Encrypted file system.** When a user at a standalone Professional desktop encrypts a file, the default Admin account is assigned the role of *Default Recovery Agent* (DRA). The DRA gets a special encryption certificate called a File Recovery certificate with a key that is included with every encrypted file. The File Recovery key permits someone logged on as Admin to open files that were encrypted by another user. See Chapter 14, "Managing File Systems Security," for more information.

When assigning the local Administrator password, make it long, unique, and cryptographically strong. See Chapter 6 for advice on password selection.

Don't lose the Administrator password, especially on a server. If the server is a member of a domain, you can log on using a domain Administrator account. If the server loses network connection, you should be able to log on using cached credentials. If something goes wrong with the server and the cached credentials are not available, however, you might find yourself locked out. There are password-cracking utilities, such as L0phtcrack from L0pht Heavy Industries, `www.l0pht.com`, that can help you recover an Administrator password.

Domains and Workgroups

Windows 2000 and classic NT use two terms that are not actually related to each other but often get confused: *domains* and *workgroups*.

- A **domain** is a security entity. Domain members obtain their authentications from special servers called domain controllers.
- A **workgroup** is a resource-location entity. Workgroup members locate each other using special servers called browsers.

If you lived through the Cold War like I did, you'll appreciate the source of the confusion of these two terms. I recall stories about the Soviet Union and its seemingly despotic leaders, such as Khrushchev and Breshnev. In reality, ultimate power in the USSR resided in two chairs, the head of the Supreme Soviet and the chairman of the Communist Party. The fact that one man appeared to be the sole head of state was because he held both positions.

In the same way, a domain appears to be both an authentication entity and a browsing entity because the same server, the *primary domain controller* (PDC), holds both the security database and the browsing database. In reality, the two services are completely different. See Chapter 5 for a discussion of browsing and resource location.

If you are installing a server or desktop that has no need for a shared security affiliation with other machines, you can make it a member of a workgroup. Members of the same workgroup on the same IP subnet share the same browser, so they can find each other's resources.

When the time comes for a user to connect to a shared resource on a workgroup server, the user must have an account in the local security database of the server. If you don't want to maintain separate authentication databases at every server and desktop, you need to create a domain. See Chapter 7 for an introduction to the Active Directory and Windows 2000 domains.

Dates and Times

One of the final steps taken by Setup is configuring the date and time at the machine. You are prompted to verify the system time and to set the time zone. This seemingly trivial operation turns out to be critical for a couple of reasons: file time stamps and Kerberos time stamps.

When a file is created, modified, or accessed, a time stamp attribute is changed in the file record. If the transaction involves a file on a server, the time stamp comes from the server clock, not the client clock. If a user in Atlanta saves a file to a server in LA, for example, the time stamp that the Atlanta user sees immediately after saving the file would be the current time in LA corrected for the time zone. If server times are not synchronized, users have difficulty sorting through similar files on different servers to see which are the most recent.

Windows 2000 uses a new authentication protocol called Kerberos that issues electronic tickets to control access to servers. These tickets contain time stamps to help thwart bad guys who might copy them and use them later to impersonate a user. Windows 2000 domain controllers issue Kerberos tickets. If the domain controllers get too far out of time synchronization, the time stamps in their Kerberos tickets would be perpetually invalid and domain authentication would fail. Windows 2000 keeps time synchronized between domain controllers using the *Windows Time Service* (WTS).

Member servers and desktops are not included in WTS time synchronization. You must configure them to synchronize using a logon script or a third-party utility. You can find details of WTS and designing logon scripts to include time synchronization in Chapter 6.

Configuration Phase

Following the completion of the graphical setup phase, the machine restarts. This marks the official end of Setup as a process; from a practical standpoint, however, a user must log on and configure the machine before it can be considered ready for production.

Initial User Logon

After the machine restarts following the graphical installation phase, a small `Welcome to Windows` window appears prompting the user to press `Ctrl+Alt+Del` to log on.

Ctrl+Alt+Del and the Trojan Horse

The three-finger logon has been a feature of NT from its inception. The intent is to reduce the possibility that a Trojan horse program could impersonate the logon window and capture the user credentials.

There are so many other avenues for trojan horse infiltrations, not to mention all those Windows 9x clients that don't have this sophisticated twist to their domain logon process, that you may wonder why it's worth the bother. "Better safe than sorry" is the rule when it comes to security, so the three-finger logon survives. Standalone Windows 2000 Professional desktops can avoid the logon requirement, but only if they are not connected to a domain.

The console logon process is controlled by a service called WINLOGON.EXE. WINLOGON works in concert with the *Local Security Authority* (LSA) to authenticate the user via authentication providers. Kerberos is the primary provider.

The window that collects the logon credentials comes from the Graphical Identification and Authentication library, MSGINA.DLL. Third-party vendors can replace this library with their own GINA. Novell replaces MSGINA.DLL with NWGINA.DLL, for example, which collects NDS, bindery, and scripting options along with the standard Windows logon information.

If the computer was joined to a domain during setup, the logon window has a drop-down box listing the domain name along with the local computer name. This gives the user the option of logging on to the domain or just to the local SAM. The user would need an account in the local SAM to log on locally. This is commonly not provided in a domain environment.

Final PnP Enumeration

Plug and Play takes advantage of the initial user logon to discover and report any devices that were missed or skipped during setup. If PnP cannot find drivers, the user is prompted to provide them. Depending on the nature of the devices, the kind of drivers they use, and the resource allocations required to get the devices working, the user may be required to restart the machine.

For example, a new video adapter may not have drivers on the CD. Installing a new video driver affects several components in the Windows 2000 Executive, so when the new drivers are loaded, the machine must restart.

This completes the installation overview. It's time to actually do the work.

Installing Windows 2000 Using Setup Disks

This section contains step-by-step details for installing Windows 2000 Server using the four Setup boot disks or the Windows 2000 CD. The steps for installing Windows 2000 Professional closely parallel this process.

Building the Setup Boot Disks

If you have misplaced the four Setup disks that came with the Windows 2000 CD, you can build a new set using the Makeboot or Makebt32 utilities located on the Windows 2000 CD in the \Bootdisk directory. You can run Makeboot from any Microsoft operating system. You can run Makebt32 from Windows 9x, NT, or Windows 2000. (Classic NT used the NT installation program, Winnt32, to build the setup disks. This feature is no longer available.)

You'll need four blank disks labeled Setup Disk 1 through 4. The first disk will be the Setup boot disk. The disks do not need to be formatted. If they contain data, the data is overwritten without warning. You must run Makeboot/Makebt32 from a command prompt so that you can specify the drive letter of the floppy drive that holds the disks with the following syntax:

```
makebt32 a:.
```

Character Phase Setup

The steps in this section assume that you are installing Windows 2000 on a new machine or reformatting the system/boot partition of an existing machine. If you are upgrading, go to Chapter 2. If you are configuring an NT server to dual-boot, check for sufficient free space in a second partition. You'll need 800MB–1000MB depending on the cluster size. Installing parallel copies of 32-bit Windows operating systems into the same partition is not recommended.

With the four Setup disks in hand and the Windows 2000 CD in the CD-ROM drive, proceed as follows:

Procedure 1.3 Installing Windows 2000 on a New Machine

1. Insert Setup Disk 1 in the floppy drive (or the bootable CD in the CD-ROM drive) and start the computer. It's a good idea to initiate Setup using a cold start. Some systems are not good about resetting every bit of hardware with a warm boot.

2. After booting to the first Setup disk, cycle through the disks as prompted. When all drivers have been loaded and the Windows 2000 Executive initializes, a Welcome To Setup screen appears.

3. There are three options. The Repair option is covered in Chapter 18. Press Enter to continue with Setup.

4. The Windows 2000 Licensing Agreement screen appears. This contains the text of the End User Licensing Agreement (EULA).

5. Press F8 to agree to the terms of the EULA. A partition management screen appears. If you are installing on a new server, the drives show a status of Unpartitioned Space.

6. If you are installing on an existing server and you want to delete the current system/boot partition, highlight the partition name and press D. Setup responds with two confirmation screens.

   The first confirmation screen appears if the partition is a system partition (flagged Active in the Master Boot Record). Press Enter to confirm.

   The second confirmation screen is standard for any partition deletion. Confirm by pressing L.

7. If you are installing on an existing server and you elect to install into an existing partition, and that partition contains another Windows operating system, Setup prompts you to confirm. If you do, a series of screens walks you through removing the existing Windows operating system. You can install a parallel copy of Windows 2000 into the partition, but you are strongly urged not to do so.

8. After you have deleted the existing system/boot partition or if this is a new drive, highlight the Unpartitioned Space entry and press C to create a partition.

   If you select the first drive on the list, it becomes the boot drive and the system drive. If you select one of the other drives, Setup will put the Windows 2000 system files in the root of the boot partition. If the boot drive does not have a bootable partition, Setup prompts you to create one to hold startup files. A 1MB partition is sufficient.

9. When you create a partition, Setup prompts you to specify the size of the partition in MB. You should make the partition at least 1000MB, with 2GB preferred.

10. When the partition has been created, Setup returns to the partition management screen. Highlight the newly created partition and press Enter to install Windows 2000 into that partition.

11. Setup now prompts you to format the partition using either NTFS or FAT. NTFS is preferred because of its security and recoverability.

12. Select a format type and press Enter. Setup formats the partition and displays a progress bar. The initial format is always FAT (or FAT32 for partitions <2GB) because the small NTFS driver used by Setup cannot format a drive as NTFS.

    If you elected to install into a separate partition on a machine that already has a copy of classic NT, you are warned that the existing NT must be running Service Pack 4 or higher. This ensures it has the NTFS.SYS driver that can read NTFS 5 volumes.

13. When the format is finished, Setup begins copying installation files from the CD to the newly formatted partition.

14. When the file copy has completed, Setup prompts you to remove any floppy disks from the floppy drive and remove the Windows 2000 CD from the CD-ROM drive and restart. You do not need to remove the CD unless you have a bootable CD-ROM drive. The system restarts automatically if you take no action.

When the system restarts, if you elected to format a new partition as NTFS, the partition is converted from FAT or FAT32 to NTFS then the system restarts again. The graphical phase begins after the second restart.

Graphical Phase

After restart, the system loads and shifts to graphics mode and begins Setup again. A Welcome window opens.

Procedure 1.4 **Installing the Graphic Mode Portion of Setup**

1. Click Next at the Welcome window or wait a while for Setup to proceed automatically. The Installing Devices window opens and PnP enumeration begins.

   Give this step lots and lots of time. The machine may seem to hang for many minutes. Some administrators report 20–40 minute delays, with some complex systems stalling here for hours. One administrator reported a 16-hour delay, but the installation went normally after that. Be patient. If you get frustrated and restart, Setup will only return to this point and begin the discovery all over again; so don't lose heart.

2. If you make it through the device installation without hangs or errors, the `Regional Settings` window opens (see Figure 1.1). You have the opportunity here to change the `Locale` and `Keyboard` settings, if necessary.

`Locale Settings` determine the *National Language Support* (NLS) files that Setup loads. These files control parameters, such as display language, decimal points, monetary units, and such.

`Keyboard Settings` control key mappings and special keystroke functions.

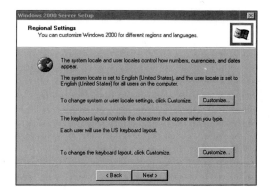

Figure 1.1 Windows 2000 Server upgrade—`Regional Settings` window.

3. Click `Next`. The `Personalize Your Software` window opens. Fill in the `Name` and `Organization` fields. These entries are for information only. The name is not used to build any accounts and the company name you enter does not affect licensing. Setup merely writes the values to the Registry where they are used by applications that want to identify the user.

Registry Tip: Changing the Registered Owner Name
You might want to avoid putting actual usernames in the `Personalize Your Software` window. When the computer goes to another user, the help desk gets a call like this, "This new computer says it's Jerry's computer. Well, it isn't Jerry's computer, it's *my* computer and I want it to say so." You can change the user information in the Registry:

Key: HKLM | Software | Microsoft | Windows NT | CurrentVersion

Value: RegisteredOwner

4. Click Next. The Licensing Modes window opens (see Figure 1.2). Refer to the "Licensing" section earlier in this chapter for details on making the decision between Per Server and Per Seat licensing.

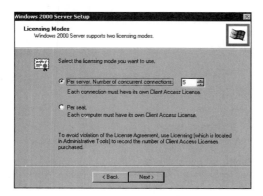

Figure 1.2   Windows 2000 Server upgrade—Licensing Modes window.

5. Click Next. The Computer Name and Administrator Password window opens (see Figure 1.3). Refer to the "Managing Administrator Passwords" section earlier in this chapter for advice on selecting server names and passwords.

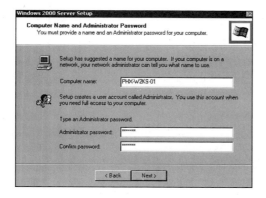

Figure 1.3   Windows 2000 Server upgrade—Computer Name and Administrator Password window.

6. Click Next. The Windows 2000 Components window opens (see Figure 1.4). Rather than installing additional components at this time, you may want to wait until after Setup has finished. If something goes wrong, you'll have less to troubleshoot. All but a few of the optional components can be installed at a later time without restarting the machine.

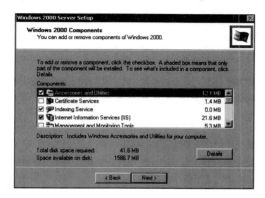

Figure 1.4 Windows 2000 Server upgrade—Windows 2000 Components window.

7. If you do choose to install components, highlight an entry and click Details. A window opens listing the optional components. The example in Figure 1.5 shows the Networking Services list.

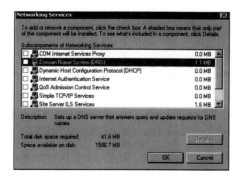

Figure 1.5 Windows 2000 Server upgrade—Networking Services window.

8. Click Next. If you have a modem in the server or an external modem that is PnP compatible, the Modem Dialing Information window opens. Enter your area code and any dial-out prefix such as 9 or 19. This information is used to make Registry entries under HKLM | System | Software | Microsoft | Windows | CurrentVersion | Telephony.

9. Click Next. The Date and Time Settings window opens. Use this window to set the date, time, and time zone. It is very important to set these values correctly because the system uses them for file and authentication time-stamping. See the "Dates and Times" section earlier in this chapter for details.

10. Click Next. The Networking Settings window opens. At this point, Windows 2000 performs additional inspections to determine the state of the network and how to configure the network hardware. If Setup discovers SAP broadcasts and accompanying IPX/SPX traffic, for example, it will load the NWLINK transport drivers. TCP/IP is always loaded.

    NOTE: If you have legacy network adapters that were not configured correctly during the device installation step, the machine may hang at this step. Give Setup lots of time, however, before restarting.

11. After the network drivers have loaded, the Networking Settings window changes to show two configuration choices: Typical Settings and Custom Settings.

    Selecting Typical Settings tells Setup to lease an address from DHCP and use the configuration information in the DHCP response packet. See Chapter 5 for information about DHCP. If a DHCP server is not available, the TCP/IP driver defaults to a random address from the 169.254.0.0 address space.

12. Select the Custom Settings radio button and click Next. The Networking Components window opens (see Figure 1.6). You can use this window to make any special configurations for network services and communication protocols.

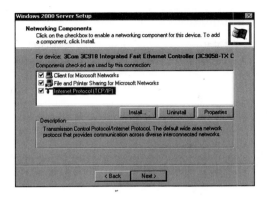

Figure 1.6   Windows 2000 Server upgrade—Networking Components window.

13. For example, double-click Internet Protocol (TCP/IP) to open its
    Properties window (see Figure 1.7). Use this window to enter an IP
    address, default gateway, and DNS server, along with advanced settings for
    WINS and security features, such as TCP/IP filtering and IPSec.

Figure 1.7   Windows 2000 Server upgrade—Internet Protocol (TCP/IP)
Properties window showing example IP address and DNS entries.

14. After you have completed entering your configuration settings, click OK to close and return to the Networking Settings window.

15. Click Next. The Workgroup or Computer Domain window opens (see Figure 1.8). If you want the machine to be in a workgroup, leave the default radio button selected and enter the workgroup name.

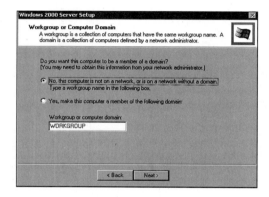

Figure 1.8 Windows 2000 Server upgrade—Workgroup or Computer Domain window.

If you want to join the machine to a domain, select the Yes, Make This Computer A Member Of The Following Domain and enter the domain name. You will need administrator privileges in the domain to complete this step.

If you get an *Unable to Locate Domain Controller* error, the problem is usually with your WINS setup for NT4 domains and DNS for Windows 2000 domains. Click Back to return to the Networking Settings window and make the necessary changes to your TCP/IP configuration.

16. Click Next. The Installing Components window opens and Setup begins copying files from the Windows 2000 CD.

17. After the file copy is complete, the Performing Final Tasks window opens and Setup begins configuring the services and components you installed.

18. After the final tasks have been finished, Setup displays the Completing the Windows 2000 Setup Wizard window. Click Finish to restart.

Final Configuration

After restart, the system boots to `Ctrl+Alt+Del` logon window. Log on and finish configuring the machine.

When you log on to a Windows 2000 domain, you are authenticated via Kerberos at a Windows 2000 domain controller. Details of this logon are in Chapter 6. During this initial logon, a service called USERINIT.EXE sets up the your working environment, creates your user profile, and starts the Explorer shell for you in your security context.

If you are logging on to a newly installed server, the `Configure Your Server` window opens (see Figure 1.9).

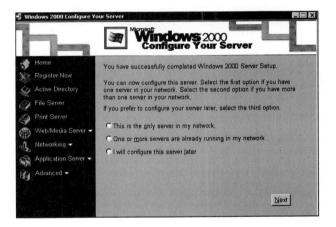

Figure 1.9   `Configure Your Server` window.

This window is controlled by the Server Configuration Wizard, SRVWIZ.DLL, a component of MSHTA.EXE, the Internet Explorer repair tool. The Server Configuration Wizard is controlled by a Registry entry under `HKCU | Software | Microsoft | Windows NT | CurrentVersion | Setup | Welcome | Srvwiz`.

You can select one of the server configuration options and click `Next`. The second window has a set of Java-based drop-down menus that can guide you through configuring the services. Figure 1.10 shows an example.

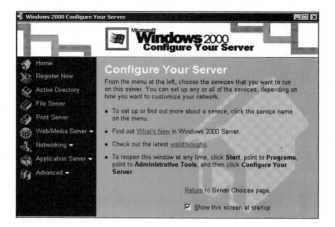

Figure 1.10   `Configure Your Server` window showing
the list of available service control options.

You can close the wizard with the option to not open it again, if you prefer
to configure your server manually. Later, if you change your mind and decide
that a wizard looks like a pretty good way to configure a server, you can
launch it again from the Control Panel using the Configure Your Server
applet.

Event Log Check

Before you begin serious server configuration, you should check the Event
log to make sure no abnormal situations came up during the boot that did
not get reported at the console.

The Event Log is maintained by a comprehensive logging service that is
an integral part of SERVICES.EXE. Event logs are stored in the
`\WINNT\System32\Config` folder along with the Registry hives. You can view the
contents of the logs using the `Event Viewer` console, EVENTVWR.MSC, or
the `Event Viewer` executable, EVENTVWR.EXE.

The `Event Viewer` console can be opened from START | PROGRAMS |
ADMINISTRATIVE TOOLS | EVENT VIEWER. Figure 1.11 shows an example of
the `Event Viewer` console showing the System Log.

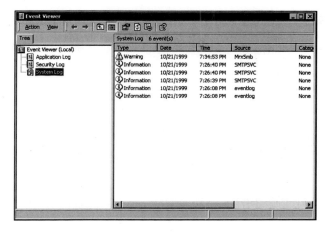

Figure 1.11   `Event Viewer` console showing System
Log entries after installing Windows 2000.

Registry Tip: Event Log Parameters
The Registry keys associated with the Event log are stored under `HKLM | System | CurrentControlSet | Services | EventLog`.

There are three primary Event logs: Application, System, and Security. In addition, a domain controller has a Directory Services log and a File Replication Service log. There is also a DNS log for DNS servers. The Security log is used only if auditing is enabled. See Chapter 14 for information on auditing file system transactions and Chapter 10, "Managing Active Directory Security," for information on auditing Active Directory.

You should get familiar with the normal Event log entries for your system. Some errors happen all the time and are benign. Others should receive your immediate attention. Each entry in the Event log has a description of the event and many have suggestions for troubleshooting.

If you have no abnormal indications and the system appears to be functioning normally, you can declare a job well done and give yourself a week off. If Setup did not complete at all, or had errors, refer to the next section, "Correcting Common Setup Problems." Figure 1.12 shows what an error looks like in the Event log.

Figure 1.12 Sample Event log entry showing error details.

The most common symptoms of problems appear during booting. Let's take a look at exactly what happens when Windows 2000 boots to get a feel for where the problems might show themselves.

This brings us to the last topic in this chapter: what to do if Setup doesn't have a happy ending, or even a happy beginning.

Correcting Common Setup Problems

The first thing to do if something goes wrong is to look for clues about what happened. Setup leaves behind several records of what it did and how it did it. If your problem is not so severe that you can't boot the machine, take a look for the following files under \WINNT:

- **SETUPLOG.TXT.** Describes in detail each driver and services that was loaded and each DLL that was registered during the character phase of setup.

- **SETUPACT.LOG.** Describes the file operations that took place during the graphical phase of setup.

- **SETUPERR.LOG.** Lists any errors that were reported by any devices or services during setup. If this log is not zero bytes, Setup offers to display it at the end of the installation.

You can also boot with the Boot Log option. This lists the drivers that are loaded by NTLDR and SCREG. To do this, press F8 at the BOOT menu and select BOOT LOGGING from the menu. This writes a NETBT.LOG file to the \WINNT directory.

Stop 0x0000007b Inaccessible_Boot_Device

Sometimes the system starts to boot following an installation, but then experiences a Kernel-mode stop (Blue Screen of Death) with a bug-check code of 0x0000007b, Inaccessible_Boot_Device. This problem occurs when the cylinder-head-sector (CHS) configuration reported by BIOS does not match the settings in the Master Boot Record. Frequently, the only way to recover the system is to format the drive and start over. A partition report from Partition Magic or System Commander can help in diagnosing this problem.

Setup Hangs

Of all the possible frustrations that can occur during setup, hangs are the worst because there are not overt symptoms. Setup just reaches a point when it seems to be thinking. And it thinks. And it thinks. You aren't sure whether it's supposed to be thinking that long. There's no benchmark to judge by, at least until you get a few installs under your belt, and you wonder what to do next.

The first rule for dealing with hangs during setup is to do nothing. Wait it out. Delays on the order of hours are not unheard of. The outcome is usually good, and any happy ending is worth waiting for.

If you get a serious hang during the device-detection portion of the graphical phase, press Shift+F10 to open a console window and check the contents of SETUPLOG.TXT. If there are entries, you know something is happening. If the progress bar doesn't move for a couple more hours and no further entries are written to the file, you can throw in the towel. I suggest waiting at least six hours, however.

While you're waiting, search the documentation for known incompatibilities. This includes a search of the following:

- Release Notes on the Windows 2000 CD
- KnowledgeBase listings at www.microsoft.com/technet
- Readme files on the CD
- Vendor Web sites

If you decide to give up and restart, take a few preliminary steps to keep from returning right back to another six-hour wait. Forget about scientific method. The idea is to get the machine running under Windows 2000. You can figure out the precise problem later.

- Go through the preinstallation checklist at the start of this chapter to make sure you didn't miss anything, such as firmware upgrades, turning off shadowing, or setting up legacy components.

- Build a fresh set of Setup disks. Many administrators have reported a successful install after doing just this step; so you might want to try it first.
- Remove the NIC.
- Remove any multimedia boards.
- If you have two monitor cards, remove one.
- Remove any legacy ISA cards.
- Move the PCI cards around to different slots.
- If your machine has multiple PCI buses, try moving all the components to one bus.
- If you have any special SCSI components, such as scanners, take them off the bus.
- If you have any new and fancy equipment, such as FireWire interface cards to your digital camera or parallel port adapters, take them off the machine.
- Turn off ACPI in CMOS, if possible.
- For laptops, take out any PCMCIA cards and remove the unit from its docking station.
- Remove USB components (use PS/2 keyboard, if available).
- Turn off MWAVE and other DSP-based components.

Now try again. If you still get an inordinate wait, on the order of multiple hours, double-check the HCL again to make sure that your system is listed. If it is, strip the machine down to hull metal with nothing more than a vanilla VGA card, a keyboard, and a mouse. Disable everything in CMOS that even smells like an advanced option. Then try again. If the system still hangs, try installing Windows 2000 on a similar piece of hardware. If you get similar results, it's time to call the vendor.

You might also try selecting a different hardware driver. Booting from the Setup disk and when you see the *Setup is inspecting your computer's hardware configuration* message, press F5. Wait until the screen changes to blue and Setup is about to begin. At that point, a list of the available hardware drivers appears. You have the opportunity to load an alternative set. Try one of the other options or get the OEM hardware drivers from your vendor.

Some Devices Fail

If you can get the operating system to load but some functions are not available, you may have device malfunctions or resource conflicts. The Device Manager shows these kinds of problems. There are several ways to open Device Manager:

- Open the Hardware Wizard in Control Panel and select View Hardware Properties.

- Open the Computer Management console by right-clicking the My Computer icon on the desktop and selecting MANAGE from the fly-out menu. Expand the tree under SYSTEM TOOLS | DEVICE MANAGER.

- Open the Device Manager console by right-clicking the My Computer icon, selecting PROPERTIES from the fly-out menu, selecting the Hardware tab, and then clicking Device Manager.

- (My personal favorite) Open the Run window, enter **DEVMGMT.MSC**, and press Enter.

If a device shows a question mark or a red X, double-click it to view the conflict. Some device failures are more common than others. Some have become downright notorious. See Chapter 2 for details on troubleshooting PnP and hardware problems.

You might need to boot to Safe mode to get to the Device Manager. Press F8 at the BOOT menu, and then select SAFE MODE from the option list.

Problems with Setup Disks

You should only use setup disks that have been prepared using MAKEBOOT.EXE or MAKEBT32.EXE. Use fresh disk media and label them clearly. Don't mix Setup disks between Windows 2000 Server, Advanced Server, Datacenter Server, or Professional

- **Unable to boot from Setup disk.** If you build a set of Setup boot disks using Makeboot or Makebt32 and the boot disk subsequently fails to work, you will get the error message *Non-system disk or disk error.* The Windows 2000 Setup disks do not use IO.SYS or MSDOS.SYS, but they are still susceptible to boot sector viruses. Do a virus scan of the disk or build a new set of disks on another machine. If the floppy disk is infected, it's likely that the hard drive will be infected, also. This will cause the subsequent restart after the initial file load to fail. This turns out to be one of the more common problems reported to Microsoft tech support.

- **Improperly prepared Setup disks.** The first Setup disk is bootable because it contains a copy of the Setup bootstrap loader, SETUPLDR.BIN. The disk must be prepared with MAKEBOOT.EXE or MAKEBT32.EXE to recognize this bootstrap loader. The standard NT/Windows 2000 floppy disk looks for NTLDR. DOS boot disks look for IO.SYS.

- **Repeated *Insert Disk 2* messages.** If the first Setup disk boots the machine but you keep getting an *Insert Disk 2* message, the change line may have failed. This is pin 34 on the floppy drive. Test this by booting to DOS, and then running DIR. Change the disk and run another DIR. If you get the same listing, the change line has failed. A common cause of change line failure is a badly seated cable connector or a cable connector that has come loose from the ribbon cable. Replace the ribbon cable with a known good cable and see whether this solves the problem. If not, swap out the floppy drive.

Failure of DHCP or WINS Database Conversion

If the Jet upgrade fails for either or both of the WINS and DHCP databases, do the following:

Procedure 1.5   Solving Failure of DHCP or WINS Database Conversion

1. Stop the service if it has started.
2. Restore the old database from tape.
3. Start the service again. This starts the Jet conversion automatically.

   If the conversion still fails, the database is probably corrupt. The best course of action at that point is to let the WINS database rebuild itself and create the DHCP scopes from scratch.

Problems Copying Files to the Hard Drive

On occasion, Windows will refuse to recognize a hard drive. If the drive is not listed in Setup's partition manager screen, NTDETECT did not recognize it for some reason. There are several possible causes.

- **Check seating for all cable connectors.** Also make sure the cables are all there. Not to mention the drive, if this is a new machine. Boot to DOS and see whether you can see the drive using Fdisk.

- **Verify that shadow RAM and write-back L2 have been disabled in CMOS.** These are also frequent causes of Kernel-mode stops and corrupted data. Windows 2000 handles all disk caching. You will get better and more reliable performance without a hardware cache unless it is certified to work with Windows 2000.

- **Supported disk translations.** Check that drives have not been configured with a special disk manager that is not compatible with Windows 2000. Some unique flavors of sector maps are not recognized.

- **Scan for viruses.** Windows 2000 will not install on an infected hard drive. Scan the drive using a DOS or Windows virus detection tool.

- **Check for proper Master Boot Record.** The Master Boot Record might be corrupt. Boot to DOS and run `Fdisk /mbr` to build a new boot record.

- **SCSI terminations.** If you have a SCSI drive, make sure that the SCSI cable is terminated correctly. Even if the drive worked fine under DOS or Windows, it might fail under Windows 2000 owing to the different nature of the SCSI driver. Also check to make sure that the SCSI drive you used for Setup is still listed on the SCSI scan that runs during POST.

- **SCSI boot settings.** Make sure that SCSI boot drive settings are correct. You may think you're booting to one drive, but are actually booting to another.

- **IDE recognized in CMOS.** If you have a large IDE or EIDE drive, make sure that the drive configuration is correct in CMOS. If the drive uses a cylinder translation utility, such as Ontrack, make sure it is certified to work with Windows 2000.

- **No older drives.** Support has been dropped for old ESDI and WD1003 drives. It's not likely that you have these in a Pentium-class production machine, but you might have done a motherboard swap.

- **Problems with new ATA66 interface cards.** Quite a few ATA66 interface cards are just now coming on the market and a few of the drivers have been rushed. If your ATA66 interface isn't recognized or causes Kernel-mode stop errors, check with the vendor for the most current driver. They are probably coding it while they talk to you on the phone.

- **No DriveSpace volumes.** Make sure that the installation volume has not been compressed using DriveSpace or DoubleSpace. These compression utilities are not supported by Windows 2000.

- **No legacy dynamic partitioning.** Some partitioning utilities may cause Setup to fail. If you use a partitioning utility, check it for compatibiltiy with Windows 2000. The most current version of Partition Magic for example, will work with Windows 2000.

Missing or Incorrect CD-ROM Drives

If Setup prompts you over and over and over again to insert the Setup CD-ROM, you know you have an unsupported or misconfigured CD-ROM drive.

- **Verify supported drive.** Some CD-ROM drives are not supported by Windows 2000, especially older drives with proprietary interfaces. Some drives that worked in NT4 were retired and are no longer supported in Windows 2000. As with all hardware, check to make sure your CD-ROM drive is on the HCL.

- **Timing problems.** CD-ROM drives that work fine under DOS/Windows or Windows 95/98 sometimes fail to work under Windows 2000 because of tighter timing specifications. If you have a SCSI or modified SCSI interface, using the interface BIOS routines to check the device.

- **SCSI terminations.** If you have a SCSI CD-ROM drive, check the device list displayed during the POST scan. If the drive does not appear, check the power connections, ribbon or external cable connections, bus terminations, and possible conflicts with SCSI ID. If the SCSI ID is listed with no name or vendor information, the drive might not be supported by the SCSI BIOS or the drive might be defective.

- **IDE configuration.** If the CD-ROM drive is on an IDE bus that is shared with a hard drive, check for proper master/slave configuration. Check CMOS to make sure the controller interface is enabled.

- **Workaround for unsupported CD-ROM drives.** If your CD-ROM drive is not supported but you still want to load Windows 2000 on the machine, boot to DOS, load the ASPI drivers and MSCDEX, then use Winnt /b to begin Setup. You can't use the CD-ROM after loading Windows 2000, but you can always swap out the drive later or wait for the vendor to write Windows 2000 drivers.

Missing or Non-Functioning Network Adapters

Network adapters are a common cause of Setup hangs and PnP disasters. This is not as true for newer adapters with current WDM (Windows Driver Model) drivers, but older cards and legacy cards that were revised right up until the very last second before pressing the CD might just be a little on the touchy side.

- **Windows 95 operation no guarantee.** Don't assume that the PnP features of a network adapter will work on Windows 2000 because they work on Windows 95. Windows 2000 PnP is much more aggressive about changing resources and much less tolerant of shared resources.

- **Incorrect resource allocation.** Use Device Manager to check the resources that have been assigned to the adapter. If there is a conflict, the adapter icon will have either a yellow circle with an exclamation point or a red circle with an X. Double-click on the network adapter to open the `Adapter Properties` window. Select the `Resources` tab.

- **Improper PCI resource sharing.** PCI adapters rarely have a problem with RAM base conflicts, but they can get I/O base and IRQ conflicts if the system BIOS attempts to share resources or if HAL changes the PCI settings. If this happens, disable PnP in CMOS, and then assign the resources manually. If you have a fleet of machines with this same motherboard, BIOS, and network adapter, either look for a different driver or think about hiring help for your deployment.

- **Verify the physical layer.** If the network drivers load but you cannot see the network, you may have a plain old bad adapter (POBA). See whether you can ping the loopback address, 127.0.0.1. This checks the IP stack down to the NDIS MAC driver, which implies that the ASIC controller on the network adapter is functioning properly. The problem could then be with the transceiver, the cables and connectors, or the hub or switch. Use known good cable or test the port connection from another computer. Make sure you don't have crossover cable installed; that is, cable that swaps the 1-2 and 3-6 pairs for use in connecting hubs together.

- **Duplex mismatches.** A very common problem when using 10/100Mbps adapters and switches is a mismatch between duplex settings at the adapter and the switch. In full-duplex mode, collision detection is turned off. This permits the port and the NIC to transmit and receive at the same time. If the switch is still in half-duplex mode, however, it will interpret full-duplex transmissions as a collision and reject the frame. The network response turns to molasses and the CRC/alignment check error rate at the switch skyrockets. If you have an autosensing 10/100 NIC, make sure the hub is properly configured. Don't trust the link lights. Try another computer in the same port.

Video Problems

If Setup can't detect the make and model of video adapter installed in the machine, it will fall back on standard VGA drivers. Video problems are another common cause of Setup hangs. You may also get Kernel-mode stop errors. Check the HCL to see whether the adapter is supported.

- **Loss of video sync.** If you change video settings and lose the display as soon as you accept the changes, do nothing. The system returns to its old configuration after 15 seconds. If this does not happen, restart and press F8 at the BOOT menu. Select SAFE MODE from the ADVANCED OPTIONS menu. This loads standard VGA drivers and gives you the chance to poke around for a different configuration or driver that works. Avoid the VGA MODE option in the ADVANCED OPTIONS menu. This also loads stock VGA drivers, but does so with persistent Registry entries rather than the transient ones used by Safe mode.

- **Unable to get full range of video options.** Windows 2000 relies totally on PnP to discover the video adapter and monitor. If PnP gets the wrong driver, or if the driver on the CD is not recent enough, you may not get the full set of horizontal sweep rates or color densities that the card is advertised to have. Check the vendor's Web site for updated drivers.

Inappropriate Hardware Profiles

If you upgrade an NT4 laptop that is configured to use hardware profiles, the profiles are retained even though you should not need them in Windows 2000 thanks to PnP. You should delete the old hardware profiles and see whether the laptop properly recognizes its docked and undocked conditions. This is likely to work, even on older laptops, but some of the power management features may be unavailable.

Moving Forward

Installing a new operating system of any kind is easiest when starting from a clean slate. Upgrades are much more complex. The next chapter covers upgrading to Windows 2000 from NT4 Server, NT4 Workstation, and Windows 9x. It also covers planning and executing a deployment of Windows 2000 Professional using the new Remote Installation Service (RIS) in Windows 2000.

2

Performing Upgrades and Automated Installations

Chapter 1, "Installing and Configuring Windows 2000," covered the prerequisites and preparations for installing Windows 2000 and detailed steps of a clean installation. This chapter continues the discussion of installations, but the focus shifts to upgrades.

There is a clear upgrade path from nearly all Windows implementations to Windows 2000. Most organizations have made the leap to a 32-bit desktop of one form or another, so the most common upgrades are from some flavor of NT4 or from some flavor of Windows 9x. This chapter includes the following details:

- Functional overview of an NT4 upgrade

- Step-by-step description of an NT4 upgrade

- Functional overview of a Windows 9x upgrade

- Step-by-step description of a Windows 9x upgrade

- Automating Windows 2000 deployments using cloning, Remote Installation Services, and scripted installs

No discussion of installing or upgrading Windows 2000 would be complete without a look at the most useful administrative tool in the product, the capability to remotely manage using Terminal Services.

Before concentrating on upgrades, however, it's important to get a feel for how Windows 2000 boots and initializes. Aside from hardware incompatibilities, which were covered in the preceding chapter, the most common problems encountered during upgrades involve changes made to the system that affect the way it starts.

Functional Description of the Windows 2000 Boot Process

Computers are like airplanes: They are most prone to accidents during take-off and landing. This topic contains a detailed analysis of the Windows 2000 boot process for use in troubleshooting upgrade and setup problems.

Power On Self Test (POST)

When you turn on any Intel-based computer, the system starts out with a *Power On Self Test* (POST). Specific actions during the POST vary from system to system. A short beep at the end indicates a successful completion.

The final step in the POST is a handoff to an INT13 routine in BIOS that checks for a bootable device. Usually this routine starts at the A: drive followed by the C: drive, which is either the master IDE drive on the primary IDE controller or a SCSI drive identified in the SCSI BIOS as bootable. Some systems also support CD-ROM booting.

Initial Bootstrap Loading

If the system finds a *Master Boot Record* (MBR) on the C: drive, it loads the executable code in the MBR and uses it to scan the partition table at the end of the MBR to find the sector/offset of the active boot partition.

If the MBR cannot find suitable entries in the partition table, it displays the error *Invalid Partition Table*. If it finds a partition table but cannot locate the start of the active partition, it displays either the error *Error Loading Operating System* or the error *Missing Operating System*.

When the executable code in the MBR finds the active partition, it loads the first sector (512 bytes) into memory at location 0x700h. This is called the partition boot sector, or more commonly just the boot sector. The boot sector contains executable code designed to find and load a secondary bootstrap loader. On a DOS machine, this is IO.SYS. On a Windows 2000/NT machine, the bootstrap loader is NTLDR. The executable code in the boot sector cannot read a file system, so NTLDR must be in the root of the boot drive.

If NTLDR is missing or will not load, the boot sector code displays error messages, such as *A disk read error has occurred* or *NTLDR is missing* or *NTLDR is compressed*. In any event, the message includes the instructions *Press Ctrl+Alt+Del to restart*.

NTLDR Versions

The Windows 2000 version of NTLDR can load the NT4 boot files, but the opposite is not true. The 4.x version of NTLDR will not load Windows 2000. Keep this in mind if you apply an NT4 service pack or do an emergency repair on a dual-boot machine while booted to NT4. If you overwrite NTLDR, you cannot boot to Windows 2000.

If you accidentally overwrite NTLDR on a dual-boot machine, you can replace it with a copy of NTLDR file from another Windows 2000 machine. The same file is used for Server and Professional.

NTLDR

When NTLDR executes, it initializes the video hardware and puts the screen in 80x25 mode with a black background. It then switches the processor to Protected mode to support 32-bit memory addressing and initializes miniature versions of the NTFS and FAT file system drivers contained in the NTLDR code itself. These file system drivers permit NTLDR to see enough of the drive to load the remaining Windows 2000 system files.

Now NTLDR locates a file called BOOT.INI, which contains the Windows 2000 BOOT menu. See "Working with BOOT.INI" later in this chapter for details about the entries in BOOT.INI. If NTLDR cannot find BOOT.INI, it displays the error *Windows 2000 could not start because the following file is missing or corrupt: BOOT.INI*. If BOOT.INI is present but does not contain valid entries, any number of errors can appear. Generally they indicate a problem with ARC paths or ARC firmware.

If you install Windows 2000 in addition to an existing operating system, such as Windows 9x or DOS, the boot sector from the previous operating system is saved in file called BOOTSECT.DOS. The alternate operating system becomes a selection in the BOOT.INI menu. If the alternate operating system is selected at boot time, NTLDR loads the contents of BOOT-SECT.DOS into memory at file location 700h, shifts back to Real mode, and turns control over to the executable code in the boot sector image.

If a Windows 2000 partition is selected from the BOOT menu, NTLDR checks the partition for a copy of the Windows 2000 operating system kernel, NTOSKRNL.EXE, and its associate Hardware Abstraction Layer driver, HAL.DLL and video driver, BOOTVID.DLL. If it finds these files, it loads their images but does not execute them quite yet. If NTLDR does not find

NTOSKRNL.EXE, it gives the error *Windows 2000 could not start because the following file is missing or corrupt:\<winnt root>\system32\ NTOSKRNL.EXE.* The most likely cause of this error is an incorrect BOOT.INI entry, although corruption of the file system on the volume can also be the culprit.

Before NTLDR can execute the kernel image, it needs to know something about the hardware. This is the cue for NTDETECT.COM.

Alternative SCSI Driver

Under most circumstances, if a system uses SCSI hard drives, the SCSI interface has a BIOS that determines which devices on the bus are mass storage. It reports these devices in order by SCSI ID. If a SCSI adapter does not have a BIOS, or if the BIOS is disabled, NTLDR needs a way to determine the drive location specified by the ARC path in BOOT.INI.

When Setup detects that a SCSI interface does not have a functioning BIOS, it takes the SCSI interface driver, copies it to the root of the boot partition, and renames it as NTBOOTDD.SYS. If the BOOT.INI entry indicates that the mass storage device is a SCSI drive handled by an interface without a BIOS, NTLDR can load NTBOOTDD.SYS and use the minidriver to communicate with the drive.

NTDETECT.COM

NTLDR uses a hardware recognizer, NTDETECT.COM, to gather the same kind of information on an Intel machine that a RISC machine has in firmware. Don't confuse NTDETECT with the Plug and Play Manager. PnP enumeration happens much further along in the boot process.

NTDETECT looks for the following hardware configurations. (The CPU type and FPU type are detected later on by NTOSKRNL.EXE and HAL.DLL.)

- Machine ID
- Bus/adapter type
- Video
- Keyboard
- Communication port
- Parallel port
- Floppy drive
- Mouse

NTDETECT uses this information to build a data structure in memory that is used later on by the kernel driver to construct a Registry hive called Hardware.

Now the scene shifts back to NTLDR, which has been waiting in the wings to start loading service drivers.

Service Driver Loads

NTLDR opens the System hive in the Registry and checks the Select key to find the CurrentControlSet. It then scans the list of Services keys in the CurrentControlSet looking for devices with a Start value of 0, indicating Service_Boot_Start, and 1, indicating Service_System_Start. It loads these drivers in the order specified by the Group value under Control | Service Group Order.

At this point, the console shows a *Starting Windows 2000* message along the bottom of the screen with a progress bar that slides along as the drivers load. When this is complete, NTLDR initializes NTOSKRNL.EXE and hands over the images in memory.

Kernel Initialization

When NTOSKRNL starts, it initializes HAL.DLL and BOOTVID.DLL. The screen now shifts to Graphic mode. Then NTOSKRNL initializes the drivers prepped by NTLDR. It also uses the information from NTDETECT.COM to create a volatile Hardware hive in the Registry and calls on the Session Manager, SMSS.EXE, to do a little preliminary housekeeping.

Session Manager

Session Manager reads its own key in the System hive under HKLM | System | CurrentControlSet | Control | Session Manager to find entries under BootExecute. By default, this includes AUTOCHK, a boot-time version of CHKDSK. Session Manager also sets up the paging file, PAGEFILE.SYS, to hold memory pages swapped out of RAM.

Registry Tip: Forcing AUTOCHK to Repair

AUTOCHK normally runs in Read-Only mode, so it reports problems but does not repair them. You can force AUTOCHK to repair file system problems (similar to running Chkdsk /f) by putting a /p after the entry in the Registry.

Key:	HKLM | System | CurrentControlSet | Control | Session Manager
Value:	BootExecute
Data:	Autochk * /p

After Session Manager finishes its chores, it does the following two things simultaneously:

- Loads the console logon service, WINLOGON.EXE, to start the authentication verification process. WINLOGON starts the Local Security Authority Subsystem, LSASS.EXE, and the print spooler, SPOOLSS.EXE, along with their supporting function libraries.

- Loads the Services Controller, SCREG.EXE, to finish loading the rest of the devices and services.

Users are sometimes mystified by the long delay between entering their credentials at the logon window and getting to the desktop. If the system has quite a few background processes to start, it takes SCREG a while to finish up. Meanwhile, WINLOGON has done its job and is twiddling its thumbs waiting. So is the user.

If SCREG loads the drivers and starts the services without incident, and WINLOGON can authenticate a user at the console, then the boot is considered successful. Happy ending. Bring up the violin music. Fade to credits.

If it cannot start a device or service, it takes action as defined in the associated Registry key. This runs the gamut from putting a simple message in the Event Log to crashing the system with a stop error. If the problem is not catastrophic, SCREG displays a console message telling you that a problem occurred and that you should check the Event Log. This console message does not always appear, so you should always check the log when you start a server. Histories of abnormal starts should be investigated and the problem isolated and corrected.

Working with BOOT.INI

As shown in the previous discussion, the Windows 2000 bootstrap loader, NTLDR, relies on BOOT.INI to locate the Windows 2000 boot directory. This section contains details about the structure of BOOT.INI. If you encounter strange behavior during restart following an upgrade, or when adding new mass storage hardware, you can start your investigations with a look at BOOT.INI.

System File Attributes and Superhidden Definition

The BOOT.INI file attributes are set to System and read-only by default. This prevents a casual user from modifying or deleting the file. If you need to modify the contents of BOOT.INI, use Attrib to toggle the read-only attribute.

The remaining system files, such as NTLDR, NTDETECT.COM, and NTBOOTDD.SYS, are in a superhidden state. This is a new configuration in Windows 2000 and is defined as having both the System and Hidden attributes set.

Here is an example BOOT.INI file:

```
[boot loader]
timeout=30
default=multi(0)disk(0)rdisk(0)partition(1)\WINNT

[operating systems]
multi(0)disk(0)rdisk(0)partition(1)\WINNT="Microsoft Windows 2000 Server" /fastdetect
c:\= "MS/DOS"
```

The long, inscrutable entry under `[operating systems]` is the *Advanced RISC Computing* path (ARC path). The ARC path is a pointer that leads NTLDR to a Windows 2000 partition. ARC syntax uses this convention:

```
controller()disk()rdisk()partition()\systemroot="menu listing"
```

Here is what each entry means:

`controller()`—Interface Type

The three possible entries are

- `multi()`. Indicates IDE drives and SCSI drives with an onboard BIOS. The number in parentheses is the ordinal ID of the IDE or SCSI controller. If Windows 2000 is installed on a drive connected to the secondary IDE controller, the ARC entry would be `multi(1)`.

- `scsi()`. Indicates a SCSI controller with no onboard BIOS or a BIOS that has been disabled. This is a legacy entry from classic NT and no longer used in Windows 2000.

- `signature()`. Indicates that the drive is not accessible by standard INT13 calls and requires special handling by NTLDR. See the section titled "Special Arc Paths for Non-INT13 Drives" at the end of this section for more information. The number in parenthesis is a signature written to the MBR of the disk when it is partitioned during setup.

If the controller type is `signature()` and the drive is on a SCSI bus with an interface that does not have a BIOS, NTLDR uses the SCSI miniport driver in NTBOOTDD.SYS to read the drives and find the matching signature.

`disk()`—SCSI ID

The `disk()` entry was used in conjunction with the `scsi()` controller type to indicate the SCSI ID of the disk where the boot files are located. It is no longer required in Windows 2000 because the `signature()` entry identifies the drive uniquely without the SCSI ID. For controller designations of `multi()`, the value for `disk()` is always 0.

rdisk()—Relative Disk Location

The rdisk() entry is used in conjunction with multi() to indicate the relative disk location. For IDE drives, the relative disk location is determined by the master/slave designation. For example, the slave drive on the first IDE controller would have an ARC designator of multi(0)disk(0)rdisk(1).

For SCSI drives, the relative disk location is determined by the device scan performed by the SCSI BIOS during POST. Generally, the scan order matches the SCSI ID order. If the BIOS reports that there are three drives on the bus, for example, the ARC designator for the third drive would be multi(0)disk(0)rdisk(2) regardless of the SCSI ID. If you select a drive other than 0 to be the boot drive, the relative disk locations would change.

For controller designations of signature(), the value for rdisk() is always 0 because the system uses the MBR signature to find the drive.

partition()—Boot Partition Sequence Number

This is the sequential number of the boot partition. Note that this sequence starts with 1, not 0. See the sidebar titled "Partition Number Changes" for curious aspects to the numbering sequences.

\systemroot—Windows 2000 System Directory

The system directory is \WINNT by default, and that is the directory used in all examples in this book. A different name can be chosen during setup. The environment variable %systemroot% displays the name of the system directory. You should have only one system root directory on any given partition. Microsoft strongly discourages having multiple 32-bit Windows installations in the same partition because files affect system operation in locations other than %systemroot%.

"menu listing"—Menu Text

The text in quotation marks is displayed as the menu listing in the BOOT menu. You can change this text if it helps your users to navigate to the correct entry; under normal circumstances, however, users could really care less and don't want to see the menu anyway.

ARC Path Examples

Assume, for example, that you have a machine configured with several versions of Windows 2000 and NT along with a dual-boot to DOS. The drives and partitions are set up as shown in Table 2.1.

Table 2.1   **Example Partition Tables**

SCSI ID #	Drive #	Partition #	OS
ID 0	C	1	DOS
ID 0	D	2	NTW 4.0
ID 1	E	1	NTS 4.0
ID 2	F	1	W2KP
ID 2	G	2	W2KS

Here are the ARC paths for each boot partition:

```
multi(0)disk(0)rdisk(0)partition(2)\WINNT="Windows NT Workstation Version 4.0"
multi(0)disk(0)rdisk(1)partition(1)\WINNT="Windows NT Server Version 4.0"
multi(0)disk(0)rdisk(2)partition(1)\WINNT="Windows 2000 Professional" /fastdetect
multi(0)disk(0)rdisk(2)partition(2)\WINNT="Windows 2000 Server" /fastdetect
c:\="MS/DOS"
```

Partition Number Changes

There are a few subtleties to the way ARC paths are derived. It is possible to cause a change in the partition numbering without realizing it and, thus, cause the system to fail to boot.

Putting aside dynamic drives under Logical Disk Manager for the moment, a basic drive can have up to four primary partitions. The primary partitions are numbered sequentially; any logical drives in the extended partition are numbered. If a drive has one primary partition and an extended partition containing two logical drives, for example, the ARC path for a Windows 2000 installation on the second logical drive in the extended partition would have a partition() entry of partition(3).

Let's say there is still lots of free space left at the end of this disk so the user installs a second copy of Windows 2000 in that free space and partitions it as a primary partition. This is the only option because a disk can have only one extended partition.

When the second primary partition is created, it gets an ARC designator of partition(2) because it is the second primary partition.

The partition() entry for the first Windows 2000 installation is now invalid. Its entry should be partition(4) because it is in the second logical drive in the extended partition. When the user attempts to boot to that entry in BOOT.INI, NTLDR fails to find a copy of NTOSKRNL and displays an error.

This can be fixed by booting to the new Windows 2000 installation and modifying the BOOT.INI.

BOOT.INI Switches

Here are the options and switches used in BOOT.INI:

- **Timeout.** This determines the pause duration before NTLDR goes to the default partition. The default is 30 seconds. See the sidebar titled "Setting BOOT Menu Delay Times" for information on changing the default delay.

- **Default.** This determines the partition that will be used to boot the system if no action is taken.

- **[Operating Systems].** Lists the bootable partitions by their ARC paths.

- **/fastdetect.** Skips PnP enumeration of serial interfaces until the graphic portion of the system loads.

- **/pcilock.** Disables most of the automatic resource allocation functions of HAL. This prevents HAL from changing resource allocations made by the PnP BIOS. This is a useful tool for correcting system hangs.

- **/sos.** Displays the name of the drivers as they load along with the results of the AUTOCHK scan that is done at each system boot. Think of this switch as "Show Our System."

- **/maxmem.** Used for troubleshooting memory-related problems. This switch limits the amount of real memory the system will use. If you think you have a bad bank of memory, set this value below the second bank. If your problems disappear, replace the memory. You can also use this switch for testing memory-related performance issues.

- **/scsiordinal:x.** Differentiates between identical SCSI controllers. If you add a second controller and boot to a Blue Screen stop, the SCSI driver may be binding to the wrong controller. Set the x value to 1 if the Windows 2000 files are on the second controller.

- **/cmdcons.** Used in conjunction with loading the Recovery Console.

- **/win95dos** and **/win95.** These switches emulate the dual-boot features in Windows 9x. They are used in conjunction with BOOTSECT.DOS files that contain Windows 95 bootstrap.

Setting Boot Menu Delay Times

Users often want to change the BOOT menu delay time. "It takes the darned thing long enough to boot as it is," goes the call to the help desk. If you are the technician taking the call, you probably don't want to talk someone through editing BOOT.INI to change the Timeout value. Instead, use the user interface as follows:

Procedure 2.1   Changing the Boot Menu Delay Time

1. Right-click the My Computer icon and select PROPERTIES from the fly-out menu. The System Properties window opens.

2. Select the Advanced tab.

3. Click Startup and Recovery.

4. Select a new top entry for the Default Operating System under System Startup.

If you want to skip the menu completely, set Timeout to 0 by editing BOOT.INI or uncheck the setting in the user interface. You can still use the F8 key to bring up special boot selections, but you have to be quick. It's better to leave the time at 1–3 seconds.

If you want to disable the countdown timer completely, so that the menu displays forever until a selection is made, edit BOOT.INI and change the Timeout setting to –1. You cannot make this change from the user interface.

Special ARC Paths for Non-INT13 Drives

When the user selects an entry in BOOT.INI, NTLDR reads the ARC path to find the drive and partition and then makes an INT13 BIOS call to load the boot sector. In three instances, this INT13 call could fail in a supported configuration:

- The boot partition is larger than 7.8GB.
- The boot partition geometry has more than 1,024 cylinders.
- The SCSI BIOS has disabled under PnP.

In classic NT, the first two instances are not supported at all. The entire contents of the boot partition in classic NT must fall within the 24-bit addressing scheme of a standard INT13 call, which limits the size of the boot partition to approximately 7.8GB. Classic NT handles the lack of a SCSI BIOS by including the `scsi()` controller entry in the ARC path. This was a trigger for NTLDR to load the SCSI miniport driver in NTBOOTDD.SYS and look for the drive specified by the `disk()` entry.

Windows 2000 supports all three special INT13 configurations. In the case of the large drives or drives with non-standard geometry, it uses newer INT13 extensions that are part of the PC97 specification. These extensions permit access beyond the 7.8GB limit.

The case of SCSI drives on an interface with no BIOS is a little trickier because the controller ID used by the classic NT ARC path could be changed by PnP. A way of uniquely identifying the SCSI drive without using the interface number is needed.

To signal NTLDR that it needs to use INT13 extensions or NTBOOTDD.SYS, Windows 2000 introduced a new ARC controller type called `signature()`. Here is an example ARC path using this controller type:

```
signature(ea1aa9c7)disk(0)rdisk(0)partition(1)\WINNT="Microsoft Windows 2000 Professional"
/fastdetect
```

When NTLDR sees a `signature()` entry in an ARC path, it scans the mass storage devices looking for a drive with an MBR that contains the signature. The signature is placed in the MBR by Setup when the partition is created. Classic NT also marked drives with an MBR signature. During an upgrade, if the original BOOT.INI has a `scsi()` controller entry, it is replaced with a `signature()` entry and the existing MBR signature is inserted in the parentheses.

The Windows 2000 Logical Disk Manager also uses the MBR signature when creating the LDM database for a dynamic disk. See Chapter 12, "Configuring Data Storage," for details.

If the drive designated by `signature()` entry has a boot sector beyond the 7.8GB limit, NTLDR can find the boot sector using INT13 extension calls. The maximum boot partition size in Windows 2000 is 32GB, based on the FAT32 volume size limit.

If the `signature()` entry points at a SCSI drive with an interface that has no BIOS, NTLDR loads the SCSI miniport driver in NTBOOTDD.SYS and uses it to locate the drive.

This `signature()` method of identifying drives in BOOT.INI has its drawbacks. If the disk signature is overwritten by a virus or the MBR is corrupted and must be overwritten, NTLDR will be unable to locate the drive and it will give the error *Windows 2000 could not start because of a computer disk hardware configuration problem.*

If you encounter this problem, you must boot from a fault-tolerant boot disk to get the system up. See Chapter 3, "Adding Additional Hardware," for instructions on booting to Windows 2000 from a floppy disk. The boot disk must have a copy of the BOOT.INI from the system with the large drive so that the signature will be the same. If you are an NT administrator accustomed to having a generic boot disk for your servers and workstations, you will need to change your recovery strategies somewhat.

After you have gotten the system up, you can use the `Disk Management` console to write a new signature. Then you must read the signature using a hex editor, such as Disk Probe from the Resource Kit and modify the BOOT.INI file accordingly.

NT4 Upgrade Overview

When you upgrade, you can expect Setup to do the following:

- Preserve the Explorer shell configuration or convert a Program Manager shell to Explorer format along with all local and roaming user profiles stored.

- Retain the computer's SID and domain membership.

- Retain the contents of the SAM and LSA databases so that existing user accounts remain intact along with their group memberships and the system security policies. The network authentication mechanism changes to Kerberos rather than NT LAN Manager Challenge-Response, but this is transparent and does not affect the structure of the security databases.

- Maintain the Registry entries affecting application configuration. There may still be issues regarding application compatibility with Windows 2000 to contend with after the upgrade is complete.

- Upgrade network drivers to the new NDIS 5 drivers while retaining current IP and IPX addresses, transport driver settings, drive mappings, printer captures, and remote access configurations.
- Upgrade base NT services, such as DNS, DHCP, WINS, IIS, and *Services for Macintosh* (SFM). New features and functionality are incorporated and the management interfaces change to MMC consoles.

Upgrade Paths

Windows 2000 supports upgrading the following Windows platforms:

- **NT4 Workstation.** You can only upgrade NT4 Workstation to Windows 2000 Professional. There is no direct upgrade path to Windows 2000 Server.
- **NT4 Server.** You can only upgrade NT4 Server to Windows 2000 Server or Advanced Server. There is no downgrade path to Professional. Upgrade paths to Windows 2000 Datacenter Server have not been published. Watch Microsoft's Web site for further information.
- **Domain controllers.** When you upgrade a domain controller, the contents of the security databases in the Registry are migrated to the Active Directory. There is a long list of prerequisites and precautions to consider before doing this upgrade. Refer to Chapter 9, "Deploying Windows 2000 Domains," for details.
- **NT3.51 Server.** You can upgrade NT3.51 Server to Windows 2000 Server, but not Windows 2000 Professional.
- **NT3.51 Workstation.** You can upgrade NT3.51 Workstation to Windows 2000 Professional, but not to Windows 2000 Server.
- **Windows Terminal Server.** You can upgrade directly to Windows 2000 Server or Advanced Server. All WTS functionality is now part of the Terminal Services feature in the core operating system.
- **BackOffice 4.5 and Small Business Server.** Microsoft plans on releasing a series of service packs to the various components of BackOffice, enabling them to run on Windows 2000. Get more information at www.microsoft.com/backofficeserver/prodinfo/windows2000.htm.
- **NT4 Enterprise Edition.** You must upgrade to Windows 2000 Advanced Server to retain the same functionality.

- **NT4 Windows Terminal Server.** The Terminal Services in Windows 2000 are a complete replacement for WTS. If you are running Citrix MetaFrame on top of WTS to get *Independent Computing Architecture* (ICA) support, you must upgrade to MetaFrame 1.8 for Windows 2000. Get more information at the Citrix Web site, www.citrix.com.
- **Citrix WinFrame.** You cannot upgrade from any version of WinFrame to Windows 2000. You must do a fresh install of Windows 2000 and then install MetaFrame 1.8 for Windows 2000.

NT4 and Windows 3.51 can be running any combination of service packs and hot fixes. If you plan on dual-booting with NT4, you must install Service Pack 4 or higher to get the updated NTFS.SYS driver. You cannot dual-boot between NT3.51 and Windows 2000.

All features in the NT4 Option Pack have been incorporated into the core Windows 2000 product. Certain functions of *Routing and Remote Access Services* (RRAS) are implemented differently, and dial-up changes significantly.

Upgrade Preliminaries

The installation prerequisites and checklists in Chapter 1 are equally valid for upgrades. If you have incompatible hardware or unsupported configurations or applications that are not certified to run under Windows 2000, you can expect to have problems. Do a thorough inventory of hardware and software before upgrading.

If you are upgrading an existing NT4 server or workstation, don't assume that the machine will work fine under Windows 2000. It doesn't matter how stable the machine has been in the past. Vendors tend to push the performance envelope by tuning the mix of processor, cache, chipset, BIOS, memory, bus, and peripherals to run a particular way under NT4. That same box might turn into a support nightmare when asked to run Windows 2000. This is especially true for older machines that were built before *Advanced Configuration and Power Instrumentation* (ACPI) features were common.

This is not to say that you shouldn't upgrade an older machine. Just be aware that administrators like yourself have lost many hours and millimeters of stomach lining chasing compatibility problems. Don't assume that you can upgrade a server over a lunch hour and have it ready for the afternoon shift.

You should take a few additional steps to help ensure a smooth transition.

Prepare WINS and DHCP Databases

Windows 2000 includes a newer version of the Jet database technology used to support services, such as WINS and DHCP. When you upgrade, Setup runs a JETCONV utility to convert the Jet databases to the new format. This conversion does not always proceed smoothly. If the existing Jet databases are corrupt or unstable, the upgrade could fail and leave you without WINS or DHCP services. Before upgrading, compact and clean up the Jet databases as follows:

Procedure 2.2   **Preparing DHCP and WINS for Upgrade**

1. If you have no secondary WINS or DHCP server, you might want to set one up just in case. It is much easier to recover a database by replicating it than restoring it from tape and rerunning JETCONV.

2. Scavenge the WINS database and make sure that there are no tombstones or other inconsistencies.

3. Reconcile the DHCP database and make sure there are no address inconsistencies.

4. Stop WINS.

5. Stop DHCP.

6. Run JETPACK.EXE on each database to compact it, clean out any old entries, and re-index. Use this syntax:

```
jetpack -40db wins.mdb
```

   or

```
jetpack -40db dhcp.mdb
```

   The -40db tells the packer that this is a version 4.0 database. If you are upgrading an NT3.51 server, use -351db instead.

7. Start WINS and verify normal operation.

8. Start DHCP and verify normal operation.

9. Begin the Windows 2000 upgrade.

Prepare to Upgrade IIS Web Services and IE

Windows 2000 ships with the most current version of IE 5. If you upgrade a system running an older browser, Setup should retain proxy settings, history files, cookies, and temp files.

Microsoft responds to new forms of Internet attack very quickly. Often the patch is out within hours. There is very little regression testing done, either to the base OS or for any upgrades. If you install an NT4 hot fix just before upgrading, you might lose the hot fix or it might not work correctly. Keep close tabs on the trade magazines and Microsoft's Security Advisor Web site, www.microsoft.com/security. Don't upgrade a production Web server until you are sure all fixes and features have been synched.

If you are running NT4 Workstation Peer Web Services, it is upgraded to IIS 5 in Windows 2000. This is not the case for Peer Web Services running on Windows 95/98. They will not be upgraded. If you have Web Services loaded on Windows 95/98, uninstall it before upgrading. You can elect to install Peer Web Services during the upgrade.

Prepare for Possible Service Interruptions

If you are upgrading a server that runs a large number of network support services, you might want to build a temporary server to host at least some of those services until you get a satisfactory upgrade. A minor upgrade glitch might render the server unavailable for a considerable period of time.

If you have a server that is running Exchange, WINS, DNS, DHCP, TCP/IP printing, and maybe even acting as a *Remote Access Service* (RAS) server and RRAS direct-dial router, you'll lose a lot of functionality if the upgrade fails.

Moving these services can require some work because they involve changing IP addresses at the clients, so you may want to configure a standby server with the same name and running the same services. Keep it off the wire until you need it. If you have to use this standby server, you may need to delete the old server name from the domain and rejoin the new server.

Upgrade Differences Between Server and Professional

The setup steps for Windows 2000 Server and Professional are virtually identical. In fact, the core code of both products is the same. Microsoft imposes limits on Windows 2000 Professional to differentiate it and justify the price difference. Table 2.2 lists these differences.

Table 2.2 **Windows 2000 Server and Professional Differences**

Feature	Server	Professional
Concurrent connections	Unlimited	10
Concurrent dial-up connections	256	1
Concurrent FTP connections	Unlimited	10
Web services	IIS	PWS (licensed for intranet use only
Maximum CPUs	4 (Server) 8 (Advanced)	2
TCP/IP services	All	ICS, IIS
Virtual Web sites	Yes	No
Terminal Services	Yes	No
Services for Macintosh	Yes	No
Fault-tolerant disk configurations	Mirroring RAID 5	None
Quantum timeslice tuning processes	Background processes	Foreground

Upgrading NT4 Server or Workstation

The steps in this section apply to upgrading an NT4 server or workstation. The upgrade is divided into two phases.

- **Initial assessment.** In this phase, the Windows 2000 installation management utility, WINNT32.EXE, asks a few questions about your plans for the machine and gathers information about the current installation. The result of this effort is a *Setup Information File* (SIF) called WINNT.SIF, which acts as a script for the actual upgrade.

- **Upgrade implementation.** In this phase, the setup utilities outlined in the preceding chapter take over and perform the installation based on the WINNT.SIF script and the contents of the Registry.

Performing the Initial Assessment Phase

You must have administrator privileges on the NT4 machine to do the upgrade. You can be logged on to the domain or the local workstation. When ready, proceed as follows:

Procedure 2.3 Performing Initial Setup Assessment for NT4 Upgrade

1. Insert the Windows 2000 CD in the CD-ROM drive. AUTORUN initiates SETUP.EXE, the Windows 2000 CD management utility. Setup prompts you to upgrade with the message *This CD-ROM contains a newer version of Windows than the one you are presently using. Would you like to upgrade to Windows 2000?*

2. Click Yes to initiate the upgrade. Setup launches WINNT32.EXE, the Windows 2000 installation management utility. The `Welcome to the Windows 2000 Setup Wizard` window opens.

   - The `Upgrade to Windows 2000` option replaces the current NT4 installation with Windows 2000.

   - The `Install a New Copy of Windows 2000` initiates a clean installation as covered in the preceding chapter. This creates a dual-boot machine. If you select this option, be sure to install into a new partition.

3. Click Next. The `License Agreement` window opens. You really have no choice other than selecting I `Accept This Agreement`. WINNT32 will not let you proceed if you don't accept the licensing agreement.

4. Click Next. WINNT32 loads the Setup Information File, TXTSETUP.SIF, from the CD. Following a short lookup in the Registry, the `Report System Compatibility` window opens and displays components or devices that are not Windows 2000 compatible (see Figure 2.1).

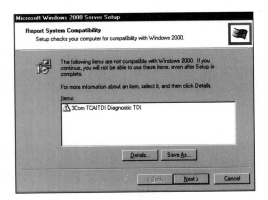

Figure 2.1 Windows 2000 Server Setup—`Report System Compatibility` window showing examples of incompatible services and drivers.

5. Click Next. The Copying Installation Files window opens. WINNT32 now copies the installation files to the local drive under a temp folder named \$Win_nt$.-1s. By default, this temp folder goes in the same volume as the \I386 folder. Setup also creates a \$Win_nt$.~bt directory at the root of the boot partition that contains the WINNT.SIF script.

Upgrade Implementation Phase

Following the restart, Setup proceeds without any further user intervention. The four stages are

- **Device installation.** Setup performs a PnP enumeration and loads the necessary drivers either from the \$Win_nt.~1s folder or the CD.
- **Networking installation.** Setup performs an additional scan for network devices and protocols and then installs and initializes the appropriate drivers.
- **Component installation.** Setup uses the WINNT.SIF script and current Registry settings to determine what components are or should be installed and then upgrades the drivers.
- **Final tasks.** Setup installs the START menu items, registers components, saves final settings and removes the temporary files.

The same caveats apply to the device installation stage during this upgrade as for an initial installation. It can take a long, long time. A delay of several hours is not unheard of, although 20 or 30 minutes is more common. See the troubleshooting tips at the end of Chapter 1 if you think Setup has stopped.

After the upgrade finishes, the machine restarts one last time and you can log on. The domain affiliations should be the same, so you can use your normal credentials.

After you have logged on, verify that all services that were operational under NT4 are still operational under Windows 2000. Check the Event Log to see whether there are any errors. If you have applications that start automatically, they may fail if they are not fully Windows 2000 compatible. If you disabled any services prior to upgrading, enable and start them now to verify that the new drivers work correctly.

At this point, you can take your Setup disks and CD and move on to the next machine and do it all over again. If the thought of doing this hundreds or thousands times for all the servers and desktops in your enterprise gives you the willies, take heart. The CD and the Resource Kit contain several tools for automating an installation or upgrade—and third parties are just aching to help you out, too. Details are in the "Automating Windows 2000 Deployments" section later in this chapter. First, however, it's important to review what's involved in upgrading Windows 9x.

Windows 9x Upgrade Functional Overview

Here's the good news: You can upgrade a Windows 9x computer directly to Windows 2000 Professional and retain all your environment settings and application configurations.

Here's the bad news: Upgrading doesn't always carry over the configuration settings in exactly the way they worked before. This is generally because of hardware incompatibilities, although some legacy and special-purpose applications do not run on Windows 2000.

The Windows 9x upgrade is divided into the same two phases as the NT4 upgrade.

- **Initial assessment.** In this phase, the Windows 2000 installation management utility, WINNT32.EXE, asks many questions and performs a detailed set of diagnostic and evaluation tests to determine the current state of hardware and applications. This results in a WINNT.SIF installation script and an evaluation report.

- **Scripted install.** In this phase, the system boots using the Windows 2000 Setup utilities and the information in the WINNT.SIF script is used to migrate the Registry and make all necessary changes to turn the machine into a Windows 2000 desktop while retaining as much of the old configuration as possible.

The Windows 9x upgrade is much more elaborate than an NT4 upgrade because the Registries are not directly compatible. Also, the upgrade involves migrating PnP devices between systems that use fundamentally different PnP architectures. This is a tricky matter. If something goes wrong, the system might be left betwixt and between, as we say in southern New Mexico, and you might find yourself reinstalling from scratch.

During the initial assessment phase, you are asked pointed questions about your current configuration and your planned configuration. This includes questions about the ultimate domain affiliation for the newly created Windows 2000 computer, new entries for any local passwords, whether to use any upgrade packs from the system vendor, and whether to convert the disk volumes to NTFS.

Domain Affiliation

If the Windows client on the Windows 9x machine is configured to use domain security, WINNT32 will offer you the opportunity to join the computer to the same domain after it is upgraded to Windows 2000. This can be done in one of two ways:

- **Preregistration.** You can enter the computer name manually into the domain database prior to doing the upgrade. For an NT4 domain, you would use Server Manager. For a Windows 2000 domain, you would use the AD Users and Computers console to create the computer account in the Computers container. When the Windows 9x computer attempts to join the domain, it sees that the account has already been created and uses it to establish the trust to the domain.

- **Concurrent registration.** If you do not want to preregister the computer, you can elect to create the computer account during the upgrade. To use this option, you provide administrative credentials during the WINNT32 interview that are added to the upgrade script. The name and password is stored in clear text in the script, so use appropriate security precautions.

During the upgrade, if Setup cannot locate a domain controller, it prompts for permission to skip the account creation and proceed. This is usually the easiest path to take. Troubleshooting in the middle of setup is difficult because you have no tools at your disposal. Wait until after setup and register manually.

Passwords

A Windows 9x computer has a password file in the \Windows directory for each user who logs on to the machine. These files have the user's logon ID as a filename with a .PWL extension. The password in a PWL file is encrypted using a one-way algorithm that differs from the Windows 2000 algorithm. Setup cannot read this password. When the computer is upgraded to Windows 2000, here is how Setup handles the PWL files:

- Every account with a PWL file in the Windows directory gets a user account in the local SAM database. The passwords are left null for a short time.

- On the first boot following the upgrade, the user is prompted for a password that is assigned to every new account in the SAM derived from a PWL file. The passwords can be changed at a later time using either the Computer Management console or the Users and Passwords icon in Control Panel.

Windows Upgrade Packs

You'll be prompted during the WINNT32 interview to provide vendor upgrade packs, if you have any. An upgrade pack is a way for a vendor to include updates to their proprietary software or to add additional drivers.

NTFS Conversion

The existing Windows 9x boot partition will be formatted either as FAT or FAT32. During the WINNT32 interview, you elect to convert it to NTFS. It is nearly always a good idea to use NTFS. You get better reliability, security, and manageability.

    If you ordinarily leave the boot/system partitions in classic NT machines formatted as FAT to simplify recovery in the event of a problem with a system file, you can do the same thing in Windows 2000 with the Recovery Console, even for NTFS partitions.

Upgrading Windows 9x

When you're ready to begin the upgrade, proceed as follows. The steps in this section apply to both Windows 95 and Windows 98. The upgrade starts with the initial assessment phase.

Initial Assessment Phase

The following steps explain how to perform an initial setup assessment for a Windows 9x upgrade.

Procedure 2.4 **Performing Initial Setup Assessment for Windows 9x Upgrade**

1. Insert the Windows 2000 CD in the CD-ROM drive. AUTORUN initiates SETUP.EXE, the Windows 2000 CD management utility. You are prompted to upgrade with this message: *This CD-ROM contains a newer version of Windows than the one you are presently using. Would you like to upgrade to Windows 2000?*

2. Click Yes to initiate the upgrade. Setup launches WINNT32.EXE, the Windows 2000 installation utility. The Welcome to the Windows 2000 Setup Wizard window opens.

   - The Upgrade to Windows 2000 option replaces the current Windows 9x installation with Windows 2000.

   - The Install a New Copy of Windows 2000 initiates a clean installation as covered in the preceding chapter. This creates a dual-boot machine. Be sure to install to a new partition.

3. Click Next. The License Agreement window opens. Select I Accept This Agreement. WINNT32 will not let you proceed if you don't accept the licensing agreement.

4. Click Next. The Preparing to Upgrade to Windows 2000 window opens (see Figure 2.2). The window lists the functions WINNT32 is about to perform. You can use the hyperlink to check the Microsoft Web site for late-breaking news.

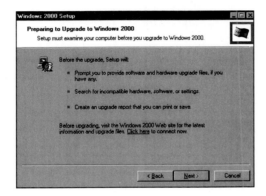

Figure 2.2   Windows 2000 Setup—Preparing to Upgrade to Windows 2000 window.

5. Click Next. The Hardware Check window opens. WINNT32 examines the system to determine whether any hardware incompatibilities might interfere with the upgrade. This examination takes about 5–10 minutes.

6. When the system examination is complete, the Domain Logon window opens if the computer is configured to authenticate users to a domain. If Windows 9x was not configured to use domain authentication, skip this step.

   The recommended option is to keep the domain logon. This requires that the computer join the domain during setup.

   If you choose not to keep the domain authentication, select the No option. The computer will be made a member of the workgroup for which is it currently configured.

7. Click Next. If you elected to join the computer to a domain, the Computer Account window opens (see Figure 2.3). The example shows the computer joining a domain called Company.com.

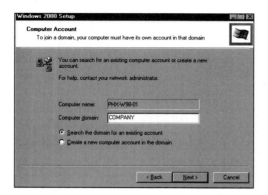

Figure 2.3   Windows 2000 Setup—Computer Account window showing domain selection.

The upgrade overview discusses the options for joining a client to a domain. The options are preregistering the computer or registering during the upgrade.

If you intend to preregister the computer in the domain, select Search the Domain for an Existing Account.

If you do not intend to preregister the computer, select Create a New Computer Account in the Domain.

8. Click Next. If you selected the Search the Domain for an Existing Account option, WINNT32 queries the domain database for a computer account matching the computer name in the Computer Account window. If it does not find the name, it displays an informational message. Click OK to return to the Computer Account window. Correct the problem and proceed.

   If you selected the Create a New Computer Account in the Domain option, an Account Information window opens to collect credentials for the administrative account to use when registering the computer. Enter the name and password of an administrative account. This information is written in clear text in the TXTSETUP.INF script, so take appropriate security precautions.

   If you did not select Create a New Computer Account in the Domain, skip this step.

9. Click Next. The Provide Upgrade Packs window opens (see Figure 2.4). The example assumes that you have no upgrade packs.

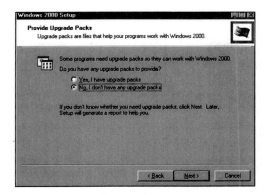

Figure 2.4   Windows 2000 Setup—Provide Upgrade Packs window showing default selection.

10. Click Next. The Upgrading to the Windows 2000 NTFS File System window opens. The upgrade overview has information to help you decide which file system to choose.

11. Click Next. WINNT32 prepares an upgrade summary, which lists possible problems that might occur. This process takes 5 to 10 minutes. If it finds hardware that needs special drivers that are not available on the Windows 2000, a Provide Updated Plug and Play Files window opens (see Figure 2.5).

    You can click Provide Files to load the drivers at this time or you can wait until after setup. If the device is critical for operation, you should load the driver now.

    If WINNT32 finds no incompatible devices, skip this step.

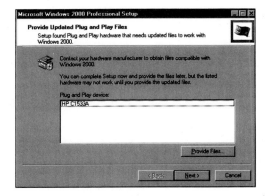

Figure 2.5   Windows 2000 Setup—Provide Updated Plug and Play Files window showing an example device that requires additional drivers.

12. Click Next. The Upgrade Report window opens (see Figure 2.6). This window contains a list of the incompatible drivers and services running on the machine with hotlinks to Microsoft's Web site for more information. If nothing on the report looks like it would cause the upgrade to fail or be unstable, proceed.

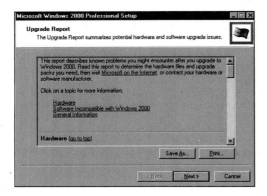

Figure 2.6   Windows 2000 Setup—Upgrade Report window.

13. Click Next. The Ready to Install Windows 2000 window opens. The window explains that Setup takes about an hour and a half and requires no intervention.

14. Click Next. The Copying Installation Files window opens. WINNT32 copies the installation files to a temporary directory and then restarts the machine.

Assessment Phase Results

Here are the actions that WINNT32 takes after the upgrade interview is complete:

- Collects the interview responses into a Setup Installation File, WINNT.SIF, that acts as a script for automating the upgrade.
- Copies boot files to a temporary directory called Win_nt.~bt. These are the same files that are on the Setup disks. WINNT.SIF is placed in this directory, as well.
- Copies the installation files to a temporary directory called Win_nt.~ls. This includes all the nearly 4,000 files from the \I386 directory on the CD. The two temporary directories are deleted after the upgrade. The two directories together require about 200MB of free disk space in addition to the 850MB or so required to perform the upgrade itself.

- Places a copy of the standard Windows 2000 secondary bootstrap loader, NTLDR, into the root of the boot partition.
- Places a copy of the Setup bootstrap loader, SETUPLDR.BIN, in the root of the active drive and renames it LDR.
- Copies the contents of the boot sector to a BOOTSECT.DOS file at the root of the boot partition.
- Overwrites the boot sector with code that loads NTLDR.
- Places a special boot sector file called BOOTSECT.DAT in the Win_nt.~bt directory. This alternate boot sector contains executable code that loads the Setup bootstrap loader, LDR.
- Creates a BOOT.INI file at the root of the boot partition with entries that point BOOTSECT.DAT in c:\Win_nt.~bt and the root of the boot partition, which automatically loads BOOTSECT.DOS. Here are example BOOT.INI entries at this stage of the installation:

```
[Boot Loader]
Timeout=5
Default=C:\$WIN_NT$.~BT\BOOTSECT.DAT
[Operating Systems]
C:\$WIN_NT$.~BT\BOOTSECT.DAT="Microsoft Windows 2000 Professional Setup"
C:\="Microsoft Windows"
```

With these changes in place, the system is ready to perform an unattended installation following the restart.

Performing the Implementation Phase

When the system restarts, the new boot sector loads NTLDR, which reads the BOOT.INI and finds the default entry pointing at the BOOTSECT.DAT file in c:\$Win_nt.~bt. It loads this alternative boot sector, which starts Setup.

The executable code in the alternative boot sector loads LDR, the Setup secondary bootstrap loader. LDR uses NTDETECT.COM to do a hardware scan and then starts extracting the setup files in $Win_nt.~bt into memory. From this point forward, the character phase of the setup proceeds as described in the preceding chapter, except that all entries are scripted so that no input is required.

If you elected to format the boot/system partition as NTFS, the system converts the file system following restart and then restarts again. The graphical phase also proceeds automatically.

During the graphical phase, if the machine cannot find a domain controller or if the credentials you gave were insufficient to create the computer account, Setup will prompt for permission to continue. Click Yes and create the account later.

When the system restarts for the final time, it boots to the standard Ctrl+Alt+Del logon window unless this is a standalone workstation, in which case the system boots right to the Explorer desktop.

At this point, the system should be ready for the user. Refer to Chapter 1 for the post-installation checkouts and any troubleshooting that you might need to do.

Both the NT4 and Windows 95 upgrades can be deployed automatically using predefined scripts rather than the script created by WINNT32. This is covered in the next section.

Automating Windows 2000 Deployments

This section contains the details for preparing an automated deployment of Windows 2000 Professional. You can use the same steps to churn out servers, as well. Three general types of automated deployments methods:

1. Disk cloning

2. Remote Installation Services

3. Distributed scripts

Of the three, disk cloning is the fastest but the most complex to deploy because it involves dealing with many possible hardware combinations. Distributed scripts are the simplest to deploy, but require the most work at the desktop. Remote Installation Services is a new feature in Windows 2000 that also uses scripts, but deploys them more efficiently if you have suitable hardware. Let's start with a look at cloning.

Disk Cloning

The idea behind cloning is to configure a master desktop to have exactly the content, look, and feel that you want for your users, and then to duplicate it to a few hundred or thousand desktops. This deployment method seems to be ideal. Build a box and dupe it off. Bada-bing, bada-bang. You have a thousand-node deployment done in an afternoon.

Unfortunately, it's not quite that easy. First of all, Microsoft does not officially condone cloning of fully installed machines. It supports only cloning of a system that has been installed up to the point of the graphical phase of setup. Beyond that, the OS and application installations must be scripted. This is due to three factors:

- Unique PnP identifiers
- Hardware incompatibilities
- SID duplication

Before getting into the grimy details of the problems, it should be said that many, many organizations use cloning to deploy full installations with great success. Microsoft does not include a cloning package in Windows 2000; so if you want to do a cloned deployment, you must purchase a third-party utility. Several are on the market.

The oldest and best, in my opinion, is Norton Ghost from Symantec, `www.symantec.com\ghost`. A runner-up from a feature perspective, although it is less expensive and easier to use, is ImageCast Deluxe from Microhouse at `www.microhouse.com\frame_deluxe.htm`.

Both of these products permit you to send an image to multiple machines using IP multicast, a highly efficient way to use bandwidth. Multicasting an image to 100 machines is as fast as imaging one. The packages also include NTFS support, dynamic updates, automated partition sizing, and a last but very important feature, the capability to change the *security ID* (SID) code of cloned machines.

Which brings up one of the three major problems with fully cloned deployments. Let's now look at them in detail.

Security ID (SID) Duplication

Every Windows 2000 and NT computer has a unique SID buried deep in the Registry. The SID forms the basis of secure communications with other Windows 2000 and NT computers. The local computer SID is used to build SIDs for user and group accounts created at a server or desktop. Domain accounts are based on the domain SID.

If you have 100 cloned computers, each one will have the same administrator SID. If you put those computers in a workgroup, you have security issues. It is simple to gain unauthorized access to a computer from another computer with the same SID.

The cloning tools previously mentioned have a SID-changing apparatus that guarantees a unique local SID. You can also find a SID changer at Mark Russinovich's SysInternals Web site, `www.sysinternals.com`. Microsoft supplies one too, but it is not nearly as easy to use.

PnP Identifiers

When the Plug and Play Manager enumerates the devices on a machine, it assigns unique identifiers to the bus interfaces and the components they contain, along with every major and most minor component in the system. These identifiers become part of a Registry subtree called Enum under `HKLM | System | CurrentControlSet`. This is commonly called the Enum tree.

When you swap out a component, Plug and Play Manager knows that the component changed because the unique ID doesn't fit the new component. It modifies the Enum tree accordingly. If you change out a major subassembly, such as a motherboard, the Plug and Play Manager may become hopelessly lost and will probably refuse to recognize the drive interfaces or memory.

When you clone a machine, you clone the contents of the Enum tree as well. Placing this image on a machine that is not completely identical to the master machine may send Plug and Play Manager into enumeration spasms. Be sure to test your cloned configuration on every subset of hardware you have to see whether this is going to be a problem for you.

Hardware Incompatibilities

Even without special PnP identifiers, Windows 2000 is not very forgiving of hardware differences. Think of cloning as performing an organ transplant. You have the fewest troubles when transplanting from an identical twin. Fraternal twins and siblings work fairly well, but you can get rejection problems when transplanting between total strangers.

When cloning between different types of machines, you never know when a small difference in processor, motherboard, and memory might be dramatic enough to make the desktop unstable. If you are sitting in your office and surveying a database that lists 73 different makes and models of desktops and laptops in your organization, the glories of cloning get a little tainted.

If you have 100 or 1,000 each of those 73 models, cloning might be worthwhile. If you have three each, you might be better off with a scripted deployment.

SYSPREP and SIDWALKER

For many years, Microsoft adamantly refused to countenance cloning of NT computers because of the security implications of duplicating the SID. Microsoft still does not provide any cloning utilities in Windows 2000, but it does provide a SID-changing utility called SIDWALKER. Unfortunately, SIDWALKER is more of an OEM tool and much clumsier to use than the third-party tools already mentioned.

SIDWALKER is used in conjunction with SYSPREP, an OEM distribution tool. SYSPREP clears out the Registry information associated with the computer ID, including the computer SID, and puts the system in the state you would find just after the text-based portion of Setup.

SYSPREP is designed for hardware vendors who want a quick way to erase individual computer settings prior to duping 10,000 copies of a hard drive. It is not suitable for a corporate deployment where efficient use of administrative resources is tremendously important. If you want to take a look at SYSPREP, it is located on the Windows 2000 CD in the `\Support\Reskit\Netmgmt\Deploy` directory.

Remote Installation (RI)

If you look at all the pluses and minuses of cloning and decide that the potential problems outweigh the benefits, you might want to move on and look at scripted installations.

In a scripted installation or upgrade, you create an answer file that eliminates the need to be at the console of the machine to answer questions during the WINNT32 evaluation phase. The script handles all the questions and you just come back in a while and make sure that everything went all right.

You can distribute scripted installation in a couple of ways. One is to use a new service in Windows 2000 called the *Remote Installation Service* (RIS).

In theory, RIS is an administrator's dream. It promises to combine the easy installation of disk cloning with the hardware specificity of a scripted install. It's like getting beer *and* fudge for dinner. Unfortunately, you have to eat your Brussels sprouts first. Here's why.

Functional Overview of RIS

RIS consists of a server and a client component. The server component is the Remote Installation Service itself, which manages a boot image capable of installing Windows 2000 Professional. The RIS server listens for client machines that use remote booting to connect to the RIS server and download the image.

The remote booting process takes advantage of two events that happen during POST: a ROM scan and an INT13 call for a bootable device. The ROM scan permits a device with a ROM signature of 55AAh to run executable code that initializes the associated device. Network adapters equipped with a remote boot PROM have executable code that enables them to obtain a boot image from a host server.

Very few network adapters nowadays have a remote boot PROM, so RIS also comes with PROM emulator software that can be loaded from a boot floppy disk when the POST starts the final boot process.

Whether the RIS client uses hardware PROM or a PROM emulator, the sequence of events is the same.

Procedure 2.5 **Sequence of Events for Remote Installation Service Client Connection**

1. The client gets an IP address and a configuration packet from a DHCP server.

2. It uses this information to locate a DNS server.

3. It uses the DNS to find a domain controller.

4. It makes an LDAP call to locate a RIS server.

5. It uses the remote booting protocol to connect to the RIS service on the server and begin downloading the bootstrap image.

6. The bootstrap image copies a full suite of installation files to the local drive.

7. An installation script in the installation files walks through an unattended installation at the client.

8. The next time the client boots, it is running Windows 2000.

Handling Multiple RIS Servers

A RIS server can be configured to respond only to known clients. A "known client" is one that has been preregistered in Active Directory. If a RIS server gets an image request from a client that is not registered in the directory, it does not respond. This feature permits using RIS to handle installations for two or more domains on a single broadcast segment.

RIS Requirements

To get RIS to work, you need the following services running somewhere on your network:

- Active Directory
- Dynamic DNS
- DHCP
- A RIS server that is either a domain controller or a member of a Windows 2000 domain
- A RIS client with either a remote boot network adapter (NDIS-style PROM, not ODI) or a network adapter that supports a PROM emulator

You can build such a floppy disk using the Remote Boot Floppy Generator utility on the Windows 2000 Server CD. The executable name is RBFG.EXE. It is located under \WINNT\System32\Reminst after you install the RIS service.

Usable Card Types

The RIS boot disk works with only a select few network adapters. As of this writing, that list includes the following:

- 3Com 90x(B) (900/905) series of PCI cards (B, Combo, TPC, TPO, T4 and TX)
- Hewlett-Packard DeskDirect 10/100TX PCI NIC
- SMC 8432, 9332, and 9432 Epic PCI NICs
- AMD PCnet adapters
- Compaq NetFlex 100, 110, and 3
- DEC DE450, DE500
- IntelPro 10+, 100+, 100B

You can try another card type and it might work. Only PCI cards are supported in any event. ISA and EISA cards may initialize and see the network and load the initial RIS screens, but they will not load an RIS image and you'll get a *Failure to authenticate* error of one form or another.

RIS Volume Requirements

Like any remote booting service, RIS depends on an image file loaded across the network to the remote boot clients. RIS gets persnickety about the disk volumes that hold the boot image.

- The volume cannot be the same as that holding the Windows 2000 system files.
- The volume must be formatted NTFS.
- You'll need at least 800MB–1000MB of free space.

If you do not meet these requirements, RIS will not work correctly and you'll end up redoing a lot of work.

Installing RIS

Here's how to install the RIS driver files:

Procedure 2.6 **Installing Remote Installation Services**

1. Select a server to host the RIS boot images. The server does not need to be a domain controller, but it must be a member server of a Windows 2000 domain.
2. Open `Control Panel` | `Add/Remove Programs`.
3. Click `Configure Windows`. The `Add or Remove Windows Components` window opens.
4. Click `Components`. The `Windows 2000 Components` window opens.
5. Select `Remote Installation Services` and click `Next`. The device installer does its work and then prompts you to restart, which you should do.

RIS Image Configuration

After restart, configure a remote installation image as follows:

Procedure 2.7 **Configuring a Remote Installation Services Image**

1. Insert the Windows 2000 Workstation CD in the CD-ROM drive.
2. From the `Run` window or a command prompt, launch RISETUP.EXE. This starts the Remote Installation Wizard.
3. The `Welcome` window opens. If the server is not a member of a Windows 2000 domain, or cannot find the domain controller in DNS, RISETUP will fail with an error telling you that the domain could not be located. If the directory configuration for the RI server is incorrect, the client may not be able to find the RIS, and you will get a similar error.

4. Click Next. The Remote Installation Server Directory Location window opens. Enter the drive letter of the volume that will hold the installation files and the directory name.

5. Click Next. The Initial Remote Installation Server Settings window opens. If you want the RI server to service clients immediately, select Respond to Client Computers Requesting Service.

RIS Service Management

If you have existing remote boot clients in your network, or you have another RIS server, you may want to leave the RIS service disabled until you're ready to initiate deployment.

Also, you must stop and start RIS every time you make the slightest change in the image or the RIS configuration. You'll be making lots of changes at first, so it's easier to leave the service disabled until you're ready to use it.

6. Click Next. The Location of the Windows Workstation Installation Files window opens. As the name implies, enter the path to the I386 directory on the CD. If you enter the path wrong, you'll get an error and a prompt to browse for the correct directory. As a general rule, Windows 2000 is much better about letting you browse for installation files than NT4.

7. Click Next. The Windows 2000 Professional Directory Name window opens. Enter the name of the directory to hold the installation files. Remember that you have already designated the volume name, so all you need to do here is identify the directory. You must use an 8.3 name so that the client computer can see it. Use the default name unless you have more than one image on the server.

8. Click Next. The Friendly Description and Help Text window opens. You can configure different images for different situations, such as one for a group of clients or different types of hardware.

   The RIS clients get a list of the images that you create, so make sure the Friendly Description gives enough detail to choose. Put explanatory information in the Help Text window. The contents appear at the remote boot client when the user selects Help while choosing an image.

9. Click Next. The Remote Installation Server Summary window opens. If you made a mistake in any of the previous windows, now is the time to change it.

10. Click Finish. RISETUP now copies files from the Windows 2000 Workstation CD to the RIS directory. You'll get an informative checklist showing the progress. The last item on the checklist is "Starting the Remote Installation Service." This will not occur if you did not select the option to start the service automatically.

Configure the RIS Server

When Setup finishes copying files, configure the RIS server. This requires a bit of juggling in Active Directory:

Procedure 2.8   **Configuring a Remote Installation Services Server**

---

1. Load the AD Users and Computers console from START | PROGRAMS | ADMINISTRATIVE TOOLS.

2. Find the computer icon for the server that is running RIS.

3. Right-click the icon and select PROPERTIES from the fly-out menu. The Properties window opens.

4. Select the Remote Install tab. Note that some RIS configuration settings were made during the image installation.

5. Click Advanced Settings. The Remote Installation Service Properties window opens.

6. In the New Clients tab, under Automatic Computer Naming, click the combo box under Generate Client Computer Names Using.

7. Under Computer Account Location, select A Specific Directory Service Location.

8. Click Browse and select a container. This enables you to pick a container other than the one holding the server. If necessary, build a container for workstations. You don't want workstation objects cluttering your Domain Controllers container.

Computer and Usernames

RIS has several options for automatically naming computers. Some of them involve associating a computer name with a username. This is rarely a good idea in large organizations where computers get traded regularly between users. A better choice, if you want automatic naming, is to use the MAC address. This is a clean way to get a unique name that will not change unless you change the network adapter.

The default naming format prefixes the MAC address with the letters NP. This two-character prefix is important because some TCP/IP utilities, such as Ping, do not work if the host name starts with a numeral.

Instead of NP, you might want to preface the MAC address with two or three letters that designate the workstation's location. Click Advanced to change the prefix. Prefixes help sort out workstations on Browse lists. They aren't required for directory browsing because you'll probably put workstations into local containers; until you have completed the transition to Active Directory, however, you should make provisions for classic NT browsing.

9. Select the OS Images tab. The list contains the name of the image you configured with RISETUP.

   If you want more than one image, run RISETUP at the server again and
   build a second image in a different distribution directory with a different
   "friendly name." Then use the Add button at this window to put the new
   image on the list.

10. Click OK to return to the Remote Install tab under Properties.

11. Click Manage Clients. The Client Computers window opens.

12. Click Add. The Pre-Stage Client Computers window opens. Use the entries
in this window to preregister a computer account in the directory.

Registering Computers in the Directory

Without preregistration, you must have someone with administrator credentials at the remote boot client the first
time it makes connection so that the Active Directory account can be added.

Frankly, however, it's a lot of trouble to prestage a client. You have to create a unique GUID/UUID, and that means
horsing around trying to figure out what number to use, and then you must type it without error. It's much simpler to register from the client.

13. Click Close to return to the Remote Install tab.

14. Under Client Servicing, select Respond to Clients Requesting Service.

15. Click OK to save all changes and close the window.

16. Go to a command prompt. Stop and start the BINLSVC service as
follows:

```
NET STOP BINLSVC
NET START BINLSVC
```

   You'll end up doing this a lot. Take my advice and build a batch file.

Establishing Privileges

Here's where things get a little complicated, as if they weren't complicated
enough already. The logon account used at the RIS client needs a couple of
special domain privileges. It must have the Log on as Batch Job privilege in
the domain and permission to create objects in the directory container that
holds the workstation object for the RIS clients. Configure this as follows:

Procedure 2.9 **Establishing Directory Privileges to Support Remote Installation Services**

1. Configure a group policy to change the system privilege for the user account. See Chapter 16, "Managing the User Operating Environment," for directions on using group policies.

2. Load the Group Policy snap-in.

3. Open the Local Computer policy.

4. Expand the tree to Computer Settings | Local Policies | User Rights Assessment.

5. Under the Attribute list in the right pane, double-click Log On as a Batch Job. This opens the Log On as a Batch Job window.

6. Click Add. The Add Users and Groups window opens.

7. Add the Administrators group, or whatever group you create to support the RIS deployment.

8. Click OK to save the changes and return to the Log On as a Batch Job window. The group is now on the list.

9. Click OK to save the list and return to the Group Policy snap-in.

10. Close the Group Policy snap-in.

11. Open the AD Users and Computers console.

12. Right-click the container you are going to use to hold the workstation accounts for the RIS clients and open the Properties window. This is the container you specified in step 8 under Configure RIS Server.

13. Select the Security tab.

14. Give domain admins and administrators Full Control permissions.

15. Click OK to save the changes.

16. Close the AD Users and Computers console.

17. If you have a large domain or several domain controllers, wait for the changes to propagate.

Configure RIS Client Boot Disk

This horse is just about ready to saddle and ride. All that's left to do is configure a client boot disk. Build the boot disk using the Remote Boot Floppy Generator, RBFG.EXE. This is located in the \WINNT\System32\Reminst directory at the RIS server.

Procedure 2.10   **Configuring a Remote Installation Services Boot Disk**

1. Launch RBFG.EXE. The Remote Boot Floppy Generator window opens.

2. Put a formatted floppy in the A: drive (or the B: drive). It does not need to be a system floppy disk. RBFG puts a special driver called RISCLIENT on the disk and makes appropriate changes to the boot sector.

3. Click Create Disk. About 20 seconds later, you have your RIS boot disk.

Booting the RIS Client

Before booting the RIS client, if you've made any changes, any at all, to the RIS properties at the server, stop and then start the BINLSVC service. Then proceed as follows:

Procedure 2.11   **Booting a Remote Installation Services Client**

1. Start a computer with the RIS client disk in the floppy disk drive.

2. Log on using the account you configured to have Log On as a Batch Job permissions.

3. The RIS CONFIGURATION menu opens. Select Automatically Setup This Computer. This launches a standard Windows 2000 Setup that uses a SIF created by RISETUP called RISTDRD.SIF.

4. The client completes an unattended installation using the RISTDRD.SIF as the script. You may need to do minor surgery on this SIF file to make it work the way you want.

RIS Client Boot Events

When the RISCLIENT driver loads, it broadcasts for a DHCP server.

When the RIS client gets an IP address from DHCP, it looks in the configuration packet for the address of a DNS server. It uses this address to query DNS for a domain controller. It then sends an LDAP query to the domain controller looking for the RIS server.

If all that works and the client can connect to the RIS server, the client loads a couple of introductory screens and eventually prompts you to log on.

RIS Summary

Here's the bottom line on RIS: It is a fast and convenient way to deploy large numbers of Professional desktops, but only if you meet a relatively long list of prerequisites:

- You have a supported network adapter.
- You already have a Windows 2000 domain in place.
- You need only a fairly standard installation with no requirement to upgrade instead of having to perform a new installation.
- You don't want to roll out lots of applications along with your deployment.

If you don't meet any of the requirements of this list, you should try using a scripted installation instead.

Scripted Installations

Any action and option that you can specify at the user interface during setup, you can specify in a script that can be used to automate the process.

The Windows 2000 CD has tools for building these deployment scripts. You can even use them to install applications. If you have more than a few applications, however, you might want to use more sophisticated deployment tools, such as the software distribution features in Windows 2000, *Systems Management Server* (SMS), or WININSTALL.

The unattended setup script is most commonly used to perform a net-work installation of Windows 2000 Professional. The distribution server that hosts the installation files needs a little over 300MB to hold the 7,500+ files in I386.

Here is a quick breakdown of the overall steps for scripting an unattended installation and performing the deployment:

Procedure 2.12 **Task List for Setting Up Scripted Installations**

1. Create an unattended setup script that automatically answers configuration questions presented by Setup.

2. Copy the Windows 2000 installation files and scripts to a distribution server and share the directory.

3. Build a boot disk that connects a target client to the shared installation directory.

4. Use the unattended setup script to install Windows 2000 on a master workstation.

5. Create a pre-application profile of the workstation.

6. Install applications.

7. Create a difference script that runs after the unattended setup script to install applications.

8. Initiate unattended setup across the network making use of all installation scripts.

9. Verify that the target workstation works correctly.

Creating an Unattended Setup Script

This section covers creating unattended setup scripts using the Setup Manager utility, SETUPMGR.EXE, from the Windows 2000 Resource Kit. The setup script is formatted much the same as an INI file, with entries that correspond to the information obtained by WINNT32 and Setup when you install or upgrade Windows 2000.

In addition to building the setup script, Setup Manager can automate the creation of the distribution share point. If you want to take advantage of that option, launch Setup Manager at the console of the server where you want the distribution files to be located. When you're ready, proceed as follows:

Procedure 2.13   **Using Setup Manager to Create an Unattended Installation Script**

1. Launch SETUPMGR. The Windows 2000 Setup Manager Wizard starts.

2. Click Next. The New or Existing Answer File window opens.

- Create A New Answer File walks you through a set of interview screens to collect information to build an unattended installation script.

- Create An Answer File That Duplicates This Computer's Configuration fills in information from the local machine as you walk through the interview screens.

- Modify An Existing Answer File provides a graphical way to edit an existing script. Some modifications must be done with a text editor, but the Setup Manager is extremely flexible.

3. Select the `Create A New Answer File` option and click `Next`. The `Product to Install` window opens. Select one of the three types of scripted installation.

   - `Windows 2000 Unattended Installation` builds an INF script that contains the entries collected in this interview phase along with a batch file that can be included along with WINNT or WINNT32 to initiate the unattended setup.

   - `SYSPREP Install` builds an INF script that handles the local installation after the cloned distribution of the package has been completed. This permits OEM vendors to distribute machines that have been pre-installed up to the point of starting the graphic phase of setup. The script completes the graphic phase automatically.

   - `Remote Installation Services` builds an SIF file for use in the RIS image.

4. Select the `Windows 2000 Unattended Installation` option and click `Next`. The `Platform` window opens. Select the platform you want to install, Professional or Server. The example steps are for Professional.

5. Click `Next`. The `User Interaction Level` window opens (see Figure 2.7). The default action for each option is displayed in the `Description` field when you select the radio button.

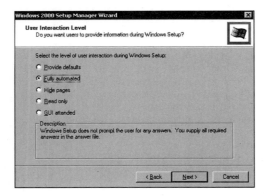

Figure 2.7 Windows 2000 Setup Manager Wizard—`User Interaction Level` window.

6. Select `Fully Automated` and click `Next`. The `License Agreement` window opens. This is your acknowledgement that the automated installations using this script comply with the *End User License Agreement* (EULA). If you do not agree to this here, the unattended installation will stop and prompt you for an EULA agreement.

7. Check I Accept the Terms of the License Agreement and click Next. The Customize the Software window opens. Enter a standard username, such as Admin and the organization name. This name is not used to create an account.

8. Click Next. The Computer Names window opens (see Figure 2.8). For a desktop deployment, automatic name generation makes the most sense. You can also enter a list of names or import them from a text file.

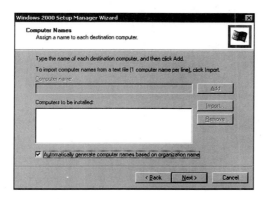

Figure 2.8 Windows 2000 Setup Manager Wizard—Computer Names window.

9. Click Next. The Administrator Password window opens (see Figure 2.9). You have two password options in a fully automated installation. You can either enter a password that will be assigned to the Administrator account when it is created or you can have the machine log on automatically as Administrator after setup and you can create the password then. Set the number of automatic logons to give you sufficient overhead in case you must reboot a couple of times. *Caution*: The setup script stores the local Administrator password in clear text. Use appropriate security measures.

10. Click Next. The Display Settings window opens. If you have a mix of computers with different video configurations, use the Windows Default option. This is usually 256 color, 800×600. If you choose a higher resolution or color density, the automated setup may fail, requiring intervention by a user or technician.

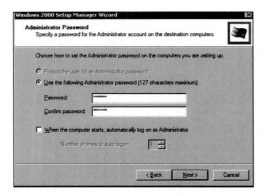

Figure 2.9   Windows 2000 Setup Manager Wizard—`Administrator Password` window.

11. Click `Next`. The `Network Settings` window opens. The `Typical` option installs TCP/IP using DHCP and uses the Microsoft client. If you want to install other clients or protocol, select `Custom` and enter the information in the appropriate window.

12. Click `Next`. The `Workgroup or Domain` window opens (see Figure 2.10). If you want to join the computer to a domain during setup, select the `Windows Server Domain` option and enter the domain name. If you have a Windows 2000 domain, enter the fully qualified DNS name. See the sidebar on the next page titled "Joining Domains During Automated Setup" for details.

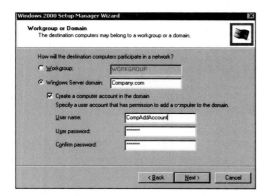

Figure 2.10   Windows 2000 Setup Manager Wizard—`Workgroup or Domain` window.

Joining Domains During Automated Setup

If you elected to use automatic computer naming, you cannot preregister the computer. Enter the name of an account with sufficient administrative privileges to add computer accounts. I recommend creating a temporary administrator account for use during deployment. Disable the account whenever it is not in use and delete it after you have completed the deployment. Use the delegation features in Active Directory to limit the privileges of this account. See Chapter 10, "Managing Active Directory Security." *Caution:* The account password is stored in the script in clear text.

13. Click Next. The Time Zone window opens. Select the correct time zone from the drop-down list. Remember to modify your setup scripts if you transport them between time zones.

14. Click Next. The Additional Settings window opens. If you elect not to edit additional settings, click Next to skip to the Distribution Folder window in step 19.

15. Select Yes | Edit Additional Settings and click Next. The Telephony window opens (see Figure 2.11). Enter the appropriate modem dialing information.

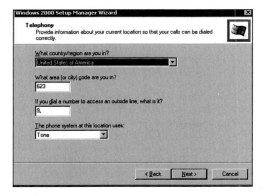

Figure 2.11 Windows 2000 Setup Manager Wizard—Telephony window.

16. Click Next. The Regional Settings window opens. Leave the Use the Default Regional Settings option selected unless you need to deploy different locale files.

17. Click Next. The Languages window opens. Select additional language, if required.

18. Click Next. The Browser and Shell Settings window opens (see Figure 2.12). Select the customization method you use in your organization, either an autoconfiguration script or a set of proxy/home page settings.

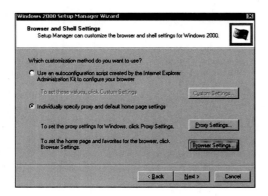

Figure 2.12 Windows 2000 Setup Manager Wizard—Browser and Shell Settings window.

19. Click Next. The Distribution Folder window opens. Enter the name of the shared folder where you want to store the installation files. The wizard copies them there automatically. Be sure that you have the Windows 2000 Professional CD in the CD-ROM drive.

20. Click Next. The Distribution Folder Name window opens. Select Create a New Distribution Folder and enter the path and name of the folder and the share name you want to use. You must do this on the distribution server. The wizard cannot create a share across the network.

21. Click Next. The Additional Mass Storage Drivers window opens. Use this window if you need to include special SCSI or ATA66 drivers in the automated distribution.

22. Click Next. The Hardware Abstraction Layer window opens. If you need to include an OEM HAL in the automated distribution, use this window to add the OEM drivers.

23. Click Next. The Additional Commands window opens (see Figure 2.13). Add any executables or scripts you want to include in the distribution. Enter the commands and add them to the Command list. You can change the order of the commands after they have been added. Make sure that you include any script engines that are not already in the Windows 2000 installation.

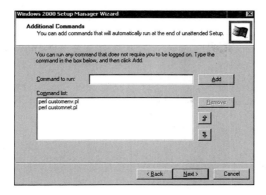

Figure 2.13   Windows 2000 Setup Manager Wizard—Additional Commands window.

24. Click Next. The OEM Branding window opens (see Figure 2.14). You can use this option for corporate installations, as well. Enter the path and name of a logo to display during setup and a wallpaper to accompany the setup background. The files you specify need to be in the specified location so that Setup Manager can copy them to the installation folder.

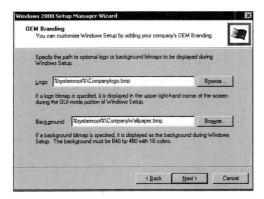

Figure 2.14   Windows 2000 Setup Manager Wizard—OEM Branding window.

25. Click Next. The Additional Files or Folders window opens (see Figure 2.15). Use this window to copy additional drivers or files to the installation folder. This creates an OEM directory in the distribution directory. You'll need this directory to deploy applications, so create it even if you have no additional files at this time.

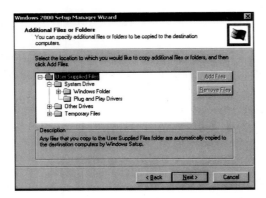

Figure 2.15 Windows 2000 Setup Manager Wizard—`Additional Files or Folders` window.

26. Click `Next`. The `Answer File Name` window opens (see Figure 2.16). Enter the name you want to assign to this unattended setup script. The default name is UNATTEND.TXT.

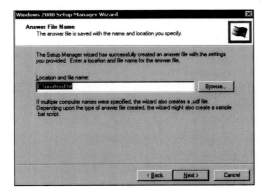

Figure 2.16 Windows 2000 Setup Manager Wizard—`Answer File Name` window.

27. Click `Next`. The `Location of Setup Files` window opens. If you have the Windows 2000 Professional CD in the CD-ROM drive, leave the `Copy the Files from CD` option selected. Otherwise, specify an alternate location.

28. Click Next. Setup Manager creates the distribution folder, shares the folder, and opens the Copying Files window. The files are copied from the CD or alternate location. After the files have copied, Setup Manager exits.

29. Copy the UNATTEND.TXT and UNATTEND.BAT files to the distribution folder.

For an example of an unattended setup script, see the next section. For methods to customize the script to install applications, see the "Using SYSDIFF" section later in this chapter.

Example Unattended Setup Script

Here's the setup script that was created based on the example screens in the preceding section. The few entries highlighted in bold require special attention:

```
;SetupMgrTag
[Unattended]
    UnattendMode=FullUnattended
    OemSkipEula=Yes ;This skips the License Agreement window.
    OemPreinstall=Yes
    DriverSigningPolicy = ignore ;Undocumented switch. Added manually
                          to avoid errors with unsigned drivers.

[GuiUnattended]
    AdminPassword=whumpa7 ;Note that local admin password is in clear text.
    OEMSkipRegional=1
    TimeZone=15
    OemSkipWelcome=1

[UserData]
    FullName=Admin
    OrgName=Company
    ComputerName=* ;This enables automatic computer naming.

[TapiLocation]
    CountryCode=1
    Dialing=Tone
    AreaCode=623
    LongDistanceAccess=9,

[SetupMgr]
    DistFolder=g:\win2000dist
    DistShare=win2000dist

[Branding]
    BrandIEUsingUnattended=Yes ;This is the Internet Explorer branding.

[Proxy]
    Use_Same_Proxy=0
```

```
[Identification]
    JoinDomain=Company.com
    DomainAdmin=CompAddAccount
    DomainAdminPassword=JabBorE# ;Domain password in clear text.

[Networking]
    InstallDefaultComponents=Yes
```

Example Unattended Setup Batch File

Setup Manager creates a batch file for initiating the unattended setup. The client maps to the shared distribution folder and executes the batch file. Here is an example:

```
@rem SetupMgrTag
@echo off
rem
rem This is a SAMPLE batch script generated by the Setup Manager Wizard.
rem If this script is moved from the location where it was generated, it may have to be
modified.
rem
set AnswerFile=.\unattend.txt
set SetupFiles=\\PHX-W2KS-03\win2000dist

\\PHX-W2KS-03\win2000dist\winnt32 /s:%SetupFiles% /unattend:%AnswerFile%
```

This batch file uses the 32-bit Windows 2000 installation management utility, WINNT32, and specifies the UNC for the distribution share and the name of the script file. If you connect to the network from a DOS client using a network boot disk, you can use the 16-bit installation manager, WINNT. If you do so, you need to add a /b switch to the command line, indicating no setup boot disks:

```
\\PHX-W2KS-03\win2000dist\winnt /b /s:%SetupFiles% /unattend:%AnswerFile%
```

If you want to specify a local drive for installing Windows 2000 other than the default boot drive, use this syntax:

```
set AnswerFile=.\unattend.txt
set SetupFiles=\\PHX-W2KS-03\win2000dist
set TargetDrive=c

\\PHX-W2KS-03\win2000dist\winnt32 /s:%SetupFiles% /unattend:%AnswerFile%
/t:%TargetDrive%
```

This scripted installation includes only the base operating system and any additional drivers and files that you included in the setup script. You can include applications in the mix of files; if you plan on deploying more than a couple, however, you might want to consider using the SYSDIFF utility on the Windows 2000 Resource Kit.

Using SYSDIFF

SYSDIFF builds a profile of the Registry and directory structure of a work-station that can be used as a blueprint for automating application installations on a target machine.

If you tried the version of SYSDIFF in the NT4 Resource Kit and found it to be nearly worthless because it did not work with long filenames, you're in for a pleasant surprise. The new SYSDIFF works with any Win32 file-name. Although the process is still complex and needs lots of doctoring to get it working, if you have a large deployment with lots of applications and you can't use cloning, SYSDIFF is worth your time.

The general steps for using SYSDIFF are as follows:

1. Do a fresh install of Windows 2000, and profile the files and Registry entries.

2. Install your applications.

3. Profile the files and Registry entries again.

Initial Installation and Profiling

Install Windows 2000 Professional on a representative desktop (hardware does not have to be identical, but it helps to be close) and configure it like you want your users to see it. Do an initial SYSDIFF profile from a com-mand prompt using this syntax:

```
Sysdiff /snap SNAP.IMG
```

where SNAP.IMG is the name of an output file. The filename must conform to DOS 8.3 naming conventions. (I usually give it an IMG extension [for image].) Save the output file to a network drive so that it will not be included in the profile. The profile can get fairly big, upwards of 10MB, so allow enough room on the server.

If you want to analyze what gets included in the profile, create a log file using the /log:*logfile* switch.

SYSDIFF /SNAP profiles three items:

- INI files
- Registry hives
- The directory tree

It takes the profile anywhere from 10 to 20 minutes to run, depending on the speed of your hard drive and network connection.

The snapshot file is binary, so you can't edit it later like you can with a scripted install.

Application Profiling

Now install the applications that you want to include in the deployment. Configure them as you would if the user had installed them locally. If you want Microsoft Word to use a network drive for the workgroup templates, for example, set it up that way.

After the master workstation is configured just the way you want it, run a SYSDIFF profile from a command prompt using the following syntax:

```
Sysdiff /diff SNAP.IMG DIFF.IMG
```

This builds a file that contains the differences between the current configuration (the one with the applications installed) and the pristine configuration in the original snapshot.

You can view the difference profile by running the following

```
Sysdiff /dump DIFF.IMG DUMPFILE.TXT
```

where DUMPFILE.TXT can be any 8.3 name. The dumpfile shows you the differences.

Profiling works best with 32-bit Windows applications. It sometimes has a problem with legacy Win16 or DOS apps. Be sure to test thoroughly before deployment.

Adding Difference Files to the Distribution Folder

The standard distribution folder built by Setup Manager does not include difference files. You use SYSDIFF to copy the difference files to the distribution folder and build the script to install them.

The easiest way to build this script is to run a SYSDIFF information file dump using the following syntax:

```
Sysdiff /inf DIFF.IMG outdir
```

where outdir is the location of the OEM directory you created using Setup Manager when you specified entries in the Additional Files or Folders window. If you did not create an OEM directory, you can use any directory for outdir. Later on, use Setup Manager to edit the unattended setup script and include the new files.

Sysdiff /inf builds an OEM directory with several subdirectories. In the root of OEM, you'll find a CMDLINES.TXT file. The file looks something like this:

```
[Commands]
"rundll32 setupapi,InstallHinfSection DefaultInstall 128 .\DIFF.INF"
```

RUNDLL32 is a general-purpose application installer. It is this installer that actually implements your script. The DIFF.INF file is too long to repeat here, but essentially it implements the differences found in the binary DIFF.IMG file.

This kind of fully scripted installation, when it works, is spooky to watch. You can boot to a network boot disk configured to communicate with the distribution server and then come back in a couple of hours and it's all done. Getting to that point takes quite a bit of fussing around with the script, the application parameters, and a bit of luck. Look for tips in the Microsoft KnowledgeBase and the Release Notes on possible problems that might come up in a profiled installation.

Building a Network Boot Disk

Whether you use disk cloning or a scripted installation, you'll need some way to boot a machine from a floppy disk and get network connection to the distribution server that has the installation files. If you are doing an upgrade and you have a network client running on the target machine, you can connect using that client. If you have a new machine with no network drivers or an existing machine that you want to format before installing Windows 2000, however, you'll need a network boot disk.

Building a Windows-based network boot disk isn't simple. Microsoft uses a proprietary open standard for network drivers called the *Network Driver Interface Specification* (NDIS). (You may see the acronym NDIS broken out as Network *Device* Interface Specification. Both are acceptable.)

Unlike its NetWare counterpart—the *Open Driver Interface* specification (ODI)—NDIS uses a chorus of support files the size of the Mormon Tabernacle Choir. You can declare yourself a true Windows networking guru if you memorize them and their correct configuration, but you probably will not have any friends.

If you're familiar with NT4, you may know that Microsoft supplied a nifty utility with NT4 Server called NCADMIN.EXE that had a feature for building NDIS boot floppy disks. Microsoft chose not to include NCAD-MIN with Windows 2000. If you need to build an NDIS boot disk, I highly recommend getting a copy of NCADMIN from an existing NT4 Server CD to build your network boot disks. It runs just fine on Windows 2000. You can also try the NETBOOT utility from the BackOffice 4.5 Resource Kit. This requires having Office 95 to enable the DAO driver.

If you can't find NCADMIN and don't want to buy the BackOffice Resource Kit, you can download the DOS 3.0 client from the Microsoft FTP site `ftp.microsoft.com/bussys/clients/msclients`. This directory contains two self-extracting executables. You'll need them both.

Using Terminal Services

Although it may seem a little tangential to the subject of installing and upgrading Windows 2000, the ability to manage a server remotely with full graphical tools is such a boon to Windows system administration that it should be covered early.

Early in the product life cycle of NT3.51, a company called Citrix licensed the NT source code from Microsoft and developed a multiuser version of NT called WinFrame. When NT4 was released, Microsoft did not license the source to Citrix. Instead, Microsoft built its own multiuser version of NT4 and sold it as a separate product called Windows Terminal Server, or WTS. Citrix continued to sell their 3.51 OEM version and added a new product called MetaFrame, which installed on top of WTS to provide key functionality that WTS lacked, most importantly a special ICA protocol developed by Citrix that improves many aspects of multiuser operations.

Windows 2000 uses the same basic multiuser architecture as WTS and exposes the multiuser functionality with a new feature called *Terminal Services* (TS). The TS service can be loaded just as easily as loading DNS or TCP/IP Printing. With TS running, you can connect to the server and get a complete Windows 2000 environment just as if you were at the console of the server.

Even if you have no intention of using TS to provide thin-client support, TS provides administrators with an extremely useful tool for remotely managing a server. In fact, TS is about the *only* way to access all the management features in Windows 2000 short of loading a remote-control program.

The licensing restrictions for TS permit administrators to connect to the TS service for purposes of administration without the need to purchase additional licenses. If users are permitted access to run applications, they require a special *Terminal Services Client Access License* (TSCAL). At the time of this writing, Microsoft has not published a price sheet for TSCALs, but the average price of a WTS CAL was around $150, a combination of the base NT Workstation OS license and a network CAL. Users who are running Windows 2000 Professional desktops do not require a CAL to access TS. You've already paid for the two licenses. This does not apply to applications. Check with your vendor for multiuser licensing details.

Complete coverage of TS falls outside the scope of this book. For a wide ranging look at installing, managing, configuring, and troubleshooting Windows 2000 TS, get *Windows 2000 Terminal Services*, by Ted Harwood.

This section covers the essential steps to get the service installed and available for server administration, including the following:

- Installing TS
- Configuring TS clients
- Connecting to TS
- Giving access to non–administrative users

You should not install TS on a server with less than 128MB of RAM. If it is a heavily used server that is already starved of resources, you should upgrade the hardware before installing TS. Connecting to the server with one administrative account requires approximately 8MB of RAM; if you use this session to do a lot of work, however, the memory requirements increase quickly. TS clients use *Remote Desktop Protocol* (RDP) to communicate with the TS server. RDP is based on the ITU T.120 multichannel conferencing protocol. RDP is perfectly acceptable for remote administration from Windows clients; if you want to use non–Windows clients or thin-client boxes, such as a Wyse Winterm, however, you'll need the Citrix MetaFrame upgrade for Windows 2000 to get the ICA client.

Installing Terminal Services

You must be logged on with administrative privileges to install TS. You'll need the Windows 2000 Server CD. This process requires that server to be restarted.

Procedure 2.14 **Installing Terminal Services**

1. From the Control Panel, open the Add/Remove Programs applet.
2. Click Add/Remove Windows Components.
3. Click Components. The Windows Components window opens.
4. Click Next. The Terminal Services Setup window opens (see Figure 2.17). Select the Remote Administration Mode option. This minimizes impact on the server and does not require special licensing.

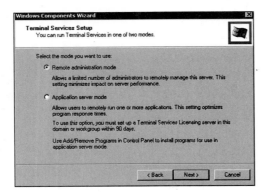

Figure 2.17 Windows Components Wizard—Terminal Services Setup window showing default Remote Administration Mode selection.

5. The Configuring Components window opens and the files are copied from the CD.

6. After the wizard has finished loading Terminals Services, you are prompted to restart—do so.

Configuring a Terminal Services Client

When Terminal Services is installed, it creates a Clients folder under \WINNT\System32. This folder contains 16-bit and 32-bit client drivers. Any Windows client with an IP stack can connect to Terminal Services with one of these sets of client drivers.

You can either share the \WINNT\System32\Clients folder or you can copy the folder to a data volume and share it there.

A Windows client connects to the folder over the network and then initiates setup as follows:

Procedure 2.15 **Configuring a Terminal Services Client**

1. Double-click Setup in the appropriate Tsclient folder. The Terminal Services Client Setup window opens. The client setup application is 16 bit, so the window appears inside another window of the same name.

2. Click Continue. The Name and Organization window opens. Enter a standard username and your organization name. This username is not used to create accounts.

3. Click OK. Confirm when prompted.

4. The License Agreement window opens. Click I Agree to accept the terms.

5. A Client Setup window opens showing the proposed local path for storing the client files. Change this path if you want to.

6. Click the big button next to Start Install. An informational window opens asking whether all users should get the same initial settings. Click Yes or No, depending on whether you want the installation to go in the All Users profile or the local user's profile.

7. The client drivers install and a Successful Completion window opens.

8. Click OK to complete the client installation.

You're ready to connect to a server running Terminal Services.

Connecting to a Terminal Services Server

The TS client installation adds an item to the START menu for launching the client.

Procedure 2.16   Connecting to a Terminal Services Server

1. Launch the TS client using START | PROGRAMS | TERMINAL SERVICES CLIENT. The Terminal Services Client window opens (see Figure 2.18).

Figure 2.18   Terminal Services Client window showing selection of TS server.

2. Enter the name of the TS server or select it from the list of all servers in the domain. If you enter the name, be sure to use the fully qualified DNS name.

3. Select a screen area that is either the same or smaller than the resolution on the local screen. This opens the remote session in a window. Leave the Data Compression and Cache Bitmaps options at their default.

4. When the client connects to the TS server, a Windows logon window displays, just as if you were logging on at the console. Because the Administrative option was selected, the logon credentials must be for a member of the Administrators local group.

5. Use the Start button to log off just as you would at a console. Be sure not to select the Shutdown option unless you really do want to shut down the server.

You can manage TS clients who are connected to a TS using the Terminal Services Manager console. Launch this from START | PROGRAMS | ADMINISTRATIVE TOOLS | TERMINAL SERVICES MANAGER. Figure 2.19 shows an example console window with one account connected.

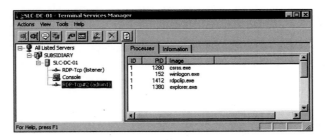

Figure 2.19 Terminal Services Manager console showing one connected user.

Giving Terminal Services Access to Non–Administrator Clients

If you want to enable users other than administrators to connect to the TS server, you must reinstall TS and select the Application Server mode.

After you have reinstalled, you can set permissions associated with TS to permit connections by users other than administrators. Reset permissions as follows:

Procedure 2.17 **Giving TS Access to Non-Administrator Clients**

1. At the TS server (or a TS client session), launch the `Terminal Services Configuration` console using START | PROGRAMS | ADMINISTRATIVE TOOLS | TERMINAL SERVICES CONFIGURATION. Figure 2.20 shows an example.

Figure 2.20 `Terminal Services Configuration` console window.

2. Expand the tree to the Configurations icon.
3. Right-click the RDP-Tcp Connection icon in the right pane and select PROPERTIES from the fly-out menu. The `Properties` window opens.
4. Select the `Permissions` tab.
5. Add groups to the list of accounts that are granted access permission. You should only grant Full Access permissions to administrators. Grant User permissions to all other users.

Adding Multiuser Applications

If you want to install an application on the TS server that can be used by multiple administrators or users, you need to set up the system to place the Registry entries and application files in a common area. This is done with the `Change User` command.

Before installing a multiuser application, open a command prompt or the `Run` window and enter the following:

```
change user /install
```

After you have completed installing the application, enter the following command:

```
change user /execute
```

If you forget to issue the `change user` command appropriately, you may cause applications to become unusable.

Moving Forward

The plan of this book is to move methodically through a complete deployment of Windows 2000 in an entire enterprise. Getting the OS installed on a few servers and a few hundred desktops is a good start, but there's still a long way to go. There's TCP/IP support services, such as DNS and DHCP to configure, security to set up, Active Directory domains to deploy, shared resources to make available, users to manage, and disasters to plan for.

Before jumping too far ahead, however, a few final touches regarding hardware need attention. Installing or upgrading a machine is only half the job. The other half is making modifications later on. The next chapter covers installing and configuring Plug and Play and legacy hardware and troubleshooting any problems that might come up along the way.

3

Adding Additional Hardware

AFTER YOU HAVE SUCCESSFULLY INSTALLED OR UPGRADED A machine to Windows 2000, you may need to expand your storage or move from IDE to SCSI or Fibre Channel drives. Or you might finally talk the boss into springing for a second processor for the Web server. Or you want to try out a new fault-tolerant network adapter. Or you might want to swap hard drives between laptops. These and other hardware issues come up all the time.

This chapter begins with a quick overview of the Windows 2000 architecture as it pertains to hardware operability, including PnP operation, followed by steps for installing various kinds of hardware. This is not intended to be a PC maintenance guide, but rather to give you a feel for how devices are installed and configured using Windows 2000. There are also workarounds and warnings about problems that have caused other administrators to seek midlife career changes into fast food or insurance sales.

Finding Hardware Standards

Much of the information in this chapter came from the various hardware standards that are either implemented or supported by Windows 2000. You can find a list of the top 150 hardware standards supported in some way by all Windows platforms at msdn.microsoft.com/standards/top150/hardware.asp. The list includes hyperlinks to the respective standard holders.

Functional Description of Windows 2000 Architecture

Let's start with a peek behind the curtain to see how Windows 2000 is built. This topic focuses on areas affecting stability and performance, including memory allocation, memory protection, process protection, I/O handling, and PnP. Other aspects of Windows 2000 architecture are covered in the chapters relating to the associated features. For example, see Chapter 15, "Managing Shared Resources," for a description of the Windows 2000 printing architecture.

Memory Allocation

Windows 2000 is a 32-bit operating system. As such, it can directly address 2^{32} bytes of memory, or about 4GB. This 4GB address space is divvied into two 2GB parcels. The upper 2GB is given to the operating system and is called kernel memory. The lower 2GB is given to applications and is called user memory. Separating memory into kernel space and user space keeps badly behaved applications from crashing the system.

A machine ordinarily doesn't have 4GB of physical memory, but that doesn't stop Windows 2000 from using the entire 4GB address space. An Executive process called the *Virtual Memory Manager* (VMM) makes use of special features in the x86 CPU to map virtual addresses to physical addresses.

But VMM is not content to keep one memory map. It acts like a shady land dealer who sells the same plot of land several times. VMM gives every process running on the machine its own 4GB of memory, each with the same half-for-the-kernel/half-for-you split. VMM cooks the books in this way by shuffling virtual memory so that processes are completely ignorant of each other. That slide presentation you're working on in PowerPoint has no idea that a Gantt chart in Primavera is occupying a neighboring area of physical memory.

DOS applications also get their own memory space thanks to a special piece of 32-bit code called the NT Virtual DOS Machine, or NTVDM.EXE. NTVDM builds a virtual 16-bit environment for the DOS application that emulates the BIOS function calls and memory handling on a standard DOS machine and provides a 16-bit command interpreter similar to

COMMAND. It's possible to configure *Terminate-and-Stay-Resident* (TSR) applications to share the same memory space, just as they would on a DOS machine. See Chapter 16, "Managing the User Operating Environment," for details.

16-bit Windows applications are the exception to this separation of virtual memory rule. Win16 applications are designed to share a common memory space. Windows 2000 accommodates this by erecting a *Windows-on-Windows* (WOW) subsystem where the Win16 applications can reside together. Again, see Chapter 16 for more information.

Paging Files

VMM would be very busy indeed if it had to map every single byte of physical memory to virtual memory. To improve performance, memory is made more granular. Instead of tracking every byte, VMM divides memory into chunks called *pages*. Paging is a function of hardware. Each memory page in the Intel x86 architecture is 4KB.

Physical memory is a scarce commodity, and the VMM shenanigans that give a separate memory space to every application make physical memory even scarcer. VMM relieves the pressure on physical memory by moving seldom-used memory pages to disk. For this purpose, VMM uses a special file called PAGEFILE.SYS. This is a superhidden file, but you see it by changing the folder options under TOOLS | FOLDER OPTIONS | VIEW. Deselect the Hide Protected Operating System Files option.

VMM always uses a paging file, even if the machine has more than enough memory to handle all the running processes. If you make the paging file too small, smaller than available physical memory, you can get *Out of Virtual Memory* errors even if you have only one application running.

If the paging file is accidentally deleted on a dual-boot machine or becomes corrupt, the system uses a temporary paging file and prompts the user to create a new one. There is a risk of system instability and possible Kernel-mode stops if the user persists in running without a properly constructed paging file. See the sidebar on the next page titled "Paging File Parameters" for more information.

Paging File Parameters

The size and distribution of the VMM paging files can be modified using System Properties as follows:

Procedure 3.1   Changing Paging File Configuration

1. Right-click the My Desktop icon and select PROPERTIES from the fly-out menu. The System Properties window opens.

2. Select the Advanced tab.

3. Click Performance Options.

4. Under Virtual Memory, click Change to open the Virtual Memory window (see Figure 3.1).

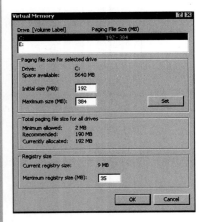

Figure 3.1   Virtual Memory window showing default paging file on the boot partition.

If you want to change the size of the existing paging file, highlight the entry and change the Initial Size and Maximum Size. If you want to build an additional paging file on a second drive, highlight the drive and enter the size values. Here are the paging file limits:

- Maximum paging file size: 4095MB.

- Maximum number of paging files: 16, with one paging file on any given partition.

- Default paging file size: RAM + 64MB.

- Registry parameters: HKLM | System | CurrentControlSet | Control | Session Manager | Memory Management.

- Virtual memory settings: All Registry parameters are set to 0, giving VMM latitude to assign memory using its own heuristics.

Unlike a Windows 3.x swap file, the Windows 2000 paging file does not occupy a contiguous chunk of disk. In fact, a very common cause of performance degradation is fragmentation of the paging file. See Chapter 13, "Managing File Systems," for ways to limit paging file fragmentation.

Kernel Memory Pools

To prevent user applications from starving the operating system of physical memory, a certain amount of physical memory is set aside for the exclusive use of kernel processes.

Physical memory is allocated to the kernel in the form of two pools: *paged pool* memory and *non-paged pool* memory. Memory in the paged pool can be swapped to the paging file. Memory in the non-paged pool must stay resident in RAM.

You should take regular statistics of kernel memory use on all servers to get a feel for trends in case you should encounter a memory leak. See the section "Tracking Kernel Memory Use" at the end of this chapter.

Paged Pool Memory

The total memory assigned to the paged pool is based on available physical memory. The paged pool limit is 192MB regardless of the available RAM.

If the system runs out of paged pool memory, it can become unstable and report *Out Of Resources* errors and RPC errors. This occurs even if there is plenty of physical memory. The most common cause for running out of paged pool memory is a large Registry. The Registry can take a maximum of 80% of paged pool memory. That doesn't leave much room for other processes.

The Registry in Windows 2000 no longer contains user and group accounts. That information is contained in the Active Directory. The number of Registry-related memory problems should therefore drastically diminish after you upgrade your domain controllers.

Non-Paged Pool Memory

The total memory assigned to the non-paged pool is a calculation based on the size of the paged pool. The limit for non-paged pool memory is 128MB regardless of the available physical memory. The paged pool and non-paged pool occupy a common memory area, and the two pools together cannot total more than 256MB.

You can view the non-paged and paged pool sizes using Task Manager. Right-click the status bar and select TASK MANAGER from the fly-out menu. Select the Performance tab and look at the Kernel Memory entries. Figure 3.2 shows an example.

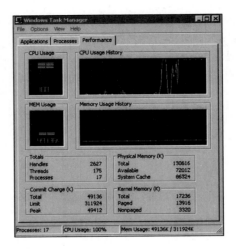

Figure 3.2 Task Manager showing kernel memory use.

Use of non-paged memory is tightly controlled because it cannot be swapped to disk and is therefore a costly resource. Non-paged pool memory is reserved for processes, such as *interrupt service requests* (ISRs) and protection code entries that cannot survive a page fault.

Applications can request non-paged memory, but Microsoft strongly discourages this. It is possible to crash the system by overcommitting the non-paged pool. This isn't a common problem, but it has been known to occur when loading and unloading applications or services that make use of non-paged pool memory. These so-called *memory leaks* are relatively rare, but can cause lots of strange problems when they occur.

Memory Leaks

One example of a non-paged pool memory leak involved the Services process in NT4. When network clients access a member server, the server validates the users' credentials by using pass-through authentication to a domain controller. The member servers were not freeing up the name of the last domain controller they contacted, so over a period of weeks the available memory would get smaller and smaller to the point that applications and services would become erratic. This problem was resolved with Service Pack 4.

4GB Tuning (4GT)

The 2GB dividing line between user memory and kernel memory is completely arbitrary, like the old DOS 640KB limit. An engineer picked a point and that was that. The kernel/user memory line was drawn at the halfway point because this permitted the use of a simple "signed bit" algorithm to designate pages as belonging to user space or kernel space (see Figure 3.3).

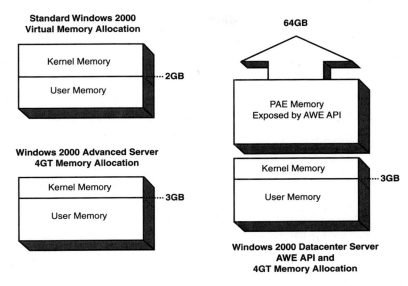

Figure 3.3 Diagram of virtual memory allocation options
for various Windows 2000 Server versions.

Just as the 640KB application memory limit in DOS seemed enormous in 1983 but gradually got more and more confining, the 2GB line in Windows 2000 is starting to pinch a little. With memory prices hovering around $1/MB with motherboards that can handle all that memory also falling in price, it's going to become more and more common to find standard production machines that can handle 4GB of memory.

Even at $1/MB, however, you'll pay several thousand dollars to put 4GB of memory in a machine. It is a shame to waste half that money by giving memory to the operating system above 2GB where most of it sits unused. If you are running standard Windows 2000 Server, don't bother adding memory above the 2GB point. Tests show that the benefits are negligible.

On the other hand, if you have an application capable of using memory above 2GB, Windows 2000 Advanced Server has an option called *4GB Memory Tuning* (4GT) that frees an additional 1GB of physical memory for use by applications by taking it away from the operating system. 4GT does this by implementing a different method of tagging pages. You must add memory above the 2GB point to take advantage of 4GT, so don't buy Advanced Server unless you plan on shelling out the cash for a machine that can take advantage of it.

RAM and L2 Cache

The Windows 2000 Virtual Memory Manager uses the onboard L2 cache in the CPU to store its memory maps. If you add too much physical memory in relation to the size of the L2 cache, you can cause system performance to worsen because VMM is forced to go onto the system bus.

Microsoft has not published any general rules for ratios of L2 cache to total memory, but you can't go wrong by allowing 256KB of L2 cache for every 256MB of physical memory. This is not too difficult when you consider that a machine capable of taking advantage of 4GB of main memory is bound to be an SMP machine. You can spec out four Xeon processors with 1MB of L2 cache or two Xeon processors with 2MB of L2 cache.

Address Windowing Extensions

Not only is the arbitrary 2GB line between kernel and user memory getting to be a constraint, the very notion of 32-bit addressing is starting to feel a little antiquated. Eight-way Xeon servers with 16GB of memory are affordably priced, and companies, such as Data General, have been pushing the envelope to 64 processors and 64GB of RAM. Running on that kind of machine, 4GB of memory looks truly puny.

The Pentium processor could always address memory beyond 4GB using a feature set called *Physical Address Extensions* (PAE). The PAE provides a 36-bit address line, making it possible to handle 64GB of physical memory. Intel has long provided a software developer's kit that included a PSE36 utility to take advantage of the PAE feature. PSE36 essentially configures all that memory above 4GB as a big RAM disk so that the system can use it as a paging file.

Windows 2000 Advanced Server and Datacenter Server make better use of PAE memory by incorporating a new API called *Address Windowing Extensions* (AWE). Using the AWE API, an application can place memory pages into real memory above 4GB, if it is available. The trick to AWE is that the application must do more of its own memory management than is typical for standard Win32 programming. Look for some vendors with products that need lots of memory to start releasing AWE versions sometime after the release of Datacenter Server in mid-2000, but this is only a stopgap until the Merced (IA-64) processor and 64-bit Windows 2000 come on-stream. Until then, if you have purchasing decisions to make that involve large, multi-processor platforms, you should get into the Datacenter Server beta so that you can evaluate your applications.

Process Protection

Windows 2000 takes advantage of special hardware protection elements built in to the Intel x86 architecture. This hardware protection takes the form of a ring protection scheme. There are four rings, 0 through 3, with Ring 0 being the most privileged. Each successive ring has lower privileges. Windows 2000 uses only Ring 0 and Ring 3 to maintain compatibility with RISC processors that have only two levels of protection (see Figure 3.4).

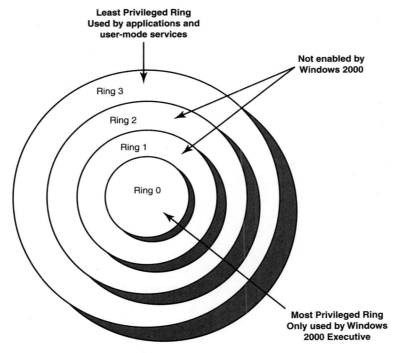

Figure 3.4   Diagram of ring protection scheme.

Processes running in Ring 0 can communicate directly with the hardware and with processes running in Ring 3. In DOS, for example, all code runs in Ring 0. In Windows 2000, only privileged system components in the Windows 2000 Executive are permitted to run in Ring 0. User applications are relegated to Ring 3.

Legacy Application Compatibility

Windows 9x also takes advantage of the Intel ring protection scheme, but legacy applications are permitted to run in Ring 0 for backward compatibility. This is never permitted in Windows 2000. There is no *MS-DOS mode*. If an application absolutely insists on writing to hardware, it absolutely will not work on Windows 2000.

Privileged Windows 2000 OS components permitted to run in Ring 0 are collectively called the Windows 2000 Executive (see Figure 3.5).

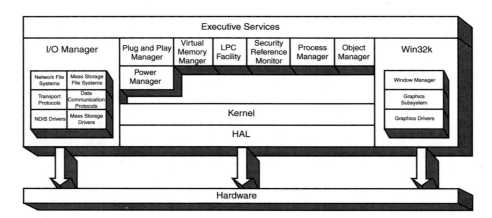

Figure 3.5   Diagram of the Windows 2000 Executive.

The Executive consists of a kernel driver, a *Hardware Abstraction Layer* (HAL), and a set of system services. The kernel driver converts hardware devices into objects that can be understood by the rest of the services in the Executive. The kernel driver is an executable, NTOSKRNL.EXE, and relies on the HAL.DLL function library for routines that manipulate devices. For this reason, the kernel driver and HAL library are not platform independent.

The remaining Executive services are grouped together based on the processes or data structures they control or use. With a couple of exceptions, these groupings are called managers. Here is a list of the managers and other service providers in the Windows 2000 Executive:

- **Executive Support.** Services that provide pool memory allocation and special queue and thread handling not provided by the kernel driver.

- **Plug and Play Manager.** *New to Windows 2000.* Services that enumerate and define the capabilities of hardware devices. See the section "Overview of Windows 2000 Plug and Play" later in this chapter.

- **Power Manager.** *New in Windows 2000.* Services that control device power operations and define hibernate/wakeup policies. These services support the *Advanced Power Management* (APM) and *Advanced Configuration and Power Interface* (ACPI) features in the machine's BIOS.

- **I/O Manager.** Services that control data flows to external storage and network devices. This includes device drivers that communicate directly to hardware without using the kernel or HAL.

- **Object Manager.** Services that control symbolic links and data structures in the object's namespace.

- **Security Reference Monitor.** Services that control access to Windows 2000 objects. See Chapter 10, "Managing Active Directory Security," and Chapter 14, "Managing File Systems Security," for more information on how Windows 2000 uses the SRM to control access to Active Directory objects, files, folders, and Registry keys.

- **Process Manager.** Services that provide structured handling for device threads.

- **Local Procedure Call Facility.** A high-level client/server interface between user processes and system services. Used by the 32-bit Windows subsystem, WIN32.DLL, the Posix subsystem, POSIX.EXE, and the OS/2 subsystem, OS2SS.EXE.

- **Virtual Memory Manager.** Services that map virtual memory to physical memory and control contiguous memory allocation.

- **Win32K.** Services that control graphics and window handling. This includes drivers that communicate directly to video and print hardware without using the kernel or HAL.

All Executive components run in Kernel mode, giving them the capability of exchanging data freely. Hardware drivers for video devices, network adapters, and mass storage also run in privileged memory space. For this reason, they are subjected to more scrutiny and testing than user-side device drivers. See www.microsoft.com/hwtest for a description of the testing requirements. See the *Driver Development Kit* (DDK) documentation for a complete description of I/O handling in Windows 2000.

Loading Specific PC Hardware Drivers

Different classes of hardware require different iterations of the kernel and HAL drivers. Windows 2000 ships with several sets of PC hardware drivers and OEMs provide others, especially if they sell SMP and NUMA machines. You can view and change the PC hardware drivers using Device Manager. See the section "Using Device Manager" later in this chapter for more details.

Procedure 3.2   **Loading PC Hardware Drivers**

1. Open Device Manager by selecting START, RUN, and then entering DEVMGMT.MSC and clicking OK. The `Device Manager` console opens.

2. Expand the tree under Computer and open the `Properties` window for the PC device (could have several different names depending on the name of the driver set) by right-clicking the icon and selecting PROPERTIES from the fly-out menu.

3. Select the `Driver` tab.

4. Click `Driver Details`. The `Driver File Details` window opens. Figure 3.6 shows an example for a uniprocessor PC.

Figure 3.6   `Driver File Details` window showing the three hardware driver files.

5. Click `Update Driver`. This launches the Upgrade Device Driver Wizard.

6. Click Next. The `Install Hardware Device Drivers` window opens.

7. Select the `Display a List of the Known Drivers for This Device` option.

8. Click Next. The `Select a Device Driver` window opens (see Figure 3.7). Select `Show All Hardware of This Device Class`. This displays the Manufacturer and Model of the kernel drivers and HAL files listed in `\WINNT\INF\HAL.INF`.

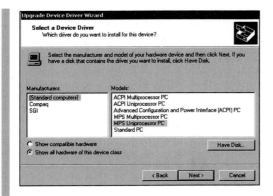

Figure 3.7 Upgrade Device Driver Wizard—Select A Device Driver window.

9. If you want to change your hardware driver, select an alternate or provide a set of OEM drivers. *Caution*: If these drivers are not correct for your machine, the system can fail to boot or can behave erratically.

10. Click Next. The drivers are copied and existing drivers are overwritten.

11. Click Finish to close the wizard and return to the Properties window.

12. Click OK to close the Properties window. The system prompts you to restart—do so.

If you select the wrong driver, the system will hang or crash with a Kernel-mode stop error. You cannot recover using the Last Known Good Configuration Boot option because changes are made outside of the Registry. Recover as follows:

Procedure 3.3 **Recovering from Loading Incorrect Hardware Drivers**

1. Boot to the Recovery Console. See Chapter 18, "Recovering from System Failures," for details.

2. Extract the following files from the \WINNT\Driver Cache\I386\DRIVER.CAB:

HAL.DLL

NTKRNLPA.EXE

NTOSKRNL.EXE

3. Copy the files to \WINNT\System32.

4. Copy the Registry files from \WINNT\Repair to \WINNT\System32\Config.

5. Restart.

Process Separation

Applications are not permitted to make direct use of system services in the Executive. Instead, applications make API calls that are handled by the 32-bit Windows subsystem, Win32. Win32 communicates these requests to the Executive using the *Client/Server Runtime Subsystem* (CSRSS). Service requests are packaged and delivered in bulk to improve performance, like a semi-tractor trailer waiting for a full load before taking off across the country.

The server-side processes on the other side of CSRSS live in the privileged space of the Executive. They call on the Executive services to fulfill requests and package the results into responses that go back to the client side where Win32 is waiting. If the request causes an illegal operation, the system forces the application to fail with a *General Protection Fault* (GPF). If the Executive never gets around to responding, CSRSS twiddles its thumbs waiting and then eventually discards the messages and tears down the connection. This may cause the application to fail, or at least be unresponsive for a time. The decision interval for CSRSS varies. See the following for more details.

Handling Unresponsive Applications

If an application stops responding to keystrokes or mouse clicks, it is either waiting for a response from Win32, which is waiting for a response from the CSRSS, or it might have gotten a response that it cannot digest. In the second instance, the application may hang forever or it may fail with a protection fault.

If the application faults, stack and process information is captured by the DrWatson utility—DRWATSON.EXE or DRWTSN32.EXE. DrWatson saves its log files in \WINNT\DRWATSON.

If an application hangs without faulting, you can kill the process from Task Manager as follows:

Procedure 3.4   **Killing Processes**

1.   Open Task Manager by pressing `Ctrl+Alt+Del` and clicking the `Task Manager` button.

2.   Select the `Applications` tab.

3.   Highlight the application that is not responding and click `End Task`.

4.   If the offending application is running a background process, you may need to use the `Processes` tab to kill the process.

Task Manager is like a responsible hunter. It may refuse to kill a process if it thinks it cannot make a clean job of it. If this happens, jot down the *process ID* (PID) in Task Manager, and then use the Kill utility from the Windows 2000 Resource Kit to kill the process. You may need to use `kill  -f` to complete the job. Kill nearly always works, but it is a dirty way to cut off a process and it can make the machine unstable. You may want to restart after using Kill just to clean up memory.

Handling Win32 Faults

If an application really misbehaves, it can cause Win32 to fault. If this happens, the operating system survives because it is protected in kernel space. Network services continue to function, as do background processes that do not interact with Win32. From the console, however, the machine will appear to go into an autistic state where it refuses to respond to any mouse clicks or keystrokes.

Because background processes continue to function, a Win32 failure on a server can go unnoticed for days or even weeks. On a desktop, however, it is immediately apparent. If a user calls to complain that a Windows 2000 machine has stopped responding, urge the user to wait while the system recognizes that a fault has occurred and works to repair the damage. The time it takes to do this varies based on the fault, but generally 15–20 minutes is more than adequate.

If it looks as if the system has truly hung, wait for a complete cessation of hard drive activity, and then press the Restart button. If AUTOCHK runs in the foreground during the graphical portion of the restart, you know that something was left in the I/O cache. This isn't likely to cause a system failure because Windows 2000 takes steps to double-protect vital components, but the data loss could affect application integrity. Take a while to check out the applications the user had open at the time of the fault. Don't assume that just because they launch and load that they will continue to work. Damage may have been done to the data.

I/O Handling

Windows 2000 is a multitasking operating system, but not even Bill Gates and Andy Groves can overcome one fundamental limitation of computing: a single CPU can only do one thing at a time. Windows 2000 gives the impression of doing many things simultaneously in the same way that a motion picture gives the impression of continuous movement by running through a series of discrete events very, very quickly.

Windows 2000 uses preemptive multitasking as opposed to the cooperative multitasking used by Windows 3.x. Anyone who has attended a parent-teacher society meeting understands the limitations of cooperative multitasking. One person can talk and talk and use up all the time. Preemptive multitasking, on the other hand, takes a sterner role. A particular thread is given a certain time span to run. When that time elapses, the thread is put aside so that another thread can have its turn.

The Windows 2000 Executive uses a trap handler to coordinate activities. The trap handler gets its input from interrupt handlers. Interrupts come in two flavors: software and hardware. Hardware interrupts are issued by devices that need the attention of the CPU. Software interrupts are issued by applications that also need attention.

Software Interrupts and Time Quantum

Software interrupts divert the CPU's attention from one stream of code to another. They originate from within the application or from the operating system. Without OS-generated software interrupts, the CPU would focus its attention on one thread until that thread relinquished control. Software interrupts are handled based on a *time quantum* and a set of *priority levels*. The time quantum is the interval that the operating system permits a single thread to run before cutting it off and moving on. Windows 2000 Server uses a long time quantum, 120 milliseconds by default, so that each background process gets lots of time to do useful work. Windows 2000 Professional uses a shorter time quantum because users want fast response when moving among applications. For more information about the time quantum, see `www.sysinternals.com/nt5.htm`.

Software Interrupts and Priority Levels

When an application issues an interrupt, it requests a priority from the thread handler in the Executive. The thread handler in turn assigns an *interrupt request level* (IRQL) to the thread. There are 32 IRQLs, from 0 to 31, with the lower numbers having the higher priority.

When the CPU sets to work on a thread at a particular IRQL, it masks any lower IRQLs. This forces threads with a lower priority to queue up until the CPU has finished working on all higher-priority threads. To keep from starving a thread completely, Windows 2000 has routines that raise the priority of waiting threads until they get attention.

For the most part, IRQL prioritization lies outside the control of an administrator. However, you can request a general IRQL priority using the Start command. There are four priority classes: Low, Normal, High, Realtime, and two prioritization levels: Abovenormal and Belownormal. If you have power users—Why do accountants come to mind?—who want applications to run at a high priority, you can have them launch the application as follows:

```
Start /High /Abovenormal APP.EXE
```

Frankly, I have done lots of fiddling with Start priorities and have rarely found them worth the trouble. Performance boosts only come into play when the thread dispatcher is starved of CPU cycles and must begin triage. Not many workstations get near this point. Generally, users start closing down applications instead of figuring out ways to launch apps that hog all the available cycles.

Adjusting the Time Quantum

The user interface provides a single control for setting the time quantum. Set it as follows:

Procedure 3.5   Adjusting the Time Quantum

1. Right-click the My Desktop icon and select PROPERTIES from the fly-out menu. The System Properties window opens.

2. Select the Advanced tab.

3. Click Performance Options.

4. In the Application Response section, select either to optimize performance for Applications or Background Services.

The Application option sets a shorter time quantum; Background sets a longer time quantum.

Hardware Interrupts

Devices use hardware interrupts to divert the attention of the CPU when they want something done. Without hardware interrupts, the CPU would be oblivious to the system clock, network adapter, mouse, keyboard, and other peripherals.

Hardware interrupts summon the CPU the same way that butlers are summoned in an English mansion. Say, for example, that you and a few cronies are playing billiards and you want a little Scotch and a few cigars to help while away the time. You pull a rope in the corner of the billiard room. This rope loops through the walls of the mansion and ends up in the pantry, where it rings one of many little bells dangling from springs. The butler hears the bell and looks up to see which bell is shaking. In this case, it's the bell for the billiard room. The butler takes out a 3×5 card labeled Billiard Room and finds instructions on it that say, "Deliver Scotch and cigars to the billiard room." The butler interrupts whatever he was doing (polishing the silver, watching *Masterpiece Theatre*, whatever) and carries out these instructions.

Here's how the process works for a computer (see Figure 3.8). A single-processor computer has two *Programmable Interrupt Controllers* (PICs) chained together to control a single interrupt line. When an interrupt arrives, the PIC raises the INT line. When the CPU sees the INT line go high, it checks the INTA line for a number indicating which interrupt caused the signal. The CPU then carries out the Interrupt Service Routine (the instructions on the butler's 3×5 card) associated with that interrupt number. See the sidebar titled "IRQ Conflicts" for details about what happens if those instructions are not correct.

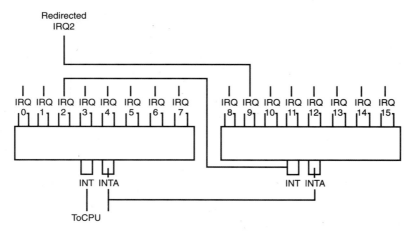

Figure 3.8 Programmable Interrupt Controller diagram.

Hardware interrupts get more complex in latter-day machines that have multiple processors and newer PCI buses. Windows 2000, along with Windows 98 and Windows 95 OSR2, supports shared PCI interrupts using extensions called *IRQ Steering*.

IRQ Conflicts

There is a possibility that the interrupt service routine associated with an interrupt is not appropriate for the device that issued it because more than one device has laid claim to an interrupt. Continuing with the English mansion example, it's as if the butler heard the bell, saw that it came from the billiard room, but accidentally pulled out the instruction card for the parlor, which says "Bring scones and tea to the parlor." When the butler carries out the action, the Madam in the parlor is perplexed, and the Master in the billiard room waits in mounting irritation.

Another potential cause of erratic I/O behavior is improper prioritization of IRQs. The CPU does not get one hardware interrupt at a time. It is constantly bombarded with them. The more peripherals you have in the machine, the more hardware interrupts you'll get. To put order into this chaos, the Programmable Interrupt Controller assigns a priority to each interrupt based on the IRQ: the lower the IRQ, the higher the priority. That's the reason the system timer is assigned Interrupt 0.

The cascaded interrupts from the second PIC complicate the prioritization. A device at IRQ15 has a higher priority than a device at IRQ5 thanks to the cascade to IRQ2. If you add a legacy device that makes the system unstable, try changing its interrupt to one with a lower priority. Also, check the vendor to see whether they report performance or stability issues with certain IRQ settings. PIO network adapters, for example, generally do not like being at a low priority IRQ.

PCI IRQ Steering

Machines that support PCI IRQ Steering maintain a special table in BIOS that lists PCI resources and their interrupts. This table acts as a small interrupt router that can be configured by the operating system to point at different interrupt service requests. This enables multiple PCI devices to share the same interrupt, a big plus when there are only 15 IRQs from which to choose. (IRQ2/IRQ9 are shared.)

You may need to disable IRQ Steering to get a particular device to work correctly. (See the section "Changing the IRQ Steering Options" at the end of this chapter.)

For more information about the PCI specification and IRQ Steering, see the PCI SIG Web site at `www.pcisig.com/tech/index.html`. Take your credit card along. A copy of the specification costs $50.

PCI IRQ Steering requires PnP to work, which brings up the final topic in this architectural overview.

Overview of Windows 2000 Plug and Play

From a hardware perspective, the most significant change in Windows 2000 is Plug and Play. Thanks to PnP, many of the traditional chores required to configure and troubleshoot hardware just evaporate. In their place come chores required to configure and troubleshoot PnP. This is progress, you see, because it demands more sophisticated diagnostic skills on the part of the administrator.

The Windows 2000 Executive has two new components to handle PnP services: the Plug and Play Manager and the Power Manager.

- **Plug and Play Manager** discovers PnP devices using a process called *enumeration*. It then loads an appropriate driver and makes Registry entries based on INF scripts written either by Microsoft or the hardware vendor. Plug and Play Manager also allocates resources, such as IRQs, I/O ports, and DMA channels.

- **Power Manager** handles dynamic interaction with devices to conserve battery life or limit wear and tear on components. Power Manager can be set to spin down a hard drive, for example, after a certain interval of inactivity.

Both the Plug and Play Manager and Power Manager depend on PnP-compatible hardware. Two standards for PnP hardware are APM and ACPI.

- **Advanced Power Management.** This is a fairly old initiative, dating back to 1991, on the part of Intel and Microsoft to define power management strategies in BIOS. APM consists primarily of a set of timeout registers. The operating system can set values to control the timeout intervals, but that's about it.

- **Advanced Configuration and Power Interface (ACPI) standard.** This standard was jointly developed by Microsoft, Intel, and Toshiba. It defines power management specifications for system BIOS, interfaces, and devices along with a policy-based API for implementing those features.

The remaining portion of this section discusses how APM and ACPI are supported on Windows 2000 and gives an overview of the Windows Driver Model, which defines a common set of drivers for consumer and business Windows.

APM Support in Windows 2000

Over the years, APM has become an amalgam of so-called green machines and smart batteries and so forth, which all require separate support in software to manage effectively. Microsoft chose to implement only a bare APM feature set in Windows 2000 Professional, and that only after an uproar from beta testers when the original product specifications eliminated APM support entirely.

The restrictions for APM support in Windows 2000 are as follows:

- APM is implemented by Windows 2000 Professional only, not Windows 2000 Server.

- APM is not implemented if ACPI support is enabled.

- APM does not expose full power management functionality, such as CPU speed reduction and CRT brightness controls.

- APM is disabled automatically on machines that have been identified as incompatible by the *Windows Hardware Quality Lab* (WHQL) suite of tests.

See "Configuring Power Management Features" later in this chapter for details on enabling and configuring APM support, if it is available.

Using APMSTAT

A tool in the Windows 2000 Resource Kit called APMSTAT tests the APM BIOS in a machine and reports whether it is suitable for Windows 2000. Here is a sample report using the -v (verbose) switch:

```
C:\Program Files\Resource Kit>apmstat -v
This computer appears to have an APM legal HAL
This machine has an APM bios present that looks OK, and it is
not on the list of machines known to have APM problems.
Check the power applet in the control panel to see if APM is enabled
APM Registry Data Dump
Major = 0001  Minor = 0002
InstallFlags = 0003
Code16Segment = f000  Code16Offset = 56c4  DataSeg = 0040
Signature = APM
Valid = 0001
Detection Log Data:
44 45 54 4c 4f 47 31 00 00 00 00 00 00 00 00 00
   D  E  T  L  O  G  1
```

If APCI is enabled, APMSTAT reports the following:

```
This is an ACPI machine. APM is NOT relevant on this machine.
```

ACPI Support on Windows 2000

The stated goal of Microsoft is get the marketplace moved on to ACPI machines so that Windows 9x and Windows 200x can use a single set of functions to control the computer's power state with the assurance that all devices recognize the machine's waking and sleeping state and react accordingly. If you're the parent of a one-year-old, you'll appreciate this goal. For more information about ACPI, get a copy of the ACPI specification from www.teleport.com/~acpi. (This is the Microsoft authorized site, despite the tilde in the URL.) You can also get lots of information about ACPI implementation and design from the nearly 40 white papers at www.microsoft.com/hwdev/onnow.

Putting design niceties aside, the power management features that are available on any given machine running Windows 2000 depend on the age of the hardware, the status of the firmware, and the quality of the ACPI implementation. Windows 2000 beta testing has uncovered many, many systems that cause problems when ACPI is enabled. Check the HCL and scour the Microsoft KnowledgeBase before deploying Windows 2000 onto laptops or manageable desktops. You should be able to install Windows 2000 on a four-year-old laptop as long as it is a Pentium machine, but you might not get the same power management features that Windows 95 OSR2 or Windows 98 would give you.

Windows 2000 has its problems even with relatively new ACPI machines. The ACPI specification is evolving and machines that met the PC97 specifications for ACPI don't necessarily meet the PC99 or the PC2001 specifications required to fully support Windows 2000. Microsoft drew a line at 1/1/99 and tested machines built prior to that date using the hardware compatibility tests developed for ACPI. The result is a Good BIOS List. An INF file called BIOSINFO.INF on the first Setup disk and in the \I386 directory on the Windows 2000 CD contains the Good BIOS List.

There is also a Non-Compliant ACPI List in the same INF that contains specific makes and models of machines with BIOS dated 1/1/99 or later that do not meet the ACPI test specifications. Setup ignores the ACPI configuration in CMOS on these machines and installs Standard PC hardware drivers instead of ACPI hardware drivers.

See "Configuring Power Management Features" coming up next for details on enabling and configuring ACPI support, if it is available.

Forcing ACPI Support

If you think your particular machine would be perfectly fine running the ACPI hardware drivers, but Setup refuses to load them, try putting ACPIEnable = 1 in the TXTSETUP.SIF on the first Setup disk. This forces Setup to enable ACPI and load the ACPI hardware drivers. This has the potential to cause the machine to crash with a Kernel-mode stop or do other gymnastics, such as continually rebooting or seizing up inexplicably; therefore, I do not advise trying this on anything other than a personal machine.

Determining Hardware Drivers Selected by Setup

You can use Device Manager to find out what hardware drivers Setup chose for a particular machine. Expand the tree under Computer to see the name of the hardware driver set. Other than OEM drivers that you installed during Setup or were installed for you by the vendor, there are eight possibilities:

- Standard PC
- ACPI Multiprocessor PC
- ACPI Uniprocessor PC (one processor in a multiprocessor machine)
- Advanced Configuration and Power Interface (ACPI) PC
- MPS Multiprocessor PC (MPS stands for MultiProcessor Standard, an Intel specification)
- MPS Uniprocessor PC (one processor in a multiprocessor machine)
- Compaq SystemPro Multiprocessor or 100% Compatible
- SGI MP (Silicon Graphics Muliprocessor)

Classic NT included hardware drivers for 486, EISA, and MCA machines. These are not included in Windows 2000.

Configuring Power Management Features

You may want to enable additional power management features for a particular machine that were enabled by Setup. Do this as follows:

Procedure 3.6 **Configuring Power Management Features**

1. From Control Panel, double-click the `Power Options` applet. The `Power Options Properties` window opens. Figure 3.9 shows an example window with the `Power Schemes` tab selected. There are six options available under `Power Schemes` with various combinations of time intervals for monitor and hard disk power-downs.

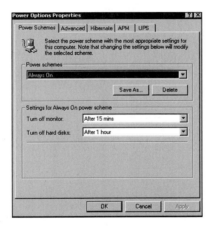

Figure 3.9 `Power Options Properties` window with `Power Schemes` tab selected.

2. Select the `Advanced` tab. The options include showing the power management icon in the System Tray, which is enabled by default on laptops, and prompting for a password when recovering from Standby mode.

   If you have an ACPI BIOS and Setup installed ACPI hardware drivers, you will also see an option in the Power Buttons field to set the action of the power button. You can set it to turn the machine off or put it in standby.

   If you enable standby operations and the hardware is configured with `Wake On LAN`, the user can leave the machine turned on all the time so that you can access it in the evenings if you need to do software distribution or access the local disk for maintenance.

3. Select the Hibernate tab. If you select the Enable Hibernate Support option, you will need sufficient disk space to dump the entire contents of memory. This option is highly recommended for laptops, but only if a similar feature has not already been enabled in hardware.

4. Select the APM tab. This tab will not be present if Plug and Play Manager did not detect an APM BIOS, if ACPI is enabled, or on Windows 2000 Server. There is one option: to Enable Advanced Power Management support. This option is not enabled by default, even if your hardware has an APM BIOS. Check the Microsoft KnowledgeBase before enabling APM. There may be known incompatibilities that did not make it into the BIOS-INFO.INF file.

5. Select the UPS tab. Use this window to enable UPS support in Windows 2000 for a compatible UPS. You must first connect the UPS to the machine using a serial connector.

6. Click OK to save the changes. If you elected to enable APM support, additional drivers may be loaded.

After you have enabled power management features, you should get more options on the Power Schemes tab. For laptops, this includes the capability of defining separate standby and spin-down policies for powered and battery operation.

Windows Driver Model (WDM)

At some distant point in the future, Microsoft intends on consolidating the consumer-friendly Windows 9x with the business-friendly Windows 200x to come up with a market-friendly single operating system.

One of the key requirements for this consolidation is a common set of device drivers, and the blueprint for those drivers is the Windows Driver Model (WDM). If you are interested in the architecture of WDM drivers or how they are developed, here are a few good references:

- *Developing Windows NT Device Drivers: A Programmer's Handbook,* **by Edward Dekker and Joseph Newcomer.** This is an excellent book for a system administrator who wants a lucid description of the world of WDM and doesn't mind sifting through a little complex jargon.

- *Windows NT Device Driver Development,* **by Peter Viscarola and Anthony Mason.** Considered the definitive book on NT device drivers. This book is geared more for the older NT Driver Model, but has solid coverage of WDM.

- **Windows 2000 Driver Development Kit (DDK).** The documentation in the DDK is terse, but you can't get much more authoritative. Load the DDK documentation on your laptop and browse it on your next long plane flight.

WDM and PnP are inextricably linked in Windows 2000, so here is a brief overview just to get the vernacular.

Bus

The WDM view of I/O starts with a bus. A bus is an interface that controls one or more devices. An IDE controller is a bus, for example, because it provides the interface to one or more hard drives. Other buses include the following:

- Personal Computer Interface (PCI) Bus
- RS–232 Serial Bus
- Parallel Port
- Advanced Configuration and Power Interface (ACPI)
- Small Computer Interface (SCSI)
- PC Card (formerly Personal Computer Memory Card International Association, or PCMCIA)
- Universal Serial Bus (USB)
- Serial Storage Architecture (SSA)
- IEEE 1394 Firewire

Bus Drivers

A bus is controlled by a bus driver. In prior versions of NT, bus drivers were integral parts of HAL.DLL. In Windows 2000, bus drivers were moved into the Plug and Play Manager and the HAL.DLL was rewritten.

A bus driver enumerates devices on its bus and builds a *Physical Device Object* (PDO) for each device it finds. The PDO virtualizes the device, rendering it into a digital form that can respond to commands from the Executive. Other duties of the bus driver include hall monitor, errand boy, receptionist, and gofer. In other words, it does the following:

- Keeps track of events on its bus and reports them to the Plug and Play Manager.
- Responds to I/O request packets (IRPs) from the Plug and Play Manager and Power Manager.

- Improves I/O performance by multiplexing bus access requests.
- Performs administrative chores required to keep the devices on the bus running smoothly.

Functional Device Objects

A bus driver generally does not communicate directly to devices on its bus unless the devices use *raw I/O*. Instead, the bus driver virtualizes the physical device objects still further into data constructs called *Functional Device Objects* (FDO). These FDOs are controlled by *function drivers*. The Plug and Play Manager loads one function driver for each device.

Function Drivers

A function driver is implemented as a set of drivers: a *class driver*, a *minidriver*, and one or more *filter drivers*.

- **Class drivers** provide basic functionality for a device type, such as a mouse or a scanner or a hard drive. Microsoft usually writes class drivers.
- **Minidrivers** determine specific operational functions. Vendors write minidrivers for their hardware.
- **Filter drivers** layer above or below the function driver and provide additional services. Microsoft encourages vendors to write filters rather than build entirely new custom minidrivers.

WDM Functional Example

Here is an example of how WDM sorts itself out in operation:

1. You insert a new PC Card SCSI controller with an attached JAZ drive into the PCMCIA slot of a laptop.
2. The PCMCIA driver discovers the new card and creates a Physical Device Object (PDO) for it. It informs Plug and Play Manager about the new PDO.
3. The Plug and Play Manager looks up the correct driver for the new PDO, loads the driver, and passes the PDO over to the SCSI driver.
4. The SCSI driver builds a Functional Device Object (FDO) and attaches it to the driver stack for the PC Card bus.
5. Plug and Play Manager instructs the SCSI driver to enumerate the bus.
6. The SCSI driver enumerates the bus, finds the SCSI drive, and creates a PDO for the drive.

7. Plug and Play Manager looks up the driver for the new PDO, loads the driver, and passes control of the PDO over to the new driver.

8. The disk driver builds an FDO for the drive and attaches the FDO to the device stack for the SCSI bus.

9. The file system drivers in I/O Manager can now communicate with the drive via the SCSI bus interface.

One of the end results of all this PnP discovery, enumeration, and object building is a set of Registry keys under HKLM | System | CurrentControlSet | Enum. This is called the Enum Tree and is used as a reference for loading services during startup.

This concludes the overview of Windows 2000 hardware architecture. It's time to start adding devices.

Installing and Configuring Devices

If your work area is anything like mine, you have stacks of PC catalogs sitting on shelves next to your desk. I have thick volumes from Ingram Micro, Tech Data, and Gates Arrow, as well as books from a dozen or so other wholesalers, not to mention mounds of mailers from retailers and hundreds of spam messages every day from resellers and jobbers and manufacturers.

No book could hope to detail the installation steps for all those different components, and I am certainly not going to try to do so in this section. The installation steps outlined here are intended to give you an idea of how the system reacts when new devices are added and where to find the configuration tools. A troubleshooting topic at the end of the chapter has hints for diagnosing and correcting problems that might arise.

PnP takes most of the work out of installing new hardware. For the most part, PnP works as advertised, at least for devices on the HCL. If you have one that's not, you might be in for a long session. If you are installing legacy adapters, follow common practices for verifying resource allocations so that you do not encounter IRQ or IOBase conflicts.

The following sections discuss installation steps for:

- Using the Device Manager
- Adding or changing CPUs
- Adding IDE hard drives
- Installing SCSI adapters and drives
- Adding removable media drives

- Adding network adapters and configuring bindings
- Configuring high-speed Internet connections
- Configuring ISDN adapters
- Configuring multiport serial adapters
- Using multiple displays

Using Device Manager

The Device Manager is an MMC console that displays the devices enumerated by PnP in a format that is easily viewed and sorted. In general, if you have hardware problems or want to configure a device, the first place to go is the `Device Manager` console. There are several ways to open the console:

- Open the Hardware Wizard in Control Panel and select `View Hardware Properties`.
- Open the `Computer Management` console by right-clicking the My Computer icon on the desktop and selecting Manage from the fly-out menu. Expand the tree under SYSTEM TOOLS | DEVICE MANAGER.
- Open the `Device Manager` console by right-clicking the My Computer icon, selecting PROPERTIES from the fly-out menu, selecting the `Hardware` tab, and then clicking `Device Manager`.
- Open the Run window, enter **DEVMGMT.MSC**, and press `Enter`.

Figure 3.10 shows an example of the device tree displayed by the `Device Management` console.

Figure 3.10 `Device Management` console showing device tree.

The device list can be sorted by device or by resource and in order of type or connection. You select one of the four options using the VIEW option in the console menu. You can also use VIEW to SHOW HIDDEN DEVICES if you want to see non-PnP devices and storage volumes.

To see the configuration information for a particular device, right-click the device icon and select PROPERTIES from the fly-out menu. If Device Manager does not list a device that you know is installed in the system, the device might either be misconfigured or it is a legacy device not recognized by Windows 2000. Legacy devices can be installed manually using the Hardware Wizard in Control Panel.

An exclamation point or question mark next to a device indicates a problem of some sort, usually a resource conflict. A big red X indicates that the problem was severe enough to force disabling of the device. To assess the problem, open the `Properties` window for the device, and then check the `Device Status` to find the nature of the problem. If the properties indicate a resource conflict, use the Resource view to see what other devices are contending for the same resource. For example, a legacy *multiple-document interface* (MDI) device might have taken the IRQ5 claimed by a second LPT port.

To clear a conflict, try deleting the device. Right-click the entry and select UNINSTALL from the fly-out menu. It may take a while for the system to make the change, but eventually the device will be removed from the tree. Then initiate a rescan by highlighting the `Devices` entry under Device Manager and selecting VIEW | SCAN FOR HARDWARE CHANGES. PnP will rescan and add the device back to the list, hopefully with a different set of resources. If this fails, delete the device again and restart. This gives PnP more options for reassigning resources.

If the resource conflict persists for a legacy device, try taking manual control of the resource allocation for the device as follows:

Procedure 3.7 **Changing Legacy Device Resource Settings**

1. Open the `Properties` window for the device.
2. Select the `Resources` tab.
3. Uncheck `Use Automatic Settings`.
4. Assign resources manually.

Avoid assigning resources that are already in use by another device. Use the RESOURCES BY TYPE option under VIEW in the console menu to sort out the devices by resource to check for possible conflicts.

After you have manually allocated resources, restart the machine. If the error persists, check that the legacy PnP options in CMOS are set according to the vendor's instructions. If the problem is with an embedded peripheral, try disabling PnP for the entire system if CMOS has that option.

Adding or Changing CPUs

If you have a multiprocessor system with one CPU, Setup installs a uniprocessor version of the PC hardware drivers. If you add a second processor at a later time, NTDETECT.COM may recognize it but the hardware drivers will not use it. You must update the following files to fully support multiprocessor operation:

- NTDETECT.COM
- HAL.DLL
- NTOSKRNL.EXE
- NTDLL.DLL
- KERNEL32.DLL
- WINSRV.DLL
- WIN32K.SYS

This is most easily accomplished using a utility in the Windows 2000 Resource Kit called UPTOMP.EXE. The UPTOMP utility is a miniature device loader that uses an INF script to give you a choice of hardware files, and then replaces the system files based on your choice.

Make sure that you have the most current firmware revision before installing a new CPU. After running UPTOMP, restart the machine and use Device Manager to check that you have the proper number of processors.

You can also open the Task Manager and select the Performance tab. If the system is using both CPUs, there will be two windows under CPU Usage History.

Adding IDE Hard Drives

The most difficult part of adding a new IDE drive is getting the right master/slave jumper combinations on the devices. If the new drive displays in CMOS with the correct size and drive geometry, Windows 2000 should have no problem finding it using the existing IDE bus drivers. You can see the new drive using the Disk Management snap-in in the Computer Management console. Open the Computer Management console via START | PROGRAMS |

ADMINISTRATIVE TOOLS | COMPUTER MANAGEMENT. See Chapter 12, "Configuring Data Storage," for the steps to configure a new disk and allocate its storage space.

If you add an additional drive on the same IDE controller with the intention of striping the drives with RAID 0, you will not get a performance improvement. An IDE interface can write to only one device at a time. Put the devices on separate controllers. The same applies to Windows 2000 Server if you are going to mirror the drives. You also get additional fault tolerance in the event of controller failure.

If you are adding ATA66 drives, you must install an ATA66 controller. It may be difficult to find an ATA66 controller on the HCL because the technology is just coming onto the scene. The major ATA66 vendors are developing Windows 2000 drivers, so be sure to get the most current driver from their Web site. You may need to use beta drivers. The performance improvement can be dramatic, so it's worth the time and trouble to work with their betas.

Installing SCSI Adapters and Drives

You can improve I/O performance considerably by changing from IDE to SCSI. Part of this is due to the faster SCSI bus, although ATA66 closes this gap considerably. Modern UltraSCSI III controllers deliver a full 80MB per second of asynchronous bandwidth. More importantly, SCSI uses asynchronous communication so that the interface can multiplex data packets. SCSI also consumes fewer CPU cycles per MB transferred, so it is more efficient and therefore gives faster overall throughput.

When installing a SCSI controller, use a PCI adapter with bus-mastering capability. Avoid the less-expensive *programmed I/O* (PIO) adapters. They put a tremendous load on the CPU because each byte or small DMA call involves a hardware interrupt. Bus-mastering adapters interrupt the CPU just once to nab a starting address and memory range, and then stream the data to memory independently. For this reason, there are no PIO SCSI adapters on the HCL.

When you install the adapter and start the machine, the Plug and Play Manager detects the new adapter and loads the appropriate drivers. You may need Windows 2000 drivers from the vendor if they are not on the CD. The drivers come with an INF that defines the configuration and Registry entries. The INF format changed in Windows 2000, so older NT4 drivers will not install correctly.

If PnP does not recognize the new adapter or devices on the bus, see the section "Resolving SCSI Problems" at the end of this chapter.

Adding Removable Media Drives

Windows 2000 has a new service called the *Removable Storage Manager* (RSM). The RSM service simplifies managing removable media if you have large CD-ROM jukeboxes or a robotic tape library, but it can make simple interfaces, such as small CD disc changers more difficult to handle.

In classic NT, each disk in a jukebox or disc changer got a separate drive letter. This caused much frustration when configuring big CD libraries because there aren't enough letters to accommodate a 100-disc library. RSM solves this problem by assigning a single drive letter to the device itself and manipulating the CDs in the background.

But for small 4x and 6x CD changers, the separate drive letters actually added to the convenience of using the product. A user who wants a particular CD can go to a drive letter and find it. Higher-end changers cache the CD contents so that the drives can be browsed quickly without causing the changer to move them around. This is not possible with RSM. Each disk must be mounted by name using the RSM Mount command. This requires that you know the logical media ID assigned to the CD by RSM. This information is available in the RSM snap-in within the Computer Management console.

Removable media drives come in three general types:

- Fast oversized floppy disk drives: ZIP, Sony, and so on
- Slow undersized hard disk drives: JAZ, Shark, and so on
- Fussy plastic burners: CD-R and CD-RW drives and magneto-optical drives

Most of these drives have parallel port and SCSI models. All major vendors have models supported by Windows 2000. The Plug and Play Manager detects the drive during enumeration and loads the appropriate driver. It then turns control over to RSM. For single-media devices, there is no need to use the RSM snap-in. The media is presented to Explorer with an appropriate icon and set of properties.

In theory, the Windows 98 WDM driver should work, but make sure that you have the Windows 2000 driver because the Registry entries differ and the developer who wrote the INF may not have included the Windows 2000 entries.

If you have a SCSI model, be sure to select a SCSI ID for it that doesn't conflict with other devices on the bus. Also, remember that the results of the SCSI bus scan determine the relative disk location for the ARC path in BOOT.INI. If the removable storage device has a SCSI ID lower than that of the primary drive, it will insert itself into the scan list ahead of the boot drive and you'll get an *Unable to Locate NTOSKRL.EXE* error.

Adding Network Adapters

Even if you disregard all the other features in PnP, the way it simplifies adding and configuring network adapters makes it worth the price of admission.

The *Network Driver Interface Specification* (NDIS) drivers used to support Windows networking have a well-deserved reputation for being difficult to handle. PnP, coupled with a properly prepared INF and a WDM driver written by someone who really knows how to code a device driver, makes installing a new network adapter a five-minute operation.

After installing the adapter and restarting the machine, the Plug and Play Manager discovers the device during enumeration. If it is a PCI PnP adapter, it is assigned resources and initialized. If it is a legacy adapter with Windows 2000 drivers on the CD or in the \WINNT\Drivers directory, PnP installs the drivers and assigns the resources based on the adapter settings. If the adapter requests an IRQ that was previously assigned to another PnP device, the Plug and Play Manager will attempt to assign a new IRQ to the PnP device. If two legacy devices conflict, there will be errors in Device Manager and possibly console errors from the Event Log.

As slick as PnP is about recognizing adapters and installing their drivers, it is not a comprehensive configuration tool, especially when it comes to installing multiple network adapters. The next few sections cover special configurations you may need to perform.

Changing Transport Binding Order

You can see the new interface by right-clicking My Network Places and selecting PROPERTIES from the fly-out menu. This opens the Network and Dial-up Connections window. Figure 3.11 shows an example with two connections.

Figure 3.11 `Network and Dial-up Connections` window showing two local area network connections.

To view the bindings for the adapters, select ADVANCED | ADVANCED SETTINGS from the menu. The `Advanced Settings` window opens with the focus set to the `Adapters and Bindings` tab. Highlight each connection to show its bindings.

If you have more than one transport protocol, adjust the binding order so that the most heavily used protocol is first. Do this by highlighting a protocol, and then clicking the up or down arrows.

Any settings you changed are saved when you click OK to close the `Advanced Settings` window.

Changing Provider Binding Order

If you have multiple network clients, also called network providers, you can change the provider order. Select the `Providers` tab. Figure 3.12 shows an example with two network providers and three print providers.

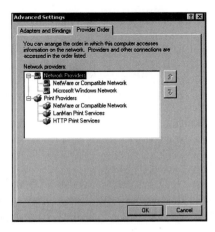

Figure 3.12 `Advanced Settings` window—`Provider Order` tab.

In a mixed Windows 2000/NetWare environment, always bind to the NetWare client provider first, even if most of your servers are Windows 2000 or NT. The *Multiple UNC Router* (MUP) that handles the internal client table must poll the interfaces when deciding which redirector owns a particular UNC path. The NetWare interface reacts more quickly with a negative response when polled for a Windows 2000 resource.

Any settings that you changed are saved when you click OK to close the Advanced Settings window.

Configuring Additional Networking Components

To install additional transports, clients, or network services to bind to the network adapters, right-click one of the connection icons and select PROPERTIES from the fly-out menu. This opens the Properties window for the connection. Any components added to one connection affect all connections.

Use the Properties window to set the TCP/IP properties, such as IP address, gateway, and DNS server if you do not use DHCP.

If you install a second adapter and you use NWLink as one of your transport protocols, you must assign a network number to both connection interfaces. This provides a unique ID for internal routing purposes. The IPX internal network number is set to all zeros (00000000) by default.

If you select a particular frame type rather than using AUTODISCOVER, you can leave the Network Number entry at all zeros. The system will discover the network address. If you have several IPX networks in the same broadcast domain, set the address manually.

Any settings that you changed are saved when you click OK to close the Advanced Settings window.

Configuring High-Speed Internet Connections

A new wave of broadband and xDSL adapters is now coming to market as cable companies and telephone companies vie for domination of the digital services to the home and office.

Cable modems are usually implemented as broadband transceivers with a standard network adapter in the PC. In this case, no special drivers are required. If the broadband adapter is inserted directly in the PC, make sure that the company has Windows 2000 or Windows 98 drivers.

xDSL support is another matter altogether. Some xDSL splitters are also just transceivers with a standard NIC in the PC. Others have boards that go into the PC. As of this writing, the list of supported xDSL adapters is limited to a very few models from 3Com, Lucent, and Texas Instruments. If you can find a representative at the telephone company who can help you with technical details—not always an easy person to find—see whether the company has tested their adapters with Windows 2000.

Configuring ISDN Adapters

ISDN adapters install just like network adapters. After the ISDN line is properly provisioned, getting the adapter to work should be the least of your hassles. You may need to tell the telco what brand of adapter you have. Often they limit you to an ála carte selection from adapters that they have already tested and have provisioning data for.

If you use an external NT1 connected to the PC via a serial interface, be sure to buy a high-speed serial port designed for this kind of connection. A standard RS-232 port can deliver only 115Kbps, which starves a 128Kbps ISDN adapter when both bearer channels are going full-bore.

If you want to configure the interface as a demand-dial Internet router, or if you need to troubleshoot PPP connections, see Chapter 17, "Managing Remote Access and Internet Routing."

Configuring Multiport Serial Adapters

If you plan on installing more than a couple of modems in a machine, you need a multiport serial adapter of some sort. The most famous of these come from Digi, although quite a few vendors sell this type of technology. Models from six manufacturers are represented on the Windows 2000 CD.

Multiport serial adapters come in two general styles: One has the connection ports built in to the adapter; the other uses an octopus cable that connects to a port box, modem rack, or terminal adapter. Neither type is inherently superior. Pick a device on the HCL from a quality vendor and you should get trouble-free services. Make sure the vendor supplies Windows 2000 drivers.

When you install the adapter, the PnP enumeration will discover any serial connections it exposes. If enumeration fails to turn up the adapter, you can use the Hardware Wizard to install the driver. After the system can see the bus, it should find the COM ports.

Once installed, the system displays additional COM ports based on the adapter model. Check Device Manager in the Computer Management snap-in to see the ports. Each port can be connected to a modem or ISDN adapter or any other type of RS-232 device.

Using Multiple Displays

If you are a CAD operator or graphic designer, you probably either have a big 21-inch monitor or dual monitors, or both. Dual-display support on classic NT required special video adapters and drivers. Windows 2000 supports dual displays as long as the adapters are AGP or PCI. You can mix the two buses, but you might lose some functionality. For example, the video speed might default to the slower of the two interfaces.

Configure the second video adapter as follows:

Procedure 3.8 **Configuring a Second Video Adapter**

1. Install the second adapter according to the manufacturer's specifications. If your machine supports AGP, chances are that it already has a video adapter in the AGP slot, so make sure the second adapter is PCI. You may experience problems with adapters from the same manufacturer that are identical except for the bus interface, AGP or PCI. The two adapters tend to have the same driver names although the contents differ slightly. You may need to use adapters from a different vendor.

2. Start the machine. The Plug and Play Manager finds the second adapter and prompts you for the Windows 2000 CD or a disk with the vendor's drivers. If the adapter is not PnP, use the Hardware Wizard to install the legacy drivers or use the stock VGA drivers.

3. The second monitor is not enabled automatically. Open the Display Properties applet in Control Panel or right-click the desktop and select PROPERTIES from the fly-out menu.

4. Select the Settings tab. The mock display window shows a graphical representation of the two monitors (see Figure 3.13).

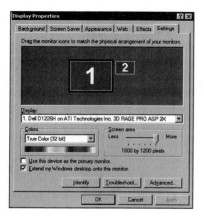

Figure 3.13 Display Properties window showing dual monitors.

5. In the drop-down box under `Display`, select the second monitor.

6. Select the `Extend My Windows Desktop onto This Monitor` option.

7. Click `Apply` to save the change. The system reconfigures and the second monitor is activated. If you do not accept the change in 15 seconds, the system reverts back to a single active monitor. If the system stalls or the video becomes unstable, restart.

8. If you want the primary display (`START` menu, System Tray, and messaging pop-up) to be the second window, select the `Use This Device as the Primary Monitor` option.

The default orientation puts the logical monitors side by side. You can move the display monitors to change that orientation.

`Display Properties` permits you to position the displays in relation to each other. This determines which borders are shared by the displays. If you put Display 1 on top of Display 2, you can drag windows and icons up and down between monitors.

Troubleshooting New Devices

When you install a new device, you always take the chance that a stable machine will suddenly cease to function or become erratic. Basic diagnostic procedures always apply. If possible, undo what you just did and see whether the problem goes away. If not, begin analyzing what changes were made and correlate them to the symptoms you're seeing. This topic contains some common tools to help you diagnose problems caused by adding components.

Building a Windows 2000 Boot Disk

It is very common when adding new mass storage devices or interfaces that the machine refuses to boot. This is generally caused because the additional drive or interface changed the ARC path to the Windows 2000 boot partition. Other reasons for failure to boot include the following:

- The Windows 2000 system files at the root of the boot partition have been corrupted or deleted.

- The boot sector has been corrupted by a virus.

- A user ran SYS against the C: drive in an attempt to make the machine dual-boot.

- The primary drive in a mirrored set has failed (software RAID only).

- The NTBOOTDD.SYS driver has been deleted or been corrupted on a system with a SCSI interface that has no BIOS.

In all these situations, the core Windows 2000 files in the \WINNT directory are probably just fine. You can bypass the problem files and disk structures by booting from a floppy disk that has been configured with the Windows 2000 system files used for booting. This is often called a fault-tolerant boot disk.

When building this boot disk, it's important to use a disk that has been formatted on a machine running Windows 2000. This ensures that the boot sector on the floppy disk looks for the Windows 2000 secondary bootstrap loader, NTLDR. Here is how to configure the disk to boot Windows 2000:

> **Comparing Fault-Tolerant and Windows 2000 Boot Disks**
>
> Don't confuse a fault-tolerant boot disk with Windows 2000 boot disk. You are not actually booting the operating system from the floppy disk. You are booting the initial system files that then turn around to load the operating system. See the section titled "Functional Description of the Windows 2000 Boot Process" in Chapter 2, "Performing Upgrades and Automated Installations," for details.

Procedure 3.9 **Creating a Fault-Tolerant Boot Floppy Disk**

1. Use Attrib to remove the read-only and hidden attributes from the following system files at the root of the boot drive:
```
NTLDR
NTDETECT.COM
BOOT.INI
NTBOOTDD.SYS (if present)
```

2. Insert a blank floppy disk into the floppy disk drive and format it. You can use the Quick Format option if you're sure that there are no disk defects.

3. When format is complete, copy the files listed in step 1 to the floppy.

4. Use Notepad to edit the BOOT.INI file on the floppy disk.

5. Change the Time Setting entry to −1. This disables the countdown timer. (You do not have to do this, but I find it helpful to keep the counter from ticking down when I'm troubleshooting.)

6. Save the changes and close Notepad.

7. Restart the computer and boot from the fault-tolerant boot floppy disk.

8. When the BOOT menu appears, highlight the entry representing the partition containing the Windows 2000 system files and press Enter to finish the boot.

    The ARC path in BOOT.INI tells NTLDR on the floppy disk where to find the Windows 2000 files on the hard drives. The remainder of the boot process should proceed normally.

9. At this point, the floppy disk is no longer needed. Remove it from the drive.

Keep a fault-tolerant boot disk handy for booting workstations and servers in the field. If the boot partition has more than 7.8GB or a non-standard geometry or is on a SCSI drive with an interface that has no BIOS, the ARC path will have a `signature()` entry. The number in the parentheses is a unique ID written to the MBR of the boot drive. The BOOT.INI for this machine will not work on another machine. Clearly label the boot floppy disk and keep it in safe place.

Primary Drive Failure

If you have mirrored drives and the primary drive fails, you can use the fault-tolerant boot floppy disk to boot from the mirrored partition. If the mirrored drive is the second disk on a SCSI chain, for example, the arc path would be `multi(0)disk(0)rdisk(1)partition(1)\WINNT)`.

Changing the IRQ Steering Options

You may need to change or disable the IRQ Steering option to get a particular PCI card to operate correctly with a shared IRQ.

IRQ Steering cannot be disabled on machines that have ACPI enabled. See Microsoft KnowledgeBase article Q232824 for more information. Disabling steering may produce undesirable effects. Without PCI IRQ sharing, you may not have sufficient IRQs for all your devices. If you want to try it, proceed as follows:

Procedure 3.10 **Disabling PCI IRQ Steering**

1. Open the `Device Manager` console.

2. From the console menu, select VIEW | RESOURCES BY TYPE.

3. Expand the tree under `Interrupt Request (IRQ)`. See Figure 3.14 for an example. This shows the devices that share the same IRQ. If you have a device that is not working because of this IRQ sharing, it will be flagged with a yellow question mark or a red X.

4. From the console menu, select VIEW | DEVICES BY TYPE.

5. Expand the tree under `Computer`. The device listed is the HAL/kernel combination selected by Setup. Unless you have a multiprocessor PC or an ACPI unit, the listing will more than likely be `Standard PC`.

6. Right-click the PC icon and select PROPERTIES from the fly-out menu. The `Properties` window opens.

7. Select the `IRQ Steering` tab (see Figure 3.15). If the tab is not there, your machine does not support IRQ Steering.

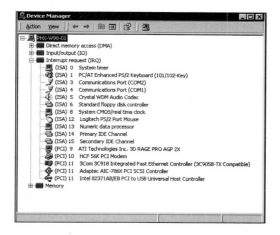

Figure 3.14 Example list of components listed by IRQ.
Note that three PCI devices share the same IRQ.

Figure 3.15 PC Properties showing IRQ Steering tab
with a readout of the current IRQ Routing Status.

If your machine supports PCI IRQ Steering and Setup did not disable it
for some reason, the Use IRQ Steering option is already selected. The IRQ
Routing Status field shows a history of the IRQ routing activity.

8. Uncheck the Use IRQ Steering option.

9. Click OK to save the change and return to the main Device
Manager window.

10. After you have finished, close the Device Manager.

11. Restart the machine and recheck the Device Manager for errors.

Resolving SCSI Problems

If Plug and Play Manager does not recognize the controller or the disks on the controller, or you get data corruption or a significant number of errors in the Event Log relating to the SCSI devices on that interface, the single most likely cause is improper termination or excessive cable length. The following can cause improper termination.

- Mixing active and passive terminations.
- Mixing cable types, which can cause impedance matching and timing problems.
- Having too many terminations, such as having the SCSI controller in the middle of the bus with active termination enabled on the controller and terminators at either end of the cable.
- Forgetting to attach the resistor pack.
- Attaching a resistor pack when active termination is enabled.
- Thinking that you have enabled active termination on a device but actually putting the jumper on the wrong pins.
- Thinking that you have disabled active termination on a device but actually removing the jumper from the wrong pins.

The cable and terminator configuration might have worked in NT4, but Windows 2000 puts much greater demand on the hard disk interface to boost performance. Weaklings break down quickly. Replace the interface with one on the HCL. If it is built in to the motherboard, get a PCI adapter and disable the motherboard interface.

If you already have a SCSI adapter and you add a second one of the exact make and model, you may need to disable the BIOS on the second adapter to keep it from squabbling with the first adapter. This does not affect Windows 2000 functionality; if you put an installation of Windows 2000 on a disk connected to the second adapter, however, Setup will copy the SCSI miniport driver to the root of the partition and name it NTBOOTDD.SYS so that NTLDR can use the driver to scan the SCSI bus. Setup will also use a `signature()` controller ID in the ARC path in BOOT.INI to identify the drive. The parameter in the parentheses of `signature()` is a special signature in the Master Boot Record placed there by Setup.

You may get an *Unable to Locate Operating System* error after adding a second SCSI controller. You can thank PCI for that. In most cases, the SCSI adapter with the lowest IOBase address is assumed to be the boot host adapter. In PnP systems, the PCI slot closest to the CPU normally gets the lowest IOBase address. Therefore, if you installed the second adapter in a slot closer to the CPU (lower number), you changed your active drive designation. Try swapping PCI slots. Plug and Play Manager assigns component identifiers based on their PCI slot; therefore, by swapping slots, you'll force a new PnP enumeration.

Correcting Non-PnP System Hangs

If the system hangs while NTDETECT is running, you probably have a problem with the motherboard or memory or hard drive interface. The function of NTDETECT is to recognize hardware. If it cannot do its job, it stalls.

You can't resolve this error until you know what component is causing the hang. There are a couple of ways to find this out. One is to press F8 at the BOOT menu and select the BOOT LOGGING option. This writes a Boot Log to the hard drive; if you can't get booted, however, you can't read the log.

The second alternative is to use a debug version of NTDETECT.COM called NTDETECT.CHK. The NTDETECT.CHK file is located on the Windows 2000 CD in the \SUPPORT\DEBUG\I386 directory. Use NTDETECT.CHK as follows:

Procedure 3.11   **Using NTDETECT.CHK**

1. Make a duplicate of Setup disk 1 using Diskcopy (or some other disk-duplicating utility).
2. Copy NTDETECT.CHK onto the duplicate disk.
3. Rename NTDETECT.COM to NTDETECT.OLD.
4. Rename NTDETECT.CHK to NTDETECT.COM.
5. Reboot using the disk with the renamed NTDETECT.CHK.

The debug version of NTDETECT works just like the regular version except that it displays what it detects as each component is encountered. When the system hangs, the last component on the screen is the one causing the problem. Look for IRQ or IOBase conflicts.

Correcting PnP Problems

Plug and Play is like the little girl with the little curl right in the middle of her forehead. When it is good, it is very, very good. When it is bad, it is downright awful. Because PnP has toasted its share of machines since its introduction with Windows 95, you might be hesitant to use a PnP-based operating system to configure a server. If you're looking for a "No PnP" option in Windows 2000, however, you're out of luck. PnP required extensive changes to the PC hardware drivers, especially the HAL. Although you can disable PnP options on the server, in general hardware vendors are accustomed to dealing with PnP problems and have engineered many of the early bugs out of their gear.

If the system hangs during the latter stages of restart after installing a new device, you either have a problem with the device driver, a resource conflict, or both. The testing requirements to get the "Ready for Windows 2000" logo do not require extensive compatibility tests with other hardware. Your new network adapter might run foul of your video accelerator, but only when a certain brand of multimedia adapter is present.

Windows 2000 comes with a "Safe mode" option similar to Windows 9x that disables most PnP enumeration. When the BOOT menu displays, press F8 to bring up the WINDOWS 2000 ADVANCED OPTIONS menu. Here are the options:

- SAFE MODE. Loads a bare version of Windows 2000 with no devices enabled except for the keyboard, mouse, and video.

- SAFE MODE WITH NETWORKING. Same as regular Safe mode but with network drivers loaded. Use this option if the problem is not network related and you need to access a server to get drivers.

- SAFE MODE WITH COMMAND PROMPT. Does not load the Explorer shell. This is *not* the same as booting to DOS. There is no hidden DOS in Windows 2000 like there is in Windows 9x. The command prompt is a full 32-bit environment. If you run a graphical application, Explorer will launch.

- ENABLE BOOT LOGGING. Select this option to write a log listing the drivers loaded during startup. The log is named NTBTLOG.TXT and is located in the \WINNT directory. This option replaces the \sos switch in a classic NT ARC path.

- ENABLE VGA MODE. This option replaces the video drivers with standard 16-color VGA drivers. This option replaces the \basevideo switch in a classic NT ARC path.

- **LAST KNOWN GOOD CONFIGURATION.** This option replaces the Registry entries for system drivers and controls for loading those drivers.

- **DIRECTORY SERVICES RESTORE MODE.** This option puts a domain controller in Safe mode and permits repairing and recovering the Active Directory information store. See Chapter 11, "Managing Active Directory Replication and Directory Maintenance," for a complete discussion of this option.

- **DEBUGGING MODE.** Enables automatic recovery and restart. Replaces the /crashdebug switch in a classic NT ARC path.

See Chapter 18, "Recovering from System Failures," for details on recovering a system if the problem lies deeper than a simple PnP resource allocation error.

If the problem is with a laptop or a manageable desktop, check the ACPI configuration. An incompatible machine or system board may have slipped through testing. You may need to disable ACPI, APM, and even some basic PnP functionality in CMOS to get the system to behave.

Token Ring and PCMCIA network adapters use a RAMbase. Make sure that all memory-mapped legacy components are set for different memory addresses.

Sometimes combo PCMCIA cards cause PnP troubles because of driver problems, or race conditions set up a circumstance where resources are not assigned the same way each time. If the combo card is on the HCL, contact the laptop vendor.

Another cause of system hangs is resource overlap between PCI devices caused by IRQ Steering or adjustments made by HAL early in the system boot. If you have a system that works fine one day and is unstable the next, especially if you have just added a new PCI device, try disabling IRQ Steering (see the earlier section "Changing the IRQ Steering Options") and disabling HAL resource allocation functions. This is done by adding a /pcilock switch to the ARC path in BOOT.INI. The syntax is as follows:

```
[boot loader]
timeout=30
default=multi(0)disk(0)rdisk(0)partition(1)\WINNT
[operating systems]
multi(0)disk(0)rdisk(0)partition(1)\WINNT="Windows 2000 Server" /fastdetect /PCILOCK
```

Finally, you always have the option to reinstall Windows 2000 to a separate partition on the same machine. If Setup goes well with the new device installed, you know that there was a Registry entry of one form or another that was causing the problem. You can compare the Registries and Device Manager resource allocations to see where the difference lies.

Tracking Kernel Memory Use

You should try to keep long-term statistics for kernel memory use on your servers so that you can spot abnormal trends. The most convenient tool for doing this is Performance Monitor. Open the `Performance Monitor` console using START | PROGRAMS | ADMINISTRATIVE TOOLS | PERFORMANCE. Figure 3.16 shows an example.

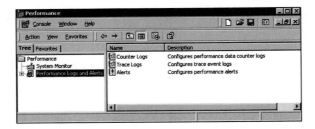

Figure 3.16 `Performance` console showing Performance Logs and Alerts icon.

The `Performance` console contains two snap-ins. The `System Monitor` snap-in is an ActiveX control designed to display performance counters in graphical format. The `Performance Logs and Alerts` snap-in is designed to collect performance statistics and write them to a log or send alerts to a console or Event Log. Logs are the best way to collect long-term performance statistics. Configure a log to collect kernel memory statistics as follows:

Procedure 3.12 **Configuring Performance Monitor to Collect Kernel Memory Statistics**

1. Expand the tree under `Performance Logs and Alerts` and highlight `Counter Logs`.

2. Right-click a blank area in the right pane and select NEW LOG SETTINGS from the fly-out menu. The `New Log Settings` window opens.

3. Enter a name for the log, such as **Long-Term Kernel Memory Use**.

4. Click OK. A management window opens for the log. The window name matches the log name you assigned in step 3.

5. Click Add. The Select Counters window opens. Figure 3.17 shows an example.

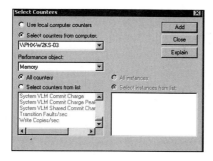

Figure 3.17 Select Counters window with the Memory object selected and the All Counters option set.

6. Under Performance Object, select Memory from the drop-down box.

7. Select the All Counters radio button. Long-term performance data collection involves taking snapshots at infrequent intervals, such as once an hour, so collecting all available counters will not be too much of a burden on the server.

8. Click Add to add the counters to the log, and then click Close to return to the main log management window.

9. Set the Sample Data Every value to 1 Hour.

10. Select the Log Files tab. The default location of the log is a folder called \Perflog at the root of the system partition. You can change this location using the Browse button.

11. The default filename uses the name you assigned to the log plus a six-digit number. If you stipulate a Log File Size Limit at the bottom of the window, a log fills up, then closes, and another begins filling.

12. Click OK to save the selections and return to the Performance console.

Collect statistics for a few days, and then view the contents of the log using the System Monitor snap-in. To do this, select the log as the source for the chart as follows:

Procedure 3.13 **Charting Performance Monitor Logs**

1. Highlight the System Monitor icon. An empty chart appears in the right pane.

2. Right-click the chart and select PROPERTIES from the fly-out menu. The `Properties` window opens.

3. Select the `Source` tab.

4. Select the `Log File` radio button.

5. Click `Browse` to open the `Select Log File` navigation tool. The focus is set automatically to the `\Perflog` folder.

6. Double-click the name of the counter log you configured to select it and return to the `System Monitor Properties` window.

7. Click `OK` to save the selections, close the window, and return to the main `Performance` window. Nothing happens quite yet.

8. Right-click the right pane again and this time select ADD COUNTERS from the fly-out menu. The `Add Counters` window opens.

9. Select the `All Counters` radio button, and then click `Add` followed by `Close`. This adds all the counters to the chart. If that makes the chart too busy, you can delete counter entries.

The chart shows the statistics you collected in the log. Up to 100 data points can be displayed. Figure 3.18 shows an example. Press `Ctrl+H` to turn on highlighting so that any counter you select in the lower part of the window turns into a white line in the chart.

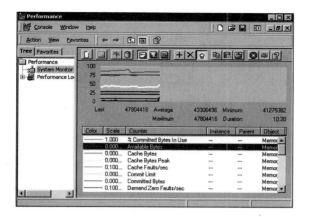

Figure 3.18 The `Performance` console showing chart display of memory statistics collected in a counter log.

Moving Forward

The first three chapters covered installing, modifying, and troubleshooting Windows 2000. Now that the machines are in place, it's time to start setting up the network resources necessary to support users. First, however, it's worth taking some time to look at Windows networking with particular attention to name resolution, because some of the biggest changes in Windows 2000 center around the way computer names are resolved and located.

4

Understanding NetBIOS Name Resolution

FOR THE MOST PART, WINDOWS 2000 IS A TCP/IP product. Microsoft has worked feverishly to finish pulling Windows 2000/NT out of the LAN Manager tide pool where it first evolved. You may argue that the job isn't quite done yet, that Windows 2000 isn't ready to swim in the deep waters where the UNIX sharks live, but it seems to me that Microsoft takes its survival lessons from the piranha rather than the shark: If you can't beat them with size and speed, overwhelm them with numbers and ferocity.

Even with the extensive use of TCP/IP-based protocols in Windows 2000, there are still a few vestiges of its NetBIOS ancestors. Some of the more awkward traits involve computer naming and name resolution. Windows 2000 can use Dynamic DNS (covered in Chapter 5, "Managing Domain Name System (DNS) Services and Dynamic Host Configuration (DHCP) Services") for all name resolution tasks, but backward compatibility requires some allowance for classic name resolution.

This chapter starts with an overview of Windows 2000 networking with a focus on the addresses and ports used by various networking protocols. This overview includes details of the *Server Message Block* (SMB) protocol that Windows uses to carry networking commands and the NetBIOS naming conventions that go hand in hand with SMB. Then the focus shifts to more practical matters and includes the following topics:

- Network diagnostic utilities
- Resolving NetBIOS names using broadcasts, LMHOSTS, and WINS

- Installing WINS
- Configuring and managing WINS replication
- Disabling NetBIOS name resolution

Network Names and NWLink

The name resolution mechanisms discussed in this chapter concentrate on TCP/IP. Both Novell and Microsoft are moving toward a purely TCP/IP networking environment, so I think this is appropriate.

Like classic NT, Windows 2000 includes NetWare support by providing a *NetWare Core Protocol* (NCP) client redirector, NWRDR.SYS, and an IPX/SPX-compatible network stack, NWLINK.SYS. NetBIOS name resolution over NWLINK uses a NetBIOS-over-NWLINK helper, NWLNKNB.SYS. The function of these drivers has not changed from classic NT.

Overview of Windows 2000 Networking

This topic covers the methods used by Windows 2000 to determine the proper address or port at each network layer, using the OSI model as a road map. Windows networking doesn't precisely follow OSI, but the structure is close enough to permit parallels (see Figure 4.1).

OSI		Windows 2000
Application		LanManServer.dll and Srv.sys (Server) LanManWorkstation.dll and Mrxsmb.sys (Client) Afd.sys (Sockets) Netbios.sys (NetBIOS emulator)
Presentation		Not Separately Implemented
Session		Tdi.sys (Transport Driver Interface) Tcpip.sys (TCP/IP, includes ARP, ICMP, IGMP) Netbt.sys (NetBIOS-over-TCP/IP)
Transport		
Network		
Data Link	Logical Link Control	
	Media Access Control	Ndis.sys (Network Driver Interface Specification) <miniport>.sys (Adapter driver)
Physical		

Figure 4.1 Diagram of OSI layers and Windows 2000 network drivers.

Data Link Layer

In the OSI model, the data link layer defines the methods for packaging data to be transmitted over the physical media. The OSI data link layer is further divided by IEEE 802.1 into a *Media Access Control* (MAC) layer and a *Logical Link Control* (LLC) layer. Windows networking does not implement separate MAC and LLC drivers. Instead, the network layer drivers handle LLC duties while the MAC duties are handled by NDIS.SYS, the Network Driver Interface Specification driver, along with a set of miniport and filter drivers. Vendors typically write the miniport driver for their adapters.

Adapter miniport drivers do not communicate directly with the Windows 2000 Executive. The NDIS.SYS driver is the sole mechanism for a miniport driver to obtain system services. Windows 2000 does not have any "monolithic" drivers. Adapter miniport drivers come in the form of SYS drivers stored under \WINNT\Drivers. A driver is installed with the help of an associated INF file located in \WINNT\INF. The network INF files are prefixed with NET*.

The NDIS miniport driver works with the controller chip on the network adapter and with the NDIS.SYS class driver to build transmission frames. These frames require the MAC address of their intended destination. NDIS cannot discover this address automatically. A higher-level protocol must supply it.

Loading Alternative Windows 2000 Network Drivers

The \WINNT\Drivers and \WINNT\INF folders contain all the drivers and installation routines that are on the Windows 2000 CD. If you install an adapter that does not have an INF file in \WINNT\INF, the installer will prompt you for drivers. I recommend obtaining the Windows 2000 drivers from the vendor's Web site instead of using any disk that accompanies the adapter unless you verify that they are the same driver version.

When searching for network adapter drivers, look for drivers specifically written for Windows 2000 or NDIS5. These drivers conform to the *Windows Driver Model* (WDM) and should incorporate features, such as power management, *Windows Management Instrumentation* (WMI), and *Web-Based Enterprise Management* (WBEM). It is theoretically possible to use older NDIS4 drivers in Windows 2000; but because the INF format has changed, the driver probably will not install.

Network and Transport Layers

A little further up the OSI stack is the network layer, which is responsible for traffic management, and the transport layer, which is responsible for connection management. In TCP/IP, network layer functions are assigned to the *Internet Protocol* (IP) and transport layer functions are assigned to either the *Transport Control Protocol* (TCP) or the *User Datagram Protocol* (UDP). Windows 2000 uses a single driver, TCPIP.SYS, to implement both layers.

Addressing at the network layer takes the form of an IP address, a 32-bit number normally shown in dotted-decimal notation, such as 10.1.50.233. Every IP packet must contain the IP address of the destination host unless it is a broadcast or multicast packet. A key responsibility of TCPIP.SYS is to determine the correct IP address of a packet's destination.

Addressing at the transport layer takes the form of a port number. Most high-level network applications that make use of TCP/IP have been assigned well-known port numbers. RFC 1700, "Assigned Numbers," lists these. FTP uses TCP port 21, for example, and HTTP uses TCP port 80. It is the responsibility of the high-level application to provide a port number if a well-known port is not used.

The combination of an IP address and a port number is called a *socket*. If the high-level protocol specifies a socket, TCPIP.SYS breaks down the name into its component parts.

Some high-level applications do not use TCP or UDP. Windows 2000 supports these so-called raw IP applications. The application is responsible for either providing the IP address, or a resolvable host name, to TCPIP.SYS.

Session Layer

The standard OSI session layer is responsible for handling connection-oriented communications. In TCP/IP, the TCP protocol implements session layer functionality by handling datagram sequencing and guaranteeing datagram delivery. High-level applications at layer seven are free to use their own session-control methods, as well.

UDP, in contrast, supports sessionless applications, typically broadcasts/multicasts, brief messages, and other data streams where sequencing and guaranteed delivery are not important. Sessionless applications resemble dysfunctional relationships where one computer listens only as long as the other computer has something interesting to say.

Presentation Layer

Presentation layer functionality, such as encryption and data translation, is not implemented as a distinct set of drivers in Windows 2000. Applications must provide this service, if they require it.

Application Layer

At the top of the OSI model sits the application layer. This is where the Windows 2000 network services live. An example is the LAN Manager Workstation service and its complimentary file system driver, MRXSMB.SYS. This service communicates with the LAN Manager Server service and its file system driver, SRV.SYS, running on another Windows 2000 station.

Network applications can use any method they desire for identifying their peers. Windows networking components, such as LAN Manager Workstation and LAN Manager Server use computer names. These are often called NetBIOS names because the underlying command protocol, SMB, has its roots in NetBIOS. See the sidebar on the next page titled "SMB and NetBIOS Names" for more information.

A NetBIOS name consists of a unique 15–byte name and a 1–byte service identifier. If the computer name has fewer than 15 characters, the NetBIOS name is padded to 15 bytes before appending the service ID. For example, the Messenger service on computer `PHX-W2KP-027` would identify itself in an SMB message as `PHX-W2KP-027      <03>`. The number in angle brackets is the service ID.

NetBIOS naming does not have a hierarchy. NetBIOS names must be unique regardless of their domain or workgroup affiliation if they share the same segment. A computer in the `LOX` domain with an IP address of 10.1.1.1/16 cannot have the same name as a computer in the `BAGEL` domain with the IP address 10.1.1.2/16. This is not true of TCP/IP host names. DNS is perfectly happy saying, "This is my brother Darrell and this is my other brother Darrell."

NetBIOS Scope Options

Quite a while back, Microsoft and IBM tried to introduce a form of hierarchical domain naming called *scope options* into NetBIOS, but these scopes were clumsy to use and never really caught on. The design simulated DNS naming hierarchies in a very limited way, but was too convoluted to be effective.

NetBIOS names can contain any ANSI character, including spaces, with the following exceptions: `/\[]":;¦<>+=,?*`. Acceptable NetBIOS names include the following:

```
MYSUPERCOMPUTER
MY   COMPUTER
MY#1COMPUTER
MY_COMPUTER
MY-COMPUTER
MY!COMPUTER
```

Several characters permitted in NetBIOS names, such as spaces and under-scores, are not included in standard DNS naming. See RFC 952, "DOD Internet Host Table Specification, and RFC 1123, Requirements for Internet Hosts—Application and Support," for more information. Because Windows 2000 computers live in both the TCP/IP world and the NetBIOS world, you may want to avoid characters not supported by DNS.

SMB and NetBIOS Names

SMB-based applications use NetBIOS naming, but they are not NetBIOS applications. NetBIOS is a high-level net-work protocol just like sockets. Windows network applications, such as LAN Manager Workstation, do not use NetBIOS. They use network file system drivers, such as MRXSMB.SYS. Windows 2000 does provide a NetBIOS emu-lator, NETBIOS.DLL, that exposes NetBIOS functionality if a legacy application needs it; but they are becoming rare.

The reason that NetBIOS naming and SMB appear related harkens back to their early days. IBM co-developed NetBIOS with Sytek for their PC Network program and it became a de facto standard for network interfaces. At the same time, IBM and Microsoft were working with 3Com to develop a networking command language that eventually became SMB. In early versions of OS/2 LAN Manager, SMB applications would use NetBIOS as their net-work interface with NetBEUI as the transport protocol.

Beginning with NT Advanced Server and later versions of OS/2 LAN Manager and Warp from IBM, SMB matured to a network protocol-independent command language. But because SMB and NetBIOS grew up together, and back-ward compatibility was (and still is) important, quite a few NetBIOS conventions were retained in SMB. This includes NetBIOS naming and NetBIOS name resolution.

The bottom line of all this history is that SMB does not use NetBIOS as a networking protocol, but does follow NetBIOS naming restrictions.

Name Resolution at Each Network Service Layer

The last topic worked its way up the OSI model and identified the addresses, ports, and names used at each layer. Table 4.1 lists them. Processes running at each layer communicate with their peer processes at other stations using these addresses, ports, and names.

Table 4.1   **Addresses and Names Used at Each Windows 2000 Network Layer**

Layer	Protocol	Name or Address
Application	SMB	NetBIOS name
Transport	TCP or UDP	Port number
Network	IP	IP address
Data link	NDIS	MAC address

Let's now work our way down the OSI stack to see how each layer resolves the NetBIOS name supplied at the application layer into an address that can be used to communicate with its peer.

Application Layer and Server Message Block (SMB)

Windows client redirectors and servers use the SMB protocol to communicate with each other. A variety of SMB dialects represent different maturity states of the protocol. One of the first things that happens in an SMB transaction is a negotiation between the parties to agree on a common dialect. Windows 2000 uses the NT LM 0.12 dialect.

In the absence of a locator mechanism, such as the Browser service (covered Chapter 15, "Managing Shared Resources") or DNS (Chapter 5), SMB applications can use broadcasts to find each other. This works something like a CB radio. When the Workstation service on one station wants to communicate with the Server service on another station, for example, the Workstation service puts out a broadcast that essentially says, "Breaker on that Ethernet. This here's the Workstation service on PHX-W2KP-027 looking for that Server service on PHX-W2KS-01. Come on back, PHX-W2KS-01 Server service." When the Server service on PHX-W2KS-01 gets this message, it returns a response such as, "You got that PHX-W2KS-01 Server service, good buddy. Come on back." The two services agree on a dialect, assign a unique ID to the session, and begin communications.

When a Windows 2000/NT computer that is a member of a domain establishes SMB communication with a domain controller, it also establishes a secure *Remote Procedure Call* (RPC) session. This RPC session uses SMB, but encrypts the traffic using a password created for the computer account, also known as an *LSA Secret*. This secure channel is used to exchange user authentication information and to do other domain-related housekeeping. The LSA Secret contains the NetBIOS name of the server, not its IP address. If a domain member cannot resolve the domain controller name into an IP address, it cannot build a secure RPC channel and users cannot get authenticated in the domain.

SMB and System Integration

SMB is the lingua franca for a variety of network operating systems, not just Windows 2000. It is used by all versions of Windows, from Windows for Workgroups through Windows 9x and classic NT. OS/2 Warp uses SMB because Warp and NT share a common ancestor in OS/2 LAN Manager. SMB is also used by Samba, a UNIX port of SMB that is widely available on most platforms. Samba is also available as a set of NLMs on NetWare.

Different SMB-based applications can talk to each other, although you may not get full functionality. It's like a conversation between a Portuguese merchant and an Italian tourist. The general ideas might get across just fine, but there may be problems with the details of the transaction. SMB applications on non-Windows platforms most commonly have problems with authentication.

A few years ago, Microsoft rechristened SMB as the *Common Internet File System* (CIFS). The new name is purely market positioning. The CIFS/SMB dialect used by Windows 2000 is the same dialect used by all versions of NT since 3.51.

Transport Layer

SMB is a session-oriented protocol. Peer SMB applications running on two stations must establish a link with each other prior to exchanging SMB messages. For this reason, SMB traffic is always carried in TCP datagrams. TCP takes responsibility for divvying up application messages into datagrams, sequencing those datagrams, and tracking them to ensure delivery.

The well-known port for SMB traffic is TCP port 139. Windows 2000 computers can also use TCP port 445 if they do not require NetBIOS-over-TCP/IP support. See the section "Disabling NetBIOS-over-TCP/IP Name Resolution" at the end of this chapter for more information.

Windows computers can also exchange sessionless traffic. Examples include name resolution/registration and NetBIOS broadcasts. Because these messages do not require sessions and are generally quite small, they use UDP. Windows uses UDP port 137 for NetBIOS name resolution/registration and UDP port 138 for NetBIOS broadcasts and unidirectional traffic. When you use the net send command to pop up a message on a user's console, for example, the message goes out over UDP port 138.

Restricting SMB Traffic Through Firewalls

If you want to restrict SMB communications from outside the local network, configure your firewall or TCP/IP filter to block traffic over TCP port 139 and UDP ports 138 and 137. If you want to block Windows 2000 SMB traffic, also block TCP port 445.

Network Layer

The IP protocol takes the UDP and TCP datagrams and packages them for delivery to the NDIS driver waiting at the MAC layer. IP can also carry so-called raw IP traffic from applications that bypass TCP and UDP to talk directly to IP.

The IP layer is the first layer where serious NetBIOS name resolution occurs. The TCPIP.SYS driver is responsible for determining the IP address of the destination based on the NetBIOS name in the SMB message. For this name resolution work, TCPIP.SYS can either use its own internal DNS resolver or it can rely on the *NetBIOS-over-TCP/IP* helper, NETBT.SYS.

As finite-element mathematicians would say, name resolution at this point becomes a non-trivial task. The bulk of the remainder of this chapter is taken up with how NETBT.SYS and TCPIP.SYS do this chore. In brief, these drivers have the following tools at their disposal:

- **LMHOSTS.** This file contains a static lookup table consisting of IP address entries and corresponding NetBIOS computer names.
- **HOSTS.** This file contains a static lookup table consisting of IP address entries and corresponding host names.
- **Broadcasts.** This method uses UDP datagrams sent as IP multicasts that request a response from the destination station that contains the station's IP address.
- **WINS.** This method uses a central database that contains NetBIOS names and IP addresses.
- **DNS.** This method uses a central database that contains host names and IP addresses.

Using one or more of these methods, TCPIP.SYS and NETBT.SYS determine the IP address of the destination station, which enables TCPIP.SYS to build the header of the IP packet. But TCPIP.SYS isn't done yet. It has another network layer driver that is involved with name resolution. It is the *Address Resolution Protocol* (ARP). The following section covers this protocol.

Internet Control Management Protocol (ICMP)

Another network layer protocol implemented by TCPIP.SYS is the *Internet Control Management Protocol* (ICMP).

The most familiar use of ICMP is in diagnostic programs, such as Ping and TRACERT. When you ping a host, for example, the result is a series of ICMP Echo Request and ICMP Echo Reply transactions.

ICMP is also used to communicate network connection problems between physical layer entities. If an IP packet exceeds the *Maximum Transmission Unit* (MTU) value for a router interface, for example, the router discards the packet and sends back an ICMP message with the correct MTU.

Media Access Control Layer

The original SMB message has now been sliced and diced and is almost ready for transmission to the destination station. There is just one thing lacking: The NDIS drivers at the MAC layer don't know diddly about NetBIOS names, TCP/UDP ports, or IP addresses. Down in the basement of the OSI stack, only one thing counts, and that is the MAC address associated with the physical device.

MAC Address Components

The MAC address is branded into the adapter's ROM. It consists of a unique six-octet number. The first three octets identify the manufacturer. (For example, the machine I'm using has a NetGear adapter branded with 00A0CC for the manufacturer's ID.)

The final three octets of the MAC address are assigned in sequence by the manufacturer. These three octets give enough room for little more than 16.5 million unique numbers. Most major manufacturers have several MAC IDs.

NDIS cannot discover the MAC address of a remote station. The network layer driver is responsible for determining the address and passing it over to NDIS. This is where ARP comes into the story.

TCPIP.SYS uses ARP to broadcast the destination stations' IP address. Then it waits for a response. The destination station processes the broadcast, sees that the ARP contains its IP address, and returns the packet directly to the sender with its MAC address. TCPIP.SYS plucks the MAC address out of the ARP response and gives it to NDIS. The NDIS drivers, NDIS.SYS and the adapter miniport driver, use the MAC address to build the header of a transmission frame. TCPIP.SYS caches the IP address/MAC address pair, so it doesn't need to do another broadcast for a while. ARP cache entries are removed after 10 minutes unless they are not being used, in which case they are deleted after 2 minutes.

ARP broadcasts succeed even in routed environments, because IP routers are programmed to act on ARP requests for IP addresses in their network range. The router responds by returning the MAC address of the router interface associated with the network number in the IP address. This fools the originating station into thinking that it is talking to the destination station. The router then repackages the packet and sends it either to the destination network (if it is in the routing table) or to its own gateway for further processing.

Viewing MAC addresses

You can see the MAC address associated with the network adapters in your machine by opening a command prompt and entering IPCONFIG /all. This also shows the IP information associated with the interfaces. Here is an example:

```
C:\>IPCONFIG /all

Windows 2000 IP Configuration

        Host Name . . . . . . . . . . . . : PHX-W2KP-001
        Primary DNS Suffix . . . . . . . : Company.com
        Node Type . . . . . . . . . . . : Hybrid
        IP Routing Enabled. . . . . . . . : No
        WINS Proxy Enabled. . . . . . . . : No

Ethernet adapter Local Area Connection 2:

        Connection-specific DNS Suffix . . : Company.com
        Description . . . . . . . . . . : NETGEAR FA310TX Fast Ethernet Adapter
(NGRPCI)
        Physical Address. . . . . . . . : 00-A0-CC-AA-AA-AA
        DHCP Enabled. . . . . . . . . . : No
        IP Address. . . . . . . . . . . : 10.1.200.1
        Subnet Mask . . . . . . . . . . : 255.255.0.0
        Default Gateway . . . . . . . . : 10.1.1.254
        DNS Servers . . . . . . . . . . : 10.1.1.1
```

You can view the contents of the ARP cache using the arp -a command at a command prompt:

```
C:\>    arp -a
Interface: 10.1.10.3 on Interface 0x2000003
        Internet Address      Physical Address            Type
        10.1.1.1                08-00-09-aa-aa-aa    dynamic
```

You can delete a particular host from the ARP cache using arp -d as follows:

```
c:\>arp -d 10.1.1.1
```

or

```
c:\>arp -d *
```

Server Message Block Details

You can get a good feel for the way SMB traffic is handled by TCPIP.SYS using the Network Monitor service that comes with Windows 2000 Server. Load the Network Monitor service using CONTROL PANEL | ADD/REMOVE PROGRAMS | NETWORK COMPONENTS. When the service is loaded, launch the Network Monitor program via START | PROGRAMS | ADMINISTRATIVE

TOOLS | NETWORK MONITOR. Figure 4.2 shows an example of the `Network Monitor` window. The monitor can display traffic only on a local interface. For a Promiscuous-mode version, get a copy of SMS for Windows 2000 or a third-party sniffer, such as Sniffer Pro from Network Associates.

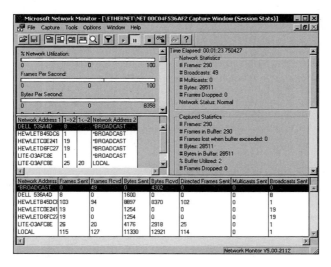

Figure 4.2 `Network Monitor` window showing captured traffic on a small network.

The following list shows the contents of a captured frame that contains an SMB message. The various layer protocols are expanded so that you can see their control structures and payload. The entries of particular interest are bolded and explained here:

```
FRAME: Base frame properties
      FRAME: Time of capture = Dec 12, 1997 7:57:30.317
      FRAME: Time delta from previous physical frame: 1 milliseconds
      FRAME: Frame number: 13
      FRAME: Total frame length: 203 bytes
      FRAME: Capture frame length: 203 bytes
      FRAME: Frame data: Number of data bytes remaining = 203 (0x00CB)
  ETHERNET: ETYPE = 0x0800 : Protocol = IP:  DOD Internet Protocol
      ¹ETHERNET: Destination address : 080009AAAAAA
      ²ETHERNET: Source address : 006097BBBBBB
      ETHERNET: Frame Length : 203 (0x00CB)
      ETHERNET: Ethernet Type : 0x0800 (IP:  DOD Internet Protocol)
  IP: ID = 0x7B26; Proto = TCP; Len: 189
      ³IP: Protocol = TCP - Transmission Control
      ⁴IP: Source Address = 10.1.1.40
      ⁵IP: Destination Address = 10.1.1.10
```

```
      TCP: .AP..., len:  149, seq: 356803238-356803386, ack:  76085993, win: 8756, src: 2365
dst:  139 (NBT Session)
      TCP: Source Port = 0x093D
      ⁶TCP: Destination Port = NETBIOS Session Service
      ⁷TCP: Sequence Number = 356803238 (0x154462A6)
      TCP: Acknowledgement Number = 76085993 (0x488FAE9)
   ⁸NBT: SS: Session Message, Len: 133
      NBT: Packet Type = Session Message
      NBT: Packet Flags = 0 (0x0)
      NBT: Packet Length = 133 (0x85)
      NBT: SS Data: Number of data bytes remaining = 133 (0x0085)
   ⁹SMB: C negotiate, Dialect = NT LM 0.12
      SMB: NT status code = 0x0, Facility = System, Severity = Success, Code = (0)
STATUS_WAIT_0
      SMB: Header: PID = 0xFEFF TID = 0x0000 MID = 0x0000 UID = 0x0000
      SMB: Command = C negotiate
         ¹⁰SMB: Dialect Strings Understood
            SMB: Dialect String = PC NETWORK PROGRAM 1.0
            SMB: Dialect String = LANMAN1.0
            SMB: Dialect String = Windows for Workgroups 3.1a
            SMB: Dialect String = LM1.2X002
            SMB: Dialect String = LANMAN2.1
            SMB: Dialect String = NT LM 0.12
```

1. & 2. Ethernet: Destination and Source addresses. These are the MAC addresses of the network cards in the sending and receiving computer. A few packets before this one, the system used ARP to discover the MAC address for the destination IP address.

3. IP: Protocol. This line shows the payload classification. In this case, the IP packet holds a TCP datagram. It could also hold a UDP datagram or it could be a raw IP packet, in which case this line should include the application that built the payload.

4. & 5. IP: Source and Destination addresses. This entry contains the IP address for the source computer and the destination computer. This information came from the NetBIOS helper, NETBT.SYS, which sent out a broadcast earlier in the trace.

6. TCP: Destination port. The TCPIP.SYS driver uses well-known TCP port 139 for session-oriented traffic. The capture program decoded port 139 as the NetBIOS Session service. When NETBT.SYS sent out its name resolution packet, it used UDP port 137. Any datagrams would use UDP port 138. Well-known TCP and UDP ports are contained in the SERVICES file under \WINNT\System32\Drivers\etc.

7. **TCP: Sequence Number.** TCP sequences its datagrams so that they can be reassembled at the destination. If a piece ends up missing, TCP tells the sender to transmit it again without bothering the application level protocol. SMB–based services use TCP because of this feature.

8. **NBT: SS: Session Message.** The *SS* stands for Session service. This tells TCPIP.SYS at the receiving station that the enclosed message is a NetBIOS session message so that it can act accordingly.

9. **SMB: C negotiate, Dialect = NT LM 0.12.** As SMB matured, the language got richer and more powerful, like auld Ænglishe turning into modern street jive. A modern SMB client may need to talk to an older SMB peer; so like polite wayfarers, they first decide on a common dialect. The most current dialect is NT LM 0.12. The *LM* stands for LAN Manager; but Windows 2000/NT also uses this dialect.

10. **SMB: Dialect Strings Understood.** This lists the dialects the sender can interpret.

NetBIOS Services

A hidden 16th byte in the NetBIOS computer name designates a service, such as Workstation, Master Browser, and so forth. The combination of a NetBIOS name in the first 15 bytes and a service ID in the 16th byte forms a unique identifier, similar to the way an IP address and TCP/UDP port number combine to form a socket. Table 4.2 shows the NetBIOS service designators for reference.

Table 4.2 **NetBOIS Service Designators**

NetBIOS Name	Svc #	Service Name
Username	03	Messenger service
Domainname	00	Domain Name
Domainname	1B	Domain Master Browser
Domainname	1C	Domain Controllers
Domainname	1D	Master Browser
Domainname	1E	Browser Service Elections
Inet~Services	1C	IIS
IS~computer name	00	IIS
Computername	00	Workstation service
--__MSBROWSE__	01	Master Browser

NetBIOS Name	Svc #	Service Name
Computername	03	Messenger service
Computername	06	RAS Server service
Computername	1F	NetDDE service
Computername	20	File Server service
Computername	21	RAS Client service
Computername	22	Microsoft Exchange Interchange (MSMail Connector)
Computername	23	Microsoft Exchange Store
Computername	24	Microsoft Exchange Directory
Computername	30	Modem Sharing Server service
Computername	31	Modem Sharing Client service
Computername	43	SMS Clients Remote Control
Computername	44	SMS Administrators Remote Control Tool
Computername	45	SMS Clients Remote Chat
Computername	46	SMS Clients Remote Transfer
Computername	87	Microsoft Exchange MTA
Computername	6A	Microsoft Exchange IMC
Computername	BE	Network Monitor Agent
Computername	BF	Network Monitor Application

The combination of NetBIOS name and service identifiers are classified into NetBIOS name types. The NETBT.SYS driver uses NetBIOS name types to handle name registration. Here are the registration-handling methods:

- **Unique.** The associated name/service combination can use only one IP address. If another computer tries to register the same name/service combination with a different IP address, it will be challenged. If one Windows 2000 computer named BORIS is already on the network, for example, a second computer named BORIS will not be permitted to register the same NetBIOS service.

- **Group.** Multiple computers can use the associated name/service combination. The NETBT.SYS driver uses the Group type to define multicast groups. An SMB message directed at a multicast group in network 10.1.0.0, for example, would use an IP multicast address of 10.1.255.255. Multicasting reduces the processing load on computers in the network because only members of the multicast group need to examine the packet.

- **Multihomed.** This name/service combination must be unique, but can be associated with multiple IP addresses. The NETBT.SYS driver uses the Multihomed type to designate services registered by a machine with multiple network adapters. The computer's name/service combination is registered with the IP address of each adapter.

- **Internet.** This special group designation identifies primary and backup domain controllers. A PDC normally replicates with its BDCs using multicasts for efficiency. Some routers block multicast packets. This is where WINS takes over. The WINS server takes the multicast replication packets and directs them as unicast packets directly to the IP addresses of BDCs in its database. These unicast packets make it through intervening routers to their respective BDCs.

Multihomed NetBIOS Registrations and Single Adapters

The Multihomed NetBIOS name type is not assigned to name/service combinations originating from a computer with multiple IP addresses bound to the same adapter. Only the first IP address bound to the adapter is registered. If a Web server has 20 IP addresses bound to the network adapter to represent 20 different virtual Web sites, for example, only the first IP address would be used to register the File Server, Messenger, and Workstation NetBIOS services.

Even though the other addresses do not appear as multihomed registrations, they are available for SMB connections. If a server has two IP addresses, 10.1.1.1 and 10.1.1.2, assigned to the same adapter, for example, it is possible to connect to either address with a net use command. This is a change from classic NT. In classic NT, only the first address could be used for SMB connections.

Network Diagnostic Utilities

Windows 2000 comes with several command-line utilities to help troubleshoot IP-related problems. They are IPCONFIG, NETSTAT, TRACERT, PATHPING, NBTSTAT, and NETDIAG. The following sections describe their functions and most commonly used options.

IPCONFIG

The IP parameters for an interface are set and configured using the Network and Dial-up Connection window. You can view these settings from the command line using IPCONFIG. Run IPCONFIG /all to display detailed information for each interface. Here is an example:

```
Ethernet adapter :
    Host Name: . . . . . . . . . . . : PHX-W2KP-023.company.com
        Description . . . . . . . . . . : NETGEAR FA310TX Fast Ethernet Adapter (NGRPCI).
        Physical Address. . . . . . . . : 08-00-09-AA-AA-AA
```

```
DHCP Enabled. . . . . . . . . : Yes
IP Address. . . . . . . . . . : 10.1.60.1
Subnet Mask . . . . . . . . . : 255.255.0.0
Default Gateway . . . . . . . : 10.1.254.254
Primary WINS Server . . . . . : 10.1.100.254
Secondary WINS Server . . . . : 10.1.100.253
Lease Obtained. . . . . . . . : Saturday, November 29, 1999 6:35:06 PM
Lease Expires . . . . . . . . : Sunday, November 30, 1999 6:35:06 PM
```

Here are the switches associated with IPCONFIG and their functions. All but the first two switches are new in Windows 2000. The three DNS switches are absolutely essential troubleshooting aids.

- **IPCONFIG /release.** If an adapter is configured for DHCP, this option releases the currently leased address. Use this switch to force the client to give up an address that you want to assign to another adapter.

- **IPCONFIG /renew.** If the adapter is configured for DHCP, this option releases the current lease and immediately renews the lease. Under most circumstances, the client will obtain the address that it had previously leased. Use this option to download a new DHCP configuration packet.

- **IPCONFIG /displaydns.** This option shows the records in the local DNS cache.

- **IPCONFIG /flushdns.** This option clears the local DNS cache.

- **IPCONFIG /registerdns.** This option registers the client with Dynamic DNS.

- **IPCONFIG /showclassid.** Lists the allowable DHCP class IDs for the adapter.

- **IPCONFIG /setclassid.** Modifies the DHCP class ID.

NETSTAT

This utility comes straight from UNIX. It displays data collected from any interfaces configured for TCP/IP.

- **NETSTAT -a.** Displays the various TCP and UDP sessions established on an interface. Use this switch when you want a quick check for potential teardrop attacks or other possible problems that could cause a server to accumulate excessive TCP listens and sessions:

```
TCP     ATL-DC-01:3269         ATL-DC-01.subsidiary.com:0      LISTENING
TCP     ATL-DC-01:6548         ATL-DC-01.subsidiary.com:0      LISTENING
TCP     ATL-DC-01:nbsession    ATL-DC-01.subsidiary.com:0      LISTENING
TCP     ATL-DC-01:389          ATL-DC-01.subsidiary.com:1065   ESTABLISHED
TCP     ATL-DC-01:389          ATL-DC-01.subsidiary.com:1095   ESTABLISHED
TCP     ATL-DC-01:389          ATL-DC-01.subsidiary.com:1103   ESTABLISHED
```

- **NETSTAT -e.** Displays Ethernet statistics including problem packets:

```
Interface Statistics
                              Received      Sent
Bytes                         870327        9569847
Unicast packets               6729          10074
Non-unicast packets           2345          725
Discards                      0             0
Errors                        0             2
Unknown protocols             0
```

- **NETSTAT -n.** Displays local addresses and port numbers for the various sessions and listens:

```
Active Connections
   Proto  Local Address        Foreign Address       State
   TCP    10.1.100.1:445       10.1.1.1:1160         ESTABLISHED
   TCP    10.1.100.1:445       10.2.1.1:1313         ESTABLISHED
   TCP    10.1.100.1:445       10.3.1.2:1047         ESTABLISHED
   TCP    10.1.100.1:2261      10.1.1.254:3389       ESTABLISHED
```

- **NETSTAT -p [tcp] [udp] [ip].** Similar to -n, but lists by host name. The list includes a protocol represented by p. The example is for NETSTAT -p tcp. (The microsoft-ds entry is a translation of TCP port 445.)

```
Proto  Local Address               Foreign Address       State
TCP    phx-w2kp-01:microsoft-ds    PHX-DC-01:1160        ESTABLISHED
TCP    phx-w2kp-01:microsoft-ds    HOU-DC-01:1313        ESTABLISHED
TCP    phx-w2kp-01:microsoft-ds    ALB-DC-01:1047        ESTABLISHED
TCP    phx-w2kp-01:2261            PHX-NT4S-30:3389      ESTABLISHED
```

- **NETSTAT -r.** Displays the contents of the local routing table. The listing also includes the active ports:

```
===========================================================================
Interface List
0x1 ......................... Internal loopback interface for 127.0.0.0 network
0x2 ......................... Internal RAS Server interface for dial in clients
0x3 ...08 00 09 aa aa aa ...... NETGEAR FA310TX Fast Ethernet Adapter (NGRPCI)
===========================================================================
===========================================================================
Active Routes:
Network Destination        Netmask           Gateway       Interface    Metric
10.1.0.0                   255.255.0.0       10.1.30.1     10.1.30.1    1
10.1.30.1                  255.255.255.255   127.0.0.1     127.0.0.1    1
10.255.255.255             255.255.255.255   10.1.30.1     10.1.30.1    1
127.0.0.0                  255.0.0.0         127.0.0.1     127.0.0.1    1
127.0.0.1                  255.255.255.255   127.0.0.1     127.0.0.1    1
224.0.0.0                  224.0.0.0         10.1.30.1     10.1.30.1    1
255.255.255.255            255.255.255.255   10.1.30.1     10.1.30.1    1
===========================================================================
```

- **NETSTAT -s.** Displays statistics for each protocol. Use the -p switch to select a particular protocol:

```
TCP Statistics
   Active Opens                   = 1103
   Passive Opens                  = 1204
   Failed Connection Attempts     = 1
   Reset Connections              = 34
   Current Connections            = 22
   Segments Received              = 23942
   Segments Sent                  = 27209
   Segments Retransmitted         = 134
```

TRACERT

This utility is similar to the UNIX traceroute. It reports the IP address and name of each interface between the client and the target. If Ping fails, TRACERT can tell you where the responses have stopped.

TRACERT works by sending out a series of ICMP Echo Requests to the destination host, similar to Ping, except that TRACERT controls the *Time-To-Live* (TTL) value in the ICMP packet to get a response from each intervening router.

TRACERT sends the first ICMP Echo Request with a TTL of 1, so the first router responds but the second times out with a *TTL Exceeded in Transit* error. The next ICMP has a TTL of 2, then 3, and so forth until the ultimate host finally responds. Each request is repeated three times and the output is presented as a series of router names and IP addresses. By default, TRAC-ERT does a reverse DNS query to get the name associated with each IP address. Here is a sample TRACERT report:

```
C:\>TRACERT www.metacrawler.com
Tracing route to v16.go2net.com [206.253.217.16] over a maximum of 30 hops:
  1    136 ms   134 ms   146 ms   ts03.bur.primenet.com [207.218.32.23]
  2    132 ms   132 ms   131 ms   fe2-0.cr1.BUR.globalcenter.net [207.218.32.1]
  3    147 ms   211 ms   129 ms   fe0-1.cr2.BUR.globalcenter.net [207.218.173.35]
  4    138 ms   137 ms   138 ms   pos0-3-155M.cr1.NUQ.globalcenter.net [206.251.1.49]
  5    138 ms   138 ms   138 ms   pos1-0-622M.cr1.SNV.globalcenter.net [206.251.0.74]
  6    139 ms   140 ms   156 ms   pos5-0-0-155M.br3.SNV.globalcenter.net [206.132.150.30]
  7    144 ms   145 ms   141 ms   sl-gw1-sj-12-0.sprintlink.net [144.228.110.9]
  8    143 ms   139 ms   140 ms   sl-bb10-sj-0-2-155M.sprintlink.net [144.232.3.29]
  9    147 ms   145 ms   144 ms   sl-bb21-stk-7-0.sprintlink.net [144.232.8.194]
 10    160 ms   159 ms   157 ms   sl-bb10-sea-1-0.sprintlink.net [144.232.8.30]
 11    161 ms   163 ms   160 ms   sl-gw4-sea-8-0-0.sprintlink.net [144.232.6.54]
 12    160 ms   158 ms   157 ms   sl-internap-1-0-0-T3.sprintlink.net [144.228.96.14]
 13    158 ms   162 ms   161 ms   border3as.fe0-1-fenet2.sea.pnap.net [206.253.192.199]
 14    168 ms   166 ms   160 ms   v16.go2net.com [206.253.217.16]

Trace complete.
```

Here are the TRACERT switches:

- **TRACERT -d.** Turns off host name lookups. This significantly speeds up traces. Highly recommended.
- **TRACERT -h.** Increases the maximum hop count. The default is 30.
- **TRACERT -j host-list.** This option is used to force TRACERT to use a specific router via source routing. For a detailed look at how to use this option in a large production environment, take a look at `boardwatch.internet.com/mag/96/dec/bwm38.html`.
- **TRACERT -w.** Increases the maximum timeout.

PATHPING

TRACERT can take a long time to start producing a listing because it waits for the echo response from the final host. Windows 2000 has a faster trace diagnostic called PATHPING. This utility sends out a series of ICMP Echo Requests with incremented TTLs, just as TRACERT does; instead of analyzing them during the initial transaction, however, it displays the results immediately and then waits until the ultimate host is contacted before calculating statistics. Highly recommended.

NBTSTAT

When a Windows TCP/IP client resolves a NetBIOS name, it caches the results in a NetBIOS Name Cache table. The entry stays in the cache for 600 seconds (10 minutes) by default. You can view and manipulate the contents of NetBIOS Name Cache using NBTSTAT. Here are the NBTSTAT switches and their functions. The switches are case sensitive.

- **NBTSTAT -c.** Displays the local name cache. Use this switch when you want to verify that a computer has the correct IP address cached for a particular host name. The -c switch can keep you from spending hours troubleshooting a Ping failure whose real cause is a bad name in the name cache.

  The following code listing shows a sample name cache. The header says `Remote Name Cache`, but it actually means a "cache of remote names." The `Type` column is the 2-byte hex ID of the NetBIOS service. The first three entries were preloaded from a local LMHOSTS file, which gives them a life of 60 seconds rather than the default 600 seconds.

```
Node IpAddress: [10.1.1.10] Scope Id: []
            NetBIOS Remote Cache Name Table

      Name              Type          Host Address    Life [sec]
  ----------------------------------------------------------------
  COMPANY-DC-02         <03>  UNIQUE     10.1.1.20       60
  COMPANY-DC-02         <00>  UNIQUE     10.1.1.20       60
  COMPANY-DC-02         <20>  UNIQUE     10.1.1.20       60
  COMPANY-NTS-01        <00>  UNIQUE     10.1.1.101      600
```

- **NBTSTAT - a.** Displays the name cache on a remote computer given its NetBIOS name. This option also displays the MAC address of the remote network adapter. Example syntax: `NBTSTAT -a phx-dc-01`.

- **NBTSTAT -A.** Displays the name cache on a remote machine given its IP address. Also displays the MAC address of the remote network adapter. Example syntax: `NBTSTAT -A 10.1.1.1`.

- **NBTSTAT -n.** Displays the NetBIOS names associated with the local computer. This includes the computer name with all services, the locally logged-on user with all services, the workgroup or domain of the computer, and any browser services running:

```
Node IpAddress: [10.1.10.3] Scope Id: []
            NetBIOS Local Name Table

      Name              Type          Status
  -----------------------------------------------
  PHX-W2KP-001          <00>  UNIQUE     Registered
  COMPANY               <00>  GROUP      Registered
  PHX-W2KP-001          <03>  UNIQUE     Registered
  PHX-W2KP-001          <20>  UNIQUE     Registered
  COMPANY               <1E>  GROUP      Registered
  .._MSBROWSE__.        <01>  GROUP      Registered
```

- **NBTSTAT -r.** Lists the names in the name cache and how they were resolved. This is handy when you are trying to determine whether a computer used broadcasts or WINS to get an IP address.

```
    NetBIOS Names Resolution and Registration Statistics
    ------------------------------------------------------

    Resolved By Broadcast     = 2
    Resolved By Name Server   = 5
    Registered By Broadcast   = 32
    Registered By Name Server = 8


    NetBIOS Names Resolved By Broadcast
    -----------------------------------------------
          PHX-DC-01      <00>
          PHX-DC-01      <00>
```

- **NBTSTAT -R.** Purges the name cache and loads the preload (#PRE) items out of the LMHOSTS file. See the section "Resolving NetBIOS Names Using LMHOSTS" later in the chapter.

- **NBTSTAT -S.** Displays the current sessions on the local machine showing the IP addresses of the connected machines. This is very useful when you want a quick display of the services that have active connections:

```
NetBIOS Connection Table
Local Name                State    In/Out  Remote Host          Input   Output
- - - - - - - - - - - - - - - - - - - - - - - - - - - - - - - - - - - - - - - -
PHX-W2KP-001     <03>     Listening
PHX-W2KP-001              Connected  In     10.1.100.3          2KB     3KB
ADMINISTRATOR    <03>     Listening
```

- **NBTSTAT -s.** Same as -S, but with the name of the connected machine rather than the IP address:

```
NetBIOS Connection Table
Local Name                State    In/Out  Remote Host          Input   Output
- - - - - - - - - - - - - - - - - - - - - - - - - - - - - - - - - - - - - - - -
PHX-W2KP-001     <03>     Listening
PHX-W2KP-001              Connected  In     PHX-DC-01           2KB     3KB
ADMINISTRATOR    <03>     Listening
```

- **NBTSTAT -RR.** Releases the name registration in WINS and then reregisters. Introduced in NT4 SP4, it is extremely useful for correcting WINS errors. A bad record can be deleted manually from WINS, and then the client can be reregistered with this option.

If you discover during all this pinging and tracing and name cache scanning that everyone else in the area is working fine and only this machine is having problems, try opening the Network and Dial-up Connections window and checking the status of the connection icon. If it has a big X on it, the interface has lost communication with the network. Check the Event Log to see whether there is some reason for the failure. Then try the next utility, NETDIAG.

Registry Tip: Location of NetBIOS Cache Control Keys
The Registry key that contains the configuration parameters, such as cache timeouts and broadcast counts, is located in HKLM | System | CurrentControlSet | Services | NETBT.

NETDIAG

This utility, new to Windows 2000, does a comprehensive set of tests on just about every network function. The following is a list of all the network services tested by NETDIAG. The report is usually too long to read in a console. Pipe it to a file for review.

Autonet	IpLoopBk	NetBTTransports
Bindings	IPX	NETSTAT
Browser	Kerberos	NetWare
DcList	LDAP	Route
DefGw	Member	Trust
DNS	Modem	WAN
DsGetDc	NbtNm	WINS
IPCONFIG	Dis	Winsock

If you have a network problem that goes beyond a simple connectivity glitch, NETDIAG is the first place to turn. It will either find the source or give you a set of good clues to continue troubleshooting. It may take a while to sort through the report, but the root cause should be buried in there somewhere.

Resolving NetBIOS Names Using Broadcasts

The name resolution overview at the start of this chapter laid out a series of methods for resolving a NetBIOS name into its associated IP address. The earliest method, but one that is still in common use today in small networks, uses broadcasts. (Non-broadcast alternatives using LMHOSTS and WINS are covered in subsequent sections.)

Name resolution based on broadcasts makes a fundamental assumption that all stations have a unique address. After all, a broadcast is no different from just leaning your head out a screen door and yelling, "John Henry, when y'all get a second, come on over here and give me a hand. Y'hear?" For that kind of broadcast-based name calling to work, there can be only one John Henry in town. In the same way, when a computer broadcasts for a computer named PHX-DC-01, there had better only be one on the wire.

Windows computers that use broadcasts to resolve names also use broadcasts to ensure the uniqueness of their names. This is called name registration, and it works like this:

Procedure 4.1 **Functional Sequence for NetBIOS Name Resolution Using Broadcasts**

1. When a Windows computer named PHX–W2KP–002 is booted and comes onto the network, it first checks to make sure that no other computer is using its name. It does this by sending out a *NetBIOS Name Registration* broadcast. This application layer broadcast is placed into an IP multicast packet at the network layer and directed at the client's subnet. For example, a client with the IP address 10.1.3.150, subnet 255.255.0.0, would send out a name registration multicast addressed to 10.1.255.255. Stations that are in the broadcast space but not in network 10.1.0.0 can ignore the multicast.

2. If another computer with the name PHX–W2KP–002 hears the multicast, it sends back a challenge to the computer that originated the broadcast saying, in effect, "Back off. I'm using that name, and here's my IP address to prove it."

3. The newcomer doesn't meekly retreat in the face of this challenge, however. It verifies the identity of the challenger by sending out an ARP broadcast containing the challenger's IP address. If the ARP gets no response, the newcomer uses the name anyway. If the ARP gets a response, the newcomer gives up, refuses to bind network services to the adapter, and informs the user of the duplicate name. It also puts a warning in the Event Log.

4. If the newcomer satisfies itself that its name is unique, it binds the application layer protocols, such as Workstation, Server, and Browser, to the TCP/IP stack and initializes the network drivers.

5. When the network applications can see the network, the SMB redirector—LAN Manager Workstation in the case of Windows 2000—prepares to communicate with a server. If it needs to access a domain controller to authenticate the member computer, for example, call it PHX–DC–01. The redirector knows the domain controller's NetBIOS name because it is in the Registry under LSA Secrets, but it doesn't know the server's IP address or MAC address. It builds an SMB message destined for PHX–DC–01 and sends it to the TCPIP.SYS driver.

6. When TCPIP.SYS gets the SMB message, it uses NETBT.SYS to send out a *NetBIOS Name Resolution* multicast looking for the IP address of the destination server. The multicast says, in effect, "I'm looking for server PHX–DC–01." NETBT.SYS sends out the multicast every half second for three tries and then gives up if it does not get a response.

7. If PHX-DC-01 hears the multicast, it responds with an acknowledgement that contains its IP address. The acknowledgement is sent directly back to the client because PHX-DC-01 learned the client's NetBIOS name, IP address, and MAC address from the name resolution multicast.

8. TCPIP.SYS nabs the IP address from the name resolution response and sends out an ARP to confirm the address. When it is confirmed, NETBT.SYS caches the name and IP address of the server in a *NetBIOS name table* where it can be used in subsequent transactions.

This small-town method of shouting out names and waiting for responses doesn't work very well in the bright lights and big city of a routed TCP/IP network where routers and Layer 3 switches and intelligent bridges are configured to stop broadcasts. The next two sections cover how to use LMHOSTS and WINS to handle name resolution and registration in a routed environment.

Resolving NetBIOS Names Using LMHOSTS

In the early days of NetBIOS, Microsoft borrowed an idea from UNIX for resolving host names in a routed environment by using a static lookup table in a HOSTS file. Because the Microsoft team was working on OS/2 LAN Manager at the time, the NetBIOS name lookup table was called LMHOSTS with no extension. It carries the same name today.

TCP/IP-Related File Locations

The LMHOSTS file is located in the \WINNT\System32\Drivers\etc directory along with several other TCP/IP-related files. This directory is defined by the following Registry entry :

    Key: HKL | SYSTEM | CurrentControlSet | Services | Tcpip | Parameters
    Value: DataBasePath

This directory also contains a sample LMHOSTS file called LMHOSTS.SAM. You can rename this to LMHOSTS and modify it to suit your purposes.

The \WINNT\System32\Drivers\etc directory holds these other TCP/IP-related files:

- **HOSTS.** Used to provide TCP/IP host name lookups.
- **SERVICES.** Contains well-known TCP and UDP ports and their uses.
- **PROTOCOL.** Contains the list of IP protocols used on the computer in accordance with RFC 1060.
- **NETWORKS.** Contains a quick lookup of network names and their corresponding gateway IP addresses.
- **QUOTES.** Supports the ever-popular Quote of the Day protocol. The default entries lean rather heavily on George Bernard Shaw and Charles Dickens, but you're free to add more.

Configuring LMHOSTS

The idea behind LMHOSTS is to have a place where NETBT.SYS can quickly find the IP address associated with a NetBIOS name. The LMHOSTS file is a text file consisting of IP addresses and host names. Here is an example LMHOSTS file listing three servers, two of which are domain controllers for a domain called COMPANY:

```
# LMHOSTS file for Domain COMPANY
10.1.1.10        PHX-DC-01          #PRE      #DOM:COMPANY
10.1.1.20        PHX-DC-02          #PRE      #DOM:COMPANY
10.1.1.30        PHX-W2KS-01        #PRE
10.1.1.100       PHX-W2KS-02        #PRE

#BEGIN_ALTERNATE
#INCLUDE         \\PHX-DC-01\PUBLIC\ETC\LMHOSTS
#INCLUDE         \\PHX-DC-02\PUBLIC\ETC\LMHOSTS
#END_ALTERNATE
```

The pound sign (#) has two functions:

- Precedes a switch, such as #PRE, #DOM, and #INCLUDE.
- If not followed by a recognized switch, the sign indicates a remark, such as that used in the first line.

Here are the switches used in LMHOSTS. The switch name must be upper-case, otherwise the entry is considered a remark.

- **#PRE.** This switch loads the contents of the LMHOSTS file into the NetBIOS name cache at boot time. This speeds up the initial lookup.

- **#DOM:.** This switch flags the station as a domain controller. The entry after the colon is the domain name. If you use LMHOSTS in a domain environment, this switch is a necessity because it tells the local client where to go to get authenticated.

- **#INCLUDE:.** Tells TCPIP.SYS to load the LMHOSTS file from another computer. The #INCLUDE option enables you to maintain a single, central LMHOSTS file that can be referenced by other workstations in a work-group. The entry uses a UNC name, \\PHX-DC-01\PUBLIC, where PUBLIC is a share name. There is a subtle Catch-22 at work here. The UNC path contains a NetBIOS name. You must make sure the LMHOSTS file has an entry for that name.

- **#BEGIN_ALTERNATE and #END_ALTERNATE.** Use these statements to bracket multiple entries under a single #INCLUDE statement. If you have only one #INCLUDE statement, you do not need bracketing statements.

Using LMHOSTS

LMHOSTS should be used only as a last resort. Those little static mappings become ticking bombs that follow you around like the crocodile that chased Captain Hook in *Peter Pan*. One day you'll forget they're out there and *snap*.

That being said, there are some common uses for LMHOSTS. For instance, some administrators use LMHOSTS to resolve names over dial-up connections. There is an option to use WINS over dial-up, but very often it is ineffective or takes too long to work. A quick-and-dirty LMHOSTS entry at the dial-up client with an entry for a domain controller and any servers associated with persistent mappings does the trick.

Rather than use LMHOSTS in this situation, however, you may want to consider just entering the IP address of the server in the UNC path. Instead of entering `\\PHX-W2KS-03\Users\LLuthor` in the `Map Network Drive` window and using an LMHOSTS entry to map the server name to an IP address, for instance, just enter a UNC name of `\\10.1.1.43\Users\LLuthor` or whatever the server's IP address might be. If you change the server's IP address, the users must remap, but this is usually easier for them than reconfiguring LMHOSTS.

Resolving NetBIOS Names Using WINS

There is an alternative to statically mapping names and IP addresses in LMHOSTS. The venerable *Windows Internet Name Service* (WINS) maintains a database of NetBIOS names and IP address mappings that WINS clients use to register their own NetBIOS services and to find the IP addresses of the services running on other WINS clients.

WINS is based on protocols and services defined in RFC 1001, "Protocol Standard For A NetBIOS Service On A TCP/UDP Transport: Concepts And Methods," and RFC 1002, "Protocol Standard For A NetBIOS Service On A TCP/UDP Transport: Detailed Specifications." These are public standards but, in practice, Microsoft WINS is the only commercial NetBIOS name service.

WINS works like a bridal registry. In a bridal registry, happy couples go to Nordstroms or Wal-Mart and *register* their wedding. Their friends go to the same store to *resolve* their gift-buying decisions. With WINS, clients go to a WINS server and *register* their NetBIOS services with the corresponding IP addresses. Other WINS clients send queries to the WINS server to *resolve* NetBIOS names into IP addresses.

For all its seeming simplicity, WINS is the single most pernicious cause of weird, inexplicable behavior in a classic NT network. Managing WINS in a large network is without question one of the most complex duties of a classic NT administrator. Thankfully, much of the need for WINS goes away in Windows 2000 thanks to Dynamic DNS. As covered in the next chapter, Dynamic DNS provides much the same service as WINS. It gives a way for clients to automatically create host records in DNS and to use DNS to do lookups for other dynamically registered host names.

Dynamic DNS has several advantages over WINS. The first is that DNS is a hierarchical namespace as opposed to the flat world of NetBIOS names. Computer names still need to be unique within the same Windows 2000 domain, but locating them in a hierarchical namespace is much easier. Another advantage is that Dynamic DNS is an open standard that is being implemented on all major NOS platforms. There is no need to maintain a separate, all-but-proprietary WINS database. And finally, Dynamic DNS can be integrated into Active Directory to get automatic replication handling.

Because Windows 2000 is the only Windows platform currently capable of Dynamic DNS registration, it will probably be a while before you can get completely away from needing WINS. Even if you plan on deploying strictly Windows 2000 servers and desktops, you should lay out a WINS strategy on paper just in case you run into DNS snags and need temporary help in resolving NetBIOS names.

This section provides an overview of installing, configuring, and troubleshooting WINS on Windows 2000. If you currently manage a classic NT network that uses WINS, you'll find no new functionality in Windows 2000 compared to NT4 Service Pack 5. If you are running NT4 WINS with SP4 or lower, I recommend you either upgrade to Windows 2000 or install SP4 to get the updated WINS features. They are a significant improvement over classic WINS.

WINS Functional Overview

Every computer in a domain must have a unique name. As shown previously, this can be accomplished with broadcasts in small networks, but a routed network needs a central repository of name registrations that is consistent throughout a domain so that clients can resolve NetBIOS names to IP addresses across router boundaries. Those are the two functions of WINS, name registration and name resolution. Let's look at registration first.

Name Registration Using WINS

A WINS client is configured with the IP address of at least one WINS server. This enables the client to find the WINS server in a routed environment. Here is a typical sequence of events when a client registers itself with its WINS server:

1. When the WINS client comes up on the network, it sends a *name registration request* to its WINS server. The client sends a registration request for each of its SMB-based services. If the client is running Server, Workstation, and Messenger services, for example, it submits three registration requests to WINS.

   If the client has multiple network adapters (also known as a *multihomed* WINS client), it submits registration requests for each service on each adapter.

2. If the WINS database at the server contains no other records that use the name or IP address that the client is requesting, the WINS server returns a *positive name registration response* and adds the records to its database along with a *renewal interval* after which the registration expires. The client must renew the registration within this period. By default, the renewal interval is six days.

3. If the WINS database at the server contains a record with the same name but different IP address, the WINS server tells the client to wait for a short time (five minutes) while it sends a *name query request* to the client that already has the registration. If the existing client responds, the WINS server sends a *negative name registration response* to the requesting client.

4. If the existing client does not respond to the name query request, the WINS server returns a positive response to the client, adds the records to the database, and assigns a renewal interval.

5. At the halfway point of the renewal interval, the client sends a renewal request to the WINS server for each registered service. The server responds and the renewal interval clock is reset.

6. When the WINS client goes off the network using a standard shutdown process, it sends a *name release* to its WINS server.

7. The server marks the associated records as released and assigns an *extinction interval* to the record. During the extinction interval, the released record is not replicated. The owner server is free to reassign the name or address to another client, but replication partners are not. This interval simplifies reregistration when the client comes back online.

In short, the name registration cycle for a WINS client consists of the following:

- A registration request followed by a registration response
- A period of active status during which the client renews its registrations periodically
- A release request followed by a node release
- A period of released status during which the client can be reregistered quickly

Name Registration Failure Handling

The WINS name registration process includes the following several features for handling common failure modes:

- **Failure to reregister.** If a client releases a registration and does not subsequently reregister, the server waits until the end of the extinction interval and then assigns a status of *tombstoned* to the record. Tombstoned records are replicated so that other WINS servers know that the name and IP address are available should another client attempt to register using them. An extinction timeout interval is assigned to the tombstoned record. The default interval is six days. After this interval, the record is removed from the database during scavenging.

- **Failure to renew.** If a client does not renew a registration within the renewal period, the record is assigned a status of *released*. The server assigns an extinction interval to the record after which it is tombstoned.

- **Failure to release.** If a client does not release a registration within the renewal period, the record is released automatically. The server assigns an extinction interval to the record, after which it is tombstoned.

- **Unable to contact primary WINS server.** If the primary WINS server is unavailable when the client attempts to renew a registration, the client can renew with its secondary WINS server, if one has been configured. This could lead to an awkward situation where the primary server has an active record and the secondary server has a released record. To prevent this, if the client releases a registration to a WINS server that is not the owner, the record is immediately tombstoned.

- **Client crash.** The WINS server has no way of knowing whether a client goes offline abnormally until the end of the renewal interval. The client record stays active and the server continues to hand out the client's IP address in response to query requests. If a client gets the address for a crashed client and attempts to use it, the connection attempt will fail. The client reports this failure to the WINS server, which checks the status of the client using a name query request. If the WINS server gets no reply, it releases the record with an extinction interval.

In a small network with one WINS server, this relatively simple sequence of events is sufficient to maintain database integrity, ensure name uniqueness, and give rapid response to lookup queries. In a big network with several WINS servers configured for interserver replication, the situation becomes much more complex. Details are discussed in the section "Functional Description of WINS Replication" later in the chapter. First, let's see how name resolution works.

Name Resolution Using WINS

When a WINS client needs to resolve a NetBIOS name associated with a service, the NETBT.SYS driver sends a *name lookup query* to the WINS server. If the name contains a dot or is longer than 16 characters, it is considered a DNS host name and the TCPIP.SYS driver uses DNS, not NETBT, to resolve the name.

When a WINS server receives a lookup query, it locates the record. If a record exists and if it is marked *active*, the WINS server returns a *name lookup response* with the IP address.

If a client is configured to use two WINS servers, a primary and a secondary, the client will query the secondary server if the primary server is unavailable.

Client Name Resolution Options

A Windows client can be configured to register and resolve NetBIOS names in one of two ways, broadcast or WINS. There are several combinations of these two methods. The combination used by a client is determined by the NetBIOS node type. There are four node types:

- **b-node (broadcast).** The NETBT driver uses IP multicasts to register and resolve names. If there is a router, L3 switch, or intelligent bridge between the client and server, the name registration is heard on the local subnet only and name resolution for any stations off the local subnet fails. This results in user complaints, such as, "I'm looking in My Network Places and I can see the servers in my building, but I can't see the servers in Building 303." B-node is the default node type if WINS is not enabled.

- **p-node (point-to-point).** This method uses WINS exclusively. If a p-node client cannot find its WINS server, all registrations and resolutions fail.

- **m-node (mixed).** This method avoids the complete reliance on WINS by first using broadcasts to resolve a name on a local subnet and contacting the WINS server if the broadcast fails.

- **h-node (hybrid).** This method is not defined in RFC 1001 or 1002. Microsoft introduced it to reduce the broadcast traffic produced by m-node clients. An h-node client contacts WINS first, and then falls back on local broadcasts only if the WINS query fails. This is the default node type if WINS is enabled.

Choosing a node type is a matter of balancing convenience, fault tolerance, and operational stability. b-node is generally a poor choice in all but the smallest networks. If you have at least one Windows 2000/NT server, you should use WINS. m-node is inadvisable for pretty much the same reason. Why broadcast if you have a WINS server.

The real choice, then, is between p-node and h-node. Here you have to weigh your alternatives. h-node seems like the rational alternative; in practice, however, h-node clients frequently generate broadcasts even when a WINS server is available. Also, h-node clients exhibit a tendency to hang a long time at logoff because they insist on deregistering both with WINS and by broadcast.

p-node clients, on the other hand, generate no broadcast traffic and break off the wire cleanly after they deregister at the WINS server, which takes a negligible amount of time. The problem with p-node is that you lose all NetBIOS name resolution if the WINS server goes down or is otherwise unavailable.

If you have a secondary WINS server and the staff to respond quickly in case the servers are unavailable for some reason, you should choose p-node. If you have only one WINS server in a particular location and want to maintain service continuity when the WINS server goes down, opt for h-node.

Functional Description of WINS Replication

It is theoretically possible to handle NetBIOS name resolution for an entire global enterprise with a single WINS server equipped with only moderately powerful hardware (Pentium 400, 64MB RAM, 10Mb NIC.) Such a server can handle thousands of registrations a minute, enough to support a client community of 30,000 or so nodes. But raw processing power is not the whole story. Issues of fault tolerance and WAN traffic must also be considered. Generally, you should distribute WINS servers to each major office or LAN installation. If you have hundreds of small networks, such as a retail business, however, you do not need a WINS server in each location. Set up regional WINS servers and use the WAN for name registration/resolution.

Each WINS server maintains a database of the registration records requested by its clients. The server is said to be the *owner* of those records. A WINS server can replicate its database entries to other WINS servers that are configured as its replication partners. The servers each have a single database. The records are identified by owner. When a new replication partner is added, its database records are merged with the existing entries.

WINS uses two replication modes, somewhat reminiscent of Dr. Doolittle: a Push mode and a Pull mode.

- **Push mode.** When accumulated changes reach a preset level, the WINS server contacts its replication partners and sends them the updates. *Push replication is event driven.*

- **Pull mode.** A particular WINS server's replication partners periodically poll for updates. *Pull replication is time driven.*

You can establish a rudimentary form of multiple-master replication by configuring two WINS servers as push-pull partners with each other. Name registrations in the WINS databases of both partners are replicated to each other as they accumulate and at intervals throughout the day. WINS clients can use either these servers, or both of them with one configured as a primary and the other as a secondary.

Only updated records are replicated between replication partners. This minimizes network traffic. Each record has a version ID that increments when the record is updated. In push replication, the server sends records with a version ID higher than the last batch that was sent to that particular partner. In pull replication, the pull partner sends a replication request containing the highest version ID it has received from that partner. The partner then sends updates with a higher version ID.

Push-pull replication is the preferred configuration. If you have a slow or expensive WAN link, you can use pull by itself and set the replication interval relatively long. There are other possible combinations of pushes and pulls, but for the most part they exist for certification exam scenarios only.

When you set up replication between multiple WINS servers, you should try to create a defined replication topology. You can use a ring, similar to Active Directory replication, where each WINS server replicates to the server on either side. Or you can use a hub and spoke, where all WINS servers replicate to a central master, which then distributes the updates to the other servers. Or you can set up a meshed topology where all servers replicate to each other. This last gives you the fastest convergence, but is the most prone to database anomalies. Regardless of the topology, be careful not to set yourself up for replication loops.

This concludes the WINS functional overview. Let's get to work installing WINS and getting clients configured to use it.

Installing WINS

If you do not presently use WINS on your network and you are deploying only Windows 2000 servers and clients, you can avoid WINS entirely. Windows 2000 clients use Dynamic DNS for resolving both TCP/IP host names and NetBIOS names. Classic NT and Windows 9x clients also have the capability, but the feature is too difficult to manage in a peer networking environment without Dynamic DNS.

If you have an existing WINS infrastructure in place, you can upgrade the existing NT4 WINS servers to Windows 2000. This automatically migrates the WINS database to a new version of the Jet engine while preserving the current configuration settings and database mappings. See Chapter 2, "Performing Upgrades and Automated Installations," for steps to take if the database conversion does not complete successfully.

If a particular WINS server is also a domain controller, you should consider transferring WINS to another server unless you are ready to migrate your domain to Active Directory at the same time that you upgrade WINS. See Chapter 9, "Deploying Windows 2000 Domains," for more information.

If you want to configure WINS on a Windows 2000 server for the first time, proceed as follows:

Procedure 4.2   Installing WINS on a Windows 2000 Server

1. From Control Panel, double-click the Add/Remove Programs applet. The Add/Remove Programs window opens.

2. Click Add/Remove Windows Components. The Windows Components Wizard starts.

3. Highlight Networking Services and click Details.

4. Select the Windows Internet Name Service (WINS) option and click OK to return to the main window.

5. Click Next to accept the change and proceed with the installation.

6. When the drivers finish loading, the wizard displays a completion window. Click Finish to close the wizard and return to the Add/Remove Programs window.

7. Click Close. The services starts automatically. There is no need to restart.

WINS is configured and managed from an MMC console, WINS.MSC. Open the console using START | PROGRAMS | ADMINISTRATIVE SERVICES | WINS. There's nothing to configure at the moment because no clients are using the server. Let's set up a few clients, and then come back to see how the WINS Management console works.

Configuring WINS Clients

Any Windows network client can be directed at a Windows 2000 WINS server. If the client uses DHCP, see the Registry Tip earlier in this chapter titled "Configuring the NETBT Node Type" for configuration information. If the client is statically mapped, you must configure it locally. Configure WINS at a Windows 2000 client as follows:

Procedure 4.3 **Configuring a WINS Client**

1. Right-click My Network Places and select PROPERTIES from the fly-out menu. The Network and Dial-up Connections window opens.
2. Right-click Local Area Connection and select PROPERTIES from the fly-out menu. The Local Area Connection Properties window opens.
3. Double-click the Internet Protocols (TCP/IP) entry. The Internet Protocol (TCP/IP) Properties window opens.
4. Click Advanced. The Advanced TCP/IP Settings window opens.
5. Select the WINS tab (see Figure 4.3). Ensure that the Enable NetBIOS over TCP/IP option is selected. If you disable this option, the client will not use WINS, even if you configure it with the address of a WINS server.

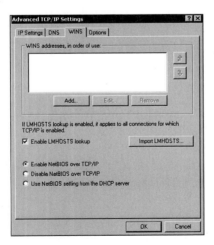

Figure 4.3 Advanced TCP/IP Settings window—WINS tab.

6. Click Add. The TCP/IP WINS Server window opens. Enter the IP address of a WINS server and click Add to save the change and return to the Advanced TCP/IP Settings window. You can add the address of a backup WINS server, if there is one. The WINS client queries the backup server if the primary server is unavailable.

7. Click OK to save the changes and return to the Internet Protocol (TCP/IP) Properties window.

8. Click OK to close the window and return to the Local Area Connection Properties window.

9. Click OK to close the window.

10. Open a command prompt.

11. Enter **NBTSTAT -RR** to register the client with the WINS server.

Repeat this for the remainder of your statically mapped clients. Then go back to the WINS server to check the registration listings and to manage the records.

Managing WINS Records

Once a Windows client has been configured to use a WINS server, the name registration and resolution process happens automatically. You can see the results by opening the WINS console using START | PROGRAMS | ADMINISTRA-TIVE SERVICES | WINS.

If you are an NT administrator accustomed to the standard WINS Management executable, you'll find the MMC console to be much different. When you open the console the first time, the right pane contains instructions to select a display option of Find by Owner or Find by Name. The "owner" in this case is the WINS server that holds the database. The selection steps are covered in this section. Figure 4.4 shows the WINS console after it has been configured to sort by owner.

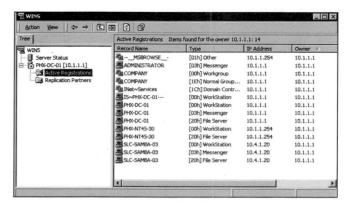

Figure 4.4 WINS console showing a list of active registrations sorted by owner.

Selecting WINS Records by Owner

Right-click the server icon and select VIEW | FIND BY OWNER from the fly-out menu, a `Find by Owner` window opens (see Figure 4.5).

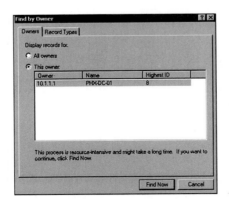

Figure 4.5 `Find by Owner` window—Owners tab showing one available WINS server.

The window cautions that this process is resource intensive. In a big network with thousands of WINS clients, listing every record in the WINS database can take a while. The resulting dataset is very difficult to manage, as well. You can limit the dataset somewhat by selecting the `Record Types` tab and choosing only those record types that you want to view, such as domain controller registrations. Figure 4.6 shows an example.

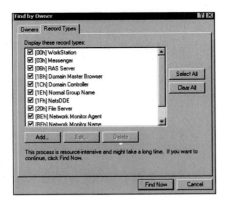

Figure 4.6 `Find by Owner` window—Record Types tab showing list of available record types.

Selecting WINS Records by Name

If you have a truly enormous WINS database, it is much more convenient to select the records by name. Right-click the server icon and select VIEW | FIND BY NAME. A Find by Name window opens where you can enter the first few letters of the computer- or username you're searching for.

After making your selection, the right pane lists only those records that start with the letters you selected. There is no flag that you have selected a partial listing; so if you are using a console that is already open, be sure to check select criteria if you can't find a record you're looking for.

Viewing WINS Record Properties

To view the contents of a WINS record, right-click the record icon in the right pane of the console window and select PROPERTIES from the fly-out menu. The Properties window for that record opens. Figure 4.7 shows an example.

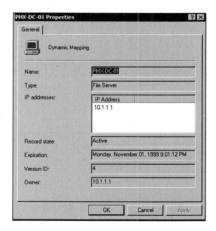

Figure 4.7   Properties of WINS registration.

The Type entry shows the service that was registered. This corresponds to the service ID at the end of the NetBIOS name.

The Record State can be Active, Released, or Tombstoned, as follows:

- **Active.** The WINS client is online with a current record in the WINS database.
- **Released.** The WINS client has notified the server that it is going offline, or that the record has expired without being renewed.

- **Tombstoned.** The expiration timeout period has elapsed and the client has not renewed the registration.

The Expiration is determined by the default extinction timeout. It is six days, by default.

The Version ID is the sequential number assigned by the record owner.

Statically Mapping WINS Records

If you have servers that are not WINS clients, either because you do not want to configure them as such or because they are not Windows-based servers, you can add a static record to the WINS database. This static mapping is equivalent to adding a host record to a DNS database. Add a static mapping as follows:

Procedure 4.4   Adding a Static WINS Mapping

1. Open the WINS console and expand the tree to Active Registrations.

2. Right-click Active Registrations and select NEW STATIC MAPPING from the fly-out menu. The New Static Mapping window opens. Figure 4.8 shows an example.

Figure 4.8   New Static Mapping window showing sample server entry.

3. Enter the name and IP address of the server. The example entry is for a UNIX server running Samba. Leave the NetBIOS Scope field blank. Leave the Type entry at Unique.

4. Click OK to save the entry and return to the main WINS console.

5. Refresh the Active Registrations list. The new entry appears with three listings, one each for File Server, Workstation, and Messenger. This is standard for all static registrations.

6. From a WINS client, make a network connection to the new host using the flat NetBIOS name. The connection will succeed if the host has SMB resources available.

Deleting Records

One of the many improvements in Windows 2000 WINS (and NT4 SP4) is the capability to selectively delete or tombstone records. A WINS database tends to accumulate clutter. It is not unusual to see many duplicate records, tombstoned entries, and records for defunct workgroups (and static client mappings) that were put in place when the "Macarena" was a hit.

To delete a particular entry, right-click the entry and select DELETE from the fly-out menu. A Delete Record window opens giving you two options:

- **Delete the Record Only from This Server.** This option is appropriate when an incorrect record or records exists at only one server. For instance, a server may have been experiencing replication problems. You have fixed the problem, but not before the database accumulated a few dozen bad entries. Use this option to delete those entries.

- **Replicate Deletion of the Record to Other Servers (Tombstone).** This option does not delete the record immediately, but rather it marks the record for deletion by giving it a tombstone status. This tombstone record is replicated, informing all the other servers that this record is no longer valid. At the end of the extinction interval, it is deleted.

Configuring WINS Replication

Before you configure WINS replication, you should have a diagram of the replication topology you plan to use. With this diagram in hand, use these steps to configure replication:

Procedure 4.5   **Configuring WINS Replication**

1. Open the WINS Manager console from START | PROGRAMS | ADMINISTRATIVE TOOLS | WINS.

2. Right-click Replication Partners and select NEW REPLICATION PARTNER from the fly-out menu. The New Replication Partner window opens.

3. Enter the IP address of the WINS server that you want to use as a replication partner. Enter the server's NetBIOS name only if it is on the same network segment, which is virtually never the case.

4. Click on OK to save the change. The WINS service contacts the replication partner and establishes the replication connection. If this completes successfully, the replication partner is added to the list in the right pane of the WINS console.

5. Right-click the icon for the replication partner and select PROPERTIES from the fly-out menu. The Properties window opens.

6. Select the Advanced tab (see Figure 4.9). The default replication configuration is Push/Pull. This is the preferred replication method. Use a simple push or a simple pull only when configuring replication across slow or unreliable WAN links.

Figure 4.9 Replication Partner Properties window—Advanced tab showing partner type, replication interval, and persistent connection.

7. Under both Pull Replication and Push Replication, select the Use Persistent Connection for Replication option. This option, new to WINS in NT4 SP4 and Windows 2000, avoids a problem in classic WINS where the connection would only be made long enough to replicate. This limited the number of long-term connections across a WAN, but it added to the replication delay. With modern data communications equipment, it makes sense to improve performance by using persistent connections.

8. Under `Pull Replication`, select a replication interval. The default is 30 minutes, which is generally sufficient unless you are making a lot of changes to your network configuration. You can force replication using the REPLICATE NOW option in the fly-out menu for the Replication icon.

9. Under `Push Replication`, leave the `Number of Changes in Version ID Before Replication` set to 0 so that changes propagate as soon as they are made. The WINS database engine has its own governing rules, so there is no need to accumulate changes unless you have infrastructure equipment such as a demand-dial interface or ISDN connection that is used more efficiently by delivering large volumes of data less frequently.

10. Repeat the same process at the replication partner.

11. After you have finished configuring replication at both partners, check the System Log using the Event Viewer to verify that replication has completed.

12. Open the WINS console at one partner and change the `Find by Owner` option to include all owners. Figure 4.10 shows an example of a WINS console with two owners listed who are replication partners.

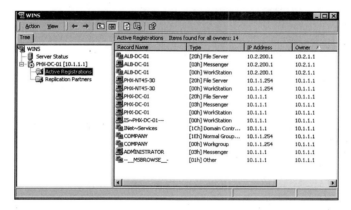

Figure 4.10 WINS console showing database entries from two owners who are replication partners.

See the next section for steps to manage replication after you have verified that the databases have replicated.

Managing WINS Replication

After you have configured WINS database replication, you can control the replication options as follows:

Procedure 4.6   **Managing WINS Replication**

1. Open the WINS console.

2. Right-click the Replication Partners icon and select PROPERTIES from the fly-out menu. The Replication Partners window opens.

   Replicate Only with Partners is selected by default. This option prevents a rogue server from pulling a copy of the WINS database from an existing server.

   Overwrite Unique Static Mappings at This Server (Migrate On) is disabled by default. This option is intended to enable you to change clients configured as broadcast nodes (b-node) over to WINS nodes (p-node or h-node). The assumption is that the b-node client had a static mapping in WINS. The Migrate On option prevents the new dynamic registration from overwriting the static mapping. This option makes it possible to overwrite any static mapping, however, so it should not be enabled except for node type migration.

3. Use the Push Replication tab and Pull Replication tab to change any settings that you made during the initial configuration.

4. Select the Advanced tab.

   The Enable Automatic Partner Configuration option permits the server to establish replication connections with other WINS servers.

   All WINS servers announce themselves on the network using the *Internet Group Management Protocol* (IGMP). This announcement takes the form of IGMP multicasts sent to IP address 224.0.1.24. If you set the Enable Automatic Partner Configuration option and the WINS server picks up one of these IGMP multicasts, it configures itself as a push-pull partner of the server that sent out the IGMP announcement with a replication interval set at the default 30 minutes.

   The automatic partner configuration feature is supposed to simplify WINS replication setup, but in practice you nearly always want to have specific control over replication. Automatic partner configuration is recommended only for smaller networks with very few subnets.

Setting Replication Intervals

If you have slow WAN links, you may be tempted to set a very long replication interval, on the order of once every several hours. Be sure to experiment first. It's possible to set the replication interval so high that it affects daily operations.

If you bring up a server in Houston, for example, a user in Denver will not see it in Explorer until the WINS server in Houston replicates the update to the WINS server in Denver. If you set the replication interval too long, the users in Denver will start calling the help desk.

On the other side, it's a mistake on a large network to set replication intervals too short, say every minute or so. If the WINS servers are spending all their time replicating between each other, performance degrades and help desk calls also start pouring in. Experiment to find the right replication interval for your network. If a user gets impatient, manually initiate replication.

Managing WINS Services

In addition to configuring options for viewing records and controlling replication, a set of features associated with the WINS service itself control database and record handling. These are accessed by right-clicking the server icon in the WINS console and selecting PROPERTIES from the fly-out menu. The Properties window opens for the server with the focus set to the General tab (see Figure 4.11).

Figure 4.11 WINS Server Properties window—General tab.

The `Automatically Update Statistics Every` option is selected by default. It refreshes a set of WINS server statistics that can be viewed by right-clicking the server icon and selecting DISPLAY SERVER STATISTICS. The `WINS Server Statistics` window opens. Figure 4.12 shows an example. This window is useful for determining replication problems, name registration errors, and for gauging whether the service is overloaded.

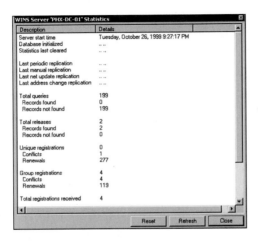

Figure 4.12 `WINS Server Statistics` window.

The `Backup Database During Server Shutdown` option is not selected by default. This option closes down the Jet database engine, and then makes a copy of the WINS.MDB file any time the server shuts down. If you are performing normal backups using a Windows 2000–compliant backup utility, you do not need to enable this feature.

Setting Renewal and Extinction Intervals

Select the `Intervals` tab (see Figure 4.13). There are four interval settings controllable in this window. Under most circumstances, the default settings deliver optimized results. Changing the values without first analyzing their interrelation can seriously affect database consistency.

- **`Renewal Interval.`** This is the interval during which a client must renew its registrations. Clients ordinarily renew halfway through the renewal interval. The renewal interval also determines the periodic scavenging frequency for the server. During scavenging, the system deletes tombstoned entries and compacts the database. Frequent scavenging is good preventative medicine and improves performance. You can manually initiate scavenging by right-clicking the icon for the WINS server in the WINS console and selecting SCAVENGE DATABASE from the fly-out menu.

- **Extinction Interval.** This value is assigned to a released record. During the extinction interval, the record owner does not replicate the record. It is waiting for the client to reregister. After the extinction interval, if the client has not reregistered, the record is tombstoned.

- **Extinction Timeout.** This value is assigned to a tombstoned record. If a client does not claim the name or IP address associated with the record by the end of the extinction timeout, the record is removed at the scavenging.

- **Verification Interval.** This value is assigned to a replicated record. During scavenging, if the record age exceeds the verification interval, the server queries its replication partner to determine whether the record is still valid. If not, it is deleted. If so, the record gets a fresh time stamp and a new verification interval. The default verification interval is 24 days.

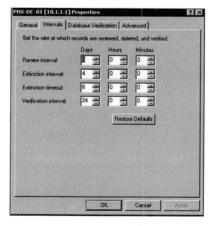

Figure 4.13 WINS Server Properties window—Intervals tab.

Ensuring Database Consistency

Select the Database Verification tab (see Figure 4.14). This window exposes to the UI a feature that was available in classic WINS only by making manual Registry entries. A database consistency check consists of copying the contents of the database at a replication partner and verifying that it matches the local database.

The `Begin Verifying At` option sets the start time for the verification check. The default is 2 a.m.

This check is enabled by default and should be left enabled unless you have a very large WINS database that consumes too much time to verify every night. In that case, select the `Randomly Selected Partners` option to do a portion of the database verifications each night.

Figure 4.14 `WINS Server Properties` window—`Database Verification` tab.

Controlling Log and Database Location and Burst Handling

Select the `Advanced` tab (see Figure 4.15). This tab contains three options.

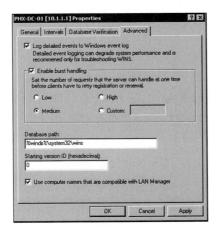

Figure 4.15 `WINS Server Properties` window—`Advanced` tab.

The `Log Detailed Events to Windows Event Log` results in a log entry whenever just about anything occurs in the WINS database. The window warns you that this will fill up the log quickly and it isn't kidding. Use this option for diagnostic purposes only.

The `Enable Burst Handling` option controls the way the WINS service handles multiple registration requests. When you first put a WINS server online in a large network and point many thousands of clients at it, the database can get overwhelmed with building new records. Ordinarily, the system starts dropping requests if the request queue gets full. With `Burst Handling` enabled, the clients are given a positive registration response with a short renewal interval, five minutes. This is equivalent to a quick "come back when Daddy isn't busy." If the server really gets busy, it starts assigning longer and longer renewal intervals.

The four radio buttons control the `BurstQueSize` value in `HKLM | System | CurrentControlSet | Services | WINS | Parameters`. The presets are as follows:

Low – 300

Medium – 500

High – 1,000

If you have a dedicated WINS server with lots of horsepower and a fast hard drive, you can push `Custom` up to 2,500.

The `Database Path` option is useful if you want to change the location of the WINS database to get it out of the system partition and onto a faster drive or a volume with more space. Stop the service before moving the database. Be sure to move the log files as well.

Setting Default *WINS* Console Properties

A few options affect the `WINS` console itself. In the `WINS` console, right-click the WINS icon at the top of the tree and select PROPERTIES from the fly-out menu. The `WINS Properties` window opens.

Using this window, you can elect to display the servers by `Name` Or by `IP Address`.

The `Show DNS Names for WINS Servers` option displays the fully qualified DNS name for the server rather than the flat NetBIOS name. This option is a little misleading, because the fully qualified name is pulled from the DNS suffix entry in System properties rather than the TCP/IP properties. If the WINS server has not been joined to a domain, it's likely that the DNS suffix is blank.

To check the DNS suffix setting, open the System icon in Control Panel and select the Network Identification tab. If the Full Computer Name entry does not have a DNS suffix, click Properties, and then click More to add one. You must restart the machine after saving the entry.

Selecting the Validate Cache of WINS Servers at Startup option causes WINS to query the list of WINS servers you have loaded into the console. If one or more are offline, the system displays a console message and makes an Event Log entry.

Do's and Don'ts of WINS

When managing a large WINS installation, a bit of advice from my grandfather, an old-time New Mexico cowboy, is appropriate. Granddad was fond of saying, "Don't get in front of the herd, don't make any sudden moves, and remember that you can always shoot the troublemaker." Here is how that advice applies in the context of wrangling WINS:

- **Don't put a WINS server in every LAN segment.** WINS replication has a well-deserved reputation for skittishness. WINS clients can find a name server through many intervening routers. Install server in strategic locations and use the WAN to route registrations and queries.

- **Don't set up independent WINS servers.** WINS replication in an organization needs to be carefully coordinated. Working around authority figures is a prized American right, and is even laudable at times; but in the case of WINS, it can cause real problems.

- **Map your replication topology carefully.** Be especially watchful for replication circularities.

- **Check database statistics regularly.** Don't wait for a database corruption problem to catch you off-guard. The new Jet database engine in Windows 2000 is much less likely to corrupt a WINS database than its predecessors; the possibility still exists, however, and you should be watchful.

- **Avoid using WINS proxies.** Proxies are used to support Windows clients who do not have a Microsoft IP stack. A WINS proxy listens for address resolution broadcasts from non-WINS clients and forwards them to a WINS server on behalf of the client. When the resolution returns from the WINS server, the proxy forwards it to the client. WINS proxies are very slow, have a limited cache, and crash often. If you have older Windows 3.x machines, upgrade the operating system instead of deploying WINS proxies.

- **When all else fails, delete and start over.** If a particular WINS server seems to be causing problems, your best course of action is to stop the WINS service, delete the files in `\WINNT\System32\Wins`, and then start all over again. This is especially true if the server has replication partners. It's better to repopulate a local WINS database and re-create any static mappings than to pollute an entire WINS infrastructure.

Disabling NetBIOS–over–TCP/IP Name Resolution

After you have completed the transition to Windows 2000 servers and desktops, you can disable NetBIOS–over–TCP/IP name resolution and use DNS exclusively. Windows 2000 computers can exchange SMB traffic over TCP port 445, a well-known port originally set aside for Microsoft-DS. SMB traffic over TCP port 445 uses NETBT for encapsulating SMB into TCP datagrams, but avoids the lengthy and complex name resolution strategies covered in this chapter.

The biggest advantage to using port 445 and eliminating NetBIOS–over–TCP/IP name resolution is the substantial reduction in network traffic. Here's a small but telling example you can try yourself. Load a Promiscuous-mode sniffer, such as the Intel sniffer in SMS or Sniffer Pro from Network Associates. Configure it to monitor all traffic.

With NetBIOS–over–TCP/IP name resolution enabled on all machines, open My Network Places, and then open Computers Near Me. This initiates a flood of traffic as the computer communicates with the Master Browser, checks for NetBIOS services on any servers that are touched, verifies its own name registration, and so forth. In a three-node network, this operation results in 30–50 frames, 80% of which are broadcasts. Multiply those 30–50 frames by 1,000 or 2,000 nodes on a good-sized flat network and you can see the traffic problem.

Now disable NetBIOS–over–TCP/IP name resolution using the steps at the end of this section and do the same operation; open My Network Places, and then open Computers Near Me. This results in a grand total of zero frames. Multiply 0 by 1,000 or 2,000 nodes and you get a good idea of the benefits in disabling classic NetBIOS name resolution. Not only does it drastically reduce network traffic, but you'll notice that windows react much more quickly without the need to wait for broadcast results.

Practically speaking, you can't get rid of NetBIOS–over–TCP/IP name resolution completely until you've purged all down-level Windows clients and servers from your network. Several classic services, such as Browser,

Messenger, and basic file and printer mapping, no longer function without port 138 and 139 services. When you're ready to make the transition, proceed as follows:

Procedure 4.7   Disabling NetBIOS-over-TCP/IP Name Resolution

---

1. Open the `Network and Dial-up Connections` window by right-clicking `My Network Places` and selecting `Properties`.

2. Right-click the Local Area Connection icon and select PROPERTIES from the fly-out menu. The `Local Area Connection Properties` window opens.

3. Highlight `Internet Protocol (TCP/IP)` and click `Properties`. The `Internet Protocol (TCP/IP) Properties` window opens.

4. Click `Advanced`. The `Advanced TCP/IP Settings` window opens.

5. Select the `WINS` tab.

6. Select the `Disable NetBIOS over TCP/IP` radio button. Note that this setting can also be distributed by DHCP clients.

7. Click `OK` to save the change and return to the `Internet Protocol (TCP/IP) Properties` window.

8. Click `OK` to return to the `Local Area Connection Properties` window.

9. Click `OK` to save all changes and close the window.

The NetBIOS options configured at the UI can also be changed in the Registry as follows:

```
Key:     HKLM | SYSTEM | CurrentControlSet | Services | NETBT | Parameters | Interfaces |
         Tcpip_{classid}
Value:   NetbiosOptions
Data:    0 - DHCP selected; 1 - enabled; 2 - disabled
```

Moving Forward

This chapter covered classic NT name resolution using broadcasts, LMHOSTS, and WINS. The next chapter leaves the classic NT/NetBIOS world behind and moves on to the name resolution using Dynamic DNS. The next chapter also covers DHCP to prepare for simplified deployment of Windows 2000 desktops.

5

Managing Domain Name System (DNS) Services and Dynamic Host Configuration (DHCP) Services

THE PRECEDING CHAPTER COVERED THE CLASSIC NT mechanisms for resolving computer names into IP addresses. Windows 2000 can use any of those methods—broadcasts, LMHOSTS, and WINS—but the preferred name resolution method is the *Domain Name System* (DNS). More specifically, Windows 2000 uses Dynamic DNS as described in RFC 2136, "Dynamic DNS." With Dynamic DNS, computers and services automatically register their resource records without manual intervention on the part of a DNS administrator.

Dynamic DNS is a tremendously important component of Windows 2000. Without a solid DNS infrastructure, you cannot deploy Active Directory–based domains, the cornerstone of the product, and Kerberos, the distributed authentication service in Windows 2000. Both of these services depend on DNS to guide clients to domain controllers. Other features, big and small, also depend on DNS to function correctly.

Windows 2000 DNS contains many other improvements over NT4 DNS. Like dynamic resource record registrations, these new features incorporate provisions that have recently become part of Internet standard DNS. The following are some of the more important improvements:

- **Notification-driven zone transfers.** Standard DNS requires secondary name servers to poll a master name server for updates. Windows 2000 DNS incorporates notification features that let the master server inform its secondaries when an update has occurred. The secondaries then replicate immediately, greatly shortening convergence times. This feature is based on RFC 1996, "A Mechanism for Prompt Notification of Zone Changes.

- **Incremental Zone Transfers.** Standard DNS replication transfers the entire contents of a zone table from the master to its secondaries for every update. In Windows 2000, secondary DNS servers request incremental zone transfers so that only changes to the zone table are replicated. This significantly reduces replication traffic, making it possible to locate secondary DNS servers at the end of network connections even in large networks. This feature is based on RFC 1995, "Incremental Zone Transfer In DNS."

- **Active Directory–integrated zone tables.** DNS resource records can be stored in the Active Directory, where they can be updated by any domain controller running DNS. This eliminates the bottleneck of a single primary master server in standard DNS. This feature is proprietary to Windows 2000 DNS.

- **Secure DNS updates.** Dynamic DNS updates can be limited exclusively to trusted clients. This helps prevent attacks designed to populate a zone table with false resource records that could send users or user data to unsecured locations. See the section "Dynamic Update Security" later in this chapter for details on the Internet documents used to design this feature.

If you want general information about DNS, try the DNS Resource Directory at www.dns.net/dnsrd. You can also get specific DNS questions answered by Dr. DNS at www.acmebw.com/askmr.htm. If you have a small network and don't want to bother with DNS, you can use DNS services from your ISP. Generally this service has a price tag, so you might want to check out the free public DNS service available at soa.granitecanyon.com. You will not be able to dynamically register resource records with general-access DNS services, so they are unsuitable if you are going to AD-based domains.

DNS Domains and Windows 2000 Domains

Before getting too far into DNS domains, it's important to deal with the ongoing confusion of Microsoft's use of the word *domain* and the way the term is used in DNS.

- A DNS domain defines a shared namespace. The boundaries of this namespace are determined by the contents of the DNS database, which is called a *zone table*.

- A Windows 2000 domain defines a shared security structure. The boundaries of this structure are determined by the contents of the AD information store, in Windows 2000, and the SAM REGISTRY hive in classic NT.

Even though DNS domains and Windows 2000 domains are technically separate entities, the two share a common boundary in Windows 2000 because Active Directory relies on DNS to define its namespace. An AD domain follows the outline of a DNS domain like a school district overlaying a township.

Overview of DNS Domain Structure

As its name implies, the Domain Name System defines a naming structure based on structures called *domains*. A domain defines a region in a hierarchical namespace, similar to the way folders define nodes in a hierarchical file system. Figure 5.1 shows a typical DNS namespace.

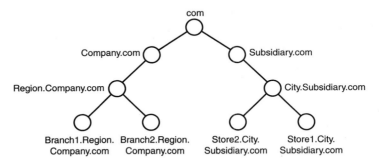

Figure 5.1 Typical DNS namespace.

Instead of top-down path names like those in a file system, DNS uses a bottom-up naming system. The full path to a host name in DNS that includes the chain of domains leading to it from the root is called the *fully qualified domain name* (FQDN). The FQDN of a host is unique anywhere in the DNS namespace. The FQDN of the server in the bottom domain in Figure 5.1 would be `alb-dns-01.branch1.region.company..`

You may have noticed an extra dot (.) at the end of the FQDN in the last sentence. This dot serves the same purpose in DNS as the leading slash in a file system path. It indicates the root of the tree and tells the system where to start parsing. The only way that a DNS client or server can know for sure that a name is fully qualified is if it sees a trailing dot. For typographic simplicity, trailing dots are omitted from FQDNs in this book. However, you should make it a point to include them when troubleshooting DNS problems.

Private and Public DNS Namespaces

The domain at the top of a DNS namespace is the *root domain*. The name of the root depends on whether a DNS namespace is internal to the organization, a private namespace, or extends out to the Internet, a public namespace. Figure 5.2 shows examples of both.

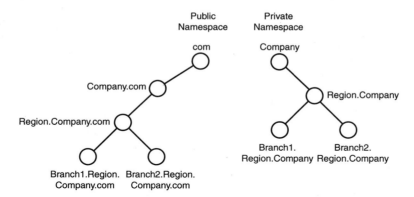

Figure 5.2 Comparison of public and private DNS namespaces.

The root of a public DNS namespace is one of the *top-level domains* assigned to the organization by the naming agency that manages the namespace. The top-level domains managed by InterNIC include com, gov, mil, and org among others. InterNIC also assigns domains to organizations outside the United States based on ISO 3166 country identifiers.

Zones

As previously defined, a DNS domain defines a namespace. The contents of that namespace are determined by a database called a *zone table*. The terms *domain* and *zone* often get used interchangeably, but there is a distinction. The same kind of distinction marks the difference between a family name and a family tree. When someone in the Jones family has a new baby, for example, Great-Grandmother Jones opens the big family Bible and inks in the baby's name at the correct point in the family tree. If little Freddie asks Great-Grandmother Jones about his relationship to the new baby, she peeks at the tree and says, "She's your third-cousin twice removed." She might also remark that your chins look alike. If someone has already asked her the same question recently, she may remember the answer without looking it up.

A zone table is usually an ASCII text file. Windows 2000 zone tables have a .DNS extension and are located in \WINNT\System32\DNS. The zone table contains the names of computers, users, services, and other entities that require mappings between their names and their IP addresses. For example, the ubiquitous com domain defines a namespace containing commercial entities that have registered themselves with InterNIC and obtained a unique second-level domain name.

A zone can contain more than one DNS domain in the same way that a family tree can contain more then one last name. For example, a single zone could contain the records for the `company` domain, the `region.company` domain, and the `branch1.region.company` domain. These domains could also be divided into different zones, each with its own zone table.

A single DNS server can store multiple zone tables in the same way that one Bible can be used to document family trees for different families. One server could host the zone table for the `company` domain and the `branch1.region.company` domain, for instance, while another server hosted the zone table for the `region.company` domain.

DNS servers that host different zones in a contiguous namespace can use a simple referral mechanism to find entries in each other's zone tables. They do so by searching the DNS tree starting at the root of the tree. They find the root using a special table called the *root hints*.

Root Hints

A root hints table is a text file that contains the names and IP addresses of the name servers at the root of the DNS namespace. Windows 2000 stores the root hints in a file called CACHE.DNS located in `WINNT\System32\DNS`.

For a private DNS namespace, the root hints table specifies the name or names of internal DNS servers that host the zone table for the root domain. For example, the root hints for the private DNS namespace in Figure 5.2 would contain a listing for the name server `phx-dns-01.company`.

For a public DNS namespace, the root hints contain the names and IP addresses of the InterNIC root servers. (You can add other servers to the list if you register your domain with an alternative naming service.)

InterNIC maintains 13 root servers to handle DNS queries on the Internet. The server names are listed in CACHE.DNS. Here are the first few lines to show what the root hint entries look like:

```
;       This file is made available by InterNIC registration services under anonymous FTP as file
;       domain/named.root on server  FTP.RS.INTERNIC.NET  -OR- under Gopher
;       at  RS.INTERNIC.NET under menu InterNIC Registration Services (NSI)
;       submenu   InterNIC Registration Archives file     named.root
;
;       last update:    Aug 22, 1997
;       related version of root zone:   1997082200
;
; formerly NS.INTERNIC.NET
;
.                               3600000  IN  NS     A.ROOT-SERVERS.NET.
A.ROOT-SERVERS.NET.             3600000      A      198.41.0.4
++++++++truncated for brevity++++++++
; End of File
```

Root Server Selection

If the root hints table contains multiple servers, the local DNS server must decide which one to use for root queries. It does this by trying each root server in turn during the normal course of handling queries. When it receives the first query for a host outside its zone, for example, it sends that query to the first root server. The next query it receives goes to the next root server and so forth until it has sent a query to each of the root servers in sequence.

When it sends these queries, the DNS server measures the *round-trip time* (RTT) of the responses. After it has collected RTT data on all the root servers, it picks the one with the shortest RTT and uses it for subsequent queries.

If the RTT degrades at some point in the future, the DNS server polls again to re-evaluate and may select a new root server.

Resource Records

A zone table consists of *resource records*, which are just lines of text in the zone table file, one line per record. RFC 1183, "New DNS RR Definitions," defines more than a dozen record types, but only a few are used with any frequency. See "Format of Common Resource Records" later in this chapter for details on the commonly used records in Windows 2000 DNS.

When a DNS client needs information from a name server, it queries its DNS server for a particular resource record. If a DNS client needs the IP address corresponding to a server called `alb-w2ks-01.branch1.region.company`, for example, it sends a request to its DNS server asking for the A, or Host, record for that server. The server handles that request differently depending on whether it is *authoritative* for that zone.

Authoritative Query Responses

A DNS server that holds a copy of a zone table is said to be *authoritative* for that zone. When tracing a DNS query, the buck always stops at an authoritative server for the zone specified in the query.

When a query arrives for a record within a name server's zone of authority, the server performs an *authoritative lookup*. Here is how it handles that authoritative lookup:

- If the server finds the requested record in its zone table, it responds with a copy of the record contents.

- If the server has recently done a lookup on the same record, it responds with a cached copy of the record. This is much faster than doing a file lookup from disk.

- If the server cannot find the requested record, it returns a *Record Not Found* response to the client.

Non-Authoritative Query Responses

If a DNS server does not have a copy of the zone table for a requested zone, it has three alternatives when handling the query:

1. Respond to the query with a cached copy of the record that has been stored following a previous lookup. This is called a *non-authoritative reply*.

2. It attempts to respond to the query by querying other name servers until it locates one that has a copy of the requested record.

3. Respond with a referral to a name server further up the tree that might have a copy of the record.

The last two methods are based in large part on a *search type* flag included in the client query. The flag has two possible states:

- **Recursive.** This tells the DNS server to respond with a copy of the requested resource record no matter what. If the server has to consult with other DNS servers to find the record, so be it. A recursive query is like a Spartan mother sending her son into battle saying, "Come back carrying your shield or lying on it."

- **Iterative.** This request permits the DNS server to return a referral to another DNS server that is likely to have a copy of the record rather than chasing down the referral itself. An iterative search puts the workload on the client to follow up on the referral.

DNS clients typically set the recursive flag in their queries on the assumption that the DNS server has more capacity for handling the search. Recursive queries from thousands of clients can put a great deal of load on a DNS server, so it is not uncommon to find servers configured to reject recursive queries. For example, the InterNIC top-level root servers are configured to reject recursive queries. Even if a name server permits recursive queries, it is good etiquette to get permission from the administrator prior to sending recursive queries to it. See the section "Configuring Advanced DNS Server Parameters" later in this chapter for the steps to disable recursive queries on Windows 2000 DNS servers.

DNS servers typically use iterative queries when they do searches on behalf of clients. A local server can handle referrals, so it doesn't make sense to put an unnecessary burden on upstream DNS servers. Windows 2000 DNS servers default to iterative queries and there are no adjustment parameters.

Primary and Secondary DNS Servers

In standard DNS configurations—ones that do not use Active Directory integration—only one name server can have a read/write copy of a zone table. That server is called the *primary name server*. All changes to the zone table must be funneled to the primary name server. By definition, the primary name server is authoritative for its zone.

For fault tolerance and performance, it is a good idea to install one or more *secondary name servers*. A secondary has a read-only copy of the zone table. A secondary name server is authoritative for a zone because it has a copy of the zone table, but it must forward any zone changes to the primary.

Windows 2000 has a feature that avoids the bottleneck of having a single read/write copy of the zone table. A zone table can be integrated into Active Directory, making resource records into Directory objects that can be modified by any Windows 2000 domain controller in the domain. The domain controller must be configured as a DNS server. See the section "Integrating DNS Zones into Active Directory" later in this chapter for the steps to perform this integration.

Forward and Reverse Lookup Zones

A standard DNS zone table is called a *forward lookup zone* because it searches by the name of the record until it either finds the entry or reaches the end of the zone table. But what if a user knows the IP address of a host and wants the associated name? An example of this kind of reverse lookup occurs when you use Ping with the -a switch. This tells Ping to display the host name along with the ICMP Echo Reply, like this:

```
E:\>ping -a 10.1.1.254
Pinging router.company.com [10.1.1.254] with 32 bytes of data:
Reply from 10.1.1.254: bytes=32 time<10ms TTL=128
```

DNS found the host name in this example by performing a search of a *reverse lookup zone*. This seems simple enough, but it turns out to be something of an exercise. DNS forward lookup zone tables are structured around host names, not IP addresses. Extracting a host name based on an IP address from a forward lookup table would require an incredibly expensive full table scan that could encompass all the millions of zones scattered on DNS servers all over the planet. DNS avoids this impossible situation by creating a separate zone table based on IP address. This is called a *reverse lookup zone*.

Structure of a Reverse Lookup Zone Table

A reverse lookup zone table is built using one record type, the PTR record. A PTR record contains the octets from the host ID in reverse order. The following listing contains examples of zone table entries from a reverse lookup zone for the 10.1.0.0 network:

```
; Database file 1.10.in-addr.arpa.dns for 1.10.in-addr.arpa zone.
; Zone version:  8
;  Zone records
1.1         PTR      phx-dc-01
21.1        PTR      phx-w2ks-12
254.1       PTR      phx-rtr-01
```

Note that the network address, 10.1.0.0, is reversed to make 1.10. If the network address were 222.100.93.0, the start of the zone table name would be 93.100.222.

This reversal is necessary because the dotted-decimal notation used by IP addresses puts the most significant octet to the far *left*, whereas the referral mechanism used by DNS assumes that the most significant field is at the far *right*. Following the DNS referral method to its logical conclusion, if the inverted IP addresses form a contiguous tree, there would need to be 255 root domains with 255 separate primary name servers, one each for the 255 available addresses in the upper octet of the dotted-decimal IP address format.

To avoid this mess, the *Advanced Research Project Administration* (ARPA), which was in charge of the Internet at the time this naming scheme was devised, decreed an artificial root for the reverse lookup zone and dubbed it in-addr.arpa. The InterNIC root servers are authoritative for in-addr.arpa.

Function of the *in-addr.arpa* Root

With the artificial in-addr.arpa root in place, a single primary name server can own the whole reverse lookup zone with 255 nodes at the second level, a paltry number compared to the kazillions of second-level nodes in the com namespace.

What this means to you as a DNS administrator is that you must build a reverse lookup zone rooted at in-addr.arpa for every IP network in your organization. The name for each of these zones would start with the reverse of its network ID followed by the suffix in-addr.arpa. For example, the network ID 209.12.73.0 would have a reverse lookup zone of 73.12.209.in-addr.arpa. The zone could have any DNS server as a primary name server, but it is typically the primary server for the root of the associated forward lookup zone.

DNS Client Resolvers

The purpose of all these forward lookup zones and reverse lookup zones and the name servers that host them is to provide a quick and reliable place for clients to find the IP address corresponding to a host name or service name. The client service responsible for finding this IP address is called a *resolver*. In Windows 2000, the DNS resolver is part of the main TCP/IP driver, TCPIP.SYS.

When a Windows 2000 application specifies the name of a particular server, the resolver inside TCPIP.SYS first looks in a local Hosts table. The Hosts table is a text file containing a series of entries that specify IP addresses and their associated host names. Here is an example Hosts table. The pound sign (#) denotes a comment:

```
10.1.1.1     phx-dc-01.company.com          #Phoenix domain controller
10.1.1.2     phx-dc-02.company.com          #Phoenix domain controller
10.3.1.27    slc-w2ks-31.branch1.company.com   #Salt Lake City general purpose server
10.2.1.12    hou-web-04.subsidiary.com        #Houston web server in subsidiary company
```

The host name specified by the application must exactly match the entry in the Hosts table for the resolver to perform a successful lookup. If the application specifies a fully qualified name, the Hosts table must specify fully qualified names like those in the example. The Hosts table can also contain flat computer names, such as phx-dc-01, in which case the application must specify the flat name, not the fully qualified name.

Registry Tip: Hosts Table Location

The Hosts file is located in WINNT\System32\Drivers\Etc along with other TCP/IP-related files, such as LMHOSTS, Protocols, Networks, and Services. This directory is specified by the following Registry value:

```
Key:     HKLM | SYSTEM | CurrentControlSet | Services | TCPIP | Parameters
Value:   DataBasePath
Data:    \WINNT\System32\Drivers\Etc\
```

If the resolver does not find an entry in the Hosts table, it then queries its DNS server. Like a good *Jeopardy* contestant, the DNS resolver always submits its requests to a name server in the form of a question. When a TCP/IP-based application needs to communicate with a particular host, the resolver submits a *DNS query* to its name server.

When the resolver gets a response to its query, it caches the results in memory to speed up subsequent queries for the same host name. DNS servers that obtain records in response to queries on behalf of users also cache the results. A name cache could get very large if the entries were never removed. To prevent unbridled cache growth, every DNS resource record contains a *Time-To-Live* (TTL) setting that tells the resolver how long to cache the entry.

If you want to clear the resolver cache at a client, use IPCONFIG with the following syntax: IPCONFIG /flushdns. If you want to clear the DNS cache at a server, you can use the DNS console or the DNSCMD utility from the Resource Kit with this syntax: DNSCMD /clearcache. The only adverse consequence of clearing a cache is that you force the client resolver or server to slowly accumulate the entries again, and performance will suffer until they do so.

Automatic FQDN Construction

If a user or an application specifies a flat host name, such as alb-dc-01, the client resolver must have some way of determining a DNS domain for the name. Flat names cannot be submitted to DNS because server will not know what zone table to use for the lookup.

When the Windows 2000 resolver is given a flat name, it appends the DNS domain name of the client to the name to form a FQDN. It can be quite complex.

The ability to generate a FQDN from a flat name is an important convenience for users. If a user in the region.company DNS domain needs to map a drive, for example, he enters a UNC name, such as \\alb-dc-01\datashare, in the Map Network Drive window. The resolver automatically appends the DNS domain of the client and queries DNS for alb-dc-01.region.company. Because most user requests are for servers in the local zone, the automatic FQDN assignment makes the network simpler to use. Not necessarily simpler to manage, however.

Determining DNS Domain Names

When a user or application specifies a flat computer name rather than an FQDN, the TCP/IP driver uses the domain name as a suffix to build an FQDN to use when querying DNS. The DNS domain name is also used by the TCP/IP driver to register the computer with Dynamic DNS.

The Registry stores values for the host name and domain that are used to define the FQDN for the computer. Unfortunately, host name/domain pairs are stored in several different places and used in different ways. Figure 5.3 shows a Registry Editor window with the focus on HKLM | System | CurrentControlSet | Services | Tcpip to show the keys where the host name/domain entries are located. Table 5.1 lists the locations and their functions. Step-by-step details for setting the values using graphical management tools follow the table.

Special Parsing for Host Names

If NetBIOS-over-TCP/IP name resolution is enabled, TCPIP.SYS works in conjunction with NETBT.SYS, the NetBIOS-over-TCP/IP helper, to resolve the host name. The two resolvers work in parallel, with NETBT.SYS sending out a WINS query or a broadcast while the DNS resolver in TCPIP.SYS sends out a DNS query. If the user's DNS domain name is set incorrectly, the DNS query will fail because of an improper FQDN; the WINS query may succeed, however, if the flat name is in the WINS database. The user doesn't know or care why it works, only that it works. If you make a configuration change sometime down the road and the connection stops working, however, it can be tricky to troubleshoot.

Keep this sequence in mind when tracing name resolution problems:

- A Windows 2000 WINS client queries both WINS and DNS simultaneously. It uses the first positive response it receives.

- A Windows 2000 b-node client broadcasts and queries DNS simultaneously. It uses the first positive response it receives.

- A Windows 2000 client that has NETBT disabled queries only DNS.

There is another special situation regarding the mixed use of a DNS resolver and NetBIOS name resolution that can make troubleshooting difficult. If the user specifies a name with an embedded dot but does not provide a trailing dot, the resolver first appends a dot and tries the name. If that fails, the resolver appends the entire domain name and tries again.

If a user in the Branch1.Company DNS domain enters `net use * \\alb-dc-01.branch1\datashare`, for example, the resolver would first send DNS a query for `alb-dc-01.branch1.` with the trailing dot. When that fails, as it will because Branch1 is not the root domain, the resolver would query for `alb-dc-01.branch1.branch1.region.company`, which would also fail.

As you move away from NetBIOS naming to DNS naming, it's important to train your users to enter the correct fully qualified name if they are attempting to connect outside of their local namespace.

Finally, there is a minor difference in the way Windows 2000 handles a DNS host name compared to classic NT. In classic NT, if a name had embedded periods or was longer than 16 characters, the resolver assumed that the name was a DNS host name and bypassed NETBT.SYS. In Windows 2000, NETBT.SYS uses the invalid name to query WINS and broadcast.

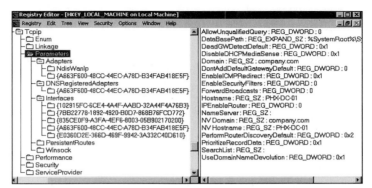

Figure 5.3   Registry Editor showing Tcpip keys and values.

Table 5.1   **Hostname/Domain Values and Functions**

Keys	Values	Functions
HKLM | System | CurrentControlSet | Services | Tcpip | Parameters	NV Hostname and NV Domain	The *non-volatile* (NV) values are set by an administrator using the System Properties window in the UI. The NV values control other Hostname/Domain pairs, but are not used by the TCP/IP driver directly.
HKLM | System | CurrentControlSet | Services | Tcpip | Parameters	Hostname and Domain	These values are set to match the NV value with the same name. The Domain value is copied to the PrimaryDomainName value in DNSRegisteredAdapters (described next), where it determines the DNS domain used for Dynamic DNS registration.

continues ▶

Table 5.1 **Continued**

Keys	Values	Functions
		The `Domain` value is also used by the TCP/IP driver as a primary suffix when building an FQDN to submit to DNS.
`HKLM	System	CurrentControlSet	Services	Tcpip	Parameters DNSRegisteredAdapters	{Class ID}`	`HostName, DomainName, and and PrimaryDomainName`	The `DNSRegisteredAdapters` key stores information used to register the computer with DNS. The `Hostname` value matches the `Hostname` value in the `Parameters` key. The `PrimaryDomainName` value matches the `Domain` value in the `Parameters` key. The `DomainName` value matches the `Domain` value assigned to an interface if that interface has been designated to use for DNS registration (described next). The `DomainName` and `PrimaryDomainName` values are both used to control DNS registration. If they have different values, the computer will register in two different DNS domains and get a Host record in both domains.

Keys	Values	Functions
HKLM | System | CurrentControlSet | Services | Tcpip, Parameters | Interfaces | {Class ID}	Domain	This value is set by an administrator using the TCP/IP Properties window in the UI. The Domain value is used by the TCP/IP driver as a secondary suffix when building FQDNs. If the interface has been designated to use for DNS registration, the Domain value is copied to the DomainName value under DNSRegisteredAdapters.
HKLM | System CurrentControlSet | Services | Tcpip | Parameters | Interfaces | {Class ID}	DHCPDomain	If the machine is a DHCP client that receives a DNS domain name as a part of a DHCP configuration packet, the DHCPDomain value is copied from the configuration packet. If the Domain value for the interface has a setting, the DHCPDomain value is ignored. If the Domain value for the interface is blank, the DHCPDomain value is used by the TCP/IP driver as a secondary suffix for building FQDNs.

continues ▶

Table 5.1 **Continued**

Keys	Values	Functions
		If the `Domain` value is blank and the interface has been designated for use in DNS registration, the `DHCPDomain` value is copied to the `DomainName` value under `DNSRegisteredAdapters`.

As you can see from Table 5.1, it is possible for a computer to be registered in more than one DNS domain and to use different FQDNs when querying DNS, if a flat name is given to the DNS resolver. It is important to use consistent entries when setting these values from the user interface. The best route is to leave one set or the other blank. The next few sections detail how the values are set and which should be used.

Non-Volatile (NV) Names

The NV values for Hostname and Domain are set using the `System Properties` window. Hostname is derived from the computer's NetBIOS name and Domain is taken from an entry called `DNS Suffix`. Set these parameters as follows:

Procedure 5.1 **Setting DNS Suffix in the *System Properties* Window**

1. Right-click `My Computer` and select PROPERTIES from the fly-out menu. The `System Properties` window opens.

2. Select the `Network Identification` tab (see Figure 5.4). The `Full Computer Name` entry shows the current settings that are derived from the `NV Hostname` and `NV Domain` entries in the Registry.

Figure 5.4 `System Properties` window—Network Identification tab.

3. Click `Properties`. The `Identification Changes` window opens (see Figure 5.5). The Computer Name entry is saved to the `NV Hostname` value in the Registry.

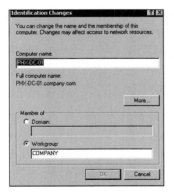

Figure 5.5 `Identification Changes` window showing Computer name (NV Hostname).

The Domain/Workgroup entries under Member Of are not saved to NV Domain. The next window contains an option to change NV Domain automatically based on domain affiliation.

4. Click More. The DNS Suffix and NetBIOS Computer Name window opens (see Figure 5.6). The Primary DNS Suffix entry determines the value for NV Domain.

The Change Primary DNS Suffix When Domain Membership Changes option is selected by default. This is an important option because NV Domain is used to register the machine with Dynamic DNS. If the name does not change when the domain membership changes, the client cannot find a domain controller in the proper domain.

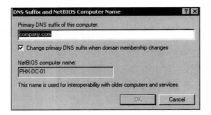

Figure 5.6   DNS Suffix and NetBIOS Computer Name window showing primary DNS suffix (NV Domain name) and NetBIOS computer name (NV Hostname).

5. Close all windows.

If you change the computer's name or DNS suffix, you must restart the machine. A domain controller's name and DNS suffix cannot be altered from the UI and should never be changed in the Registry.

TCP/IP Interface Names

The Domain value for an interface is set with the TCP/IP Properties window for the interface. The value is called *DNS Suffix* in the UI. Set the value as follows:

Procedure 5.2   **Setting DNS Suffix in the TCP/IP Interface**

1. Right-click My Network Places and select PROPERTIES from the fly-out menu. The Network and Dial-up Connections window opens.

2. Right-click the Local Area Connection icon and select PROPERTIES from the fly-out menu. The Local Area Connection Properties window opens.

3. Double-click Internet Protocol (TCP/IP). The Internet Protocol (TCP/IP) Properties window opens.

4. Click Advanced. The Advanced TCP/IP Settings window opens.

5. Select the DNS tab. See Figure 5.7 for an example. The entry for DNS Suffix for This Connection determines the setting of the Domain value in the Registry for the interface. See the sidebar titled "Choosing a DNS Suffix Source" for reasons why you might want to leave this blank.

The Use This Connection's DNS Suffix in DNS Registration option designates whether this interface will be used for registering a computer with Dynamic DNS. As shown in Figure 5.7, Dynamic DNS registration uses the DNS Suffix from both the TCP/IP Properties and System Properties windows.

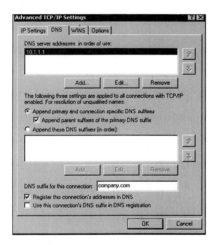

Figure 5.7 Advanced TCP/IP Settings window—DNS tab.

6. Close all windows. Any changes are written to the Registry and take effect immediately.

Choosing a DNS Suffix Source

There are two places in the UI to set a DNS suffix: System Properties window and the TCP/IP Properties window for an interface. The Registry settings made in these two windows are not kept in sync. This means it is possible to register the computer in two domains.

The DNS Suffix entries in System Properties and TCP/IP Properties are used to build FQDNs for use when querying DNS. The System Properties suffix is the primary suffix and is used first when querying DNS. If that query fails, the suffix from TCP/IP Properties is used. You can verify this by setting two different values and then using IPCONFIG /all to view the DNS Suffix Search List.

Because the DNS suffix entries in System Properties and TCP/IP Properties have the potential to conflict with each other, you should use one or the other, but not both, to assign a domain name to a client. Because you must use System Properties to join a computer to a domain, and because the System Properties is the primary suffix for FQDN queries, it makes sense to use the System Properties suffix. In a workgroup environment where the System Properties suffix is superfluous, use the TCP/IP Properties suffix and remember to leave the System Properties suffix blank.

If the client is configured for DHCP, keep in mind that the DNS Domain value in the configuration packet is used in lieu of a DNS Suffix entry if the static entry is blank. If you use DHCP in a domain, it is important to make sure the domain name in the DHCP scope matches the name of the authoritative zone used by the clients. See "Configuring DHCP to Support DNS" at the end of this chapter for details.

Secondary DNS Servers

The traditional method for improving lookup performance and fault tolerance in DNS is to install secondary DNS servers. Secondary servers answer queries from users based on zone information they obtain from master DNS servers. The primary DNS server acts as the first master with a first layer of secondaries. A secondary server can also be a master with its own collection of secondaries. The deeper the structure, the longer it takes to achieve convergence.

Secondary servers come in two general categories, based on whether they have a local copy of the zone table:

- **Standard secondary servers.** These servers have a read-only copy of the zone table pulled from a master server. A standard secondary is authoritative for its zone.

- **Caching-only servers.** These servers have no zone table of their own. They forward all client queries to an authoritative server and then ship the server responses back to the clients. They also store the responses in a local cache for reuse should that client or another one asks for the same record.

The advantage of a standard secondary is that most queries are handled right at the server. The disadvantage is the replication traffic involved with transferring the zone information to the secondary.

The advantage of a caching-only server is that it provides address resolution without the zone transfer traffic involved with a standard secondary. The disadvantage is that it is not authoritative for any zone, so it can take a while to build up a useful cache and the cache goes away if the server is restarted.

The steps for installing and configuring secondary servers are in "Configuring Secondary DNS Servers" later in this chapter. You should consider the following several factors when deploying DNS secondaries, especially if you are just starting to deploy your DNS infrastructure:

- **Distribute query traffic.** If you now have only a few secondary name servers located around your network, you may want to increase that number substantially. Between Dynamic DNS and Active Directory, a big Windows 2000 deployment can increase the number of DNS queries by several orders of magnitude. Windows 2000 clients use DNS constantly to locate network resources. If they are forced to send queries across a slow or unpredictable WAN, you will encounter difficulties with authentication and resource access.

- **Design for fault tolerance.** Windows 2000 clients and servers depend heavily on DNS. A downed DNS server could result in a complete loss of access to network resources. Install enough secondary servers so that a single failure, even to the primary server, will not interrupt service.

- **Monitor statistics.** Features such as incremental zone transfers and Active Directory integrated zones that are discussed in the next few sections help to reduce replication traffic considerably, but they are not a complete panacea to DNS performance issues. Special DNS counters in Performance Monitor can tell you very precisely what your replication and query traffic looks like at a particular server. You should consider logging performance continuously until you get a solid baseline to use for troubleshooting.

Zone Table Replication

A DNS secondary can obtain a copy of a zone table either from the primary DNS server or another secondary. The act of copying a zone table is called a *zone transfer*.

Windows 2000 incorporates two RFC-based provisions, update notification and incremental zone transfers, designed to improve zone table consistency and minimize bandwidth. In addition, zone information in Windows

2000 DNS can be stored in the directory, eliminating the need for special-ized zone transfer mechanisms completely. The following sections provide the details on these three options.

Update Notification

In a standard zone transfer, the secondary name server polls its master peri-odically to see whether the zone table has changed. The polling interval is set by a Refresh Interval in the *Start of Authority* (SOA) record. Figure 5.8 shows an example SOA record. See "Format of Common Resource Records" for more information on the structure and function of the SOA record.

Figure 5.8 Zone Properties window showing the Start of Authority (SOA) tab. The Refresh Interval determines the polling time between zone transfers.

When a secondary server reaches the end of its refresh interval, it asks its master for a copy of its SOA record. This record contains a serial number—a sequence number that is incremented each time the zone table is updated. If the serial number in the SOA record copy held by the secondary is lower than the serial number in the SOA record polled from the master, the sec-ondary initiates a zone transfer.

Polling is an inefficient method for controlling replication. Windows 2000 DNS implements an addition to the traditional polling method based on the provisions of RFC 1996, "A Mechanism for Prompt Notification of Zone Changes." This RFC defines a new DNS opcode called DNS Notify. This notification adds one key step to standard polling. Here is how it works.

Procedure 5.3 **Functional Description of Standard Polled Zone Transfer**

1. When an update is made to the zone table at the master name server, the server sends out a DNS Notify message to its secondary name servers. It must be configured with the IP addresses of these servers.

2. The secondary name servers respond to the DNS Notify message by returning a standard update request for the SOA record.

3. From this point forward, the zone transfer proceeds in a traditional fashion.

Notification Differences from NT4

NT4 DNS implemented the DNS Notify opcode, but the administrator was required to manually initiate the notification by selecting UPDATE SERVER DATA FILE from the zone's PROPERTY menu. This was required because NT4 DNS used standard zone transfers, which copies the entire zone table.

Because Windows 2000 supports incremental zone transfers, notification is done automatically and the updates are copied as quickly as the secondaries can pull them down.

Incremental Zone Transfers

A standard DNS zone transfer copies the entire contents of the zone table from the master name server to its secondaries. This causes excessive network traffic and puts an undue load on the name servers. Windows 2000 avoids this problem by implementing the provisions of RFC 1995, "Incremental Zone Transfer in DNS."

In an incremental transfer, the secondary server supplies the serial number from its copy of the SOA record when it requests a zone transfer. The master server sends only those updates that have been made in the meantime.

Windows 2000 DNS defaults to doing incremental zone transfers. If a Windows 2000 name server is a secondary to a master that does not support incremental transfers, it falls back to using full zone transfers. The same is true if a non–Windows 2000 name server that does not support incremental transfers is configured as a secondary to a Windows 2000 name server. The secondary uses the opcode for a standard transfer and the Windows 2000 server complies.

Active Directory Integration

In addition to the two RFC-compliant zone transfer methods, Windows 2000 DNS zone tables can also be integrated into Active Directory. This eliminates the need for conventional zone transfers because the directory is replicated using its own multiple-master replication scheme.

Active Directory integration also makes it possible for any Windows 2000 domain controller that is running DNS to update zone entries. The DNS service requires very little overhead, so you can easily deploy DNS on every domain controller. Using this feature, you can eliminate the single primary name server of traditional DNS along with the single primary domain controller in classic NT.

In terms of performance, bandwidth utilization, and manageability, integrating DNS into Active Directory is a win. There are a few caveats, however:

- **No ASCII zone tables.** Directory-integrated zones store resource records as directory objects. There are no ASCII files that you can just copy to another name server and use. You can, however, pull a standard zone from a directory-integrated DNS server, so it's fairly simple to get a boot file if you need one.

- **Relies on Active Directory availability.** If the directory is unavailable, DNS goes away with it. This is a double-edged sword, because clients and domain controllers in other domains rely on DNS to find Active Directory services; so if DNS is unavailable, you might not be able to reach the domain controllers to fix them. I strongly advise maintaining at least one conventional secondary DNS zone to use in case of emergency.

- **Only primary zones can be Directory-integrated.** If you plan on Directory-integrating a zone, the primary master name server must be running Windows 2000. This may cause you discomfort if you are an administrator who currently runs UNIX or NetWare DNS and are hesitant about cutting over to Windows 2000. You may want to leave Directory integration alone for a while, but watch out for security issues with Dynamic DNS. See "Dynamic Update Security" later in this chapter for more information.

- **Delegated zones can be hosted by non-Windows 2000 DNS servers.** You can migrate the primary master name server in the root zone to Windows 2000 and Directory integrate the zone while keeping your child zones on BIND or NetWare.

- **Only domain controllers have read/write access to Directory-integrated zones.** Windows 2000 member servers, NT4 DNS, and third-party name servers can only be secondary name servers after the zone has been integrated into the Directory.

Using Forwarders

When a DNS server gets a query for a record in another zone that it does not have in cache, it checks its root hints table to find a root server, and then uses iterative queries to "walk the tree" until it finds a name server that has the record. This process is detailed in "Functional Description of DNS Query Handling" later in this chapter. There is an alternative to doing all that grunt work, and that is to check with another server that might have already done the grunt work first. This is called forwarding, and the server that is referenced is called a *forwarder*.

A forwarding server can be either a primary or a secondary. It has a local copy of a zone table and a root hints table, so it is equipped to handle requests for hosts inside or outside its zone of authority. But it also has a list of forwarders that it uses when it gets a query that is out of zone and not in cache. The forwarding server is betting that the forwarder has already located the record and has it in cache. By doing a quick check with the forwarder, a lot of time and energy is saved.

If the forwarder does not have the record cached, it starts locating it. This takes a period of time, during which the forwarding server can give up and do the lookup itself. The forwarder also finds the record and caches it so that the next time the record is right there for the taking.

A server configured to use a forwarder exclusively for out-of-zone lookups is called a *slave server*. Slave servers depend completely on their forwarder. If the forwarder cannot find the record, the slave sends a "No Record" response back to the client.

The most common use of forwarders is to resolve Internet addresses from inside a firewall. The forwarder is placed in the DMZ or it might even be at an ISP. The forwarding server is in the private network. When a client sends the internal name server a query for an Internet host (or any host that is not in the zone), the forwarding server sends the request to the forwarder. The forwarder builds up a cache of records, so overall query performance gradually gets better.

No special configurations are required at the forwarder. The steps to set up a server to use a forwarder are in "Configuring a DNS Server to Use a Forwarder" later in this chapter.

Dynamic Zone Updates

Windows 2000 supports dynamic zone updates as described in RFC 2136, "Dynamic Updates in the Domain Name System." This RFC defines new opcode called DNS Update that can add records to a zone table automatically. The DNS Update message contains the type of record to add, the name of the zone where the record should be added, and any prerequisite records that must or must not be present. As a minimum, Windows 2000 clients register an A (host) record and a PTR (reverse lookup pointer) record.

Dynamic DNS clients register their records at boot time, and then refresh them every 24 hours. DHCP clients refresh their records when renewing their lease. Non-RFC 2136 clients, such as down-level Windows clients, can dynamically register their A and PTR records by proxy through DHCP. See "Configuring DHCP to Support DNS" later in this chapter for details.

You can force dynamic registration using a new IPCONFIG option called /registerdns. The syntax is IPCONFIG /registerdns. This option sends a DNS Update message to the client's DNS server.

Certain stipulations apply when dynamically registering a resource record:

- When a client attempts to register a record that does not already exist, the DNS server adds the new record updates to the zone.

- If a record exists with a different name but the same IP address, the new record is added and the old record is left in place.

- If a record exists with the same host name but different IP address, the original record is overwritten with the new address value.

Keep this last instance in mind when you get to the section "Dynamic Update Security." Important DNS entries can be easily overwritten if you aren't careful.

Although the primary master DNS server has the only read/write copy of the zone table, the DNS client can be configured to point at any authoritative server for the zone. The secondary servers pass the DNS Update messages from the clients up to the primary master. The primary master notifies the secondaries of the change, and the secondaries pull an incremental zone transfer.

If the client is configured to point at a non-authoritative server, such as a caching-only server, the dynamic updates are not passed on to the authoritative server and the client is not registered.

Dynamic registration carries the risks that your nice, clean DNS zone tables might start to look like something best described as an aftermath. To avoid this, implement scavenging for the zone using the steps in "Configuring Scavenging" later in this chapter.

Another potential problem with dynamic updates is security. If it is easy to add records to a zone table, it's a sure bet that some bad guy will take advantage. The next section discusses this further.

Dynamic Update Security

DNS servers make particularly enticing targets for intruders. They hold the IP address of every host in your network, and that kind of information can be damaging in the wrong hands. DNS servers are also likely candidates for denial-of-service attacks because the network so utterly depends on them. As Windows 2000 DNS servers get field exposure, security holes are bound to show up. Be sure to install security patches as soon as they become available (after testing them, of course.)

One of the most important security measures you can take regarding dynamic updates is to control the stations permitted to register resource records. The current standards-track document for this type of security is RFC 2137, "Secure Domain Name System Dynamic Update." Microsoft began designing Directory-integrated zones before this RFC went on standards-track, so the security implementation in Windows 2000 follows earlier Internet Draft proposals and not RFC 2137.

To secure the DNS zone, you must integrate it into Active Directory. Standard primary zones do not have dynamic update security protection. After you have integrated the zone into the directory, the resource records are secured using standard Windows 2000 object security. See Chapter 10, "Managing Active Directory Security," for details on Active Directory security.

Figure 5.9 shows a partial list of users and groups who are usually on the access control list for a DNS zone. The key players are the Everyone group, which has read access to the records, and the Authenticated Users group, which has the Create Child Objects permission necessary to build new resource records. There are no computers or groups containing computer accounts on this list. A user in one of the security groups that are authorized to create new DNS objects (Authenticated Users, Domain Admins, and DNS Admins) must log on at the console before the resource record is created.

Speaking of the DNS Admins group, this group is created in the domain when DNS is installed on a domain controller or member server. Its function is to provide a standard administrative group with a controlled set of access rights strictly to administer DNS servers and directory-integrated resource records. No accounts are placed in the group by default.

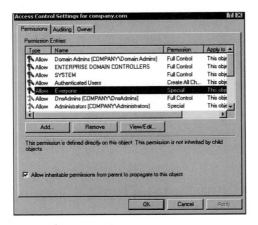

Figure 5.9 Access list for directory-integrated DNS zone showing some of the security principals who have access to the records.

RFC 2137 and Windows 2000 Dynamic DNS Security

The current standards-track document that addresses the issue of Dynamic DNS security is RFC 2137, "Secure Domain Name System Dynamic Update." Windows 2000 DNS update security methods were designed prior to RFC 2137 being placed on standards-track. The DNS update security in Windows 2000 is based on the following Internet Drafts:

- Draft-ietf-dnsind-tsig-09.txt, "Secret Key Transaction Signatures for DNS (TSIG)"

- Draft-ietf-dnsind-tkey-00.txt, "Secret Key Establishment for DNS (TKEY RR)"

- Draft-skwan-gss-tsig-04.txt, "GSS Algorithm for TSIG (GSS-TSIG)"

Record Scavenging

If you have ever managed a large WINS installation, you know how messy a dynamically updated registration database can become. Before letting your DNS zone tables get overwhelmed by old and superceded resource records, take steps to do some regular housekeeping. Windows 2000 has a scavenging option that time stamps dynamically registered resource records with an aging value and then clears out the unused records on a regular basis.

Scavenging is not enabled by default. It can be enabled for a particular zone or for every zone on a DNS server. Scavenging affects primary zones and directory-integrated zones only. Secondary zones are read-only. If you scavenge the master zone, the secondary zones get cleaned up during the zone transfers.

Because scavenging works by including an aging value in the dynamically registered resource records, it changes the format of the zone table, making it incompatible with non–Windows 2000 name servers. Zone transfers are unaffected because the DNS service filters out the aging value, but you can't take a copy of the .DNS file for the zone and load it onto an NT4 or BIND name server.

Scavenging uses two intervals, the *non-refresh interval* and the *refresh interval*, to determine when a particular record should be removed from the zone table. Both intervals are set for seven days by default. Here is how they work.

When a resource record is first dynamically created, DNS assigns an aging value based on the 7-day non-refresh interval. During this 7-day interval, DNS does not accept refreshes to the record. This prevents the system from being overwhelmed every morning with refreshes from thousands of machines as they are turned on.

After the initial seven-day non-refresh interval, the record is free to be refreshed. DNS clients refresh their records at boot time and every 24-hours if they are left on. The refresh interval lasts for another seven days. At the end of the seven-day refresh interval, if the aging value has not been refreshed, the record will be removed during scavenging.

Scavenging can be initiated manually from the PROPERTIES menu of the zone icon or by scheduling it to run periodically as part of the DNS server properties (see "Configuring Scavenging").

If a user goes on vacation for more than two weeks and leaves her machine off, the DNS registration for her A and PTR records will age out and periodic scavenging will remove them from the zone table. This is not a catastrophe. The user does not lose any security privileges or functionality. When the user starts up the machine after coming back from vacation and logs on, the system will reregister with DNS and build a new resource record.

WINS Forwarding

Windows 2000 DNS continues to support the WINS forwarding feature first introduced in NT4. WINS forwarding makes use of two special resource records, the WINS record and the WINS-R (reverse) record, that point at WINS servers where DNS can forward queries if they cannot be located in the zone table.

Dynamic DNS eliminates the need for WINS forwarding in a purely Windows 2000 environment, but forwarding is still necessary as long as you have down-level clients that do not take advantage of Dynamic DNS registration.

It is possible to eliminate the need for WINS forwarding if all your down-level clients are DHCP clients. A special proxy feature in Windows 2000 DHCP can perform DNS registration for clients that do not support the feature. See "Configuring DHCP to Support DNS" later in this chapter for more information.

Format of Common Resource Records

This section covers the contents, functions, and zone table entries for the resource records commonly used in Windows 2000 DNS. I realize that analyzing database record structures is about as enjoyable as chewing boiled tennis racket strings, but familiarity with structure of these records can come in handy when you need to tweak the system or troubleshoot problems. The following records are described in this section:

- Start of Authority (SOA)
- Host (A)
- Name Server (NS)
- Alias (CNAME)
- Pointer (PTR)
- Service Locator (SRV)

For a complete list of the Windows DNS resource records and a description of their functions, I recommend taking a look at *Windows NT DNS*, by Michael Masterson, Herman Knief, et al.

Start of Authority *(SOA)*

Every DNS domain tree has a *Start of Authority* (SOA) server that holds the primary zone table. The SOA record identifies the root server along with additional information, such as the e-mail address of the responsible administrator and TTL data. Figure 5.8 shows an example SOA record.

Here is a copy of the text listing for the SOA record along with the beginning lines of the zone table:

```
;   Database file company.com.dns for company.com zone
;     Zone version:  1
;
@   IN  SOA phx-dc-01. administrator.company.com  (
                1          ; serial number
                900        ; refresh
                600        ; retry
                86400      ; expire
                3600       ) ; minimum TTL
```

Here are the SOA record entries and their functions:

- **@.** Indicates that this is the root domain.
- **IN.** Designates this record as an "Internet" record class. This is the most common record class. Other classes, such as the Hesiod class, are used in specialized or academic environments. Windows 2000 DNS assumes an IN class if one is not specified.
- **Serial number.** This is an increment counter that tracks changes to the database. This counter controls zone transfers. The zone version number in the header of the zone file must match the serial number in the SOA record.
- **Refresh interval.** This option specifies the time a secondary DNS server waits before polling for updates. The default interval is 15 minutes.
- **Retry interval.** The time a secondary DNS server waits after failing to find its master before trying once again to make contact. The default time is 10 minutes.
- **Expire time.** The interval during which a secondary DNS server continues to respond to queries after failure to pull a zone transfer. The default time is 24 hours. This means that you can take your primary DNS server down for a while as long as the clients are configured with the IP address of a secondary.
- **Minimum TTL.** Clients and other DNS servers cache resource records to speed up subsequent queries for the same record. The minimum TTL setting determines the default cache time for a record. Individual resource records can specify different TTL values. The individual TTL settings take precedence over the SOA default on a Windows 2000 DNS server.

Host (A)

The most common DNS query is for the IP address of a host. The A record contains this information. Figure 5.10 shows an example of an A record. Microsoft chose to name this record Host rather than use its RFC name of Address, but the format is the same and the zone table entries are interchangeable between Windows 2000 and BIND.

Figure 5.10 Host (A) record showing the host name and IP address.

Here is an example zone table listing:

```
;  Zone records
phx-dc-01           1200        A     10.1.1.1
phx-w2kp-002        1200        A     10.1.200.223
phx-w98-001         1200        A     10.1.10.3
www                 1200        A     10.1.10.103
                                A     10.1.10.104
                                A     10.1.10.105
```

- Column 1 specifies the host name. Windows 2000 DNS does not specify the IN record class. If it were included, the A record would look like this:
  ```
  phx-dc-01   IN    1200    A    10.1.1.1.
  ```

- Column 2 specifies the TTL value for the record. This TTL over-rides the default TTL in the SOA record. That is not standard BIND functionality.

- Column 3 specifies the record type.

- Column 4 specifies the IP address of the host. A host can have several IP addresses, in which case the host name is listed once with one or more lines after it containing alternative IP addresses.

DNS and Round-Robin

If you have more than one host record (A record) with the same IP address, DNS rotates through the addresses when responding to queries. This evens out the load on the servers.

For example, you might have two intranet servers with the same HTML files. The server names are www1.company.com and www2.company.com. By putting two A records called www.company.com in DNS, each with the IP address of one of the servers, incoming hits from client browsers are distributed evenly between the two machines.

If you want DNS to return the same IP address regardless of the number of host records pointing at other addresses, disable this option as follows:

Procedure 5.4   **Disabling Round-Robin Host Selection**

1. Open the DNS console.

2. Right-click the DNS server icon and select PROPERTIES from the fly-out menu. The Properties window opens.

3. Select the Advanced tab.

4. Under Server Options, deselect Enable Round Robin.

5. Click OK to save the changes and close the window.

6. Close the console.

Name Server *(NS)*

In addition to the SOA and A records, every zone file has at least one NS record. The NS record contains the name and IP address of the primary DNS server and any delegated servers. Delegation enables one name server to ask another for help with a query. Windows 2000 provides a special wizard for setting up delegation. The steps for using the wizard are listed under "Configuring Hierarchical Zones" later in this chapter.

The list of NS records can be viewed and modified by opening the Properties window for a domain and selecting the Name Servers tab. Figure 5.11 shows an example containing a primary name server, phx-dc-01.company.com, and a delegated name server in a child domain, alb-dns-01.branch1.company.com.

Figure 5.11 NS records from the zone Properties window.

The name server records for delegated domains appear in a special format within the zone table. Here is an example:

```
;  Zone NS records
@                      NS     phx-dc-01.company.com.
;
;  Delegated sub-zone:  branch1.company.com.
;
branch1                NS     alb-dns-01.branch1.company.com.
alb-dns-01.branch1     A      10.2.1.1
;  End delegation
```

Alias (CNAME)

The need often arises to use an alternate name for a host. The RFC term for this record type is the *Canonical Name* (CNAME). Microsoft chose to call it an *alias*, which is actually a better description and easier to pronounce. An alias record points at the A record for the host.

When a client requests an A record for a certain host name, if a CNAME record exists with the same name, DNS returns both the CNAME record and the associated A record. See Figure 5.12 for an example alias (CNAME) record.

Figure 5.12   Example alias (CNAME) record.

Here is the text listing in the zone table for a CNAME record:

```
dns        CNAME     phx-dc-01.company.com.
```

The example uses dns as an alias for a domain controller that is also a DNS server. The advantage to using CNAME records rather than using several A records with different host names and the same IP address is that with aliases, you have to change only one record if you decide to change the IP address of the host.

Pointer (PTR)

A reverse lookup zone table uses PTR records to sort the listings by IP address rather than by name. Reverse lookup zones are described earlier in this chapter under "Forward and Reverse Lookup Zones." In brief, a reverse lookup zone stores host IP addresses in reverse format so that DNS can search for them using the same right-to-left hierarchy that it uses to parse out DNS domain names. The reverse lookup namespace is rooted in a special domain called in-addr.arpa. Figure 5.13 shows a PTR record.

Figure 5.13   PTR record showing reversed IP address under Subnet
and the standard dotted-decimal address under Host IP Number.

The graphical display of the PTR record shows the reversed IP address under
the Subnet field and the standard IP address format under the Host IP
Number field. The actual PTR record entry contains only the reversed IP
address. Here is a reverse lookup zone table excerpt for 1.10.in-addr.arpa.
showing several hosts:

```
200.1       PTR     www.company.com.
150.1       PTR     phx-w2ks-03.company.com.
30.1        PTR     phx-w2kp-021.company.com.
```

Service Locator (SRV)

The service locator record is a relatively new record type compared to the
standard A and CNAME records. The SRV record was introduced in RFC 2052,
"A DNS RR for specifying the location of services (DNS SRV)." It provides
a general record type for identifying hosts that run special services.

In Windows 2000, the SRV record is used to locate Active Directory and
Kerberos services such as LDAP at TCP port 389, Kerberos at TCP port 88,
Kerberos Change Password Protocol at TCP port 464, and Global Catalog
services at TCP port 3286 along with UDP ports for the same services for
clients that need to send only connectionless datagrams.

Figure 5.14 shows an example SRV record. Chapter 7, "Understanding
Active Directory Services," contains details of how the SRV record is used to
support client access to Active Directory services.

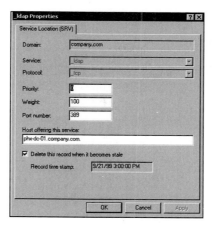

Figure 5.14 SRV record for _ldap service on TCP port 389.

The following excerpt from a zone table shows SRV records for a few Active Directory listings. The leading underscores are due to a change in the SRV format in RFC 2052 and are slated to disappear in future iterations.

```
_gc._tcp              600        SRV      0 100 3268     phx-dc-01.company.com.
_kerberos._tcp        600        SRV      0 100 88       phx-dc-01.company.com.
_kpasswd._tcp         600        SRV      0 100 464      phx-dc-01.company.com.
_ldap._tcp            600        SRV      0 100 389      phx-dc-01.company.com.
```

The three columns after SRV need a little explanation. They are for priority, weight, and port.

- **Priority.** If several servers offer the same service, they can be assigned different priorities based on their capability. The client resolver chooses among them. The lower the number, the higher the priority. Active Directory SRV records all use priority 0.

- **Weight.** When several hosts have the same priority, the client chooses among them using a weighting factor. Active Directory SRV records all use a weighting factor of 100.

- **Port.** The TCP or UDP port used by the protocol. The example _ldap entry uses well-known TCP port 389.

When a client needs to know the server that hosts a particular service, it sends a query to its DNS server requesting the SRV records for that service. The DNS server goes through all the SRV records and returns any that fit the request. If there is more than one server on the list, the client uses the priority and weighting factors to make a selection. If all factors are equal, the client picks a host at random.

With the structure and function of the resource records in mind along with the details of how Windows 2000 DNS stores and manages those records, let's take a look at query handling to see how clients use the records to resolve names into IP addresses.

Functional Description of DNS Query Handling

This section contains step-by-step descriptions of DNS queries using several scenarios:

- A query handled by an authoritative server
- A query handled by a non-authoritative server
- A reverse-lookup query

Knowing how DNS queries are handled helps when designing a DNS system and when integrating Windows 2000 name services into an existing DNS infrastructure.

Queries Handled by Authoritative Servers

Assume, for example, that a user at a Windows 2000 computer in the company.com DNS domain opens Notepad and tries to access a file on a file server called phx-w2ks-02. Here's what happens from the point of view of DNS:

Procedure 5.5   Function Description of Query Handling by an Authoritative Name Server

1. The Microsoft client redirector, LAN Manager Workstation, along with its network file system, MRXSMB.SYS, builds an SMB message to initiate a session with phx-w2ks-02.

2. The redirector hands the SMB message over to the TCP/IP driver, TCPIP.SYS, for packaging and transport. TCPIP.SYS works with its NetBIOS-over-TCP/IP helper, NETBT.SYS, to build a datagram for the SMB message. Session-oriented SMB traffic uses TCP port 139.

3. TCPIP.SYS needs the IP address of phx-w2ks-02 so that it can build an IP packet. To get this address, TCPIP.SYS uses its internal DNS resolver. The remainder of this discussion refers to this resolver as if it were a separate service.

4. The resolver fires off a query to its associated DNS server. The query contains the following:

> The fully qualified DNS name of the target computer; in this case, `phx-w2ks-02.company.com`.
>
> The resource record type being requested. This is a simple host name lookup, so the query is for an A record.
>
> The resource record class being requested. This is nearly always the IN, or Internet, class. Other classes are used only in very limited circumstances.

5. When the DNS server receives the query, it parses the host name from right-to-left to find the DNS domain, `company.com`.

6. In this instance, the DNS server is authoritative for the requested zone, so it does a zone table lookup to find the requested resource record.

7. When the DNS server finds the A record for `phx-w2ks-02`, it sends the entire contents of the record back to the client in the form of a *DNS Query Response*. If the A record does not contain a TTL value, the DNS server inserts the minimum TTL value from the SOA record for the zone. The default TTL is one hour, or 3,600 seconds.

   If the DNS server cannot find the requested record, it returns a *Record Not Found* response. An authoritative DNS server does not consult another DNS server when it cannot resolve a query within its zone of authority. When the resolver gets a *Record Not Found* response from an authoritative name server, it returns an error to the application without attempting further lookups.

8. Now that the resolver has obtained the IP address, TCPIP.SYS has some work to do. It uses the IP address from the A record to build an IP packet, then it uses *Address Resolution Protocol* (ARP) to find the MAC address associated with the IP address. TCPIP.SYS then hands over the packet and the MAC address to NDIS, which builds a transmission frame and sends it to the target server.

9. TCPIP.SYS also hands the A record over to the *DNS Resolver Cache* service. The Resolver Cache service holds onto the A record for the time period specified in the TTL.

DNS Packet Contents

It can be instructive to view the contents of the DNS messages involved in a name query transaction. The Network Monitor service that comes with Windows 2000 Server is a great tool for capturing and examining packets as long as the traffic is on the local network interface. Figure 5.15 shows a capture packet containing the response to a Host query (A record) request returned by an authoritative DNS server. The following are the key items to examine:

- **UDP entry.** Indicates that DNS query uses UDP port 53. This is the well-known port for DNS.

- **DNS flags.** The server indicates that it is authoritative for the domain, it supports recursive queries, and there was no error in the response.

- **DNS question section.** This contains a copy of the original DNS query asking for a host record for phx-dc-01.company.com.

- **DNS answer section.** The response contains the A record information for phx-dc-01.company.com, including its IP address and the default TTL value from the SOA record.

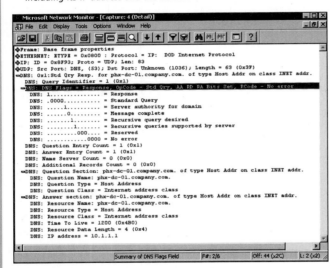

Figure 5.15 Captured packet showing DNS standard query response.

If you have a DNS server inside a firewall and you need to send queries to an InterNIC root server or some other public name server, you must either enable UDP port 53 at the firewall or configure your DNS server to use NAT or a proxy to access the Internet. Windows 2000 DNS servers answer a DNS query on the same interface that receives the query, so enabling UDP port 53 is adequate to support DNS queries and their responses.

Working with the DNS Resolver Cache Service

Windows 2000 introduces three very useful new options to the IPCONFIG utility that are designed to help work with DNS.

- `IPCONFIG /flushdns` This option flushes the contents of the DNS cache without forcing you to stop and start the Resolver Cache Service.

- `IPCONFIG /displaydns` This option lists the current contents of the resolver cache. It is extraordinarily useful when trying to diagnose a lookup error.

- `IPCONFIG /registerdns` This option registers the computer name with Dynamic DNS. See the section titled "Dynamic Zone Updates" for a description of the way DNS domain names are selected for this registration.

One of the reasons the /flushdns switch is so important for troubleshooting is that Windows 2000 implements the provisions of RFC 2308, "Negative Caching of DNS Queries (DNS NCACHE)." This means that failed lookups are cached right along with successful lookups. If you are troubleshooting, this means you'll continue to get a *Bad IP Address* error even after you fix the problem until you flush the cache.

Queries Handled by Non–Authoritative Servers

Consider the situation if the user, instead of trying to access a file on a server on the internal network, tries to access a file on an external network, such as the Internet. For example, the user opens a browser and points it at www.whitehouse.gov. In this trace, let's skip the OSI Layer 7 details and get right to the DNS query.

Procedure 5.6 **Functional Description of Query Handling by Non-Authoritative Name Server**

1. The DNS resolver sends off a recursive query to its DNS server asking for an A record for www.whitehouse.gov. A recursive query tells the DNS server to do all the work in resolving the address.

2. The local DNS server in the company.com DNS domain has no zone table for whitehouse.gov. The recursive query tells the server to refer the request to another DNS server, but which one? This is where the root hints in the CACHE.DNS file come into play. The root hints identify servers at the top of the domain. Because the company.com DNS domain is rooted in an InterNIC domain, com, the root hints has a list of the InterNIC root servers. See "Configuring Root Hints" later in this chapter for more information.

3. After consulting the root hints file, the DNS server fires off an iterative query to an InterNIC root server saying, in effect, "Give me an A record for www.whitehouse.gov or tell me the name of a server that can help me."

4. In every likelihood, the InterNIC root server does not have an A record for www.whitehouse.gov. However, the InterNIC root servers are SOA for the domain gov, and that means they have Name Server (NS) records pointing at the DNS servers delegated to hold the zone tables for the domains directly under gov.

5. The root server consults its NS records and discovers an authoritative server for whitehouse.gov. It returns the A record for sec1.dns.psi.net along with its IP address of 38.8.92.2.

Trace Names

If you're wondering where I got the specific names in this trace, skip ahead to the section on "Examining Zone Tables with NSLOOKUP".

6. The company.com DNS server now sends an iterative query to sec1.dns.psi.net asking for an A record for www.whitehouse.gov. The resolver at the client is still waiting patiently.

7. Because the DNS service on sec1.dns.psi.net is SOA for whitehouse.gov, it does a zone table lookup and returns an A record with the IP address 198.137.240.92.

8. When the company.com DNS server receives the A record for www.whitehouse.gov in answer to its query, it forwards the record to the client that originally sent the query. It also caches a copy in case another client sends a similar query. This cache is handled by TCPIP.SYS, DNS Resolver Cache, but the aging times are still determined by the TTL value in the record.

The key point to remember about the actions of the non-authoritative server is that the root hints file is used to find the name and IP address of a root server. If this had been a private DNS namespace with an internal root server that did not have the InterNIC root servers in root hints, the query would have failed.

Reverse Lookup Queries

Here is how DNS handles a reverse lookup request. Assume, for example, that a user in the company.com domain, address 10.1.0.0, uses ping -a to find the host name for 209.12.73.4.

Procedure 5.7   **Functional Description of Reverse Lookup Query**

1. The resolver sends a reverse lookup query, called a *Domain Name Pointer* request, to its DNS server. The resolver requests a PTR record for `4.73.12.209.in-addr.arpa`.

2. The local DNS server is not SOA for the `73.12.209.in-addr.arpa` zone, so it refers the query to one of the InterNIC root servers, which are SOA for the `in-addr.arpa` zone.

3. The InterNIC root server does not have a zone table for `73.12.209.in-addr.arpa`, but it has an NS record for the name server that holds the zone for `209.in-addr.arpa`. It returns a referral containing the IP address of the name server.

4. The `company.com` DNS server now sends the same reverse lookup query to the name server in the referral. This server does not have a zone table for `73.12.209.in-addr.arpa` either, but it has an NS record for a name server holding the zone for `12.209.in-addr.arpa`. It returns a referral.

5. The `company.com` DNS server now sends the same reverse lookup query to the name server in the referral. This server *does* hold the zone table for `73.12.209.in-addr.arpa`. It performs a zone lookup for the PTR record for `4` and returns the contents along with the associated A record, which contains the host name, `www.newmexico.com`.

6. TCPIP.SYS gives the host name information to Ping, which displays it along with the ICMP Echo Response information in the console listing. The DNS Resolver Cache service caches both the PTR record and the A record for future reference.

Reverse lookup queries are uncommon, so many DNS administrators just don't create reverse lookup zones. Active Directory uses reverse lookups on occasion to help find SRV records, and they aid in troubleshooting, so they are worth the small effort to build and maintain them.

Configuring DNS Clients

It's about time to install DNS, but first let's configure a few DNS clients so that they will be ready to use the server after it is in operation. Windows 2000 clients need two pieces of information about DNS:

1. The IP address of the DNS server or servers where they will send queries.

2. The default zone name to use when sending queries. (This is also called the DNS Suffix.)

The IP address information is configured in TCP/IP Properties. The DNS Suffix information is configured in two places: the TCP/IP Properties for the network interface and System Properties for the computer. These entries are stored in separate places in the Registry. See "Determining DNS Domain Names" earlier in this chapter for details on how these entries are used. Start with configuring the TCP/IP properties.

Configuring DNS Information in *TCP/IP* Properties

When you have the information you need to configure a client's DNS settings, proceed as follows:

Procedure 5.8 **Configuring DNS Information for TCP/IP Interface Properties**

1. Right-click My Network Places and select PROPERTIES from the fly-out menu. The Network and Dial-up Connections window opens.

2. Right-click the Local Connection icon and select PROPERTIES from the fly-out menu. The Local Connection Properties window opens.

3. Double-click the Internet Protocol (TCP/IP) entry to open its Properties window.

4. Click Advanced. The Advanced TCP/IP Settings window opens.

5. Select the DNS tab.

6. Under DNS Server Addresses, click Add. The TCP/IP DNS Server window opens.

7. Enter the IP address of the DNS server and click Add to add it to the list. You can add several servers to the list.

8. Leave the DNS Suffix for This Connection field blank. Do not select the Use This Connection's DNS Suffix in DNS Registration option. Wait for the next section to configure these settings in System Properties.

9. Click OK to retain the change and close the window.

10. Click OK to return to the TCP/IP Properties window.

11. Click OK to close the window and update the Registry with the changes.

Using Multiple DNS Servers

You can configure a client to query multiple DNS servers. If the first server on the list does not respond, the resolver consults the next server. If the first server responds authoritatively with a *Record Not Found* error, the client does not consult additional servers.

Configuring DNS Information in *System* Properties

The DNS Suffix information in System Properties is used as the primary suffix for building FQDNs and is used to register the computer in Dynamic DNS. You will get best results by putting suffix information here rather than TCP/IP Properties. View and modify the DNS Suffix information in System Properties as follows. A system restart is required if you make changes.

Procedure 5.9 Configuring DNS Information in the *System Properties* Window

1. Right-click My Computer and select PROPERTIES from the fly-out menu. The System Properties window opens.

2. Select the Network Identification tab.

3. Click Properties. The Identification Changes window opens.

4. Click More. The DNS Suffix and NetBIOS Computer Name window opens.

5. Enter the DNS domain name. Be sure to check the Change Primary DNS Suffix when Domain Membership Changes option. This ensures that the server's DNS domain matches its Active Directory domain.

6. Click OK to save the change.

7. Click OK to return to the System Properties window. The system prompts you that the change requires a restart.

8. Click OK, and then OK again to close the System Properties window. The system prompts again to restart. Do so.

After you have completed configuring clients, use IPCONFIG /all to double-check the configuration, and then proceed with installing DNS at the server.

Installing and Configuring DNS

I'm sure that you're thinking that it's long since time to actually install and configure DNS, the service, after having worked through DNS, the theory. I agree. Let's go.

If you have existing NT4 DNS servers, you can upgrade them to Windows 2000. Upgrading preserves the existing DNS server configuration and zone tables. Upgrade the primary DNS server first, and then upgrade any secondary masters. This enables incremental zone transfers automatically. The number of DNS records will increase dramatically after you begin to distribute Windows 2000 clients who register automatically in Dynamic DNS. The incremental zone transfers will help conserve bandwidth.

If you have non–Windows 2000 DNS servers, they must support RFC 2136, "Dynamic DNS," and RFC 2052, "A DNS RR for Specifying the Location of Services (DNS SRV)." NetWare 5.0 DNS fits the bill, as does BIND 8.1.2 and higher.

Command-Line Management of DNS

This is as good a place as any to talk about command-line management tools for DNS. The new DNS console in Windows 2000 represents quite an improvement over the NT4 DNS Manager; when the time comes to do serious work across a network, however, it is always good to have a command-line utility. The Windows 2000 Resource Kit includes a CLI tool for DNS management called DNSCMD.

You can do virtually any action with DNSCMD that you could do from the DNS console. This includes adding and deleting resource records, listing the contents of zones, resetting the DNS service, directory-integrating a zone, scavenging old dynamic records, and clearing the DNS cache. Armed with a little time and some scripting tools, you can tailor a set of utilities that can do just about any operation that needs doing.

The tool comes with command-line help for options and syntax with extensive examples in the Resource Kit online help. This is a tool worth learning to use if you are going to manage a number of DNS servers.

When you're ready to install the DNS service, proceed as follows. Install the drivers and support files first. You'll need the Windows 2000 Server CD-ROM.

Procedure 5.10 **Installing DNS Drivers**

1. From Control Panel, open the Add/Remove Programs applet.

2. Click Add/Remove Windows Components. The Windows Components Wizard starts with the focus set to the Windows Components window.

3. Highlight Networking Services and click Details. The Networking Services window opens.

4. Select Domain Name System (DNS) and click OK to save the change and return to the Windows Components window.

5. Click Next. The Configuring Components window opens and the drivers begin loading. When the drivers have loaded and the configuration is complete, the wizard displays a successful completion window.

6. Click Finish to close the window and return to the Add/Remove Programs window.

7. Close the Add/Remove Programs window.

At this point, you can begin configuring the service. There is no need to restart. Start by creating a forward lookup zone for the top of your DNS namespace and one or more reverse lookup zones for the network IDs. These steps are covered in the next sections.

DNS Boot Information

The DNS service starts automatically at boot time. You can start and stop the service using the DNS console or from the command line using net stop dns and net start dns.

If the DNS service is configured as a standard primary or secondary, it initializes the zone tables based on Registry entries located at HKLM | System | CurrentControlSet | Services | DNS | Zones. Each zone has a separate key with values that define the name of the database file, whether it allows dynamic updates, and whether updates must be from secure clients.

When a directory-integrated DNS service starts, it initializes the zone tables based on entries in the Registry and in Active Directory.

Creating a Forward Lookup Zone

The first forward lookup zone you create should be for the root of your DNS namespace. In the Company public namespace used in these examples, for example, the first zone would be for the company.com DNS domain. Proceed as follows:

Procedure 5.11   Creating a Forward Lookup Zone

1. From the START menu, select START | PROGRAMS | ADMINISTRATIVE TOOLS | DNS. The DNS console opens. The DNS tree shows the local server and two empty branches for forward and reverse lookup zones.

2. Right-click the Forward Lookup Zone icon and select NEW ZONE from the fly-out menu. This starts the New Zone Wizard.

3. Click Next. The Zone Type window opens (see Figure 5.16). Leave the default selection at Standard Primary.

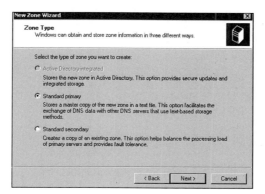

Figure 5.16 New Zone Wizard—Zone Type window showing default selection of Standard Primary.

4. Click Next. The Zone Name window opens (see Figure 5.17). Enter the name of the zone. The example shows a zone for a public DNS namespace.

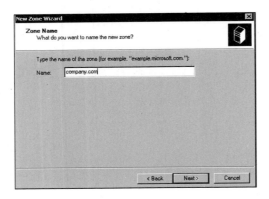

Figure 5.17 New Zone Wizard—Zone Name window.

5. Click Next. The Zone File window opens. The zone table name should match the zone name with a .DNS extension. If you have an existing zone table file, you can import it at this point with the Use This Existing File option.

6. Click Next. The wizard displays a completion window.

7. Click Finish to close the window and return to the DNS console. The new zone appears as a folder under the Forward Lookup Zones icon in the left pane of the window. When that zone icon is highlighted, the associated resource records are displayed in the right pane (see Figure 5.18).

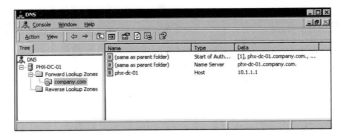

Figure 5.18 DNS console showing new forward lookup zone.

Creating Reverse Lookup Zones

The forward lookup zone handles standard queries such as A record and SRV record requests. The reverse lookup zone will handle those few queries where the client knows the IP address and wants a host name. You can get by without creating reverse lookup zones, but they come in very handy for troubleshooting (and I highly recommend installing them).

Procedure 5.12   **Creating a Reverse Lookup Zone**

1. Right-click the Reverse Lookup Zone icon and select NEW ZONE from the fly-out menu. This starts the New Zone Wizard.

2. Click Next. The Zone Type window opens. Leave the default selection at Standard Primary.

3. Click Next. The Reverse Lookup Zone window opens (see Figure 5.19). Under Network ID, enter the network portion of the subnet the zone will service. The examples in this book use the 10.x networks with a 16-bit subnet mask, so the entry shows 10.1 with the last two octets empty. Each unique number in the second octet requires a separate reverse lookup zone.

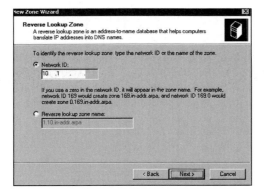

Figure 5.19   New Zone Wizard—Zone File window.

4. Click Next. The Zone File window opens. Leave the default setting. The zone table name should match the zone name with a .DNS extension. If you have an existing zone table, you can import it at this point with the Use This Existing File option.

5. Click Next. The wizard displays a completion window.

6. Click Finish to close the window and return to the DNS console.

After the reverse lookup zones are in place, create a few test host records to make sure the associated PTR records are created successfully. Then test the zone from a client by Pinging the test records and the DNS server.

Configuring Hierarchical Zones

After you have installed your first DNS server and created the first zone, you can now install additional zones if you are building a hierarchical DNS namespace.

If you have a small network, you can probably get along nicely with a flat namespace that keeps all resource records in the same domain. If you are a medium-sized organization just now deploying TCP/IP on a large scale to make way for Windows 2000, you should consider defining a namespace hierarchy that matches your Windows 2000 domain strategy. See Chapter 8, "Designing Windows 2000 Domains," for details on Active Directory and DNS design.

If you are in a large organization with a structured network that uses TCP/IP, you probably already have a DNS hierarchy in place. A big accounting firm might assign servers by functional unit, for example, then by region, then vertical organization, then the company, yielding an FQDN of oracle-w2ks-1379.sap.northamerica.it-consulting.bigacctfirm.com.

If you decide to build a hierarchical DNS namespace, you must choose whether to put a particular child domain in its parent's zone or give it a zone of its own. Giving a child domain its own zone has the advantage of speeding zone table lookups and reducing zone transfer traffic, although this is less critical in Windows 2000 thanks to incremental zone transfers. Usually the decision to split a subdomain into a separate zone is a management decision based on the reporting relationships of the administrative teams.

If you use separate zones, you need to configure the name servers to resolve queries between the zones. You need to plan for two primary situations:

1. Queries from DNS clients in a child zone for records in its parent zone. This requires configuring the root hints file.
2. Queries from DNS clients in a parent zone for records in a child zone. This requires configuring delegation.

Configuring Root Hints

Queries from DNS clients in a child zone for records in its parent zone are resolved by configuring root hints on the DNS server in the child zone to include an authoritative server or servers in the parent zone. Figure 5.20

shows a parent-child DNS domain with each domain contained in a separate zone table.

Figure 5.20 DNS console showing parent-child domains as separate zones.

Start by installing DNS on two servers and creating the zones. The objective of the following steps is to make it possible for a user in the child domain to resolve an address in the parent domain by querying only the DNS server in the child domain. Proceed as follows:

Procedure 5.13 **Configuring Root Hints**

1. Open the DNS console.

2. Right-click the DNS server icon and select PROPERTIES from the fly-out menu. The Properties window opens.

3. Select the Root Hints tab. If the tab isn't there, see the following sidebar.

Recovering Root Hints

If you open the server Properties window and do not find a Root Hints tab, the server may be configured as a root server. If you have a folder with a dot next to it at the top of the DNS tree, this is a root server.

A root server, by definition, cannot have root hints. The server still has a CACHE.DNS file, but it only contains the NS and A record of the root server itself.

You can restore the standard Root Hints tab by deleting the root zone (the folder with the dot next to it). After doing this, open the server Properties window again. The Root Hints tab should be there.

4. Click Add. The Create New Record window opens.

5. Enter the fully qualified DNS name of the root server, with or without the trailing dot, under Server Name.

6. Enter the IP address of the server under Server IP Addresses, and then click Add to put it on the list. If the server has multiple IP addresses, you can add each of them to the list. If you prefer that the queries use one of the addresses preferentially, use the Up and Down buttons to adjust the search list.

7. Click OK to retain the changes and return to the Properties window. Make sure that the root server is at the top of the list.

8. Click OK to save the changes and close the window.

9. Test the configuration by Pinging a host in the parent domain from a client in the child domain. The Ping may take a while, but eventually it will succeed.

Configuring Delegation

The preceding section showed how to get a successful query for a host in a domain higher in the DNS namespace. Getting a successful query for a host lower in the namespace takes a bit more work. Assume, for example, that you are in the company.com DNS domain and you want to Ping a server called alb-w2ks-11 in the branch1.bompany.com DNS domain. The Ping sends the resolver into action and results in a query to DNS for alb-w2ks-11.branch1.company.com.

For this Ping to succeed, the DNS server in the company.com domain must find the A record for the server. But the company.com DNS server has only a copy of the company.com zone table. It must refer the query to a name server in the branch1.company.com domain. This is called *delegation*.

DNS servers, like military brass, always delegate down, not up. Therefore, when configuring delegation in your DNS namespace, start at the root and work your way down as follows:

Procedure 5.14 **Configuring Delegations**

1. Open the DNS console.

2. Right-click the zone name and select NEW | DELEGATION from the fly-out menu. This starts the New Delegation Wizard.

3. Click Next. The Delegated Domain Name window opens.

4. Enter the flat name of the child domain under Delegated Domain. The fully qualified name is built automatically.

5. Click Next. The Name Servers window opens.

6. Click Add. The New Resource Record window opens.

7. Under Server Name, enter the fully qualified name of an authoritative server for the child zone. See the sidebar titled "Lame Delegations" for the reason it is so important to select an authoritative server.

8. Under IP Address, enter the IP address of the name server in the child domain, and then click Add to put it on the list.

9. Click OK to retain the changes and return to the Name Servers window. The server appears on the Server Name list.

10. Click Next. The wizard displays a completion window.

11. Click Finish to save the changes and close the wizard.

The DNS tree in the left pane of the DNS console shows the child domain listed under the parent. The right pane shows an NS record for the child domain name server. Test the delegation by Pinging a host in the child domain from a DNS client in the parent domain. The Ping should succeed nearly immediately. A packet trace shows the referral to the child domain.

Lame Delegations

A common error when configuring delegation is specifying a server that is not authoritative for the specified domain. This results in what is called a *lame delegation*.

A lame delegation is a ticking time bomb. The system appears to work just fine until one day when the non-authoritative server returns the wrong record out of its cache. The DNS server in the parent domain forwards the faulty response to the querying client and puts it in its own cache where other clients get it.

Remember the way you felt when you found out your parents weren't infallible? Well, DNS clients who get faulty responses from lame delegations feel the same way. Make sure that you always delegate to an authoritative server.

Configuring Secondary DNS Servers

This section covers the configuration steps for a secondary DNS server. Secondary servers have a local read-only copy of a zone table that is pulled from a master name server. Secondary servers are authoritative for their zones, but cannot make changes to the zone. This section also covers the steps necessary to configure a master DNS server to accept zone transfer requests from a secondary and to notify the secondary when zone updates have occurred.

The initial service installation for a secondary DNS server is the same as for a primary server. Only the zone configuration steps differ. Load the service drivers using the steps in "Installing and Configuring DNS" earlier in this chapter and then return here.

Enabling Zone Transfers and Update Notifications

A secondary server cannot pull a zone until zone transfers and notifications are enabled at the master DNS server. To enable these options, proceed as follows:

Procedure 5.15 **Enabling Zone Transfers and Notifications**

1. Open the DNS console.

2. Right-click the zone icon and select PROPERTIES from fly-out menu. The Properties window opens.

3. Select the Zone Transfers tab. Select the Allow Zone Transfers option. There are three notification options.

   To Any Server. This is self-explanatory and not recommended. This permits any server or user to pull a zone from your name server. A comprehensive list of host names and IP addresses is not something that you want in unauthorized hands.

   Only to Servers Listed in the Name Servers Tab. This option limits zone transfers to servers with NS records in the zone table. This is the preferred option because it does not involve keeping two lists of servers (actually three lists, because you must also maintain a notification list). If you delegate to untrusted domains, however, you may not want to select this option because it permits administrators of the delegated name server to pull a zone.

   Only to the Following Servers. This option gives you the most control over zone transfers by identifying each authorized secondary individually. This does not prevent an intruder from spoofing the IP address of a secondary to pull a zone, but its better than leaving the door wide open.

4. Click Notify. The Notify window opens.

   Update notification is enabled by default in Windows 2000. This ensures that the zone tables on the secondary name servers are kept current. You have the option in this window of automatically notifying servers in the NS list or specifying servers. If you chose the Only to the Following Servers option in the previous window, you must also individually select secondary servers for notification.

5. Click OK to save the notification settings and return to the Properties window.

6. Click OK to save the zone transfer settings and return to the DNS console.

7. Close the DNS console.

Test both the zone transfer setting and update notification by adding a test record at the primary. After refreshing the DNS console at the secondary, the record appears on the list. If this does not occur, check the IP addresses and notification settings.

Configuring a Secondary DNS Server

An authoritative secondary name server maintains a local copy of the zone table. It uses root hints or a forwarder to handle queries that are outside of the zone.

If you have configured the master server to do zone transfers with only selected secondaries, you must first add the IP address for this server to the list. You should also include the new secondary on the list of secondary servers to notify for updates.

Procedure 5.16 **Configuring a Secondary Server**

1. Open the DNS console.
2. Right-click the Forward Lookup Zone icon and select NEW ZONE from the fly-out menu. The New Zone Wizard starts.
3. Click Next. The Zone Type window opens. (For an example, see Figure 5.16.)
4. Click Next. The Zone Name window opens. Enter the FQDN name of the zone you are going to transfer to this server. For example, enter **company.com**.
5. Click Next. The Master DNS Servers window opens.
6. Enter the IP address of the master name server that you designated for use by this secondary and click Add to add it to the list. You can pull zones from several masters.
7. Click Next. The wizard displays a completion window.
8. Click Finish to close the wizard and return to the DNS console. The zone is transferred automatically.
9. Verify by expanding the tree that the zone transferred correctly. If you get a big red X with a *Zone Not Loaded* error, press F5 to refresh. If the red X persists, you possibly forgot to enable zone transfers at the master server and add the secondary to the zone transfer list.

After the secondary server is operational, configure clients to use it and verify by Pinging hosts inside and outside the zone. If Pings outside the zone do not work, check your root hints at the primary and secondary.

Integrating DNS Zones into Active Directory

When a zone is integrated into the Directory, the ASCII zone table is abandoned and Directory objects are created for each resource record. You must run DNS on a domain controller to Directory-integrate the zone. You can only Directory-integrate a primary zone. See "Active Directory Integration" earlier in this chapter for details on Directory-integrated operations. When you meet the conditions for integrating zone and are ready to migrate a primary zone to a Directory-integrated zone, proceed as follows:

Procedure 5.17   Integrating Primary Zone into Active Directory

1. Open the DNS console.
2. Right-click the zone that you want to integrate into the directory and select PROPERTIES from the fly-out menu. The Properties window opens.
3. At the General tab, adjacent to the Type entry, click Change. The Change Zone Type window opens.
4. Click OK to make the change. A confirmation window appears.
5. Click OK to confirm and return to the Properties window. The Type now shows Active Directory—integrated.
6. Click OK to close the window and return to the DNS console.

Verify that the zone entries were transferred to the Directory as follows:

Procedure 5.18   Verifying Resource Record Integration

1. Open the Active Directory Users and Computers console via START | PROGRAMS | ADMINISTRATIVE TOOLS | ACTIVE DIRECTORY USERS AND COMPUTERS.
2. From the CONSOLE menu, select VIEW | ADVANCED VIEW. This exposes the System folder, among other items.

3. Expand the tree to `System`, `MicrosoftDNS`. The zone table displays as a folder containing dnsNode objects. Each of these objects represents a resource record. Figure 5.21 shows an example.

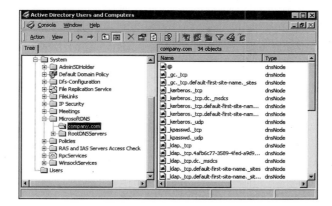

Figure 5.21 `Active Directory Users and Computers` console showing contents of `company.com` zone table under MicrosoftDNS container.

The dnsNode objects are not manageable as resource records from the `Active Directory Users and Computers` console. DNS zone management is still done from the `DNS` console or by using the DNSCMD utility.

Configuring a Caching-Only Server

Caching-only servers are used to speed up query response by collecting a large number of cached records in response to client lookups. A caching-only server does not have a copy of a zone table and is therefore not authoritative. It obtains resource records from other DNS servers on behalf of clients.

The name cache is kept in memory, so make sure that the machine has lots of RAM. If you want to flush the cache, you can stop and start the DNS service or use the DNSCMD utility from the Windows 2000 Resource Kit. The syntax is `DNSCMD /clearcache`. Purging defeats the purpose of a caching-only server, however; so if you find yourself purging frequently to maintain performance, consider getting more memory.

A caching-only server does not pull zone transfers, so there is no need to add it to the list of secondaries at the master DNS server.

The initial DNS service installation is the same as for a primary DNS server. Only the configuration steps differ. Load the service drivers using the steps in "Installing and Configuring DNS," and then return here to configure the service.

Procedure 5.19 **Configuring a Caching-Only Server**

1. Open the DNS console.

2. Right-click the server icon and select PROPERTIES from the fly-out menu. The Properties window opens.

3. Select the Root Hints tab.

4. Delete the InterNIC root servers from the list (if they are there) using the Remove button.

5. Click Add. The New Resource Record window opens with the Name Server (NS) tab showing.

6. Enter the FQDN of the master name server and its IP address. Click Add to add the IP address to the list. You can configure multiple name servers. They do not need to be in the same zone.

7. Click OK to save the entries and return to the Properties window.

8. Click OK to save the list and return to the DNS console.

9. Close the console.

Verify that the caching-only server works by Pinging a remote server name from a client that is configured to use the server for DNS. Ping several host names to stock up the cache, and then try the same names from another desktop. The response time should be much quicker.

Configuring a DNS Server to Use a Forwarder

A DNS server can be configured to send an out-of-zone query to another on the chance that the server has already located the record and has it in cache. If the bet fails and the record is not available, the forwarding server walks the tree to find the record on its own.

Before configuring a server to send queries to a forwarder, it is considered good manners to inform the administrator. A forwarding server has the potential for sending many thousands of queries to the forwarder.

The example steps assume that you are configuring an existing DNS server inside a firewall and using a forwarder outside the firewall to resolve Internet addresses. Configure the forwarding option as follows:

Procedure 5.20 **Configuring a DNS Server to Use a Forwarder**

1. Open the DNS console.

2. Right-click the server name and select PROPERTIES from the fly-out menu. The Properties window opens.

3. Select the Forwarders tab.

4. Select the Enable Forwarders option.

5. Enter the IP address of the forwarder and click Add to add it to the list.

6. Leave the Forward Time-Out (seconds) option set for five seconds. The forwarder should answer out of its cache, which doesn't take very long. If the forwarder takes longer than five seconds to respond, it is probably doing a search.

7. Click OK to save the settings and return to the DNS console.

8. Stop and start the DNS service by right-clicking the server icon and selecting All Tasks, Stop, and then All Tasks, Start.

Verify that the forwarder works by Pinging an Internet host name from a DNS client. The Ping succeeds after a short time delay. If the Ping does not succeed, check the IP addresses to make sure that you are pointed at the correct server.

Managing Dynamic DNS

Keeping a traditional DNS zone table updated with new resource records requires lots of manual work. A large network with thousands of servers needs a full-time administrator just to manage DNS. With Dynamic DNS, clients and servers can register their A records automatically at boot time. Application servers can register SRV and other specialized records. Outdated records can be scavenged periodically to prevent clutter. It's a fairly automated process. Dynamic DNS probably will not do away with the need for full-time DNS management in a big network, but it should help rescue the administrator from a little of the tedium.

This section covers how to enable Dynamic DNS in Windows 2000, how to configure security so that only trusted clients can register their resource records, and how to maintain the zone table to prevent accumulating outdated records.

Configuring a Dynamic Zone

After you have installed and configured a Windows 2000 DNS server, enable Dynamic DNS for a particular zone as follows:

Procedure 5.21 **Configuring a Dynamic Zone**

1. Open the DNS console.
2. Right-click the zone that you want to configure for Dynamic DNS and select PROPERTIES from the fly-out menu. The Properties window opens.
3. In the Allow Dynamic Updates drop-down box, select Yes.
4. Click OK to save the change and return to the DNS console.
5. Verify that dynamic registration works by opening a command prompt at a Windows 2000 client that is configured to use this DNS server and enter IPCONFIG /registerdns. The host record is added to the zone table automatically. You may need to refresh the console to see it.

You must configure the reverse lookup zones for dynamic updates, as well. If you fail to do this, DNS will add A records but not PTR records when new clients come online.

Managing Dynamic DNS Security

If you enable Dynamic DNS with no security options, it is possible that a computer can come online with the same name as a host that is already in the zone table and overwrite the A record. This has the potential to be very disruptive. Imagine that your company post office has the name MAIN-PO. A user could bring a workstation online called MAIN-PO and DNS would obediently overwrite the A record of the post office. If it is a malicious user doing this, you have a real problem.

The only way to avoid this behavior in Windows 2000 Dynamic DNS is to Directory-integrate the zone and require that Dynamic DNS clients be members of the domain. This avoids the A record overwrite problem because two computers are not permitted to have the same name in an Active Directory domain. See "Integrating DNS Zones into Active Directory" earlier in this chapterfor the steps to convert a primary zone to a Directory-integrated zone.

After a zone has been integrated into the Directory, the resource records are protected by Windows 2000 object security. DNS clients that are not domain members cannot dynamically register their host records. Figure 5.22 shows a System Log error from the DSNAPI service on a Windows 2000 DNS client that has attempted to register a host record when it is not a member of the domain.

Figure 5.22 Event Properties from System Log showing rejected registration attempt by client that is not a domain member.

The disadvantage to this security method, of course, is that not all your desktops are running Windows 2000. Many of them aren't even running Windows. You can dynamically register down-level Windows clients using Windows 2000 DHCP. See "Configuring DHCP to Support DNS" later in this chapter for details. For non-Windows clients, you must add the names manually to the zone table. This situation may change after Windows 2000 incorporates the provisions of RFC 2137.

Disabling DNS on an Interface

If you do not Directory-integrate a dynamic zone, you can at least take steps to prevent outsiders from registering records on your server. If you have a DNS server with two network interfaces, for example, one connected to the public network and the other connected to the local network, you can disable DNS (and Dynamic DNS registrations) on the public interface. Do this as follows:

Procedure 5.22   Disabling DNS on an Interface

1. Open the DNS console.
2. Right-click the server icon and select PROPERTIES from the fly-out menu. The Properties window opens with the Interfaces tab selected.
3. Under Listen On, select the Only the Following IP Addresses option.
4. Use the Remove button to delete all but the private interface.
5. Click OK to save the new settings and return to the DNS console.
6. Close the console.

> **Registry Tip: Dynamic Updates**
>
> The Listen On option sets the following Registry value:
>
> ```
> Key:      HKLM | System | CurrentControlSet | Services | TcpIp\Parameters |
>           ➟Interfaces | {GUID}
> Value:    DisableDynamicUpdate
> Data:     0x1 disables updates; 0x0 enables updates
> ```

Configuring Scavenging

Dynamically registered records can become obsolete when machines crash or come on and off the network at infrequent intervals, as laptops are prone to do. When scavenging is enabled, DNS applies an aging value to dynamically registered resource records. Scavenging removes records that have not been refreshed for more than 14 days.

If you enable scavenging, the format of the zone table changes to allow room for the aging value. This is a proprietary change, so you cannot move the zone file to a non-Windows 2000 name server. You can pull a zone to a standard secondary, which filters the aging information and writes a standard zone table. This also means third-party name servers can be used as secondaries.

Scavenging can be enabled for a single zone or for all zones on the server. Enable scavenging for a zone as follows:

Procedure 5.23 **Configuring Scavenging**

1. Open the DNS console.

2. Right-click the zone icon and select PROPERTIES from the fly-out menu. The Properties window opens.

3. At the General tab, click Aging. The Zone Aging/Scavenging Properties window opens.

4. Select the Scavenge Stale Resource Records option.

5. Leave the default seven-day values for No-Refresh Interval and Refresh Interval.

6. Click OK to save the settings. A warning message appears informing you that the zone table record format will be changed.

7. Click Yes to acknowledge the warning and apply the change.

8. At the Properties window, click OK to save the changes and close the window.

From this point forward, any new dynamic registrations are assigned an aging value. Old records will be purged when scavenge runs. Set scavenging to run periodically as follows:

Procedure 5.24 **Setting Periodic Scavenging**

1. Right-click the server icon and select PROPERTIES from the fly-out menu. The Properties window opens.

2. Select the Advanced tab (see Figure 5.23).

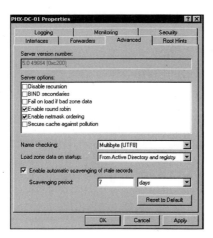

Figure 5.23 DNS Server Properties window—Advanced tab showing automatic scavenging enabled.

3. Select the `Enable Automatic Scavenging of Stale Records` option.

4. Leave the `Scavenging Period` set for the default of seven days.

5. Click `OK` to save the settings and close the window.

You should arrange to check the status of the zone table periodically to make sure that scavenge is working. If you see many old records that should have been scavenged, try scavenging them manually. If that succeeds, check your periodic scavenging settings. If it does not succeed, make sure that you have correctly configured scavenging to work for the zone.

WINS Forwarding

Although WINS forwarding is not strictly a Dynamic DNS feature, it is covered here because it provides essentially the same service.

In NT4 DNS, Microsoft introduced a couple of new DNS resource records, WINS and WINS-R, that contain the IP address of a WINS server to use in the event that a host address cannot be located in the local zone table. This record is added and configured using a special properties page in the zone properties. Access the page by right-clicking the zone icon and selecting PROPERTIES from the fly-out menu and then selecting the WINS tab. A similar page for the WINS-R record is present in the `Properties` window for a reverse lookup zone. Figure 5.24 shows an example.

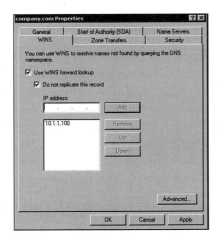

Figure 5.24 `Zone Properties` window showing `WINS` tab.

The Use WINS Forward Lookup option is disabled by default. When selected, it creates a WINS resource record. A Windows 2000 DNS server recognizes this WINS record and uses it to locate a WINS server to use for forwarding.

If you elect to use WINS forwarding, add the IP address of at least one WINS server to the list by entering the IP address and clicking Add. You can specify more than one WINS server for fault tolerance, but be careful of selecting too many. This option can seriously delay a name query because WINS is slower than DNS. Adding lots of WINS servers is a sure way to degrade lookup performance.

The Do No Replicate This Record option is not selected by default. It prevents replicating the WINS record to DNS servers that do not recognize the record type.

Configuring Advanced DNS Server Parameters

Several DNS server options are collected under the Advanced tab in the DNS server Properties window. Several of these options are covered elsewhere in the chapter. This section covers the remaining options.

The advanced options access these as follows:

Procedure 5.25 Accessing Advanced Server Parameters

1. Open the DNS console.
2. Right-click the server icon and select PROPERTIES from the fly-out menu. The Properties window opens.
3. Select the Advanced tab

The following options are available in this window:

- Disable Recursion. A default Windows 2000 server accepts recursive queries. This enables the server to do DNS searches on behalf of clients and is the preferred configuration. Select the Disable Recursion option if you want the server to accept only iterative queries.

- BIND Secondaries. By default, Windows 2000 does a zone transfer by copying multiple records in compressed format. If you have secondary name servers running BIND versions earlier than 4.9.4, select the BIND Secondaries option to perform zone transfers one record at a time in uncompressed form.

- Fail On Load if Bad Zone Data. See the sidebar titled "Starting DNS from a BIND Boot File."

- **Enable Round Robin.** See the sidebar titled "DNS and Round-Robin" earlier in this chapter.

- **Enable Netmask Ordering.** If a zone table has multiple resource records that fit a particular query, this option causes the DNS server to sort the responses so that the records in the same subnet as the querying client are listed first. If this option is not checked, the responses are ordered as they appear in the zone table.

- **Secure Cache Against Pollution.** All name servers cache query results to speed subsequent queries for the same record. One possible attack method is to use indirection to get an improper record in the cache where it can then send users to an unsecured site. If a user browses the Internet to www.company.com and the user's name server has an alias for www.company.com that points at www.competitor.com, for example, the A record for www.competitor.com would be added to the local name server cache. Returning a record from one DNS domain in response to a query for a record in another DNS domain is called *cache pollution*. The Secure Cache Against Pollution prevents this problem by caching only query results that match the root domain of the query.

- **Name Checking.** By default, Microsoft's DNS permits any ANSI character to be used in a DNS host name. This includes special characters not included in standard DNS names as defined by RFC 1123, "Requirements for Internet Hosts—Application and Support." If you have non-Microsoft name servers, or expect to interface with non-Microsoft name servers, select the Strict RFC (ANSI) option. If you have only Microsoft DNS and you want to enable Unicode host names, select the Multibyte (UTF8) option.

- **Enable Automatic Scavenging of Stale Records.** See the "Configuring Scavenging" steps earlier in the chapter.

Starting DNS from a BIND Boot File

Windows 2000 supports file-based booting like that used by BIND. If you need to boot a Windows 2000 DNS server using a boot file from a BIND server, copy the file to \WINNT\System32\DNS, and then configure the boot method as follows. (The \WINNT\System32\DNS\Samples directory contains a boot file you can use for a template.)

Procedure 5.26   Starting DNS from a BIND File

1. Open the DNS console.

2. Right-click the DNS server icon and select PROPERTIES from the fly-out menu. The Properties window opens.

3. Select the Advanced tab.

4. Under Load Zone Data on Startup, select From File.

5. Click OK to save the changes and close the window.

6. Close the console.

If the BIND file contains data that is not permitted in Microsoft DNS zone files, such as giving an alias (CNAME) record the same name as the host, the DNS service will ignore the bad records, log them to the Event Log, and continue to load the zone table. If you would prefer to abort the zone table load in case of an error, proceed as follows:

Procedure 5.27   Setting the Fail on Load if Bad Zone Option

1. Open the DNS console.

2. Right-click the DNS server icon and select PROPERTIES from the fly-out menu. The Properties window opens.

3. Select the Advanced tab.

4. Under Server Options, select Fail on Load if Bad Zone Data.

5. Click OK to save the changes and close the window.

6. Close the console.

Examining Zone Tables with NSLOOKUP

When you run into problems with DNS, the NSLOOKUP utility is the tool of choice for tracking down problems. NSLOOKUP enables you to perform selective zone transfers so that you can examine resource records in the zone table. You can also use NSLOOKUP to verify that a DNS server exists, find out what zone tables it manages, verify that the DNS server has a particular resource record, and to browse the resource records as if you were browsing a directory.

NSLOOKUP has two modes: Interactive and Non-Interactive. If you run NSLOOKUP and specify parameters on the command line, you run the utility in Non-Interactive mode. To see the IP address for www.guam.net and the name servers that are authoritative for the zone that holds the A record, for example, issue the NSLOOKUP command followed by the name of the server as follows:

```
C:\>nslookup www.guam.net c.root-servers.net.
4.33.192.in-addr.arpa    nameserver = NS.PSI.NET
NS.PSI.NET       internet address = 192.33.4.10
Name:    www.guam.net
Served by:
- NS.GUAM.net
          198.81.233.2
          GUAM.net
```

To use the Interactive mode, just enter **NSLOOKUP** with no parameters. When you enter Interactive mode, you get a listing of the default name server followed by a command prompt, >:

```
U:\>nslookup
Default Server:  dns1.primenet.net
Address:  206.165.5.10
>
```

From the command prompt, enter a question mark to see the list of NSLOOKUP commands:

```
> ?
Commands:    (identifiers are shown in uppercase, [] means optional)
NAME            - print info about the host/domain NAME using default server
NAME1 NAME2     - as above, but use NAME2 as server
help or ?       - print info on common commands
set OPTION      - set an option
    all         - print options, current server and host
    [no]debug   - print debugging information
    [no]d2      - print exhaustive debugging information
    [no]defname - append domain name to each query
    [no]recurse - ask for recursive answer to query
    [no]search  - use domain search list
    [no]vc      - always use a virtual circuit
    domain=NAME - set default domain name to NAME
    srchlist=N1[/N2/.../N6] - set domain to N1 and search list to N1,N2, etc.
    root=NAME   - set root server to NAME
    retry=X     - set number of retries to X
    timeout=X   - set initial time-out interval to X seconds
    querytype=X - set query type, e.g., A,ANY,CNAME,MX,NS,PTR,SOA
    type=X      - synonym for querytype
    class=X     - set query class to one of IN (Internet), CHAOS, HESIOD or ANY
server NAME     - set default server to NAME, using current default server
lserver NAME    - set default server to NAME, using initial server
```

```
finger [USER]    - finger the optional NAME at the current default host
root             - set current default server to the root
ls [opt] DOMAIN [> FILE] - list addresses in DOMAIN (optional: output to FILE)
    -a           - list canonical names and aliases
    -d           - list all records
    -t TYPE      - list records of the given type (e.g. A,CNAME,MX,NS,PTR etc.)
view FILE        - sort an 'ls' output file and view it with pg
exit             - exit the program
```

If you want to see the default settings for NSLOOKUP, use set all. (You cannot just type **set** like a DOS command. This makes NSLOOKUP think that you are querying for a server named set.)

```
> set all
Default Server:  dns1.primenet.net
Address:  206.165.5.10
Set options:
  nodebug       defname       search        recurse
  nod2          novc          noignoretc    port=53
  querytype=A   class=IN      timeout=2     retry=3
  root=ns.nic.ddn.mil.        domain=company.com
  srchlist=company.com
```

The following sections cover the most common NSLOOKUP interactive commands and Set parameters.

server

Use this command to change the name of the DNS server that fields the NSLOOKUP queries. Be sure to use FQDNs with a trailing dot. If your default name server is phx-dns-01.company.com, but you want to troubleshoot a DNS server in the Denver office dnv-dns-01.region.company.com, for example, you would enter the following:

```
> server dnv-dns-01.region.company.com.
Default server: dnv-dns-01.region.company.com
Address: 10.5.1.10
```

lserver

The lserver command works like server, but always uses the default name server. This enables you to escape from a dead end when you use the server command to get onto a name server that is not authoritative and cannot resolve another server name. If you use server to change to a name server that has no zone table, you will not be able to use the server command to go to another server because it can't resolve the new host name. The lserver command gets you back to your home DNS server.

root

This command works like the `server` command to change the default DNS server, but it selects the name from the top of the server list in the CACHE.DNS file. This could be an InterNIC root server or, if the server is a private root server, it would be an internal name server.

ls

This command lists the resource records in a particular zone. In essence, `ls` does a zone transfer of the selected record type. You can limit the scope of the transfer by specifying a record type using the -t switch. Here is an example showing the host records (A records) in the `company.com` zone:

```
> ls -t a company.com.
[phx-dc-01.company.com]
 company.com.                        A      10.1.1.1
 gc._msdcs.company.com.              A      10.1.1.1
 alb-dns-01.branch1.company.com.     A      10.3.1.1
 phx-dc-01.company.com.              A      10.1.1.1
 phx-nt4s-30.company.com.            A      10.1.1.201
```

If you specify any as the record type, or use the -d switch with `ls`, NSLOOKUP returns the entire zone table. Use caution: This can be quite an extensive list on some name servers. Use the indirection pipe (>) to save the output of `ls` to a file.

You may be thinking that `ls` represents a security problem. You would be correct. Because `ls` works by performing a zone transfer, you can block it by controlling the servers that are allowed to pull a zone transfer. See "Enabling Zone Transfers and Update Notifications" earlier in this chapter for details.

set [no]debug

When `debug` is set, the report from an interactive command includes debugging information. This debugging information shows the results of a query including intermediate name servers included in the search. The following example is the result of a recursive query for `whitehouse.gov` that started at an InterNIC root server and worked its way down to find the associated IP address.

```
> set debug
> whitehouse.gov.
Server:  ns.nic.ddn.mil
Address:  192.112.36.4
. . . . . . . . . . . .
Got answer:
    HEADER:
        opcode = QUERY, id = 5, rcode = NOERROR
        header flags:  response, want recursion
        questions = 1,  answers = 1,  authority records = 2,  additional = 2
```

```
    QUESTIONS:
        whitehouse.gov, type = A, class = IN
    ANSWERS:
    ->  whitehouse.gov
        internet address = 198.137.241.30
        ttl = 172800 (2 days)
    AUTHORITY RECORDS:
    ->  whitehouse.gov
        nameserver = SEC1.DNS.PSI.NET
        ttl = 172800 (2 days)
    ADDITIONAL RECORDS:
    ->  SEC1.DNS.PSI.NET
        internet address = 38.8.92.2
        ttl = 172800 (2 days)
------------
Non-authoritative answer:
Name:    whitehouse.gov
Address:  198.137.241.30
```

The debug option is especially useful for locating improper referrals caused by incorrect delegations.

Set [no]d2

Set this parameter if you aren't satisfied knowing the results of the query and you also need to know the exact format of the query itself. Here is the additional d2 information from a whitehouse.gov lookup.

```
> set d2
> whitehouse.gov.
;truncated to show differences from standard debug listing
------------
SendRequest(), len 32
    HEADER:
        opcode = QUERY, id = 10, rcode = NOERROR
        header flags:  query, want recursion
        questions = 1,  answers = 0,  authority records = 0,  additional = 0

    QUESTIONS:
        whitehouse.gov, type = A, class = IN
```

set [no]defname

You may have noticed a trailing period at the end of each server name in the example lookups. The trailing dot tells NSLOOKUP that the name is fully qualified. If you do not include the period, NSLOOKUP appends the default domain name for the client. If you have a hard time remembering to include the trailing period, you can use set nodefname to tell NSLOOKUP not to append the domain name.

set [no]recurse

If you want NSLOOKUP queries to emulate a DNS server rather than a DNS client, queries should be configured as iterative and not recursive. Use this switch to change the query type as needed.

set querytype

You can limit or change the scope of a query by setting a certain record type. If you want to query for the MX records on a name server, for example, give the following command:

```
> set type=mx
> whitehouse.gov.
Server:  whitehouse.gov
Address:  198.137.241.30

whitehouse.gov  MX preference = 100, mail exchanger = storm.eop.gov
storm.eop.gov  internet address = 198.137.241.51
```

Configuring DHCP to Support DNS

Windows 2000 is the only Windows product that currently supports Dynamic DNS registration. Microsoft may include the feature in upcoming service releases for Windows 9x. If you want to move more quickly to reduce your reliance on WINS, you can take advantage of the DHCP proxy features for Dynamic DNS registration. This proxy makes it possible to move large numbers of desktops and servers over to DNS-enabled name resolution very quickly.

The DHCP proxy feature in Windows 2000 was structured using the provisions of Internet Draft draft-ietf-dhc-dhcp-dns-10.txt, "Interaction Between DHCP and DNS." This draft outlines the use of a new DHCP option called *Client FQDN*, option 81. This option includes a new message format that a client can use to inform the DHCP server of its FQDN. The DHCP server uses this information to send a DNS Update message to the DNS server on behalf of the client.

This section includes instructions for installing DHCP, authorizing it to work in a Windows 2000 domain, and configuring the scope options necessary to support Dynamic DNS proxy. Except for the new look of the MMC console and a few provisions for vendor-specific options and class IDs, the *Dynamic Host Configuration Protocol* (DHCP) service in Windows 2000 is virtually identical to its NT4 SP4/SP5 counterpart.

If you are upgrading from NT4 SP4/SP5, the only change is an upgrade to the Jet database that holds the DHCP records. See Chapter 2, "Performing Upgrades and Automated Installations," for steps to take if the Jet upgrade fails.

Installing DHCP

Before installing DHCP, you should inventory your current IP address assignments and ensure that you know the hosts that have static addresses. Windows 2000 DHCP, along with NT4 SP4, will use ICMP to verify that an address is free before leasing it, but that verification is not comprehensive. When you are ready to install DHCP and set aside addresses to lease, proceed as follows:

Procedure 5.28 **Installing DHCP Service Drivers**

1. From Control Panel, open the Add/Remove Programs applet.
2. Click Add/Remove Windows Components. The Windows Components Wizard starts with the focus set to the Windows Components window.
3. Highlight Networking Services and click Details. The Networking Services window opens.
4. Select Dynamic Host Configuration Protocol (DHCP) and click OK to save the change and return to the Windows Components window.
5. Click Next. The Configuring Components window opens and the drivers begin loading. When the drivers have loaded and the configuration is complete, the wizard displays a successful completion window.
6. Click Finish to close the window and return to the Add/Remove Programs window.
7. Close the Add/Remove Programs window.

At this point, you can begin configuring the service. There is no need to restart.

Authorizing a DHCP Server

After the service drivers have been loaded, open the DHCP console (see Figure 5.25). The server icon shows a red down arrow, meaning that the service has not started. If you are installing the service on a domain controller or domain member server, the status in the right pane will show Not Authorized. If you are installing in a workgroup, press F5 to refresh the console. The server status should change to Running.

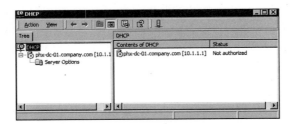

Figure 5.25 DHCP console showing newly installed
DHCP server in a pre-authorized state.

Windows 2000 DHCP has a feature that attempts to prevent rogue DHCP
servers from coming on the wire and leasing improper IP addresses. This feature requires a DHCP server to be *authorized*. An authorized DHCP server
has a DHCPClass object in Active Directory. This object can be viewed
using the AD Sites and Services console. It is stored under Services,
NetServices. Figure 5.26 shows an example.

Figure 5.26 AD Sites and Services console
showing authorized DHCP server.

Authorize a DHCP server by right-clicking the server icon in the right pane
and selecting AUTHORIZE from the fly-out menu. The DHCP object is added
to the directory automatically. Then refresh the console with F5. The server
status changes to Running.

Verify that the server is issuing addresses by renewing an existing DHCP
client. If you are in a routed network that uses DHCP helpers, you need to
configure the BOOTP relay agents at your routers to point at the new
DHCP server. After you have verified basic operability, take the server out of
production by deactivating the scope while you configure the scope options.

Configuring Scope Options

While the scope is deactivated, select the scope options that you want to include in the DHCP ACK packet that is returned to the clients along with their leased address. The list of scope options does not include the new option 81, FQDN Client option. This option is configured separately as part of scope properties. It is covered in the next section. At this point, you need to configure options for DNS server(s), a DNS domain name, and a default gateway. You may have other options you want to include, but these are the basics. To configure scope options, proceed as follows:

Procedure 5.29   **Configuring Scope Options**

1. Right-click the server icon and select NEW SCOPE from the fly-out menu. The New Scope Wizard starts.

2. Click Next. The Scope Name window opens. Give the scope a name and description that can help you identify it when it displays in the console.

3. Click Next. The IP Address Range window opens (see Figure 5.27). Enter an address range and subnet mask for the scope. The example shows the private network of 10.1.0.0 with a 24-bit subnet mask.

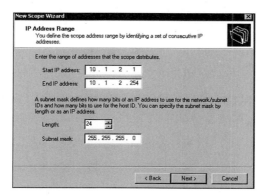

Figure 5.27   New Scope Wizard—IP Address Range window.

4. Click Next. The Add Exclusions window opens. If you have addresses within the scope that are already assigned to hosts or need to be set aside for static assignment, exclude them here.

5. Click Next. The Lease Duration window opens. The new default lease duration is eight days, up from three days in NT4. This gives enough time for a user to go on a week's vacation and still get the old address back. If you have a shortage of addresses, you can cut the lease duration back to eight hours.

6. Click Next. The Configure Your DHCP Options window opens. Let's skip the rest of the wizard and configure the options from the DHCP console. It's faster. Select No, I WILL Configure These Options Later.

7. Click Next. The wizard displays a completion window.

8. Click Finish to close the wizard and return to the DHCP console. The console now shows the new scope with its address pool and exclusions (see Figure 5.28).

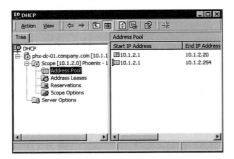

Figure 5.28   DHCP console showing new scope and address pool.

9. Right-click the Scope Options window and select NEW SCOPE OPTIONS from the fly-out menu. The Scope Options window opens (see Figure 5.29).

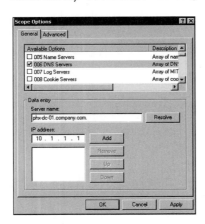

Figure 5.29   Scope Options window showing selection for DNS servers.

10. Select Option 006 DNS Servers. Enter the FQDN of the DNS server that you want to use for this scope and click Resolve to get its IP address. (I prefer this method because it quickly validates that the DNS configuration is correct.)

11. Select `Option 015 DNS Domain Name`. Enter the DNS domain name (same as DNS Suffix) you want to distribute to clients in this scope. This name must exist as a DNS zone on the server selected in option 006.

12. Select other options you want to include in the configuration packet. Typical entries are `Option 003 Router`, `Option 046 WINS/NBNS Servers`, and `046 WINT/NBT Node Type`.

13. Click `OK` to set the options and close the window.

14. Right-click the `Scope` icon and select ACTIVE. This permits the DHCP service to respond to DHCP requests and makes the address pool in the scope available. The status of the scope changes to `Active` in the right pane of the console.

When a DHCP client leases an address from this server, it gets the IP address of one or more DNS servers. If the client is running Windows 2000, the client registers its leased address, both the `A` and `PTR` record, with DNS. You can verify this by checking the DNS console to see whether new addresses are appearing as Windows 2000 DHCP clients that were not DNS clients before get their new DHCP configuration packets.

Dynamic Client Icons

If you highlight the `Address Leases` icon and look at the list of active DHCP clients, you will notice that the icons for dynamically registered clients have fountain pen emblems.

FQDN Scope Option Configurations

If a DHCP client is not running Windows 2000 or some other client that supports Dynamic DNS updates, it will not register its leased DHCP address in DNS. This limits the effectiveness of DNS as a name repository in a peer networking environment, at least if you want to get away from running WINS.

The new `Client FQDN` option is exposed as a properties page for a scope or the DHCP server as a whole. View and configure the new options by opening the `Properties` window for the scope icon and selecting the `DNS` tab. The `Automatically Update DHCP Client Information in DNS` selection enables option 81, `Client FQDN`, for all addresses in the scope. The remaining options are dimmed if this is deselected. Here is a list of the functions for the various configuration options:

- `Update DNS Only if DHCP Client Requests`. This is the preferred option. If the client has selected the `Register This Connection's Addresses in DNS` option under `TCP/IP Properties`, the client takes responsibility for updating DNS and the DHCP server bows out.

- Always Update DNS. This option overrides the Register This Connection's Addresses in DNS setting at the client and uses the FQDN message from the client to register. If this option is selected, a flag is toggled in the option 81 message to the client telling it not to update DNS.

- Discard Forward (Name-to-Address) Lookups When Lease Expires. This option is selected by default. It removes the A record when the lease expires. The DNS scavenger does this, too, but it's better to keep the zone tidy day by day.

- Enable Updates for DNS Clients That Do Not Support Dynamic Updates. This option is not set by default. It provides a way for down-level clients to dynamically register their resource records. If you are prepared to have a couple of thousand resource records appear in your zone table during tomorrow morning's logon, select this option.

If you select the last option that registers down-level clients by proxy, you'll see the icons appear as dynamic registration icons (fountain pen emblem) as the clients renew their leases. As clients renew their leases, they renew their Dynamic DNS registrations, as well.

Trace of DHCP

Figure 5.30 shows a DHCP ACK packet captured by Network Monitor. The Option field at the bottom of the listing shows the new Dynamic DNS option entries along with the other options configured for the scope. If you ever experience DHCP pains that will not go away, Network Monitor is a good way to fluoroscope your network to find the problem.

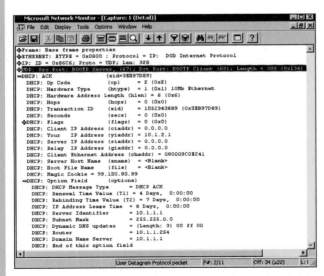

Figure 5.30   Network Monitor capture of DHCP ACK packet containing configuration options that include Dynamic DNS settings.

Moving Forward

This chapter covered a lot of ground, but it's worth taking time to get a solid DNS infrastructure that can handle dynamic record registrations and resolve addresses throughout the namespace. A reliable and fully functional Dynamic DNS system is critical to the success of a Windows 2000 deployment. It is not an exaggeration to predict that you will save a week of troubleshooting and downtime as you roll out Active Directory–based domains for every day you spend refining and testing the DNS design that underpins them.

No deployment strategy is complete without security as a top item on the agenda. Before setting up for a domain deployment, therefore, it's important to take a look in the next chapter at the new distributed authentication security used in Windows 2000, Kerberos.

6

Understanding Network Access Security and Kerberos

EVERY ORGANIZATION HAS VALUABLE RESOURCES it must protect from theft, vandalism, and even innocent clumsiness. Whether those resources take the form of cartons in a warehouse or files on a hard drive, the fundamental aspects of security remain the same:

- **Authentication.** Individuals must be verified to have authorized access to controlled areas.
- **Access control.** All possible entry points must be blocked and guarded. Sensitive areas may need additional internal access controls.
- **Audit.** Access must be monitored and responsible personnel informed immediately if an access infraction occurs.

This chapter covers the authentication and audit features available in Windows 2000. Access control is covered in Chapter 14, "Managing File Systems Security," and Chapter 15, "Managing Shared Resources." Additional authentication and access control information pertaining specifically to remote access is covered in Chapter 17, "Managing Remote Access and Internet Routing."

Access Security Overview

Since its inception, classic NT has used a proprietary authentication scheme called *NT LAN Manager* (NTLM) *Challenge-Response.* With Windows 2000, Microsoft adopted a public domain authentication scheme called *Kerberos.* Kerberos was developed at MIT as part of Project Athena. It takes its name from the mythological three-headed hound that guarded the gates of the underworld in Roman mythology. (If you're a humanities scholar making the transition to Information Technology, you may wonder why Project Athena picked a Roman mythic creature rather than the Greek counterpart, Cerberus. I can't help you. Computers and classics just don't mix.)

Windows 2000 uses version 5 of Kerberos as defined by RFC 1510, "The Kerberos Network Authentication Service V5." Many Kerberos implementations also use an API library described in RFC 1964, "The Kerberos Version 5 Generic Security Service Application Programming Interface (GSS-API) Mechanism." Windows 2000 does not use the GSS-API directly. Instead, it uses a similar set of function calls exposed by the Security Support Provider Interface (SSPI).

Because the authentication mechanism is designed to be as transparent as possible, it isn't all that obvious that Kerberos is at work rather than the classic NTLM Challenge-Response. Windows 2000 uses Kerberos in the following circumstances:

- Authenticating users logging on to Windows 2000 domain controllers
- Authenticating users logging on to Windows 2000 servers and workstations that are members of a Windows 2000 domain
- Authenticating users logging on to standalone Windows 2000 servers and workstations
- Authenticating users accessing a Windows 2000 server or workstation from a Windows 9x client configured with the Active Directory add-on

NTLM Challenge-Response authentication is used in the following instances:

- Authenticating users logging on to Windows 2000 servers and workstations that are members of a classic NT domain (or accessing a classic NT domain from a Windows 2000 domain via a trust relationship)
- Authenticating users accessing a Windows 2000 server or workstation from a classic NT server or workstation
- Authenticating users accessing a Windows 2000 server from a standard Windows 9x or 3.1x client

If you find yourself wondering how to verify this, you can enable auditing and examine the logged transactions, because a user logs on both at the console of a member workstation and the console of the server. See the "Auditing" section later in this chapter.

Functional Description of NT Security Architecture

It's difficult to point your finger at one place in the Windows 2000 architectural model and say, "Here is where you find security-handling services." Security is integrated into every aspect of the operating system. The majority of security decisions are controlled by the *Local Security Authority* (LSA). The LSA calls upon *logon services,* such as WINLOGON and NETLOGON, to obtain *security credentials* from users. After it has obtained the user's credentials, the LSA performs its authentication chores with the help of *security providers*. After a user has been authenticated, he or she receives an *access token* that identifies all processes initiated by the user. The token identifies the user's security code along with any groups and special privileges associated with that user.

Microsoft makes it possible for third-party vendors to extend and modify the base authentication mechanism for console logons. Normally, the user provides credentials in the form of a name/password combination, but other packages use thumbprints, voiceprints, retinal scans, answers to nosey questions, and someday probably even invasive surgery. Companies go to great lengths to keep unauthorized users from running Solitaire on their networks. These third-party packages can also work by relying on Microsoft's standard authentication engine with modifications to the credential-handling mechanism. This is done using a special library of security routines that make calls to the *Graphical Identification and Authentication* (GINA) library. A common example is the NWGINA used by the NetWare client for Windows 2000.

Local Security Authority (LSA)

The LSA uses a typical NT/Windows 2000 client/server subsystem arrangement consisting of a User-mode portion running in Ring 3 and an Executive portion running in Ring 0. The User-mode side consists of the *Local Security Authority SubSystem,* or LSASS.EXE. The Executive side consists of the *Security Reference Monitor* (SRM). The LSASS includes two services that collect user credentials: WINLOGON and NETLOGON, and a set of security providers, part of the SSPI, that process these credentials to verify that the user is authorized to access the computer or domain or both. In the Registry, these security providers are called *security packages*.

Security Providers and the SSPI

The SSPI provides a configurable and flexible way for Windows 2000 to interact with security systems. The SSPI enables programmers to use a single set of API calls to handle authentication chores instead of forcing them to make provisions for any and all types of local, network, Internet, public/private key, and proprietary authentication mechanisms. SSPI provides the same flexibility for authentication systems that Network Device Interface Specification (NDIS) provides for network systems and Open Database Connectivity (ODBC) provides for database management systems.

Security providers take the form of DLL libraries that snap into the LSASS executable. Third-party vendors who want to develop new and nifty security packages can write their own providers. As Windows 2000 matures, look for more and more third-party SSPI providers as vendors look for ways to leverage this new feature to their advantage. The following provider packages come with Windows 2000:

- **Kerberos (KERBEROS.DLL).** This provider supports Kerberos clients. When a Windows 2000 client attempts to access a Windows 2000 server, the client calls on KERBEROS.DLL to handle the authentication. As discussed in the next topic, the server side of this Kerberos transaction is controlled by the Kerberos Key Distribution Center service, KDCSVC.DLL, running on a Windows 2000 domain controller

- **NTLM Challenge-Response (MSV1_0.DLL).** This provider supports classic NTLM Challenge-Response authentication. A complementary implementation of NTLM Challenge-Response for Internet services is provided by WINSSPI.DLL. This provider supports WWW services that use WINSSPI to authenticate users who initiate server-side scripts running CGI, ActiveX, or Windows Script Host.

- **LSA Negotiate (LSASRV.DLL).** This provider interacts with WINLOGON and NETLOGON to pass security credentials to the security providers.

- **Distributed Password Authentication (MSAPSSPC.DLL).** The DPA provider supports the Microsoft Network (MSN) and other large content providers.

- **MSN authentication (MSNSSPC.DLL).** This provider supports an older, proprietary authentication used by MSN before DPA.

- **Secure Socket Layer/Private Communications Transport (SSL/PCT) (SCHANNEL.DLL).** This provider supports secure Internet communications. For example, this provider is used when Internet Explorer secure API calls are made to WININET.

- **Digest authentication (DIGEST.DLL).** This provider supports a new method for authenticating WWW users. It is an extension of the standard basic Web authentication, but does not require transfer of the user's password.

Registry Tip: Security support providers

The list of security support providers is located in HKLM | System | CurrentControlSet | Control | SecurityProviders.

Control parameters for the LSA and its security support providers are contained in HKLM | System | CurrentControlSet | Control | LSA.

Account and Security Databases

The various security support providers need a way to store credentials for users, groups, and computers. Classic NT and standalone Windows 2000 computers store security information in three Registry-based security databases. Windows 2000 domain controllers store security information in the Active Directory.

The three classic NT security databases are as follows:

- **Builtin.** This database contains the two default user accounts, Administrator and Guest, along with various default groups such as Domain Users for domains and Power User for workstations and stand-alone servers. The Builtin database is part of the SAM Registry hive in the HKEY_Local_Machine (HKLM) subtree. This and other Registry hives (except for user profiles) are located in the Winnt\System32\Config directory. The structure of the Builtin database differs between standalone servers and domain controllers. This is one of the reasons that a classic NT server requires reinstallation to upgrade it to a domain controller. A Windows 2000 domain controller migrates the Builtin accounts to the Active Directory when it is promoted.

- **Security Account Manager (SAM).** This database contains classic NT user and group accounts created after the initial installation of Windows 2000. This database is contained in the SAM Registry hive. Each user, group, and computer is assigned a security ID (SID). The Security Reference Monitor uses SIDs to control access to security objects such as files, Registry keys, and Active Directory objects. See the "Security ID Codes" section later in the chapter for details on SID construction.

- **LSA.** This database contains the password rules, system policies, and trust accounts for the computer. It is kept in the SECURITY Registry hive, also under the HKEY_Local_Machine subtree. The SECURITY hive also contains a copy of the SAM database.

Peeking Inside the Hives

Ordinarily, you cannot view the contents of the three classic security databases because the Registry keys permit full access by the System account only. If you want to take a peek inside these hives, you can set the permissions on the Registry keys to give your account or the Administrators group account full control access. *Do not do this on a production computer.* You will not necessarily wreck the security database, but you take a big chance of corrupting an entry. All data in the security databases is encrypted and stored in binary format. Refer to Figure 6.1 for an example of the hive structure.

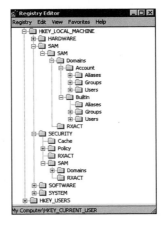

Figure 6.1   SAM database viewed by the Registry Editor after changing security permissions.

Computer Accounts

The SAM database contains accounts for computers as well as users and groups. Computer accounts create miniature trust relationships with a domain controller. These trusts are used to establish secure communications links using MS Remote Procedure Call (MSRPC), which the local LSA uses to pass through the user's authentication request to a domain controller. The Windows 2000 computer account prevents someone from plugging an unauthorized computer on to the network and getting access to the domain.

Every computer account has a password associated with it that is generated when the computer joins the domain. You can't see this password from the UI. It changes every 28 days via a secure negotiation between the computer and a domain controller.

Expired Password

It sometimes happens that a user cannot connect to the domain after an extended absence because the local computer account password has expired. If this happens, you must take the workstation out of the domain, delete the computer's domain registration, and then rejoin it to the domain. You must also re-register a workstation if you change its name. This gives the computer a new domain SID. If you attempt to join a computer to a domain and give it the same name as an existing computer, the domain controller will reject the registration request, even if the existing computer is no longer on the network. Be sure to delete old computer registrations.

Passwords

Neither the SAM nor the Active Directory stores a clear-text copy of a user's password. Instead, the password is encrypted using RSA MD4 encryption. The MD4 algorithm takes a variable-length password and encrypts it using a secret key to produce a fixed-length result called a *message digest.* The message digest is a one-way function, meaning that it cannot be decrypted back to its original form. This one-way function is often called a hash function, or sometimes just a hash. This is because MD encryption permits mixing together discrete elements when forming the message digest.

The more bits there are in the message digest, the harder it is to break. Domestic versions of Windows 2000 use a 128-bit message digest, considered unbreakable by anyone but the National Security Administration (NSA), and only then with a great deal of expensive supercomputer time. Windows 2000 increases the complexity of the message digest by using case-sensitive Unicode characters. Export versions of Windows 2000 are limited to a 40-bit message digest, considered easily crackable by folks whose job it is to do such deeds.

The security picture is much bleaker when you look at the support for down-level clients, such as Windows 9x and Win31. Older versions of Windows use a LAN Manager–compatible password encrypted using the U.S. Data Encryption Standard (DES). Not only is DES encryption not nearly as secure as MD4, the LAN Manager password itself is more easily determined because it is not case sensitive and uses only ANSI characters. A number of tools have bubbled up in the Internet that can scan a classic SAM database, nab LAN Manager passwords, and use them to open a system. Starting with Windows NT 4 SP3 and continuing into Windows 2000, the SAM can be protected with special encryption to protect these LAN Manager passwords. This requires generating a special system key that is used to encrypt the password store. As of this writing, no one has successfully cracked the SAM or the Active Directory on a Windows 2000 computer. Still, you should carefully guard access to the security databases just in case some bright 14-year-old devises a hack. This includes protecting backup tapes and anything else that holds backup copies of the Registry, such as RDISK or REGBACK. Network access to the server does not expose the SAM or the directory because they are locked on a running server. A potential backdoor exists because the RDISK utility saves an unlocked copy of the SAM in the `WINNT\Repair` directory.

LAN Manager passwords also represent a security hole because they are transmitted over the wire during the authentication process. Even if you do not have down-level clients, this makes it possible for an unauthorized person to collect the DES-encrypted passwords. You can prevent a Windows 2000 server from challenging for a LAN Manager password, and disable Windows 2000 clients from sending them, so long as you do not have down-level Windows 9x or 3.1x clients in your network. Use the following Registry entry to disable LAN Manager passwords:

```
Key:     HKLM \System\CurrentControlSet\Control\LSA
Value:   LMCompatibilityLevel
Data:    2 (REG_DWORD)
```

Security ID Codes

All Windows 2000 and NT computers, both servers and workstations, get a unique SID during initial setup. Standalone servers and workstations use the local computer SID to build SIDs for users and groups stored in the local SAM. Domain controllers use the SID assigned to the domain SID for building user, group, and computer account SIDs.

A SID consists of a series of 48-bit (6-byte) components that identify the issuing authority, the identity of any sub-authorities that determine how an account bearing this SID can interact with the operating system, and a random number that uniquely identifies the computer or domain. The binary content of the SID is rendered into alphanumeric format when exposed to the user interface. Here is an example of a computer SID:

S-1-5-21-1683771067-1221355100-624655392

The bold portion uses the format: **S-R-IA-SA**

- **S** represents the **SID Identifier**. It flags the number as a SID rather than some other kind of long, obscure number.
- **R** represents the **Revision**. All SIDs generated by Windows 2000 and classic NT have a revision level of 1.
- **IA** represents the **Issuing Authority**. Nearly all SIDs use the NT AUTHORITY as the issuing authority. The NT AUTHORITY designator is 5.
- **SA** represents one or more the **Sub-Authorities**. These authorities designate special groups or functions.

A user's SID consists of the SID of the computer or domain holding the user's account, followed by a sequential number called a relative ID (RID). Here is an example of a user SID. The bold portion is the RID:

S-1-5-21-1683771067-1221355100-624655392-**500**

Every user, computer, and group in a domain is given a RID by the primary domain controller (PDC) when the account is created. The default Administrator account gets RID 500 and the Guest account gets RID 501. RIDs for other users, groups, and computers are doled out in sequence on a first-come, first-served basis starting with decimal 1000, or hex200. The SAM stores user and computer accounts in the same database. It differentiates between them by appending a dollar sign to the computer names. A registered domain member computer with the name PHX-W2K-003, for example, would have a computer account name in the SAM of PHX-W2K-003$. In the Active Directory, user accounts and computer accounts are assigned different object classes that have different attributes, but even then the classes are virtually identical.

If you're new to NT/Windows 2000, this business of SIDs and RIDs might seem like geek-level stuff that no one really cares about except design engineers. Nothing could be further from the truth. Understanding how SIDs are generated, stored, and manipulated is absolutely vital to troubleshooting otherwise inexplicable security events. Just like Deep Throat telling Bob Woodward to follow the money, when you troubleshoot Windows 2000 security problems, you must follow the SIDs. What if Nancy Atchison in Accounting marries Bill Topeka in Engineering, for example, and they decide to hyphenate their last names and insist that you change their logon names? When you change natchison to natchisontopeka and btopeka to batchisontopeka, the change has no impact on their user rights because the underlying SIDs remain the same. If, on the other hand, you delete their accounts and built new ones with their new names, they would lose their access rights and group memberships. Not a pleasant prospect when you consider that these two users might be members of dozens and dozens of groups in addition to having their individual accounts included on file and directory access lists in resource domains all over the world.

SIDs

Certain SIDs represent standard local and global groups. These are called *well-known SIDs*. The groups represented by these SIDs have special significance to the operating system. For example, a special local group called *Interactive* has a SID of S-1-5-4. Any user who logs on at the console of a Windows 2000 computer is made a member of the Interactive group and is given whatever rights have been assigned to that group. On Windows 2000 Professional desktops, the Interactive group is a member of the Power Users group, giving a local user even more system rights.

Some well-known SIDs represent accounts rather than groups. For example, SID S-1-5-18 represents the Local System account, which provides a security context for background services. This Local System account is important to keep in mind because it comes into play when processes running on one computer need to access resources on another computer. Table 6.1 shows the well-known SIDs and their functions

Table 6.1   **Well-Known SIDs and Their Functions**

SID	Function
S-1-0-0	A memberless group used to represent an account with no known SID. This is also called a *null SID*.
S-1-1-0	This is the World SID, which is known in Windows 2000 and NT as the *Everyone* group. This group includes all users who log on to the domain, including anonymous users accessing resources from the Internet.
S-1-2-0	The *Local* group. This group includes users who have physically logged on to the console of the computer.
S-1-3-0	The *Creator/Owner* group. This group designates the user or service that created a security object or currently owns a security object. This number acts as a placeholder and is normally not displayed in the user interface.
S-1-3-1	A special form of the *Creator/Owner* group that contains the primary group for an account. Windows 2000 uses the primary group to support Macintosh users in a domain. The default primary group for users in a local SAM is Users. The default primary group for users in the Active Directory is *Domain Users*. The primary group can be changed, if necessary.

SID	Function
S-1-5	The *NT AUTHORITY*. SIDs for special groups issued by this authority start with S-1-5
S-1-5-1	Dial-up
S-1-5-2	Network
S-1-5-3	Batch
S-1-5-4	Interactive
S-1-5-5	Logon used to control process access between sessions
S-1-5-6	Service
S-1-5-7	Anonymous logon
S-1-5-8	Proxy
S-1-5-9	Server logon (also called the Domain Controllers or Enterprise Controllers account)
S-1-5-10	Self
S-1-5-11	Authenticated user (added in NT4 SP3, to differentiate S-1-1-0 *Everyone* users who have received network authentication from S-1-1-0 *Everyone* users who are touching the network as anonymous users)
S-1-5-12	Restricted code
S-1-5-13	Terminal server
S-1-5-20	Built-in global
S-1-5-21	Non-unique IDs
S-1-5-32	Built-in local

RIDs

Maintaining a sequential list of RIDs is automatic in classic NT because only the PDC can add new users, groups, and computers to the domain SAM database. The situation gets a bit more complicated in a Windows 2000 domain because every domain controller can write to the Active Directory.

A Windows 2000 domain has a single *RID pool* that is passed around among domain controllers like kids sharing a Tootsie Roll. Each domain controller carves off a chunk of 100,000 RIDs from the RID pool and uses them when it needs to add a new user, group, or computer to the Active Directory. This means that a Windows 2000 domain could have nonsequential RIDs. Classic *Backup Domain Controllers* (BDCs) will refuse to replicate if they see that the RIDs do not conform to standards.

To provide backward compatibility for classic BDCs, a Windows 2000 domain has a special operating configuration called *Mixed mode*. In a Mixed-mode domain, one Windows 2000 domain controller is designated as the RID master and retains exclusive use of the RID pool. By default, the RID master is the upgraded PDC. This server also becomes a PDC master to support the classic domain requirement that replication must come from a single server. The PDC master and RID master do not necessarily need to be the same server, but that configuration makes the most sense. The PDC master and RID master can be transferred to another Windows 2000 domain controller. From the perspective of the classic BDCs on the network, this appears to be a promotion of a BDC to a PDC. They acknowledge the change and begin replicating from the new domain controller.

When all classic NT domain controllers have been upgraded or retired so that every domain controller is running Windows 2000, the network can be shifted to *Native mode*. This is a one-time event and cannot be reversed. No classic NT domain controllers can ever again be introduced into a Native mode domain. The RID master releases the RID pool to other Windows 2000 domain controllers and the PDC master becomes irrelevant.

Access Tokens

After a security provider authenticates a user, LSASS calls on the Security Reference Monitor (SRM) in the Windows 2000 Executive to assemble the user's *access token*. The access token accompanies the threads of all processes spawned by the user. The token contains the user's SID along with the SID of any groups to which the user belongs. If a user logs on at the console of a standalone Windows 2000 Professional desktop, for example, the user gets an access token containing the user's SID, the S-1-2 local group, the S-1-5-4 Interactive group, and the SID for the Power Users group to which the Interactive group belongs. Each of these SIDs has certain defined permissions bestowed on the user because they are in the access token. The token also contains security restrictions that apply to the user, such as logon hours and password expiration.

An access token does not accompany the user across the network. Access permission, like politics, is always local. When a user attempts to connect to a server, or initiates a process that attempts a connection, the local security authority first authenticates the user using processes described in this chapter, and then *impersonates* the user to obtain an access token that accompanies any processes initiated by the user.

Limitations of Classic NT Security

Classic NT Registry-based security has the following eight major limitations:

- Restricted SAM size
- Multiple logon IDs
- PDC represents single point of failure
- Poor operational performance
- Poor replication performance
- Lack of management granularity
- Security databases differ between servers and domain controllers
- Nontransitive trust relationships

Restricted SAM Size

The total number of users, computers, and groups in classic NT is limited because the SAM cannot grow much above 80MB or so. This is due to restrictions on overall Registry size, called the *Registry size limit* (RSL), which keeps the Registry from consuming all the available paged pool memory. Generally speaking, paged pool memory represents the total available RAM less about 4MB set aside for the non-paged pool memory used by the Executive. You can view the settings for the various memory pools in `HKLM | System | CurrentControlSet | Control | Session Manager | Memory Management`. The default values for these memory pools are zero, indicating that they are calculated dynamically. You should not change any values unless you have specific directions from Microsoft Technical Support.

One setting that can be adjusted is the RSL. This is usually done automatically by the system when the Registry grows to the point that it is about to exceed the RSL. You can also adjust the RSL manually using the System applet in Control Panel. Select the `Advanced` tab, click `Performance`, and then click `Change` to open the `Virtual Memory` window. The value in the `Maximum Registry Size` field is the RSL. This is not the amount of memory actually set aside for the Registry, but the maximum size that the Registry is permitted to grow. The default RSL is 25% of paged pool memory. The RSL is permitted to grow to 80% of paged pool memory with a ceiling of about 108MB. The SAM is only one component of the Registry, so it is restricted further to about 80MB. Each user account uses 1KB, with 0.5KB for each computer account and 4KB for each group account. A typical SAM has enough room for about 40,000 users if you count the groups you'll need to manage them. In practical terms, poor replication performance and slow logon times cut the maximum number of users to about 15,000.

Multiple Logon IDs

In an ideal universe, the domain logon account would provide access to all server-based applications. In the real world, client/server application designers have been slow to use the flat-file security database in classic NT. This forces users to have separate logon IDs for the domain, email, host access, groupware, Internet proxies, and so forth.

Single Point of Failure

Updates to the classic NT security databases can only be done by contacting the PDC. If the PDC in the master domain crashes, users cannot change their passwords and you cannot add new users or domain global groups anywhere in the world. To correct this problem, an administrator must promote a BDC to PDC somewhere in the domain. If the promoted BDC doesn't have the horsepower of the original PDC, worldwide performance suffers. A worse situation occurs if the WAN connection that connects the PDC to the rest of the domain goes down. In this situation, you don't dare promote a BDC because when the WAN connection returns, you'll have two PDCs with slightly different security database contents. This forces you to make a Solomon decision, keeping one PDC and killing the other. In short, you have the makings of a real disaster.

Poor Operational Performance

The single PDC in a classic NT domain also imposes practical limits on daily operations. Assume, for example, that you are an administrator of a global NT network with 30,000 users. You are stationed in Omaha, but the PDC for the master security domain is Boston. You open User Manager for Domains to add a new user. Depending on the speed of the WAN link, it can take a long, long time to read the huge, flat-file SAM database across the WAN from Boston to Omaha. Most administrators in large NT domains learn to use command-line utilities to avoid this irritation.

Poor Replication Performance

The hub-and-spoke replication model of classic NT imposes operational limits beyond the problem with limited SAM size. A large network with many BDCs imposes a great deal of load on the PDC to keep the databases replicated. By default, replication occurs when 200 updates accumulate or every seven minutes or at a random interval between one and seven minutes. If you don't want to wait for replication to carry an update to a remote BDC, you must use Server Manager to force replication. This means opening still another tool and waiting another period of time.

Security Databases Differ Between Servers and Domain Controllers

The SAM database has a different structure on a domain controller than on a regular server. A classic NT server cannot be promoted directly to domain controller, and it cannot be demoted from a domain controller back to a server. The difference in the security database structure makes it necessary to completely reinstall NT if you want to change the server's security role.

Lack of Management Granularity

Administrators in one location in the domain have administrator privileges everywhere in the domain. Assume, for example, that a user forgets his password one morning and, after trying a few different entries, eventually picks up an intruder lockout. This happens all the time, right? Who can the user call for help? A local administrator? No. Local administrators have no rights in the master security domain. Only administrators in the master domain can perform password resets and intruder lockout resets and other routine daily services.

The central staff in a big network generally lift their noses at this kind of work, however, and try to delegate responsibility back to the local administrators. Unfortunately, there is no such thing in classic NT as a "Regional Domain Admin" or "Limited Domain Admin." There is an Account Operator group, but the management privileges of this group extend throughout the domain. This means an administrator hired and managed by the IT group in one city can make changes to accounts in another city. (Most IT managers I know tend to frown and get red in the face and make calls to their CIOs when they find out about this kind of situation.)

Several third-party tools have become popular to overcome this lack of management granularity in NT. Examples include Enterprise Administrator from Mission Critical Software, www.missioncritical.com, and Trusted Enterprise Manager from MDD, Inc., www.mddinc.com. These products filled a need in classic NT and they might find their way into the Windows 2000 market, but they carry their own replication and management baggage that might not be suitable for your environment. They are worth a look, however.

Nontransitive Trust Relationships

Several domains can be linked together to form *trust relationships*. In classic NT, however, these trusts come strictly in pairs. If Domain A trusts Domain B, and Domain B trusts Domain C, then Domain A does not trust Domain C or vice versa. Managing a large network with many interlocking trusts can turn highly competent administrators into slobbering maniacs. You know when you walk into the operations center of a big classic NT shop because there's butcher paper on the walls with circles and arrows going everywhere.

Windows 2000 Kerberos Authentication

In light of all the functional and operational limitations in classic NT security, it was imperative that Microsoft improve the situation in Windows 2000. Rather than try to incrementally fix the classic NT security structure, Microsoft chose to adopt entirely different security methods while maintaining backward compatibility with classic NT. The LDAP-based Active Directory replaced the old flat-file Registry databases and, to replace the aging NTLM Challenge-Response authentication, Microsoft chose another open standard, Kerberos.

Kerberos, the mythological hound, had three heads so that it could guard all ways in and out of Hades. Kerberos, the modern authentication mechanism, uses the following three parties to validate authorized users:

- A user who is trying to gain access to resources on a target server
- The target server that needs to validate the user's identity before giving access
- A special server that holds credentials for both the user and the target server so that it can perform the necessary authentications to authorize the user's access

The three-way nature of Kerberos authentication resolves nearly all the authentication-related limitations in classic NT security. Kerberos supports fully transitive trusts between domains, making it possible for administrators in Domain A to use groups from Domain C via a trust to Domain B. This sets the stage for more elaborate domain trust configurations without additional management overhead. Kerberos also provides mutual authentication and periodic re-authentication, making it a more secure protocol than NTLM Challenge-Response. And best of all, Kerberos is much faster than NTLM.

The functional overview portion of this chapter covers how the three-way Kerberos authentication takes place. Kerberos has its own lexicon, so the overview also introduces a lot of new vocabulary. The remaining topics cover how to use the new security policies in Windows 2000.

Kerberos Overview

Kerberos transactions resemble a scene from a John Le Carre spy novel. Imagine that a mole needs to contact her parent spy organization. She sends a prearranged signal, and the parent organization agrees to send a runner to meet her. The mole has never seen the runner before. The runner has never seen the mole before. How does each know that the other is genuine? Simple. They have a common acquaintance, the Chief back at headquarters. Here's how it works:

Procedure 6.1 **Kerberos Authentication Transaction**

1. The mole calls the Chief and says, "Give me a secret that only you and the runner know."

2. The Chief, always security-conscious, verifies that the mole is genuine by asking for a special signal known only to members of the secret service.

3. If the mole gives the correct sign, the Chief gets out the personnel files for the mole and the runner. A personnel file contains a secret encryption key known only to that spy.

4. The Chief then builds a message to the mole. The message has two parts:

   - Part one contains a random number thought up by the Chief and encrypted with the mole's secret key.

   - Part two contains the same random number, the mole's name, the time the Chief made the note, and a duration beyond which the note is not valid, all encrypted with the runner's secret key.

   Anyone reading this message would not glean any useful information from it. Only the Chief can read the whole thing, and he's so absent-minded that he forgets the random number as soon as he gives the message to the mole. No one could torture him to obtain it.

5. The mole uses her secret key to decode the random number in her portion of the message. If the result is gibberish, she assumes that someone has impersonated the Chief and given her a fake message. If the number looks right, she puts the runner's portion of the message in her purse for safekeeping.

6. That afternoon the mole and the runner meet. They exchange names. The mole gives the runner the second part of the Chief's message. She watches him closely. This is a moment of truth.

   - If the runner cannot decode the Chief's message, the mole knows the runner is bogus and shoots him.

   - If the runner can decode the message, but the contents inside are scrambled, the runner knows the mole has fiddled with the message and he shoots her.

- If the runner decodes the message and the mole's name in the message is different from the name she gave when they met, he shoots her.

- If the runner has ever seen the random number before, he shoots her.

- If the time of day exceeds the allowable duration of the Chief's message, the runner throws away the message and walks on.

7. If none of these unfortunate circumstances occur, the mole hands the runner another message. The mole devised this message. It contains her name, the current time, and the total number of letters in the message. The mole coded this message using her copy of the Chief's random number as an encryption key.

8. The runner uses the random number he obtained from his part of the Chief's message to decode the mole's message. If the result is garbled, one of them is an imposter, but they don't know which one. The scene comes to a Quentin Tarantino ending: The mole shoots the runner and the runner shoots the mole.

9. If the runner can decode the mole's message, the three-way authentication is complete and they begin sharing information.

I know extended metaphors make for slippery examples, but this game of *I Know A Secret, Do You?* follows a Kerberos authentication under Windows 2000 fairly closely. The actual transactions are a bit more complicated only because the principals can't meet face to face, so to speak. They send out their messages over a public network and so must assume that a bogeyman is out there capturing packets and using them to infiltrate the network.

Before examining Kerberos transactions in detail, it's important to understand the terms and expressions used by Kerberos. They differ significantly from those used by NTLM.

Kerberos Vocabulary

Kerberos has existed in the public domain for years and has a colorful language all its own. The mix of this terminology with those used to describe classic NT authentication makes for a hodge-podge of lingo that is dense, even by network systems standards. The following list of Kerberos terms explains their meaning and maps them to their classic NT counterparts.

Security Principal

Any authentication mechanism must be able to validate entities—whether they are users or computers or other devices that desire access to local or network resources. The Kerberos term for these entities is *security principals*, or often just *principals*. Security principals in Windows 2000 are *users*, *groups*, and *computers*. Each of these security principals is assigned a SID for use in the Windows 2000 object-based security system.

Realm

Every authentication system—Kerberos is no exception—requires a database to hold credentials. A Kerberos *realm* is defined by the contents of the database that holds the credentials for its security principals. The terms *domain* and *realm* are synonymous in Windows 2000. All objects in a domain, including those representing security principals, are contained in a single Active Directory database.

Ticket

The *ticket* is the fundamental unit of currency in Kerberos transactions. The ticket contains encrypted information used by the three parties in a Kerberos transaction to authenticate a security principal. When a security principal attempts to access a server, a ticket for that server must be presented. How that ticket is obtained, submitted, and validated is covered in the "Analysis of Kerberos Transactions" section a little later in this chapter.

Key Distribution Center

The central service that distributes Kerberos tickets is called the *Key Distribution Center* (KDC). A *key* and a ticket represent the same concept, but the term *key* is rarely used in contexts other than the KDC. The KDC has two primary functions: an authentication service and a ticket-issuing service. Some Kerberos implementations use separate servers for these two services, but this is not a requirement. Windows 2000 uses a single Key Distribution service, KDCSVC, to both authenticate security principals and issue their tickets. The KDCSVC runs only on domain controllers. Other Windows 2000 computers and Windows 9x computers with the Active Directory add-on have client services that are used to communicate with the KDCSVC using Kerberos protocols.

Kerberos is an open protocol, so, theoretically, Windows 2000 clients can get Kerberos tickets from a KDC on any platform and vice versa. In practice, however, subtle differences between Kerberos implementations make interoperability a challenge. So far, Microsoft has stipulated compatibility only with MIT Kerberos 5.

Ticket-Granting Service

The Ticket-Granting service is one of the two functions of a KDC. Whenever a security principal reaches out across the network to touch a server, it must present a Kerberos ticket for that server. The security principal obtains this ticket from a Ticket-Granting service. In Windows 2000, the Ticket-Granting service is incorporated into the KDCSVC service on a domain controller. It is not listed separately on a process list.

A ticket authorizes a user to access only a specific server. If a Windows 2000 user maps a drive to a shared folder on five servers, for example, the Kerberos client service must contact the KDCSVC service on a domain controller and obtain tickets for each of those servers on behalf of the client. The ticket is submitted to the target server as part of the initial server message block (SMB) connect command.

Authentication Service

Authentication is the second function of a KDC. Before a user can obtain a ticket, he must be verified to be an authorized security principal in the realm of that KDC. The Authentication service performs this function by checking the security principal's credentials against the contents of the security database. Windows 2000 uses the Active Directory for this database. When the KDCSVC on a Windows 2000 domain controller authenticates a user, it issues a *ticket-granting ticket* (TGT). The TGT speeds up the ticket-granting process by preauthorizing the user. In subsequent transactions when the user wants to access a specific server, the Kerberos client server submits the TGT to the KDC to quickly get a ticket for the target server. It's like eating Thanksgiving dinner at your grandmother's house. You must first get permission to eat at the family table. Only later do you get permission to dig in.

Validating Server

The validating server is the third party in the three-way Kerberos transaction. A Kerberos *validating server* is equivalent to a Windows 2000 *member server.* When a user attempts to access a member server, the Kerberos client submits a ticket for that server obtained from the KDC. The member server *validates* that ticket by checking the contents for encrypted messages that only an authorized security principal could possibly put there. A validating server must belong to the same Kerberos realm as the KDC that issues its tickets.

Transitive Trusts

Kerberos transactions in Windows 2000 are called *transitive* because KDCs in trusted domains work together transparently to point Kerberos clients at the proper domain controller to obtain tickets. A classic NT domain trust relationship could only be established between pairs of domains because the SAM was limited in what it could store about a trusted domain. Using Kerberos, the classic trust relationship can be expanded to include trusts between remote domains.

Assume, for example, that Domain B trusts Domain A and Domain C trusts Domain B. In classic NT, administrators from Domain C could not add users and groups from Domain A to their local access control lists. In Windows 2000, users and groups from any of the three domains can be added to groups and access control lists in any other domain.

The complexities of classic NT trust relationships have always caused migraines for administrators. Most big NT shops have multicolored trust interconnection diagrams hanging on the walls of their server rooms; the administrators use these when creating groups and assigning access rights. Kerberos transitive trusts won't eliminate the need for those drawings; after you have fully migrated to Windows 2000, however, they should look more like engineering diagrams and less like Dr. Seuss illustrations.

KRBTGT Account

Kerberos uses a special identifier to differentiate ticket-granting tickets issued by KDCs in different realms. This identifier is a combination of the realm name and the password associated with a special account called `krbtgt`. The KDC uses a hash of the `krbtgt` password to encrypt a random number called a *nonce* that it includes in the data field of all TGTs. This nonce makes it difficult to hijack or copy authentication tickets because the `krbtgt` key is known only to the original domain.

The `krbtgt` account is built automatically when the first server in the domain is promoted to domain controller. The account cannot be deleted and the name cannot be changed. You can change the password, but this is not recommended. Changing the password has no adverse effect, per se. It does invalidate any outstanding TGT tickets, however, and so forces the client processes holding these tickets to request new ones from the KDC. This is done transparently to the user, so there is no service interruption. However, the problem with changing the `krbtgt` password is that now *you* know the password, and if you know it then somebody else might find out what it is. This could result in a security breach.

Kerberos Ticket Details

There are two types of Kerberos tickets: a TGT and a standard ticket. The two tickets have the same structure. The only difference is the way that they're used. A TGT is issued during an Authentication service exchange. A standard ticket is issued during a Ticket-Granting service exchange.

Both Kerberos ticket types consist of a clear-text portion and an encrypted portion. The clear-text portion includes the following:

- **Ticket version number.** Windows 2000 uses Kerberos version 5.

- **Validating server name.** This is the name of the server that the user wants to access. In Windows 2000, this is the NetBIOS computer name, which doubles as the TCP/IP host name.

- **Validating server realm.** This is the name of the Kerberos realm—Windows 2000 domain—that contains the validating server. This field is necessary because the security principal may be in a different domain from the server he is attempting to access.

The encrypted portion of the ticket includes the following:

- **Flags.** A series of flags assigned by the KDC determines how the ticket can be used. This includes permission to forward the ticket to another realm, which permits users in one domain to access servers in a trusted domain. A KDC can also put a flag on a ticket that authorizes a server to use it as a proxy for the original client when accessing another server. In Windows 2000, this is called *delegation of trust*.

- **Session key.** A random number generated by the KDC when it builds a ticket. The session key is the shared secret that the KDC, the client, and the validating server have in common. Keep your eye on the session key when tracing Kerberos transactions.

- **Client's name and realm.** A Kerberos ticket forms only one part of the initial message sent to a validating server. Another portion of the message includes the user's name and domain (realm) in clear text. The validating server matches the encrypted information in the ticket against the clear-text information to make sure that they match. This prevents hijacking a ticket issued to one user and presenting it on behalf of another user.

- **Transited realms.** If a user needs to access a server in a different realm (domain), the local KDC cannot grant a ticket. Instead, it gets a ticket on behalf of the user from the KDC in the server's realm. If the KDC does not know the name of the server's realm, it refers the ticket request to a

KDC in a neighboring realm in hopes that the neighboring KDC knows the right realm. There may be several realms between the user and the validating server. The *transited realms* portion of the Kerberos ticket stores the names of these intervening realms so that the validating server can verify that they are all trusted. Without this check, a seemingly valid ticket might actually be a Manchurian Candidate submitted by an untrusted realm.

- **Time stamp.** There are two entries in this field: the date and time that the ticket was issued and the date and time that it expires. Kerberos tickets are supposed to be impossible to impersonate, but they are programmed to die automatically just in case a bright bad guy figures out how to do the ticket. The expiration time is determined by a Time-To-Live (TTL) value configured at the KDC. For Windows 2000, the default TTL is eight hours. For the time stamp to work correctly, all Kerberos clients in a domain must have their times roughly in sync. Windows 2000 uses W32TIME service to synchronize time between domain controllers. Windows 2000 Kerberos allows a good bit of slop in time stamping. The recommended deviance is about two minutes. Windows 2000 allows five minutes.

- **Authorization data.** Windows 2000 uses this field in two ways: In a TGT ticket, it includes an encrypted random number called a *nonce* that acts as a backup validation between the domain controller and its client. If a domain controller cannot decrypt the nonce, it knows immediately that the user's credentials are invalid. In a regular Kerberos ticket, Windows 2000 uses this field to store the user's SID and the SIDs of any groups to which the user belongs. This SID information is used by the validating server to construct an access token for the user.

Analysis of Kerberos Transactions

Windows 2000 uses Kerberos authentication in the following two situations:

- **Initial logon.** A Windows 2000 computer or a Windows 9x computer with the Active Directory add-on uses Kerberos to verify that a user has authorization to access the local computer.

- **Domain server access.** A Windows 2000 server that is a member of a Windows 2000 domain uses Kerberos to verify that a user has authorization to access the domain.

It is important to understand the details of these two authentication transactions so that you can troubleshoot password problems, trace the source of access denials, and determine whether a computer trust or domain trust has failed.

Let's look at initial logon authentication first.

Logon Authentication

The following example traces the Kerberos transaction that occurs when a user logs on to a domain from the console of a Windows 2000 computer that is a member of the domain. Refer to Figure 6.2. Here are the key points to watch for:

- The user must present domain credentials to get access to a domain member computer.

- The user's plain-text and encrypted password is never transmitted over the wire.

- The user can log on to any domain that is transitively trusted by the client computer's domain. The user must have an account in that domain.

- The authentication results in obtaining a TGT, which can be submitted at a later time to get tickets to specific servers.

- The Kerberos transaction must use IP because DNS is required to locate a domain controller.

- The end result of a successful logon is obtaining local access to the Windows 2000 computer and a TGT that can be used to access servers in the domain.

Domain Member Trust

When a computer is a domain member, it also uses Kerberos to authenticate with a domain controller via the NETLOGON service. The domain controller uses the computer's account in the Active Directory to validate the computer's identity. This account is virtually identical to a user account, including the SID and any group memberships associated with the computer.

Because the computer is an authorized security principal in the domain, any communication links it makes to its domain controller can be trusted by the user. One example of this is the secure RPC connection used to carry MSRPC messages between the computer and its domain controller. In the example, a successful computer domain logon is assumed. The Kerberos authentication for the initial computer logon works the same as the initial user authentication traced in the example.

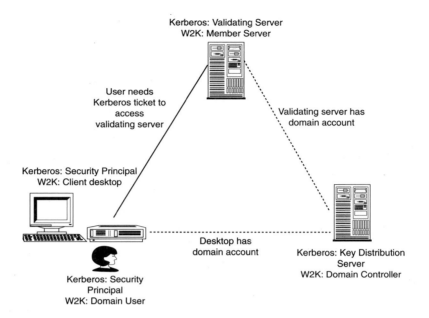

Figure 6.2 Domain configuration for example logon transaction.

Procedure 6.2 **Kerberos User Logon Transaction**

1. After the local computer has completed its domain authentication, the WINLOGON service presents a `Welcome` window.

2. The user initiates a logon sequence by pressing Ctrl+Alt+Del. This is meant to foil any Trojan horse programs that may be impersonating the operating system at this point. Both Windows 2000 and classic NT trap the Ctrl+Alt+Del interrupt and use it to initiate a security sequence. In the case of an initial logon, the result is to have WINLOGON display a logon window.

3. The user enters an account name and password and selects a domain in the Domain field of the logon window. The Domain field can contain the following types of entries:

   ■ **Domain name(s).** The list includes the name of the domain to which this computer belongs and any domains trusted by that domain or other domains trusted transitively by those domains. The user must have an account in the chosen domain. The user is not required to specify a logon context—that is, the name of the organizational unit (OU) containing the user account. The names of all security principals in a domain must be unique.

- **Local computer name.** This option permits the user to log on to the local computer without authenticating in the domain. To do this, the user must have an account in the local SAM database on the computer. Local logons still use Kerberos, but they do not involve calls to the KDC service on a domain controller. The local logon option is not available on domain controllers. The user must log on to the domain to access the console of a domain controller.

- **Internet name.** This enables the user to enter his or her universal service name, which has this format: username@company.com. This shortcut provides a consistent access nomenclature. You can tell your users, "Log on using the same name as your email address."

4. WINLOGON takes the user's credentials and passes them over to the LSA SubSystem, LSASS, which works with the Kerberos security provider to encrypt the user's password into an MD4 hash function. The clear-text password disappears as soon as it is encrypted.

5. Because the user entered a domain name in the WINLOGON window, LSASS passes control over to NETLOGON. NETLOGON works with the Kerberos security provider to construct a request for a TGT. The TGT request contains the

- User's logon ID name.
- KDC name (Windows 2000 domain controller name).
- Random number called a *nonce* which is encrypted using the hash of the user's password.

The nonce serves a couple of purposes. First, it enables the KDC service at the domain controller to quickly determine whether the user entered a proper password. If the KDC service cannot decrypt the nonce using the user's hashed password stored in the Active Directory, it immediately sends back an error. The nonce also acts as a laundry mark for mutual authentication. The client uses it to validate that the message is truly a response to its original message and not a bogus response generated by an impersonator.

The TGT request from the client includes a request for a particular *ticket type*. There are many ticket types, but a Kerberos client most often requests a *proxiable* TGT. Later on, if the client redeems the TGT for a ticket to a server in trusted domain, the local domain controller can use the proxiable TGT to obtain a ticket from a domain controller in the trusted domain.

6. After NETLOGON has the TGT request, it uses DNS to determine the name of a domain controller in the target domain. This query takes the form of an SRV record request for services on TCP port 88, the well-known Kerberos port. When NETLOGON gets the name and IP address of a domain controller, it sends the TGT request using Kerberos protocols.

    Let's stop here for a second and review the status so far. At this point, the user is still waiting at the WINLOGON window of the client computer for something to happen. The NETLOGON service has asked LSASS to produce an authentication request, and LSASS has complied with a Kerberos TGT request. NETLOGON has located a domain controller in the user's domain and sent the TGT request to the domain controller. It is now waiting for a response.

7. The NETLOGON service at the domain controller receives the TGT request and passes it to the LSASS. The LSASS uses the Kerberos Key Distribution service, KDCSVC, to look up the user's name in the Active Directory. If the name exists, and if the hash of the client's password successfully decrypts the nonce provided by the client, the user's SID and the SIDs of any groups to which the user belongs are retrieved from the Active Directory and used to build a TGT.

    The TGT includes a time stamp and a TTL interval along with a *session key*, a random number that uniquely identifies this particular ticket. The KDC also includes a nonce encrypted with the password hash of the krbtgt account. The client must include this nonce when it uses the TGT to request a specific ticket. If the TGT that comes back from the client does not have the nonce, or if the nonce is scrambled, the KDC knows that someone is trying to impersonate the user.

    The KDC service encrypts the coded portion of the TGT using the hash of the user's password obtained from the Active Directory. This hash matches the hash calculated by LSASS at the client computer. Note that neither the user's password nor the hash function is ever transmitted on the wire.

8. The LSASS now takes the TGT and passes it to the NETLOGON service, which sends it as a reply to the NETLOGON service at the client.

9. The NETLOGON service at the client passes the TGT to the local Kerberos security provider, which decodes the encrypted portion using the hash of the user's password. If it cannot decode the ticket—that is, the decrypted message does not match a CRC included in the encrypted portion—Kerberos discards the TGT on the assumption that it came from a bogus domain controller or was damaged in transit.

   If Kerberos can decode the ticket, it checks the copy of the client nonce to makes sure it matches the nonce it put in the TGT request. If the nonce does not match, the Kerberos provider assumes that a bogus domain controller has returned a TGT and it is discarded.

   If the TGT appears valid, Kerberos extracts the session key from the ticket and puts it in a cache along with the TGT. All subsequent ticket requests to the domain controller must be accompanied by this TGT. When it expires, the client must request a new one.

10. Kerberos turns the Authorization Data portion of the message containing the user's personal and group SIDs over to the LSASS, which uses the Security Reference Monitor in the Windows 2000 Executive to build an access token for the user. At this point, the console logon is complete. The system launches the Explorer shell, attaches the access user's token to this process thread, and the workday begins. Any subsequent processes spawned by the user are run in the user's security context and get the user's access token.

Network Resource Access Authentication

At this point, the user has access to the local machine. Now take a look at what happens when the user tries to access a resource on another server. The key points to watch for are as follows:

- The local client must go back to its domain controller to get a specific Kerberos ticket for the target server.
- The Kerberos ticket is included in the standard SMB messages between the client and server.
- The client presents the Kerberos server ticket in all transactions, making it nearly impossible for an impersonator to step in and take over the session.

The following steps describe the process for Kerberos authentication of a user attempting to access a remote server.

Procedure 6.3   **Kerberos Authenticating User Accessing Remote Server**

1. The user opens My Network Places, navigates to the name of a server, and double-clicks the server icon.

2. The TCP/IP driver converts the server's NetBIOS name to an IP address via a call to DNS or WINS. See Chapter 4, "Understanding NetBIOS Name Resolution" for more details.

3. After the client has an IP address for the target server, the network redirector builds an SMB message to create a session and connect to the server. It can't send this SMB yet, however, because it does not have a Kerberos ticket for the server. It calls on LSASS to provide this information.

4. LSASS calls on the Kerberos security provider to use its TGT to build a *ticket request*. The ticket request specifies the name of the target server, the name of the user, an encrypted random number for a nonce, and the provider's cached copy of the TGT. The Kerberos provider encrypts its portion of the ticket request using the session key it got from the TGT as an encryption key.

5. LSASS sends the Kerberos ticket request to the KDC service on its domain controller.

6. The KDC service at the domain controller quickly validates the TGT by checking the nonce and then double-checks the user's identity. It then builds a ticket for the target server. The ticket includes the name of the server, time stamp and TTL information, and a session key for this ticket. The KDC service encrypts part of the ticket using the password hash for the target server. It then bundles the server ticket into a *ticket reply*. The reply contains a copy of the session key for the ticket encrypted with the user's password hash along with the nonce supplied by the user.

7. The Kerberos service at the client computer obtains the ticket reply and decodes its portion of the reply to check the nonce and extract the session key for the ticket.

   It uses this information to build an *access request*. The access request contains the server ticket (which contains a copy of the session key encrypted with the server's password hash) and a copy of the session key encrypted with the session key itself. This encrypted session key as an *authenticator*. It is designed to stymie impersonators who might try intercepting server tickets and using them to gain unauthorized access. The impersonator would need to build its own access request that included the server ticket, but it would not know the session key so it could not include a valid authenticator.

8. LSASS hands the access request over to the Windows client redirector, which includes the request in the initial SMB that it sends to the target server.

9. The target server (also called the validating server in Kerberos) extracts the access request and passes it to its own LSASS, which calls on the local Kerberos provider to validate the ticket.

10. The local Kerberos provider decodes the portion of the ticket encrypted with the server's password hash. If the decoded message does not match the CRC in the message, it is discarded. From the decoded message, the provider extracts the session key for the ticket. It uses the session key to decode the authenticator. If the session keys match, the provider checks the time stamp to verify that the ticket is still valid.

11. If all this checks out, the target server grants access to the user. The client caches its copy of the ticket and its associated session key. It uses the cached ticket for all Kerberos transactions with the target server until the ticket expires. At that point, the client gets a new ticket from the KDC. This ongoing re-authentication is one of the major strengths of Kerberos.

Kerberos Implementation Details

For all the great features that Kerberos enables, very few operational requirements are involved with using it. Windows 2000 computers always use Kerberos when authenticating to other Windows 2000 computers and to a Windows 2000 domain. No actions are required on the part of an administrator to configure or manage these transactions.

Transitive trusts are enabled via Kerberos without any additional configuration required. In a Native-mode Windows 2000 domain, groups and users from domains that are trusted by the client's domain are made available on pick lists for access control lists and group memberships lists automatically. Windows 2000 servers and clients in Mixed-mode domains use a combination of Kerberos and NTLM Challenge-Response, depending on the computer they are accessing. There is no indication in the user interface about the authentication mechanism used by a particular connection.

The KDC service and the Kerberos client service do not have their own executables and are not shown on process lists. They are loaded as a part of LSASS. The Registry parameters that control the KDC service are located in HKLM | System | CurrentControlSet | Services | KDC, but this key contains no special control values.

The Windows 2000 Resource Kit contains two utilities, KSETUP and KTPASS, for use in configuring a domain controller to act as an MIT Kerberos 5 key distribution center. As of the time of this writing, no additional tools are included for managing Kerberos.

It's hard to talk about Kerberos without sounding like a Madison Avenue flak. Kerberos is quick, quiet, and won't upset your stomach. Unfortunately, the same cannot be said for the security policies that take effect after Kerberos has done its duties. The following section discusses those policies.

Configuring Security Policies

Microsoft defines a *policy* as a "set of rules that determine the interaction between a subject and an object." The rules associated with security policies are part of an overall policy configuration mechanism called *group policies*. These group policies are the next generation of policies in Windows, successors to the system policies introduced in Windows 95 and NT4. System policies consisted of a set of Registry entries controlled by a single management vehicle, the System Policy Editor, or Poledit. For example, a classic NT policy combines various Registry keys and values that change the Explorer shell into a single *desktop policy.*

These classic system policies have serious limitations, especially when it comes to distributing security configurations.

- System policy updates permanently change the local Registries. This is called *tattooing.* These Registry changes can cause serious problems. If you accidentally distribute a security update that locks users out of their computers, for example, you might end up doing 10,000 desktop visits to correct your mistake.

- System policies can only be distributed in one file, the NTCONFIG.POL file. This hampers the ability to create security policies tailored to specific user communities. System policies can be targeted at specific groups, but this creates a large NTCONFIG.POL file that is cumbersome to maintain.

- The range of Registry entries that can be changed using system policies is limited because of backward compatibility with classic NT.

System policies are still supported by Windows 2000, but have been superceded by *group policies.* Any system parameter that relies on a Registry entry can be controlled by group policies. These changes are made in a volatile manner and do not tattoo the local Registries. If the group policy is removed, the original Registry entries take effect.

Group policies can be used to control a wide variety of configurations, including security settings, system services, user interface parameters, and application settings. In addition, group policies can be used to control the following:

- Disk quota policies
- Encrypted file system recovery policies
- Folder redirection policies
- Logon/logoff scripts
- Software installation

Registry-based group policies that affect computer settings are applied to entries in the HKEY_Local_Machine hive. Policies that affect user settings are applied to HKEY_Current_User. These policies are applied each time the computer or user logs on, and are refreshed every 90 minutes by default until the user logs off. Some policies can be set to apply only at logoff, as well. Group policies are delivered to computers in one of two ways:

- **Local policies.** These policies are stored on the local drive in \WINNT\System32\GroupPolicy. They affect the local computer and users who log on to that computer.
- **Active Directory policies.** These policies are stored in two places. The majority of the policies are located in the \WINNT\Sysvol\Sysvol\ <domain_name> directory on every domain controller. The second Sysvol directory is shared with the name SYSVOL. The remainder of the policies are stored in the directory in a set of Group Policy Containers (GPCs). These policies can be associated with the Domain container, a Sites container, or any OU container. See Chapter 7, "Understanding Active Directory Services," for details on these containers.

The \WINNT\Sysvol\Sysvol\<domain_name> directory is replicated to all domain controllers by the File Replication service (FRS). See Chapter 13, "Managing File Systems" for details on FRS operation. In brief, the FRS is a general-purpose data synchronization service designed to replicate file updates to targeted servers. Only updated files are copied, and a database of file operations is kept to prevent accidental erasures and overwrites. FRS requires the use of NTFS5 on all replicated volumes.

The initial release of Windows 2000 includes eight group policy types. Each policy type is configured by a server-side extension in the Group Policy snap-in. When a client receives a policy configured by a particular snap-in extension, it processes the contents using a complementary client-side DLL. Table 6.2 contains the policy snap-in extensions and their client-side DLLs.

Table 6.2 **Group Policy Extensions and Client-Side DLLs**

Server-Side Extension	Implementing DLL
Registry Administrative Templates	USERENV.DLL (Computers and Users)
Folder Redirection Editor	FDEPLOY.DLL
Scripts (Computers and Users)	GPTEXT.DLL
Security Settings	SCECLI.DLL
Software Installation	APPMGMTS.DLL (Computers and Users)
Disk Quota	DSKQUOTA.DLL
Encrypting File System Recovery	SCECLI.DLL
Internet Explorer Branding	IEDKCS32.DLL
IP Security (IPSEC)	GPTEXT.DLL

Registry Tip: Client-side extension list
The client-side extension list can be found at HKLM | Software | Microsoft | Windows NT | CurrentVersion | Winlogon | GPExtensions.

The server-side extension for security policy handling, SCESRV.DLL, is part of the Services suite. The client-side extension, SCECLI.DLL, is part of the LSASS.

This chapter covers managing security settings group policies. It includes a functional overview of the operation of the Security Settings snap-in extension and how to configure the templates used by that extension to tailor the security policies delivered to clients in your system. Group policies affecting other user configuration parameters are covered in Chapter 16, "Managing the User Operating Environment." Software distribution, other than automated deployment of Windows 2000, lies beyond the scope of this book. Automated deployment policies are covered in Chapter 2, "Performing Upgrades and Automated Installations."

Although details about the Active Directory are not covered until chapters 7 to 10, you need to understand one AD concept before looking at the way group policies are distributed in a domain. That is the concept of *containers*.

The Active Directory is an object-oriented database. A file system is an example of such a database. Object-oriented databases are structured into hierarchies in which some objects can contain other objects. In the case of a file system made up of directory objects and file objects, a "directory" is an object that can contain other objects, whereas a "file" is an object that cannot. Objects that can contain other objects are often called container objects.

Active Directory Is an LDAP Directory Service

If you are a NetWare administrator, you are accustomed to thinking of Directory Service objects in terms of them being either container objects or leaf objects. The Active Directory is an LDAP Directory Service and does not make this distinction. Any object class in LDAP can be a container.

Each object in the directory represents a real-world item, such as a user named Gwashington, a computer named PHX-DC-01, a group named Phx_Sales, and so forth. Each of these objects is derived from a particular *object class*. A class defines a collection of *attributes* (sometimes called *properties*). When an object is created based on object class, it is said to be an *instance* of the class. If an object class included the attributes of being a near-sighted system administrator with flat feet and a paralyzing coffee addiction, the author would be an instance of that class.

The directory is structured so that objects from a given object class can contain only objects from specific classes. The basis for this determination generally derives from what makes most sense in terms of database operations. For example, it makes sense that an object of the class Subnet-Container can contain objects of the class Subnet. It does not make sense for it to contain objects of the class Computer. These *structure rules* determine what an Active Directory tree can look like.

The directory has four significant container classes: the Domain-DNS class, the Site class, the Organizational Unit (OU) class, and the Container class. There can only be one instance of the Domain-DNS class in a domain, and that object represents the top of the domain. There can be multiple instances of the Site class, but the use of these objects is restricted to defining directory replication boundaries. The generic Container class can be created by the system only and cannot be linked to group policies. This leaves only the OU class for use as a general-purpose container for structuring a directory.

The OU, Domain, and Site containers in a directory can be linked to group policies. When a policy is linked to a container, all computer and user objects under that container inherit the policy. It is possible to modify the same Registry setting in policies linked to different containers. Local group policies can also change settings, as can legacy system policies from NTCONFIG.POL. The following policy hierarchy is used to set precedence for conflicting policy entries:

- OU policies. These are applied last and have the highest precedence.
- Domain policies
- Site policies
- Local policies
- System policies

If you are a domain user who sets your Local policy to have a green desktop background but there is a Site policy that sets a blue background and a Domain policy for a yellow background and an OU policy for purple, you will get a purple desktop.

Every Active Directory has two default group policies (unless they have been deleted after installation): the *Default Domain Policy* linked to the Domain container, and the *Default Domain Controller* policy linked to the domain controller OU. You can modify these policies to set your own security entries or create new policies of your own. You can have as many policies as you want, constrained only by your willingness to manage them all.

If multiple policies are linked to the same container, they are normally applied in the order that they were created. The order can be changed in the management console by moving a particular policy in relation to the others on the list.

The files used to support group policies are not actually stored in the directory database. They are stored as discrete policy folders under `\WINNT\SYSVOL\SYSVOL\<domain_name>`. This is not necessarily the same \WINNT as %systemroot%. The location of the SYSVOL directory is selected when a server is promoted to a domain controller.

The second SYSVOL in the path is shared as SYSVOL. Client computers and users access the SYSVOL share on their authenticating domain controller to find policies. The directory contains special objects that have pointers to these policy folders in SYSVOL. These objects are instances of the class `GroupPolicyContainer`, so they are sometimes called GPC objects. GPC objects have attributes that contain the UNC path of its associated policy, the snap-in extensions used to create it, and the client-side extensions necessary to handle it.

When Windows 2000 clients log on to the domain, they query the directory for GPC objects. If any of the GPC objects are applicable to the client, the associated policy folder contents are downloaded from SYSVOL. If the policy affects Registry entries, and most of them do in one way or another, the policy entries overlay the existing Registry entries. If the policy is removed or changed, the underlying Registry entries take effect again.

Here are the key points to remember about directory-based group policies:

- The directory holds pointers to group policies stored in SYSVOL on each domain controller.
- Group policies are downloaded automatically by Windows 2000 domain members.
- Policies are applied using a hierarchy in which the OU user or computer's OU has the highest precedent.

Before looking at specific details for group policies that affect security settings, take a look at how to view and configure those policies using the Group Policy Editor.

Group Policy Editor Overview

Policies are configured using the Group Policy Editor snap-in, GPEDIT.MSC. This snap-in relies on the Group Policy Editor support file, GPEDIT.DLL. This snap-in is part of several different consoles, depending on the location of the policy to be edited.

- GPEDIT.MSC is loaded into its own console to edit local policies.
- AD Users and Computers, DSA.MSC, is used to create and edit profiles associated with the Domain container and any OU containers.
- AD Sites and Services, DSSITE.MSC, is used to create and edit profiles associated with Site containers.

The Group Policy Editor has several snap-in extensions corresponding to the policy types that can be edited. All extensions are loaded by default. This procedure covers how to selectively load snap-in extensions to tailor a console to a specific purpose.

Procedure 6.4 **Editing Local Policies Using the *Group Policy Editor* Console**

1. Open the Run command using Start | Run.
2. Enter GPEDIT.MSC and click OK. The Group Policy console opens as shown in Figure 6.3.

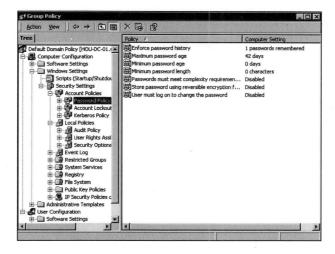

Figure 6.3 `Group Policy` console showing Password policies.

3. Expand the tree to find the entries under the Computer Configuration icon and the User Configuration icon. These entries contain the security settings as well as the other policy paraphernalia, such as logon/logoff scripts and administrative templates for controlling the Registry configurations.

The Registry updates associated with *Computer Configuration* entries are applied when the computer starts and affect settings in `HKEY_Local_Machine`. The Registry updates associated with *User Configuration* entries are applied when a user logs on to the computer and affect settings in `HKEY_Current_User`.

Computer Configuration entries associated with Registry entries are applied when the computer starts and normally affect settings in `HKEY_Local_Machine`. User Configuration entries are applied when a user logs on to the computer and normally affect settings in `HKEY_Current_User`.

To edit just the Security Settings for a local computer, load the `Security Policy` console from the START menu using START | PROGRAMS | ADMINIS-TRATIVE TOOLS | LOCAL SECURITY POLICY. The `Security Policy` window opens. The Security Settings are the same as those loaded by GPEDIT.MSC.

To edit domain group policies, you must first know which container you want to associate with the policy. The following example uses the `AD Users and Computers` console to open the default domain group policy associated with the Domain-DNS container. You can use the same steps to open or create group policies for an OU container. You can also use the AD Sites and Services console to access group policies associated with Site containers. The policy options are the same. Only their place in the hierarchy differs.

Procedure 6.5 **Editing Domain Policies on Domain Controllers**

1. Open the AD Users and Computers console or the AD Sites and Services console using START | PROGRAMS | ADMINISTRATIVE TOOLS.

2. Right-click the Domain container at the top of the tree and select PROPERTIES from the fly-out menu. The Properties window opens. If you wanted to open or create a policy for an OU, right-click the OU icon. You cannot create policies for any other object class in this console.

3. Select Default Domain Policy and click Edit. The Group Policy console window opens.

4. Check the list of options under each of the Settings objects. Along with the same options that were listed for a standalone computer, there are additional entries for application deployment and central control of profile information. Set the focus on the Security Settings under Computer Configuration.

If you only want to configure one or two options, you can build a custom Group Policy console and load only those snap-in extensions you want to manage. You can use custom consoles to help farm out your administrative tasks. You may want to give security policy administration to one group, for example, and application distribution policy administration to another group. You can create a custom console for each set of tasks. Chapter 10, "Managing Active Directory Security," covers how to delegate object rights to limit administrative privileges to conform to the custom console you build. The following example describes how to build an MMC console.

Procedure 6.6 **Building an *MMC* Console**

1. Open an empty MMC console using START | RUN | MMC.

2. From the MMC CONSOLE menu, SELECT CONSOLE | ADD/REMOVE SNAP-IN.

3. Click Add at the Add/Remove Snap-in window. The Add Standalone Snap-in window appears.

4. Select Group Policy and click Add. The Select Group Policy Object window appears.

The default Group Policy Object is the `Local Computer`. This is not a GPO as such, but looks directly at the local policy database in `\WINNT\System32\GroupPolicy` (see Figure 6.4).

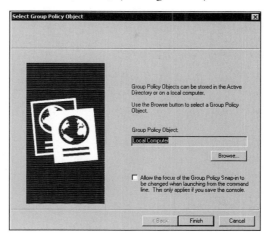

Figure 6.4 Select `Group Policy Object` window showing the Local Computer policy.

5. Click `Browse` to open the `Browse for a Group Policy Object` window. By default, all GPOs in the directory are kept in a container called Policies, but for purposes of display they are shown under their associated OU. GPOs are linked to containers via attributes in the container objects (see Figure 6.5).

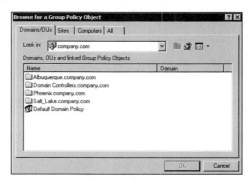

Figure 6.5 Browse for a `Group Policy Object` window showing several available OUs along with the Default Domain Policy.

6. Select the Default Domain Policy and click OK to return to the Select Group Policy Object window. The Default Domain Policy now appears under Group Policy Object.

7. Click Finish to add the policy and return to the Add Standalone Snap-In window.

8. Click Close to close the window and return to the Add/Remove Snap-in window.

9. Select the Extensions tab. Figure 6.6 shows an example.

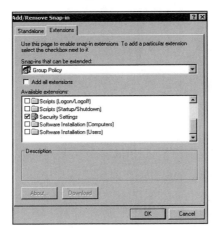

Figure 6.6 Add/Remove Snap-in window showing list of available extensions.

10. Uncheck the Add All Extensions option and check only the Security Settings option.

11. Click OK to save the change and return to the console.

12. From the MMC CONSOLE menu (right below the title bar), select CONSOLE | OPTIONS. The Options window opens.

13. Verify that Always Open Console Files in Author Mode is unchecked. Author mode permits a user to add and delete snap-ins from the console.

14. Select the Console tab. Give the icon a descriptive name, such as Domain Security Policy Editor. This does not name the associated MSC file. That comes later.

15. In the Console Mode combo box, select User Mode Full Access, Single Window. This option prevents the user from loading additional snap-ins and

extensions, but gives the user the ability to change the window's focus. `Limited Access` maintains the look and feel of the console by preventing the user from opening new windows.

The `Do Not Save Changes To This Console` option does not preserve the user's icon selections and tree expansions between sessions.

16. Click `OK` to save the changes and return to the console.

17. Close the console. You'll be prompted to save it. Give the console a file-name that is descriptive but short, such as DOMSECEDIT.MSC. Save the file to the All Users profile if you want it to show in the menu for anyone logging on to this computer.

18. Open the console you just saved. See that the `Console` menu is not visible. This means the console has not opened in Author mode. If you find yourself wanting to make changes to the console at a later time, you can open it in Author mode from the command line as follows: `mmc domsecedit.msc /a`. This trick works only if you have administrator privileges.

19. Close the console.

Functional Overview of Security Policies

Local security policy settings are stored on the local drive in the Security Editor database, SECEDIT.SDB. This database is located in `\WINNT\Security\Database`. The SECEDIT database uses Jet technology but cannot be edited with standard Jet database tools such as Microsoft Access. The Jet support files, such as transaction logs and the checkpoint file, are located in the parent directory, `\WINNT\Security`.

The SECEDIT database gets its initial configuration settings from one of several template files. These default templates are stored in `\WINNT\INF`.

- **DEFLTSV.INF**. Default server template
- **DEFLTWK.INF**. Default workstation template
- **DEFLTDC.INF**. Default domain controller template
- **DCUP.INF**. Domain controller upgrade template used when upgrading NT4 domain controllers

In addition to the default templates, additional templates are stored under `\WINNT\Security\Templates`. These templates contain prepackaged settings for basic, secure, and high security configurations. Any of these security templates can be loaded into the SECEDIT database and used to modify the system settings.

When you view the security entries in the Group Policy Editor, each icon under Security Settings represents a discrete section of the SECEDIT database. The template files are also divided into these sections. Figure 6.7 show these icons and the settings.

Figure 6.7 Custom GPE Console showing major Security Setting icons.

When you make a change to a policy setting in the Group Policy Editor, the update is written to the SECEDIT database. The WINLOGON service uses these settings to update the appropriate Registry entries. Under normal circumstances, WINLOGON would not perform this function until logoff or again at logon. If you want to force WINLOGON to load a policy change, you can use the command-line Security Editor utility, SECEDIT. The syntax is as follows:

```
secedit /refreshpolicy machine_policy (user_policy)
```

The machine_policy option flushes the Computer Configuration settings from SECEDIT to the HKEY_Local_Machine hive. The user_policy option flushes the User Configuration settings to HKEY_Current_User. This policy flush can take a minute or so. Watch the hard drive light. You can also check the Event log for an entry from SCECLI that the Group Policy entry was successfully applied.

Any changes to the SECEDIT database are also written to the associated template file so that the database can be reinitialized with the same settings, if necessary.

Registry Tip: Current template file
The name of the current template file is stored in the Registry under HKLM | Software | Microsoft | Windows NT | CurrentVersion | Secedit | TemplateUsed.

In addition to the local security settings, domain member servers and workstations download group policy updates from the domain during logon and logoff. When a Windows 2000 member computer authenticates, it queries the Active Directory for any GPC objects. These GPC objects have attributes that point to disk-based group policy folders stored on the domain controller under the SYSVOL share, \\<domain_name>\Sysvol\ <domain_name>\Policies. The policy folder names use the globally unique identifier (GUID) assigned to the policy.

Security settings policy files for are stored in the associated policy folder under \WINNT\Sysvol\Sysvol\<domain_name>\Policies\Machine\Microsoft\ Windows NT\SecEdit. The policy filename is GPTTMPL.INF. (You may also see a GPTTMPL.PNF file, which is a compiled version of the INF.)

Configuring User Security Settings
A limited number of user security settings can also be configured using the Group Policy Editor. These settings are stored in \WINNT\Sysvol\Sysvol\<domain_name>\Policies\User\Microsoft\Windows NT\SecEdit and are downloaded to the user's personal profile under \Documents and Settings\<logonID>\My Documents\Security\Database. Personal settings can also be configured in a SECEDIT.SDB file and put in this folder.

SYSVOL can hold a long list of policy folders. The folders are tracked in the local Registry under the key HKLM | Software | Microsoft | Windows | CurrentVersion | Group Policy | Shadow. Each policy is assigned a sequential number starting with zero. This sequence determines the order in which policies linked to a particular container are applied, so the higher number has the higher precedence. You can change this order using the MMC console associated with the group policies you are managing.

When a client computer logs on to the domain, it downloads the GPTTMPL.INF security settings from each policy that includes that computer. For example, a domain controller would download the GPTTMPL.INF file from the Default Domain policy and the Default Domain Controller policy.

The client copies the file to the local drive under \WINNT\Security\ Templates\Policy. Each file is first copied to a TMPGPTFL.INF file, and then renamed with a sequential number that matches the policy sequence number in the local Registry. The Default Domain policy is given a .DOM extension, and all other policy files get an .INF extension.

By default, the policy files are downloaded at logon and then refreshed every 90 minutes. You can use `secedit /refreshpolicy machine_policy` to force a download, but the security settings will not take affect until the next logon.

After the security setting policy files have been downloaded, they are layered on top of the settings in SECEDIT.SDB and applied to the Registry. This is done in a volatile manner so that the local Registry is not tattooed with permanent policy changes. You can see the difference between the local settings and the downloaded settings by opening the local Group Policy Editor, GPEDIT.MSC, or by launching the Local Security Policy console from START | PROGRAMS | ADMINISTRATIVE TOOLS. If a downloaded group policy is in force, two columns appear in the right pane, one labeled `Computer Setting` and one labeled `Effective Setting`.

Registry Tip: Security hive settings

Most of the security settings updated by group policies involve keys in the hidden and locked Security hive in the Registry. If you are following along in the Group Policy Editor, you may have noticed the Kerberos Policy settings under Account Policies. These settings are also stored in the Security hive under SECURITY\Policy.

You can view the keys in the Security hive on a non-production system by changing the permissions on the Security key to Administrators | Full Control and flowing the changes down the tree.

Here are the key points to remember about the way security policies are applied to local systems:

- Security policies for a local machine are stored in the Security Editor database, `\WINNT\Security\Database\Secedit.sdb`.

- Group policies, including those involving security settings, are downloaded from a domain controller when a Windows 2000 computer authenticates to the domain.

- Group policies are applied in order of precedence, with the OU containing the computer account taking priority, followed by the computer's domain affiliation then its site. Local policies come next with legacy system policies falling in place dead last.

- Group policies downloaded from a domain controller do not permanently alter local Registry settings. If the policy changes are removed, the original Registry entries take affect once again.

- The next few sections include details on the available security setting options and how to use them to control access to local computers and domains.

Configuring Access Security Policies

Some security policies have become so firmly entrenched that it would be nearly unthinkable not to use them. This includes periodic password changes, disallowing blank passwords, imposing a lockout out after a series of unsuccessful logon attempts, and so forth. It's possible to argue the merits of these and other policies, but for the most part it is safe to say that too much security is better than too little. This section covers the various security policies available in Windows 2000 and how to implement them, starting with password and lockout policies.

Access by Non-Microsoft Computers

The encrypted authentication passwords stored in the Active Directory can be used only by Windows clients and clients configured to use Windows authentication mechanisms. Active Directory clients authenticate using Kerberos. Classic NT clients authenticate using NTLM Challenge-Response. Down-level Windows 9x and 3.1x clients use LAN Manager authentication.

The world is not comprised of purely Windows clients, as you well know. Windows 2000 supports access by UNIX clients running SAMBA, a public-domain SMB package that has ports to virtually every flavor of UNIX imaginable. Older SAMBA versions may not work with Windows 2000 because the reversibly encrypted LAN Manager password is no longer enabled, at least in a default Windows 2000 configuration. Newer SAMBA versions understand the NTLM Challenge-Response protocol and can even act as servers in a classic domain.

Macintosh users running OS versions earlier than 7.1 will also be unable to access a Windows 2000 server without reversible passwords. Microsoft provides a custom user authentication module (UAM) for Macintosh version 7.1 and above, but the package has a history of instability on earlier clients. The UAM exposes NTLM authentication only, not Kerberos. Windows 2000 supports the native Random Number Exchange UAM that has been part of AppleTalk File Protocol (AFP) since version 2.1, but you must enable reversible passwords for it to work. This also applies to Macintosh remote access via *AppleTalk Remote Access Protocol* (ARAP). As with SAMBA, the best course of action is to upgrade if your system can handle version 7.1 or above.

Enabling reversibly encrypted LAN Manager passwords (also called *clear-text* passwords) is not recommended because of their extreme vulnerability. If you have no other alternative, you can choose between enabling them for all users in a domain or for individual users to limit your security exposure. Configure the domain policy as follows:

Procedure 6.7 **Enabling Reversible Passwords for a Domain**

1. Open the AD Users and Computers console using START | PROGRAMS | ADMINISTRATIVE TOOLS.

2. Right-click the Domain icon at the top of the tree in the left pane and select PROPERTIES from the fly-out menu. The Properties window opens.

3. Select the Group Policy tab.

4. Double-click the Default Domain Policy listing to open the Group Policy console.

5. Expand the tree to Computer Configuration | Security Settings | Account Policies | Password Policy.

6. In the right pane, double-click Store Password Using Reversible Encryption for All Users in the Domain. The Security Policy Setting window opens.

7. Click OK to save the change and return to the Group Policy console.

8. Clients can now log on using their clear-text passwords. Users with pre-existing Windows 2000 accounts must log off, then log on again to create the reversible password.

If you want to enable reversibly encrypted passwords for selected users, proceed as follows:

Procedure 6.8 **Enabling Reversible Passwords for Selected Users**

1. For domain users, open the AD Users and Computers console using START | PROGRAMS | ADMINISTRATIVE TOOLS. Expand the tree to show the Users container or an OU you have configured to hold user objects.

2. For user accounts on a standalone server or workstation, open the Computer Management Console using START | PROGRAMS | ADMINISTRATIVE TOOLS. Expand the tree to System Tools | Local Users and Groups | Users.

3. Double-click the user object to open the Properties window.

4. Select the Account tab.

5. Under `Account` `options`, check `Save` `password` `as` `encrypted` `clear` `text`. Figure 6.8 shows an example.

6. Click `OK` to save the change and return to the console. The user must log off, and then log on to create the reversible password.

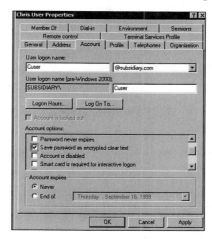

Figure 6.8 `User` `Properties` window showing clear-text option enabled.

Password Synchronization

Nothing seems to irritate users more than passwords. Users are human—not always patient, kind, and calm humans, but humans nonetheless—and whether out of forgetfulness or sheer perversity, humans do not like populating their memory with random scraps of information such as passwords. Anything administrators can do to keep users out of multiple password purgatory saves them consternation and saves administrators hours of support time.

Under normal circumstances, Windows 2000 users need only deal with one operating system password, that for their domain account. A user who has authenticated in the domain is given the Authenticated User SID, S-1-5-11, as part of his access token. By default, the Authenticated User account is a member of the Local Users group. This gives the user access to the local computer. Windows 2000 Professional also adds the Authenticated User account to the Power Users local group, a departure from classic NT4. Members of the Power Users group can install local software and create printers and do a variety of other privileged tasks not permitted to mere users.

This Authenticated User alternative to getting local access works only if the computer itself is a member of the domain. Standalone workstations and servers are not trusted to access the Active Directory on a domain controller. They can authenticate users using accounts in the local SAM only. This can be a challenge for laptop users who take their machines off the network and need to log on locally. Rather than give the user multiple accounts, one for the local computer and one for the domain, Windows 2000 caches the domain account credentials in the local SAM. This permits the user to log on locally and retain the same system privileges as if the authentication had occurred at a domain controller. This has the added benefit of retaining the user's local environment settings. Otherwise, the user would have two sets of local configurations, one associated with the domain SID and one with the local SID.

This begs the question of what to do if the computer cannot contact a domain controller and a field administrator needs to log on locally to fix the problem. Many organizations give their Windows 2000 desktops the same password for the local Administrator account. This is a questionable practice, not because it gives too much access to administrators who know the password—they could log on locally if the computer were on the network—but because the password never changes. A disgruntled ex-employee or contractor could come back a year or two after being fired and find desktops to access, either locally or across the network using the default C$ or ADMIN$ share points.

One alternative is to use random passwords for the local Administrator account and forego local troubleshooting if the computer cannot communicate with the network. Most field technicians take a dim view of this alternative. It can turn a simple network driver glitch into a time-consuming reinstallation.

Another alternative is to put a scheduled process in place at the workstations that changes the local Administrator password regularly using a file distributed to the local desktops in the background. This could be as simple as running NET USER <username> <password> in the context of the current local Administrator account or as complex as coding a special applet in Perl or Windows Script Host that does the job. You might want to take a look at *Windows NT Shell Scripting*, by Tim Hill (published by Macmillan Technical Publishing, 1998), for great ways to do intricate tricks like this.

Users can change their passwords on a Windows 2000 computer in the following three ways:

1. Wait for the domain password to expire and change it when prompted. Domain passwords expire every 42 days by default. The user is notified 14 days prior to password expiration to change the password. Both of these settings can be changed using group policies. To change the expiration interval, open the Group Policy Editor and look for Computer Configuration | Windows Settings | Security Settings | Account Policies | Password Policy | Maximum Password Age. To change the notification interval, look for Computer Configuration | Windows Settings | Security Settings | Local Policies | Security Options | Prompt User To Change Password Before Expiration.

2. Press Ctrl+Alt+Del to bring up the Windows Security window, and then click Change Password. The user must enter the existing password, and then the new password with a confirmation. If the user has logged on to a remote domain using a transitive trust, the correct domain should be displayed under Log On To. If the computer is configured with a second network client in addition to the Windows Networking client, such as Client Services for NetWare, both passwords can be changed at once.

3. Open a command session and enter NET USER username password /domain. This option is available to administrators only, and it is the fastest way to change a password. No confirmation is required, so be sure you spell correctly.

Users at down-level computers such as Windows 9x and Windows 3.1 can log on to a domain, but their computers do not have a domain, so the local system must authenticate them locally. Password changes initiated using the Password applet in Control Panel will keep the local and domain passwords in sync so long as the user keeps the default options in the Change Password window. If the passwords get out of sync, the user is forced to enter two passwords in the morning. If the user forgets one, he will not get access. Local Windows passwords are encrypted and then stored in a PWL file in the Windows directory. If the user's local password gets out of sync with the domain password, the simplest fix is to delete the PWL file, log off, and then have the user log on. The system prompts for a Windows password and saves it in a new PWL file.

If the user presses the pesky Esc key to bypass domain logon, the Password Change option in Control Panel is disabled. This is good news because it prevents the user from changing only one of the passwords. Your troubles aren't over, however. Now it's time to learn how to configure the domain to require complex passwords. Instead of choosing a password such as *Schlamiel3*, the user might enter the name of a pet dog, *Sam*, instead. The domain rejects this password, but Windows 9x is much more forgiving and changes the local Windows password. The next time the user logs on, he becomes as disoriented as a visitor from Sirius. He pounds at the keyboard in mounting frustration, eventually picking up an intruder lockout. He then gets on the phone to the Help Desk to complain about his ★&^% password and your ^★& system.

Complex Passwords

On the *X-Files*, a hacker can guess a DoD password in two or three tries. In a production network, it's just about that easy to guess a user's password. Users don't generally assign tough passwords when left to their own discretion.

In response to several successful hacks of the SAM database, Microsoft provided a strong password filter in NT4 SP3 to enforce a complex password policy. This policy and the filter are included in Windows 2000. Complicated passwords are tough to remember and often find their way onto yellow sticky notes under mouse pads, if not right there on the side of the monitor, but they do help prevent outsiders from staging successful dictionary attacks across the network.

NT Crack Engines

The most popular NT crack engine attacks passwords in groups of seven characters. It works on the groups simultaneously; so if a password is 11 characters long and the last four characters happen to be letters, they will be revealed almost instantly. Then they can often be used to guess the first seven characters. Similarly, putting a non-alphanumeric character at the end of an eight-character password leaves the first seven characters open for an easy crack if they are simple characters. Once they are guessed, it doesn't take long to figure out the complex character. Keep this in mind when defining your password strategy. The best passwords are 7 or 14 characters long.

Complex passwords must be at least six characters long, cannot contain the username or any part of the user's full name as entered in the directory or SAM, and must contain characters with any three of the following attributes:

- Uppercase letters (A, B, C, and so on)
- Lowercase letters (a, b, c, and so on)
- Arabic numerals (0, 1, 2, and so on)
- Special characters and punctuation symbols (#!&^+)

These example passwords would make it through the complex filter:

- #RedDog
- Jabber8wocky@%
- Spinoza#ROCKS! (Unless the user's name is Spinoza, in which case you might have someone with a lot to say about complex names and password duality.)

There are no facilities, either in the UI or the Registry, for changing the filter settings, even if you want to make them tighter. In TechNet article Q161990, which describes the strong password filter, Microsoft states, "If you wish to raise or lower these requirements, you must write your own .DLL." Enable complex passwords as follows:

Procedure 6.9 **Enabling Complex Passwords**

1. Open the `Group Policy` console for the Active Directory container or local computer that you want to configure. Use the steps outlined in "Group Policy Editor Overview."

2. Select `Computer Settings` | `Security Settings` | `Account Policies` | `Password Policy`.

3. Double-click `Passwords Must Meet Complexity Requirements of the Installed Password Filter`. The `Policy Setting` window for this option appears.

4. Select the `Enabled` radio button.

5. Click `OK` to save the change and return to the `Group Policy` console.

6. The next time the users change their passwords, any non-complex passwords will be rejected. Be sure to brief them before implementing the policy.

Lockout Policies

If you do not like the idea of the bad guys hammering away at your network trying to guess user passwords, you'll want to institute a lockout policy that disables a user's account after repeated invalid logon attempts. A lockout policy has three elements:

- **Lockout count.** The number of invalid logon attempts permitted before the account is locked out.
- **Lockout reset time.** The interval between invalid attempts after which the lockout count is returned to zero. For example, a lockout reset time of 10 minutes would cause the lockout counter to continue incrementing for invalid logon attempts made every nine minutes.
- **Lockout duration.** The interval following a lockout after which the lockout is automatically cleared and the user can try to log on again.

Lockout policies create administrative burdens because users have a hard time remembering their passwords. If you set the lockout count too low, you or your poor colleagues at the Help Desk will get lots of phone calls. If you set the value too high, you reduce the effectiveness of the policy. By the same token, if you set the lockout reset time too short, the bad guy can set his daemon to try multiple accounts with sufficient wait between attempts to foil your lockout strategy. It's up to you to come up with a combination of settings that gives you adequate security without imposing too much of a hardship on your user support staff.

A domain account lockout policy is enforced by the LSASS on a domain controller. It applies both to console logon attempts and network logon attempts at any member computer. A console logon is the initial domain authentication performed when a user enters credentials at the console of a member computer. Console logons in Windows 2000 are handled by the WINLOGON service. A network logon occurs when a user attempts to connect to a shared resource on a server using network protocols. Windows 2000 uses the NETLOGON service to handle network logons. Both WINLOGON and NETLOGON are part of the LSASS.

LSASS also imposes the lockout policy on other services that accept network connections. This includes FTP, Telnet, and HTTP. Repeated invalid logon attempts using any combination of these services will trip the lockout.

The lockout policy has very few exceptions. The Built-In Administrator account cannot be locked out, but this exception does not apply to other accounts with administrator privileges. Computer accounts cannot be locked out, neither can domain trust accounts.

Before you put a lockout policy in place, here's a little something to consider. Under normal circumstances, when a user enters incorrect credentials during a console logon attempt, the system rejects the attempt without giving a clue whether it was the name or the password that was incorrect. If you put a lockout policy in place, an unauthorized user who picks up a lockout knows that he at least got the logon name right. Most organizations have logon names that follow a recognizable pattern, so this revealing clue doesn't really make much difference, but it's worth knowing.

You can set a lockout policy for an entire domain or particular workstations. Configure the policy as follows:

Procedure 6.10   **Lockout Policy for a Domain**

1. Open the Group Policy console for the Active Directory container or local computer that you want to configure. Use the steps outlined in "Group Policy Editor Overview."

2. Navigate to Computer Settings | Security Settings | Account Policies | Account Lockout Policy.

3. Double-click Account Lockout Counter and set the value for the number of attempts you're willing to give a user before locking out the account. Five is a good number.

4. Click OK to save the setting. The system automatically sets default values for Lockout Account Duration and Reset Account Lockout Count After to 30 minutes apiece. You can leave these settings at their defaults or choose values that make sense for your system. If you try to set the lockout duration shorter than the reset duration, the system will prompt you to at least make them equal values.

5. Close the Group Policy console.

6. From a command prompt, run secedit /refreshpolicy machine_policy to apply the changes to the Active Directory or local SAM.

7. Verify that a lockout occurs by attempting invalid logons using any account but the Administrator account.

Auditing

As sanitation engineers and quantum physicists have long known, just because you can't see something doesn't mean it isn't really there. You must assume that bad guys are constantly trying to get on your network. Even if you aren't connected to the Internet, you have to be careful of insiders, even if your company is one big happy family where everyone goes to baseball games and Nine Inch Nails concerts together.

Any activity involving Windows 2000 security objects can be audited. Logging a lot of activity puts a load on the affected server, so choose your audit points carefully. Audit reports are written to the Security log, which can be viewed by the `Programs | Administrative Tools | Event Viewer`. The associated Event log, SECEVENT.EVT, is located in the `WINNT\System32\Config` directory. You must have Administrator privileges to open this log.

The default Event log size is 512KB, which might be too small for the Security log if you audit many events. The default behavior of the log is to overwrite older entries when the log fills up, which might obscure old sins. You can change these and other log file settings as follows:

Procedure 6.11   **Log File Settings**

1. Open the `Event Viewer` console using START | PROGRAMS | ADMINISTRA-TIVE TOOLS | EVENT VIEWER. You only need one option.

2. Right-click the `Security Log` object and select PROPERTIES from the fly-out menu. The `Properties` window opens.

3. Change the entry for `Maximum Log Size` to a value large enough to accommodate several days' logging.

4. Under `Event Log Wrapping`, set the logging behavior when the log file gets full. (I usually select `Do Not Overwrite Events`.) Don't forget to save the log and clear it manually every week or so. You can set a system policy that causes the server to refuse connections if the Security log gets full.

5. Click `OK` to save any changes and close the `Properties` window.

You can make the Event log configurations part of an Event Log Settings policy and push them out to member servers and workstations. This gives you a standard set of log parameters when you collect your audit information.

You can read the Security logs across the network, but you must do this one at a time unless you use a third-party tool to collect Event log entries. One of the better tools for this kind of work is Event Admin from Midwest Commerce, Inc. It puts the Event log entries into an ODBC-compliant database for viewing and reporting.

Enable auditing and set audit policies as follows:

Procedure 6.12   **Audit Policies**

1. Open the `Group Policy` console for the Active Directory container or local computer that you want to configure. Use the steps outlined in "Group Policy Editor Overview."

2. Select `Computer Configuration | Windows Settings | Security Settings | Local Policies | Audit Policy`. The following events can be audited:

- **Account Logon.** This monitors network access to a computer via network logon and logoff. Use this policy when you want a record of accounts that access the server and what privileges they have been assigned.

- **Account Management.** This monitors an administrator who adds, deletes, or modifies the attributes of any security principal such as users, groups, or computers. This is especially useful if you have a large and diverse IT group and you're still getting used to the way Active Directory delegation works. You might want to make sure that the new administrator in the Chemistry lab isn't adding the entire freshman class to the SENIOR_FACULTY group, which has access to the grade spreadsheets.

- **Directory Services Access.** This monitors administrative access to the Active Directory.

- **Logon Events.** This monitors console logon/logoff. This is different from Account Logon, which monitors network access.

- **Object Access.** This monitors access to security objects such as files, directories, Registry keys, and directory objects. In most circumstances, you must also configure the individual object classes for auditing. NTFS files, for example, must be enabled for auditing via the Properties window, opened by right-clicking the file in Explorer.

- **Policy Change.** This monitors changes in any of the policies you've set. With so many policies flying around in Windows 2000, I leave this audit point on all the time because it shows any user and machine policy updates that come from the domain.

- **Privilege Use.** This monitors privileged access to resources by the system or accounts that have system privileges. For example, only administrators can open the Security log. When you open the Security log, an entry is made in the log under Privilege Use that shows your account name and what you did that exercised a system privilege.

- **Process Tracking.** This monitors access to executable code such as EXE, DLL, and OCX files. This is handy for figuring out who is accessing a particular file. It can also help track down viruses, although most virus scanners offer better tools.

- **System Events.** This monitors the various system updates that occur during operation. If you're troubleshooting a pesky service that refuses to work for some inexplicable reason, this is a great trace to follow. Used in conjunction with Process Tracking, you can follow the service to see whether it performs an illegal or disallowed activity or asks the system to perform such an activity. The trace also shows you how the various security providers get initialized.

3. Double-click the policy you want to enable. This opens the Security Policy Setting window for the policy. For example, you may want to enable Audit Account Logon Events and Audit Logon Events to see the kind of reports that auditing provides.

4. Select Define These Policy Settings, and then select Success and/or Failure under Audit These Attempts.

5. Click OK to save the change and return to the Group Policy console.

6. Close the console.

7. Refresh the policy by opening a command session and entering secedit /refreshpolicy machine_policy. The audit policy takes effect immediately. There is no need to restart.

8. Test the audit policies you set by performing an auditable activity. For example, with Audit Account Logon Events and Audit Logon Events enabled, log on at a member server or workstation. Figure 6.9 shows the Event Viewer console with a set of logon/logoff events under Security Log.

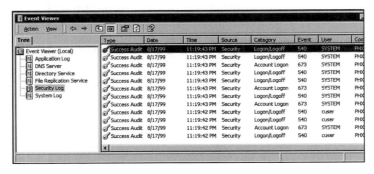

Figure 6.9 Event Viewer showing Security Log with various auditing events displayed.

9. Double-click one of the entries to see the information supplied by the auditing policy. Figure 6.10 shows an example of the audit report for a user console logon. Notice that the user was granted an Authentication ticket that was validated by the krbtgt account.

Figure 6.10   Event log entry for a user console logon.

10. Close all windows and consoles.

If you don't see any entries in the Event log after enabling auditing and running SECEDIT, press F5 or select REFRESH from the console menu. If you still do not get entries, and the server is a member of a Windows 2000 domain, the Default Domain Controllers group policy might have a No Auditing option set. The OU policy takes precedence over the domain policy you just set. Open the Group Policy console for the Domain Controller OU and verify that there are no Audit policies in place. If this is not the problem, make sure that Block Policy Inheritance is not selected at the Domain Controllers Properties window, Group Policy tab. This would prevent the Default Domain policy from being inherited by the domain controller.

Assigning System Rights

Many Windows 2000 operations come accompanied by the caveat, "You need Administrator rights to do this" or "This requires Backup Operator permissions" and so forth. System-level rights are assigned using security groups that define privileges ranging from the ability to create a paging file to permission for logging on at the console of a server. Users and groups get these system rights by being associated with the applicable security group. If you are an experienced NT administrator, you're accustomed to configuring rights with User Manager. In Windows 2000, these rights are configured with the Group Policy Editor.

Before examining the list of rights in detail, take a look at how to configure the policies that control access to them.

Procedure 6.13 **Configuring User Rights Policies**

1. Open the `AD Users and Computers` console and navigate to `Windows Settings | Security Settings | Local Policies | User Rights Assignment`. The available policies are listed in the right pane of the window. Figure 6.11 shows an example.

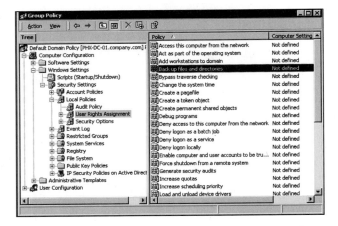

Figure 6.11 `Group Policy` console showing list of User Rights policies.

2. Double-click a policy to open its `Security Policy Setting` window.
3. Click `Add`. The `Group Name` window opens.

   Click `Browse`. The `Select Users or Groups` window opens.
4. Double-click on groups and users from the list to add them to the name list in the bottom pane of the window.
5. Click `OK` to save your selections and return to the `Group Name` window. The names appear as a semicolon-delimited list under Audit Policy.

   Click `OK` to close the window. The group list is put in the main pane of the `Security Policy Setting` window.
6. Click `OK` to save this configuration and return to the `Group Policy` console.

Now take a look at how to apply the User Rights policies. Some of these policies deal with obscure memory and process handling that lie beyond the scope of this book. Here is a quick list of the commonly configured rights followed by details for each one along with the default groups assigned to the policy. The name starting with *Se* in parentheses next to each policy is the formal privilege name. You will see these names in command-line interfaces and Event log entries:

- Access this computer from the network
- Act as part of the operating system
- Add workstations to domain
- Backup files and directories
- Create a pagefile
- Bypass traverse checking
- Change system time
- Log on locally
- Shut down the system
- Force shutdown from a remote system
- Load and unload device drivers
- Manage auditing and Security log
- Take ownership of files and other objects
- Log on as a batch job and log on as a service

Access this computer from the network. (SeNetworkLogonRight) (Administrators, Everyone, Power Users, IUSR, IWAM) This right gives users network access to resources such as shared folders, printers, and Web services. The Internet User (IUSR) and Internet Web Application Manager (IWAM) accounts are added to this list when IIS is installed. Some administrators with Windows 2000 workstations that are configured as peer servers (the default) often use this privilege to restrict peer file sharing. For example, you could delete the Everyone and Power Users groups and create a group called PEER_ADMINS to put on list for this right. By controlling the membership of PEER_ADMINS, you control who has the right to share files locally at their workstations. You can also use this right to restrict file-and-print access to NT servers that are supposed to be used only for application servers. User files tend to show up in the darndest places, but to find them tucked away on your big Oracle server is aggravating. Remove the Everyone and Power Users group from this right to prevent that from happening. Users can still access the client/server application via the client.

Act as part of the operating system. (SeTcbPrivilege) (Empty by default) Ordinarily you would never give this privilege to a regular user account. It is designed primarily for services that run in the background (daemons in UNIX jargon, NLMs for you NetWare folks). Vendors of these service packages, which are usually either utilities or client/server applications, design their installation routines to create a special user that is then used to control the background processes kicked off by the package. The installation routine should add that special account to the list of users with the Act As Part Of ... privilege automatically, but some are not quite that sophisticated. This is especially true of home-brew applications. Designers in your organization might be whiz-bangs with Win32 code, but not so savvy about NT system administration.

Add workstations to domain. (SeMachineAccountPrivilege) (Empty by default) As discussed Chapter 1, "Installing and Configuring Windows 2000," a workstation must be joined to a domain before users log on to that computer with their domain passwords. This is true of both classic NT and Windows 2000. New computers come on to a network regularly, and old computers often get renamed, so it becomes a logistical problem keeping track of computer registrations. You might want to give the right to register computers to technicians at the loading bay or to department power users who receive the computers. For example, you could create a group called DEPT_GURUS and put that group on the access list for Add Workstations To Domain. You could then put selected users in this group and they would then inherit the right to register workstations into the domain without having any other system or domain privileges. This right is only effective when enabled at domain controllers; if you maintain a separate GPO for the Domain Controllers OU, you should configure this policy for that GPO.

Back up files and directories / restore files and directories. (SeBackupPrivilege, SeRestorePrivilege) (Administrators, Backup Operators) The privilege of performing backups and restores is not necessarily an honor, but it is a key security assignment. The person who can copy confidential files from a server onto backup tape, and put those files back on some other server, essentially becomes the most trusted person in that organization. It's surprising to find organizations that require rigorous background checks for people who touch money at the front desk but perform only the most cursory review of the people doing their backups. At any rate, all third-party backup applications for Windows 2000 require you to create a special account that is put on the access list for these two rights and controls access to the files while the backup runs. If the backup fails, often it is because someone changed the password for this account or changed the name or deleted it because he didn't know what CHEY_AGENT was used for.

Create a pagefile. (SeCreatePagefilePrivilege) (Administrators) Windows 2000 Setup creates a paging file that should be sufficient for most users. One problem that often arises, however, is fragmentation of the paging file. This has a tremendous impact on performance, much more than fragmentation of the other files on the system. The defragger that comes with Windows 2000, a pared down version of Executive Software's Diskeeper, does not defrag the paging file. The commercial version of Diskeeper does defrag the paging file, but that costs money. One workaround is to configure a security option (covered later) that automatically deletes the paging file whenever the user logs off, and then create it anew at logon. This is also a good way to preserve security if you are concerned about one user pawing through another user's paging file with a sector reader. If you implement this policy, you will need to add the Everyone group to the member list for this privilege.

Bypass traverse checking. (SeChangeNotifyPrivilege) (Everyone) It is not uncommon to have a highly restricted directory nestled partway down a directory tree. Many servers have restricted folders that run like limestone layers across many different directory trees in a volume. This usually happens in a panic after an audit. By bypassing traverse checking, users can skip over these restricted folders and get to unrestricted folders further down the tree. POSIX compatibility demands that the Everyone group be removed from the access list for this right. (C2 configuration requirements does not require any change to the default configuration. You must disable POSIX for C2.) Don't take the Everyone group off the access list for this right until you are thoroughly familiar with the directory structure on the server and have ferreted out all pockets of highly restricted folders and moved them to discrete locations.

Change system time. (SeSystemtimePrivilege) (Administrators, [Server Operators] [Power Users]) Quite a few network processes and procedures depend on a single coordinated time source, so you might ask yourself why Microsoft didn't incorporate an automatic time sync into a domain client, a la NetWare. This remains one of the great secrets of the ages. You must run a logon script with a NET TIME command to sync the local workstation time with a domain controller. The syntax is net time /domain:dom_name /set /yes. The /yes bypasses the confirmation prompt. You must make your users a member of the Power Users group on their local workstations for this to work. Rights are always local. You can configure a domain policy to give the Users security group `SeSystemTimePrivilege`.

Log on locally. (`SeInteractiveLogonRight`) (Administrators, Account Operators, Backup Operators, Print Operators, Server Operators, IUSR, IWAM, LDAP_Anonymous, [Power Users], and [Users]) This right says, in effect, "You have permission to log on at the console of this computer." Obviously, the list for this privilege doesn't exactly define an exclusive club. The only default use of this privilege is to keep Users and Power Users from logging on at the console of server. If they try, they get a *Insufficient Privileges* error. This is also a common error for administrators new to trust relationships. Just because you can select your home domain from the pick list in WINLOGON doesn't necessarily mean you have local logon permissions in a trusting domain. Administrators in the trusting domain must give you `SeInteractiveLogonRight` permission by adding your account or a group containing your account to the Log On Locally list in their domain.

The special accounts IUSER, LDAP_Anonymous, and IWAM are given `SeInteractiveLogonRight` because of an interesting quirk in NETLOGON. The NETLOGON service works cheek-by-jowl with the network redirectors to pass along authentication requests to either MSV1_0 or Kerberos, depending on the client. But a user who browses a Windows 2000–hosted Web site or does an LDAP lookup for an ILS connection doesn't have an account in the domain or on the host server. He or she is given access via one of the special accounts. Because these accounts do not access the server via NETLOGON, they cannot be authenticated via the network. They come in the front door as if they did a console logon. Be very careful when granting other system privileges to these accounts. You might find yourself opening a security hole without realizing it. The IUSR account is also a member of the Guests group, for example; so if you or your colleagues have a habit of enabling the Guest account and giving the Guests group access to certain directories, you might end up inviting the great Internet bourgeoisie on to your network.

Shut down the system. (`SeShutdownPrivilege`) (Administrators, Backup Operators, [Power Users], [Users]) Under most circumstances, you do not want an average user to walk up the console of a server, press Ctrl+Alt+Del and select `Shutdown`. For this reason, only Administrators and Backup Operators have this permission for servers.

Force shutdown from a remote system. (`SeRemoteShutdownPrivilege`) (Administrators, Server Operators, [Power Users]) It's often necessary to reboot a system. Windows 2000 is much less obnoxious in this regard, but you'll still find yourself rebooting a server to clear out memory or free up a seized application. And you might need to restart a user's system if the user isn't in the area to give a manual three-finger salute. You can use the Shutdown utility that comes in the NT Resource Kit (there's a graphic version, SHUTGUI, for those of you who don't like command-line utilities), but you first need to have the Force Shutdown right at the target computer.

Load and unload device drivers. (SeLoadDriverPrivilege) (Administrators) If there were ever a right that you do not want to distribute to the average user population, this is it. Enough said.

Manage auditing and Security log. (SeSecurityPrivilege) (Administrators) This right gives permission to view, save, and clear the Security log and to establish audit policies. If you want to give your corporate or campus security officers the right to manage auditing on your Windows 2000 servers without giving them wide-ranging powers, you can put them on this access list.

Take ownership of files and other objects. (SeTakeOwnershipPrivilege) (Administrators) Every security object in NT has an owner. This is a fundamental tenet of C2 that is implemented right at the gut level of Windows 2000. An owner can do anything with the object he or she owns. Period. End of story. As an Administrator with SeTakeOwnershipPrivilege, you can take ownership of an object away from another user. It is also possible to assign ownership to another user, but not with the standard tools in Windows 2000. One possibility is to use a utility called chown from Mortise Kerns Systems, www.mks.com. A demo version of this and other UNIX-like tools comes in the Services for UNIX toolkit from Microsoft. Using chown, you can also assign ownership groups as well as individual user. For example, you could establish an ORPHAN_DATA group to assign ownership of files and directories that have been abandoned by their original users. Such a group would be easy to search for, thereby simplifying data cleanup.

Log on as a batch job and **Log on as a service.** (SeBatchLogonRight) (SeServiceLogonRight) (Empty) These two rights are somewhat complementary. It sometimes comes to pass that applications or utilities need to launch automatically and run in the background. No process can run as an orphan, and most background services run under the auspices of SYSTEM. This has its limitations, though. You don't necessarily want SYSTEM to run a third-party application. What if the application crashes and renders SYSTEM incapable of tending to other duties? Most apps establish a user account responsible for launching and monitoring the background process. This account must get authenticated, and it does so as either a batch job or a service. The difference is one of approach. An executable must either be specially designed to be a service or parlayed into a service using a utility such as SRVANY from the NT Resource Kit. A batch job can be any BAT or CMD file, so it is much easier to set up, but you still need a host to launch it in the background. The Scheduler is just such a host. Open it from the Control Panel. You can specify a user ID to use when running the process, and Scheduler will take care of getting the correct permissions.

Assigning Security Options

The final major group of security policies exposed to the Group Policy Editor are security options. This list consists of individual Registry entries that have some passing applicability to security. Unlike the preceding policies, these entries are not associated with users. They affect general system operation. Here is a list of a few of the more commonly encountered policies. An in-depth explanation of their default security options, associated Registry keys, values, and functions follows the list.

- Allow system to be shut down without having to log on
- Audit the access of global system objects
- Audit the use of all user rights including backup and restore
- Rename Administrator account [Guest Account]
- Clear virtual memory pagefile when system shuts down
- Shut down system immediately if unable to log security audits
- Do not allow enumeration of account names and shares by anonymous users
- Disable Ctrl+Alt+Del requirement for logon
- Do not display last username in logon screen
- Secure channel: digitally sign secure channel data
- Secure channel: digitally encrypt all secure channel data
- Secure channel: digitally encrypt or sign secure channel data
- Encrypt files in the offline folders cache
- Automatically log off users when logon time expires
- Message text for users attempting to log on
- Message title for users attempting to log on
- Number Of previous logons to cache
- Restrict CD-ROM access to locally logged-on user only
- Restrict floppy access to locally logged-on user only
- Send unencrypted password to connect to third-party smb servers

Allow system to be shut down without having to log on.
(HKLM\Software\Microsoft\Windows NT\CurrentVersion\Winlogon\
ShutdownWithoutLogon) There is a Shutdown button in the WINLOGON
window that permits a user to shut down the computer without logging
on. This discourages users from just shutting off the machine, although
it has been my experience that few people get this message. The
ShutdownWithoutLogon feature is disabled on servers so that the system can tell
you whether users are accessing the server or deliver other pronouncements
before you initiate the shutdown. If you find this annoying, enable this option.

Audit the access of global system objects. (HKLM | System |
CurrentControlSet | Control | Lsa | AuditBaseObject) The interior of
Windows 2000 is like the Pentagon. There are many places you don't really
want to see and most of them are pretty dull, even if you could see them.
Ordinarily, if you enable object access auditing using an audit policy, these
obscure internal objects will be excluded from the list. Enabling this option
adds them to the list. For the most part, this is only useful to driver and
system-level programmers.

Audit the use of all user rights including backup and restore.
(HKLM | System | CurrentControlSet | Control | Lsa | FullPrivilegeAuditing)
This is one of those "why bother" features. Under normal circumstances, if
you enable auditing of privileged object access, the Security log would fill as
soon as you performed your first backup and the exercise of the Backup
Operator privilege is logged over and over again. This auditing is ordinarily
bypassed. When you set this option, the exercise of Backup and Restore will
be logged. Only use this when you think that someone is misusing his or
her privileges. And be sure to make the Security log very large to accommodate the entries and be prepared for a very slow backup.

Rename Administrator account [Guest Account]. (Registry or
Directory entry locked) You have to assume that the bogeyman lurks everywhere, and you can be sure that the bogeyman is after your Administrator
password. You cannot delete Built-In accounts and groups—they are as fixed
as the Statue of Liberty—but you can change their names, and many administrators do to make it that much more difficult for the bogeyman to try dictionary attacks. This security option can make the change for you and propagate
it throughout your enterprise. If you decide to implement this policy, make
absolutely sure you have several other accounts with full administrative privileges, and then change the names to something long and incomprehensible.
Then, write down the new names and passwords and keep them safe. You may
need them. Not the Guest account, certainly, but NT treats the Administrator

account, or rather the SID that represents that account, with special respect. He's like a J.R.R. Tolkien wizard. There are some privileges hidden from view that only the one true Administrator can wield.

Clear virtual memory pagefile when system shuts down. (HKLM | System | CurrentControlSet | Control | Session Manager | Memory Management | ClearPageFileAtShutdown) As discussed earlier in this chapter, clearing out PAGEFILE.SYS is a good way not only to enforce security but to prevent performance-robbing fragmentation of the paging file. It requires some extra time to clear out the file, but not much. This option is highly recommended, especially if you do not deploy a third-party defragger that works on the paging file.

Shut down system immediately if unable to log security audits. (HKLM | System | CurrentControlSet | Control | Lsa | CrashOnAuditFail) If you choose to audit a system, you might object to someone logging on if that audit stream is not tracking. If the Security log fills, the bad guy might sneak on unnoticed. The ultimate stop to this problem is to shut down the system as soon as the Security log runs out of room. This may strike you as somewhat self-destructive way to enforce security audits, but hey, you have to grant the effectiveness. If you choose to enable this option and the system crashes, you can restart and logon as Administrator—not an account with Administrator privileges, mind you, only the Administrator account will work. If you renamed the Administrator account, this is one situation where you'll need the special account.

Do not allow enumeration of account names and shares by anonymous users. (HKLM | System | CurrentControlSet | Control | Lsa | RestrictAnonymous) Consider this scenario. You've created a classic NT one-way trust relationship between a resource domain and an account domain. Standard stuff for a master domain model. You're an administrator in the resource domain and you want to put a global group from the master domain on to the access control list on a local directory. You have logged on to the local resource domain with your administrator password. You make contact with the master domain using the NTFS permissions tool to get a list of users and groups. At that point, you are not logged on with an account from the account domain. How do you get that user list? Well, the domain controller gives domain special permission to anonymous members of the resource domain to enumerate the user list. You can disable this permission using this option if you don't want to give the resource domain administrators a list of users. This is most commonly done when the trust is established to a client's domain.

Disable Ctrl+Alt+Del requirement for logon. (HKLM | Software | Microsoft | Windows NT | CurrentVersion | Winlogon | DisableCAD) This new addition to Windows 2000 was intended to give workstation users who are not members of a domain the ability get right to the Explorer shell without a logon. It should not be enabled for member workstations or servers.

Do not display last username in logon screen. (HKLM | Software | Microsoft | Windows NT | CurrentVersion | Winlogon | DontDisplayLastUserName) It's handy not to be forced to type in your username each time you log on, but some users (and some security-conscious administrators) object to leaving the name exposed so that the bad guy can guess at a password.

Secure channel: digitally sign secure channel. (HKLM | System | CurrentControlSet | Services | Netlogon | Parameters | SealSecureChannel) This and the following two settings are designed to deal with a very specific potential security breach in Windows 2000. Member workstations and servers communicate to their domain controllers over a secure RPC link. This link is not checked for integrity, so a bright bad guy could conceivably impersonate a machine on the wire and divert secure traffic. The digital signing identifies each packet coming over the secure link. It slows down communications somewhat. (I do not have statistics.)

Secure channel: digitally encrypt all secure channel data. (HKLM | System | CurrentControlSet | Services | Netlogon | Parameters | SignSecureChannel) Same as the preceding description, but with the addition of encryption for all traffic, not just passwords.

Secure channel: digitally encrypt or sign secure channel. (HKLM | System | CurrentControlSet | Services | Netlogon | Parameters | RequireSignOrSeal) Same as preceding description, but forces secure traffic instead of letting the members auto-negotiate. Only set this option if every domain controller is set the same way.

Encrypt files in the offline folders cache. (HKLM | Software | Microsoft | Windows | CurrentVersion | NetCache | EncryptEntireCache) Client-side caching speeds network communication by holding copies of executables and other read-only files at the local machine. A bad guy could conceivably nab these saved files and steal valuable secrets. Encrypting the files slows performance, but improves security. You may have noticed a trend.

Automatically log off users when logon time expires. (HKLM | System | CurrentControlSet | Control | Session Manager | ProtectionMode) You can define a specific time of day after which a user or group of users is denied access. This is useful when you have a group of users who have specific duties from 8 to 5, but should not be messing around on the network after hours. Many managers find this option attractive in the era of Internet browsing. The question becomes, what happens to the user who is on the network when the fatal hour approaches. If you do not set this option, the user is warned repeatedly that their time has expired but they can continue to use network resources. If you enable this option, the user is warned several times and then, at the scheduled time, all network access is cut off. If you use this option, be sure to warn your users that the warnings mean business. They had best save their work or it will be lost. The users are not forced off the local machine. This policy affects network access only.

Message text for users attempting to log on. (HKLM | Software | Microsoft | Windows NT | CurrentVersion | Winlogon | LegalNoticeText) This and the next option define parameters for a special window that appears after the user presses Ctrl+Alt+Del but before the WINLOGON credentials window. It is most often used to display boilerplate HR text like "You are using COMPANY equipment and must obey COMPANY policies that are available in COMPANY offices."

Message title for users attempting to log on. (HKLM | Software | Microsoft | Windows NT | CurrentVersion | Winlogon | LegalNoticeCaption) This option specifies the title bar text in the window configured by LegalNoticeText.

Number of previous logons to cache. (HKLM | Software | Microsoft | Windows NT | CurrentVersion | Winlogon | CachedLogonsCount) If a Windows 2000 workstation cannot contact its domain controller, a user can still be logged on via cached credentials. The cache is set for 10 by default. If you have a workstation at which many people log on, some of them may have been aged out of the cache. You can set this option to as many as 50 logons.

Restrict CD-ROM access to locally logged-on user only. (HKLM | Software | Microsoft | Windows NT | CurrentVersion | Winlogon | AllocateCDRoms) C2 security requirements include a specification to exclude removable media from network access. This and the following option meet that requirement. You may be wondering about your Jaz or Zip drive or CD-R unit. The answer is, don't do it if you C2 it.

Restrict floppy access to locally logged-on user only. (HKLM | Software | Microsoft | Windows NT | CurrentVersion | Winlogon | AllocateFloppies) See preceding item.

Send unencrypted password to connect to third-party smb servers. (HKLM | System | CurrentControlSet | Control | Lsa | LmCompatibilityLevel) Windows 3.1x and Windows 9x clients who connect to a Windows 2000 server participate in NTLM Challenge-Response but do not use MD4 hash to share encrypted information. Instead, they use an older DES encryption with a password that actually travels along the wire. You can stop this behavior by setting this option, but only if you have no down-level clients remaining on your network.

Loading Custom Security Templates

The security settings in SECEDIT.SDB are initialized by a template file. Templates used to initially configure a system are stored in \WINNT\INF. Additional templates are stored in \WINNT\Security\Templates. You can modify these templates or build new ones and load them into SECEDIT.SDB using the Security Templates snap-in.

You can also use a template to analyze your existing security configuration to determine whether any security problems exist. This is done using The Security Configuration And Analysis snap-in.

This section covers the steps for using both of these security snap-ins to configure system security. First, take a look at how to modify an existing template or build a new one and apply it to the local security database. This should only be necessary if you have a standalone server or workstation. A domain member computer should be managed using group policies.

Procedure 6.14 **Configuring Security Templates**

1. Open an empty MMC console by entering MMC at the Run window.

2. From the console menu, select CONSOLE | ADD/REMOVE SNAP-IN. The Add/Remove Snap-in window opens.

3. Click Add. The Add Standalone Snap-in window opens.

4. Select both the Security Configuration and Analysis snap-in and the Security Templates snap-in.

5. Close the window to return to the Add/Remove Snap-in window. The two snap-ins are on the list. There are no extensions.

6. Click OK to save the additions and return to the MMC console.

7. Select CONSOLE | SAVE AS and save the console with a descriptive name such as SECCONF.MSC.

8. Expand the tree for both snap-ins. Security Templates contains a list of files from \WINNT\Security\Templates. Security Configuration and Analysis shows a set of instructions for performing an analysis. Figure 6.12 shows an example.

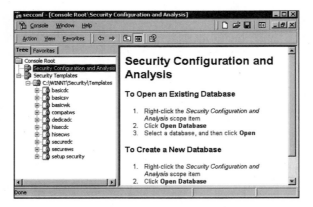

Figure 6.12   Custom MMC console showing Security Templates
and Security Configuration and Analysis snap-ins.

9. Expand the tree under one of the templates and examine the Account Policies and Local Policies settings. Each template packages a set of policy options designed to simplify security configuration.

10. To modify an existing template, expand the tree under the template icon and modify the settings.

11. To build a new template, right-click the template path and select NEW TEMPLATE from the fly-out menu. A window opens with fields for Template Name and Description. Enter this information and click OK to create the template. The template is added to the template list and contains no special settings. Configure it based on your requirements.

After you have configured a template with the settings you think are appropriate for your system, apply it to the local system by importing it into the security database. Do this as follows:

Procedure 6.15   **Applying a Custom Security Template**

1. Open the local Group Policy editor, GPEDIT.MSC.

2. Expand the tree to the Security Settings icon.

3. Right-click the Security Settings icon and select IMPORT POLICY from the fly-out menu. The Import Policy From window opens.

4. Double-click the name of your new template to load it into the security database.

5. Verify that the local settings reflect the options you selected in the `Template Settings` console.

6. Close the Group Policy editor.

If the computer is a domain member, the settings you apply to the local database will not override group policies downloaded from the domain. If you want to check the current security settings for a computer, including those in the downloaded group policies, you can run an analysis using a copy of the Security Configuration database, SECEDIT.SDB. This database is locked when the system is in operation, so you must make a copy of it. The copy can be any name and can remain in the same \WINNT\Security folder.

Procedure 6.16 **Performing a Security Analysis**

1. Load the custom console that contains the Security Configuration and Analysis snap-in.

2. Right-click the Security Configuration and Analysis icon and select OPEN DATABASE from the fly-out menu. The `Open Database` window opens.

3. Navigate to `\WINNT\Security\Database` and load the copy of SECEDIT.SDB. If you try to load the SECEDIT.SDB file itself, you will get an *Access Denied* error.

4. With the database loaded, right-click the Security Configuration and Analysis icon and select ANALYZE COMPUTER NOW from the fly-out menu. The `Perform Analysis` window opens with a path for the analysis log. The default path goes to the `Temp` directory in your local user's profile.

5. Click OK. The analysis is performed. The `Analyzing System Security` window charts the progress. The event should not take long to complete unless your configuration includes a complex list of file and Registry security entries.

6. When the analysis is complete, expand the tree under Security Configuration and Analysis. It shows the standard set of security settings icons and policies. When you highlight a policy, the right pane shows a comparison of the settings in the copy of the SECEDIT database you loaded and the current computer settings. Figure 6.13 shows an example. Any differences between the Database Setting entries and the Computer Setting entries are attributable to group policies that have been downloaded from the domain.

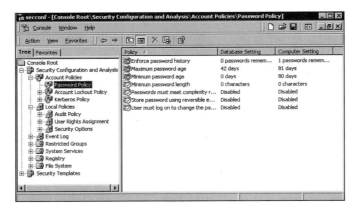

Figure 6.13 Analysis results after running Security Configuration Analysis.

7. Scan the contents of the analysis and decide how you want to handle any discrepancies. The best course of action for a domain member is to modify the group policies. For a standalone server, if the database contents are correct, you can right-click the Security Configuration and Analysis icon and select CONFIGURE COMPUTER NOW from the fly-out menu. This will overwrite any local configuration policies with the contents of the configuration database.

8. If you want to do just the opposite, to update the configuration database with an existing template, right-click the Security Configuration and Analysis icon and select Import Template. Select the template from the list and click OK to apply it.

Configuring Secondary Logon

UNIX administrators often sneer, perhaps rightfully so, at the inconvenience of the admin tools in Windows 2000 and NT. If you really want to use grep and awk and those other utilities that sound like my grandfather coughing up phlegm while he watched the Ed Sullivan show, get the Services for UNIX add-on pack. Before you pop for the extra tools, however, you might find a few in the Windows 2000 shrink-wrap that will serve your needs.

One tool addresses a security issue and a nagging problem for field technicians. The security issue is that Windows 2000/NT administrators spend too much time logged on with administrator privileges. This exposes the network to all kinds of bad germs. The administrator needs a way to stay logged on with normal system privileges but to quickly get administrator rights to perform specific functions.

The nagging problem for technicians concerns desktop visits. Let's say you sit down at a user's desktop and you need to perform a few diagnostic routines or install a piece of software. The user doesn't have admin rights. You don't want to log on with your ID because of the change in profile.

In both cases, what is needed is the ability to exercise administrative privileges—to do a quick superuser logon, if you will—without logging off first. Windows 2000 enables this feature with the *Secondary Logon Service*, SECLOGON. The SECLOGON service permits you to kick off a process in an administrator's context. The SECLOGON service is one of the suite of services loaded and managed by the Services executable. The SECLOGON service starts automatically at logon.

Call up the SECLOGON service to launch a program by using the `runas` command. The syntax for `runas` is: `runas /user:<domain or computer name>\username   app_name`.

For example, log on to a Windows 2000 workstation as a standard user without admin rights. Open a command prompt and run the `Time` command. Try to change the system time. You'll be denied access. Users cannot change the system time. This requires administrator privileges. Now enter the following command (the example uses a domain name of company):

```
runas /user:company\administrator  cmd
```

You'll be prompted for the password for Administrator. Enter it. A command session opens in the context of Administrator. Look at the title bar to verify this. Any applications launched from this session use the administrator's access token and system privileges. Now try to change the system time again. You will succeed.

You can also use the `runas` command to open MMC snap-ins from a user's desktop. If you want to load the Computer Management console to check the partitioning of a user's drive, for example, you can use the following command to launch the console in the Administrator's context:

```
runas  /user:company\administrator  "mmc  c:\winnt\system32\compmgmt.msc"
```

After you have finished your administrative chores, be sure to close any programs and sessions you opened with `runas`. You don't want to leave a door open for the user.

Moving Forward

At this point in the Windows 2000 migration odyssey, the preliminaries have been completed. We've installed a few Windows 2000 servers and configured name resolution with WINS and DNS. We have good control over IP addressing with DHCP. And we have control of access security and security policies. Now we're ready to start designing the architecture of the network, and to do that we need to know a lot more about the Active Directory.

7

Understanding Active Directory Services

IMAGINE THE NIRVANA OF NETWORK OPERATING SYSTEMS. It would consist of fully compatible hardware that runs and runs without constant attention and adjustment. It would provide a stable, scalable, secure, and flexible environment for users that would run virtually any application with an absolute minimum of management chores. And it would run these applications on every type of computing device, file server, app server, Web server, database server, workstation, storage attached network device, laptop, handheld PC, remote access portal, mainframe gateway, coffee maker, and soda pop machine.

Classic NT teased us with this dream of a global unified system. Sure, NT wasn't as stable as NetWare, as scalable as UNIX, as manageable as Banyan, or as cheap as LANtastic, but you sure couldn't fault it for flexibility. Classic NT runs just as reliably on a 486 clone laptop as it does on a $200,000 Data General behemoth. This flexibility made classic NT the darling of corporate IT managers as they began balking at expensive, proprietary solutions and were demanding a commodity operating system that could run on commodity components, and the marketplace pretty much got what it wanted in classic NT. The CEO gets her email from an NT server. The CFO runs financials on an NT server. The COO manages intelligent factories with NT servers. Middle managers get information from a cornucopia of business automation toys hosted by NT servers. And users get basic file and print services and Internet access from NT servers.

As for the administrators of these classic systems, well, managing classic NT isn't exactly Nirvana. That's because all this applause for classic NT's flexibility begs the question of its *scalability*. A network operating system cannot be considered scaleable if the management chores necessary to keep it running increase geometrically with the number of servers and users. Theoretically, a single classic NT domain can support 20 or 30 thousand users and their workstations. A meshed multiple-master domain can support four or five times that number. Microsoft has this kind of huge NT network, as do many other large organizations, but take it from me, the administrators of those systems know the difference between *scalability* and *stretchability*.

Classic NT has many eccentricities, big and small, which limit its scalability. Many of these eccentricities stem from NT's clumsy, flat-file, Registry-based security system. If you've ever taken any NT certification exams, you've had to memorize those arcane NT domain models with their Byzantine trust topologies and soap opera implementation scenarios. "Sales trusts Personnel but does not trust Accounting, so how do you give the CFO access to the sales forecasts so she can approve the hiring requests from the HR director?"

What is lacking in classic NT is a true *Directory Service* capable of handling the management chores for a network containing hundreds of thousands, if not millions, of users. That's what Microsoft has delivered in Windows 2000 with Active Directory. Let's sneak under the ballyhoo surrounding Active Directory and look at the details of its architecture, nomenclature, and interfaces.

Directory Service Components

Directory Services are like SAABs. You never notice them until you think about owning one, then you see them everywhere. For example, I have a Directory Service of sorts sitting near my phone in a big book called the Yellow Pages. This Yellow Pages Directory Service contains entries for every business in my dialing region. Each entry has certain attributes such as Name, Address, and Phone number, with additional attributes that give details about the business such as products, maps, and slogans.

Every Directory Service has rules that govern what information can be placed in the Directory and how that information is stored. Entries in the Yellow Pages Directory Service fall under categories like "Attorneys," "Theaters—Movies," and "Restaurants—Outrageously Overpriced." There are also rules that determine how the information in the Directory Service can be accessed. For example, there is a rule in the Yellow Pages Directory

Service that states, *If the user attempts to access this directory after breaking down on the freeway and hiking five miles to get to a rest stop where this is the only Directory because all the rest have been stolen and the user has just a single quarter to his name, then all entries under "Automobile—Repair & Service" must be ripped out.*

A network Directory Service is a bit more complex than the Yellow Pages, but the concepts remain the same. The Directory stores, organizes, and retrieves information about objects of interest in a network. This means it contains entries for users and groups, workstations and servers, policies and scripts, printers and queues, switches and routers, and just about anything else that relates to computing. For example, distributed applications now store user and desktop information in Directory Services so that the application can be deployed seamlessly to thousands of desktops across a galaxy of desktops. Group collaboration tools rely on Directory Services for users to locate each other and to locate tools to facilitate information sharing. Infrastructure components now look to a Directory Service to find policies that control access, protocols, flow-paths, and quality of service. And while all this exciting technology zizzles and swizzles around the network, we administrators can just sit back in the comfort of our swivel chairs like George Jetson and manage the whole shebang with controls that are themselves part of the Directory Service.

All hype? For the most part, sure. George Jetson doesn't have to diagnose and fix a corrupted database that sends the entire system into meltdown. But the potential is certainly there to build networks of galactic proportions, so let's get down to some basic questions. How does a Directory Service work? Why does it work that way? How does it break and how is it fixed? Let's start with a look at the history of Directory Services as it pertains to the Active Directory.

Brief History of Directory Services

The story of the great Mississippi River starts with a smallish lake in upstate Minnesota. The store of global Directory Services starts with a smallish document called X.500, *Data Networks and Open System Communications—Directory*. The dramatis persona for the Directory Service story includes standards bodies and vendors from all over the world. First and foremost of these players is the *International Telecommunication Union* (ITU). The ITU is a United Nations agency that acts as a forum for governments who want to achieve a consensus on global telecom issues. The ITU membership includes manufacturers and service providers from over 130 countries.

The branch of the ITU specifically tasked with making Directory Service recommendations is the Telecommunication Standardization Sector, or ITU-T. The ITU-T was formerly called the *Comité Consultatif International Téléphonique et Télégraphique* (CCITT). The ITU-T issues recommendations in many areas, from broadcast requirements and measuring equipment to faxing. These recommendations are grouped into lettered series. For example, the V series covers data communication over telephone networks and includes such famous standards such as V.34, *Wideband Analog Modem Communication*, and V.90, *Connecting Analog to Digital Modems*. The X series recommendations, which include the X.500 recommendations for Directory Services, cover a variety of data network and open system communication technologies, such as X.25 packet-switched networks and X.400 messaging systems. For a complete listing of ITU recommendations, see `www.itu.int/publications/itu-t/itutx.htm`.

The ITU-T does not set standards, it only makes recommendations. Getting an international standard approved requires the consent of the *International Organization for Standardization* (ISO). Unlike the ITU, whose membership comes from industry vendors, ISO members come from national standards bodies. The U.S. member is the *American National Standards Institute* (ANSI). The ISO Web site is located at `www.ISO.ch`. The ch indicates that the site is in Switzerland, just in case you are not up on your ISO 3166 two-letter country codes.

Source of the ISO Name

You may be wondering why the initials ISO do not match the name "International Organization for Standardization." Actually, the letters are not initials at all. They come from the Greek word *isos*, meaning equal. These letters were used to avoid the hodgepodge of acronyms that would have resulted if the various member countries translated International Organization for Standardization into their own language with their own initials.

The ISO is responsible for achieving consensus and standardization almost every area, from the quality standards of ISO 9000 to the standard paper sizes of ISO 216. In the networking industry, it is most famous for ISO 7498, *Information Technology—Open System Interconnection—Basic Reference Model*, better known as the OSI Model. ISO standards that affect data communication technology are often jointly published with the ITU-T. For example, the ISO standard that parallels the ITU-T X.500 recommendations for Directory Services is ISO 9594, *Information Technology—Open Systems Interconnection—The Directory*. Because the ISO issues standards and the ITU-T issues recommendations, it is actually a misnomer to refer to the "X.500 Standard," but this is commonly done because the two documents are identical. In this book, I'll refer to the X.500/9594 Standard.

The ISO is the senior standards body in the world, but it certainly is not the only one. Many agencies dip their spoons in the Standards soup bowl, and they sometimes slosh on each other. In the data communications field, there is overlap between standards published by the ISO and standards published by the *International Electrotechnical Commission* (IEC). The IEC deals with international standardization for electronics, magnetics, electromagnetics, electroacoustics, telecommunication, and energy production/distribution. They promulgate terminology, symbols, measurement standards, performance standards, dependability, design, development, safety, and environmental standards. The U.S. member of the IEC is also ANSI. The ISO and IEC have joined with the ITU in publishing Directory Service standards. The IEC Web site is located at `www.IEC.ch`.

In the United States, there is one senior Standards body, ANSI, with many, many advisory bodies. This should come as no surprise in a country where millions of people regularly call television talk shows to give advice to total strangers about their sex lives. The advisory body with the most influence over implementation of the X.500/9594 standard is the *Internet Engineering Task Force* (IETF). Their Web site is located at `www.IETF.org`. The IETF is an amalgam of developers, researchers, designers, and crazed individuals of all stripes who have an interest in the workings of the Internet. Special working groups within the IETF ride herd on Internet workings by using a collaborative process called the Internet Standards Process, a unique and somewhat lengthy operation that consists of thrashing a good idea mercilessly until it breaks into pieces that can be easily digested by the collective organism.

The Internet Standards Process is facilitated by documents called *Request for Comments* (RFCs). To give you an idea of how long it takes to assimilate new ideas into Internet standards, out of the hundreds and hundreds of standards-track RFCs listed in RFC 2400, "Internet Official Protocol Standards," only about three dozen have been elevated to the lofty status of Official Standard. The rest are still squirming somewhere in the approval process. This doesn't stop vendors from implementing particular RFCs, but the stipulations in those RFCs are elective, a fine oxymoron. Copies of RFCs, Standards, Standards Track documents, Internet Drafts, and other working papers can be found at the IETF site and at various mirrored sites around the Internet. I prefer the search engine at the Internet Engineering Standards Repository, `www.normos.org`.

The IETF and its teeming throngs can circumvent many of the ISO/IEC standards and ITU recommendations if they deem it necessary to send useful protocols out into the world. An example of this is the *Lightweight Directory Access Protocol* (LDAP). LDAP is a pared-down version of the X.500 Directory Service. It forms the basis of Active Directory, as well as Netscape

Directory Services and other Directory Service products. There is no LDAP standard from the ISO and no LDAP recommendation from the ITU. LDAP is purely an Internet concoction. Active Directory implements the most current version of LDAP, version 3, as documented in RFC 2251, "Lightweight Directory Access Protocol v3." This RFC expands and augments the original LDAP Standards Track document, RFC 1777, "Lightweight Directory Access Protocol."

Although LDAP is not precisely an X.500 implementation, a great deal of the design basis of LDAP comes from X.500. Before describing LDAP in detail, let's take a look at its parent, X.500.

X.500 Overview

The goal of ITU Recommendation X.500/ISO-IEC Standard 9594 is to cut through the babble of competing user database repositories and provide a universal methodology for storing, distributing, and accessing user information. An X.500/9594 Directory Service contains a distributed information store that can contain almost any useful information about the users of an Information System and the infrastructure that supports that system.

The *distributed* nature of the information store in a Directory Service is important because a fundamental purpose of the Directory is to give access to any authorized client anywhere in the network. This would be virtually impossible to do on a grand scale with a single database replicated to many servers. In an X.500 Directory Service, servers contain pieces of the overall information store and use a complex set of referrals to guide users to the server that holds the particular information they are looking for.

The framework for the distributed information store in a Directory Service conforms to the functional outlines of the implementing organization. Properly designed Directory Services are equally at home in colleges, governmental entities, corporate enterprises, non-profit organizations, and international telecommunications oligopolies. A Directory Service is probably not suited to bowling leagues and bridge clubs, but nothing in its fundamental organization precludes that use. You also would probably not implement a Directory Service to manage a point-of-sale system in a local video store. A Directory Service is not a general-purpose database. But you most certainly would consider implementing a Directory Service to manage the three thousand salespeople who log on at those point-of-sale terminals.

The magic of X.500 comes from the flexible way it compartmentalizes management of its information store. An organization with strict corporate policies governing computer use and stiff penalties for violating those polices would be equally comfortable deploying an X.500 Directory Service as a rock-and-roll organization with virtually no computer control policies at all. This flexibility comes at the cost of complexity, not the least of which is a thicket of nomenclature rife with obscure computing jargon and Three Letter Acronyms (TLAs). The operations described by these terms and acronyms crop up quite a bit in the documentation of LDAP and Active Directory, though, so it pays to give them a Quick Run Through (QRT). See Figure 7.1 for a roadmap.

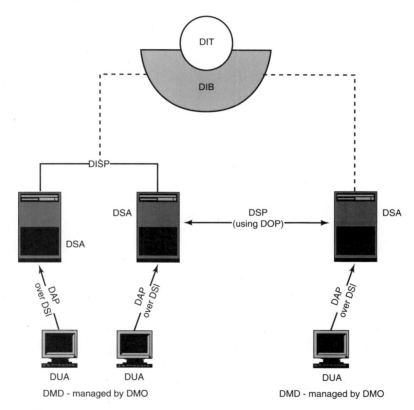

Figure 7.1   X.500 Components and their communication protocols.

- Information in an X.500 Directory is stored in a *Directory Information Base* (DIB).

- The DIB is divided into pieces that are structured into a hierarchy called a *Directory Information Tree* (DIT).

- Each piece of the DIB is stored on a server called a *Directory Service Agent* (DSA).

- A user who needs information from the Directory submits queries via an application interface called a *Directory User Agent* (DUA).

- A DUA communicates with a DSA using the *Directory Access Protocol* (DAP).

- One DSA communicates with another using the *Directory System Protocol* (DSP).

- Administrative information exchanged between DSAs is controlled via policies defined by the *Directory Operational Binding Management Protocol* (DOP).

- A single *Directory Management Organization* (DMO) takes charge of a *Directory Management Domain* (DMD) that contains one or more DSAs.

- Information held by one DSA is replicated to other DSAs in the same DMD using the *Directory Information Shadowing Protocol* (DISP).

- DAP, DSP, DISP, and all other high-level communication protocols in X.500 use OSI networking as defined in ITU Recommendation X.200/OSI-EIU Standard 7498.

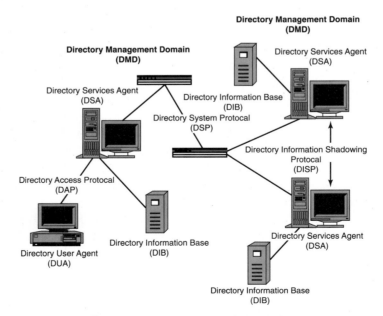

Figure 7.2 Diagram of sample X.500 layout.

Here's an example of how these elements tie together in a production X.500 Directory. Refer to Figure 7.2. Let's say that the secondhand car dealers in America decide to form an association that uses X.500 to store information about vehicles sold by each member. The DIB for this Directory Service would include makes, models, years, vehicle identification numbers, and unbeatable prices. Each dealer is assigned a DMO that controls a DMD. The DIB in each DMD is hosted by at least one DSA, which exchanges administrative information with DSAs in other DMDs using DOP. Dealerships in the same region have individual DSAs that replicate their copy of the DIB between each other via DISP. The pieces of the DIB are joined into a single DIT, the root of which is hosted by a DSA at association headquarters. Why go through all this trouble? Well, if a customer at a dealership in Kankakee wants a cherry-colored Cherokee, the salesperson can sit at a DUA and submit a query to the local DSA via DAP. First, DSA would check its copy of the local DIB. If it failed to locate a record locally, the DSA would use DSP to query other DSAs until it either found a match or exhausted all possibilities. In the latter case, the DUA is programmed to suggest alternatives, like cream-colored Chevelles.

Why LDAP Instead of X.500?

There are several pedigreed X.500 Directory Services commercially available, but few have achieved widespread popularity. The problem with pristine X.500 implementations is the overhead represented by all those protocols. When you get an army of DUAs all talking DAP over ISO to DSAs that refer queries to other DSAs using DSP while at the same time mirroring their DIB to other DSAs in their DMD via DISP, my friend, you've got a whole D★★ lot to go wrong.

In the early 90's, a few bright folks at the University of Michigan wanted to build a Directory Service to handle their 100,000+ students, staff, and faculty. They gave up on the complexities of X.500 and came up with a scheme that retained the X.500 directory structure, but gave it a streamlined access protocol based on standard TCP/IP instead of ISO. In addition, they came up with a pared-down referral mechanism, a more flexible security model, and no fixed replication protocol. They called it the *Lightweight Directory Access Protocol* (LDAP). The rest, as they say, is history. If you want to read more, take a look at www.umich.edu/~dirsvcs. Be sure to wear your blue and gold.

When Microsoft decided to replace the clumsy Registry-based security system in classic NT with a true Directory Service, rather than devise a proprietary Directory Service of their own, they chose to adopt LDAP. Even more importantly, from our perspective as administrators, Microsoft chose to deliver this LDAP Directory Service using two proven technologies. For a database engine, they used a revved-up version of the *Extensible Schema Engine* (ESE), first introduced with Exchange. Microsoft chose ESE over their SQL Server database engine because a SQL engine does not work efficiently with the structure of an LDAP directory. The ESE engine, on the other hand, was primarily designed as an object-oriented database. It's not unreasonable to say that Exchange has been an extensive, three-year beta for Active Directory. There should be an Easter Egg in Windows 2000 containing the names of the Exchange administrators who contributed hundred of thousands of hours to this unofficial beta.

Active Directory Drivers

The ESE engine driver is ESENT.DLL, loaded as part of the SERVICES suite. It is ESENT that reads and writes the ISAM files in the information store. Another term for ESENT is a *table manager*.

Most of the high-level functionality discussed in this chapter is handled by the Directory Services Agent, NTDSA.DLL, which runs under the Local Security Authority SubSystem, LSASS. The NTDSA driver identifies objects in the database, handles transaction processing and authentication, and constructs referrals to other DSAs.

There is a third part of the Directory that is not handled by a driver, as such. It is the *database layer*. This layer sits between ESENT and NTDSA and mediates transactions between them. The database layer turns the flat ISAM information store into a hierarchical database that the Active Directory can understand. It also exposes the Jet API so that NTDSA can make calls to the ESENT table manager. It also converts an object's LDAP distinguished name into an integer that is keyed to the object's entry in the ISAM table.

For a Directory location service, Microsoft chose to abandon the phenomenally quirky and just-this-side-of-proprietary WINS (Windows Naming Service) in favor of another open standard, *Domain Name System* (DNS). Not only did Microsoft throw in their lot with DNS, they made use of a relatively new DNS technology, Dynamic DNS, documented in RFC 2136, "Dynamic Updates in the Domain Name System."

This combination of LDAP for the Directory Service, ESE for the Directory database engine, and Dynamic DNS for locating Directory Services makes Windows 2000 the most open of all Microsoft's networking systems to date. However, good ingredients don't necessarily guarantee a palatable product, as anyone who has tasted my cooking will attest. Active Directory has proven itself admirably in the lab and in limited production in several large networks that are part of a special Rapid Deployment

Opportunity program. Even so, a Directory Service is a complex animal and there are gotchas by the bucketful to watch out for. We'll cover as many as possible in this and the next three chapters.

Active Directory Information Structure

At its most fundamental level, a Directory Service is just a big database. It may be a bit fancier than the database you use to tally the overtime pay you've lost since taking your salaried administrator position a few years back, but the principles are pretty much the same. In X.500 terminology, the Directory Service database is called a *Directory Information Base* (DIB). If you think of an old-style library card catalog system as a kind of Directory Service, then one of those oak cabinets with rows of drawers is a DIB.

The X.500 Directory Service structure was developed at a time when *object-oriented* databases represented leading-edge technology. If your only exposure to database technology has been with more modern relational databases, the design constraints of an object database can look a little strange. In a relational database, a record is formed by the intersection of a row and a column in a table. A record can be uniquely identified by a table name and a cell ID. Tables can be linked so that information in them can be accessed by a single query.

This is not the case for object-oriented databases. In an object-oriented database, each record (object) occupies a unique position identified by a name and a path. The location of the object can be traced back to the top of the database by using its full name, like a Daughter of the American Revolution tracing her forebears back to the Mayflower. A file system is an example of an object-oriented database.

Object databases consist of big, structured sequential files connected by a set of indexes that are themselves nothing more than big, structured sequential files. The underlying database technology for Active Directory is *Indexed Sequential Access Method* (ISAM). You'll see this term in the Event Log and other reports. The ESE database engine exposes the flat ISAM structure as a hierarchy of objects. In addition, Microsoft makes extensive use of COM technology with Active Directory objects represented as COM objects via *Active Directory Services Interface* (ADSI).

Container and Leaf Objects in LDAP

Traditional X.500 Directory Services classify objects as either *container* objects or *leaf* objects. Only container objects can hold other objects. This is not true of LDAP directories such as Active Directory. In LDAP, just about any object can be used as a container. There are very few leaf objects in the strictest sense of the word, fewer than ten in the Active Directory. Rigid guidelines constrain what class of objects another object can hold, though, so anarchy does not reign.

The Directory contains information about specific types of objects, such as user objects, computer objects, and so forth. These are called object *classes*. A class is a bundle of *attributes* with a name. Figure 7.3 shows how attributes and classes are related.

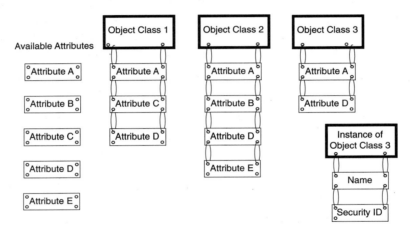

Figure 7.3   Classes and attributes in a Directory Service.

Attributes and Properties

Attributes are also often called *properties*. There is a difference between these two terms, but it is so subtle that most reference manuals, including this one, use them interchangeably.

The attribute list associated with a particular object class differentiates it from all other object classes. For example, user objects have different attributes than computer objects or IP Security objects. Using the library card catalog example, there are different color cards that represent different classes of items that can be found in the library, such as Books, Periodicals, and Tapes. A card for Books has entries for Title, Author, ISBN, and so forth. A card for Tapes would have these entries plus additional entries for Reader and Play—Time. Not every attribute needs to have a value. This saves storage space and reduces replication traffic.

Classes also define the scope of a Directory. You would not expect to find cards in a library card catalog representing Off-The-Road Vehicles or Double-Meat Hamburgers. The initial scope of the Active Directory database is defined by Microsoft, but the underlying design can be expanded to include objects defined by vendors or yourself, if you want to tailor a few items for your organization.

Designers strive to limit the complexity of a Directory by defining a minimum number of classes and making attributes as widely applicable as possible. For example, in the library card catalog example, it would be a mistake to create a class called *Somewhat-Less-Than-Riveting-Early-20th-Century-American-Novels*, even though it seems like quite a few objects would fit that class. In relation to the overall scope of a library, though, this classification would be too narrow. The Active Directory has only about 200 object classes for a directory store capable of handling 10 million objects. The classes include common objects like *User, Group,* and *Computer* along with more esoteric objects like *Protocol-Config-HTTP-Server* and *MSMQ-Enterprise-Settings.*

Each individual object in the Directory database is derived from a specific object class. Another way of saying this is that an object represents an *instance* of a class. Each instance of an object class differs from another instance by having different values for its attributes. This gets a little fuzzy if you look at it too hard, so it helps to have a visual. Remember the movie *Elephant Man*? In a great scene, the lead character, John Merrick, stands in front of a curious mob and exclaims, "I am not an elephant. I am a human being." Had Mr. Merrick been a Directory Services designer, he could have clarified his point even further by adding, "What I mean to say is, I am an instance of the Human Being class, not the Elephant class. The only difference between you and me is a relatively minor attribute of mine that has a different value from yours. So lay off, will you?"

Defining the attribute list for an object class can be slippery. Subtle differences may force a designer to create a new class. If you were designing a library card catalog, you might start out by defining a class called Tape with an attribute called Type that has two permitted values, *Audio* and *Video*. This decision forces you to define attributes for the Tape class that fully define both audiotapes and videotapes. After months of agonizing, you might decide that the properties of audio and video tapes are so different that they warrant creating two classes, *Audio Tape* and *Video Tape*, each with their own unique attribute sets. There are many instances in Active Directory and LDAP where two object classes differ by only one or two attributes.

The objects in a Directory Service fit together based on an *Information Model*. The model acts as a blueprint that defines the eventual layout. Models are not design specifications, but without a model, you could start out with a pile of automobile parts and end up building a go-cart. Let's take a look at the LDAP Information Model and see how Active Directory conforms and departs from it.

Directory Information Model

A Directory Service, as defined by the X.500/9594 standard, defines a technology capable of cataloging information about every user in every institution on every continent in the entire world. The goal of X.500 was to define a single source of information where users from all nations could go to locate each other and learn about each other and discover common likes and dislikes and eventually communicate freely to find a path to universal peace and brotherhood and the dawning of the Age of Aquarius. For this reason, many of the components of the X.500 information model have a distinctly geopolitical flavor.

LDAP has somewhat more modest ambitions than X.500, (although I'm sure a single universal Directory Service running Active Directory would appeal to Bill Gates), but it still makes sense to use a political model when examining the structure of a Directory Service. Take a federation as an example. In a federation, autonomous regions levy local taxes and take charge of local security and generally defer to a central authority only when they need something from one another, like a standard size for railroad tracks or a common set of baseball rules. Autonomous regions can be subdivided into even smaller regions called localities. An X.500 Directory Service for the United States would have just over fifty localities representing states and territories and the District of Columbia. Each of these localities could be further divided into organizational entities, such as counties and cities and townships. These subdivisions need not be completely autonomous, although a visit to the New Mexico State House while the legislature is in session may convince you otherwise.

In Active Directory, an autonomous region is called a *domain*. Each domain has an independent security structure, an independent namespace, and independent management.

DNS Domains and Active Directory Domains

It has always been unfortunate that Microsoft chose to snarl together NT terminology with DNS terminology by using the name *domain* to define a management area in the SAM. This confusion only deepens in Windows 2000 because Active Directory domains and DNS are so intimately entwined. In case you skipped the DNS chapter, here's a quick review of the differences between DNS domains, classic NT domains, and Windows 2000 domains:

- A DNS domain is a collection of hosts and services that occupy a common namespace. The database for DNS domain is a *zone table*.

- A classic NT domain is a collection of users, groups, and computers that share a common security framework. The databases for a classic NT domain are contained in the SAM and Security hives in the Registry.

- A Windows 2000 domain is a collection of network entities that share a common security framework and namespace. The database for a Windows 2000 domain is the Active Directory.

Active Directory is capable of holding millions of objects in a single domain, but a big domain is like an NBA center. He may be the key to winning, but only if he doesn't have to move too fast or too often. The Directory database, NTDS.DIT, can get very big, very quickly. The DIT for a domain with 150,000 objects can be difficult to replicate and manage. For this reason, big organizations need to break up their Active Directory into several domains and knit those domains together with trust relationships. There are four different types of trust relationships. Figure 7.4 shows how they are constructed.

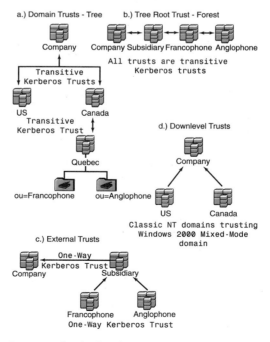

Figure 7.4   Structures for the four basic Windows 2000 trust relationships.

- **Domain Trusts.** This style of trust exists between domains that share a common schema, configuration context, global catalog, and occupy the same DNS namespace. Domain trusts are used to build *trees*. A tree is made up of *parent* and *child* domains. A parent domain can have more than one child domain, with a Domain Trust relationship between them. Each of those child domains can have Domain Trust relationships with their own child domains. Trees of more than seven to ten levels are discouraged for performance reasons.

- **Tree Root Trusts.** This style of trust exists between domains that share a common schema, naming context, and global catalog but occupy different DNS namespaces. Tree Root trusts are used to build *forests*. A forest is made up of peer domains with no hierarchical relationship. Forests provide a way to connect domains between organizations that want to maintain separate management boundaries and DNS namespaces but share common security principals and LDAP referral mechanisms.

- **External Trusts.** Domains that do not have Directory elements in common but share common security principals can be connected by external trusts. External trusts resemble classic NT trusts. Users and groups from an external trusted domain can be used as security principals in a trusting domain, but LDAP searches will not cross the trust boundary so directory objects are not visible to users in the trusting domain. External trusts provide a quick way to configure access lists on resources that must be made available to users from outside domains.

- **Downlevel Trusts.** A trust between a Windows 2000 domain and a classic NT domain is a downlevel trust. This style of trust exists for backward compatibility. It uses classic NT challenge-response security instead of Kerberos, so it is not transitive.

I have not yet discussed several of the terms used in the preceding list, so here are a few quick definitions.

- **Naming Context.** A Directory object that forms a replication boundary is called a naming context. Another term for naming context is *partition*.

- **Schema.** The schema defines the contents and structure of the Directory and the rules that relate objects in the Directory with each other. These rules come in the form of schema objects that are themselves part of the Directory in the same way that the definition for the word "dictionary" is contained in a dictionary. The expression 'share a common schema' means that a tree or forest contains only one copy of the schema. This copy is replicated to all domain controllers.

- **Global Catalog.** Each Windows 2000 domain defines a separate LDAP Directory. There is no facility in LDAPv3 for referring queries between separate Directories. Microsoft finesses this limitation by providing an index to every object in every domain in a Directory tree or forest. This index is called the *Global Catalog* (GC). The GC contains many commonly used attributes. Clients can avoid deep LDAP searches up and down the Directory tree by doing a quick lookup in the GC. The GC also contains the names of superior and subordinate domains and the names of the domain controllers which host copies of the Directory, so that every domain controller knows the name of every other domain controller in every domain in the forest.

In the initial version of Windows 2000, Domain trusts and Tree Root trusts can only be formed when a domain is created. There are no tools for consolidating domains (grafting) or prying them apart (pruning) after the domains are in place. Objects can be moved between domains using a command-line utility called Movetree. See Chapter 9, "Deploying Windows 2000 Domains," for details on using Movetree.

External trusts can be broken while leaving the domains intact, but breaking any other trust requires demoting every domain controller in the trusting domain.

Even though trust relationships join domains in such a way that LDAP queries can succeed across domain boundaries, trusted and trusting domains remain separate entities from a management perspective. Active Directory management consoles, such as AD Users and Groups, can focus only on one domain at a time. Users can browse for objects across domains thanks to the Global Catalog, but when the time comes to fulfill a lookup request, if the attribute is not in the GC, the query must be referred to a domain controller in the target domain. If the domain controller in that domain is at the wrong end of a 56k line that is oversubscribed with users downloading the Dancing Baby AVI clip, your Directory lookups will take a while.

Directory Naming Conventions

The Directory Information Base for Active Directory and all LDAP and X.500 Directory Services is an object-oriented database. Object-oriented databases rely on a rigorous naming convention to locate entries in the database. A file system is an example of an object database. To find a file called MYFILE.TXT, you must know the entire path from Root to the file. You can tell the operating system to search for a particular file in the file system, but that search is expensive in terms of cycles and I/O.

This reliance on structured naming has given X.500 and LDAP a reputation for inscrutability. Actually, the X.500 naming scheme is relatively straightforward—at least compared to human genome research.

Refer to Figure 7.5. In X.500 and LDAP terminology, the simple name of an object is its *Common Name* (CN). The CN designator applies to all but a couple of object types. Objects with their own designators include:

- **Domain objects.** These objects carry *Domain Component* designators (DC). For example, the LDAP name for an Active Directory domain with the DNS name Company.com would be `dc=Company,dc=com`.

- **Organizational Unit objects.** These objects carry the OU designator, such as `ou=Accounting`.

A couple of Active Directory objects carry more traditional X.500 designators. I'll point them out as they come up.

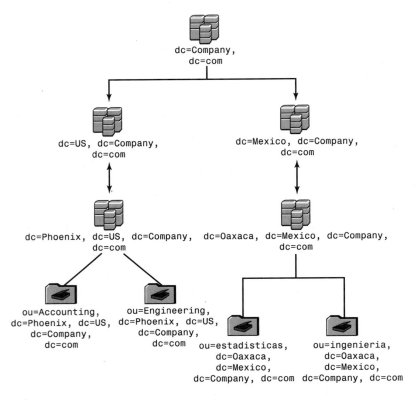

Figure 7.5 LDAP names and their relationship to Directory locations.

Case Sensitivity of LDAP Names

LDAP names in general, and Active Directory specifically, are not case sensitive. In most instances, the case you specify when you enter a value is retained in the object's attribute. Feel free to mix cases based on your corporate standards or personal aesthetic.

An object name that includes its full path from the root of the Directory is called a *Distinguished Name* (DN). The distinguished name is a concatenation of the common names for each of the objects in the path. An example distinguished name for a user named CSantana whose Directory object is stored in the default cn=Users container in a domain named Company.com would be cn=CSantana,cn=Users,dc=Company,dc=com.

One identifying characteristic of LDAP distinguished names, other than the way they get long and clumsy and hard to read, is their little-endian path syntax. As you read from left to right, you travel up the Directory tree. This is in contrast to file system paths, which run down the tree as you read from left to right.

An object name without a path, or a partial path, is called a *Relative Distinguished Name* (RDN). The common name cn=CSantana is an example of an RDN. The RDN serves the same purpose as a path fragment in a filename. It is a convenient navigational shortcut.

The combination of an object's name and its LDAP designator is called a *typeful* name. Example typeful names include cn=Administrators and cn=Administrators,cn=BuiltIn,dc=Company,dc=com. You are not necessarily required to use typeful names when specifying LDAP DNs and RDNs. Some applications parse for periods or semicolons between the common names. For example, an application may permit you to enter Administrators.BuiltIn.Company.com rather than the full typeful name.

Some applications that permit *typeless* names need a period at the end of the name to signify that the name is a distinguished name. In this case, the trailing dot represents the root of the Directory. For example, an application may parse group_name.users.company.com as a relative distinguished name instead of a distinguished name. This could cause the application to do an inappropriate lookup because the distinguished name is the only sure way of locating an object in the Directory.

When entering typeless names, it is important to place the delimiters properly. Also, because periods and commas can act as LDAP delimiters, avoid using them in server names, user names, share names, or other entities that are represented by Directory objects. This is not an absolute requirement—Windows 2000 administration tools do a good job of parsing true periods from delimiters—but if you plan on writing scripts or using the LDAP API or ADSI to write code, you'll find that periods in your object names can give you devilish bugs.

If you are writing code and you need to allow for periods in object names, precede the period with a backslash in an LDAP query to tell the parser that the period is a special character, not a delimiter. For example, if your user names looked like `tom.collins`, then a typeless name in a script would look like this: `tom\.collins.Users.Company.com`. The same is true for user names that have embedded commas and periods, such as Winston H. Borntothepurple, Jr. An ADSI query for this name would look like this: `winston h\. borntothepurple\, jr\.`

Directory Domain Structures

Figure 7.6 shows a tree diagram for a single Windows 2000 domain. At the top is an entity called *RootDSE*. This is not a Directory object, as such. It is a construct with attributes that point the way to important Directory containers, like a signpost at a rural intersection. LDAP clients use information from RootDSE to configure their lookups.

RFC 2251, "Lightweight Directory Access Protocol (v3)," specifies that RootDSE must exist outside of the Directory naming contexts and be excluded from any tree searches that start at Root. For this reason, RootDSE has no Distinguished Name. RootDSE is like the eye above the pyramid on the back of a dollar bill. It sits apart from the structure but knows all about it. Underneath RootDSE is a Domain-DNS object that represents the start of the Directory namespace. This object class carries the Domain Component designator, `dc`. RFC 2377, "Naming Plan for Internet Directory-Enabled Applications," requires that the common name of a Domain-DNS object match an associated DNS domain name. This enables LDAP clients to use DNS to locate Directory Services. Organizations with public DNS domains, such as `Company.com` and `University.edu`, would have Domain-DNS objects with distinguished names, such as `dc=Company,dc=com` and `dc=University,dc=edu`.

You cannot build a Windows 2000 domain with a single `dc` component as the name for the Domain-DNS object. When a server is promoted to domain controller to create a new domain, Windows 2000 parses the DNS domain name looking for at least one period. If it does not find one, it refuses to promote the server. Organizations with private DNS namespaces such as `US.Company` or `Undergrad.University` would have Domain-DNS objects with distinguished names like `dc=US,dc=Company` and `dc=Undergrad,dc=University`.

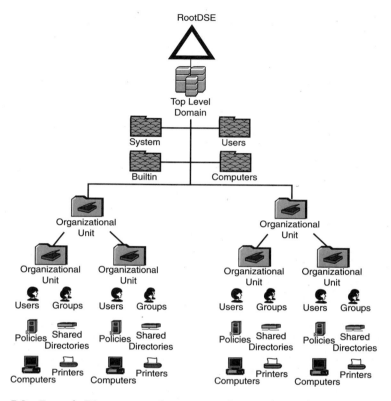

Figure 7.6   Example Directory container structure for a single Windows 2000 domain.

The next level down in the Directory is populated by containers used to organize objects in the domain. These container objects are derived from two classes:

- **Container objects.** These are generic container objects reserved exclusively for use by the system. `cn` objects cannot be created by MMC snap-ins or command line tools. An example distinguished name for one of the default Container objects is `cn=Users,dc=Company,dc=com`.

- **Organizational Unit (OU) objects.** These container objects are used to build structures that hold objects, such as Users, Groups, and Computers. An OU can be a subordinate of another OU, making it possible to arrange OUs into hierarchies, like a standard file system directory. For example, all the objects for an office could be collected under `ou=Office,dc=Company,dc=com`. You could then put additional OUs under the `ou=Office` container to separate User objects into different containers by department.

Objects in the same container are called *siblings*. Sibling common names must be unique, even if the entries are derived from different classes and, therefore, represent different objects. For example, you cannot have a Computer object and a User object with the same name in the same container. Also, Active Directory requires that objects with names derived from NetBIOS, such as Computers, Users, and Groups, must have unique names no matter what Active Directory container they reside in. For example, you cannot have a User object with a dn of cn=JDurante,ou=Phoenix,dc=Company,dc=com and an object with the dn of cn=JDurante,ou=Houston,cn=Computers,cn=Company,dc=com.

You are permitted to use the same name on different object classes as long as the objects are not siblings, but this is discouraged. It is very confusing to have a group in one container with the same name as a user in another container. Figure 7.7 shows three domains in a tree/forest arrangement. Notice that the names of the users, computers, and groups are the same in the three domains. This is a permitted configuration within Active Directory, *but it is not recommended*. Allowing identical names to proliferate is a ticket to confusion, both for users and administrators. For example, it is possible to reach through the Kerberos transitive trust and use the Phx_Acct group from Branch.Company.com to control access to an NTFS folder on a server in the Phoenix OU under Company.com. Administrators in Phoenix would have to constantly remind themselves that the group came from a different domain. My personal preference is to use distinct names on all objects of the same class throughout a forest.

These and other subtle details of Active Directory design are covered in Chapter 8, "Designing Windows 2000 Domains." Now let's take a closer look at the structure of the Active Directory as defined by the Directory schema.

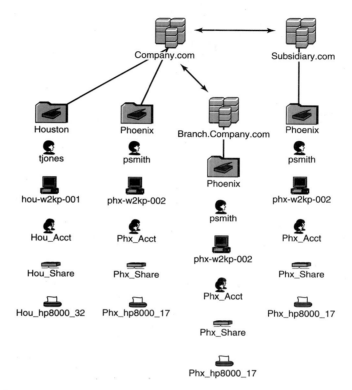

Figure 7.7   Domains as namespace partitions. This configuration is not recommended.

Active Directory Schema

The object-oriented database underlying Active Directory is composed of individual instances of various object classes. Each object class is defined by a unique set of attributes or properties. These object classes and their attributes, along with the rules for arranging and managing them, is called the *schema* of the Directory.

To visualize how the schema works, consider a simple, paper-based directory. Every month or so I get a catalog from Land's End, the clothing retailer. This catalog is a database of sorts, similar to a Directory Service except that it guides the user to a garment instead of a network entity.

- The schema for this directory defines a set of object *classes* with the scope of "Garments Sold by Land's End." These garment classes represent objects of interest in the real world, such as Sweaters, Suits, Blazers, Accessories, and so forth.

- The schema also defines the available *attributes* that can be associated with the various object classes, such as Size, Color, Inseam-Length, and Price along with more subtle attributes specific to the directory itself, such as Picture-Of-Garment.

- The schema has *content rules* that define what attributes can be associated with a class. Some attributes, like Size and Color, might be associated with nearly every class. An attribute like Inseam-Length, however, might only be associated with classes like Slacks and Jeans, not Sport-Coats or Shoes.

- Some garment classes have attributes that are nearly identical. For example, the attributes that define the Polo-Shirts class differ only slightly from the attributes that define the Sport-Shirts class. In the database that is the Land's End catalog, it is possible to *derive* one class from another then tack on just the attributes that are different. The child object class *inherits* the attributes associated with its parent.

- This capability to derive one garment class from another makes it important to have certain *structure rules* that keep the directory aligned with the real world. For example, a structure rule would prevent placing an object from the Bathrobe class under a container from the Shoe class.

- A particular garment is an *instance* of its garment class. For example, an instance of the Blazer class would be the solid red blazer with green plaid lining that I gave my brother for Christmas last year. (The snide thank you note I received in return came from the Hallmark Directory Service as an instance of the Ungrateful-Sibling class.)

- The schema also has *syntax rules* that define the type of value that can be associated with an attribute. For example, the Size attribute must have whole integer values while the Shoe-Size attribute can have real number (fractional) values. Syntax rules also stipulate special requirements that vary depending on the class to which an attribute is associated. For example, the Land's End directory apparently has a schema rule that operates when the Inseam-Length attribute associated with the Slacks class has a value of 34—the length that happens to fit the author. This rule filters the Price attribute so that only those instances with prices of three digits or more are available for shipment.

- Because garment classes and attributes in the Land's End directory can change, the Land's End directory is *extensible*. For example, an attribute called Number-Of-Sleeve-Buttons could be added to the schema and the Blazers class could be modified to include this attribute.

I know this was a long example, so here are the key terms and concepts:

- **Object Classes.** Define the objects that can appear in the Directory and their associated attributes.

- **Class Derivations.** Define a method for building new object classes out of existing object classes.

- **Object Attributes.** Define the available attributes. This includes extended attributes that govern actions that can be taken on object classes.

- **Structure Rules.** Determine possible tree arrangements.

- **Syntax Rules.** Determine the type of value an attribute is capable of storing.

- **Content Rules.** Determine the attributes that can be associated with a given class.

Object Classes and Class Derivations

An object class is nothing more than a bundle of attributes with a name. The User class, for example, has certain attributes that, taken together, make it distinct from the Organizational-Unit class or the Server class. The X.500/9594 standard, as modified by RFC 2256, "A Summary of the X.500(96) User Schema for use with LDAPv3," defines 21 classes and 55 attributes in a standard LDAP directory schema. The Active Directory schema extends this list quite a bit, out to nearly 200 classes and just under 1500 attributes. If you want a complete list, check out the Windows 2000 Platform SDK or look at the MSDN Web site, msdn.microsoft.com.

Standard LDAP Classes and Attributes Not Used in Active Directory

The Active Directory schema includes all RFC 2256 classes, except for Alias and Strong-Authentication-User, and all attributes, except for Aliased-Object-Name. The exclusion of Alias was deliberate. Aliases are a notorious source of performance difficulties and integrity problems in Directory Services. In addition, most of the object classes that would normally be given aliases are required to have unique names in Active Directory. This includes users, computers, and groups.

The Active Directory schema also includes six standards-track attributes associated with the Internet-Organizational-Person class based on *draft-smith-ldap-inetorgperson-01.txt* and four Netscape attributes involving mail handling.

The attributes associated with a particular class often overlap. For example, the attribute list for the Mailbox class includes all the attributes associated with the Mail-Recipient class with one addition, the Delivery-Mechanism attribute. There are hundreds of classes and many hundreds of attributes in the Directory. If the attributes in each class had to be separately defined, the sheer number of perturbations would make the Directory look less like a tree and more like an example of German expressionism.

The list of attributes that must be specifically defined for an object class is limited because an object class *inherits* the attributes from its parent class. The designer need only stipulate the few additional attributes that make the subordinate class unique.

The class that another class inherits its attributes from is called its *superior*. If a designer puts a class under several superiors, then it inherits the attributes of all those superiors. Attributes flow down the hierarchy of object classes like genes in a family tree. Here is an example of class inheritance for the Computer object class:

```
Top
    Person
        Organizational-Person
            Contact
            User
                Computer
```

Figure 7.8 shows the same inheritance in a diagram. The Computer class has attributes for Operating-System and Network. It inherits Logon and Access-Control attributes from the User class, Physical-Location from the Organizational-Person class, User and Password attributes from the Person class, and a myriad of operational attributes from the Top class.

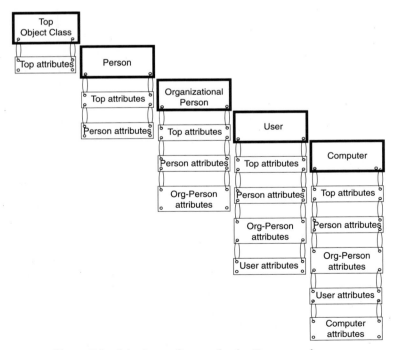

Figure 7.8   Inheritance diagram for the Computer class.

All classes derive from *Top*, so all classes share the Top attributes. This makes it possible to define certain attributes that are common to every class. For example, every class has a Common-Name attribute. You won't find objects of the class Top in the Directory, not like you will find User objects and Server objects. Think of Top like a director who never actually appears on camera but leaves a distinctive mark on the production. Top is an *Abstract* class, one of three types of object classes in the Directory. These object classes are defined in the following list.

- **Abstract.** Classes that exist solely to derive other object classes. There are 14 abstract classes in the Active Directory. Examples include Top, Leaf, Connection-Point, Device, Person, and Security Object.
- **Auxiliary.** Used to extend the definition of an abstract class for specialized purposes. There are only four of these classes in the Active Directory: Mail-Recipient, Sam-Domain, Sam-Domain-Base, and Security-Principal.
- **Structural.** Classes that have objects in the Directory. Examples include User, Group, Computer, and Server.

These three class types are like assembly line robots designed to produce things called "objects." The Abstract classes are the mill workers and pattern makers which build the tools and dies used on the assembly line. The Structural classes are the tools and dies themselves that stamp and shape the objects. The Auxiliary classes are the custom shops at the end of the line where special versions of standard objects are turned out.

It's not enough to define schema components as things, actions, and relationships. Laws and customs are also necessary to avoid anarchy. These take the form of *schema rules*.

Schema Rules

Directory Service designers build certain rules into the schema that determine how classes and attributes are used, what kind of values they can have, and what relationship they have to each other. These rules fall into three categories:

- Structure Rules
- Content Rules
- Syntax Rules

Structure Rules

Frank Lloyd Wright established the design paradigm for twentieth century architecture by declaring that form should always follow function. He was a building architect rather than Directory Services architect, of course, but Active Directory is as much of a monument to form and function as a prairie house, and it is the *structure rules* that accomplish this.

There is really only one structure rule: Each object class has only certain classes that can be directly above it, called *Possible Superiors*. This structure rule is very important in an LDAP directory because most of the object classes are containers, as opposed to an X.500 directory where you can count the number of container classes on one hand. The list of possible superiors for a particular class is contained in the Poss-Superior attribute of the SchemaClass object that defines the class.

This structure rule prevents putting an instance of the User class under an instance of a totally unrelated container class, like IPSEC-Base or NTDS Settings.

Content Rules

Every object class has certain attributes with values that cannot be left blank when an object is instantiated. These are called *must-contain* attributes. For example, every instance of the User class must have a value for the Common-Name attribute. Other attributes are optional and are designated *may-contain* attributes. For example, in the User class, it is up to the administrator's discretion whether to assign a value to the Fax-Phone attribute. When an object class inherits attributes from a superior, it also inherits the must-contain and may-contain designation for those attributes. For example, the Top class defines four must-contain attributes. Because all object classes derive from Top, instances of all object classes have these four attributes.

- **NT-Security-Descriptor.** The basic security data structure for all Windows 2000 objects.

- **Object-Category.** Specifies the DN of the base schema object from which the object class was derived. For example, the object category for a User object will always be `cn=person,cn=schema,cn=configuration,dc=company,dc=com`. See the "Schema Definition Objects" section later in this chapter for details about how schema objects are stored.

- **Object-Class.** Specifies the Directory hierarchy for the class from which the object was derived. For a user object, this would be Top | Person | OrganizationalPerson | User.

- **Instance–Type.** Specifies the type of instantiation used to derive the object. All objects, with the exception of the Domain Component object, have an instance-type of 4. The value for domain component objects is 5.

All LDAP applications (and this includes the directory management MMC snap-ins) that create an instance of an object must supply values for all mandatory attributes. Some attributes, like Common-name and the logon name (aka SAM-Account-Name), can be defined by the user of the application. Others, like Object-SID and Instance-Type, are created by the system in response to API calls from the application. Most general-purpose ADSI and LDAP browsers are not programmed to derive values for these must-contain attributes, and they cannot be used to create these kinds of objects.

The list of must-contain attributes is small compared to the total number of attributes associated with an object class. For example, the User class has over four dozen possible attributes inherited from a variety of superior classes but only six of these attributes are mandatory.

This brings up an important design principle of the Directory. Only attributes that have values are stored in the Directory along with their associated objects. This greatly reduces the Directory size. If every attribute for every instance of every object were included in the Directory, the database would be monstrous for no good reason because 99% of the attributes would have null values. Because attributes can be added after an object is created and then later removed if they are not required, the ESE database engine must constantly pack and repack the data. One key operational parameter to watch if you are an early adopter of Windows 2000 is database fragmentation.

Syntax Rules

Attributes store data. Data must have a data type to define the storage requirements. Real numbers have a different form from integers, which are different from long integers, which are different from character strings. An attribute can have only one data type. An attribute cannot hold a string when associated with one object class and an integer when associated with another. For example, the Common-Name attribute can only store a Unicode String data type. The values associated with the various attributes are defined by the *syntax rules* for the schema. Table 7.1 lists the possible syntax options.

Table 7.1 **Common Active Directory Syntax Options**

Syntax	Description
Boolean	TRUE or FALSE value. Commonly used to define decision points. Examples include printing options such as Print-Collate and Print-Color.
Integer	A 32-bit number.
Large Integer	A 64-bit number. Big numbers take up memory and demand more processing power, so it isn't reasonable to use Large Integer types for all numbers. Attributes such as the Update-Status-Number (USN) that are used to control Directory operation have Large Integer values. So do time/date values, which count 100-nanosecond intervals from an epoch point, which is Jan. 1, 1900 for Win32 systems.
Object(DS-DN)	Values conforming to LDAP requirements for a Distinguished Name. For example, dc=Company,dc=com.
Object(OR Name)	The O/R address of an X.400 mail recipient.
Object(Replica-Link)	Special octet string used to represent replication sites. Examples: Reps-To, Reps-From, Reps-To-Ext.
String(Generalized Time)	Special form of time marker used for attributes like Create-Time-Stamp and Modify-Time-Stamp
String(IA5)	Special type of case-insensitive strings used for RADIUS and Ascend applications.
String(NT-Sec-Desc)	An NT security descriptor, a special data structure used by Windows 2000 to identify security principals and their access rights for an object. Only three attributes in the Active Directory use this syntax: **FRS-Root-Security**—Used to identify security principals with access to the root of a file replication system structure. **PKI-Enrollment-Access**—Used to identify security principals with access to public key encryption integration applications. **NT-Security-Descriptor**—Used to identify security principals with access to Directory objects.
String(Numeric)	A series of numerals. This syntax is used only in the International-ISDN-Number attribute and the X.121-Address attribute.
String(Object Identifier	An Object ID (OID). An OID uses dotted decimal notation with many potential iterations. Used only in the OID-Type attribute.
String(Octet)	A big-endian byte. Examples include the Globally-Unique-Identifier attribute and other security-related attributes such as CA (Certificate Authority).

Syntax	Description
String(Printable)	A string used when applications need clear text information stored in the Directory. This includes DHCP, DXA, and NNTP applications, among others.
String(SID)	A representation of the set of 48-bit numbers that make up a Security ID, or SID.
String(Teletex)	A case-insensitive character string. Example: Computer-Name.
String(Unicode)	A string of 2-byte Unicode characters. Most names and strings in the Directory are stored using this syntax. The only exceptions are attributes that must be understood by non-Unicode clients.
String(UTC Time)	A value that measures the number of seconds since 1/1/1970. This syntax only uses a 32-bit number, which can't count all that many seconds, leaving a looming Year 2106 problem that will probably be fixed in Windows 2107 SP5.

Schema Definition Objects

Individual objects are always instances of an object class. Achieving this design principal involves using a template that defines the attributes, schema rules, and class hierarchy for the objects within an object class. The same applies for attributes, which require a template to define the syntax rules. This suite of templates makes up the *schema definitions* for a Directory Service information store.

Some Directory Services put the schema definitions into a separate file that is loaded at boot time or whenever the schema requires changing. In contrast, the Active Directory schema is *self-referential.* That is to say, all class definitions, attribute definitions, and schema rules are part of the schema itself. An appropriate title for an Active Directory schema self-help book would be *Everything I Need to Know I Learned From Myself.*

The Directory schema contains two schema object classes, *ClassSchema* and *AttributeSchema,* that act like patterns in a lathe to turn out objects. The ClassSchema objects have attributes that define the class hierarchy and schema rules for their associated classes:

- **Possible-Superior.** This defines the structure rules for the object.

- **Must-Contain** and **May-Contain.** These define the attributes that can be associated with the object.

- **Sub-Class-of.** This defines the hierarchy for the class.

AttributeSchema objects have two attributes that define the associated syntax rules:

- **Attribute-Syntax.** This defines the type of value an attribute may possess.
- **OM-Syntax.** Used in conjunction with OM-Object-Class to further refine the attribute type. This designator is based on X/Open Object Model definitions.

ClassSchema and AttributeSchema objects are stored in the Directory in a special container called Schema, which is stored in a container called Configuration. Figure 7.9 shows the location. You cannot see these containers using the standard Directory management console snap-ins. The figure comes from a tool in the Resource Kit, the ADSI Editor. See the "Using LDAP Browsers" section later in this chapter for details.

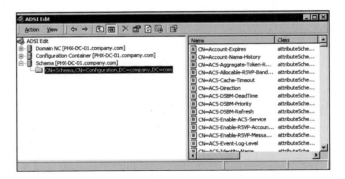

Figure 7.9　Location of Schema and Configuration containers in the Directory.

Aggregate Object

In addition to ClassSchema and ClassAttribute classes, the Schema container holds a class called *SubSchema* with one instance, an object called *Aggregate*. The distinguished name of this object is `cn=aggregate,cn=schema,`
`cn=configuration,dc=company,dc=com`. The purpose of Aggregate is to provide a single point for LDAP clients to discover information about the Directory

schema. Without this object, clients would be forced to perform expensive scans of the entire Schema container. The Aggregate object contains several attributes that define the schema parameters:

- **Extended–Class–Info.** Lists the ClassSchema objects in the Schema container. There are over 200 classes in Active Directory.

- **Extended–Attribute–Info.** Lists the AttributeSchema objects in the Schema container. There are nearly 1500 attributes in Active Directory, 60 of which are flagged as INDEXED. This tells the ESE engine to include those attributes in its indexing operations to speed lookups. Nearly 80 attributes are flagged as SYSTEM-ONLY, meaning that they cannot be changed with MMC snap-ins or standard ADSI library calls.

- **DIT–Content–Rules.** Lists a small set of special object classes that affect security and mail.

This completes the overview of the schema structure, function, and rules. Before moving forward, let's look at a couple of attributes that are associated with every object class and are crucial to understanding the more advanced tools in the Windows 2000 Resource Kit. The attributes are the *Object Identifier* (OID) and the *Globally Unique Identifier* (GUID).

Object Identifier (OID)

Every entry in the Directory is assigned an OID. The ISO defines the structure and distribution of OIDs in ISO/IEC 8824:1990, *Information Technology— Open Systems Interconnection—Specification of Abstract Syntax Notation One (ASN.1)*. The thrust of ASN.1 is to provide a mechanism for standards bodies in various countries to enumerate standard data items so that they do not conflict with each other. ASN.1 governs more than just Directory Services classes and attributes. For example, OIDs are used extensively in SNMP to build hierarchies of Management Information Base (MIB) numbers. They are also assigned to many items associated with the Internet. If you're interested in the list of organizations that assign OID numbers and their hierarchy, it is available at `ftp.isi.edu/in-notes/iana/assignments/enterprise-numbers`.

Figure 7.10 shows the OID hierarchy that leads down to Directory Service entries. There are two series of numbers formatted in dotted decimal notation:

- Series 1 numbers are passed out by the ISO to countries which assign the next series to standards bodies, which in turn give the next sequence to vendors, who use them as they see fit. The series starts at the OSI, which assigned 1.2.840 to ANSI, which assigned 1.2.840.113556 to Microsoft. Any Directory Service class or attribute developed by Microsoft carries an OED in the 1.2.840.113556.1.5 series. For example, the User entry has an OID of 1.2.840.113556.1.5.9.

- Series 2 numbers are reserved for use by the Joint ITU–T/ISO. These numbers are universal. Every vendor who builds a Directory Service that uses classes and attributes specified in X.500 must use the OID numbers for them assigned in Series 2.

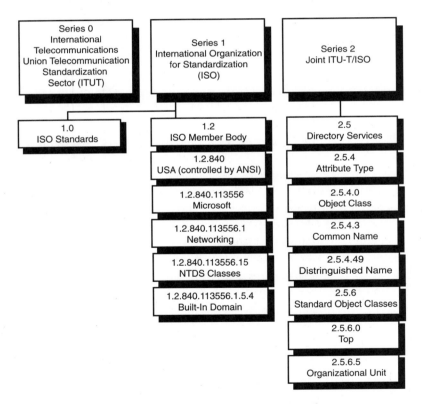

Figure 7.10 OID hierarchy showing common classes.

Finding OID Hierarchy Information

Many thanks to Harald Alvestrand, who made good use of a long winter in Trondheim, Norway, to build a hyper-linked tree showing many of the common OID registrations. His information is now slightly out of date but the structure is still valid and very instructive. Visit his Web site at www.alvestrand.no/objectid.

The OID for a class or attribute is stored in the GovernsID attribute of the SchemaClass object that defines the class or attribute. For example, the OID for any User object in the Active Directory is 1.2.840.113556.1.5.9.

Globally Unique Identifier (GUID)

Directory objects are also COM objects, and all COM objects are given a Globally Unique Identifier (GUID). The GUID is a proprietary data structure and does not appear in the ITU-T or OSI literature. A GUID is a 128-bit number generated in a way that virtually guarantees its uniqueness regardless of the system that issues it. The GUID consists of a 60-bit time stamp, a version number, a variant, and the 48-bit MAC address of the issuing system. The decimal format of the GUID is:

```
4 bytes time_low
2 bytes time_mid
2 bytes time_hi+version
2 bytes clock_hi+variant
1 byte clock_low
6 bytes MAC
```

The GUID also goes by the names *Universally Unique Identifier* (UUID), and *Class ID* (CLSID). You may see these designators used to identify *controls* sent by clients to the Active Directory to facilitate queries. Controls take the form of COM objects. For example, an application might send a lookup to a domain controller requesting the Common-Name attribute for all users with the last name of Montoya. In my home state of New Mexico, this query is likely to result in a pretty long list. Rather than have the Directory send back hundreds of names, the application could send a control that tells the Directory to sort the names alphabetically and then return them 10 at a time.

GUIDs and Security

GUID numbers have gotten lots of press lately thanks to a few high-profile privacy reports. Because the GUID includes the MAC address of the originating system, it is relatively easy to ferret out the source of a COM object or any other file that includes a GUID.

Naming Contexts

The success of any Directory Service hinges on its ability to respond quickly and reliably to client queries. Because Active Directory is the sole source of authentication both for network access and access to shared resources on network servers and workstations, not to mention a repository for a pile of application-related objects put there by Microsoft and third-party vendors, the information store has the possibility of growing very large.

The contents of an Active Directory define the boundaries of a Windows 2000 domain. A big company with thousands and thousands of users, computers, and groups is tough to fit into a single Directory. Even if you put aside the political squabbles that inevitably erupt when trying to build a single, coordinated information management structure, the information store for a large domain gets too unwieldy for practical use. Some mechanism for reducing the size of the information store is needed.

In X.500 and LDAP, the Directory Information Base can be divided into separate chunks with each chunk replicated as a separate unit. X.500 calls these *partitions*. LDAP calls them *naming contexts*. Both the Microsoft documentation and LDAP-related RFCs use the two terms interchangeably. The Resource Kit tools favor the term *naming context*, and that is the term I use throughout this book. Figure 7.11 shows the naming contexts in a three-domain network.

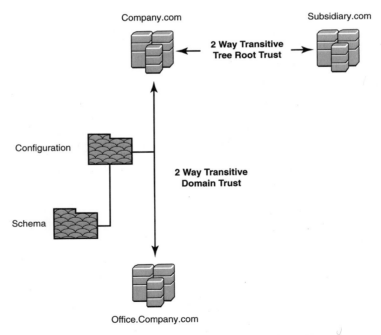

Figure 7.11 Domains and containers that form separate naming contexts.

A naming context defines a separate portion of the Active Directory information store that holds the objects in that naming context. For example, if the `dc=Branch,dc=Company,dc=com` container defines the border of a naming context, then the portion of the information store defined by that naming context would hold the object `cn=MGibson,cn=Users,dc=Branch,dc=Company,dc=com`. Changes to the `cn=MGibson` object would be replicated separately from changes to objects in the `dc=Company,dc=com` naming context.

Domain controllers hold copies of the naming context for their domains. They use this copy to satisfy lookup requests on the part of clients in their domain and trusted domains.

The only containers in Active Directory that can be used as naming context boundaries by administrators are Domain containers. This is purely an artificial requirement imposed by Microsoft. LDAP permits any container to form the top of a naming context. In fact, Active Directory itself has two containers, Configuration and Schema, that form separate naming contexts.

As Windows 2000 begins moving into big networks with hundreds of thousands of users, it may be that Microsoft's initial strategy of limiting naming contexts to the domain containers will not hold up. Subsequent releases of Windows 2000 may give administrators more flexibility in choosing where to create new naming contexts.

The key point to remember about naming contexts is that they are stored as distinct entities on domain controllers and are replicated as distinct entities between domain controllers. Each of the domain controllers in the Company.com domain holds a full replica of the `dc=Company,dc=com` naming context.

The domain structure in Figure 7.11 shows the naming contexts in a fairly typical Windows 2000 tree/forest arrangement. There are five naming contexts. Here are their names and the objects they contain:

- **`dc=Company,dc=com`**. This container holds objects that represent security principals (users, groups, and computers) in the `Company.com` domain along with objects that support system-level functions in the domain such as policies and security certificates.

- **`dc=Office,dc=Company,dc=com`**. Holds security principals and system objects in the `Office.Company.com` child domain.

- **`dc=Subsidiary,dc=com`**. Holds security principals and system objects in the `Subsidiary.com` peer domain.

- `dc=Configuration,dc=Company,dc=com.` Holds objects that define the structure of Sites and Services for the entire forest.

- `dc=Schema,dc=Configuration,dc=Company,dc=com.` Holds objects that define the structure of the Directory schema for the entire forest.

Separating domains into discrete naming contexts accomplishes two purposes in Active Directory. First, Active Directory uses these naming contexts to define a *hierarchy of knowledge*. Each naming context has at least one superior naming context and may have one or more subordinate naming contexts. There are pointers in the Directory that indicate to clients where to find these superior and subordinate naming contexts. Clients use this information to formulate lookups. For example, if a client wants a list of users in the `Subsidiary.com` domain, the lookup can be directed at a domain controller that holds a copy of the `dc=Subsidiary,dc=com` naming context.

Second, naming contexts define separate replication units. The major purpose for dividing a network into several domains is to reduce the size of the information store on the domain controllers. The more objects in a given naming context, the more work a domain controller has to do to store and replicate those objects. This generates traffic and work for the other domain controllers, as well.

Let's look at role of naming contexts in defining a Directory hierarchy first, then take a look at their role in defining replication boundaries.

Naming Contexts as Namespace Partitions

Windows 2000 knits together domains using transitive Kerberos trusts. Kerberos only facilitates authentication, though; it does not enable LDAP Directory searches. LDAP clients request information about objects in a trusted domain by querying domain controllers in that domain. They find these domain controllers using objects in the Directory that point at the outside naming contexts.

Some LDAP implementations tie together naming contexts using Superior References and Subordinate References. This only works in a tree topology. Windows 2000 uses a different method to enable support for trusted domains in a forest topology. The Windows 2000 method involves storing a set of CrossRef objects in the Directory that store location information about all available naming contexts. Figure 7.12 shows these CrossRef objects in their parent container, `cn=Partitions,cn=Configuration`.

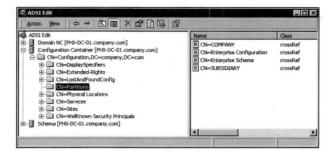

Figure 7.12   ADSI Editor showing CrossRef objects that store information about naming contexts in a set of trusted domains.

When a domain controller receives a lookup request for an object, it first checks to see if it has a replica of the associated naming context. The object's distinguished name indicates that naming context. For example, an object with a distinguished name of cn=User_name,cn=Users,dc=Company,dc=com can be found in the dc=Company,dc=com naming context.

If the domain controller has a replica of that naming context, it performs the lookup and returns the requested information. If the domain controller does not have a replica, it checks the CrossRef objects to see if the naming context is available in a trusted domain. If it is, the domain controller either returns a *referral* to the client, telling it to look for a domain controller in the correct naming context, or it performs a *chain* operation that contacts a domain controller in that naming context on behalf of the client.

In either case, referrals or chaining, the request is said to *walk the tree*. This is actually a misnomer in Active Directory because the request might "walk the forest" instead, but the concept is the same. Referrals and chaining operations route LDAP requests to the domain controller that holds a copy of the correct naming context.

Naming Contexts as Replication Units

Naming contexts also define separate replication units. This is not quite the same as saying that a naming context represents a replication boundary. In Windows 2000, replication boundaries are formed by Sites, not by naming contexts. A Site is an area of high-speed network connectivity associated with one or more discrete IP subnets. For a more complete explanation of Sites, see the Sites heading under the description of objects in the Configuration container section later in this chapter.

Each naming context can have replicas on multiple domain controllers, and each domain controller can host replicas of multiple naming contexts. The Windows 2000 Resource Kit includes a utility called the Replication Monitor, or Replmon, that is used to view and manage naming contexts and their replication. Figure 7.13 shows an example `Replication Monitor` window for the naming context diagram in Figure 7.13.

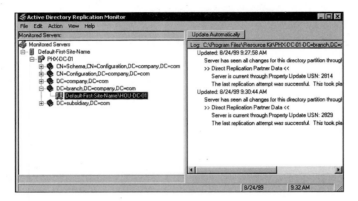

Figure 7.13 `Replication Monitor` console showing naming contexts which correspond to the forest in Figure 7.11.

In Figure 7.13, the domain controller named `PHX-DC-01` hosts the following replicas:

- Read–write replica of `dc=Company,dc=com`
- Read–only replica of `dc=Office,dc=Company,dc=com`
- Read–only replica of `dc=Subsidiary,dc=com`
- Read–write replica of `cn=Configuration,dc=Company,dc=com`
- Read–write replica of `cn=Schema,cn=Configuration,dc=Company,dc=com`

There is only one Configuration naming context and one Schema naming context in an entire forest. These naming contexts are replicated to every domain controller in the forest. This is what the Microsoft documentation means when it says that trusting domains share a common schema and configuration-naming context with their trusted partners.

The domain controller has read–only replicas of other naming contexts because it is a Global Catalog server. This is explained in the next section.

Naming Contexts and Global Catalog Servers

Each domain controller in a domain holds a full replica of the naming context for that domain. Using that naming context, the domain controller can satisfy any lookup request that involves objects in that particular domain. For example, what if domain controller HOU-DC-01 in Figure 7.13 gets a lookup request for a user with the distinguished name `cn=HOlajuwon,cn=Users,dc=Branch,dc=Company,dc=com`?

HOU-DC-01 hosts replicas of these naming context replicas:

- Read-write replica of `cn=Schema,cn=Configuration,dc=Company,dc=com`
- Read-write replica of `dc=Subsidiary,dc=com`
- Read-write replica of `cn=Configuration,dc=Company,dc=com`

Because it has a replica of `dc=Branch,dc=Company,dc=com`, HOU-DC-01 can dive right into its information store and satisfy the lookup. But what if it gets a lookup request for `cn=JKidd,cn=Users,dc=Company,dc=com`? Because HOU-DC-01 has no replica of the naming context `dc=Company,dc=com`, it must either refer or chain the request to a domain controller in Company.com.

But what if the situation was reversed? What if PHX-DC-01 got a lookup request for `cn=HOlajuwon,cn=Users,dc=Branch,dc=Company,dc=com`? In this case, the lookup request could be satisfied without a referral or a chain because PHX-DC-01 has a local replica of the `dc=Branch,dc=Company,dc=com` naming context. It has this replica because it is a *Global Catalog* server.

The Global Catalog is an index of every object in every domain in the forest. It contains only a few (60 or so) of the 1500 available attributes for those objects, but the ones it contains are those that are used the most often. By putting a partial replica of every naming context on every GC, Windows 2000 is able to resolve most lookups without the necessity of a referral or chain across a slow WAN link.

Better yet, as a Global Catalog server, PHX-DC-01 can satisfy lookup requests for non-GC servers in its local site. This means one or two GC servers in an office or on your campus can eliminate virtually all WAN traffic generated by Active Directory lookups.

The next few chapters contain details for managing Global Catalog servers in a production environment. Here are a few preliminary operational requirements to keep in mind:

- Every Global Catalog server has a copy of every naming context from every domain, but these replicas hold only a few selected attributes.
- If a domain controller receives a query for an object in its own naming context, then it can fulfill the query immediately.

- If a domain controller that is *not* a Global Catalog server receives a query for an object in the naming context of a trusted domain, it cannot fulfill the request. It returns a referral that directs the client to the domain of origin for that naming context.

- If a domain controller that *is* a Global Catalog server receives a query for an object in the naming context of a trusted domain, and the requested attributes are part of the Global Catalog, then it can fulfill the query immediately.

- If a domain controller that is also a Global Catalog server receives a query for an object in the naming context of a trusted domain, and the requested attributes are *not* part of the Global Catalog, then it cannot fulfill the request. It returns a referral that directs the client to the domain of origin for that naming context.

This completes the discussion of generic LDAP and Active Directory components. It's time to weld those components together into an actual Active Directory structure. First, though, let's take a look at a couple of tools that help illustrate the interior structure of Active Directory.

Active Directory Browsing Utilities

Windows 2000 comes with three MMC consoles for viewing and managing Active Directory objects. These are:

- **AD Users and Computers.** This console is used to manage individual security principals such as users, groups, and computers as well as to structure those objects into Organizational Units where they can be managed with Group Policies. The console file name is `Dsa.msc`.

- **AD Sites and Services.** This console is used to manage Sites, the replication entity for Active Directory, and enterprise services such as DNS, DHCP, and Certification Authorities. The console filename is `Dssite.msc`.

- **AD Domains and Trusts.** This console is more of a navigational aid for a big organization. It provides a consolidated console that lists all domains in the forest in their appropriate hierarchy and permits launching the `AD Users and Computers` console to manage any remote domain. The console file name is `Domain.msc`.

These consoles are all launched from the `Start` button at Windows 2000 server using START | PROGRAMS | ADMINISTRATIVE TOOLS | <CONSOLE NAME>. The workings of these consoles are explained through this and the other Active Directory chapters. But many of the most interesting pathways within the inner sanctum of the Active Directory are not visible using these consoles. This requires special tools from the Resource Kit. They are the *ADSI Editor*, adsiedit.msc, and the *LDAP Browser*, ldp.exe. You can also download the Platform SDK from the Microsoft Developer's Network, MSDN, at msdn.microsoft.com. The SDK has ADSI libraries that you can use to write your own applications to view and modify objects in the Directory.

Before seeing how these tools work, there are a few preliminaries that you need to know about the way clients communicate with the Active Directory.

When an AD client needs information from the Directory, it submits an LDAP lookup request to the domain controller at which it authenticated. This request takes the form of a TCP datagram containing the LDAP request. Figure 7.14 shows a captured frame containing an LDAP lookup request. The request is for Group Policy Link objects and Group Policy Option objects in the cn=System,dc=Company,dc=com container. This request was sent to TCP Port 389. You can see that at the end of the TCP line, the fourth protocol in the list. TCP Port 389 is the well-known port for LDAP.

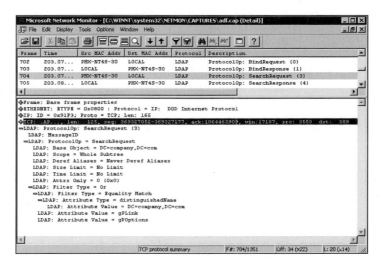

Figure 7.14   Captured frame showing TCP datagram
containing LDAP request sent to Port 389.

This request went to the standard LDAP port. But what if the application needs to do a quick check of items that might not be in the same naming context as the user's domain? It could do this via a lookup to the Global Catalog port. Figure 7.15 shows a more general request that has been sent to TCP Port 3268 on the domain controller. This is the Global Catalog port.

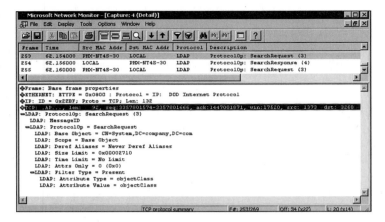

Figure 7.15 Captured frame showing TCP datagram
send to Port 3268, the Global Catalog port.

Lookup requests sent to a Global Catalog server via TCP Port 3268 are handled by searching the partial replicas of the domain naming contexts hosts by the GC. The Platform SDK advises developers to use a Global Catalog for LDAP lookups whenever possible.

Instead of specifically directing a lookup request at a particular TCP port, the application can formulate a lookup request with a general ADSI query header. These headers take the general form of a URL:

`LDAP://<server_name>:<port#>/<object DN>`.

The DN stands for Distinguished Name. The letters LDAP must be in all caps. The `<server_name>:<port#>` portion is optional. If it is not included, the AD client sends the request to a domain controller selected out of DNS. An example ADSI header to open the Configuration container in the Company.com domain would be: `LDAP://cn=Configuration,dc=Company,dc=com`.

The first part of any URL is a protocol ID, which converts to a port number, so instead of addressing the URL to the LDAP port, the address could be to the Global Catalog port as follows:

`GC://cn=Configuration,dc=Company,dc=com`.

The LDAP line tells the AD client to find a computer in DNS that has a Service Record (SRV record type) indicating that it is a domain controller capable of responding to LDAP requests on TCP Port 389. The GC line tells the AD client to find a computer in DNS that has an SRV record indicating that it is a GC server capable of responding to LDAP requests on TCP Port 3268.

The two ADSI tools in the Resource Kit do a fairly good job of hiding LDAP addressing complexities. Just keep the two different ports in mind— 389 for standard LDAP requests and 3268 for Global Catalog requests— along with the structure of the ADSI header in case you need to formulate a specific query.

ADSI Editor

The more convenient of the two LDAP tools is the ADSI Editor. It is a general-purpose Active Directory browser that can be used to display the actual format of the Directory, not just the pre-packaged views in the AD management consoles. Here's how to load and use it:

Procedure 7.1   **Loading the ADSI Editor**

1. Open the Resource Kit using START | PROGRAMS | RESOURCE KIT | TOOLS MANAGEMENT CONSOLE.

2. Expand the tree to show `Microsoft Resource Kits` | `Windows 2000 Resource Kit` | `Tool Categories` | `Tools A to Z`. Figure 7.16 shows an example.

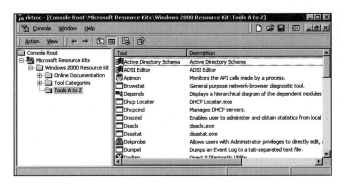

Figure 7.16   Windows 2000 `Resource Kit Tools Management` console window showing the `Tools A to Z` option.

3. Launch ADSI Editor from the pick list. This opens the `ADSI Edit` console showing the three standard naming contexts, Domain NC, Configuration, and Schema. See Figure 7.17.

Figure 7.17 `ADSI Editor` console showing three standard naming contexts for a domain.

4. If you do not see the naming contexts, or you want to view a different naming context on another domain controller, right-click the `ADSI Edit` icon and select CONNECT TO from the fly-out menu. The `Connection` window opens. See Figure 7.18.

Figure 7.18 ADSI Editor `Connection` window showing the selection of a domain controller in the `Subsidiary.com` domain to view the Subsidiary domain naming context.

5. Under Computer, select the `Select or Type a Domain or Server` radio button.

6. In the combo box, type the fully qualified DNS name of a domain controller. The example shows a domain controller `HOU-DC-01` in the `Subsidiary.com` domain. When you make this entry, the Path automatically changes. Other LDAP tools are not this friendly when it comes to specifying LDAP connections.

7. Click Advanced. The Advanced window opens. See Figure 7.19.

Figure 7.19 ADSI Editor Advanced window showing alternative credentials, specific port number, and protocol selection.

The options in this window are used as follows:

- **Credentials.** If you are connecting to a Directory in another domain, or you are currently logged on using an account that does not have administrator privileges, you can specify a set of administrator credentials.

- **Port Number.** If this field is left blank, ADSI Editor uses well-known TCP port 389 for LDAP. You can specify a different port if you are browsing a non-standard implementation. You could also use this option to browse the Global Catalog through TCP port 3268, but it is more convenient to use the Protocol feature.

- **Protocol.** Select whether you want to browse the full Directory or the Global Catalog. If you specify a particular domain controller and it does not host a copy of the GC, you will get an error.

8. Click OK to save the changes and return to the Connections window.

9. Click OK to save the changes and return to the main ADSI Editor window. The display refreshes to show the new settings, if you made any changes.

Whether you decide to use the default domain controller or select a new one, the following steps show how to get information about the Directory using ADSI Editor.

Procedure 7.2 **Using the ADSI Editor to Obtain Directory Information**

1. Expand the tree to show the top of the naming context you want to view. You can open several naming contexts, making the ADSI Editor a handy way to view a big enterprise with many domains. See Figure 7.20.

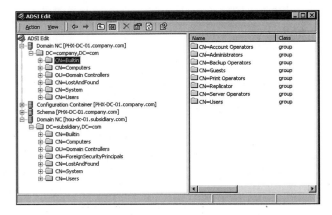

Figure 7.20 ADSI Editor showing second-level containers for local domain naming context and trusted domain naming context.

2. You can also view the attributes associated with an object along with their values. For example, expand the Domain NC tree to show the list of objects under cn=Users then right-click cn=Administrator and select PROPERTIES from the fly-out menu. The Properties window opens for this object (see Figure 7.21.)

Figure 7.21 Properties for the Administrator object, distinguished name cn=Administrator,cn=Users,dc=Company,dc=com.

The Path field in the window indicates the connection syntax used to find this object. The Class field indicates that this object is an instance of the User class.

3. In the `Select Which Properties to View` drop-down box, select `Both`. Browse the list of attributes in the `Select a Property to View` box. If you have adequate privileges, you can use the `Edit` field to change the value of the attribute, but I do not recommend doing so unless you are absolutely sure of how the attribute is used and validated. You may find yourself making a change that renders the object useless to the system. Experiment with inconsequential attributes like Company, Department, and Description. Click `Set` to save the changes when you're finished, then `OK` to close the window.

You can also use the ADSI Editor to create objects, but this is not recommended. Using the AD management consoles gets you the benefit of entry forms, validations, and automatic insertion values for system attributes such as GUID and Security Descriptors. For bulk work, you can use the command-line alternatives in the Resource Kit. See Chapter 10 for details.

LDAP Browser

The Resource Kit also comes with a generic LDAP browser called LDP. This tool is less convenient to use than the ADSI Editor, but it provides more information with a single mouse click. Some LDAP operations hidden by ADSI Editor are exposed in the LDAP browser. Let's go over them before we use the browser.

When an LDAP client needs information from an LDAP server, it first *binds* to the server. The bind operation authenticates the user via one of the methods supported by that server's LDAP implementation. The supported methods are specified in the RootDSE object. They are:

- **GSS-API.** This authentication method is described in RFC 2078, "Generic Security Service Application Program Interface, Version 2." The GSS-API is essentially an abstraction and handshaking mechanism that enables a client and a service to start the authentication process. After the two of them have used GSS-API to determine a common security mechanism, they are free to use that mechanism to authenticate. Windows 2000 uses the Security Support Provider Interface (SSPI) to expose GSS-API so that underlying security support providers such as NTLM and Kerberos can be used. The Kerberos implementation complies with RFC 1964, "The Kerberos Version 5 GSS-API Mechanism."

- **GSS-SPNEGO.** This is not a security provider, per se, but a mechanism that permits GSS-API clients of different flavors to negotiate a suitable provider. The SPNEGO interface is described in RFC 2478, "The Simple and Protected GSS-API Negotiation Mechanism." Windows 2000 clients default to using GSS-SPNEGO when binding to Active Directory and the server will pick Kerberos as the preferred authentication method.

Binding versus Connectionless Browsing

Binding is not an absolute requirement to view the contents of a Directory. Connectionless browsing is permitted by the LDAP specifications. This is done by sending datagrams to UDP port 389. Under nearly all circumstances, Windows 2000 security will prevent connectionless access to Directory objects.

After it has finished binding, the client can perform several types of operations if the user has sufficient access rights:

- **Search (browse).** Looks for specific objects or objects with specific attributes. Accepts wild cards and filters.
- **Compare.** Checks to see whether an object matches a set of requirements. This is similar to search but faster.
- **Modify (add, delete, move).** Put new objects in the Directory, remove existing objects, change the attributes of objects, and change the distinguished name, which is the same as moving the object.
- **Abandon.** This tells a domain controller to stop working on a request.

When the client has completed its transactions, it unbinds from the server, releasing the connection. The process of binding and unbinding is the most time-consuming part of the transaction, so developers of LDAP applications often leave the connection in place to speed up subsequent transactions. If the server does not get Directory queries from a particular client for a period of time, it closes the connection automatically. These settings are specified by the LDAP-Admin-Limits attribute of the Default-Query-Policies object in the Services container of the Directory. See the "Standard Directory Contents" section later in this chapter for details.

When you use the LDAP Browser, you must walk through various steps to bind, query, and unbind. Here's how it works:

Procedure 7.3 **Using the LDAP Browser**

1. Open the Resource Kit using START | PROGRAMS | RESOURCE KIT | TOOLS MANAGEMENT CONSOLE.

2. Expand the tree to show Microsoft Resource Kits | Windows 2000 Resource Kit | Tool Categories | Tools A to Z.

3. Launch LDP from the pick list. This opens the LDP window.

4. Select Connection | Connect to open the Connect window. Figure 7.22 shows an example.

Figure 7.22 LDP utility showing the Connect window for connecting to a domain controller through well-known TCP port 389 for LDAP.

5. Under Server, enter the fully qualified DNS name of a domain controller. Under Port, specify either 389, the well known port for standard LDAP queries, or 3268, the proprietary port for Microsoft's Global Catalog service.

6. Leave the Connectionless option unchecked.

7. Click OK. The right pane of the window shows the result of the connection. See Figure 7.23. If the connection is successful, the attributes associated with RootDSE appear. RootDSE attributes are detailed in the "Standard Directory Contents" section later in this chapter.

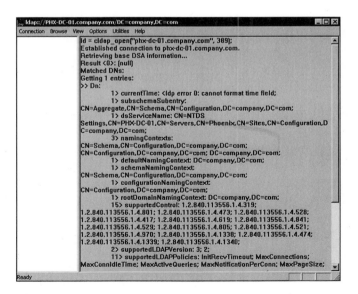

Figure 7.23 LDAP browser window showing successful connection and RootDSE attributes.

8. From the menu, select VIEW | TREE. This opens the Tree View window.

9. Under BaseDN, enter the distinguished name of the container you want to browse. For example, you can enter dc=Company,dc=com to see the domain naming context. You can also specify a container lower in the Directory if you wish. For example, you could select the Users container by entering cn=Users,dc=Company,dc=com.

10. Click OK to submit the query. If successful, the left pane of the window shows any subordinate naming contexts and the right pane shows attributes of the target object (see Figure 7.24.)

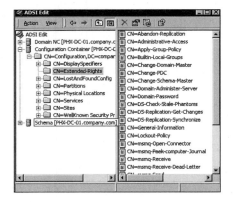

Figure 7.24 LDAP browser showing tree view of Company.com domain naming context and partial list of attributes for the Domain–DNS object dc=Company,dc=com.

11. If you want to view the attributes for a specific object, use the options under the BROWSE menu.

There are quite a few more options in the LDAP browser, but let's cover more about the Directory structure and LDAP operations first.

Other LDAP Tools

Because Active Directory is an RFC-compliant implementation of LDAP, you can use virtually any LDAP tool for browsing objects and collecting information. Here are a few sources of LDAP tools and related information:

- **University of Michigan (www.umich.edu/~dirsvcs/ldap/index.html).** The origin of LDAP and still a primary source of LDAP tools. The documentation is sparse and the tools in Windows 2000 are more comprehensive, but it's worth a look.

- **Novell (`www.novell.com/products/nds/ldap.html`).** NetWare 5 boogies on IP and so does NDS. Novell is putting lots of calories into doing the "Internet thing" right. Also take a look at `developer.novell.com` for LDAP and X.500 tools that might be useful in a mixed network.

- **Innosoft (`www.innosoft.com`).** This company has been in the LDAP and X.500 business for quite a while and their expertise shows. Their Directory Product Architect, Mark Wahl, played a critical role in LDAP v3 development.

- **OpenLDAP (`www.openldap.org`).** If you are an open source kind of a person, you should take a look at the latest wares from that community. These toolkits are not for the fainthearted and there are no compiled packages to play with, but it's worth a peek if you want to build your own administration tools to replace those clumsy MMC snap-ins.

- **Boldon James (`www.bj.co.uk`).** If you are not an open source fanatic and don't mind spending a few dollars to get a polished toolkit, these folks are worth a visit. A class act.

Standard Directory Contents

This section covers the function of naming contexts and their contents. Let's start at the top of the Directory with RootDSE. You might recall that RootDSE is a special container that has no distinguished name and does not represent a naming context. Each domain controller builds its own copy of RootDSE that it uses to store information about the replicas of the naming contexts it hosts and functional information about its copy of the Directory.

LDAP RootDSE and NDS [ROOT]

NetWare administrators, don't confuse RootDSE with the [Root] object in NDS. [Root] is an X.500 construct that obeys the standard partitioning rules in the NDS tree. Client queries that "walk to root" in NDS actually generate NCP traffic to a server that holds a partition of [Root]. This is not the case with RootDSE. Each domain controller has its own iteration of RootDSE created on-the-fly based on the contents of the naming context replicas it hosts.

Table 7.2 lists the critical attributes of RootDSE and their functions along with example values.

Table 7.2 **RootDSE Attributes, Their Functions and Example Values for a Domain Controller in the Domain *Office.Company.com***

Attribute Name	Attribute Function	Example Value
Default-Naming-Context	Contains the distinguished name of the Domain-DNS object that defines the top of the local domain namespace.	dc=Office,dc=Company,dc=com
Root-Domain-Naming-Context	Contains the distinguished name of the Domain-DNS, object that represents the top of the Directory namespace.	dc=Company,dc=com
Configuration-Naming-Context	Contains the distinguished name of name of the Configuration container.	cn=Configuration,dc=Company,dc=com
Schema-Naming-Context	Contains the distinguished name of the Schema container.	cn=Schema,cn=Configuration,dc=Company,dc=com
Naming-Contexts	Contains the distinguished names of all naming contexts with replicas on the domain controller hosting this instance of RootDSE.	dc=Company,dc=com dc=Office,dc=Company dc=com cn=Configuration,dc=Company,dc=com cn=Schema,cn=Configuration dc=Company,dc=com
DNS-Host-Name	Contains the fully qualified DNS name of the domain controller hosting this instance of RootDSE.	alb-dc-01.Office.Company.com
LDAP-Service-Name	The UPN (User Principal Name) of the domain controller hosting this instance of RootDSE. Computer objects are just special forms of User objects, so they can have UPNs. The dollar sign is Microsoft shorthand dating back to classic NT and SAM. It indicates a hidden or secret object.	Company.com:phx-dc-01$@Company.com

Attribute Name	Attribute Function	Example Value
Server-Name	Contains the distinguished name of the Server object that represents the domain controller holding this instance of RootDSE. The DN of the server object helps clients to find the server's site, which is key for locating the server in DNS.	cn=alb-dc-01,cn= Server,cn= Albuquerque, cn=Sites, cn=Configuration, dc=Company,dc=com
DS-Service-Name	Contains the distinguished name of the NTDS Settings object associated with the domain controller hosting this instance of RootDSE. The NTDS Settings object has attributes that control Directory replication.	cn=NTDS,Settings, cn=alb-dc- 01,cn=Servers, cn=Albuquerque, cn=Sites,cn= Configuration, dc=Company,dc=com
SubSchemaSubEntry	Contains the distinguished name of the Aggregate object.	cn=Aggregate,cn= Schema, cn=Configuration, dc=Company,dc=com
Supported-Capabilities	Contains the OID that describes the basic capability of the Directory Service.	1.2.840.113556.1.4.800
Supported-Control	Lists the OIDs of special LDAP controls. These controls extend the base functionality of an LDAP client by permitting it to request special client/server operations, such as OIDs of various controls. For example, OID 1.2.840.113556.1.4.319 indicates that the Directory supports the Paged-Results Searches control, a control that returns the results of a query in bite-sized chunks.	

continues ▶

Table 7.2 **Continued**

Attribute Name	Attribute Function	Example Value
Supported-LDAP-Policies	Contains LDAP policies that affect connections, idle time table size, and so on.	InitRecvTimeout; MaxConnections; MaxConnIdleTime; MaxActiveQueries; MaxNotificationPerConn; MaxPageSize; MaxQueryDuration; MaxTempTableSize; MaxResultSetSize; MaxPoolThreads; MaxDatagramRecv
Supported-LDAP-Version	Contains the major LDAP versions supported by this release of Active Directory.	Currently Active Directory supports LDAP v3 as described in RFC 2251, "Lightweight Directory Access Protocol (v3)," and LDAP v2 as described in RFC 1777, "Lightweight Directory Access Protocol."
Supported-SASL-Mechanisms	Contains the names of the Simple Authentication and Security Layer (SASL) providers supported by Active Directory. There are only two entries in a standard Active Directory implementation, GSS-API and GSS-SPNEGO. **GSS-API.** This API permits services and clients to select a mutual security method for authentication. **GSS-SPNEGO.** This is a method for clients and services of different flavors to negotiate a mutual security provider for authentication. This is the default selection for Windows 2000 clients. The result of the SPNEGO negotiation is Kerberos.	

Domain-DNS

Underneath RootDSE is a Domain-DNS object that represents the beginning of the domain namespace. A Domain-DNS object has several attributes that describe the structure of the domain. Table 7.3 lists these attributes and their functions. The examples are for a server named ALB-DC-01 in the Albuquerque site of the Office.Company.com domain.

Table 7.3 Domain-DNS Object Attributes and Functions

Attribute	Function	Example Value
Domain-Replica	Contains the flat NetBIOS name of the classic NT PDC that was promoted to initiate this Windows 2000 domain.	`alb-dc-01`

FSMO-Role-Owner	Contains the distinguished name of the NTDS Settings object for the server hosting this replica of the naming context. The NTDS Settings object contains the list of FSMO role masters for the domain. FSMO stands for *Flexible Single Master Operations*.	`cn=NTDS Settings,`
		`cn=alb-dc-01,cn=`
		`Servers,cn=`
		`Albuquerque,`
		`cn=Sites,cn=`
		`Configuration,`
		`dc=Company,dc=com`

GP-Link
GP-Options
	These attributes specify the GUID of the default group policy object for this domain and any group policy options. See Chapter 10 for information about group policies.	`GP-Link: cn=`
		`{31B2F340-016D-11D2-`
		`0945F-00C04FB984F9},`
		`cn=Policies,cn=System,`
		`dc=Company,dc=com`
		`    GP-Options: 0`

Lockout-Duration Lockout-Observation-Window Lockout-Threshhold Max-Pwd-Age Min-Pwd-Age Modified-Count PWD-History-Length Pwd-Properties	Contains values that control password policies and intruder lockout policies. These settings are equivalent to the classic lockout policies. These settings are equivalent to the classic NT polices contained in the LSA database inside the SECURITY hive in the Registry. Password policies are configured using the Group Policy editor.	Varies with policy settings. The only default setting is Max-Pwd-Age of 42, which is the same setting used by classic NT.

continues ▶

Table 7.3 **Continued**

Attribute	Function	Example Value
Creation-Time Modified-Count Modified-Count-At-Last-Prom Builtin-Creation-Time Builtin-Modified-Count LSA-Creation-Time LSA-Modified-Count UAS-Compat	These attributes are equivalent to entries in the SAM, Builtin, and LSA databases from a classic PDC Registry. They exist for backward compatibility only. The UAS-Compat attribute indicates that the user and group entries are compatible with LAN Manager 2.2 User Accounts Subsystem modules.	Varies
RID-Manager-Reference	Specifies the distinguished name of the RIDManager$ object.	The RID Manager is the first domain controller promoted in the domain. This role is passed on automatically when the RID Manager is demoted, or it can be transferred manually.
Next-RID	This object contains the pool of available Relative ID codes for the domain. A domain controller uses Relative ID codes to build Security ID codes (SIDs) for security principals, such as users, groups, and computers.	The value of the Next-RID attribute varies with current RID levels in the domain.
NT-Mixed-Domain	Designates whether the domain is operating in "mixed mode," meaning that it supports classic NT domain controllers, or "native mode," with no classic support.	Default is 1 for mixed-mode. Changes to 0 when the domain is promoted to native mode.
Repl-Up-To-Date-Vector Reps-From Reps-To	Contains replication control information.	Varies
Sub-Refs	Contains the distinguished name any trusted child domains.	N/A for the child domain in our example. The root domain, Company.com, would have an entry for Office.Company.com.

Attribute	Function	Example Value
SubSchema SubEntry	Contains the distinguished name of the Aggregate object, a special object in the SubSchema class that contains the names of all classes and attributes in the schema.	cn=Aggregate,cn=Schema, cn=Configuration, dc=Company,dc=com

Configuration Container

The Configuration container is also a naming context, meaning that it is replicated separately from the Domain naming context. Configuration is one of the two containers holding structural information about the Directory (the Schema container is the other). The Configuration object itself is rather bland. It represents a naming context, so it contains replication control attributes. It also has a SubRefs attribute that points to the Schema container. The really interesting parts are the containers under Configuration. There are eight major containers under Configuration. Two of these, Sites and Services, are exposed through the Active Directory Sites and Services snap-in. The rest are hidden except when viewed with ADSI or LDAP browsers. Here are their contents and functions.

DisplaySpecifiers

This container holds objects from the display Specifiers class. Each instance of this class is associated with a structural object class for which it alters the viewable attributes. This is called *shadowing*. For example, the user-display specifier shadows the user class.

Display specifiers simplify many programming tasks. One of these is *localization*, the task of producing foreign language versions of an application. It would be horrendously complex to develop even a basic FIGS (French, Italian, German, Spanish) version of the Directory if that effort entailed translating every class and attribute, then tracking changes to each translated object individually through change control. Multiply that effort by the number of versions that will eventually be available with character sets from Cyrillic, Kanji, Szechwan, Arabic, Korean, Hebrew, Thai, and so on, and you can see the magnitude of the problem.

Rather than translate each object, a localization team can develop a set of display specifiers based on the *National Language Support* (NLS) files that already exist for Windows 2000. These NLS files are grouped and numbered by *code page*. The United States English code page is number 1033. The code pages for FIGS countries are *French*, 1036; *Italian*, 1040; *German*, 1031; and *Spanish*, 1034. In the Directory, you will see references to code pages by hex rather than decimal. The United States English code page, decimal 1033, corresponds to hex 409. Application designers build their code to obtain attribute values from a base object, then overlay them with localized property pages using GUID values taken from the associated display specifier. For example, the Domain-DNS object class has an attribute called *Name*. If this attribute is viewed through the filter of a German code page, hex 407, the attribute would be listed as *Firma*.

Display specifiers can also define separate context menus, property pages, and icons based on whether or not the user accessing the object has administrator privileges. For example, consider the fly-out menu that appears when you right-click a Directory object comes from a context menu. The display specifier permits the designer to put a basic set of menus in the Explorer shell for the user, and a menu with a wider array of management options for an administrator. These specialized context menus and property pages come in the form GUID values contained in these display specifier attributes:

- Admin-Context-Menu
- Admin-Property-Pages
- Attribute-Display-Names
- Shell-Property-Pages

The display specifier objects are stored under a container named 409, if you are using the US English code page.

Extended-Rights Container

Directory objects are also Windows 2000 security objects. This makes it possible to assign permissions to the Directory object itself as well as the properties associated with the object. This is a powerful feature, but actually using it can be tedious. For example, let's say you want to grant permission for Help Desk personnel to modify the list of members for a Group, but that's it. Picking through the list of security permissions and trying to guess exactly which ones can do the job without granting too much access is difficult and time consuming. Also, a particular task might require several permissions, so you would have to try various combinations.

The schema includes a special set of rights designed to modify multiple object permissions simultaneously to simplify assigning management duties. These are called *extended rights*. For example, an extended right called

Membership grants the ability to modify the membership of a single group, selected groups, every group in a container, or every group in a container and its subordinate containers.

Extended rights come in the form of Directory objects derived from the Control-Access-Right class. These objects are stored in the Extended-Rights container. Figure 7.25 shows this container and a few of the Control-Access-Rights objects.

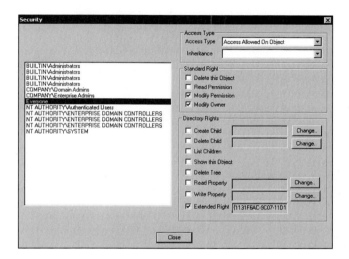

Figure 7.25 Extended-Rights container showing some of the extended rights that can be associated with structural object classes.

Like the display specifier objects mentioned above, the Control-Access-Right objects are associated with the structural objects they modify. For example, there are extended rights called Personal-Information and Public-Information that are associated with User and Contact classes.

Figure 7.26 shows how these extended rights are displayed in the Security settings for a user object.

There are over 50 extended rights covering a wide assortment of management operations, such as changing passwords, changing domain configurations, resetting user lockouts, and managing Backoffice services. The Applies-To attribute in the Control-Access-Right object defines the associated structural object class to which the extended right applies. If you view this attribute, you'll discover that it takes the form of a Globally Unique Identifier (GUID). This GUID corresponds to the Schema-ID-GUID attribute of an object class. Refer to the help file in the Platform SDK or query the MSDN Web site, msdn.microsoft.com, if you want to find the object class associated with a particular GUID.

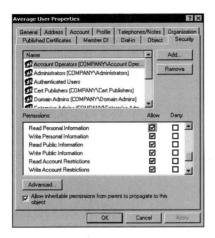

Figure 7.26 Properties windows for a user object showing extended rights under Permissions.

LostandFoundConfig

This container holds orphaned objects that get lost during Directory database replication or repairs. During repair operations, the ESENT engine has mechanisms that search out orphaned entries and attempt to fix them. If they cannot be fixed, they are placed in this container where they can be deleted or moved where they belong. See Chapter 10, "Managing Active Directory Security," for more information about Directory repair procedures.

Partitions

This container holds the cross-reference objects that point at the naming contexts of trusted domain. Table 7.4 lists the attributes that contain information about these naming contexts. Because the Configuration container is replicated to every domain controller in every domain in the forest, the contents of the Partitions container can be used to build a referral or a chained response to any trusted domain.

Table 7.4   **Contents of Cross-Ref Objects Used to Locate Domain
Controllers Hosting Replicas of Naming Contexts**

Attribute	Function	Example Value
DNS-Root	Contains the fully qualified DNS name of the root of the domain associated with the naming context. This is what tells a client where to look for SRV records in DNS.	office.company.com
NC-Name	Contains the distinguished name of container at the top of the Naming Context.	dc=Office,dc=Company,dc=com
NetBIOS-Name	Contains the flat NetBIOS name of the domain. This is used to register the domain name in WINS and to respond to downlevel clients who are searching for a domain using broadcasts.	OFFICE
Trust-Parent (tree only)	Contains the distinguished name of the superior domain in the tree. This is functionally the same as the Superior-Reference attribute used in standard LDAP.	dc=Company,dc=com
Trust-Root (forest only)	Contains the distinguished name of the domain that is at the root of a forest.	N/A for this example.

Physical Locations

This container holds Physical-Location-DN objects associated with DEN.
For example, a DEN-aware router can place a locator object in this container. Because DEN makes use of standard LDAP functionality, this is the
only object class in Active Directory that uses the Location attribute.

The DEN initiative has developed a set of policies for controlling network parameters affecting Quality of Service (QoS), IP Security (IPSec), and other core networking functions. All leading routing and infrastructure vendors have pledged support for DEN, and many have allied themselves with both Microsoft and Novell for the "Directory" part of DEN. Visit the Web site of your favorite vendor to see their DEN-aware products and find out their plans for Active Directory integration.

Services

This container is exposed in the AD Sites and Services console by selecting VIEW | SHOW SERVICES option from the menu. Think of the contents of the Services container as a kind of enterprise-wide Registry. The default entries include configuration parameters for the Extensible Authentication Protocol, Microsoft Message Queue Services, Network services such as DHCP, Public Key Encryption, Routing and Remote Access Services, Remote Access Dial-Up Services, and Directory query policies. Application vendors are sure to put lots of entries in this container as Windows 2000 takes hold.

Most of the containers and objects in the Services container have only one or two attributes of any interest. For example, the Directory Service object has an attribute called SPN-Mappings, which stands for Service Principal Name. This attribute holds the name of every service offered by the domain controller. Another interesting object is Default Query Policies, which has an attribute called LDAP Admin Limits that lists the network parameters to be used by LDAP clients when querying domain controllers. The following list shows these parameters and their default settings:

```
MaxDatagramRecv=1024
MaxPoolThreads=4
MaxResultSetSize=262144
MaxTempTableSize=10000
MaxQueryDuration=120
MaxPageSize=1000
MaxNotificationPerConn=5
MaxActiveQueries=20
MaxConnIdleTime=900
InitRecvTimeout=120
MaxConnections=5000
```

At the time of this writing, Microsoft has not provided information about the optimal settings for these parameters for heavily trafficked domain controllers. If your Directory performance seems slow and all other performance indicators (CPU utilization, I/O, and network) seem to be acceptable, you might try bumping these numbers up gradually.

Sites

The Sites container is also exposed in the AD Sites and Services console. The objects in this container control Directory replication and other Site-specific functions.

In Windows 2000, a Site represents an area of high-speed network interconnections. For example, the local area network in the Phoenix office of Company.com would be a Site. The Houston office would be another site. Under normal circumstances, physical networks are connected by slow WAN links, such as T-1, fraction T-1, ISDN, or 56K leased lines. Active Directory represents these physical connections with Site Links.

During replication, all domain controllers in the same Site replicate at every five minutes or when a given number of changes have accumulated. Domain controllers in different sites replicate at much longer intervals (as long as six hours, by default) and only replicate using a schedule regardless of the number of accumulated changes.

A Site can contain more than one domain. For example, a forest for a university might contain separate domains for each school, but they are all in the same campus network so the domains are in the same site. Figure 7.27 shows a typical Site configuration.

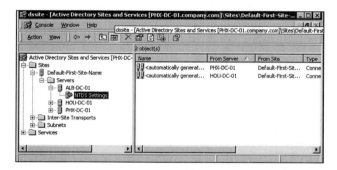

Figure 7.27   Active Directory Sites and Services
snap-in showing NTDS settings objects.

Chapter 11 covers Active Directory replication. The interesting Directory objects at this stage are the NTDS Settings objects associated with each site. These objects control replication of naming contexts between domain controllers. These objects have several attributes that influence Directory operation:

- **DMD-Location** (DMD is X.500 shorthand for Directory Management Domain). Contains the distinguished name of the Schema container. The reason for the name is that the Schema container is an instance of the DMD class.

- **Invocation-ID.** A GUID that uniquely identifies a domain controller for purposes of replication control. Changes to a Directory object made at one domain controller are replicated to its neighboring domain controllers. These DCs replicate to their neighbors. The Invocation-ID identifies the domain controller that did the original write.

- **Has-Master-NCs.** This attribute contains the distinguished name of every naming context with a replica on a particular domain controller. For example, a domain controller in the `Office.Company.com` domain that is not a Global Catalog server would have the following replicas: `dc=Office,dc=Company,dc=com; cn=Schema,cn=Configuration,dc=Company,dc=com;` and `cn=Configuration,DC=Company,DC=com`.

- **Has-Partial-NCs.** A partial naming context refers to the limited-attribute naming context replica kept by a Global Catalog server. Only a GC would have entries in this attribute. Figure 7.28 shows how this option is set using the `AD Sites and Services` console. Access the option by opening the console and navigating to `Default-First-Site-Name | Servers | <server_name>` and opening the `Properties` window for the `NTDS Settings` object.

Figure 7.28 DSSITE.MSC snap-in showing the `Global Catalog` option in the NTDS Settings properties for a domain controller.

Well-Known Security Principals

The object-based security used by classic NT and Windows 2000 assigns a unique Security Identifier (SID) to every security principal. There is a set of well-known SIDs that represents special purpose groups. This includes groups like *Interactive*, which designates users who are logged on at the console of a machine; *Network*, which designates users who have logged onto the domain; and *Everyone*, which designates every user in a domain. Objects that represent well-known security principals are stored in the Directory as instances of the Foreign-Security-Principal class. See Chapter 6, "Understanding Network Access Security and Kerberos," for details on how these SIDs are used to control access security.

Schema

This container starts a separate naming context. The Schema container holds ClassSchema and AttributeSchema objects that represent the various classes and attributes in the Directory. If this sounds like a circular definition, it's meant to be. Unlike some Directory Services that load the schema in a separate file, the Active Directory schema is completely self-referential.

The Schema container object is an instance of the Directory Management Domain (DMD) class. This is a holdover from Exchange, which uses X.500 terminology to define the information store. Because the Schema object represents a naming context boundary, it also contains replication control attributes similar to those in the Configuration object and the Domain-DNS object.

If you search through the objects in the Schema container, you'll come across one that doesn't seem to fit the pattern. This is a special object called Aggregate. This lone instance of the LDAP SubSchema class in the Active Directory has attributes that contain the names of all classes and attributes in the Directory. Active Directory and LDAP clients can request the contents of the Aggregate object and get the full schema without querying for the entire contents of the Schema container.

Active Directory Support Files

The X.500/9594 standard does not specify a specific database design or base file structure. Microsoft chose to use a new-and-improved version of its *Extensible Storage Engine* (ESE), similar to the Jet design used in Exchange 5.5.

The ESENT engine is theoretically capable of handling 10 million Directory objects with a maximum storage capacity of 17 terabytes. The shipping version of the database has proven to be stable and reliable, but early adopters should take care when ramping up. Watch performance closely and don't ignore replication or retrieval anomalies.

The files that make up the Active Directory information store are located under \WINNT\NTDS on a volume specified during domain controller promotion. The following list contains the Active Directory support files and their functions:

- **NTDS.DIT.** This is the main information store. NTDS stands for *NT Directory Services*. The DIT stands for *Directory Information Tree*. The NTDS.DIT file on a particular domain controller contains all naming contexts hosted by that domain controller, including the Configuration and Schema naming contexts. There is no separate data dictionary or metadirectory.

- **SCHEMA.INI.** This file is used to initialize the NTDS.DIT during the initial promotion of a domain controller. It is not used after that has been accomplished.

- **EDB.LOG.** This is the primary transaction log for the Directory. Any changes made to objects in the Directory are saved to the EDB.LOG before being committed to the main NTDS.DIT database. Entries in EDB.LOG that have not been committed to NTDS.DIT are kept in memory to improve performance. The EDB.LOG file is always 1000 KB. When it fills, the updates are flushed to the DIT and the log fills again.

- **EDBxxxxx.LOG.** These auxiliary transaction tracking logs are used to store changes if the main EDB.LOG file gets full before it can be flushed to the DIT. The xxxxx entries stand for sequential numbers in hex. When the EDB.LOG file fills up, it is renamed to EDB00001.LOG and a new EDB.LOG file is created. The fifteenth log file would be EDB0000F.LOG and so forth. The system builds as many EDBxxxxx.LOG files as needed to store changes.

- **EDB.CHK.** This is a *checkpoint* file. It is used by the transaction tracking system to mark the point at which updates are transferred from the log files to the DIT. As the commits are flushed, the checkpoint moves forward in the EDB.CHK file. If the system terminates abnormally, the pointer tells the system how far along a given set of commits had progressed before the termination. This speeds up recovery dramatically for big systems with many updates in the log.

- **RES1.LOG** and **RES2.LOG.** These are reserve log files. If the hard drive fills to capacity just as the system is attempting to create an EDBxxxxx.LOG file, the space reserved by the RES log files is used. The system then puts a dire warning on the screen prompting you to take action to free up disk space quickly before the Directory gets corrupted. You should never let a volume containing Active Directory files get even close to being full. File fragmentation is a big performance thief, and fragmentation increases exponentially as free space diminishes.
- **TEMP.EDB.** This is a scratch pad used to store in-progress transactions and to hold pages pulled out of the DIT file during compaction.

Chapter 11 covers database recovery and information store management.

Functional Description of LDAP Lookups

Previously, I used a Land's End catalog as an example of a static Directory Service. In actuality, Active Directory is less like a mail-order firm than a well-run department store. For instance, in a department store, you can sidle up to the fragrance bar and ask, "How much is the Chanel No. 5?" and be sure of getting an immediate reply, especially if you already have your credit card in hand. But what if you ask, "Where can I find a size 16 chambray shirt that looks like a Tommy Hilfiger design but doesn't cost so darn much?" The fragrance associate probably doesn't know, but you get directions to the Men's Wear department. You make your way there and ask an associate your question. That associate may not know the answer, either, but now you get directions to the Bargain Men's Wear department in the basement behind last year's Christmas decorations. You proceed to that area and ask an associate your question again. This time you'll either be handed a shirt or given an excuse why it isn't available.

LDAP uses a similar system of referrals to point clients at the DSA that hosts the naming context containing the requested information. These referrals virtually guarantee the success of any lookup, as long as the object exists inside the scope of the information store. Referrals put the burden of searching on the clients, though, as opposed to X.500, which gives all that messy search work to the DSAs. LDAP is Wal-Mart to the Nordstroms of X.500.

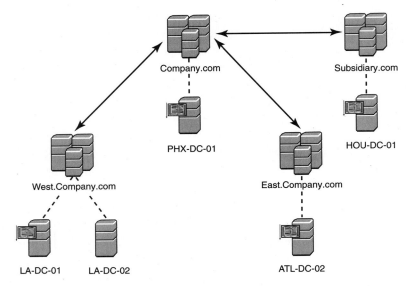

Figure 7.29 Directory forest with five domains to demonstrate LDAP lookups.

Here is how an LDAP lookup operates. Figure 7.29 shows a forest with five domains. The domain controllers for the various domains are shown in the diagram and listed in Table 7.5.

Table 7.5 **Domains and Their Domain Controllers**

Domain	Domain Controller	Global Catalog Server
Company.com	PHX-DC-01.Company.com	Yes
West.Company.com	LA-DC-01.West.Company.com	Yes
West.Company.com	LA-DC-02.West.Company.com	No
East.Company.com	ATL-DC-01.East.Company.com	Yes
Subsidiary.com	HOU-DC-01. Subsidiary.com	Yes

Consider a PC that is an Active Directory client in the LA office. The user of this PC initiates a Directory search for a user named Tim Smith with the distinguished name `cn=tsmith,cn=Users,dc=Subsidiary,dc=com`. (It's a little far-fetched to imagine that a user would enter a typeful DN, but let's assume that the application developer collects the information in a friendlier way and does the formatting in the background.)

If the user's PC authenticated with domain controller LA-DC-02, the application sends an LDAP lookup to LA-DC-01 asking for the specified Directory object. This domain controller is not a Global Catalog server, so when it checks its list of naming contexts, it discovers that it has no replica for dc=Subsidiary,dc=com. LA-DC-01 has a couple of ways to proceed, depending on how the client application flagged the request.

- If the request is flagged for chaining, LA-DC-01 can forward the request to a domain controller hosting a replica of dc=Subsidiary,dc=com. It knows that Subsidiary.com is a trusted domain by checking the Cross-Ref objects under cn=Partitions,cn=Configuration,dc=company,dc=com. It will find the HOU-DC-01.subsidiary.com domain controller when it queries DNS.

- If the request is flagged for referral, LA-DC-01 could return the request to the client with the identity of the correct naming context. The client then performs the DNS lookup to find a domain controller in the remote domain and submits its request to that server.

- The Global Catalog server, LA-DC-01, offers a third alternative. Rather than chain to the remote DC in Houston or referring the client to the remote domain, LA-DC-02 submits the lookup to the GC server. The GC holds a partial copy of the Subsidiary.com naming context. As long as the request is for one of the attributes in the GC, the lookup is fulfilled without WAN traffic. Both the client (in the case of referrals) and the domain controller (in the case of chaining) locate domain controllers in trusted domain using DNS. Let's take a closer look at how that works.

How LDAP Clients Locate Active Directory Services

Active Directory clients use DNS to locate Windows 2000 domain controllers and their respective Active Directory Services. They do this by querying for Service Locator (SRV) records that point at Directory Services, Kerberos services, and Global Catalog services. SRV records are designated Resource Record type 33. See Chapter 5, "Managing Domain Name System (DNS) Services and Dynamic Host Configuration (DHCP) Services," for a description of the SRV record, and refer to RFC 2052, "A DNS RR for specifying the location of services (DNS SRV)."

SRV Functional Overview

The SRV record is a recent addition to the DNS stable. It is a derivative of the Mail Exchange (MX) record. SRV records give clients a way to locate servers that host protocol-specific services. For example, consider an SRV record for a hypothetical protocol called RAD that runs over TCP port 999. If a DNS client in the Company.com zone needs the name of a RAD server, it can query DNS for SRV records associated with tcp.RAD. The DNS server responds with all SRV records listed under that heading. It does not use round robin, as it would in response to an A record query. The client is free to choose from the list like a prom queen picking a dance partner.

Here is an example of what the SRV records for the RAD protocol would look like:

```
RAD.tcp      SRV 1 0 999 primary-RAD-server
RAD.tcp      SRV 2 1 999 sec-RAD-server-1
RAD.tcp      SRV 2 2 999 sec-RAD-server-2
RAD.tcp      SRV 2 1 999 sec-RAD-server-3
```

The SRV entry designates the resource record type and the name at the end of the record designates the name of the host that is running the RAD protocol. The DNS server also returns the A records for these hosts, so the client does not need to send out another query to find their IP addresses.

The three numbers in the resource record refer to *priority, weight,* and *port* (in that order). Here are explanations for those values:

- **Priority.** When several servers offer the same service, they can be assigned different priorities. The client resolver chooses among them using the priority setting. The host with the lowest number has the highest priority. If that host is unavailable, the client proceeds to the next highest priority host. In the tcp.RAD list, the client would choose primary-RAD-server first.

- **Weight.** When several hosts have the same priority, the client chooses among them using a weighting factor. The chance of it picking a particular host is higher if the host has a higher weighting factor. The weighting factor is calculated based on the ratio of a host's weight value in relation to the sum of the weights for the other hosts with the same priority. Weighting factors give the client the ability to say, "Host sec-RAD-server-1 is twice as fast as the others." The odds of a client picking that server are 2 out of 4, or 50% higher.

- **Port.** The TCP or UDP port used by the protocol. The example RAD protocol used TCP port 999. LDAP uses TCP port 389 for standard queries. Microsoft uses TCP port 3268 for LDAP queries directed at Global Catalog servers. Kerberos uses TCP port 88 for authentication and TCP port 464 for the kpasswd service. Windows 2000 Kerberos also accepts connectionless requests over UDP 88 and 464 for clients that can squeeze an authentication request into 1500 bytes.

SRV Records for Active Directory

When a Window 2000 server is promoted to domain controller, it registers a boatload of SRV records with its associated DNS server. Figure 7.30 shows a DNS zone table for the Company.com domain. The zone table contains SRV records for LDAP services, Kerberos KDC services, and Global Catalog services, as well as SRV records pointing at the PDC role master, the Kerberos password port, and connectionless options for Kerberos using UDP.

Function of kpasswd

The kpasswd SRV records associated with TCP and UDP port 464 are used to support the Kerberos Change Password Protocol (KCPP) currently in Internet draft.

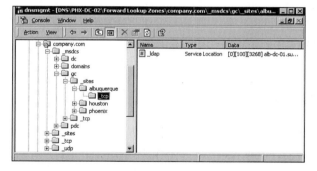

Figure 7.30   DNS Management snap-in showing
zone tables for the Company.com domain.

Format of SRV Record Names

The leading underscores in the SRV record names are part of a transition from an older SRV format to a new format as specified in RFC 2052, "SRV Record Format and Use." At some point in the future, the underscores will be discarded.

The SRV record syntax uses little-endian notation. A Windows 2000 DNS server reverses the order to display SRV records as a hierarchy of folders. The top folder represents the right-most entry in the SRV record. The following list has excerpts from the Company.com.dns zone table showing the structure of the associated SRV records:

```
kerberos._tcp.phoenix._sites.dc._msdcs        600      SRV     0 100 88     phx-dc-01.company.com._
kerberos._tcp.phoenix._sites                  600      SRV     0 100 88     phx-dc-01.company.com.
kerberos._tcp.dc._msdcs                       600      SRV     0 100 88     phx-dc-01.company.com.
kerberos._tcp                                 600      SRV     0 100 88     phx-dc-01.company.com.
kerberos._udp                                 600      SRV     0 100 88     phx-dc-01.company.com.
kpasswd._tcp                                  600      SRV     0 100 464    phx-dc-01.company.com.
kpasswd._udp                                  600      SRV     0 100 464    phx-dc-01.company.com.
ldap._tcp.phoenix._sites.gc._msdcs            600      SRV     0 100 3268   phx-dc-01.company.com.
gc._tcp.phoenix._sites                        600      SRV     0 100 3268   phx-dc-01.company.com.
ldap._tcp.gc._msdcs                           600      SRV     0 100 3268   phx-dc-01.company.com.
gc._tcp                                       600      SRV     0 100 3268   phx-dc-01.company.com.
ldap._tcp.phoenix._sites.dc._msdcs            600      SRV     0 100 389    phx-dc-01.company.com._
ldap._tcp.phoenix._sites                      600      SRV     0 100 389    phx-dc-01.company.com._
ldap._tcp.dc._msdcs                           600      SRV     0 100 389    phx-dc-01.company.com.
ldap._tcp.{guid of domain}.domains._msdcs     600      SRV     0 100 389    phx-dc-01.company.com.
ldap._tcp                                     600      SRV     0 100 389    phx-dc-01.company.com.
ldap._tcp.pdc._msdcs                          600      SRV     0 100 389    phx-dc-01.company.com.
phx-dc-01                                     1200     A       10.1.1.1
gc._msdcs                                     600      A       10.1.1.1
{GUID of DC invocation}._msdcs               600      CNAME   phx-dc-01.company.com.
```

Here are the functions of the SRV records based on their groupings in the DNS Management snap-in:

- **_MSDCS.** This heading collects together SRV records based on their status as Domain Controllers, Domain invocations, Global Catalog servers, and Primary Domain Controllers. Domain controllers and Global Catalog servers are broken down by site. This tells Active Directory clients very quickly where to find local services. Domain invocations support replication. Each domain controller gets a GUID that it uses when invoking replication. The PDC entry contains the SRV record for the domain controller assigned to be the PDC Flexible Single Master Operation (FSMO) role master. The PDC record tells Windows 2000 clients where to find the PDC emulator in a mixed-mode domain.

- **_SITES.** A Site represents an area of high-speed connectivity associated with one or more distinct IP subnets. By indexing domain controllers based on their Site affiliation, clients can look in _SITES to find local services rather than sending their LDAP lookups across the WAN.
- **_TCP.** This heading collects all domain controllers in the DNS zone. The _TCP grouping acts as a catchall for clients who can't find their specific site or who need to find a domain controller elsewhere in the network if none of those with local SRV records respond.
- **_UDP.** Kerberos v5 permits clients to use connectionless services to get tickets and change passwords. This is done via UDP ports that correspond to the TCP ports for the same services, UDP port 88 for ticketing and UDP 464 for password changes.

Operational Description of SRV Record Queries

Here is an example sequence of events that occurs when a Directory-enabled client searches for a domain controller. In the example, the domain is named Company.com. There are two domain controllers, PHX–DC–01 and PHX–DC–02. The domain controllers are in a Site named Phoenix.

Procedure 7.4 **Searching for a Domain Controller**

1. When a user initiates a process that requires a Directory lookup, the client DNS resolver sends a query to DNS for SRV records. If the client has cached its site name, the client will query DNS for SRV records in _ldap._tcp.Site_name._sites.dc._msdcs.company.com. If no name is cached, the client queries DNS for records in _ldap._tcp.company.com and works down from there.

> **Registry Tip**
>
> The client cache of site information is in the following Registry location:
>
> Key: HKLM | System | CurrentControlSet | Services | Netlogon | Parameters
>
> Value: DynamicSiteName
>
> Data: Flat name of the last domain controller authenticating the client.
>
> Example, phx-dc-01.

2. Separate sites have separate IP subnets. The client chooses among the SRV records to find a domain controller that shares its subnet. If it cannot find one, it chooses at random. All SRV records for Active Directory Services have the same priority and weighting factor.

3. After a client discovers the name of a domain controller in its site, it performs an LDAP "ping" by sending a brief query to UDP port 389. Based on the client's IP address, the domain controller may return a response referring the client to another site. If this happens, the client goes back to DNS for a domain controller in the new site and eventually ends up back at this point again.

4. After a client finds a domain controller, it behaves like a lonely kid who has finally found a friend. It hounds the domain controller with LDAP requests, Kerberos ticket requests, and referrals to other domains. LDAP requests go to the port specified in the SRV record, which is TCP port 389 for standard lookups and 3268 for Global Catalog lookups. Kerberos requests go to TCP port 88 with password changes going to port 464.

5. The first LDAP lookup performed by the client is a request for NULL, which the Directory interprets as a request for RootDSE. The client uses RootDSE to find supported SASL security mechanisms.

   SASL stands for *Simple Authentication and Security Layer*. The primary SASL mechanism submitted by Windows Active Directory clients during the initial bind is GSS-API SPNEGO. GSS-API stands for *Generic Security Service API*. SPNEGO stands for *Security Negotiation*. In a SPNEGO transaction, the client presents a list of its available authentication mechanism and the service picks the one that is most likely to succeed. Windows 2000 clients use SPNEGO, and the resulting authentication method is inevitably Kerberos.

   Active Directory also supports NTLM challenge-response authentication negotiated through SPNEGO (although not all features are exposed to downlevel clients) and Secure Sockets Layer (SSL) transactions over TCP Port 636.

6. The client now requests all the ObjectClass attributes in RootDSE. This is a healthy list containing virtually everything there is to know about the structure and access controls of the Directory. Now the client knows how to find its way around in the Directory so it can query for specific items. Let's say, for instance, that the user double-clicked the Directory icon in My Network Places. This would initiate an LDAP lookup request to display naming context information.

7. To fulfill this request, the LDAP client requests the contents of the Partitions container, which gives it a copy of all the CrossRef objects that denote the various naming contexts in the Directory. (Recall that the Partitions container is under Configuration, so it holds the naming vcontexts for the entire forest, not just the naming contexts hosted by the domain controller being queried.) With only one domain, the search returns a single distinguished name. In our example, that would be
`cn=Company,cn=Partitions,cn=Configuration,dc=Company,dc=com`.

8. The client uses the information it finds in this CrossRef object to get the DNS Name of the root domain and the distinguished name of the naming context.

9. If the user decides to drill down further in the Directory portion of My Network Places, the LDAP requestor will query for the Aggregate object, which contains the names of schema and attribute objects that the client will need to build a graphical display.

This example has only one domain, so any further LDAP lookups work the same way. But if there were multiple domains configured in trees or forests, and the user sent lookup requests for objects in those trusted domains, the domain controller would generate referrals or chain the request to the target domain on behalf of the user, depending on the way the application developer set the LDAP flags. After the client has the referral, the lookup uses the same mechanism as described in the example.

LDAP File Interchange Format

No discussion of LDAP would be complete without covering the movement of large blocks of data into and out of the Directory. The Active Directory complies with *LDAP Data Interchange Format* (LDIF). This format is still in Internet draft stage but with the backing of Netscape and the support of Microsoft, it's likely to survive to a standards-track. The following example shows the LDIF format for the attributes of the Administrator account in the `Company.com` domain.

```
dn: CN=Administrator,CN=Users,DC=company,DC=com
memberOf: CN=Group Policy Admins,CN=Users,DC=company,DC=com
memberOf: CN=Enterprise Admins,CN=Users,DC=company,DC=com
memberOf: CN=Schema Admins,CN=Users,DC=company,DC=com
memberOf: CN=Administrators,CN=Builtin,DC=company,DC=com
memberOf: CN=Domain Admins,CN=Users,DC=company,DC=com
accountExpires: 9223372036854775807
adminCount: 1
```

```
badPasswordTime: 125693193676075896
badPwdCount: 0
codePage: 0
cn: Administrator
countryCode: 0
description: Built-in account for administering the computer/domain
isCriticalSystemObject: TRUE
lastLogoff: 0
lastLogon: 125693891796993128
logonCount: 109
distinguishedName: CN=Administrator,CN=Users,DC=company,DC=com
objectCategory: CN=Person,CN=Schema,CN=Configuration,DC=company,DC=com
objectClass: user
objectGUID:: gLgtb/ju0hGcKADAT1NqTQ==
objectSid:: AQUAAAAAAUVAAAAoF4uDLI/DAf7Cwgn9AEAAA==
primaryGroupID: 513
pwdLastSet: 125681556744344992
name: Administrator
sAMAccountName: Administrator
sAMAccountType: 805306368
userAccountControl: 66048
uSNChanged: 1532
uSNCreated: 1410
whenChanged: 19990410040835.0Z
whenCreated: 19990410034956.0Z
```

Here are a few items to notice about this example:

- LDIF files use simple ASCII characters. If you have high-order Unicode values in some of the attributes, they might not survive the translation.

- Long integers that represent time and dates will be represented in decimal format and, as such, will not survive reimport. Fortunately, these items are discarded and created afresh when the entry is imported and the new object is created.

- Octet strings are converted to Base64 format. This is indicated by a double-colon after the attribute name. ObjectGUID is an example. These values would withstand a reimport, but for the most part this syntax is used for values that are unique for an object so the input values would be ignored.

- The attributes conform to the Active Directory schema for this forest, which has not been modified from the standard schema shipped in Windows 2000 v0. If you attempt to import these values into a foreign Directory Service, many of the attributes and syntax rules may not match. At the very least, you'll need to change the distinguished name, as it is unlikely that the foreign Directory Service will use the same namespace.

Windows 2000 comes with a command-line tool for importing and exporting LDIF files. It is the LDIF Directory Synchronization Bulk import/export tool, ldifde.exe. The output in the previous example was produced with ldifde. Run ldifde with no switches to get a list of parameters.

The purpose of including a utility like ldifde was to simplify importing large amounts of data into the Directory, but it is also handy for making quick checks of Directory entries without opening up a pesky MMC snap-in. If you prefer, you can specify -f con to put the output on the tube. For example:

- To know the group membership of a user, use Ldifde -d cn=username,cn=Users,dc=company,dc=com -f con

- To check the entries in a trusted domain, use Ldifde -s alb-dc-01.office.company.com -d dc=Office,dc=Company,dc=com -f con

- To find all the printers in an organizational unit, use Ldifde -d ou=Phoenix,dc=Company,dc=com -r "(objectclass=printers)" -f con

The more complex situations are where ldifde really shines. You can import staggering amounts of information into the Directory very quickly. It doesn't take much coding to build an LDIF file from another database, either.

For example, let's say you are the administrator for a school district and you want to add 5000 new students into the Directory. You probably have the student list in a dusty old mainframe or AS400 or maybe even a big UNIX box of one form or another. You can write a little JCL or a custom data dump and output the student list to a delimited file. Then, use an existing LDIFDE dump as a template and structure the import file accordingly.

Many of the attributes for user and group objects are owned by the system and will not accept input from an LDIF import. Here's a trick. Run an export on a user account with the -m switch. This enables "SAM Logic" on the export, which is another way of saying that it skips the attributes that are owned by the system. This gives you a template to use when building your JCL or database export. You might be able to get away with something as simple as a looping grep that inputs the student's name from a comma-delimited file.

Speaking of comma-delimited files, you may want to take a look at the *CSV Directory Synchronization Bulk Import/Export* tool, CSVDE.EXE. It works exactly like LDIFDE but with comma-delimited files for input and output instead of LDIF files. Personally, I get a headache looking at CSV files, but they are compatible with a wider range of database tools than LDIF, so this might be the more useful tool for large-scale database operations.

Moving Forward

This chapter covered the structure and operation of Active Directory. The next four chapters describe how to design, deploy, and manage Active Directory-based domains and how to repair and recover the Active Directory database in the event of a problem.

8

Designing Windows 2000 Domains

THE PRECEDING CHAPTER COVERED THE STRUCTURE OF ACTIVE Directory. This chapter covers how to use Active Directory to build Windows 2000 domains. Before diving into complex design issues, however, it's important to discuss the need to even have a design in the first place.

I'll be honest. When I read reference manuals about new technologies, this is generally the chapter I skip. I'm usually convinced that the problems I'll face will be so unique that I'm better off diving into implementation, at least in a lab environment, so I can get a feel for the magnitude of my challenges. Many colleagues of mine feel the same way. For early adopters of Windows 2000, the adventure begins with an upgrade CD, not a drawing board. For that reason, I'll keep the advice in this chapter short and practical. Skim through it quickly. Return at your leisure.

Design Objectives

Active Directory is a fine piece of technology, or at least a darned good one, but it's a little like Lego blocks. You can build just about anything with them, but for what purpose? Any administrator knows that a network does not exist purely as a stage for technology. It exists for all those users out there who demand simple, reliable, high-performance access to files, printers, and client/server applications. Users want their network resources to be accessible with the least possible fuss. If a resource is more than two clicks away, it might as well be in the Magellanic Clouds. Every help desk operator and network administrator has a book of war stories about wildly impatient users who babble and scream when faced with what are, to them, completely inscrutable network operations, such as mapping drives and connecting to printers and finding their email and so forth.

Users also don't want to deal with complex security requirements. Sure, most users recognize the value of security—especially if they store sensitive personal information on a server—but they want security to be as unobtrusive as possible. They don't generally care about technological niceties, such as comprehensive Directory Services and sophisticated authentication systems. They want to memorize one password, two at the most, and they want that password to work in as many situations as possible. They don't want to hear about arcane stuff, such as namespace partitions and organizational unit contexts.

So, proper domain design should make access to resources as intuitive as possible. Fine. But there is more to good design than simplicity. From the perspective of a system administrator, domain designs must meet a host of objectives. Here are some of the major ones:

- **Security.** The security protocols used to control access to the domain and domain resources must be strong enough to protect millions or billions of dollars of data and hardware. Security is paramount. The domain design must make it as difficult as possible to gain unauthorized access and as simple as possible to gain authorized access. It must support auditing so that abuse is discovered early before extensive damage is done. It must do its work as quickly and unobtrusively as possible.

- **Stability.** No network operating system is acceptable that presents network resources in an unpredictable manner or demonstrates oddball behavior when called on to do its chores. The services controlled by the domain must operate the same way every minute of every day.

- **Reliability.** A good design does not have single points of failure. If a single point of failure is unavoidable, the design incorporates contingencies that are straightforward to implement and have a high probability of successful execution.

- **Manageability.** After a domain is in place, it should not take a platoon of system engineers working around the clock to keep it working. Ideally, a single administrator in a central location should be able to manage the entire domain, delegating authority as necessary to simplify housekeeping.

- **Interoperability.** No administrator can avoid having a variety of hardware running multiple operating system. A good design should minimize the friction when information is forced to go from one system to another.

- **Recoverability.** A Windows 2000 domain relies, body and soul, on the Active Directory database. No database is safe from corruption, bugs, and bad Karma. Repairing or rebuilding a corrupted directory database and restoring full operability must be well documented and deliver reliable results.

- **Efficiency.** Domains' operations take a toll on network resources, such as communication bandwidth and server hardware. The design should localize directory data streams whenever possible and direct nonlocal data streams into the fastest pipeline at the lowest cost. The design should minimize infrastructure costs, or at least make those costs so incontestably necessary that only the most miserly executive would dare slash the budget.

In addition, there is a less definable, but equally compelling set of design influences generally grouped under headings, such as *ooomph*, *juice*, *pull*, and *politics*. These influences can take an otherwise elegant design and mash it up beyond all recognition. With this in mind, although the initial foray into domain design begins with a broad set of guidelines based on practical engineering rules, it also includes a generous sprinkling of caution in places where you might encounter squabbles.

DNS and Active Directory Namespaces

Windows 2000 domains require TCP/IP. There is no alternative and no workaround. If you use a transport protocol other than TCP/IP, you can stop right here and start redesigning your infrastructure. A few years ago, this would be a tall order; thanks to Mr. Internet, however, it is now rare to find an organization that cannot route and manage TCP/IP traffic. Still, they do exist. Many small businesses with no need for a full-time Internet connection often rely entirely on IPX or a nonroutable protocol, such as NetBEUI or LAT or DECnet or LANtastic's AILANBIO. If you own or are employed by such a business and you buy a new Windows 2000 server, or you let a vendor sell you one, you just decided to deploy TCP/IP and DNS and probably DHCP on your network whether you like it or not. You must either pay your vendor to configure those IP services for you or start studying.

Active Directory uses DNS as a skeleton for its namespace. Again, there is no alternative and no workaround. Any Windows 2000 domain you build must have a name that matches a corresponding DNS domain. Figure 8.1 shows an example DNS tree and a corresponding Windows 2000 domain tree.

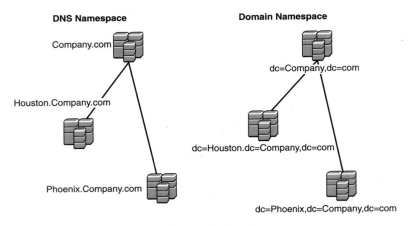

Figure 8.1   DNS and Windows 2000 domain name mappings.

External versus Internal DNS

You must be absolutely certain of reliable connectivity between the servers that will be your Windows 2000 domain controllers and your DNS servers. Nearly all problems involving Active Directory deployment are traceable in one way or another to a DNS failure. Also, your DNS servers must be running a version of DNS that supports dynamic host registrations as defined in RFC 2136, "Dynamic Updates in the Domain Name System (DNS UPDATE)." A Windows 2000 server won't let you promote it to domain controller unless it can communicate with a DNS zone that accepts RFC 2136 dynamic updates.

If you do not already have DNS deployed in your network, your task is relatively simple. Determine what you want your Windows 2000 domain to look like and plan your DNS design accordingly. If you already have a DNS namespace, however, you need to get the answers to a few questions. First, do you control the DNS servers internally or do you subscribe to DNS services through an *Internet service provider* (ISP) or a *network service provider* (NSP), such as MCI/Worldcom or Sprint-Paranet? If you rely on an outside provider, its DNS servers probably do not support dynamic DNS. And even if they do, the service provider will probably not permit your servers to register themselves. The ISP/NSP community has a great deal of concern about the security of dynamic DNS.

Even if you find an ISP that permits you to register hosts on its dynamic DNS servers, you may not be comfortable relying on that WAN connection to keep your Windows 2000 domain alive. It's one thing to lose access to Yahoo! or AOL when your ISDN or fractional T-1 line goes down. It's quite another to lose all your Active Directory services and thus lose access to your network. I highly recommend that you set up your own Windows 2000 DNS server in-house before deploying a Windows 2000 domain. Even if this server just stores the *Service Locator* (SRV) records for your domain and forwards every other query to your service provider's DNS server, it's still worth the trouble of building it.

If you have only one server and it is either the classic NT server you intend on upgrading or a third-party server you plan on replacing, you can install and configure DNS concurrently with the Windows 2000 installation. If you neglect to do this, the Domain Controller Promotion Wizard will prompt you to install DNS as part of the promotion. See Chapter 5, "Managing Domain Name System (DNS) Services and Dynamic Host Configuration (DHCP) Services," for details.

Private or Public Namespace

If you have a DNS infrastructure that you control, your next concern is the DNS namespace. Your company may not want to use their public DNS zone to support internal network systems, such as Active Directory. They may prefer to use a private DNS namespace protected behind a firewall. Figure 8.2 shows a diagram of a private DNS namespace.

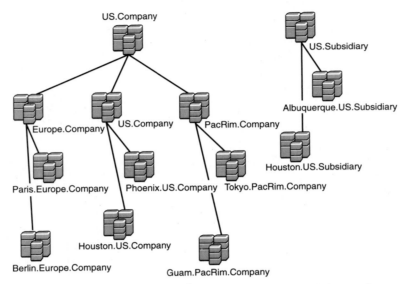

Figure 8.2 Private DNS namespace for a company with a global network.

This private DNS namespace may not be as good a fit for a Windows 2000 domain structure as the one in the figure. If you have a flat DNS namespace, for example, it would be acceptable only if you plan on deploying a single Windows 2000 domain. If you want a hierarchy of domains in a tree, however, you must have the corresponding DNS domains in place first. The domain diagram in Figure 8.2 corresponds to the DNS namespace design in Figure 8.3.

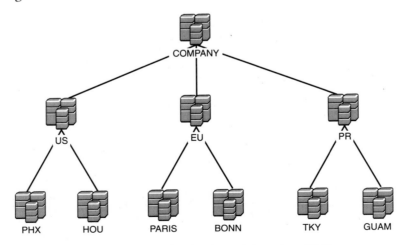

Figure 8.3 Active Directory design using existing private DNS namespace.

The marriage of Active Directory and DNS might not be a happy one in your organization. You may have a multitude of highly competitive IT groups, not to mention departments and branches that are not even part of the IT organization, which have fractured your DNS namespace into many zones that forward and delegate in ways that would give a chess champion a headache. The DNS namespace for a university, for example, might have separate management zones for Academic Services, Administration, Alumni, Biology, Chemistry, Physics, Fine Arts, Physical Education, Facilities, Math-Physics, Humanities, Bookstore, Union, and the Library, with subdomains under each for Undergrads, Grads, Law, Medical, and Hospital, not to mention more subbranches for outlying campuses and extended campuses and minicampuses and walk-in learning centers and on and on and on.

Here's the point. If your organization has an internal DNS architecture, by all means use it as a starting point for your Windows 2000 domain design; be certain, however, that the namespace is adequate for your needs. For example, a company's private DNS namespace system might exist solely to support a small corporate intranet with a few Web servers in a small DNS zone called ourweb.inc. If you try to hang an Active Directory on this DNS namespace, you'll be stuck with a flat architecture and a root name that makes no sense for your purposes. You don't want to get deeply committed to a domain design only to discover that the naming standard it imposes doesn't fit the expectations of your user community. Seemingly trivial namespace issues can cause big troubles later on. If you are forced to change your naming conventions during deployment, you will have to demote your entire fleet of Windows 2000 domain controllers to change the domain name. This can make you decidedly unpopular.

Use Existing DNS Zone or Build New Zone

You may decide to avoid the existing DNS namespaces in your organization and create a new one just for Windows 2000. If you go this route, you face a two design challenges at the outset and several in the future. Assume, for example, that the client machines in an office are configured to use a DNS server with the address 10.1.1.1 as their primary DNS server. If this server is running a version of DNS that does not support dynamic registrations, your first challenge is to either upgrade it or decommission it and install one that does. This can be Windows 2000 DNS or NetWare 5 DNS or any of the third-party products mentioned in Chapter 5.

Next, because you're building a new DNS namespace for your Windows 2000 domain, you must make allowance for the existing DNS namespace. Ideally, you should have a copy of both zone tables, the existing zone and the new zone supporting your Windows 2000 deployment, on the dynamic DNS server. In this way, clients can point to a single DNS server to get resolution for hosts in both DNS domains. If you want to keep the existing zone on a separate server, you have two choices. You can configure one of the DNS servers to forward to the other, but this has the potential to be unstable and difficult to manage. Alternatively, you can configure the DNS clients to point at both servers, in which case you have a reconfiguration problem if you decide to change DNS servers.

Finally, you face a future design challenge involving convergence. You are already faced with marrying intranet, Internet, email, telephony, remote access, IP voice, and network technologies. Who knows what the next five years will bring? Users are sure to demand a single identity in this converging technological universe. Just think how much happier they will be if you take a firm stand at the beginning of your Windows 2000 deployment and insist on a unified DNS namespace and therefore a unified Windows 2000 domain namespace for your entire organization. You might not have any friends left at the end of this negotiation, but that's the subject of another book.

Even if your current DNS namespace seems suitable for a Windows 2000 domain, ask yourself what the rest of the company is doing. One local branch office might be perfectly happy to create a Windows 2000 domain at their fork in the company's private DNS namespace, call it `Phoenix.Company`; another branch office, however, might figure that the public namespace is a better fit and build their Windows 2000 domain around `Houston.US.Company.com`. Meanwhile, the central IT group is putting together grand plans for three global Windows 2000 domains rooted in the public namespace at `US.Company.com`, `Europe.Company.com`, and `Pacrim.Company.com`. The administrators in the subsidiary business line hear about this and lay plans to root their domain at `Subsidiary.com` because they think they can form a tree with `Company.com` at the common root, `com`. Disaster looms on several fronts. Here's why:

- The administrators in the `Phoenix.Company` domain cannot make their domain a child of `US.Company.com` because the DNS namespaces differ.

- The administrators in `Houston.US.Company.com` avoid the namespace problem by using the public DNS name, but they can't join their existing domain to `US.Company.com` because Windows 2000 has no "grafting" tool. They would be forced to build a new child domain under `US.Company.com`, manually move their users and groups and computers to the new domain, and then demote all domain controllers in their old domain and promote them back into the new child domain. (Details on merging domains are covered in the next chapter.)

- The Subsidiary.com administrators also get a rude surprise when they find out that an InterNIC domain doesn't count as a root for forming a Windows 2000 tree. Windows 2000 will refuse to configure a domain with a single name at the root. This includes InterNIC domains, such as com, org, and gov, as well as private domains, such as Company. The DNS domain that roots a Windows 2000 domain must have a fully qualified name containing at least two components (for example, US.Company, Company.com, University.edu).

Deployment Lessons from NDS

Some NetWare administrators will recognize this inability of Windows 2000 to easily modify a directory namespace from their experiences with early versions of NDS. More than a few NDS 4.0 deployments ended up with massive restructuring because of name changes or poor partition planning. Until the Windows 2000 naming-context management tools get better, the lesson is clear: It's better to delay deployment than to get partway through it and then stop and start again with new domain names.

In the previous examples, you may argue that the Subsidiary.com domain has the alternative of forming a tree-root trust with US.Company to form a forest. This is true, but only when it first deploys its domain. A domain can join a forest only when the first domain controller is promoted. There is not even a rudimentary set of tools in Windows 2000 to form a forest from two independent Windows 2000 domains.

Also, forests have limitations for deep LDAP searches that make them a less-than-optimal solution. Mixed-domain namespaces also cause trouble for users when they search for resources in trusted domains. Users tend to get irritable when the help desk operator explains, "The share you're looking for is on a server in the Salt Lake City office. They're in the Company domain, so you have to open the directory in My Network Places and expand the tree starting at Company rather than Subsidiary. Yes, we know it's confusing. Yes, we know that you have better things to do than figure out all this computer junk. Thank you for calling the Company, Inc., help desk. Have a nice day."

"And so it goes," to quote my favorite author, Kurt Vonnegut, Jr. Mr. Vonnegut might also point out that deploying Windows 2000 is a lot like passing through a chronosynclasticinfidibulum. You end up being everywhere and nowhere at the same time. After you think you have a DNS namespace design you can use, let people kick it around for a while before you proceed with the Windows 2000 domain design.

Initial Design Strategies

Figure 8.4 shows the default structure of a Windows 2000 domain naming context. The standard containers have the advantage of simplicity, but that's about it. Using them is acceptable for small organizations, but they fall short of the mark for organizations that have separate IT groups or a significant number of users with distinct operational needs. You'll also want to avoid the standard containers if you expect to delegate management functions to individuals outside of the IT department, such as contractors or outsource firms or department power users. If you start off with the standard containers, you'll know it's time to tailor a new container design when administrators start pointing fingers at each other when directory objects or rights "mysteriously" appear and disappear.

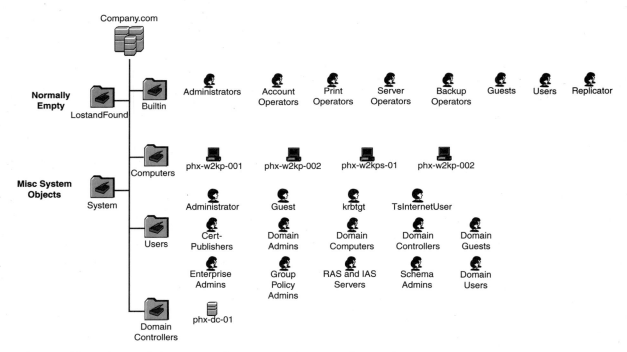

Figure 8.4 Default containers for a new Windows 2000 domain naming context.

The only general-purpose object at your disposal for creating new directory containers is the *Organizational Unit* (OU). The more generalized *Container* class is available only to the system. The *Country, Organization,* and *Locality* classes are present in the schema, but Active Directory does not use them.

The OU plays several roles in Active Directory design. It hosts Group Policy objects that contain security restrictions, logon/logoff scripts, software distribution packages, and that control the desktop environment. It acts as a natural boundary for assigning specialized management rights over the objects it contains. In addition, it helps keep the directory tidy, not a trivial thing when you have thousands and thousands of objects to manage. Speaking of tidiness, if you decide to use your own containers to structure the directory, you may want to delete the standard containers. Don't bother. Not only can't they be deleted, they are fixed in place. The best you can do is learn to ignore them.

Single Domain Strengths and Weaknesses

As you doodle your initial domain design, start out by looking for ways to use a single domain. Do this even if you have a strong feeling that a single domain would not be feasible for your organizations thanks to the number of users or the political turmoil that might ensue when deploying a single, comprehensive domain. Several good reasons justify taking this approach, including the following:

- A single domain is easier for users to navigate. Users look at network structures with all the fear and suspicion of medieval serfs gaping up at a comet. The simpler you can make it for them, the greater chance your design has of being successfully implemented in anything like its original form.

- DNS is much simpler to configure when you have a single Active Directory domain. AD clients rely on SRV records to locate domain controllers and AD services. If you have multiple domains in complex parent-child configurations, the resulting DNS zone referrals might get a little tricky to configure. DNS causes the majority of Active Directory problems. The simpler the DNS design, the better.

- Managing replication is much more straightforward in a single domain because you are not mixing sites and domains in your replication topology.

- Many of the complexities in Active Directory involve the handling of LDAP lookups in different naming contexts. The placement of *Global Catalog* (GC) servers is critical in a multiple-domain deployment. Users may not even be able to log on unless there is a GC server available in their site. A single domain does not depend on access to a GC server because every domain controller has a replica of all naming contexts.

- Finally, security is simpler to implement in a single domain. Transitive Kerberos trusts make it possible to access trusted domains seamlessly; just because a feature is transparent, however, doesn't mean it's simple to manage. An administrator's worst nightmare is sifting through the membership list for hundreds of groups when trying to resolve a problem with file and directory access permissions. This can be especially difficult in Windows 2000 because there are three different types of groups with many ways to nest and mingle them.

The only drawback to having a single domain is the size of the Active Directory database. The more objects you pack into a single domain, the more likely you are to encounter stability and replication problems. The initial challenge to the limits of a single, unified Windows 2000 domain in terms of raw numbers of users and machines will probably come from large universities, big secondary school districts, and high-tech companies with many thousands of knowledge workers. Storing, updating, replicating, and searching an Active Directory information store for a 100,000-user domain can suck cycles and memory from a domain controller like teenagers at a beer party. Globally replicating updates to this big information store across a WAN can tax data communication links to their breaking point.

Microsoft has tested a domain with 1.5 million users in their labs, but only time and experience will reveal what the optimum size of a Windows 2000 domain should be in a production environment. The alternative to having one large information store is to partition the directory into separate domains. Each domain becomes a distinct naming context that is separately replicated. GC servers host a replica of all domains in a forest, but the GC contains only 60 or so attributes, which makes the information store much more manageable.

For networks with 10,000 users or fewer, a single domain is perfectly feasible. If you have a network with more than 20,000 users or so, take a look at the "Multiple Domain Strengths and Weaknesses" section later in this chapter. If you are in that in-between area of 10,000 to 20,000 users, lay out designs using both single and multiple domains and decide which would work best from a management perspective. I think you'll find that politics will partition the directory long before you reach any architectural limits.

AD Information Store Sizes

Calculating the projected size of an Active Directory information store is not nearly as critical in Windows 2000 domain design as calculating SAM sizes were for NT4 domain design. Here are some numbers to use as a rule of thumb:

- User objects with standard mandatory attributes: 3.5KB

- User objects will full suite of attributes: 4.5KB

- OU objects: 1KB

- Group objects: varies with group membership

The information store for a domain with half a million users and computers along with a full compliment of groups, servers, sites, and policies to support them would approach 2.5GB.

Multiple Domain Strengths and Weaknesses

Any domain design effort should begin with the hope of fitting the entire organization into one domain. The bigger the domain, however, the bigger the Active Directory database, and there comes a point where size affects durability. Ask the designers of the *Hindenberg* and the *Titanic*.

The ESENT database engine that underlies Active Directory can hold 10 million objects in a 17-terabyte information store. Theoretically, this provides enough capacity for a few million users along with their computers, groups, infrastructure components, and any application objects that developers might want to toss in the mix. Theory, however, is the province of software engineers. Administrators must concern themselves with practicality, and the practical size of Windows 2000 domains has yet to be fully explored. Every growth curve has a knee, but it's going to take a year or two for field reports to show where that knee lies for Windows 2000.

The very largest companies—Fortune 500 lists the U.S. Postal Service as the largest employer with nearly 900,000—are not likely to move to Active Directory in a big way any time soon. National ISPs with their millions of users won't jump either, at least not until the technology has been around for a while—neither will NetWare administrators with mature NDS infrastructures or UNIX administrators with megamultiprocessor boxes hosting proprietary authentication services of one form or another. This is not to say that Microsoft won't work very hard to sell Windows 2000 into these organizations, but it's likely that the deployments will proceed from the bottom up rather than the top down, which makes design a challenge.

Domain Design Rule: Use separate domains if your directory is going to be very large, but minimize their number.

The only way to limit the size of the directory database is to partition it into separate domains. As an early adopter of Windows 2000, you will not know at the outset if a single domain for your organization will become too large to manage effectively. Here is my recommendation. If you have more than 15,000 users, you may want to consider using separate domains. If you have more than 50,000 users, you will almost certainly want separate domains. If you have any doubt, by all means use separate domains. It's better to live with a partitioned directory than to watch an unexpected shimmy turn your domain into a Galloping Gertie, tossing users off the network and sending management looking for a new network architect. Just remember that domains represent separate naming contexts, which complicates replication, and the domain hierarchy shown in the Explorer interface can confuse users. Don't go overboard.

Unless you are in a huge Fortune 100 company, a single domain will probably do quite nicely, at least from an architectural standpoint. You may find that your single domain fractures, however, because of balkanization rather than engineering limitations. Current classic NT administrators and their managers may be comfortable with autonomous trusted domains. They will view consolidation attempts with suspicion. Even if you offer to make them a child domain in the directory tree, you may encounter resistance. Child domains smack of capitulation to central IT. You may find that local administrators want a wide forest rather than a tall tree.

Depending on your personal force of will and your backing from management, you may end up with more domains than you really need. You should not let local administrators carry their independence too far at the expense of reliability and performance. And if you are a local administrator trying to get your voice heard in the domain design, try to rein in your suspicions. There is room for a great deal of autonomy in a single domain, and not that much more flexibility in a forest. There can only be one schema and one configuration-naming context in a forest, for instance, so you can't make any radical departures involving the directory structure itself. Furthermore, LDAP searches across tree-root trusts are not as efficient as in a single domain or down a domain-root trust. See Chapter 7, "Understanding Active Directory Services," for details on LDAP searches.

Figure 8.5 shows an example of a directory tree where global regions have been compartmentalized into separate child domains. In addition, large offices have been made into child domains rather than OUs. If you decide to use this domain design, watch out for DNS namespace deployment issues. It's one thing to put a little box labeled `Phoenix.US.Company.com` on a sketch pad, and it's quite another to convince local administrators to build new DNS zones and modify their host files and client configurations accordingly.

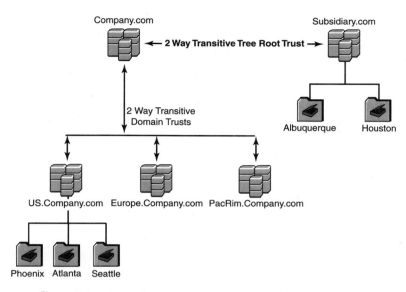

Figure 8.5 Upper directory containers using multiple domains.

As you lay out your OUs, think about possible namespace boundaries that you may need if you are forced to partition an office or department into a separate domain. And watch out for long names. Rather than use full city or department names, you may want to abbreviate to shorten the fully qualified DNS names. Users rarely encounter LDAP-distinguished names; if their logon context is `user@Albuquerque.NewMexico.United States.NorthAmerica.Company.com`, however, they may get a little irritated.

Just because users can log on and see network resources around the globe via transitive Kerberos trusts doesn't mean that they can access all those resources. At this point, we need to leave behind the top of the directory and start to focus on simplifying access for users by laying out containers at the bottom of the directory. This is where your powers of diplomacy as well as your design skills will be tested.

Strategies for Upper-Level Designs

A directory service is supposed to facilitate network management based on the functional boundaries within an organization. At least, that's the gist of the X.500 specification. The object class names tend to lead you in the direction of using organizational charts to design the Directory. Before putting in that call to HR to get the most current organizational charts, though, you may want to reconsider this approach. Let's see why.

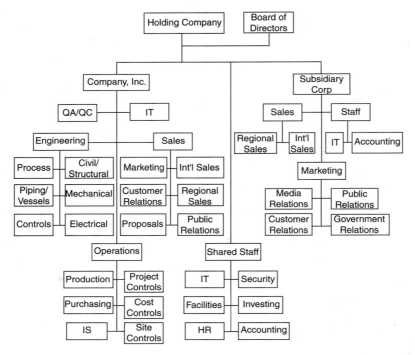

Figure 8.6 Typical organization chart for a moderate-sized company.

Figure 8.6 shows an organization chart for a company with two business lines. The primary business line carries the company's principal name, Company, Inc. The second business line is a wholly owned company named Subsidiary Corp. These two business lines share common offices in a couple of cities; other than the fact that their employees eat lunch in the same cafeteria and bank at the same credit union, however, they are completely separate operating entities.

This applies to the IT departments, as well, and with a vengeance. Not only do the Company and Subsidiary IT departments have their own staff and budgets, their administrators pride themselves on managing their part of the network a thousand times better than those dunderheads on the other side of the basement. The company also maintains a small corporate IT staff, but these folks are forced to spend their time doing five-year return-on-investment projections and distributing long reports in Lotus Notes instead of centrally managing technology deployments.

The problem with using an organization chart like the one in Figure 8.6 to design a directory is that organization charts show only general executive and management reporting relationships. They don't reveal the functional hierarchies, regional hierarchies, and business-line cross-matrix hierarchies that affect the way computers are used in the organization. Even modern, forward-thinking companies dedicated to empowerment and individual ownership have some sort of hierarchical relationship among groups, if only to determine who gets first dibs on the parking spaces. Ask any SAP implementer. Trying to map out these interlocking responsibilities and relationships can be a devilish piece of work. If you try to design a domain based solely on organization charts, you're destined to spend many, many days in long and arduous meetings just trying to get an initial consensus that the organization charts are even correct. Then you will have to rework your domain design every time a department has a quality-circle meeting that changes their operations.

This leads to one of the foremost rules of Windows 2000 domain design:

Domain Design Rule: Make sure the domain structure works for the IT organization.

Don't be overly concerned about other departments in the early stages of the design. If you build it, they will come. Structure your initial design on the IT organization; those are the people who will be using the management tools and interfaces inside Windows 2000.

Even by tightly narrowing the focus, however, you are still going to have to work hard to achieve consensus. It's not likely that you'll get any two IT organizations to agree on a common domain structure. Even if the managers come to a collegial agreement, squabbling at the working level could put an end to any arrangements fairly quickly. So don't design in a closed office. Determine how your IT organization divides the management duties, either vertically by business unit or horizontally by region, and then put on your detective hat and search out all the administrators and their managers and see how they interact on a day-to-day basis.

Don't just look for people with job titles that say *Administrator*. Look for hidden lines of responsibility within computer and network operations. You'll find power users and department gurus outside of the formal IT structure who have wide-ranging administrative responsibilities. Search for corporate IT staff who have been matrixed into the local organizations and who have brought with them a variety of administrative rights. You are bound to find a few consultants who have administrative or management duties that are integral to daily operations. In short, find anyone who might need or want administrative privileges in the domain.

After you have outlined the true IT administrative hierarchy, not the one in the formal organization charts, you need to know how the staff members interact with each other. You must define the administrative privileges required by each administrator to do his or her job. After you have done that, you can separate the IT users into groups based on the administrative privileges they exercise and who they administer. Finally, lay out the top of the directory so that the administrative groups you defined during your research can be assigned access rights over the OUs that contain the users and computers and shared resources that they manage.

Chapter 10, "Managing Active Directory Security," takes a detailed look at Active Directory security. Windows 2000 uses groups in quite a few different ways, however, so it's worth taking a few minutes for a quick overview here.

Functional Overview of Windows 2000 Security Groups

Windows 2000 has two group types: security groups and distribution groups. Distribution groups are used solely to manage software distribution and cannot be used to control access to security objects.

There are three classes of security groups, each with its own special functions and somewhat peculiar limitations. Before listing the groups, let's take a look at an operational characteristic of Windows 2000 domains that affects the way groups are handled. This characteristic comes from the need for backward compatibility with classic NT.

A classic NT domain consists of a single PDC that can write to the security database and one or more BDCs that replicate security updates from the PDC. In Windows 2000, the Active Directory replaces the SAM. Active Directory objects that represent security principals, such as users, computers, and groups, have attributes with values that simulate their SAM counterparts. A Windows 2000 domain controller can replicate these attributes to classic BDCs so that they can continue authenticating users and computers. This support for classic NT replication is vital to managing a deployment of Windows 2000 into an existing NT network.

Classic BDCs can replicate only from the PDC defined in a special secret trust within the *Local Security Authority* (LSA) database inside the Security hive in the Registry. In Windows 2000, however, any domain controller can write to the Active Directory. Therefore, to maintain compatibility, a single Windows 2000 domain controller is designated as a PDC role master, one of several *Flexible Single Master Operations* (FSMO) role masters designated in Windows 2000 to control domain operations.

The PDC role master is ordinarily the original NT PDC that has been upgraded to Windows 2000, although it is possible to transfer the PDC role master to another Windows 2000 domain controller. The operation is similar to the way a classic BDC is promoted to PDC. All Active Directory updates affecting SAM attributes are written only at the PDC role master, and the classic BDCs replicate from this role master.

A domain that still has classic BDCs replicating from a PDC role master is said to be in *Mixed mode*. In a Mixed-mode domain, security groups are limited to their classic NT restrictions. Global groups cannot be nested in other global groups, local groups cannot be nested in other local groups, and local groups from a trusted domain cannot be used as security principals in a trusting domain.

Interaction of Security Groups in Native-Mode Domains

When all classic BDCs have been upgraded or decommissioned, the Windows 2000 domain can be shifted to *Native mode*. After this has been done, domain member computers can participate fully in transitive Kerberos trusts, opening the way for a much more flexible group management system. The following list contains the group management rules for a Native-mode Windows 2000 domain:

- **Domain local groups.** Used for backward compatibility with classic NT. Domain local group members can be users from the local domain along with users and global groups and universal groups from trusted domains. A domain local group can be used only to control access to security objects in its local domain. For example, a domain local group in the Company.com domain cannot be delegated control over an OU in the Branch.Company.com domain.

- **Global groups.** Used to control access to local resources within a domain. Global group members can be users and global groups from its local domain only. A global group can be used to control access to security objects in the local domain and trusting domains. For example, a global group in the Company.com domain can be delegated control over an OU in the Branch.Company.com domain, assuming that a domain trust relationship is in place.

- **Universal.** Used to control access to resources across domain boundaries. Universal groups are available only in Native-mode domains. A universal group can have individual members from any domain along with global and universal groups from trusted domains. A universal group can be used to control access to security objects in any trusting domain.

The distinction between global groups and universal groups lies in the way the directory stores group membership information. The Directory object for a security principal (users, groups, and computers) has an attribute called Member-Of. This attribute contains the distinguished name of every domain local and global group to which the user belongs. Here is a list of the

Member-Of entries for a user named Company User who is a member of three groups. The list was obtained using LDIFDE, introduced in the preceding chapter.

```
dn: CN=Company User,CN=Users,DC=company,DC=com
memberOf: CN=Phx_Eng,OU=Groups,OU=Phoenix,DC=company,DC=com
memberOf: CN=Account Operators,CN=Builtin,DC=company,DC=com
memberOf: CN=Users,CN=Builtin,DC=company,DC=com
```

When the user logs on, the LSA checks the Member-Of attribute for user group memberships and also scans the local naming context looking for groups that have the user as a member. This information is contained in a `Member` attribute associated with the group object. Here is an example LDIFDE dump for the Administrators group:

```
dn: CN=Administrators,CN=Builtin,DC=company,DC=com
member: CN=Phx Admin,CN=Users,DC=company,DC=com
member: CN=Domain Admins,CN=Users,DC=company,DC=com
member: CN=Enterprise Admins,CN=Users,DC=company,DC=com
member: CN=Administrator,CN=Users,DC=company,DC=com
```

Backlinking

The pairing of Member/Member-Of for group membership is not uncommon in the directory. There are many instances of such pairs. The information store actually keeps a second database, the Link database, to track this type pairing. One of the database consistency checks that run on a scheduled basis in the background and can also be performed manually using NTDSUTIL as a backlink consistency check.

Operational Overview of Windows 2000 Security Groups

Figure 8.7 shows a diagram of a forest of Native-mode domains. If the domains in this forest were classic NT domains or Mixed-mode Windows 2000 domains, the trust between the Subsidiary domain and the Office domain would not be seen by Branch and Company. The Auditor would need an account in the Company domain to get access to the shared folder in the Branch child domain. After the domains have been shifted to Native mode and the Kerberos trusts have become fully transitive, an administrator in Branch could put the Auditor from Office on the ACL for the shared folder or a local group in the Branch domain.

When you click the button that shifts you to Native mode, you cast away the last remaining lifeline to classic NT. If your Active Directory deployment goes south for some reason, you won't have a comfortable old PDC and BDC to fall back on unless you restore them from tape. See Chapter 11, "Managing Active Directory Replication and Directory Maintenance," for details on handling Active Directory disasters.

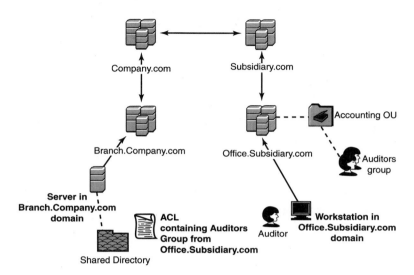

Figure 8.7   Forest of Native-mode domains.

As you formulate your domain strategy, keep in mind that local administrators will be assigning local access permissions using groups from trusted domains. If you create many domains, it turns administration of these permissions into a detective search through a web of interlocking group memberships that make it nearly impossible to determine whether a particular user has proper rights. This is sure to send auditors and data owners alike into a tizzy.

Here is a quick description of how group membership is used to control access to directory objects. Chapter 10 includes a more complete description.

When LSA scans the naming context for group memberships, it also looks up the SID corresponding to each of the groups associated with the user. When it has this information, it hands over the SIDs to the Kerberos *Key Distribution Center* (KDC) service, which includes the SIDs in the *ticket-granting ticket* (TGT) it issues to the user.

The Member-Of attribute in the user object in the local naming context does not contain membership information for groups in trusted domains. LSA must use another mechanism for discovering group memberships in trusted domains. If it does not do this, the user might be given inappropriate access to a resource that was protected by a group from a trusted domain.

To avoid this situation, LSA also scans the GC looking for universal groups that have the user as a member. It looks there because the GC has a copy of every naming context in the domain. This means that each time a user is issued a TGT by a KDC, the LSA must do a full scan of the entire

GC looking for any universal groups that contain the user or any of the user's groups. Including the groups in the scan is necessary because universal groups can nest universal and global groups from any Native-mode domain.

If the LSA finds any universal groups containing the user or a user's group as a member, it adds the SID of the universal group (also obtained from the GC) to the list of SIDs that it passes to the KDC for inclusion in the user's TGT. The SIDs in this TGT are used to construct local access tokens at member servers anywhere in the forest. Putting all this together, you can say the following: Universal groups can be used to control access to local domain resources by security principals anywhere in the forest.

If the relationship between domain local groups, global groups, and universal groups is still a little unclear, try doing an LDIFDE dump of the same user object from a domain controller in the user's domain that is not a GC, a GC server in the user's domain, and a GC server that is not in the user's domain. The results you see will follow these guidelines (after the updates have replicated):

- The LDIFDE dump of the user object at the non-GC domain controller lists just the domain groups (local, global, and universal).

- The dump at the GC in the user's domain will show all groups from all domains in the forest.

- The dump at the GC in the trusted domain will show only universal groups from any domain in the forest.

The universal group objects in the GC must have their full Member attribute, and this attribute must be replicated to every GC in the forest. This is not an inconsequential feat if you have thousands of users in dozens and dozens of locations around the world. Keep a couple of rules in mind when defining groups to control directory access and to delegate administrative privileges:

- Only use universal groups when security principals from a trusted domain will access the object.

- Avoid individual users as members of universal groups. The membership changes too often. Assign global groups from each trusted domain and modify the membership list of the global group.

Delegation and Inheritance of Access Permissions

If you've ever laid out a server file system, you know how tricky it can be to arrange directories so that access rights don't turn into a haphazard sprawl. The situation is even more complex for the directory.

Classic NT and Windows 2000 share a common object-based security model. Data structures such as NTFS files and directories, Registry keys, and Active Directory entries are *security objects*. Security objects have special access control structures called *security descriptors*. A security descriptor contains an *access control list* (ACL) that defines the security principals who are authorized to access the object. The ACL also defines the *access permissions* granted to the security principal. The basic access permissions for directory objects are as follows:

- **List.** The right to browse objects in a container
- **Read.** The right to view the properties (attributes) of an object
- **Write.** The right to modify an object's properties
- **Create.** The right to create a new object
- **Delete.** The right to delete an object
- **Extended.** Special rights unique to specific object classes
- **Permissions.** The right to change the permissions on an object

When a user accesses a server, the user is assigned an *access token*. The token contains the *security ID* (SID) that represents the user and the SIDs for any groups to which the user belongs. When the user attempts to access a security object, the *Local Security Authority SubSystem* (LSASS) checks the security descriptor in the object and the user's access token and validates that one or more SIDs in the token matches one or more entries in the object's access control list. The user is given or denied access permission for the object based on this validation.

This security function has not changed from classic NT. What's new in Windows 2000 is the concept of *delegation* and *inheritance*.

- **Delegation.** Access permissions assigned by a higher authority are associated with a group or individual, and are then applied to a container.
- **Inheritance.** Access permissions assigned to a container flow down the directory and are applied to subordinate objects and containers.

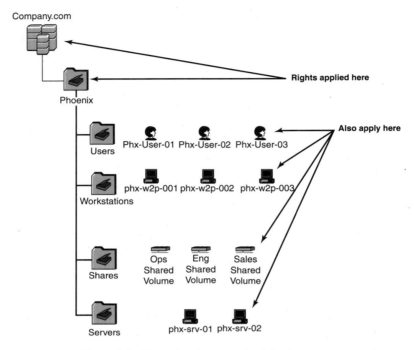

Figure 8.8 Example of access rights inheritance.

Delegation and inheritance are two of the most significant influences on directory design, so it's worth taking a detailed look at how they operate (see Figure 8.8). Consider a medium-sized company that wants you to design the directory for a single Windows 2000 domain. You begin by determining its IT management structure.

You discover that the company sanctions individual empowerment by promulgating a highly decentralized information management paradigm with emphasis on taking personal responsibility for maximizing shareholder value. (I'm quoting the company's internal Web site.) This roughly translates into, "The company's information system is managed by independent support groups with no budget to deploy any meaningful technology and no central direction except for random reprimands." Based on this policy, you find that most departments demand and get their own servers, infrastructure, and IT staff, and they are about as likely to welcome a directory designer with plans for consolidated domain management as an Appalachian sharecropper is to welcome a Bureau of Alcohol, Tobacco, and Firearms agent. Undaunted, you start with the upper container structure for the directory.

Example Upper Container Structure

Your job at this point is to design a container structure that segments users according to the administrative groups who manage them. This enables you to delegate administrator permissions so that inheritance affects only specific segments of the user population.

Figure 8.9 shows the top-level container structure for a single domain. The domain encompasses a good chunk of the western United States, Mexico, and a bit of Central America. The company has two business lines. A wholly owned subsidiary shares facilities in two of the company offices and has separate facilities in two remote cities.

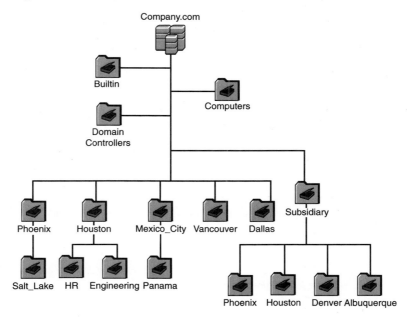

Figure 8.9 Upper container structure for North American company with two business lines and a single domain.

The company has several departments with quasi-independent computing staff. The HR department, for example, insists that the confidential nature of the data on their servers and local hard drives (no, they still don't quite trust the network) makes it imperative that only members of their own administrative staff manage their equipment. Other departments and office managers demand similar autonomy. Even managers who are willing to make use of a central IT group have made specific demands that might cause them to splinter off if they aren't satisfied with their piece of the domain design.

The upper container structure for this domain divides along geographic lines because each office has its own IT staff. Departments with independent computing staff get separate containers under their office. This permits local IT personnel to administer the subordinate containers instead of relying on a central IT group. The Salt_Lake OU is an example of the opposite situation. The local IT staff would be perfectly content being in the Phoenix OU but the Phoenix staff didn't want them to have administrative rights.

Display Specifiers and Localization

The preceding chapter introduced display specifiers, special directory objects that provide local language and punctuation overlays to other directory objects. Thanks to display specifiers, the fields and options for directory objects in Mexico City will be displayed in Spanish rather than English.

The design puts nearly all the OUs at or near the top of the directory. No performance penalty accrues for having a wide directory structure. In fact, the opposite is true. You should avoid going too deep with your OU structure. The indexing and caching features in the ESENT engine can handle 10 levels with ease, but going deeper is not recommended. Highly decentralized organizations might have trouble maintaining a shallow container structure, so you might want to consult with Microsoft field engineers to determine an optimal configuration for your situation.

The container structure for this company would be radically different if it were to have an omnipotent central IT department with a closely bound office staff subject to frequent audits and performance appraisals. In such a case, you could eliminate an entire upper stratum of the directory. Figure 8.10 shows an example.

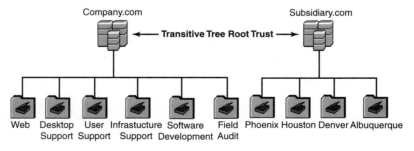

Figure 8.10 Upper containers for highly centralized IT organization with subsidiary business line configured as peer domain in a forest.

The container layout for a highly centralized IT organization distributes management rights among autonomous groups in the central IT organization.

These containers hold the users, groups, computers, printers, and shared folders controlled by that group regardless of the office where they are located. The directory is replicated everywhere, so a container, such as User Support, can hold user objects from Phoenix, Houston, and Mexico City. Notice that the administrators in the Subsidiary business unit didn't trust the central IT group and insisted on having a separate namespace joined to the forest with a tree-root trust.

Dividing high-level OUs by IT work processes rather than department work processes does not affect user functionality so long as you stay within the confines of a single domain. If you have a single global domain, a user can travel from Phoenix to Seoul and see the same domain on the WINLOGON pick list and use the same logon ID to access the network. Before you put this preliminary design through the review-and-approval gauntlet, it's time to think about whether you might need more than one domain.

Design Strategies for Lower Directory Levels

The rules for container layout at the lower levels of the directory change a bit from the upper levels. At this phase of the design, you have two concerns that sometimes conflict: You want to simplify management for administrators, and you want to simplify resource access for users. Let's start with management.

Good management implies a good delegation strategy. It doesn't take a Wharton MBA to figure out that you want to push management authority as low in the organization as possible. This leads us to the third rule for domain design:

> *Domain Design Rule: Design for centralized control of the Directory structure and localized control of Directory objects.*

Implementing management controls at the lower levels of the directory requires an understanding of *group policies*. Chapter 10 covers this subject in detail. A look here at a couple of high points, however, will help you to understand the impact of group policies on directory design.

Functional Overview of Group Policies

Classic NT and Windows 95 introduced the concept of System Policies as a way to distribute Registry updates. Those System Policies were a collection of Registry keys and values collected into an NTCONFIG.POL file (or CONFIG.POL, in the case of Windows 9x) and distributed at logon by downloading from the NETLOGON share point on the authenticating domain controller.

Windows 2000 *Group Policies* are a more sophisticated form of policy distribution mechanism that includes a wider range of Registry entries along with logon/logoff scripts, automatic software downloads, security configurations, folder redirections, and cryptographic certificate options.

Group policies that affect Registry settings are stored in REGISTRY.POL files. These files are downloaded at logon and applied to the local Registry. Group policies that affect Computer Configuration settings are applied to entries in the HKEY_Local_Machine hive. Policies that affect User Configuration settings are applied to HKEY_Current_User.

One important difference between Group Policies and classic System Policies is that Group Policies are applied in a volatile fashion. They do not "tattoo" the Registry as System Policies do. If a Group Policy is removed, the original local Registry settings take effect again. Group Policies are refreshed every 90 minutes at the client until the user logs off. Some policies can be set to apply at logoff only.

Group Policies are stored in different places depending on whether they affect the local system only or are distributed from a domain controller to domain member computers:

- **Local Policies.** These policies are stored on the local drive in `\WINNT\System32\GroupPolicy`. They affect the local computer and users who log on to that computer.

- **Active Directory Policies.** These policies are stored in two places. The majority of the policies are located in the `\WINNT\Sysvol\Sysvol\ <domain_name>` directory on every domain controller. The second Sysvol directory is shared with the name SYSVOL. The remainder of the policies are stored in the directory in a set of Group Policy containers, or GPC objects. These policies can be associated with the Domain container, a Sites container, or any OU container. See Chapter 7 for details on these containers.

The `\WINNT\Sysvol\Sysvol\<domain_name>` directory is replicated to all domain controllers by the *File Replication Service* (FRS). See Chapter 13, "Managing File Systems," for details on FRS operation. In brief, the FRS is a general-purpose data synchronization service designed to replicate file updates to targeted servers. Only updated files are copied, and a database of file operations is kept to prevent accidental erasures and overwrites. FRS requires the use of NTFS5 on all replicated volumes.

Group Policies distributed by domain controllers have objects in the directory point at the folders in SYSVOL. These objects are instances of the GroupPolicyContainer class, or GPC. Windows 2000 clients automatically do a lookup for GPC objects and load the associated policy files. A group policy can be linked OU containers, the Domain-DNS container, and the Sites container. There is a hierarchy that determines the precedence of policies if a particular entry conflicts. OU Policies have the highest precedence, followed by Domain Policies, and then Site Policies with Local Policies taking precedence only over any legacy System Policies that the client might download.

A container can have multiple Group Policies linked to it, and a single Group Policy can be linked to more than one container. The policies are listed by their GUIDs, which doesn't give you much useful information.

Operational Overview of Group Policies

Group Policies are configured using the Group Policy console. This console relies on the Group Policy Editor support file, GPEDIT.DLL, so the console is sometimes called the Group Policy Editor. The Group Policy Editor is loaded by several different consoles, depending on the location of the policy to be edited:

- The Group Policy Editor console, GPEDIT.MSC, is used to edit Local Policies.

- AD Users and Computers, DSA.MSC, is used to create and edit profiles associated with the Domain container and any OU containers.

- AD Sites and Services, DSSITE.MSC, is used to create and edit profiles associated with Site containers.

The Group Policy Editor has several snap-in extensions corresponding to the policy types that can be edited. All extensions are loaded by default. You can also create a custom Group Policy console, which is handy if you want to distribute it to users with delegated administrative rights. Do this as follows:

Procedure 8.1 **Creating a GPE Console**

1. From the Start | Run window, enter **MMC** and click OK. An empty MMC console window opens (see Figure 8.11).

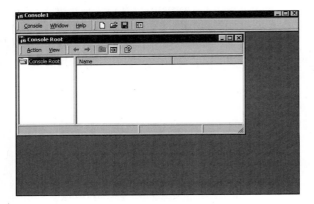

Figure 8.11 Empty MMC console ready for adding a snap-in.

2. From the CONSOLE menu, select CONSOLE | ADD REMOVE SNAP-IN. (Use Ctrl+M for a shortcut). The Add/Remove Snap-in window appears.

3. Click Add. The Add Standalone Snap-in window appears (see Figure 8.12.)

Figure 8.12 Add Standalone Snap-in window showing Group Policy selection.

4. Select Group Policy from the pick list and click Add. The Select Group Policy Object window appears. In the Group Policy Object box, the local computer is the default entry.

5. Click `Browse`. The `Browse for a Group Policy Object` window appears (see Figure 8.13).

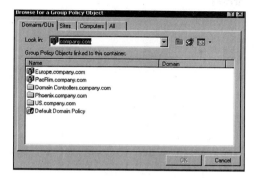

Figure 8.13 `Browse for a Group Policy Object` window showing the list of GPOs available for a particular domain.

- The `Domains/OUs` tab shows the policies that have been created and linked to an OU container or a Domain-DNS container.
- The `Sites` tab shows the policies that have been created and bound to the Sites container.
- The `Computer` tab shows the policies that have been created and bound to a particular Computer object.

6. From the `Domains/OUs` tab, double-click an OU. The associated Group Policy Object appears on the link list.

7. If there is no object listed, a GPO has not yet been created for this OU. Right-click the white area under `Name` and select NEW from the fly-out menu. A policy icon appears on the list with a default name of `New Group Policy Object`.

8. Change the name to something descriptive, like the name of the OU or the purpose of the GPO.

9. Click `OK` to save the selection and return to the `Select Group Policy Object` window.

10. Click `Finish` to save the changes and return to the `Add Standalone Snap-in` window.

11. Click `Close` to return to the `Add/Remove Snap-in` window. The GPO will be on the list of policy objects available for this snap-in.

continues ▶

Procedure 8.1 **continued**

12. Select the `Extensions` tab.

13. Ensure that the `Add All Extensions` option is checked to display all available GPO options (see Figure 8.14).

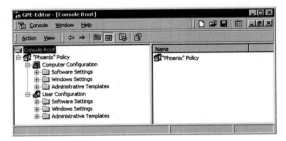

Figure 8.14 Group Policy Editor snap-in with the default domain GPO loaded.

14. Click `OK` to save the changes and return to the `Console` window. The new policy will appear under `Console Root` in the left pane of the window. If you want to retain these settings for this `MMC` console, select CONSOLE | SAVE AS and give the console a name like `GPE-Editor`. It will be saved with an .MSC extension.

15. The new console will be saved in the `My Documents` folder on the desktop. You can access it through the folder icon or by using START | DOCUMENTS | MY DOCUMENTS.

Assigning Group Policies to Containers

As you gather information about departments and groups in your organization, ask yourself whether they need separate policies. The Sales department manager might want every desktop nailed down tight, for example, so that the salespeople will focus on their quotas instead of fooling with their PCs. "Get rid of that darned Solitaire game, too, while you're at it," she demands. On the other hand, the field construction superintendent might consider even mild restrictions to be too confining and barks when his users are put in the same container as the general population back at the home office.

When deciding on policy boundaries, don't overlook sites. A university might enforce a certain policy on the main campus, for example, which does not apply to satellite campuses. Rather than apply the policy to five different domains on the main campus, you can link the policy to the Site object. This applies it to all computers and users who log on in the associated IP subnet. Figure 8.15 shows an example global site configuration. Each of the sites has a different IP subnet, which guides client PCs to the correct local domain controllers.

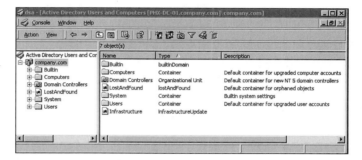

Figure 8.15   Active Directory Sites and Services snap-in showing example site configuration for global directory.

Example Lower-Level Directory Design

By applying the lower-level domain design rule to the example company, the container design for the lower levels of the Company.com domain ends up looking like Figure 8.16. The intention of this diagram is to show one potential design and the thoughts behind it. You may have devised a different design, given the scenario. There are thousands of possible design permutations. After all, NetWare 4.x has been on the market for many years, with a few million nodes under management, and I think I'm safe in saying that no two NDS trees look exactly alike. Windows 2000 domain designs will be equally as diverse.

The top of the directory retains the container structure presented in the preceding section. The lower containers are laid out as follows:

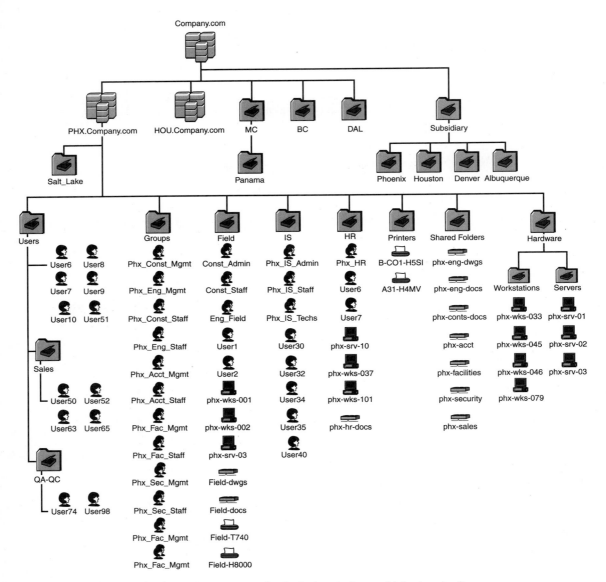

Figure 8.16 Lower-level container structure for single domain in a multiple–domain directory.

- **Users.** This container holds the accounts for all users in the Phoenix office except for HR and field personnel, who attach to the network via a home run to the Phoenix LAN. Putting all users in a single container makes it possible to delegate an administrative group for that container.

The subordinate container for Sales accommodates their request for a different Group Policy. In theory, every department could have its own OU with highly tailored Group Policies for specific needs. That kind of support takes time and staff.

- **Groups.** This container reflects a certain tidiness on my part that you might not share. Keeping group objects in one container makes it easier to find them. This is not a trivial problem if you have an office with a few thousand groups to manage. No performance penalty is involved with putting a group in a different container from its members.

- **Field.** This container provides a place to put objects for remote locations, such as job sites and temporary quarters. The separate container accomplishes two things. First, group policies for field personnel are usually much less restrictive than office policies. Second, field operations often have local technicians who are not full-fledged administrators. The separate container provides a way to assign them limited administrative rights over their users and machines.

- **IS and HR.** These containers provide discrete management units that satisfy the need for autonomy on the part of the staff. The danger, of course, is that the department administrators in the HR container will somehow bollix up their part of the directory and no one from the main IT group will be able to rescue them.

- **Printers and Shared_Folders.** These containers place items that users search for near the top of the container structure. The fewer containers a user has to negotiate to find a shared item in the directory, the more likely they are to use it. If you don't make directory access drop-dead simple, you'll never wean users away from browsing.

- **Hardware.** This container puts Computer objects into two separate containers, one for workstations and one for servers, where they can be managed as distinct units. The desktop administrators or break/fix technicians can be given admin rights over the Workstation container while only network administrators have rights over the Server container. There is no operational advantage to putting Computer objects in the same container as their users. It's much easier to find objects in a container that isn't cluttered with different object classes.

After you decide on a design for the lower levels, it's time to get input from users, managers, and other administrators. Plan on this taking a while, even in a small organization. You might want to set up a small lab environment so that you can walk users through logons and resource searches to see how they react to the container structure.

If you work for a smaller organization, or you are a consultant with a practice that focuses on small and medium-sized companies, you may find the design in Figure 8.16 to be a bit too much. Figure 8.17 shows a directory for a smaller organization.

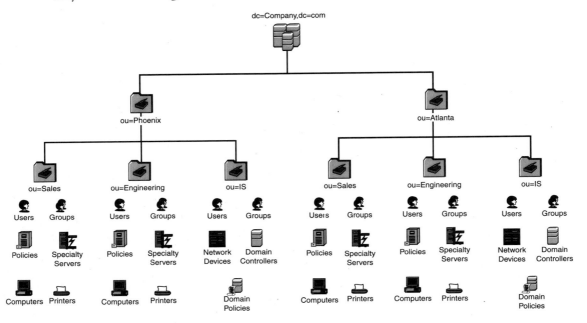

Figure 8.17   Directory design for a small company.

When IT staff is limited, local department gurus and power users tend to take on more administrative duties. For this reason, the design in Figure 8.16 divides the lower containers along functional lines. A group in each OU can be assigned management rights for the OU and you or a central administrator can modify the group memberships based on requests from the department managers.

Whatever design method you choose, and however your container layouts end up, the best you can hope for is a work in progress. Leave yourself room for changes and don't be afraid to shake up the design quite a bit in response to changes in the IT work processes. So long as you don't split off a new domain and you don't get too creative with your Group Policies, modifications to the container structure should not affect your users too much.

This just about takes care of the design preparations. Now you need to attend to a few housekeeping chores, and those involve placing special-function servers.

Placing Special-Function Servers

After you've arrived at a final domain design, you need to decide where to place a few special servers. These include the domain controllers for the various domains, Global Catalog servers, DNS secondaries, and FSMO role masters. Of this group, FSMOs are the most exotic; so let's deal with them first.

FSMO Role Masters

Multiple-master replication makes it possible for all domain controllers to be peers. Still, a few duties, for one reason or another, must remain in the hands of a single domain controller. These are called *Flexible Single Master Operations* (FSMO) (pronounced FizzMohs). A domain controller that has a particular FSMO assignment is called a *role master*.

Role masters are chosen automatically by the system. It is possible to transfer a role master to a different domain controller. This normally requires communication with the existing role master; if the role master fails, however, a role can be transferred manually. This is called *seizing a role*. As a general rule, you do not seize a role unless the old role master is permanently lost. See Chapter 10 for details on changing or seizing role masters.

The identity of a particular FSMO role master is designated by an attribute called `FSMORoleHolder` in the associated Directory object for that role. The roles and their Directory objects are included in the following list:

- **Domain Naming Master.** The Domain Naming Master controls the addition and removal of domains in a forest.
- **Schema Master.** The Schema Master controls read/write access to the schema naming context. All other domain controllers in a forest have a read-only replica of the schema naming context.

These two role masters must be unique for a forest and must reside on the same domain controller. Their functions are quite different, however. The first domain controller promoted in a forest becomes the Domain Naming Master and Schema Master. If this role master becomes unavailable, normal operations are not impaired, but you cannot add or remove domains and you cannot modify the schema. Both of these are relatively rare occurrences, so you have lots of time to recover the failed server. The two roles require very little overhead and generate virtually no traffic, so they should only be moved if a domain controller in a more appropriate location comes online. Always assign the two roles to the same domain controller. Failure to do so can cause data integrity problems with the directory.

The identity of the Domain Naming Master is stored in the `FSMORoleMaster` attribute of the Partitions object. The Partitions object is stored under the Configuration container. The object itself is not visible using standard AD management consoles, but you can view the identity of the role master as follows:

Procedure 8.2   **Viewing the Identity of the Role Master**

---

1. Open the AD Domains and Trusts snap-in.
2. Right-click the Domains and Trusts icon at the top of the tree.
3. Select OPERATION MASTER from the fly-out menu.

The identity of the Schema Master is stored in the `FSMORoleMaster` attribute of the Schema container. This object also is not visible using the standard AD management consoles. You can easily load the console as follows:

Procedure 8.3   **Loading the Standard AD Management Console**

---

1. From the Run window, enter `SCHMMGMT.MSC`. This launches the `Schema Management` console.
2. Right-click the Schema Manager icon at the top of the tree.
3. Select OPERATIONS MASTER from the fly-out menu.

RID Master

All security objects in Windows 2000 have a SID. The SID is a combination of the SID of the domain and a sequential number called the *relative ID* (RID). Domain controllers in a Windows 2000 domain pass around the RID pool and carve off 100,000-number slices to affix to security objects created by that domain controller. In a Mixed-mode domain, only one domain controller can assign RIDs, the PDC emulator. This ensures that all RIDs are sequential, a necessity for classic NT BDCs. In a Native-mode Windows 2000 domain, any domain controller can assign a RID to a security principal.

In a Native-mode domain, the RID pool is passed from one domain controller to another. When a domain controller needs more RIDs, it becomes the RID master, gets the RID pool, and carves off a hunk of addresses. It stores the numbers in a Directory object called RID Set using an attribute called `RIDAllocationPool`. The RID Set object is located under the domain controller's Computer object in the Domain Controllers container. This object also holds the value for the next RID and the number of the last allocation pool held by that domain controller.

The identity of the Domain Naming Master is stored in the FSMORoleMaster attribute of the RID Manager$ object under the System container. This attribute contains the distinguished name of the NTDS Settings object that points at the server, such as the following:

`Ntds Settings,cn=phx-dc-01,cn=Servers,cn=Phoenix,cn=Sites,cn=Configuration,dc=Company, dc=com.`

This object is not visible using standard directory management snap-ins. To view or change the identity of the RID master, open the Active Directory Users and Computers snap-in, right-click the Users and Computers icon at the top of the tree, and select OPERATIONS MASTERS from the fly-out menu.

PDC Master

In a Mixed-mode domain, the classic NT BDCs can only pull replication updates from a primary domain controller. Like ducks waddling after their mother, classic BDCs insist on using the original PDC and no other. They have a special SAM object called an LSA Secret, which connects them via secure RPC to the PDC.

For this reason, the classic NT PDC is always the first domain controller to be promoted when deploying Windows 2000. It becomes the PDC role master. If you transfer this role to another role master, it appears to the down-level BDCs as if a BDC had been promoted to PDC. They begin replicating from the new role master as soon as they can set up an RPC connection with the NETLOGON service. The PDC role master can be assigned only to a Windows 2000 domain controller. After you have begun the deployment of Windows 2000 in an existing classic NT domain, you cannot return to a classic PDC without demoting your Windows 2000 domain controllers and starting over.

The identity of the Domain Naming Master is stored in the FSMORoleMaster attribute of the Domain-DNS object, such as dc=Company,dc=com. This attribute contains the distinguished name of the NTDS Settings object that points at the server, such as the following:

`Ntds Settings,cn=phx-dc-01,cn=Servers,cn=Phoenix,cn=Sites,cn=Configuration,dc=Company, dc=com.`

This attribute is not displayed as a property of the object in the AD Users and Computers console, but you can view it as follows:

Procedure 8.4   **Viewing the *FSMORoleMaster* Attribute**

1. Right-click the AD Users and Computers icon at the top of the tree.
2. Select OPERATIONS MASTERS from the fly-out menu. The PDC Role Master window opens.

Infrastructure Master

Rapid dissemination of group membership in a large network is important. Users get impatient when they are added to a group that is supposed to give them access to a directory and it takes a long time for that change to take effect. Windows 2000 assigns the job of coordinating and replicating group membership changes within a domain to a single FSMO, the Infrastructure Manager.

The identity of the Domain Naming Master is stored in the `FSMORoleMaster` attribute of the Infrastructure object under the Domain-DNS container, such as `cn=Infrastructure,dc=Company,dc=com`. This attribute contains the distinguished name of the NTDS Settings object that points at the server.

This object is not displayed by default on the `AD Users and Computers` console. You can view the settings as follows:

Procedure 8.5   **Viewing the *FSMORoleMaster* Attribute**

1. Right-click the AD Users and Computers icon at the top of the tree.
2. Select OPERATIONS MASTERS from the fly-out menu. This opens the `Infrastructure Role Master` window.

Domain Controllers

Each Windows 2000 domain controller has a read/write replica of the domain naming context and a read-only replica of the schema and configuration naming contexts. Unlike NetWare, member servers in a Windows 2000 domain do not host external replicas of the directory. When users access a particular server, the initial authentication is handled by Kerberos and the users are given access tokens that the LSA on the member server uses to grant or deny access to security objects. There is very little authentication performance gain by making a member server into a domain controller, and you might even hurt performance by unnecessarily taking cycles for replication and directory management.

Calculating the number and placement of domain controllers is as much of an art as a science. Fault tolerance demands that you have at least two in a domain. After that, performance and reliability are the primary criteria. Field reports from large beta sites indicate that query handling on a single domain controller is fast enough so that there is no perceptible performance improvement by increasing the number of domain controllers until the network I/O starts to become a bottleneck. DNS assists in divvying the load among domain controllers.

So, plan on putting at least two domain controllers in every large office for fault tolerance and one in every small remote office where you don't want users authenticating over the WAN. A remote office with only a few users and a network that stays well connected to the WAN over the course of a day can get away without a domain controller. Be sure the local users understand that a failure of their WAN connection means a complete loss of access to their local server. Without a Kerberos KDC to authenticate users and pass out tickets, a member server will reject connections. This won't happen immediately, but you'll see the effects accumulate as older Kerberos tickets expire.

In most cases, people tend to err on the other side, deploying too many domain controllers. Thanks to multiple-master replication, all domain controllers share the burden of passing along updates to their copy of the directory. Theoretically, a bottleneck should not occur at a single server. The more replicas of a naming context that you have on the wire, however, the more likely you are to encounter a replication trauma that causes other domain controllers to fidget or fail. Watch your NTDS statistics in Performance Monitor as you ramp up the number of domain controllers. If you see network traffic or disk activity start to zoom up, you know that you've reached the knee of the growth curve.

Global Catalog Servers

Standard domain controllers do not host copies of naming contexts from other domains. Without a local copy of the naming contexts from the trusted domains, clients from those domains must authenticate over the network to reach a domain controller in a trusted domain. Global Catalog domain controllers solve this problem by hosting a partial replica of all domain naming contexts in a forest. The size of this database would be monstrous for a big network, so only around 60 attributes are included in the GC. A search for any other attribute is referred to a domain controller holding a full replica.

If there is no GC domain controller available, users will not be allowed to log on to the domain. This is because the membership list for universal groups in trusted domains is available only at GC servers. Because users might be members of universal groups with a Deny Access security setting on important security objects, Microsoft considered it prudent to block their access entirely if a GC were not available to verify their group memberships. This restriction does not apply to administrators. GC servers also facilitate LDAP lookups by providing an index of the most commonly used attributes in every trusted domain. This reduces lookup traffic among trusted domains and significantly improves performance.

Designating a domain controller as a GC server can significantly increase the hardware requirements for the server in a big network. A child domain with 300 users might have an NTDS.DIT of 15 or 20MB, but the overall GC for the company might be 10 or 20 or 100 times that size. It doesn't make sense to require the office manager of a small branch to buy a fire-breathing server just to get GC services. Spend your money on a reliable Frame Relay connection with a hefty committed information rate and let the clients authenticate across the WAN. Small offices do not generate much authentication traffic. If you think certain processes may generate exceptional traffic levels, use the Network Monitor to check packet traffic and audit the traffic levels through the CSU/DSU.

DNS Secondaries

The stability and reliability of a Windows 2000 domain absolutely depends on the stability and reliability of the dynamic DNS system that provides name resolution services for that domain. It does no good to put a domain controller in a branch office to achieve fault tolerance without placing a dynamic DNS secondary for the zone in the same office.

The most straightforward way to distribute DNS services in conjunction with the directory is to use directory-integrated DNS (see Chapter 5 for details). Directory-integrated DNS places zone table information directly in the Directory where every domain controller can reach it. All you need to do is install DNS services on a domain controller and configure it as a directory-integrated secondary and that's that. Configure local clients to use this domain controller as a DNS server or set the configuration in DHCP.

A few caveats apply when using directory-integrated DNS. Foremost is that the DNS server must also be a domain controller. If you are accustomed to hosting your DNS services on a workstation or low-end server, you might not be able to continue this practice if you have a large network with a big directory database.

If you have a mix of Windows 2000 dynamic DNS along with dynamic DNS servers from other sources, such as BIND or NetWare, you can use directory-integrated DNS on your Windows 2000 servers. Just be certain that they are configured to send zone transfers via normal methods to non-Windows 2000 DNS servers (see Chapter 5 for details).

Finally, if you are just starting your Windows 2000 domain deployment and you have only one or two domain controllers up and running, you might want to install DNS on a non-domain controller and configure it as a standard DNS secondary pulling zones from one of the directory-integrated primaries. This becomes your backup in the event that you lose the directory-integrated zones. You do not need to point any clients at this server. It's just there for backup until you are confident of your Active Directory configuration.

Moving Forward

If you're a "measure twice, cut once" type of administrator, you're probably comfortable with the approach I've taken to designing domains. If you've had good success in the past by diving into the deep end of technology and figuring out how to stay afloat, you may have skipped this chapter entirely. In any case, it's time to begin deploying Windows 2000 domains. The next two chapters cover installation details for Windows 2000 domain controllers, managing users and groups in Windows 2000 domains, and troubleshooting Active Directory problems.

9

Deploying Windows 2000 Domains

THE TIME FOR TALK IS OVER. YOU'VE ASSAYED THE alternatives, written the reports, drawn the drawings, consumed cups of coffee, met in meetings, parlayed plans, fought fights, arrived at agreements, and now you're ready to do the deed and deploy a Windows 2000 domain. Here's a quick rundown of the planning and preparation done so far:

- Deployed IP infrastructure, if not already done.
- Verified proper classic NT NetBIOS name resolution and installed a Windows 2000 WINS server, if required. (Chapter 4, "Understanding NetBIOS Name Resolution")
- Designed a DNS namespace and deployed dynamic DNS. (Chapter 5, "Managing Domain Name System (DNS) Services and Dynamic Host Configuration (DHCP) Services")
- Got acquainted with Kerberos and Active Directory technologies. (Chapter 6, "Understanding Network Access Security and Kerberos," and Chapter 7, "Understanding Active Directory Services")
- Laid out a plan for Directory containers and domain partitions. (Chapter 8, "Designing Windows 2000 Domains")
- Determined placement of FSMO role masters, global catalog servers, and DNS secondary servers. (Chapter 8, "Designing Windows 2000 Domains")
- Contacted next of kin.

Chapter 1, "Installing and Configuring Windows 2000," covered installing Windows 2000 servers and upgrading classic NT servers to Windows 2000, but it deferred discussing domain controller upgrades to this chapter. The upgrade of a classic NT domain controller to a Windows 2000 domain controller proceeds in two stages. Stage one involves upgrading the basic NOS and any services associated with the NOS. The classic accounts and domain configurations remain in the SAM and are available for local logon, but NET-LOGON is disabled. Stage two involves promoting the server to a Windows 2000 domain controller and migrating the SAM and Security database entries out of the Registry and into the newly created Active Directory.

The reason for the two-stage upgrade goes to the heart of the way Windows 2000 handles domain controllers. In classic NT, a server could either be a domain controller or a standard server, but not both. You had to reinstall NT to change its security role. In Windows 2000, a standard server can be promoted to a domain controller and demoted back to a standard server as many times as you like. The domain controller services become just another item in a list of services a server can provide along with DNS, DHCP, Terminal Services, and Certificate Authority services. Because any Windows 2000 server can be made into a domain controller, the only thing that makes a classic NT domain controller special is the account and policy information in the SAM and Security Registry hives.

Review the deployment prerequisites in this chapter before upgrading any domain controllers. The sequence of the upgrades is important. Then, when you're ready to begin, refer to Chapter 1 for details on upgrading the NOS. After you've performed the initial stage of the upgrade on a classic domain controller, return to this chapter for the steps to perform the domain controller promotion.

If you have a WAN, it's important to preview the section "Introduction to Sites and Site Replication" at the end of this chapter and the details in Chapter 11, "Managing Active Directory Replication and Directory Maintenance," prior to starting your Windows 2000 deployment. Replication between LANs depends on a structured set of IP subnets. If you spend half your time at a telnet console reconfiguring your routers and the other half yelling at service providers about why the configurations don't work, you may want to defer your Windows 2000 deployment for a while until your IP infrastructure is stable.

At this point, there are two ways to proceed. If you're tossing out whatever classic NT infrastructure you have and starting fresh by rebuilding all domain controllers, skip to the "Let the Upgrades Begin" section. If you have classic NT domains in place and you want to preserve those accounts and access permissions, you need to make a few more preparations. Proceed to the next section.

Preparing Classic NT Domain Controllers for Upgrade

Figure 9.1 shows a classic NT multiple-master domain. All the trust relationships from the resource domains to the three account domains are the result of the intransitive nature of interdomain trusts in classic NT. For example, let's say you're an administrator in a local resource domain, such as the Phoenix domain in Figure 9.1. Your users log on to the US account domain. They gain access to local resources in the Phoenix domain because they are members of local groups that have been populated with global groups and individuals from the US master domain.

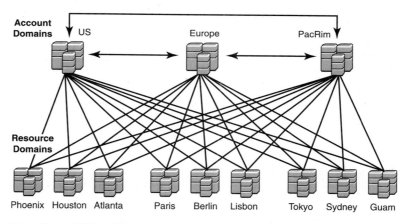

Figure 9.1   Classic NT multiple-master domains showing fully meshed trust relationships.

Because classic NT domains are not transitive, you cannot simply select a user account from another master account domain, say Europe, and put it into a local group in Phoenix. By the same token, you can't take a user or group account from the Europe or PacRim account domains and put it on the ACL of an NTFS folder in the Phoenix domain.

Administrators in the US account domain are equally limited. They can only populate US groups with users from the US domain. If a user from Guam in the PacRim account domain wants to access files in the Phoenix domain, the US domain administrator must create an account for that user in the US domain. The user in Guam can log on to the US domain, using that US account from a computer in the Guam resource domain, because of the mutual trusts between the two account domains.

The domain diagram in Figure 9.1 is a textbook case of a fully meshed, multiple-master domain. Most NT domain architectures in large organizations don't have trusts that are quite so clearly defined. Classic NT domains tend to come into existence in a haphazard way. A set of local administrators builds a domain to handle a specific situation. A little later, they find that they need resources from other domains, so they create trusts. The trusts multiply until someone in a central IT organization creates a master trust. But unless the central organization is overwhelmingly supported, other master trusts come into existence along with the resource trusts until a cluttered configuration results, such as that in Figure 9.2.

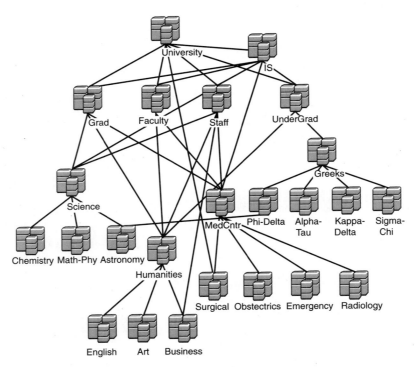

Figure 9.2   Cluttered classic NT multiple-master domain architecture.

If you follow the trade magazines, you've probably seen articles touting the advantages of "flattening your Windows NT domains" in preparation for deploying Windows 2000. The structure in Figure 9.2 probably needs thermonuclear detonation rather than flattening, but you get the idea. You should make every attempt to simplify your classic NT domain configuration before migrating to Active Directory-based Windows 2000 domains. But domain architectures don't turn into Escher drawings all by themselves. The politics and compromises that created the mess in Figure 9.2 will be the same politics and compromises you'll face as you start a Windows 2000 deployment.

If you have the job of bringing order into classic NT domain chaos, your best approach may *not* be to fight for collapsing the existing NT domains. Rather, you may want to campaign for a centrally managed, contiguous DNS namespace. It's my experience that the reverence for DNS naming and DNS architecture makes this mission more likely to succeed than getting folks to agree on a uniform classic NT domain architecture. And if you win the DNS namespace battle, you've all but won the Windows 2000 domain consolidation war.

That being said, if you do plan on reconfiguring your domains, it's much easier to do this *before* you upgrade to Windows 2000. For one thing, you're dealing with known technology in classic NT, however creaky. Second, the Windows 2000 tools for moving accounts and groups between domains aren't nearly as mature as those available for reconfiguring classic NT domains. Finally, you'll get the chance to shake the cobwebs out of the domain plan before actually starting the Windows 2000 deployment. If the administrators in Europe, for example, decide that they need a domain of their own and that's all there is to say about it, you need to know this well in advance of the Windows 2000 rollout.

Here's a checklist of the domain reconfiguration chores you may need to perform in preparation for migrating classic NT domains to Windows 2000:

- Migrate user accounts to the new domain, including local and centralized user profiles and all Registry entries that affect local software configuration. This migration must include updating ACL lists with the new user SIDs.

- Migrate domain and local group accounts to the new domain, including user membership. Like the user migration, this one must include updating all ACL lists.

- Migrate computer accounts to the new domain. User domain authentication relies on a secure RPC connection between the member workstation and its domain, so this computer account migration is extremely important. It's also the hardest part of the domain restructuring because it involves touching every desktop, unless you invest in a third party tool that does the work for you.

- Tear down the old domain controllers and reinstall classic NT to bring them into the new domain.

Accomplishing all this with the standard admin tools in classic NT is a tedious process. If you have hundreds or thousands of accounts to migrate, it's nearly impossible to complete a standard migration to a single domain quickly enough to meet any practical Windows 2000 implementation schedule. You may want to consider shelling out a few dollars to buy domain reconfiguration tools such as:

- **Virtuosity, Aelita Software, www.aelita.com.** This is fairly inexpensive at about $1000 per license. It uses either Access or SQL Server to store migration information. The configuration interface is relatively straightforward to use and the results are predictable.

- **DM/Reconfigurator, FastLane Technology, www.fastlanetech.com.** This tool is considerably more expensive than Virtuosity at $15/seat migrated, but the array of tools is much more comprehensive. If the thought of pushing a button that changes the domain configuration of 10,000 users makes you nervous and you want the most control possible, check out this tool.

- **Direct Admin, Entevo, www.entevo.com.** The core strength of this tool is its ADSI interface. The Entevo designers worked on the initial design of Active Directory and COM+, and their experience shows. The cost was not available at the time of this writing but probably hovers around $1000. Entevo also has a DirectMigrate 2000 tool that promises to simplify the entire upgrade process. There is also an NDS management product that provides a single MMC console for managing Windows 2000, classic NT, and NetWare networks. Nifty stuff if you're moving away from NetWare.

- **NDS for NT, Novell, www.novell.com.** If you're not moving away from NetWare (and this is usually an emphatic NOT, if my experience is any judge), then you might want to use NDS for NT to move user accounts between domains. You won't get the same ACL support as you would from one of the NT packages, but you leverage your existing NDS commitment and give your users the least hassle. As of the time of this writing, you'll need to reverse migrate your accounts out of NDS for NT before upgrading to Windows 2000. That may change if Novell is able to ship an Active Directory-compatible version of NDS.

If you decide to wait until after the Windows 2000 upgrade to reconfigure your domains, there are two tools in the Resource Kit for moving, importing and exporting objects. These are Movetree for user and group accounts and Netdom for computer accounts. These tools are covered in the "Special Domain Operations" section later in this chapter.

Final DNS Namespace Checks

Before you upgrade your domain controllers, you need to have already deployed Windows 2000 DNS servers or upgraded your existing DNS servers to support RFC 2136, "Dynamic DNS," and RFC 2052, "A DNS RR for Specifying the Location of Services (DNS SRV)." Chapter 5 has the details on configuring Windows 2000 DNS servers, and Chapter 8, "Designing Windows 2000 Domains," has recommendations for designing DNS namespaces that support Windows 2000 domains.

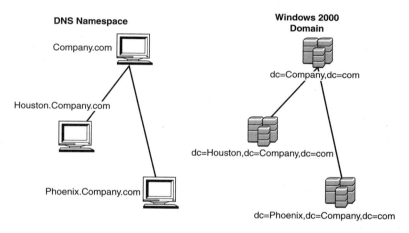

Figure 9.3 Example DNS namespace and Windows 2000 domain name mappings.

Figure 9.3 shows a simple DNS namespace and its corresponding Windows 2000 domain name mappings. Here are a few items that are often over-looked when preparing to migrate to these Windows 2000 domains:

- Configure the TCP/IP properties of every classic NT domain controller to point at a DNS server that is either running Windows 2000 or some other RFC 2052–compliant version of DNS. The DNS server should be hosting the zone table for the Windows 2000 domain you're about to create. In other words, the domain controller should always be configured to point at a DNS server that is SOA for the zone that contains the Windows 2000 domain. For example, if you are going to promote the domain controller and create a Windows 2000 domain named Company.com, then the DNS server for the domain controller needs to host the company.com zone. Don't forget to check for alternate DNS servers in the configuration list. Sometimes a standby server in another location has not yet been upgraded to dynamic DNS.

- If your classic NT domain name does not match the DNS domain name you're going to use, *change the NT domain name before upgrading.* There is no utility in the initial release of Windows 2000 to change a domain name.

- Make absolutely certain that your DNS server and zone configurations are correct. Root hints and delegations must be configured correctly, especially if the domain controller will be a child domain of another Windows 2000 domain. For example, when you promote a domain controller in a child domain in a tree or a peer domain in a forest, it must be able to contact a domain controller in the root domain to replicate the Configuration and Schema naming contexts. If you have a private DNS namespace, but your root hints point at the InterNIC DNS root servers, then the child domains will not be able to find the Windows 2000 domain controllers in the root domain. If you promote a domain controller and receive an *Unable to locate suitable domain controller* error, this is one possible cause.

- If you have a WAN, review the replication topics in Chapter 11 and develop a Site plan for replication that matches your IP routing and DNS naming. If you need to make changes to either one, be sure to do so prior to upgrading the domain controllers. The Active Directory Installation Wizard makes DNS and Active Directory entries based on the IP address of the server. You're much more likely to get a successful upgrade and a correct replication topology if you have the correct IP addresses on all the domain controllers right from the start.

- You'll need WINS until all Windows computers in your network have been upgraded to Windows 2000. This might take until the year 2005, so don't let your NetBIOS name resolution go slack just yet. Check your WINS database to make sure that the host records for all domain controllers match their DNS records. This sometimes goes unnoticed because servers don't look at DNS if they get a proper response from WINS. But a Windows 2000 machine queries DNS first, and this can cause unexpected failures if the names and IP addresses are not consistent.

- For the same reason, check for LMHOSTS files and HOSTS files at every domain controller. It's easy to forget these static files. They lie there quietly, like a Stephen King character lurking under a bridge, waiting...to...pounce. You should find the LMHOSTS and HOSTS files in \WINNT\System32\Drivers\Etc unless someone has changed the Registry setting for the default location. This is HKLM | System | CurrentControlSet | Services | TCPIP | Parameters | DataBasePath.

- If the domain controller is a DHCP client (not a common configuration), then be sure to check the DHCP scope options to verify that the DNS configurations are correct. Check the static TCP/IP settings, as well. It sometimes happens that an administrator, rushing to solve a problem, puts a static DNS or WINS entry into the local TCP/IP configuration for a DHCP client. This overrides the DHCP scope options.

- If your domain controller has multiple network cards, or multiple IP addresses bound to the same network card, you may experience problems with NetBIOS name resolution. The NetBIOS helper uses only the first address in the IP address sequence. This is not usually a problem in Classic NT because clients use WINS to find the domain controller, and only the first IP address will be registered in WINS. But the TCPIP driver in Windows 2000 registers all addresses with dynamic DNS, so Windows 2000 clients may fail when they make an SMB connection to the domain controller. In general, it is a bad idea to have a multihomed Windows 2000 domain controller.

Hardware Preparations

Chapter 1 lists the NOS requirements for a Windows 2000 Server, including CPU speed, system memory, L2 cache, I/O performance, disk capacity, and network connections. Depending on the size of your network, a domain controller should be sized more for I/O performance and reliability than for raw CPU speed. Give it lots of memory, too, just as you would any application server.

A domain controller can also act as a file-and-print server and even run small applications, but it should not be used for heavy-duty client/server applications. This is not so much a limitation of the hardware or Active Directory as it is a logistical decision. If you are running an email application and that application crashes so that you must restart the server, you don't want that evolution to affect the services provided by a domain controller.

You must have at least one NTFS version 5 volume on the domain controller to hold the SYSVOL folders. The NTFS 5 volume is required because the folders make use of NTFS reparse points, a feature only available in NTFS 5. If your classic domain controller has only FAT partitions, it's best to convert them to NTFS prior to the upgrade. That way, if something goes wrong, you aren't trying to diagnose two problems, the upgrade and the file system conversion.

I recommend that you run NTFS on all domain controller volumes, if for no other reason than to take advantage of NTFS security and recoverability. If you prefer to leave your system partition formatted as FAT so you can boot to a floppy and access the system files, this is no longer necessary in Windows 2000. You can boot to a special Recovery Console that gives you access to NTFS volumes. If you still prefer to leave the system files on a FAT partition, you can do so without interfering with the domain controller upgrade. The SYSVOL folders can be placed on another volume. During the Windows 2000 NOS upgrade, you'll be prompted to convert any existing FAT, FAT32, and NTFS 4 partitions to NTFS 5. You can decline this conversion for the system partition.

SYSVOL and Reparse Points

Reparse points act as soft links to other file systems or to other points on the same file system. SYSVOL is a shared folder that contains two reparse points that connect back to folders higher in the directory tree than the SYSVOL share. This permits placing highly restrictive permissions on the shared SYSVOL folder, while giving administrators a place to make changes in the linked folders.

You should always use separate drives for the main Active Directory files, the Active Directory log files, and SYSVOL. There are several reasons for this:

- Separating the Active Directory log files from the main information store, NTDS.DIT, is critical if you want to repair a corrupted database.
- Putting SYSVOL on its own volume helps to improve performance if you have many users downloading profiles and logon/logoff scripts.
- Keeping the main Active Directory information store on a separate disk maximizes read performance.
- In a big domain with thousands of users in the Directory, you should give the information store lots of elbowroom. The default Directory size is 10MB, but it grows like a weevil from there. The log files consume at least 30MB and can grow to ten times that size. The more attributes you assign to each user and computer, and the more groups you have that have lots of members, the faster the Directory grows.

It is possible to change the location of the Directory files after you promote a domain controller, but it isn't fun. See Chapter 11 for more information.

As for network connectivity, reliable data communication lines are important at all times, of course, but they are especially critical during upgrades of backup domain controller. If you have an office with a BDC at the wrong end of an oversubscribed 56K line or, worse yet, an analog line that is prone to hang up without warning, you may want to rig an alternate path for stable communications before upgrading the BDC, or do the upgrade in the evening when the line is clear. After the Directory has replicated to the newly upgraded server, the bandwidth demands are much lower.

Choosing a PDC to Upgrade

The first domain controller to be upgraded must be the Primary Domain Controller (PDC). If you have a single classic NT domain, then the choice is simple. If you have a master domain architecture with one account domain and one or more resource domains, always upgrade the PDC in the account domain first. This preserves the hierarchy of the Directory. If you have a multiple-master domain architecture, choose an account domain to upgrade by using the following criteria:

- If you are eventually going to collapse all classic account domains into a single Windows 2000 domain, start with the PDC in the domain that is slated to be at the top of the Directory.

- If you intend to turn the account domains into children of a single root domain, start with the PDC in the domain that is slated to form the top of the namespace.

- If you intend to turn the account domains into a forest with separate DNS namespaces, upgrade the PDC in the domain that you want to host the two enterprise FSMOs, Domain Name Master and Schema Master. See Chapter 8 for details about FSMO Role Masters.

Check Time Synchronization

Active Directory uses loose time stamping to resolve collisions when the same property is changed at more than one domain controller. Kerberos also uses loose time stamping to validate tickets and to set the expiration time of tickets and ticket-granting tickets. It's important that the clocks on all Windows 2000 domain controllers stay within about 5 minutes of each other, corrected for time zone.

Possible Time Synchronization Errors

The difference between times on two domain controllers is called the *skew*. The allowable skew is 5 minutes. If the local time on a domain controller is outside the acceptable skew in relation to the other domain controllers, you will either get an *API Return Buffer Too Small* error or an *Unable to locate members of forest, extended error* message when attempting to promote the domain controller.

The Windows Time Service (WTS) handles time synchronization between domain controllers. The service driver is W32TIME.EXE, part of the Services suite. W32Time is normally set to manual. It is started during the domain controller promotion. If the domain controller being promoted cannot synchronize with the domain controller to which it is attached, the promotion will fail.

You won't have a time sync problem when upgrading the first domain controller, of course, but you may get errors when promoting subsequent servers. It's a good practice to always sync the time manually prior to upgrading.

The fastest way to synchronize time is to use the Net Time command. The syntax is Net Time /domain:domain_name. Because the PDC is the first domain controller to be upgraded, the time returned by this NetTime command will be the time at the Windows 2000 DC.

You must have administrator privileges (or at least the Change System Time privilege) in the domain to run Net Time against a domain time source. It's important to sync the time before the NOS upgrade. You won't be able to sync afterward because you will not have administrator privileges in the domain from the BDC until you complete the domain controller promotion. If you forget to sync prior to the NOS upgrade, you can set the time manually using the time icon in the System Tray. Be sure to set the time zone.

Prepare for Upgrade Disasters

The most valuable machine in an NT domain is probably the PDC. You can make a case that Exchange or Notes servers are more critical, given the fact that executives tend to thump on the IT staff very quickly following email failures, but the PDC hosts the only read-write copy of the security databases for the entire domain, so keeping it up is a fairly high priority. Unfortunately for those of us who like to ease into something as complex as a big NOS upgrade, when you migrate from classic NT domains to Windows 2000 domains, the very first domain controller you must upgrade is the PDC. You have no choice. This protects the integrity of the security databases.

A classic PDC has a read-write copy of the SAM and Security Registry hives, which hold the three security databases: SAM, BuiltIn, and LSA. When a classic PDC is promoted to Windows 2000, the contents of these databases are migrated into Active Directory. The Local Security Authority (LSA) on the domain controller, working through the MSV1_0 security provider, exposes the SAM attributes of the security principals to downlevel clients. Every Windows 2000 domain controller has a read-write copy of the Active Directory database. If a BDC were upgraded first and made into a Windows 2000 domain controller, the classic PDC could not replicate changes with it. The PDC must be replicated first so that the only live copy of the security databases resides in the Active Directory.

When you promote a classic PDC to a Windows 2000 domain controller, it becomes the PDC Role Master for the domain. This is a special Flexible Single Role Operations (FSMO) designation that identifies the one and only Windows 2000 domain controller that is allowed to function as a downlevel PDC. The PDC Role Master replicates to all downlevel BDCs in the domain. If you open `User Manager for Domains` on a downlevel server in this domain, you will be looking at the SAM-related contents of the Active Directory at the PDC Role Master.

There is another FSMO role that affects upgrades. The first Windows 2000 domain controller also acts as RID Master for the domain. A *Relative ID* (RID) is a sequential number appended to the SID of the domain to form unique SIDs that are assigned, in sequence, to all security principals, such as users, computers, and groups. In classic NT, all RIDs come from the PDC because it has the only read/write copy of the SAM. In Windows 2000, each domain controller is capable of assigning a RID from its share of a floating RID pool. While classic BDCs are still on the network —this is called a mixed-mode domain—the PDC Master and the RID Master must be the same machine.

If something goes wrong while you are upgrading your PDC, your best friend is, of course, a reliable tape backup that you have tested by restoring to a test server so you know, beyond the shadow of a doubt that it works. Rapid recovery is paramount, though, so you may want to consider making a few special arrangements.

First, you can make an image backup of the domain controller. Image backups store an exact replica of a drive. They can restore a system very quickly. You boot from a set of floppies, start your recovery, and in a few minutes you're back on line.

A couple of products have good reputations for saving image backups to tape. Replica from Legato Software (`www.legato.com`) is one. UltraBac from BEI Corporation (`www.ultrabac.com`) is another. You can also image the disk to a file using utilities like Norton Ghost from Symantec (`www.symantec.com`) or DriveImage from Powerquest (`www.powerquest.com`).

Image recovery gets a little clumsy if you recover to different hardware, so you should have a spare server with similar hardware, just in case.

Even if you choose not to do an image backup, a standard backup is essential. If you are forced to do an upgrade of an NT4 server without doing a full backup first, you should at least make a backup of the Registry using an Emergency Repair Disk (ERD). If something goes wrong with the upgrade, you can reinstall NT and use the ERD to recover the Registry settings. Be sure to generate the ERD using `rdisk /s` to include the SAM and Security hives. You can also use REGBACK from the NT4 Resource Kit. In a large network with many user accounts, the files generated by `rdisk /s` may not fit on a floppy. If you have a system this big, though, you *really* need a tape backup! You can also use RDISK /S to skip the emergency repair disk and save the repair files, including the large SAM, to `\WINNT\Repair`. You can then copy the files to another server or a ZIP drive.

If your PDC runs other mission-critical services, like a SQL database or a third-party client/server application, I highly recommend promoting a BDC with no client/server apps to PDC and upgrading this server to Windows 2000 first. If you are forced to do major surgery on your newly upgraded PDC, you don't want to move vital body parts like SQL tablespaces out of the way. All it takes is one stray DLL that you missed in your testing to crash the server and wreck a perfectly good Saturday morning.

If your PDC is also your primary WINS server, you should seriously consider putting WINS on a different machine, even if that means going through some reconfiguration pain with your client computers. The Jet databases for WINS and DHCP are modified during the upgrade to Windows 2000. They have been known to not be revived again.

You may also want to consider having a small, standby BDC that you take off the wire just prior to upgrading the PDC. If you experience problems, you can put the standby BDC back on the network while you fix the problem with the production PDC. The standby BDC is like a spare tire. It doesn't need to be a full-bore dual-Pentium monster, but it should mimic the hardware of the PDC as closely as possible so that you can do an image restore of the PDC to it, if necessary. Be sure to statically map the address of this BDC in WINS before taking it off the wire. It may take weeks for you to get all the classic domain controllers in your network upgraded to Windows 2000, WINS will tombstone the registration after a while.

A few potential, maybe even likely, disasters that you should include in your recovery planning follow.

Scenario 1—Local Disaster

Let's say that, during the upgrade of the PDC, the server goes to domain controller heaven. In this case, your classic BDCs are still functional so the users are still able to authenticate. You cannot add any new users or register new computers or change passwords, but at least the domain is functioning. Here's the fallback plan. Promote a BDC that is in the same office as the PDC, or a BDC in an outlying office if the local BDC is unavailable. You can also use the little standby BDC if you don't want to promote your real BDC. After you get full access to the SAM once again, recover the original NT PDC from tape and start over again (after you figure out what went wrong, of course). You cannot promote a classic BDC to PDC if the Windows 2000 PDC is online and functional. If the domain becomes unstable, you'll need to take the Windows 2000 PDC offline, then promote a BDC.

Scenario 2—Widespread Disaster

In this scenario, the PDC does the big chill during the upgrade and corrupts the security databases. The corrupted entries propagate to the classic BDCs, making the domain inaccessible and rendering the BDCs useless for promotion. Here's the fallback plan—Take the classic BDCs offline so they don't confuse member servers and workstations. Put the standby BDC online and promote it to PDC. Put the BDCs back online and force the PDC to replicate to them. The PDC has the only read-write copy of the security databases, so it will overwrite the corrupted SAM on the BDCs. Then, recover the original PDC from tape while it's off the wire, demote it to BDC, put it back on the wire, then promote it to PDC again. That puts you back to status quo ante. Correct the problem, then start your upgrades over again.

Scenario 3—Weasel Disaster

This is an insidious failure. The PDC upgrade goes fine, but while you're doing the BDC upgrades, the Active Directory database gets corrupted and that corrupts the replicated copies to the BDCs, some of which are now full-fledged Windows 2000 domain controllers. Here's the fallback plan: Repair the Active Directory database or recover an uncorrupted copy from tape using the steps in Chapter 11. If the Directory cannot be repaired or recovered, take the Windows 2000 domain controllers offline and put the standby BDC on the wire. From here, the work proceeds like that in Scenario 2. If you've already deployed Windows 2000 into resource domains, the recovery might get very ugly because you might lose the trust relationships. Ideally, you should have no user accounts in your resource domain, so that as soon as you get a BDC promoted to PDC, you can remake the trusts.

Scenario 4—Ultimate Disaster

In the scariest of all scenarios, the Active Directory craters after all classic BDCs have been upgraded. The poisoned Directory entries propagate to the Windows 2000 domain controllers as fast as you can say "multiple-master replication." If you can't repair the Directory database, your fallback plan is to recover it from tape, make the restoration server authoritative for the domain, and propagate the changes to the other domain controllers. (See Chapter 11 for details.)

If the backup tapes are also corrupt, and you still have your little standby BDC, you can take all Windows 2000 domain controllers offline and put the standby BDC back online, then restore the classic PDC from tape. All passwords and computer accounts created since the start of the Windows 2000 upgrade would be lost. You'll have to take your lashings, but you'll probably keep your job/assignment/career.

Plan to Promote Classic BDCs and Shift to Native Mode

You won't really see the benefit of a Windows 2000 domain until you either upgrade or decommission all downlevel BDCs. At that point, you can shift the domain to native mode and get fully transitive trust relationships, nested global groups, Directory-Integrated DNS, and fully transitive dial-up authentication. Depending on the size of your network, it could take weeks or months for you to completely upgrade all classic NT domain controllers in your network. Two situations might hamper your progress.

If you have Citrix WinFrame domain controllers running the Citrix OEM version of NT3.51, and you want to retain them as domain controllers, you're faced with two upgrades. You must upgrade the server to Windows 2000 and Terminal Server, then install the MetaFrame upgrade from Citrix. Yes, I know the ICA client licenses are expensive. If you want to save the money, you can reinstall WinFrame and make the server a member server instead of a domain controller.

If you run client/server applications on your classic NT domain controllers, you may encounter significant upgrade delays as you wait for vendors to come out with Windows 2000 versions of their products. You might have to wait years for some of the niche vendors. If you don't want to wait that long to get into a native mode configuration, you might find yourself in the unenviable position of de-installing the application, rebuilding the server as an NT4 member server, then reinstalling the application.

Support for Classic NT4 RAS Servers

When a classic NT RAS server that is a member of a Windows 2000 domain authenticates a dial-up user, it must validate the user's credentials and check dial-up permissions. The Directory objects that contain this information are usually only available to Kerberos clients. For this reason, some of the security permissions on objects in the Directory must be set to permit downlevel servers to check their attributes.

This is accomplished using a new Builtin Local group called *Pre-Windows 2000 Compatible Access*. This group is given the following security settings for User objects:

- Read Remote Access Information
- Read General Information
- Read Group Membership
- Read Account Restrictions
- Read Logon Information

The Pre-Windows 2000 Compatible Access group also has these permissions for Group Objects:

- Read All Properties
- List Contents
- Read Permissions

During domain controller promotion, you are asked if you have classic NT4 RAS servers on your network. If so, you are instructed to set the permissions for Pre-Windows 2000 Access. This option places the Everyone group in the Pre-Windows 2000 Compatible Access group. The net effect of this action is that the classic NT RAS servers can now check the dial-up permissions for any user or group of users using standard NTLM authentication.

After you have upgraded your NT4 RAS servers, you can put security back to normal by removing the Everyone group from the Windows 2000 Compatible Access group.

Prepare to Support Classic System Policy and Logon Script Replication

Classic NT replication is not supported by Windows 2000. If you have system policy files, such as CONFIG.POL (Windows 9x) or NTCONFIG.POL (NT4), or logon scripts that you have been replicating from your PDC to its BDCs, these files will not be replicated after you upgrade.

Classic NT replication used the NT File Replication service, Lmrepl, to replicate files from the $REPL share on a PDC to its BDCs. (The replication primary could be any server, but normally it is a PDC because the reason for using replication is to handle logon scripts and policies.) The BDCs pull the contents of the REPL$ share to their \WINNT\System32\Repl\Import directory, which is shared as NETLOGON. All Windows clients are hard-coded to look in the NETLOGON share at boot time to see if there are policies and scripts to load.

This classic replication based on Lmrepl has been replaced in Windows 2000 by the *File Replication Service* (FRS). Files and folders controlled by FRS can only be replicated between Windows 2000 servers. Microsoft suggests the following workaround to push files on a Windows 2000 PDC Role Master out to its BDCs. Do the first two steps prior to upgrading the PDC to Windows 2000.

Procedure 9.1 **Pushing Files to a PDC Role Master Workaround**

1. Use Server Manager to remove the current replication configuration between the PDC and BDCs.

2. Configure replication between one of the BDCs and the remaining BDCs. In essence, you are designating a BDC to act as a replication primary. The remaining BDCs, acting as replication secondaries, pull files from the REPL$ share at the replication primary. In a standard replication configuration, this requires no additional work at the BDCs. In this configuration, you will need to use Server Manager to manually configure each BDC to pull from the replication primary.

3. Now upgrade the PDC to Windows 2000. When you do so, the contents of the \WINNT\System32\Repl\Export directory are copied to \WINNT\Sysvol\Sysvol\<domain_Name>\Scripts. The second Sysvol directory is shared as SYSVOL for Windows 2000 clients. The Scripts directory is shared as NETLOGON for downlevel clients.

4. Now create a batch file that copies the contents of the \WINNT\Sysvol\Sysvol\<domain_Name>\Scripts directory at the PDC to the \WINNT\System32\Repl\Export directory at the BDC acting as the replication primary. This is the directory that the replication secondaries are pulling from. Microsoft calls this a *FRS->Lmrepl Bridge*, which is a pretty fancy name for a batch file with a single xcopy command in it.

5. Configure Task Scheduler at the PDC to run this batch file periodically. This refreshes the files at the replication primary.

Using this workaround, you can continue to use classic System Policies and logon scripts for your downlevel clients as you deploy Windows 2000 domain controllers. You don't want to have to perform this configuration more than once, so when you select the BDC to be the replication primary, make sure it's the last BDC to be upgraded. Otherwise, you'll have to go through this whole process again.

Additional Deployment Issues

Here are some additional concerns you may have when faced with upgrading a PDC:

- **What happens to the SAM database?** All user, group, and computer accounts are copied from the SAM into the Directory. All secrets, such as passwords, LSA secrets for trust relationships, computer account passwords, group memberships, and so forth, are copied.

- **What about special security settings such as password histories and intruder lockouts?** The Security hive is migrated into the Directory, and the domain policies and user rights policies are implemented as Group Policies.

- **What about trust relationships to other domains?** Classic NT trust relationships are converted to Downlevel Trusts in Windows 2000. There should be no indication at all in the trusting domains that the account domain has been upgraded.

- **What about ACLs?** User SIDs in the local domain do not change when the accounts are migrated into Active Directory, so all ACL entries on security objects, such as NTFS directories and files and Registry keys, remain intact. Users and groups from trusted domains are also still recognized through the Downlevel Trust.

- **When should I perform the upgrade?** The first thing you need to know when scheduling the upgrade is that the NETLOGON service is disabled at the domain controller from the time you start the NOS upgrade until you successfully promote the PDC to a full-fledged Windows 2000 domain controller. The server cannot authenticate users or accept changes or replicate to BDCs without NETLOGON. If this will not impact operations, then by all means do the upgrade during working hours. If it will, budget time in the evening or weekends. If the upgrade goes smoothly, you'll be out in the sunshine in about an hour. But if there were ever a situation where Murphy is waiting to pounce, this is it. Plan accordingly.

- **Who can perform the upgrade?** Anyone with full administrator privileges in the classic NT domain can perform the upgrade. Be absolutely sure you have the password of the classic NT Administrator account and at least one other account with administrator privileges. After the NOS upgrade, before the Directory is operational, only administrators are permitted to log on at the console. If the upgrade fails because the SAM is corrupted, you might not be able to log on at all. In that situation, you must recover the classic NT PDC from tape, and try again.

- **Should I defrag first?** I recommend using a commercial defragger on all NTFS partitions prior to upgrading. Your NT server may have been operating for years without a defrag. This can cause upgrade problems and domain controller promotion failures. Run the defragger several times until you have a clean volume.

- **Can I upgrade a PDC that is running NDS for NT?** As of this writing, no. You must first reverse-migrate to rebuild the local SAM, then upgrade to Windows 2000. You can leave NDS for NT running on the classic BDCs until their time comes for upgrading, but this is not recommended.

- **How does the upgrade affect browsing?** The newly upgraded Windows 2000 PDC remains the Domain Master Browser and NetBIOS over TCPIP (NetBT) is enabled. Any Backup Browsers in the same subnet continue to get their browse lists from the Windows 2000 PDC, as do Master Browsers in other subnets. As you proceed with the Windows 2000 deployment, the new Windows 2000 servers will win browse elections over classic NT servers and workstations in their subnets to become Master Browsers. Eventually, when you have upgraded your desktops and your servers, you can turn off NetBT services, say goodbye to WINS, and use DNS exclusively.

- **Can I change a domain name during the upgrade?** Always use the classic NT domain name for the Windows 2000 domain. The Domain Controller Installation wizard will let you change the name, but it retains the old NetBIOS name, which causes much confusion. For example, if you are upgrading a domain controller in the COMPANY domain (NetBIOS name), the Domain Controller Upgrade wizard would allow you to use a Windows 2000 domain name of NewCompany.com, but the old COMPANY flat name continues to appear in the Registry and on domain lists at downlevel clients.

Let the Upgrades Begin

At this point, you should have a clear roadmap of your deployment plans. You should know which classic domain controllers you are going to upgrade and in what order. All the prerequisite lists should be completed and you have brewed a big pot of coffee. Let's take the plunge and start the upgrade of the PDC in the master account domain.

Upgrading and Promoting the Initial PDC

Figure 9.4 shows an example domain diagram that I'll use to describe upgrade options. Here's a quick list of pertinent features about the company and its domains:

- The company has four offices. The headquarters is in Phoenix with a branch in Salt Lake City. A wholly owned subsidiary has its headquarters in Houston with a branch in Albuquerque. Only the WAN components applicable to this discussion are shown.
- The domain architecture uses multiple-master account domains. COMPANY and SUBSIDIARY are the master domains sharing a two-way trust.
- The BRANCH domain in Salt Lake City is a resource domain with a one-way trust to COMPANY. Servers and workstations in Salt Lake are members of BRANCH.
- Users in Salt Lake log onto COMPANY via a BDC located in the office. The only user accounts in the BRANCH domain are admin accounts for the local IT staff.
- The SUBSIDIARY domain has no resource domains. The NT servers and workstations in Albuquerque are members of SUBSIDIARY. Users in Albuquerque log onto SUBSIDIARY via a BDC located in the office.
- Users in both the COMPANY domain and the SUBSIDIARY domain access a shared folder on a member server in Salt Lake City. This shared folder has an ACL with one entry for a local group in the BRANCH resource domain. This local group has two members, the Administrator account in BRANCH and a global group from COMPANY called GLOBAL_COMPANY.
- SUBSIDIARY users who need to access to the shared folder in Salt Lake must log onto COMPANY using an account provided for them in the COMPANY domain. The two-way trust allows them to select the COMPANY domain from the pick list in the WINLOGON window.

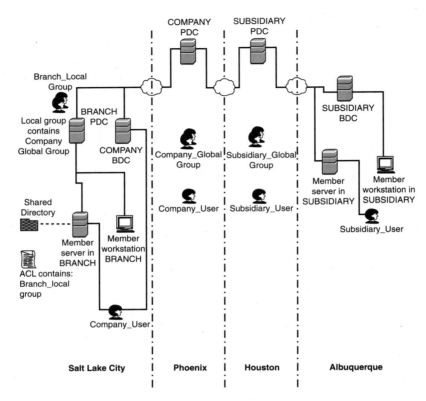

Figure 9.4 Classic NT Multiple-Master Domain with two
account domains and a single resource domain.

A full deployment of Windows 2000 to all domain controllers in both
domains consists of the following steps, each of which is detailed in this
section.

Procedure 9.2   **Overview of Windows 2000 Domain Deployment**

1. There are two master account domains, so the first step is to choose a PDC. The COMPANY domain will eventually be the parent of the BRANCH domain and the start of the forest for the SUBSIDIARY domain, so the PDC in COMPANY is the place to start.

2. Upgrade the COMPANY PDC, then verify user access, Dynamic DNS updates, classic replication to BDCs, and operation of classic trust relationships.

3. Configure the default first Site with the proper name and IP links.

4. Upgrade BDCs in the domain and verify peer-to-peer Directory replication.

5. Assign Global Catalog servers and verify Global Catalog replication.

6. Upgrade the PDC in the resource domain, BRANCH, then verify Dynamic DNS updates, operation of transitive trust relationships, Directory replication, and replication to classic BDCs.

7. Upgrade BDCs in the resource domain and verify peer-to-peer replication.

8. If transitioning to a single domain, create OUs and move accounts from child domain to root domain.

9. Upgrade remaining resource domains under first account domain.

10. Repeat for second account domain.

11. Shift all domains to Native Mode.

12. Celebrate!

The PDC in the COMPANY domain is slated as the first domain controller to upgrade. Get the Windows 2000 Server CD and start the NOS upgrade as follows:

Procedure 9.3   **Upgrading and Promoting an Account Domain PDC**

1. Insert the Windows 2000 Server CD. Autorun automatically starts the Setup Wizard. If this doesn't happen, someone might have disabled Autorun. Open My Computer and double-click the CD-ROM drive icon. This starts the Setup Wizard manually.

2. Click Next and kick back. Barring any hardware problems, in about an hour you'll have an upgraded Windows 2000 server ready to promote to a domain controller. Refer to Chapter 1 for detailed installation and troubleshooting instructions for the NOS upgrade.

3. After the server restarts for the final time following the NOS upgrade, log on as Administrator or an account with administrator privileges in the old domain. The Active Directory Installation Wizard starts automatically.

4. Don't proceed yet. It's important to do a few DNS hygiene checks or you may not enjoy a successful domain controller promotion. Put the wizard window to one side for a while. You can even close it, if you wish. Restart the wizard by opening a Run window and entering DCPROMO.

5. Check the DNS server to make sure the newly upgraded server registered its Host record in the proper DNS zone. If the Host record is missing, refresh the display and check again. If the record is still missing, try registering the server manually by opening a command session at the server and running ipconfig /registerdns. Refresh the DNS console and check to see if the Host record appears. If not, take a look at any other DNS zones hosted by that domain controller. The Host record may be listed under the wrong zone due an incorrect TCP/IP setting at the server. Refer to Chapter 5 for DNS troubleshooting details.

6. At the newly upgraded server, open a command session and run Nslookup.

   If you connect right away to the DNS server, you know that the local and remote configurations are correct.

   If you get a *Can't find server name...*error, you may have lost network connection, or you may not have properly configured the reverse lookup zone at the DNS server. Check for a PTR record in the zone representing the server's IP address. Remember that the address is reversed and depends on your subnet masking. A server with an IP address of 10.6.3.150 mask 255.255.255.0 should have a PTR record of 150 in the 3.6.10.in-addr.arpa zone. If you're using Windows 2000 DNS, the DNS Management console displays the actual IP address, which may seem counterintuitive if you are accustomed to other DNS products.

7. While in Nslookup, if the DNS server is configured to permit zone transfers, use ls -d <domain_name> to make sure that the record list includes the host record for the newly upgraded server. For the example, the command would be ls -d company.com. If the host list you pull with the zone transfer does not match the list displayed at the DNS snap-in, you either have a problem with the zone table or the local server is pointing at the wrong DNS server.

8. Exit Nslookup. If the DNS checks are satisfactory, proceed with the domain controller promotion. Go back to the wizard.

9. Click Next. The Create Tree or Child Domain window appears.

10. Select `Create a New Domain Tree`. All subsequent domains must either be children of this domain in a tree or peers in a forest.

11. Click `Next`. The `Create or Join Forest` window appears.

12. Select `Create a New Forest of Domain Trees`. This makes the domain the Domain Naming master and the Schema master for the forest. All other domains in the forest must build a Trust Root relationship to this domain when they are created.

If you neglected to configure the TCP/IP properties of this server to point at a DNS server, a window would appear at this point prompting you to configure the DNS client. Ideally, you should never see this window.

13. Click `Next`. The `New Domain Name` window appears. See Figure 9.5.

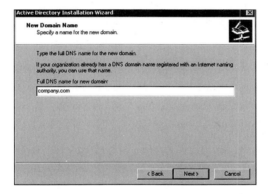

Figure 9.5 `Active Directory Installation Wizard`—`New Domain Name` window.

14. Enter the full DNS name for this domain. Use the existing NetBIOS name of the domain as the initial portion of the DNS domain name. For example, the classic COMPANY domain becomes `Company.com`. The entry is not case sensitive and you do not need to enter a trailing dot.

15. Click `Next`. The system verifies that the NetBIOS domain name is not in use elsewhere. It derives the flat NetBIOS name by parsing the fully qualified DNS name to extract the left-most string. For example, if you enter a fully qualified DNS name of `Branch.Region.Company.com`, then the flat name would be `Branch`. If no other Windows domain challenges the name, the `Database and Log Locations` window appears. See Figure 9.6.

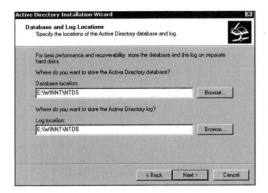

Figure 9.6 `Active Directory Installation Wizard—Database and Log Locations` window.

16. Enter the drive and path where you want to store the Directory database, NTDS.DIT, and its log files. You'll get better performance by storing the log files on a separate drive. You also need to have the log files on a separate drive if you want to rebuild the Directory following a crash of the drive holding NTDS.DIT. Do not put the files in the default WINNT directory on the system drive. Keep the Directory separate from the NOS, both for the sake of tidiness and to avoid losing both the system and the Directory in the same disk crash.

    The example shows the NTDS.DIT files and the log files on the same drive because the underlying hardware is high-performance hardware RAID with a standby drive.

17. Click `Next`. The `Shared System Volume` window appears. The `SYSVOL` directory contains login scripts, policies, and other replication-dependent files used by clients. This directory must reside on an NTFS 5 volume because it uses reparse points. Enter a drive and path for the `SYSVOL` directory. You can put it on the same drive as the Directory database or logs if you have a small network, but if hundreds of users will be accessing the login script and policies from the SYSVOL share, consider putting it on a separate drive. If you point the wizard at a FAT or FAT32 volume, you will get the error shown in Figure 9.7.

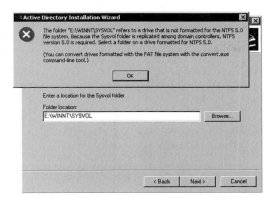

Figure 9.7   Error message when attempting to put SYSVOL on a volume that is not formatted NTFS 5.

18. Click Next. The wizard now queries DNS to register the domain name. If it is unable to locate a DNS server or if the server is not running Dynamic DNS for the target zone, the Wizard informs you of the problem. Check your DNS server, then click Back to check and correct any IP configuration problem at the local server. You can change IP configurations on the fly if you made a mistake in the IP address or zone name.

    If you forgot to build a DNS server, you have a couple of options at this point. My recommendation is to stop right here, cancel the promotion, upgrade a member server, and configure it for DNS. If you only have a few NT servers and this is the only one available for DNS (it might already *be* your DNS server), then you'll be offered the opportunity to install DNS as part of the domain controller promotion. This is a viable option, and it works most of the time, but keep in mind that if something doesn't go right, you might find yourself unable to promote the server to domain controller and unable to go back to NT4 without recovering from tape.

19. If you get the DNS warning, click OK to acknowledge it. The Configure DNS window appears. Select Yes | Install and Configure DNS on this Computer. You'll need the Windows 2000 Server CD in just a moment to install the DNS files. The configuration doesn't start right away, though.

20. If you didn't get the DNS warning, the wizard takes you directly to the window in the next step.

21. Click Next. The Windows NT 4.0 RAS Servers window appears. See Figure 9.8. The wizard notifies you that it must weaken permissions slightly if you want to allow dial-in users to access the domain through a classic NT RAS server. The RAS server must be a member of this domain or a trusted domain. See the "Preparing to Support Classic RAS Servers" section for details.

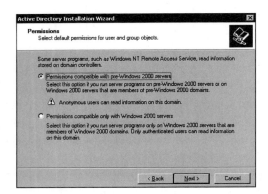

Figure 9.8   Active Directory Installation Wizard—Windows NT 4.0 RAS Servers window.

The example shows a selection of No, do not change the permissions. If you have classic RAS servers on your network, select Yes, weaken the permissions. Later, after all your classic NT RAS servers have been upgraded to Windows 2000, run NETSH.EXE on the PDC Master to reset security.

22. Click Next. The Directory Services Restore Mode Administrator Password window opens.

Use this window to enter a password for a special Administrator account to be placed in the local SAM of the domain controller. The original Administrator account will be migrated to Active Directory. This account is used when booting to Directory Services Restore Mode, a special form of Safe Mode used to restore the AD information store. This account is also used when booting to the Recovery Console, a special command interpreter designed to facilitate file maintenance on an unstable machine. Don't forget this password. When you need it, you will *really* need it. I recommend you write it down on a slip of paper and put that paper inside the locked case of the server.

23. Click Next. The Summary window appears. Review the selections and make sure you are about to do what you planned to do.

24. Click Next. The Configuring Active Directory window appears and the promotion begins. See Table 9.1 a little further in the chapter for details of the promotion process.

If you chose to install DNS, you'll be prompted to do so during the promotion.

25. After the domain controller promotion is finished, the wizard displays the Completing the Active Directory Installation Wizard window. Click Finish to close the window. Restart the machine when prompted.

If you already had a DNS server installed and you are watching it to see if the SRV records register properly, wait just a few minutes. The server must successfully start—all drivers load, all services start, and a user does a successful console logon—before SRV records are registered.

After the server restarts, you should be able to log on using any account that existed in the old domain. As with any console logon at an NT or Windows 2000 server, the account must have local logon privileges.

Troubleshooting Promotion Problems

The Configuring Active Directory window gives you a running report of what actions the wizard is taking. The system also writes a report to a file called DCPROMOUI.LOG located in \WINNT\Debug. There is also a log for what goes on behind the scenes, DCPROMO.LOG.

The most common cause of domain controller promotion problems is improper DNS configuration. If you get an inexplicable failure during promotion, check your DNS setup carefully. Even if you're absolutely sure it's correct, check it again. There are lots of subtle ways that DNS can derail the promotion.

If you are promoting a second or subsequent domain controller, you might encounter a problem initializing the W32Time service. If the promotion hangs at that point, or if you get an error such as *API Return Buffer Too Small* or *Unable to locate members of forest, extended error,* then cancel the promotion and check your time sync.

If DNS is not the cause of the promotion failure, it may be attributable to:

- Corrupt SAM or Security hives
- Registry corruption or improper Registry settings that involve a critical service, such as time synchronization or NTFS security

- Failure to point the wizard at an NTFS 5 volume for SYSVOL
- Running out of memory or drive space during the promotion (more often due to massive fragmentation than actual drive space limitations)
- Network connection problems
- Drive or file corruption

Table 9.1 shows a typical sequence of events during a domain controller promotion as logged by the AD Installation Wizard in DCPROMO.LOG. Check this list if you have a failure and you want to see what a successful promotion looks like.

Table 9.1 *DCPROMO.LOG* **Entries for a Successful Domain Controller Promotion**

Action	Explanation
DsRolerDcAsDc: DnsDomainName COMPANY.COM	The AD Installation Wizard begins impersonating the invoker and uses this account to make configuration changes. The first change is to set the Registry entries. The DNS name for this domain will be COMPANY.COM.
FlatDomainName COMPANY	This is the NetBIOS name derived from parsing out the leftmost portion of the fully qualified DNS name. Because you are upgrading a domain controller in an existing domain, it isn't likely that you'll have problems registering this name.
SiteName Default-First-Site-Name	The first site is always named Default-First-Site-Name. Subsequent domain controllers will place themselves in sites based on their IP address and the IP address associated with the site.
SystemVolumeRootPath H:\WINNT\SYSVOL DsDatabasePath G:\WINNT\SYSVOL DsLogPath H:\WINNT\NTDS	These are the drives and paths of the various domain controller directories. The SYSVOL directory actually contains another directory also named SYSVOL, and it is this second SYSVOL that is shared.

Action	Explanation
Validating path `H:\WINNT\SYSVOL` for 0×3 Validating path `H:\WINNT\NTDS` for 0×3 Validating path `H:\WINNT\SYSVOL` for 0×7	These tests verify that the volume is formatted as NTFS 5 and is valid for storing Directory files.
DisplayUpdate Stopping service NETLOGON DsRolepConfigure Service NETLOGON to 1 returned 0	The system stops NETLOGON to prevent the domain controller from authenticating users or replicating during the promotion.
DisplayUpdate Creating the System Volume `H:\WINNT\SYSVOL` DisplayUpdate Preparing for system volume replication using root `H:\WINNT\SYSVOL`	The SYSVOL directory and subdirectories are created and prepped for the File Replication System.
DisplayUpdate Copying initial Directory Service database file `C:\WINNT\system32` `ntds.dit` to `H:\WINNT\NTDS\ntds.dit`	An initial Directory database, NTDS.DIT, is copied from the system directory. This acts as a skeleton for updating from the SAM and Security hives.
DisplayUpdate Installing the Directory Service	Configures the ESENT engine.
Calling NtdsInstall for `COMPANY.COM` NtdsInstall for `COMPANY.COM` returned 0 DsRolepInstallDs returned 0	Begins and completes the installation routine.

continues ▶

Table 9.1 **Continued**

Action	Explanation
Setting AccountDomainInfo to: Domain: COMPANY Sid: S-1-5-21- 1202660629- 1214440339- 1644491937	Establishes the flat name of the domain and prepares a SID for the domain. Because this is an upgrade, the system will adopt the existing domain SID.
DisplayUpdate Configuring service RPCLOCATOR DsRolepConfigureService RPCLOCATOR to 4 returned 0	The RPC Locator service is a run-time service that is used to establish Remote Procedure Call connections between RPC end-points. All communication between domain controllers takes place over secure RPC connections. If an RPC connection cannot be made to all BDCs, promotion will fail.
DisplayUpdate Configuring service NETLOGON DsRolepConfigureService NETLOGON to 20 returned 0 DsRolepSetRegString Value on SYSTEM\ CurrentControlSet\ Control\Lsa\MSV1_0\ Auth2 to RASSFM returned 0 DisplayUpdate Setting the LSA policy information from policy (null)	The system performs a series of security manipulations to prepare for conversion to Kerberos from the default MSV1_0, NTLM Challenge-Response.
DisplayUpdate Configuring service kdc DsRolepConfigureService kdc to 4 returned 0	Configures the Kerberos Key Distribution Center service. This service is part of the Local Security Authority SubSystem (LSASS) and does not appear as a separate item on the Task List. You can find the service on the list of Services in the Computer Management snap-in.

Action	Explanation
DisplayUpdate Configuring Service IsmServ DsRolepConfigureService IsmServ to 4 returned 0	Configures the Intersite Messaging Service, a required component for Directory replication.
DisplayUpdate Configuring service TrkSvr DsRolepConfigureService TrkSvr to 4 returned 0	This is the server side of the Link Tracking Service. This service keeps track of moved files so that shortcuts and COM/DCOM links can be updated.
DisplayUpdate Configuring service w32time DsRolepConfigureService w32time to 4 returned 0	This service keeps the domain controller in sync with other domain controllers. If this is the first domain controller to be promoted, its time becomes the standard time for all other systems.
Updated InstalledSiteName To Default-First-Site-Name	An internal setting has been configured for the default site name.
DisplayUpdate Setting the computer's CNS computer name root to COMPANY.COM	This announces that the namespace has been set.
DisplayUpdate Setting security on the domain controller and Directory Service	Now that Directory objects have been exposed as security principals, some critical files and Registry keys are updated with new group names.
SetProductType to 2 [LanmanNT] returned 0	An internal setting has been configured for the product. LAN MAN NT is the legacy name for Windows 2000.

continues ▶

Table 9.1 **Continued**

Action	Explanation
DisplayUpdate The attempted domain controller operation has completed DsRolepSetOperation Done returned 0	You're finished.

Verifying Network Resource Access

Following the server NOS upgrade and promotion, perform a quick set of checks to make sure users can still access shared resources on the upgraded server.

- Log on at a downlevel workstation in the account domain, open Network Neighborhood, and verify that you can see the newly upgraded server. Double-click the server to see the shared resources.

- Log on at a downlevel workstation in a resource domain, open Network Neighborhood, and verify that you can see the newly upgraded server. Double-click the server to see the shared resources. Do this in each resource domain to verify that the trusts are intact.

- Verify that the contents of the \WINNT\System32\Repl\Import\Scripts file are copied to the \WINNT\SYSVOL\Sysvol\domain_name\Scripts directory, which is shared as NETLOGON. Then, verify that downlevel users continue to download these system policies and logon scripts. This includes CONFIG.POL for Windows 9x clients, NTCONFIG.POL for NT4 clients, and classic logon scripts in the form of batch files or KIX or Perl scripts. The REPL$ share and the classic NT file replication that went with it are no longer supported. See the "Prepare to Support Classic System Policy and Logon Script Replication" section for more information.

- The standard NT hidden shares, C$ and other drive letters, ADMIN$, and IPC$ are still used by Windows 2000. The usual restriction applies that only members of the Administrators group can access them.

- Roaming profiles hosted by the domain controller should not be affected. Verify this by logging on as a roaming user and checking that the profile is downloaded as usual.

Verifying DNS Updates

After you restart the domain controller and logon, check the DNS server to verify that the SRV records for the server have been added. Figure 9.9 shows an example. If the local DNS server is a secondary, you may need to force a zone transfer to see the records.

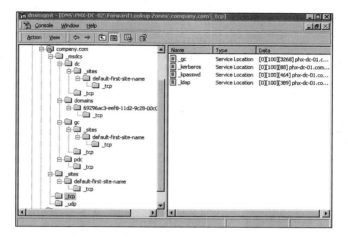

Figure 9.9   DNS Management Snap-in showing SRV records for newly promoted domain controller.

The wizard would have refused to promote the domain controller if it could not find a dynamic DNS zone, so if the SRV records do not appear in the zone table, you may have lost communication with the DNS server during restart. Also, check to make sure the server was pointed at the correct DNS server. You might be looking at a secondary that has not pulled a zone transfer yet.

If you lost connection to the DNS server between the time you promoted the DC and the time you restarted, the SRV records will automatically register when you get the DNS server back on line. You can either restart the domain controller again or open a command session and refresh the DNS registration by entering `ipconfig /registerdns`. During this troubleshooting, the classic BDCs will handle authentication, but password changes will not be accepted and you won't be able to add new users or groups.

Verifying Classic Replication

A Windows 2000 domain controller acting as a PDC in a mixed domain must convert Directory attributes to SAM entries that can be replicated to classic BDCs. Following the PDC upgrade, you should verify that the BDCs are getting these updates. There are two ways to do this. The simplest way is to make a change such as adding a new user account. Then, open Server Manager at a classic BDC, highlight the PDC, and select COMPUTER | SYNCHRONIZE ENTIRE DOMAIN from the menu. This starts a replication cycle. Wait a while, then check the Event Log at each BDC to verify that the replication occurred. Try logging on as the new user from a resource domain, just to make sure.

Server Manager and Windows 2000

You can run Server Manager from a Windows 2000 server and use it to manage a Windows 2000 server, but some of the features will not work. You can run User Manager for Domains from a Windows 2000 server but you can only use it to manage a classic NT domain. On the other hand, you can run User Manager for Domains from a classic NT server or workstation and use it to add accounts and groups to a Windows 2000 domain, but only classic NT features will be visible.

You should probably let the system stabilize for a while just to make sure the server doesn't experience unexpected crashes before you proceed. Apply the same rule of thumb that cardiologists apply to heart attack victims—if the patient remains stable for 72 hours, the next ten years look pretty good.

Configuring Sites and Verifying Replication

At this point, you need to think about paving the way for Active Directory replication, and that means configuring Sites. The "Overview of Sites and Site Replication" section at the end of this chapter has an overview, and details are in Chapter 11. It's easy to ignore Sites because if you don't configure them, everything still works. All domain controllers are placed in the Default-First-Site-Name site, and replication occurs under the assumption that all domain controllers are connected by high-speed links. You may not be happy with the effect this has on your WAN.

High-Speed Connection Definition

Connection speeds are tested dynamically by the system using a series of pings. If the connection speed is faster than 500 Kbps, the connection is considered high-speed. Anything under 500 Kbps is considered low-speed. By these criteria, a full T1 is not considered a "low-speed" connection, although a heavily trafficked T1 can introduce significant delays during peak periods. Also, the speed checker makes no allowance for Committed Information Rate (CIR), so a small frame relay pipe might be declared a high-speed connection if the latency happens to be low during the test.

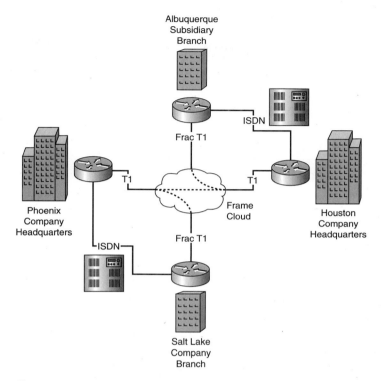

Figure 9.10   WAN layout for use in designing Windows 2000 site plan.

Figure 9.10 shows a portion of a sample wide area network including frame relay PVCs and point-to-point ISDN lines. In this configuration, each office is a separate Site in the Directory.

A Site must be associated with an IP subnet. The Directory uses this, in conjunction with DNS, to guide clients to a local domain controller. A Site can contain more than one subnet. Each subnet is defined by a special IP Subnet object in the Directory that is associated with one, and only one, Site. A site plan like the one in Figure 9.11 becomes a guide to creating those objects.

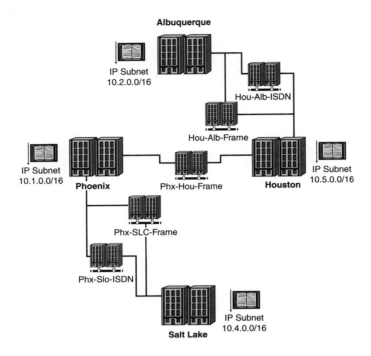

Figure 9.11 Site plan corresponding to WAN layout in Figure 9.10.

Chapter 11 contains the guidelines for creating a Site plan. After you promote your first domain controller, you should implement that plan by creating the various Site objects, IP Subnet objects, and Site Link objects. The
tool for doing this work is the AD Sites and Services console, Dssite.msc. You
must have administrative rights in the root domain to use this console. Figure
9.12 has an example of the AD Sites and Services console with Site-related
objects that correspond to the site plan in Figure 9.11.

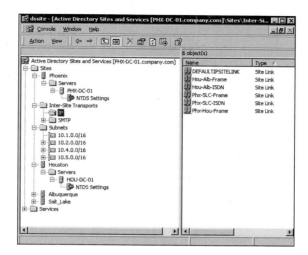

Figure 9.12   Sites and Services snap-in showing Sites, Site Links, and IP Subnets for example wide area network. The focus of the right pane is on the IP Intersite Transports.

As you deploy your domain controllers, it's important to ensure that they are properly inserted into the Replication topology and that replication is taking place. A special service, the Knowledge Consistency Checker (KCC), is responsible for building the connections between existing domain controllers and new domain controllers.

If you check the Event Log and see an entry like the one in Figure 9.13, you know you did everything right. If you see NETLOGON errors, such as the one in Figure 9.14, you know you have more work to do. The entry shows a Windows 2000 client that is a member of the domain but has a different IP subnet. This happens when you forget to build Sites and configure them with the correct IP Subnets or when you have misconfigured a subnet assignment.

Figure 9.13 Event Log entry showing KCC acknowledgment that replication has been configured correctly.

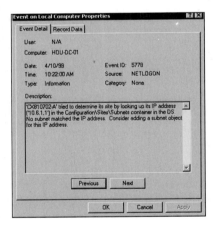

Figure 9.14 Event Log entry showing NETLOGON error resulting from incorrect Site configuration.

After you've built the Sites and site links according to your Site plan, it's time to promote the remaining BDCs in the master account domain.

Upgrading Account Domain BDCs

You can operate for a while in mixed-mode, but it is not a suitable configuration for the long term. If the Windows 2000 PDC fails and you have other Windows 2000 domain controllers, you can use one of these DCs to seize the PDC role and become the PDC Role Master, but the classic BDCs might get confused and stop replicating. You could also promote a classic

BDC to PDC, but you won't be able to bring the Windows 2000 domain controller back online, and you must demote the remaining Windows 2000 domain controllers. Neither of these two alternatives is very appealing. You should complete the exodus from classic NT domain controllers to Windows 2000 domain controllers as quickly as possible.

As you deploy Windows 2000 to each BDC, it replicates the entire Directory database from some other Windows 2000 domain controller. The AD Installation Wizard does not use the local copy of the SAM and Security database in the BDC's Registry. If you have a big Directory that must be replicated over a slow line, or worse, a dial-up connection, it may take quite a while to complete the domain controller promotion. Plan on promoting remote domain controllers in the evening or on the weekend to avoid peak loads on the WAN. You can also configure a Windows 2000 domain controller at a central location and ship it to the remote site, but most companies don't have spare servers just lying around for this purpose.

When you're ready to upgrade and promote an account domain BDC, proceed as follows:

Procedure 9.4 **Upgrading and Promoting an Account Domain BDC**

1. Perform the NOS upgrade exactly as you did for the PDC. Insert the Windows 2000 Server CD and let Autorun start the process.

2. After the final restart, the Active Directory Installation Wizard starts automatically. Perform the DNS and time sync hygiene checks outlined in the PDC installation.

   At the `Active Directory Installation Wizard Welcome` window, click `Next`. The `Additional Domain Controller or Member Server` window appears.

3. Select `Make a domain controller`. You'll be prompted for administrator credentials in the domain. After a final confirmation, the server is joined to the domain as a member server and the classic BDC trust to the PDC is broken. If you decide later that you made a mistake, you must reinstall classic NT and configure the server to be a BDC.

4. Click `Next`. The `Network Credentials` window appears. Enter a name and password with administrator credentials in the domain.

5. Click `Next`. Give the path for the main Directory files and log files.

6. Click `Next`. Give the path for the `SYSVOL` directory. If you expect to have lots of profiles and login scripts and group policy objects, put this directory on a separate drive from the main Directory files. In a small network, you can get away with putting `SYSVOL` on the same drive as the Directory files.

7. Click `Next`. Check the summary to make sure you made all the right selections.

8. Click Next and watch the wizard go to work. If you are upgrading a BDC in a remote office and it appears that replication has swamped the WAN connection, you can click Replicate later. The wizard does a few chores then prompts you to restart so it can complete the replication. You can leave the system running until you can reduce the WAN traffic, then restart so that replication can finish. During this time, the domain controller is not available to handle authentication requests.

9. After replication has completed and the wizard reports a successful promotion, proceed to the next sections to verify operation.

Verifying Peer Active Directory Replication

When you promote the second and subsequent domain controllers in an existing Windows 2000 domain, the AD Installation Wizard calls upon the KCC to build a replication connection to another Windows 2000 domain controller. This connection is used both for the initial DIT replication and for ongoing replication of updates once the domain controller is in operation. The KCC also builds at least one other connection to fully integrate the domain controller into the replica ring. Watch for Event Log warnings from the KCC, such as *The Attempt To Establish A Replication Link failed with the following status....* This is your clue that something is wrong.

The usual cause for these failures, as you might expect, is our old friend DNS. If the KCC cannot locate the appropriate SRV records for other domain controllers in the same site, it cannot build connections to those domain controllers. The failure may have other causes, including hardware failures, network driver failures, incorrect site configuration, or lack of WAN connectivity, but don't look at those until you've verified that DNS is configured correctly.

After you've resolved the problem, you should see Event Log messages such as the one in Figure 9.15.

Figure 9.15 Event Log entry showing successful connections to a new domain controller.

You can verify that the domain controller has been fully inserted into the replica ring as follows:

Procedure 9.5 **Verifying Directory Replication Between Domain Controllers**

1. At the newly promoted domain controller, open the `Active Directory Sites and Services` snap-in.

2. Expand the tree to show the site for the domain controller and its NTDS Settings (see Figure 9.16.)

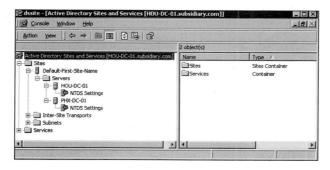

Figure 9.16 Active Directory Sites and Services snap-in showing new site and connections.

3. If you find that the server object representing the domain controller is not under the correct site, verify that the proper subnet has been assigned to the site. Refer to a site map like the one shown in Figure 9.15. Replication should work even if you have the wrong site configuration, but queries from client PCs might be directed out over the WAN instead of being kept locally with their own subnet. After you correct the IP problem, you can move the server object and its associated links to the correct site. See Chapter 11 for details.

4. Verify that at least one replication connection is present for the domain controller. The KCC will build additional connections, but this takes a while. Return in a couple of hours or wait overnight, then check the status.

5. A simple way to check replication is to change a property and see if the other domain controllers get the update. A convenient change is the description of the Connection object associated with the new domain controller. Right-click the Connection object (it has a tag that says <automatically generated>) and select PROPERTIES from the fly-out menu. This opens the Properties window for the connection.

6. At the Active Directory Service Connection tab, enter a new description. Click OK to save the change.

7. Right-click the connection again and select REPLICATE NOW from the fly-out menu.

8. Shift the focus of the snap-in to the domain controller at the other end of the connection by right-clicking the Active Directory Sites and Services icon and selecting CONNECT TO DOMAIN CONTROLLER from the fly-out menu. Choose the domain controller using the navigational window.

9. By the time you change the focus of the snap-in to the other domain controller, the update for the Connection description should have replicated. When you open the Properties window for the connection, you'll see the new description. It may take longer for replication to work if you are crossing a site connection. In that case, you'll get a message telling you that the replication will occur at the next opportunity.

10. If proper replication stubbornly continues to elude you, or if the domain controller refuses to authenticate users (indicating a failure at a more basic level), you might want to demote the domain controller and try again. You won't lose any Directory information in doing so. The other domain controllers have an identical copy. Local clients may be forced out onto the WAN to get their authentication and Directory lookups, so prepare them to expect slow performance for a while.

Assigning Global Catalog Servers

The AD Installation Wizard does not automatically make a new domain controller into a Global Catalog server. This is a good thing, not a bad thing, as I used to tell my kids when they still listened to me. By default, a Windows 2000 domain controller only holds a replica of the naming context for its own domain along with the Schema and Configuration naming contexts. If you configure the domain controller to be a Global Catalog server, it then holds a partial replica of every domain naming context in the entire forest. This is not an insignificant chore if you have a big network with hundreds of thousands of users in several domains. Consider your Global Catalog server placements carefully. When in doubt, install one. Users can experience logon errors and problems accessing shared resources via global group memberships if they cannot contact a Global Catalog server. Plan on putting a GC at each major location. Configure a domain controller to be a Global Catalog server as follows:

Procedure 9.6   Configuring a Domain Controller to Be a Global Catalog Server

1. Open the Active Directory Sites and Services snap-in.
2. Expand the tree to find the server that you want to make into a GC.
3. Right-click the NTDS Settings object and select PROPERTIES from the fly-out menu.
4. Select Global Catalog Server. You might also want to take this opportunity to fill in a description for the object.
5. Click OK to save the change. The new status takes effect immediately, but it might take a while for replication to finish. Verify that the domain controller now has GC status in one of the following ways.
6. Look in the Directory Services event log for an NTDS General entry, event 1119, indicating that the server is now a Global Catalog server.
7. Look in DNS under Root_domain | _msdcs | gc. At the top of gc, you'll see a series of host records (type A) with the name gc. This is a DNS shortcut that takes advantage of round-robin load sharing. Further down, under _sites, you'll see an entry for each site that has a Global Catalog server and the SRV record for that server under _tcp (see Figure 9.17.)

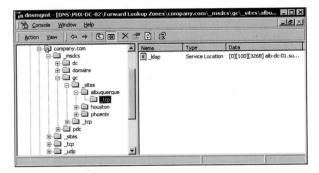

Figure 9.17   DNS Management snap-in showing SRV record for new
Global Catalog server.

8. Launch the ADSI Editor snap-in and point it at TCP port 3268 of the
   domain controller. If you get a response, it's a Global Catalog server.

9. Use the Replication Administration command line tool, REPADMIN,
   from the Resource Kit. The syntax is `repadmin /kcc <dsa>` where `<dsa>`
   is the fully qualified DNS name of the domain controller. For more
   information about this tool, see Chapter 11.

Upgrading Resource Domain

You've now finished the first stage of the migration, upgrading the account
domain while preserving the classic trust relationships to the resource
domains. Now you need to upgrade the resource domains and get them into
the Directory tree. Just like the account domains, you must start with the
PDC of the domain. It doesn't matter which domain you start with as long
as they are all children at the same level under the top domain. Do not
upgrade a domain that will not be a child or a peer of an existing domain
unless you intend it to be the root domain.

The NOS upgrade works exactly like the PDC upgrade in the account
domain, but the domain controller promotion is a bit different because you'll
be forming a child domain. Make sure your DNS namespace is correctly
configured with the child domain either configured as a new zone or a
domain in an existing zone. If it is a new zone, make sure the zone is set for
dynamic updates. And make sure the zone name matches the flat NetBIOS
name. For example, the classic NT resource domain called BRANCH that
will be a child of the Windows 2000 domain Company.com needs a DNS
zone named `Branch.Company.com` or a child domain of Branch in the
`Company.com` zone.

If you have a multi-tiered classic NT domain structure where classic resource domains also act as account domains for resource domains further downstream, you must upgrade the middle domains first. This maintains a contiguous namespace.

When you're ready to upgrade the PDC in the Resource domain, proceed as follows:

Procedure 9.7   **Upgrading and Promoting a Resource Domain PDC**

1. Upgrade the NOS using the Server CD. After the final restart, the Active Directory Installation Wizard starts automatically.

2. Perform the DNS and time sync hygiene checks outlined in the PDC promotion procedure.

3. Return to the AD Installation Wizard and click Next. The Create Tree or Child window appears.

4. Select the Create New Child option to incorporate the new domain into the existing Directory tree.

5. Click Next. The system thinks for a while, then the Network Credentials window appears.

6. Enter the name, password, and fully qualified domain name of the root domain. In the example, this would be Administrator, the administrator's password, and the domain name of Company.com.

7. Click Next. The Child Domain Installation window appears.

8. Enter the fully qualified DNS name of the root domain and the single name of the child. In our example, the root domain would be Company.com and the child domain would be Branch.

9. Click Next. The Database and Log Locations window appears. Enter the path to the database and log locations. As noted in the other promotions, you'll get better performance and fault tolerance by putting the log files on separate drives.

10. Click Next. The Shared System Volume window appears. Enter a path where you want the wizard to put the SYSVOL directory.

11. Click Next. The Windows NT 4.0 RAS Servers window appears. If you have a RAS box running classic NT, you must elect to "weaken" the permissions. Otherwise, leave the default radio button selected.

12. Click Next. The Directory Services Restore Mode Administrator Password window opens.

Use this window to enter a password for a special Administrator account to be placed in the local SAM of the domain controller. This account is used when booting to Directory Services Restore Mode, a special form of Safe Mode used to restore the AD information store.

13. Click Next through the final few informational windows. The promotion begins. Go grab a cup of coffee. When the wizard finishes, restart the machine and proceed to the "Verifying Transitive Trust Relationships" section.

Upgrading Additional Master Account Domains

At this point, you've completed the migration of an entire classic NT domain, including the account domain and all resource domains. Now you need to upgrade the remaining multiple-master account domain. you have two choices: You can put the domain under the first Windows 2000 domain as a child, or you can make it a separate Directory tree to form a forest. If you choose to make it a child domain, follow the same procedure as you did for upgrading a resource domain. The DNS domain name you select for the child domain must be contiguous with the existing namespace.

If you choose to form a forest, proceed with the steps in this section:

Procedure 9.8 **Creating a Forest of Trusted Domains**

1. Upgrade the NOS on the PDC in the second account domain. After the final restart, the DC AD Installation Wizard appears.

2. Perform the DNS and time sync hygiene checks outlined in the PDC promotion procedure.

3. Return to the AD Installation Wizard and click Next. The Create Tree or Child window appears.

4. Select Create new domain tree to start a new Directory tree that you will join into a forest.

5. Click Next. The Create or Join Forest window appears.

6. Select Place this new domain in an existing forest.

7. Click Next. The New Domain Tree window appears.

8. Enter the fully qualified DNS name of the new domain. In the example, the domain name is Subsidiary.com. The name is not case sensitive, and you do not need to include the trailing dot. If you enter the root domain name Company.com by mistake, you'll receive an error.

9. Click Next. The system issues a NetBIOS name registration broadcast and does a WINS check in the background to verify that the flat name does not exist elsewhere. If no domain challenges the registration, the Database and Log Locations window appears.

10. Enter the path to the database and log locations. As noted in the other promotions done so far, you'll get better performance and recoverability by putting the log files on a separate drive. Avoid putting any Directory files in the system partition.

11. Click Next. The Shared System Volume window appears. Enter a path where you want the wizard to put the SYSVOL directory.

12. Click Next. The Windows NT 4.0 RAS Servers window appears. If you have a RAS box running classic NT, you must elect to "weaken" the permissions.

13. Click Next. The Directory Services Restore Mode Administrator Password window opens. Use this window to enter a password for a special Administrator account to be placed in the local SAM of the domain controller. This account is used when booting to Directory Services Restore Mode, a special form of Safe Mode used to restore the AD information store.

14. Click Next through the final few informational windows. The promotion begins. Go grab another cup of coffee. When the wizard finishes, restart the machine and proceed to the verification checks in the next section.

Verifying Transitive Trust Relationships

Now that you have a Windows 2000 domain that has joined another Windows 2000 domain tree or forest, verify that users on both sides of the trust can access their accounts and make use of shared resources using the access rights that were granted prior to the upgrade.

Procedure 9.9   **Verifying Transitive Trust Accessibility**

1. First, open the AD Domains and Trusts console at the newly promoted domain controller. The console shows the domains in the forest and their hierarchy.

2. Right-click the new domain and select PROPERTIES from the fly-out menu. The Properties window opens. Select the Trusts tab. Figure 9.18 shows an example.

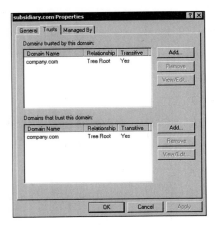

Figure 9.18   `Properties` window for `Subsidiary.com` domain showing Tree Root trust.

The classic two-way trust is now a transitive Kerberos trust of the type *Tree Root*. If you do not create a tree root trust during initial domain controller promotion, you cannot form one later.

3. Highlight the trusted domain and click `Edit`. The `Properties` window appears. The `General` tab shows the status of the trust. Figure 9.19 shows an example. The `SPN Suffixes` tab is useful only when you have an External Trust (similar to a classic NT trust) in which the principals do not have the same name as their DNS name. The SPN Suffix is basically an alias that permits finding the domain controller in the externally trusted domain.

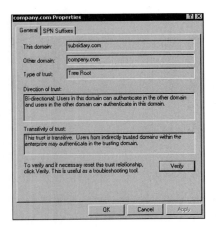

Figure 9.19   `Properties` window for tree root trust showing the direction and transitive nature of the trust.

4. Click Verify. You might be prompted for credentials, depending on the direction of the trust. The Verify option tests that the passwords for the trust are synched and the RPC connection is in place. If it finds an error, the system will take corrective action after asking for permission. This may include resetting the trust passwords. Don't do this until you verify that you have a good network connection between the domain controllers. A quick ping is sufficient to verify connection. If the passwords go out of kilter and can't be realigned, you will lose the trust.

5. You should also verify that users in trusting domain can still access resources. The pick list of domains at the Winlogon window should be the same as in the classic NT configuration. The user should be able to log a trusted domain using an account in that domain.

6. Once logged on, verify that the user has retained the same access rights to directories, Registry keys, and so forth. If the account has admin rights, verify that it can see all the members of local groups that have global groups from the account domain as members. If an ACL shows a bare SID, you have communication problems to the Global Catalog server. This will prevent you from logging on as a standard user.

When these checks show that you have full functionality in the resource domain, promote the remaining domain controllers using the same procedure as you used in the account domain. At this point, if you are building a tree or forest of trusted domains, you're finished. If you want a single domain, you need to move user and group accounts to the root domain then transfer your member servers and workstations to the root domain. Proceed to the next sections.

Shifting to Native Mode

A mixed-mode Windows 2000 network supports classic domain controllers by providing a single RID master, a single PDC, and classic NT group restrictions. After you shift to native mode, you get full multiple-master replication, a floating RID pool, nested global groups, fully transitive trusts, transitive dial-up authentication, and Directory-enabled DNS.

If none of these features particularly excite you, you still may want to shift to native mode to get access to Universal groups. If you have multiple domains, you must use Universal groups to give access to users from domains in the forest that are not directly trusted. Universal groups are not available in mixed-mode domains. See Chapter 15, "Managing Shared Resources," for more details about the workings of Universal groups and the Global Catalog.

First and foremost, before you shift the domain to native mode, you must complete the Windows 2000 domain controller upgrades. After you switch to native mode, all classic NT replication ceases. You can continue to introduce classic NT servers into the native mode domain as member servers—this includes UNIX SAMBA servers—but not classic NT domain controllers. Run through your checklist of domain controllers again and again, like Santa Claus checking for bad little children. Did you forget that backup domain controller in Jakarta? Johannesburg? Jersey City? Are you sure you're done?

What about your resource domains? Theoretically, you can shift the root domain to native mode while its trusting domains are still in mixed mode, but practically speaking, you will encounter difficulties. The classic domain controllers in the trusting domains will not recognize groups or users from a Native Mode domain, so you will not be able to access security principals from the trusted domain. All in all, it's best to wait until everyone is wearing their swim trunks before opening the gate to the pool.

When you shift a domain to Native Mode, you must restart each domain controller. You say you have 200 domain controllers scattered all over the world? There's no need to host a global restart festival. The domain continues to operate normally while the stragglers restart their machines. Until everyone completes this chore, do not implement any Native Mode features. When you're sure that you've made all preparations, shift the domain to native mode as follows:

Procedure 9.10   **Shifting a Domain to Native Mode**

1. Open the Active Directory Domains and Trusts snap-in.

2. Focus the snap-in on the root domain if it is not already there. Do this by right-clicking the top of the tree and selecting SELECT DOMAIN from the fly-out menu.

3. Right-click the domain object and select PROPERTIES from the fly-out menu. The Properties window opens for the domain (see Figure 9.20.)

Figure 9.20   Properties window for a Windows 2000 domain showing the current Mixed Mode state.

4. Click Change Mode. You'll receive a warning that this is a non-reversible operation. After you make the change, there is no turning back. The change won't take effect until you click OK in the next step. Acknowledge the warning.

5. Click OK to save the change. An informational message appears notifying that this domain controller and every other domain controller in the domain must be restarted after the Domain | Properties | General tab shows Native Mode.

6. Acknowledge the warning. The window closes but the system does not restart automatically. Restart it manually.

Delayed Effects of Native Mode Shift

You may notice, if you poke around the AD Users and Computers console before downing the server, that you are able to exercise a few native mode features before restarting. For example, you can create Universal groups and access security principals from other native mode domains. There are more fundamental changes that are not enabled until you restart. Be sure to let your colleagues in outlying offices know that they must still restart their servers.

7. After restarting, verify that you have native mode functionality by creating a Universal group, nesting a Global group in it, and using it as a security principal on a Directory object. If the native mode shift has not taken effect, you'll get an Active Directory internal error. Do this with each domain controller as you restart it.

8. Repeat the native mode shifts in each child domain and peer domain in the forest.

After you've made the shift to native mode and propagated it to all domains in the forest, you can say that the migration to Windows 2000 domains is officially FINISHED! Apply for a pay raise or a pension payment, depending on your emotional state.

Special Domain Operations

Even after you have established your domain configuration, the Directory contents will change constantly. If you have multiple domains, some of those changes will involve jockeying objects between domains. For example, you may have defined separate domains for different offices. If a user gets transferred between offices, his or her user object must be moved to a new domain.

You also face the prospect of interdomain object moves if you decide that you want to consolidate or divide domains. There are no slick "prune and graft" tools in the initial release of Windows 2000. These kinds of operations must be done manually from the command line using tools from the Windows 2000 Resource Kit.

The tool for moving users, groups, and computers from one domain to another is Movetree. The tool for changing the domain affiliation of member servers and workstations is Netdom. Neither of these tools is what you'd call "administrator friendly." Let's take a look at their operation and syntax before putting them into action.

Using Movetree to Transfer User and Group Accounts

Recall that a domain forms a separate naming context in the Directory. If you are accustomed to NetWare and NDS, think of naming contexts as partitions. When you move an object from one container to another within the same naming context, the change is relatively trivial. Only the distinguished name changes along with a few pointers in the Directory database. Refer to Figure 9.21, for example. If a user account were moved from the Accounting OU to the Sales OU in the Branch.Company.com domain, the DN of the user object would change from ou=Accounting,dc=Branch,dc=Company,dc=com to ou=,Sales,dc=Branch,dc=Company,dc=com but the user's SID, group memberships, and password would be unaffected.

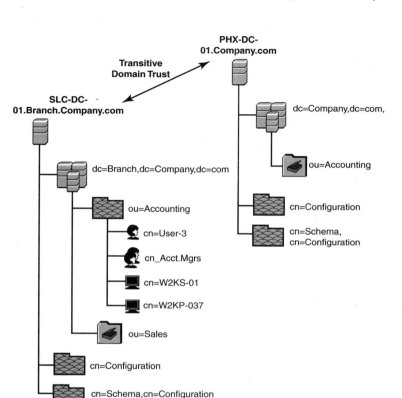

Figure 9.21 Two-domain tree showing naming
contexts as example for Movetree operation.

On the other hand, when you move an object between domains, you do
more than simply change the distinguished name; you change the placement
of the object within the Directory database itself by changing its naming
context. In essence, the system must build an entirely new object in the
destination–naming context and delete the object from the source–naming
context. This new object must have the same SID or the user will lose all
access rights. The same is true for group objects and computer objects. Not
only that, the operation must be done in a fail-safe manner so that if something goes wrong, the object is not lost or damaged or duplicated.

Here is how Movetree meets these criteria. When you use Movetree, you
specify enough information so it can establish communications between
domains, authenticate the administrator doing the move, and verify that the
operation can proceed without error. There are examples in the
"Consolidating Domains" section later in this chapter that show how to

move entire OUs and their contents. For now, let's move just one object. The following example shows how to move a user called `User-3` from the Accounting OU in the `Branch.Company.com` domain to the Accounting OU in the `Company.com` domain. Here are the terms you'll need to specify for Movetree:

- **Source DSA.** This is the fully qualified DNS name of a domain controller that holds a replica of the naming context that contain objects you want to move. In other words, it is a domain controller in the child or peer domain. The source DSA in the example is `SLC-DC-01.Branch.Company.com`.

- **Destination DSA.** This is the fully qualified DNS name of a domain controller that holds a replica of the naming context where you want to move the objects. In other words, it is a domain controller in the parent or root domain. The destination DSA in the example is `PHX-DC-01.Company.com`.

- **Source DN.** This is the distinguished name of the object or container that you're going to move to the new domain. The source DN in the example is `cn=User-3,ou=Accounting,dc=Branch,dc=Company,dc=com`.

- **Destination DN.** This is the distinguished name of the object or container that will become the new object in the new domain. Movetree works a little differently than a file move. You must always specify the name of the target object. If you are moving a container and the objects under it, you only need to specify the container name. The destination DN in the example is `cn=User-3,ou=Accounting,dc=Company,dc=com`.

- **User account and password.** This is an account with administrative privileges in both domains. If you are in one domain and you're using an account from the target domain, separate the domain and the account name with a backslash. For example, `/u company\administrator /p whumpa3`. If you don't want to put your password in clear text, you can leave it out of the initial command. You'll be prompted for a password when Movetree begins processing the command line arguments.

This makes for a long command line. The following puts the elements on several lines for clarity. The actual command would be a single line.

```
movetree /check
/s slc-dc-01.branch.company.com
/d phx-dc-01.company.com
/sdn cn=User-3,ou=Accounting,dc=Branch,dc=Company,dc=com
/ddn cn=User-3,ou=Accounting, ,dc=Company,dc=com
/u company\administrator
/p whumpa3
```

If the command line is formatted correctly and all the information is correct, the check run will display a listing similar to the following:

```
ReturnCode: 0x0
The operation completed successfully.
MoveTree established connections to source and destination servers
Result: 0x0
The operation completed successfully.
MoveTree check destination RDN conflict for object: cn=userone,ou=stuff,dc=subsidiary,dc=com
MOVETREE PRE-CHECK FINISHED.
MOVETREE IS READY TO START THE MOVE OPERATION.
```

If you get an error, it will be displayed as an error code above the operation. The check does not perform a comprehensive verification of the process, though, so you won't really know if the move will be successful until you actually do it. To actually perform the move, use the /start switch instead of the /check switch. The utility performs the premove checks again then performs the move:

```
ReturnCode: 0x0
The operation completed successfully.
MoveTree cross domain move object cn=user one,ou=stuff,dc=subsidiary,dc=com to container
cn=users,dc=company,dc=com
ReturnCode: 0x0
The operation completed successfully.
MoveTree deleted entry (null)
ReturnCode: 0x0
The operation completed successfully.
MoveTree deleted entry (null)
MOVETREE FINISHED SUCCESSFULLY.
```

The two deleted entries are temporary containers used by Movetree to hold objects while they are in transition. The temporary containers are stored in the LostandFound container. If the transfer hangs, and it sometimes does, you can kill the Movetree process using Task Manager and then move the objects out of the LostandFound container to a local OU and begin the transfer again. Figure 9.22 shows the AD Users and Groups container (Advanced View) with the temporary holding containers under LostandFound.

Movetree works the same way when moving OUs and groups as it does with users. It will move computer objects too, but it does not update the local Registry at the member computers. This is done with the Netdom utility. Do not use Movetree to migrate computer accounts to new domains.

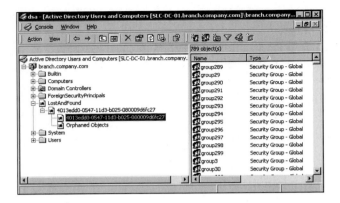

Figure 9.22 Temporary container built by
Movetree in the LostandFound container.

Using Netdom to Transfer Computer Accounts

Member computers in a domain (this includes member servers) maintain a
Computer account in the Directory exactly like that of a user. In fact, the
Computer object is derived from the User object in the schema and only has
a few attributes that are different. You can move the computer object to a
new domain manually by disjoining the computer from its current domain
then joining it to the new domain, but who wants to visit hundreds of desktops just to change a domain name? There's a utility that does this grunt
work. It's called Netdom.

Netdom has more switches and special functions than Times Square has
pickpockets. You can use it to do quite a few tricks with domain trust relationships and Kerberos. This section focuses on moving member computers
between domains. Here are the chores Netdom takes care of when moving
computer accounts:

- It communicates with the member workstation or server to make the
  necessary Registry changes to point at a new host domain.

- It builds an account in the new host domain and deletes the account from
  the old host domain.

- It reboots the member computer so the changes will take effect.

- It retains the computer's SID so that no access permissions are lost.

Here is the syntax for executing Netdom and a list of the required switches:

```
netdom machine_name /domain /ud /pd /uo /po /ou /verbose /reboot
```

- **domain.** Give the fully qualified DNS name of the destination domain. For example, /domain:Company.com. The flat NetBIOS name will work if you still run NetBIOS support and have a WINS server operational.

- **ud.** Enter an administrative account in the destination domain. If you are logged onto a different domain, preface the user name with the flat NetBIOS name of the destination domain followed by a backslash. For example, ud:company\administrator.

- **pd.** Enter the password of the account specified by /ud. You can enter * if you don't want to type the password on the screen or in a batch file. Example: /pd:whamma3 or /pd:*.

- **uo.** Enter an administrative account in the source domain or for the local machine. Preface the name with the flat NetBIOS name of the source domain if you are logged on from a different domain. Example: uo:branch\administrator.

- **po.** Enter the password of the account specified by /uo. Use * if you wish to type the password in later.

- **server.** Enter the fully qualified DNS name of a specific domain controller in the destination domain. This is not required unless you want to make sure you use a local DC. Example: /server:phx-dc-01.company.com.

- **ou.** Enter the distinguished name of the OU where you want the computer account. If you leave this switch out, the account is created in the Computer container. Example: ou=Accounting,dc=Company,dc=com.

- **verbose.** Puts more information on the tube. It's a good idea to use this switch in case something goes wrong.

- **reboot.** The change to the local Registry at the target workstations does not take effect until the computers restart. This switch forces that restart. This option is not recommended if you are running the batch file in the middle of the workday, of course, but you can include a parameter to delay restart for a given number of minutes. Example, /reboot:30.

Here's a Netdom command that moves a member computer from the Branch.Company.com domain to the Company.com domain. (The actual command would be on a single line):

```
netdom move alb-w2kp-01.branch.company.com
/domain:company.com
/ud:company\administrator
```

```
/pd:*
/uo:branch\administrator
/po:*
/verbose /reboot
```

After you get the hang of Netdom, you can build batch files that can move large numbers of workstations to a different domain. The workstations and servers have to be online when you issue the command, so you have to communicate to your users not to turn their machines off. Somebody is sure to forget, so you might have to schedule the work over two or three nights.

With Movetree and Netdom batch files firmly in hand, you're ready for wholesale domain changes. Proceed to the next section to see what else is involved.

Consolidating Domains

Figure 9.23 shows sketches of a three-domain forest that needs to be consolidated into a single Windows 2000 domain. The procedure steps use parent-child terminology but you use the same steps when collapsing a peer domain into another domain in a forest. The sequence of operations is as follows:

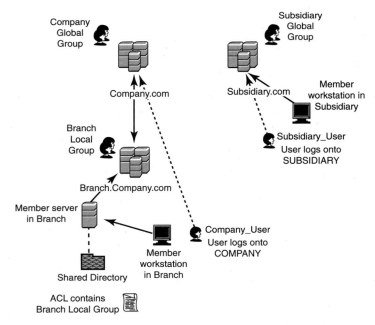

Figure 9.23   Directory structure prior to consolidation.

Procedure 9.11   **Overview of Domain Consolidation**

1. Define OUs you will need in the parent domain for accounts and groups from the child domain. Do not create them. The utilities do that automatically.

2. Move user and computer objects out of the Users container into a temporary OU in the child domain. This avoids duplicate account errors that will keep Movetree from working.

3. Use Movetree to migrate users and groups to the parent domain while retaining all access rights.

4. Use Netdom to migrate computer accounts for servers and workstations to the parent domain and modify local Registry settings.

5. Demote domain controllers in the child domain to eliminate old domain.

The example consolidates users, groups, and computers from the Branch.Company.com child domain and the Subsidiary.com peer domain in the root Company.com domain. Figure 9.24 shows a sketch of the Directory structure after the consolidation is complete. Here are the prerequisite steps:

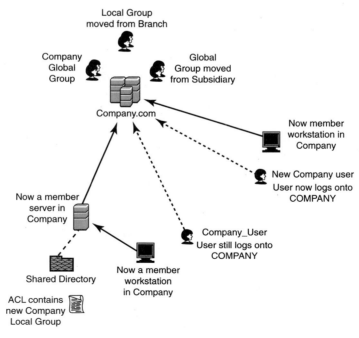

Figure 9.24   Directory structure following domain consolidation.

Procedure 9.12 **Domain Consolidation Prerequisite Actions**

1. Shift the parent domain to Native Mode. This is required to get the non-sequential RID support necessary to keep the same SID associated with the moved accounts. *Shifting to Native Mode is a non-reversible action that completely disables classic NT replication and renders classic BDCs inoperative.*

2. Install the Windows 2000 Resource Kit on at least one domain controller in either the child or the parent domain. This installs the Movetree and Netdom utilities.

3. Create or configure an administrative account with privileges in all domains.

Define OUs in the Trusted Domain

When consolidating domains, it's likely that there are management boundaries that you want to retain. For example, the old domain might have been created by a department or a local office where the administrators still want to control user accounts, printers, and assign ACL rights. To get this same management granularity in a single domain, you'll need to define Organizational Units in the consolidated Directory structure. Figure 9.25 shows what these OUs might look like.

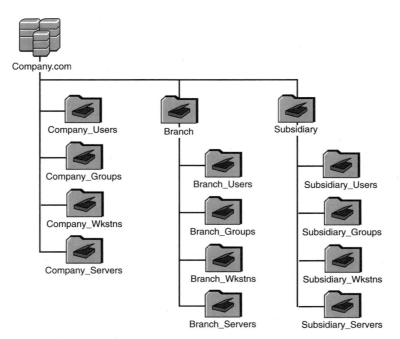

Figure 9.25 Organizational Units for consolidated domain.

Create the OUs using the AD Users and Groups console. You do not need to make any special configurations to accommodate the objects that you will move into them, but remember that the users might already have group policies in their home domains. You will need to create policies that either mimic or replace their existing policies.

Create Temporary OUs in the Child Domain

One of the shortcomings of Movetree is that it takes an "all or nothing" approach to moving objects under a container. If you try to move the contents of the Users container to another domain, for example, you'll encounter many instances of duplicate accounts and a duplicate object stops Movetree in its tracks. If you use the default Users container to store user and group accounts, it's best to create a temporary OU in that domain and move the accounts to the temporary OU. Otherwise, you'll be forced to move user and group objects one at a time. This is not a pleasant way to spend the sunshine of your youth.

I recommend creating an OU called XFER just under the Domain-DNS object that defines the top of the child domain. Move the accounts and groups out of the Users container into this one using the MOVE command from the console menu or right-click the selected objects and select MOVE from the fly-out menu.

This does not apply to OUs you've already built for your users unless you have an OU by the same name in the destination domain. If so, you can transfer the objects to an OU of a different name to keep Movetree happy then move the user objects around once they're in the new domain. For example, if you have Accounting OUs in each domain, tell Movetree to use a name of ACCT_TEMP to move the objects. After they have been transferred to the new domain, move them into the Accounting container.

Move User and Group Accounts to the Trusted Domain

Moving user and group accounts is done with Movetree. It's probably easiest to use Movetree from the console of a domain controller, but there's no reason why you can't do the work from a member workstation so long as you have good network connectivity to the domain controllers. Keep the syntax straight if you are logged into a domain different than the domains you're working with.

Procedure 9.13 **Moving User and Group Accounts Between Domains**

1. Log on using an account that has admin rights in both domains. You may want to create a temporary account and put it in the Enterprise Admins group. I do not recommend using Enterprise Admins on a permanent basis, because the group has too many privileges associated with it. Delete the temporary group account after the migration is finished, or at least take it out of the Enterprise Admins group. (Only the cynical among you are sneering that the account will never be deleted or moved.)

2. Create the XFER container and move the group and user accounts out of the Users container.

3. At this point, all user and group accounts in the Branch domain are in three OUs: Accounting, Sales, and XFER. Each of these OUs can now be moved to the parent domain, Company.com. Because Company.com already has an Accounting OU, you will need to specify a temporary name with Movetree. This is shown in the next step.

4. Open a command session. Here is the Movetree syntax for moving the Accounting OU to its temporary OU in Company.com. (Each switch is on a separate line for clarity. Use one line to issue the command.)

```
movetree /start
/s slc-dc-01.branch.company.com
/d phx-dc-01.company.com
/sdn ou=Accounting,dc=Branch,dc=Company,dc=Com
/ddn ou=Acct-Temp,dc=Company,dc=com
/u company\adminstrator
/p whumpa3
```

5. After Movetree reports successful completion, verify that the operation was a success using the Active Directory Users and Groups snap-in. Movetree will often mislead you and give a successful result when absolutely nothing happened. If this occurs, you more than likely have a syntax error somewhere. If you get an error code on the screen, the messages are usually very clear as to the problem.

Movetree Execution Times

In a lab environment using 400Mhz Pentium II servers on a 10Mbps network, it took Movetree approximately ten minutes to transfer 4000 accounts to their new container in the parent domain.

6. Verify that users can now log on using the new domain name from the pick list in Winlogon.

7. Verify that the access rights lists on your NTFS files show the new names. This is the function of the Infrastructure Master, so it might take a while for folks at the wrong end of a slow link to show the changes. Until then, the bare SIDs may appear on the access lists.

8. Now move the other two OUs. After all the users and groups have been moved and you've verified operations, it's time to move the computer objects.

Move Computer Accounts to the Trusted Domain

The syntax and methods for moving computer accounts with Netdom is the same whether you move one or a thousand. You can create a batch file that loops through a comma-delimited list of computer accounts and moves them to the new domain. The easiest way to obtain that comma-delimited file is to use `Csvde`, an LDAP utility included in Windows 2000 that dumps the contents of the Directory to a comma-delimited file. The syntax is:

```
csvde -d <dn of container> -f <output_file_name>
```

To dump the contents of the Computer container in the Company.com domain, the entry would be:

```
csvde -d "cn=computers,dc=company,dc=com" -f complist.ldf
```

After you have the file, load it into a database program or spreadsheet and delete all but the computer names then use those to write your batch script for Netdom.

Demote Domain Controllers in Trusting Domain

You cannot move Domain Controller objects to the new domain as you did for member servers and workstations. You must demote the domain controllers, move them to the new domain, and then promote them as peer domain controllers in the parent domain.

When you demote the last domain controller in a domain, you lose all accounts in the domain. I'll say this again with emphasis. When you demote the last domain controller, *you lose every single solitary user and computer and group account that you've ever created since the domain was first installed*. If you do this by mistake, you must recover the Directory from tape. The loss isn't catastrophic, but you'll feel foolish.

Another thing to watch out for when demoting a domain controller is to not lose your last Global Catalog server. The system warns you if you demote a GC, but it's easy to ignore a warning. If you remove the last GC, users will not be able to log on. You can log on as Administrator and correct the problem by configuring a domain controller as a GC server, but there's bound to be confusion for a while. After you've made sure at least one other domain controller configured as a GC is on the wire, proceed as follows:

Procedure 9.14 Demoting a Domain Controller

1. At the console of the domain controller, log on with an account that has administrator rights in the domain.

2. From the Run window, launch DCPROMO. The Active Directory Installation Wizard opens.

3. The wizard notifies you that this server is already a domain controller and offers to demote it.

   The Wizard looks for a functioning Directory Service in memory. If you boot to Safe Mode or Directory Service Repair mode, the Directory Service does not start, so if you run DCPROMO, you would end up reinstalling the Directory. Don't do this. You will corrupt your existing Directory.

4. Click Next. The Remove Active Directory window appears.

   Leave This server is the last domain controller in the domain unchecked. This ensures that the domain controller will become a member server after it is demoted.

5. If this is the last domain controller in the domain, and you've made arrangements to preserve your user accounts and group accounts and you're sure you won't lock yourself out of a directory structure by losing the access control rights, select This server is the last domain controller in the domain. The wizard will prompt you for credentials in the parent domain or the root domain in the forest so it can break the trust. It will also prompt you for local Administrator credentials so it can rebuild the local SAM.

6. Click Next. The Summary window appears. Review it to make sure you got everything right.

7. Click Next to carry out the demotion.

8. During the demotion, the wizard transfers any FSMO roles held by this server to other owners. You may want to verify the identify of the new FSMO. Refer to Chapter 8 for details about FSMOs and Role Masters.

9. The wizard also does housekeeping with DNS and the Directory metadata that points at trust relationships. It's fairly easy to verify that the DNS records have been whisked away cleanly. To verify that the trust has been broken cleanly, open the AD Domains and Trusts console, open the Properties window for the domain, and go to the Trusts tab. If the trust remains, you will need to remove it manually and clean up the metadata.

10. When the server restarts, it will be a member server of the existing domain or, if it were the last domain controller in the domain, a stand-alone server in a workgroup of the same name as the now-defunct domain.

Dividing Domains

The sequence of events for splitting an existing domain into two domains is as follows:

- Create a new DNS domain. This does not necessarily have to be a separate zone, but it's likely that you'll want to delegate DNS management along with Windows 2000 management.

- Either demote an existing Window 2000 domain controller in the domain or promote a server to a domain controller in the new domain. Establish a trust during the promotion.

- Configure at least one more domain controller for the new domain to get fault tolerance.

- Create OUs in the new domain for the accounts and groups you're going to move from the parent or peer domain.

- Use Movetree to migrate user and group accounts to the new domain.

- Use Netdom to migrate computer accounts to the new domain.

- Verify access to resources in the new domain.

Adding New Domains to a Tree or Forest

You may want to add additional domains into a tree or a forest after the initial deployment of Windows 2000. This is easily done if the Windows 2000 domain you want to add does not already exist. For example, let's say Company, Inc., buys another company, call it Affiliate, Inc. If the new company has not yet migrated to Windows 2000, you can create a new Windows 2000 domain that is either a child of the existing domain, call it `Affiliate.Company.com`, or a peer domain called `Affiliate.com` joined to the `Company.com` forest.

If, on the other hand, the `Affiliate.com` domain already exists, you have a lot of work ahead of you. In the initial release of Windows 2000, you cannot form Tree Root trusts or Domain Trusts between existing Windows 2000 domains. You are forced to demote every Windows 2000 domain controller in the `Affiliate.com` domain then rebuild the domain from scratch with the appropriate trust relationship. If you do decide to do this, you probably will not want to retype hundreds of user and group names. See Chapter 7 for tips on using LDIFDE to dump user lists into a form that you can import back into the new domain.

If rebuilding domains seems like too much work just to get access to a few files from another domain, there is a partial alternative. You can build an External Trust between the two domains. This works like a classic NT trust relationship. Users from Affiliate.com could be placed on access control lists for resources in Company.com, and vice versa, so they could share files and work processes. The trust is not transitive, though, so if you have multiple domains under Company.com, users from Affiliate could not be added to access lists in the child domains. It's probably only a matter of time before an enterprising third party develops a tool for merging two domains. Who knows, it might even be Microsoft. Until then, you can use the External Trust as a bridge.

To add a new domain to a tree or forest, install Windows 2000 on a server, then promote it using Dcpromo. The steps from that point on are the same as those following an upgrade, so refer to the section in this chapter that parallels what you want to accomplish. For example, if you want to add a child domain, refer to the "Upgrading Resource Domains" section. If you want to add a peer domain to a forest, refer to the "Upgrading Additional Master Account Domains" section.

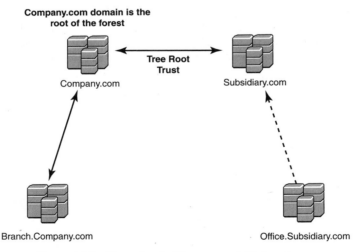

Figure 9.26 Example of adding a new child domain to a tree that is not the root of the forest.

If you want to add a new child domain to a domain tree that is not the root of a forest, you'll have to make one small change to your procedure. Refer Figure 9.26 for an example. The `Company.com` domain is the root of the forest that includes `Subsidiary.com`. This means any change to the domain structure of the forest can only be done using an account that has administrative privileges in the `Company.com` domain. During the domain controller promotion, you'll be prompted for credentials of an account that has the privilege of adding new domains. Instead of specifying an administrative account in `Subsidiary.com`, you'll need to specify an administrative account in the `Company.com` domain.

From that point forward, the procedure for completing the promotion is the same. The new domain will be added to the list of CrossRef objects in the `cn=Partitions,cn=Configuration,dc=Company,dc=com` container.

Unsupported Domain Operations

There are several operations involving domains that are either not supported at all or require a great deal of work to accomplish. They are:

- **Renaming Domains.** There is no utility in Windows 2000 or the Resource Kit for renaming a domain. The Netdom utility only works with classic NT domains. You must demote all domain controllers then rebuild the domain from scratch using a new name.

- **Breaking trusts.** In the initial release of Windows 2000, you cannot break a Domain Trust or a Tree Root trust to form an independent domain. If you want to separate domains, you must demote all domain controllers in the child domain or the peer domain then rebuild the domain from scratch as an independent domain.

- **Renaming Domain Controllers.** There is no utility in Windows 2000 or the Resource Kit to rename a domain controller. You must first demote it to a standard server, rename it, and then promote it back to a domain controller.

- **Moving Domain Controllers Between Domains.** There is no utility in Windows 2000 or the Resource Kit to move a domain controller between domains. You must demote it to a standard server, join it to the new domain, and then promote it to a domain controller in the new domain.

Introduction to Sites and Site Replication

Chapter 11 covers Directory replication and replication topologies in detail. The purpose of previewing this topic now is to ensure that your domain design does not include presumptions about replication that might not be justified.

In classic NT, only the Primary Domain Controller has read-write access to the security databases. All changes to users, groups, computers, and trusts go across the network to the PDC and then are replicated from the PDC out to the BDCs. When an administrator in a remote site opens User Manager for Domains, the information on the screen comes from the PDC, even if there is a BDC within arm's reach. In Windows 2000, all domain controllers are peers. One domain controller is designated as a PDC Master and it replicates to the classic BDCs. Because each Windows 2000 domain controller is capable of writing to the Directory, the replication process must propagate changes from all domain controllers to all domain controllers. This is called *multiple master replication*.

Multiple master replication is a complicated affair. As the Directory grows larger, the number of updates that must be replicated increases. As the network itself gets larger, there is the need for more domain controllers and they make additional replication demands. Replicating Directory updates happens quickly at LAN speeds, even for a very large Directory, but replication of a large information store can easily swamp a slow WAN connection. The replication topology defines areas of high-speed interconnections as Sites. Refer to Figure 9.27. Replication between Sites is performed at longer intervals with special configurations for compression and notification.

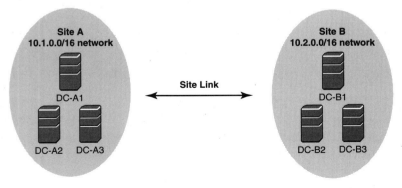

Figure 9.27   Sketch of domain controllers for two sites
showing site link for intersite replication.

Sites and domains have no relation to each other. A site can have many domains. A domain can be stretched across many sites. This can be a little confusing if you're accustomed to systems like Novell Directory Services or Netscape Directory Services where the partition boundaries also serve as replication boundaries.

Site boundaries in Windows 2000 are defined by IP subnets. You can have more than one IP network in a site, but each site must be on a different IP network or subnet. This permits sites to perform a second function in addition to controlling replication. Client computers use sites to find their local domain controllers. They do this by searching for SRV records stored in DNS that reference the site or sites associated with a particular IP network. The SRV records contain the names and port numbers of the domain controllers in that site. For example, clients in the Salt_Lake site of the `Branch.Region.Company.com` domain query DNS for SRV records in `_ldap._tcp.branch._sites.branch.region.company.com`. These SRV records point the way towards the domain controllers in that site.

The replication system has a special service called a *Knowledge Consistency Checker* (KCC) whose job it is to weave domain controllers into a replication topology where no server is more than three hops away from any other server. The KCC uses parameters in the Site Link object to determine how often to replicate between any two domain controllers, but the number of connections between domain controllers in different sites is not related to the number of site links. Think of a Site Link as a multiplexed connection that can carry many communication channels. Figure 9.28 shows the connections between domain controllers based on the two-site diagram in Figure 9.27.

One of the final domain design checks is to define replication boundaries based on sites. These boundaries should be fairly simple to determine. If you have a WAN map, roll it out and begin making marks. Every LAN is a candidate for a site and every WAN connection is a candidate for a site boundary. If you have multiple WAN connections to a single site, you can define several site links with different costs so that the KCC can make additional connections for fault tolerance.

If you have WAN connections that are T-1 speeds or greater, you'll have to estimate whether your replication traffic, combined with all the other traffic on the wire, will be within your bandwidth tolerance. Put an SNMP sniffer on the WAN ports and look at traffic patterns. I wish I could tell you how much traffic to expect for a given number of Directory objects, but that varies too much by usage. A university with a user population that logs on and off continually throughout the day will generate more replication traffic than a large office where everyone comes in at 7:00 and turns on their PC.

If you use high-traffic items like certificates, RADIUS, and Smart Cards, you'll generate more traffic than with standard Kerberos. If you feel that a fat WAN pipe is already heavily subscribed, you should define a site boundary. Refer to Chapter 11 for more information about how to configure sites, site links, and monitor replication.

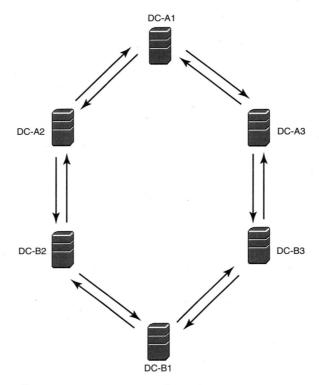

Figure 9.28   Domain controller replication connections for the two-site diagram shown in Figure 9.27.

Moving Forward

At this point, you have a full compliment of Windows 2000 domains but no user accounts. The next chapter covers Directory security and how to manage users and groups after you give them access to the domain.

10

Managing Active Directory Security

BIG PROJECTS LIKE WINDOWS 2000 DEPLOYMENT GENERALLY go through several stages that more or less follow a musical theme. First comes the "Itsy-Bitsy Spider" stage where lots of good ideas rise up and get washed away. Then comes the Benny Goodman stage where everyone starts to get in the swing of things. We have now arrived at the Jerry Lee Lewis stage where there's a whole lot of shakin' going on. During this stage, we need to come to terms with the security challenges in the Active Directory so that we can prepare for the final, Led Zeppelin stage where we climb our "Stairway to Heaven" and actually begin operating the network. (If we don't do things right, we go to the Grateful Dead stage in the next chapter.)

The information in this chapter covers the following topics:

- Introduction to access control rights and an overview of Directory security
- Delegating management rights and controlling rights inheritance
- Creating and managing user and group objects
- Using groups to manage Directory objects
- Using the Secondary Logon Service and the Runas command

Overview of Directory Security

Any strategy for managing the Directory must be based on a viable security framework. Before looking at the details of user and group management, it's a good idea to get familiar with Windows 2000 security as it applies to Directory objects. If you are an experienced NT administrator, you can skip most of this section. Windows 2000 uses the same object-based security mechanism as classic NT. You should, however, read the sections on delegation and managing groups because Windows 2000 has a few new features in these areas.

Security Principals

A security principal is someone or something that is permitted to access a Windows 2000 security object. Security objects include Directory objects, NTFS files and directories, and Registry keys. Security principals include users, groups, and computers. Security principals are distinguished from other objects because they have a *security ID* (SID) that uniquely identifies them to the security subsystem.

NDS OU Compared to AD OU

NetWare administrators should take note that Windows 2000 OUs cannot be used as security principals. An OU has no SID. When it comes to Windows 2000 security, an OU is a bridesmaid, never a bride.

Windows 2000 has two types of groups, only one of which is a security principal. These are *security groups*. The other type is the *distribution group*, a new addition in Windows 2000. Used in conjunction with group policies, a distribution group determines which users or computers get a particular software package.

Computers are also security principals. Administrators rarely assign rights to computers, but the system uses computer accounts extensively. A member computer has an account in the Directory that is assigned a random password when it is created. The password is automatically updated every 28 days via secure communication between the member computer and a domain controller. The computer account is authenticated using Kerberos.

The computer account is part of a miniature trust relationship formed between a member computer and the domain. The system uses this trust relationship to build *Remote Procedure Call* (RPC) connections that handle user authentications and other secure transactions.

Security Descriptors and Access Control Lists

Every security object in Windows 2000 has a special data structure within it called a *security descriptor* that identifies the security principals who can access the object and defines what they can do after they've gained access. Figure 10.1 shows a block diagram of a security descriptor.

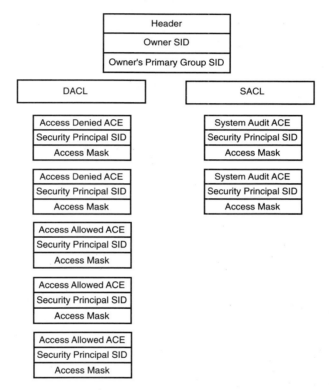

Figure 10.1   Block diagram of security descriptor showing ACE entries, DACL, and SACL tables.

A security descriptor has six components:

- **Header.** This describes the contents of the security description. The header also has a control structure that defines whether the object can inherit rights from its parent.

- **Owner's SID.** All Windows 2000 security objects have an owner. Except for administrators, the owner's SID will be the SID of the user who creates the object. Objects created by members of the Administrators group are assigned an owner of Administrator.

- **Primary group SID for the owner.** This is not used for Directory objects, but is applicable to NTFS objects. See Chapter 13, "Managing File Systems," for more information.
- **Discretionary access control list (DACL).** An access control list identifies security principals who have either been granted access or denied access. The "discretionary" in DACL means that owners and administrators can make changes to the access control list.
- **System access control list (SACL).** This is an additional access control list used solely by the auditing system. The SACL cannot be modified using standard management tools. It is available only through programming interfaces.

An access control list contains one or more *access control entries* (ACE). An ACE consists of two parts:

1. A SID representing a security principal
2. An access mask defining permissions for that security principal

When users log on, they are assigned an access token that contains the user's SID and the SIDs of any groups to which the user belongs. When a process spawned by that user attempts to access a security object, the Security Reference Monitor in the Windows 2000 Executive checks the SIDs in the user's token against each ACE on the object's access control list. Armed with this information, it determines whether the user has access permission. It also knows what rights to give the user for that particular object. This is a core operating capability of the system and occurs very quickly.

Viewing Access Control Entries

You can view the security descriptor for a Directory object using any of the Active Directory management consoles. For example, open the `Active Directory Users and Groups` console and expand the tree. Right-click on an object and select PROPERTIES from the fly-out menu. Then select the `Security` tab. This shows the access control entries for the object. The example in Figure 10.2 shows the access control entries for a user object named `Average User`.

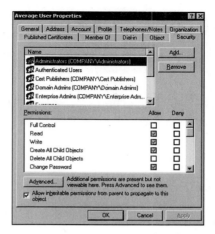

Figure 10.2   Security properties for a sample user showing
names and access rights of access control entries.

Chapter 14, "Managing File Systems Security," has a full list of the standard
security principals in Windows 2000 and their functions. Here is a brief
description of the security principals listed in Figure 10.2 to give you an idea
of the typical cast of characters:

- **Authenticated Users.** A special well-known SID assigned to any user
  who has authenticated in the domain.
- **System.** Another well-known SID, this one representing the System
  account.
- **Self.** Another well-known SID, this one representing a group with one
  member, the user. The Self group is different from the Authenticated Users
  group because the user might have logged on to the local machine but
  not the domain.
- **Domain Admins.** A global security group created when the first
  Windows 2000 domain controller is promoted. The Domain Admins
  group appears on virtually all access lists. This is how central administrative
  privileges are propagated to the member servers and workstations in the
  domain.
- **Enterprise Admins.** A Global/Universal group inherited from the
  Domain-DNS object dc=Company,dc=com. The Enterprise Admins group has
  the same sort of privileges as Domain Admins, but extended to the entire
  forest.

- **Account Operators.** A built-in Global group that has limited privileges specifically designed for handling user accounts.

- **Cert Publishers.** A Global group used to manage public/private key (X.509) certificates. It is on a user's ACL to permit reading and writing the certificate information in the user's object.

- **RAS and IAS Servers.** A Global group used to manage remote access and Internet authentication services. Accounts for *Remote Access Servers* (RAS) and *Internet Authentication Servers* (IAS) are placed in this group so that the server can do Directory lookups to verify user permissions.

- **Pre-Windows 2000 Compatible Access.** This group provides support for NT4 RAS servers that need additional permissions to check user permissions in the Directory. See the sidebar titled "Pre-Windows 2000 Compatible Access."

Some of the security principals listed in the main `Properties` window have more than one ACE. When you select one of these entries, the system informs you that additional permissions are present by putting a message next to the `Advanced` button. Click `Advanced` to see a more comprehensive view of the security list. Figure 10.3 shows an example.

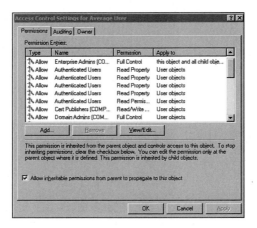

Figure 10.3 `Access Control Settings` window showing that each security principal can have more than one access right.

Pre-Windows 2000 Compatible Access

When a user establishes a dial-up session with a RAS server, the server must do a series of Directory lookups to authenticate the user and establish the user's access permissions. These Directory lookups require Kerberos authentication. An NT4 RAS server, using classic NTLM authentication, cannot view the contents of the Directory objects. Neither can a Windows 2000 RAS server that is a member of a classic NT domain.

The Pre-Windows 2000 Compatible Access group has been given a set of permissions in the Directory that permit an NT4 RAS server, or another NT4 service that requires user information in the Directory not available via NTLM, to read user and group information. The specific rights granted to this group are as follows:

- Read Remote Access Information

- Read General Information

- Read Group Membership

- Read Account Restrictions

- Read Logon Information

- Read All Group Properties

- List Group Contents

- Read Group Permissions

To use this group to grant permissions to NT4 RAS servers, Windows 2000 RAS servers in an NT4 domain, or other NT4 services requiring access to user information, make the Everyone group a member of the Pre-Windows 2000 Compatible Access group.

Types of Access Rights

Fifteen standard access rights can be applied to any Windows 2000 security object, including Directory objects. In addition, Windows 2000 has nearly 50 extended rights, of which about a dozen are applicable to Directory objects. The standard access rights take on different meanings and actions when applied to different types of security objects. The *Local Security Authority Subsystem* (LSASS) works in conjunction with the *Security Reference Monitor* (SRM) to interpret the rights based on their associated object type.

Most access rights can be applied to individual attributes (also called properties) within a Directory object as well as the Directory object itself. For example, a user object has an attribute called Street that stores the user's street address. It is possible to assign permissions specifically to read but not write the Street attribute for a given user object. Using delegation as discussed in "Access Rights Delegation," you could delegate permission to read the Street attribute on all user objects in a domain or OU.

Here are the standard object types as they apply to directory objects:

- **Access System Security.** Permits reading and modifying the object's SACL (used for auditing only).
- **Add/Remove Self as Member.** Permits the user to put herself on the member list of the object.
- **Control Access.** Permits an application to apply extended rights to an ACE. This ACE is not available in the Directory management tools. It is applied programmatically. The Object-Type field in this ACE contains a GUID that identifies the extended right.
- **Create All Child Objects.** Permits creating additional objects in a container. The Object-Type field in this ACE contains a GUID that identifies the type of objects that can be created. If this field is blank, any subordinate object type can be created.
- **Delete All Child Objects.** Permits deleting objects in a container. If the Object-Type field contains a GUID, only objects of that type can be deleted. Otherwise, any subordinate object type can be deleted.
- **Delete.** Permits deleting an object.
- **Delete Subtree.** Permits deleting subordinate objects when deleting an object above them in the Directory hierarchy. This right enables subtree deletion even if the subordinate objects have permissions to the contrary.
- **List Object.** Permits listing an object when browsing the Directory. Without this right, the object is hidden.
- **List Contents.** Permits listing subordinate objects. If you deny the List Contents right, a user can see an object but not objects under it. This can be used to hide objects in an OU when you want only certain administrators to see and manage those objects.
- **Modify Owner.** Permits taking ownership of the object. Object owners have the right to do anything with an object. If you were to accidentally delete every entry in the access list for an object, only the owner could open the security descriptor and put them back. Ownership is assigned to the Administrators group when any administrator creates an object. This ensures that another can modify objects created by one administrator.
- **Read All Properties.** Permits reading the properties of an object. If the Object-Type field contains a GUID, only objects of that type can be read. Generally, users must have Read All Properties access so that their LDAP lookups can succeed.

- **Write All Properties.** Permits modifying the properties of an object. If the Object-Type field contains a GUID, only properties of that type can be modified.
- **Read Permissions.** Permits reading the contents of the security descriptor. If you remove this right, the user can browse the objects in the Directory but not look at the access permissions on those objects.
- **Modify Permissions.** Permits modifying the contents of the security descriptor.
- **Right Synchronize.** Permits using the object to signal a process thread. This is applied programmatically only and is not exposed in the management tools.

In addition to the 15 standard rights, there are four generic templates. These templates are standard for all Windows 2000 security objects. They take special meaning when applied to Directory objects:

- **Generic Execute.** Permits listing the object and all subordinate objects. Equivalent to List Object and List Contents.
- **Generic Read.** Permits reading an object's properties and security descriptors as well as the properties and security descriptors of all subordinate objects.
- **Generic Write.** Permits modifying an object's properties and its DACL. Also permits adding and removing subordinate objects.
- **Generic All.** Combines privileges granted by all generic masks. This is the template used by the Full Control option.

Access Control Entry Classifications

An ACE can either allow or deny a particular right or it can enable Auditing to log the use of that right. Here are details:

- **Access Allowed.** This specifically grants a particular privilege. When you grant read and modify permissions on a Directory object, for example, the system builds an Access Allowed ACE for those permissions and puts it on the ACL for that object along with the SID of the security principal.
- **Access Denied.** This ACE revokes a particular privilege. You can block a security principal from modifying an object, for example, but permit the principal to read the object. In this case, there would be an Access Denied ACE for the modify option and an Access Allowed ACE for the read option on the ACL for the object.

- **System Audit.** This ACE identifies a particular action as an auditable event. A System Audit ACE is listed on a Security ACL. It only becomes effective if Auditing has been enabled for that object class. If you enabled Auditing for user objects, for example, resetting a user's password would result in an entry in the Security Log.

Access Control Entry Rules

If you think of object security as a card game, the various access rights are just cards in the deck. They have no real function without rules to govern how they are used. Four rules determine precedence of access rights and accumulation of rights:

- **Rule 1.** The system always evaluates Access Denied ACEs first. If a user belongs to a group with an Access Allowed ACE and another group with an Access Denied ACE on the same object or property, the denial takes precedence. In the game of object security, a denial ACE always trumps.
- **Rule 2.** Having no ACE is equivalent to a denial. If a user's SID does not appear on an Access Allowed ACE for an object and the user does not belong to a group that has an Access Allowed ACE, the user is denied access. It's important to remember this rule. If you delete all entries from an access list, you will lose access to the object. If it is a container, you will lose access to the subordinate objects.
- **Rule 3.** Rights granted by Access Allowed ACEs are cumulative unless overridden by an Access Denied ACE. For example, consider two groups. One group has read privileges to an object. The other group has write privileges to the same object. Access Allowed ACEs are cumulative, so a user in both groups would get read and write access to the object.
- **Rule 4.** An ACE applied to a Directory object also applies to the object's properties unless overridden by an ACE for a specific property (see Figure 10.4).

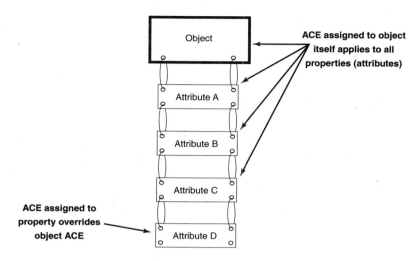

Figure 10.4 ACE entries apply to an object and all object properties unless overridden by specific property rights assignment.

If a group has Full Control rights to an object, the group has Full Control rights to all properties of that object. If an Access Denied ACE is applied to a specific property, however, the Access Denied ACE takes precedence.

You should keep in mind a few corollaries to these ACE rules as you manage directory security:

- **Don't associate an Access Denied ACE with an administrative group.** You might accidentally lock yourself and your colleagues out of an important container.

- **Don't associate an Access Denied ACE with the Everyone group.** The same applies to any of the other well-known groups such as Interactive or Network or System. This can have unexpected consequences. If you don't want everyone to have access to an object, remove the Everyone group from the ACL.

These access control rules determine how different ACEs on the same ACL interact with each other. They do not determine how ACLs on one object apply to ACLs on subordinate objects. For that, we need inheritance rules.

Access Control Inheritance

When you assign an ACE to a container object, the permissions associated with the ACE flow down the tree in a process called *inheritance*.

Rights inheritance is not a new concept in Windows 2000. Classic NT has always used inheritance to assign default access rights to files, directories, and Registry keys. When a new object is created, it inherits the security descriptor from its parent. This feature continues in Windows 2000.

What is new is the concept of *dynamic* inheritance. When an inheritable ACE is added to the access list of a container object in the Directory, the security descriptors of the subordinate objects are updated automatically. This is similar to the "Apply to All Subfolders" option in classic NT NTFS permissions; instead of overwriting the security descriptors in the child objects, however, the new ACE is added to the list.

The dynamic inheritance in Windows 2000 is not exactly dynamic. It is actually a form of dynamic/static inheritance. When you add an ACE to the security descriptor of a container object and set the inheritance to flow down the tree, the security descriptors of all child objects are updated with the new ACE. If you have 500 user accounts in an OU and you add an inheritable ACE to the ACL of the OU, for example, the security descriptors of the 500 user accounts are modified. The Directory engine is tuned for this type of work, but it still takes a little time.

Modifying the security descriptor on an object generally triggers a replication of that object. In the case of dynamic inheritance, only the object with the inheritable ACE is replicated. When the copy of the object on the other replicas is updated, the database engine takes over to apply the changes to the security descriptors of the child objects based on the inheritance option.

Inheritance Differences Between Active Directory and NDS

There is quite a controversy between Novell and Microsoft concerning their different approaches to inheritance. Novell implements true dynamic inheritance in NDS. Inheritable ACLs in NDS are not actually applied to individual objects. Each time you touch an object, the system scans up the Directory to calculate the effective rights assigned to the object. Microsoft's method, in contrast, emulates dynamic inheritance by updating the static ACLs whenever a change is made.

There are advantages and disadvantages to both approaches. Microsoft's approach yields faster lookups, all other things being equal, because there is no need to wait for the system to calculate effective rights. Its disadvantage is that it takes a while to update the child objects when an ACL changes. Novell's approach does not involve quite so much object manipulation, but calculating effective rights can be slow in a big tree with lots of levels.

In both cases, the time difference is negligible unless you have a truly huge number of objects in a container. Neither Novell nor Microsoft encourage such a practice.

You can specify permissions to be either inheritable or non-inheritable. You can also define whether the permissions apply to subordinate objects directly under a container or to all subordinate objects in all containers. When the system evaluates ACE listings, it groups them by how they are applied. Directly applied ACE listings take precedence over inherited ACE listings, and Access Denied ACEs always take precedence.

The following example uses the `Active Directory Users and Computers` console to apply inheritable rights to a test OU.

Procedure 10.1 **Applying inheritable rights to a directory container.**

1. Open the `Active Directory Users and Computers` console.

2. From the menu, select VIEW | ADVANCED FEATURES. This enables you to view the contents of the security descriptors for the Directory objects.

3. Create a test OU to practice on. This prevents you from making an innocent mistake that mangles a production container. Create a couple of user objects under this OU. See "Managing User and Group Accounts" for details on creating user accounts. If this is a production server and your corporate policies prohibit creating user IDs, you can create contact objects. They act the same as user objects, but they have no security rights.

4. Right-click the new OU and select PROPERTIES from the fly-out menu.

5. Select the `Security` tab (see Figure 10.5). You'll see a list of access control entries.

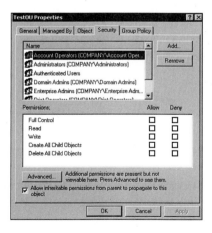

Figure 10.5 `Properties` page for an example OU showing the Security tab with access control entries.

6. Deselect `Allow Inheritable Permissions`. You'll be prompted to either copy the currently inherited ACE entries as permanent entries in the security descriptor or to remove them.

7. Click `Remove`. Only the dynamically inherited entries for the Administrators, Enterprise Admins, and Pre-Windows 2000 Compatible Access groups disappear. All other permissions were applied statically when the object was created.

   You may want to take advantage of the `Copy Previously Inherited Permissions` option when deselecting inheritance. Having no ACE is the same as having a Deny ACE. If you do not copy the existing permissions, be certain that you do not remove inherited rights from a container or object without first statically adding an administrative group.

8. In addition to selecting whether this object will inherit permissions from its parent, you can set inheritance options for the entries on this object to determine whether they will propagate to subordinate objects. Click `Advanced`. The `Access Control Settings` window opens (as shown in Figure 10.6).

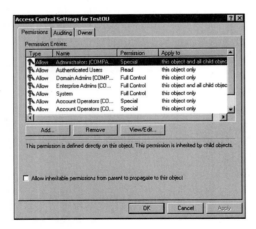

Figure 10.6 `Access Control Settings` window for TestOU object showing the ACE type, associated security principal, the type of permission, and the inheritance options.

Figure 10.6 shows the access control settings for the TestOU. Each line represents an ACE. Security principals can be associated with several ACEs. Remember that the rights associated with Access Allowed ACE entries are cumulative, so the security principal associated with multiple ACEs gets all the rights assigned by those entries.

9. Highlight one of the ACE listings and click View/Edit. The Permission Entry window opens (see Figure 10.7). The Apply Onto drop-down box lists the inheritance options that can be associated with the ACE. There are three general options and a host of specific options for various object types. The three general options are as follows:

- **This Object Only.** The ACE will not be inherited by any subordinate objects.

- Subobjects Only. The ACE does not affect this object but will be inherited by subordinate objects.

- This Object and All Subobjects. The ACE affects this object and will be inherited by subordinate objects.

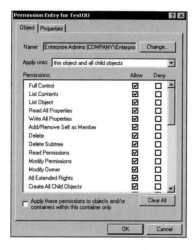

Figure 10.7 Permission Entry window for TestOU showing the inheritance option and the associated permissions.

10. Close the windows you have open and return to the Active Directory Users and Groups console.

You can assign permissions and inheritance options to individual properties as well as entire objects. You do not need to pore over the list of property options trying to figure out which ones to assign and how they should be inherited. You can use a Delegation Wizard to assign a prepackaged set of permissions. See the next section for details.

Granular Control of Access Permissions

The three inheritance options, coupled with the ability to assign an ACE to a specific property, gives you an immense amount of flexibility in assigning access rights. For example, you can grant someone Full Control rights to computer objects in a container while leaving that person with standard rights on every other object class.

This granularity can get downright microscopic. If you want to give the Web_Operators group in Houston permission to modify the Home-Page property for users everywhere in the network except for the Sales group in La Jolla, for example, partner, you can do it.

Access Rights Delegation

Windows 2000 uses delegation to assign the right mix of access permissions and inheritance options to achieve a desired set of management options. There is a fairly subtle distinction between *delegation* and *inheritance*. Inheritance is a mechanism for applying changes to security descriptors based on the contents of a parent's security descriptor. Delegation involves selecting the right access permissions to inherit. It's something like setting up a beach umbrella. The umbrella casts a shadow (delegation) and you sit in its shade (inheritance).

Sometimes you get unexpected consequences when you delegate. In *Catch 22*, for example, Milo Minderbinder was able to use his delegated authority as a supply officer for a small Air Corps detachment to effectively take over the war effort in Italy. You may have had similar experiences when delegating administrative privileges to a power user in a department.

Rather than trying to pick through nearly 200 different properties associated with users, groups, and computers trying to figure out which ones to assign, and maybe getting some of those unexpected consequences, you can use a tool in the `Directory Management` console called the Delegation Wizard.

I'm not generally a fan of admin wizards. For the most part, I think they complicate simple chores. For specifying and controlling rights inheritance, however, the Delegation Wizard comes close to being a tool of choice. It consolidates the extensive range of permissions and sub-permissions involved with managing Directory objects and delivers them in a concise set of windows. The Delegation Wizard uses these steps to assign access rights and inheritance options:

- You start by selecting the security principal (user, local group, global group, universal group, or computer) to whom you want to grant access rights.

- Then you select the object types over which the security principal will exercise control.

- Then select the rights you want to delegate to the security principal.
- Finally, select the types of subordinate objects that will be affected by the delegation.

The next steps show how this works. You can use access rights delegation from any of the Directory management consoles. The example uses the `Active Directory Users and Groups` console because this is where most of the delegations are required.

Procedure 10.2 **Delegating Access Rights**

1. At the Active Directory Users and Groups snap-in, right-click the test OU and select DELEGATE CONTROL from the fly-out menu. The `Delegation Control Wizard` starts.

2. Click `Next`. The `Active Directory Folder` window opens. The name of the object you're managing displays.

3. Click `Next`. The `Group or User Selection` window opens.

4. Click `Add`. The `Select Users, Computers, or Groups` window opens (see Figure 10.8).

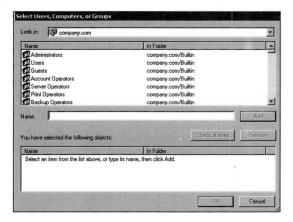

Figure 10.8 `Select Users, Computers, or Groups` window showing the list of security principals in the Company.com domain.

5. Double-click a user or group to add it to the list (or highlight several and add them with the `Add` button), and then click `OK` to save the change and return to the Delegation Wizard. The selected groups or users will be listed.

6. Click Next. The Predefined Delegations window opens (see Figure 10.9).

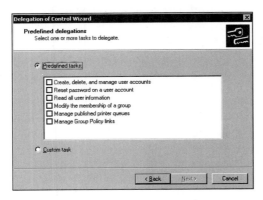

Figure 10.9   Delegation of Control Wizard—Predefined Delegations window

7. You can select any or all of the options under Predefined Tasks or build a Custom Task. If you select a predefined task and click Next, you'll be presented with a summary window. Click Finish and the rights will be applied. Select Custom Task just to see what this option looks like.

8. Click Next. The Active Directory Object Type window opens (see Figure 10.10).

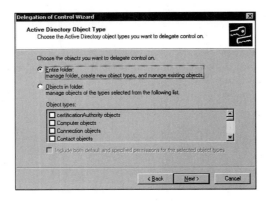

Figure 10.10   Delegation of Control Wizard—Active Directory Object Type window.

9. If you select Entire Folder, the rights you select in the next window will be assigned to all subordinate objects regardless of their type. If you select Objects in Folder, you can select one or more object types that will inherit the rights you assign.

10. Scroll down the list under Object Types and select User Objects.

11. Click Next. The Permissions window opens (see Figure 10.11).

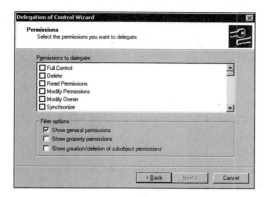

Figure 10.11   Delegation of Control Wizard—Permissions window.

With the Show General Permissions option checked, the list of rights under Permissions to Delegate includes both the standard access rights covered in the "Types of Access Rights" section as well as a host of extended rights applicable to the User object class. The list of extended rights will differ for different object classes. Refer to Chapter 7, "Understanding Active Directory Services," for an explanation of extended rights.

The Show Property Permissions option displays a list of all properties associated with the User object class and the option to permit reading or writing or both for each property. This is probably not something you'll use all that often, but it's good to know that you can grant the right to read a user's middle name and nothing else.

The Show Creation/Deletion of Subobject Permissions option is only applicable for the Entire Folder option from the preceding window. It lists the object types associated with the container with the option to create or delete them. This is useful if you want to define rights for a special group so that they can create object types such as groups or users but not delete them.

12. Select the right or rights you want to grant, and then click Next. The wizard will display a summary window. Click Finish to apply the changes. Remember that the update will be applied to every object of the type you selected.

Delegating Extended Rights

Many of the rights displayed in the Delegation Wizard are derived from special Directory objects called Extended-Rights objects. These extended rights act as templates, of a sort, that simplify assigning property rights.

Here's an example. Assume, that a company operates a central help desk that takes calls from internal users all over the country. The help desk technicians do not have administrative rights in the Directory so they cannot help when users call to complain that they have lost or forgotten their passwords. The help desk technicians, in turn, complain to you that it takes too long to get a systems administrator to solve the problem. They want the ability to reset passwords and create new passwords for users throughout the company. You can give them this right without granting other administrative privileges by using extended rights.

Many extended rights are associated with user objects. Two of these, User-Force-Change-Password (display name *Password Reset*) and Update-Password (display name *Change Password*) can be used to delegate password rights to the help desk technicians. It's best to assign rights to administrative groups instead of assigning them to individual user accounts, so the example uses a group called HelpDesk Admins (see Figure 10.12).

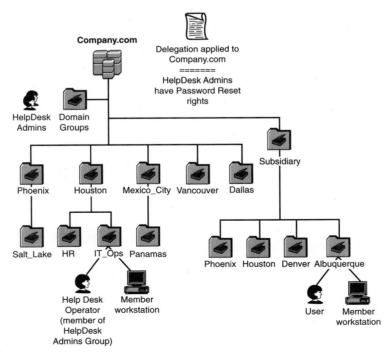

Figure 10.12 Directory structure showing operation of extended rights delegation.

Procedure 10.3 **Assigning Extended Rights**

1. Open the `Active Directory Users and Groups` console.

2. Right-click the domain object, `Company.com`, and select DELEGATE CONTROL from the fly-out menu. The `Delegation Wizard` window opens. Let's zip through the selections to make sure we get the right configurations for this situation.

3. Click `Next`. The `Active Directory Folder` window opens showing the name of the folder. In this case, the name would be `Company.com`.

4. Click `Next`. The `Group or User Selection` window opens.

5. Click `Add`. The `Select Users, Computers, or Groups` window opens.

6. Double-click the `HelpDesk Admins` group and click `OK` to save the change and return to the preceding window.

7. Click `Next`. The `Predefined Delegations` window opens. There is a predefined option for password resets, but none for modifying existing passwords. Select `Custom Task`.

8. Click `Next`. The `Active Directory Object Type` window opens.

9. Select `Objects in Folder`.

10. Scroll down the Object Types list and select `User Objects`.

11. Click `Next`. The `Permissions` window opens. Under `Permissions to Delegate`, select `Change Password` and `Reset Password`.

12. Click `Next`. The wizard displays a summary window. Check the entries to make sure that they are correct, and then click `Finish` to apply the changes.

13. Verify the new delegation settings by checking the security properties of a user account in the domain. You will find the HelpDesk Admins group on two inherited ACEs with special rights to do the two functions you delegated.

Managing Access Lists with DSACLS

The previous examples use the `Active Directory Users and Groups` console to manage permissions for Directory objects. If you're the type to sneer at graphical admin tools, or you want to build batch files or scripts to do your work, you will be interested in a command-line utility in the Windows 2000 Resource Kit called the *Directory ACL Editor* (DSACLS).

The DSACLS syntax for viewing a security descriptor for a Directory object is `dsacls <object's distinguished name>`. To see the contents of the security descriptor for the Administrator object in the Company.com domain, enter the following:

```
dscacls cn=administrator,cn=users,dc=company,dc=com
```

Figure 10.13 shows a security properties window for a sample user object. All but three entries have been deleted for brevity. The following example shows the DSACLS listing corresponding to the access control entries in the figure:

```
C:\>dsacls "cn=average user,cn=users,dc=company,dc=com"
Displaying ACTRL_ACCESS list: AccessList
        Entries: 1
                Flags: 1
                        cEntries: 3
                        Entry 0:
                                Trustee.Name: COMPANY\Domain Admins
                                fAccessFlags: 1
                                Access: 0x780001ff
                                ProvSpecificAccess: 0
                                Inheritance: 0x2
                                lpInheritProperty:
                        Entry 1:
                                Trustee.Name: NT AUTHORITY\SELF
                                fAccessFlags: 1
                                Access: 0x780001ff
                                ProvSpecificAccess: 0
                                Inheritance: 0x0
                                lpInheritProperty:
                        Entry 2:
                                Trustee.Name: NT AUTHORITY\SYSTEM
                                fAccessFlags: 1
                                Access: 0x780001ff
                                ProvSpecificAccess: 0
                                Inheritance: 0x0
                                lpInheritProperty:
DSACLS succeeded
```

Figure 10.13 Security properties for Average User account
corresponding to DSACLS list shown in Procedure 10.3

The Access entry in each of the listings holds an eight–digit hex number
called an *access mask*. There are four types of access masks, some of which are
the same for all Windows 2000 security objects and some only applicable to
Directory objects:

- **Standard.** Masks that apply standard security access rights. These rights
  are the same for all Windows 2000 security objects. The WRITE_DAC
  right is a standard access mask that permits its associated security principal
  to change an object's security descriptor, for example.

- **Generic.** Masks that act as templates for a list of specific rights. For
  example, the GENERIC_READ mask permits its associated security
  principal to read an object's properties and security descriptor along with
  the properties and security descriptors of the object's children.

- **Specific.** Masks that have special meaning when applied to Directory
  objects. For example, the DS_CREATE_CHILD mask permits its associated security principal to create objects under a container object.

- **Extended.** A GUID for a special right that has been associated with one
  or more Directory objects. You've seen already in this chapter how this
  operates for the Reset Password right applied to user objects.

Table 10.1 lists the standard access rights and their associated access mask.
The masks are listed because you may see them in command–line utilities
and Error Log entries.

Table 10.1 **Access Mask Types and Mask Numbers**

Access Mask Type	Mask
Delete	08000000
Read Properties	00000010
Read Permissions	10000000
Modify Properties	00000020
Modify Permissions	20000000
Delete Subtree	00000040
Modify Owner	40000000
List Object	00000080
Generic Delete (inherited only)	80000000
Control Access	00000100
Create a Child Object	00000001
Delete a Child Object	00000002
List Contents	00000004
Add/Remove Self as Member	00000008

Here is an example of how the system combines individual access mask values to form a single mask. Assume, for example, that you assign a certain security principal Full Control rights. The access mask for this ACE would be 0x780000ff, the sum of the following:

```
Delete              (08000000)
Read Permissions    (10000000)
Modify Permissions  (20000000)
Modify Owner        (40000000)
Create Child Object (00000001)
Delete Child Object (00000002)
List Contents       (00000004)
Add/Remove Self     (00000008)
Read Properties     (00000010)
Modify Properties   (00000020)
Delete Subtree      (00000040)
List Object         (00000080)
Control Access      (00000100)
```

If you assign an access right to a particular property, the DSACLS listing will include the name of property, as follows:

```
Property: Change Password
         Flags: 1
                 cEntries: 1
                 Entry 0:
```

```
Trustee.Name: COMPANY\HelpDesk Admins
fAccessFlags: 1
Access: 0x100
ProvSpecificAccess: 0
Inheritance: 0x2
  lpInheritProperty:
```

In this instance, the HelpDesk Admins have been given Control Access rights (00000100) to the Change Password property for the object.

The inheritance configuration for the access rights associated with each ACE is controlled by the Inheritance option. This option has three possible values:

- **This Object Only.** 0×0 as displayed by DSACLS.
- **Subobjects Only.** 0×a as displayed by DSACLS.
- **This Object and All Subobjects.** 0×2 as displayed by DSACLS.

You can use DSACLS to modify rights as well as read them. If you wanted to assign Full Control access rights to a group called Daily Operations for all objects in an OU called Sales and all subcontainers under Sales, for example, you would do so with the following command:

```
dsacls ou=Sales,dc=Company,dc=com /s:co /g "Daily Operations":780001ff
```

For normal workday activities, DSACLS is probably too clumsy to use. If you have many rights to dole out or read, however, it can come in very handy. You can use the information from a DSACLS dump to configure other tools, too, such as any VBScript/JavaScript tools you want to build. At this point, you have the security tools in place, so you're ready to invite in the customers.

Managing User and Group Accounts

This section covers the three most common Directory-related activities involving users:

1. Creating and modifying user accounts
2. Creating and modifying group accounts
3. Assigning and modifying group memberships

This section covers the first two items. The next section, "Using Groups to Manage Directory Objects," covers the third. Other user management work involving users and groups such as creating and distributing group policies and controlling desktop environments is covered in Chapter 15, "Managing Shared Resources."

Tools for Managing SAM-Based Users and Groups

Because this chapter covers Active Directory, this topic covers creating users and groups in the Directory. Windows 2000 servers that are not domain controllers along with Windows 2000 Professional desktops also have user and group accounts stored in the local SAM. These groups are added, deleted, and modified using the Computer Management console. There are three ways to open this console:

1. Launch from the START menu using START | PROGRAMS | ADMINISTRATIVE TOOLS | COMPUTER MANAGEMENT.

2. Right-click the My Computer icon on the desktop and select MANAGE from the fly-out menu.

3. From the Run window, enter **COMPMGMT.MSC** and press Enter.

In addition to the Computer Management console, Windows 2000 Professional has a special Control Panel applet called Users and Passwords that provides an alternative way to manage users and groups. This interface is a little easier to use than an MMC console.

Creating User Accounts

As a general rule, you should create user, group, and computer accounts under an OU rather than in the default Users and Computers containers. Part of this is tidiness. You don't want to see dozens or hundreds or thousands of accounts hanging off these two containers like bananas in a bunch. Even more important is the need to corral accounts into discrete units to simplify administrative chores.

Figure 10.14 shows the lower-level container structure built in Chapter 9, "Deploying Windows 2000 Domains." By putting user and group and computer accounts into separate containers at the lower level, you can delegate administrative rights over the accounts and assign separate group policies to the containers.

Compartmentalizing users by OU does not change their logon context. All users in the domain are managed as if the Directory were a flat namespace where every username must be unique. This can have unexpected consequences in a big domain. Referring to Figure 10.14, assume that the administrators in the Phoenix OU install a backup application. Backups generally run as a background process, so the application needs a security context with Backup Operator permissions. To get it, the application generally creates a default user account, such as ProductUser, and puts that account in the Backup Operators group. If the administrators in Houston try to install the same application, the automatic account creation will fail because the account already exists in the Phoenix OU. The Houston administrators may not be able to see it if they don't have rights in the OU, so this kind of problem can be frustrating.

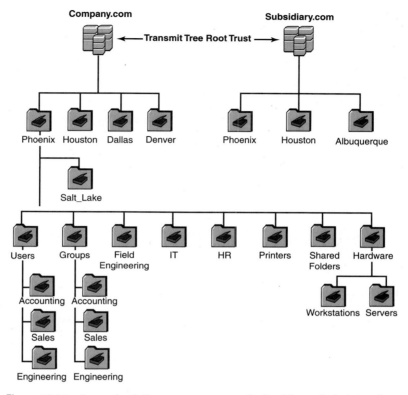

Figure 10.14 Lower-level directory structure ready for delegated administration.

Creating User Accounts with the Net User Command

If you don't like graphical management tools, you can create user accounts quickly from the command line, and then move them later to their proper location in the Directory.

A new account is created with the Net User command. Here is the syntax:

```
net user jjones * /add /fullname:Jim Jones
```

The new account is added to the cn=Users,dc=Domain,dc=root container.

Several additional options are available by typing **Net Help User**.

When you have a system for assigning unique usernames, add new accounts as follows.

Procedure 10.4 **Creating a User Account**

1. Open the Active Directory Users and Groups console and expand the tree to view the containers under the Phoenix OU.

2. Right-click the Users container under the Phoenix OU and select NEW | USER from the fly-out menu. The Create User window opens (see Figure 10.15).

Figure 10.15 Create New Object — (User) window showing new account for help desk technician Rita Manuel.

3. Fill in the blank fields. The Next button will not activate until you enter a Last Name and a Logon Name. The requirement for a logon name should be obvious. The last name requirement comes from LDAP. See the section "Managing User and Group Accounts" for a description of how the entries in this window are saved in the Directory and used by the system.

   If you select a logon name that is already in use, you'll be warned as soon as you click Next. If you enter a full name that is already in use, you'll be warned as soon as you try to save the record. If you enter a logon name or full name that matches an existing group name, you'll also get an error.

4. Click Next. A second window with additional information concerning passwords opens (see Figure 10.16). Enter a password for the user and confirm it. Select User Must Change Password at Next Logon to force the user to select a password that is not known to you. See Chapter 6, "Understanding Network Access Security and Kerberos," for information about strong passwords and access security. The remaining options are self-explanatory.

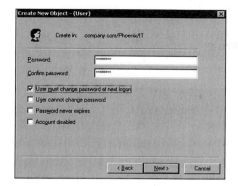

Figure 10.16   Create New Object — (User) password information window.

Forcing Password Changes May Cause Problems for Windows 9x Users

The User Must Change Password at First Logon option may cause problems for down-level Windows 9x/WFWG clients. These clients store a Windows password locally in a PWL file. The users may have logged on to their local computers several times before being configured to log on to a domain.

If the users are forced to change passwords, the user may enter "two-password purgatory," with one password for the domain and one for the local Windows desktop. You'll need to walk the user through deleting the old PWL files in the \WINDOWS directory and reconfirming his new password.

One way around this problem is to uncheck the User Must Change Password at First Logon option; but this means the administrator who created the account now possesses the user's password. This is often not an acceptable policy.

5. Click Next. A summary screen opens highlighting the change you're about to make.

6. Click Finish. The object is created.

7. Double-click the new user object to open the Properties window. Take this opportunity to fill in the pertinent information about the user (see Figure 10.17).

8. Select the Account tab (see Figure 10.18). This is where you change the user's logon name. The Account Options field has several options that affect the user's ability to log on and use network resources. A few of these options require additional information. See the sidebar titled "Logon Options" for more information.

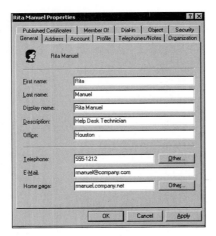

Figure 10.17 User properties showing `General` tab.

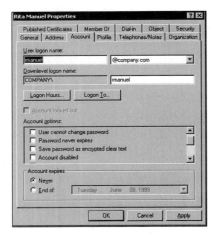

Figure 10.18 User properties showing `Account` tab.

Logon Options

The Account tab in the user properties window has several account options that affect user logon and resource use. Here is a partial list and recommended settings.

User Must Logon Using a Smart Card. This forces the user to key in the PIN and token from a SecureID card so that a Security Dynamics ACE server can perform the authentication. You must install a SecureID client for this option to be worthwhile. If you are not familiar with this technology, check out the Security Dynamics Web site at www.securitydynamics.com.

Account Is Trusted for Delegation. Kerberos has an option that permits a host to forward a ticket to another host if the ticket as been marked as "forwardable." This is typically enabled when the client talks to a middleware application, CORBA app, or other three-tier client/server applications. It is also used when using the File Encryption Service to encrypt files on a server. This option should not be selected unless necessary to support an application. It opens a way for sophisticated tricks on the part of trojan horse programs that impersonate the user. Chapter 14, "Managing File Systems Security," has a more extensive discussion of account delegation under the "Encrypted File System" section.

Account Is Sensitive and Cannot Be Delegated. If you have an account that you absolutely do not want to be delegated by a server when it contacts another server, select this option.

Use DES Encryption Types for This Account. By default, Windows 2000 uses MD4 encryption from RSA for logons and MD5 for MS-CHAPv2 in remote dial up. RSA is an arm of Security Dynamics, Inc. If you have a non-Windows client that cannot use an NTLM MD4 password hash, you can enable this option to permit the system to use DES.

Don't Require Kerberos Preauthentication. A Kerberos client has the option of including an encrypted time stamp in a Preauthentication field inside a Kerberos TGT request or authentication request. The time stamp is encrypted using the user's password hash as a key. The KDC gets the TGT request and decrypts the time stamp using its copy of the user's hash from the Directory. If the decrypted time stamp fails CRC, the TGT request is immediately rejected. If the Don't Require Kerberos Preauthentication option is set for a user, the KDC ignores the encrypted time stamp if one is present. This feature provides support for Kerberos applications that do not include encrypted preauthentication time stamps.

9. After you have made your entries, click OK to save the changes and close the Properties window.

10. Go to a Windows 2000 Pro workstation or down-level client that is a member of the domain and try to log on with the new account. If you get an *Unknown User* error and you're sure that you entered the credentials correctly, you may have to wait for replication to transfer the updates from the domain controller where you made the change to the domain controller where the workstation has its secure connection. This should happen very quickly within the same site, but can take as long as six hours between sites.

Username Information in the Directory

Before describing how to change a username, it's necessary to take a look at all the different usernames that Windows 2000 keeps in the Directory. At least nine different renditions of a user's name are derived from attributes stored in the user object. These attributes are combined and displayed differently depending on the circumstance. Figure 10.19 shows the name fields in the UI when adding a new user account. Table 10.2 lists the Directory attributes where each of these fields are saved and the most common occurrence or use of the attribute.

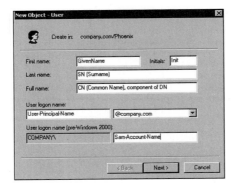

Figure 10.19 New Object - User window showing the
fields that become Directory attributes for the user.

Table 10.2 **Username Attributes and Their Uses**

Directory Name	New Object—User Field	Commonly Appears In
SAM-Account-Name.	Copied from User Logon This name does not change when users are moved between containers. All logons are context-free within a domain. Limited to 20 characters.	Logon ID.
DN (Distinguished Name)	Combination of First Name, Initials, and Last Name along with the full LDAP path to user object.	LDAP and ADSI applications.

Directory Name	New Object—User Field	Commonly Appears In
Distinguished Name	Same as DN.	ADSI variant used for programming, but not shown directly in UI.
CN (Common Name)	Part of DN. Limited to 64 characters. The CN remains the same when user objects are moved between containers. Container changes may not be transparent if the new OU has a different set of group policies.	Most common Attribute used when showing names in the UI. Examples include the user list in `Active Directory Users and Computers` and the user lists in `Find Users, Contacts, and Groups`.
User-Principal-Name	Derived from User Logon Name (pre-Windows 2000). Must be unique. Filled in automatically with `User Logon Name` `unless changed manually`.	Entered at WINLOGON or using CLI Utilities. Syntax: `username@domain.root` Example: `wcoyote@speedbump.com` The system accepts either the SAM Account Name or the User Principal Name for logon if the two entries become different.
Name	Same as CN.	LDAP attribute not used in Windows 2000 UI.
Initials	Copied from Initials field.	Not shown separately from DN or CN.
GivenName	Copied from First Name field.	X.400 attribute used by MAPI applications.
DisplayName	Same as DN. Fullname attribute from classic SAM is migrated to DisplayName.	Press `Ctrl+Alt+Del` while logged on. The logon information in The `Windows Security` window comes from DisplayName.
SN (Surname)	Copied from Last Name field.	X.500 attribute not used in Windows 2000 UI.

Renaming a User Account

Keeping Table 10.2 in mind, you have to know what functionality you want to change when you change a user's name. Here are the steps for changing names using the `Active Directory Users and Computers` console:

Procedure 10.5   **Renaming a User Account**

1. Open the `Active Directory Users and Computers` console.

2. Expand the tree to show the list of users. Figure 10.20 shows a list with three users, all named Jim Jones, that were added using the `Net User` command. The logon IDs were kept unique with suffix numbers.

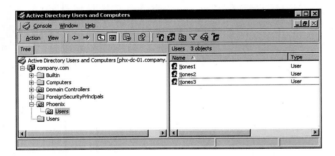

Figure 10.20   `Active Directory Users and Computers` console showing three users with similar names.

3. Highlight an account and press `F2` to rename it. An edit boundary appears around the name.

4. Change the name to the user's full name, something like Jim R. Jones or James Ronald Jones and press `Enter`. The `Rename User` window opens. Most of the fields are blank because the accounts were added from the command line.

   The new name you assigned to the user is shown in the Full Name field. Whatever you enter in this field is written to the CN attribute in the user object as well as the CN, which is derived from the DN. It does not change the user's logon ID or UPN. You must enter that information manually.

5. Using Table 10.2 as a guide, enter the remaining information. The final window should look something like Figure 10.21.

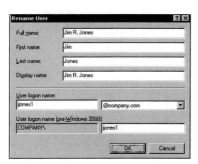

Figure 10.21   Rename User window after updating user information.

6. Click OK to save the changes and return to the Active Directory Users and Computers console. The name listed in the window comes from the CN attribute.

You can change any of the names associated with a user object without affecting the user's access rights because the SID remains the same. You may see some delay in seeing the new name in the Security window at remote domains and the update to the user object replicates to the other domain controllers.

Now that users and groups exist in the Directory, it's time to learn how to use them to manage access to Directory objects from all domains in a forest.

Creating Groups

Group accounts are created using the same tools as user accounts. You can keep the user and group accounts together in the same OU or separate them if you want to assign different policies or management rights.

Group names must be unique in a domain, and cannot be the same as usernames. Groups also have several Directory attributes associated with names, but only two appear in the UI: SAM-Account-Name and CN. When creating and renaming groups, be sure to keep these two names in sync. Down-level clients see the SAM-Account-Name. The Directory searches for the CN (or the DN, of which it is a component).

Several types of groups have complicated interrelationships. These are covered in the next section. For now, let's create a group, and assign group members, and wait to decide the best form of group to use.

Procedure 10.6   **Creating a Group**

1. Open the `Active Directory Users and Computers` console.

2. Expand the tree to the OU where you want to create the group.

3. Right-click the OU icon and select NEW | GROUP from the fly-out menu. The `New Object — Group` window opens (see Figure 10.22).

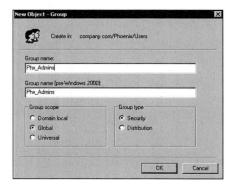

Figure 10.22   `New Object - Group` window showing name entries for new group.

4. Enter a name for the group under Group Name. This name becomes the CN for the group object. The name you enter is mirrored to the Pre-Windows 2000 field. This is the field that becomes SAM-Account-Name. Leave the `Group Scope` as `Global` for now.

5. Click `OK` to save the settings and create the group. The new group appears in the list of objects under the OU. You may need to press `F5` to refresh.

Adding Group Members

Members can be added to a group in one of two ways:

1. Right-click the user you want to put in a group and select ADD MEMBERS TO A GROUP from the fly-out menu. A `Select Group` window opens and you can double-click the group where you want to add the user. You use the same steps to add a group as a member of another group.

2. Double-click the group icon to open its `Properties` window, and then select the `Members` tab. Click `Add` to add users and groups to the group.

The "Using Groups to Manage Directory Objects" section contains the rules for assigning users and groups from other domains.

Renaming Groups

A group object is a security principal, just like a user object. It has a SID that can be made part of an ACE in the security descriptor of an object. Renaming a group has no effect on its access rights because the SID is unchanged. Make sure that you keep the SAM-Account-Name and Group Name in sync.

There is an added piece of complexity for renaming groups that did not exist for users. When you assign a user to a group, the group's DN is included in a list of groups stored in the user object under the Member-Of attribute. The *Local Security Authority* (LSA) uses this attribute to determine the user's group membership so that the correct SIDs can be included in the user's Kerberos tickets and access tokens.

This leads to a potential problem, because access lists contain SIDs, not group names. When you change a group name, or move the group to a new container so that the DN changes, the name change must be communicated quickly to all replicas in the forest so that the domain controllers can correlate the name to the SID when building Kerberos tickets.

The speedy transmission of this group information falls to a *Flexible Single Master Operations* (FSMO) role master, the *Infrastructure Master.* You can identify this server from the `Active Directory Users and Computers` console. Right-click the Users and Computers icon at the top of the tree and select OPERATIONS MASTERS from the fly-out menu. This opens the `Operations Master` window. Select the `Infrastructure Master` tab to find the name of the server. There is one Infrastructure Master in each domain. It will be the first domain controller promoted unless changed.

If the Infrastructure Master goes down, you should stop renaming groups or adding new groups until you can get the server back up again or seize the role with another domain controller. This is covered in Chapter 11, "Managing Active Directory Replication and Directory Maintenance."

The next section covers the group types used in Windows 2000 and how they are used to control access to Directory objects.

Using Groups to Manage Directory Objects

It is nearly always a good practice to aggregate users into groups based on common business functions or operational roles. Not only are groups easier to manage, but you also get a distinct performance improvement by using groups rather than individual users to control object security. It takes much longer to examine an ACL with 200 or 300 users on it than it does to check for a single SID that represents a group with 200 or 3000 members.

Windows 2000 has two group categories: *security* groups and *distribution* groups. Only security groups have a SID and can act as security principals. Distribution groups are used for software distribution.

Within the security group category are four group types: Local, Domain Local, Global, and Universal. The Domain Local type has a subtype called Builtin. The purpose of all these different group types is not just to make Windows 2000 administrators turn to self-medication, although they will probably have that effect. Used correctly, the different group types make it easier to manage security objects in a multiple domain environment.

The initial portions of this section focus on how groups are used to control access to security objects, including details on Kerberos and LSA transactions. This information acts as a foundation for the second part of this section, which covers the following areas:

- Guidelines for using Global groups and Universal groups
- Managing Universal group members
- Guidelines for placing Global Catalog servers
- Guidelines for using groups as security principals
- Allowable groups based on platform
- Group scope limitations
- Membership limitations
- Group scope improvements and downgrades
- Group nesting rules
- Examples of using groups to manage directory objects

Group Categories

Windows 2000 has four types of security groups. Three of these are inherited from classic NT and one is new in Windows 2000.

Local Groups (SAM-Based)

Windows 2000 Professional desktops and servers that are not domain controllers have Local groups that are stored in the SAM. Some of these groups are installed by default and occupy a special place in the SAM called the Builtin database. Local administrators can create additional groups to control access to local resources.

Builtin groups have inherent system privileges. For example, members of the Backup Operators group have the necessary system permissions to transfer files to and from backup tape regardless of the file's ownership or access rights settings. Most system privileges are granted to these local groups by local system policies contained in the LSA database, part of the System hive in the Registry. Other group-based privileges are buried in the source code deeper than the batcave under Bruce Wayne's mansion.

Local groups created by administrators have no inherent system privileges. They are created to provide a convenient repository for user accounts that have a common function. For example, a local server administrator might create a local group called Sales and put it on the access control list for a folder called Sales, and then put accounts representing members of the sales team into the Sales group so that they can access the Sales files.

Domain Local Groups

Domain Local groups are equivalent to SAM-based Local groups but are stored in Active Directory and are therefore held in common by all domain controllers. The classic Builtin groups with their system privileges are subclasses of the Domain Local group. They are called Builtin Local groups. Builtin Local groups have the same privileges as their SAM counterparts.

Global Groups

Global groups are repositories of user accounts. They have no inherent system privileges. Global groups can be added to Domain Local groups and Local groups, giving their members system privileges on domain controllers and local systems.

Unlike classic NT, Global groups in Windows 2000 can be placed directly into the ACL of local security objects at member servers and desktops. Global groups are intended to be the primary means for controlling access to security objects in a Windows 2000 domain. For example, the administrators of the Company.com domain can use delegation to grant administrator permissions over the Phoenix OU to a Global group called Phx_Admins. The members of the Phx_Admins group, in turn, could create other groups to control access to NTFS folders and files, local desktops, and other Directory objects.

Universal Groups

Universal groups are new in Windows 2000. They are disabled until the domain is shifted to Native mode so that support is no longer required for classic domain controllers.

Like Global groups, Universal groups have no inherent system privileges. Unlike Global groups, which are restricted to a single domain, Universal groups can be put on the ACL of any security object in the forest. The next section details the reason why the two groups are necessary and how they are handled differently by the Windows 2000 security system.

Comparison of Global Groups and Universal Groups

At first glance, Global and Universal groups appear to be identical. To understand their differences, and to see exactly why Universal groups are necessary, let's take a detailed look at the way the LSA on domain controllers uses Kerberos to distribute group membership information to member servers and desktops.

User objects have an attribute called Member-Of that contains the distinguished names of the domain groups to which the user belongs, including Builtin Local, Domain Local, Global, and Universal groups. Figure 10.23 shows the list of groups in the Member-Of attribute for the Administrator account in an example domain. The tool used to get this information was the ADSI Editor from the Windows 2000 Resource Kit.

Figure 10.23 `700 ADSI Editor` console showing Member-Of attribute for Administrator account.

The next few sections show how the LSA and Kerberos work together to use the group information in the Member-Of attribute to determine whether a user should get access to a particular object. These details will help you troubleshoot problems with object management and security issues. The sections cover three scenarios:

- Protecting a shared folder using a Global group
- Protecting a Directory object using a Domain Local group
- Protecting a Directory object using a Universal group

The initial scenario uses a folder object rather than a Directory object to more clearly illustrate the way LSA works in a domain environment.

Local Admin Rights in a Domain

Throughout the following discussion, the administrators who make local changes to member servers have local system privileges because they are members of the Domain Admins Global group. Both classic NT and Windows 2000 automatically add the Domain Admins Global group to the local Administrators group on member servers and desktops when they are joined to the domain. This gives members of the Domain Admins Global group sweeping powers in a domain, something like being on the Louisiana Highway Patrol.

Protecting a Shared Folder Using a Global Group

Refer to Figure 10.24. In this diagram, a user in the Company.com domain wants to access a shared folder on a member server in the Company.com domain. The user is a member of a Global group in the Company.com domain.

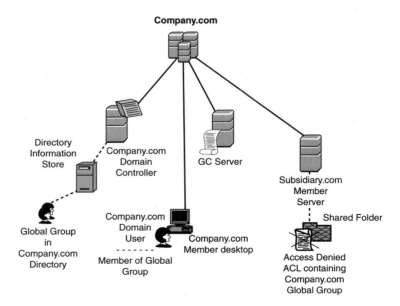

Figure 10.24 Diagram showing shared folder on member server accessed by user in Local domain.

An administrator has placed a Global group on the ACL of the shared folder with Deny All permissions. The security descriptor for the folder now contains an ACE with the Global group's SID and an Access Denied mask.

The administrator has also made the user a member of the Global group. The user should be denied access when attempting to open the folder. The steps in this section show how this is accomplished.

To summarize, a user who is a member of a domain is trying to access a shared folder on a member server in that same domain. The user is a member of a Global group that has been denied access to the folder. Here is the sequence of events that block the user when he attempts to access the shared folder:

Procedure 10.7 **Functional Description of User and Group Validation Within a Single Domain**

1. After a user logs on to the domain and authenticates to a domain controller, the LSA on the domain controller scans the user object to get the user's SID from the Object-SID attribute. The LSA must collect this and other SIDs so that it can pass them to the Kerberos KDC to include in a TGT that will be issued to the user.

2. The LSA now checks the list of group names in the Member-Of attribute in the user object. This tells LSA what domain groups the user belongs to. LSA does a quick lookup in the Directory to get the SIDs corresponding to each of the group names.

3. The Member-Of attribute in the user object contains only groups from the local domain. The LSA also needs to know whether the user is a member of Universal groups in other domains in the forest. One of these groups might be on an ACL for a security object in the local domain. LSA determines the user's Universal group membership in outside domains by querying a *Global Catalog* (GC) server. See the sidebar on the next page titled "Global Catalog Lookups for Universal Groups" to get more information.

   The LSA searches the membership lists on the GC looking for instances of the user's SID and the SID of any domain groups to which the user belongs. This ensures that it will find instances where a group containing the user has been nested with a Universal group. If the GC search turns up a group name from another domain, the LSA adds the group's SID to the list it is assembling for the KDC.

Global Catalog Lookups for Universal Groups

Any administrator who has Object Create rights in the Directory can create Universal groups. Users and groups from any domain can be members of Universal groups in any other domain. (There are a few limits to the types of groups that can be assigned as members of a Universal group. For purposes of this discussion, however, it's enough to know that users and groups from other domains can be found on the member list.)

A standard domain controller hosts only a replica of its local naming context. Using this naming context, it can only determine group memberships in the local domain. A Global Catalog server, on the other hand, hosts a partial replica of every naming context in the forest. These replicas contain a copy of every object in the naming context but only a few attributes. One of those attributes is the member list for Universal groups.

If the domain controller doing the search is also a GC, the LSA has an easy job. It does a scan of all the naming contexts in its information store and that's that. If you use the `Active Directory Users and Groups` console or the ADSI Editor from the Resource Kit to look at the Member-Of attribute for a user object on a GC, you'll see Universal groups from other domains. If you look at the same attribute for the same user on a replica of the naming context hosted by a non-GC, you will only see groups from the user's domain.

If the domain controller is not a GC, LSA sends an LDAP lookup request to a GC server with instructions to do the group member scan. The LSA locates a GC server by querying DNS to get SRV records associated with _ldap TCP port 3268.

4. After LSA has collected all the SIDs it needs, it gives them to the KDC service. KDC includes the SIDs in the Authorization Data field of the Kerberos TGT that it issues to the user. See Chapter 6 for details on the structure of this ticket.

5. When the network client at the user's machine receives the TGT from the domain controller, it places the TGT in a cache for use when it needs a ticket to access a member server. Kerberos tickets are issued for specific servers.

6. When the user contacts the member server in an attempt to access the shared folder on that server, the network client submits the TGT to the KDC on its domain controller to get a ticket for the member server.

7. The KDC copies the Authorization Data field from the TGT to the Authorization Data field of the ticket it issues for the member server. This field contains the SIDs collected by LSA. KDC then issues the ticket to the network client. (Keep your eye on this field. It's like the little girl in the red dress in *Schindler's List*.)

8. The network client presents the Kerberos ticket to the member server during the initial connection transaction. The LSA on the member server validates the ticket by decrypting it with its password hash. It then extracts the list of SIDs from the Authorization data field and uses them to build a local access token for the user. It also does a scan of the SAM to see

whether the user or any of the user's groups are members of Local groups. If so, the SIDs for those groups are added to the SIDs from the Kerberos ticket in the access token. The access token accompanies any processes initiated by the user on that server.

9. When the user attempts to open the shared folder on the member server, the local LSA on the server compares the SIDs in the user's access token to the SIDs in the security descriptor for the folder. It discovers a match between the global group SID and the SID on the Access Denied ACE. The LSA denies access to the user.

In short, the ability of a user to access resources on a member server in the same domain depends on the contents of a Kerberos ticket issued by a domain controller in that same domain. The domain controller builds this Kerberos ticket using a list of SIDs obtained by LSA based on the contents of the Member-Of attribute in the user object and a scan of the Universal groups in the Global Catalog.

Now let's expand the scope a bit and see what happens when the user tries to access a Directory object in another domain. This demonstrates how the LSA and KDC in the two domains exchange group information.

Well-Known SIDs and Group Memberships

To simplify the examples in this discussion, I omitted the well-known SIDs that LSA includes in the list it gives to the KDC. These well-known SIDs represent special groups that have system privileges. Examples of these well-known SIDs include the Authenticated Users SID, the Everyone SID, and the Network SID. See Chapter 6 for a list of the well-known SIDs and their functions.

Protecting a Directory Object Using a Domain Local Group

Refer to Figure 10.25. A user in the Company.com domain wants read/write access to an OU in the Subsidiary.com domain. This user could be a corporate auditor who wants to check the configuration of the OU or it might be a consultant who is trying to help resolve a problem. A Domain Admin in Subsidiary.com has placed a Domain Local group on the ACL of the OU and given the group read/write permissions. The ACE for that listing contains the user's Company.com SID and a generic read/write mask.

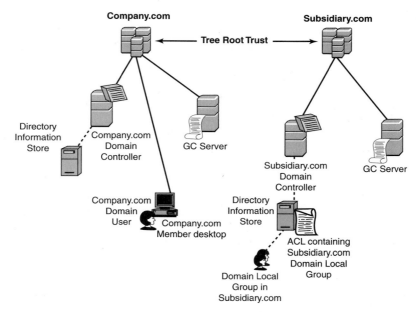

Figure 10.25   Diagram showing Directory object on domain controller in trusting domain being accessed by user in trusted domain.

Trust Directions

The two domains, Company.com and Subsidiary.com, are connected in the forest by a *tree-root trust*. This is a two-way transitive Kerberos trust, so the distinction I'm making between "trusting" and "trusted" domains is a little arbitrary.

The focus in the example is on the user in Company.com who is accessing an object in Subsidiary.com. The administrator is protecting an object in Subsidiary.com using an account from Company.com, so the Subsidiary.com domain is the "trusting" domain and Company.com is the "trusted" domain. Trusts always flow in the opposite direction of the way they are used.

The administrator was able to modify the security descriptor of the OU in Subsidiary.com because she is a member of the Domain Admins group in Subsidiary.com. The Domain Admins group has read/write access to Directory objects in their domain.

To summarize, a user from a trusted domain, Company.com, is attempting to access a Directory object in a trusting domain, Subsidiary.com. The object is protected by a Domain Local group in the Subsidiary.com domain.

The user is a Company.com user and a member of that group. Here is the sequence of events that validates the user when she attempts to access the OU using the `Active Directory Users and Computers` console:

Procedure 10.8 **Functional Description of User and Group Validation Across Domains Using Domain Local Group**

1. When the user logs on to Company.com, the LSA builds a SID list for the user based on the Member-Of attribute in the user object and a scan of the Universal groups in the GC.

   The LSA does not find the Domain Local group membership of the user in the Subsidiary.com domain. The partial copy of the naming contexts in the GC does not include the membership list for Domain Local groups. Therefore, the TGT issued by the KDC in Company.com contains only the user's SID and the SID for any Company.com groups to which the user belongs.

2. When the Company.com user opens the `Active Directory Users and Computers` console and shifts the focus to the Subsidiary.com domain, the network client on the user's machine must submit a Kerberos ticket to a domain controller in Subsidiary.com so that it can get permission to send it LDAP lookups. Active Directory does not accept connectionless lookup requests.

   To get a Kerberos ticket for a server in the Subsidiary.com domain, the network client must have a TGT for the Subsidiary.com domain. The KDC in Company.com can't issue this TGT. It must be issued by a KDC on a Subsidiary.com domain controller.

   The KDC in Company.com helps out a little, however, by getting a TGT for the Subsidiary.com domain from a domain controller in Subsidiary.com on behalf of the user. The KDC in Subsidiary.com issues this TGT based on the tree-root trust that exists between the two domains.

3. When the LSA on the Subsidiary.com domain controller builds the TGT for the Company.com user, it performs a group scan of its local naming context to see whether the user or any of the user's groups are members of Domain Local groups. LSA finds the user account in the Domain Local group where the administrator put it. It adds the SID for this group to those from the Company.com TGT and builds a new TGT for the Subsidiary.com domain. It then issues the ticket to the Company.com domain controller, which forwards it to the network client at the user's PC.

4. The network client immediately cashes in the Subsidiary.com TGT to get a ticket for a Subsidiary.com domain controller. The network client chooses a domain controller in Subsidiary.com based on SRV records for that domain in DNS.

5. The KDC on a Subsidiary.com domain controller issues the Kerberos ticket to the domain controller that the network client selected. The ticket contains a copy of the Authorization Data field from the Subsidiary.com TGT. This field contains the Domain Local group SID from Subsidiary.com along with the group SIDs from Company.com.

6. The network client submits this Kerberos ticket to the Subsidiary.com domain controller that it chose to use when accessing the Directory. The domain controller validates the ticket by decrypting it with its password hash. The LSA on the domain controller does not perform a SAM scan because a domain controller is not permitted to have local groups in the SAM. The LSA builds a local access token for the user with the SIDs from the Authorization Data field.

7. When the user attempts to access the OU in the Subsidiary.com domain, the LSA on the Subsidiary.com domain controller compares the SIDs on the ACL for that OU to the SIDs in the user's access token. It finds the Domain Local group SID that matches the SID on the ACL and gives the user read/write access to the object.

In short, when users from trusted domains are made members of Domain Local groups in trusting domains, the LSA on domain controllers in the trusting domain can validate the users' access rights based on the contents of the Kerberos ticket issued by a domain controller in their domain.

It isn't necessary to go through any Kerberos machinations for Global groups. Users from one domain cannot be added to the Global group in another domain regardless of the trust configuration. Global groups can only have members from their domain. For the same reason, Domain Local groups cannot be nested into Global groups because users from trusting domains might be members of the Domain Local group.

So the stage is set to look at the more complex situation when a user from one domain who is a member of a Global group in that domain tries to access a Directory object in another domain when that object is protected by a Universal group.

Protecting a Directory Object Using a Universal Group

Refer to Figure 10.26. In this example, users from both the Company.com domain and the Subsidiary.com domain are accessing an OU in the Subidiary.com domain. Instead of using a Domain Local group containing the user accounts, an administrator in the Company.com domain took advantage of several new features in Windows 2000 to do the following:

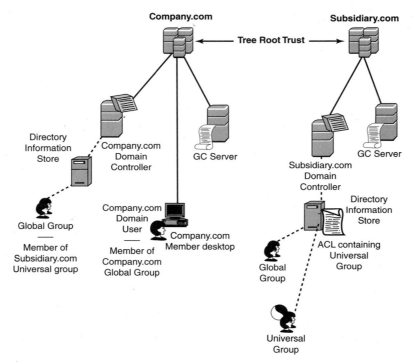

Figure 10.26   Diagram showing directory object on domain controller in trusting domain being accessed by user in trusted domain.

- **Create Global groups in both domains to use for interdomain administration.** The ability to make changes to any object anywhere in a forest is given to one group, the Enterprise Admins group. By default, the Administrator account in the root domain of the forest is a member of this group. The Company.com administrator either logged on using that Administrator account or used the Administrator account to make his own account a member of Enterprise Admins.

- **Create a Universal group in the Subsidiary.com domain.** Universal groups are available only in a domain that has been shifted to Native mode. Because the administrator created the Universal group in Subsidiary.com, the Company.com domain can remain in Mixed mode.

- **Place the Universal group on the ACL for the OU with read/write permissions.** Universal groups can be used as security principals on any object anywhere in the forest.

- **Place the Global groups as members of the Universal group.** Windows 2000 has extensive capabilities to nest groups. See "Guidelines for Using Groups as Security Principals" for details.

The following example traces the sequence of events that validates a user from Company.com who tries to access the OU in Subsidiary.com. The user is a member of the Global group that the administrator created in Company.com. This is the Global group that is nested with the Universal group in Subidiary.com. Here is the sequence of events that validates the user when she attempts to access the OU using the `Active Directory Users and Computers` console:

Procedure 10.9 **Functional Description of User and Group Validation Across Domains Using Universal Group**

1. When the user logs on to Company.com, the LSA on the Company.com domain controller finds the user's Global group membership in the Member-Of attribute. When LSA does the GC scan, it finds the Universal group membership for the Global group. LSA turns these SIDs over to the KDC, which builds a TGT that has the SIDs in the Authorization Data field.

2. When the user opens the `Active Directory Users and Computers` console and sets the focus to the Subsidiary.com domain, the network client obtains a TGT from the Subsidiary.com domain and a ticket for the domain controller using the process outlined in the preceding section.

   The end result of that process is a Kerberos ticket for a specific domain controller in the Subsidiary.com domain. The ticket contains the SIDs of the user's Global group membership in Company.com and the Universal group membership in Subsidiary.com.

3. The domain controller receiving the Kerberos ticket validates it, and then builds a local access token with the SIDs in the Authentication Data field.

4. When the user attempts to access the OU object in Subsidiary.com, the LSA on the domain controller checks the SIDs in the user's access token against the list of SIDs in the security descriptor for the OU. It finds a match for the Universal group SID with an ACE mask of read/write. The LSA gives the user appropriate access.

In short, if a user is a member of a universal group, the LSA on a member server in any domain can validate the user based on the contents of a Kerberos ticket issued by a domain controller in that server's domain.

Summary of Group Functions

It took a long time and a lot of steps to get to this point, so let's draw together the examples into a few general principles:

- Security objects on domain controllers that are accessed exclusively by users within that domain can be protected by Domain Local groups or Global groups.

- Security objects on member computers that are accessed exclusively by users within that domain can be protected by Global groups.

- Security objects on any domain controller or member computer that are accessed by users from multiple domains can be protected by Universal groups.

- The requirement that every domain controller in a forest have access to a Global Catalog server, with the stipulation that the GC must contain the membership list of every Universal group in the forest, becomes the limiting factor when laying out interdomain object security.

Choosing Between Global and Universal Groups

Based on the principles outlined in the summary from the preceding section, deciding whether to create a Universal or a Global group to control access to a particular object depends on who will access it. For the most part, users tend to be parochial. They keep their files on local servers. Global groups are fine for most situations. Why waste bandwidth and GC storage replicating Universal group members between domains if they won't be used? If an object starts off as local and then the scope expands, you can either convert the Global group to a Universal group or create a new Universal group. See "Group Scope Improvements and Downgrades" for details.

Universal groups can be a significant contributor to Directory bulk on a GC server. If you make every group a Universal group in a network with tens of thousands of users, you'll end up storing a *lot* of group members in the GC. This doesn't tax the AD database engine excessively—ESENT can handle 10 million objects—but the GC is supposed to be a place to do quick lookups, not some behemoth that has to be loaded onto a domain controller with a forklift.

Even more important than the size of the information store on the GC is the work necessary to replicate objects in the store. Try to minimize situations that trigger replication of a Universal group. Avoid putting individual users in Universal groups. User populations tend to change often. Each update forces the system to replicate the group. Put users in Global groups within a domain, and then nest the Global groups into the Universal groups that are on the ACLs. This enables you to modify the Global group membership without changing the Universal group members.

If central accounting has a Universal group called Audit_Team, for example, the Phoenix office could maintain a Global group called Phoenix_Auditors and the Houston office could maintain a Global group called Houston_Auditors and so on. Local administrators in each office would control the membership list for the Global group. The Universal group membership would stay relatively stable.

Guidelines for Placing Global Catalog Servers

The LSA has only one way of knowing whether a user has been added to a Universal group in another domain or is a member of a Global group that has been nested into a Universal group in another domain. It must check the membership list on a GC server. For this reason, it is vital that every domain controller be able to find a GC.

A domain controller finds a GC by looking for SRV records in DNS. Under normal circumstances, it selects a GC from its own site. If no GCs are associated with the local site, or if that GC is down, the domain controllers find a GC at another site. If you have no GCs in a site and the WAN link to the other sites goes down, users cannot log on. LSA imposes this restriction because it cannot verify the user's Universal group membership. The symptoms of having no GC available are as follows:

- Users attempt to log on to the domain and get the error *The system could not log you on because a domain controller could not be contacted…* even though the local domain controller is operating normally. The Administrator account is exempt from this restriction.

- When adding users to an ACL or modifying group memberships, you open the Select User window to browse a trusted domain and get the error *No objects are available at this time.*

- When adding users, the Active Directory Users and Computers console gives the error *The uniqueness of this user's proposed user logon name could not be validated....* If you get this message, you can still add the user account but it will be verified for uniqueness after the GC comes back online.

As you can see, loss of access of a GC isn't an unmitigated disaster, but it certainly ranks up there in the top 10 for reasons why administrators don't have good days. Have at least two GCs at every large site and one at remote offices, possibly more if the GC gets overloaded. Use the NTDS counters in Performance Monitor to establish a baseline and spot trends.

Guidelines for Using Groups as Security Principals

With only three group types in a domain—Domain Local, Global, and Universal—you would think the rules for managing groups could not get too complicated. Well, *au contraire*, as we say in southern New Mexico. When Windows 2000 plays Three Card Monte with groups, it can shuffle and deal and shift them in ways that make W. C. Fields look like a Baptist preacher. Here are the rules for Windows 2000 group management:

- **Allowable groups based on platform**
  Workstations and standalone servers can have only Local groups. These groups are stored in the SAM.

  Mixed-mode domain controllers can have Domain Local groups and Global groups.

  Native-mode domain controllers can have Domain Local, Global, and Universal groups.

- **Group scope limitations**
  Local groups on member servers and desktops can only be put on the ACL of local security objects.

  Domain Local groups can only be put on the ACL of security objects on domain controllers in that domain. This also applies to system rights associated with Builtin Local groups. If Jane_Admin is a member of the Administrators group in the Company.com domain, for example, she gets local administrator privileges on domain controllers but not on member computers.

  Global groups can be put on the ACL of any security object in the domain, including member computers and domain controllers.

Universal groups can be put on the ACL of any security object in any domain in the forest.

- **Group membership limitations**

  Local group members can be: users from the local SAM; users, Global and Universal groups from the local domain; and users, Global and Universal groups from domains trusted explicitly by the local domain. In Native mode, the trust extent expands to any domain in the forest.

  Domain Local group members can be: users, computers, Local, Global, and Universal groups from the local domain; and users, computers, Global, and Universal groups from explicitly trusted domains. In Native mode, the trust extent expands to any domain in the forest.

  Global group members can be users, computers, and Global groups from the local domain only.

  Universal group members can be users, computers, Global groups, and Universal groups from the local domain and any other domain in the forest.

- **Group scope improvements and downgrades**

  A Domain Local group can be improved to a Universal group if it does not have a Local group as a member.

  A Global group scope can be improved to a Universal group at any time.

  A Universal group can be downgraded to a Global group if it has no cross-domain members.

  A Universal group can be downgraded to a Local group, but the action must be performed on a GC server.

  A Global group cannot be downgraded.

  If the last domain controller in a domain is demoted to a standard server, Directory accounts are not migrated to the local SAM. New accounts for Administrator, Guest, and Builtin groups are created in the SAM.

- **Group nesting rules**

  Local groups (SAM-based) cannot be nested.

  Domain Local groups cannot be nested.

  Global groups can be nested into Universal groups, but not vice versa.

  Universal groups can be nested into Domain Local groups and Local groups.

Examples of Managing Directory Objects Using Groups

If Thoreau were a systems administrator, he would urge us to simplify, simplify. It may seem to you that to "simplify systems management" is an oxymoron, and you're probably right; but we can at least strive for elegance and economy. (We can also take lessons from Thoreau on burying the real costs of projects in budget reports.)

So, let's ask the question, can we use just one group to manage an entire Directory structure including all child domains in a tree and peer domains in a forest? Microsoft provides such a group, the Enterprise Admins group.

Managing the Directory with the Enterprise Admins Group

When you install the first Windows 2000 domain controller and use it to define the top of the Directory namespace, the AD Installation Wizard creates the Enterprise Admin group. This group is put on the Domain-DNS object at the top of the tree with something just shy of Full Control access rights. The inheritance flag is set so that these rights propagate down the structure to all subordinate containers. This gives the Enterprise Admins group carte-blanche access to all objects in the Directory.

In addition, when new domains are joined to the tree, either as child domains or as trust-root domains in a forest, the Enterprise Admins group is nested with the Administrators group in the trusting domains, giving the Enterprise Admins group members system-level privileges everywhere in the network.

You must admit, this certainly centralizes Directory administration, which was one of the initial goals of Directory design. Perhaps, however, it centralizes administration a bit too much, something like turning over control of all three branches of the federal government to the Bureau of Mines. If you decide to use the Enterprise Admins to manage your network, I suggest that you grant membership only to a select few administrators with special logon IDs that they use only when they need *übermensch* privileges.

The same problem applies, although to a lesser extent, to the *Domain Admins* global group within a domain. This group is added automatically to the ACL of Directory objects. It is also automatically added to the local Administrators group on member workstations and servers when they are joined to the domain.

If you compartmentalize your Directory with domains, it might make sense to use the Domain Admins group. If you decide to have a single domain with a hierarchy of OUs, however, you should forgo the simplicity of the Domain Admins group and create your own administrative groups to handle desktop and Directory tasks. This requires an extra step when deploying member workstations and servers because you must add the group to the local Administrators group, but you can automate this very easily from the command line (net localgroup Desktop_Admins /add, for example) and this bit of extra work is well repaid by added security and flexibility.

Managing the Directory with Custom Admin Groups

It looks as if it might take more than one group to properly manage a domain. The question is, how many groups are required? The answer is the same as Mozart gave Prince Leopold in *Amadeus*. "I use just as many notes as I need, your Majesty, no more and no less." Let's walk through a couple of typical scenarios.

The forest in Figure 10.27 shows a domain called Company.com that was designed for management by a single IT organization. The focus is on the Phoenix OU. Administrators in Phoenix are divided into three groups to handle the various systems and to respond to user needs.

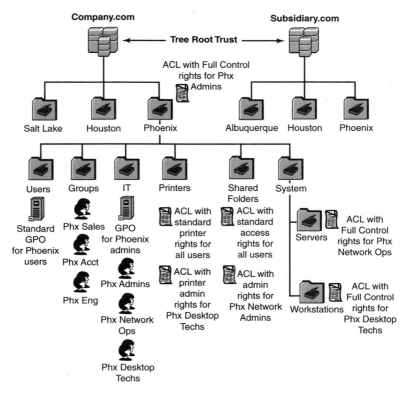

Figure 10.27   Example forest with lower-level OUs in Company.com designed for support by a single IT organization.

The Groups container in Phoenix holds security groups for NTFS and Share permissions. The group names include a Phx designator because this is a single domain, so there must be a quick way to identify groups from the various office OUs. The groups under the Phoenix OU in the Subsidiary.com domain would also use a Phx designator. Because they are separate domains, there is no need to differentiate between the two group names.

The company has a relatively large and vocal Sales department. The salespeople work on commission and they aren't exactly reticent about putting demands on the IT staff when they think their computers are getting in the way of sales. They also aren't slow about sending emails to company executives when they don't think they're getting quick and efficient solutions.

To make a long story short, the Sales Manager decided to break free the surly bonds of centralized computing and hire his own administrators to run his servers and desktops. He insists that the IT department give his administrators access to the Directory so that they can manage users and computers. He also wants certain end users—he calls them gurus—to have admin rights so that they can play a more active role in user support. An unpaid role, I might add, which was probably one of the reasons for the separation.

Computer Gurus and Directory Management

Just about every department has a computer guru. You might even be one yourself. Many system administrators got their start as department computer gurus. It's the latter-twentieth-century version of the Horatio Alger story, except that instead of fame and wealth, you get a 24×7 pager and an eye twitch.

One of the best parts of Windows 2000 rights delegation is the ability to grant extensive but controlled admin rights to trusted department personnel. By laying out lower-level OUs with an eye toward distributed management, you can easily turn over a great deal of day-to-day operations to individual departments without compromising security higher in the Directory.

The IT manager responds to the Sales manager by authorizing her administrators to do what it takes to accommodate the request but then to leave the sales administrators alone to sink or swim on their own merit. Figure 10.28 shows one way to do this.

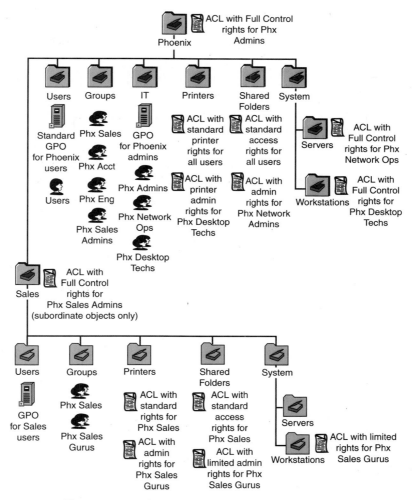

Figure 10.28   Phoenix OU showing new Sales container
with rights assigned to Sales administrators and gurus.

The Phoenix IT administrators start by creating an OU for the Sales department. They place the OU under the Phoenix container. They build a container structure similar to that used in the main office container for consistency. If the new administrators choose not to retain that structure, so be it.

After the Sales containers are built, the Phoenix IT admins populate it with users and groups from the Sales department. This includes users, groups, computers, printers, and any servers that the Sales staff insists on controlling.

Now the Phoenix IT administrators create a Global group called Phx Sales Admins. They do not make this a Universal group because it will not be used to control access to resources in Subsidiary.com. If at some future date the Sales departments in the two domains decide to work together, the group scope can be improved to a Universal group.

The Phoenix IT administrators populate the Phx Sales Admins group with members from the Sales administrative staff after their user objects have been moved to the Sales container. Instead of putting the Phx Sales Admins group under the Sales container, however, they leave it in the main Phoenix container. If they put it under Sales, members of Phx Sales Admin could turn around and assign more members to the group, possibly users from outside the Sales department. As with any policy decision, this was not done without some wrangling.

The Phoenix IT administrators also created a Phx Sales Guru group with no members. They placed this group in the Sales container where the Phx Sales Admins group has full access rights to it. The Sales administrators can add members to this group. The Phx Sales Admins group can also create other groups under the Sales OU to use for assigning NTFS permissions on their servers and workstations.

Now comes the most contentious decision, the inheritance selection for the Phx Sales Admins group at the Sales container. The IT administrators have Full Control access rights at the Phoenix container, which gives them Full Control rights to the Sales OU via dynamic inheritance. The Sales administrators want them to disable this inheritance at the Sales container so that only the Phx Sales Admins group has Full Control access to objects in Sales. The IT administrators insist that they need Full Control access so that they can help out in case of trouble.

The debate rages back and forth. If the Phx Sales Admins group is given Full Access control rights to the Sales container, they will probably disable inheritance. The IT administrators would see this change and use their Enterprise Admins rights to change it back. Instead of carrying on a feud, however, the IT administrators decide to block access to the Sales object by giving Full Control permissions to the Phx Sales Admins group but setting the inheritance to apply only to child objects and containers under Sales. This prevents the Phx Sales Admins group from changing the inheritance setting. See Figure 10.29 for an example.

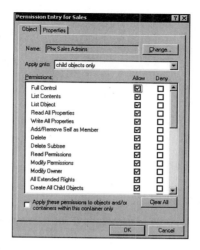

Figure 10.29   Permissions list for the Sales container
showing the `Child Objects Only` option.

If you are designing a Directory tree partitioned into multiple domains
rather than multiple OUs, you may encounter the same contentious situations. The details are a bit more complicated because it is more difficult to
move objects between domains, but the basic operations are the same. Set the
access rights on the uppermost domain so that the administrators higher in
the tree have Full Control access with inheritance set to flow all the way
down the tree. At each domain, set up the rights so that the local administrators do not have rights to the domain object itself, just the objects under it.

Using the Secondary Logon Service and RunAs

The examples throughout this chapter have shown local administrators going
about their daily work while logged on using their administrative accounts.
This is generally not a good practice. Quite a few bad things can happen
when a user logs on with full administrative rights. Viruses get activated.
Mistakes can be made with the Delete key. The list goes on and on.

Windows 2000 comes with a *Secondary Logon Service* (SLS) that makes it
possible to use a standard user account for logon and then launch an administrative console with elevated permissions to perform administrative tasks.
The console can be closed when it is not in use. This is philosophically similar to the su (superuser) command in UNIX, but is implemented somewhat
differently.

The SLS is installed by default and starts at boot time. The service is hosted by SERVICES.EXE. The code is contained in SECLOGON.DLL. The service is accessed using the RunAs utility either from a command line or the Run window. The syntax for RunAs is: runas /u:domain\user exe or runas /u:user@domain.root exe.

One of the easiest ways to use the SLS is to open a command console window using RunAs and then launch applications from there in the same security context that you used to open the window. To do this, open a Run window and enter **runas /u:administrator@company.com cmd**. When the command console window opens, the title bar shows the ID you used to open it. From this console window, if you want to change a user account or add a group or do some other chore in the Directory, you can enter **dsa.msc** at the command prompt to open the Active Directory Users and Computers console in the administrator's security context.

The SLS is also a convenient way to perform administrative tasks at a user's desktop. You can open a command session at elevated permissions while you work on the machine and then close the console after you've finished. If you want to preserve the user's existing environment variables to assist you in troubleshooting from the console, use the /env switch: runas /env /u:administrator@company.com cmd.exe.

If you initiate a network connection from the console, you can access the connection through the console but not through the shell. For example, you can map a drive to the admin shares of another server while you are at elevated permissions by entering **net use y: \\server_name.company.com\c$**. The connection succeeds because you have sufficient credentials. If you go to the My Computer window and look at the drive you just mapped, however, it shows an X and denies access if you try to use it because the shell is still running with your logon permissions.

If you want to run the shell at elevated permissions, too, you can shut down Explorer and then restart it using RunAs from the Task Manager. Do this as described in Procedure 10.10.

Procedure 10.10 **Starting Explorer Shell Using RunAs**

1. Open Task Manager by pressing Ctrl+Alt+Del and then clicking Task Manager.

2. Select the Processes tab.

3. Highlight Explorer and click End Process. Confirm when prompted.

4. When Explorer shuts down, select FILE | RUN from the TASK MANAGER menu and start Explorer as follows:

```
runas /u:administrator@company.com explorer.exe
```

This starts Explorer at elevated permissions. Some components, such as the status bar and System Tray, continue to run in your logon context and are unavailable.

If you try this, you'll notice that the shell loads the Default User profile when you start it with RunAs. If you want to run the shell at elevated permissions with your own local profile, use the /profile switch as follows:

```
runas /profile /u:administrator@company.com explorer.exe
```

If you're not the command-line type, you can use a shell shortcut. Hold down the Shift key, then right-click an icon for an executable, and then select the RUN AS option from the fly-out menu. A Run As Other User window opens with fields to enter administrator credentials.

Moving Forward

This completes the discussion of access rights and groups, at least as far as the Directory is concerned. See Chapter 14 for more information on NTFS file system permissions and Chapter 6 for a discussion of group policies as they relate to security. The next chapter covers setting up sites, replicating Directory objects, and fixing the Directory if something goes wrong.

11

Managing Active Directory Replication and Directory Maintenance

OF ALL THE ENHANCEMENTS, IMPROVEMENTS, and home decorating ideas that went into Windows 2000, a prime candidate for the Best Supporting Actor award is *multiple-master replication*. Active Directory may be fancy technology, but it is the capability to put a read-write copy of the Directory on every domain controller (DC) that really sets Windows 2000 apart from classic NT. No more primary and backup DCs. In Windows 2000, every DC is a peer of every other DC. That's both advantageous and challenging.

In terms of advantages, a single Windows 2000 DC can authenticate users and computers, and it can audit virtually every aspect of their activity on the network. It can also accept password changes, deliver group policies and software updates, respond to LDAP lookups, update the Directory database in response to LDAP modification requests, support a host of security providers, accept authentication requests from down-level clients and remote access clients, and support RADIUS, TACACS, and certificate services. In addition, it can replicate DNS zone information, update its replication partners, and collect and disseminate information to and from directory-enabled infrastructure components. What's more, it does all this while keeping its neighboring DCs apprised of its current state via replication, and it provides backward compatibility with all versions of classic NT and Windows.

As for challenges, managing those super-powered DCs while they exchange updates via multiple-master replication is vastly more complicated than managing classic NT replication. Recovering the information store in the event of a problem is much more difficult, as well.

In classic NT, if the SAM gets corrupted, you swallow hard, recover the Registry on the PDC, then let it replicate out to the BDCs. It takes a few minutes. The hardest part is explaining to users why their password changes reverted back. Not fun, but not a major career hiccup, either.

Recovering from the loss or corruption of an Active Directory database is not nearly that simple. This chapter covers how to recognize and repair Directory integrity problems before they get out of control. Keeping integrity problems from occurring is preferable, though, so let's start with an overview of Windows 2000 replication, and then discuss how to configure it to keep the Directory healthy.

Replication Overview

A DC stores the Active Directory objects in a file called NTDS.DIT. (DIT stands for Directory Information Tree.) The file is located in the \WINNT\NTDS directory that was created when the server was promoted to a DC. A few log files and checkpoint files are also in this directory. They provide fault tolerance and help to improve performance.

NTDS.DIT is divided into separate logical partitions called *naming contexts*. Every DC holds a replica of at least three naming contexts: the Domain-DNS naming context for that domain, the Configuration naming context for the forest, and the Schema naming context for the forest. The DIT on a GC server also contains a read-only replica of the Domain-DNS naming contexts for the other domains in the forest.

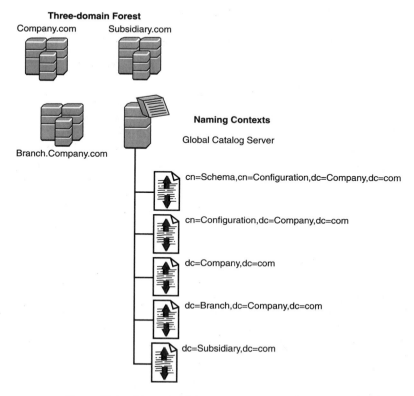

Figure 11.1 Diagram of three-domain forest and the
naming contexts on a GC in that forest.

Figure 11.1 shows a three-domain forest and the naming contexts that would be found in the NTDS.DIT of a GC server in that forest. Figure 11.2 shows how the naming contexts in Figure 11.1 would be distributed among the DCs in the forest.

Replication connections between DCs always represent inbound data flows. All Directory replication is pull replication. The only outbound traffic is a notification from one DC to its replication partners that updates are ready to transfer.

The default replication topology is a loop. Each DC has inbound connections from at least two different replication partners, assuming that the forest has more than two DCs. The replication system may create additional connections to mesh the topology. It uses a spanning tree algorithm to make this decision.

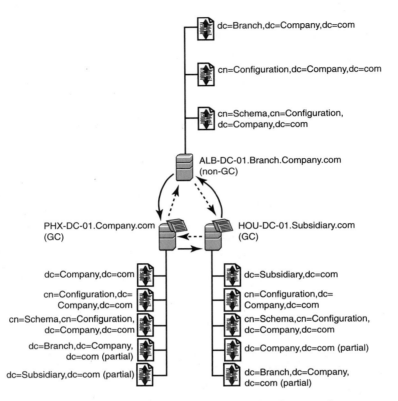

Figure 11.2 Diagram of naming context distribution and
replication connections for the forest shown in Figure 11.1.

The "Detailed Analysis of Replication Transactions" section later in this
chapter traces each step in a replication event, but before getting to that level
of detail, let's take a brief look at the high-level replication transactions just
to get a feel for how they work.

Overview of Intrasite Replication Transaction

Refer to the diagram in Figure 11.3. The particulars of the configuration
that affect replication are as follows:

- The forest in the diagram has two domains: Company.com and
  Subsidiary.com. The domains share a Tree Root trust.

- The computers in the Company.com domain are located in Phoenix. The
  Subsidiary.com domain computers are located in Houston.

- The Company.com domain has two DCs. PHX-DC-01 is a GC server, and PHX-DC-02 is not. One DC, HOU-DC-01, is in the Subsidiary.com domain; it is also a GC server.
- All DCs are in the same site. This is acceptable because the two local networks are linked by a high-speed WAN connection.

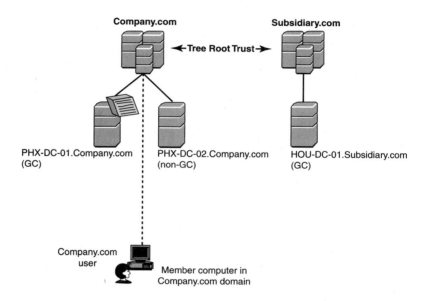

Figure 11.3   Diagram of two-domain forest in a single site.

The trace starts with a user turning on a desktop in Company.com.

Procedure 11.1   **Functional Description of Intrasite Replication**

1. When Windows 2000 loads, the network client in the local system authenticates to one of the two DCs in the Company.com domain. The client locates these DCs using SRV records in DNS. If the client authenticates at PHX-DC-01, all subsequent user authentication and LDAP traffic from that client is directed at PHX-DC-01.

Identifying a Client's Logon Server
You can identify the DC that authenticated a client computer by opening a command prompt and typing SET. Look for the LOGONSERVER variable.

2. At some point during the day, a user takes advantage of a shareware LDAP application she found that lets her access information stored in databases, such as Active Directory. She uses this tool to change her job title. This action sends an LDAP message to PHX-DC-01 that modifies the Title attribute in the user's Directory object.

3. Assuming that all appropriate security requirements are met, PHX-DC-01 makes the change to the user's Directory object. In a few minutes, PHX-DC-01 informs its replication partners that it updated its copy of the dc=Company,dc=com naming context and that it is ready to replicate those changes.

4. The replication partners respond with a demand that PHX-DC-01 send its updates. This is the "pull" part of the replication transaction. (The replication requests include special values designed to prevent redundant updates. These are covered in the "Detailed Analysis of Replication Transactions" section later in this chapter.)

5. PHX-DC-01 responds to the replication requests from its partners, but it does so a little differently depending on the nature of the partner:

   PHX-DC-02 is a DC in the Company.com domain. As such, it hosts a full replica of the dc=Company,dc=com naming context. PHX-DC-01 sends PHX-DC-02 the updated Title attribute, which PHX-DC-02 uses to modify the copy of the user object in its replica of dc=Company,dc=com.

   HOU-DC-01 is a GC server in a different domain. It has a replica of the dc=Company,dc=com naming context, but the Title attribute is not one of the 60 or so attributes contained in the GC. PHX-DC-01 responds to the replication request from HOU-DC-01 with only an acknowledgment.

6. After PHX-DC-02 applies the updates, it notifies its replication partners that it made changes to its replica of the dc=company,dc=com naming context and is ready to replicate them. In this example, the replication stops at that point.

In a larger network with other DCs in the replica ring, PHX-DC-02 passes its update to another DC, and so on, until the update propagates to all replicas of the naming context.

Intrasite Replication Summary

Keep in mind the following important points concerning the high-level transactions in Active Directory replication:

- The contents of the Directory database are partitioned by naming context. Each naming context forms a separate replication unit.
- Only properties are replicated, not entire objects. This cuts down replication traffic and reduces the load on the Directory engine.
- DCs replicate to specific partners, not to every other DC.
- Properties that are not in the GC are replicated only to DCs in the same domain.
- Properties in the GC are replicated to every GC server in every domain in the forest.

Replication Topology

When a Windows 2000 server is promoted to DC, a special service called the *Knowledge Consistency Checker* (KCC) is given responsibility for weaving the server into the replication topology for the forest. The KCC gets its name from X.500, where the Directory contents are sometimes referred to as *knowledge.*

The KCC runs in the context of the *Local Security Authority SubSystem* (LSASS). It does not appear as a separate process on the Task List. After the KCC establishes connections between DCs, the *Directory Replication Agent* (DRA), takes over to do the grunt work of propagating updates to replication partners. The DRA treats each naming context as a separate replication entity, even though all the objects in those naming contexts are stored in the same NTDT.DIT file.

Active Directory Replication and LDAP

The replication mechanism used by Active Directory is proprietary to Microsoft. LDAP v3 does not define a replication methodology, although several schemes are working their way through the acceptance process. Microsoft stated that it is considering reworking Active Directory replication in future versions of Windows 2000, if and when a specific LDAP replication method is finalized as a standard.

When the KCC builds a replication topology, it starts with a simple ring such as that shown in Figure 11.4. Each DC in the ring gets inbound connections from at least two other DCs. These DCs can be in different domains, but as long as they are in the same forest, they share a common replication topology.

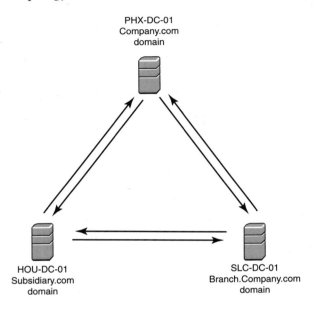

PHX-DC-01
Company.com
domain

HOU-DC-01
Subsidiary.com
domain

SLC-DC-01
Branch.Company.com
domain

Figure 11.4 Simple replication ring.

When a new DC is promoted, the KCC integrates its information store into the replication topology in much the same way that aliens invade Earth in grade C sci-fi movies. During the DC promotion, the KCC snakes out a single tendril between an existing DC and the new one. It uses this connection to replicate the Directory to the new DC during promotion.

When the DC restarts following promotion, the KCC builds a second connection to the same replication partner so that updates from the new DC can replicate outward. The KCC then analyzes its topology map and builds additional connections for the new DC that tie it to at least one other DC. This inserts the new server into the replica ring.

As the number of DCs increases, the KCC adds connections and meshes them together to keep the hop count between DCs to three or fewer. This minimizes replication latencies and shortens the convergence time should a DC fail. An example of a meshed topology is shown in Figure 11.5. For simplicity, the figure shows only one set of inbound connections at each DC.

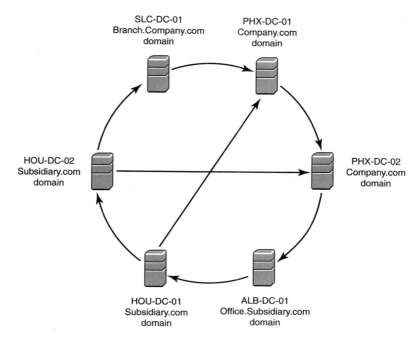

Figure 11.5 Meshed replication topology.

If a DC stops responding to repeated replication requests by the DRA, the KCC takes over and builds new connections to bypass the failed DC. This is a lot like a heart muscle healing itself after a heart attack by bypassing damaged coronary capillaries with new ones.

If the DC comes back online again, the KCC either tears down the bypass or restructures the topology to accommodate the new connections. You can build manual connections, but for the most part, the best course of action is to be patient and enable the KCC to do its work without interruption.

Functional Overview of Sites

Unlike other Directory Services, such as NDS and Netscape Directory Services, Active Directory does not use naming contexts to define replication boundaries. Instead, replication boundaries are defined by areas of high-speed interconnection called *sites*. An administrator builds a Directory object that identifies a site and associates it with a distinct IP subnet so that the site can be uniquely identified in DNS.

A site is usually a LAN or MAN. A site can encompass a wide area connection if the link performance meets the criteria (see the following sidebar), and if sufficient bandwidth is available to support full-speed replication at standard intervals. This includes a T1 or fractional T1 connection if the lines are not heavily subscribed.

Measuring Link Performance

Unlike classic NT, Windows 2000 measures link performance to determine whether a slow or fast link exists. The calculation goes like this:

1. Ping a server with 0 bytes of data, and time the round trip. If the time is less than 10 ms, it's a fast link.

2. Ping the same server with 4KB of data, and time the round trip.

3. Calculate the delta between the 4KB round trip and the 0KB round trip. This results in the time necessary to move 4KB of data.

4. Repeat 3 times and get an average 4KB transfer time.

5. Convert to bits-per-second and compare to benchmark. The default benchmark is 500Kbps.

You can put an entire Windows 2000 forest in one site. This yields the least convergence delay, which is important if you are trying to support a global network and you don't want to wait a long time for replication to effect a change at a remote replica.

You might opt for using multiple sites instead of a single site for two reasons: to localize replication traffic and to localize Directory access.

Using Sites to Localize Replication Traffic

Replication within a site (intrasite replication) is handled differently from replication between sites (intersite replication) in the following ways:

- Intersite replication intervals are much longer than intrasite intervals. Intersite replication occurs during 15-minute windows every 6 hours. Intrasite replication occurs at least once every 5 minutes.

- DCs in the same site notify each other that updates occurred requiring replication. Update notification is disabled between sites.

- Intersite replication traffic is compressed. Compression is turned off within a site.

- Intersite replication uses IP by default. Intrasite replication uses Remote Procedure Call (RPC) connections, which support synchronous communications.

- Intersite replication can be packaged as mail and sent between sites by using SMTP. This is handy if the Directory is very small, changes are infrequent, and the remote site has a demand-dial connection.

As you can see, if you decide to use sites and intersite replication, you are going to experience lengthy delays in getting information transferred between the sites. On the other hand, if you do not define separate sites, the replication traffic might swamp a wide area link and cause the DCs in that location to fall out of sync.

The next section gives an overview of intersite replication. This information can help you decide whether to use a single site or multiple sites for your network.

Functional Description of Intrasite Replication

This section describes the replication flowpaths when DCs are configured to be in different sites. Because a single domain can span multiple sites, and a single site can span multiple domains, replication can sometimes be a little difficult to follow. Refer to Figure 11.6 for an example of how a mix of domains and sites within a network might look. The particulars for this configuration are as follows:

- Two local area networks exist: one at Headquarters and one at a local store. A 56K leased line connects the networks.

- Two sites exist: HQ and STORE. Each site represents an area of high-speed interconnection.

- Two domains exist: DomA and DomB. DomA is the corporate domain. DomB is a small regional domain used to support local stores. The domains share a Domain Trust. The domain hierarchy does not affect replication.

- Two DCs exist in each domain. The DomB DC in the Store network is a GC server. It provides fault tolerance in case the 56K line goes down, which happens fairly often.

- The core router at Headquarters is in network 10.3.20.0. An additional subnet at Headquarters, 10.3.21.0, is set aside for a warehouse which is on the other end of the campus.
- The Store network uses the 10.3.22.0 subnet.

Figure 11.6 also shows the replication flowpaths based on the site configuration. Recall that replication connections always represent inbound data flows.

- The HQ site encompasses all DCs in DomA and DomB at Headquarters, so the three DCs in that location form a replica ring. Replication among these three servers occurs at least every 5 minutes, with update notifications to minimize latency.
- The replication between DC DomB-01 at the HQ site and DC DomB-02 at the STORE site is much less frequent. The default interval is a 15-minute window every 6 hours, with no update notifications.

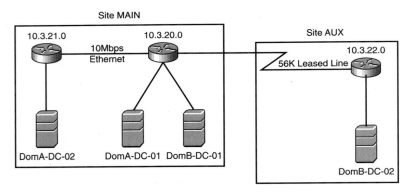

Figure 11.6   Two sites with mixed domains and subnets.

The decision to make the Store network into a separate site had a dramatic impact on the replication latency. The intervals can be changed, but the net effect still has a much higher latency. You may look at this and decide that sites are something to avoid and upgrade your wide area connections instead. But you may not have a choice about using sites because of their second function, which is to localize client queries.

Using Sites to Localize Active Directory Access

Sites are used to direct client LDAP queries and Kerberos authentications to local DCs. This is accomplished with the help of DNS.

Active Directory clients use SRV records stored in DNS to find DCs. DCs store these SRV records in a hierarchy based on their domain and site affiliation. Figure 11.7 shows a DNS zone table with SRV records divided among several sites.

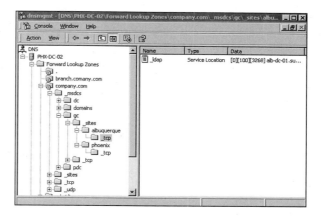

Figure 11.7 DNS zone table showing sites and SRV records.

SRV records in DNS are sorted from the bottom up as follows (the underscore prefixes are required by RFC 2052, "A DNS RR for Specifying the Location of Services"):

- **Network service type.** This includes _kerberos, _ldap, _kpasswd, and _gc.
- **Transport protocol.** This is either _tcp or _udp.
- **Site name.** This is the name of the Site object in the Directory that is used to define the relationship of the site to other sites.
- **The Microsoft-specific DNS path.** _sites.dc._msdc
- **DNS domain name.** This is the name of the DNS domain that corresponds to the Active-Directory-based domain.

Each site has an IP subnet assigned to it by an administrator when the Site object is created in the Directory. When DCs are promoted, their server objects are placed in a site based on their IP addresses. The placement of the server object determines how the DC registers its SRV records. A DC in the STORE site, for instance, registers its SRV records under
STORE._sites.dc._msdcs.DomB.com.

By sorting the SRV records by site, Active Directory clients can identify their local DCs. Without this sorting mechanism, a client in Tuscaloosa could end up authenticating on a DC in Toronto.

A network client is assigned a site at boot time by the DC that authenticates it. The DC determines the site based on the client's IP address and the list of IP subnets assigned to Site objects in the Directory. For example, in Figure 10.5 in Chapter 10, "Managing Active Directory Security," the site named STORE is assigned an IP subnet of 10.3.22.0/24. A client with an IP address of 10.3.22.17 is assigned to the STORE site.

When the network client queries DNS for SRV records, it looks for records based on the network service it requires, the site it was assigned, and the DNS Suffix stored in the TCP/IP Registry key. For an authentication transaction, the network client gets SRV records under
`_kerberos._tcp.<sitename>._sites.dc._msdcs.<domain>.<root>`.

When DNS receives this query, it returns all SRV records that meet the query criteria, sorting them by priority and weight. See Chapter 5, "Managing Domain Name System (DNS) Services and Dynamic Host Configuration (DHCP) Services," for more complete details of this sorting.

When the network client receives the SRV records, it fires off an LDAP ping over UDP port 389 to every DC on the list. It sends these pings in rapid succession, every one-tenth of a second. The first DC to respond wins the race after the client verifies that the DC is from the correct domain. The next section contains an example showing how a Windows 2000 client locates a local DC in the local site.

Functional Description of Intersite Authentication

Refer back to the diagram in Figure 11.6. Let's say a user in the Store network travels to Headquarters and plugs in a laptop that is a client of DomB. The laptop gets an address in the 10.3.20.0 network from DHCP. When the client machine authenticates, this is what happens:

Procedure 11.2   Client Authentication Across Site Boundaries

1. The network client queries DNS looking for SRV records under
   `_kerberos._tcp.STORE._sites.dc._msdcs.DomB.com`. The client includes the
   STORE site because the last site name is kept in the Registry under HKLM
   | System | CurrentControlSet | Services | Netlogon | Parameters |
   DynamicSiteName.

2. DNS returns the Kerberos-related SRV records for the STORE site in the DomB domain. In this case, only one record exists, that of DomB-02.

3. The client does an LDAP ping to DomB-02.

4. DomB-02 gets the LDAP ping from the client and notices that the client's IP subnet is wrong for the STORE site. It responds with an LDAP message telling the client to use the HQ site.

Distributed Knowledge of Sites

The DomB-02 DC knows about the HQ site and its associated IP subnet because it has a copy of the Configuration naming context. All DCs have a copy of this naming context. The Configuration naming context stores the container where site information is kept:

`cn=Sites,cn=Service,cn=Configuration,dc=Company,dc=com`.

5. The network client goes back to DNS and queries for SRV records under `_kerberos._tcp.HQ._sites.dc._msdcs.DomB.com`. This turns up any DCs in the HQ site.

6. DNS returns the requested SRV records. In this case, only one record exists, that of DomB-01.

7. The client does an LDAP ping to DomB-01.

8. DC DomB-01 responds, and the two machines use Kerberos and LSA to establish a secure RPC session.

If the network client cannot contact any DCs in its original site, it queries DNS for SRV records under `_kerberos._tcp.dc._msdcs.DomB.com`. This locates all DCs in the domain. It then uses LDAP pings sent to all those servers to find one that responds. If it turns out that the first DC to respond is in Anchorage or Guam, the user may notice some performance degradation.

You cannot configure a "preferred DC" for a client. If you have a large LAN and you want to compartmentalize your clients based on their area of a campus LAN or MAN, you must structure your replication topology around multiple sites, even if all interconnections meet the definition of "high speed."

Site Objects in Active Directory

Directory objects that control replication are stored in the Sites container in the Configuration naming context. When you promote the first Windows 2000 server to DC in a forest, a site called `Default-First-Site-Name` is created.

All subsequent DCs in the forest are put in that site until an administrator builds additional sites. Figure 11.8 shows a view of the AD Sites and Services console with the tree expanded to show site-related objects.

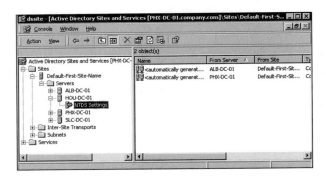

Figure 11.8 Active Directory Sites and Services console showing objects used to control replication.

The following is a list of the Directory objects used to configure and manage Sites:

- **Site.** This object defines a site and acts as a placeholder for the objects underneath.

- **Specific site.** This object contains a Site-Object-BL attribute that points to a Subnet object such as 10.3.20.0/24. Every site must be matched up with at least one subnet.

- **Subnet.** This object contains a Site-Object attribute that points at the specific Site object that references the subnet, such as CN=Store, CN=Sites,CN=Configuration,DC=DomB,DC=com. Every subnet must be unique.

- **Specific server.** This object contains the DNS Host Name of the server and its Globally Unique Identifier (GUID), which is used to uniquely identify the server for replication purposes.

- **NTDS Settings.** This object lists the Naming Contexts in the DIT of the associated Server. For example, the DomB-02 DC has these entries:

```
hasPartialReplicaNCs: DC=DomA,DC=com
hasMasterNCs: CN=Schema,CN=Configuration,DC=DomA,DC=com
hasMasterNCs: CN=Configuration,DC=DomA,DC=com
hasMasterNCs: DC=DomB,DC=com
```

The NTDS Site Settings object also contains a Server-Reference-BL attribute that specifies the location of replicated volumes on the associated server. For example, every DC replicates SYSVOL, so the attribute contains:

```
CN=DOMB-02,CN=Domain System Volume (SYSVOL share),CN=File Replication
Service,CN=System,DC=DomB,DC=com
```

- **NTDS Site Settings.** This object contains an attribute called Intersite-Topology-Generator that points at the NTDS Settings objects for the servers in the site. The KCC uses this information to build replication connections. The NTDS Site Settings object also contains a Schedule attribute that determines the default replication schedule for Connection objects.

- **Site Link.** This object contains a Site-List attribute that shows the sites that use a particular transport. For example, the system defines an initial IP Site Link object called Default-IP-Site-Link. This is the only required entry, because the KCC supports transitive replication over a single link.

- **Connection.** This object defines parameters for the inbound replication to the DC. It uses a From-Server attribute to identify the replication partner, a Transport-Type attribute to specify the name of the associated transport object, and a Schedule attribute to define how often to poll for updates. An MS-DS-Replicates-NC-Reason attribute lists the reason for the inbound replication of each naming context.

The "Configuring Intersite Replication" section later in this chapter describes how these objects are used when configuring sites and intersite replication. But first, let's take a more detailed look at replication transactions to see how the system keeps the replicas in sync.

Detailed Analysis of Replication Transactions

The replication mechanism used by Active Directory is *loosely coupled*. This means an interval of some duration exists between the time a modification is made to an object at one replica of the Directory and the time the modified object appears in all replicas. During this interval, an LDAP query to one DC could produce a different result than the same query submitted to another DC.

The time it takes for an update to propagate to all DCs is called *convergence*. Application designers are warned repeatedly in the Windows 2000 Platform SDK documentation and in MSDN articles to take convergence into account when writing code. Still, it's possible that a Directory-enabled application might mistakenly read information from a replica on one DC and write to the replica on another DC. Or it might read and cogitate for a while before writing, during which time the property changes. There is no help or workaround for this. Keep the loosely coupled behavior of the Directory in mind when troubleshooting problems.

Active Directory uses multiple-master replication to propagate changes. Every DC has a read-write replica of three naming contexts: one for its own domain, one for Configuration, and one for Schema. GC servers also keep a partial, read-only copy of the domain naming contexts for all domains in the forest.

Schema Modifications and the Schema Master

Writing to the Schema is a Flexible Single Master Operation (FSMO). Only one DC can have Write access to the Schema at a time. This is the Schema role master. Any DC can be assigned as Schema role master. For details, see the section "Managing the Loss of an FSMO Role Master" later in this chapter.

The combination of multiple-master replication and loosely coupled update propagation raises the possibility that a change made to an object's property at one DC might propagate and overwrite a later change made to the same property at another DC. Also, updates could circulate back through the replication loop to the originating DC without a mechanism to choke feedback.

The replication system propagates updates to individual properties, not entire objects, so data integrity safeguards are incorporated into each property. These safeguards come in the form of special values that are stored with the property as a single atomic transaction, meaning that if one isn't written, none of them is written. These values are:

- **Update Sequence Number (USN).** This is a sequence number assigned to the property when it is created or modified. Each property contains two USNs. One is assigned by the DC that did the original modification. One is assigned by the DC hosting the replica of the naming context that stores the property.

- **Globally Unique Identifier (GUID).** This number represents the DC that originally modified the property.

- **Property Version Number (PVN).** This is a sequence number that identifies how many times the property was modified.
- **Time stamp.** This is a date–time stamp that marks when the property was modified.

The PVN and time stamp are used to negotiate precedence if two or more updates are received in the same replication cycle. In addition, the GUID of the originating DC and the USN associated with that originating write are used to calculate a value called the Up-to-Date Vector (UTD Vector). A DC maintains a UTD Vector list for its replication partners to ensure that updates do not circle around and get reapplied to the same property.

The next few sections cover the operation of these control values in detail. The examples use a three-node replication ring in a single domain and in a single site, as shown in Figure 11.9. The GC status of the DCs does not matter, because only one domain exists.

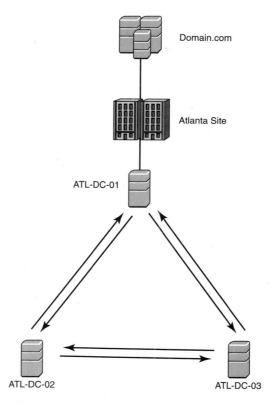

Domain.com

Atlanta Site

ATL-DC-01

ATL-DC-02   ATL-DC-03

Figure 11.9   Three-node replication ring with all DCs in the same domain and site.

The examples trace changes to the properties of a user object with the common name cn=Al Bondigas. The property lists in the examples show only a few selected items. Actually, more than three dozen properties are commonly associated with a user object. For example, the following is a list of properties for the cn=Al_Bondigas object taken from naming context replica on DC ATL-DC-01. The sequence numbers for the Title property are different from the others because it was updated after Al's user object was created.

Loc. USN	Originating DSA	Org.USN	Org.Time/Date	PVN	Attribute Name
1416	Atlanta\ATL-DC-01	1416	1999-03-01 01:20.50	1	objectClass
1416	Atlanta\ATL-DC-01	1416	1999-03-01 01:20.50	1	cn
1416	Atlanta\ATL-DC-01	1416	1999-03-01 01:20.50	1	description
14D3	Atlanta\ATL-DC-01	14D3	1999-03-02 12:14.31	2	title
1416	Atlanta\ATL-DC-01	1416	1999-03-01 01:20.50	1	department

Property Lists and Repadmin

The listings in the examples come from the Replication Administration utility, Repadmin. You can find more information about using this utility in the section "Using the Replication Administrator" later in this chapter.

Use of the Update Sequence Number (USN)

Each DC maintains a counter called the *Update Sequence Number* (USN). The USN counter increments by one whenever a DC does an update (or batch of updates) to its copy of the Directory. The system uses this number to minimize replication traffic by filtering out all but the most current updates between replication partners. This is how it works.

USN Size

The USN is a 64-bit number, making it possible to assign 2^{64} unique USNs. This makes it possible for a DC to assign 10,000 USNs per second for 66 million years, which should last until the next version of Windows.

Procedure 11.3 **Detailed Replication Trace Showing USN**

1. In this series of examples, we'll modify the Description property of the cn=Al Bondigas object. The following is the property listing taken from the replica on ATL-DC-01:

Loc. USN	Originating DSA	Org.USN	Org.Time/Date	PVN	Attribute Name
1416	Atlanta\ATL-DC-01	1416	1999-03-01 01:20.50	1	description

2. The following is the listing taken from the replica on ATL-DC-02.

```
Loc. USN   Originating DSA    Org.USN   Org.Time/Date      PVN   Attribute
=======    ================   ====      ==============     ===   =========
2F5        Atlanta\ATL-DC-01  1416      1999-03-01 01:20.50  1   description
```

The only difference in the ATL-DC-02 listing is the value for *Local USN*. If the two DCs were in different time zones, the time stamp display would be corrected for time zone. The actual number is an octet string based on Greenwich Mean Time (also called Universal Time).

3. Now let's modify the Description attribute for Al's object. The easiest way to do this is by using the `Active Directory Users and Groups` console. We'll assume that the change is first made to the replica on ATL-DC-01. The following is the modified attribute:

```
Loc. USN   Originating DSA    Org.USN   Org.Time/Date      PVN   Attribute
=======    ================   ====      ==============     ===   =========
15B1       Atlanta\ATL-DC-01  15B1      1999-04-21 02:35.33  2   description
```

The Local USN and Originating USN values remain the same, because the update was done at the same DC where the object was created. Note that the Property Version Number (PVN) was incremented by one.

4. When ATL-DC-02 eventually replicates this change, the listing in its replica after the update looks like this:

```
Loc.USN    Originating DSA    Org.USN   Org.Time/Date      PVN   Attribute
=======    ================   ====      ==============     ===   =========
3AC        Atlanta\ATL-DC-01  15B1      1999-04-21 02:35.33  2   description
```

The Local USN value reflects the state of the USN counter on ATL-DC-02 when the update arrived.

5. When ATL-DC-02 received the update, it also took note of the USN assigned by ATL-DC-01. It put this in a table called the *USN Table* where it keeps USN entries for all its replication partners. It uses these entries to request only new updates from those partners. Now that we know this, let's look at another replication event, this one for the Department property. The information from the ATL-DC-01 replica prior to any changes looks like the following:

```
Loc.USN    Originating DSA    Org.USN   Org.Time/Date      PVN   Attribute
=======    ================   ====      ==============     ===   =========
1416       Atlanta\ATL-DC-01  1416      1999-03-01 01:20.50  1   department
```

6. Now we modify the Department attribute at ATL-DC-01. The new listing looks as follows:

```
Loc.USN   Originating DSA      Org.USN   Org.Time/Date        PVN   Attribute
=======   ================     ====      ==============       ===   =========
15B2      Atlanta\ATL-DC-01    15B2      1999-04-21 02:37.15    2   department
```

7. We now force replication. (See the "Forcing Replication" section later in this chapter.) ATL-DC-01 notifies ATL-DC-02 that it has waiting updates. ATL-DC-02 responds by requesting replication, but it includes a stipulation. It refers to its USN Table and says, in effect, "Only send updates with a USN higher than 15B1, if you please."

8. ATL-DC-01 sifts through its list of waiting updates and sees that it has only one with a USN higher than 15B1, the update it just made to Al's Department property with USN 15B2. It packages this update and sends it to ATL-DC-02.

9. ATL-DC-02 applies the change. The property listing after the update looks like this:

```
Loc.USN   Originating DSA      Org.USN   Org.Time/Date        PVN   Attribute
=======   ================     ====      ==============       ===   =========
3AD       Atlanta\ATL-DC-01    15B2      1999-04-21 02:37.15    2   department
```

10. In a couple of minutes, ATL-DC-02 notifies ATL-DC-03 that it has waiting updates. (The standard replication schedule has 5-minute intervals.) ATL-DC-03 consults its USN Table for ATL-DC-02 and requests updates that have USNs higher than 32A, the USN associated with the last update it got from ATL-DC-02.

11. ATL-DC-02 packages the newest updates to Al's object and sends them to ATL-DC-03.

These transaction traces get a little convoluted. If you didn't want to bother going through them, I don't blame you. The bottom line is that USNs reduce replication traffic by letting DCs request only the updates that they need from each replication partner. Remember these important points about how USNs operate:

- Each DC generates its own USN by incrementing a 64-bit counter each time it updates its copy of any naming context.

- Each DC maintains a table of the last USN it received from each replication partner.

- When a DC modifies a property, it includes the current USN along with a time stamp, a version number, and a GUID. These are all saved as a single atomic operation.

- When a DC requests updates from a replication partner, it includes the last USN it received from that partner. Only properties with higher USNs are pulled from a replication partner.

Use of the Up-To-Date Vector (UTD Vector)

The circular nature of Directory replication makes it possible for updates to propagate back to their origin. For example, when ATL-DC-02 updated the Description attribute for Al's object, it applied a USN of 3AC. At some point in the future—5 minutes at the most—ATL-DC-02 notifies ATL-DC-01 that it has updates. This triggers a replication request from ATL-DC-01.

The USN that accompanies this request is sure to be lower than the 3AC that ATL-DC-02 applied to the Description property of Al's object, so we expect ATL-DC-02 to return the update. If it does, though, ATL-DC-01 applies the update to its copy of the property and uses the next value of its local USN.

When the time comes for the ATL-DC-01 to replicate to ATL-DC-02, it gives the property right back because the local USN is higher than the one requested by ATL-DC-02, and the whole ugly cycle begins again. Unchecked, updates keep circulating and circulating like a case of the Ebola virus until the entire network hemorrhages with replication traffic. Positive feedback such as this calls for a dampener of some sort. In the case of Active Directory, the feedback dampener is called the *Up-to-Date Vector*, or UTD Vector. It works like this.

Every property includes the identity of the *originating server*. When a DC receives a stream of new property updates in a replication transaction, it takes note of the GUID of the originating write server and the USN assigned by that server in each property. It uses this information to improve the highest USN value in a table called the UTD Vector Table. When the replication partner receives the replication request, it does two things:

- First, it collects all the objects with properties that have a higher local USN than the value requested by the replication partner.
- Then, it runs through the list and filters out any properties with UTD Vectors that indicate the property originated with the replication partner.

This second operation, the filtering based on UTD Vectors, prevents sending redundant updates back to the originating server. The following is an example of how the UTD Vector, works using the update to the cn=Al Bondigas object in the preceding section.

Procedure 11.4 **Detailed Replication Trace Showing UTD Vector**

1. The Description attribute at ATL-DC-01 replicated to ATL-DC-02 looks as follows:

Loc. USN	Originating DSA	Org.USN	Org.Time/Date	PVN	Attribute
15B1	Atlanta\ATL-DC-01	15B1	1999-03-21 02:35.33	2	description

2. The listing at ATL-DC-02 after it received the update looks like this:

Loc.USN	Originating DSA	Org.USN	Org.Time/Date	PVN	Attribute
3AC	Atlanta\ATL-DC-01	15B1	1999-03-21 02:35.33	2	description

When ATL-DC-02 applied the update, it also improved the USN Table for ATL-DC-01 to 15B1 as we saw in the previous section. It also improved the UTD Vector table entry for ATL-DC-01 to reflect the 15B1 USN because the property change originated with ATL-DC-01.

3. Now, consider what happens when ATL-DC-02 replicates the updated Description property to ATL-DC-03. The property at ATL-DC-03 before and after the update looks like this.

Before:

Loc.USN	Originating DSA	Org.USN	Org.Time/Date	Ver	Attribute
101	Atlanta\ATL-DC-01	1416	1999-03-01 01:20.50	1	description

After:

Loc.USN	Originating DSA	Org.USN	Org.Time/Date	Ver	Attribute
1B9	Atlanta\ATL-DC-01	15B1	1999-03-21 02:35.33	2	description
...					

4. When ATL-DC-03 applies the update, it also improves the USN table entry for ATL-DC-02 to 3AC to reflect the highest USN received from that source. It then improves the UTD Vector table entry for ATL-DC-01 to the 15B1 USN associated with the originating write.

5. At some point in the future, DC ATL-DC-01 requests replication from ATL-DC-03. When it sends its replication request, ATL-DC-01 includes the value of the last USN it received from ATL-DC-03. This is sure to be less than the 1B9 that ATL-DC-03 applied to its copy of Al's Description property.

6. Now, as the carnival magician says, watch the cards, not my hands. Ordinarily, ATL-DC-03 replicates the update to Al's Description property because the local USN is higher than that requested by ATL-DC-01. But, first, it compares the property's UTD Vector—the combination of Originating Server and USN—with the UTD Vector it has for ATL-DC-01. This vector is `ATL-DC-01/15B1`. Because the UTD Vector values are equal, ATL-DC-03 does not send the update. The feedback loop is broken. Civilization is saved. Cut to commercial.

The UTD Vector is a critical component in preventing replication storms. Remember these important points about the UTD Vector:

- The UTD Vector is a combination of the GUID of the server that made the original change to a property and the USN that it applied to the property when it made the change.

- Each DC maintains a table listing the highest UTD Vector value associated with every server in the replication topology.

- When a DC sends updates to properties, it filters the list based on the UTD Vector associated with the properties and the UTD Vector stored in its table for the target server.

Use of Property Version Numbers and Time Stamps

We've seen how the USN and UTD Vector form a tag team that wrestles with update propagation issues. They do not, however, ensure data integrity. An administrator or user might change a property multiple times in quick succession, or two administrators might change the same property at the same time. The USNs and UTD Vectors will increment and the changes will circulate until they meet at a DC, potentially resulting in an earlier change overwriting a later change and compromising data integrity. The Active Directory has another tag team to battle this problem: the *Property Version Number* and the *time stamp*.

The Property Version Number (PVN) is incremented by 1 whenever the property is changed directly by a DC. When the property is updated via replication, the PVN assigned by the originating server is applied to the local copy of the property. The time stamp applied by the originating server is also saved when a property is replicated.

Let's go back to our example of updating the Description property for the cn=Al Bondigas object. The property listing from the replica on ATL-DC-01 looks as follows:

```
Loc.USN   Originating DSA    Org.USN   Org.Time/Date        Ver   Attribute
=======   ===============    =======   ==============       ===   =========
  15B1    Atlanta\ATL-DC-01   15B1     1999-03-21 02:35.33   2     description
```

Consider the arrival of this update at ATL-DC-02 when it replicates from ATL-DC-01. So far in our discussion, we've assumed that a DC blindly applies replicated updates. In reality, the DC behaves more like a shrewd shopper in a flea market. When it receives an update, it compares the PVN in the updated property with the PVN in its local copy of the property. If the local PVN is higher than the PVN in the update, the update is not applied. This keeps updates that take different tracks around the replication loop from stepping on each other.

The PVN doesn't help, though, if the incoming update has the same PVN as the PVN in the local copy. This is called a *collision*. The Directory Replication Agent uses the originating time stamp to resolve collisions. The update with the most current time stamp is written to the Directory.

You might think this is the end of the collision story, but it's not. Time stamping in Windows 2000 is very loose. Skews of 5 minutes are permissible. If two updates collide and their time stamps are within the permissible skew, the system really doesn't know which property should have priority by simply examining the time stamps. When time stamps are within the permissible skew, *the update with the most data is saved*. So, if two administrators change the Description property for the cn=Al Bondigas object at the same time from different DCs, the one with the longer description takes precedence. Maintaining the DCs within this 5-minute skew is the job of the Windows Time Service. Let's take a look at this service before proceeding onward with our discussion of replication.

Use of the Windows Time Service

The time on individual DCs is kept in sync using the *Windows Time Service*, (WTS). The WTS is a standard implementation of the Simple Network Time Protocol (SNTP) as promulgated in RFC 2030, "Simple Network Time Protocol (SNTP) Version 4 for IPv4, IPv6 and OSI." The function library for WTS is W32TIME.DLL, part of the Services.exe suite.

Every Windows 2000 DC is an SNTP time server, but very little built-in SNTP functionality exists, other than keeping in sync with other Windows 2000 DCs. You can see the Windows Time Service on the service list by opening a Run window and entering services.msc. This opens the Services console.

Registry Hint: Windows Time Service

The Registry settings for the Windows Time Service are stored as follows:

Key: HKLM | SYSTEM | CurrentControlSet | Services | W32TIME | Parameters

Value / Data: LocalNTP / 0

Value / Data: Period / SpecialSkew

Value / Data: Type / NT5DS

A domain has one primary time server. This is the first DC promoted. Other DCs check incoming time stamps from the primary server against their own system clock to see if they are still in sync. If a DC finds itself outside the acceptable skew, it performs an SNTP transaction with the primary time server to reset its local clock.

You should not manually set the time on a DC. If you do, it puts incorrect time stamps on the updates it makes to Directory properties. This can cause integrity problems when the objects are replicated. Always change time by synchronizing the DC with the time standard server. The easiest way to do this is by using the Net Time command as follows:

```
net time \\computer_name /SET
```

You can manually sync the time at a member server or workstation using net time /domain or net time /rtsdomain. Don't bother doing this on a DC. It merely looks at its own clock and is satisfied. A net time /setsntp option updates the Registry with the names or IP addresses of SNTP time servers. The target time server is checked when the server boots. If you use net time or net time /set, the /setsntp switch has no effect.

If you want to sync your primary time server with a time standard such as the U.S. Naval Observatory, you need a third-party product. Two shareware products with minimal license costs are widely used in NT networks. They also work with Windows 2000. One is AtomTime, available at www.atomtime.com. The other is Tardis, available at www.kaska.demon.co.uk.

AtomTime is noteworthy for its convenience. Simply load it and set it for an update interval and you're done. It defaults to the Atomic Clock in Boulder, Colorado. Tardis has the most features, and costs only a couple of dollars more than AtomTime.

You can include the Net Time command in logon scripts so that desktops sync with their local DC at boot time. No periodic polling occurs afterward. If you do time-sensitive work, invest in one of the third-party SNTP tools.

Controlling Replication Parameters

The default replication intervals are set by entries in the NTDS Site Settings object and are usually adequate to support most operations. This section covers ways to adjust the default replication intervals if you want to tune your system, and it shows how to force replication if you want to hurry the process along.

Setting Replication Intervals

Within a site, DCs send out replication announcements within 5 minutes after receiving an update. This does not apply to replication between sites. Replication between sites is controlled solely by fixed polling schedules.

When a DC receives a replication notification from a replication partner, it responds by sending a replication request to that partner. If the DC that sent the notification has more than one replication partner, it receives more than one replication request. It deals with the requests in order by sending an update package to the first partner, waiting 30 seconds, and then sending an update package to the next partner.

Registry Tip: NTDS Replication Parameters

The values that control Directory replication are stored as follows:

Key: HKLM ¦ System ¦ CurrentControlSet ¦ NTDS ¦ Parameters.

Value: Replicator notify pause after modify (secs)

Data: 300 secs (x12c)

Value: Replicator notify pause between DSAs (secs)

Data: 30 secs (x1e)

If you want a shorter notification interval, you can reduce the Replicator notify pause after modify interval, but keep an eye on utilization levels. Under normal circumstances, you're better off leaving the default setting and using the Active Directory Sites and Services console to force replication when you need to propagate an update more quickly. See the "Forcing Replication" section later in this chapter for more information.

In addition to update notifications, DCs replicate with their partners at fixed intervals. The purpose for this fixed schedule is to check for broken connections. The value for the fixed replication interval is stored in the Connection object. You can access these objects to view or change the fixed schedule using the `Active Directory Sites and Service` console. See Figure 11.10 for an example.

Figure 11.10 Connection object properties showing the default transport and name of replication partner.

If you click `Change Schedule`, a `Schedule` window opens to show the default replication schedule. See Figure 11.11.

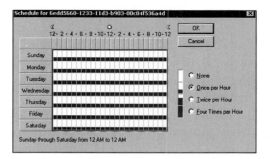

Figure 11.11 `Schedule` window showing default fixed replication schedule between DCs in the same site.

The default intrasite polling interval is 1 hour. You can make this more frequent, but it does not improve replication performance. The only situation that requires a shorter interval is when you are having problems with your network connections and you want the system to check connection integrity more often. The default intersite polling schedule is a 15-minute window every 6 hours.

Forcing Replication using MMC Tools

If you want a particular update to replicate sooner than the default interval, you can force replication. One way to do this is by using the AD Sites and Services console as follows:

Procedure 11.5 Forcing Replication with the *AD Sites and Services* Console

1. Expand the tree to the server to which you want to replicate. (Connections represent inbound data flows.)

2. Find the NTDS Settings object and its associated Connection objects under the Server icon.

3. Right-click the connection from the replication partner and select REPLICATE NOW from the fly-out menu. You get a message indicating that the replication commenced. If the link is broken, you get a message saying that the RPC connection is unavailable. If the connection is an intersite connection, the replication request will be queued.

You can check the Event Log to verify that replication is complete. Alternatively, you can check the properties of a target object to verify that they changed.

Forcing Replication from the Command Line with Repadmin

If you prefer to use command-line tools, you can force replication using the Replication Administrator utility, Repadmin, in the Windows 2000 Resource Kit. The syntax is:

```
repadmin /syncall <DSA> <NC>
```

<DSA> is the fully qualified domain name of the server to which you want to replicate. <NC> is the distinguished name of the naming context you want to replicate. For example:

```
repadmin /syncall phx-dc-01.company.com dc=company,dc=com
```

Listing the server GUID followed by the distinguished name of the naming context when it replicates indicates a successful replication.

Diagnosing RPC Problems

Intrasite replication takes place over secure RPC connections. A failed RPC connection can result in Event Log errors, such as *There are no more endpoints available from the RPC Endpoint Mapper.*

This is generally caused by network hardware failure, either a bad switch port or bad router table or a failed network adapter. It could also be caused by another RPC application that decided to interfere with the RPC Endpoint Mapper and the TCP ports it uses. The Microsoft RPC Runtime service selects TCP ports above 1024 at random to make its connections. If another process steps on one of those ports, you will get replication errors.

Another possible cause of an RPC failure is a failure of the RPC Locator service. This service uses TCP port 135 to reach out to an RPC server. Sometimes a rogue application uses TCP port 135 and steps on the Locator Service. More often, though, losing this port is the result of a zealous firewall administrator.

If you think you are getting a failure of the RPC Locator service, try using the Rpcping utilities from the Resource Kit. These were originally designed for Exchange, but they are just as useful for Active Directory.

Two components to RPC tracing by using Rpcping exist. At the server, you start the *RPC Listener* by running `RpingS32`. From the client, generate RPC traffic by running `Rpings` and specifying the fully qualified DNS name of the server. If you get a response, you know that the RPC Locator service is working at the client end and the RPC Run-Time is properly configured at the server.

If Rpcping fails, check your network connections and configurations. Try restarting the server. You may have a problem with the network adapter driver, so always make sure you have the most current Windows 2000 driver from the vendor.

Configuring Intersite Replication

If you take no action to create Site objects within the Directory, all newly promoted DCs are put into the same site as the first DC. This is called the Default-First-Name-Site. The KCC automatically builds and configures connections between DCs in the same site, so all DCs in the Default-First-Name-Site are part of the same replica ring. This may not be appropriate if one or more of those servers are connected by slow wide area links. You need to create and configure additional sites to break up the replica ring.

Sites and site planning were introduced in Chapter 9, "Deploying Windows 2000 Domains," during the initial stages of domain design. The purpose at that time was to make sure the designer anticipated the possibility of slow intrasite replication when locating DCs and Flexible Single Master Operations servers (FSMOs). This section takes that initial sketch and uses it to create sites, build replication links between sites, and troubleshoot problems that might arise.

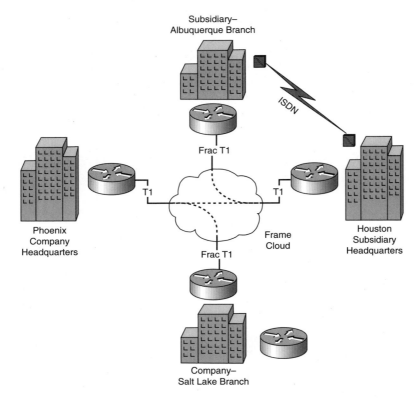

Figure 11.12 WAN layout for offices in four cities.

Figure 11.12 shows a WAN layout similar to the one used in Chapter 9. It shows four offices scattered around the Southwest. The office networks are connected using moderately high-speed WAN connections through an unmeshed frame relay network. A fallback ISDN line between Houston and Albuquerque exists for emergency use if the frame relay goes down.

Figure 11.13 shows a site plan for configuring intersite replication between the offices in Figure 11.12. The site plan uses the name of the city for the site name, but this is not required. A retail organization could use store names, such as Store2332. A university could use campus names, such as UC-Irvine, UC-Davis, and so forth. The site configuration does not necessarily parallel the domain configuration, but it might. If so, it is not a good idea to name the sites after the domains. The Directory enables you to do this because the objects are in different containers, but you'll confuse yourself later because you might end up with several domains sharing the same site connections.

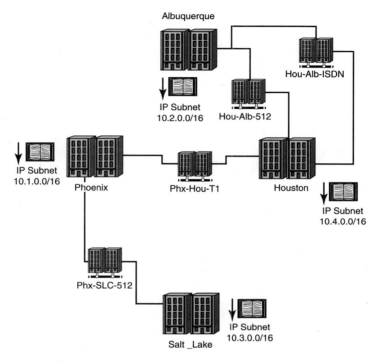

Figure 11.13 Site plan showing replication connections corresponding to WAN layout in Figure 11.12.

The next few sections cover creating and configuring the Directory objects that represent the various elements of the site plan. The general course of action is as follows:

- Rename the Default–First–Site–Name object.
- Create new Site objects.
- Create Subnet objects.
- Create Site Link objects (if required).
- Create Site Link Bridge objects.
- Designate Bridgehead servers.

After you complete this work, the KCC should be able to automatically handle any changes you make to the distribution of DCs and GC servers in the network with no further intervention. If the KCC has a problem with connections, you can deal with it manually.

Renaming the Default–First–Site–Name Object

The default name for the first site is a little long and clumsy for most uses. The steps to rename it are as follows.

Procedure 11.6 **Renaming the Default–First–Site–Name Object.**

1. Open the Active Directory Sites and Services console.
2. Right-click the Default-First-Site-Name object and select RENAME from the fly-out menu. The object name gets a bounding box and a blue background.
3. Change the name to the name of the site in your site plan and press Enter.
4. Leave the console open. You need it to perform the next steps.

The name change is registered with DNS automatically. You should verify this because it is an important element in getting the rest of the sites to work properly.

The older site name remains in DNS until the change replicates to all DCs and they register the new site with DNS. If the DNS server is off-line when you change the name, or if you lose network connection while the change is replicating, you may need to delete the old site manually from the zone table.

Creating a New Site Object

After you rename the first site, create site objects for the remaining sites in your plan. Do this using the Active Directory Sites and Services console as follows:

Procedure 11.7 **Creating a New Site Object**

1. Right-click the Sites object and select NEW SITE from the fly-out menu. The Create New Object - (Site) window appears. See Figure 11.14.
2. Under Name, enter the name of the site. The example uses a site name of Houston.
3. Under Link Name, highlight DefaultIPSiteLink. This is the only link required. Windows 2000 supports transitive replication through a single link.
4. Click OK to create the Site object. Leave the console open.

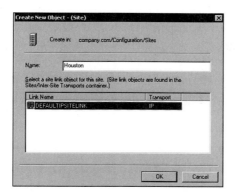

Figure 11.14 `Create New Object - (Site)` window.

When you create the Site object, the system automatically creates a Server container and two Settings objects, `Licensing Site Settings` and `NTDS Site Settings`. The system also adds several SRV records to DNS that point at the new DC. These records are grouped under the _msdcs and _sites headings.

Creating a Subnet Object

Active Directory uses subnets to differentiate between sites. Create Subnet objects for each IP subnet in your WAN as follows:

Procedure 11.9 **Creating a Subnet Object**

1. Right-click the `Subnets` object and select NEW SUBNET from the fly-out menu. The `Create New Object - (Subnet)` window appears. See Figure 11.15.

2. Under `Name`, enter the subnet address and the number of bits in the subnet mask. The example uses a private 10-space network, 10.1.0.0, with a 16-bit mask corresponding to 255.255.0.0. If you have a single class C address that you got from an ISP, you need to subnet it down to route between offices. For example, you might have 206.223.141.0/27 where the bitmask corresponds to a dotted-decimal mask of 255.255.255.224.

3. Select a Site object to associate with the Subnet object. The example uses the Phoenix site. If you have more than one subnet in a Site, you can create multiple subnet objects and associate them with the same site.

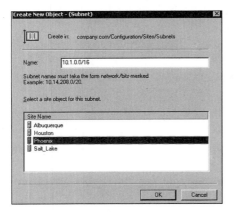

Figure 11.15 `Create New Object - (Subnet)` window showing subnet for the Phoenix site.

4. Click OK to create the subnet object and return to the main console window. Leave the console open.

Use the same procedure to create Subnet objects for all the subnets in your network. These objects determine where DCs place themselves in the Site topology during promotion, so be sure not to miss any addresses.

Creating a Site Link Object

A Site Link object represents the physical link between sites. The KCC uses the Site Link objects to construct a spanning tree map of the network for use when it builds Connection objects between sites. Under most circumstances, you can assign all sites to the default link, titled DefaultIPSiteLink. Windows 2000 replication takes advantage of transitive replication so that the KCC can build its topologies looking through one DC to its neighbors.

If the automatic topology generation used by KCC doesn't give you ideal results, indicated by synchronization problems or complete failures to replicate, you might need to define Site Links and manually assign sites to them. Again, this should not be necessary. You should consult with Microsoft technical support to resolve replication problems prior to using nontransitive links.

If you build Site Links, you define them in a way that mirrors the topology of your network. If you have a mixture of link types and link speeds, you define a Link Object for each link type and define the costs so that the KCC uses the fastest links when building Connection objects. If you have several connections between LANs, you can create a Site Link object for each one and assign costs based on bandwidth and availability.

When assigning costs, the links with the lowest cost are most likely to get a connection. If you leave the costs at their default of 100, the KCC might build direct connections between two very slow branch office sites instead of building a series of connections between high-speed sites. In the example network, costs are assigned as follows:

- 1 to the T1 frame relay connections between Phoenix and Houston
- 20 to the fractional T1 connections between the branch offices
- 100 to the ISDN connections

The KCC can use a Site Link to carry replication over IP or SMTP or both. You can use message-based SMTP if you have a site that makes periodic connection with the network, such as a dial-up connection or an expensive ISDN line. When you've laid out your network infrastructure and defined the necessary connections that represent your WAN to the KCC, you are ready to create and configure the necessary Site Link objects. Proceed as follows:

Procedure 11.9   **Creating and Configuring Site Link Objects**

1. Expand the tree to find the IP object under Sites | Inter-Site Transports.

2. Right-click the IP object and select NEW SITE LINK from the fly-out menu. The Create New Object - (Site Link) window appears. See Figure 11.16.

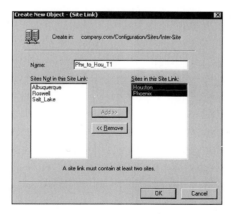

Figure 11.16   Create New Object - (Site Link) window.

3. Under Name, enter a name for the Site Link object.

Naming Site Links

When assigning names to Site Links, it's a good idea to include the names of the end-points in the name so that you can tell at a glance where the link goes. This works like the names of rural highways in the Midwest. If you've ever tried to find your way around Cincinnati, you know exactly what I'm talking about. The Carmel-Tabasco road connects the town of Carmel to the town of Tabasco.

You can also include the connection type in the name to differentiate multiple links between the same sites. For example, the primary connection between the Houston office and the Albuquerque office is a frame relay PVC with a Committed Information Rate (CIR) of 512Kbps, so the name could be Hou_To_Alb_512. Another way of designating the names is by the preference of the link. In our example network, backup ISDN lines exist. The Site Link object for the primary connection could be named Hou_To_Alb_Primary while the ISDN line could be named Hou_To_Alb_Standby.

4. Select two sites and click Add to put them in the Sites In This Link list. You must have at least two sites associated with a Site Link.

5. Click OK to create the object.

6. Open the Properties window for the new Site Link object. See Figure 11.17.

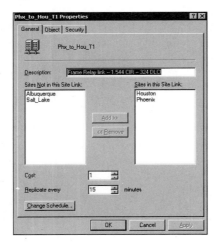

Figure 11.17 Site Link Properties for the Phoenix to Houston link showing description, cost, and interval.

7. Enter a Description for the link. You might want to include the type of connection, the bandwidth, and any helpful information that helps you isolate problems if you have trouble with the link.

8. Assign a `Cost` to the link. This is the highest-speed link in the example network, so it gets a cost of 1. For the 512K links to the branch offices, assign a cost of 20. For the emergency ISDN line, assign a cost of 100. Keep the options to a minimum. The KCC uses these numbers to build a spanning tree map. If you use too many values, you'll confuse matters rather than help them.

9. Shorten the default `Replication` interval unless the link is especially slow or heavily subscribed. The shortest interval that the system accepts is 15 minutes. If you enter a shorter interval, the change is accepted, but the interval is set to 15.

10. Click `Change Schedule`. The `Schedule` window opens for the link. See Figure 11.18.

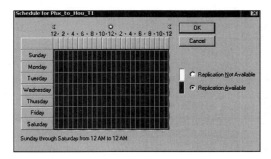

Figure 11.18   `Schedule` window for the Phoenix to Houston Site Link showing that replication is available 7x24.

11. If the connection is up at certain times, clear the blue for the intervals where it is not available. Use this option if you have a slow link that experiences peak traffic at certain times and you don't want to add replication traffic to the mix. When you play games with replication intervals, keep in mind that you're affecting latency.

12. Click `OK` to save the change and return to the `Properties` window.

13. Click `OK` to save the changes and return to the console.

14. Close the console.

Now create Site Link objects for the remaining connections between sites. Figure 11.19 shows the list for the example WAN. Remember, you are mapping out the network for the benefit of the KCC, so you need a link for every WAN connection.

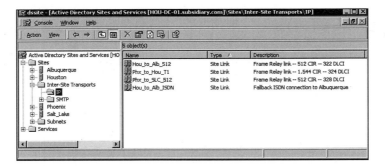

Figure 11.19 Final list of site links for the example network.

You might find after building the links that the KCC needs just a bit more information about your network to lay its plans effectively. You might need to tell the KCC about the preferred routes you want it to take when building connections between sites. You do this with Site Link Bridges.

Creating Site Link Bridge Objects

A Site Link Bridge defines a preferred route for replication traffic between sites. The example network doesn't have enough routes to make a Site Link Bridge worthwhile. A better example is a frame relay network with home runs to various global offices, and different connection bandwidths and reliability ratings on the various connections to the cloud.

In a meshed network, there might be three or four possible routes that a hypothetical replication path could take to get from a site in Kuala Lumpur to a site in Kalamazoo. The KCC does not make cost estimates based on combinations of Site Links. It simply asks, "What is the least cost for the next hop?", and then derives its spanning tree accordingly. If you have a preferred route you want a replication stream to take, you must define a Site Link Bridge object that collects the Site Links that represent these routes.

Using Site Link Bridges is completely optional. You can leave the site link configuration in its default transitive configuration and watch to see what happens. You may be perfectly satisfied. But you may also find that the KCC makes poor connection choices and you start getting Event Log messages saying that the DRA is unable to keep up with Directory updates, or the DCs at a particular site may continually lose sync with their replication partners.

Before a Site Link Bridge can take effect, you must disable the transitive bridging that is turned on by default. After you do this, you might find yourself in the position of creating Site Link Bridges for all your major routes. If you have a big network and you've already defined a large number of Site Link objects, be prepared to spend some time on this chore.

When you are deciding what links to add to a bridge, picture the traceroute you want to see for your replication traffic. Assign the Site Links to the Site Link Bridge accordingly. Follow these steps to disable global transitive bridging and to build a Site Link Bridge object to define a preferred route in our example network:

Procedure 11.10 **Building a Site Link Bridge Object**

1. Open the `Active Directory Sites and Services` console.

2. Right-click the `IP` object and select PROPERTIES from the fly-out menu. The `IP Properties` window opens. See Figure 11.20.

Figure 11.20 `IP Properties` window showing the global bridging option.

3. De-select the `Bridge All Site Links` option. This removes the global transitive bridging for site links.

4. Right-click the `IP` object and select NEW SITE LINK BRIDGE from the fly-out menu. The `Create New Object - (Site Link Bridge)` window appears. See Figure 11.21.

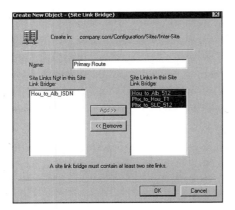

Figure 11.21 `Create New Object - (Site Link Bridge)` window

5. Select the links you want to define for the preferred route and click Add to put them on the list.

6. Click OK to save the changes and return to the console. The `Site Link Bridge` object is added to the list of IP link objects.

7. Monitor your Event Log and Connection object status carefully over the next few hours to see how the KCC reacts to the change.

Only a few more hygiene items to take care of and then the job is complete. One of those items is making sure that efficient use is made of the DCs when it comes to propagating replication traffic. To do that, we may need Bridgehead servers.

Designating Bridgehead Servers

Under normal circumstances, the KCC knits together a replication topology that uses the lowest-cost links while maintaining a hop count of 3 or fewer. This can result in some convoluted replication topologies in a large network with many sites.

You can reduce the complexity of intersite replication between DCs and possibly improve performance by designating a *Bridgehead server* to act as a replication gateway between sites. The Bridgehead acts as a replication gateway. The DRA on the Bridgehead server accepts incoming replication from partners at other sites using slow IP intersite replication, and then distributes the updates to its replication partners at its local site using high-speed RPC replication.

The disadvantage to using a Bridgehead server is the single point of failure. A Bridgehead server should have fast and reliable LAN and WAN connections and be as stable as possible.

Bridgehead Servers and Firewalls

One of the most common uses for Bridgehead servers is to replicate through a firewall. By assigning one server and one server only to act as the replication point for a site, you can configure the firewall to pass traffic only for that server.

Using Bridgehead servers is optional. Enable your network to operate for a while without them and monitor performance. Or you may decide not to wait because you don't like the hassle of wondering what part of your intersite replication topology will be adversely affected when bringing down a particular DC. Using a Bridgehead server makes outage work much easier to plan. Designate a Bridgehead server and configure other DCs to use it as follows:

Procedure 11.11 **Designating a Bridgehead Server**

1. Open the `Active Directory Sites and Services` console.

2. Expand the tree to show the Server object representing the DC you want to use for a Bridgehead server.

3. Right-click the Server object and select PROPERTIES from the fly-out menu. The `Properties` window opens. See Figure 11.22.

Figure 11.22 `Properties` window for server showing transports that have been added to the Bridgehead list.

4. Select the transports you want to bridge, and click Add to move them to the Bridgehead side of the window. It doesn't do any harm to move the SMTP transport, even if you don't use it.

5. Click OK to save the changes.

6. Now you must configure at least two DCs in the site to replicate from the Bridgehead server. Open the properties page for a DC in the same site as the Bridgehead server. The Computer field has Computer and Domain fields. By default, these show the local server. Click Change to open a Select Computer window.

7. Select the Bridgehead server and click OK to save the change and return to the Properties window.

8. Click OK to save the changes. The KCC sees that you designated a Bridgehead server and adjusts the Connection objects accordingly. If you built your own connection objects manually, make sure they do not bypass the Bridgehead server. If they do, you risk a spanning tree loop that could cause performance to degrade.

Special Replication Operations

After you set up your sites and deploy your DCs, there shouldn't be much else to do but bask in a job well done. One or two things may crop up, though, that demand your attention.

For instance, you may have included a wide area connection within a site thinking that the connection could handle normal replication. You may start seeing errors in the Event log about missed replications or complete replication failures. Or, the performance at the link may get very bad during the replication intervals. If this happens, you need to create a new site and move the server into that site.

You may also find that the KCC selects inappropriate replication partners in spite of all your good work in designing and costing the site links the aggregating them with Site Link Bridges. Don't get impatient. It takes a long while for the KCC to do its job and even longer for the updates to replicate out to other DCs in the forest.

While the KCC builds connections, you may get error messages in the Event Log saying that Directory lookup requests at the new DC have failed, but you can safely ignore them while the KCC builds a stable replication topology. In a large network with intersite connections, it may take 6 hours or more for the new connections to show up at all DCs. Sometimes, though, nothing else can be done to get replication moving other than changing a DC's replication partner or manually building a new connection.

If a DC goes down, it may take a while for the KCC to recognize the problem and begin work to heal the replication ring. If you follow the KCC's progress in the Event Log, you will see it notice the replication failures to the downed server and then watch as it builds new connections between the remaining DCs. If the KCC fails to respond in time to forestall an emergency, you can intervene and do a manual bypass.

When you build a manual connection, you interfere with the automatic operation of the KCC. This isn't necessarily a bad thing. The network will not melt down if you make a mistake. But you may find that a DC gets into unexpected replication difficulties caused by your actions. Consider all manual interventions carefully before proceeding.

Moving Server Objects Between Sites

You may be part of a central IT group that builds new servers for remote locations and then ships them for installation by a local tech or an outsourcing agent. During the DC promotion, the local IP address of the server defines its site affiliation. This site may not be correct for the ultimate destination.

If you change the IP network of a DC, or build a new site that is assigned the IP network of an existing DC, you need to move the Server object for the DC to a new Site container along with the NTDS Settings object and the connection objects. This is done using the AD Sites and Services console as follows:

Procedure 11.12 Moving a Server Object to a New Site

1. Open the Active Directory Sites and Services console.

2. Right-click the server object you want to move and select MOVE SERVER from the fly-out menu. The Move Server window opens.

3. Highlight the site where you want the Server object to go and click OK. The window closes and returns you to the console.

4. Check the Servers container under the site to verify that the object and its associated NTDS Settings and Connections objects made it to the correct location.

After moving a Server object to a new site, give the KCC lots of time to set up the new replication topology. If you move a Server object out of a site where it has high-speed connection to its replication partners, the KCC also automatically changes the replication transport from RPC to IP. After you see connections between the DC and at least one other replication partner, right-click the connection object and force replication. If you get an error, the KCC has not yet finished its work. Wait a good, long time and try again. If it still fails, check the Event Log. You may see an error such as the one in Figure 11.23.

If you get a connection error, make sure you didn't accidentally associate the site with the wrong IP address. Check DNS to ensure that the SRV records are in their proper places and that the server is configured to point at a functioning DNS server.

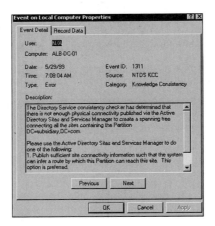

Figure 11.23   Event Log entry showing failure
of the KCC to build a connection.

Manually Selecting a New Replication Partner

When the KCC builds a connection, it selects two end-point DCs and places a Connection object into the NTDS Settings container for those servers. Connection objects always represent inbound data flows. You cannot change the inbound target of a Connection object, but you can change its replication partner. Make absolutely sure that you don't inadvertently put the DC into a loop or place the end-point at a DC in the forest that does not communicate directly with other DCs holding replicas of the same naming contexts. When you are ready to select a new replication partner, proceed as follows:

Procedure 11.13 **Selecting a New Replication Partner**

1. Open the Active Directory Sites and Services console.

2. Expand the tree to find the target server, and highlight its NTDS Settings icon.

3. Double-click the Connections object from the DC you want to change. This opens the Properties window for the connection. See Figure 11.24.

Figure 11.24 Properties window for <automatically generated> connection showing its replication partner.

The Replicate From field contains the name of the replication partner, the partner's site, and the domains that are replicated from that partner. In the example, the target server is in the Subsidiary.com domain and is not a GC server, so it does not replicate any other naming contexts.

4. In the Replicate From field, click Change. The Find DCs window opens. If you have an extensive forest, this list might be fairly long.

5. Double-click the DC that you want to be the server's new replication partner. This closes the window and returns you to the Properties window. The new replication partner is listed in the Server field.

6. Click OK to save the changes and close the window. The DRA sees the change and begins replication from the new partner. If this is an inter-site connection, it may take a while for replication to occur.

Manually Building a New Connection

If the normal KCC machinery doesn't build the connections necessary to keep a DC in sync, you need to manhandle a connection into place. Do this as follows:

Procedure 11.14   Building a New Replication Connection

---

1. Open the Active Directory Sites and Services console.

2. Expand the tree to show the contents of the NTDS Settings container under the server for which you want to build a connection. There should already be at least one Connection object designated <automatically generated>. This was built by the KCC.

3. Right-click the NTDS Settings object and select NEW NT DS CONNECTION from the fly-out menu. The Find DCs window opens.

4. Select the DC from which you want to build a connection. Remember that Connection objects always represent inbound data flows.

5. Click OK. The Create New Object - (Connection) window opens. The name of the DC you selected is inserted in the Name field.

6. Click OK to save the change and return to the console. The new con-nection object appears on the list. You should keep an eye on the Event Log to make sure the DRA sees the new connection and replicates across it. You may need to enable Directory diagnostics to do this. See the next section.

Troubleshooting Replication Problems

Active Directory replication involves a series of complex transactions. If one of these transactions fails, the problems it causes tend to be...well...complex. In general, replication problems are caused by unstable server hardware, poor network connections, and DNS errors.

The symptoms usually are a series of Error Log messages about failed replication. The logged message tells you the cause of the failure, but it doesn't necessarily tell you the cause of the problem. Several tools are available to help you get more information. They include:

- Special diagnostic traces that put more information in the Event Log
- Command-line replication administration utility, Repadmin
- Graphical Replication Monitor utility, Replmon

Directory Diagnostics Traces

One tool for tracing replication problems is hidden in the Registry. A variety of Diagnostics settings under HKLM | System | CurrentControlSet | Services | NTDS | Diagnostics dump information into the Event Log. Three possible settings exist for each diagnostic trace (in addition to 0 for disabled):

1. Minimum reporting
3. Moderate reporting
5. Full reporting

Full reporting gives the most information but can fill up the Directory Services log quickly in a production environment. This doesn't hurt anything, but you may miss an important piece of data. Figure 11.25 shows an example Event Log report for a diagnostics trace of replication:

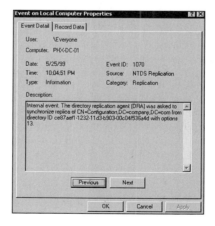

Figure 11.25 Event Log entry showing a replication event logged as a result of enabling Replication Diagnostics.

The contents of an Event Log can be exported to a CSV or TXT tab-delimited file and then imported into a database or spreadsheet. From the EVENT LOG menu, select FILE | SAVE AS and then select the file type and location for the export.

An EXPORT option also exists, but it has the same functions as SAVE AS. In addition, you can use a tool in the Resource Kit, called Dumpel, for the three standard logs—application, security, and system. As of this writing, Dumpel does not work with the Directory Services log or the File Replication log.

Using the Command-Line Replication Administrator, Repadmin

Microsoft supplies a command-line Resource Kit utility, called the Replication Administrator, or Repadmin, for managing the inner workings of replication. A graphical tool, Replmon, shows much of the same information. For details, see the section "Using the Graphical Replication Monitor" later in this chapter.

The online help (repadmin /?) shows the syntax for options and switches. What follows is a brief rundown of the nomenclature, in case the terms are unfamiliar:

- DSA is X.500 terminology for Directory Services Agent. In Windows 2000, a DSA is a DC.

- When entering the name of a DSA, use the fully qualified DNS name. For example, enter slc-dc-01.branch.company.com.

- GUID stands for Globally Unique Identifier. This is an octet string that is assigned to a DC. A DC actually has two GUIDs: an object GUID and an invocation GUID. The object GUID designates the DSA itself. The invocation GUID designates the Directory replica hosted by that DSA.

- The naming context designates one of the Directory partitions hosted by the DSA. Only GC servers host copies of all domain naming contexts, and those are read-only.

- Object DN designates the LDAP Distinguished Name of the object you want to list.

In some respects, the functions in the Replication Administrator duplicate those in the AD Sites and Services console. For example, if you want to know whether a DC is configured as a GC server, you can open the console, navigate to the NTDS Settings object for that server, and check the properties. Or you can open a command prompt and type repadmin /options.

The AD Sites and Services console lacks many of the details available in Repadmin. The following are a few of the questions that Repadmin can answer:

- What is the status of knowledge consistency for this replication ring?

```
repadmin /kcc
Consistency check on local host successful.
```

- Where and when was an object first created, what attributes does it have values for, and what are the USN values associated with those attributes?

```
repadmin /showmeta cn=sites,cn=configuration,dc=company,dc=com phx-dc-01.company.com
```

```
10 entries.
Loc.USN   Originating DSA      Org.USN   Org.Time/Date          Ver   Attribute
=======   ================     =======   ==============         ===   =========
   1165   Phoenix\PHX-DC-01      1165    1999-05-23 17:48.40      1    objectClass
   1165   Phoenix\PHX-DC-01      1165    1999-05-23 17:48.40      1    cn
   2765   Phoenix\PHX-DC-02      2843    1999-05-24 18:14.10      3    description
   1165   Phoenix\PHX-DC-01      1165    1999-05-23 17:48.40      1    instanceType
   1165   Phoenix\PHX-DC-01      1165    1999-05-23 17:48.40      1    whenCreated
   1165   Phoenix\PHX-DC-01      1165    1999-05-23 17:48.40      1    showInAdvancedViewOnly
   1165   Phoenix\PHX-DC-01      1165    1999-05-23 17:48.40      1    nTSecurityDescriptor
   1165   Phoenix\PHX-DC-01      1165    1999-05-23 17:48.40      1    name
   1165   Phoenix\PHX-DC-01      1165    1999-05-23 17:48.40      1    systemFlags
   1165   Phoenix\PHX-DC-01      1165    1999-05-23 17:48.40      1    objectCategory
```

- What was the result of the last replication event from each replication partner? (This listing shows the results for the Schema naming context at the PHX-DC-01 DSA.)

```
repadmin /showreps

Phoenix\PHX-DC-01
DSA Options : IS_GC
objectGuid  : 61d9fcd2-1172-11d3-b902-00c04f536a4d
invocationID: 61d9fcd2-1172-11d3-b902-00c04f536a4d


==== INBOUND NEIGHBORS ======================================
CN=Schema,CN=Configuration,DC=company,DC=com

Phoenix\SLC-DC-01
    DEL:604ba650-124d-11d3-b903-00c04f536a4d via RPC
        objectGuid: 85e37932-124d-11d3-b903-00c04f536a4d
        Last attempt @ 1999-05-26 19:53.35 failed, result 1722:
            The RPC server is unavailable.
        Last success @ 1999-05-25 17:45.37.
        27 consecutive failure(s).
```

```
Phoenix\PHX-DC-02 via RPC
        objectGuid: ce87aef1-1232-11d3-b903-00c04f536a4d
        Last attempt @ 1999-05-26 19:53.35 was successful.
Phoenix\HOU-DC-01 via IP
        objectGuid: fba7a044-1176-11d3-b903-00c04f536a4d
        Last attempt @ 1999-05-26 19:53.35 was successful.


==== OUTBOUND NEIGHBORS FOR CHANGE NOTIFICATIONS ============

CN=Schema,CN=Configuration,DC=company,DC=com
    Phoenix\HOU-DC-01 via RPC
        objectGuid: fba7a044-1176-11d3-b903-00c04f536a4d
```

Without a connection, the system can report only the GUID of the failed replication partner, not its name. You can interrogate the DCs to find their GUIDs and then figure out which one failed. A glance at the Event Log is helpful because it lists the GUIDs in the context of the server that caused the error. The showreps listing for a site with many DCs can be difficult to interpret. If you want to look at just the failures, use the /unreplicated switch.

- What is the current value of the Up-To-Date Vector for a given DC? (As a quick review, the UTD Vector is a combination of the GUID of the originating server and the USN assigned by that server. The DRA uses this information to filter out redundant updates.)

```
repadmin /showvector cn=schema,cn=configuration,dc=company,dc=com

Phoenix\PHX-DC-01        @ USN 6126
Phoenix\PHX-DC-02        @ USN 4820
Phoenix\HOU-DC-01        @ USN 5685
```

- How do I force a connection to update?

```
repadmin /syncall phx-dc-01.company.com cn=schema,cn=configuration,dc=company,dc=com

        CALLBACK MESSAGE: The following replication is in progress:
            From: fba7a044-1176-11d3-b903-00c04f536a4d._msdcs.company.com
            To  : 61d9fcd2-1172-11d3-b902-00c04f536a4d._msdcs.company.com
        CALLBACK MESSAGE: The following replication completed successfully:
            From: fba7a044-1176-11d3-b903-00c04f536a4d._msdcs.company.com
            To  : 61d9fcd2-1172-11d3-b902-00c04f536a4d._msdcs.company.com
        CALLBACK MESSAGE: The following replication is in progress:
            From: ce87aef1-1232-11d3-b903-00c04f536a4d._msdcs.company.com
            To  : 61d9fcd2-1172-11d3-b902-00c04f536a4d._msdcs.company.com
```

```
CALLBACK MESSAGE: The following replication completed successfully:
    From: ce87aef1-1232-11d3-b903-00c04f536a4d._msdcs.company.com
    To  : 61d9fcd2-1172-11d3-b902-00c04f536a4d._msdcs.company.com
CALLBACK MESSAGE: SyncAll Finished.

SyncAll terminated with no errors.
```

Using the Graphical Replication Monitor, Replmon

In addition to the command-line tool, Repadmin, the Windows 2000 Resource Kit has a graphical tool for managing replication called the Replication Monitor, or Replmon. This tool most definitely falls into the "must-have" category. Repadmin is a great utility and quick to use, but Replmon puts a lot of information on the screen in a highly useful format. Open the Replication Monitor and select a DC to monitor as follows:

Procedure 11.15   Using Replication Monitor to Select a DC

1. Open the Replication Monitor from the RESOURCE KIT menu. Although it is not an MMC console, it has the same look and feel.

2. When the main window opens, right-click Monitored Servers and select ADD MONITORED SERVERS from the fly-out menu. The Add Monitored Server Wizard starts.

3. Select the Search the directory for the server to add option. After a brief pause while the server does a Directory lookup, the name of the server's domain is inserted into the dropdown box field.

4. Click Next. The Add Server To Monitor window opens. The top pane shows the list of available sites in the forest. Select a server by expanding the tree and double-clicking a Server icon. You can also select the Enter the name of the server... option at the bottom of the window, and enter the name of the server you want to monitor. You can enter the flat name.

   If you are going to monitor a server in another domain and you are not logged on with administrative rights in that domain, select the Use alternate credentials option, click Change, and enter suitable credentials in the target domain.

5. Click Finish. The server is added to the main Replication Monitor window. Expand the tree to show the naming contexts (see Figure 11.26 for an example). Highlight one of the servers in the tree to view the replication log for that connection.

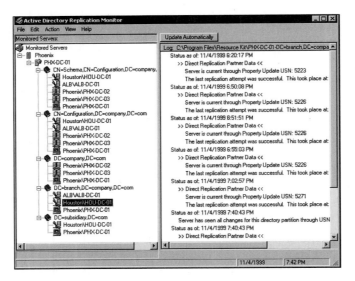

Figure 11.26 `Replication Monitor` (Replmon) main window showing naming contexts on server PHX-DC-01.

6. Initiate replication of a naming context by right-clicking the icon representing a replication partner and selecting SYNCHRONIZE WITH THIS REPLICATION PARTNER from the fly-out menu. This action sends a pull replication request.

7. Press F5 (Refresh). The log updates with the results of the replication.

The following is a quick rundown of the information shown on the main `Replication Monitor` window, as shown in Figure 11.26.

- **Naming Contexts.** Each naming context hosted by the server is listed. If the server is a GC server, the list includes every domain in the forest. If the server is a standard DC, the list includes the domain naming context and the Schema and Configuration naming context from the root domain.

- **Replication partners.** The tree under each naming context lists the inbound replication partners for that naming context. The names are listed by site and then by flat name. In the example, PHX-DC-01 has four replication partners for the Schema and Configuration naming contexts.

- **Server icons.** The double-server icon with a link indicates an intrasite replication partner. A server icon that looks as though it is talking on a futuristic phone represents an intrasite connection. A miniature PC indicates the local server.
- **Log entries.** The right pane lists the replication history for the connection. New entries are added to the end.

Registry Tip: Replication Monitor Settings

The Replication Monitor parameters are stored in the following location:

Key: HKCU | Software | VB and VBA Program Settings | Active Directory
        Replication Monitor | Settings

Values: View Menu Options

Replmon View Options

After you configure Replmon to monitor a DC, set viewing options by selecting VIEW | OPTIONS from the menu. The Active Directory Replication Monitor Options window opens with the focus set to the General tab. See Figure 11.27 for a sample of this window.

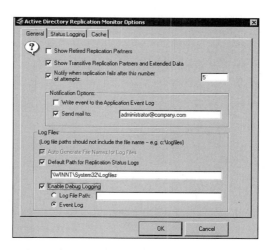

Figure 11.27   Active Directory Replication Monitor Options window.

Most of the options in this window are self-explanatory. Some that might be a little obscure include the following.

- **Show Retired Replication Partners.** These are server objects that were tombstoned but not yet deleted by the ESENT database engine. They are usually deleted over time. The Ntdsutil utility has an option for cleaning up metadata that can delete these old entries. For more information, see the section "Removing Out-of-Use Server Objects from the Directory" near the end of this chapter.

- **Show Transitive Replication Partners and Extended Data.** This option enables Replmon to show USN and metadata information from servers outside the local site that are multiplexed on the same Site Link.

- **Notify When Replication Fails After This Number Of Attempts.** This option, coupled with the Notification Options entry in the next field, can be used to send email if a connection fails to replicate. Set the attempt number at 3-5 to account for a couple of missed attempts that might happen in the ordinary course of operations.

- **Log Files.** This changes the default path for the log files. The default location is the Resource Kit directory.

- **Enable Debug Logging.** This option is for debugging Replmon, not for debugging replication. Debug Logging writes a great deal of information about the Replmon application to the Application log. The log fills very quickly.

Replmon Connection Properties

You can view a great deal of information about a particular replication connection by opening the Properties window for the connection. Figure 11.28 shows an example.

The General tab shows the connection type and information about the connection itself. The important statistics are the last three lines, which show whether replication attempts failed and the associated error message.

The Update Sequence Numbers tab shows the current USN and the USN receives from the replication partner. This option requires you to select the Show transitive replication partners and extended data option in the View options menu. Figure 11.29 shows an example of the Update Sequence Numbers tab. The USN information is useful when you compare it to the same numbers as the replication partner.

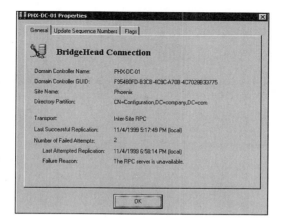

Figure 11.28   Replication connection
Properties window—General tab.

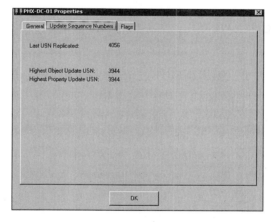

Figure 11.29   Replication connection Properties
window—Update Sequence Numbers tab.

The Flags tab lists the configuration settings for the replication connection. The flags shown in the example are standard for an intersite connection.

Replmon Naming Context Properties

Right-click a Naming Context icon and select Show change notifications to replication partners. This opens a window by the same name. The window displays a list of servers that are notified when changes are made to this Naming Context. Figure 11.30 shows an example. Notification is only applicable for intrasite replication, so the list of servers only includes those in the local site. You can save the list to a log file for comparison to other servers in the same replica ring.

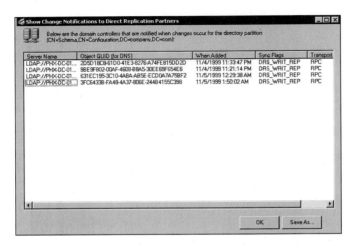

Figure 11.30 `Show Change Notifications to Direct`
`Replication Partners` window showing list of notification partners.

Replmon Replica Synchronization Options

Right-click a `Naming Context` icon and select `Synchronize this directory partition with all servers`. This opens a window of the same name. Figure 11.31 shows an example. This list of options enables you to override the default replication behavior in a variety of ways.

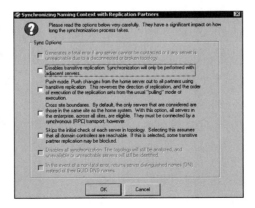

Figure 11.31 `Synchronizing Naming Context`
`with Replication Partners` window.

- **Disable Transitive Replication.** By default, all intersite replication uses the same default Site Link, and the KCC is free to build connections between DCs regardless of their site affiliation. If you are troubleshooting problems with replication loops or failed replication to a particular server, you can disable transitive replication when initiating a replication event to see if it succeeds.

- **Push Mode.** By default, Windows 2000 replication is pull only. This selection enables push mode for this replication transaction.

- **Cross Site Boundaries.** This option enables you to directly initiate an intersite replication, but it is effective only for RPC connections. The default intersite connection transport is IP. You can use the Properties window for a connection to change the transport to RPC and then select this option. If you change the transport for a connection, the connection status changes to a static connection that requires manual control.

- **Skip Initial Topology Check.** This speeds up replication across a slow network with many DCs. It takes the chance that a server or link is down.

- **Generate Fatal Error On Unreachable Server.** Not enabled.

- **Disable All Synchronization.** Not enabled.

- **Return Server DN.** Not enabled.

Replmon Server Property Menu Selections

When you right-click the server icon in Replication Monitor, a fly-out (properties) menu appears. Several of the options in this menu can give you highly useful information about replication in particular and the DC status in general.

- **Generate Status Report.** Select this option to get a comprehensive report on the DC's Directory configuration. The list of items in the report is selected from a Report Options window that opens prior to running the report. Figure 11.32 shows an example.

- **Show Group Policy Status.** Lists all the Group Policy objects for the domain and whether the object was synced. Use this information if users on some DCs are getting policies and other users aren't.

- **Show Trust Relationships.** This option shows the same information as the AD Domains and Trusts window, but much more conveniently.

- **Display Metadata properties.** When you select this option, you are prompted to enter a set of alternate credentials, if necessary, and then the distinguished name of an object whose replication data you want to view. This is equivalent to `repadmin/showmeta`. Figure 11.33 shows an example. Metadata information is invaluable when trying to isolate a problem with a corrupt property or corrupt user object. By comparing the Metadata on various replicas, you can discover whether you have a corruption problem and how extensive the problem has become.

Figure 11.32 `Report Options` window for Replmon server status report.

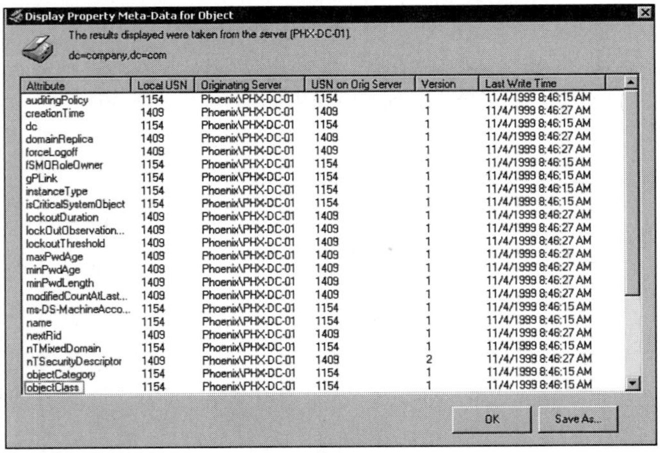

Figure 11.33 `Display Property Meta-Data for Object` window showing metadata properties for `dc=Company,dc=com`.

Server Properties

Right-click the server icon in the Replmon window and open the Properties window. The tabs in this window give you an update of the server's replication status.

- **Server Flags.** Lists special DC options including GC status, KDC status, and W32Time status.

- **FSMO Roles.** This tab lists all the FSMO role masters by name and site with a Query button for each to verify that the server is still online. Figure 11.34 shows an example.

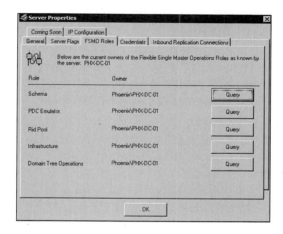

Figure 11.34 Replmon Server Properties
window—FSMO Roles tab.

- **Inbound Replication Connections.** This tab answers the Who, Why, and How for each inbound replication connection. Figure 11.35 shows an example.

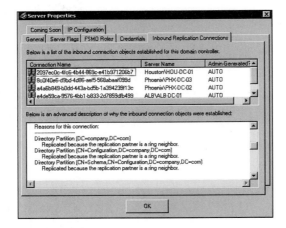

Figure 11.35 Replmon Server Properties window —Inbound Replication Connections.

Using the *Performance* Console to Monitor Active Directory Statistics

The Performance console provides a way to collect short-term and long-term operating statistics on Directory Service operations in general, and replication in particular. Open the Performance console using START | PROGRAMS | ADMINISTRATIVE TOOLS | PERFORMANCE.

The Performance console contains two snap-ins. The System Monitor snap-in is an Active X control designed to display performance counters in graphical format. The Performance Logs and Alerts snap-in is designed to collect performance statistics and write them to a log or send alerts to a console or Event Log.

Overview of Active Directory Performance Counters

To get a quick look at the monitoring options available for the Directory, right-click the empty chart in the Performance console and select ADD COUNTERS from the fly-out menu. The Add Counters window opens. See Figure 11.36 for an example.

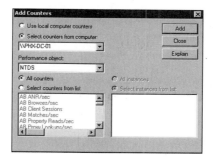

Figure 11.36 Add Counters window showing NTDS counters.

Performance monitoring in Windows 2000 uses *objects* and *counters*. An object points at a high-level process or services, such as Processor, Memory, or DNS. Each object has a list of counters that represent specific functions that can generate statistics.

Registry Tip: Performance Counter DLL

Performance monitoring counters for a particular service are contained in a special DLL for that service. The performance counter library for the NTDS object is NTDSPERF.DLL.

Performance counter libraries are identified in the Registry under a Performance key for the service. The Registry entry for the NTDS performance counters is HKLM | System | CurrentControlSet | Services | NTDS | Performance.

The NTDS object has an extensive list of counters for monitoring Directory Service operation as well as replication. The counters fall into these general categories:

- **DRA traffic (inbound/outbound).** These counters show the number of objects, properties, values, and bytes flowing into and out of the NTDS.DIT database. These statistics are extremely useful when evaluating the operation of a DC in a replica ring. A single slow DSA can slow the entire ring. Compare these statistics between DSAs to see where the bottleneck lies.

- **AB operations.** These are Address Book operations such as browses, lookups, reads, matches, and Ambiguous Name Resolution (ANR) events. You can ignore these entries unless you are using a Directory-enabled mail program, such as Exchange Server.

- **DS client operations.** These counters show things, such as bind rates and name translation rates, for Directory clients. Use these counters in conjunction with the KCC counters, LDAP counters, and a selection of Processor and Memory counters to see whether you have too many clients trying to access a single DC.

- **LDAP operations.** These counters help you to differentiate between raw Directory Service activity and activity caused by LDAP binds, searches, reads, and writes. Comparing these statistics between DCs helps you to get a feel for where the clients are sending their queries. You can spot a misconfigured site or DNS entry, too, if you see that a DC is getting too few queries.

- **DS server operations.** These counters show reads, writes, searches, and the cache hit rate for the Directory store itself. This gives you an idea of how heavily trafficked a particular DC is compared to its peers. Use these counters when you're trying to decide whether to bring another DC on line.

- **DS security descriptor operations.** These counters show the propagation of ACL updates down the Directory. Active Directory uses static access control lists. These ACLs can be subjected to massive updates in response to delegation. Use these counters if you want to see how the ACL propagation affects performance. Figure 11.37 shows an example of delegating rights for User objects in a container that has 20,000 user objects.

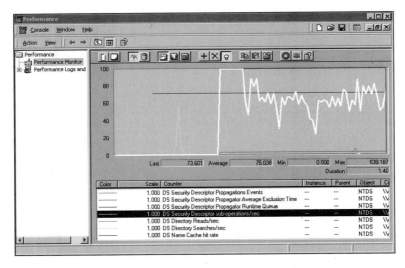

Figure 11.37 DS Security Descriptor propagation rates after delegating rights in a container with 20,000 user objects.

- **KCC operations and LSA operations.** These counters give you an indication of how busy your DC gets while carrying out its authentication chores. Use these counters if you are trying to decide whether you need an additional DC to help speed up morning logon. Authentication requests also put a demand on the Local Security Authority SubSystem (LSASS), so you might want to include that process thread in your logging.

- **NSPI operations.** The Name Server Provider Interface (NSPI) is included in Windows 2000 for backward compatibility with Exchange Server. If you are not integrating Windows 2000 and Exchange, you can ignore these counters. If you are doing an Exchange Server migration, the NSPI counters help you to identify misconfigured DCs.

- **NTLM operations and SAM operations.** These counters help to identify how much activity down-level clients generate. As you deploy Windows 2000 professional to the desktop, you should see this activity drop off considerably.

- **XDS operations.** These counters monitor X/Open Directory Services activity through the SSPI interface. If you have no DCE clients configured to point at Windows 2000 DCs, you can ignore these counters.

Logging Active Directory Performance Counters

The charting feature in the `Performance` console is handy for looking at a snapshot of a few counters, but logs are definitely the preferred method for collecting performance statistics, because they give you a long-term look with records suitable for trend analysis. Configure a Performance log to collect Directory Service statistics as follows:

Procedure 11.16 **Configuring Performance Monitor to Collect Directory Service Statistics**

1. Expand the tree under Performance Logs and Alerts and highlight `Counter Logs`.

2. Right-click a blank area in the right pane and select NEW LOG SETTINGS from the fly-out menu. The `New Log Settings` window opens.

3. Enter a name for the log, such as `Replication Stats`.

4. Click OK. A management window opens for the log. The window name matches the log name you assigned in Step 3.

5. Click Add. The Select Counters window opens.

6. Under Performance Object, select the object you want to monitor. You can collect statistics from more than one object at a time.

7. With the performance object highlighted, select the All Counters radio button. Long-term performance data collection involves taking snapshots at infrequent intervals, such as once an hour, so collecting all available counters is not too much of a burden on the server.

8. Click Add to add the counters to the log, and then click Close to return to the main log management window.

9. Set the Sample Data Every value to 1 Hours.

10. Select the Log Files tab. The default location of the log is a folder called \Perflog at the root of the system partition. You can change this location using the Browse button.

11. The default filename uses the name you assigned to the log plus a 6-digit number. If you stipulate a Log File Size Limit at the bottom of the window, a log fills up and then closes, and another begins filling.

12. Click OK to save the selections and return to the Performance console.

Viewing Performance Logs

Collect statistics for a few days and then view the contents of the log using the System Monitor snap-in. To do this, select the log as the source for the chart as follows:

Procedure 11.17 Charting Performance Monitor Logs

1. Highlight the System Monitor icon. An empty chart appears in the right pane.

2. Right-click the chart and select PROPERTIES from the fly-out menu. The Properties window opens.

3. Select the Source tab.

4. Select the Log File radio button.

5. Click Browse to open the Select Log File navigation tool. The focus is set automatically to the \Perflog folder.

6. Double-click the name of the counter log you configured to select it and return to the System Monitor Properties window.

7. Click OK to save the selections, close the window, and return to the main Performance window. Nothing happens quite yet.

8. Right-click the right pane again and this time select ADD COUNTERS from the fly-out menu. The Add Counters window opens.

9. Select the All Counters radio button and then click Add, followed by Close. This adds all the counters to the chart. If that makes the chart too busy, you can delete counter entries.

The chart shows the statistics you collected in the performance log. Up to 100 data points can be displayed.

Using Performance Logs to Isolate Replication Problems

The Performance console can help answer some of the trickier questions regarding the Directory, such as "What size server do I need for a DC?" and "Is replication working adequately?"

For example, you might have been given a Pentium 400 with 128MB of memory and a 10Mbps Ethernet card for a DC in a remote office that connects to the network via frame relay with a 128K CIR. You are concerned that the DC is not adequate, and the pipe to the network is too small to handle replication along with all the user traffic.

For the sake of example, Figure 11.38 shows a Performance Monitor trace of what happens when a server is configured to be a GC server in a network with 30,000 users in the trusted domains. Granted, this isn't the sort of thing you do every day, but it gives you an idea of how much load you can put on a DC in certain situations. The spikes in this graph are the result of a periodic pause for security authentication using the BONE protocol. (BONE stands for Bloodhound-Oriented Network Entity.)

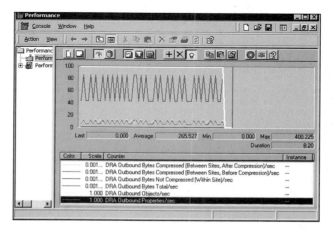

Figure 11.38 Performance Monitor trace showing large replication following conversion to GC server in a large network.

The following are a few statistics from the trace of this event that might be of interest to you. These outbound traffic statistics should match the inbound statistics at the target server:

- Average Outbound bytes/sec: 8248 bytes/sec
- Average Outbound Objects/sec: 9.4
- Average Outbound Properties/sec: 281.3
- Average Outbound Network Traffic: 8835 bytes/sec
- Average Processor utilization: 9.2%

Compare these intersite replication statistics to those for intrasite replication of the same naming contexts using the same class of machine and connection:

- Average Total Inbound bytes/sec: 138814 bytes/sec
- Average Inbound Objects/sec: 30.2
- Average Outbound Properties/sec: 397.3
- Average Outbound Network Traffic: 141839 bytes/sec
- Average Processor Utilization: 14.8%

As you can see, the intrasite RPC connections are much more efficient than the intersite IP connections. Also, the intrasite transactions are not interrupted every 6 seconds for a BONE transaction. It took approximately 40 minutes to replicate the naming contexts of a 58MB DIT across a 10Mbps Ethernet link using intersite replication. It took approximately 15 minutes for that same wave of updates to make it across an intrasite connection using the same network speeds. Keep this in mind as you consider whether to create a new site and go to intersite replication. Put off that decision as long as possible unless your WAN performance is so heavily impacted that you have no choice.

Managing the Loss of a FSMO Role Master

All Windows 2000 DCs are peers when it comes to replicating their naming contexts among each other, but a few tasks are not suitable for multiple-master operation and must be handled by a single server. These tasks are called Flexible Single Master Operations (FSMOs). The server that is assigned a FSMO is called the FSMO Role Master.

Chapter 8, "Designing Windows 2000 Domains," discussed the jobs assigned to FSMOs. The following is a quick overview:

- **Domain Naming Master.** This FSMO is responsible for updating the cross-reference objects in the Sites container and verifying that the names are unique.
- **Schema Master.** This FSMO designates the DC with the read-write copy of the Schema container. The DC does not enable modification to the contents of the Schema container without a change to the Registry. Refer to Chapter 7, "Understanding Active Directory Services," for more information.
- **RID Master.** This FSMO holds the master copy of the Relative ID numbers that are appended to the Security ID (SID) of the domain to form SIDs for the security principals in the domain.
- **PDC Master.** This FSMO replicates updates to classic BDCs. It also acts as a clearinghouse for password updates. If a DC cannot verify a user's password in its copy of the Directory, it forwards the request to the PDC Master.
- **Infrastructure Master.** This FSMO is responsible for the rapid transmission of group memberships and changes in group names to GC servers. This ensures that Universal group memberships are kept current so that users get the proper access rights. See Chapter 10 for details.

A short outage of a FSMO Role Master does not warrant special action, but if you take a Role Master down for an extended period, you should transfer its role or roles to another DC. This is especially true if the server is going under the knife with little hope of recovery.

If a FSMO Role Master crashes and cannot be recovered, you must seize its roles and give them to another DC. Anyone who has gone through a change in corporate ownership probably knows the difference between "transferring" a role and "seizing" a role.

- In a FSMO role transfer, the existing role master relinquishes its role to the target server. Both servers ensure that the proper Directory objects get updated in each other's replica of the naming context that contains the role object.
- In a FSMO role seizure, the target server asks permission first, but takes the role anyway regardless of the answer. The DC that seizes the role makes the necessary changes to the Directory objects in its replica of the naming context that contains the role object.

Because the contents of the naming context stored by the original role master are now invalid, it is important that it not be brought back online again. After a role is seized, treat the superceded role master server like Smokey Bear treats a campfire. Drown it, stir it, and drown it again. The only exception is the PDC Role Master. A superceded PDC Master can be brought back on the line and then forced to relinquish its role in an action very similar to bringing a classic PDC back online after a BDC is promoted.

You have the option of using a Directory management console or a command-line utility to do role transfers. This section examines both methods, starting with the console method. The console selection depends on the role you're transferring. Refer to Table 11.1 for a list of the roles and their consoles along with precautions for placing the role.

Table 11.1   **FSMO Transfer Information**

FSMO Role	Console	Precautions
Domain Naming Master	`Active Directory`	Keep this and the Domains and Trusts Schema Master on the same DC. These two roles are unique in the enterprise, so make sure the servers are well connected to the WAN.
Schema Master	`Schema Management`	See previous.
PDC Master	`Active Directory`	The PDC Master replicates User, Group, and Computer attributes to all classic BDCs. Ensure that it has speedy I/O and is well connected to the network. If you have a domain that spans a WAN, make sure the PDC Master has a fast connection to the boundary router.
RID Master	`Active Directory Users and Computers`	Put this role master on the same server as the PDC Master unless you have a very large domain with a great deal of load on the PDC. In this case, you can use separate servers, but make sure they stay connected to each other.

FSMO Role	Console	Precautions
Infrastructure Master	`Active Directory Users and Computers`	Put this role master on a GC server.

Changing a Role Master Using a Directory Management Console

Refer to Table 11.1 to find the applicable console and then proceed with the transfer as follows:

Procedure 11.18 **Changing a Role Master Using a Directory Management Console**

1. Open the applicable console for the FSMO that you are going to transfer. The examples use the PDC Master.
2. Right-click the very top icon, the one with the same name as the console. Select CONNECT TO DOMAIN CONTROLLER from the fly-out menu.
3. Select the name of the DC you want to be the new role master. This satisfies an LDAP requirement to bind to the server so that you can be authenticated to and open its replica of the Configuration naming context.
4. Click OK to connect to the DC.
5. Right-click the top icon again. This time, select OPERATIONS MASTER from the fly-out menu. The `Operations` window appears.
6. Select the tab associated with the role you want to transfer. The example shows the `PDC` tab.
7. Verify that the DC listed under Current Focus is the name of the server where you want the role to be transferred.
8. Click `Change`. You are prompted to verify.
9. Click OK. After a short wait, you'll be informed that the Operations Master was successfully transferred. The `Operations` tab now shows the new name under Current Operations Master.
10. Click OK to close the window.

At this point, you can verify that the role was transferred using the ADSI Editor. Navigate to the container corresponding to the console you used to make the change (the Domain DNS container for the PDC Role Master, for example) and check the value associated with the FSMO-Role-Owner attribute. It should show the distinguished name of the new role master you selected.

The change you made to the role master now replicates out to the other DCs in the domain or the forest, depending on the location of the FSMO object. If you changed the role master for the two enterprise FSMOs, the Schema Master, or the Infrastructure Master, avoid making any changes that affect the schema or adding any new DCs to the forest until the change is fully replicated. If you have a large network with many intersite connections, it may take several multiples of 6 hours for the updates to converge completely.

Transferring a Role Master Using Ntdsutil

You can also use Ntdsutil to do normal role transfers if you don't like using graphical tools. You must use Ntdsutil if you are going to seize a role. Role seizures are covered in the next section.

You can run Ntdsutil from any member Windows 2000 computer in the domain. The DC that becomes the new role master must be online. Proceed as follows:

Procedure 11.19 **Changing a Role Master Using Ntdsutil**

1. Log on using an account with administrator privileges in the domain. If the transfer involves either of the enterprise roles, Schema Master or Domain Naming Master, you must also have administrator rights in the Configuration naming context.

2. Open a command session and run `ntdsutil`.

3. Enter `Roles` at the `ntdsutil:` prompt. This opens the `FSMO Maintenance:` prompt.

4. Enter `?` to get the options list.

```
fsmo maintenance: ?

?                               - Print this help information
Connections                     - Connect to a specific Domain Controller
Help                            - Print this help information
Quit                            - Return to the prior menu
Seize domain naming master      - Overwrite domain role on connected server
Seize infrastructure master     - Overwrite infrastructure role on connected server
Seize PDC                       - Overwrite PDC role on connected server
Seize RID master                - Overwrite RID role on connected server
Seize schema master             - Overwrite schema role on connected server
```

```
Select operation target           - Select sites, servers, domains and roles
Transfer domain naming master     - Make connected server the domain naming master
Transfer infrastructure master    - Make connected server the infrastructure master
Transfer PDC                      - Make connected server the PDC
Transfer RID master               - Make connected server the RID master
Transfer schema master            - Make connected server the schema master
```

5. Type `Connections`. This opens the `Server Connections` prompt.

6. Type `?` to get the options list.

```
server connections: ?
```

```
?                       - Print this help information
Clear creds             - Clear prior connection credentials
Connect to domain %s    - Connect to DNS domain name
Connect to server %s    - Connect to server, DNS name or IP address
Help                    - Print this help information
Info                    - Show connection information
Quit                    - Return to the prior menu
Set creds %s %s %s      - Set connection creds as domain, user, pwd. Use "NULL"
for null password
```

7. Enter `Connect to Server %s` where `%s` is the fully qualified DNS name of the DC where you want to transfer the role. For example, enter `Connect to Server company.com`. If successful, you get the following report:

```
server connections: connect to server phx-dc-02.company.com.
Binding to \\PHX-DC-02.company.com ...
Connected to \\PHX-DC-02.company.com using credentials of locally logged on user
```

8. If you want to use another account, use the `Set Creds` command prior to issuing the `Connect to Server` command.

9. Enter `q` to exit the module and return to the `FSMO Maintenance` prompt.

10. Select a role to transfer. The example transfers the PDC Master. This is the equivalent of promoting a backup DC and demoting the primary DC.

11. Enter `Transfer PDC`. A window appears requesting that you verify this operation. Click `OK` to initiate the role transfer.

12. If the transfer operation fails, you get an error message and the role remains with its original master. For example, if the target server is already the role master, you are notified of this. If the transfer operation proceeds without error, Ntdsutil responds with a list of the current role masters, indicating a successful end to the operation.

```
fsmo maintenance: transfer pdc
Server "phx-dc-01.subsidiary.com." knows about 5 roles
Schema - CN=NTDS Settings,CN=PHX-DC-
01,CN=Servers,CN=Phoenix,CN=Sites,CN=Configuration,DC=company,DC=com
Domain - CN=NTDS Settings,CN=PHX-DC-
01,CN=Servers,CN=Phoenix,CN=Sites,CN=Configuration,DC=company,DC=com
PDC - CN=NTDS Settings,CN=PHX-DC-
02,CN=Servers,CN=Phoenix,CN=Sites,CN=Configuration,DC=company,DC=com
RID - CN=NTDS Settings,CN=PHX-DC-
01,CN=Servers,CN=Phoenix,CN=Sites,CN=Configuration,DC=company,DC=com
Infrastructure - CN=NTDS Settings,CN=PHX-DC-
01,CN=Servers,CN=Phoenix,CN=Sites,CN=Configuration,DC=company,DC=com
```

Seizing a Role Master Using Ntdsutil

If the DC hosting an FSMO role master crashes or otherwise becomes unavailable, you cannot use the management consoles to transfer roles. You must seize the role using Ntdsutil.

As a reminder, if you seize a role from its designated role master, you must not reintroduce the superceded role master back onto the network. You take the chance of corrupting the Directory. The only exception to this is the PDC Role Master.

As with transferring a role, you can run Ntdsutil from any member Windows 2000 computer in the domain. The DC that becomes the new role master must be online. Proceed as follows:

Procedure 11.20   **Seizing a FSMO Role**

1. Log on using an account with administrator privileges in the domain. If the seizure involves either of the enterprise roles, Schema Master or Domain Naming Master, you must also have administrator rights for the Configuration naming context.

2. Open a command session and run `ntdsutil`.

3. Select `Roles` from the prompt. This opens the `FSMO Maintenance` prompt.

4. Type `Connections`. This opens the `Server Connections` prompt.

5. Enter `Connect to Server %s`, where `%s` is the fully qualified DNS name of the DC where you want to transfer the role. For example, `Connect to Server company.com`. If successful, you get the following report:

```
server connections: connect to server phx-dc-03.company.com.
Binding to \\PHX-DC-03.company.com ...
Connected to \\PHX-DC-03.company.com using credentials of locally logged on user
```

6. Enter q to exit the module and return to `FSMO Maintenance`.

7. Select a role to seize. The example seizes the RID Master.

8. Enter `Seize RID Master`. A window appears requesting that you verify this operation. Click `OK`.

9. If the seizure fails, you get an error message and the role remains with its original master. If the transfer operation proceeds without error, Ntdsutil responds with a list of the current role masters. See the previous section for an example listing.

Be sure you take steps to ensure that the superceded role master is not reintroduced. Formatting the hard drive is not too extreme.

Restoring Replication to a Failed DC

When a DC fails, its attached clients become aware of the loss when their Directory lookups fail and their Kerberos tickets time out and are not renewed. The client queries DNS for alternative DCs, gets reauthenticated, and the client is none the wiser, as long as he or she has no open files on the server or no print jobs holding in a print queue on that server. If the client's site has no more DCs, the next DNS query asks for all DCs. This might land the client at a disadvantageous spot in the WAN from a performance point of view, but the user should still be able to get useful work done.

When you return the failed DC to service, the Directory Replication Agent (DRA) communicates with its replication partners and gets any updates. This could take time if the server was down a while, especially if it is at the wrong end of a slow WAN link. But if you're patient, you should eventually see a note in the Event Log that the DRA was able to sync up.

I successfully reintroduced a DC into a forest after a week with no adverse consequences. This applies even if you performed a schema modification or changed the replication topology. Every DC has a replica of the Configuration and Schema naming context, and this is updated before the Active Directory Services are initialized. The only caveat is that you should not reintroduce a DC that you suspect of having file corruption. A corrupted local DIT may propagate corrupt values to other DCs.

If you change the replication topology while a DC is off the tree, you can either wait for the KCC to find a suitable replication partner before the machine begins to sync up, or manually create a connection for the DC to use. During this time, the Directory-based services are disabled, so client PCs that happen to find the DC in DNS don't use it to authenticate or get incorrect Directory information via LDAP.

If the DC loses touch with its replication partners and no longer responds to Kerberos or LDAP queries after you put it back on the wire, remove it from the network immediately. You can refresh the DIT by doing a tape restore to the DC. See the section "Performing an Authoritative Directory Restoration" later in this chapter.

If the server was out of touch for weeks or underwent major surgery while it was out of commission, you may not want to introduce it back into the tree. Unfortunately, you cannot demote a DC while it is disconnected from the network. The Active Directory Installation Wizard, which is also responsible for deinstallation, refuses to demote unless it can contact the Infrastructure FSMO Role Master. If you do not want to put the server on the network or restore the Directory from tape, you have no choice but to reinstall Windows 2000. If the server hosts a client/server application or two, this might be painful. The best solution I can offer is prevention. Don't put client/server applications on DCs.

Backing Up the Directory

The good old days of classic NT where you could capture the entire Registry on a single emergency repair floppy are gone. The only method for backing up the Registry and the Active Directory is by using Windows 2000 Backup, Ntbackup. The new and improved Ntbackup enables backing up to a network drive and removable media as well as to tape.

No Support for RDISK

The classic RDISK utility that saves a compressed copy of the Registry hives is not included in Windows 2000. Ntbackup has an option called Create Emergency Repair Disk, but this option saves only the AUTOEXEC.NT, CONFIG.NT, and SETUP.LOG files. No options exist for saving the Registry files to floppy.

The Create Emergency Repair Disk option in Ntbackup saves a backup copy of the Registry hives to \WINNT\Repair\Backup for use if you need to recover an individual hive.

One drawback to the new backup strategy in Windows 2000 does exist. You cannot back up or restore just the Registry or just the Directory or just the boot files. You must back up and restore all system files at once. Microsoft calls these the *System State* files. They include:

- The Active Directory database, NTDS.DIT, and its associated log and checkpoint files
- Selected Internet Explorer and shared files from the Program Files directory
- All Registry hives from the \WINNT\System32\Config directory
- The COM+ class registration database
- All files in the \WINNT directory and the system files NTDETECT.COM, BOOTSECT.DAT, Ntldr, and BOOT.INI
- The Certificate Services files
- The contents of the \SYSVOL directory

This backup strategy maintains consistency between the various data storehouses, but it means that if you make a minor mistake that affects a portion of the Registry out of reach of the Last Known Good Configuration rollback, you might be forced to restore all System State files, including the Directory. Rather than do a Directory recovery, you can use the Recovery Console to restore the hive. See Chapter 18, "Recovering from System Failures," for details.

This section covers backing up the System State files using Ntbackup. Restoring the System State files is covered a little later in the "Performing an Authoritative Directory Restoration" section of this chapter. The authoritative restore requires using Ntdsutil, which is covered in that section, as well. Proceed with the System State backup as follows:

Procedure 11.21 **Performing a System State Backup**

1. If you are backing up to tape, PnP should have found the tape drive when you booted the system and installed the drivers for it. If you are using the Removal Storage Manager, you may need to juggle your media pools to do the backup. This is done using the Computer Management console. Figure 11.39 shows a view of the consoles and the Removable Media information. See Chapter 18 for details.

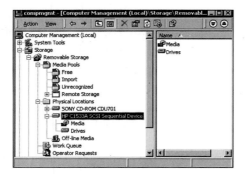

Figure 11.39 `Computer Management` console showing Removable Storage media and its configuration.

2. If you are backing up to tape, make sure you have a fresh backup tape installed in the tape drive. You can choose to append data onto existing media, but why confuse yourself when the time comes to restore. With one backup on the media, you can't be led astray.

3. If you are backing up to removable media, make sure you have a formatted drive with enough capacity for the System State files. You should assume you need 1GB, which puts you in the Jaz or ORB categories of removable media.

4. Start Windows 2000 Backup via START | PROGRAMS | ACCESSORIES | SYSTEM TOOLS | BACKUP. The `Backup` window opens.

5. Select the `Backup` tab.

6. Expand the tree, if necessary, to reveal the `System State` option, which is the last option under the drive letters.

7. Place a check next to the `System State` option.

8. Under `Backup Destination`, select the tape unit you are using for the backup. If you are backing up to a file, select `File`, and then enter the path and filename under `Backup Media or File Name`. Be sure to save the files on reliable removable media or on a network drive that is sure to be available if you need to recover. Don't back up to the local hard drive.

9. From the menu, select TOOLS | OPTIONS. The `Options` window opens.

10. Select the `Backup Type` tab.

11. Under `Default Backup Type`, select the `Copy` option. This keeps the system from resetting the archive bit so that you'll be sure to capture the System State files on your normal nightly backup.

12. Select the `Backup Log` tab.

13. Select the `Detailed` radio button. This gives lots of information, including the name of every file included in the backup. Normally, this gives too much information to be useful, but it is worth doing at least once to see exactly what is included in the System State backup.

14. Click OK to save the changes and return to the main `Backup` window.

15. We want to run this backup job interactively rather than scheduling it, so click `Start Backup`.

16. If this is the first time you've used this tape, you may get a message stating that *There is no unused media with the selected type, but unrecognized media is available.* You might also be prompted to confirm the overwrite of existing data if the tape is recognized. If you're sure you haven't inserted a tape with valuable data on it, click OK. Different tape systems have different formatting and retrieval schemes, so the messages may vary. Refer to your system documentation for specific instructions. Ntbackup uses the Microsoft Tape Format (MTF).

17. When the system can see the tape or the file location, if you are using removable media, the backup begins. The `Backup Progress` window opens to show you what's happening. See Figure 11.40.

Figure 11.40 `Backup Progress` window showing file transfer and time information.

18. When the backup is complete, you get a final window showing the statistics. The Status field will probably state that files were skipped. Click Report to view the backup log. The most likely culprit is the `DO_NOT_REMOVE_NtFrs_Preinstall_Directory` under SYSVOL. This folder holds files that were copied as part of the initial migration of files and folders into the File Replication System database. It can be skipped.

Review the list of files in the log to see what is included. Note that the Directory files do not appear on the log, but they are captured in the backup. Also, the Registry files are backed up out of a special folder called \Registry instead of their actual location in \WINNT\System32\Config. The \Registry folder is a temporary volatile folder used to capture a snapshot of the Registry for backup. This prevents a file lock during backup from blocking access to the Registry.

Restoring the Directory from tape or file backup is a two-step process. You cannot simply restore the files and overwrite the existing Directory files. The naming context replicas on the other DCs have properties with time stamps and version numbers that are later than those on the backup. These properties are propagated to the DC, and you may get back the corruption or error that you wanted to cleanse out. You must first restore the files from tape and then use Ntdsutil to do an Authoritative Restore of the files. Refer to the "Performing an Authoritative Directory Restoration" section later in this chapter.

Performing Directory Maintenance

Active Directory is like any other database when it comes to needing attention. Sometimes it gets filled with gaps and needs compacting. Sometimes it gets messy and needs reindexing. Sometimes it gets corrupted and needs repair. And sometimes it gets completely zonked and needs restoration. The tool for doing this work is the NT Directory Service Utility, Ntdsutil.

Ntdsutil is actually a set of canned instructions for another utility, Esentutl, the grandchild of the Eseutil database utility designed for Exchange. Esentutl has a large number of switches that can be very difficult to sort through when performing database operations. Ntdsutil resolves this usability problem by providing a menuing system with clear options (OK, mostly clear options) that correspond to Esentutl commands.

This section covers the following Ntdsutil operations:

- Performing Directory integrity checks
- Removing out-of-use server objects from the Directory metadata
- Compacting and reindexing the Directory
- Repairing the Directory database
- Performing an Authoritative Directory Restoration

All these operations require that you run the server in DS Repair mode. This is one of several special diagnostic boot options in Windows 2000. Access these options by pressing F8 at the boot menu.

Checked and Free Builds

When running in any of the Safe modes, the Desktop shows the Windows 2000 version and build number along with the term *free*. This does not refer to price of the software. It indicates that you're running a build that is free of debug symbols. A *checked* build contains the necessary debug symbols used for kernel-mode debugging. The checked build runs more slowly and takes more memory, so it is not loaded by default.

All these options, with the exception of Directory Services Repair Mode, are covered in Chapter 18. The following is a brief list to compare the options:

- **Safe Mode.** This mode avoids PnP and loads a bare set of peripheral drivers. This includes drivers for the mouse and keyboard, 16-color VGA video, SCSI and IDE interfaces and drives, floppy interface and drives, and a few system services. Safe Mode does not load network services, so you may get application errors from client/server apps running on the machine. This mode sets SAFEBOOT_OPTION=MINIMAL.

- **Safe Mode with Networking.** This option loads network drivers, including the Workstation and Server service, along with server-based services, such as DNS, DHCP, and WINS. This mode is useful when you want to test network connections on a workstation without loading a long list of peripheral drivers. Do not use this mode on a DC. This mode sets SAFEBOOT_OPTION=NETWORK.

- **Safe Mode with Command Prompt.** This option does not load the Explorer shell. Use this mode if corruption in Explorer or the Registry causes the machine to blue screen or behave abnormally with the UI loaded. In this mode, the system boots to a standard CMD window. You can run programs. Avoid graphical programs because Explorer when a graphical program is launched. This mode sets SAFEBOOT_OPTION=MINIMAL.

- **Enable Boot Logging.** Use this option if you want to write a log of the kernel service drivers as they load. The output goes to a file called NTBTLOG.TXT in the \WINNT directory.

- **Enable VGA Mode.** This option replaces the currently loaded video drivers with standard 16-color VGA drivers. This is useful for troubleshooting video problems, but after using this option you must manually reload the correct drivers. If you aren't sure of the correct drivers, you might find yourself searching the vendor's Web site. Use only if standard Safe Mode does not work.

- **Last Known Good Configuration.** The System hive in the Registry stores control and services information in a special key called CurrentControlSet. It maintains a backup of the last control set that successfully started the machine. This option enables you to start with that last known good control set. This comes in handy if you install an application that makes a Registry change that causes the system to become unstable.

- **Debugging Mode.** Sends boot information to another computer via a serial connection.

- **Directory Service Restore Mode (Windows 2000 DCs only).** This is a special version of Safe Mode. While booted in this mode, the network drivers are loaded and the Server service starts, but the Directory is left inactive. See the following sidebar for more information. This mode sets SAFEBOOT_OPTION=DSREPAIR.

Logging On in DS Repair Mode

When the system is running in DS Repair mode, the Directory is not available. Console logon is handled by MSV1_0 in conjunction with the SAM.

When a server is promoted to DC, all accounts are migrated from the SAM to Active Directory. Copies of the accounts are not left behind. During the promotion to DC, a new Administrator account is created in the SAM to enable console logon in DS Repair mode and when running the Recovery Console (covered in Chapter 18).

If you forget the password to this special Administrator account, you cannot boot to DS Repair mode. You may be able to recover the password using a password cracker, but that takes time, and time is usually short when you need to use DS Repair mode.

I recommend writing down the special Administrator recovery password on a slip of paper and locking it inside the server case.

Performing Directory Integrity checks

You can pull several information screens using Ntdsutil prior to performing any update operations. They give you a rough idea of how the Directory is structured.

At the DC where you want to check database integrity, boot to DS Repair mode and run Ntdsutil. This opens the Ntdsutil: prompt. Then, refer to the following set of steps.

Procedure 11.22 **Performing Directory Integrity Checks**

1. Enter `Files`. This opens the `File Maintenance:` prompt.

2. Enter `info`. This lists the following information:

`Drive Information:`

```
C:\ NTFS (Fixed Drive ) free(459.9 Mb) total(1.1 Gb)
E:\ NTFS (Fixed Drive ) free(456.5 Mb) total(502.0 Mb)
```

`DS Path Information:`

```
Database   :      e:\WINNT\NTDS\ntds.dit - 10.1 Mb
Backup dir :      e:\WINNT\NTDS\dsadata.bak
Working dir:      e:\WINNT\NTDS
Log dir    :      e:\WINNT\NTDS - 30.0 Mb total
                              res2.log - 10.0 Mb
                              res1.log - 10.0 Mb
                              edb.log - 10.0 Mb
```

A big domain with tens of thousands of users and computers and groups might have an NTDS.DIT file of 100- or 200MB, depending on how much information is stored for each user. There should not be a large number of log files if the database was relatively stable for a while.

3. Enter `header`. This lists the following information (important items are in bold):

```
Executing Command: C:\WINNT\system32\esentutl.exe /m "e:\WINNT\NTDS\ntds.dit" /! 10240 /8


Microsoft(R) Windows(TM) Database Utilities
Version 6.0
Copyright (C) Microsoft Corporation 1991-1999.  All Rights Reserved.


Initiating FILE DUMP mode...
Database: e:\WINNT\NTDS\ntds.dit


Format ulMagic: 0x89abcdef
Engine ulMagic: 0x89abcdef
Format ulVersion: 0x620,2
Engine ulVersion: 0x620,2
DB Signature: Create time:4/8/1999 11:44:41 Rand:372018 Computer:
cbDbPage: 8192
dbtime: 117616
```
State: Consistent
```
Log Required: 0-0
Shadowed: Yes
```

```
Last Objid: 124
Repair Count: 0
Repair Date: 0/0/1900 0:0:0
Last Consistent: (1,16610,148)  5/28/1999 11:08:20
Last Attach: (1,38,435)  5/27/1999 19:32:27
Last Detach: (0,0,0)  0/0/1900 0:0:0
Dbid: 1
Log Signature: Create time:5/27/1999 19:32:23 Rand:334873607 Computer:
OS Version: (5.0.2031 SP 0)

Previous Full Backup:
Log Gen: - 2-2
Mark: (2,41,492)
Mark: 5/20/1999 23:17:23

Current Incremental Backup:
Log Gen: - 0-0
Mark: (0,0,0)
Mark: 0/0/1900 0:0:0

Current Full Backup:
        Log Gen: - 0-0
        Mark: (0,0,0)
        Mark: 0/0/1900 0:0:0

Operation completed successfully in 0.78 seconds.
Spawned Process Exit code 0x0(0)
```

A lot of information is in this listing. The important points are these: The database state is consistent, it has not been repaired, and it has been backed up. If the state were inconsistent, this would indicate that the memory cache and the Directory files were not in sync. A soft recovery should solve that problem. See the section "Repairing the Database" a little later in this chapter.

4. Enter integrity to run the integrity checks. The output looks like this (index list shortened for brevity):

```
Opening database [Current].
        Executing Command: C:\WINNT\system32\esentutl.exe /g "e:\WINNT\NTDS\ntds.dit" /!
        10240 /8 /v /x /o

        Initiating INTEGRITY mode...
        Database: e:\WINNT\NTDS\ntds.dit
        Temp. Database: INTEG.EDB
        got 4072 buffers
        checking database header
```

```
checking database integrity

              Scanning Status  ( % complete )

     0    10   20   30   40   50   60   70   80   90   100
     |—--|----|----|----|----|----|----|----|----|----|
             checking SystemRoot
             SystemRoot (OE)
             SystemRoot (AE)
     checking system table
             MSysObjectsShadow
             MSysObjects
             Name
             RootObjects
             rebuilding and comparing indexes
     checking table "datatable" (6)
             checking data
             checking long value tree (24)
             checking index "INDEX_000901FD" (122)
   <<…index list shortened for brevity>>
             rebuilding and comparing indexes
     checking table "hiddentable" (16)
             checking data
             rebuilding and comparing indexes
     checking table "link_table" (14)
             checking data
             checking index "backlink_index" (15)
             rebuilding and comparing indexes
     checking table "MSysDefrag1" (123)
             checking data
             checking index "TablesToDefrag" (124)
             rebuilding and comparing indexes
     checking table "sdproptable" (17)
             checking data
             checking index "clientid_index" (19)
             checking index "trim_index" (18)
             rebuilding and comparing indexes

integrity check completed.
Operation completed successfully in 19.125 seconds.


Spawned Process Exit code 0x0(0)

If integrity was successful, it is recommended
you run semantic database analysis to insure
semantic database consistency as well.
```

If the integrity check shows errors, such as corrupted pages in the tables, the integrity checker attempts to correct them on-the-fly. One potential unrecoverable error is the inability to read pages from the database, indicating that the database is corrupt. This requires a hard restore. If the check performed satisfactorily, follow the onscreen recommendation and perform a semantic database consistency check, as well.

5. Enter q to move back to the Ntdsutil: prompt.

6. Enter Semantic database analysis. This opens the Semantic Checker prompt.

7. Enter Verbose On to turn on verbose logging. This only affects the output of the semantic checker and does not impact performance.

8. Enter Go Fixup to initiate the checker in fixup mode. The output looks something like this:

```
Fixup mode is turned on
Opening database [Current].....Done.

Getting record count...1327 records
Writing summary into log file dsdit.dmp
Records scanned:        1300
Processing records..Done.
```

9. The real news is in the output file, DSDIT.DMP. Look for it wherever you launched Ntdsutil. An example follows:

```
WARNING: Phantom object 11 has old time stamp[04/08/1630]
INFO: UpToDate vector found for NC head 1149(Company)
INFO: UpToDate vector found for NC head 1150(Configuration)
INFO: UpToDate vector found for NC head 1166(Schema)
INFO: UpToDate vector found for NC head 1416(Subsidiary)
INFO: Partial Attributes List found for NC head 1416(Subsidiary)
WARNING: Deleted object 2521 has time stamp[12/29/9999] later than now
Warning SE_DACL_PROTECTED for 2536({31B2F340-016D-11D2-945F-00C04FB984F9})
Warning SE_DACL_PROTECTED for 2539({6AC1786C-016F-11D2-945F-00C04FB984F9})
Warning SE_DACL_PROTECTED for 1370(AdminSDHolder)
Warning SE_DACL_PROTECTED for 1375(Enterprise Admins)
Warning SE_DACL_PROTECTED for 1396(Domain Admins)
1327 total records walked.

Summary:
Active Objects       1277
Phantoms               13
Deleted          37
```

Phantom Records

References to objects by other objects in the Directory are entered by Distinguished Name. If the DN refers to a naming context that is not contained in the information store, a phantom record is created. NetWare administrators recognize these as external references. When the reference is renamed or deleted, the Infrastructure Role Master cleans up the phantom object.

The 12/29/9999 time stamp for the deleted object is normal. This is done automatically for all deleted objects. Objects flagged for deletion are said to be *tombstoned*. Another way to spot a tombstoned object is to look for the Boolean property *Is-Deleted* set to 1.

You will (or should) see an Up-to-Date Vector value for each naming context hosted by the DC. There will be a `partial attributes` finding for each replica that is part of the GC.

The `SE_DACL_PROTECTED` warnings indicate that the semantic checker was not able to open the objects.

10. If you want to see details on an object, use the Get command. For example, `Get 1416` for the listing shown in the previous step yields the following result:

```
Opening database [Current]......Done.

Data for DNT 1416
RDN = subsidiary
PDNT = 11
RefCount = 15
DNT of NC = 2
ClassID = 0xa0043
Deleted? No
Object? Yes
Instance Type = 0x1
Security Descriptor Present [Length 496].
2  11  1416
```

In this listing, DNT stands for Distinguished Name Tag, one of the elements of the data store in NTDS. DIT. PDNT stands for Parent DNT.

This is the last of the information listings. Let's move on to fixing anything that was broken.

Removing Out-of-Use Server Objects from the Directory

When you demote a DC, the system does not automatically remove the associated Server object from the Sites container. Ordinarily, the easiest way to delete the object is by using the `Active Directory Sites and Services` console. You can also do the work using Ntdsutil. You do not need to down the system to perform the work in either case. In our example, the server we want to remove is SLC-DC-01.Subsidiary.com, a DC that was recently removed from service in the Salt_Lake site of the Subsidiary.com domain. Proceed as follows:

Procedure 11.24   **Cleaning Directory Metadata**

1. At any Windows 2000 server in the domain, run Ntdsutil.

2. From the Ntdsutil: prompt, enter Metadata Cleanup. This opens the Metadata Cleanup: prompt.

3. Enter ? for an options list.

```
Connections                                - Connect to a specific DCHelp
                  - Print this help informationQuit                           -
Return to the prior menuRemove selected domain          - Remove DS objects for
selected domain
Remove selected server         - Remove DS objects for selected server
Select operation target        - Select sites, servers, domains and roles
```

4. Enter Connections and then enter ? for an options list.

```
Clear creds                               - Clear prior connection credentialsConnect to
domain %s               - Connect to DNS domain nameConnect to server %s         -
Connect to server, DNS name or IP addressHelp                                -
Print this help information
Info                                 - Show connection information
Quit                                 - Return to the prior menu
Set creds %s %s %s           - Set connection creds as domain, user, pwd (Use "NULL"
for null password)
```

5. If you are working from a member server and you are not logged on with administrator credentials, use the Set Creds command to define your binding credentials.

6. Enter Connect to Server <dsa> to bind to a server, where <dsa> is the fully qualified DNS name of the DC where you want to make the update to the Directory. Any functioning DC will do, but if you want the change to be propagated quickly, you might want to select the Bridgehead server, if you use one. The entries and transaction results so far look like this:

```
server connections: set creds subsidiary.com administrator pw
server connections: connect to server hou-dc-01.subsidiary.com
Binding to hou-dc-01.subsidiary.com as user(administrator) in domain(subsidiary.com) ...
Connected to hou-dc-01.subsidiary.com as user(administrator) in domain(subsidiary.com) .
```

7. Enter Select Operation Target. This opens the Select Operation Target: prompt. Enter ? for an options list.

```
Connections                          - Connect to a specific DC
Help                                 - Print this help information
List current selections              - List the current site/domain/server
List domains                         - Lists all domains which have Cross-Refs
List domains in site                 - Lists domains in the selected site
List roles for connected server      - Lists roles connected server knows about
List servers for domain in site      - Lists servers for selected domain and site
List servers in site                 - Lists servers in selected site
List sites                           - List sites in the enterprise
Quit                                 - Return to the prior menu
Select domain %d                     - Make domain %d the selected domain
Select server %d                     - Make server %d the selected server
Select site %d                       - Make site %d the selected site
```

8. Enter List Sites. An example output looks like this:

```
select operation target: list sites
Found 4 site(s)0 - CN=Phoenix,CN=Sites,CN=Configuration,DC=company,DC=com1 -
CN=Houston,CN=Sites,CN=Configuration,DC=company,DC=com2 -
CN=Albuquerque,CN=Sites,CN=Configuration,DC=company,DC=com
3 - CN=Salt_Lake,CN=Sites,CN=Configuration,DC=company,DC=com
```

9. Enter Select Site <#> where <#> is the number of the site containing the server you want to remove.

```
select operation target: select site 1
Site - CN=Salt_Lake,CN=Sites,CN=Configuration,DC=company,DC=com
No current domain
No current server
```

10. Enter List Domains in Site. An example output looks like this:

```
select operation target: list domains in site

Found 1 domain(s)
0 - DC=subsidiary,DC=com
1 - DC=company,DC=com
```

11. Enter Select Domain <#> where <#> is the number of the domain containing the server you want to remove.

```
select operation target: select domain 0

Site - CN=Salt_Lake,CN=Sites,CN=Configuration,DC=company,DC=com
Domain - DC=subsidiary,DC=com
No current server
```

12. Enter List Servers for Domain in Site. An example output looks like this:

```
select operation target: list servers for domain in site

Found 1 server(s)
0 - CN=SLC-DC-01,CN=Servers,CN=Salt_Lake,CN=Sites,CN=Configuration,DC=company,DC=com
```

13. Enter Select Server <#> where <#> is the number of the server you want to remove. An example output looks like this:

```
select operation target: select server 0

Site - CN=Salt_Lake,CN=Sites,CN=Configuration,DC=company,DC=com
Domain - DC=subsidiary,DC=com
Server - CN=SLC-DC-01,CN=Servers,CN=Salt_Lake,CN=Sites,CN=Configuration,DC=company,DC=com
DSA object - CN=NTDS Settings,CN=SLC-DC-01,CN=Servers,CN=Salt_Lake,CN=Sites,
    CN=Configuration,DC=company,DC=com
DNS host name - SLC-DC-01.subsidiary.com
Computer object - CN=SLC-DC-01,OU=DCs,DC=subsidiary,DC=com
```

14. We've now targeted the server object we want to delete. Enter q to return to the Metadata Cleanup: prompt.

15. Enter Remove Selected Server. A message window appears prompting you to verify your request.

16. Click Yes and the deed is done. An example output looks like this:

```
Metadata cleanup: remove selected server
"CN=SLC-DC-01,CN=Servers,CN=Salt_Lake,CN=Sites,CN=Configuration,DC=company,DC=com"
        removed from server "phx-dc-01.company.com"
```

17. Quit out of Ntdsutil and wait for the change to replicate.

You can use the same technique to remove a domain that was not fully deleted when the last DC was removed from service. If you demote the last DC normally, this should not happen. If the last DC gave up the ghost, you must remove all unwanted metadata before re-creating the domain. Needless to say, be very careful that you don't delete any operational domains.

Compacting and Reindexing the Active Directory Database

If you are an experienced Exchange Server administrator, you know how fragile the old ESE database could be. It needed frequent compacting and reindexing to keep the post office running. The new-and-improved ESENT engine in Windows 2000 should not require nearly this much work, but sometimes it is prudent to do a little housekeeping.

If you wait for the system to respond slowly to authentication requests or LDAP lookups, it might be too late to solve the problem. Just to be on the safe side, it's best to do preventative maintenance and pack every so often. Unfortunately, you have to down the server to do this work. Packing the database affects only the local information store, so if you have 20 DCs, you need to pack the Directory on each one. This requires lots of down time. As of this writing, the job cannot be automated.

Ntdsutil compacts a database by copying the contents of the existing NTDS.DIT to a new copy of NTDS.DIT in a temporary directory of your, naming. If the directory does not exist, it is created on-the-fly. When the compacting is finished, you either copy the new file over the old file or point the system at the new directory. You do not need to mess with the log files. When I do this work, I rename the existing \NTDS directory after I'm done, move the temporary directory into the same volume, and rename it to NTDS. If you keep the log files on a separate drive—a good practice—you do not need to delete or move them.

Procedure 11.24 **Compacting and Reindexing the Directory**

1. Boot the DC to DS Repair mode and run Ntdsutil.

2. At the Ntdsutil: prompt, enter files. This opens the File Maintenance prompt.

3. Enter Compact to <directory> where <directory> is the name of the temporary directory to store the compacted NTDS.DIT. An example of the result follows:

```
file maintenance: compact to c:\ntdstemp
Opening database [Current].
Creating dir: c:\ntdstemp
Using Temporary Path: C:\
Executing Command: C:\WINNT\system32\esentutl.exe /d "e:\WINNT\NTDS\ntds.dit" /8
 /o /l"e:\WINNT\NTDS" /s"e:\WINNT\NTDS" /t"c:\temp\ntds.dit" /!10240 /p


Initiating DEFRAGMENTATION mode...
Database: e:\WINNT\NTDS\ntds.dit
Log files: e:\WINNT\NTDS
System files: e:\WINNT\NTDS
Temp. Database: c:\temp\ntds.dit

          Defragmentation Status ( % complete )
```

```
   0   10  20  30  40  50  60  70  80  90  100
   |----|----|----|----|----|----|----|----|----|----|
   ...............................................
```

```
Note:
   It is recommended that you immediately perform a full backup
   of this database. If you restore a backup made before the
   defragmentation, the database will be rolled back to the state
   it was in at the time of that backup.

Operation completed successfully in 22.172 seconds.
Spawned Process Exit code 0x0(0)
```

4. Copy the new NTDS.DIT to the original \NTDS directory. If you want, you can leave the new directory where it is and redirect the Directory pointers:

```
Set Path Backup <directory>
Set path DB <directory>
Set path logs <directory>
Set path working dir <directory>
```

If you normally keep your logs on a different drive, you can leave that pointer alone.

Repairing the Active Directory Database

If the system encounters a problem caused by corrupted pages in the database, a corrupt index file, or a combination of the two, you need to repair the database. You get a console message if the damage is severe, and the machine might even reboot with an error that the LSA is no longer functioning. You can boot to the DS Repair mode, as long as the damage is to the Directory and not to the LSA itself.

The two stages of repair are a soft recovery and a hard repair. A soft recovery rebuilds the entries using the logs and checkpoint file and then rebuilds the indexes. A hard repair covers the same ground as the soft recovery but also deletes any corrupted pages. This can cause loss of data, so don't do a hard repair unless you have no other alternative. You should always get a backup of the Directory prior to performing any database repair. Proceed as follows:

Procedure 11.25   **Backing up the Directory**

1. Boot the DC to DS Repair mode.

2. Run Ntdsutil.

3. At the prompt, enter files. This opens the File Maintenance: prompt.

4. Enter Recover. An example output looks like this:

```
Executing Command: C:\WINNT\system32\esentutl.exe /r /8 /o /l"e:\WINNT\NTDS" /s"
e:\WINNT\NTDS" /!10240Initiating RECOVERY mode...Log files: e:\WINNT\NTDSSystem files:
e:\WINNT\NTDS

Performing soft recovery...
Operation completed successfully in 6.985 seconds.
Spawned Process Exit code 0x0(0)

If recovery was successful, it is recommended
 you run semantic database analysis to insure
 semantic database consistency as well.
```

As you can see, this operation proceeds relatively painlessly as long as nothing is wrong. If performing the soft recovery does not resolve the problem, you need to perform a hard repair. You may want to consider contacting Microsoft Technical Support before proceeding. They may have other suggestions that are not as drastic.

5. From the File Maintenance: prompt, enter Repair. An example output looks like this:

```
Opening database [Current].
Executing Command: C:\WINNT\system32\esentutl.exe /p "e:\WINNT\NTDS\ntds.dit" /! 10240 /8 /v
/x /o

Initiating REPAIR mode...
Database: e:\WINNT\NTDS\ntds.dit
Temp. Database: REPAIR.EDB
got 3910 buffers
checking database header
forcing database to consistent state

checking database integrity
<<result of integrity check deleted for brevity>>

integrity check completed.
Warning:
You MUST delete the logfiles for this database

Note:
```

```
It is recommended that you immediately perform a full backup
of this database. If you restore a backup made before the
repair, the database will be rolled back to the state
it was in at the time of that backup.
```

```
Operation completed successfully in 4.336 seconds.
Spawned Process Exit code 0x0(0)
```

If a problem is encountered during the repair, the error is written to the REPAIR.TXT file in the \WINNT\NTDS directory where the NTDS.DIT file resides. You should also check the Event Log for any errors.

6. Perform a full backup of the System State files using the procedure outlined in the "Backing Up the Directory" section earlier in this chapter.

Performing an Authoritative Directory Restoration

If you cannot restore Directory operation by soft recovery or hard repair, you are forced to restore from backup tape or file. You might also encounter the need for a tape restore if a well-intentioned administrator turns loose an ADSI-based script that deletes every user with a last name starting with S. Nothing in the standard Ntdsutil options saves you from this kind of mistake. Even if you are willing to key in the names again, the SIDs are different, so the users lose their ACL rights. You must restore from tape.

You can't simply run a tape restore to recover the System State files. That updates only a single replica of the Directory. The other DCs will quickly act to replace the properties you just restored with their own that are more recent. You avoid this by performing an *Authoritative Restore*. This operation adds 100000 to the Property Version Number of every property on every read-write replica on the DC. This huge increase makes absolutely sure that this copy of the property overwrites the copies in the other replicas. The big number, 100000, is easy to track and simplifies comparing PVNs from different replicas.

The following is a sample REPADMIN listing showing how a user object looks after an authoritative restore. The ObjectClass attribute is not touched by the authoritative restore because it is a special attribute used for indexing.

Loc.USN	Originating DSA	Org.USN	Org.Time/Date	Ver	Attribute
2562	Houston\HOU-DC-01	2562	1999-05-23 21:21.29	1	objectClass
28905	Houston\HOU-DC-01	28905	1999-05-29 19:59.32	100002	cn
28905	Houston\HOU-DC-01	28905	1999-05-29 19:59.32	100002	sn

```
28905   Houston\HOU-DC-01   28905     1999-05-29 19:59.32   100001   description
28905   Houston\HOU-DC-01   28905     1999-05-29 19:59.32   100001   givenName
28905   Houston\HOU-DC-01   28905     1999-05-29 19:59.32   100001   instanceType
...
```

Because these are all originating writes with brand-new USNs and big PVNs, the properties replicate outward and overwrite the properties in every replica on every DC. For this reason, performing an authoritative restore can result in massive replication traffic in a big Directory. Schedule it after hours and pay particular attention to DCs at the wrong end of slow WAN links. When you're ready to start, proceed as follows:

Procedure 11.26   Performing an Authoritative Restore

1. At the DC where you have the corrupted files (or any DC if you're recovering from an accidental object deletion), restart the system in DS Repair mode.

2. Insert the backup tape or removable media with the System State files.

3. Run NTBACKUP via START | PROGRAMS | ACCESSORIES | SYSTEM TOOLS | BACKUP.

4. Select the Restore tab.

5. Expand the tree to show the drive and list of previously submitted jobs. When you expand the tree at the tape icon, you may need to wait a while for the tape to rewind so that the system can read the catalog.

6. Place a check next to the System State option.

7. Click Restore Now. You are prompted with a message warning that the System State files will always overwrite the existing files unless restoring to an alternate location. I do not recommend restoring to an alternate location because too many files and too many variables are involved if you try to copy them by hand. Hold your breath and enable the system to overwrite where it wants.

8. Click Yes to acknowledge the message and proceed. The Restore Progress window opens, and the tape drive or removable media begins responding.

9. When the restore is complete, click Report, and review the log to make sure that all files were restored without error.

10. Close Notepad and return to the Restore Progress window. Click Close to finish the restore. You are prompted to shut down the system. DO NOT RESTART. Instead, click No to bypass the restart option and close the Backup program.

11. Open a command session.

12. Run Ntdsutil.

13. From the Ntdsutil: prompt, enter Authoritative Restore. This opens the Authoritative Restore: prompt.

    Just a reminder on what the Authoritative Restore does: The system increases the Property Version Number by 100000 for all properties on all objects in all naming contexts hosted by this DC. (This does not include read-only replicas of trusted domains hosted by GC servers.) This drastic increase in PVN ensures that this copy of the DIT takes precedence in all collision detection events.

14. Enter Restore Database. A message window opens prompting you to verify the action.

15. Click Yes to begin the Authoritative Restore. An example output looks like this:

```
Opening DIT database…………. Done.
The current time is 05-29-99 03:59:37.
Most recent database update occurred at 05-29-99 14:27.52.
Increasing version numbers by 100000.

Counting records that need updating…
Records found: 0000020292
Done.

Found 20292 records to update.
Updating records…
Successfully updated 20292 records.
Authoritative Restore completed successfully.
```

    If the restore does not complete successfully, you may have a corrupted DIT. Try doing a soft restore and then a hard repair, retrying the Authoritative Restore each time. If it still refuses to work, try restoring from tape one more time and trying again. Then call Microsoft Technical Support for advice. You should start thinking about an alternate DC you can use to do the tape restore.

16. Quit out of Ntdsdit and restart the DC. When it comes back online, manually force replication to its replication partners and then baby-sit the system until replication ceases and the Directory reaches convergence. The easiest way to follow this around the forest is to use Performance Monitor. Point it at a remote DC and set the counters for inbound DRA. Believe me, you'll know when it starts.

Moving Forward

At this point in the Windows 2000 deployment, the domain configuration is complete. The system is ready to start accepting member servers. The next few chapters cover how to prepare these servers for production, including configuring data storage and file systems, securing file systems using NTFS permissions and the Encrypted File System, and sharing the file and print resources so that users can access them easily and reliably.

12

Configuring Data Storage

A COMPUTER WITHOUT THE CAPABILITY TO STORE INFORMATION is an expensive and somewhat unglamorous piece of furniture. The list of potential storage options for servers and workstations has grown spectacularly in the past few years. The proliferation in removable media options alone is enough to give administrators fits, as we try to please users while retaining some control over their operating environment.

Configuring all this storage requires a knowledge of the devices themselves along with their interfaces, connectors, firmware options, software options, PnP options, and their interrupt and I/O port and DMA requirements. Then they need to work with all the rest of the peripherals already loaded on the machine, not to mention any utilities or system applications that make use of storage devices.

As if matters were not complicated enough already, there is always the question of the reliability and stability of the equipment itself. Anyone who has spent a long evening trying to get a supposedly world-class CD-ROM drive to work in a supposedly world-class PC will attest to the spotty reliability of many products on the market, even those that find their way onto the Windows 2000 Hardware Compatibility List.

Much of the fabled 20 million lines of code in Windows 2000 is for the drivers that handle this cornucopia of interface and storage options. This includes, but is certainly not limited to:

- Hard drive interfaces and media, such as IDE, EIDE, UltraATA, SCSI, SCSI2, and SCSI3 in their standard, ultra and ultra-wide forms, IEEE 1394 Firewire, Fibre Channel, and USB
- Floppy interfaces and floppy drives, including the new crop of ultrafloppies
- Large-capacity removable media, such as Jaz and Orb drives, along with medium-capacity removable media, such as Zip and Superdisk drives
- Plastic-based media, such as CD-ROM, CD-R and CD-WR, DVD and DVDx, and MO hybrids
- Silicon-based media in the form of flash memory drives
- Tape drives and tape media, such as 4mm, 8mm, AdicDLT, ExabyteDLT, Travan, ADR, AIT, LTO, and DAT

The *Removable Storage Manager* (RSM) handles tape-based storage. This service also handles removable media, such as CDs and DVDs, but not floppy disks. The RSM assigns a *library* to each removable media device. The library allows the system to track different media elements associated with the same drive by forming a *media pool*. A CD jukebox would represent a single library, for example, with the mounted CDs being members of the media pool. Chapter 13, "Managing File Systems," covers how RSM works with the *Remote Storage Service* (RSS) to provide hierarchical storage management features. Chapter 18, "Recovering from System Failures," covers the use of RSM to control backup systems.

The *Logical Disk Manager* service (LDM) handles disk-based storage in Windows 2000. The LDM has two methods for configuring disk storage. It can use classic partitions, such as those used by DOS and Windows 9x, but it also provides an entirely new way of configuring disks that Microsoft licensed from Veritas. This new disk configuration does away with classic disk partitions and replaces them with an LDM database stored in a special partition at the end of the disk. The LDM database is replicated between disks and makes the storage system self-configuring. Think of LDM as a kind of Active Directory for disks.

This chapter covers configuring disk–based storage using the Logical Disk Manager. The following section discuss:

- Functional description of LDM
- Disk changes made by LDM
- Performing initial disk configurations
- Creating partitions and volumes
- Recovering failed fault-tolerant disks

Functional Description of LDM

LDM supports two different types of disk partitions:

- **Basic disks.** Space on a classic disk is apportioned using the classic disk partitioning methods that have been around since DOS 3.2 and modified slightly by Windows 9x. Disk divisions on basic disks are called *partitions*.
- **Dynamic disks.** Space on a dynamic disk is apportioned using a special LDM database stored in a 1MB partition at the end of the drive. Disk divisions on a dynamic disk are called *volumes*.

A disk that was originally configured as a basic disk and then converted to a dynamic disk retains its classic partitioning. Partitions on this kind of disk are called *hard-linked*. Hard-linked partitions can be used to boot the system and can be read by DOS and Windows 9x.

Volumes (partitions) created on a dynamic disk and stored in the LDM database are called *soft-linked* partitions. Soft-linked partitions can be accessed only by Windows 2000. They cannot be used to boot the system.

Logical Disk Manager Drivers and Registry Keys

The LDM service is contained in DMSERVER.DLL, part of the Services suite. LDM uses the classic NT fault-tolerant driver, FTDISK.SYS, to handle basic disks and a new driver, DMIO.SYS, to handle dynamic disks.

The disk subsystem has a bus extender called DMBOOT.SYS and a filter driver, DMLOAD.SYS, that controls data flow to and from the disk drivers.

The Registry values that control the LDM service and its drivers are located under HKLM | System | CurrentControlSet | Services | LDM.

All dynamic disks on a machine share a copy of the LDM database. This makes it possible to create volumes that use space from more than one disk. The LDM can be used to configure the following volume types:

- **Simple volume.** This is the equivalent to a classic partition. When you create a simple volume, you set aside a certain portion of a disk, measured in MB, which can be used to create a file system. There is room in the LDM database for thousands of simple volumes on a disk, but it's not likely you'll want more than a handful.

- **Spanned volume.** This volume type links together free space from more than one disk, or areas of free space on the same disk, to form a single logical unit. Spanned volumes provide a simple and quick way of expanding storage capacity without adding drive letters or formatting volumes. Spanned volumes are equivalent to classic NT volume sets.

Limitations of Spanned Volumes

Spanned volumes that include multiple disks cannot be mirrored, at least in software, so spanning volumes across multiple physical drives is not recommended because of the lack of fault tolerance.

One use for volume spanning that does not increase the risk of disk failure is expanding a logical volume after adding storage space to a hardware array. The additional free space provided by the RAID controller can be spanned into an existing logical volume.

An alternative to using spanned volumes is to use NTFS mount points. See the next chapter for more information.

- **Striped volume.** This is a RAID 0 configuration. The data stream is divided into chunks and written to multiple disks simultaneously. Striped volumes have performance advantages, especially when used with a high-speed data bus, but they increase the likelihood of data loss because a single drive failure disables the entire volume.

- **Mirrored volume.** This is a RAID 1 configuration. The same data stream is directed onto two disks simultaneously. The file systems on the mirrored volumes remain available if either disk fails. Mirrored drives that are driven by different controllers are said to be *duplexed*. Mirrored volumes have fast seek times because either disk can respond to a read request. They are slower than single disks for writing because data must be written to two disks simultaneously, although duplexed drives are theoretically faster in this regard.

- **RAID 5 volume.** A configuration in which the data stream is divided into chunks written to multiple disks along with parity information that can be used to reconstitute a lost disk should one fail. RAID 5 represents a compromise between performance, fault tolerance, and flexibility. It is slower than mirroring, but makes more effective use of storage capacity because a higher percentage of total storage is available for file systems. It is slower than striping or spanned volumes but provides fault tolerance.

Functional Description of RAID 5 Storage

If you are not familiar with RAID configurations or terminology, you might want to take a look at the *Windows 2000 Hardware Companion* by Rob Marsh (ISBN: 1-5787-0079-5) or any of the many Windows NT study guides. Here's a quick overview.

In RAID 5, the Logical Disk Manager divides the data stream going to the disks into 64KB chunks. It then calculates parity information on two of the chunks to arrive at a third chunk that is also 64KB in size. This parity calculation uses a XOR, or exclusive OR function. The XOR calculation is like a party game used to break up couples: If two values match, you get a logical 0; if two values don't match, you get a logical 1. Table 12.1 shows a XOR truth table:

Table 12.1   **XOR Truth Table**

A	B	C
0	0	0
0	1	1
1	0	1
1	1	0

To see the magic of XOR, cover up any column. You can quickly figure out the contents of each cell in the missing column based on whether the other two cells match or don't match. In the same way, if you remove a disk from a RAID 5 array, the system can quickly calculate the missing contents by doing a XOR on the data on the other disks.

You must have at least three disks to make a RAID 5 array because the system must have at least two chunks of data to calculate a parity chunk. The parity chunks are spread across the three drives so that one drive's worth of storage capacity is lost. If you have four drives, 25% of the capacity is lost. If you had an ultrawide SCSI 3 bus populated with 15 drives, you would lose only 6.7% of the total capacity. You would also lose performance due to bus saturation, but that's beyond the scope of this book. A regular striped volume does not calculate parity information, so its performance is dramatically better, but you lose fault tolerance.

Restrictions on Special LDM Volumes

A few restrictions apply when using the special volume configurations provided by LDM. Most of these restrictions relate to the way volumes can be mixed together. You do not need to memorize this list. In general, if a particular configuration is unsupported, the option will not be available in the management tools.

- All special disk configurations must use dynamic disks.
- Spanned volumes that include multiple disks cannot be mirrored.
- Striped and RAID 5 volumes cannot be mirrored.
- Fault-tolerant disk sets in classic NT machines will be upgraded to dynamic disks during setup, but you cannot move a classic NT fault-tolerant disk set to a Windows 2000 machine. There is no DISK key or binary image structure in Windows 2000 to support FTEDIT, the Fault-Tolerant Disk Editor.
- The system partition must reside on a standard partition, a simple volume, or a mirrored volume. It cannot reside on a striped, RAID 5, or spanned volume. The boot partition can reside on any type of volume.

Boot and System

In case you are not familiar with Microsoft's awkward and unintuitive definition of "boot" partitions and "system" partitions, here it is:

- The *boot partition* contains the Windows 2000 system files. When the Microsoft documentation (and this book, for consistency) refers to the "boot disk," it refers to the disk containing the Windows 2000 system files. This is not necessarily the disk with the active partition that is used to boot the system.

- The system partition contains the files that Windows 2000 uses to load the operating system: NTDLR, NTDETECT.COM, BOOT.INI, BOOTSECT.DOS, and NTBOOTDD.SYS. These must reside in the root of the drive that is used to boot the system. When Microsoft refers to the "system disk," it means the disk that boots the operating system.

Confusing? You bet. Will it change? Not likely. I'm certain that by the time today's magnetic storage has been replaced by crystal matrix storage, the Windows OS of the day will designate the lattice holding the operating system files as the boot stratum.

The storage subsystem is transparent to the file system. All the disk configurations support the three native Windows 2000 file systems—FAT, FAT32, and NTFS—along with third-party file systems such as the *Andrew File System* (AFS) and the *Network File System* (NFS). You can use the stripped-down version of Diskeeper that comes with Windows 2000 to defragment file systems on any disk configuration. Diskeeper does not move data between disks in a striped or mirrored volume, but it defragments the clusters that belong to a particular file on each disk so that they are contiguous. You can also use NTFS mount points for any of the volumes. You can create a RAID 5 volume and mount it at a directory on an existing drive, for example, so that the users don't need to map an additional drive letter.

Windows 2000 Professional continues Microsoft's practice of artificially limiting the functionality of the workstation product by eliminating mirroring and RAID 5 from the list of available volume types. If you create a mirrored group or a RAID 5 group on a Windows 2000 Server and transfer the disks to a machine running Windows 2000 Professional, then you can import them and use them. (I do not recommend this practice, but it is an available option. See the "Moving Dynamic Disks Between Computers" section later in this chapter for more information.)

Object Namespace

Before configuring disks, partitions, and volumes, it's important to take a brief look at the inner workings of the Windows 2000 Executive as it relates to disk storage. The various elements of the storage system are represented in the Windows 2000 Executive by objects in the *Object Namespace*. Physical storage is virtualized in the Object Namespace, and logical storage is represented by handles with pointers called *symbolic links*. The symbolic links connect logical devices to physical devices.

You can view the Object Namespace in a couple of ways. One is to use the *Object Viewer*, WINOBJ, from the Platform SDK. A better tool comes from Mark Russinovich and the gang at System Internals, www.sysinternals.com. This tool is also called WINOBJ, but Mark's version is 50% smaller than Microsoft's and more accurate. I recommend using it. Figure 12.1 shows an example of the WINOBJ display for disk devices.

Figure 12.1 Windows Object Viewer from www.sysinternals.com showing the Device list in the Object Namespace.

The design of the Object Namespace is helpful to system administrators because it defines a map that describes data flows and data repositories in the system.

Using Disk Probe

The initial portion of the next section examines the structure of the Master Boot Record and partition tables on drives that have been configured as basic disks and dynamic disks. This information helps to define the operational parameters and limitations of the two storage alternatives. It also helps in diagnosing problems when an LDM drive does not behave like a classic drive. LDM fundamentally alters the way storage is managed. By understanding how those changes are implemented as disk structures, you'll have a much better idea of how to handle operational problems.

I made use of a tool called Disk Probe from the Windows 2000 Resource Kit to get the MBR listings. Disk Probe can also be used to save copies of the MBR and the boot sector so that you recover them if they get corrupted. Disk Probe can write to disks as well as read from them, so use it with caution.

Here is a quick set of instructions for loading and using Disk Probe if you want to follow along with the text.

Procedure 12.1 **Using Disk Probe**

1. Install the Resource Kit if you have not already done so.
2. Open the Resource Kit tool list and launch Disk Probe. This opens the `Disk Probe` main window in an uninitialized state (see Figure 12.2).

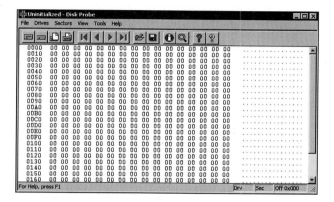

Figure 12.2 `Disk Probe` main window with no drives initialized.

3. Select DRIVES | PHYSICAL DRIVE from the menu. The `Open Physical Drive` window opens (see Figure 12.3).

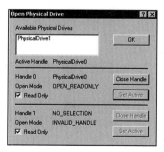

Figure 12.3 Disk Probe—`Open Physical Drive` window showing Physical Drive 0 selected and active.

4. Double-click a physical drive to assign it to the next available handle. You may have handles for two drives, either logical or physical, available at a time.

5. Click Set Active to make the drive available to the probe. This only initializes Disk Probe. It does not make the drive active in the FDISK sense.

6. Click OK to save the choices and close the window.

7. From the main menu, select SECTORS | READ. The Read Sectors window opens.

8. Enter a Starting Sector of **0** and a Number of Sectors of **1**. Because a physical drive was selected, this reads the Master Boot Record. If you select a logical drive, the first sector would be the partition boot sector.

9. Click Read to read the sectors. The main Disk Probe window shows the contents. If you select an invalid sector number, you'll get an error. If you select an invalid number of sectors (the buffer limit is 4,096), you'll get an error. If you select a sector near the end of the disk and specify a number of sectors that puts the buffer beyond the end of the disk, the program will fault and close. If you did everything right, you'll see the contents of the Master Boot Record in hex and byte format (see Figure 12.4).

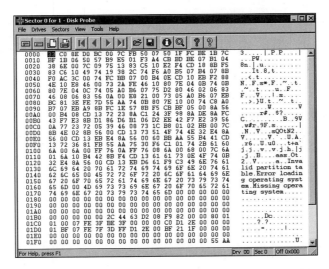

Figure 12.4 Disk Probe window showing the contents of the Master Boot Record.

10. From the menu, select VIEW | PARTITION TABLE. The display now shows content of each entry in the partition table (see Figure 12.5).

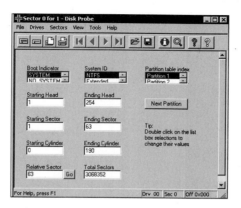

Figure 12.5 Disk Probe window showing the partition table.

11. If you want to search out a particular entry in a range of sectors, select TOOLS | SEARCH SECTORS from the menu. This opens the Search Sectors window (see Figure 12.6).

Figure 12.6 Search Sectors window showing a search for the string NTLDR in the first 64 sectors of the physical drive.

12. Under Search Type, select Exhaustive Search and Ignore Case.

13. Under Character Type, select ASCII Characters, unless you are searching for entries in a file that uses Unicode.

14. Under First and Last Sector to Search, enter a range. Ordinarily, you would want to limit your search to a few sectors. A full scan of an entire disk can take a very long time.

15. Under Enter characters to search for, enter a short string. (I use this feature to find sector headings when I'm looking for the start of a file entry or a heading in a disk structure.)

16. After you have finished probing, be sure to release the active handle and close Disk Probe.

Disk Changes Made by LDM

LDM makes several changes to the Master Boot Record when a basic disk is converted to a dynamic disk, especially to the structure of the partition table. LDM also adds special pointers to the reserved space following the MBR and adds a partition to the end of the disk to hold the LDM database. These changes significantly impact the way the storage system operates. The best way to understand this impact is to take a detailed look at the standard disk structures before and after LDM modifies them.

Master Boot Record

Both basic and dynamic disks make use of the *Master Boot Record* (MBR). The MBR occupies the first sector (512 bytes) of a disk. It contains executable code that the system BIOS loads into memory via a standard INT13 BIOS call at boot time. The executable code scans the last four lines of the MBR to find a *partition table*. Each entry in the partition table points at the location of a partition on the disk.

A flag just before the partition table designates one partition as *active*, or bootable. The first sector of a bootable partition is called the *partition boot sector* (PBS). The PBS contains executable code designed to launch a bootstrap loader. In the case of Windows 2000 on an Intel platform, the bootstrap loader is NTLDR. The drive configuration does not affect the PBS.

Fault–Tolerant Signature

The first MBR change made by LDM is the addition of a *fault-tolerant signature* to the body of the MBR. The fault-tolerant signature is a series of bytes starting either at offset 1B8 (classic NT) or 1B5 (Windows 2000.) There is no special intelligence in this number. You can write one yourself using a hex editor, if you like. The only requirement is that it be unique among the disks in that computer.

The system uses the fault–tolerant signature as an index to disk information stored in a Registry key called `HKLM | System | Mounted Devices`. This key replaces the `HKLM | System | Disk` key used in classic NT. The Mounted Devices key is also called the *Mount Manager database*. See the sidebar titled "Mount Manager and Drive Selections" for more information. Figure 12.7 shows a sample Mounted Devices key.

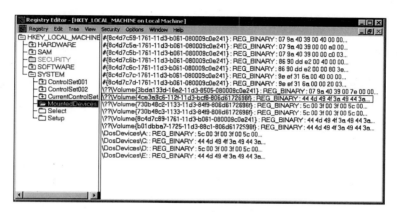

Figure 12.7   Registry Editor showing the values in the Mounted Devices key.

Take a look at the entries for drives F, H, I, and J. See how they all have the same starting sequence? This sequence comes from the fault–tolerant signature in the MBR. The entries prefixed by `\??\Volume` are symbolic links. The Object Namespace uses symbolic links to point at disk structures such as partitions and volumes, as well as file system structures. Symbolic links representing disks are indexed by the fault–tolerant signature in the MBR.

Mount Manager and Drive Selection

The `HKLM | System | Mounted Devices` key is also called the Mount Manager database. The Mount Manager driver, MOUNTMGR.SYS, uses this database to assign drive letters at boot time.

When a new volume or partition is added, Mount Manager selects a drive letter to assign. There are a number of criteria for assigning drive letters. These are outlined in KnowledgeBase article Q234048, "How Windows 2000 Assigns, Reserves, and Stores Drive Letters." Briefly, partitions are scanned in the following order:

- **Legacy fault-tolerant disk sets.** These FTDISK-based partitions have a drive letter stored in the partition. This drive letter should be assigned to the disk set if at all possible to ensure access to the disk set. That's why they get first priority.

- **Dynamic disks with legacy partition table.** These are called "hard-linked" partitions because the volumes have entries in the partition table and are therefore bootable.

- **Dynamic disks with no legacy partition table.** These are called "soft-linked" partitions because they only exist in the LDM database.

- **Basic disks and removable disks.** These are disks that do not have an LDM database, and therefore have a standard partition table. Basic disks are scanned by first primary partition, then logical drives in extended partitions, and then remaining primary partitions.

- **CD-ROM drives.**

The system writes the fault-tolerant signature the first time you run the Disk Management snap-in. This is described in "Using the Disk Management Snap-In" section a little later in the chapter. If an MBR is not present when the signature is written, LDM writes an MBR and then writes the signature.

MBR put the following example in place by the Disk Management snap-in after installing a SCSI drive that has just been low-level formatted. The bold entries before the partition table are the fault-tolerant signature:

```
00000000   33 C0 8E D0 BC 00 7C FB-50 07 50 1F FC BE 1B 7C   3.....¦.P.P....¦
00000010   BF 1B 06 50 57 B9 E5 01-F3 A4 CB BD BE 07 B1 04   ...PW...........
00000020   38 6E 00 7C 09 75 13 83-C5 10 E2 F4 CD 18 8B F5   8n.¦.u..........
00000030   83 C6 10 49 74 19 38 2C-74 F6 A0 B5 07 B4 07 8B   ...It.8,t.......
00000040   F0 AC 3C 00 74 FC BB 07-00 B4 0E CD 10 EB F2 88   ..<.t...........
00000050   4E 10 E8 46 00 73 2A FE-46 10 80 7E 04 0B 74 0B   N..F.s*.F..~..t.
00000060   80 7E 04 0C 74 05 A0 B6-07 75 D2 80 46 02 06 83   .~..t....u..F...
00000070   46 08 06 83 56 0A 00 E8-21 00 73 05 A0 B6 07 EB   F...V...!.s.....
00000080   BC 81 3E FE 7D 55 AA 74-0B 80 7E 10 00 74 C8 A0   ..>.}U.t..~..t..
00000090   B7 07 EB A9 8B FC 1E 57-8B F5 CB BF 05 00 8A 56   .......W.......V
000000A0   00 B4 08 CD 13 72 23 8A-C1 24 3F 98 8A DE 8A FC   .....r#..$?.....
000000B0   43 F7 E3 8B D1 86 D6 B1-06 D2 EE 42 F7 E2 39 56   C..........B..9V
000000C0   0A 77 23 72 05 39 46 08-73 1C B8 01 02 BB 00 7C   .w#r.9F.s......¦
000000D0   8B 4E 02 8B 56 00 CD 13-73 51 4F 74 4E 32 E4 8A   .N..V...sQOtN2..
000000E0   56 00 CD 13 EB E4 8A 56-00 60 BB AA 55 B4 41 CD   V......V.`..U.A.
000000F0   13 72 36 81 FB 55 AA 75-30 F6 C1 01 74 2B 61 60   .r6..U.u0...t+a`
00000100   6A 00 6A 00 FF 76 0A FF-76 08 6A 00 68 00 7C 6A   j.j..v..v.j.h.¦j
00000110   01 6A 10 B4 42 8B F4 CD-13 61 61 73 0E 4F 74 0B   .j..B....aas.Ot.
00000120   32 E4 8A 56 00 CD 13 EB-D6 61 F9 C3 49 6E 76 61   2..V.....a..Inva
00000130   6C 69 64 20 70 61 72 74-69 74 69 6F 6E 20 74 61   lid partition ta
00000140   62 6C 65 00 45 72 72 6F-72 20 6C 6F 61 64 69 6E   ble.Error loadin
00000150   67 20 6F 70 65 72 61 74-69 6E 67 20 73 79 73 74   g operating syst
00000160   65 6D 00 4D 69 73 73 69-6E 67 20 6F 70 65 72 61   em.Missing opera
00000170   74 69 6E 67 20 73 79 73-74 65 6D 00 00 00 00 00   ting system.....
00000180   00 00 00 00 00 00 00 00-00 00 00 00 00 00 00 00   ................
00000190   00 00 00 00 00 00 00 00-00 00 00 00 00 00 00 00   ................
000001A0   00 00 00 00 00 00 00 00-00 00 00 00 00 00 00 00   ................
000001B0   00 00 00 00 00 00 00 00-08 4C 74 AC 00 00 00 00   ......,Dc..n.....
```

`<<inserted remark — partition table entries>>`

```
000001C0   00 00 00 00 00 00 00 00-00 00 00 00 00 00 00 00   ................
000001D0   00 00 00 00 00 00 00 00-00 00 00 00 00 00 00 00   ................
000001E0   00 00 00 00 00 00 00 00-00 00 00 00 00 00 00 00   ................
000001F0   00 00 00 00 00 00 00 00-00 00 00 00 00 00 55 AA   ..............U.
```

The last four lines of the MBR comprise the partition table. This is a freshly formatted drive, so there are no partitions in the table. The next section covers the standard format of a partition table both before and after the disk has been configured as a dynamic disk.

The 55AA flag indicates the end of the MBR. The sectors between the end of the MBR and the start of the first partition (which normally starts at sector 63) are usually left blank. The Logical Disk Manager uses this area for pointers and disk information when the disk is upgraded to a dynamic disk.

Partition Table Prior to LDM Updates

The partition table can hold a maximum of four entries, so there are a maximum of four partitions on a basic disk. Here is an example partition table with four partitions. The fourth partition is an extended partition:

```
000001B0   00 00 00 00 00 00 00 00-08 4C 74 AC 00 00 80 00     .........Lt.....
000001C0   21 00 07 46 05 01 20 00-00 00 E0 4F 00 00 00 00     !..F.. ....O....
000001D0   01 0A 06 3F 20 3B 00 50-00 00 00 90 01 00 00 00     ...? ;.P........
000001E0   01 3C 06 3F 20 6D 00 E0-01 00 00 90 01 00 00 05     .<.? m..........
000001F0   38 0E 05 FE 3F 15 00 70-03 00 96 F4 01 00 55 AA     8...?..p......U.
```

Because the LDM makes changes to several key elements in the standard partition table, here is a listing of the partition table elements to use when analyzing those changes. The partition table starts at offset 1B14. Here is the first table entry spread out to show the constituents:

```
80 00 21 00 07 46 05 01 20 00 00 00 E0 4F 00 00
```

- **80.** This indicates that the partition is active, which means it is bootable.
- **00 21 00.** The starting cylinder, head, and sector of the partition.
- **07.** The partition type, also called media type. These are 01=FAT12, 04=FAT16, 05=Extended Partition, 06=BIGDOS FAT, 07=NTFS, 0B=FAT32 < 512MB, 0C=FAT32>512MB, and 42=Logical Disk Manager. The system passes this information on to the bootstrap loader so that it knows what file system driver to use.
- **46 05 01.** The ending cylinder, head, and sector of the partition.
- **20 00 00 00.** The relative offset of the start of the partition in numbers of sectors.
- **E0 4F 00 00.** The number of sectors in the partition. Both the sector counts use little-endian format, so reverse the octets before making the decimal conversion. For example, 00 02 becomes 0200h, or 512 decimal.

Partition Table After LDM Upgrade

When LDM converts a basic disk to a dynamic disk, the upgrade process changes the partition table. Here is the partition table after conversion to a dynamic disk:

```
000001B0   00 00 00 00 00 00 00 00-08 4C 74 AC 00 00 80 00   .........Lt.....
000001C0   21 00 42 46 05 01 20 00-00 00 E0 4F 00 00 00 46   !.BF.. .....O...F
000001D0   06 01 42 A5 1E 07 00 50-00 00 00 90 01 00 00 A5   ..B....P........
000001E0   1F 07 42 05 37 0E 00 E0-01 00 00 90 01 00 00 05   ..B.7...........
000001F0   38 0E 05 FE 3F 15 00 70-03 00 96 F4 01 00 55 AA   8.B.?..p......U.
```

The second partition was changed to point at the LDM partition at the end of the disk. Ordinarily, this change would be made to the first partition; but in this case, the first partition was marked as active, or bootable. If a bootable partition is in place, LDM leaves it in place as a "hard-linked" partition so that it can boot an operating system. A "soft-linked" partition pointing at the LDM database cannot boot an OS.

The second change affects the media type entries for the first three partitions at offset 1C2, 1D2, 1E2. These entries were changed to 42. (There's nothing in the documentation to indicate whether this number was selected by a Douglas Adams fan.) Type 42 indicates an LDM partition.

The media type for an extended partition is left at type 05, but the logical drives in the extended partition are converted to LDM volumes with appropriate entries in the LDM database. Because the original type 05 entries are undisturbed, these become "hard-linked" partitions and can be read by DOS and Windows 9x.

Changes to Reserved Disk Area

The dynamic disk conversion also adds new entries at sector 6, where it creates a Private Heading (PRIVHEAD) sector. This sector contains information about the disk including the *Globally Unique Identifier* (GUID) that represents this disk in the LDM database. It also contains the sector offset of the start of the LDM partition, the sector offset of the start of the LDM database itself, and other information about the disk configuration:

```
00000000   50 52 49 56 48 45 41 44   00 00 13 4F 00 02 00 0B   PRIVHEAD...O....
00000010   01 BE AC 79 54 5E 0B 4A   00 00 00 00 00 00 00 01   ._¬yT^.J........
00000020   00 00 00 00 00 00 07 FF   00 00 00 00 00 00 07 40   .......ÿ.......@
00000030   39 31 31 32 39 64 35 39   2D 31 38 36 63 2D 31 31   91129d59-186c-11
00000040   64 33 2D 62 30 36 35 2D   30 38 30 30 30 39 63 30   d3-b065-080009c0
00000050   65 32 34 31 00 00 00 00   00 00 00 00 00 00 00 00   e241............
00000060   00 00 00 00 00 00 00 00   00 00 00 00 00 00 00 00   ................
00000070   00 00 00 00 00 00 00 00   00 00 00 00 00 00 00 00   ................
00000080   00 00 00 00 00 00 00 00   00 00 00 00 00 00 00 00   ................
```

```
00000090  00 00 00 00 00 00 00 00  00 00 00 00 00 00 00 00   ...............
000000A0  00 00 00 00 00 00 00 00  00 00 00 00 00 00 00 00   ...............
000000B0  00 00 00 00 00 00 00 00  00 00 00 00 00 00 00 00   ...............
000000C0  00 00 00 00 00 00 00 00  00 00 00 00 00 00 00 00   ...............
000000D0  00 00 00 00 00 00 00 00  00 00 00 00 00 00 00 00   ...............
000000E0  00 00 00 00 00 00 00 00  00 00 00 00 00 00 00 00   ...............
000000F0  00 00 00 00 00 00 00 00  00 00 00 00 00 00 00 00   ...............
00000100  00 00 00 00 00 00 00 00  00 00 00 00 00 00 00 00   ...............
00000110  00 02 00 00 00 00 00 00  00 00 00 00 00 00 00 00   ...............
00000120  00 00 20 00 00 00 00 00  20 29 70 00 00 00 00 00   .. ..... )p.....
00000130  20 29 90 00 00 00 00 00  00 08 00 00 00 00 00 00    )_............
00000140  00 00 01 00 00 00 00 00  00 07 FE 00 00 00 01 00   .............._..
00000150  00 00 01 00 00 00 00 00  00 05 C9 00 00 00 00 00   ..........É.....
00000160  00 00 E0 00 00 00 00 00  00 00 00 00 00 00 00 00   ..à............
00000170  00 00 00 00 00 00 00 00  00 00 00 00 00 00 00 00   ...............
```

LDM Database Construction

The LDM database is located in the last 1MB of the physical drive. It starts with a Table of Contents, or TOCBLOCK, sector that contains a small amount of configuration information and then several KB of space for log files. There are two TOCBLOCK sectors in case one gets corrupted:

```
00000000  54 4F 43 42 4C 4F 43 4B  00 00 08 C1 00 00 00 00   TOCBLOCK...Á....
00000010  00 00 00 04 00 00 00 00  00 00 00 00 00 00 00 00   ...............
00000020  00 00 00 00 63 6F 6E 66  69 67 00 00 00 00 00 00   ....config......
00000030  00 00 00 00 00 11 00 00  00 00 00 00 05 C9 00 06   .............É..
00000040  00 01 00 00 00 00 6C 6F  67 00 00 00 00 00 00 08   ......log.......
00000050  00 00 00 00 00 00 05 DA  00 00 00 00 00 00 00 E0   .......Ú.......à
00000060  00 06 00 01 00 00 00 00  00 00 00 00 00 00 00 00   ...............
```

The Volume Manager Database, or VMDB, starts a few sectors after the TOCBLOCK. (Volume Manager is the Veritas name for Logical Disk Manager.) The VMDB sector includes the Disk Group (DG) number, which is a concatenation of the computer's name, the letters *Dg*, and a sequence number. The default sequence number is 0. The VMDB sector also contains the GUID of the disk that appears in the PRIVHEAD sector:

```
00000000  56 4D 44 42 00 00 16 B0  00 00 00 80 00 00 02 00   VMDB...°........
00000010  00 01 00 04 00 0A 53 6C  63 2D 77 32 6B 70 2D 30   ......Slc-w2kp-0
00000020  30 31 44 67 30 00 00 00  00 00 00 00 00 00 00 00   01Dg0...........
00000030  00 00 00 00 00 37 37 63  64 66 32 39 62 2D 31 37   .....77cdf29b-17
00000040  32 33 2D 31 31 64 33 2D  39 37 30 62 2D 30 38 30   23-11d3-970b-080
00000050  30 30 39 63 30 65 32 34  31 00 00 00 00 00 00 00   009c0e241.......
00000060  00 00 00 00 00 00 00 00  00 00 00 00 00 00 00 00   ...............
00000070  00 00 00 00 00 00 00 00  00 00 00 06 92 00 00 00   ............'...
00000080  00 00 00 06 92 00 00 00  01 00 00 00 01 00 00 00   ....'...........
00000090  01 00 00 00 05 00 00 00  00 00 00 00 00 00 00 00   ...............
000000A0  00 00 00 00 01 00 00 00  01 00 00 00 01 00 00 00   ...............
```

```
000000B0    05 00 00 00 00 00 00 00   00 00 00 00 00 01 BE B1    .............._±
000000C0    4D D9 19 66 27 00 00 00   00 00 00 00 00 00 00 00    MÙ.f'..........
000000D0    00 00 00 00 00 00 00 00   00 00 00 00 00 00 00 00    ...............
000000E0    00 00 00 00 00 00 00 00   00 00 00 00 00 00 00 00    ...............
000000F0       00 00 00 00 00 00 00 00   00 00 00 00 00 00 00 00    ...............
```

The rest of the LDM partition is divvied up into 128-byte areas called *virtual blocks* (VBLKs). These form the contents of the LDM database. Some of these virtual blocks represent this and the other physical drives on the machine that have been configured as dynamic disks:

```
00000280    56 42 4C 4B 00 00 00 05   00 00 00 06 00 00 00 02    VBLK............
00000290    00 00 00 34 00 00 00 78   02 06 91 05 44 69 73 6B    ...4...x..'.Disk
000002A0    35 24 31 35 37 38 32 31   62 61 2D 31 64 34 31 2D    5$157821ba-1d41-
000002B0    31 31 64 33 2D 61 33 39   34 2D 30 38 30 30 30 39    11d3-a394-080009
000002C0    63 30 65 32 34 31 3D 53   43 53 49 5C 44 49 53 4B    c0e241=SCSI\DISK
000002D0    26 56 45 4E 5F 53 45 41   47 41 54 45 26 50 52 4F    &VEN_SEAGATE&PRO
000002E0    44 5F 53 54 35 31 30 38   30 4E 26 52 45 56 5F 30    D_ST51080N&REV_0
000002F0       39 34 33 5C 33 26 31 42   33 43 31 35 31 33 26 30    943\3&1B3C1513&0
```

If you examine the data on your own system, you may see that the VBLK has less information than the one shown in the example. This depends on what the system can glean from the drive's BIOS. The disk numbers in the metadata do not correspond to the disk numbers in the Disk Management snap-in. Other virtual blocks represent logical volumes that include this disk. Here is the default volume that includes this disk:

```
00000480    56 42 4C 4B 00 00 00 09   00 00 00 34 00 00 00 01    VBLK.......4....
00000490    00 00 02 51 00 00 00 53   02 04 0F 07 56 6F 6C 75    ...Q...S....Volu
000004A0    6D 65 31 03 67 65 6E 00   41 43 54 49 56 45 00 00    me1.gen.ACTIVE..
000004B0    00 00 00 00 00 00 03 01   05 00 A0 00 11 01 01 00    .......... .....
000004C0    00 00 00 00 00 04 91 00   00 00 00 00 00 04 68 03    ......'.......h.
000004D0    25 81 1A 00 00 00 00 07   B0 1D BB A6 17 25 11 D3    %_......°.»_.%.Ó
000004E0    88 C1 80 6D 61 72 69 6F   02 43 3A 00 00 00 00 00    ^Á.mario.C:.....
000004F0       00 00 00 00 00 00 00 00   00 00 00 00 00 00 00 00    ...............
```

There are also VBLK entries designating the volume type, such as RAID 5, striped, mirrored, and so forth. Taken together, these database entries give the Logical Disk Manager a wide range of control over the volume structure on the disks. Add-on products from Veritas and other vendors will capitalize on this database.

The jury is still out on performance of the new software-based RAID in Windows 2000. It is nearly impossible to get an apples-to-apples comparison between software RAID and hardware RAID due to tuning differences. If your budget has room, you're better off with hardware RAID because you get extra features such as hot-swappable drives and the ability to dynamically resize an array. For a few more dollars, you get a RAID controller, lots of onboard memory, and a battery backup so that you can use write-back caching.

Performing Initial Disk Configurations

If you're an experienced NT administrator, you may be skeptical about dynamic disks. At first glance, they appear to be a fix looking for something broken. You do not need a dynamic disk on a system with only one disk. Because most workstations have only one disk, you can use a basic disk configuration for everything except servers. There is no performance advantage and no increase in stability or reliability of a dynamic disk over a basic disk. The file systems on dynamic disks are just as susceptible to viruses as those on basic disks because the partition boot sector is unchanged. The LDM supports SCSI sector sparing on both basic and dynamic disks so that is not a reason to upgrade, as it was on classic NT. Sector sparing protects data on a SCSI drive by automatically moving data from a failed sector to a spare sector.

The only time you need to use dynamic disks is if you want to use any of the special volume configurations such as mirroring, volume spanning, striping, or RAID 5. Classic fault-tolerant disk sets are supported only if they existed prior to upgrading to Windows 2000.

Dynamic disks have several advantages over classic NT fault-tolerant disk sets, including the following:

- Disk reconfigurations do not require rebooting.
- Disk sets can be remotely managed.
- Volumes have greater flexibility, especially when configuring volume spans. Volume spans on the same logical drive can be mirrored. This simplifies upgrading hardware. You can add a drive in an emergency to extend a volume, and then come back later to add a bigger drive and mirror it to the two spanned volumes. You can then either leave the system in that configuration for increased fault tolerance, or remove the small drives and leave behind the big one with a single volume. Volume spanning is much more stable under LDM.
- The LDM database is replicated to each dynamic disk. If a volume includes multiple drives, you can remove the drives, and then replace them and get them out of order. The volume will still work because the database is on the drive, not the Registry. For the same reason, the volume structure is retained even if the Registry gets corrupted or is otherwise unavailable.
- You can boot from a fault-tolerant boot floppy disk to the secondary drive of a mirrored volume without breaking the mirror. This was not possible in classic NT using FTDISK because the Registry on the mirrored disk was locked.

- Dynamic disks are extensible, so third parties can add value. This sounds like an advertising claim, but there are lots of companies looking to offer great features if there were only hooks in the system. Dynamic disks provide this kind of hook.

Changing Drive Orders in Disk Arrays

I'm usually somewhat dubious of feature lists, and you probably are too. In this case, the dynamic disk features perform as advertised. The ability to change drive order is especially handy because it corrects a weakness of classic fault-tolerant disk arrays. Using dynamic disks, you can change SCSI ID numbers and disk controllers, and IDE master/slave configurations and disk controllers at random, and the system will function just fine. The Disk Management display gets a little messy, but the system continues to operate without a hitch.

LDM and dynamic disks do not provide the same kind of comprehensive feature sets found in hardware RAID controllers. There is no support for hot-swappable disks, hot-standby disks, or dynamic growth when adding new disks. Also, the LDM version that comes with Windows 2000 does not include partition management features such as volume resizing, although an add-on pack from Veritas will have this feature. Also be on the lookout for products from PowerQuest, Paragon Software, and V Communications that take advantage of LDM.

Precautions for Converting Basic Disks to Dynamic Disks

Dynamic disks have their little eccentricities. Getting used to them is a little like getting used to the metric system—the basic system makes lots of sense, but there's pain in the transition. You'll find a host of prerequisites and restrictions when converting basic disks to dynamic disks. If one of these prevents you from converting to dynamic disks and you need a special feature they provide, your only alternative is to remove the existing partition, convert the disk to a dynamic disk, configure a volume, and then restore the data from tape. The following restrictions and prerequisites apply:

- You cannot convert a disk with existing partitions if there is no room for the LDM database at the end of the disk. The database takes approximately 1MB. The system attempts to make room by redefining the partition boundaries. If you have SCSI drives, the system will make use of the spare sectors set aside for hot fixes. This can dramatically reduce the cushion you have for sector sparing, so you're better off leaving a little bit of free space during initial setup, if you have that flexibility. About the only time you should run into problems is if you have a disk with a Linux partition or another third-party file system.

- In general, dynamic disks are not supported on laptops. There are exceptions, depending on how Windows 2000 interprets the BIOS. This limitation should not be a problem, because laptops seldom use multiple drives.

- You might not be able to convert a disk with sector sizes larger than 512 bytes. This is not a strict limitation. I have successfully converted disks with a variety of sector sizes. Nevertheless, this limit is in the documentation, so don't count on doing a successful conversion for disks containing large sectors. If you are running FAT, you may need to convert to NTFS prior to converting to dynamic disks to get the smaller sector size.

- If you have a classic NT server or workstations with an existing fault-tolerant disk assembly, you can convert the disks to dynamic disks after setup to take advantage of LDM volumes. You cannot convert just one disk out of a classic fault-tolerant disk set. You must convert all the disks *en toto* or not at all.

- You cannot convert removable media. This is true even if your BIOS permits you to designate a removable media drive as fixed media.

- A disk can only be bootable if it is upgraded from a basic disk with an active partition. Ordinarily, this is not a problem because all disks are basic before they are upgraded, but you can encounter difficulties when working with mirrored volumes. See the "Breaking a Mirrored Volume" section later in the chapter.

- After you convert a drive containing an active (that is, bootable) partition, say goodbye to dual-booting the machine to any operating system other than Windows 2000. You cannot boot to DOS, Windows 9x, or classic NT from a dynamic disk. If you keep the boot disk configured as a basic disk so that you can boot to an earlier OS, or if you boot from floppy disk, you cannot view any dynamic disks in the system even if they have FAT or FAT32 file systems. If you dual-boot between Windows 2000 installations, you can view the contents of dynamic disks created by the partner installation, but you may have problems managing volumes because the computer name in the LDM database differs.

- If you try to install Windows 2000 on a computer configured with dynamic disks, you may run into problems finding free disk space. This is because the partition manager loaded by the Setup program cannot read the LDM database.

- You cannot convert back to a basic disk without first removing all volumes. If the partition table was kept intact during the dynamic disk conversion, you will retain your original partitions when you convert back to a basic disk; but you'll lose your data because the file systems are removed when you remove the dynamic disk volumes. You must format the partitions and restore data from tape. There is no guarantee that the partition table will be retained in its original form; so if you want to revert back to the original basic disk configuration, use Disk Probe or Disk Save from the Resource Kit to preserve the MBR before you convert to dynamic disk.

- The system files (NTDLR, NTDETECT.COM, BOOT.INI, BOOTSECT.DOS, and NTBOOTDD.SYS) can reside on a dynamic disk, but they must reside on a simple volume.

- Both the boot disk and the system disk (if they reside on different disks) can be converted to a dynamic disk; because the conversion must unmount the file system, however, the boot disk cannot be converted while the operating system is running.

Converting a Boot Partition to a Dynamic Disk

If you elect to convert a disk containing a Windows 2000 boot partition, the following occurs:

- An `Encapsulation Info` key is placed in the Registry under HKLM | System | CurrentControlSet | Services | DMIO with a binary value of FDISK Data showing the structure of the partitions on the disk.

- An EncapsulationPending key is put under HKLM | System | CurrentControlSet | Services | DMLOAD with no keys. It acts as a flag to notify the system to make the change to the Master Boot Record, and construct the LDM database using the information in the Encapsulation Info key.

- The system restarts, makes the change, and then you are prompted to restart again.

- After the second restart, the conversion is complete, and the system runs with its system files on a dynamic volume.

- On rare occasions, you may be forced to reboot when you start creating volumes on a disk following conversion. This happens most often when you had several partitions on the disk prior to conversion. Apparently, it is caused when the LDM needs to write to the partition table in the MBR in such a way that the system must reinitialize the disk. Fortunately, this does not happen often.

- You cannot install Windows 2000 to a dynamic disk that was not upgraded from a basic disk and then boot directly to that disk. The partition table will not point at a classic boot sector. See the following sidebar for more information.

Soft-Linked Partitions Cannot Boot the System

Assume, for example, that you have a Windows 2000 server that has a system/boot drive on a basic disk, and three or four data volumes that you configured on dynamic disks. These disks have never been basic disks.

A problem occurs that forces you to reinstall Windows 2000 so that you can fix the problem. You don't want to overwrite the existing system files, so you install Windows 2000 to one of the data volumes. Because the data volume resides on a dynamic disk with no hard-linked boot partition, you must boot from a fault-tolerant boot disk to load the operating system.

As of this writing, no utility takes the contents of the LDM database and uses it to write a partition table, and build a boot sector at the required location.

This is a long list but, for the most part, the conversion itself is a straightforward affair. The next couple of sections cover the specific instructions. After conversion, operational factors affect your handling of failed disks. You may want to take a look at the "Recovering from Failed Fault-Tolerant Disks" section to get a feel for what you need to do to prepare for problems.

Using the Disk Management Snap-In

The graphical tool used to configure disk storage is the Disk Management snap-in, DISKMGMT.MSC. This snap-in is part of a suite of snap-ins contained in the Computer Management console. You can open the Computer Management console via START | PROGRAMS | ADMINISTRATIVE TOOLS | COMPUTER MANAGEMENT.

The Disk Management snap-in does not manipulate the disk configuration directly. It communicates with the Logical Disk Server service via the Logical Disk Manager Administrator program, DMADMIN. The DMADMIN program launches as soon as the Disk Management snap-in loads. The first time you do this, the system notices that you do not have fault-tolerant signatures in the MBR of the hard drives, and that the disks are configured as basic disks. It launches a wizard to help you make these changes. Here's how it works:

Procedure 12.2 **Configuring Disk Signatures with DMADMIN**

1. Open the Computer Management console via START | PROGRAMS | ADMINISTRATIVE TOOLS | COMPUTER MANAGEMENT. Expand the tree to show the Storage options (see Figure 12.8).

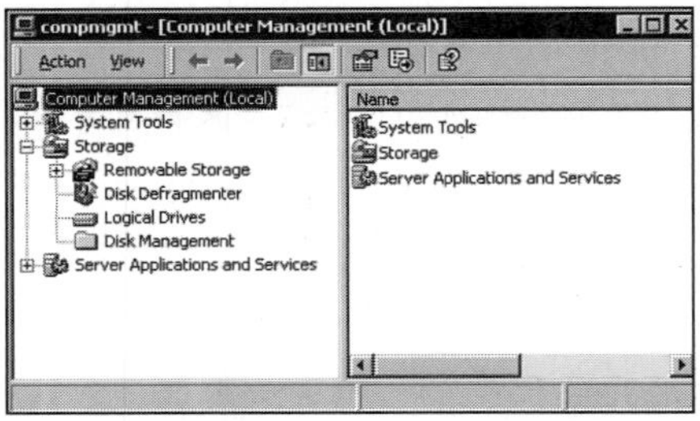

Figure 12.8   Computer Management console showing the four Storage options.

2. Click on the Disk Management icon. This opens the Disk Management snap-in, which in turn launches DMADMIN in the background and gets information from the LDM Server service. The results display in the right pane of the window.

3. When DMADMIN loads, it checks the MBR on each disk looking for a fault-tolerant signature and pointers at an LDM database. If it sees no signature and/or LDM pointers, it launches the Write Signature and Upgrade Disk Wizard. You can opt not to upgrade to dynamic disks, but writing a fault-tolerant signature is not optional. The storage system must have this signature to build the Registry entries it needs to manage the disks, regardless of whether they are dynamic or basic.

4. Click Next. The Select Disks to Write Signature window opens.

5. Put a check next to all the disks.

6. Click Next. The Select Disks to Upgrade window opens.

7. Deselect any disks that you do not want to upgrade to dynamic disks. You can upgrade them later, if you want. See the next section for details.

8. Click Next. The system writes the fault-tolerant signatures to the disks and upgrades any that you selected. A final window summarizes what was done.

9. Click Finish to close the window. The disk configuration shows in the right pane of the Disk Management snap-in (see Figure 12.9).

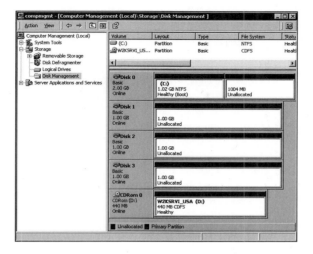

Figure 12.9   Disk Management snap-in showing disk configurations.

Additional Disk Management Snap-In Options

Before creating partitions and volumes, let's take a look at a few other options in the Disk Management snap-in. The text portion at the top of the Disk Management snap-in window shows each logical partition and volume represented by a drive letter along with information about the volume or partition, such as its file system and status. The graphical portion of the window shows each disk represented by a long bar with a status box to the left. The bar shows the approximate amount of the disk apportioned to a partition or volume. The status box shows the disk number, the configuration (basic or dynamic), the capacity, and the status (online, offline, failed, or missing).

- For IDE disks, the disk number depends on the order of the disk on the IDE or EIDE bus and the number of the controller. The master drive on the primary controller would be disk 0 and the slave drive (if there were one) would be disk 1. These would be followed by the master drive on the secondary controller followed by the slave on the secondary controller. This does not apply to CD-ROM drives, which will always display last.

- For SCSI disks, the disk numbers represent the scan order of the SCSI controller, not the SCSI ID itself. Ordinarily, disks are scanned by SCSI ID so that the disks' numbers will be in the same order as their SCSI IDs. If someone changed the scan order, however, the sequence of disk numbers will differ from the sequence of SCSI IDs.

If you right-click the graphical bar associated with an empty disk, you'll get options to create a partition on a basic disk or create a volume on a dynamic disk. If you right-click on an existing partition or volume, you'll get options to format with a file system, assign or change a drive letter, or delete the volume or partition. You can also view the properties of the disk. Proceed as follows:

Procedure 12.3 **Viewing Disk Properties**

1. Right-click the unallocated space on any drive and select PROPERTIES from the fly-out menu. The Properties window opens (see Figure 12.10).

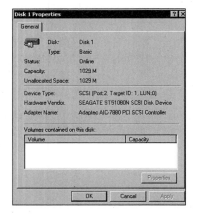

Figure 12.10 Properties window for a disk with unallocated space.

The Properties window shows you the same information as the status block in the graphical display plus information about the disk vendor and the SCSI ID or port/target ID for IDE/EIDE disks.

2. Click OK to close the window.

3. Right-click an allocated partition on the system disk and select PROPERTIES from the fly-out menu. The Properties window opens with the General tab displayed first. This gives information about the file system. The next chapter covers these options (see Figure 12.11).

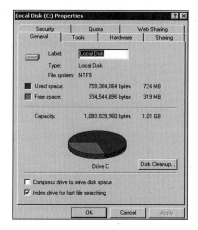

Figure 12.11 `Disk Properties` window for allocated space showing `General` tab with file system properties.

4. Select the `Hardware` tab. This tab is a good source of quick, comprehensive information about the storage available on a system (see Figure 12.12).

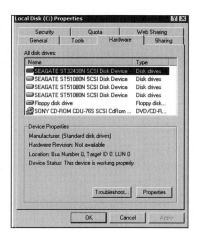

Figure 12.12 `Disk Properties` window for allocated space showing `Hardware` tab with system disk properties.

5. Highlight a drive and click `Properties`. The `Properties` window for the drive opens with the `General` tab selected.

   If you want the system to avoid using a particular drive, such as a secondary CD-ROM or a standby hard disk, you can select `Do not use this device` under Device Usage.

The `Disk Properties` tab typically has a `Write Cache Enabled` option. Microsoft discourages the use of hardware caching unless the controller and disk assembly are specifically tested and listed in the HCL. If you enable hardware caching, be sure to check this option. Otherwise, you risk data corruption that could result from the loss of synchronization of the Windows 2000 cache and the hardware cache.

A CD or DVD player may have an option under Disk Properties to enable `Digital Audio Playback for CDs`. Experiment with this. Your CD or DVD may not support direct digital audio. You'll know right away if you enable this option, and the drive doesn't support the feature. The sound will skip, and the quality will be awful. You may need to restart to enable the feature.

If you have a SCSI drive, the SCSI `Properties` tab generally contains options to disable `Tagged Queuing` and `Synchronous Transfers`. Both of these features are important to achieving high SCSI performance and should only be disabled for troubleshooting and if specifically advised by the hardware vendor.

6. Click `OK` to save changes and close the window.

It's important to cover just a few more preliminary operations before configuring storage. These are: creating a separate management console for the Disk Management snap-in, manually writing a fault-tolerant signature, manually upgrading to a dynamic disk, reverting back to a basic disk, and changing drive letters.

Creating a Custom Disk Management Console

Most of the default management consoles in Windows 2000 have one or two snap-ins. The `Computer Management` console has several. This can make it inconvenient to use if you do a lot of disk management activities. This section contains steps for building a custom `Disk Management` console.

Procedure 12.4 **Building a Custom *Disk Management* Console**
_____

1. From the `Run` command or a command line, open an empty `MMC` console by entering `MMC`.

2. From the CONSOLE menu, select CONSOLE | ADD/REMOVE SNAP-IN. The `Add/Remove Snap-in` window opens.

3. Click `Add`. The `Add Standalone Snap-in` window opens.

4. Select the Disk Management snap-in and click `Add`. The `Choose Computer` window opens.

5. Leave the `Local Computer` radio button selected and click `Finish` to add the snap-in to the list.

6. At the `Add Standalone Snap-in` window, click `Close`.

7. At the `Add/Remove Standalone Snap-in` window, click `OK`.

8. The console now shows the snap-in. Select CONSOLE | SAVE and give it a short name that's easy to type from a command line, such as DM. The system adds the .MSC extension for you.

You can add additional snap-ins if you frequently manage other servers.

Manually Writing a Fault–Tolerant Signature

If you decide to skip writing a fault-tolerant signature using the wizard, or you add a new disk to the system and the wizard does not appear because someone selected the `Do not show this wizard again` option, the disk may show a red Stop bar with a warning that the disk type is *Unknown*. I say "may," because to verify their drives some manufacturers and VARs use test routines that put a Master Boot Record and an NT fault-tolerant signature on the disk. If you get the red Stop and an Unknown status, write a fault-tolerant signature as follows:

Procedure 12.5 **Manually Writing a Fault–Tolerant Signature**

1. Open the Disk Management snap-in using the special console or the `Computer Management` console.

2. Expand the window to show the Stop bar for the Unknown disk type that needs a fault-tolerant signature.

3. Right-click the status block where the Stop bar is located (see Figure 12.13).

4. Select WRITE SIGNATURE from the fly-out menu. The `Write Signature` window appears listing the disk you selected.

5. The system writes a fault-tolerant signature to the disk. The `Disk Management` window now shows the status as Basic. If the disk did not have a Master Boot Record, the system writes one along with the FT signature. The disk is now ready to upgrade or to create a partition for a file system.

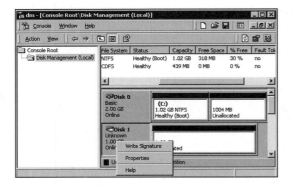

Figure 12.13   `Disk Management` console showing Unknown disk and WRITE SIGNATURE menu option.

Manually Upgrading to a Dynamic Disk

If you upgrade a classic NT server or workstation with an existing fault-tolerant disk set, LDM leaves the disks configured as basic disks and uses FTDISK.SYS to access the disk set. It builds a Registry key called HKLM | System | Disk with a subkey of FTState to store information about the disk set. This does not apply if the NT server had mirrored boot disks. You must break the mirror prior to upgrading to Windows 2000.

FTEDIT No Longer Supported

The classic NT term "fault-tolerant disk set" is something of a misnomer because it includes configurations that are not fault tolerant, such as the stripe set without parity and volume set. These configurations used the fault-tolerant driver FTDISK, so they were called fault-tolerant disk sets.

The classic NT Fault-Tolerant Disk Editor, FTEDIT, will not work on a Windows 2000 machine even if a classic fault-tolerant disk set is present. The DISK key in the Registry has a different configuration that FTEDIT does not understand.

When the system is restarted following the upgrade, the fault-tolerant disk set may take a long time to initialize because FTDISK is not as efficient as DMIO. The file system will be available for use during this initialization but access to it will be slow. When the disk set shows Healthy in the Disk Management snap-in, it's time to upgrade to dynamic disks. When you do this, the fault-tolerant disk set will be converted to the corresponding volume. For example, a stripe set with parity will be converted to a striped volume. Proceed as follows:

Procedure 12.6 **Manually Upgrading to a Dynamic Disk**

1. Open the Disk Management snap-in using the special console or the `Computer Management` console.

2. Expand the window to show the basic disk or disks that you want to upgrade.

3. Right-click the status block for one of the disks and select UPGRADE TO DYNAMIC DISK from the fly-out menu. The `Upgrade to Dynamic Disk` window opens listing all the basic disks with a check mark next to the one you right-clicked.

4. Check the other disks if you have a fault-tolerant disk set, or (if you want to) prep more basic disks for a shared volume.

5. Click OK to initiate the upgrade. If you have existing partitions with active file systems on the disks, you'll be prompted to confirm the change and warned that the file system will be dismounted. Acknowledge these messages.

6. As the LDM upgrades the disks, their status changes to Dynamic in the Disk Management snap-in. After it has finished, the disks are ready to create volumes and file systems. See the "Creating Partitions and Volumes" section later in this chapter.

Reverting Back to a Basic Disk

You cannot just go back to a basic disk configuration after upgrading to a dynamic disk. Volumes created after the upgrade will not have entries in the Master Boot Record. For this reason, you must remove all volumes from the dynamic disk before reverting it to a basic disk. If the dynamic disk has volumes shared with other disks, those volumes must be removed from all the disks. There is a workaround to this "remove the volume" rule. (I'll discuss it after first doing the job in the approved way.) Proceed as follows:

Procedure 12.7 **Removing Shared Volumes Using Standard Techniques**

1. Load the Disk Management snap-in.

2. Delete all volumes using the instructions in the "Deleting a Volume" section. If the disk contains volumes from other disks, those volumes must be deleted as well (see Figure 12.14).

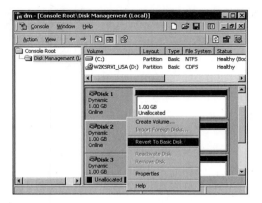

Figure 12.14 Disk Management snap-in showing empty Dynamic Disk to Revert to Basic Disk.

3. When the disk is empty, right-click the status block and select REVERT TO BASIC DISK from the fly-out menu. There is no intermediate menu. The disk reverts and the disk type changes to Basic in the status block. At this point, you can create partitions and install file systems on the disk.

As you can see, it doesn't take long to make the change, but it can be a lot of work getting to that point and recovering afterward. Assume, for example, that a user converts the boot disk on a workstation to a dynamic disk and then realizes later that he cannot boot the system into DOS, a function necessary to support a legacy application. Using the standard procedure, you are forced to delete the boot volume and revert to a basic disk, and then reinstall DOS and Windows 2000, and then reinstall all the user's apps. Not a pleasant experience.

A workaround to this requirement is not supported by Microsoft, but it can help you recover without doing a massive reinstall. The workaround applies only if you had a single boot partition on the original basic disk, and you have not created new volumes after upgrading (so the original partition table is still intact).

Caution When Using Disk Probe

The steps described in this section make direct changes to the Master Boot Record of a production machine. Use care when making these changes. It is possible to put the disk in an unrecoverable condition.

If you meet these requirements, you can change the media type in the partition table from 42 back to the original setting. This permits you to boot from the disk without error. You'll need a tool that can read and write to the

Master Boot Record. This can be done using the Disk Probe utility from the Resource Kit.

Procedure 12.8 **Removing Shared Volumes Using Nonstandard Technique**

1. Launch Disk Probe.

2. From the menu, select DRIVES | PHYSICAL DRIVE. The Open Physical Drive window opens.

3. Double-click the drive you want to manually revert to a basic drive. Be very sure that you get the correct drive. You can lose data if you make a mistake.

4. Deselect the Read Only flag for the Handle assigned to the drive.

5. Click Set Active to assign the handle to the physical drive. The window should look like that in Figure 12.15.

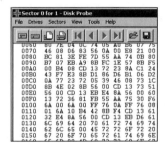

Figure 12.15 Open Physical Drives window set to write to PhysicalDrive 0.

6. Click OK to save the settings and close the window.

7. From the menu, select SECTORS | READ. The Read Sectors window opens.

8. Leave the settings at their defaults (Starting Sector = 0, Number of Sectors = 1) and click Read. The window closes and the main Disk Probe window shows the context of the MBR (see Figure 12.16).

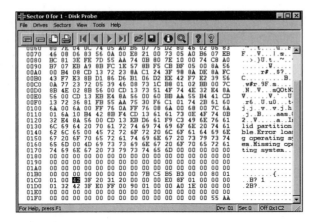

Figure 12.16 `Disk Probe` window showing the partition table prior to manual conversion.

9. Look for the byte at offset 1C2. This is the media type for the first partition. Change it from 42, the Logical Disk Manager type, to the type that represents the format of the file system that is on the volume. This would be 01=FAT12, 04=FAT16, 05=Extended Partition, 06=BIGDOS FAT, 07=NTFS, 0B=FAT32 < 512MB, and 0C=FAT32 >= 512MB.

10. From the menu, select SECTORS | WRITE. The `Write Sector` window opens to identify the drive to which you're writing and the starting sector of the write. You read only one sector, so you'll only write one sector.

11. Click `Write It`. You're prompted to confirm. Click `Yes`.

12. Close the window and exit the program. This releases the lock on the sector.

13. Restart the machine if you changed the MBR of the boot disk.

14. Once restarted, open the Disk Management snap-in and confirm that you now have a basic disk and that the volume or volumes now display as partitions.

15. If you have other dynamic disks in the machine, the Disk Management snap-in may display the old volume with a status of Missing. It gets this information from the LDM database on the other drives. Right-click the status block of the missing drive and select REMOVE DISK from the fly-out menu.

At this point, you can use the disk just as you normally would. If you want to make it back into a dynamic disk at some time in the future, the upgrade will proceed without error and the partition information will be retained.

Changing Drive Letters

Windows-based machines have always been cantankerous in the way they assign logical drive letters, and Windows 2000 is no exception. Drive letters can change in response to disks coming on- and offline. Removable media drives are a common culprit, as are CD-ROM jukeboxes. You might also get an awkward drive letter assigned to a new volume or partition because you forgot you had network drives mapped to drive letters just below the last physical drive. If you want to change the drive letter associated with a particular drive, you can do this in the Disk Management snap-in. You must, however, consider a few cautions:

- You cannot change the letter of the boot partition (volume) or the system partition (volume). The system will refuse to make this change. This differs from classic NT, where you could make this change and then had to clamber through the Registry looking for drive letters that needed to be changed.

- Changing the letter of a drive that hosts an application can cause the application to fail. This is especially true for complex client/server databases.

- Changing a drive letter causes all shared directories on that volume to fail. The Registry entries for shares are hard-coded to the drive letter. They are stored as share names in the Registry key HKLM | System | CurrentControlSet | Services | LanManServer | Shares.

- If you have shortcuts to files and directories on NTFS volumes and partitions, the Distributed Link Tracking system automatically changes the shortcuts if the files are moved or renamed. If you change the drive letter, the link tracking system will not automatically update its database. However, clients who access shortcuts that include the old drive letter may still function. The system gives a "best-guess" response the first time they use the shortcut. That guess usually includes the new drive letter. This is not a 100% sure thing, however, so changing the drive letter of a production file server is not something to do on a whim.

The example shows how to change the drive letter of a CD-ROM. You can use the same technique to change the drive letter for a fixed disk or removable media disk.

Procedure 12.9   **Changing Drive Letters**

1. Open the Disk Management snap-in.

2. Right-click the drive icon in the text section or the bar or the status block in the graphic section and select CHANGE DRIVE LETTER AND PATH from the fly-out menu. The Drive Letter and Path window opens.

3. Click Modify. The Modify Drive Letter or Path window opens.

4. Select a new drive letter from the Assign a Drive Letter drop-down box.

5. Click OK to save the change. You'll be prompted to confirm. Click Yes. Changes are made to the Registry that appear in the Disk Management snap-in.

> **Registry Tip: Mount Point Information**
> The Registry values affected when changing mount point information are stored under HKCU | Software | Microsoft | Windows | CurrentVersion | Explorer | MountPoints.

It's finally time to create partitions and volumes.

Creating Partitions and Volumes

A variety of disk configurations are available in Windows 2000. Choosing the one that's right for your needs can be a puzzle if you are new to configuring hardware. For basic disks, you have two options:

- **Primary partition.** Use this option if you have a single disk that you want to divide into one or more logical drives. The partition boot sector of a primary partition can be used to load an operating system. Ordinarily, if you do not include the Windows 2000 boot/system disk in a mirrored set, you will want to leave it as a basic disk and use some or all of that disk as a single primary partition. If you use hardware RAID with very large logical disks, you may want to use several partitions, or an extended partition with several logical drives. Creating a single partition for a 100GB disk, for example, would force the file system to use large sectors that might not be an efficient use of the disk.

- **Extended partition.** Use this option if you want to boot from DOS or Windows 9x and see files in a partition other than the primary partition that boots the operating system. If you use Windows 2000 or NT exclusively, you do not need extended partitions.

If you use dynamic disks, you have many additional options, including the following:

- **Simple volume.** Use this option if you have a single dynamic disk that you want to divide into one or more logical drives. A simple volume cannot boot an operating system other than Windows 2000, even if that OS was on the disk before it was converted from a basic disk. You can, however, read the disk if you boot from floppy disk if the file system is FAT16 or FAT32. If ERD Commander from www.sysinternals.com has been upgraded to read NTFS5. By the time you read this, you'll be able to read an NTFS volume.

- **Spanned volume.** Use this option if you have a hardware RAID array that you've expanded with additional drives and you want to keep the same volume name and drive letter. You should not span volumes between physical drives, because it increases your likelihood of losing all data in the volume with a single drive failure.

- **Striped volume.** Use this option if you don't care about fault tolerance and want fast I/O. This is popular with CAD and desktop publishing workstations where the work files are saved locally throughout the day, and then copied to a file server at night for backup. You will not see much of a performance improvement on IDE unless you use separate controllers. You can also improve performance on SCSI by using separate controllers if you have several drives in the striped volume.

- **Mirrored volume.** Use this option as the most secure way to protect your file system and other sensitive files. You can use mirroring for standard data volumes, but it is more expensive than RAID 5 with only a marginal performance improvement. Use separate controllers for maximum fault tolerance. This also improves performance if you have IDE drives. This option is not available on Windows 2000 Professional.

- **RAID 5 volume.** Use this option when you want fault tolerance and large logical drives. This option is not available on Windows 2000 Professional.

The next few sections contain the steps for creating these partition and volume configurations.

Creating Primary Partitions

The disk must be configured as a basic disk. If you create a primary partition on a disk that already has a primary partition containing DOS or Windows 9x, the down-level operating systems cannot see the partition when you boot into them. There is a maximum of four primary partitions on a disk.

You do not necessarily need to use the Disk Management snap-in to do this partitioning. You can boot to DOS and use FDISK, if you think that's easier.

Procedure 12.10 **Creating Primary Partitions**

1. Open the Disk Management snap-in.

2. Right-click the graphic bar representing the disk you want to partition and select CREATE PARTITION from the fly-out menu. The Create Partition Wizard opens.

3. Click Next. The Select Partition Type window opens.

4. Select the Primary Partition radio button.

5. Click Next. The Specify Partition Size window appears.

   Enter a size for the partition in MB. The minimum size displayed in the window is only a guideline. You should not create very small partitions, except for testing. Very large partitions should be formatted as NTFS to get the smallest cluster size.

6. Click Next. The Assign Drive Letter or Path window appears.

   There are several options for mounting the volume. Under normal circumstances, you would select the next available drive letter and be done with it. The Mount this volume at an empty folder… option makes use of *NTFS reparse points* to mount the partition at a folder in an NTFS partition or volume. These are covered in the next chapter. You also have the option to wait until later to make a decision.

7. Click Next. The Format Partition window opens. Select a file system to format the partition. See the next chapter for recommendations.

8. Click Next. A window summarizes your selections.

9. Click Finish to create and format the partition. The Disk Management snap-in now displays the partition with its file system and available space. Figure 12.17 shows a disk with four unformatted primary partitions. Drive letters E and F were skipped because they were mapped to network drives.

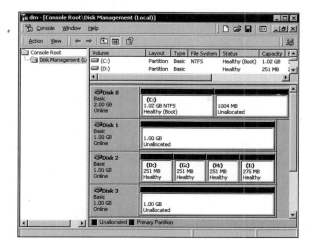

Figure 12.17 Disk Management snap-in showing Disk 2 with four unformatted primary partitions.

Creating Extended Partitions and Logical Drives

To do this work, the disk must be configured as a basic disk. There can only be one extended partition on a disk. The entire disk can be configured as an extended partition, but Windows 2000 cannot boot from an extended partition. Proceed as follows:

Procedure 12.11 **Creating Extended Partitions and Logical Drives**

1. Open the Disk Management snap-in.

2. Right-click the graphic bar representing the disk you want to partition and select CREATE PARTITION from the fly-out menu. The Create Partition Wizard opens.

3. Click Next. The Select Partition Type window opens.

4. Select the Extended Partition radio button.

5. Click Next. The Specify Partition Size window appears. Enter a size for the partition in MB. The minimum size displayed in the window is only a guideline. You should not create very small partitions except for testing. Very large partitions should be formatted as NTFS.

6. Click Next. A window summarizes your changes.

7. Click Finish to save the configuration and create the extended partition.

8. When the partition has been created, all the space in the extended partition is free space. You must create at least one logical drive to get useful storage. Right-click the green area in the graphic representing the extended partition and select CREATE LOGICAL DRIVE from the fly-out menu. The Create Partition Wizard opens.

9. Click Next. The Select Partition Type window opens. The Logical Drive radio button is selected by default.

10. Click Next. Assign a value to Amount of disk space to use. Ordinarily, you would select something less than the full partition size. Otherwise, you would have created a primary partition.

11. Click Next. The Assign Drive Letter or Path window opens. Assign a drive letter or select a volume and directory to use as a mount point.

12. Click Next. The Format Partition window opens.

13. Select a file system to format the partition. See the next chapter for recommendations. The example uses NTFS.

14. Click Next. A window summarizes your selections.

15. Click Finish to accept the settings and create and format the logical drive. The Disk Management snap-in now displays the extended partition and its logical drive. You can create additional logical drives to the extent that you have free space available. The only limit to the number of logical drives is the number of drive letters that you have a available, and even that isn't a limit if you use mount points.

Creating Simple Volumes

To do this work, the disk must be configured as a dynamic disk. Several simple volumes can be created on a single disk. A simple volume can be extended later using Volume Spanning. Proceed as follows:

Procedure 12.12   **Creating Simple Volumes**

1. Open the Disk Management snap-in.

2. Right-click the graphic for the disk on which you want to create the simple volume, and select CREATE VOLUME from the fly-out menu. The Create Volume Wizard opens.

3. Click Next. The Select Volume Type window opens.

4. Select the Simple Volume radio button.

5. Click Next. The Select Disks window opens (see Figure 12.18). The example shows creating a second volume using free space on the boot/system disk, which is a dynamic disk. The existing volume cannot be spanned because it is a system volume.

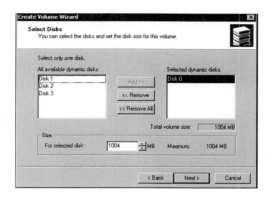

Figure 12.18   Create Volume Wizard—Select Disks window.

6. Click Next. The Assign Drive Letter or Path window opens. Assign a drive letter or mount the volume at an empty folder on an NTFS drive or choose to defer the drive assignment for another time.

7. Click Next. The Format Volume window opens. Select a file system to format the volume.

8. Click Next. A window summarizes the options you selected.

9. Click Finish. The volume is created and formatted. The Disk Management snap-in displays the results. The example in Figure 12.19 shows a second volume on the same disk that holds the boot volume. This keeps data separate from the operating system.

Figure 12.19 Disk Management snap-in showing new simple volume while it is formatting.

Spanning Volumes

Under a couple of circumstances, you may need to create spanned volumes. One is when you need to add more storage but you don't want to add an additional drive letter. The other is when you know from the start that you need more storage than you can get from a single disk, and you don't want to use striping. The example here shows how to expand an existing simple volume. If you want to create a spanned volume right from the start you can create a volume, select the Spanned Volume option, and assign the drives that you want to span. You cannot extend the boot volume or the system volume.

You must have a dynamic disk to use spanned volumes. If the data is in a partition on a basic disk, you must convert the disk to a dynamic disk before spanning the volume. After doing so, proceed as follows:

Procedure 12.13 Configuring a Spanned Volume

1. Open the Disk Management snap-in.

2. Right-click the graphic for the simple volume you want to extend and select EXTEND VOLUME from the fly-out menu. The Extend Volume Wizard starts.

3. Click Next. The Select Disks window opens. Select the disk you want to include in the span. Only dynamic disks appear on the list. You can span to any dynamic disk that has free space, but it is recommended that you use an empty disk to simplify recovery should the disk fail.

4. Click Next. A window summarizes the options you selected.

Click Finish. The volume is created and quick formatted with the file system on the existing volume. The Disk Management snap-in displays the results. In the example, three disks have been included in the volume span (see Figure 12.20).

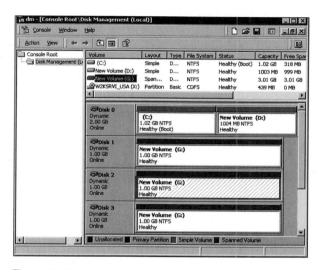

Figure 12.20   Disk Management console showing a three-disk volume span.

Creating Striped Volumes

If you want lots of storage space with great performance and you aren't concerned about fault tolerance, you might want to configure a striped volume. You must have at least two dynamic disks in the striped volume with an upper limit set by the specifications of the bus you're using. A fast, wide ultra SCSI bus can have 15 drives. An SSA bus can have dozens. You can mix disks from different buses, but this is not recommended because of the difference in performance and operating characteristics. If you have only IDE or EIDE drives, you will not get a performance boost by striping two drives on the same controller. Duplex the drives to get maximum performance. When you're ready, create a striped volume as follows:

Procedure 12.14   **Creating Striped Volumes**

1. Open the Disk Management snap-in.

2. Right-click the graphic for one of the disks that you want to include in the striped volume and select CREATE VOLUME from the fly-out menu. The Create Volume Wizard opens.

3. Click Next. The Select Volume Type window opens.

4. Select the Striped Simple Volume radio button.

5. Click Next. The Select Disks window opens. Select at least one other disk that you want to include in the volume. Only dynamic disks will appear on the list. You can stripe span to any dynamic disk that has free space. The total space given to any disk will equal the smallest free space on any selected disk. If Disk 1 has 500MB of free space and Disk 2 has 300MB of free space, for example, the striped volume will take 300MB on each disk, leaving 200MB of free space remaining on Disk 1. If you want to take less, select a Size value in the For All Selected Disks option.

6. Click Next. The Assign Drive Letter or Path window opens.

7. Assign a drive letter or an empty volume on an NTFS volume.

8. Click Next. The Format Volume window opens. Select a file system to use for the volume.

9. Click Next. A window summarizes the options you selected.

10. Click Finish. The volume is created and formatted with the file system you selected. The Disk Management snap-in displays the results.

Creating Mirrored Volumes

When creating mirrored volumes, both of the disks must be dynamic disks. The secondary disk must have at least as much free space as the size of the primary volume. See the following sidebar for more information. Proceed as follows:

Allow For Manufacturing Tolerances on Mirrored Drives

In the examples, I left a small amount of free space at the end of the drive. This allows for small differences in capacity between the two drives.

Drives with the same specs, even drives from the same manufacturer, often have different useful capacities depending on manufacturing tolerances and the total number of bad sectors identified during low-level formatting. If the secondary disk is just one sector shy of the primary, the system will refuse to mirror.

Procedure 12.15 **Creating Mirrored Volumes**

1. Open the Disk Management snap-in. Figure 12.21 shows an example disk configuration prior to mirroring.

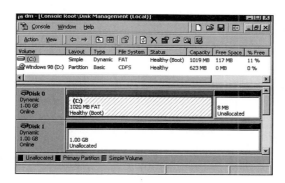

Figure 12.21 Disk Management snap-in showing dual disks prior to mirroring.

2. Right-click the graphic on the volume you want to mirror and select ADD MIRROR from the fly-out menu. The Add Mirror window opens.

3. Select the disk you want to use for a mirror and click Add Mirror.

If you mirror the boot disk, the system sends a message prompting you to add a line to your BOOT.INI file to enable booting from the mirrored disk. For example, the BOOT.INI file entry you might use for the configuration in Figure 12.21 would be as follows:

```
multi(0)disk(0)rdisk(1)partition(1)\WINNT="Windows 2000 Mirrored Secondary Disk"
/fastdetect
```

This is an advantage of LDM over the classic FTDISK. In previous versions of NT, you couldn't boot to the mirrored secondary without breaking the mirror. Using LDM, there really is no "primary" and "secondary" drive. The volume you use to boot is the primary volume. *If the mirrored drive has never been configured with a classic bootable partition prior to the mirroring, however, you cannot use it to boot the system.* See the next section for more information.

4. Click OK to acknowledge the message. The system has already begun building the mirror. This is indicated by a *Regenerating* status in the graphic for the two disks. Regeneration copies the contents of the primary disk to the secondary disk sector by sector. This can take a long time for a big volume. For a fast SCSI bus, figure about 10 minutes per GB. If you allow users to access the file system while it is regenerating, this time estimate can double or even quadruple. After the volume has regenerated, it shows as Healthy in the Disk Management snap-in.

Breaking a Mirrored Volume

If you need to break a mirrored volume for one reason or another, you have the choice of breaking the mirror or removing it. If you break the mirror, here's what happens:

- The file system is left intact on both disks, so you have two exact replicas.
- The volume on the secondary disk is given the next available drive letter.
- If the boot disk was one of the mirrored disks, the primary disk contains the paging file.
- If the file system on the mirrored volume was mounted at an NTFS folder, when you break the mirror the primary drive remains mounted to the file system. The volume on the secondary drive is given its own drive letter.
- If you have shared directories in the file system on the mirrored volume, the shares will be retained on the primary drive after you break the mirror.

If you choose to remove the mirror, you can delete the volume on one or both disks. The volume you retain keeps the same drive letter or remains mounted to an NTFS mount point, depending on the original configuration.

Breaking the mirror is the easy part. It's recovering afterward that can get tricky. If the mirror includes the boot volume, you may encounter a couple of subtle problems after you break the mirror. First, here are the steps to break a mirror:

Procedure 12.16   **Breaking a Mirrored Volume**

1. Load the Disk Management snap-in.

2. Right-click the mirrored volume and select BREAK MIRROR from the fly-out menu.

3. The system prompts for verification and reminds you that the volumes will no longer be fault tolerant. Click Yes to acknowledge.

4. If you break the mirror of the boot disk, the system also warns that the volume is in use and prompts for verification that you want to proceed. Click Yes.

5. The system breaks the mirror and assigns the next available drive letter to the volume on the secondary disk.

Now that the mirror is broken, here are the problems with trying to boot from the second disk:

- **Soft-linked partitions are not bootable.** The dynamic disk upgrade process places an entry in the partition table pointing at the LDM partition. This entry does not make the disk bootable. *Only disks with hard-linked partitions can be bootable.* You can get around both problems by using the Disk Management snap-in to create a bootable partition on the second disk while it is still a basic disk. Then, upgrade the disk to a dynamic disk, delete the volume, and mirror the drive. You can also boot using a fault-tolerant boot floppy disk.

- **Drive letter incorrect.** When you break the mirror, the drive you used to load the operating system becomes the C: drive. If you boot to the secondary drive using a fault-tolerant boot disk and then break the mirror, the secondary disk becomes the C: drive. This disk may not be bootable (see first bullet), and the first disk won't load the operating system from an alternative drive letter.

Resolve the second problem as follows:

Procedure 12.17   **Making the C: Drive Bootable After Breaking a Mirror**

1. Use the fault-tolerant boot floppy disk to boot to the original primary drive. This will have some letter other than C. For example, call it the H: drive. You'll get an error message warning you that there is no paging file. Don't create a paging file.

2. Use the Disk Management snap-in to change the drive letter of the secondary drive to a letter other than C. Call it the J: drive, for example.

3. Use the fault-tolerant boot floppy disk to boot to the new J: drive. You will get errors because you changed the letter of the boot volume, but the system should start.

4. Use the Disk Management snap-in to change the drive letter of the original primary, which is now the H: drive, back to C: drive.

5. Restart again and let the system boot directly from the primary drive.

Does this sound like a lot of work? It is. And the situation gets worse if the primary drive fails. If you have not taken the precaution of making the secondary drive bootable with a hard-link partition, you are stuck booting from floppy forever; that is, unless you are willing to delete the volume on the remaining disk, revert it back to a basic disk, partition the disk, reinstall Windows 2000, and then restore the original contents of the disk from tape.

Your only alternative is probably to take a snapshot of the MBR on the primary disk and save that on a floppy disk somewhere. If the primary disk crashes, use that snapshot to write a new MBR to the secondary disk. This works only in some cases because the volume on the secondary disk may not start at the same place as the primary. You may need to make some changes using a hex editor. This is better than booting from a floppy disk for the remaining life of the server. Hopefully either Microsoft or Veritas will address this problem soon after the release of Windows 2000.

Creating RAID 5 Volumes

If you have at least three dynamic disks with free space, you can configure them as a single RAID 5 volume. The maximum volume size is limited by the available free space on the smallest disk. If you have two 4GB disks and one 2GB disk, for example, the maximum size of the volume on each disk will be limited to 2GB. The remaining space on the 4GB disks will be left as free space. I do not recommend using this free space because it complicates recovery in the event of a failed disk. The maximum storage capacity of a RAID 5 volume is always one disk less than the overall disk space that is used. If you have a five-disk volume with 2GB per disk, for example, the maximum available storage is 8GB.

Procedure 12.18 **Creating RAID 5 Volumes**

1. Open the Disk Management snap-in.

2. Right-click the graphic for one of the disks you want to include in the striped volume and select CREATE VOLUME from the fly-out menu. The Create Volume Wizard opens.

3. Click Next. The Select Volume Type window opens.

4. Select the RAID 5 radio button.

5. Click Next. The Select Disks window opens. Select at least two other disks you want to include in the volume.

6. Click Next. The Assign Drive Letter or Path window opens.

7. Assign a drive letter or an empty volume on an NTFS volume.

8. Click Next. The Format Volume window opens. Select a file system to use for the volume.

9. Click Next. A window summarizes the options you selected.

10. Click Finish. The volume is created and formatted with the file system you selected. The Disk Management snap-in displays the results.

It takes a short while for the system to generate the volume (the system uses the word *regenerate* because it uses the same process in subsequent regenerations) and format it with a file system. For a fairly fast 4GB drive, expect to wait 5 to 10 minutes for the regeneration and at least that long for the formatting. If you have 18GB drives, take a long lunch.

Deleting a Volume

The LDM version that ships with Windows 2000 does not permit dynamically changing the size of a volume. If you have to change the allocation of space on a disk, you may need to delete a volume and rebuild it. It may seem obvious, but before you delete the volume, make sure the data has been copied or backed up. Even third-party file recovery utilities will fail if you delete a volume. The files aren't deleted and you can contract with a data recovery vendor to get the files back, but that's expensive. When you're sure you're ready, proceed as follows:

Deleting Volumes Containing Mount Points

If you delete a volume that contains an NTFS mount point, the data in the mounted volume is not affected. You can go back later and mount the volume to another folder or give it a letter of its own.

Procedure 12.19 **Deleting a Volume**

1. Open the Disk Management snap-in.

2. Right-click the volume you want to remove, and select DELETE VOLUME from the fly-out menu.

3. The system prompts to verify the action. Click Yes.

4. If you get an error saying that the volume is currently in use, you should cancel out of the action and locate the open files. If you don't spot anything obvious, look for processes in the Task List that might have a lock on the volume. Antivirus programs are notorious for this.

5. After the volume has been deleted, the Disk Management snap-in shows free space on the disk.

Recovering Failed Fault-Tolerant Disks

If you have your data on a single drive or a non-fault-tolerant volume, such as a spanned volume or a striped volume, you expect that you will lose data if a drive fails. Because disk failure is an unavoidable fact of computer life, I assume that you have a good backup system and a plan for restoring data quickly during the workday. If a single disk in a striped volume fails, for example, you must delete the volume from the remaining disks, replace the disk, and rebuild the volume.

On the other hand, if you don't want to deal with masses of panicked users and their crazed managers who will gather outside the server room like enraged French revolutionaries looking for guillotine fodder, you'll want to put your data on a fault-tolerant system of one form or another. Hopefully by doing so, a single disk failure will not be the cause of a service outage. This section covers putting a system back in a stable condition following a disk failure and then recovering the system to normal operation. This includes the following operations:

- Replacing a failed disk in a RAID 5 volume
- Building a fault-tolerant boot floppy disk
- Replacing a failed disk in a mirrored volume
- Moving dynamic volumes between computers

Replacing a Failed Disk in a RAID 5 Volume

When a disk fails in a RAID 5 volume, you will get a console message when the system attempts to write to the volume and LDM can't find the disk. The error message states *A disk that is part of a fault-tolerant volume can no longer be accessed.* This message comes from a process called FT Orphan. This is a special process that logically disconnects the drive from the system to eliminate the possibility of data corruption.

The file system on the volume with the failed disk continues to be active. Your only indication of the failure (unless you have configured the system to alert you of problems) is a slight decrease in I/O performance. When you get the message that you have a failed disk, open the Disk Management snap-in. You'll get a display that looks something like that in Figure 12.22. Each disk for the volume shows a Failed Redundancy status, and the failed drive shows a red Stop indicator.

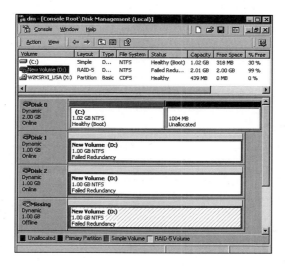

Figure 12.22 Disk Management snap-in showing failed disk in RAID 5 volume.

Thanks to the fault-tolerant nature of RAID 5, the system remains operational but you have now entered a twilight zone (apologies to Rod Serling) where the next drive crash causes data loss. You do not need to take immediate action, but you should not wait for days and days, either. Get a spare drive that has at least as much capacity as the drive you are replacing. It should also be configured for the same SCSI ID to simplify installation, although this is not a requirement.

You can use the Disk Management snap-in to check the SCSI ID assigned to the drive even when the drive is dead. Right-click the status block, and select PROPERTIES from the fly-out menu. The SCSI ID (called the Target ID) and the *Local Unit Number* (LUN) are listed. I recommend that you paste a screen print of this window on the server so that you have a reference when you replace the disk. That snarl of SCSI cables inside the machine can lead you astray unless you have a map. Nothing is quite so embarrassing as replacing the wrong drive.

After you have the replacement drive in your hands and your users have left for the day, you're ready to get to work. Down the server and replace the drive. Test the drive operability using the IDE or SCSI hardware utilities the come with the machine, if any. Restart and let the operating system load. The RAID 5 volume will initialize and the file system should mount. Open the Disk Management snap-in. The display should look something like that in Figure 12.23.

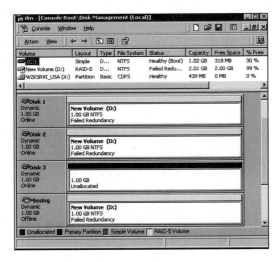

Figure 12.23 Disk Management snap-in showing replacement disk with Unknown status and the RAID 5 array with a Failed Redundancy status.

The RAID 5 volume still shows a Failed Redundancy status. A status block for the missing disk appears because its information is contained in the LDM database on the other disks. The replacement disk is brand new, so it does not have a fault-tolerant signature or a Master Boot Record. The system lists its status as Unknown. Proceed as follows:

Delays in Updating Disk Management Display

It sometimes happens that the LDM does not initialize correctly when loading the Disk Management snap-in. The RAID 5 volume may show Healthy even though it is not. If this happens, select ACTION | RESCAN DISKS from the menu, and then close the Disk Administrator snap-in and open it again. You may need to do this a couple of times to get the display to show a Failed Redundancy status.

Procedure 12.20   **Replacing a Failed Disk in a RAID 5 Volume**

1. Write a signature to the new disk using the instructions in Procedure 12.5, "Manually Writing a Fault–Tolerant Signature."

2. Upgrade the disk to a dynamic disk using the instructions in Procedure 12.6, "Manually Upgrading to a Dynamic Disk."

3. Right-click the RAID 5 volume, and select REPAIR VOLUME from the fly-out menu.

4. Select the new disk to use as a replacement for the failed disk. The new disk now becomes part of the RAID 5 volume, and the system begins regenerating. This can take a long time. A 4GB drive might take an hour to regenerate. This time gets significantly longer if users access the drive while it regenerates. Figure 12.24 shows an example of the Disk Management snap-in during this regeneration period. The small portion of the disk that shows "Unalloc" is due to a slight discrepancy between the storage capacity of the new drive and the failed drive.

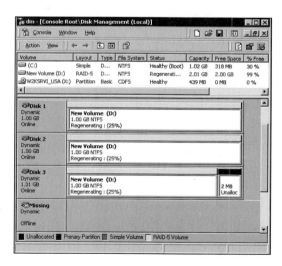

Figure 12.24   Disk Management snap-in showing RAID 5 volume during regeneration.

5. While the regeneration is in progress, right-click the status block for the missing disk and select REMOVE DISK from the fly-out menu. The status block disappears and the graphic display rearranges.

Building a Fault-Tolerant Boot Floppy Disk

If you mirror your boot volume—the most popular fault-tolerant choice— one of the most important tools you have for recovering from a failure is a fault-tolerant boot floppy disk. The secondary drive is not necessarily bootable, so you need a way to boot the system to the mirrored volume on the secondary drive if the primary drive fails. Even if the secondary drive is bootable, you may have forgotten to modify the BOOT.INI file to point at the correct relative disk location. Even if you don't mirror your boot volumes, a boot floppy disk is handy to have because you may experience problems with the MBR or PBS that prevent the machine from booting.

The fault-tolerant boot floppy disk does not boot the system to a floppy disk. This can only be done using the Repair Console. What the fault-tolerant boot floppy disk does is put the system files on a disk so that you can use the secondary bootstrap loader, NTLDR, to load the boot files from the \WINNT partition on the hard drive.

Detailed steps for creating a fault-tolerant boot floppy disk are in Chapter 3, "Adding Additional Hardware," Procedure 3.9. Here is a brief set of steps for your convenience. Chapter 3 also contains information about ARC paths and BOOT.INI entries.

Procedure 12.21 Building a Fault-Tolerant Boot Floppy Disk

1. Format a floppy disk. You cannot use a preformatted floppy disk because the boot sector must look for NTLDR. You can use a disk formatted on an NT4 machine.

2. Copy the system files to the root of the A: drive. These files are as follows:

```
NTLDR
NTDETECT.COM
BOOT.INI
NTBOOTDD.SYS (if required)
```

3. Use ATTRIB to remove the read-only attribute from BOOT.INI.

4. Edit the BOOT.INI file on the floppy disk to include the ARC path of the boot volume on the second drive. This would look something like this:

```
multi(0)disk(0)rdisk(1)partition(1)\WINNT="Windows 2000 Mirrored Secondary Disk"
/fastdetect
```

You might also want to change the time setting to -1. This disables the counter.

5. Restart the computer and boot from the fault-tolerant boot floppy disk.

6. When the BOOT menu appears, select the second disk. The system will boot from the secondary disk. At this point, the floppy disk is no longer needed. Remove it from the drive.

Replacing a Failed Disk in a Mirrored Volume

If you lose a disk that is part of a mirrored volume, the system responds as it did for a failed disk in a RAID 5 volume. When the system attempts to write to the volume and fails to get a response from the disk, the FT Orphan process disconnects the system from the drive and announces this to the console. In a mirrored volume that includes the boot files, the orphaning process also locks the Registry on the failed drive. Even if you can get the failed drive back in service, the system will refuse to load the operating system from it.

When you open the Disk Management snap-in, you'll get a display like that in Figure 12.25. The failed drive has a Missing status. The mirrored volume shows a Failed Redundancy status. The secondary drive moves to the top of the drive list. This may be different in your system, depending on your SCSI ID configuration.

As you can see in the figure, it can be difficult to determine exactly which drive failed in a two-disk mirrored volume. You should keep careful records of the SCSI IDs or IDE controller numbers. (The unallocated space in this figure differs from the previous mirroring figures because I used a different system to force a disk failure.)

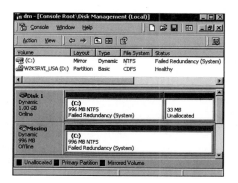

Figure 12.25 Disk Management snap-in showing failed primary drive in a mirrored volume.

As with the RAID 5 failure, you do not need to take immediate corrective action. As many administrators will attest, however, you take a big chance if you wait too long. Very often a system comes with drives that are sequentially numbered off the assembly line. If one drive fails, the other might not be far behind.

Obtain a new disk that is at least the size of the one you're replacing. You should configure it for the same SCSI ID or IDE master/slave configuration to simplify recovery. When you're ready to replace the drive, proceed as follows:

Procedure 12.22   **Replacing a Failed Disk in a Mirrored Volume**

---

1. Down the server and replace the drive.

2. Restart and boot from the fault-tolerant boot floppy disk. If you replaced the drive using the same SCSI ID, pick the BOOT.INI menu item corresponding to the original rdisk() value of the secondary drive. If you used a different SCSI ID, you need to figure out the right rdisk() value and modify the BOOT.INI file on the boot floppy disk accordingly.

3. After the operating system finishes loading, open the Disk Administrator snap-in. The display looks something like that in Figure 12.26. In the example, I used a higher SCSI ID for the replacement drive so that the illustration would clearly show the new disk and the failed (now missing) disk. The diagram also shows the new disk after it has been given a fault-tolerant signature.

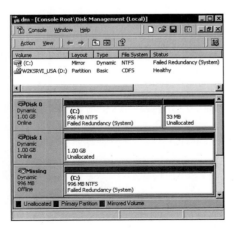

Figure 12.26   Disk Management snap-in following disk replacement of mirrored drive showing failed disk and new disk.

4. Write a fault-tolerant signature to the new disk using the instructions in Procedure 12.5, "Manually Writing a Fault-Tolerant Signature."

5. Upgrade the disk to a dynamic disk using the instructions in Procedure 12.6, "Manually Upgrading to a Dynamic Disk."

6. Right-click the mirrored volume and select REMOVE MIRROR from the fly-out menu. The Remove Mirror window opens.

7. Select the missing disk from the list and click Remove Mirror. The system prompts for verification. Click Yes. The remaining disk now shows a Healthy status.

8. Right-click the status block for the missing disk and select REMOVE DISK from the fly-out menu. The disk disappears immediately.

9. If you have verified that the new primary disk is bootable, remirror the volume to the new drive using the instructions in Procedure 12.15, "Creating Mirrored Volumes." If the new primary disk is not bootable, you'll need to get a good backup and then reinstall the operating system and recover from tape to get a bootable primary disk. After this is done, remirror the volume.

Moving Dynamic Disks Between Computers

It sometimes happens that a server or workstation goes to that big byte bucket in the sky. (This usually happens about a half hour before your plane is due to leave on that vacation you've been planning for the past year.) If the problem is not with the storage system, one quick recovery method that might get you to the plane on time is to move the data disks to a new machine.

Moving Windows 2000 boot and system disks between machines can cause problems because the operating system so heavily depends on the type of hardware. If you move the boot disk (the disk with the Windows 2000 system files) to a different platform, expect to see lots of PnP activity when you start the machine. You may also need to supply the hardware drivers for the new platform. This can be difficult if the boot partition or volume is formatted as NTFS. You must boot to the Repair Console and copy the file manually. See Chapter 18, "Recovering from System Failures" for more information.

Moving basic disks between machines is usually a simple matter. The system sees the new disk, reads the partition table, and assigns the next available drive letters to the partitions it finds. Moving dynamic disks, however, especially dynamic disks that contain volumes that span disks, can be a challenge. The Logical Disk Manager database on the disks you're moving differs from the LDM database that exists on the disks in the machine. A disk with an LDM database from another computer is called a *foreign disk*. You must carry out steps to import the configuration information on the foreign disks into the LDM database. If this is not done, the system cannot see the volumes on the disks and can't mount the file systems.

In addition to these concerns, you might also run into problems if you move disks between a server and a workstation. Windows 2000 Professional does not support fault-tolerant volumes. You can, however, move an existing fault-tolerant volume to a Windows 2000 Professional computer and it will work. Managing that volume after it is installed is difficult. I do not recommend this action, but you need to know that you have the option. The example in this section moves a set of three adapters configured with a RAID 5 volume from one server to another server.

Procedure 12.23 **Moving an Existing Fault-Tolerant Volume to a Windows 2000 Professional Computer**

1. Down the two servers and transfer the drives. This can be a relatively easy operation, such as moving an external cage with its own SCSI or Firewire or SSA adapter. It can also be a real nightmare. You might have to make room in a small box for three new drives, build a new SCSI cable because the old one doesn't have enough connectors, solve termination issues, rework the SCSI IDs, and so forth and so on.

2. After the drives have been installed, test them to make sure that they are connected and that you know the order of their installation. The LDM permits the sequence of disks to be changed, but your job is more difficult if the Disk Management snap-in display has the foreign disks distributed willy-nilly.

3. Boot the operating system and make sure that the system loads. The data on the new drives will not be available until you import the disks. Also, any share points you have for directories on the drives will need to be recreated.

4. Open the Disk Management snap-in. After initialization, the graphical display looks something like that in Figure 12.27. The disks from the other computer are flagged as Foreign.

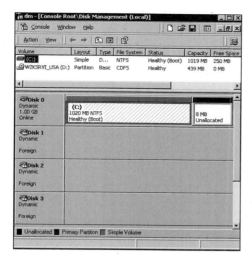

Figure 12.27 Disk Management snap-in showing disks moved from another machine as foreign disks.

5. Right-click the status block of any of the foreign disks and select IMPORT FOREIGN DISKS from the fly-out menu. The Import Foreign Disks window opens, showing the name of the original server from where the disks came. This information comes from the LDM database at the end of the disks.

6. Click OK. The system analyzes the disks, and then the Verify Volumes on Foreign Disks window opens.

   The system may report the Data Condition as Data Incomplete. This indicates that you did not move all the disks in the disk group. This is expected if the boot/system disk in the original server was a dynamic disk, or if there were other dynamic disks in the original server that you intentionally didn't move. Make sure that you have all the disks that are in the shared volume. You are permitted to move a subset of a disk group, but you'll need to do a few more steps.

7. Click OK. The system warns you that it might not be able to recover data if you had a Data Incomplete status in the preceding window.

8. Click OK to acknowledge the warning. The system imports the disks and then attempts to build the volumes and initialize the file system. The status may go to Failed on the disks. Don't worry (at least not yet). This is normal if you did not include all disks in the disk group in the transfer.

9. Right-click the status block for any of the new disks, and select REACTIVATE DISK from the fly-out menu. The system will think a long time and you'll hear lots of disk activity. If the reactivation is successful, a drive letter for the volume appears and the status changes to Regenerating. This regeneration takes a long time and consumes many CPU cycles. The file system is active during this time and you can access files, but this is not recommended because it slows down regeneration. After regeneration has completed, the new volumes show a status of Healthy.

10. There is a chance that any existing dynamic disks in the new machine will show an Error status after the import in the status block of the disk. This is because their copy of the LDM database has values that they cannot interpret. If this happens, right-click the status block for the disk, and select REACTIVATE DISK from the fly-out menu. This should immediately correct the problem.

Moving Forward

Now that the disk storage is in place, it's time to configure a file system. The next chapter covers how to configure and manage the three alternatives in Windows 2000: FAT, FAT32, and NTFS. After the file systems are in place, it's on to Chapter 14, "Managing File Systems Security," which deals with file system security and the Encrypting File System. Then it's on to Chapter 15, "Managing Shared Resources," which covers sharing files and printers. After that work is complete, the backroom portion of the Windows 2000 deployment is just about done. The focus then shifts to the desktop.

13

Managing File Systems

IN A PRIOR LIFETIME, BEFORE I GOT INTO INFORMATION TECHNOLOGY, I was a nuclear power plant operator and Navy submariner. Despite what you may read in Tom Clancy novels, the struggle to keep the world safe for democracy during the Cold War had its quiet interludes. You should not think for one second, though, that professional submariners wasted their precious time watching movies or playing pinochle. Oh, no. We spent what little free time we had quizzing each other constantly on power plant theory and submarine design and operational procedures. (Okay, maybe we played a *little* pinochle.)

During these quizzes, a favorite question went like this: "Trace the path of a drop of water from the ocean through the reactor core and back into the ocean, and describe the operation of each component it goes through along the way." If you could answer that question, you had a pretty good integrated knowledge of the systems on the boat. If you could answer that question while winning at pinochle, well, you were a real hotshot.

You can play similar games with file system design. For example, try tracing a byte from the hard drive of a computer to the monitor and describe each driver that moves the byte along its way. As system administrators, we don't need to know the answer to that kind of question in anything near the level of detail required of a hardware engineer or system designer, but it can be very valuable to at least be familiar with the details of the file system structures. This helps to anticipate problems, plan for emergencies, and troubleshoot odd behaviors.

The last chapter described how the Logical Disk Manager (LDM) created raw data storage. When the storage is available, Windows 2000 uses Installable File System (IFS) drivers to turn that raw storage into something capable of storing and retrieving data in a useful format. The IFS drivers that control access to disk-based storage are as follows:

- **FASTFAT.SYS.** FAT driver (also supports FAT32).
- **NTFS.SYS.** NT File System.
- **CDFS.SYS.** CD-ROM File System. This file system supports ISO 9660 disks with long filenames to a maximum of 32 characters.
- **UDFS.SYS.** Universal Disk Format file system driver. This file system supports DVD drives with standard long filenames.
- **PINBALL.SYS.** HPFS file system driver. This file system is no longer supported.
- **EFS.SYS.** Encrypting File System.
- **RSFILTER.SYS.** Remote Storage System driver. Although not specifically for disks, this file system provides near-online access to files stored on tape.

A complete description of these IFS drivers lies outside the scope of this book. For more information, I highly recommend *Developing Windows NT Device Drivers* by Edward Dekker and Joseph Newcomer.

Beyond the intricacies of file system driver design, aspects pertaining to the operation of the file systems themselves warrant our attention as system administrators. This chapter contains detailed functional and operational descriptions of the three core Windows 2000 file systems: FAT16, FAT32, and NTFS, including practical advantages and limitations of each system. It also contains step-by-step instructions for configuring and managing the following file system features:

- Compression and Sparse file handling
- Reparse Points and Mount Points
- Distributed Link Tracking
- Disk Defragmenter
- Fault-tolerant features, including log tracking and the new Change Journal
- Quota Management
- Remote Storage Services

Overview of Windows 2000 File Systems

Several important disk structures support file system operations. They are:

- **Sectors and Clusters.** These form the basic divisions of data on a disk. The sectors are determined by the disk geometry and are fixed by the manufacturer. Drives made for the U.S. market generally have 512-byte sectors. Clusters are logical groupings of sectors. A file system uses clusters to make the disk appear more granular, which reduces processing overhead.

- **Partitions and Volumes.** A logical division of a disk or collection of disks that forms a boundary for a file system. The last chapter made careful distinction between *partitions* and *volumes* because the LDM uses the two terms differently. At the level of abstraction represented by a file system, however, volumes and partitions represent the same thing.

- **Partition Boot Sector.** The first sector of a partition that contains information about the file system and a small amount of bootstrap code to help load the file system.

- **BIOS Parameter Block.** A subset of the boot sector that contains specific file system information.

- **File Allocation Table (FAT).** A map of the clusters on the disk that contain files. The standard FAT uses 16-bit addresses for clusters. The newer FAT32 uses 32-bit addresses for expanded capacity.

- **Master File Table (MFT).** An object-oriented file database used by NTFS.

- **Directories.** An index of filenames used to structure the file system into a hierarchy.

- **Additional indexes.** NTFS supports indexing of any attribute in the MFT database. The structure and operation of these indexes comprise a good deal of the additional features described in this chapter.

This chapter examines each of these structures and uses them to compare the functionality of the three native Windows 2000 file systems: FAT, FAT32, and NTFS. Highlights at the end of each section summarize the information presented.

Sectors and Clusters

Data on a disk is stored in sectors. Each sector is 512 bytes. Sectors form concentric tracks on the disk. A 10GB drive formatted as a single volume has approximately 20 million sectors.

Requiring a file system to number and track so many sectors would cause quite a strain. To improve performance, the disk is made to appear more granular by collecting the sectors into clumps called *allocation units,* or *clusters.*

The term *cluster size* indicates the number of sectors in the cluster. If a disk is formatted with an 8-sector cluster size, each cluster holds 4KB of data. If a file does not completely fill a cluster or set of clusters, the extra space is wasted, so the most effective use of the hard disk is obtained when the cluster size equals one sector.

As cluster size grows, disk utilization gets worse. All the file systems supported by Windows 2000 strike a compromise between disk utilization and file system efficiency.

FAT

The standard FAT file system uses a 16-bit address scheme. This pegs the maximum number of clusters at 2^{16}, or 65,535. If cluster size were to equal one sector on a FAT volume, the volume could reach only a maximum of 65536×512 bytes, or 32MB. FAT supports volume sizes larger than 32MB by increasing the cluster size.

Due to real-mode memory limits, FAT under DOS and Windows 9x is limited to cluster size that is a power of 2 less than the address limit. Therefore, the maximum cluster size is 2^{15} bytes, or 32KB. The maximum size of a FAT partition under DOS and Windows 95, then, is 65535×32KB, or about 2GB. FAT under Windows 2000 has a cluster size limit of 2^{16} bytes, or 64KB, thanks to protected-mode memory addressing.

A FAT volume under Windows 2000 can grow up to 4GB. If a FAT volume has cluster sizes larger than 32KB, DOS or Windows 95 cannot access it. Keep this in mind if you have a dual-boot machine. For the same reason, the classic NT setup program defaults to a maximum volume size of 2GB, with 4GB available using the ExtendPartition option in Unattended Install. Windows 2000 supports system partitions larger than 2GB by first formatting with FAT32.

FAT32

In Windows 95 OSR2, Microsoft introduced a file system called FAT32. This file system uses 32-bit FAT entries, making the maximum file size 2^{32} bytes, or about 4GB. DOS, standard Windows 95, and classic NT cannot read a standard FAT32 partition. Cluster addressing in FAT32 uses a truncated 32-bit address with the high four bits reserved. Therefore, a FAT32 volume can have up to 2^{28} clusters.

With a minimum cluster size of 4KB and a maximum of 32KB, this puts the theoretical maximum volume size for FAT32 at 8TB. Current industry standards for disk geometry and translation put a limit of 2^{32} sectors, or 2TB, on the capacity of a single disk or disk array. Windows 2000 limits the size of FAT32 volumes still further. The maximum FAT32 volume size under Windows 2000 is 32GB. This enables the system to cache the entire FAT in memory to speed performance.

NTFS

The NT File System, NTFS, uses a 64-bit addressing scheme. This gives individual files a theoretical limit of 2^{64} bytes, or about 16 exabytes. Industry standards limit the maximum volume size to 2TB.

Sector and Cluster Highlights

These are the key points to remember about the way the three file systems use sectors and clusters:

- The maximum FAT cluster size is 32KB.
- The maximum FAT partition size under DOS and Windows 95 is 2GB.
- The maximum FAT partition size under Windows 2000 is 4GB. DOS and Windows 9x cannot access partitions larger than 2GB.
- Windows 2000 supports system partitions larger than 2GB by first formatting with FAT32.
- A maximum FAT32 volume size is 8TB. Industry standards limit the maximum volume size to 2TB.
- Windows 2000 limits the size of FAT32 volumes to 32GB.
- The maximum NTFS volume size is 16 exabytes. Industry standards limit the maximum volume size to 2TB.

Partition Boot Sector and BIOS Parameter Block

The last chapter described how the LDM carves off all or part of a hard drive for a file system. The LDM can also combine several drives into a single logical volume. When the file system formats this volume, it sets aside the first sector for a special structure called the *Partition Boot Sector*, or simply the *boot sector*. This is done even if the partition is not actually used to boot the system. The boot sector contains information that identifies the file system and the location of critical data structures that support the file system.

Jump to Bootstrap Loader

The boot sector contents differ depending on the file system, but the first few entries are consistent. A listing follows:

```
<<First 16 bytes of a FAT boot sector>>
EB 3C 90 4D 53 44 4F 53 35 2E 30 00 02 04 01 00  .<.MSDOS5.0.....
```

The first 3 bytes of the boot sector contain a jump instruction that skips to another portion of the boot sector that contains executable code called the *bootstrap loader*. This bootstrap code is just barely smart enough to locate and execute the *secondary bootstrap loader*, which does the grunt work of actually loading the operating system. For DOS and Windows 9x, the secondary bootstrap loader is IO.SYS. For classic NT and Windows 2000, it is NTLDR. For Alpha machines, no boot sector exists. Instead, the ARC locator in ROM is configured to look for a secondary bootstrap loader called OSLOADER.

The next 8 bytes of the boot sector contain an OEM file system name and an optional version number. Windows 2000 uses the name MSDOS5.0 for both FAT and FAT32. This keeps legacy applications from getting upset if they check the boot sector to find the file system and see a version they don't recognize. Windows 2000 supports using SETVER in a Virtual DOS Machine (VDM), but why force administrators to mess around with SETVER if you can avoid the problem by lying about the file system version right from the start.

Following these first 11 bytes come two sets of entries called the *BIOS Parameter Block* (BPB), and the *Extended BPB*. The contents of these structures differ depending on the file system.

FAT BPB

The BIOS Parameter Block in a FAT partition is 25 bytes long, and it's followed by 26 bytes that form the Extended BPB. The following listing shows both structures and a description of their contents. Intel machines use little-endian notation, so reverse the words and double-words to get their actual value. For example, 00 02 becomes 0200h, or 512 decimal.

```
<<BPB and Extended BPB for a FAT16 volume. The first 11 bytes of the boot sector are
included for context.>>
EB 3C 90 4D 53 44 4F 53 35 2E 30 00 02 04 01 00  .<.MSDOS5.0.....
02 00 02 00 00 F8 C8 00 20 00 40 00 20 00 00 00  ........ .@. ...
E0 1F 03 00 80 00 29 20 24 ED 64 4E 4F 20 4E 41  ......) $.dNO NA
4D 45 20 20 20 20 46 41 54 31 36 20 20 20 33 C9  ME    FAT16   3.
```

- **Bytes per Sector (00 02).** 200h or decimal 512. Most drives made for the U.S. market have 512-byte sectors.

- **Sectors per Cluster (04).** 4h or decimal 4. At 512 bytes per sector, this yields 2048 bytes per cluster. This partition is only 100MB, a relatively tiny partition by today's standards. FAT's limited address space results in inefficient use of the hard drive.

- **Reserved sectors before start of FAT (01 00).** 0001h or 1. This indicates that one sector exists between the start of the partition and the start of the FAT. The boot sector is one sector long, so the FAT starts right after the boot sector. This starting point is a requirement for FAT16 partitions, and one of its key weaknesses. The fixed location of the FAT in relation to the boot sector makes it susceptible to failure in the event of a bad sector. It also limits the flexibility of the file system to store additional metadata.

- **Number of FAT copies (02).** All FAT16 partitions have two copies of the FAT. One copy is primary and the other is a mirror. If the file system cannot read a particular entry from the primary, it falls back on the secondary. The Windows 2000 FASTFAT driver puts an error in the Event Log if this happens. No capability exists within the FAT file system to move the FAT to a good sector. If the file system driver notifies you of a failure to read or write to the primary FAT, plan on reformatting the drive and restoring the data from tape as soon as possible.

- **Maximum number of entries in the root directory (00 02).** 200h or 512. The Root directory of FAT16 file system is limited to a fixed size that can hold only 512 directory entries. This presents a problem for long filenames, because each of the additional 13 characters in the filename takes an additional directory entry.

- **Number of sectors (00 00).** This is sometimes called the *small sector* value, and it is used only for partitions of 32MB or smaller. This is based on being able to directly number 2^{16} sectors when the cluster size equals one sector, as it did for DOS 3.0 and earlier. The small sector value is set to 0 for partitions greater than 32MB.

- **Media Descriptor (F8).** F8 indicates a hard disk, including removable media devices. Other values exist for floppies.

- **Sectors per FAT (C8 00).** 00C8h or 200 sectors. Given a sector size of 512 bytes, this particular FAT is 100K. Double this number to account for a mirrored copy of the FAT, and the ratio of file system size to partition size is about .2%. This is fairly lean for a file system, much leaner than FAT32 or NTFS, but this leanness comes at the expense of large cluster sizes and inefficient disk use.

- **Sectors per Track (20 00), 20h or 32, and Number of Heads (40 00),** 40h or 64. Taken together, these values constitute the virtual disk geometry that the file system uses to locate clusters.

- **Hidden sectors (20 00 00 00).** 20h or 32 hidden sectors. This is the number of sectors between the physical start of the disk and the start of the partition. This reserved area leaves room for the operating system to store additional data about the disk. The small number for this partition, 32, indicates that it is the first partition on the disk.

- **Sector Count (E0 1F 03 00).** 31FE0h or 204768 sectors. At 512 bytes per sector, this yields approximately 102MB. The partition size displayed in the Disk Management console only approximates this size. Windows 2000 can format FAT16 partitions with 64K clusters, so the maximum partition size is 4GB. The installation partition in classic NT was limited to 2GB because the FAT driver on the installation disks could read a maximum of 32K clusters. Windows 2000 automatically formats an installation partition to FAT32 if it exceeds 2GB.

- **Drive Type (80) – 80h (decimal not applicable).** From an operating system perspective, drives are numbered sequentially from 80h, so the second drive is 81h, and so on. The corresponding BPB entry is nearly always 80h regardless of the actual disk location.

- **Special use (00).** The two lowest bits in this entry are used as flags. The low order bit is called the "dirty flag." If the dirty flag is set, it indicates that the file system was shut down abnormally. Windows 2000 runs a boot-time version of Chkdsk called Autochk if the dirty bit is set. The next bit is a "scan" bit that tells the system to do a full sector scan at boot time. This bit is usually set along with the dirty bit.

- **Disk signature (29) – 29h (decimal not applicable).** A value of 29h indicates that an extended BPB is present. Windows 2000 recognizes values of 28h or 29h.

- **Serial number of the volume (20 24 ED 64) – 64ED-2420 (decimal not applicable).** This number uniquely identifies the volume. Don't confuse this number with the Globally Unique Identifier used by LDM. The hardware partitioning information is stored at a different location.

- **Legacy volume label (4E 4F 20 4E 41 4D 45 20 20 20 20).** The name NO NAME with trailing blanks is always assigned to FAT16 partitions. The actual volume label is contained in the first entry of the root directory.

- **File system descriptor (46 41 54 31 36 20 20 20).** These 8 bytes contain the file system name. Partitions formatted by Windows 2000 have names such as FAT12, FAT16, FAT32, or NTFS. A FAT12 partition is smaller than 32MB and uses 12-bit FAT entries.

FAT32 BPB

The first thing you notice about the FAT32 entries in the boot sector is that they're longer. That is because FAT32 includes new features that require more space to implement. The official name for this larger structure is the *Big FAT BIOS Parameter Block*. (I was a tubby as a child, so I don't particularly like this nomenclature, but there it is.)

A *Big FAT BOOT FS Info* sector comes right after the boot sector. This sector contains special lookup information to make it easier for the file system to locate unused clusters. A listing of the BPB and BFBPB follows. The first 11 bytes at the start of the boot sector are shown for context.

```
EB 58 90 4D 53 44 4F 53 35 2E 30 00 02 02 20 00  .X.MSDOS5.0... .
02 00 00 00 00 F8 00 00 20 00 40 00 20 00 00 00  ........ .@. ...
E0 1F 03 00 1A 03 00 00 00 00 00 00 02 00 00 00  ................
01 00 06 00 00 00 00 00 00 00 00 00 00 00 00 00  ................
80 00 29 D9 F7 56 DC 4E 4F 20 4E 41 4D 45 20 20  ..)..V.NO NAME
20 20 46 41 54 33 32 20 20 20 33 C9 8E D1 BC F4   FAT32   3.....
```

- **Bytes per Sector (00 02).** The same 200h or 512 bytes per cluster that is pretty much standard for all U.S. drives.

- **Sectors per Cluster (02).** This is half the number of sectors per cluster as FAT16, but still more than the 1 sector/cluster that you might expect. We'll see why in just a minute after finishing this list.

- **Reserved Sectors (20 00).** Now 20 sectors exist between the boot sector and the first FAT. This is one of the improvements of FAT32. The FAT does not need to be in a fixed location. The extra room enables the system to put information between the boot sector and the start of the file system itself. This includes the *File Information Sector* and the *Boot Sector Copy* described later in this list.

- **Number of FATs (02).** FAT32 also uses a mirrored fat, but it is optional in Windows 9x. Windows 2000 does not have an option to forgo the mirror FAT.

- **Maximum Entries in Root Directory (00 00).** The Root directory under FAT32 was freed from the 512-file limit of FAT16. The FAT32 root directory can contain up to 65,532 files and directories. FAT32 also supports long filenames with additional directory entries, so the increased number of handles greatly enhances long filename support.

- **Small Sectors (00 00).** This entry is always 0. Windows 2000 does not enable formatting a FAT32 partition with fewer than 65526 clusters.

- **Media Descriptor** (F8). This entry is always F8. Windows 2000 can format only a hard drive as FAT32. Floppies continue to be formatted as regular FAT.

- **Sectors per FAT (00 00).** This is a legacy value that is not applicable in FAT32. Setting this value to 0 acts as a "FAT32 Flag" to the operating system.

- **Sectors per Track (20 00) – 20h, decimal 32, and Number of Heads (40 00) – 40h, decimal 64.** These entries are the same as their FAT16 counterparts. Both file systems recognize the same logical disk geometry.

- **Hidden Sectors (20 00 00 00) – 20h, or decimal 32.** This entry means the same as in FAT16—the number of sectors between physical start of the partition and the boot sector.

- **Sector Count (E0 1F 03 00) – 31FE0h, or decimal 204768.** This entry has the same meaning as FAT.

- **Sectors per FAT (1A 03 00 00) – 31Ah, or 794 sectors in the FAT.** *This is a new entry.* Compare this value to the 200 sectors taken up for the FAT under FAT16 for the same partition. The weight gain occurs for two reasons. One is that each FAT entry takes 4 bytes instead of 2. The second is that the volume contains more clusters. Together with the mirrored FAT, a total of 794KB is taken up by the file system in this 100MB volume. This is about a .8% ratio, four times the size of FAT16, but still slim compared to NTFS.

- **Flags (00 00).** *This is a new entry.* Two possible values exist for this entry. If the high bit is set to 1, the contents of the primary FAT are mirrored to a secondary FAT. If this mirroring is enabled, the low four bits indicate the number of the FAT secondaries. Windows 2000 supports only one mirror.

- **File System Version (00 00).** *This is a new entry.* Used only by Windows 9x. The high-order byte indicates the version and the low byte indicates the incremental version. Both bytes are set to 0 in Windows 2000.

- **Root Cluster (02 00 00 00) — 02h.** *This is a new entry.* It indicates the cluster number of the root directory in the FAT. This entry makes it possible to place the root directory anywhere in the partition.

- **File System Information Sector (01 00) — 01h.** *This is a new entry.* It points at a sector that contains the total free clusters and the number of the most recently allocated cluster. This enables the file system to report these values without doing a complete scan of the FAT. Ordinarily, this sector is positioned immediately after the boot sector in the reserved sectors.

- **Backup Boot Sector (06 00) — 06h.** *This is a new entry.* It specifies the offset location of the backup boot sector. This backup boot sector corrects another deficiency in FAT16. If the boot sector gets corrupted, the system can read configuration information from the mirrored copy. The mirrored boot sector is placed in the reserved sectors, just after the primary boot sector.

- **Reserved (00 00 00 00 00 00 00 00 00 00 00 00).** Set aside for future expansion.

- **Drive Type (80).** Same as FAT16.

- **Special Use (00).** Same as FAT16.

- **Signature (29).** Same as FAT16. Indicates that an extended BPB is present.

- **Volume Serial Number (DA 2F BB 58). Same as FAT16.**

- **Volume Label (4E 4F 20 4E 41 4D 45 20 20 20 20).** Same as FAT16. Set to NO NAME   . The trailing blanks are part of the name.

- **File System (46 41 54 33 32 20 20 20).** Set by Windows 2000 to FAT32. The trailing blanks are part of the name.

NTFS BPB

The NTFS file system does not need to see much information in the boot sector. This is a listing of the 61 bytes that form the NTFS BPB and Extended BPB.

```
<<BPB and Extended BPB for an NTFS partition. The first 11 bytes of the boot sector are
shown for context.>>
EB 52 90 4E 54 46 53 20 20 20 20 00 02 01 00 00 .R.NTFS    .....
00 00 00 00 00 F8 00 00 20 00 40 00 20 00 00 00 ........ .@. ...
00 00 00 00 80 00 80 00 DF 1F 03 00 00 00 00 00 ...............
56 06 00 00 00 00 00 00 D6 30 02 00 00 00 00 00 V........0......
02 00 00 00 08 00 00 00
```

- **Bytes per Sector (00 02).** 200h or 512, standard for U.S. drives.

- **Sectors per Cluster (01).** NTFS strives to keep one sector per cluster until the volume size gets fairly large, about 500MB, with the cluster size doubling with each doubling of volume size. For example, a 1GB volume has a default cluster size of 2K. A 2GB volume has 4K clusters, and so forth. The largest cluster size under NTFS is 64K, the default for volumes in excess of 32GB. Compared to FAT32, NTFS supports volumes four times as large with the same cluster size.

- **Reserved (00 00).** NTFS puts the boot sector right at the start of the partition.

- **Number of FATs (00).** Not used.

- **Max Entries in Root (00 00).** Not used.

- **Small Clusters (00 00).** Not used.

- **Media Descriptor (F8).** Same as FAT. F8 indicates a hard drive.

- **Sectors per FAT (00 00).** Not used.

- **Sectors per Track (20 00) – 20h, and Number of Heads (40 00) – 40h.** Same meanings as FAT and FAT32.

- **Hidden Sectors (20 00 00 00) – 20h, or decimal 32.** Same meaning as FAT and FAT32.

- **Sector Count (00 00 00 00).** Not used. This legacy entry is too small for the big address space of NTFS. Another entry by the same name, which appears a little further down in this list, accommodates 64-bit addressing.

- **Sectors per FAT (80 00 80 00).** Not used.

- **Sector Count (DF 1F 03 00 00 00 00 00).** This new entry uses a double-word that is big enough to address 2^{64} sectors, although the practical limit is 2^{32} sectors, or 2TB, based on industry standards. Now, 2TB may seem like a lot of space today, but wait until you see the beta of Office 2002.

- **Logical Cluster Number for Master File Table (56 06 00 00 00 00 00 00) – 656, or decimal 1622.** Like FAT and FAT32, NTFS uses clusters rather than sectors to locate files. Each cluster is numbered with a *Logical Cluster Number* (LCN). For example, the MFT in this volume starts at cluster 1622. Ordinarily, you find the MFT as close to the beginning of the volume as possible to get a throughput advantage from the higher disk velocities. This partition was converted from FAT32, and there was no room for the MFT at the start of the disk.

- **Logical Cluster Number of MFT Mirror (FF 8F 01 00 00 00 00 00) − 018FFFh.** The file system puts a mirrored copy of the MFT near the center of the partition. If the system is unable to read the primary $MFT record, which contains the location of the other MFT records, it looks in the BPB to find the mirrored copy. The file system puts an error in the Event Log if this happens.

- **Clusters per MFT Record (02 00 00 00) − 2h, or 1024 bytes per MFT record.** This is the default record size for Windows 2000 and NT4. Earlier versions of NT used 2K and 4K records. A large record size makes more efficient use of the disk when saving small files, because the file's data can reside entirely in its MFT record. Those were happier days, though, when applications actually created small files. Nowadays, 4K is hardly enough to store the header on a data file. Microsoft rethought its MFT strategy and opted for leanness.

- **Clusters in MFT Index (08 00 00 00) − 8h.** The MFT index is a binary table that shows the layout of the MFT. This information is contained in an MFT metadata record called $Bitmap.

- **Volume Serial Number (C2 8D 68 AC CB 68 AC F0).** Same as FAT.

- **Checksum (00 00 00 00).** A 32-bit checksum of the MFT to validate that it is free of corruption.

One of the primary advantages of NTFS over FAT or FAT32 is its efficient use of the drive by having small cluster sizes in relation to the size of the volume. You can recover literally hundreds of megabytes on a drive simply by converting from FAT to NTFS. Table 13.1 lists the default cluster sizes based on volume size.

Table 13.1 **NTFS Cluster Sizes as a Function of Volume Size**

Volume Size	Cluster Size
< =512MB	512 bytes
513MB − 1GB	1K
1GB − 2GB	2K
2GB − 4GB	4K
4GB − 8GB	8K
8GB − 16GB	16K
16GB − 32GB	32K
>32GB	64K

You may wonder why NTFS needs to have cluster sizes larger than a single sector with so many addresses at its disposal. This has to do with performance. For example, consider a 32GB volume formatted as a single volume. If the volume were formatted with one sector/cluster, the file system would need to track the contents of 64 billion clusters. The enormity of these calculations would slow performance to a crawl and force the file system database to grow to monstrous proportions. The default cluster sizes represent a compromise between performance and efficient use of disk space.

That being said, the default NTFS cluster sizes were put in place quite a few years ago. A modern server with fast-wide SCSI or fast ATA disks, bus-mastering disk interface cards, and fast CPUs can handle cluster sizes that are one or even two steps smaller than the default.

For example, you can safely format a 32GB volume to have 32K or 16K clusters with no performance degradation. You select a specific cluster size by using the `Disk Management` console or by using a switch on the Format command. For example, to format an NTFS volume with a 16K cluster size, enter `format d: /fs:ntfs /a:16K`.

You must reformat the volume if you want to change the cluster size. You are not restricted on the cluster size for NTFS volumes containing Windows 2000 boot or system files. When converting to NTFS, the default cluster size is set to 1 sector, 512 bytes, and cannot be changed.

Compression Requires Smaller Clusters

NTFS file compression is not available at cluster sizes larger than 4K, so if you want to use compression on a big drive, you have to format with small clusters. The small cluster size on a big volume, coupled with the additional drag of NTFS compression, can exact a significant performance penalty.

The cluster size is set based on the size of the volume, not the size of the disk. If you create a large NTFS volume on a RAID array, the default cluster size is set according to the logical size of the volume.

Boot Sector Highlights

The following are the key points to remember about the boot sector structures for the three file systems:

- The FAT boot sector fixes the location of the FAT. If a sector containing the FAT fails, the file system becomes inoperable. The FAT32 file table location is not fixed.
- The file table is mirrored on both FAT and FAT32 volumes.
- The number of files at the root of a FAT partition is limited to 512. The FAT32 limit is 65,532 files.

- FAT and FAT32 volumes support long filenames using additional directory entries.

- The limited addressing space of FAT16 wastes drive space by using large cluster sizes. FAT32 volumes have smaller cluster sizes, and NTFS volumes have the smallest cluster sizes.

- FAT32 uses 4-byte entries that are not compatible with legacy DOS disk utilities.

- The FAT32 file table is much larger, and the mirrored table makes it even larger. Windows 2000 limits FAT32 volumes to 32GB so that the FAT32 file table can be cached in memory.

- A File System Information sector in FAT32 speeds cluster allocation.

- Both FAT32 and NTFS mirror the boot sector for fault tolerance.

- NTFS uses a Master File Table to store file records.

- FAT and FAT32 volumes can be converted to NTFS, but NTFS volumes cannot be converted to FAT or FAT32.

- The MFT location is not fixed in an NTFS volume. A partial copy of the MFT is mirrored at the center of the disk for fault tolerance.

- NTFS can withstand a loss of a sector containing MFT records.

FAT and MFT Structures

The whole purpose of a file system is to track files. DOS introduced a *File Allocation Table* (FAT), as the structure that defined the layout and structure of the files on a volume. A FAT is essentially a map showing which clusters are in use and which aren't. The files associated with each item on the map are indexed in directory records. Windows 9x OSR2 expanded the FAT to support 32-bit addressing but retained its basic design of cluster map and directory indexing.

NTFS uses an entirely different approach based on a hierarchical database called the *Master File Table* (MFT). Files and directories are represented in the MFT by records containing attributes that describe their contents. Because the MFT is a database rather than a simple cluster map, its entries can contain more information than a FAT and can be indexed in more ways than simply by filename. The following two sections contain functional descriptions of the FAT and MFT. The MFT is covered in greater detail later in this chapter.

FAT Cluster Map

FAT16 maps out the clusters in a volume using 2 bytes, or 16 bits, to address each cluster. FAT32 uses 4 bytes to get 32-bit cluster addresses. A listing of a standard FAT looks like this:

```
<<FAT16 File Allocation Table with 23 files. ASCII renderings are not relevant and have been
omitted. Entries in bold represent a file that takes up 12 clusters.>>
F8FF FFFF FFFF FFFF FFFF FFFF FFFF FFFF
0900 FFFF 0B00 FFFF 0D00 FFFF 0F00 FFFF
1100 1200 1300 FFFF FFFF FFFF FFFF FFFF
FFFF FFFF FFFF FFFF FFFF FFFF 1F00 2000
2100 2200 2300 FFFF 2500 2600 2700 2800
2900 2A00 2B00 2C00 2D00 2E00 2F00 FFFF
```

The first byte in the FAT, F8, is the media type. The following 3 bytes are reserved. Each subsequent 2-byte entry contains either a cluster number or one of the following entries:

- **FFFF.** End of a file
- **FFF7.** Bad cluster (FFF7)
- **FFF5.** Reserved cluster (FFF6)

Consecutive FFFF entries mean that the associated file or directory fits completely into one cluster. Files that spill over into additional clusters are identified by a series of numbers called the *cluster sequence number.* The bold portion of the listing shows a file starting at cluster 0025 (remember to reverse the little-endian notation) and ending at cluster 3000 (shown by the FFFF end-of-file marker). You cannot determine the actual file size from the FAT listing, but you know that the file used 12 clusters. If the cluster size were 32K, the file would take up 394K on the disk.

A mirror of the FAT is positioned immediately after the primary FAT. If a sector in the primary FAT fails, causing the associated cluster to be unreadable, the system can read from the secondary FAT. The mirrored FAT takes the same amount of disk space as the primary FAT.

FAT excels by dint of its compactness and speed. After all, a FAT is really nothing more than a digitized drawing of the disk showing the location and extent of every file. A lookup in a bitmap index takes only a split-nanosecond if the bitmap is fairly small in relation to the size of the disk. A 1GB volume with 32K clusters has just more than 32,000 FAT entries. Each entry takes 2 bytes, so the FAT takes about 64K.

FAT32 Cluster Map

The layout of a FAT32 cluster map is the same as a FAT16 map, except that each entry uses 4 bytes (32 bits) instead of 2 bytes (16 bits) to describe a cluster location. A FAT32 listing looks like this:

```
<<FAT32 File Allocation Table containing 16 files.>>
F8FFFFFF FFFFFFFF FFFFFF0F FFFFFF0F
FFFFFF0F FFFFFF0F FFFFFF0F FFFFFF0F
09000000 0A000000 0B000000 FFFFFF0F
FFFFFF0F 0E000000 FFFFFF0F FFFFFF0F
FFFFFF0F FFFFFF0F FFFFFF0F FFFFFF0F
15000000 16000000 17000000 FFFFFF0F
19000000 1A000000 1B000000 1C000000
1D000000 1E000000 1F000000 20000000
21000000 22000000 23000000 24000000
25000000 26000000 27000000 FFFFFF0F
```

The first byte, F8, is the media descriptor with the next 7 bytes reserved. The subsequent double-word entries (4 bytes each) represent clusters. An FFFFFF0F entry is an EOF marker.

The increased address space in FAT32 makes it possible to have truly huge volumes, but relatively large cluster sizes are still required to keep the FAT from growing too large. For example, consider an 8GB disk, not so big by today's standards. If this disk were formatted as a single FAT32 volume with a 2-sector cluster size, the FAT would contain 8 million entries at 4 bytes apiece. Add this to the mirrored FAT—optional in Windows 9x, but required in Windows 2000—and the overall space taken up by the file system is 64MB, plus the clusters used by the directories.

The operating system tries to keep the entire FAT in memory to speed lookups, but that is out of the question in this case. Not only do lookups in such a monster structure take a long time, the chances of corruption approach near certainty, especially when the drive becomes fragmented.

Directories Used as Index for FAT

Both FAT and FAT32 use directories to index the cluster map in the FAT. A directory record stores the names of the files and directories directly underneath that directory. A directory can be stored anywhere on the disk, and it is assigned a FAT cluster just like a file. The file system doesn't differentiate between the two. A listing for a directory on a FAT16 volume looks like this.

```
<<Root directory on FAT16 volume. Bold numbers represent the starting cluster number in the
FAT.>>
4E 45 57 20 56 4F 4C 55 4D 45 20 08 00 00 00 00 NEW VOLUME .....
00 00 00 00 00 00 45 A4 CE 26 00 00 00 00 00 00 ......E..&......
4F 4E 45 20 20 20 20 20 54 58 54 10 08 79 BD A4 ONE     TXT..y..
CE 26 CE 26 00 00 C0 A4 CE 26 02 00 00 00 00 00 .&.&.....&......
```

```
54 57 4F 20 20 20 20 20 54 58 54 10 08 BB C0 A4 TWO     TXT.....
CE 26 CE 26 00 00 C1 A4 CE 26 08 00 00 00 00 00 .&.&.....&......
E5 48 52 45 45 20 20 20 54 58 54 10 08 A2 C1 A4 .HREE   TXT.....
CE 26 CE 26 00 00 C2 A4 CE 26 12 00 00 00 00 00 .&.&.....&......
```

Each entry represents a file or subdirectory. It contains the corresponding cluster number from the FAT (shown in bold). This particular directory is the Root directory, so the initial entry is the volume name. If this were a standard directory, the first two entries would be the proverbial (.) and (..), representing the directory itself and its parent directory.

The bottom entry, the one that starts with .HREE   TXT, is a deleted file. As you are doubtlessly aware, the FAT file system does not delete files, it merely replaces the first letter with the σ character, which is decimal 229 or hex E5. Undelete programs recover files by putting a character back in that spot, and then doing some creative searches to determine whether the chain of FAT entries for that file can be reconstituted.

Structure of a FAT/FAT32 Directory Listing

The following extract of the directory listing shows a single file entry. Remember to reverse the bytes for words and double-words.

```
<<Extract of directory entry for a file.>>
54 57 4F 20 20 20 20 20 54 58 54 10 08 BB C0 A4 TWO     TXT.....
CE 26 CE 26 00 00 C1 A4 CE 26 08 00 00 00 00 00 .&.&.....&......
```

- **Name (54 57 4F 20 20 20 20 20 54 58 54).** The first 11 bytes are set aside for the filename. The name of this file is TWO   .TXT. The filename is padded to make 8 bytes and the extension is padded to 3 bytes. Long filenames are supported in Windows 2000 and classic NT by adding directory entries to hold the extra characters.

- **Attribute (10).** This entry contains bits that define the standard DOS attributes of read-only, hidden, system, and archive.

- **Reserved (08 BB C0 A4 CE 26 CE 26 00 00).** The next 10 bytes are reserved.

- **Date and Time Stamp (C1 A4 CE 26).** Four bytes represent the date and time the file was created.

- **FAT entry (08 00).** 08h. These 2 bytes represent the cluster number in the FAT. The example entry, 08h, shows that the file starts at the eighth cluster. A FAT32 directory looks the same but uses a long integer (32-bit) to accommodate the larger FAT. It uses one of the reserved bytes to get the additional 2 bytes.

- **File Length (FE 0F 00 00).** 0FFE, or 4094 bytes. This is the file length in bytes. The file system compares this number to the chain of clusters in the FAT to check for corruption. If the chain is two clusters long in the FAT, but the File Length entry corresponds to four sectors, the system knows a problem exists.

This method of indexing files has disadvantages on big volumes. The file system must first find the filename in its directory record. Directories are scattered everywhere, so a deep search might involve scanning the entire hard drive. When the directory record is found, the only useful bit of information in the file entry is the cluster sequence number from the FAT. So now the file system must move the drive heads back to the start of the volume to read the FAT (or read from a cached copy in memory) to find the remaining cluster numbers. Only then can it move the heads out to the start of the file on disk.

Fragmentation makes this search process even more disk-intensive. The directory entries are 32 bytes long, which is fairly trim, but the directory itself takes a whole cluster on the disk. That accentuates waste on a big disk with many directories and subdirectories. Directories can also become fragmented if the entries fill a cluster and do not have an adjacent cluster to handle the overflow.

FAT/FAT32 File Record Structure

The least interesting component of the FAT file system is the file record itself. Let's look at one just to round out the story. Files start at cluster boundaries.

```
<<Start of cluster containing a file.>>
7468 6973 2069 7320 6120 736D 616C 6C20 this is a small
6669 6C65 2E20 0000 0000 0000 0000 0000 file. .........
0000 0000 0000 0000 0000 0000 0000 0000 ................
```

If the cluster size for this volume is 32 sectors, this 22-byte file consumes 16KB. This is a fairly poor utilization ratio. FAT32 makes better use of a disk, thanks to its larger address space, which enables smaller cluster sizes.

MFT Functional Description

Unlike the cluster map used by FAT and FAT32 to locate files, NTFS uses a hierarchical object-oriented database called the MFT. The MFT consists of fixed-length records, 1KB apiece, stored in tabular format. Each record consists of a set of attributes that, taken together, uniquely identifies the location and contents of a corresponding file or directory. (A few minor exceptions to this "one record, one file" rule do exist, but these are encountered only when a file gets very large and very fragmented.)

MFT records are also Windows 2000 objects, so they get protection from the same Executive security system that protects Active Directory records, Registry entries, and virtual hardware devices.

Three classes of MFT records exist:

- **File records.** These records store information typically thought of as "data," such as application files, driver files, system files, database files, and so forth.

- **Directory records.** These records store and index filenames. Directory records also index other attributes, such as reparse points, security descriptors, and link tracking information.

- **Hybrid records.** These records contain attributes associated with both file and directory records. They are used to support specialized services or features.

The MFT is a self-referential database. That is, it contains information that defines its own structure. This information is stored in special records called *metadata* records. NTFS4 set aside the first 16 MFT records to hold metadata, but it actually used only 11 of them. The remainder was reserved for future use. NTFS5 sets aside the first 26 MFT records for metadata and uses 15 of them. Interestingly enough, it does not use any of the five records reserved in the classic MFT format.

NTFS5 Metadata Files Completely Hidden

Under NT4, you could see the metadata files from the command line using dir /a:h $filename.

NTFS5 completely shields the metadata files from view. You know the files are there, though, because they take up room on the volume. You can see the space set aside for the metadata files by running Chkdsk`:

```
635008 kilobytes total disk space.
535691 kilobytes in 8206 user files.
1894 kilobytes in 592 indexes.
14176 kilobytes in use by the system.
83247 kilobytes available on disk.
```

As you can see, the NTFS system files take a significant chunk out of a small volume. On volumes in excess of 10GB or so, though, the percentage of total space consumed by the NTFS file system is smaller than FAT32 when cluster sizes are equal.

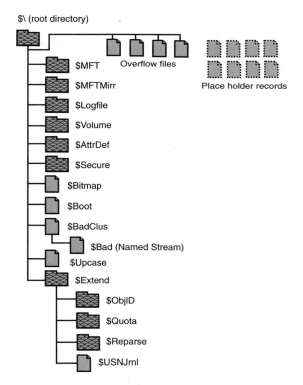

Figure 13.1   MFT record structure shown in standard file-and-folder hierarchy.

Figure 13.1 shows a diagram of the metadata record structure if you could see it as directories and files. MFT metadata records start with a dollar sign, $. Their order and structure is rigorously controlled, because the secondary bootstrap loader, Ntldr, runs in real mode and cannot deal with lots of complexity.

Ntldr finds the MFT using information in the boot sector. It then loads the first few metadata records, uses them to find the operating system files, and continues loading the operating system.

MFT Metadata Records and Their Functions

A quick list of the MFT metadata records and their functions follows. More details are provided later in this chapter.

- **$MFT.** NTFS treats everything on the disk as a file, including the MFT itself. $MFT is the file record for the MFT. The MFT record structure is a hybrid of a file record and a directory record. The data portion contains pointers at the MFT itself and at MFT fragments, if any exist. The directory portion contains a bitmap attribute that lays out the MFT structure and shows which records are in use and which aren't. The bootstrap loader finds the $MFT record by using a pointer in the boot sector.

- **$MFTMirr.** NTFS mirrors the first few MFT records out at the halfway point in the volume. If the cluster holding the primary $MFT record goes bad, the system can use the mirror to find the remaining portions of the MFT. The $MFTMirr is a standard MFT file record with a pointer at the location of the mirrored file.

- **$LogFile.** This record contains the location of the log files used to support NTFS transaction tracking. NTFS enables disk writes to be cached prior to committing them to disk. This so-called *lazy write* feature significantly improves performance, but it has the potential to corrupt the file system if the information on the disk gets out of sync with the records in the MFT. NTFS guards against this by using a *Log File Service* (LFS), to write critical MFT information to a log file, before transferring it to the MFT. If the system crashes, NTFS re-establishes file system integrity by applying entries out of the log file to the MFT. This avoids a lengthy full system rebuild after an abnormal shutdown. The $LogFile record uses a standard file record structure with a data attribute that points at two log files, one primary and one mirror, located at the middle of the volume.

- **$Volume.** This record contains the name of the NTFS volume, its size, and the version of NTFS used to format it. The $Volume record uses a unique format with specialized attributes.

- **$AttrDef.** This record contains an Attribute_Definition file that lists the attributes supported by NTFS along with information about them, such as whether they must remain in the MFT or can be stored elsewhere on the disk. The $AttrDef record uses a standard file record format.

- **$\.** This record contains the root directory of the file system. Like FAT and FAT32, directories are used to index the file system by filename. The root directory is a metadata record because its location and contents are critical for finding everything else in the file system. The $\ record uses a standard directory record format.

- **$BitMap.** Just like FAT and FAT32, NTFS maintains a cluster map of the volume so that it can quickly determine the location of unused clusters. The NTFS cluster map, however, uses individual bits, so even huge volumes can be mapped in a compact structure. The $BitMap record uses a standard file record format.

- **$Boot.** This file, which holds the location of the secondary bootstrap loader, NTLDR, is a metadata record, because the primary bootstrap code needs to be able to find the secondary bootstrap code. It can't do this without referring to the MFT. The NTLDR file itself is generally located immediately after the reserved sectors that follow the boot sector. The $Boot record uses a standard file record format.

- **$BadClus.** This file contains the location of any bad clusters identified during initial formatting or subsequent operation. If you choose the *quick format* option, the system does not scan for bad clusters. NTFS supports native SCSI sector sparing, so a cluster is not marked as bad unless all the spare sectors are exhausted from those set aside on the drive. The $BadClus record uses a standard file record format.

- **$Secure.** This is a new record in NTFS5. It contains the security descriptors for the MFT records. Aggregating the security descriptors rather than placing them in their own MFT records improves performance and enables mirroring for fault tolerance. The $Secure record uses the standard file record format.

- **$UpCase.** This file contains a map of lowercase Unicode characters to their uppercase equivalents. The $UpCase record uses the standard file record format.

- **$Extend.** A new record in NTFS5, this directory contains additional metadata records beyond the base 16 records in NTFS4. The $Extend directory has entries for four metadata records: $Quota, $ObjID, $Reparse, and the Change Journal, $UsnJrnl, if one is used on the volume. The $Extend record uses a standard directory record format.

- **$Quota.** The $Quota record is a directory that holds records for user SIDs and the files they own. It supports assigning space on a volume based on quotas. The $Quota record has existed in NTFS since its inception, but it is only now being implemented. The $Quota record uses a standard directory structure.

- **$ObjID.** A new record in NTFS5, this directory record contains pointers to files containing Globally Unique Identifiers (GUIDs) associated with COM files, shortcuts, and other links. This forms a central repository of link information that is used by the Link Tracking Service to discover the location of the base files when they are moved. This enables administrators to move files between NTFS5 volumes without the need for manually changing the shortcuts or COM links pointing at that file.

- **$Reparse.** This is also a new record in NTFS5. It stores information about files that contain *reparse points.* A reparse point is a new attribute in NTFS5. Essentially, it redirects an application to another data repository and provides code for interpreting the byte stream from that new data repository. Windows 2000 uses reparse points to support mount points and Remote Storage, but you can expect third-party vendors to take advantage of them, too.

- **$UsnJrnl.** A new record in NTFS5, this is a standard file record containing Change Journal entries. The Change Journal is used to quickly recover the additional indexes in NTFS5, including any third-party entries that may have a special index.

Individual records in a database are meaningless unless you are familiar with their associated attributes. NTFS5 defines 16 attributes for the MFT, just a couple more than NTFS4. Some attributes, such as $File_Name, are used by all record types. Others, such as $Volume_Version, are used by only one record type.

The NTFS database is theoretically extensible, but to my knowledge, no widely available commercial product modifies the MFT. The vendor of such a product needs to regression-test any proprietary MFT extensions against thousands and thousands of other commercial applications, just as Microsoft is doing to support the changes in NTFS5.

FAT and MFT Structure Highlights

The key points to remember about the structure of FAT and MFT are as follows:

- The FAT and FAT32 file table is a map of the on-disk clusters.

- NTFS uses a database, the MFT, to locate files and directories, rather than a cluster map.

- FAT and FAT32 directories are an index of the clusters on the map. The directories are scattered throughout the disk.

- NTFS directories are an integral part of the MFT and are placed on disk in large segments to improve performance and consistency checking.

- The FAT and FAT32 file system has a rigorous structure. The MFT structure is defined by hidden metadata records that are themselves part of the MFT. The record structure can be expanded with different record types and indexes.

- Deleted files are not removed from the FAT. The index entry in the directory is marked with a special symbol that frees the associated clusters. Fragmentation is a severe problem. The MFT structure resists the effects of fragmentation.

- NTFS file and directory records are Windows 2000 security objects and are protected by the integrated security system. FAT and FAT32 files and directories have no security.

- Maintaining file system consistency in a big FAT or FAT32 volume is difficult because of the random distribution of directory structures.

New NTFS Features

The next section contains a description of these attributes and their function in the MFT. Several of the new features in NTFS5 are implemented by modifications to the MFT metadata records, the attribute list, and the standard record structure. These new features and their attributes are:

- **Distributed Link Tracking.** Automatically tracks the location of records for source files used in links to shortcuts and OLE objects. This feature relies on a new attribute, $Object_ID, and a new metadata record, $ObjID.

- **Reparse Points.** Enables mounting file systems from other volumes such as hard drives and CD-ROM drives at a folder on an NTFS file system. Also enables replacing a file with pointers and special handling code to support features such as hierarchical storage management. This feature relies on a new attribute, $Reparse, and a new metadata record, $Reparse_Point.

- **Quota Tracking.** Enables limiting the total space a user can have on a volume. This feature relies on an existing attribute, $Quota, that was never before implemented, and on a new metadata record, $Quota.

- **Change Log.** Provides a quick way for applications that index the MFT to update their indexes quickly without rescanning the entire MFT. The feature relies on a new metadata record, $UsnJrnl.

- **Encrypted File System.** Enables encrypting files so that only the user who encrypted the files can read them. This feature relies on a new MFT attribute, $Logged_Utility_Streams. See Chapter 15, "Managing Shared Resources," for more information.

The first four features are covered in this chapter. The Encrypted File System is covered in Chapter 14, "Managing File Systems Security."

NTFS Detailed Operating Description

The MFT is an object-oriented database. Objects are derived from classes that contain certain attributes. For example, a file record contains a $Data attribute and a directory record contains an $Index_Root attribute.

All attributes have two portions: a header portion and a data portion. The header portion contains descriptive information about the attribute itself, such as the total number of bytes in the attribute, the number of bytes in each portion of the attribute, the offset from the start of the attribute where the data portion is found, time stamps, flags, and so forth.

The data portion of the attribute has the information that the attribute is designed to hold. For example, the data portion of the $File_Name attribute contains a filename. This is a listing of the $File_Name attribute for a file named `FileName.txt`. The bold text is the header portion. The light text is the data portion. The trailing zeros after the filename are padding.

```
<<$File_Name attribute showing header and data portions of the attribute. Data portion is in
bold.>>
30 00 00 00 78 00 00 00 00 00 00 00 00 00 02 00 0...x..........
5A 00 00 00 18 00 01 00 05 00 00 00 00 00 05 00 Z..............
F0 98 70 DB 6A BF BE 01 F0 98 70 DB 6A BF BE 01 ..p.j.....p.j...
F0 98 70 DB 6A BF BE 01 F0 98 70 DB 6A BF BE 01 ..p.j.....p.j...
00 00 00 00 00 00 00 00 00 00 00 00 00 00 00 00 ................
20 00 00 00 00 00 00 00 0C 03 46 00 69 00 6C 00  .........F.i.l.
65 00 4E 00 61 00 6D 00 65 00 2E 00 74 00 78 00 e.N.a.m.e...t.x.
74 00 00 00 00 00 00 00                          t.......
```

The attribute header structure is fairly consistent between attribute types. It contains the following:

- The first 4 bytes (30 00 00 00 in the example) represent the type code for the attribute. Reversing the little-endian notation (long integer this time, so reverse 4 bytes, 00 00 00 30) yields a type code of 30, indicating a $File_Name attribute. The system uses type codes instead of names so that attributes can be sorted in the record. Attributes with lower type codes come first. This rule makes it unnecessary to have special metadata records defining record structures.

- The next 4 bytes (78 00 00 00) represent the byte count (120 bytes) of the attribute, including the header portion.

- The next 8 bytes are reserved.

- Next come 4 bytes (5A 00 00 00) that represent the byte count (90 bytes) of the data portion of the attribute.
- Next come 2 bytes (18 00) that represent the offset (24 bytes) from the start of the attribute header to the start of the data portion of the attribute.
- The next 10 bytes contain special flags and attributes.
- The next 32 bytes contain time stamps.
- The final 26 bytes contain locator information specific to the attribute itself.

An attribute need not reside entirely inside its MFT record. $Data attributes, for instance, rarely fit into a 1K MFT record. If an attribute gets too big, the file system keeps the header portion in the MFT record and moves the data portion out onto the disk with a pointer left behind to mark the location. Such an attribute is termed *nonresident*. Some attributes are required to stay resident to support file system operations. These attributes are flagged in the $AttrDef metadata record.

When the file system makes an attribute nonresident, it attempts to keep the data in a contiguous set of clusters called a *run*. This is easy to do on a volume with lots of free space, but as free space gets tight and available clusters get scattered around the drive, it is not possible to keep the data in a single run. In this case, the file gets fragmented into multiple runs. Each run has a pointer in the MFT record. This pointer has three elements:

- **Starting Logical Cluster Number (LCN).** Each cluster in the volume is given a sequential number called an LCN. The LCN is a 64-bit number.
- **Starting Virtual Cluster Number (VCN).** Individual clusters in a run are tracked using an offset number called a VCN. If a file is fragmented into multiple runs, the pointer for each run contains the VCN of the first cluster in that run.
- **Number of Clusters.** The number of clusters in the run.

The combination of LCN and VCN in the run pointer makes locating a particular byte in a file very simple. The file system takes the byte offset requested by the application ("Go to byte 1232 and read the next 100 bytes") and divides it by the cluster size to determine the cluster that contains the requested byte. It then does a lookup in the MFT record to find the run that contains that particular VCN.

The pointer containing that VCN also contains the LCN of the start of the run. If the file system gets busy with lots of requests, it doesn't bother sending the drive heads back and forth to the MFT to get new LCN numbers. Instead, it sweeps the heads back and forth across the drive, grabbing location information from the MFT, and then picking the requested data from the selected clusters like farmers picking grapes. This is called *elevator seeking*.

MFT Functional Concepts Highlights

The MFT concepts covered so far are as follows:

- A file or directory is actually a record in the MFT database.
- The MFT record consists of a set of attributes that collectively defines the contents of a directory or file.
- MFT attributes are normally contained in the MFT record, but they can be moved out onto the disk if they grow too large.
- Data in the nonresident portion of the attribute is placed in a set of clusters called a *run*. Runs are located by information contained in the MFT database.
- Data can be fragmented across multiple runs. File access techniques limit the impact of fragmentation. Windows 2000 has a defragmenter if fragmentation grows too severe.

With these concepts in mind, let's take a closer look at how NTFS uses these MFT record attributes to control the file system.

Functional Description of MFT Attributes

The MFT in NTFS5 uses 16 attributes to build records. The attribute names also start with dollar signs. Some of these attributes are common to every record, such as $Standard_Information and $File_Name. The others have special functions and are used by particular types of records. For example, the $Volume record contains $Volume_Name and $Volume_Information attributes. Table 13.2 contains a list of the NTFS5 attributes and their record types.

Table 13.2 **MFT Attributes Sorted by Record Type**

$Standard_Information	10
$Attribute_List	20
$File_Name	30
$Object_Id	40★★
$Security_Descriptor	50
$Volume_Name	60
$Volume_Information	70
$Data	80
$Index_Root	90
$Index_Allocation	A0
$Bitmap	B0
$Reparse_Point	C0
$Ea_Information (No longer used. HPFS compatibility dropped.)	D0
$Ea (No longer used. HPFS compatibility dropped.)	E0
$Logged_Utility_Stream (Used in encrypted files.)	100

★★ *The NTFS4 attribute called $Volume_Version is no longer used. Its type code, 40, was given to $ObjectID.*

The following sections contain extracts of the hex contents from MFT records. The intent of this analysis is to show specifics about the operation of the MFT and how it affects NTFS functionality. If you are interested in seeing more of the structures than are shown in the examples, use a hex editor capable of reading disk contents and scan for the markers shown in the listings. I used Hex Workshop from BreakPoint Software, www.bpsoft.com, to pull the listings.

Roadmap to Key MFT Attributes

The coverage of the MFT record attributes in this section is intended as a reference guide to the internal workings of the MFT. This information can help you troubleshoot NTFS problems by showing you exactly how the file and directory attributes are used by NTFS to support I/O calls from the operating system.

This is a quick list of the attributes and their features that are covered in this section. It should give you an idea of why so much detail is presented when describing their structure.

- **$Standard_Information.** Contains the common file attributes (read-only, system, hidden, and archive), along with a set of time stamps that shows when the file was created, when the data was modified, when the attributes were modified, and when the file was last accessed. This information is displayed at the `dir` command and in Explorer.

- **$File_Name.** Contains the short and long names assigned to the file. The discussion details the algorithms that create short names and discusses naming problems that arise. Filenames are also critical elements in file indexing, so a good grasp of the naming structures helps to understand why certain practices, such as putting 5000 files that all start with the same six letters in the same directory, are not a good idea.

- **$Security_Descriptor.** NTFS records are security objects. Understanding how they are stored and retrieved from their associated MFT records enhances your ability to understand the security topics in the next chapter.

- **$Data.** A great many new features in Windows 2000 take advantage of the multiple data stream capability of NTFS. This section shows how the data is stored and helps you understand how streams are used for journaling and file summaries. This section also details compression and sparse file handling.

- **Directory attributes.** The structure and operation of the three attributes associated with MFT directories are the key determinants of NTFS reliability and internal consistency. Knowing how the index structures are stored helps you understand the limitations of defragmenting, file encryption, and file-name indexing.

- **$MFT and $MFTMirr.** These sections detail the operation of the MFT itself. Using this knowledge, you can better understand the Windows 2000 boot sequence and the system recovery mechanisms outlined in Chapter 18, "Recovering from System Failures."

- **$Logged_Utility_Stream.** This attribute is associated with the Encrypted File System, and is covered in Chapter 14.

- **$Reparse_Point.** Of all the mystical and magical new features in Windows 2000, reparse points and the features that use them are some of the most misunderstood. After you see how the MFT records store and use this attribute, you'll have a good grasp of the operation of mounted points, hierarchical storage management, and the structure of the Sysvol folders used to support group policies in a domain.

Common Attribute Types

Of the 16 attributes available in NTFS5, two appear in all record types. They are $Standard_Information and $File_Name. Each record also has a 48-byte header not associated with any specific attribute type. The record header contains a sequence number that identifies the record in the MFT, a file reference number that identifies the record's offset in relation to the start of the volume, an update counter for consistency checking, and other physical parameters of the record.

$Standard_Information

The $Standard_Information attribute contains commonly used information that must remain resident in the MFT record. The following is a listing of the $Standard_Information attribute from a typical MFT record.

```
<<$Standard_Information attribute>>
10 00 00 00 60 00 00 00 00 00 00 00 00 00 00 00  ....`..........
48 00 00 00 18 00 00 00 F0 98 70 DB 6A BF BE 01  H.........p.j...
F0 98 70 DB 6A BF BE 01 F0 98 70 DB 6A BF BE 01  ..p.j.....p.j...
F0 98 70 DB 6A BF BE 01 20 00 00 00 00 00 00 00  ..p.j... .......
00 00 00 00 00 00 00 00 00 00 00 00 03 01 00 00  ...............
00 00 00 00 00 00 00 00 50 06 00 00 00 00 00 00  ........P.......
```

The 96 bytes in this attribute contain the following information:

- **Time stamps** (the F0 98 70 DB 6A BF BE 01 entries) for the following actions: creation, last access, last attribute modification, and last data modification.

- **Attribute flags** for basic attributes such as read-only, hidden, system, and archived.

- **Update counter** that increments each time the record is changed. NTFS puts a copy of this update counter in the last 2 bytes of each sector in the record and uses it for consistency checking.

- **Link counter** that tracks the number of files that point to this record. This is used for POSIX support and does not refer to the new link-tracking feature in Windows 2000.

The time stamp entries need additional explanation. The difference between "attribute modification" and "data modification" refers to the way the system tracks updates to a record. The time stamp in the $Standard_Information attribute applies to the $Data attribute if this were a file record and the $Index_Root attribute if this were a directory record. Changes to these attributes increment the Last Data Modification time stamp. Changes to any other attribute increment the Last Attribute Modification time stamp.

Also, the Last Access Time time stamp does not get updated each time a file is accessed. Rather, it is updated only once in any one-hour period regardless of the number of times a file is touched. This granularity improves performance by limiting the number of file writes caused when Explorer sweeps over a directory and looks inside the files for icons. The last access time granularity for FAT32 is set for one day.

Suppressing Last Access Time Updates

You can improve file system performance by eliminating the update to the Last Access Time time stamp. Do so with the following Registry change:

```
Key:     HKLM | System | CurrentControlSet | Control | FileSystem
Value:   NtfsDisableLastAccessUpdate
Data:    1 (REG_DWORD)
```

$File_Name

Every MFT record has a $File_Name attribute. If the filename does not meet MSDOS 8.3 naming standards, two $File_Name attributes are present, one for the long name and one for the automatically generated short name. The $File_Name attributes must stay resident. This listing shows the two $File_Name attributes for a file with the name Long File Name.txt. The attribute headers for the two attributes are shown in bold. They start with type code 30.

```
<<$File_Name attribute for short file name.>>
30 00 00 00 78 00 00 00 00 00 00 00 00 00 03 00 0...x...........
5A 00 00 00 18 00 01 00 1C 00 00 00 00 00 01 00 Z...............
5E 7B 88 9A 92 BF BE 01 5E 7B 88 9A 92 BF BE 01 ^{......^{......
5E 7B 88 9A 92 BF BE 01 5E 7B 88 9A 92 BF BE 01 ^{......^{......
00 00 00 00 00 00 00 00 00 00 00 00 00 00 00 00 ................
20 00 00 00 00 00 00 00 0C 02 4C 00 4F 00 4E 00  .........L.O.N.
47 00 46 00 49 00 7E 00 31 00 2E 00 54 00 58 00 G.F.I.~.1...T.X.
54 00 6D 00 65 00 2E 00                          T.m.e...

<<$File_Name attribute for long file name.>>
                        30 00 00 00 80 00 00 00         0.......
00 00 00 00 00 00 02 00 66 00 00 00 18 00 01 00 ........f.......
1C 00 00 00 00 00 01 00 5E 7B 88 9A 92 BF BE 01 ........^{......
5E 7B 88 9A 92 BF BE 01 5E 7B 88 9A 92 BF BE 01 ^{......^{......
5E 7B 88 9A 92 BF BE 01 00 00 00 00 00 00 00 00 ^{..............
```

```
00 00 00 00 00 00 00 00 20 00 00 00 00 00 00 00    ........ .......
12 01 4C 00 6F 00 6E 00 67 00 20 00 46 00 69 00    ..L.o.n.g. .F.i.
6C 00 65 00 20 00 4E 00 61 00 6D 00 65 00 2E 00    l.e. .N.a.m.e...
74 00 78 00 74 00 00 00                            t.x.t...
```

Several items of note are in this listing:

- The first entry in the data portion of the attribute (1C 00 00 00, in the examples) is the MFT sequence number of the directory that indexes this file. For example, this file is in a directory named Dir_One. Based on the sequence number, the MFT record for Dir_One is the 28th record in the MFT (1Ch converts to decimal 28). All files and directories in the Dir_One directory reference this sequence number. NTFS uses the number to determine a file's parent directory and to verify consistency in the database. If the Dir_One directory does not have a listing for Long File Name.txt, that entry requires repair.

- The next 4 bytes are a series of flags. One of them is a resident/nonresident flag (00 00 01 00). Filenames are always resident.

- The next four entries (5E 7B 88 9A 92 BF BE 01) are time stamps.

- The next 16 bytes are reserved.

- The 20 00 00 00 entry has an undocumented purpose.

- The last 2 bytes just prior to the start of the text portion of the filename (OC 02 for the short name and 12 01 for the long filename) have two functions. The first byte indicates the length of the filename. Because this is a single byte, NTFS long filenames are limited to 255 characters. The second byte is a flag indicating the name type. 01 indicates a long filename; 02 a short filename; and 03 a long filename that meets the requirements of a short filename.

- The remaining bytes are the text of the filename in Unicode. Unicode uses 2 bytes to represent characters. ANSI characters need only 1 byte, so the next byte is blank.

This attribute supports the following features:

- **Unicode support.** All NTFS filenames, both short and long, use Unicode characters. The system presents the Unicode characters in the short name as ANSI when a lookup request comes from a DOS client. The following is a directory listing using dir /x that shows the short and long names:

```
E:\DIR /X
Volume in drive E is NTFS
Volume Serial Number is FC46-A70C
```

```
Directory of E:\

06/21/99  10:23p     21 LONGFI~1.TXT    Long File Name.txt
           1 File(s)   21 bytes
           0 Dir(s)    104,342,528 bytes free
```

- **Special characters in filenames.** Spaces are permitted in Windows 2000 long filenames, as are multiple periods, leading periods, and all but a handful of the 65,000+ Unicode character set. For example, you can use the Alt–Numkeypad shortcut to build fancy filenames, such as hKeᵖ????©£.txt. The excluded characters are / : * ? " < > , | .

- **Mixed-case name storage.** Filenames in Windows 2000 are not case-sensitive, but the system retains the case and displays it to 32-bit clients. For example, if you save a file with the name `Multi-Case File Name.txt`, and then enter `dir multi*` at the command line, the name displays as `Multi-Case File Name.txt`.

- **Maximum filename and path lengths.** The maximum filename is 255 characters and so is the maximum path length because the directory records that index the filenames also use a single byte to define path length. For this reason, keep your directory names as short as possible, especially if you have deep structures.

Short Names and Long Names

If you have DOS or Windows 3.x clients on your network, your servers must build short names to correspond to long filenames created by 32-bit clients. Building a long name is not as straightforward as you might think. The system cannot simply take the first eight characters of the filename and the first three characters of the extension and call it a job well done. What if several files in the same directory start with the same letters?

NTFS uses two algorithms to generate short filenames. Both are based in part on the long filename to preserve the first few letters as a navigational aid. The algorithm changes if five or more files in the same directory start with the same letters. The first algorithm follows:

1. Delete all Unicode characters that do not map to standard ANSI characters.

2. Remove spaces, internal periods, and other illegal DOS characters. The name `Long.File.Name.Test` becomes `LongFileName.Test`.

3. Keep the first three characters after the last period as an extension. `LongFileName.Test` becomes `LongFileName.Tes`.

4. Drop all characters after the first six. `LongFileName.Tes` becomes `LongFi.Tes`.

5. Append a tilde (~) followed by a sequence numeral to the filename to prevent duplicate filenames. `LongFi.Tes` becomes `LongFi~1.Tes`.

6. Finally, convert the name to uppercase. The final short form of `Long.File.Name.Test` is `LONGFI~1.TES`.

The fifth and subsequent long files with the same first six letters are treated somewhat differently:

1. Drop Unicode characters, spaces, and extra periods (same process).

2. Keep the first three characters after the last period as an extension (same process).

3. Drop all characters after the first *two* instead of six. At this stage, `Long.File.Name.Test5` becomes `Lo.Tes`.

4. Append four hexadecimal numbers derived via an algorithm applied to the remaining characters in the long filename. `Long.File.Name.Test5` yields `D623` and `Long.File.Name.Test6` becomes `E623`. At this stage, the short name is `LoD623.Tes`.

5. Append a tilde (~) followed by a sequence numeral to the new filename just in case the algorithm comes up with duplicate names. `LoD623.Tes` becomes `LoD623~1.Tes`.

6. Finally, convert the name to uppercase. The final short form of `Long.File.Name.Test5` becomes `LOD623~1.TES`.

Cautions when Using Long Filenames

Long filenames have been around for years now, so I'm sure you are well aware of the standard pitfalls. Keep the following important items in mind.

- **Moving long-name files between machines.** The short name algorithm used by Windows 2000/NT, Windows 9x, and the two long namespaces on NetWare—LONGNAME.NAM for 4.1x and OS2.NAM for 3.x—all work differently.

- **Excessively long names slow performance.** It's a good idea to keep names shorter than 32 characters for optimal performance. Then, if a directory gets heavily fragmented, the short and long name attributes can get separated.

- **Use caution in batch files.** The CMD.EXE command interpreter in Windows 2000 does not act the same as COMMAND.COM. For example, using CMD, you do not need to enclose long names with quotes when changing directories. You can enter cd c:\dir one and go right to the directory. This is not standard for all commands, however. If you enter del dir one*, you'll delete every file starting with dir and every file starting with one.

- **Special handling for file extensions.** File extensions also affect the operation of wildcards. Consider Long.File.Name.Test1.htm and Long.File.Name.Test2.html as examples. If you go to the command prompt and do a directory listing for *.htm, you get both files in the list instead of just the htm file. This seems like a fairly innocuous bug, but what if you enter del *.htm, thinking to get rid of only old htm files. You also delete the html files, as well.

- **DOS applications delete long names.** If a DOS application changes a short name, the long name is deleted. For example, if a user changes the name LONGFI~1.TXT to HOLYMOLY.TXT using a DOS-based network client, the dir /x listing looks like this at the console of the server:

```
E:\DIR /XVolume in drive E is NTFS
Volume Serial Number is FC46-A70C
Directory of E:\

06/21/99  10:23p    21       HOLYMOLY.TXT

2 File(s)   21 bytes
0 Dir(s)    104,342,528 bytes free
```

Filtering Filename Extensions on Long Filenames

You can use a Registry entry to force the system to filter out long extensions when responding to command-line requests. This slows down file system response to command-line entries, so make the change only if you need it.

```
Key:    HKLM\SYSTEM\CurrentControlSet\Control\FileSystem
Value:  Win95TruncatedExtensions
Data:   0 (normally set to 1)
```

$Security_Descriptor

All NTFS records are Windows 2000 security objects. As such, they contain a security descriptor that defines who owns the object, who can or cannot access the object (the DACL), and who can or cannot audit the object (the SACL). In NTFS4, the $Security_Descriptor attribute starts off as resident, but can become nonresident if it gets too large.

In production, security descriptors can grow faster than a sumo wrestler on a rice farm. In classic NT, the big security descriptors become nonresident attributes that are scattered around the disk, degrading performance and increasing the time to propagate ACL changes.

In NTFS5, the $Security_Descriptor attributes are made nonresident by default. They are stored in a special MFT record called $Secure. Because the records are in a single location, multiple records can reference the same security descriptor. This improves performance when propagating ACL updates.

The $Secure record is a hybrid of a directory and a data record. The data attribute contains a named data stream called $SDS that holds the security descriptors. It also has two directory attributes, $SDH and $SII, one to index the descriptors and one to mirror the index.

Core metadata records retain their standard security descriptors. The bootstrap loader fails if it does not find a security descriptor for the record and it is too limited in function to handle the new $Secure folder.

$Secure Attributes and Inheritance Blocking

If ACL inheritance is turned off at some point in the directory tree, a new security descriptor is added, and you must make the appropriate change at that point in the directory if you want to grant rights further down the tree.

Even with centralized security descriptors, each MFT record is touched as ACL changes propagate down the tree, because the file system updates time stamps and change counters in the individual records. NTFS is tuned for this kind of work, though, and it happens quickly, with very little performance degradation.

If a file is moved from an NTFS4 volume on a classic NT machine to an NTFS5 volume on a Windows 2000 machine, the security descriptor accompanying the file is converted to the new format and moved to nonresident status. This also applies to classic NT files restored from tape to a Windows 2000 machine.

File Records and the $Data Attribute

Files are represented in the MFT by a record type that contains the three common attributes, $Standard_Information, $File_Name, and $Security_Descriptor, along with a fourth attribute called $Data. The $Data attribute contains a header portion that describes the location and size of the attribute and a data portion that contains the data itself.

It's unfortunate that the attribute name, $Data, and the thing the attribute contains, data, have the same name. I'll differentiate between them by referring to the attribute itself as $Data and the contents of the data portion of the attribute as small-d data.

The data portion of the $Data attribute can be modified by compression and encryption, as well as by being replaced completely by a reparse point. The data within the attribute is handled differently if it is set up as a special file type called a *sparse file*. These features are covered in specific sections later in this chapter. For now, let's concentrate on the format of a standard $Data attribute.

$Data Attribute Structure

All file records have at least one $Data attribute. If the data portion of the attribute is small enough—fewer than 500 bytes or so, depending on the length of the filename—it fits right into the MFT record. This listing for a $Data attribute shows where the data fits into the MFT record. The $Data attribute is type code 80 and is shown in bold. The listing includes the $Standard_Information and $File_Name attributes for context.

```
<<$Standard_Information attribute>>
46 49 4C 45 2A 00 03 00 1D 09 30 00 00 00 00 00 FILE*.....0.....
01 00 01 00 30 00 01 00 60 01 00 00 00 04 00 00 ....0...`.......
00 00 00 00 00 00 00 00 03 00 02 00 00 00 00 00 ...............
10 00 00 00 60 00 00 00 00 00 00 00 00 00 00 00 ....`..........
48 00 00 00 18 00 00 00 02 24 47 7C 31 BB BE 01 H........$G¦1...
02 24 47 7C 31 BB BE 01 02 24 47 7C 31 BB BE 01 .$G¦1....$G¦1...
02 24 47 7C 31 BB BE 01 20 00 00 00 00 00 00 00 .$G¦1... .......
00 00 00 00 00 00 00 00 00 00 00 00 02 01 00 00 ...............
00 00 00 00 00 00 00 00 00 00 00 00 00 00 00 00 ...............


<<$File_Name attribute>>
30 00 00 00 70 00 00 00 00 00 00 00 00 00 02 00 0...p..........
54 00 00 00 18 00 01 00 05 00 00 00 00 00 05 00 T..............
02 24 47 7C 31 BB BE 01 02 24 47 7C 31 BB BE 01 .$G¦1....$G¦1...
02 24 47 7C 31 BB BE 01 02 24 47 7C 31 BB BE 01 .$G¦1....$G¦1...
00 00 00 00 00 00 00 00 00 00 00 00 00 00 00 00 ...............
20 00 00 00 00 00 00 00 09 03 73 00 68 00 6F 00  .........s.h.o.
72 00 74 00 2E 00 74 00 78 00 74 00 00 00 00 00 r.t...t.x.t.....


<<$Data attribute with header portion shown in bold. Attribute has type code 80.>>
80 00 00 00 58 00 00 00 00 00 18 00 00 00 01 00 ....X...........
40 00 00 00 18 00 00 00 54 68 69 73 20 69 73 20 @.......This is
61 20 73 68 6F 72 74 20 66 69 6C 65 20 74 6F 20 a short file to
75 73 65 20 66 6F 72 20 61 20 73 61 6D 70 6C 65 use for a sample
20 6F 66 20 61 6E 20 4E 54 46 53 20 66 69 6C 65  of an NTFS file
20 65 6E 74 72 79 2E 20 FF FF FF FF 82 79 47 11  entry. .....yG.
```

The four FF FF FF FF entries followed by the double-word 11 47 79 82 (reversing the little-endian notation) at the end of the listing is the end-of-record notation in NTFS5, not part of the $Data attribute.

If the $Data attribute gets too big, it outgrows the 1K MFT record and the system moves the data portion out onto the hard drive. The header portion of the attribute stays resident along with a small piece of the data portion containing information about the nonresident portion and pointers to the nonresident data runs. This is what the resident header portion looks like after the data portion is made nonresident.

```
<<last part of $File_Name attribute, shown for context>>
20 00 00 00 00 00 00 00 0B 03 62 00 69 00 67 00  .........b.i.g.
66 00 69 00 6C 00 65 00 2E 00 74 00 78 00 74 00  f.i.l.e...t.x.t.

<<Resident header portion of non-resident $Data attribute. The bold section contains
information about the file and pointers to the non-resident data runs. This file has six
fragments.>>
80 00 00 00 50 00 00 00 01 00 00 00 00 00 03 00  ....P..........
00 00 00 00 00 00 00 00 5D 00 00 00 00 00 00 00  ........].......
40 00 00 00 00 00 00 00 00 BC 00 00 00 00 00 00 00  @..............
80 BB 00 00 00 00 00 00 80 BB 00 00 00 00 00 00  ..............
11 0A 16 21 02 F7 2F 11 0C 08 21 46 0C DA 00 FD  ...!../...!F....
FF FF FF FF 82 79 47 11 00 00 00 00 00 00 00 00  .....yG.........
```

The data portion of the listing contains the following information:

- **Number of Clusters.** 5D, or decimal 93. This is the total number of clusters containing the file, including any fragmented runs.

- **Reserved.** The next 4 bytes are reserved.

- **Size on Disk.** BC00, or decimal 48,128. This value includes the unused part of the final cluster, so it is always an even multiple of the cluster size.

- **File size.** BB80, or decimal 48,000 bytes. This value is what the UI and the command line report as the "file size."

- **Flags.** 00 00 00 40. Sets flags for features such as compression and encryption.

- **Location pointer.** Contains the following information in packed form: Logical Cluster Number of the start of the run, Virtual Cluster Number of the start of the run, and number of clusters in the run.

Over time, as users add more and more information to a file, it grows and becomes even more fragmented. This adds more pointers to the MFT record. If the number of pointer entries outgrows the 1K MFT record—as would happen if the file gets extremely fragmented—the system takes another MFT record to hold the additional pointers.

When the attributes are split between records, NTFS puts an $Attribute_List attribute in the first MFT record to track the additional MFT records and their mappings. This happens very rarely. In packed form, the pointer needs only 4 bytes, so a 1K MFT record can hold pointers to more than 200 runs. Under normal circumstances, you defrag the drive long before files get 200 fragments. But a volume can get so fragmented that you find several instances of a file record having an $Attribute_List attribute. If you don't believe me, talk to any consultant who tried to service a machine in production since the release of NT 3.51 without any defragging.

Multiple $Data Attributes

The default $Data attribute has no name. When an application issues an API call to read or write a file, NTFS delivers the contents of the unnamed $Data attribute. You can add more $Data attributes to a file record. These additional $Data attributes must have a name. The data portion of a $Data attribute is called a *stream*, so you will hear these named $Data attributes referred to as *named data streams*. An example of how named data streams work follows:

1. Build a file named `Superman.txt` by echoing a few characters from the command prompt as follows:

```
C:\>echo It's a bird. > Superman.txt
```

This creates an MFT record for a file named `Superman.txt` with an unnamed data attribute that contains the characters `It's a bird`. This is a listing of the unnamed $Data attribute.

```
<<Last part of $File_Name attribute, shown for context>>
20 00 00 00 00 00 00 00 0C 03 53 00 75 00 70 00   .........S.u.p.
65 00 72 00 6D 00 61 00 6E 00 2E 00 74 00 78 00   e.r.m.a.n...t.x.
74 00 00 00 00 00 00 00                           t.......

<<Unnamed $Data attribute with data portion shown in bold.>>
                        80 00 00 00 28 00 00 00         ....(...
00 00 18 00 00 00 01 00 0F 00 00 00 18 00 00 00   ................
49 74 27 73 20 61 20 62 69 72 64 2E 20 0D 0A 00   It's a bird. ...
FF FF FF FF 82 79 47 11 00 00 00 00 00 00 00 00   .....yG.........
```

2. Add a second data attribute by echoing different text to a named stream as follows:

```
C:\>echo It's a plane. > superman.txt:stream1
```

3. Now add a third data attribute with a different data stream name:

```
C:\>echo It's SUPERMAN. > superman.txt:stream2
```

This listing of the file record shows the three $Data attributes. Look for the three Type 80 attributes. The first named attribute is in bold and the second is in italic.

```
<<Last part of $File_Name attribute, shown for context>>
20 00 00 00 00 00 00 00 0C 03 53 00 75 00 70 00  .........S.u.p.
65 00 72 00 6D 00 61 00 6E 00 2E 00 74 00 78 00  e.r.m.a.n...t.x.
74 00 00 00 00 00 00 00                           t.......

<<Unnamed $Data attribute>>
                        80 00 00 00 28 00 00 00      ....(...
00 00 18 00 00 00 01 00 0F 00 00 00 18 00 00 00  ................
49 74 27 73 20 61 20 62 69 72 64 2E 20 0D 0A 00  It's a bird. ...

<<First named $Data attribute with name, stream1, shown in bold.>>
80 00 00 00 38 00 00 00 00 07 18 00 00 00 03 00  ....8..........
10 00 00 00 28 00 00 00 73 00 74 00 72 00 65 00  ....(...s.t.r.e.
61 00 6D 00 31 00 00 00 49 74 27 73 20 61 20 70  a.m.1...It's a p
6C 61 6E 65 2E 20 0D 0A                           lane. ..

<<Second named $Data attribute with name, stream2, shown in bold.>>
                        80 00 00 00 40 00 00 00      ....@...
00 07 18 00 00 00 04 00 11 00 00 00 28 00 00 00  ............(...
73 00 74 00 72 00 65 00 61 00 6D 00 32 00 00 00  s.t.r.e.a.m.2...
49 74 27 73 20 53 55 50 45 52 4D 41 4E 2E 20 0D  It's SUPERMAN. .
0A 00 00 00 00 00 00 00 FF FF FF FF 82 79 47 11  ............yG.
```

Very few applications support named streams. The simplest way to view the contents of this file is by piping the various named streams through the MORE command as follows:

```
C:\>more < superman.txt
It's a bird.

C:\>more < superman.txt:stream1
It's a plane.

C:\>more < superman.txt: stream2
It's SUPERMAN.
```

At first glance, you would think that named data streams are enabling tech-nology for lots of new and innovative applications. This is what Microsoft thought, too. In point of fact, though, only one program has ever made sig-nificant use of data streams, and that is Microsoft's own *Services for Macintosh* (SFM). An SFM volume uses streams to support dual-fork Macintosh files.

Summary Information Database and Data Streams

A new feature in Windows 2000 uses named data streams in a slightly less ambitious way than SFM. You may notice when you open the `Properties` window for files that a `Summary` tab is behind the `Security` tab. Figure 13.2 shows an example.

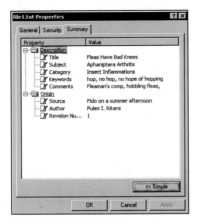

Figure 13.2   Summary information tab from typical file.

When you make entries into the Summary fields, the information is saved as a series of named $Data streams in the file record. This listing shows the unnamed $Data attributes for Summary Information. This is a long listing because the stream names are long.

```
<<unnamed $Data attribute>>
00000000 80000000 48000000 00001800 00000100 ....H..........
00000016 2D000000 18000000 54657874 206F6620 ·.......Text of
00000032 66696C65 3120696E 20746865 20756E6E file1 in the unn
00000048 616D6564 20244461 74612061 74747269 amed $Data attri
00000064 62757465 2E000000              bute....
```

<<First named $Data attribute, DocumentSummaryInformation. The bold number near the end of the attribute is the pointer to the non-resident portion.>>

```
                               80000000 80000000            ........
00000080 011B4000 00000D00 00000000 00000000  ..@.............
00000096 00000000 00000000 78000000 00000000  ........x.......
00000112 00020000 00000000 9C000000 00000000  ...............
00000128 9C000000 00000000 05004400 6F006300  .........D.o.c.
00000144 75006D00 65006E00 74005300 75006D00  u.m.e.n.t.S.u.m.
00000160 6D006100 72007900 49006E00 66006F00  m.a.r.y.I.n.f.o.
00000176 72006D00 61007400 69006F00 6E000000  r.m.a.t.i.o.n...
00000192 11011F00 1F000000            .........
```

<<Second named $Data attribute. This one is a standard marker used for all summary information entries. It is an acronym for a Windows development engineer.>>
```
                               80000000 80000000            ......
00000208 011B4000 00000700 00000000 00000000  ..@.............
00000224 00000000 00000000 78000000 00000000  ........x.......
00000240 00020000 00000000 A8000000 00000000  ...............
00000256 A8000000 00000000 05005300 65006200  .........S.e.b.
00000272 69006500 73006E00 72004D00 6B007500  i.e.s.n.r.M.k.u.
00000288 64007200 66006300 6F004900 61006100  d.r.f.c.o.I.a.a.
00000304 6D007400 79006B00 64004400 61000000  m.t.y.k.d.D.a...
00000320 21010E30 00300000            !..0.0
```

<<Another named $Data attribute. This one contains the GUID (also called the Class ID, or CLSID) for the file. This helps track the file if it is copied to another location.>>
```
                               80000000 68000000            h...
00000448 00261800 00000300 00000000 68000000  .&..........h...
00000464 7B003400 63003800 63006300 31003500  {.4.c.8.c.c.1.5.
00000480 35002D00 36006300 31006500 2D003100  5.-.6.c.1.e.-.1.
00000496 31006400 31002D00 38006500 34003100  1.d.1.-.8.e.4.1.
00000512 2D003000 30006300 30003400 66006200  -.0.0.c.0.4.f.b.
00000528 39003300 38003600 64007D00 00000000  9.3.8.6.d.}.....
00000544 FFFFFFFF 82794711            .....yG.
```

The nonresident portion of each named stream is stored in special buffers that are indexed by the Summary Information Database. These buffers are prefixed by 2 bytes, FEFF, if you are scanning the disk with a hex editor. The following is a listing for a buffer:

```
<<Summary Information buffer showing an items entered in a Summary window.>>
FEFF0000 05000200 00000000 00000000 ................
00000000 00000000 01000000 02D5CDD5 ................
9C2E1B10 93970800 2B2CF9AE 30000000 ........+,..0...
6C000000 03000000 01000000 28000000 l..........(...
00000080 30000000 02000000 38000000 ....0.......8...
00000000 00000000 02000000 B0040000 ................
13000000 09040000 1E000000 2A000000 ............*...
49006E00 73006500 63007400 20004900 I.n.s.e.c.t. .I.
6E006600 6C006100 6D006D00 61007400 n.f.l.a.m.m.a.t.
69006F00 6E007300 00000000 00000000 i.o.n.s........
```

The Summary entries for one file become pick list items for all other files thanks to the Summary Information Database. For example, let's say a user works all night on an Excel spreadsheet. After closing the file, he opens the PROPERTIES | SUMMARY window and makes an entry in the Category field like this: *Miserable Stinking Report for a Miserable Stinking Boss.* This entry now appears in the Category drop-down on all files accessed from that workstation by that user.

The Summary Information Database controls access to entries based on the user's GUID, not the ACLs for the associated files. The "Stinking Boss" category that is applied to a particular file is visible to other users with access to the file, but the "Stinking Boss" pick list item appears only for the originating user.

If you copy a file containing summary information to a classic NT server, the named streams containing the summary information are also copied. They are visible to Windows 2000 clients who access the files, but they are not visible from NT4, because the UI is not coded to recognize them.

Other, more ambitious, attempts to use named data streams foundered because of interoperability problems. For example, a Windows 2000 feature that didn't quite make it through beta testing was called *Native Structure Storage* (NSS). This feature used named data streams in combination with reparse points (a way to redirect the file to another point in a file system—see the section by the same name a little later in this chapter) to store compound documents from Microsoft Office.

Unfortunately, when an NSS document was moved to a platform that did not support streams and reparse points, including classic NT servers, the data disappeared. There were so many cries of protest from beta testers that NSS was dropped from the product. The lesson from that experience is clear. If you have mixed operating environments with different file systems, don't use features that are not transportable.

Data Streams and Internet Security

Data streams got some attention in early 1999 because of a security hole associated with IIS. Using this hole, it was possible to expose the underlying data inside an ASP or CGI script rather than simply running the script. You did this by entering the URL of the script and then specifying the $DATA attribute at the end of the address, such as `http://www.anyserver.com/somescript.asp::$DATA`.

Seeing the contents of a script, rather than executing the script itself, is not something many Webmasters appreciate. This wasn't much of a "hole" as security breaches go, because the user must have Read access to the directory holding the scripts, which is not a normal configuration. The hole was patched in SP4 and remains patched in Windows 2000.

Before continuing on to the other MFT attributes, let's look at two special features associated with the $Data attribute: compression and sparse file support. File encryption also affects $Data attributes, but that subject is covered in Chapter 14.

File Compression

As the saying goes, when it comes to disk storage, you can never have too much and it can never be too fast. Even in an era when 50GB fast-wide SCSI drives with more on-board intelligence than Apollo carried to the moon can be had for less than two grand, many times new storage is not easy to come by or to incorporate into a production system. And besides, who wants to spend a precious weekend rebuilding a RAID cage and babysitting the data transfer from tape just because users want to save five years worth of email with graphics attachments?

On the server side, compression is not the answer to storage problems, by any means, but it can help pull you out of a scrape until you can get new storage online and available. For workstations, compression is a more viable alternative. It can save you the money and hassle of deploying new disks to older machines. Of course, you probably had to deploy new disks just to hold the system files for Windows 2000 Professional, but it's the principle that counts.

Functional Description of File Compression

NTFS can compress one individual file, all files in a directory, or all files on a volume. The compression algorithm balances speed and disk storage. For example, the algorithm in Windows 9x DriveSpace scans every 2 bytes looking for a match. NTFS scans every 3 bytes. This is a little less aggressive, but much faster. Also, the NTFS compression algorithm works on 16-cluster pieces at a time rather than scanning and compressing an entire run. This enables the system to analyze stretches of data to see if they are even worth compressing.

Compression is set by means of a bit in the file header. When the bit is set, the system compresses the file when it is saved and decompresses the file on the fly to read it. Directories have a compression bit, as well. When this bit is set, all files created in that directory have their compression bit set. Thus, new files created or copied to this directory are compressed. Existing files are not compressed unless a special option is selected in the UI.

An additional flag in the $Data attribute header indicates the manner of compression used. This makes it possible to define new compression algorithms at some future date. Details about the inner workings of the compression algorithm used in Windows 2000 are beyond the scope of this book. I recommend the NTFS chapters of *Inside Windows NT* by David Solomon (Microsoft Press; ISBN: 1572316772) for more information.

Enabling Compression

No controls are available in the UI or Registry hacks to change the compression mechanism. The only setting is to turn the compression bit on or off. This can be done using Explorer or a command-line utility called COMPACT. Let's look at Explorer first.

Procedure 13.1 **Enabling Compression**

1. Open Explorer or My Computer and navigate to the file or directory.
2. Right-click the icon and select PROPERTIES from the fly-out menu. The Properties window opens. See Figure 13.3.

Figure 13.3   Properties window showing information about a big file in an uncompressed state.

3. In the Attributes field, click Advanced. The Advanced Attributes window opens. This window controls the various attribute bits in the MFT record. See the sidebar titled "Using Advanced File Attributes" for more information.

Figure 13.4   Advanced Attributes window showing status of file attributes, such as compression and encryption.

Using Advanced File Attributes

The Advanced Attributes window for a file or folder, as shown in Figure 13.4, has several options that affect file storage. This is what they do:

- The Archive bit comes from classic NT and DOS. It signals that the file was changed but not backed up.

- The Index bit is new to Windows 2000 and indicates that the *Content Index Service*, (CISVC), should scan the file. This service began life as an add-on indexer for Internet Information Server and has now burrowed its way into the operating system. Fortunately, this option is turned off by default.

- The Compress attribute causes the system to compress the file.

- The Encrypt attribute causes the system to encrypt the file.

The Compress and Encrypt attributes are mutually exclusive. This happens for two reasons.

- Encrypted files have very few similar characters, so Microsoft does not consider them good candidates for compression.

- The system cannot restore compressed encrypted files from tape. The Restore process recovers a compressed file from tape by reading the header to find the starting cluster on the drive where the file was originally located. The Restore process, running in the context of a Backup Operator, cannot read the encrypted file to find the destination cluster.

4. Select Compress Contents to save disk space, and then click OK to save the change and close the window.

5. Click OK to apply the change and close the Properties window. Depending on the size of the file, it may take a while to compress.

6. Close the Properties window, and then open it again. The Size on Disk value shows you the new compressed size.

Compressing Files Using the Compact Utility

If you prefer command-line tools, use the Compact utility to compress and decompress files. To set the compression bit, run compact /c. To reset the bit, run compact /u.

If you want to set the compression bit on a directory and compress all the files in that directory and its subdirectories, run compact /c /s.

To list files and their compression information, run compact with no switches. For example, this is a list of the standard BMP files that come with Windows 2000 in their compressed state:

```
C:\TestDir\compact
 Listing C:\TestDir\
 New files added to this directory will not be compressed.

    1272 :      1024 = 1.2 to 1 C Blue Lace 16.bmp
   17062 :     17062 = 1.0 to 1 C Coffee Bean.bmp
```

```
16730 :     15872 = 1.1 to 1 C FeatherTexture.bmp
17336 :     13312 = 1.3 to 1 C Gone Fishing.bmp
```

```
Of 4 files within 1 directories
4 are compressed and 0 are not compressed.
46,310 total bytes of data are stored in 32,430 bytes.
The compression ratio is 1.2 to 1.
```

Compression and Performance

Compression exacts a significant performance penalty on file and print servers. Microsoft publishes numbers ranging from a 5% to 15% reduction in end-to-end data transfer times. My own experience points to much higher throughput degradation.

Exact numbers are difficult to quantify because busy production servers have hundreds of connected users doing who-knows-what with applications, personal databases, and data files from 1000 different vendors, and so on and so forth. Imposing compression on this mishmash generally makes you unpopular. Compressing personal files on a server makes better use of the feature than wholesale compression. Because users can compress their own files, take this into account when moving data.

File Compression Highlights

Working with compressed files in a production environment can result in some surprises. Keep these general operational guidelines in mind:

- Setting the compression bit on a directory affects files created in that directory only.

- The compression bit is in the header of the $Data attribute, not in the data itself. Any operation that creates a new file inherits the compression bit setting from the parent directory. *Copying* a file creates a new $Data attribute, so a copied file inherits the compression setting of its new directory. *Moving* a file retains the $Data attribute, so a moved file retains its compression bit setting regardless of the setting of its new directory.

- When moving a file between NTFS volumes, a new file is created. The compression setting is inherited from the new folder.

- The same compression algorithm is used in NTFS4 and NTFS5. If you dual-boot and choose to leave a volume formatted with NTFS4, the compressed files on it are visible from Windows 2000.

- DriveSpace compression is not compatible with NTFS compression. Windows 2000 cannot read DriveSpace volumes. If a file is moved over the network from a Windows 9x DriveSpace volume to a Windows 2000 NTFS directory, it inherits the compression bit from the parent directory.

- When copying or moving files, the file always decompresses first, even if it is going to a compressed directory. Backup programs use standard file system API calls to open files; therefore, files are decompressed as they go to tape. This avoids compatibility problems with tape systems that do compression in hardware or software, but it also slows backup performance.

- Compressed files retain their compressed bit while on tape. When they are restored, they are recompressed regardless of the compression setting of the parent directory.

- Restoring compressed files can be a challenge. The file comes off the tape in uncompressed form. It takes the system a finite period of time to compress the file. If the volume has limited free space, the restore may fail because the system can't shoehorn the files onto the volume fast enough to keep up with the tape unit. The only way around this problem is to restore to a location with lots of disk space and then copy the files manually.

- Be careful of the disk statistics reported by Explorer. The list of files in a directory shows the compressed files in blue (if you enabled this feature in Folder Properties), but the file size parameter is the uncompressed size, not the compressed size.

- Compressed volumes can become heavily fragmented. The Disk Defragmenter does a poor job of defragging compressed volumes, so it's common to see administrators resolve fragmentation problems on compressed volumes by purchasing new storage and restoring from tape.

Sparse Files

Database and imaging applications typically allocate large amounts of disk space that they don't necessarily fill right away. The new SDK that accompanies Windows 2000 has a special set of API calls that build structures called *sparse files*. A sparse file specifies a certain size for itself, but does not actually claim the disk space until the file begins to fill up. Because sparse files are handled at the application level, the disk savings come with no performance penalty, as there is with regular file compression.

You cannot create a sparse file simply by filling a text file with 0s. Nor do you necessarily get a sparse file when you build huge databases with lots of wasted space in the records. Sparse files require special API calls in the application. Because this feature is new to Windows 2000, it will probably be a while before applications take advantage of them. The most significant application that uses sparse files in Windows 2000 is the Content Indexer, which stores its catalog information in sparse format.

No settings or Registry hacks are available for sparse file handling, making this the most transparent feature in NTFS5. One of the ways sparse files come to light is with quotas. If you impose quotas on users, the allocated disk space in the sparse file counts against the user's quota, even though the file size might report something much smaller than the quota setting. This might cause users to squawk, especially if you charge for storage by the megabyte.

You can try explaining to the user the nature of sparse file handling and the special qualities of the file. You can also bump up the user's quota because you know that the sparse file is not actually taking up space. Watch out, though. Today's sparse file is tomorrow's 300MB monster.

Directory Records

A database needs an index to speed lookups. All file systems supported by Windows 2000—and just about any general-purpose file system, for that matter—index the database by filename. NTFS keeps this index in a record type called a *directory*. This record contains the common attributes as a file record, but instead of a $Data attribute, it contains three special attributes used to list, sort, and locate files and subdirectories. These attributes are $Index_Root, $Index_Allocation, and $Bitmap.

$Index_Root

The $Index_Root attribute holds a copy of the $File_Name attribute from all files and subdirectories. Don't confuse the $Index_Root attribute with the "Root" directory, $\. The "Root" directory is a special instance of a directory record type. The directory is located with the other critical metadata records in the MFT so that the bootstrap loader can find it without groping around.

Consider a directory, \Dir_One, which holds a file called FILE_1.TXT. The $\ metadata record—the "Root" directory—has an $Index_Root attribute containing a copy of the $File_Name attribute for the Dir_One directory.

The MFT record for `Dir_One` has an $Index_Root attribute containing a copy of the $File_Name attribute for FILE_1.TXT. Each $File_Name attribute has an entry indicating the MFT sequence number of its parent directory. The system uses this information to keep the directory structure internally consistent.

Structure of the $Index_Root Attribute

The following is an MFT record listing for the `Dir_One` directory showing the $Index_Root attribute.

```
<<last part of the $File_Name attribute shown for context.>>
00 00 00 10 00 00 00 00 07 03 44 00 69 00 72 00 ..........D.i.r.
5F 00 4F 00 6E 00 65 00                          _.O.n.e.

<<$Index_Root attribute, type code 90. The heading, shown in bold, identifies the name of
the attribute stream, $I30. This attribute contains the File_1.txt entry also shown in
bold.>>
                        90 00 00 00 B8 00 00 00          ........
00 04 18 00 00 00 01 00 98 00 00 00 20 00 00 00 ............ ...
24 00 49 00 33 00 30 00 30 00 00 00 01 00 00 00 $.I.3.0.0.......
00 10 00 00 08 00 00 00 10 00 00 00 88 00 00 00 ...............
88 00 00 00 00 00 00 00 1C 00 00 00 00 00 01 00 ...............
68 00 56 00 00 00 00 00 1B 00 00 00 00 00 01 00 h.V...........
18 62 25 BF 5C C0 BE 01 18 62 25 BF 5C C0 BE 01 .b%.\....b%.\...
18 62 25 BF 5C C0 BE 01 18 62 25 BF 5C C0 BE 01 .b%.\....b%.\...
10 00 00 00 00 00 00 00 10 00 00 00 00 00 00 00 ...............
20 00 00 00 00 00 00 00 0A 03 46 00 69 00 6C 00 .........F.i.l.
65 00 5F 00 31 00 2E 00 74 00 78 00 74 00 00 00 e._.1...t.x.t...
00 00 00 00 00 00 00 00 10 00 00 00 02 00 00 00 ...............
FF FF FF FF 82 79 47 11 00 00 00 00 00 00 00 00 .....yG.........
```

The data portion of the $Index_Root attribute—don't confuse this with the $Data attribute—is always a named stream. It carries the name $I30. The data portion of the attribute contains a copy of the $File_Name attribute from FILE_1.TXT.

The underlined number at the start of the filename listing is the MFT sequence number of the `Dir_One` directory. The system uses this entry to check internal consistency. If the file had a long name, both the long and short name attributes would be included in the directory record. Duplicating these attributes from every file and subdirectory imposes a small cost in disk I/O, but significantly improves directory lookup performance.

Nonresident $Index_Root Attributes and B-Tree Sorting

For small directories, such as the one in the previous example, the $Index_Root attribute is resident because the filename entries can fit in a single MFT record. If a directory has more than about five entries—fewer if they have long filenames—the system moves the data portion of the $Index_Root attribute out onto the disk. Rather than use long runs of various lengths that can get highly fragmented, the system uses fixed-length *index buffers*, 4KB apiece, to store the nonresident portions of the $Index_Root attribute.

Depending on the length of the filenames, each 4K buffer can hold about 20 to 40 entries. This listing shows index buffer entries for files named 100.txt, 101.txt, and so forth.

```
<<Start of index buffer for non-resident portion of $Index_Root attribute.>>
49 4E 44 58 28 00 09 00 88 6B 10 00 00 00 00 00 INDX(....k......
00 00 00 00 00 00 00 00 28 00 00 00 B8 07 00 00 ........(.......
E8 0F 00 00 00 00 00 00 02 00 00 00 74 00 BE 01 ............t...
00 00 74 00 BE 01 00 00 00 00 00 00 00 00 00 00 ..t.............

<<File name entry. Portion in bold is the MFT sequence of the file record. Underlined
portion is the MFT sequence number of the file's parent directory.>>
1D 00 00 00 00 00 01 00 60 00 50 00 00 00 00 00 ........`.P.....
1B 00 00 00 00 00 01 00 CA 39 60 57 E9 BD BE 01 .........9`W....
42 C7 66 55 E9 BD BE 01 CA 39 60 57 E9 BD BE 01 B.fU.....9`W....
CA 39 60 57 E9 BD BE 01 10 00 00 00 00 00 00 00 .9`W............
0B 00 00 00 00 00 00 00 20 00 00 00 00 00 00 00 ........ .......
07 03 31 00 30 00 30 00 2E 00 74 00 78 00 74 00 ..1.0.0...t.x.t.

<<Second name entry. Note that this file was created right after the 100.txt file because it
has the next MFT sequence number.>>
1E 00 00 00 00 00 01 00 60 00 50 00 00 00 00 00 ........`.P.....
1B 00 00 00 00 00 01 00 24 9C 62 57 E9 BD BE 01 ........$.bW....
42 C7 66 55 E9 BD BE 01 24 9C 62 57 E9 BD BE 01 B.fU....$.bW....
24 9C 62 57 E9 BD BE 01 10 00 00 00 00 00 00 00 $.bW............
0B 00 00 00 00 00 00 00 20 00 00 00 00 00 00 00 ........ .......
07 03 31 00 30 00 31 00 2E 00 74 00 78 00 74 00 ..1.0.1...t.x.t.
```

The resident portion of the $Index_Root attribute contains pointers to the nonresident index buffers. The pointers act as nodes in a b-tree structure. Figure 13.5 shows a b-tree for a shallow directory structure. A b-tree lookup doesn't take much work on the part of the file system. Is the file lexicographically less than 120.txt? Go left. Otherwise, go right.

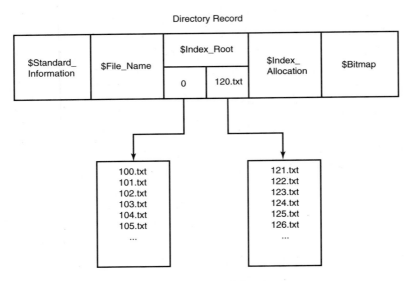

Figure 13.5 Directory record showing b-tree entries and two nonresident index buffers.

The decision of where to proceed at a b-tree node need not be a binary one. The number of index points in the $Index_Root attribute can grow as the number of entries increases. When an index buffer fills, the system copies the last half of its entries to a new buffer and puts the first filename of the run in the $Index_Root attribute as a pointer and b-tree index. This is a listing of the resident portion of the $Index_Root attribute for Dir_One.

```
<<Excerpt of $Index_Root attribute showing two b-tree nodes, 0 and 120.txt (bold). The $I30
is the name of the $Index_Root attribute. A standard directory has only one $Index_Root
attribute, but it could have more.>>
24 00 49 00 33 00 30 00  30 00 00 00 01 00 00 00   $.I.3.0.0.......
00 10 00 00 08 00 00 00  10 00 00 00 F8 00 00 00   ................
F8 00 00 00 01 00 00 00  33 00 00 00 00 00 01 00   ........3.......
68 00 50 00 01 00 00 00  1C 00 00 00 00 00 01 00   h.P.............
FC D8 FC 70 EE BD BE 01  A2 A5 35 99 ED BD BE 01   ...p......5.....
FC D8 FC 70 EE BD BE 01  FC D8 FC 70 EE BD BE 01   ...p.......p....
10 00 00 00 00 00 00 00  09 00 00 00 00 00 00 00   ................
20 00 00 00 00 00 00 00  07 03 31 00 32 00 30 00   .........1.2.0.
2E 00 74 00 78 00 74 00  00 00 00 00 00 00 00 00   ..t.x.t.........
48 00 00 00 00 00 01 00  68 00 50 00 01 00 00 00   H.......h.P.....
1C 00 00 00 00 00 01 00  16 91 8A 5B EF BD BE 01   ...........[....
A2 A5 35 99 ED BD BE 01  16 91 8A 5B EF BD BE 01   ..5........[....
16 91 8A 5B EF BD BE 01  10 00 00 00 00 00 00 00   ...[............
09 00 00 00 00 00 00 00  20 00 00 00 00 00 00 00   ........ .......
```

An index structure using b-tree is self-maintaining. Let's say a new file named 1000.txt is added to the Dir_One directory. Its filename entry goes into the first index buffer, because 1000.txt is smaller in an alphanumeric sense than 120.txt. The entry is inserted after 100.txt and before 101.txt. If a whole slew of 1000-series files are added to Dir_One, additional buffers are created with index entries added to the resident portion of $Index_Root. For example, the new index points might be **1020.txt, 1040.txt,** and **120.txt**.

As more files are added to a directory, more buffers are added to the disk with more pointers in the $Index_Root attribute. At some point, the pointers exceed the capacity of the MFT record. The system then moves the pointers out onto the disk into two INDX buffers and leaves behind another set of pointers. Essentially, this reindexes the b-tree without any additional housekeeping. Figure 13.6 shows how this new b-tree looks. This process can continue indefinitely. If the number of nonresident directory pointers gets too big for a single 4KB index buffer, the system creates another set of buffers and puts another pointer in the MFT record.

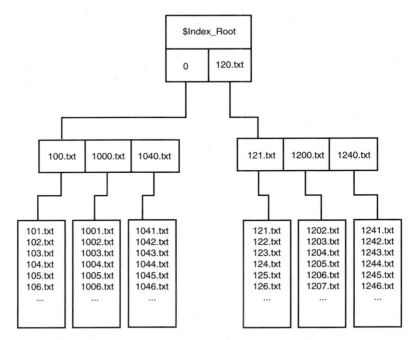

Figure 13.6 More complex b-tree with secondary indexing.

Separate Indexing for Short and Long Filename Attributes

Long filenames add complexity to this indexing scheme. The $Index_Root attribute sorts filename entries alphanumerically without distinguishing between short names and long names. For example, if you have three long names, such as Twilight of the Gods.txt, Twilight Double-Header.txt, and Twilight Zone.txt in the same directory, the short names TWILIG~1, TWILIG~2, and TWILIG~3 sort to the top of the filename list. If you have many, many long filenames starting with the same few letters, you are seriously degrading performance by forcing the system to do a full scan of all the index buffers looking for corresponding short names.

Disabling 8.3 Filename Creation

You can eliminate the performance problems caused by short names by disabling 8.3 name creation. This also reduces the disk space used to store index buffers. Do this only if you have no DOS/Win3.x clients. Use the following Registry entry:

```
Key:    HKLM\SYSTEM\CurrentControlSet\Control\FileSystem
Value:  NTFSDisable8dot3NameCreation
Data:   0
```

$Index_Allocation and $Bitmap

When the system makes a portion of the $Index_Root attribute nonresident, it adds two more attributes to the directory record to improve performance. One is the $Index_Allocation attribute. This attribute contains a count of the total number of index buffers used by the directory. (It actually stores a byte count, but index buffers come in fixed sizes, so it's the same thing.) It also stores a mapping between the Virtual Cluster Numbers in the buffers to the Logical Cluster Number of the buffer locations.

The $Bitmap attribute helps the file system to find a specific byte in a file, thereby dramatically improving performance for lookups in random-access files such as databases, word processing, and image processing. The other additional attribute is called $Bitmap. This attribute keeps a map of the unused space in the buffers so that the system knows whether it needs another buffer without scanning the entries. Both attributes must stay resident in the directory record. A listing follows.

```
<<Index_Allocation attribute, type code A0. Bold numbers are LCN-to-VCN mappings>>
A0 00 00 00 50 00 00 00 01 04 40 00 00 00 03 00   ....P.....@.....
00 00 00 00 00 00 00 00 27 00 00 00 00 00 00 00   ........'.......
48 00 00 00 00 00 00 00 00 50 00 00 00 00 00 00   H........P......
00 50 00 00 00 00 00 00 00 50 00 00 00 00 00 00   .P.......P......
24 00 49 00 33 00 30 00 **11 0A 16 21 1E F1 2F 00** $.I.3.0....!../.
```

<<$Bitmap attribute, type code B0. Bold numbers are the bitmap.>>
```
B0 00 00 00 28 00 00 00 00 04 18 00 00 00 04 00   ....(...........
08 00 00 00 20 00 00 00 24 00 49 00 33 00 30 00   .... ...$.I.3.0.
1F 00 00 00 00 00 00 00            ........
```

Remember that these two attributes are present only when the data portion of the $Index_Root attribute is moved out onto the disk. They are present to improve performance and ensure data consistency.

Directory Attributes Highlights

Remember the following key points regarding the contents and structure of an MFT directory record:

- Directories store an index of filename attributes for files and subdirectories.
- Short-name and long-name attributes are separately indexed.
- Each file and directory record has an entry indicating the MFT record of the directory that indexes it.
- Directory records contain small cluster maps to speed lookups for individual bytes in random-access files.
- Directory entries use a b-tree structure to sort filenames. This significantly improves lookup performance.
- Directory records can become fragmented, forcing the file system to do a separate disk lookup to find a file.

Additional Metadata Record Descriptions

We need to take a quick look at a few additional metadata records. They are $MFT, $Bitmap, $MFTMirr, $BadClus, and $Volume.

$MFT and $Bitmap

The MFT is a self-referential database. It contains within the database all the information needed to access the database. An external data dictionary or Schema is unnecessary. This means that the MFT itself is a file and requires a record in the MFT. This is the function of the $MFT record. The $Bitmap record holds a map of the free and used clusters on the disk, much the same as FAT, but with 1 bit per cluster rather than 2 or 4 bytes. The $Bitmap serves the same purpose as a tote board. It lets the pit boss know who's where and what they're playing.

The $MFT record should be in a specific spot because the secondary bootstrap loader, Ntldr, must be able to find it. The bootstrap loader finds the MFT by reading the location entry in the boot sector.

The key points to remember about the $MFT record are as follows:

- The $MFT contains all the files necessary to read the $MFT files.

- The $MFT holds a bitmap that describes the structure of the file table. This improves performance.

- The $MFT must be in a specific location as indicated in the boot sector so that the secondary bootstrap loader, Ntldr, can find it.

$MFTMirr

During restart following a system crash, the bootstrap loader must be able to find the first MFT record so that it can load the metadata records at the start of the MFT and initialize the file system. If the first MFT record is damaged or otherwise unreadable, the bootstrap loader must take steps to recover the file system. For this reason, copies of critical metadata records are mirrored at the middle of the volume. The $MFTMirr metadata record contains the Logical Cluster Number of the remaining MFT records.

The key points to remember about the $MFTMirr attribute are as follows:

- The mirror does not contain all the MFT records, only the critical metadata records.

- The mirror is placed at the middle of the volume.

- The secondary bootstrap loader can find the mirror, if necessary, using a locator in the boot sector.

$BadClus

When NTFS is unable to read a cluster, its first action is to wait for the SCSI driver to make a spare sector available via sector sparing. If the file system is using an IDE drive, or if no sectors are available in the spare area on disk, NTFS takes over and moves the data to a spare sector within the mounted volume. The cluster containing the bad sector is marked as bad by entering the LCN in the $BadClus database. Each of these entries takes the form of a named data stream. In essence, the system assigns a file to the bad sector so that no other file can use it.

The key points to remember about the $BadClus attribute are as follows:

- NTFS marks bad clusters independently of the drive subsystem.
- The $BadClus record contains the Bad Cluster database.
- NTFS uses its own form of sector sparing if hardware sparing is not available.

$Volume Record and Volume Attributes

The $Volume record stores information about the NTFS volume. The record has a fixed location in relation to the start of the MFT so that the bootstrap loader can find it. The $Volume record contains two special attributes: $Volume_Name and $Volume_Information. A third attribute used by NTFS4, $Volume_Version, was dropped in NTFS5 and its entries were incorporated into $Volume_Information.

This listing for a volume named Windows 2000 Volume shows the entries in the two attributes.

```
<<$Volume_Name attribute, code type 60, with the data portion containing the volume
name in bold. The data portion is limited to 32 Unicode characters, or 64 bytes.>>
60 00 00 00 40 00 00 00 00 00 18 00 00 00 04 00  `...@..........
28 00 00 00 18 00 00 00 57 00 69 00 6E 00 64 00  (.......W.i.n.d.
6F 00 77 00 73 00 20 00 32 00 30 00 30 00 30 00  o.w.s. .2.0.0.0.
20 00 56 00 6F 00 6C 00 75 00 6D 00 65 00 20 00   .V.o.l.u.m.e. .

<<$Volume_Information attribute, code type 70, showing the entry for NTFS5 in bold.
There is also a "dirty" flag, not currently set, that would initiate a volume
scan at boot time.>>
70 00 00 00 28 00 00 00 00 00 18 00 00 00 05 00  p...(..........
0C 00 00 00 18 00 00 00 00 00 00 00 00 00 00 00  ................
03 00 00 00 00 00 00 00                          ........
```

At first glance, 00 00 00 03 does not look like a version number for NTFS5. Actually, it is the combination of 03 in the data portion of the attribute and the 05 00 flag in the header that indicates NTFS5.

The key points to remember about the $Volume record and its attributes are as follows:

- The $Volume record is where the NTFS version is stored.
- The volume name is limited to 32 characters.
- The volume can be flagged as "dirty," forcing Autochk to run at boot time.

Converting from FAT and FAT32 to NTFS

You can convert a FAT or FAT32 partition or volume to NTFS, but you cannot do the reverse. The only way to go back is to reformat and restore the data from tape. You should always do a backup before converting, because the system may become unstable or refuse to restart.

Conversion uses a command-line utility, Convert. The syntax is:

```
convert volume_name /fs:ntfs
```

You can specify a volume name, drive letter, or mount point. If you specify a drive letter, you are prompted for the volume name just to verify that you have the right volume. Run VOL if you need to verify the volume name.

The default cluster size is 512 bytes to make the most effective use of the volume during conversion. You cannot change the cluster size later without reformatting the volume.

The system must be able to get an exclusive lock on all files to do the conversion. If it cannot get exclusive access, you are asked whether you want to do the conversion at the next restart. If you answer Yes, the following entry is made to the Registry:

```
Key:        HKLM ¦ System ¦ CurrentControlSet ¦ Control ¦ SessionManager
Value:      BootExecute
Data:       autochk autoconv \??\e: /FS:ntfs
```

The \\??\e: entry is the symbolic link that represents the existing volume. The symbolic link comes from the Object Namespace and can be viewed using WinObj. See Chapter 12, "Configuring Data Storage," for more information.

NTFS Conversion Algorithm

The algorithm used when converting a FAT or FAT32 volume to NTFS is designed to preserve the integrity of the FAT right up until the last moment. All temporary writes are done to free space. The MFT metadata records are placed in free space. The only thing that could happen to cause the system to fail to restart is if the update to the boot sector fails. In this case, you can boot from a fault-tolerant boot floppy.

You need plenty of free space to do the conversion. A rough computation follows:

1. Multiply the number of files and directories on the volume by 1280.

2. Divide the volume size in bytes by 100. The lower limit is 1,048,576 and the upper limit is 4,194,304. Add this to the result of Step 1.

3. Divide the volume size in bytes by 803 and add to the result of Step 2.

4. Add 196,096 to the result of Step 3.

For example, the computation for a 4GB volume with 100,000 files looks like this:

```
100,000 * 1280 = 128,000,000
4GB * 1024 = 4096E6 / 100 = 40960000
4,096,000 + 128,000,000 = 132,096,000
4096E6 / 803 = 5,100,871 + 132,096,000 = 137,196,871
137,196,871 + 196,096 = 137,392,967
```

This volume needs approximately 134MB of free space to do the NTFS conversion. That represents less than 5% of the total space.

Key Points

Remember these key points when converting a file system to NTFS:

- Conversion preserves the contents of the volume.
- Don't convert crowded volumes. The MFT can become fragmented if the conversion utility cannot find sufficient contiguous clusters. This has a serious effect on performance.
- Defrag tools do not repair MFT fragmentation.
- The default cluster size when converting is 512 bytes. You cannot change it.

Distributed Link Tracking

Do you spend hours or days, even weeks, planning data moves because of the time it takes coordinating with users who have links to files buried deep in the directory structure under a share point? Relief may be at hand in Windows 2000 in the form of the *Link Tracking Service* (LTS). This service keeps track of the location of source files for shortcuts and OLE applications. An example is a compound document in Word that contains an OLE link to an Excel spreadsheet. Typically, if the spreadsheet is moved, the compound document fails to find it. Using link tracking, the file is found automatically, even if it is moved to another server in a domain.

A shortcut or OLE application that builds a link to another file is called a *link client*. The target file for the link is called the *link source*. In NT4 and Windows 9x, Explorer falls back on a relatively clumsy search algorithm if the link client cannot find the link source. Essentially, Explorer behaves like a gopher that lost a carrot. It looks down, it looks up, it looks around, and then it gives up and goes for another carrot. The search pattern looks like this:

Procedure 13.2 **Classic NT Link Search Pattern**

1. Look down four levels.
2. Move up one and look down four levels into all directories from that location.
3. Go to the desktop and look down four levels.
4. Go to the root of each drive and look down four levels.
5. Repeat without the four-level limit as long as the client application or the user lets you.

The LTS eliminates this scrabbling around. It maintains a database on the local machine of all source files. If a file is moved, the database is updated and the link can be repaired. The LTS also maintains a central database in the Active Directory of source files that are moved. This enables the link to be repaired even if the source file is moved to another server or the share name is changed.

Link Tracking Functional Description

The LTS is a client/server application. The LTS client, TRKWKS, runs on every Windows 2000 computer, both servers and workstations. The LTS server, TRKSVR, runs on domain controllers. The LTS client is responsible for updating the local tracking database when a link source moves. It also informs the LTS server, which records the move in an Active Directory container called ObjectMoveTable. The DN for this container is `cn=FileLinks,cn=System,dc=domain_dns_name,dc=dns_root_name`. If you use the DSA console to view it, you must enable Advanced Features from the VIEW menu.

If the link source is moved to another location on the same machine that is accessible through the same share point, the LTS server is not required. When the source file is moved, the LTS client updates the local database. When the link client tries to access the link source, the LTS client finds the new location in the database and updates the link client.

If the link source moves to another share point on the same machine or to another machine in the same domain, the LTS client communicates the new location to the LTS server. When the link client tries to open the source file, the LTS client contacts the LTS server on behalf of the application and asks it to find the file. The LTS server does a lookup in the Active Directory, gets the new location information, and returns it to the LTS client, which then updates the link client.

Registry Tip

The Registry information for the LTS is stored in HKLM | System | CurrentControlSet | Services under TrkSvr and TrkWks. The values are stored as binary information, so hacking is not recommended.

Identifying Source Files

To do their magic, the two LTSs need a way of identifying source files unambiguously in an enterprise. They do this by means of a *Globally Unique Identifier*, or GUID. This is a 16-byte (128-bit) data structure created by the system and associated with the source file in a link. The algorithm that builds the GUID incorporates the system time and the MAC address of the network card to virtually guarantee uniqueness. The actual contents are:

- **4 bytes.** time_low
- **2 bytes.** time_mid
- **2 bytes.** time_hi+version
- **1 byte.** clock_hi+variant
- **1 byte.** clock_low
- **6 bytes.** MAC address of network card on originating machine

A file or directory is assigned a GUID when it becomes a link source. This is done by adding a new attribute called an $Object_ID. This attribute holds the GUID assigned to the link source. This GUID is not created using the standard GUID algorithm. Instead, a GUID is created for the host volume and this value acts as the start of a sequence for the remaining GUIDs. This enables the file system and the Active Directory to index the $Object_ID attributes by their source.

> **Using GUID Entries to Track Users**
>
> An interesting side benefit of using the GUID for an index is that the database shows the MAC address of anyone who puts a link on a file. All you need is a correlation between MAC addresses and owners, and you have a nifty way to determine who needs to be contacted when you move data in case the link tracking fails or is not applicable. For example, you may be moving data to a classic NT server or to a server running another OS.

Link Tracking Operational Description

Let's trace an example of how the LTS uses the $Object_ID attribute to track down a file. The simplest way to do this is to create a shortcut. A shortcut is an LNK file that points at a target file. In OLE terminology, the shortcut is the link client, and the target file is the link source. Proceed as follows:

Procedure 13.3 **Verifying Link Tracking Operation**

1. Create a file called WHEREAMI.TXT on an NTFS5 volume.

2. Create a shortcut to the WHEREAMI.TXT file on your desktop. When you do this, the file system adds an $Object_ID attribute to the record for the file. A listing looks like this.

```
<<file name of WhereAmI.txt>>
20000000 00000000 0C035700 68006500  .........W.h.e.
72006500 41006D00 49002E00 74007800  r.e.A.m.I...t.x.
74000000 00000000


<<$Object_ID attribute, type code 40, added when shortcut is created. GUID shown in bold.>>
                  40000000 28000000  t.......@...(...
00000000 00000300 10000000 18000000  ................
C2EB101E F232D311 A77A00C0 4F536A4D  .....2...z..OSjM
80000000 30000000 00001800 00000100  ....0...........
18000000 18000000 57686572 65206469  ........Where di
64207468 65206669 6C652067 6F3F0D0A  d the file go?..
```

3. The system also puts an entry in a new MFT metadata record called $ObjID. This record takes advantage of the natural indexing capability of NTFS directories to build an index of MFT records that have an $Object_ID attribute. This is a listing of the $ObjID record showing index entries for several source files.

```
<<$Index_Root attribute of $ObjID record>>
90000000 00010000 00021800 00000200  ................
E0000000 20000000 24004F00 00000000  .... ...$.O.....
00000000 13000000 00100000 08000000  ................
10000000 D0000000 D0000000 00000000  ................
20003800 00000000 58001000 00000000  .8.....X.......
```

```
<<GUID created by first link. Acts as seed for all further GUIDs.>>
C2EB101E F232D311 A77A00C0 4F536A4D .....2...z..OSjM
```

```
<<First index entry. The underlined number at the start of the entry
is the MFT record sequence number of the file that has the $Object_ID attribute.
Note that the last part of each entry contains the GUID for the next entry.
The low byte (underlined) is incremented by 1.>>
21000000 00000100 00000000 00000000 !...............
00000000 00000000 C2EB101E F232D311 ............2..
A77A00C0 4F536A4D 00000000 00000000 .z..OSjM........
00000000 00000000 20003800 00000000 ........ .8.....
58001000 00000000 C3EB101E F232D311 X...........2..
A77A00C0 4F536A4D
```

```
<<The next index entry. The sequence number indicates that the file is five records higher
than first index entry. The GUID was taken from the last entry. The next GUID is primed and
ready.>>
                 26000000 00000100 .z..OSjM&.......
00000000 00000000 00000000 00000000 ...............
C3EB101E F232D311 A77A00C0 4F536A4D .....2...z..OSjM
00000000 00000000 00000000 00000000 ...............
20003800 00000000 58001000 00000000  .8....X.......
C4EB101E F232D311 A77A00C0 4F536A4D .....2...z..OSjM
```

Just as a reminder, the link source file gets its GUID from the $ObjID database and is not created using the standard GUID algorithm.

4. The link client stores the GUID of the link source along with information about the link itself. This information is stored in the $Data attribute of the LNK file record. This partial listing shows the link tracking portions of the $Data attribute:

```
<<name of the link client>>
1C015300 68006F00 72007400 63007500 ..S.h.o.r.t.c.u.
74002000 74006F00 20005700 68006500 t. .t.o. .W.h.e.
72006500 41006D00 49002E00 74007800 r.e.A.m.I...t.x.
74002E00 6C006E00 6B000000 00000000 t...l.n.k.......
```

```
<<elements of the path to the source file>>
00446972 5F4F6E65 00001700 31000000 .Dir_One....1...
0000E326 6A941000 5375625F 4F6E6500 ...&j...Sub_One.
001C0032 00180000 00E3266B 94200057 ...2......&k. .W
68657265 416D492E 74787400 00000065 hereAmI.txt....e
```

```
<<full path to the source file, including a Location entry for the mapped drive>>
5C686F75 2D77326B 702D3031 5C707562  \hou-w2kp-01\pub
6C696300 463A0044 69725F4F 6E655C53  lic.F:.Dir_One\S
75625F4F 6E655C57 68657265 416D492E  ub_One\WhereAmI.
74787400 1C004C00 6F006300 61007400  txt...L.o.c.a.t.
69006F00 6E003A00 20004600 3A005C00  i.o.n.:. .F.:.\.
44006900 72005F00 4F006E00 65005C00  D.i.r._.O.n.e.\.
53007500 62005F00 4F006E00 65001200  S.u.b._.O.n.e...
46003A00 5C004400 69007200 5F004F00  F.:.\.D.i.r._.O.
6E006500 5C005300 75006200 5F004F00  n.e.\.S.u.b._.O.
6E006500 60000000 030000A0 58000000  n.e.`.......X...

<<name of computer hosting the source file>>
00000000 686F752D 77326B70 2D303100  ....hou-w2kp-01.

<<GUID of source file (listed twice)>>
1CBFBADE 8931D311 98B00800 09C0E241  .....1.........A
1CBFBADE 8931D311 98B00800 09C0E241  .....1.........A
```

> So, the stage is set. The shortcut—the link client—knows the GUID of the link source along with the source file location. Let's put the LTS to the test.

5. Move the link source file to another directory on the same volume. Make sure the directory is visible from the same shortcut. At this point, we're only testing the LTS client. Because the file only changed its directory, its MFT record does not move, so the corresponding index entry in the $ObjID database does not change. However, the path to the link source file that is stored in the LNK file is now incorrect.

6. Attempt to open the file by using the shortcut. The searching flashlight icon appears to distract you while the file system puts in a frantic call to the LTS client. The LTS client does a lookup in the $ObjID database and finds the MFT record for the link source. It does a lookup in the record and finds the new directory. It then tells the file system to update the information in the link client record, and the file opens.

7. This sequence of events gets a little more complicated if the file is moved to another machine. In that case, the LTS client informs the LTS server on its domain controller that the link source moved. The LTS server updates the Active Directory with the new location.

8. When the link client attempts to open the source file, the LTS client makes a network call to the LTS server, giving it the GUID of the link source file.

9. The LTS server sends back the information in the link table for that GUID.

10. The LTS client gives the information to the file system, which updates the location information in the LNK file. The file now opens.

11. If the LTS client cannot locate the link source, it falls back on the classic algorithm and gives the user a best guess. This is usually a wrong guess. The user has the option of deleting the link and building it again. This is nearly certain to require administrative intervention.

Link Tracking Highlights

Remember these key points concerning link tracking:

- LTS works only on NTFS5 volumes hosted by Windows 2000 computers.

- Distributed Link Tracking works reliably only within a domain. You may get what a colleague of mine calls "episodes of success" with the machines from different domains or workgroups, but the reliability you need to deploy to users is not there unless all computers are members of the same domain.

- When the LTS Client finds the new network path, only the Target entry for the link is updated, not the Start In entry. This can cause problems for DOS applications that use the Start In entry to find overlay files and for Win16 applications that need to find INI files.

- If you copy a file rather than move it, the $Object_ID attribute and its associated GUID stay with the original file.

- When you restore a file that is the source file of a link, the $Object_ID attribute is restored, as well. If you restore to a separate location, you end up with two files of the same name with the same GUID in the same domain. This may cause problems if you end up with links to the two files and the tracking system gets them confused. Treat all restores with extreme care because of this.

Reparse Points

Reparse points act like miniature "redirectors" inside individual file system records that point at volumes on other hard drives, CD-ROMs, or files inside tape storage libraries. Using reparse points, it is possible to represent an entire drive as a folder, eliminating the need for additional drive letters and share points. This is also called a *mount point*. When an application encounters a mount point, it scoots out to the other volume and continues on as if nothing happened.

You will encounter reparse points when you examine the folder structure under `\WINNT\Sysvol\Sysvol\<domain_name>` on a domain controller. A share point called SYSVOL is on the second Sysvol folder. The contents of the second Sysvol folder are actually mount points back to folders under `\WINNT\Sysvol\Domain`. See Chapter 17, "Managing Remote Access and Internet Routing," for more details.

Microsoft also uses reparse points to provide near-online storage with the *Remote Storage Service* (RSS). Using RSS, a file can physically reside on a tape library while a reparse point in the file record handles the interface between the local file system and the tape system. Figure 13.7 shows an example of how folders and files with reparse points look in a directory tree and in the MFT.

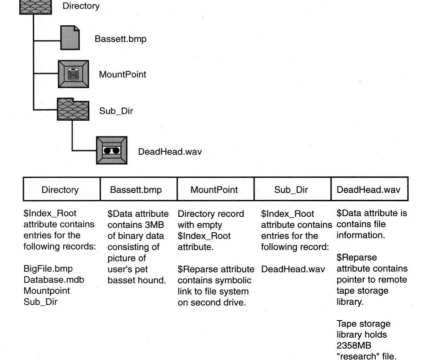

Directory	Bassett.bmp	MountPoint	Sub_Dir	DeadHead.wav
$Index_Root attribute contains entries for the following records: BigFile.bmp Database.mdb Mountpoint Sub_Dir	$Data attribute contains 3MB of binary data consisting of picture of user's pet basset hound.	Directory record with empty $Index_Root attribute. $Reparse attribute contains symbolic link to file system on second drive.	$Index_Root attribute contains entries for the following record: DeadHead.wav	$Data attribute is contains file information. $Reparse attribute contains pointer to remote tape storage library. Tape storage library holds 2358MB "research" file.

Figure 13.7   Diagram of mount points and remote storage files that make use of reparse points.

Operational Description of Mount Points

Reparse points depend on two new items in the MFT:

- **$Reparse_Point attribute.** This attribute contains information about the remote file system. If it is a disk-based file system, the attribute contains symbolic link information from the Object Namespace. You may remember the Object Namespace from the previous chapter. The \Device handle in the Object Namespace contains a list of the virtual devices managed by the Windows 2000 Executive. The symbolic link name in the $Reparse_Point points the system at the virtual device representing the CD-ROM mounted at the directory. You can view the contents of the Object Namespace using WINOBJ from the Platform SDK or from www.sysinternals.com.

- **Mount Manager Database.** NTFS maintains an index of MFT records containing $Reparse_Point attributes. This index is stored in a new metadata record called $Reparse. The system also installs a special database called $MountMgrRemoteDatabase. This hidden database is a named $Data stream in the "Root" directory—that is, the $\ metadata record. The database contains information about the remote file system, including its location and the file system filter code to use for accessing it. Vendors can specify up to 16K of code for this file system filter.

The best way to see how these two items work is to trace through an example by creating a mount point. Briefly, this involves using the Computer Management console to mount a volume to an empty folder on another volume.

The host volume—that is, the volume containing the mount point—must be formatted NTFS. The mounted volume can be another hard drive, a removable media drive, such as a Zip or Jaz drive, or even a CD-ROM or DVD.

The mounted volume can be formatted with any file system supported by Windows 2000, such as FAT, FAT32, NTFS, CDFS, or UDFS. It can contain compressed files and encrypted files. Just to be frisky, let's use a CD-ROM for an example.

Procedure 13.4   **Creating a Mount Point Using the** *Disk Management*
Console

1. First, create a folder on an NTFS volume called Mount to act as a mount point. It can be in any subdirectory. The folder must be empty. If a folder has existing file or directory entries, it cannot be used as a mount point. After a folder is made into a mount point, files or directory entries added to the mount point are added to the mounted volume.

2. Open the `Computer Management` console using START | PROGRAMS | ADMINISTRATIVE TOOLS | COMPUTER MANAGEMENT.

3. Expand the tree to `Storage` | `Disk Management`. Figure 13.8 shows the disk layout for a system with a single hard drive configured as a basic disk. It has two partitions, a boot/system partition and a data partition. The system also has a CD-ROM drive with an ISO9660 disk mounted using the CD-ROM File System (CDFS). If this were a DVD drive and DVD data disk, the display would show Universal Disk File System (UDFS).

Figure 13.8   `Disk Management` console showing disk layout for a simple system with one hard drive and one CD-ROM.

4. Right-click the graphics bar representing the CD-ROM drive and select CHANGE DRIVE LETTER AND PATH from the fly-out menu. The `Change Drive Letter and Paths` window opens. See Figure 13.9.

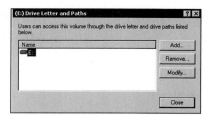

Figure 13.9 `Change Drive Letter and Paths` window.

5. Click `Add`. The `Add New Drive Letter or Path` window opens.

6. Select the `Mount this volume at an empty folder which supports drive paths` radio button and click `Browse`. The `Browse for Drive Path` window opens.

7. Navigate to an NTFS volume where you want to mount the CD-ROM. In the example, this is the folder called `Mount`. You can also click `New Folder` to create a folder on the NTFS volume. Long names are permitted.

8. Click `OK` to accept the new folder and close the window.

9. At the `Add New Drive Letter or Path` window, click `OK` to mount the drive. The `Disk Management` console does not show that a volume is mounted on another volume.

10. Right-click the graphic bar representing the NTFS volume containing the mount point—Drive F in the example—and select `Explore` from the fly-out menu. The `Explorer` window opens. (Note: If a mounted volume has no drive letter, you cannot access it directly using Explorer. You must open the parent folder from a volume with a drive letter.)

11. Navigate to the folder holding the mount point. The icon for the mount point folder changes to the icon associated with the CD currently inserted in the CD-ROM drive.

12. Right-click the mounted volume and select PROPERTIES from the fly-out menu. The `Properties` window opens for the volume. Instead of showing the properties of the CD, the window shows only that this is a `Mounted Volume`. You must click the second `Properties` button to see the properties of the mounted volume itself.

13. Close the `Properties` window. Double-click the icon for the mount point or expand the Explorer tree to show the contents. The CD opens for browsing. The AUTORUN feature does not work on mount points, which is a point in their favor.

Description of MFT Records Following Mount Point Creation

The MFT record for the folder that acts as a mount point gets a $Reparse_Point attribute, type code C0. The $Index_Root attribute is left empty. A mount point cannot be a standard directory. This is a listing of the Mount directory showing the $Reparse_Point attribute.

```
<<directory name>>
00000010 00000000 05034D00 6F007500 .........M.o.u.
6E007400 00000000


<<$Index_Root attribute - always empty for mount points>>
                  90000000 50000000 n.t.........P...
00041800 00000100 30000000 20000000 ........0... ...
24004900 33003000 30000000 01000000 $.I.3.0.0.......
00100000 08000000 10000000 20000000 ............ ...
20000000 00000000 00000000 00000000  ..............
10000000 02000000


<<$Reparse_Point attribute showing symbolic link (bold) to volume name>>
                  C0000000 90000000 ................
00000000 00000400 76000000 18000000 ........v.......
030000A0 6E000000 00006200 64000000 ....n.....b.d...
5C003F00 3F005C00 56006F00 6C007500 \.?.?.\.V.o.l.u.
6D006500 7B003100 30003500 35003900 m.e.{.1.0.5.5.9.
65006300 32002D00 32003700 32006200 e.c.2.-.2.7.2.b.
2D003100 31006400 33002D00 39003800 -.1.1.d.3.-.9.8.
61003300 2D003800 30003600 64003600 a.3.-.8.0.6.d.6.
31003700 32003600 39003600 66007D00 1.7.2.6.9.6.f.}.
5C000000 00000000 FFFFFFFF 82794711 \...........yG.
```

The important part of this listing is the symbolic link information in the $Reparse_Point attribute. Symbolic link entries always start with the prefix `030000A0`. The data portion specifies the name of a symbolic link entry in the Object Namespace. In the example, this symbolic link is named `\??\Volume{10559ec2-272b-11d3-98a3-806d6172696f}\`.

In addition to the $Reparse attribute in the directory record itself, the system also makes an entry in the $MountMgrRemoteDatabase. This database is stored as a named $Data stream in the "Root" metadata record, $\. The $\ record has no unnamed $Data stream, so giving it a named data stream effectively hides the $MountMgrRemoteDatabase from the rest of the system.

The $MountMgrRemoteDatabase holds the names of the symbolic links used by reparse points on the volume along with their Object Namespace entries and additional information about the device type. The entry stripped of its hex listing looks like this.

```
$MountMgrRemoteDatabase..
\??\Volume{10559ec2-272b-11d3-98a3-806d6172696f}
\??SCSI#CdRom&Ven_SONY&Prod_CD-ROM_CDU-76S&Rev_11c#
        3&1b3c1513&0&050#{53f5630d-b6bf-11d0-94f2-00a0c91efb8b}
```

The mounted volume in the example is a SCSI CD-ROM drive with applicable vendor information. If the volume is on a hard drive, the entry is for the LDM driver, DMIO. This tells the system what file system filter to use to read the mounted volume. If the $Reparse point is implemented by a third party, the vendor can specify up to 16K of handling code in the database to act as a file system filter.

The system also makes an index entry in the $Reparse metadata record. This is a listing of a $Reparse record with three index entries.

```
<<last portion of the file name attribute>>
26000020 00000000 08032400 52006500 &.. ......$.R.e.
70006100 72007300 65000000 00000000 p.a.r.s.e.......

<<$Index_Root attribute containing index entries for records with reparse points.>>
90000000 B0000000 00021800 00000200 ................
90000000 20000000 24005200 00000000 .... ...$.R.....
00000000 13000000 00100000 08000000 ................
10000000 80000000 80000000 00000000 ................

<<Entries starting with 1C are index entries. The underlined numbers are the MFT
sequence numbers of the indexed records.>>
1C000000 00000000 20000C00 00000000 ........ .......
030000A0 20000000 00000100 00000000 .... ...........
1C000000 00000000 20000C00 00000000 ........ .......
030000A0 21000000 00000100 00000000 ....!..........
1C000000 00000000 20000C00 00000000 ........ .......
030000A0 26000000 00000100 00000000 ....&..........
```

Using Linkd to Mount Folders

The normal volume mounting process as described in the last section is limited to mounting an entire volume at a mount point. The Windows 2000 Resource Kit contains a utility called Linkd that can be used to mount any local folder to an empty folder.

The syntax for Linkd is: linkd <empty_folder> <source_folder>.

For example, to mount the C:\WINNT folder at D:\TEST_DIR (an empty folder), enter the following:

```
linkd d:\test_dir c:\winnt
```

You cannot use Linkd to mount a folder on a network drive. Deleting the folder deletes only the link. The folder icons do not show a special mounted icon, such as that used by regular volume mount points.

Reparse Points Created by the Remote Storage Service

Windows 2000 also uses reparse points to provide pointers to offline files using the hierarchical storage management features of the Remote Storage Service (RSS). Operational details of RSS are covered in the "Remote Storage Services" section later in this chapter. From an MFT perspective, when a file is moved to tape, the $Data attribute is unaffected. The system simply adds a $Reparse attribute containing information about where the remote $Data attribute is located.

This is a listing for a file called BIGFILE2.TXT that was moved to offline storage. The contents of the $Reparse attribute are much more complex for a remote file than for a mount point. The system must store the location of the tape library, the exact location of the file in that library, and information about the library itself.

```
<<file name>>
0C036200 69006700 66006900 6C006500  ..b.i.g.f.i.l.e.
32002E00 74007800 74002000 6F006600  2...t.x.t. .o.f.

<<header of remote $Data attribute>>
80000000 50000000 01000000 00800400  ....P...........
00000000 00000000 5F070000 00000000  ........_.......
48000400 00000000 00C00E00 00000000  H...............
0FB40E00 00000000 00000000 00000000  ................
00000000 00000000 02600700 88294080  .........`...)@.

<<$Reparse attribute with RSS information>>
C0000000 10010000 00000000 00000600  ................
F8000000 18000000 040000C0 F0000000  ................
90882612 D164D011 A9B000A0 248903EA  ..&..d......$...
481D0000 65000000 01000000 01000000  H...e...........
00000000 00000000 00000000 00000000  ................
00000000 00000000 00000000 00000000  ................
00000000 00000000 00000000 00000000  ................
00000000 00000000 00000000 00000000  ................
```

```
00000000 01000080 6EC3C045 5DC3BE01 ........n..E]...
32A85EDB 402BD311 8C6100C0 4F536AF2 2.^.@+...a..OSj.
B604A272 502F0800 8C6700C0 4F536AF2 ...rP/...g..OSj.
007C1D00 00000000 00B80E00 00000000 .|..............
FA000000 00000000 0FB40E00 00000000 ................
633591FC 5CC3BE01 13AE0000 00000000 c5..\...........
01000000 00000000 00000000 00000000 ................
00000000 00000000 0FB40E00 00000000 ................
00000000 01000000 E97D397C 00000000 .........}9|....
```

Reparse Points Highlights

Remember the following concerning reparse points:

- If a folder has existing file or directory entries, it cannot be used as a mount point. After a folder is made into a mount point, files or directory entries added to it are added to the mounted volume.

- A $Reparse attribute in an MFT record precludes adding HPFS extended attributes. This is not much of a limitation because HPFS is no longer supported.

- When looking at properties of the parent volume—that is, the NTFS volume that contains the mount point—the storage capacity and current file statistics of the mounted volume(s) are not included. For example, an 8MB volume that has a 32GB volume mounted at a mount point reports 8MB as a volume size when queried by the operating system.

- A search of the parent volume—or running a DOS utility, such as TREE—includes the contents of any mounted volumes.

- A file or directory can have only one reparse point. Applications that use them have to use a workaround if some other application gets to a record first.

- A volume can be mounted at several mount points, but I recommend doing so only in special cases. Look at the problems users have with mapped logical drives. Imagine the additional confusion of having two seemingly independent mount points looking at the same data. The potential for confusion and grief is compounded by the fact that the two mount points might show up under two different share points. "I copied all my files to K:\MyData and then deleted R:\MyData and now I can't see any files in K:\MyData. What happened?"

- Copying a directory with mounted volumes also copies the contents of the mounted volumes.

- Removing a mount point using the RD command deletes only the MFT record containing the reparse point. The files on the mounted volume remain untouched. If, however, you delete a mount point using DEL or use Explorer to send it to the Recycle Bin or to delete it, all files and directories in the mounted volume are deleted.

- When backing up volumes with mount points, the backup includes files and directories on the mounted volumes. Keep this in mind when mounting a volume at multiple mount points. You could end up backing up the same volume several times. NTBACKUP has the option to skip restoration from junction points and the files under those junction points.

- If you mount a volume at a folder, the additional storage available on the volume is not reported to the operating system and the files do not appear on a tree.

File System Recovery and Fault Tolerance

The file system is the single most critical element of the operating system. If the file system gets corrupted, not only can data be lost entirely, it can be scrambled in ways that aren't immediately apparent. This can happen for a variety of reasons. A disk can crash or get large numbers of sector errors. You might lose power to the system thanks to a failed UPS (or no UPS at all) while file system information is still in the cache. A misbehaved driver might lock the system or run rampant over the file system metadata files. Or it might just be your time in the pit.

For whatever reason, recovering a consistent file system has the same urgency for a system administrator as recovering a stable pulse and vital signs has for an emergency care physician. This section covers the hygiene checks that are necessary to ensure stable operations, fault-tolerance features designed to save the day in case of catastrophe, rapid index recovery using the new Change Log, and the operation of the System File Protection system. Let's start with periodic maintenance and a familiar face, Chkdsk.

Chkdsk and Autochk

The first line of defense for preventing file system crashes is regular maintenance. The maintenance tool in Windows 2000 has a venerable name, Chkdsk. This utility analyzes the file system for corruption and consistency and repairs anything it finds that is broken.

The code that actually does the checks associated with Chkdsk is contained in the file system drivers themselves—UFAT.DLL for FAT and FAT32, and UNTFS.DLL for NTFS. This code can be initiated in several ways other than running Chkdsk. You can use Explorer by right-clicking a drive, selecting PROPERTIES from the fly-out menu, selecting the Tools tab, and then clicking Check Now under Error-Checking. Or you can initiate a consistency check at boot time using Autochk.

Comparison of Autochk and Chkdsk

You can think of Autochk as a "boot-time" version of Chkdsk. Designed to run in real mode during system startup to prevent locked files from blocking the consistency checks, Autochk cannot be run after the operating system loads. The Registry entry that controls Autochk is:

```
Key:      HKLM | System | CurrentControlSet | Control | SessionManager
Value:    BootExecute
Data:     Autocheck autochk *   <<note: "Autocheck" is a placeholder, "autochk" is the
executable.>>
```

Under normal circumstances, Autochk runs only if the so-called "dirty" flag is set, meaning that the system shut down abnormally. When Autochk runs, it checks the disk in read-only mode and reports any problems to the Application log. Check the Event Viewer for details.

Troubleshooting Frequent Autochk Operations

If you find that Autochk runs nearly every time you start a machine, and no one changed the default setting in the Registry, you have serious problems with your disk subsystem. The most common cause is using a lazy-write hardware cache that is not supported by Windows 2000. The hardware cache and the Windows 2000 software cache can get out of synchronization, causing the file system to get corrupted. Unless you are absolutely certain that your particular RAID or SCSI card uses caching that is supported by Windows 2000, disable hardware caching.

Using Chkntfs to Configure Autochk

You should run Autochk in fixup mode (equivalent to Chkdsk /f) each time the system boots so that file system problems can be caught early and corrected before they cause serious damage. You can make this change by hacking the Registry to add /p at the end of Autochk entry: for example, autochk /p *. An easier way is to use the Chkntfs utility. These are the Chkntfs settings and syntax for setting Autochk functions. In each case, **<volume>** can also be a drive letter.

- **chkntfs <volume> /c.** Sets Autochk to run in fixup mode for the specified volume or drive letter. This switch adds /m to the Autochk entry in the Registry.

- **chkntfs <volume> /d.** Returns the system to its default behavior of running Autochk in read-only mode when the dirty flag is set.

- **chkntfs <volume> /t:time.** Autochk can take a long time to finish. It runs in real mode, so very little memory exists to help it progress quickly. On a system with a big RAID array containing thousands of megabytes of files, Autochk can take several hours to finish. By using this CHKNTFS option, you add a countdown to Autochk so that you can bypass the check if you are reasonably certain that no file system corruption is present. For example, if you are going to down a server to install a new network card, you can use the /t:time option to bypass Autochk, thereby avoiding the lengthy delay. This option adds an AutoChkTimeOut value to HKLM | System | CurrentControlSet | Control | Session Manager.

- **chkntfs <volume> /x.** Excludes a disk from Autochk. Use this option with caution. If you forget you set this switch, the system does not do its necessary housekeeping checks at boot time. This option adds /k:<volume> to the Autochk entry in the Registry.

Functional Description of Chkdsk (Autochk)

When Chkdsk (or Autochk) runs, it performs a series of consistency checks. The checks as they apply to NTFS are as follows.

Pass 1

- Scans the MFT looking for active file and directory records and builds bitmaps of active MFT records and active clusters (using the LCN information in the records).

- Uses bitmaps to validate the $Bitmap file in metadata. If a record is unreadable or has an incorrect format, it is identified as a problem.

Pass 2

- Scans directory records to make sure that each file entry references an actual file record and agrees with the directory reference in the file record.

- Checks for circular references for subdirectories. A circular reference is a directory that thinks it is under the subdirectory. Circular references are very rare, but can result in the loss of a great deal of data by orphaning large chunks of the file system, so you should not take them lightly.

- Checks for consistency between filename attributes in the file records and the filename entries in the associated directory index. This pass can take many minutes, even hours, depending on the number of entries in the MFT and the complexity of the directory structure. The speed has nothing to do with volume size. A 32GB volume with 1000 files finishes in the blink of an eye. A 3GB volume with 100,000 files takes a long time.

Pass 3

- Scans security descriptors to ensure that every record references a security descriptor and that the entry agrees with the reference in the security descriptor itself. This scan changed considerably in Windows 2000 because of the change to the way security descriptors are stored. This portion of Chkdsk usually takes a long time in classic NT, but goes fairly quickly in Windows 2000.

- If a Change Log (USN Journal) is associated with the volume, the system scans the log and verifies the index entries. See the "Index Tracking and the Change Journal" section a little later in the chapter.

Pass 4

- Performs a disk scan and tries to read every sector that contains a file. Bad clusters are added to the $BadClus list. Data in the bad clusters are copied to a new cluster.

Pass 5

- Performs a disk scan of free space in the volume. Bad clusters are added to the $BadClus list.

Chkdsk Switches

Several Chkdsk switches affect how the scans are run. Two switches, /i and /c, were added in NT4 SP4 to speed up consistency checks by bypassing Passes 4 and 5. These switches also work for Autochk.

- **f**—Runs Chkdsk in fixup mode. (Autochk uses /p.)
- **/v**—Displays cleanup messages.
- **/r**—Performs a full disk scan looking for bad clusters. Any that it finds are added to the $BadClus file.
- **/1**—Displays the size of the $Logfile. When paired with a :size parameter,

such as /L:4096, changes the size of the $Logfile to the new value.

- /x—Forces a volume dismount. Any users with open files lose their data. Using this option also runs Chkdsk in fixup mode.
- /i—Skips internal consistency checks between the filename attributes in the file records and the associated filename listings in the directory index.
- /c—Skips the directory loop (cycle) checks.

Recommendations for Running Chkdsk

You should run Chkdsk periodically to find file system anomalies. You can't run Chkdsk on a volume with active files, such as the system volume or a volume containing a database, because the files are locked. You can use Chkntfs to schedule Autochk to runs in fixup mode at boot time.

If you have users who keep getting corrupted files on their Windows 2000 Professional systems, you can break them of the habit of simply turning their machine off by configuring Autochk to run in fixup mode at every boot. Make it clear that the extra boot time in the morning is necessary because they didn't down their machines correctly the night before.

File System Logging

Under most circumstances, Chkdsk or Autochk running in fixup mode can correct all file system anomalies. But what happens if the file system is in an unknown state caused by a system crash or a loss of power? Much of the active data on a Windows 2000 system stays in cache for a while before being committed to disk on the assumption that applications regularly use the same data over and over again. This so-called *lazy write* caching dramatically improves system performance, but the cost is somewhat lessened file system reliability.

If the file system is put into an unknown state following a crash or lockup, Autochk can rebuild the file system, but it goes about its work with painful slowness. This costs production time and causes enormous wear on the stomach linings and tempers of system administrators. Servers and workstations are known to crash on occasion, so it makes sense to plan for that eventuality by putting in place a way to recover a consistent file system more quickly. NTFS does this with the help of a kernel-mode service called the LFS. The LFS is a general-purpose logging service, but NTFS is currently its only client.

LFS Structure

The LFS keeps a record of all disk writes that affect the core file system. It stores these records in a file called $Logfile, one of the MFT metadata files. The $Logfile consists of a set of 4K runs stored at the midpoint of the disk. It generally starts out at 2MB with a mirrored file that is also 2MB.

User data is not protected by the LFS. If you hit the big red switch on a server or workstation, any user data in the cache is lost. In this case, it may take a while for Autochk to return the file system to a consistent state.

The $Logfile record uses a standard MFT file record format. It contains a pointer to a nonresident $Data attribute representing the log. The log itself typically starts at the middle of the volume right after the mirrored portion of the MFT. If the disk was converted from FAT or FAT32 and the middle of the disk had an existing file, the log file is placed wherever the system can find contiguous free space. If none is available, the log file is fragmented. This can hurt system performance.

Log File System Functional Overview

The $Logfile consists of two parts: the *restart area* and the *infinite logging area*. The restart area (contained in buffers prefixed by RSTR) contains location information for data in the infinite logging area. A key component of the restart area is the checkpoint information. This tells the logging system those log entries that were flushed to the MFT and those that were not. The infinite logging area (contained in buffers prefixed by RCRD) works like an 8-track tape. When the log gets full, the log service starts at the beginning again, overwriting the oldest entries.

When an update to the core file system occurs, the disk write is handed to the LFS for recording in the $Logfile. These critical updates include changes to attribute headers, security attributes, directory locations, and modifications to the MFT metadata files.

Periodically, the log entries are flushed to the MFT and the checkpoint is moved. If the system crashes during this flushing operation, the LFS can recover a consistent file system very quickly, simply by finding the checkpoint and then walking through the last $Logfile entries. The LFS then works with the file system to purge any transactions that are not completely committed and recommit them again. The final condition of the MFT reflects the status of the file system at the time of the crash, excluding any commits that are in the lazy write cache waiting to go to the log file itself.

System recovery using the log file can take a while on large volumes, but not nearly as long as a full file system rebuild using Autochk. If the log recovery fails, the file system performs a full rebuild. If this fails, the only alternative is recovery from tape. No controls and no Registry hacks are available for the LFS.

The only index that is recovered by the LFS is the filename index in the directory records. Windows 2000 has several features that require special indexing of the MFT. Recovering these indexes with a full table scan is a tedious process. To help speed things up, the system has a new feature called the Change Journal, discussed in the next section.

Index Tracking and the Change Journal

Ever since the introduction of NTFS, Microsoft has touted its ability to support third-party features that index attributes other than $File_Name. But vendors are reluctant to do so because of the dearth of documentation on the LFS, the lack of effective tools for managing the LFS, and the need to do massive reindexing following a log file recovery.

In Windows 2000, Microsoft attempted to fix this problem by adding a new feature called the *Change Journal*. The Change Journal keeps track of changes to the MFT that affect indexed entries. For example, the new reparse point feature uses a $Reparse_Point attribute and an index in a metadata record called $Reparse. Rapid recovery of this index is provided by the Change Journal.

Microsoft touts the Change Journal as enabling technology for improving the performance of applications that keep extensive indexes on the file system and depend on up-to-date records of file system changes. This includes backup programs, virus scanners, and disk utilities. If developers like what they see in the Change Journal, you'll see more and more applications use it over the next few years. The applications making use of the Change Journal in Windows 2000 are:

- **Content Indexing Service.** The Indexing Service that keeps track of data for quick retrieval and is implemented by the CISVC executable and the CIDAEMON.DLL.

- **File Replication Service (FRS).** The FRS takes data from one server and copies it to another server automatically. This process is more efficient than simply running XCOPY as a scheduled service because it replicates changes rather than the entire directory contents. The FRS supports two key Windows 2000 features: distributing group policies between domain controllers, and distributing shared files between replication partners in the Distributed File System (DFS).

- **Remote Storage Services (RSS).** This service moves files from disk to tape but makes them available as near-online storage when users select the files from disk. The Change Log improves recovery time and substantially reduces the risk of data loss caused by corrupted or inconsistent databases.

Change Journal Functional Overview

The Change Journal is a metadata record called $UsnJrnl stored under the $Extend metadata folder. Table 13.3 lists the events that trigger an entry in the Change Journal for indexed records:

Table 13.3 **Events that trigger a Change Journal entry**

Basic_Info_Change	Hard_Link_Change
Close	Indexable_Change
Compression_Change	Named_Data_Extend
Data_Extend	Named_Data_Overwrite
Data_Overwrite	Named_Data_Truncation
Data_Truncation	Object_Id_Change
Ea_Change	Rename_New_Name
Encryption_Change	Rename_Old_Name
File_Create	Reparse_Point_Change
File_Delete	Security_Change
Stream_Change	

The system keeps track of changes in the Change Journal using an *Update Sequence Number* (USN). When an entry is made or updated in the journal, it gets the next available USN. This is similar to the way that the Active Directory tracks changes. The USN is a 64-bit number, so you have enough numbers to last billions of years.

No troubleshooting tips are involved with operating the Change Journal. Rather, the Change Journal is completely transparent, just like the Log File System. No UI settings or Registry hacks are available. If the journal becomes corrupted or is accidentally deleted, the applications that rely on it are forced to do a full scan of the MFT to reindex. This might take a while. Look in the Event Log if you think restarts are taking inordinately long.

Change Journal Highlights

Remember these key points about the Change Journal:

- The Change Journal is new to Windows 2000.
- The journal speeds up recovery of features that index MFT attributes other than filenames.
- Applications that maintain MFT indexes must deliberately write to the journal.

System File Protection

A more insidious form of file corruption than system lockups or index corruption has less to do with the file system than the files that reside in it. All the various 32-bit Windows operating systems absolutely rely on a consistent set of system executables, dynamic link libraries, and supporting files that are stored in special folders in the system/boot partition. Any application programmer can modify these core systems without so much as a by-your-leave. One day you have a server that operated flawlessly for months and months. You install a seemingly innocuous application, and suddenly you enter Blue Screen purgatory.

Windows 2000 has a new feature designed to stop this kind of rampant trampling of critical system files. Called the *System File Protection* service (SFP), this service keeps a log of the critical system files and enables them to be modified in only four instances:

- Service Pack installation using UPDATE.EXE
- Hotfix installation using HOTFIX.EXE
- Operating system upgrades using WINNT32.EXE
- Windows Update service

Any attempt to modify a system file by any other means is either blocked or stymied by the SFP, which immediately overwrites the rogue file with a copy of the approved file.

The SFP system keeps a copy of controlled files in a compressed folder under \WINNT\System32\ DllCache. This folder contains a copy of every file installed from the Windows 2000 CD during Setup. When one of these files is updated using one of the four approved methods, the cached file is replaced with the updated file.

The SFP knows the protected files and their versions by comparing a signature inside the file with a signature in the NT5.CAT file, also in the DllCache folder. The protected INF files are stored in NT5INF.CAT.

Operational Description of SFP

You can test the operation of SFP as follows:

Procedure 13.5 **Verifying SFP Operation**

1. Open Explorer and navigate to the \WINNT\System32 directory. If Explorer is Web-enabled, you are prompted to verify that you have business in \WINNT and in \WINNT\System32. This is your clue that the directories are on the list of "protected" directories in SFP.

2. Scroll down to one of the critical system files installed during Setup, SOL.EXE.

3. Right-click the icon for SOL.EXE and select DELETE from the fly-out menu. Click Yes when asked to verify the deletion.

4. Don't do anything for a while. Just wait and watch. In a few seconds, the icon reappears. This is SFP at work.

SFP Elements

The SFP does not run as a separate service. Instead, it is a core feature of the operating system. The controls are kept in the Registry under HKLM | Software | Microsoft | Windows NT | Current Version | Winlogon. The values are:

- **SFCQuota.** The amount of disk space allocated for the DllCache directory. The default value is ffffffff, giving the DllCache folder a virtually limitless size of 4GB. You can get the same effect by entering −1.

- **SFCDisable.** If you set the value to 1, SFP is disabled for the next restart. It is enabled automatically on subsequent restarts. Use this switch to replace files with vendor-authorized versions or to use checked versions for debugging.

- **SFCBugCheck.** Under normal circumstances, if you attempt to replace or delete a protected file, the system warns you with a console message. If you set this value to 1, the system stops with a blue screen. This can be set on a desktop with a user who has a history of trying to change system files.

- **SFCScan.** Configures the SFP to scan the DllCache for missing files at boot time. A setting of 1 scans files at every boot. A setting of 2 scans files once.

Using the System File Checker, SFC

You do not need to hack the Registry to change the SFP settings. A command-line utility comes with Windows 2000 to set these values. Called the *System File Checker* (SFC), the utility can also rebuild the DllCache directory if files are accidentally deleted. The switches for SFC are outlined in the following sections.

sfc /scanonce

This option scans the contents of the DllCache to verify that they match the signatures in the catalog and then scans the files in the protected directories. This scan does not commence until you log in.

While the scan is running, a message appears on the console asking you to wait. You can perform other tasks and run applications, but this slows the scan. If the system encounters a file that is missing in the cache or a system file that is the wrong version, it prompts you to insert the Windows 2000 CD so that the proper file can be restored.

If you installed Windows 2000 across the network or from an I386 directory on the local hard drive, you must still have the CD to do the file protection restore. If the machine does not have a CD-ROM drive, your only workaround is to compare the contents of the DllCache with that of another machine and copy the missing files manually.

sfc /scanboot

This option performs a protected file scan at every boot. On servers administered by professionals, this is seldom necessary. Desktops, on the other hand, might need more diligent care.

Use the /scanboot option if you have consistent problems with users who delete cached files and you want to make sure they go through the tedious process of correcting their own blunders. You can also use the /SFCBugCheck switch in the Registry to blue-screen the machine if the same users insist on playing with the protected files.

sfc /quiet

This option replaces missing files without asking for permission.

sfc /cancel

Use this option if you have the system to scan at the next boot, but then you change your mind.

SFP Highlights

The key points to remember about SFP are as follows:

- SPF protects system files loaded during setup.
- SFP only enables a few authorized executables to change system files.
- Deleted or corrupt system files are replaced from an on-disk cache.
- The SFC utility can manually scan system files and repair them.

Defragmenting Files

The lack of an integrated file defragmenter is one of the most glaring deficiencies of classic NT. When NT was first released, Microsoft insisted that NTFS did not experience performance degradation when disks became fragmented. The company's recommendation was to reformat every so often and recover from tape. When asked, "What if I use FAT on my workstations?" Microsoft's answer was, "Convert to NTFS or dual-boot and run a FAT defragger."

Near the end of the NT 3.51 product cycle, a company called Executive Software came out with a native NT utility called Diskeeper that could defrag NTFS and FAT volumes. The initial release required a special hack to the file system to enable defragging. Microsoft agreed to include special API calls in NT4 at the request of Executive Software to support defrag, so the hacks were no longer required. These same API calls are used in Windows 2000, although the underlying routines are different.

The API calls provided by Microsoft for defragmentation rely on native system routines that are as safe as the file system itself. The system can restore a consistent file structure even if power is lost during defrag.

Microsoft includes a stripped-down version of Diskeeper in Windows 2000 that is managed by an MMC console called *Disk Defragmenter*, or Dfrg.msc. The utility is functionally equivalent to Executive Software's "Diskeeper Lite for NT" product, except that the Windows 2000 version works with FAT, FAT32, NTFS4, and NTFS5. The defrag engine itself consists of two executables, Dfrgfat.exe and Dfrgntfs.exe. The Dfrgfat engine works with both FAT and FAT32.

Defragmentation and Performance

It takes some doing to fragment an NTFS volume to the point where you get noticeable performance degradation. Fragmentation generally does not become a problem until you load a volume to 90% or more, use compression, or manage to fragment the paging file or the MFT.

Some people swear that defragging makes no difference at all in their performance. Others insist just the opposite. Executive Software engaged the services of NSTL, www.nstl.com, to do some performance testing comparing fragmented and unfragmented systems. Its results indicate that severe fragmentation, especially when coupled with paging file fragmentation, can seriously degrade performance. It did not run tests with the kind of mild fragmentation that happens on machines with lots of free space and a standard mix of file sizes.

Limitations of Defragmenting

Before taking a closer look at the operation of the Windows 2000 Disk Defragmenter, this is a list of what it can't or won't do.

- **Defragmenting does not affect the paging file.** A big paging file on a busy server could have hundreds of fragments, and a fragmented paging file degrades performance more so than any other single influence. It also impedes defragmenting other files by blocking defragger from getting contiguous clusters. Trying to defrag a volume with a fragmented paging file is like trying to get from one side of Boston to the other by crossing the Charles River. The few bridges that exist are nearly impossible to find.

- **Defragmenting does not affect the MFT.** You can get a fragmented MFT by converting a crowded disk or by letting an NTFS volume get to less that 25% free space. The only workaround is to reformat and recover the files from tape. See the sidebar titled "MFT Buffer" later in this chapter for more information.

- **Defragging does not affect the Registry.** If you have users who regularly install and remove applications from their workstations, the Registry can get very fragmented. Cleanup utilities such as RegClean do a moderately good job of compressing the hives, but they still leave many fragments.

- **Defragging performs poorly with compressed files.** The reason for this lies with the APIs, not the products. The MoveFile API that jockeys files to new locations works with even multiples of 16 clusters at a time, just as the compression routines do. This means a compressed volume is broken up into clumps that the defragger cannot move around effectively.

- **Disk Defragmenter does not "pack" files.** NTFS gets very little performance benefit from packing executables, DLLs, and other read–only files to the front of the drive.

- **Defragmenting cannot be scheduled.** You cannot schedule a defrag using the Disk Defragmenter that comes with Windows 2000. You also cannot use the Task Scheduler to kick off a background defrag. All defragging operations must be initiated from the `Disk Defragmenter` console. The only apparent reason for this is to differentiate the on-board product from the commercial version of Diskeeper.

All these items (with the exception of compressed files) can be handled by using commercial defrag utilities. Executive Software ships a commercial version of Diskeeper that has additional features. Other third-party defraggers are also available, most notably PerfectDisk from Raxco Software, `www.raxco.com`, and Norton SpeedDisk from Symantec, `www.symantec.com`. Under NT4, PerfectDisk did the best job of cleaning up a disk, but it was slow, slow, slow. Norton SpeedDisk ran the fastest but needed the most passes to do an effective job. Diskeeper had the best combination of speed and functionality. The jury is still out on comparative Windows 2000 performance.

Registry Tip

The controls for the Disk Defragmenter are located at the key HKLM | `Software` | `Microsoft` | `Dfrg`.

The path to the `Disk Defragmenter` console, Dfrg.msc, is stored in HKLM | `Software` | `Microsoft` | `Windows` | `CurrentVersion` | `Explorer` | `MyComputer` | `DefragPath`.

The default entry launches the console using the command %systemroot%\System32\drfg.msc %c:, which opens the console with the focus set for the C drive.

MFT Buffer

The MFT has a buffer that enables it to grow without getting fragmented. The default buffer size is 12.5% of the total volume. On an 18GB drive formatted as a single volume, the MFT has a buffer of 2.25GB. That is enough space for the MFT to hold more than 2 million files and directories without getting fragmented.

If the disk starts to get full, the file system starts encroaching on the MFT buffer. At that point, you are likely to start getting excessive file and MFT fragmentation. You should never let an NTFS volume get less than 15% free space.

You can increase the buffer size if you want. The space is set aside like a forest preserve. After the rest of the drive fills up, the system backfills into the MFT buffer like a developer building a strip mall. Add the following Registry entries to change the default buffer size:

```
Key:     HKLM | System | CurrentControlSet | Control | FileSystem
Value:   NtfsMftZoneReservation
Data:    1-4 (REG_DWORD)
```

A setting of 1 is the default, 12.5% of volume size. Entering a 2 carves out 25%. A 3 takes 50%, and a 4 takes 75%. The system works hard to keep the MFT buffer immaculate, so you are forced to defragment more often if you have a big buffer. Now that the standard MFT record size is only 1K, you rarely need to change the buffer size.

Cleaning up a Volume Prior to Defragmenting

Have you ever used the services of a housekeeper? What's the first thing you did before the housekeeper paid that first visit? You cleaned house, right? After all, you don't want a total stranger to think you're a slob, do you? The same rule applies to preparing a volume for defragmenting. It doesn't make sense to have lots of useless files on the disk that waste the defragger's time. So, do two things prior to defragging.

- Run chkdsk /f on every volume you plan on defragging. If this means restarting to get Autochk to run on the system/boot partition, so be it. I have not yet seen an instance where a system crashed or went blue-screen during defrag following a good Chkdsk.

- Get rid of deadweight files. Windows 2000 has a utility for this called *Disk Cleanup*. It comes in the form of an executable, Clnmgr.exe. Disk Cleanup scans a drive and identifies old Indexing catalogs, temporary Internet files, temporary and superceded offline files, ActiveX and Java applet downloads, and Recycle Bin contents that can be deleted without causing problems.

For workstations and specialty servers, Disk Cleanup is a quick and effective way to remove unwanted files. Run the utility as follows:

Procedure 13.6 **Using Disk Cleanup**

---

1. Launch Disk Cleanup using START | PROGRAMS | ACCESSORIES | SYSTEM TOOLS | DISK CLEANUP. The Disk Cleanup window opens.

2. Specify the drive letter for the volume you want to clean. The utility searches for files that are candidates for removal. If the disk has a mount point, the search includes the mounted volume. When finished, Disk Cleanup offers the user the results in a menu of options. See Figure 13.10.

   Choosing to delete Temporary Internet Files does not delete cookies. It does clear cached Web pages, so you may experience delays when accessing Web sites the next time you run Internet Explorer.

   Choosing to delete Temporary Off-Line Files is acceptable even if the user is offline or forgot to synchronize. Disk Cleanup only deletes offline files that are marked as synchronized with the source file.

Figure 13.10 `Disk Cleanup` window showing menu options.

3. Click the options you want to use, and then click OK to make the changes and delete the files. When Disk Cleanup finishes, it closes down without a final message.

Defragmenting an NTFS Volume

You're now ready to defrag the volume. You can open the `Disk Defragmenter` console in several ways.

- Directly from the START menu: START | PROGRAMS | ACCESSORIES | SYSTEM TOOLS | DISK DEFRAGMENTER

- From the `Computer Management` console by expanding the tree to STORAGE | DISK DEFRAGMENTER

- From Explorer or My Computer by right-clicking a drive icon, opening the `Properties` window, and selecting TOOLS | DEFRAGMENT NOW

- From the `Run` window by entering `dfrg.msc`

After you open the `Disk Defragmenter` console, you have two alternatives. You can run a fragmentation analysis of a volume, or you can jump right in and defragment the volume. Start with an analysis.

Procedure 13.7 **Performing a Defragmentation Analysis**

1. Highlight the volume, and click `Analyze`. The system looks for fragments and gives you a visual display and text report. Figure 13.11 shows an example. See the following sidebar for more information.

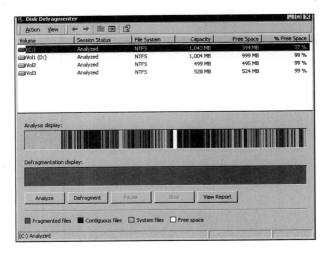

Figure 13.11 `Disk Defragmenter` window showing results of disk analysis.

Defragmentation Highlights

Volumes with no names are mounted on other volumes using mount points. Defragging a volume with mount points does not defrag the mounted volume.

You must select each volume individually. You cannot defrag more than one volume at a time using Disk Defragmenter. Third-party products have this feature.

The *System Files* referenced in the summary are not Windows 2000 system files, but NTFS system files. These consist of the MFT itself including all nonresident attributes, the paging file, and the Registry.

Don't be surprised to see lots and lots of files scattered all over the drive while the analysis tool reports that the volume does not require defragging. An NTFS volume is considered fragmented only when many nonresident data attributes are split across multiple runs. The text report for the analysis is more instructive.

---

2. Click `View Report`. The listing contains statistics for volume use, volume fragmentation, file fragmentation, pagefile fragmentation, directory fragmentation, and MFT fragmentation. Of this list, the defragger can correct file and directory fragmentation only. Expect to find nearly all the Registry hives near the top of the list for fragmentation.

3. Click Defragment. You can do this from the Report window or the main window. The system performs another analysis and then begins defragging. If it is a big volume with lots of fragmented files, the defragger may stay busy for hours. If you are defragging a server, you should do this after working hours. Not only is performance miserable, locked user files impede the defragger. Times vary depending on I/O speed, CPU speed, and bus speed.

4. Following completion, Disk Defragmenter displays a new graphical fragmentation analysis and a new report. You may need to defrag several times if you have a heavily fragmented volume.

Defragmenting FAT and FAT32 Volumes

The same Disk Defragmenter console is used to defrag FAT and FAT32 volumes, as well as NTFS volumes. The underlying engine, Dfrgfat, is different, though. If you have a dual-boot machine, you can run a Windows 9x defragger or a third-party FAT or FAT32 defragger against a Windows 2000 volume.

Both FAT and FAT32 are fundamentally more fragile than NTFS, so you are more likely—statistically speaking— to encounter file system problems during the defrag. A thorough scouring with Chkdsk before defragging is a good idea. And, as always, make sure you have a good backup.

Defragmentation Highlights

The key points to remember about using Disk Defragmenter are as follows:

- You should run Chkdsk and clean out old files prior to defragging.

- Disk Defragmenter works on all file systems supported by Windows 2000. Two different engines, DFRGFAT and DFRGNTFS, are used to defrag FAT/FAT32 and NTFS volumes.

- Defrag uses native Windows 2000 API calls to move files. These calls use standard file system protection, such as transaction logging and the change journal, to preserve file system integrity.

- Disk Defragmenter does not defrag paging files, Registry files, or other locked system files.

- It may be necessary to run the defragmenter several times to completely defrag a heavily used folder.

- Defragmentation cannot be scheduled using the Windows Scheduler.

Quotas

A deficiency in classic NT is its inability to parcel out hard-drive space. Users on classic NT servers can store three years worth of email messages in their home directories, and all the server administrator can do is gripe and send out warnings. Third-party tools for NT quota management are available, but administrators have long demanded an integrated utility that can be managed on an enterprise-wide basis. Windows 2000 tries to meet that demand with a Quota management service.

I say "tries" because the way quotas are implemented in Windows 2000 makes them less than optimal for production work. You may find that you have to change your work practices considerably if you want to use quotas. You may also decide that it's finally time to invest in one of those third-party products. Let's take a look at how quotas are implemented and then review their limitations.

Functional Description of Quotas

NTFS always had a $Quota metadata record, but it wasn't used until Windows 2000. The $Quota metadata record contains two indexes defined by two named $Index_Root streams. The first stream, $O, lists the owners of the files by SID. This is a listing of that index showing entries for two users.

```
<<end of $File_Name attribute for the $Quota record>>
26000020 00000000 06032400 51007500 &.. ......$.Q.u.
6F007400 61000000                    o.t.a....

<<start of $Index_Root attribute named $O containing index entries for owners. The
>>
                 90000000 D8000000          .......
00021800 00000300 B8000000 20000000 ............ ...
24004F00 00000000 00000000 11000000 $.O............

<<Indexed user entries with SID shown in bold. The underlined bytes in the SID are
the user's RID in hex. Converting to decimal, the first user is RID 1113 and the
second user is RID 1122.
The last underlined number in each entry is a sequence number. The first user to
access a volume with quotas or to be assigned a specific quota gets sequence number
0101. The second user gets 0201 and so forth.>>
2C000400 00000000 30001C00 00000000 ,.......0.......
01050000 00000005 15000000 5B40E770 ............[@.p
F03CDC64 4F65AB2E 59040000 01010000 .<.dOe..Y.......
```

```
2C000400 00000000 30001C00 00000000  ,.......0.......
01050000 00000005 15000000 5B40E770  ............[@.p
F03CDC64 4F65AB2E 62040000 02010000  .<.d0e..b.......
```

A second named index stream, $Q, keeps track of the default quotas, thresh-olds, and quota attributes, such as Deny Disk Space or Log Event. When a user is assigned a quota or adds files to a volume that has quota enabled, the user's SID is added to the $O index and then given an entry in the $Q index specifying the limits assigned to that user.

```
<<header information for the $Q named index attribute>>
90000000 B0010000 00021800 00000200  ................
90010000 20000000 24005100 00000000  .... ...$.Q.....
```

```
<<Flags and settings for quotas. The first bold number is the default quota
threshold. The second bold number is the default quota limit. The underlined number
contains attribute flags.>>
00000000 10000000 00100000 08000B00  ................
10000000 80010000 80010000 00000000  ................
14003000 00000000 48000400 00000000  ..0.....H.......
01000000 02000000 71000000 00000000  ........q.......
00000000 E0D12BF8 00C7BE01 00100E00  ......+.........
00000000 00A00F00 00000000 00000000  ................
```

```
<<User entries. The first bold number is a specific quota threshold assigned to the
user. The second bold number is specific quota ceiling for the user. The final line
is the user's SID. >>
14004C00 00000000 60000400 00000000  ..L.....`.......
01010000 02000000 00000000 00000000  ................
00000000 806C548A 02C7BE01 00C01200  .....lT.........
00000000 00401F00 00000000 00000000  .....@..........
00000000 01050000 00000005 15000000  ................
5B40E770 F03CDC64 4F65AB2E 59040000  [@.p.<.d0e..Y...
```

```
14004C00 00000000 60000400 00000000  ..L.....`.......
02010000 02000000 00000000 00000000  ................
00000000 80D9DCE2 02C7BE01 00100E00  ................
00000000 1F850F00 00000000 00000000  ................
00000000 01050000 00000005 15000000  ................
5B40E770 F03CDC64 4F65AB2E 62040000  [@.p.<.d0e..b...
```

When quotas are enabled, the system sets a Quota bit in the $Standard_Information attribute of each file. It also copies the file size into the $Standard_Information attribute. The $Standard_Information attribute is always resident, so this enables the quota manager to rapidly scan the MFT to index the space assigned to each user.

Quota Limitations

This method of applying the $Quota metadata record involves some awkward restrictions in the way quotas are imposed on users:

- **Quotas are assigned to a volume.** You cannot assign quotas to a directory. This affects the way you parcel out directory space. If you assign a quota of 100MB to a volume that contains files from two departments, users who work in both departments are limited to the same 100MB limit. NetWare administrators who use the DSPACE utility will miss this feature.

- **Quotas are assigned to file owners.** You cannot use quotas to parcel out disk space based on groups. For example, you cannot give the Graphic Design department more space on a volume than the Sales department, even though the graphic designers need a lot more file storage. You must assign higher quotas to individual members of the Graphic Design department if you want to keep their data on the same volume as the data of other folks.

- **Members of the Administrators group have no quota limit.** The built-in Administrators group is exempt from quotas. As an administrator, you can end up with ownership in subtle ways. For instance, you get ownership of a file if you restore it from tape to a different location than the original directory. If you copy user files to a new server to give them more room, you become the owner.

- **Quota entries are part of the file system, not Registry.** If you move a disk to another Windows 2000 machine, the quota settings move, too. If you move the disk to an NT4 machine running SP4 or better— or you have a dual-boot machine—the NTFS5 volume is accessible, but quotas do not work. Writing to the disk from NT4 may corrupt the quota index.

- **Quotas are based on the calculated file size, not on the on-disk file size.** If you compress files or use sparse files, the user may run up against a quota while still having lots of space available.

- **Quotas impact performance.** Microsoft did not release any performance statistics comparing file and print performance with and without quotas. In my own laboratory testing, I noticed an impact, but have not quantified it by using NetBench or ServerBench. The fact that the system must keep an up-to-the-minute index of all file usage on a volume should be a hint that overhead exists. Keep this in mind when deciding whether you want to implement quotas on a full-time basis. You can turn quota tracking on and off periodically to monitor space usage if you want to avoid daily performance drag.

- **You must be logged on using an account with Administrator privileges.** You cannot use the Secondary Logon Service (Runas command) to run the Quota Management console as administrator.

Assigning File Ownership with Third-Party Utilities

Standard Windows 2000 security tools only enable taking ownership, not giving it.

You can use these products to assign ownership:

- Setowner from Pedestal Software, www.pedestalsoftware.com, part of a suite of tools called NTSecTools

- Chown from MKS Software, www.mks.com, part of a suite of tools called the MKS Toolkit

  The MKS toolkit utilities are UNIX look-alikes that come in the Services for UNIX product from Microsoft. The utility suite also includes a Windows version of vi, a truly scary code combination, much like putting a Madonna mask on Don Knotts.

Quota Management Operational Description

The following steps assign quotas to a volume that is set aside strictly for user home directories. Two parameters are assigned, a threshold and a ceiling. Warnings are placed in the Event Log when users exceed either of these two values. You can also prevent users from saving files when they exceed the ceiling. You have to look closely for the Event Log warnings because they take the form of a standard blue-dot information message rather than yellow-dot or red-dot warnings.

Procedure 13.8   **Assigning User Quotas to a Volume**

1. Open Explorer. Right-click a disk you want to manage, select PROPERTIES from the fly-out, and then select the Quota tab. See Figure 13.12. (If you are managing quotas on a mounted volume, use the Disk Management console to select the volume.)

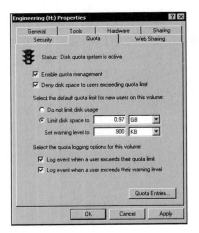

Figure 13.12 Volume properties window showing the Quota tab with options set for user home directories.

2. The default setting for quotas is disabled. Select Enable quota management to turn on quotas for the volume.

3. Select Deny disk space to users exceeding quota limit. If you like, you can leave this option unselected for a while to gather reports about users who exceed the recommended quota so that you can make arrangements with them to move or delete their files before you enforce the quota.

4. Select the Limit disk space To radio button, and enter the quota and quota thresholds you want to enforce. The system converts them to the nearest cluster boundary when you save the entry. That is why the setting in the example is .97GB instead of 1000MB.

5. Select both logging options. This records the quota offenders in the Application Log.

6. Click Apply. The system responds with a warning that the volume will be scanned to update disk usage statistics.

7. Click OK to enable quotas on the volume. The system scans the MFT to set quota bits on file records and gather ownership statistics. When the scan is completed, click Quota Entries. The Quota Entries window opens. Figure 13.13 shows an example. It may take a while for the system to resolve SIDs into user names. This is normal and does not indicate an Active Directory problem, unless the names never resolve. In that case, look for a problem communicating with a Global Catalog server.

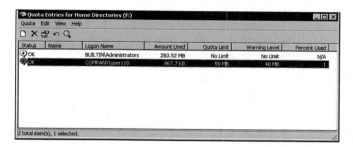

Figure 13.13 Quota Entries window showing the BUILTIN\Administrators account with no limit and a user with usage statistics listed.

8. If you open the Quota Entries window immediately after initializing quotas, the only name on the list is the Administrators local group. Users do not appear until they access the volume. The example in Figure 13.13 shows statistics for the Administrators group and the USER110 user name. Note that the Administrators group has no quota limits. The user got the default limits.

9. If you have specific users who want higher quotas, or you want to impose lower quotas selectively, you can add specific users to the quota list or select the user from the list if they already accessed the volume. From the menu, select QUOTA | NEW QUOTA ENTRY. The Select Users window opens.

10. Select the user or users to whom you want to grant individual quotas. You can select users from trusted domains anywhere in the enterprise. If you do not specify a quota for remote users, they get the default quota.

11. Click Add to put the user on the list and then OK to save the entries. The Add New Quota window opens. See Figure 13.14.

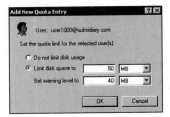

Figure 13.14   Add New Quota Entry window showing increased quotas for a specific user.

12. You can either enter special quota values for the user or choose not to impose quotas at all. Click OK to save the changes and return to the Quota Entries window. The user name now appears on the list with a current status showing the new limits.

13. If you want to change quota settings for multiple users, you can select them with the Control key pressed in normal Windows fashion and then select QUOTA | PROPERTIES from the menu.

Third-Party Quota Management Utilities

If you decide that Windows 2000 quota management doesn't meet your needs, you may want to try a third-party utility.

The two most commonly used quota management products for classic NT are QuotaAdvisor from Quinn Software, available at www.sunbelt-software.com, and Quota Server for NT from Northern Technologies in Sweden at www.northern.se. Both of these tools work with Windows 2000.

Exporting and Importing Quotas

You cannot access a "Master Quota" control from a central location such as Active Directory. If you want to impose domain-wide quotas on users, you must export and import quota settings between machines. This works only between machines in the same domain; otherwise, the target machine does not recognize the SIDs.

Procedure 13.9   **Importing and Exporting Quotas Between Machines**

1. Open the Quota tab under the Properties window for the volume with quotas you want to export.

2. Click Quota Settings. The Quota Settings window opens.

3. From the menu, select QUOTA | EXPORT. The Quota Export window appears.

4. Select a place to save the export file and give it a name. The file uses a special format.

5. From the machine where you want to import the quotas, open the `Quota Settings` window.

6. From the menu, select QUOTA | IMPORT. After a prompt to verify the action, the settings are imported. The status list now shows the new user settings.

Deleting Users from a Quota List

You cannot simply delete a user from a quota list. The user's SID is associated with files. That association must be broken before the system enables you to delete the user's entry. You have the alternative of transferring ownership of the user's files to yourself or to another user using a third-party tool. You can also delete the files, if that is a viable option.

When you attempt to delete a user, a window opens listing all the files owned by the user on the managed volume. Figure 13.15 shows an example. Using this window, you can take whatever action you deem fit to get the user off the ownership list for the files.

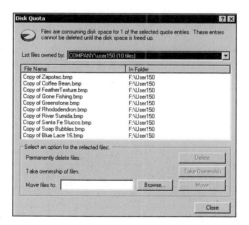

Figure 13.15 List of files owned by user on managed volume.

After you purge the user from liability, culpability, accountability, and responsibility, you can delete the entry from the quota list. If you use the `Disk Quota` window to do this, the user is removed from the list when you click OK to return to the `Quota Entries` window.

Issues and Problems with Quotas

After you impose quotas, you have to deal with user questions and frustrations. Because quotas are assigned to an entire volume, they can confuse users in several ways:

- If you have multiple shares pointed at different points on the same volume, a user might attempt to copy a slug of files from one mapped drive to another. The call to the Help Desk goes something like this: "I'm trying to copy my month-end report from my K drive to my L drive, but I'm getting 'out of disk space' errors." You can try to explain that both K and L point at the same volume and that the copy of the 30MB report exceeds the user's quota. A better solution is to eliminate redundant share points.

- If you have a single volume that contains system files and user data, a spooled print job may exceed the user's quota. The error message in this case is ambiguous—as are most printer errors—so it is difficult to diagnose. The solution is to keep data and system files separate and never impose quotas on system volumes.

- Configuring walk-up workstations (sometimes called kiosk machines) for users to get their email and file their time cards is a common practice. They often save files to the local hard drives of these machines. You can impose local quotas, but watch out for roaming profiles. If the user exceeds quota, the system refuses to download the user's roaming profile. It also refuses to build a new profile using NTUSER.DAT from the default user profile. The user is blocked from logging on. This is not necessarily a bad thing, mind you, considering that the user probably violated policy by exceeding quota, but it does require administrative intervention to resolve the problem.

- Remember that file ownership moves when a file is moved. This means that a user who is over quota can move files from another location, so long as he or she is not the owner, but that the files cannot be copied because this creates a new file with that user as owner. This typically causes no end of confusion.

- Users who are over quota and attempt to save files receive a "Drive Full" error. The consequences are uncertain. Savvy users can save the file to the local drive or to another network share. If not, they may lose the changes as they thrash around figuring out why they cannot save. The system does not broadcast a warning when a user goes over a threshold. You can configure an alert to the administrator's console.

Quotas and File Management

Quotas can cause problems for server administrators if they aren't aware that quotas are associated with file owners. For instance, Backup admins often restore files to a "landing pad" directory and then copy them to their final destination. Because an administrator copies the files, their owner becomes the Administrators local group, not the original owner. This puts the files outside the quota system, and the user gets a free ride.

You can avoid this by moving the files instead of copying them, but this risks losing the files if something goes wrong on the network, forcing you to do the restore again. The Scopy utility that comes with the Resource Kit does not preserve ownership.

Your best alternative is to copy the files and then use one of the third-party ownership management utilities to assign the original user as the owner.

Quota Highlights

The body of this section contains several extensive checklists concerning quotas. Remember the following key points:

- Quotas are applied at the volume level only.
- Quotas are applied based on file ownership.
- Members of the Administrators local group are exempt.
- Individual users can be assigned specific quotas or be exempted from quotas altogether for that volume.
- Moving and restoring files from backup retains file ownership. Copying creates a new owner. Keep this in mind when planning on the effect of quotas.
- Quotas are maintained by the file system, not the Registry. Quotas follow the disk if it is moved.

Remote Storage Services

Data storage has three metrics: cost, convenience, and performance. The most convenient media with the best performance and the highest cost is fixed hard drives. The least convenient media with the poorest performance and the least cost is tape.

Some relative prices follow. Here at the end of 1999, you can buy a 50GB fast-wide SCSI drive for just less than $2000. That's less than 4 cents per megabyte, although the real cost is closer to 10 cents when you account for housing the spindles, buying the interfaces, RAID losses, and hot standby disks. Even at this historically low price, keeping the entire data storage contents of a good-sized company—call it 50TB—on spindles for immediate access costs more than $5 million, not including ongoing maintenance and backup costs.

Compare that to the cost of tape. A DLT unit costing about $75,000 can store 3TB of data at a cost of 2.3 cents per megabyte. At that rate, storing that same 50TB of data costs about $1.2 million. But the files on that tape are slow to access and inconvenient to manage.

Technology that marries cheap tape storage to a fast, convenient file system is called *Hierarchical Storage Management* (HSM). HSM moves your old files to tape, where they can be ready to load back onto a spindle if anyone needs them.

The principles and operating logistics of HSM have a long and durable track record in the mainframe world, but the technology failed to penetrate the PC market in any significant way. The cost of spinning storage is so low and the hassle of running big tape libraries is so high that it's tough to make a business case for HSM in the PC world.

Recent advances in robotics brought automated tape libraries within the reach of the average IT department, though. Never one to ignore an opportunity to bury a feature in the OS, Microsoft contracted with Highground Technologies, www.highground.com, to produce an HSM product for Windows 2000 that takes advantage of those cheap tape libraries.

The result is *Remote Storage Services* (RSS). Don't confuse RSS with the Removable Storage Management service, RSM. The system uses RSM to control media libraries such as tape libraries and CD-ROM jukeboxes. The RSS makes use of RSM to shuffle media into and out of the library, and to call up new media from the offline pool. RSS is available only on Windows 2000 Server and Advanced Server, not on Windows 2000 Professional.

Getting Additional HSM Features

Like most other add-on technologies in Windows 2000, the Highground offering is complemented by a more comprehensive management package available at extra cost. You can download an evaluation copy from the company's Web site.

Functional Description of RSS

RSS uses two criteria to decide whether files should be moved offline: the file's last access date and the amount of desired free space on the volume. When volume loading exceeds the threshold designated by an administrator, RSS shuffles the older files off to tape faster than a corporate raider downsizing after a takeover.

RSS uses reparse points to inform the file system where the offline files are located. When a user accesses the offline file, RSS transfers the file off tape and back to disk where it can be accessed via standard NTFS. This can take a while, so the user gets a fancy animated icon for entertainment while the tape subsystem does its work.

The name *Remote Storage Services* is plural because a suite of four services work together to provide HSM support. This suite is loaded by SVCHOST. The Registry entries are located in HKLM | System | CurrentControlSet | Services. The services are:

- **Remote Storage Engine (RsEng.exe).** Coordinates the various services and provides the interface for the admin console, RsAdmin.msc.
- **Remote Storage File System Agent (RsFSA.exe).** The file system filter that acts as a go-between for the remote storage system.
- **Remote Storage Subsystem (RsSub.exe).** Controls the tape media.
- **Remote Storage User Link (RsFSA.exe).** Acts as a client interface.

Two supporting executables, RsNotify and RsMover, along with several DLLs, all start with the Rs prefix.

RSS stores information about remote files in two Jet databases under \WINNT\System32\RemoteStorage.

- An engine database, EngDB, keeps track of the file locations in the tape system.
- A File System Agent database, FsaDB, keeps track of the remote files on the disk.

Collector files at the root of the \RemoteStorage directory hold the records prior to committing them to the master database files.

Operational Considerations for RSS

A number of operational considerations affect how you implement RSS:

- Applications sometimes scan files by opening them. The infamous FindFast is one of these applications. If a scanning application touches many offline files at once, it can swamp the system with recalls. If you do not disable the application, you may be forced to stop it using Task Manager or Kill. Not all file scans result in recalls. As long as the scans involve only attributes and flags in the resident portion of the attributes, the files themselves are not opened. Context indexing and full-text searches are disabled for offline files.

- You cannot use removable media drives, such as Zip and Jaz drives, magneto-optical (MO) drives, or CD-R drives as offline media. You must use tape. If you did not already install a tape unit, refer to Chapter 2, "Performing Upgrades and Automated Installations," for instructions.

- If you have only one tape unit on a machine, it will be difficul coordinating backups and RSS. If you have only one server or cannot do backups from a workstation, you should either forgo using RSS or install a second tape unit.

- If you do not have a tape library, you must either limit your offline file list to the capacity of one cartridge or be prepared to handle cartridges manually as users touch the files. The users get a *Contact System Administrator* message if the offline file cannot be located in the tape library.

- Make sure your virus scanning software is intelligent enough to do its job without incrementing the Last Access Date. RSS never moves files offline.

- RSS is not a replacement for tape backups. Tapes can become unreadable or the catalog might be corrupted. If you are forced to reinstall Windows 2000 on a system that contains offline files, you must re-create the original volumes, recover the Remote Storage databases, and remount the original tapes before you can access the files. See "Backing Up Remote Files" later in this chapter.

Performing Initial RSS Configuration

The steps in this section load the RSS drivers and prepare a tape system for offline file storage.

The RSS drivers are not loaded as part of the standard Windows 2000 compliment of files. You need the Server CD. Installation requires restarting the system.

Procedure 13.10   **Performing Initial RSS Configuration**

1. Open `Control Panel` | `Add/Remove Programs` | `Windows Components`.

2. Select the `Remote Storage` option and click `Next`. The system installs the drivers and configures the Registry entries. You must restart after the service is installed. The `Remote Storage Management` console, Rsadmin.msc, manages the RSS. This console is loaded when the services are installed.

3. After restart, launch the Remote Storage console via START | PROGRAMS | ADMINISTRATIVE TOOLS | REMOTE STORAGE. The first time you run the console after installing RSS, a wizard walks you through configuration.

4. Click Next at the Welcome window. The wizard checks for admin privileges and the presence of suitable offline storage media, and then opens the Volume Management window. See Figure 13.16.

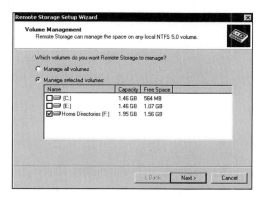

Figure 13.16 Remote Storage Setup Wizard - Volume Management window showing selection of user home directories as the managed drive.

5. Select a drive to manage. You should not select the system/boot drive. If the volume has mount points, the files on the mounted volumes are not moved.

6. Click Next. The Volume Settings window opens. See Figure 13.17. The Desired Free Space value determines when RSS begins scavenging files. The default value is 5% free space. This is a little close for comfort, so let's set it for 20%. This leaves room on the disk for reading large files back from tape. You can increase the minimum file size if you want. Just keep in mind that 1000 little files add up to a big whack of disk space, especially if you have big cluster sizes.

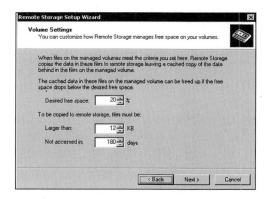

Figure 13.17 Remote Storage Setup Wizard - Volume Settings window.

7. Click Next. The Media Type window opens. If you have several tape systems installed on the server, you can select the one for RSS to use. The example shows a 4mm DAT tape.

8. Click Next. The Schedule for Copying Files window opens. The default is to copy files at 2:00 a.m. every day. This might interfere with your tape backups, or you might want to move files offline only on weekends. Click Change Schedule to modify the interval and start time. You can set multiple schedules, if you want.

9. Click Next. A summary window appears listing your choices.

10. Click Finish to accept the settings. The system configures the Registry and the file system, initializes its databases, and then opens a console containing the Remote Storage console and the Removable Storage console.

11. Leave the console open and proceed to the next section.

Assigning a Tape to the RSS Media Pool

To use tape media for remote storage, you must assign the tape to the Remote Storage media pool by using the Removable Storage Management console. This is where the process can get confusing.

If you already used the tape system to do a backup using Ntbackup or a third-party application, the tape library allocated the tape to the Backup application. If you expand the Removable Storage tree, you'll find the tape listed in the right pane of the window under Backup.

If you want to preserve the contents of that tape, right-click the media name and select EJECT from the fly-out menu. Walk through the Eject Media Wizard to retrieve the tape. Then, insert a blank tape and use the steps to prepare it for RSS.

If you want to overwrite an existing backup tape, you must first deallocate it from Backup and then prepare it as free media. Do this as follows:

Procedure 13.11 **Deallocating Previously Used Media and Preparing for RSS**

1. Right-click the media name and select ALL TASKS | DEALLOCATE from the fly-out menu. You receive a warning that the action will cause loss of the data on the media.

2. Click Yes to acknowledge the warning. You get another warning just to make sure you read the first warning. Click Yes to acknowledge the second warning and complete the deallocation. Under the State column, the media now shows Idle and Available.

3. Right-click the Media icon and select PREPARE from the fly-out menu. This action writes a Free Media label to the tape and moves it to the Free media pool. A warning informs you that all data on the media will be destroyed.

4. Click Yes to acknowledge the warning. A confirmation window appears. Click Yes to acknowledge and complete the action. The system moves the media to the Tape icon under Free.

Selecting Files to Move to Offline Storage

Now that RSS is loaded and has a tape waiting to store files, select files to move to offline storage as follows. Refer to Figure 13.18 to see the layout of the initial Remote Storage console.

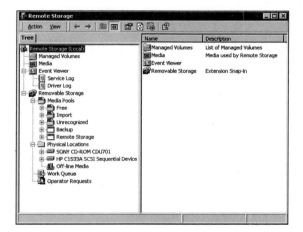

Figure 13.18   Remote Storage Setup Wizard - Remote Storage console window.

Procedure 13.12   **Selecting Files to Move to Offline Storage**

1. Right-click one of the managed volumes and select INCLUDE/EXCLUDE RULES from the fly-out menu. The Properties window opens for the managed volume. Use the General and Settings tab to change entries you made in the wizard.

2. Click Add. The Edit Include/Exclude Rule window opens. See Figure 13.19.

Figure 13.19   `Edit Include/Exclude Rule` window.

3. Enter a file extension you want to include or exclude. For example, you may want to exclude executables and DLLs. Or, you may want to include only ★.doc, ★.xls, and ★.ppt files. The rules are read from top to bottom, so if you specify to include ★.doc files from the root of the volume but later you exclude ★.doc files from a particular subdirectory, the first setting takes precedence.

4. Use drag-and-drop to move the media to the Tape icon under Remote Storage.

5. Manually initiate a file copy to offline storage. To do this, right-click the `Managed Volume` icon and select ALL TASKS | COPY FILES TO REMOTE STORAGE. An information window appears explaining that this action creates a task to do the work. See the following sidebar for more information.

Task Scheduler and RSS

When RSS is configured to periodically copy files to a remote location, it creates a script and gives the script to the Task Scheduler. You can monitor the status of the job by using the `Scheduled Tasks` icon in the Control Panel.

The `Work Queue` icon under the `Removable Storage` console gives a running history of the actions taken with the tape library itself. If you are unable to initiate an action, check the `Work Queue` to see whether the job is running, waiting, or failed.

A common cause of hangs is forgetting to put a tape in the drive or a failure of the robotic system in the library to find and load the proper tape.

If a scheduled Remote Copy job kicks off while your manual copy job is running, the scheduled job queues up and starts right after the manual job finishes. This does not present a problem because the affected files are already transferred.

6. Click OK to initiate the task.

7. Open Control Panel and launch Scheduled Tasks. A series of Remote Storage jobs are listed. The RemoteStorage_Copy job shows Running. Figure 13.20 shows an example.

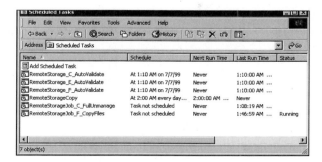

Figure 13.20 Scheduled Tasks window showing the RemoteStorageJob_F_CopyFiles job running. This is not a scheduled task, so the Next Run Time is set to Never.

8. Depending on the speed of your tape and the size and number of files you're transferring, it may take a while for the job to complete. When finished, files that are now stored offline are marked in Explorer with a little clock. Figure 13.21 shows an example. If you work from a command prompt, you'll notice that the directory listings show the size of offline files in parentheses.

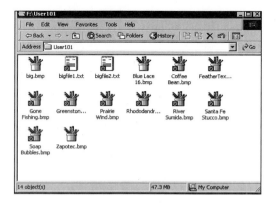

Figure 13.21 Explorer window showing remote files marked with special icons.

9. Keep in mind that Explorer and the command line show actual file sizes, not on-disk sizes. To get true loading information, view the `Properties` window for the directory or volume.

10. Open a file that is marked offline. The tape system engages to find the file. A `Recalling from Remote Storage` window opens to indicate that you need to wait.

11. When the tape library finds the file, it is transferred to disk and placed in its original directory. If the stub file is moved to a new directory, the file is restored from tape to the new location. The file retains its owner and ACLs.

Now that the file was touched, it remains on disk for the time duration specified for Remote Storage on the volume. The default is 180 days. If the tape containing the file is not in the tape library, a message appears on the console prompting the administrator to insert the proper media into the tape drive. The media name includes the server name and the sequence number of the volume.

Locating Files on Tape

The RSS system is designed to be transparent to the user. It is my experience that "transparent" technology typically comes with management tools that are clumsy, tedious, or downright insufficient for the purpose. Remote Storage just barely misses this category. The Resource Kit has two utilities designed to help work with remote files from the command line. They are the *Remote Storage Directory* utility, Rsdir, and the *Remote Storage Diagnostic* utility, Rsdiag.

Rsdir shows quite a few details that aren't included in a normal directory listing. Its strength lies in showing the exact status of a remote file. Table 13.4 shows the information included in a full Rsdir listing.

Table 13.4 **Elements of a Full Rsdir Listing**

Status	Attributes	Physical	Logical
Create Time	Last Access Time	Last Modify Time	Migrate Time
RC	Last Recall Time	HSM ID	TimeBag ID
File ID	File Version ID	Data Stream	CRC Type

Status	Attributes	Physical	Logical
Data Stream CRC	DS Size	DS Start	Data Size
Data Start	File Size	File Start	Ver Type
Ver Info	Filename		

Using this information, you can quickly determine which files were moved to tape, when they were moved, and where they were moved so that you can search for the tape and recover the files.

The companion utility, Rsdiag, provides the same function as the `Remote Management` console. Using Rsdiag, you can view, manage, recall, and copy jobs in the queue as well as dump information in the RSS databases to text files for viewing and troubleshooting. Both of these utilities are helpful for locating a tape that contains remote files.

Runaway Recalls

Other than a loss of the tapes themselves, the biggest nightmare in an HSM system is a user who accidentally recalls dozens and dozens of files from tape without realizing that it might flood the target disk. This can happen quite innocently. A tax accountant might start reviewing last year's bookkeeping records and kick off a frenzy of recalls. Or, a user might scan the contents of an old directory with a text scanner looking for a bit of information.

The system limits the files that a single user can recall by means of a *Recall Limit*. This limits the number of files a user can recall with less than 10 seconds between each touch. An administrator can adjust the ceiling as follows:

Procedure 13.13   **Setting the Recall Limit to Prevent Runaway Recalls**

1. Open the `Remote Storage` console.

2. Right-click the Remote Storage icon at the top of the tree and select PROPERTIES from the fly-out menu. The `Properties` window opens.

3. Select the `Recall Limit` tab. See Figure 13.22. The default setting for `Maximum number of successive recalls` is 60. You may want to set it for a more reasonable number, such as 20.

Figure 13.22 `Remote Storage Properties` window showing `Recall Limit` tab.

4. Check the `Exempt administrators from this limit` option, but warn the administrators of the danger of an accidental mass recall. Reduce the risk by avoiding administrator logons. Use the RunAs feature instead.

5. If a user methodically sets about opening files, reading them, and then moving on to the next file, the runaway limit is not triggered. Educating users about the meaning of that little clock icon and warning them not to recall files indiscriminately is important.

Backing up Remote Files

It may seem like a redundancy to talk about backing up files that are already on tape, but just because offline storage uses the same media as backups doesn't mean they are as reliable for data recovery. Tapes can and do become corrupt, unreadable, broken, or dirty. DLT is notorious for quirky problems that can leave an entire cartridge unraveled inside the tape unit. Other media types have their own faults.

Even if you have a tape library that is as reliable as gravity, other hazards exist. Thieves can steal the tape unit and the tapes. Fires, floods, earthquakes, and other calamities can occur. A burst of cosmic rays sent from a far, distant supernova might send the tape to that big cassette dump in the sky. In short, it is vital to protect those gigabytes or terabytes of remote data by copying them to another set of tapes.

If your tape hardware supports cloning, your best bet for assuring data continuity is to copy the entire library to a new set of cartridges and then store them offsite. If your system lacks this feature, you can use the Media Copy feature in Windows 2000 to make copies of the tapes. Figure 13.23 shows an example.

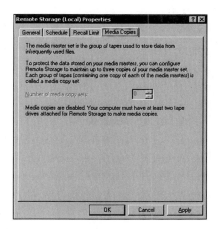

Figure 13.23   `Remote Storage Properties` showing `Media Copies` tab.

This feature is available only if you have at least one additional tape system attached to the computer. You can copy to a maximum of three tape systems at once. Files are copied to all media sets simultaneously. Set the number of copies from the `Remote Storage Properties` window as follows:

1. Open the `Remote Storage` console `Properties` window.
2. Select the `Media Copies` tab.
3. Enter the number of copies.
4. Click `OK` to save.

Removing a Volume from Remote Storage

At some point, you may decide that you no longer want to have remote files on a volume. If you decide to recall all files, you must first exempt Administrators from the runaway recall block. You can decide to leave the remote files on tape, but you need to make careful arrangements to protect the Remote Storage databases. Recovering remote files from tape without the Remote Storage databases is difficult.

If you try to remove the Remote Storage service completely by using
CONTROL PANEL | ADD/REMOVE PROGRAMS, the system offers two
alternatives:

- `Recall copied files from remote storage` is the ollie-ollie-ox-in-free
  option. Every file is copied back to disk. If you select this option, the
  `Removal Option` window shows the available free space and the space you
  need to recall all the files. If you do not have enough space, you can either
  remove existing files from the disk or copy the offline file icons to another
  disk with more capacity.

- `Maintain copied files in remote storage` option leaves the current remote
  files on tape, but does not move any more files to tape. They can still be
  recalled from tape when users open them. If you removed the tapes as part
  of deinstalling the system, you can use NTFS permissions to deny access
  to users.

In either case, full recall or simple program removal, your first step is to open
the `Remote Storage Management` console.

Procedure 13.14 **Removing a Volume from RSS**

1. Expand the tree to show Managed Volumes.
2. Right-click the managed volume you want to remove and select REMOVE
   from the fly-out menu. The `Remove Volume Management Wizard` window
   appears.
3. Click `Next` at the `Welcome` window. The `Removal Options` window appears.
   See Figure 13.24. The introduction to these steps discussed the two alternatives. This example maintains the stored files on tape just in case they
   are needed.

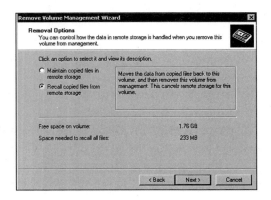

Figure 13.24 `Volume Management Wizard` — `Removal Options` window.

4. Select the `Maintain copied files in remote storage` option and click `Next`. The system prompts for confirmation.

5. Click `Yes` to acknowledge. A summary window appears describing what you just did.

6. Click `Finish` to close the wizard and return to the `Remote Storage` window. The volume is no longer managed.

If a user decides that he needs access to an offline file —this usually happens the very next day when a user demands access to a file that wasn't touched since the Watergate hearings—you can insert the tape and enable the user to open the remote file. As long as the Remote Access database is intact, the remote files continue to be available.

Recovering a Remote Storage Database

Speaking of Watergate, there is no such thing as an indestructible tape or an indestructible tape catalog. Tape durability is a function of the care with which you buy and treat the cartridges and drives. Catalog durability, on the other hand, is pretty much out of your control.

The Jet databases used by classic NT were not exactly models of reliability. Perhaps the new Jet technology is better, perhaps not. One thing is certain—if you use RSS long enough, and you use it on enough systems, you are bound to encounter a situation in which you need to recover from a lost or corrupted RSS database.

For example, a user reports that a file with a clock on the icon is no longer accessible, and you cannot open it, either, even though the tape is in the drive. Or, the server crashes and refuses to restart, forcing you to reinstall Windows 2000.

This crash took your RSS tape catalog and the volume containing the stub files. The stub files must be in their original location for the database to work, and the Windows 2000 system files must be on the same drive letter and directory. If the system crashes, you must do the following:

- Reinstall Windows 2000.
- Restore the source files from backup tape.
- Restore the RSS databases from the remote tape library.

The RSS databases are stored in the `\WINNT\System32\RemoteStorage` directory. An RSS database restoration also includes restoring the Removable Storage (RSM) database located in the `\WINNT\System32\NTMSDATA` directory. The RSS needs the RSM database so that it can find media in the media pools.

The RSS and RSM databases are both copied to the RSS tape automatically. This is done specifically to enable recovery in the event of a system crash.

The general steps for recovering the databases after a complete loss of the operating system are as follows:

Procedure 13.15 **General Steps for Data Restoration Following Loss of RSS Server**

1. Reinstall Windows 2000 without installing Remote Storage Services. You must first restore the databases.

2. If you lost the drive containing the stub files, restore the files from tape. *The drive letter and volume name must be identical.* Writing this down on the RSS tape library so that you have the information when you need it is a good idea.

3. Use the `Removable Storage Management` console to catalog the RSS tape.

4. Restore the RSS and RSM databases to their original location.

5. Move the RsEng database to a temporary location.

6. Reinstall Remote Storage Services.

7. Restore the Engine database from the backup database on the tape.

8. Verify that remote storage files are accessible.

Follow these steps when restoring the databases and regaining access to the files. If you still have the operating system but are experiencing corruption of the databases, you can restore the databases using this procedure. Proceed as follows:

Procedure 13.16 **Recovering RSM and RSS Databases from Tape**

1. Reinstall Windows 2000 and the source RSS files to their original drive letters and volume names.

2. Insert the RSS tape in the tape unit or initialize the tape library to put the first tape in the drive.

3. Launch the `Computer Management` console and expand the tree to show the elements under Removable Storage.

4. Find the RSS media under `Imported`. The media name starts with RS followed by the server name and a sequence number, such as `RS-PHX-DC-01-001`.

5. Use drag-and-drop to move the media to the Backup pool. If this pool is not available, open the Backup program using START | PROGRAMS | ACCESSORIES | SYSTEM TOOLS | BACKUP. This initializes the backup pool.

6. With the media in the Backup media area, open the Backup program using START | PROGRAMS | ACCESSORIES | SYSTEM TOOLS | BACKUP.

7. Select the `Restore` tab.

8. Expand the tree under the tape library to show the RS media.

9. Highlight the RS media. From the menu, select TOOLS | MEDIA TOOLS | CATALOG. The system scans the tape and builds a catalog. This can take a very long time. If you have gigabytes of files, be prepared to wait several hours to get a catalog.

10. When the tape is finished cataloging, an icon representing the original drive letter and volume appears under the Media icon.

11. Click the plus sign on the media to expand the tree and show the subdirectories.

12. Select the `\WINNT\System32\Ntmsdata` and `\WINNT\System32\RemoteStorage` directories. If multiple instances of these two directories occur, select the most current. Determining the date requires loading the catalogs. Put a check next to the icon to open the catalog. Opening a catalog can take a long time.

13. Find the `Restore Files To` option at the lower left of the window. It must say `Original Location`; otherwise, the system restores the files to an alternate location called RSS Managed Volume. If you accidentally restore the files to the wrong location, you can copy them manually to the correct location.

14. Click `Start Restore`. An `Advanced Options` window opens. Click `Advanced`.

15. Select `Restore Removable Storage Database`. The RSS needs the Removable Storage Database to find the original media in the media pools that are stored in this database.

16. Click `OK` to begin the restore. When the files are restored, close the restore window and close Backup.

17. Open the `Computer Management` console, and expand the tree under Removable Storage Management.

18. Verify that the media pools are restored.

Now it's time to install the Remote Storage services. Do this using CONTROL PANEL | ADD/REMOVE SOFTWARE | INSTALL WINDOWS COMPONENTS. You must reboot after the files are copied. Following restart, proceed as follows:

Procedure 13.17 **Recovering the RSS Database**

1. Open COMPUTER MANAGEMENT | SERVICES.

2. Stop the following services: Remote Storage Engine, Remote Storage Media, and Remote Storage File.

3. Open Explorer and navigate to the `\WINNT\System32\RemoteStorage\EngDB` folder.

4. Move the contents of the `\EngDB` folder to a temporary folder such as `C:\Temp\EngDB`. (Note: The EngDB database is recovered from a backup file later in this procedure.)

5. Open a command prompt.

6. Change directory to `\WINNT\System32\RemoteStorage\EngDB`.

7. Issue the following command: `rstore \WINNT\System32\RemoteStorage\EngDB.bak`. If the restore is successful, the system gives the message *Restore Succeeded*.

8. Go back to the `Computer Management` console.

9. Restart the following services: Remote Storage Engine, Remote Storage Media, and Remote Storage File.

10. Verify the restoration by opening the drive containing the stub files and recalling a file or two.

RSS Highlights

Remember the following key points about RSS:

- RSS is a suite of services designed to copy files from disk to tape and make those files available to the file system for recall.

- RSS requires a locally attached tape backup unit.

- RSS can only manage NTFS5 volumes because it uses reparse points to track file location.

- Files containing reparse points are indexed in the $Reparse database. The Change Log protects this index for rapid recovery in the event of a system crash.

- Files under a mount point are not moved to tape.
- A server should be dedicated to RSS to minimize complexity if the remote storage system must be recovered.

Moving Forward

At this stage of Windows 2000 deployment, the back room is almost ready to accept data from users. Making sure that data is stored where only authorized users can access it is the subject of the next chapter.

14

Managing File Systems Security

IF SYSTEMS MANAGEMENT WERE A THREE-RING CIRCUS—and when isn't it?—the acts attracting the most attention would be Security, Reliability, and Performance. Ideally, each act would get equal attention, but considering that the audience consists mostly of irate users, harried managers, and demanding customers, the focus usually goes to Reliability and Performance. Poor old Security is left in the back ring with the toothless tiger and the clown with a bad back. At least, that is, until an unstable employee erases the last three years of Accounts Receivables files and flees to Macedonia. Then Security is ushered into the center ring with a fanfare.

The security topics in previous chapters described strategies and steps for building strong perimeter defenses (see Chapter 6, "Understanding Network Access Security and Kerberos"), then extending that defense inward to protect sensitive information (see Chapter 10, "Managing Active Directory Security"). But after users have been authenticated and configured, they are free to wander at will through the files and folders inside any shared resources on the network. Let's shift the security emphasis from putting deadbolts on the doors to putting padlocks on the file cabinets and desks. It is time to talk about NTFS file and directory permissions.

A good defense-in-depth security strategy doesn't stop with merely controlling access to files and folders. If a file cabinet contained nothing but nonsense—such as, soundtracks from 1930s musicals and transcripts from the Federal Register—no one would bother to break into them. Windows 2000 includes a new, NTFS–based security feature called the *Encrypting File System* (EFS) that makes it possible for users to encrypt files in such a way that only the person who encrypted them can open them again.

Administrative Access to EFS Files

I know what you're thinking about EFS. You're thinking, "What has Microsoft done? They've put a tool into the hands of the average user that makes it possible to lose access to a file completely." Fortunately, this isn't quite the case. EFS incorporates a secure "backdoor" that makes it possible for trusted administrators to access encrypted files in the event that the user who encrypted them quits, dies, or simply gets too confused to know how to open them.

This chapter covers configuration and management of NTFS permissions and the Encrypting File System. The NTFS topics include:

- Functional overview of NTFS File and Directory permissions, including access control lists, standard permissions, and permission inheritance
- Strategies and specific steps for using NTFS permissions to manage file and directory structures, including command-line controls
- Enabling and configuring file and directory auditing
- Methods for changing file ownership

The Encrypting File System topics include:

- Functional overview of file and directory encryption, including details about cipher key protection using Public Key Cryptographic Services (PKCS)
- Managing personal PKCS certificates
- Recovering encrypted files when the encrypting user is no longer available
- Securing sensitive PKCS certificates to prevent compromising encrypted files
- Saving encrypted files on trusted delegation servers
- Deploying Certification Authority servers to issue PKCS certificates

Functional Overview of NTFS File and Directory Permissions

When a user logs on to a Windows 2000 computer, the Local Security Authority (LSA) builds an *access token* that contains the user's Security ID (SID) and the SID for each domain local, global, and universal security group to which the user belongs. The list also includes any well-known SIDS that apply to the user, such as the *Authenticated Users* group and the *Everyone* group.

Every process spawned by the user runs in the user's *security context*, meaning that the process carries a copy of the user's access token. When the process accesses a *security object,* such as a file, folder, Registry key, or Directory object, it presents the user's access token.

The *Security Reference Monitor* (SRM) compares the contents of the user's access token to the contents of an *Access Control List* (ACL) inside the security descriptor attached to the object. The ACL has one or more *Access Control Entries* (ACEs) that identify *security principals* who are or are not permitted to access the object. Each ACE contains a set of *permissions* that defines what can or cannot be done to the object by the security principal.

All processes run in a security context. Most background services run in the security context of the *Local System.* You can determine the security context for a service by opening the Services console, right-clicking one of the running services, and selecting PROPERTIES from the fly-out menu. With the Properties window open, select the Log On tab to see the account used by the service. Figure 14.1 shows the Log On properties for the Server service.

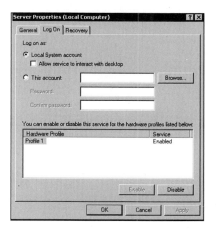

Figure 14.1 Server services properties showing that
the service runs in the Local Computer context.

You may encounter services that run in a security context other than Local System. Examples of these include backup programs and virus scanners. When these applications are installed, they create special user accounts. Those accounts provide the security context for the application. When you check the service properties for the application, you'll see the name of a user account rather than Local System. If the user account were deleted, or if the password were to change without notifying the application, then the application would cease to function.

Security Descriptor Structure

Files and folders are security objects and therefore have security descriptors attached to them. The *Master File Table* (MFT) record that defines the contents of the file or folder has a pointer to a *$Security_Descriptor* attribute that contains the following elements:

- **Owner ID.** Every security object has an owner. This is a DOD requirement, part of the C-2 security mandate. The Owner ID field in the security descriptor contains the owner's SID.

- **Group ID.** Used by POSIX only.

- **Discretionary Access Control List (DACL or Discretionary ACL).** This structure contains the ACE for each security principal. Each ACE contains the SID of the security principal and an *access mask* that describes what that principal is permitted or is not permitted to do. There are thirteen standard permissions associated with an NTFS object. An ACL can contain up to 1,820 ACEs.

- **System Access Control List (SACL or System ACL).** This structure is used to control auditing. Each ACE on the SACL gets the *SystemAudit* permission for any or all of the NTFS permissions.

Common Ownership of Administrator Objects

Under most circumstances, the SID in the Owner ID field of the security descriptor represents the user who created the file or folder. One exception is ownership of files and folders created by members of the local Administrators group.

When a member of the local Administrators group creates a file or folder, ownership is assigned to the Administrators group SID. This allows all administrators in a domain access to each other's files, folders, and Directory objects.

The access mask assigned to a security principal in an ACE includes three types of permissions: Standard, Special, and Generic.

- **Standard permissions.** These permissions apply to any Windows 2000 security object, not just to files and directories. Examples include Delete, Read_Control, Synchronize (a special programming use), Write_DAC (modify the DACL), and Write_Owner. These terms do not appear in the UI, but you may see them in error messages or when using command-line tools.

- **Special permissions.** These permissions have a specific purpose that is applicable only to NTFS objects. See the section "Standard NTFS Permissions" for a list of the permissions and their functions.

- **Generic permissions.** These permissions are templates that represent sets of standard and special permissions. Generic permissions simplify programming chores.

An ACL can contain multiple ACE listings. A security principal might have several ACEs on the same ACL and might be a member of groups represented by other ACEs. The access masks for each Access Allowed ACE are cumulative. That is, the permissions associated with each ACE add to the permissions granted by the other ACEs.

For example, let's say you have two groups, Yin and Yang. Both groups are on the ACL for a folder. The Yin group has Read access. The Yang group has Write access. If a user belongs to both groups, the user gets Read *and* Write access to the folder.

The opposite is true for Access Denied ACE masks. These masks are exclusive. For example, the Yin group has been assigned Full Control permissions. The Yang group has been assigned a Deny Access ACE to the Write permission. A user who belongs to both groups would be able to access the folder and do a file scan and read files, but could not create new files or subfolders or modify existing files.

If a security principal is not on an ACL for an object and is not a member of a group that is on an ACL, then access is denied. This is called an *Implicit Deny ACE*. The Implicit Deny is an important concept in managing NTFS permissions. If you remove all ACEs from the ACL for a folder, then no one can access the folder.

"Empty" ACL versus "Null" ACL

One nuance to the Implicit Deny ACE is that it only applies to NTFS objects that have an empty ACL. It is possible to construct an NTFS object that has no ACL in the security descriptor. A <null> ACL has the opposite effect of an empty ACL. A <null> ACL implies Full Control access to all security principals. The <null> ACL is not often encountered in a production Windows 2000 system, thanks to permission inheritance.

Standard NTFS Permissions

The contents of an NTFS object's security descriptor are exposed to the Explorer shell through the Properties window for files and folders. Open the Properties window by right-clicking the file or folder icon and selecting PROPERTIES from the fly-out menu. Then select the Security tab to see the contents of the ACL. Figure 14.2 shows an example for the \WINNT directory.

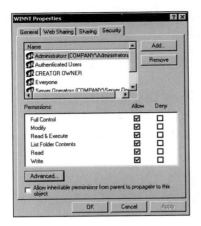

Figure 14.2 Properties window for the \WINNT folder showing
the Security tab and the access control list entries for the folder.

If you open the Properties window for a file or folder and the Security tab
is missing, the volume has been formatted as FAT or FAT32 or you do not
have permissions to view the security descriptor. If the ACL list shows bare
SIDs instead of names, see the following sidebar.

ACL Contains Bare SIDs

The list of users on an ACL may show one or more bare SIDs. This could have several causes:

- The computer was unable to contact a domain controller to resolve the SID to a user name.

- The account is in another domain and the trust relationship between the domains was broken.

- The local computer has been removed from the domain or the local trust between the computer and the
  domain has been broken.

- The user account was deleted from the domain but not removed from the local ACL.

In any case, a bare SID is always a symptom of a problem. Don't ignore one if you see it. If you are unable to
obtain access to the file or directory because of this problem, you can take ownership and put yourself or the
Administrator's group on the access list. See the "Changing File Ownership" section for details.

As you scroll down the list of names, the entries on the Permissions list
change to show the permissions assigned to the associated security principal.
Table 14.1 lists the standard permissions and their permitted actions.

Table 14.1   **Standard NTFS Permissions and Permitted Actions**

Permissions	Permitted Action—Files	Permitted Action—Folders
Full Control	Aggregate of all permissions	Aggregate of all Permissions
Modify	All actions except Delete, Change, Permissions, and Take Ownership	All actions except Delete File or Subfolder, Change Permissions, and Take Ownership
Write	Change or append data to a file	Create files and folders
Read & Execute	Open and read a file, launch an executable or batch file	Scan files in the directory, launch an executable or batch file
List Folder Contents	Not shown for Files	Combination of Read and Read & Execute

A total of thirteen permissions can be applied to a folder or a file. The standard permissions you see here are templates representing subsets of those permissions. For example, if the Permissions list for a security principal is empty, the account has been assigned special permissions that are not shown in the standard list.

When you highlight a security principal that has additional permissions, a text message appears next to the Advanced button saying *Additional permissions are present but not viewable here. Press Advanced to see them.* If you're having trouble selecting checkboxes in the main Security window, look for this message. It means that a certain combination of special permissions is not permitting you to make a selection on the generic list.

Viewing Advanced NTFS Permissions

At the Security tab for a folder or file, click Advanced to see, as Paul Harvey would say, "the *rest* of the story." The Access Control Settings window opens. Figure 14.3 shows an example.

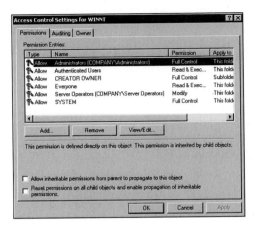

Figure 14.3 `Access Control Settings` window showing `Permissions` tab.

The `Permission Entries` list in this window contains each ACE on the ACL. Some security principals may have more than one ACE. Take a close look at the columns on the Permissions Entries list.

- **Type.** This column shows the ACE type, either `Allow` or `Deny`. A Deny ACE always takes precedence over an Allow ACE. The absence of an ACE for a particular SID is assumed to be a Deny ACE. For example, if the SID for user TJones is not on the access control list, and TJones is not a member of a group represented on the list, then TJones is denied access.

- **Name.** This column shows the account name that corresponds to the SID in the ACE. Getting this account name requires a lookup in the Directory, if the computer is a member of a domain, or the local SAM for stand-alone Windows 2000 computers.

- **Permission.** This column contains a term describing the access mask assigned to the ACE. The listing only shows permission templates. If specific permissions exist that are outside the templates, the listing shows *Special Permission*.

- **Apply To.** This column shows the inheritance method assigned to the ACE. Permission inheritance is discussed in the next section. In brief, ACE permissions assigned to a folder are inherited by files and subfolders under that folder. This inheritance simplifies the task of managing deep directory trees by propagating ACE listings automatically.

Overview of Advanced NTFS Permissions

Double-click one of the accounts in the Permission Entries list to open the
Permission Entry window for that account.

As stated previously, NTFS objects have thirteen different permissions.
Some come from standard object permissions. Others are specific to NTFS
objects. Permissions have different permitted actions depending on whether
they are assigned to a folder or to a file. Table 14.2 lists the NTFS permissions and their functions.

Table 14.2   **NTFS Permissions and Functions**

Permission	Function when assigned to a Folder	Function when assigned to a File
Traverse Folder/ Execute File	Permits the user to access a subfolder below a folder to which the user has no rights.	Permits launching an executable or running a batch file or script.
List Folder/ Read Data	Permits showing the available Files and directories in a folder using Explorer or by running `dir` from a command prompt.	Permits a file to be opened and read. Read permission implies Copy permission.
Read Attributes	Permits reading standard file and folder attributes, such as hidden, system, read-only, archive, and compression.	
Read Extended Attributes	Legacy OS/2 support. No longer applicable.	
Create Files/ Write Data	Permits creating a new file in a folder.	Permits modifying data in a file.

continues ▶

Table 14.2 **Continued**

Permission	Function when assigned to a Folder	Function when assigned to a File
Create Folders/ Append Data	Permits creating a new subfolder in a folder.	Permits adding data to an existing file.
Write Attributes	Permits modifying any of the standard file attributes.	
Write Extended	Legacy OS/2 support. No longer applicable.	
Delete	Permits deleting a subfolder or a file regardless of file permissions. This permission was called File Delete Child in classic NT. Exists for POSIX compatibility.	Not applicable.
Delete	Generic permission permits deleting files, subfolders, and their attributes.	Generic permission permits deleting the file and its attributes.
Read Permissions	Generic permission permits reading the security descriptor for a file or folder.	
Change	Generic permission permits modifying the security descriptor for a file or folder.	
Take Ownership	Generic permission permits taking ownership of a file or folder.	

Permission Inheritance

In classic NT, modifying the access list for a folder affected only that folder and the files directly under it, unless you specifically elected to flow the change down the tree. The clumsiness of this design and its lack of dynamic permission inheritance caused endless complaints among NT administrators. Windows 2000 alleviates the problem somewhat by including a feature that dynamically changes the static permissions assigned to files and folders. Microsoft has not given this feature an official name. I call it *dynamic/static inheritance*, but maybe *Inheritance 2000* would be a better choice.

The Windows 2000 object security model does not support dynamic inheritance. The *Security Reference Monitor* (SRM) only evaluates the ACEs it finds in a single security descriptor. True dynamic inheritance would require the SRM to scan up the directory tree and examine the ACL on every folder to find inheritable ACEs (or build an index of those entries that would have to be refreshed). The results of the effective rights search could not be cached because a change might occur that would affect a particular security principal.

The dynamic/static inheritance used in Windows 2000 makes use of a new ACE flag called INHERITED_ACE and an engine that automatically propagates inheritable ACEs to files and subfolders. This automatic propagation works quickly because the security descriptors are collected into one directory rather than being distributed among the various MFT records as they were in classic NT.

NTFS uses five options to determine how inheritable permissions flow down the directory tree:

- This Folder Only
- This Folder and Files
- This Folder and Subfolders
- This Folder and Subfolders and Files
- Files only

You can view and manage these options from the `Access Control Settings` window for a folder. See the next section for details.

Viewing Permission Inheritance

Open the `Access Control Settings` window for a folder (PROPERTIES | SECURITY TAB | ADVANCED) and run the cursor down the list of security principals. As you highlight an ACE, notice that the text below the `Add/Remove/View` button tells you the inheritance properties of the ACE.

For example, Figure 14.4 shows a sample subfolder with two listings under Permission Entries. The Users group has Read & Execute permissions assigned directly to the folder. The Administrators group has Full Control permissions inherited from the parent folder. The Apply To column shows that these entries will be inherited by folders, subfolders, and files.

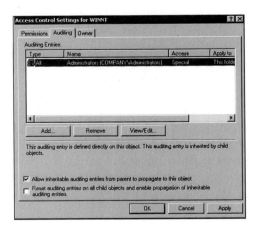

Figure 14.4 `Access Control Settings` window
showing inherited and applied permission entries.

If you highlight an inherited permission, text appears next to the `Add/Remove/View` button that explains how the inherited permissions cannot be deleted but must be blocked by clearing the `Allow inheritable permissions from parent to propagate to this object` checkbox.

If you refer to Figure 14.2, you'll see that the `Allow inheritable...` option is not checked for the `\WINNT` folder. In a default installation of Windows 2000, the Everyone group has Full Control permissions at the root directory with an inheritance option set for *This Folder, Subfolders, and Files*. By blocking inheritance of this permission, the system files in `\WINNT` are protected from accidental deletion or change by users.

The Everyone group and the Authenticated Users group are given Read & Execute permissions on the `\WINNT` f older. Inheritance for Everyone is set to *This Folder Only*. Only Authenticated Users get access further down the tree.

Removing the Everyone Group from the Root Directory

If seeing the Everyone group with Full Control access rights to virtually all folders and files in a volume makes you nervous—and it probably should—you can remove it from the Root ACL and add a group better suited to your organization. *Do not deny access to the Everyone group.* You will immediately lock yourself and everyone else (including the Local System) out of all the folders and subfolders. More than one NT system administrator has had to recover a system from tape after making this mistake.

Resetting Permissions

The dynamic/static inheritance model used by Windows 2000 makes it likely that permission changes will accumulate over the years at lower levels of the directory tree. This could cause access problems that are difficult to trace. The Reset permissions on all child objects and enable propagation of inheritable permissions option is a way to clean house. It removes all statically assigned permissions on every file and subfolder and replaces them with inheritable permissions from the folder at which you apply the option. Don't do this without giving it much thought and planning. You can wipe out years of hard work with a couple of mouse clicks.

When an ACE is added to an ACL, the Security Reference Monitor puts inherited ACEs lower in the list than directly applied ACEs. This gives the directly applied ACEs higher precedence, but it does not avoid the exclusion rule for Access Denied ACEs. If an Access Allowed ACE is directly applied to a folder and the folder inherits a Deny Access ACE, the Deny takes precedence.

When you copy files from one location to another, you create a new file at the new location. This new file inherits its ACL entries from the parent folder. If you move a file from one location to another on the same volume, the file retains its security descriptor. This could pose problems because the access list from one directory tree might not be appropriate for another. You may need to change the ACL entries after the files have been moved.

To move a file, the permissions at the original folder must permit deleting a file, because moving implies a deletion. If you move a file between volumes, the file is created from scratch in the new volume. The new file inherits the ACLs from the parent folder, just as when you copy a file to a new location.

Ownership

All files and directories have owners. The owner has full control rights. You can find the name of the owner from the Properties window by clicking Advanced and selecting the Owner tab. Figure 14.5 shows an example.

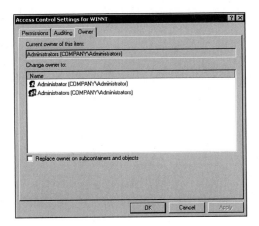

Figure 14.5 `Access Control Settings` window showing `Owner` tab with owner of \WINNT directory listed.

The Current Owner Of This Item field lists the name associated with the SID in the Owner_ID field of the security descriptor. If you see a bare SID in this field, in means the owner came from a domain that is no longer trusted by this computer.

An account with Take Ownership permissions for a file or folder can click the `Take Ownership` button and assume ownership. For example, if you let the Everyone group retain Full Control rights to folders and files, then any user can take ownership of any NTFS object. For files and folders in \WINNT, only Administrators have Take Ownership permission. The privilege does not extend to Account Operators or Server operators in a domain or to Power Users on a Windows 2000 Professional desktop.

The standard Windows 2000 tools only permit an account to take ownership, not transfer ownership. See the "Changing File Ownership" section for methods to transfer ownership using a third-party utility.

In classic NT, file and directory ownership stayed in the background. Users created, copied, moved, backed up, and restored files without much thought for the actual owner. This changes in Windows 2000 if you assign quotas to a volume. The quota management system uses ownership to track disk usage. If you impose quotas, you're likely to get very familiar with ownership requirements. See Chapter 13, "Managing File Systems," for details on quota management.

Auditing

The ability to audit security principals as they exercise their access permissions is built right into the SRM. As any IRS agent will tell you, auditing the transactions in a process can give you a great deal of information about the inner workings of that process. Not much slips past Uncle Sam and not much slips past the SRM, either.

The audit output from the SRM is saved to the Security event log, SECURITY.EVT, stored in `\WINNT\System32\Config`. You can view this log using the `Event Viewer` console, EVENTVWR.MSC. You must have administrator privileges to view and manage the Security log. Detailed steps are in the section "File and Folder Auditing."

Because auditing yields so much vital information about system operation, it represents a potential security breach and requires special controls. The security descriptor for an object has a special data structure called the *System Access Control List* (SACL) that determines who is permitted to audit an object. A user must have an Access Allowed ACE in the SACL of a file or folder to get audit information from it.

The SRM is capable of reporting on virtually all aspects of object activity, including:

- Logon / Logoff
- Account Management
- Directory Service Access
- Logon Events
- Object Access
- Policy Changes
- Privilege Use
- Process Tracking
- System Events

Auditing for each of these activities is controlled by an audit policy, either in the local computer's policies or a group policy linked to one of the three Directory containers capable of hosting policies: OU, Domain, and Site.

The audit policy of most interest for NTFS is the Object Access policy. You must enable this policy to get audit reports on file and folder activity. After the Object Access audit policy is enabled, you can elect to audit access by any security principal to any NTFS object for any of the NTFS permissions.

Using NTFS Permissions to Control Folder and File Access

Here is a fairly common scenario. A new contractor accepts an assignment at the Phoenix offices of Company, Inc. He is a structural engineer named Bob Plum. Bob is a hard worker, very skilled, and management appreciates his contribution to the team, but they don't want him—or any other contractor, for that matter—to have access to certain key documents containing budget items and personnel records. You've been tasked with blocking Bob's access to these documents.

Example of Share-level Security

One way to handle this situation is to gather the sensitive material into a separate set of folders with a share point that is not available to the general population.

The problem with this arrangement is that you end up with a flat directory structure and many, many shares. A big organization with many departments might need hundreds of shares. This causes problems because the entire share list is sent to client computers each time the users map a drive or open My Network Places.

If you have lots of shares, users are also forced to have lots of drive mappings, which irritates them and taxes your Help Desk. The conversations go something like, "Okay, are you ready? Map drive L to the CAD share to see the drawings, and map drive M to the Bridge share to see the project files under Bridges, and there's a COMMON share for using your time card, map drive H there, and an APPS share for running Office, map drive I there. You say you're on the Secret Project? Well, go ahead and map drive N to the SP share while I check on your access rights."

If you have data servers with deep directory structures, you should avoid share-level security and implement NTFS permissions instead. This allows you to keep your shares high in the tree and limit their number. The next section shows an example of this.

Example of NTFS Security

To control access to the Company, Inc., project files using NTFS permissions, start by separating the user population into groups. Then, instead of creating individual shares for each major folder, create one share for the top folder and use groups to assign NTFS permissions to the folders underneath.

For example, create a group called Phx_Eng (for Phoenix Engineering) and give it read/write access to the Engineering folder. Then create a group called Phx_Eng_Contr (for Phoenix Engineering Contractors) and deny this group access to any sensitive folders. Figure 14.6 shows an example.

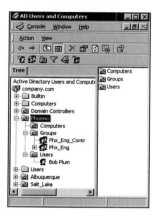

Figure 14.6 AD Users and Computers console showing new engineering user and engineering groups.

You may wonder why two groups are necessary. After all, simply leaving Bob out of the Phx_Eng group would keep him out of the sensitive because of the Implicit Deny ACE. The problem with relying on Implicit Deny is that it is not self-documenting. You are forced to keep separate records to explain why Bob was left out of the Phx_Eng group in one instance so he won't be added to the group when another administrator uses it to control access to another folder. Seeing Bob's name in a group that has been explicitly denied access to a folder makes it clear what you are trying to accomplish.

Using Groups Rather than Individuals on ACLs

It is possible to assign permissions on a user-by-user basis, but generally it's much more convenient to put one or two groups on an ACL with hundreds of users in the group than to put hundreds of users on the ACL. You'll also slow down performance considerably by having many ACL entries.

Applying NTFS Permissions

NTFS permissions can be set on a folder or on an individual file within a folder. The following example sets folder permissions to examine how those permissions are inherited.

Procedure 14.1 **Applying NTFS Permissions to a Folder**

1. Open Explorer and navigate to the folder you want to manage. The example in Figure 14.7 uses the `\Company\Engineering\Management` folder.

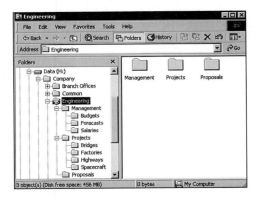

Figure 14.7 Explorer view showing an example directory structure with a share at the Engineering folder.

2. Right-click the folder and select PROPERTIES from the fly-out menu. The `Properties` window opens for the folder.

3. Select the `Security` tab. Figure 14.8 shows an example list of security principals. It's likely that the ACL will contain the Everyone group with Full Control access rights. Windows 2000 defaults to this configuration at the root of every new volume. The Everyone permissions are inherited by all subfolders and files.

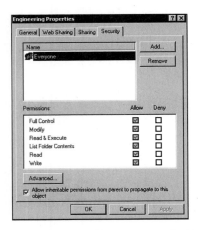

Figure 14.8 Folder properties for Engineering showing the default Everyone group with full control rights.

4. Add the Engineering group to the ACL for the Engineering folder. Click `Add`. The `Select Users, Computers, or Groups` window opens. See Figure 14.9. You have the option of choosing users and groups from the parent domain or a trusted domain. The example uses the Phx_Eng_Contr group from the parent `Company.com` domain. This group contains the account for the example contractor, Bob Plum.

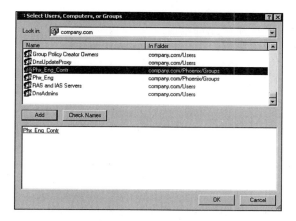

Figure 14.9 `Select Users, Computers, or Groups` window showing selection of Phx_Eng_Contr group.

5. Double-click the Phx_Eng_Contr group to add it to the list.

6. Double-click the Phx_Eng group to add it to the list. An ACL can have up to 1,820 ACEs, but you'll experience profound performance problems long before you reach that point.

7. Click `OK` to close the window and return to the `Properties` window. See Figure 14.10. The access list shows the two groups and their default access permissions.

8. Before setting permissions for the two groups, remove the Everyone group from the ACL. This group is inherited, so you cannot simply click `Remove`. If you try, an error message will appear.

   Changing the permissions for Everyone at the root directory takes some thought and planning, so the best choice for now is to de-select the `Allow Inheritable Permissions…` option at the folder. When you do this, an informational message appears asking if you want to copy the inherited permissions or remove them. See the sidebar "Be Careful of Implicit Deny" for more information.

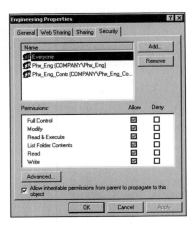

Figure 14.10 Folder properties showing new groups and default rights.

9. Click Remove. The Everyone group disappears from the access list.

10. Highlight the Phx_Eng group and select the Full Control checkbox under the Allow column. This gives the group permission to Add, Delete, and Modify any file or subfolder under the folder.

11. Highlight the Phx_Eng_Contr group and select the Full Control checkbox under the Deny column. This explicitly denies access to members of this group. At this point, you have not added an administrative group onto the ACL. When you apply these changes, you will lose access to the folder because of Implicit Deny. If you want to add more groups, do so before applying the changes.

12. Before clicking OK, click Advanced to open the Access Control Settings window. The Apply To column indicates the inheritance settings. By default, an ACE is set for full inheritance (current folder, subfolders, and files). If you want to change to another inheritance option, click View/Edit, then select the option from the Apply Onto drop-down list.

13. Click Cancel to return to the Properties window.

14. Click OK to apply the security changes. A warning message appears cautioning you about the Deny permissions you have placed in the ACL. Click Yes to acknowledge the warning and proceed with the update. The security changes are made and the Properties window closes.

Be Careful of Implicit Deny

If you choose to remove inherited permissions from a folder, be sure you have the Administrators group on the ACL, or some other group that you use for administrative purposes. Without that group, Implicit Deny would prevent you from accessing the folder.

It is not necessarily a bad thing to exclude administrators from an ACL, depending on the situation, but it makes your job more difficult if you need to help users with files in those folders. When blocking inheritance, it is usually a good idea to add an administrative group to the ACL.

The new permissions take effect immediately. Any members of the Phx_Eng group who are currently logged on can access the folder. Their access tokens already contain the SID for the Phx_Eng group. Any members of the Phx_Eng_Contr group who are currently logged on will be denied access for the same reason.

But what about Bob? If Bob logged on before you added him to the Phx_Eng_Contr group, his access token does not contain the SID for the Phx_Eng_Contr group. If he is already a member or Phx_Eng, he retains access to the Engineering folder until he logs off and then logs on again and gets a new Kerberos Ticket-Granting-Ticket (TGT) with a new set of group SIDs. The TGT is refreshed periodically, but you are better off asking the user to log off to get the update.

Using NTFS Permissions to Control File Access

There may be instances when you want to protect certain files within a folder. For example, there may be sensitive files in one of the general-access Engineering folders that should not be viewed by contractors. It is best to move these files into a separate folder, but that might not be feasible. In that case, you can assign access rights directly to the files themselves.

Assigning file permissions uses the same steps as assigning permissions to a folder. Open the Properties window for the file, select the Security tab, and use it to assign groups to the ACL and set their permissions.

When assigning file permissions, keep in mind that the user might have access permissions at the folder level that supersede the permissions you assign at the file level. The most notorious example of this is the *Delete Subfolders and Files* permission.

The Delete Subfolders and Files permission exists for compatibility with POSIX. It gives the user permission to delete a file or subfolder, *even if that permission has been explicitly denied by the file permissions.* In the example, Bob has Full Control rights in the Engineering folder. If you assign Deny All permissions to Bob for a file in that folder, he will not be able to open, move, or copy that file, but he can delete it.

The *Delete Subfolders and Files* permission is only enabled when you select the Full Control template. When assigning folder permissions to users, you should always select the Modify template rather than the Full Control template to avoid granting the *Delete Subfolders and Files* permission. The Modify template also takes away the *Change Permissions* and *Take Ownership* permissions, two other options that should not be granted to average users.

Modifying NTFS Permissions Using Xcacls

Windows 2000 comes with a command-line utility for viewing and modifying access control lists. This utility is called Cacls. The Resource Kit has an extended version of Cacls called Xcacls that has useful features. This section uses Xcacls to control permissions from the command line.

Xcacls has several switches that are useful in a variety of situations. Table 14.3 lists them.

Table 14.3   **Xcacls Switches**

Switch	Function
/t	Replaces existing ACLs to those being assigned by this command.
/e	Edits ACLs instead of replacing them.
/c	Ignores errors and continues down the list.
/g user:permission;special access	On files, use /g user:perm. The perm entry specifies the permissions that are applied to the file. On folders, use /g user:perm:spec. The perm entry specifies the permissions that are applied to the folder; spec specifies the permissions applied to the files.
	perm and spec grant the following permissions:
	R — Read C — Change F — Full control P — change Permissions O — take Ownership X — eXecute E — rEad W — Write D — Delete T — noT specified (spec only)
/r user	Revokes user's permissions.

Switch	Function
`/p user:permission;special access`	Replaces user's permissions.
`/d user`	Denies user any access whatsoever.
`/y`	Does not verify.

Xcacls Examples

Let's say you want to add a series of users to the ACL for a folder called Campaign2000. Here are a few ways to use Xcacls to do this work:

- Delete user BClinton from the ACL: `xcacls campaign2000 /r`
- Add user AGore with Full Access permission to all files and folders: `xcacls campaign2000 /g agore:f;f`
- Add user SForbes with Take Ownership permission to all files and folders: `xcacls campaign2000 /g sforbes:o;o`
- Add user GWBush with Execute rights to the folder and Delete rights to files: `xcacls campaign2000 /g gwbush:p;d`
- Deny user RPerot all rights: `xcacls campaign2000 /d rperot`

Using Xcacls to View Permissions

You can also use Xcacls to see the existing permissions for a file or folder. The listing tends to be a little inscrutable. Here is an Xcacls listing for the \WINNT folder on an example system. All but the last two entries are standard.

```
C:\>xcacls winnt
C:\WINNT NT AUTHORITY\Authenticated Users:R
        NT AUTHORITY\Authenticated Users:(OI)(CI)(IO)(special access:)
                                              GENERIC_READ
                                              GENERIC_EXECUTE

        BUILTIN\Server Operators:C
        BUILTIN\Server Operators:(OI)(CI)(IO)C
        BUILTIN\Administrators:F
        BUILTIN\Administrators:(OI)(CI)(IO)F
        NT AUTHORITY\SYSTEM:F
        NT AUTHORITY\SYSTEM:(OI)(CI)(IO)F
        BUILTIN\Administrators:F
        CREATOR OWNER:(OI)(CI)(IO)F
        Everyone:R
        COMPANY\User001:(OI)(CI)R
        COMPANY\TestGroup:(OI)(CI)F
```

The user name includes its subauthority taken from the SID. The NT AUTHORITY source indicates a SID prefix of S-1-5 with no subauthority. The two entries at the bottom of the listing were added from the COMPANY domain. The entries in parentheses define the inheritance action for the permissions.

- Inherit Only (IO) entries define permissions to be applied to any new files created in this folder.

- Container Inherit (CI) entries define permissions to be applied to any new subfolders created in this folder.

- Object Inherit (OI) entries define permissions inherited from the parent folder.

- No Propagate (NP) entries (not shown) define permissions that apply to the local folder only.

The letter at the end indicates the permission. Special Access includes any individual permissions not represented by a standard ACE mask.

Changing File Ownership

Windows 2000 complies with Department of Defense C2 requirements as defined by the "Orange Book" standards. C2 security requires that every object have an owner who wields ultimate control over the object. But what happens if the owner creates a file, limits access in some way, and then leaves the company or the country or the galaxy?

For example, what if our contractor, Bob Plum, fancies himself a writer? He's dedicated to his craft and doesn't mind indulging it on the client's time (at $120/hr billable.) Bob's workstation has been configured with redirected folders so the contents of his files are saved to a common folder on a server. Bob knows that other users can see his files, so he takes advantage of the fact that he owns the documents he creates. He sets the access permissions on his files to indicate that only he is on the ACL. Figure 14.11 shows the security properties that Bob used to protect his file. Bob can do this even if the folder holding the files has an Access Deny ACE set for Change Permissions. A file owner has a lot of flexibility.

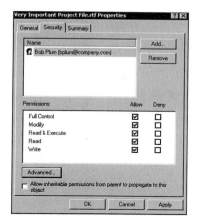

Figure 14.11 `Properties` window for user file that has specific permissions set.

When Bob's work performance deteriorates because of his extra activity, he is let go. An administrator is assigned to sift through his files. She comes across one or two files that give her an Access Denied error when she tries to open them. She is intrigued by this so she takes a look at the security properties and is given an error, *You do not have permission to view or edit the current permission settings....* She clicks past the warning and finds that the Permissions list in the `Security` tab is empty. She clicks `Advanced` and selects the `Owner` tab and sees a window like that in Figure 14.12. The current owner does not display because no one except for Bob has permission to view the security descriptor.

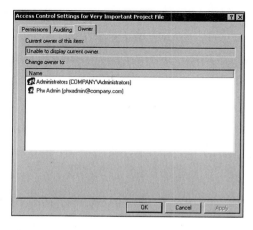

Figure 14.12 `Access Control Settings` window showing the `Owner` tab.

Because the administrator is a member of a group with Take Ownership permission, she can resolve this problem quickly. She highlights the Administrators group and clicks Apply to assume ownership. (She takes ownership on behalf of the Administrators group so her colleagues can also access the files.)

She then closes the Properties window and reopens it to refresh the contents, and now she see Bob's name on the ACL. She puts herself or the Administrators group on the ACL and takes a peek inside the file.

Up to this point, the administrator has used standard Windows 2000 tools and techniques. But what if, after evaluating the files, she decides that the true owner should be a staffer in the Legal department who is suing Bob's contract shop? There is no facility in Windows 2000 or the Resource Kit to transfer ownership. The only option is to take ownership. A third party tool for transferring ownership is called chown. It is available as a suite of utilities from Mortice Kerns Systems (MKS), Inc., at www.mks.com.

File and Folder Auditing

By auditing activities involving files and folders, you can see how users exercise their access permissions. Auditing is enabled in two stages. First, enable auditing in general by configuring a group policy. Then, configure auditing for particular folders or files. Specific steps are identified later in this section.

If you do not enable Object Access auditing before you attempt to configure NTFS audit permissions, the system responds with a warning that *The current audit policy for this computer does not have auditing turned on.* If you get this warning, you can save the audit permissions but they will not begin working until you enable the Object Access policy.

The audit output is written to the Security Log, SECEVENT.EVT, in \WINNT\System32\Config. The log contents are viewed using the Event Viewer console, EVENTVWR.MSC. You must have administrator privileges to view the Security log.

Configuring Audit Policies

The steps in this section enable Object Access auditing by modifying the Default Domain Policy. You can also set the Object Access audit policy in a custom group policy and link it to an OU or the domain or site containers.

You must have administrative rights in the Directory to modify or create group policies. If you have several existing group policies, check each one to make sure they do not specify an audit policy that might override yours. The container hierarchy for group policies places OU policies as the highest precedence, followed by Domain, then Site containers, with local policies having the lowest precedence.

The following example demonstrates how to enable system auditing.

Procedure 14.2 **Enabling System Auditing**

1. Log on using an account with administrator privileges.

2. Open the `AD Users and Computers` console.

3. Right-click the domain icon and select PROPERTIES from the fly-out menu. The `Properties` window opens.

4. Select the `Group Policy` tab.

5. Double-click the `Default Domain Policy` entry to open the `Group Policy` console.

6. Expand the tree to `Computer Configuration | Windows Settings | Security Settings | Local Policies | Audit Policy`. The right pane lists the available audit policies. Figure 14.13 shows an example.

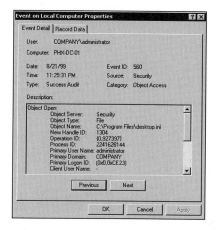

Figure 14.13 `Group Policy` console showing Audit Policy list with Audit Object Access policy enabled.

7. Double-click the `Audit Object Access` policy to open its `Security Policy Setting` window.

8. Select `Define These Policy Settings`. Under `Audit These Attempts`, select `Success` and `Failure`. This does not start auditing all object events in these two categories. It simply enables them to be used by individual object auditors.

9. Click OK to save the changes and return to the Group Policy console. The policy status changes to show the new settings.

10. Close the console.

11. It may take a while for the system to apply the new policy to the local Registry. You can run secedit /refreshpolicy machine_policy to manually refresh.

After the policy has been distributed, you can configure file and folder auditing at a member computer. Proceed to the next section.

Example Audit Configuration

The steps in this section configure auditing for the files in a specific folder. You can audit multiple folders or an entire directory tree.

Procedure 14.3   Configuring File and Folder Auditing

1. Open Explorer.

2. Right-click a folder and select PROPERTIES from the fly-out menu. The Properties window opens.

3. Select the Security tab.

4. Click Advanced. The Access Control Settings window opens.

5. Select the Auditing tab. Figure 14.14 shows an example with a set of audit entries already selected.

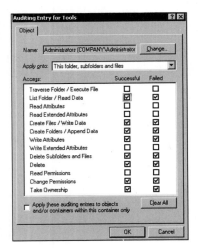

Figure 14.14   Auditing Entry for Tools window showing selected attributes for auditing.

The Audit tab includes its own option for Inheritance Settings. This is because the SACL used to control audit permissions is separate from the DACL used to control file access permissions.

6. Click Add. The Select User, Computer, or Group window opens.

7. Select a group that you want to audit for this folder. To experiment, double-click the Administrators group. The Auditing Entry window opens. Select several attributes to audit. Verify that the inheritance selection is This Folder, Subfolders, And Files.

8. Click OK to save your selections and return to the Access Control Settings window. The new ACE is now on the list.

9. Click OK to apply the changes to the security descriptors and return to the main Properties window. If you have a considerable number of subfolders and files under this folder, applying the updates may take a while.

10. Click OK to close the window and return to Explorer.

11. Open the Event Viewer console using START | PROGRAMS | ADMINISTRATIVE TOOLS | EVENT VIEWER.

12. Expand the tree to the Security Log. You must have administrator privileges to open this log. If you chose to audit a busy folder, there should already be entries on the list. Double-click an entry to see the kind of information provided by the audit trace. Figure 14.15 shows an example.

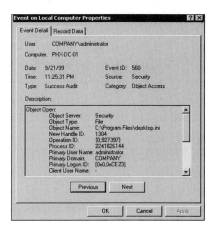

Figure 14.15 Event Log entry from the Security Log showing an audit event.

Managing the Security Log

If you audit a great many users and events, system performance will slow and the audit log will fill quickly. You can't do much about the performance problem other than to reduce the number of auditable objects. You can increase the size of the Security Log by opening its Properties window and increasing the value for Maximum Log Size.

The default Security Log size is 512KB. Do not bother setting the size larger than about 300MB. The system will not write a larger file due to memory constraints. The default action when the log file fills is to overwrite events older than seven days. You can elect a longer interval, or not to overwrite, or to overwrite only when necessary.

Using Dumpel

The Windows 2000 Resource Kit comes with an Event Log Dump utility called Dumpel. This utility dumps the contents of an event log to a file. It does not clear the log, though, so it doesn't do much good to schedule it. The syntax is: dumpel -l <log_name> -f <filename>. The default file format is the event log format (*.evt) but you can use the -t or -c switch to output to a tab-delimited or comma-delimited file.

You can use group policies to configure any of the Event Log settings, including the Security Log. This is a quick way to set up your servers and workstations for auditing. Open the Group Policy console and expand the tree to Computer Configuration ¦ Windows Settings ¦ Security Settings ¦ Event Log ¦ Settings for Event Logs. Double-click the policy you want to set, enable the policy, make the entry, and click OK to apply it.

For security reasons, you may want to prevent access to a system if the audit log fills. There is a group policy called Shut Down System Immediately If Unable To Log Security Audits under Computer Configuration ¦ Windows Settings ¦ Security Settings ¦ Local Policies ¦ Security Options. This policy will crash the system when the Security log file fills up. Only the Administrator account can log on to clear the file and recover the system, so make sure you know the Administrator password before enabling this option. Don't forget that this policy is in place.

Managing File Encryption

So far in this chapter, file access as been controlled using NTFS permissions. But what if an unauthorized user somehow manages to slither past all your carefully crafted permissions and obtain access to files? This is difficult on a server, but users are prone to share their hard drives and they do not necessarily know how to use NTFS permissions correctly. Or a user might accidentally leave a laptop in a hotel room or an airplane terminal where it is nabbed and sold for the contents of the data on the disk.

As an extra security measure, files can be encrypted so that only the user who encrypted them can obtain access. If the encryption algorithms are solid enough, and the methods used to secure the encryption keys are managed carefully enough, then this virtually guarantees security of the data.

The job of encrypting and decrypting files and folders in Windows 2000 is handled by the *Encrypting File System* (EFS). At first glance, EFS looks simple. The user sets a simple option in the file `Properties` window and whap, the file is encrypted. When the user opens the file again, it is decrypted on-the-fly. This seems perfectly reasonable and simple, but computing is rarely reasonable and simple. As soon as you take the leap of putting a file, any file, into a form that can only be accessed by one user and that user alone, a whole host of questions come to mind:

- What happens to the files if the user is not available?
- Who determines which users are authorized to encrypt files?
- What is the encryption mechanism? Is it truly resistant to attack?
- What if the file is stored on a server instead of the local hard drive? Can it still be encrypted?
- Can other users share encrypted files?
- Is there a difference between encrypting files on standalone machines and in a domain?
- Could the user potentially lock up a machine by encrypting system files?
- Can encrypted files be backed up and restored?
- What if the files are moved or copied to another folder? Do they remain encrypted? What about copying to a floppy or Zip drive?
- Can an encrypted file be deleted or renamed?
- Can encrypted files be accessed by systems other than Windows 2000?
- Can encrypted files be accessed over the Internet?

The list goes on and on. This section covers those questions along with others as it describes how the Encrypting File System works and how to manage it. Here is a brief summary of the EFS operations covered in this section:

- **Functional Overview of File and Directory Encryption.** This topic describes the mechanism used to encrypt files and the Public Key Cryptography Services (PKCS) methods used to protect the cipher keys.

- **Encrypting Files and Directories.** This section shows the steps for using Explorer and the command line to encrypt and decrypt files and folders.

- **Managing Personal Certificates.** Each user who encrypts a file on a local machine is issued a special PKCS certificate. Public and private keys derived from this certificate are used to protect the File Encryption Key (FEK) that EFS uses to encrypt a file. This section covers viewing, exporting, and importing personal certificates.

- **Recovering Encrypted Files.** EFS provides a way for trusted administrator accounts—called *Data Recovery Agents* (DRAs)—to access encrypted files without the presence of the user. This section explains the role of Data Recovery Agents and describes the policies and strategies that make data recovery possible.

- **Securing File Recovery Certificates.** DRAs make use of a special certificate called a File Recovery certificate to open files. Controlling these FR certificates is absolutely essential to maintaining a secure EFS deployment. This section describes how to export, transport, and import FR certificates.

- **Adding Data Recovery Agents.** The system automatically designates a certain account to be the DRA. This topic describes how to add other DRAs for fault-tolerance.

- **Encrypting Files On Servers**. Files accessed across the network can be encrypted. This requires enabling Kerberos delegation, with the resultant possibility of compromising security. This section shows how to configure server-based file encryption and discusses the security implications.

Functional Overview of File and Directory Encryption

The idea of encrypting personal files has a great deal of appeal to users. Most users have a touch of paranoia about computers. They read about hackers and crackers who creep through the Internet and snatch files as easily as a two-year-old filches cookies. Even if users trust that the network is safe from external attack, they know that technicians and system administrators can access personal files on servers and local machines. They like the idea of encrypting their documents.

Let's say that a user logs on to the computer and toggles the Encryption attribute to ON. The exact steps to do this aren't important right now. What's important is that this action brings the file to the attention of the EFS driver, EFS.SYS. The following sections describe how the EFS driver encrypts the file and secures the file encryption cipher.

EFS Encryption Mechanisms

EFS has two encryption responsibilities. First, it must encrypt a file. That's straightforward enough. Second, it must encrypt the key that it used to encrypt the file. That's where things get a little complicated. Let's take a look at the file encryption first.

EFS encrypts files using the *extended US Data Encryption Standard* (DESX). The DESX encryption algorithm was formulated by Ronald Rivest at RSA Data Security in an effort to shore up the relatively flaccid DES algorithm by making it more resistant to brute-force dictionary attacks while retaining its speed and exportability. Details on DESX are available in Internet draft Draft-simpson-desx-02.txt, "*The ESP DES-XEX3-CBC Transform.*"

In broad terms, standard DESX uses a three-step process to encrypt a file:

- First, it divvies a file into 64-bit portions called *blocks* and encrypts each block with a 64-bit cipher key using a simple XOR algorithm.

- Then, it uses a separate 56-bit key to encrypt the already encrypted block, this time using standard DES encryption.

- Finally, it uses a different 64-bit key to perform another XOR encryption on the same block.

The combination of these three steps results in an encrypted file that is almost on par with standard DES when it comes to resisting sophisticated decryption, but is much, much less susceptible to key-search attack.

When EFS encrypts a file, it generates a random number to use as the DESX cipher. This random number is called a *File Encryption Key* (FEK). Domestic versions of Windows 2000 use a 128-bit FEK. International versions use 56-bit keys.

The DESX algorithm is symmetrical, meaning that the same cipher is used both to encrypt and decrypt the file. This makes it ideal for use in EFS, but it also requires that the cipher be carefully protected. It does little good to encrypt a file so thoroughly that mean code-breaking machines take millions of years to muddle out the meaning if you leave the encryption key lying around in a form that anyone can read.

Microsoft protects the FEK by encrypting it using Public Key Cryptography System (PKCS) technology. PKCS also comes from RSA. It represents one of the most secure encryption technologies available in the industry.

You have to watch your scorecard carefully when you work your way through EFS. There are several encryption strategies at work.

- The file itself is encrypted using DESX with a 128-bit FEK used as a cipher key.

- The FEK is encrypted using public/private key technology where the public key is used to encrypt the FEK and the private key is used to decrypt it.

- The private key used to decrypt the FEK is itself encrypted using the MD4 hash of the user's password.

- The public/private key pairs can be exported to a portable certificate that is encrypted with a special password supplied by the user when the key pair is exported.

Each of these encryption strategies plays a role in how EFS is managed. Before getting too deeply involved with the PKCS side of EFS, let's finish looking at how the file itself is encrypted.

Why Have Two Keys?

Windows 2000 doesn't use PKCS directly for file encryption because of speed. The encryption methods used by PKCS are impressively secure but very slow and processor-intensive. The combination of moderately secure file encryption with highly secure key protection is a fairly standard way to get acceptable security and performance.

Structure of Encrypted Files

A file in an unencrypted state has a $Data attribute that faithfully reproduces the byte stream saved by the application that created the file. For example, if you open Notepad and type the word *text* several times, then save the session as a file, the $Data attribute for the file would contain the characters *text text text*.

Refer to Figure 14.16. When a user encrypts that file, the Efs.sys driver first copies the data to a temporary file, EFS0.TMP. EFS then encrypts the data and puts the result back in its original disk location. As discussed previously, EFS does this work using DESX encryption with a random 128-bit cipher key called the File Encryption Key (FEK).

The FEK must remain secure or the encrypted file can be compromised. EFS protects the FEK by encrypting it with the public portion of a public/private key pair issued to the user for this purpose.

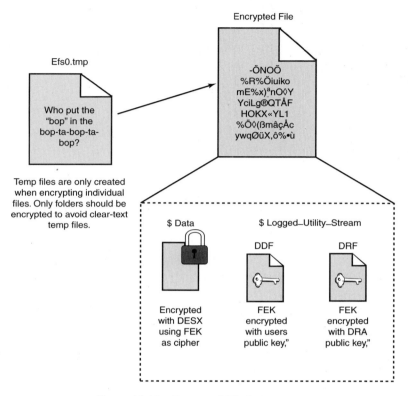

Figure 14.16 Encrypted File Structure.

When the user encrypts a file, EFS works with the LSA to get a copy of the user's public key. LSA is only too happy to cooperate. The user's public key is freely distributable. Anything encrypted by the user's public key can only be decrypted with the user's private key.

The user's public key is contained in a certificate that validates the key's authenticity. A copy of the certificate is stored along with the encrypted FEK in a special data structure called the *Data Decryption Field* (DDF).

In addition to encrypting the FEK with the user's public key, EFS also encrypts the FEK using the public key assigned to an account designated as the Data Recovery Agent (DRA). In a domain, the DRA is the Administrator account.

The DRA acts as an understudy who can rush in and decrypt a file if the user who originally encrypted it is unavailable. EFS considers the Data Recovery Agent so important that it will refuse to encrypt a file unless it has the certificate for at least one DRA. See "Recovering Encrypted Files" for more information. A copy of the DRA's public key certificate is stored along with the encrypted FEK in a special data structure called the *Data Recovery Field* (DRF).

The two EFS data fields, DDF and DRF, are stored in a special attribute of the file called the *$Logged_Utility_Stream*. This attribute resembles a named data stream that is stored along with the file. When EFS needs to decrypt the file, it locates the name of the encryptor in the DDF within the $Logged_Utility_Stream and uses that as a hint for finding the private key to decrypt the FEK. Armed with the decrypted FEK, the file's $Data attribute can be decrypted.

The fact that the public key certificates accompany the file in clear text does not present a security problem. The public key could accompany the file in searing red neon and it would not affect security in the least. Only the private key can decrypt the FEK, and that is stored in the user's profile encrypted with the user's password hash.

Here is the sequence of events the next time the user opens this file:

- EFS reads the $Logged_Utility_Stream attribute and finds the certificate information for the user.

- EFS contacts LSA to have the designated cryptographic provider access the certificate and derive the private key using secrets from the user's access token.

- EFS uses the private key to decrypt the FEK.

- EFS uses the FEK to decrypt the file in memory then delivers the clear-text byte stream to the application.

EFS sits above NTFS, so all the housekeeping that goes on at the file system level such as page files, transaction tracking logs, and USN Journals that could involve contents of the file remain encrypted.

Avoiding Temporary EFS Files

A temporary EFS file is superhidden, meaning that it has both the System and Hidden attributes and can be blocked from user view with a group policy. This does not mean that the data on the disk is hidden. The clear-text contents of the temporary file can be seen easily with a hex editor. The EFS0.TMP file is partially or completely overwritten when the next file is encrypted, but it may still leave traces that can be seen without the aid of sophisticated disk scanning equipment. For this reason, *encrypting individual files is not recommended.*

Always enable encryption at the folder level then create new files in that folder. New files are encrypted as they are saved and do not leave exposed remnants in temporary files.

On–Disk Structure of EFS Files

Here is a quick look at the $Data and $Logged_Utility_Stream attributes of a file before and after encryption. This shows how the file is changed and where the new elements are used.

This listing shows an example of $Data attribute prior to encryption. The last portion of the $Filename attribute is included for reference.

```
<<final portion of $Filename attribute for a file called file3.txt.>>
2000 0000 0000 0000 0903 6600 6900 6C00   ........f.i.l.
6500 3300 2E00 7400 7800 7400 0000 0000   e.3...t.x.t.....

<<$Data attribute - type code 80. The data portion of the attribute is resident in the MFT
record.>>
8000 0000 6800 0000 0000 1800 0000 0100   ................
5000 0000 1800 0000 7465 7874 2074 6578   p.......text tex
7420 7465 7874 0D0A 7465 7874 2074 6578   t text..text tex
7420 7465 7874 0D0A 7465 7874 2074 6578   t text..text tex
7420 7465 7874 0D0A FFFF FFFF 8279 4711   t text.......yG.
```

Here is the same record after encryption showing the $Data and $Logged_Utility_Stream attributes.

```
<<Final portion of the $Filename attribute.>>
2000 0000 0000 0000 0903 6600 6900 6C00   ........f.i.l.
6500 3300 2E00 7400 7800 7400 0000 0000   e.3...t.x.t.....

<<$Data attribute is non-resident with the packed Logical Cluster Number (shown bold)
indicating the location of the encrypted data.>>
8000 0000 4800 0000 0100 0000 0040 0500   ....H........@..
0000 0000 0000 0000 0000 0000 0000 0000   ................
4000 0000 0000 0000 0002 0000 0000 0000   @...............
7000 0000 0000 0000 7000 0000 0000 0000   p.......p.......
2101 1430 0002 0000

<<$Logged_Utility_Stream attribute - type 100 or 0001 in little-endian notation - with
packed LCN (in bold) pointing location of Data Recovery Field.>>
                    0001 0000 5000 0000   !..0........P...
0104 4000 0000 0400 0000 0000 0000 0000   ..@.............
0100 0000 0000 0000 4800 0000 0000 0000   ........H.......
0004 0000 0000 0000 7803 0000 0000 0000   ........x.......
7803 0000 0000 0000 2400 4500 4600 5300   x.......$.E.F.S.
2102 1230 0000 0000 FFFF FFFF 8279 4711   !..0.........yG.
```

Here is an excerpt of the $Logged_Utility_Stream showing the Data Decryption Field (DDF) for the user and the Data Recovery Field (DRF) for the DRA:

```
<<This excerpt from the non-resident portion of the $Logged_Utility_Stream shows the
certificate information for the user, bplum, who encrypted the file. The bold number in the
hex listing is the thumbprint from the certificate. The bold entry in the decimal listing is
the start of the user's certificate.>>
```

```
7200 0000 C800 0000 C92E 531E FBBF 079F    r.........S.....
50B7 4471 7A26 6C0C 4D3C 3F82 3400 3100    P.Dqz&l.M<?.4.1.
6500 3100 6300 3000 3000 3100 2D00 3700    e.1.c.0.0.1.-.7.
3100 3700 3300 2D00 3400 3200 3900 3600    1.7.3.-.4.2.9.6.
2D00 3900 3300 3100 3900 2D00 3200 6600    -.9.3.1.9.-.2.f.
6600 6600 3400 3200 6600 3600 6400 3800    f.f.4.2.f.6.d.8.
3100 3600 0000 4D00 6900 6300 7200 6F00    1.6...M.i.c.r.o.
7300 6F00 6600 7400 2000 4200 6100 7300    s.o.f.t. .B.a.s.
6500 2000 4300 7200 7900 7000 7400 6F00    e. .C.r.y.p.t.o.
6700 7200 6100 7000 6800 6900 6300 2000    g.r.a.p.h.i.c. .
5000 7200 6F00 7600 6900 6400 6500 7200    P.r.o.v.i.d.e.r.
2000 7600 3100 2E00 3000 0000 4F00 5500    .v.1...0...O.U.
3D00 4500 4600 5300 2000 4600 6900 6C00    =.E.F.S. .F.i.l.
6500 2000 4500 6E00 6300 7200 7900 7000    e. .E.n.c.r.y.p.
7400 6900 6F00 6E00 2000 4300 6500 7200    t.i.o.n. .C.e.r.
7400 6900 6600 6900 6300 6100 7400 6500    t.i.f.i.c.a.t.e.
2C00 2000 4C00 3D00 4500 4600 5300 2C00    ,. .L.=.E.F.S.,.
2000 4300 4E00 3D00 6200 7000 6C00 7500    .C.N.=.b.p.l.u.
6D00 0000 535E 9D13 3191 740F F2EA F70D    m...S^..1.t.....
```

<<This excerpt is the certificate information for the Data Recovery Agent, which in this case is the Administrator account for the domain. The thumbprint of the File Recovery certificate is shown in bold in the hex listing.>>

```
0000 0000 0000 0000 2800 0000 5672 B823    ........(...Vr.#
4097 749A 7949 3491 0531 30F9 478B 34AC    @.t.yI4..10.G.4.
4F00 5500 3D00 4500 4600 5300 2000 4600    O.U.=.E.F.S. .F.
6900 6C00 6500 2000 4500 6E00 6300 7200    i.l.e. .E.n.c.r.
7900 7000 7400 6900 6F00 6E00 2000 4300    y.p.t.i.o.n. .C.
6500 7200 7400 6900 6600 6900 6300 6100    e.r.t.i.f.i.c.a.
7400 6500 2C00 2000 4C00 3D00 4500 4600    t.e.,. .L.=.E.F.
5300 2C00 2000 4300 4E00 3D00 4100 6400    S.,. .C.N.=.A.d.
6D00 6900 6E00 6900 7300 7400 7200 6100    m.i.n.i.s.t.r.a.
7400 6F00 7200 0000 6C1E 6E80 C8D0 E191    t.o.r...l.n.....
```

Public Key Cryptography Services (PKCS) Used by EFS

You do not need to be steeped in the nuances of cryptography to manage EFS, but you definitely need a good understanding of the way certificates are generated, saved, and passed around. This section contains a description of the PKCS elements that are necessary to the operation of EFS.

Like DESX, PKCS encryption is reversible, but instead of being symmetrical with one key for encryption and decryption, PKCS uses two keys: a *public key* used for encryption and a *private key* used for decryption.

The first time a user encrypts a file, a public/private key pair is created for EFS by the local crypto provider.

The private key is encrypted with the user's MD4 password hash. The public key is freely distributable. Files encrypted with the public key are perfectly safe so long as no one but the key owner has access to the private key.

EFS works with the Local Security Authority to obtain the EFS keys when encrypting and decrypting files. EFS also encrypts the FEK using a key belonging to a DRA. See "Role of Data Recovery Agents" for more information.

EFS Keys and Certificates

Key management is absolutely critical to a secure PKCS system. It is a waste of time to encrypt files if the keys originate from an untrusted source.

Every Windows 2000 computer has the capability of issuing EFS keys. The keys are issued by the LSA with the help of *cryptographic providers*. The provider used to issue EFS certificates is the Microsoft Base Cryptographic Provider v 1.0.

When a user encrypts a file the first time, the crypto provider generates a public/private key pair unless a private key already exists.

The public and private keys are stored as files in the user's profile on the local machine. Figure 14.17 shows a diagram of the key and certificate locations and the internal structure of an encrypted file. The next two sections contain details about the public and private keys.

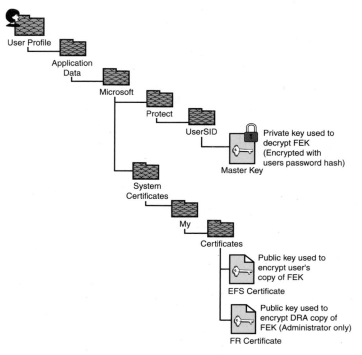

Figure 14.17   Diagram of EFS key and certificate locations.

> **Registry Tip: Cryptographic Providers**
>
> The list of cryptographic providers is in the Registry under HKLM ¦ Software ¦ Microsoft ¦
> Cryptography ¦ Defaults ¦ Provider.

Private Key Used by EFS

The private key used by EFS is located in \Documents and Settings\<userID>\Application Data\Microsoft\Protect\<userSID>. The file-name matches the header of the key inside the file.

The private key is technically not a part of EFS. It is a master key used for a variety of purposes. If a master key already exists, then it becomes the private key in the public/private pair associated with EFS.

The master key is encrypted with the user's hashed password as a cipher. When the user changes her password, the LSA works with the crypto provider to re-encrypt the private key with the new password.

The master key is essential for the proper operation of EFS. If you delete the user's profile, you also delete the master key. Without the master key, the user cannot decrypt the FEK. Without the FEK, the user cannot open an encrypted file.

Because the master key is encrypted with the user's password hash, if the user is removed from the domain or if you create a new account for the user, then the user loses access to the encrypted files. In this situation, the DRA must recover the files.

If a user logs on to the SAM of a local machine, encrypts a file, and then logs on to the domain, the user will not be able to read the encrypted file. The domain user account has a different SID and a different user profile. You should train your laptop users to use their domain accounts to log on even if they are not on the network.

Here are the important points to remember about private keys used by EFS:

- The private key is a master key used for a variety of purposes, not just for EFS.

- The master key is required to read an encrypted file.

- If a user's profile is deleted, the master key is deleted and the user can no longer read encrypted files.

EFS Public Key

Unlike the private key, which is stored in a proprietary format, the public key is stored as a PKCS *certificate*. A certificate is a file that contains the public key along with elements that verify the key's authenticity.

The public key certificate is stored in the user's profile under `\Documents and Settings\<userid>\Application Data\Microsoft\SystemCertificates\My\ Certificates`. The name of the file that holds the certificate matches the *thumbprint* of the certificate, a 128-bit message digest that provides a quick check of the certificate's identity.

EFS obtains the user's public key certificate from the crypto provider in LSA. It uses the key to encrypt the FEK, then stores the certificate in the $Logged_Utility_Stream attribute of the file. The public key certificate contains the user name of the person owning the certificate. This gives EFS the hint it needs to find the user's private key when the time comes to decrypt the file.

Certificates are issued for specific purposes, which are specified by Object Identifiers (OIDs). See the sidebar "Certificate Object Identifiers" for more information. EFS uses two certificate types: the Encrypting File System Certificate, OID 1.3.6.1.4.1.311.10.3.4, and the File Recovery certificate, OID 1.3.6.1.4.1.311.10.3.4.1.

If the EFS certificate is generated by the crypto provider on the local machine, it is termed a *self-signed certificate*. EFS certificates can also be generated by a *Certificate Authority* (CA). EFS does not require the use of a CA, but if one is available, the local crypto provider uses it. See "Managing Certificates with a Certificate Authority" for more information.

Both the master key and the public key certificate are stored in the roaming portion of the user's profile. This means that files encrypted by roaming users on different machines use the same public/private key pair. Contrast this to a user who logs on to different machines without a roaming profile. In that case, a separate EFS certificate is generated at each machine using a different master key.

The net effect is the same in either case. The user can freely access encrypted files on any of the local desktops. The advantage to having a roaming profile is that you can transfer files between the machines using Backup and not be bothered with exporting and importing the master key and EFS certificate. See "Recovering Encrypted Files" for more information.

Even though the keys and certificates are in the roaming profile, encrypted files themselves cannot be placed in a roaming profile unless the server hosting the profile is configured to be Trusted for Delegation. See "Saving Encrypted Files on Trusted Servers" for more information.

Here are the key points to remember about an EFS public key certificate:

- It is issued to a user the first time a file is encrypted on a machine.
- The public key in the EFS certificate is paired with the master private key used to decrypt the FEK.
- A copy of the public key certificate accompanies each encrypted file. EFS uses this certificate to determine the identity of the encryptor so it can locate the private key.
- The keys used by EFS are stored in the roaming portion of the user profile.

Registry Tip: Certificate ID
The thumbprint of the user's EFS certificate is stored in HKCU ¦ Software ¦ Microsoft ¦ Windows NT ¦ CurrentVersion ¦ EFS ¦ CurrentKeys ¦ CertificateHash.

Certificates

The user's public key certificate and the file containing the encrypted master key are not in transportable format. If they need to be moved to another machine, they must be exported to a certificate format that can be copied to another machine and imported. The certificate formats supported by Windows 2000 for this purpose are:

- X.509 certificates (.CER) using Distinguished Encoding Rules (DER)
- X.509 certificates (.CER) using Base-64 encoding
- PKCS #7 Cryptographic Message Syntax Standard (.P7B)
- PKCS #12 Personal Information Exchange (PFX)

Of these four certificate types, the first three are used to distribute public keys. Only the last type, the PFX certificate, can store public/private key pairs.

The PFX format uses strong encryption to store the two keys together without compromising them. For maximum security, the DRA certificate must be removed from the system when not in use, so the ability to safely store and transport certificates containing private keys is critical for formulating an EFS recovery strategy.

Certificate Object Identifiers

Certificates are issued for specific purposes as specified by an *Object Identifier* (OID) assigned to the certificate. Including an OID in a certificate is like giving it a "need to know" classification in security clearance terms. It ensures that the certificate can only be used for a designated purpose.

The OID is a unique number registered with a standards body that has been authorized by the International Standards Organization (ISO). The standards body for the U.S. is the American National Standards Institute (ANSI). The structure and distribution of OIDs is described in ISO/IEC 8824:1990, *Information Technology–Open Systems Interconnection–Specification of Abstract Syntax Notation One (ASN.1)*.

Other applications that use OIDs include Simple Network Management Protocol (SNMP) and X.500 Directory Services, such as the LDAP-based Active Directory.

Role of Data Recovery Agents

If the user who originally encrypted a file were the only person able to open it again, the stage would be set for a lot of grief. In practice, EFS includes a way for one or more accounts designated as DRA to open the file as well.

The identity of the DRA varies depending on the domain configuration:

- **Standalone Windows 2000 Professional desktop.** The default DRA is the Admin account.

- **Standalone Windows 2000 Server.** The DRA is the Administrator account stored in the local SAM.

- **Windows 2000 domain controller or domain member.** The DRA is the Administrator account stored in the Active Directory. Domain members do not have local DRAs.

The DRA is issued a certificate called the File Recovery certificate that contains a public key paired to the master key belonging to the agent. When EFS encrypts a file, it encrypts a copy of the FEK with the public key from the FR certificate and includes it along with a portion of the FR certificate in the $Logged_Utility_Stream attribute of the file.

This permits the DRA to open a file in the same way that the encrypting user would open it. There are no special "data recovery mechanisms" involved. If a user on a laptop has logged on to the local SAM and encrypted a file, you can log on as Admin and view the file. The only caveat is that the file must be on the same machine as the DRA's master key. The "Recovering Encrypted Files" section covers the system's protection of the FR certificate and DRA master key.

EFS Highlights

Here is a list of items to keep in mind as you consider how to best deploy EFS in your organization.

- EFS encrypts the data attribute in a file. It does not touch other attributes, such as the security descriptor or filename. A user with adequate NTFS permissions can rename or delete a file encrypted by another user.

- If a file is copied to a FAT or FAT32 volume, it will be saved in clear text.

- If an application opens an encrypted file and saves temp files or backup files to a non–NTFS volume, the auxiliary files will be unencrypted. Make sure you search out temporary folders used by applications and encrypt them, as well.

- EFS sits above NTFS so file contents sent to the paging file and transaction tracking logs are encrypted.

- When you set the Encryption flag on a folder, the encryption flag is inherited by files created in that folder. When a file is encrypted in this manner, it does not generate a temp file.

- Encrypting a folder does not block access to other users. When other users save their files in an encrypted folder, the files are encrypted using the public key of the user who created the file.

- Copying or moving an unencrypted file to an encrypted folder will encrypt the file.

- Encrypted files retain their encryption status when moved or copied as long as the target volume is NTFS5.

- User certificates are stored in the user's local profile. Keep this in mind when deleting "unnecessary" profiles. If the user's profile is deleted, only the DRA can get the files back. On a standalone machine, if both the user's profile and the DRA's profile are deleted, then access to the encrypted files is permanently lost.

- Under normal circumstances, you cannot encrypt files across the network. A server must be configured as Trusted for Delegation before it can store encrypted files for network users. See "Saving Encrypted Data Files on Trusted Servers" for details and precautions.

- For the same reason cited in the previous bullet, you cannot encrypt files in a roaming profile because the profile is copied to a server. The system will refuse to replicate the profile if it contains an encrypted file, unless the host server is trusted for delegation.

Here are some additional EFS limitations that are not readily apparent from the file encryption and decryption process:

- Backups of encrypted files remain encrypted. Using Backup to put an encrypted file in a backup file is the only method for moving encrypted files between machines that are not trusted for delegation.

- Compressed files cannot be encrypted. Encrypted files cannot be compressed.

- Sparse files can be encrypted and remain sparse files.

- Files with multiple data streams can be encrypted. All data streams are encrypted.

- Mount points and other reparse records cannot be encrypted. See Chapter 13 for details.

- System files cannot be encrypted. The operating system needs to read them at boot time before EFS has initialized.

- Encrypted files cannot be shared using the tools that ship with Windows 2000. There is an API call, AddUsersToEncryptedFile(), that can add additional EFS certificates to a file so that multiple users can open the same encrypted file. See the Windows 2000 Platform SDK for more information.

Encrypting Folders and Files

This section describes how to use Explorer and the command-line to encrypt and decrypt folders and files. You must have Read/Write access rights to the folder to set the encryption attribute.

An Encrypted Data Recovery Agents policy must be in effect, either at the local computer or in the domain, with at least one DRA on the list. If not, EFS will give an error and refuse to encrypt a file. See "Managing Recovery Policies" for details.

Encrypting a Folder

One of the options when encrypting a folder is to propagate the encryption down to subfolders and files. When propagating encryption settings, EFS may encounter a locked file. If this happens, a warning appears giving you the option to Retry or Ignore. Make note of the locked file to determine whether it should be encrypted.

Procedure 14.4   **Encrypting a Folder Using Explorer**

1. Open Explorer or My Computer.

2. Navigate to the folder you want to encrypt. The examples use the My Documents folder. (If you are using roaming profiles, you cannot encrypt My Documents because the system does not permit encrypting the contents of a roaming profile.)

3. Right-click the folder you want to encrypt and select PROPERTIES from the fly-out menu. The Properties window for the folder opens.

4. Click Advanced. The Advanced Attributes window opens. See Figure 14.18.

Figure 14.18   Advanced Attributes window showing Encrypt contents selection.

5. Select the Encrypt contents to secure data option. You cannot select both this and the Compress contents... option. The interface treats the two options as radio buttons even though they appear as checkboxes.

6. Click OK to save the selection and return to the main Properties window. The folder is not yet encrypted.

7. Click OK to encrypt the folder. The Confirm Attribute Changes window opens.

8. Select Apply Changes To This Folder, Subfolders, and Files. This ensures that all the contents of the folder and any subfolders the user may create are encrypted from the start. This prevents leaving unencrypted contents in the EFS temp files.

9. When the encryption attribute has been set on each file and subfolder and the affected files have been encrypted, the Properties window for the folder closes.

If the `Enable Web content in folders` option is enabled for a folder (FOLDER OPTIONS | PROPERTIES | VIEW), you can highlight the file or folder to show the encryption status in the Attributes list at the left of the window. Otherwise, there is no visual clue as to the encryption status. The name of the user who encrypted the file is not revealed.

Encrypting Individual Files

If you choose to encrypt one file instead of an entire folder, EFS issues a warning, as shown in Figure 14.19, stating that the file could become decrypted when modified. You also take the chance of exposing the clear-text contents of the file in the temporary EFS file that is used to store the file before it is encrypted.

Figure 14.19   Warning message about possible loss of decryption settings when encrypting individual files.

The default selection in the warning message, Encrypt the file and the parent folder, ensures that the file remains encrypted and that future files placed in that folder are encrypted without the use of temporary files.

Encrypting Folders and Files Using the Command Line

If you prefer a command-line alternative for manipulating files, use the Cipher command to encrypt and decrypt files and folders.

Procedure 14.5   **Encrypting a Folder and Files Using Cipher**

1. Open a command window.
2. Navigate to the folder containing the file or folder you want to encrypt.
3. Enter `cipher` to list the current encryption settings on the folder contents. There is no option to list the names of the users who encrypted the files or folders. This is promised for a maintenance release.
4. Enter `cipher /e <folder_name>` to set the encryption flag on the folder. This will cause any new files in that folder to be encrypted.

5. Enter `cipher /e /a <folder_name>\*.*` to encrypt any files and subfolders currently in the folder.

6. Enter `cipher` again to view the results. Here is a sample display:

```
C:\test\subtest>cipher \test\*.*
 Listing C:\test\
 New files added to this directory will be encrypted.

E testfile.1
E testfile.2
E subdir
```

This display indicates that the folder, `test`, was flagged for encryption, all current files were encrypted, and subfolders were flagged for encryption.

Here are additional uses for `cipher`:

- To encrypt just a folder, enter `cipher /e folder_name`. You can specify a path as well as the folder, such as `cipher /e\top_folder\middle_folder\bottom_folder`.

- To decrypt a folder, enter `cipher /d folder_name`.

- To encrypt just one file, use the `/a` switch: `cipher /e /a file_name`.

- To encrypt or decrypt all subfolders, add the `/s:<folder_name>` switch and specify the first folder in the path. This folder and all subfolders will be flagged for encryption.

- When encrypting subfolders, the encryption propagation stops if there is an error. If you want encryption propagation to continue automatically in the event of an error, add the `/i` switch: `cipher /e /i /s:\<folder_name>`.

- When propagating encryption settings, EFS skips files and folders with existing encryption settings. If you want to re-encrypt files and folders that were previously encrypted by the same user, use the `/f` switch: `cipher /e /f /s:\<folder_name>`.

- When applying or propagating encryption settings, hidden files and folders are skipped by default. If you want to encrypt hidden files and folders, add the `/h` switch: `cipher /e /h /s:\<folder_name>`.

Managing Personal Certificates

When a user encrypts a file for the first time, the local system generates a public/private key pair for the EFS if a master key does not already exist. If a master key already exists, EFS generates a public key paired to the existing master key.

The next three sections describe how to perform the following certificate operations:

- View your personal certificates.

- Export a personal certificate to another format for transport to a different machine or saving on floppy or CD. This is most often required when transferring a user's EFS keys to another computer. It is also required when exporting a File Recovery certificate prior to removing it for safe-keeping.

- Import a certificate exported at another machine. This is most often required when an encrypted file must be recovered using the File Recovery certificate.

Viewing Personal Certificates

To view the contents of a local certificate, you must log on at the console of the computer where the certificate is stored. The contents are visible when using an MMC snap-in called Certificates. The steps in this section build a custom MMC console to view the Certificates snap-in.

The Certificates snap-in shows the tickets issued to your account. If you have administrative privileges, you can also view certificates issued to the local system. You cannot view certificates issued to other users. You can also use the Certificates snap-in to export and import certificates and obtain new certificates from a Certification Authority, if one exists. See "Managing File Recovery Certificates" later in the chapter.

Procedure 14.6 **Viewing Personal Certificates**

1. Open an empty MMC console using START | RUN | MMC.

2. From the console menu, select CONSOLE | ADD/REMOVE SNAP-IN. The Add/Remove Snap-in window opens.

3. Click Add. The Add Standalone Snap-in window opens.

4. Double-click Certificates to load the snap-in. If you are logged on with an account that does not have administrator privileges, the only option is to load the user's personal certificates. This is done automatically.

5. If the account has administrator privileges, the Certificates Snap-in window opens. See the following for information on making this selection.

Certificate Selection Options

The Certificates snap-in offers these alternatives when loading a certificate viewer:

The `My User Account` option opens the certificates in the user's personal profile under `\Documents and Settings\<logonID>\Application Data\Microsoft\SystemCertificates\My\Certificates` along with personal certificates stored in the user's Directory object.

The `Service Account` option opens a `Select Computer` window then presents the list of services installed on the selected computer. Select a service that uses a certificate and it will be added to the list of certificates managed by the console. This option is useful if you are troubleshooting a Digital Signing problem.

The `Computer Account` option opens a `Select Computer` window. When you select a computer account, the snap-in opens the computer certificates stored in `HKLM | Software | Microsoft | SystemCertificates | My | Certificates`. You can view local certificates and certificates for remote computers if you have administrator rights on those computers. Under normal circumstances, a Windows 2000 Professional computer does not have a personal certificate. A Windows 2000 domain member server will have a Digital Signing certificate if you have installed a Certificate Authority. This certificate is not used by EFS.

6. With the snap-in loaded, save the console with a descriptive name, such as Cert.msc. You may want to save it in \WINNT\System32 along with the rest of the consoles so that anyone logging on to the computer can use it. The console does not point at your specific certificate. It loads the certificates of the user who launches the console.

7. Expand the tree to `Certificates—Current User | Personal | Certificates`. Any certificates issued to the user are listed in the right pane. Figure 14.20 shows an example. The Intended Purposes column lists the purpose for which the certificate was issued. This is determined by the OID associated with the certificate. The example shows two certificates, one for EFS and one for File Recovery. The example shows the domain Administrator account, which is also the default DRA for a domain. The DRA has two certificates, one for EFS and one for File Recovery.

Figure 14.20 `Certificates` console showing user's personal certificates.

8. Right-click the Certificates icon and select PROPERTIES from the fly-out menu. The Properties window opens. See Figure 14.21.

Figure 14.21 Certificate Properties window showing the File Recovery purpose and the Enable All Purposes... option selected. This is the default configuration for this certificate.

Each of the certificate's purposes is listed along with options to disable the certificate completely or to disable a particular purpose. Disabling File Recovery for this certificate would prevent Administrator from opening, copying, or moving any encrypted files other than those encrypted by the Administrator account on this computer.

9. Click OK to close the window.

10. Double-click the Certificates icon to open its Certificate window. The General tab lists pertinent information about the source and the expiration date of the certificate.

11. Click Details. Figure 14.22 shows an example. This tab shows specific entries in the certificate. Highlighting an entry displays the entire entry in the bottom pane of the window.

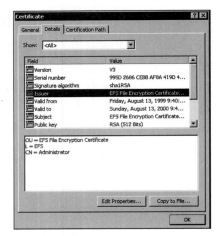

Figure 14.22   `Certificate` window—`Details` tab showing Issuer information.

The `Subject` portion of a certificate, along with the thumbprint listed at the bottom of the `Field` list, is stored in the $Logged_Utility_Stream attribute of every encrypted file. This information tells EFS which certificate to use when decrypting the File Encryption Key.

The `Copy to File` option starts the Certificate Export Wizard, which allows you to copy the certificate in a form that can be stored or transported to another computer for importing. The operation of this wizard is covered in the next section.

12. Select the `Certification Path` tab. This shows a path of Untrusted with a red X, unless the certificate is issued by a Certification Authority.

13. Click `OK` to close the window and return to the `Certificates` console.

14. Close the console. Save the console settings when prompted.

Exporting Personal Certificates

If a user changes computers and wants to transfer encrypted files from the old machine to the new one, you face a bit of work. You cannot simply copy the encrypted files over the network to the new computer. If you try, or if a user tries, the system responds with an *access denied* error and the suggestion that the source file might be in use. This is because the EFS driver runs in the security context of the Local System. The Local System running on one computer cannot access the private key in a user's EFS certificate on another computer.

You have a two-stage problem. You must somehow transfer the encrypted files to the new machine and you must transfer the user's EFS certificate to the new machine so she can read the files. Here are your general actions:

- **Backup to file.** You cannot copy the files directly, but you can take advantage of a feature in Windows 2000 Backup to copy the files to a backup file. You do not need a PKCS certificate to do the backup. Instructions for using Backup are in Chapter 18, "Recovering from System Failures."

- **Configure a roaming profile.** The simplest way to transfer a user's EFS certificate is to configure the user for a roaming profile. The EFS certificates are in the user profile, so they will copy down to the second desktop when the user logs on.

If you do not want to use a roaming profile, another alternative is to export a copy of the user's EFS certificate from the original machine and import it at the new machine. You cannot simply copy the certificate files from the user's profile. Registry parameters must be updated, which is the reason for doing the import.

Export/import operations must be performed while logged on as the user because they involve opening the user's private key. This can only be done in the user's security context because the private key is encrypted with the user's password hash. You cannot do the work from a central location.

To view and export a certificate, you will need to use the Certificate MMC snap-in. This is most easily done by loading the snap-in into a custom MMC console. See "Viewing Personal Certificates" for the steps to create a custom Certificate console.

The next steps demonstrate how to export a user's private and public keys at one machine, then import them at a second machine. The example assumes that the user's files have already been transferred using Backup. The user cannot open the files until the EFS keys have been transferred. Proceed as follows:

Procedure 14.7   **Exporting a User's EFS Public/Private Keys**

1. Log on at the console of the first computer, the one that currently has the EFS certificate.

2. Open the `Certificates` console.

3. Expand the tree to `Certificates—Current User ¦ Personal ¦ Certificates`. If no certificate exists, you are not logged on at the correct computer or you are using the wrong account. Otherwise, the user was wrong all along and had never encrypted files on this machine.

4. Right-click the `Encrypting File System` certificate and select ALL TASKS | EXPORT from the fly-out menu. This starts the `Certificate Export Wizard`. If several certificates are listed, use the `Intended Purposes` column to find the Encrypting File System certificate.

5. Click `Next`. The `Export Private Key` window opens.

6. Select `Yes, export the private key`. The certificate must contain the user's private key so EFS can use it to decrypt the FEK and extract the cipher. One common mistake is to export just the public key into an X.509 CER file. This can be imported at the second computer, but cannot be used to open encrypted files.

7. Click `Next`. The `Export File Format` window opens. See Figure 14.23. The exported file must be in PFX format because it contains the entire key pair and requires additional security. Leave the `Enable strong protection` option selected.

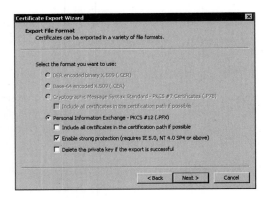

Figure 14.23 `Certificate Export Wizard—Export File Format.`

8. Click `Next`. The `Password` window opens. Enter a password and confirm. There are no complexity requirements, but the longer the password and the more non-alpha characters you use, the better.

9. Click `Next`. The `File To Export` window opens. Enter the name you want to give the exported certificate. The name has no cryptographic significance. You should include the user's logon ID. Specify a local folder for the output.

10. Click `Next`. A completion window opens.

11. Click Finish. The wizard informs you when the export has been successfully completed.

12. Close the Certificates console.

At this point, you have a PFX file containing the user's EFS certificate. Copy this file to the second computer and delete it from the first computer, just to be tidy. The contents of the file are virtually impenetrable, but you never know who might have the user's password and can obtain access to the certificate to import it.

Importing EFS Certificates

Now that you have copied the user's PFX certificate to the second computer, log on at the second computer with the user's credentials. If the user has already encrypted files at this computer, she will already have an EFS certificate. The EFS certificate you import from the first machine will work alongside the existing EFS certificate.

Procedure 14.8 **Importing EFS Certificates**

1. Log on at the console of the second computer with the user's credentials.

2. Open the Certificates console.

3. Expand the tree to Certificates - Current User ¦ Personal ¦ Certificates. If this entry does not exist, the user has not yet encrypted files on this computer.

4. Right-click the Certificates icon (or the Personal icon, if no Certificates icon is available) and select ALL TASKS | IMPORT from the fly-out menu. This starts the Certificate Import Wizard.

5. Click Next. The File To Import window opens. Click Browse and navigate to the location where you copied the PFX file and select the file.

6. Click Next. The Password window opens.

7. Enter the password you gave the file when you exported it.

8. Click Next. The Certificate Store window opens. Leave the Place all certificates in the following store radio button selected and designate a Certificate Store of Personal.

9. Click Next. A completion window opens summarizing your selections.

10. Click Finish. The wizard informs you when the certificate has been imported.

11. Highlight the `Personal` | `Certificates` icon and verify that the new certificate is listed in the right pane with an intended purpose of Encrypting File System.

12. Close the `Certificates` console.

13. Use Explorer to attempt to open an encrypted file from the other computer. The file should open, indicating that the correct certificate was imported.

Recovering Encrypted Files

If a user is unable or unavailable to open an encrypted file, the file can be opened by the DRA. The DRA is able to open the file because EFS stores a copy of the FEK encrypted with the public key from the File Recovery certificate issued to the DRA. The DRA views the encrypted file using the private key associated with the FR certificate.

There are no special recovery mechanisms or recovery applications necessary to "recover" a file. The Recovery Agent simply opens the encrypted file just as the user would open it.

This section covers:

- How default DRAs are selected.
- How the File Recovery certificate is used to recover files on standalone machines and domain members.
- How file recovery policies are configured, managed, and distributed.

Default Data Recovery Agents

EFS selects a DRA based on the domain affiliation of the machine. The FR certificate is stored in the DRA's user profile.

- The default DRA for a standalone Professional desktop is the Admin account.
- The default DRA for a standalone server is the Administrator account.
- The default DRA in a domain is the domain Administrator account.

The domain Administrator's certificate is stored under the Administrator profile on the first domain controller in the domain. A copy of the DRA certificate is stored in the Registry of every domain member computer under `HKLM` | `Software` | `Policies` | `Microsoft` | `SystemCertificates` | `EFS` | `Certificates` | `<thumbprint>`.

Data Recovery Overview

You can recover encrypted files on a standalone desktop or server by logging on using the Admin (Professional) or Administrator (Server) account and opening the file or changing its encryption attribute. For this reason, file encryption on a standalone machine is not very secure. It's possible to play all sorts of games with the local SAM accounts to obtain access to the Admin/Administrator account.

If you use encryption on standalone machines, such as laptops or user's home machines, *it is important that you remove the File Recovery certificate from the machine to prevent encrypted files from being compromised.* I cannot stress this strongly enough. There is simply no point in encrypting files if the FR certificate is left within reach. See "Securing File Recovery Certificates" for details.

In a domain, the problem of file recovery becomes a bit more complex. Here's the dilemma. The Administrator is the DRA, but you cannot simply walk up to a user's machine, log on as Administrator, and expect to open encrypted files because there is no local copy of the FR certificate and the DRA's private key. Both of these are required to open an encrypted file.

Encrypted file recovery can use one of two strategies:

- You can use Ntbackup to copy the user's encrypted files to a machine that has an FR certificate and DRA master key.

- You can export the FR certificate and DRA master key and put a copy of each on the user's machine.

Under normal circumstances, you remove the Administrator's FR certificate from the network completely, so you will need to take both actions: Copy the encrypted files to a secure server, then import the Administrator's FR certificate and DRA private key to that server to recover the files.

Data Recovery Policies

A group policy must be in place that tells each machine the identity of the DRA to use when encrypting files. This is called a File Recovery Policy. Local machines require a local File Recovery Policy.

If no group or local policy is in effect, or a DRA is not listed in the policy, EFS will refuse to encrypt files.

This notion of a "File Recovery Policy" takes some getting used to because group policies are new in Windows 2000. A group policy is nothing more than a file that is distributed to domain clients when they log on. The "File Recovery Policy" is a Registry entry containing the public key certificate of the DRA. See "Managing Recovery Policies" for more information.

The remaining topics in this section cover how to configure a file recovery policy and use it to recover files. Here are the key points to remember about recovering encrypted files to use as a road map for those actions:

- A DRA is an account that can open an encrypted file if the original user is no longer available.

- A DRA is issued a FR certificate that contains a public key. A DRA can open encrypted files because a copy of the FEK encrypted with the FR public key is included with the file.

- The default DRA is selected based on the domain affiliation of the machine.

- The identity of the DRA is specified by a group policy (domains) or local policy (standalone machines.) The policy must specify at least one DRA.

- Every encrypted file must have at least one DRA.

Managing Recovery Policies

A *recovery policy* refers to a group policy that contains the name and public key of the DRA(s). On standalone servers and workstations, the recovery policy is set in the local machine policies using the Group Policy Editor console, GPEDIT.MSC. In a domain, the recovery policy is distributed to domain member computers through a group policy.

Group policies are a set of Registry updates, logon/logoff scripts, folder redirection instructions, and software installation routines that are automatically distributed to domain member computers and users when they log on. Group policies involving the Encrypted Data Recovery Agent are saved to a REGISTRY.POL file in the associated policy folder.

Policies for standalone workstations and servers are stored under `\WINNT\System32\GroupPolicy\Machine\Registry.pol`. Group policies intended for distribution to domain member computers are stored under `\WINNT\Sysvol\Sysvol\<domain_name>\Policies\<policy_GUID>\Machine`. The second Sysvol folder in this path is shared as SYSVOL so client computers go to directly to the SYSVOL share to download policies. Figure 14.24 shows an example.

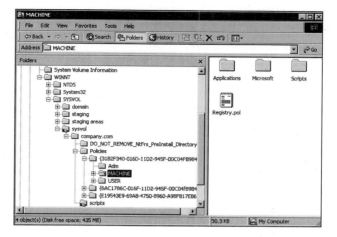

Figure 14.24 Explorer window showing path to policy files.

When domain member computers log on, they download their policy files, including the REGISTRY.POL files, from the domain controller that authenticates them. The policy files are replicated between domain controllers via the *File Replication Service* (FRS), so it doesn't matter which domain controller authenticates the client.

The Registry updates in the REGISTRY.POL file are applied immediately to the local Registry. Unlike older System Policies in NT4, group policy entries are applied in a volatile fashion. If the policy is removed, the original Registry setting takes over again.

Certificates associated with public key policies are only stored in the Registry. They do not take the form of certificate files in the user profile. The public key in a Registry-based certificate can be exported to a standard certificate format such as an X.509 certificate. The private key cannot be derived from the Registry entry.

Figure 14.25 shows the placement of the Encrypted Data Recovery Agents policy in the group policy structure. The policy is located under Computer Configuration | Windows Settings | Security Settings | Public Key Policies. The list of recovery agents is listed in the right pane when the Encrypted Data Recovery Agents policy is highlighted.

A policy entry for a recovery agent contains a copy of the File Recovery certificate issued to the agent. This certificate contains the agent's public key that EFS will use to encrypt the FEK for a file.

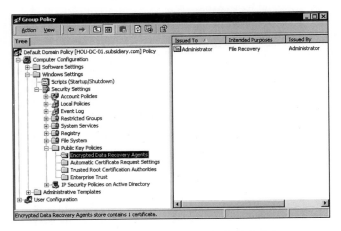

Figure 14.25   Group Policy console showing the Administrator account
listed under Encrypted Data Recovery Agents. This is the recovery policy.

Registry Tip: File Recovery Certificates

The File Recovery certificate in the REGISTRY.POL file is designed to fit in the Registry as a Binary BLOB under
HKLM | Software | Policies | Microsoft | SystemCertificates | EFS | Certificates |
<certificate_thumbprint>.

Data Recovery Policy Distribution

EFS includes a copy of a File Recovery certificate in the Data Recovery
Field of every encrypted file. It obtains the FR certificate from the domain
as part of a group policy called the Encrypted Data Recovery Agents policy.

Group policies can be linked to domains, sites, or individual OUs. The
placement of the group policy that contains an Encrypted Data Recovery
Agents policy determines the *scope of influence* of the DRA. For example, the
Default Domain Policy contains the FR certificate issued to the domain
Administrator account, the default DRA for the domain. This gives the
Administrator account a scope of influence that encompasses every domain
member computer regardless of its physical location or OU affiliation.

A local administrator can create a new group policy, link that policy to a
local OU, and assign a different Data Recovery policy. She could choose to
include the DRA from the domain or block the domain policy and use just
the OU policy.

Managing Data Recovery Policies

Group policies are configured using a Group Policy snap-in that appears in several MMC consoles. The underlying DLL for this snap-in is GPEDIT.DLL, so it is often called the Group Policy Editor. The Group Policy Editor has a long list of extensions that can be used to tailor its functions. The data recovery polices are contained in the Security extensions. These are listed in the Group Policy Editor as Security Settings.

Security Settings on standalone workstations and servers are configured using the Security Policy console, Secpol.msc.

Security Settings for domain-based group policies are managed from the AD management console that manages the associated domain object. For example, policies linked to the Domain container and any OU containers are managed from the AD Users and Computers console. Policies linked to Sites are managed from the AD Sites and Services console.

You can also build a custom console to hold the Security Settings extensions of the Group Policy snap-in. See Chapter 16, "Managing the User Operating Environment," for details on configuring a custom Group Policy console.

Configuring Recovery Agent Policies

When you open the Group Policy console, expand the tree to Computer Configuration ¦ Windows Settings ¦ Security Settings ¦ Public Key Policies ¦ Encrypted Data Recovery Agents. The right pane shows the certificate of the DRA. There must be at least one DRA, or EFS at the local clients will refuse to encrypt files.

If you set a policy that specifically lists <null> for Encrypted Data Recovery Agents (in contrast to a policy that has no entry for this policy) then users on computers affected by that policy cannot encrypt files. For example, you may want the Engineering department and the Accounting department to encrypt their files to protect product and business information, but you do not want the rest of the staff encrypting files willy-nilly. You can create a group policy, associate that policy with the Engineering and Accounting group, and assign a DRA to the data recovery policy. The default policy would have <null> under the policy. See Chapter 16 for the steps to assign group policies to groups.

The problem with implementing a group-based recovery policy is that the settings affect the Computer Configuration, not the User Configuration. This means you must associate the computer accounts with an OU or group, then assign the policy accordingly. This can be difficult to manage because it requires you to match users to their computers. In the long run, it might be easier to enable encryption and train your users to use it correctly.

Securing File Recovery Certificates

A loss of control over the File Recovery certificate for the DRA would jeopardize your entire file encryption strategy. The only sure way to maintain EFS security is to remove the FR certificate from all machines. This means lots of work if you have standalone workstations and servers.

The best strategy for deploying EFS consists of:

- Joining all desktops to the domain. This ensures that they use the domain DRA.

- Saving and removing the FR certificate from the initial domain controller. This ensures that an unauthorized person cannot get a copy of the FR and use it to access encrypted files in the domain.

- Remove the Encrypted Data Recovery Agents policy and FR certificates from all standalone machines to disable file encryption.

Before removing the FR certificate from a standalone machine or from the domain, make certain that you have a secure copy of the certificate that can be used if encrypted file recovery is required. The general actions for securing the File Recovery certificate are:

- Export the FR certificate and the master key to a certificate that can be saved to a floppy or burned to a CD.

- Delete the FR certificate from the domain controller (or standalone machine). This does not disrupt the ability of the users to encrypt files.

- Import the FR certificate only when necessary to perform a file recovery, then remove it afterward.

Exporting File Recovery Certificates

A certificate export cannot be done across the network. For a standalone Professional desktop, you must be logged on using the default Admin account. For a standalone server, you must be logged on as the local Administrator. For a Windows 2000 domain, you must be logged on at the console of the first domain controller in the domain using the domain Administrator account.

You should have a couple of blank floppies or a CD burner available to save the certificate once is has been exported. Proceed as follows:

Procedure 14.9 **Exporting a File Recovery Certificate**

1. Open the `Certificates` console.

2. Expand the tree to `Certificates - Current User | Personal | Certificates`. If this icon is not there, you are logged on at the wrong domain controller.

3. Right-click the `File Recovery` certificate and select ALL TASKS | EXPORT from the fly-out menu. This starts the `Certificate Export Wizard`. If several certificates are listed, use the Intended Purposes column to find the certificate.

4. Click `Next`. The `Export Private Key` window opens.

5. Select `Yes, export the private key`. The certificate must contain the private key to enable file recovery.

6. Click `Next`. The `Export File Format` window opens. See Figure 14.26. The exported file must be in PFX format because it contains the entire key pair and requires additional security. The dimmed selections only export the public key.

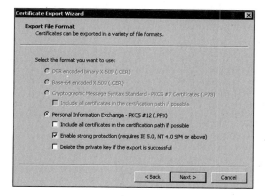

Figure 14.26 `Certificate Export Wizard—Export File Format`.

Leave the `Enable strong protection` option selected. This uses a more advanced form of encryption that is not available for pre-SP4 versions of classic NT.

7. Click `Next`. The `Password` window opens. Enter a password and confirm. There are no complexity requirements, but long passwords are better than short ones, and the more non-alpha characters you use, the better.

8. Click Next. The File To Export window opens. Enter the name you want to give the exported certificate. The name has no cryptographic significance. You should include·the user's logon ID. Specify a local folder for the output.

9. Click Next. A completion window opens.

10. Click Finish. The wizard informs you when the export has been successfully completed.

11. Close the Certificates console.

12. Copy the exported certificate to a couple of floppies. You may want to burn a copy to CD, as well. Lock the copies in a safe place. For now, keep one copy handy to perform in import check to verify that the process works. The next set of steps removes the on-disk copy of the certificate, so make sure you have a good copy.

Handling the Loss of the FR Certificate

Personally, I get a little squeamish when I read a sentence in a manual that warns me to "make sure I have a good copy" of something. So what if I don't, I usually ask. What happens then?

In this case, if you lose the FR certificate for the Administrator account, you will not be able to recover any files that users have already encrypted.

If this happens, your best course of action is to install a Certificate Authority (see "Installing Certificate Services") and create a new File Recovery certificate for the Administrator account by using the steps under "Creating Additional Data Recovery Agents."

Then, instruct users who have encrypted files to re-encrypt them. This puts the new DRA in place. If users fail to comply and later cannot open their encrypted files for some reason, you cannot help them.

Deleting File Recovery Certificates

When you have exported the FR certificate to a transportable format and safely locked away the copies, you can remove the on-disk certificate using the Certificates snap-in.

The certificate is stored in the Administrator profile under \Documents and Settings\Administrator\Application Data\Microsoft\SystemCertificates\My\ Certificates with a filename that matches the thumbprint on the certificate. Do not delete it directly. The Certificate snap-in also makes the necessary Registry updates.

Removing the FR certificate does not prevent users from encrypting and decrypting files. The public key of the DRA is still available as part of the Encrypted Data Recovery Agents policy. The only thing you lose is the ability to quickly recover files because you first need to import the certificate. When you are ready to export the FR certificate, proceed as follows:

Procedure 14.10   **Exporting a File Recovery Certificate**

1. Log on as Administrator at the domain controller that holds the FR certificate. This is the first domain controller that was promoted in the domain.

2. Open the `Certificates` console.

3. Expand the tree to `Certificates—Current User | Personal | Certificates`. If this icon does not exist, then you are not logged on at the correct domain controller or you are using the wrong Administrator account.

4. Locate the File Recovery certificate. If several certificates are listed, use the Intended Purposes column to find the File Recovery certificate.

5. Right-click the certificate and select DELETE from the fly-out menu. The snap-in sends a warning that you will not be able to decrypt data encrypted with this certificate. Click Yes to acknowledge the warning and delete the certificate.

6. You can verify that the file has been deleted by checking under `\Documents and Settings\Administrator\Application Data\Microsoft\ SystemCertificates\My\Certificates`.

7. Close the console.

If you need to recover an encrypted file, you must first import the File Recovery certificate. Refer to "Importing EFS Certificates" for details. The steps cover importing a personal EFS certificate, but they are equally valid for importing an FR certificate when logged on as Administrator / Admin.

Creating Additional Data Recovery Agents

As you probably noticed in the previous discussion, the Administrator account in the domain represents a single point of failure for EFS. Accidental loss of access to the Administrator account does occur.

In ordinary situations, loss of the Administrator account is an irritation, but it is not critical. You should have several accounts with full administrative privileges. But if you have deployed EFS in a domain, losing the Administrator account means losing the ability to recover encrypted files. Adding another DRA, then, should be high on your priority list.

Designating an alternate DRA involves issuing an FR certificate to another account. EFS will not issue this certificate. You must have a Certificate Authority. Install the CA using the steps in "Installing Certificate Services."

After you have a CA server, there are two ways to issue an FR certificate to a specific account.

- The Group Policy console has a shortcut that obtains the certificate from the CA and configures the account as a Data Recovery Agent.

- You can manually perform the same steps used by the shortcut. This would be necessary if the account already had an FR certificate and you wanted to add the certificate to the data recovery policy.

The steps in this section describe the shortcut. Refer to "Managing File Recovery Certificates" for manual methods to issue FR certificates and include them in the data recovery policy.

Procedure 14.11 Adding an Alternate DRA Using the Group Policy Shortcut

1. Log on at the console of the server where you want the File Recovery certificate to be created. Use the account you have designated as the alternate DRA. This account must have administrator privileges.

2. Open the AD Users and Computers console.

3. Open the Properties window for the Domain object.

4. Select the Group Policy tab.

5. Double-click the Default Domain Policy icon to open the Group Policy console. If you have multiple policies associated with the domain, make sure the Default Domain Policy is on top. If you do have higher priority policies, make sure they do not have policies that conflict with those that follow.

6. In the Group Policy console, navigate to Computer Configuration | Windows Settings | Security Settings | Public Key Policies | Encrypted Data Recovery Agents.

7. Right-click Encrypted Data Recovery Agents and select CREATE from the fly-out menu. This starts the Certificate Request Wizard. If you get the error *Windows cannot find a certification authority that will process the request*, you either did not install a CA server or you have not restarted this computer, so it sees the new group policy that designates the CA server. See "Managing a Certificate Authority Server" for more information.

8. Click Next. The Certificate Template window opens. The templates are stored at the CA server and in the Directory.

9. Click Next. The Certificate Friendly Name and Description window opens. Enter the requested information. Keep the name short, like File Recovery. The name has no cryptographic significance.

10. Click Next. A completion window opens. The settings list shows the Crypto Services Provider (CSP) used to create the certificate and the template used by that provider. Templates cannot be tailored or modified.

11. Click Finish. The wizard displays a successful completion message.

12. Click Install Certificate to place the certificate in the user's local profile. In the background, the wizard extracts the public key, creates a certificate, and adds the certificate to the Encrypted Data Recovery Agents list.

The recovery policy is now in place. The policy must be flushed to the local Registry and downloaded to domain member computers to take effect. You can wait for the next logon or the 90-minute periodic policy update or you can manually apply the policy using the *Security Editor* command-line tool, SECEDIT.EXE. The syntax is: secedit /refreshpolicy machine_policy.

When you run Secedit on the domain controller where you made the change, it writes the policy changes to the local Registry. When you run Secedit on a member computer, it downloads the most current policies and writes the updates to the local Registry.

It is difficult to verify directly that the new Recovery Agent policy is in effect. You can perform an indirect verification at the domain controller where you created the File Recovery certificate as follows:

Procedure 14.12 **Verifying Alternate DRA**

1. Log on as a user that has not yet encrypted a file on the server. The user must have administrator privileges to log on at the console of a domain controller.

2. Encrypt a file. You can create a test file or use an existing file. Verify that the user can open it before and after encrypting it. Don't attempt to encrypt system or compressed files. The system will refuse to comply.

3. Log off, then log on using the account of the DRA.

4. Open the encrypted file. The DRA is given access. Close the file, then use the file Properties window to toggle off the encryption attribute and convert it back to clear text. This constitutes a "recovery" from the perspective of EFS.

Saving Encrypted Files on Trusted Servers

In a default EFS configuration, a server does not permit network users to encrypt files. If a network user tries to encrypt a file, the local system returns the message, *An error occurred applying the attributes. Keyset does not exist.*

A server must be configured as Trusted for Delegation before it will permit network users to encrypt files. The reason for lies with the security context of the EFS service. The next three sections describe how this works.

Local File Encryption Sequence

Here is how a normal encryption sequence works:

- EFS is a background service. Like most background services, it runs in the security context of the Local System. This Local System account has the well-known SID S-1-5-18. Background services use this SID in their access tokens to open and modify their support files, Registry keys, and Directory attributes.

- When a user encrypts (or decrypts) a file, EFS obtains the encryption keys from the user's EFS certificate. Only a process running in the security context of the user can access this certificate because portions of it are encoded with the user's SID. Background processes like EFS are permitted to present a copy of the user's access token when acting on the user's behalf. In this situation, the process is said to *impersonate* the user.

- EFS cannot obtain the user's keys directly. It needs help from LSA. The LSA owns the CSPs that know how to locate and interpret user certificates and key files. The CSP used to support EFS is the Microsoft Base Cryptographic Provider v 1.0.

- The CSP hands the key information over to LSA, which hands it to EFS, which uses it to encrypt or decrypt the FEK. Armed with the FEK, the EFS encrypts or decrypts the file using DESX.

Network File Encryption and Delegation

When a network user tries to encrypt a file on a server across the network, the process works a little differently.

- EFS, running on the server, is responsible for encrypting the file. Encryption cannot take place directly over the network because that would expose the file to network snoops.

- EFS at the server can obtain a copy of the user's access token, but that's not enough. It must obtain access to the user's master key, which is encrypted with the user's password hash.

- EFS at the server does not know the user's password hash. It must obtain the hash from a domain controller on behalf of the user.

- EFS cannot simply request a password hash. It needs a Kerberos ticket from the client that has been marked as *forwardable* so it can pass the ticket on to the domain controller to get the password hash.

- This process of forwarding a Kerberos ticket on behalf of a client is called *delegation*. A Kerberos client will only flag a ticket as forwardable if the validating server has been designated as *Trusted for Delegation* in Active Directory.

If a server has not been configured as Trusted for Delegation in Active Directory, an attempt to encrypt a file on that server across the network will fail. Before you simply enable delegation, see the next section for the security implications. Then go to "Enabling the Trusted for Delegation Option" for the steps to configure delegation for a server.

Security Considerations for Delegation

By default, the Trusted for Delegation option is only enabled on domain controllers. The KDC service on a domain controller needs delegation so it can forward a user ticket to the KDC service on a domain controller in a trusted domain.

The Trusted for Delegation option is disabled on non-domain controllers and desktops because it leaves the machine open to Trojan horse attacks. In such an attack, a bad guy gets access to a trusted server and installs a malicious service running in the security context of a privileged user. Because the server is trusted for delegation, the subversive service can use credentials from incoming clients to replicate itself to other machines until it compromises your entire network. Then it does something despicable.

This does not mean that you should avoid the Trusted for Delegation option. It is virtually impossible to set up any reasonable implementation of EFS without one or two delegation servers. Without them, users would be forced to save their encrypted files to their local drives where they could be wiped out with a single format command or dropped machine. Just be sure you protect your delegation servers as thoroughly as you protect your domain controllers.

When a user saves an encrypted file on a delegation server, the LSA creates a local profile for the user at the server. This profile holds the user's EFS certificate and a master key for the user. The profile is derived from the Default User profile just as if the user had logged on at the console of the server.

This could pose a storage problem for the server. If 1000 users save encrypted files on the server, there will be 1000 user profiles in the \Documents and Settings folder. These profiles consume about 150KB at a minimum, so be sure you have the spare capacity in your system folder to handle the extra storage requirements. You'll also need to set up a periodic maintenance item to recover files and delete profiles of users who are no longer with the company.

Enabling the Trusted for Delegation Option

After you have determined which server or servers should be trusted for delegation, configure the option in Active Directory as follows.

Procedure 14.13 **Enabling the Trusted for Delegation Option for a Server**

1. Log on using an account with administrator privileges over the trusted server's Computer object.

2. Open the AD Users and Computers snap-in.

3. Expand the tree to the container where the computer account is stored. The default container is cn=Computers,dc=<domain>.

4. Open the Properties window for the computer. See Figure 14.27.

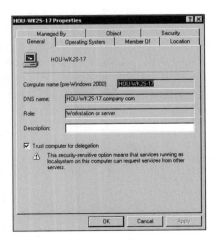

Figure 14.27   Computer account properties showing the Trust computer for delegation option.

5. Select the `Trust computer for delegation` option. The system warns you that this is a "security sensitive operation" and should not be done indiscriminately. See the introduction to this section for details on the security issues involved with delegation.

6. Click `OK` to acknowledge and return to the `Properties` window.

7. Click `OK` to apply the change.

8. Restart the trusted computer so that it can log on again to get its new configuration. You may need to restart the client computers, as well.

9. Test the configuration by logging on at a client, mapping a drive to a shared folder on the server, then encrypting a file in that shared folder. If the encryption option does not display, the volume is configured as FAT or FAT32. If the *Keyset does not exist* error persists, ensure that both the server and the client computer have been restarted and were able to contact a domain controller.

Managing a Certificate Authority Server

A *Certificate Authority* is a server that has been authorized to issue PKCS certificates. Certificates issued by a CA are based on one or more authorizing certificates in its *certificate store*. Microsoft provides the authorizing certificates for EFS and File Recovery.

A CA can also issue a certificate authorizing a *subordinate CA* to issue certificates. This subordinate CA can, in turn, issue authorization certificates to its own subordinates. Homicide detectives like to talk about a "chain of evidence" that ties a murder weapon irrefutably to the crime scene. PKCS constructs a "chain of certificates" that leads from the issuing CA to the ultimate authorizing CA.

Deploying EFS does not absolutely require the services of a CA. Each Windows 2000 Server and Professional desktop is capable of issuing self-signed EFS certificates to local users and a File Recovery certificate to the default DRA. But without a central server to issue and track certificates, EFS can be difficult to manage. In addition, you cannot issue additional File Recovery certificates to supplement the default DRA without a CA server.

Windows 2000 Server comes with a Certificate Services option that allows you to configure a CA server. It only takes a few minutes to install a CA, and it immediately begins issuing certificates to EFS users. You can also use it to issue certificates for other PKCS-enabled functions in your organization. There is much more to crafting a PKCS infrastructure than simply slapping up a CA server, but this section gives you enough information to begin layout out a deployment strategy, at least where EFS is concerned.

Functional Overview of Windows 2000 Certificate Services

A CA issues certificates on behalf of itself or a trusted parent. CA servers in Windows 2000 are arranged in a hierarchy that starts at an *Enterprise Root CA* and descends through one or more *Subordinate CAs*. Any of these CAs can issue certificates.

The certificate issued by a CA contains the chain of authorities between itself and the root CA. The arrangement resembles a domain hierarchy. You may want to install Certificate Services as a matter of course as you upgrade and deploy Windows 2000 domain controllers, just to ensure that you have fault tolerance for certificate services.

After a CA server is installed in a domain, it automatically begins issuing certificates in response to client requests. This happens because the CA server updates the default group policy associated with the Domain container to include the new CA server under a policy called Trusted Root Certificate Authorities. After member computers download this policy, they will forward user certificate requests to the CA server rather than issue self-certifications.

Users are not aware of this happening. The EFS service and LSA work in the background. Any files encrypted prior to distributing the new group policy remain visible. The user's original certificate is retained in the user's profile folder along with the new CA certificate.

Highlights on Using a Certificate Authority

Here are a few key points to remember about using a CA to issue EFS and FR certificates:

- The CA issues certificates in the background, transparently to the user. The local cryptographic provider is responsible for requesting the certificate from the CA.

- The local crypto provider knows about the CA because of a group policy put into place when the CA server is installed.

- Certificates issued by a CA are stored in the same location as certificates issued by the local crypto provider. If a user has existing certificates, they continue to work for existing documents. The user may want to run cipher to refresh the encrypted documents with the new certificate.

- A copy of a CA certificate is stored in the user's Active Directory object in an attribute called *User-Certificate*. The CA issues a separate certificate each time a user encrypts a file on a different computer. This can make the User-Certificate attribute grow very large.

- All Directory-based certificates associated with a user are downloaded and cached locally when the user logs on.

Selecting CA Servers

Any Windows 2000 member server in a forest can be the Enterprise Root CA. When selecting a root server, or any CA server, let reliability and physical security be your guide. This server will hold certificates for hundreds or thousands or tens of thousands of users and services. If it crashes and takes that information with it with no backup server and no backup files, then no recovery is possible. Make sure you install a backup CA that is at least as reliable as the Root server.

Performance should not be an issue. If you have sufficient memory and processor power to support Windows 2000, you can run a CA. The server must be running IIS, though, so you may want to add additional memory if you think that the server might eventually host additional Web services.

Another important consideration when choosing a CA server is flexibility. The certificate that authorizes the CA server to issue certificates is directly tied to the server's name and domain affiliation. If the server is renamed or disjoined from the domain, it can no longer issue or validate certificates using the original authorizing certificate. If the server is a domain controller, it can be demoted as long as it maintains contact with another domain controller.

Installing Certificate Services

You must log on as an administrator in the root domain of the forest to install Certificate Services and configure it to be an Enterprise Root CA or an Enterprise Subordinate CA. You can install the Root CA and Subordinate CAs in trusted domains by logging on using an account with administrator credentials from the root domain.

If you have an existing certificate deployment mechanism and you want certificates issued by this server to be compatible with the existing deployment method, the installation wizard has an `Advanced` option in a `Public and Private Key Pair Selection` window. You can use this option to select particular CSPs and hash algorithms. If you are using only Windows 2000 Certificate Services for your CA services, you do not need this option.

When you're ready to install Certificate Services, proceed as follows:

Procedure 14.14   **Installing Certificate Services**

1. Open the `Add/Remove Programs` applet in Control Panel.

2. Click `Add/Remove Windows Components`. This starts the `Windows Component Wizard`.

3. Select `Certificate Services` from the Components list. This loads two services, the `Certificate Services CA` and `Certificate Services Web Enrollment Support`. You do not need Web services for EFS, but CA requires that it be loaded, so install IIS, as well, if it is not already running.

4. Click `Next`. The `Certificate Authority Type Selection` window opens. See Figure 14.28. If the `Enterprise Root CA` and `Enterprise Subordinate CA` options are dimmed, you have not logged on using an account with administrative rights in the root domain of the forest.

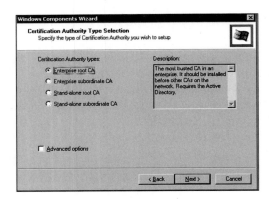

Figure 14.28   `Windows Component Wizard`—`Certificate Authority Type Selection` window showing `Enterprise root CA` selection on a domain controller.

5. Select the `Enterprise root CA` radio button and click `Next`. The `CA Identifying Information` window opens. See Figure 14.29. Fill in the requested information, keeping in mind that administrators in other domains will use this information when configuring subordinate CA servers.

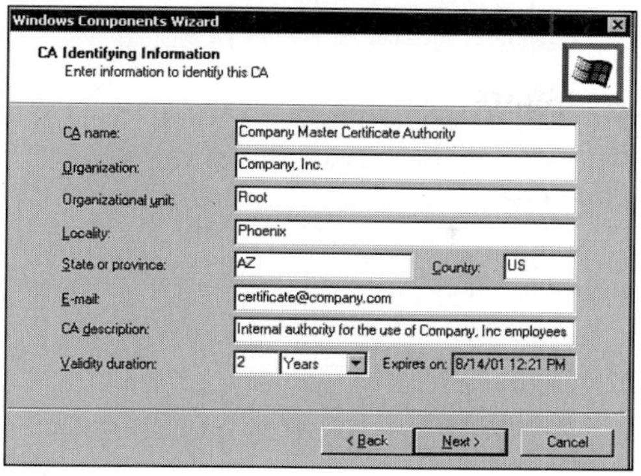

Figure 14.29 `CA Identifying Information` window.

6. Click `Next`. The `Data Storage Location` window opens. Specify a location for the Certification database.

Storing the CA Database

The default location for the CA database is in the system partition under `\WINNT\System32\Certlog`. Storing the database in the system partition is not recommended because you could lose the database if you are forced to do a complete reinstallation of Windows 2000.

If you are installing Certificate Services on a domain controller, you can put the Certlog files on the same volume as the Active Directory files or Sysvol.

The ASP files for the Web portion of Certificate Services are stored in `\WINNT\System32\CertSrv`. There is no option for an alternative location.

If you have a one CA server used by all certificate authorities, select the `Store Configuration Information in a Shared Folder` and enter the UNC path of the shared folder.

7. Click `Next`. If the paths you entered do not exist, you will be prompted to create them. Click `OK` to acknowledge.

8. If the WWW service is running on the machine, you'll be notified that it will be stopped. Click `OK` to acknowledge.

9. The wizard installs the service drivers, restarts the WWW service, and ends with a completion window. Click `Finish` to exit the wizard. There is no need to restart.

The wizard also configures a new group policy under Default Domain Policy. The policy is a copy of the Master Certificate Authority certificate under `Computer Configuration | Windows Settings | Security Settings | Public Key Policies | Trusted Root Certification Authorities`. When member computers download this policy, they start forwarding their user certificate requests to the CA server rather than issuing self-certifications. Users are not aware of this happening. Any files encrypted prior to distributing the new group policy remain visible. The user's original certificate is retained in the user's profile folder along with the new CA certificate.

Viewing Tickets Issued by a Certificate Authority

After the CA server is operational, member computers who download the CA group policy will obtain new EFS certificates from the CA server. You can view these tickets as follows:

Procedure 14.15 Viewing Tickets at a Certificate Authority

1. Open the `Certification Authority` console using START | PROGRAMS | ADMINISTRATIVE TOOLS | CERTIFICATE AUTHORITY. The console window should look like the example in Figure 14.30.

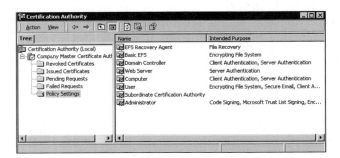

Figure 14.30 `Certification Authority` console showing Policy Settings.

2. Expand the tree to `<CA Name> | Issued Certificates`. The newly issued certificate is displayed in the left pane.

3. Double-click the certificate icon to open its `Certificate` window.

4. Select the `Details` tab. A certificate issued by a CA server has quite a bit more information in it than the ordinary self-signed EFS certificate issued locally. Scroll down the list to see the information in the lower pane. Figure 14.31 shows information for the Authority Information Access (AIA). This is the information the client uses to find the CA when it needs to validate the certificate.

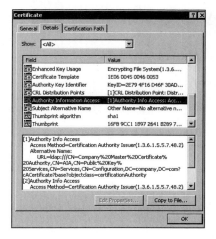

Figure 14.31 Certificate window showing Details tab and Authority Information Access details.

The Copy File button starts the Certificate Export Wizard. Use the wizard to export a certificate to a file that can be sent to a client via email or floppy. This export feature only creates a public key certificate. It cannot be used to create a certificate containing both the private and public keys. Only the certificate owner can do that.

5. Click OK to save any changes and close the console.

Verifying Certification Authority Operations

After the CA server is in place and functioning properly, it fades into the background like any good network infrastructure device. Domain users obtain EFS certificates from the CA server automatically when they encrypt files. There is no need to do any special configuration. You should verify proper operation of the CA server right at the beginning, just to make sure it is issuing certificates properly. Do so as follows:

Procedure 14.16 **Verifying CA Operation**

1. Open the AD Sites and Services console using START | PROGRAMS | ADMINISTRATIVE TOOLS | AD SITES AND SERVICES. You can open this console at the CA server even if it is not a domain controller. The console communicates with a domain controller via LDAP to get the necessary information.

2. From the menu, select VIEW | SHOW SERVICES NODE.

3. Expand the tree under Services to show `Public Key Services | Certification Authorities`. The certificate for the new CA is listed in the right pane. Figure 14.32 shows an example.

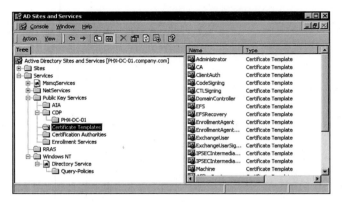

Figure 14.32 `AD Sites and Services` console showing the Certificates Templates container contents.

4. Close the `AD Sites and Services` console.

5. Open the `AD Users and Computers` console using START | PROGRAMS | ADMINISTRATIVE TOOLS | AD USERS AND COMPUTERS.

6. Open the `Properties` window for the `Domain` object.

7. Select the `Group Policy` tab.

8. Double-click the `Default Domain Policy` entry to open the `Group Policy` console. If you have multiple policies associated with the domain, make sure the `Default Domain Policy` entry is at the top of the list. If you do have higher priority policies, make sure they do not have conflicting policies.

9. In the `Group Policy` console, navigate to `Computer Configuration | Windows Settings | Security Settings | Public Key Policies | Trusted Root Certification Authorities`. The certificate for the new Enterprise Root CA is listed in the right pane. Figure 14.33 shows an example.

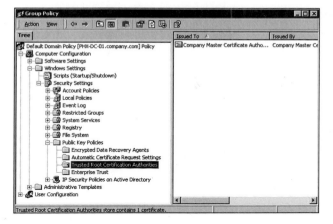

Figure 14.33 Group Policy console showing the new Enterprise Root CA under Trusted Root Certification Authorities.

10. Close the Group Policy console.

11. Open the Certification Authority console using START | PROGRAMS | ADMINISTRATIVE TOOLS | CERTIFICATION AUTHORITY.

12. Expand the tree and highlight Issued Certificates. Any issued certificates are listed in the right pane.

13. Go to a member computer in the domain and restart it so that it downloads the new group policy.

14. Log on using a domain user's account.

15. Encrypt a file.

16. At the Certification Authority console, verify that a new certificate was issued to the user.

17. Double-click the certificate to open the Certificate window and verify that the purpose is Allows data on disk to be encrypted.

18. At the client computer, open the user profile and navigate to \Documents and Settings\<logonID>\Application Data\Microsoft\SystemCertificates\My\ Certificates. The certificate issued by the CA is in the folder. Verify this by checking the filename against the thumbprint on the certificate at the CA server.

19. Close all windows and consoles.

Managing File Recovery Certificates

The CA server can issue File Recovery certificates to alternate DRAs. Designating an alternate DRA and including the certificate in the Encrypted Data Recovery Agent policy is most easily accomplished using a shortcut in the Group Policy Editor. This is described in "Creating Additional Data Recovery Agents."

You can manually issue an FR certificate for an account, then install the certificate in the Encrypted Data Recovery Agent policy as a separate step. The shortcut is a cleaner way to perform the entire process, but it's always good to have a manual backup.

The general actions to manually assign a DRA are:

- Obtain an FR certificate for the account.
- Export the certificate to an X.509 format.
- Add the certificate to the Encrypted Data Recovery Agent policy.

The steps to perform these actions are covered in the following sections.

Obtaining a File Recovery Certificate from a CA Server

These steps describe how to obtain a File Recovery certificate for an alternate DRA. The account you designate to be an alternate DRA Manual must have administrative privileges in the domain. Proceed as follows:

Procedure 14.17 **Obtaining a File Recovery Certificate**
_____

1. Log on at the console of the server where you want the File Recovery certificate to be created. Use the account designated to be the DRA.

2. Open the Certificates console.

3. Right-click the Certificates icon under Personal and select ALL TASKS | REQUEST NEW CERTIFICATE from the fly-out menu. This starts the Certificate Request Wizard. If you get the error *Windows cannot find a certification authority that will process the request,* you either did not install a CA server or you have not restarted the computer to download the group policy containing the name of the new CA server.

4. Click Next. The Certificate Template window opens. Select the File Recovery template. The templates themselves come from the CA server.

5. Click Next. The Certificate Friendly Name and Description window opens. Enter the requested information. Keep the name short and descriptive. File Recovery would do nicely.

6. Click Next. A completion window opens. The settings list shows the CSP (Crypto Services Provider), the template used to create the certificate, and the user name.

7. Click Finish. The wizard displays a successful completion message and the option to view or install the certificate.

8. Click Install Certificate to place the certificate in the user's local profile.

9. The wizard displays one more successful completion message. Click OK to acknowledge and return to the Certificate console.

10. The right pane of the console lists the new File Recovery certificate along with an EFS certificate that is also generated. If an EFS certificate is already present, you can leave them both on the list. Deleting the older one would prevent you (or the administrator whose account you are configuring) from viewing any previously encrypted files.

11. Leave the console open and proceed to the next section.

Exporting X.509 CER Certificates

The File Recovery certificate issued by the CA is not formatted for importing into the Encrypted Data Recovery Agents policy list. The certificate must be in X.509 (CER) format. Export the certificate you just created to X.509 format as follows:

Procedure 14.18   **Exporting an X.509 Certificate**

1. At the Certificate console, right-click the icon for the File Recovery certificate you just created and select ALL TASKS | EXPORT from the fly-out menu. This starts the Certificate Export Wizard.

2. Click Next. The Export Private Key window opens. Select No, do not export the private key.

3. Click Next. The Export File Format window opens. See Figure 14.34. Select one of the X.509 formats (CER). The choice of DER or Base-64 encoding does not matter in this case. Some applications only accept Base-64, but this certificate is associated with the File Recovery OID and would not be useful to any other application. Use whatever encoding method complies with your organization's crypto guidelines.

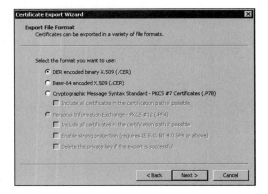

Figure 14.34 Certificate Export Wizard—Export File Format.

4. Click Next. The File To Export window opens. Enter the name you want to give the exported certificate. The name has no cryptographic significance. You should include the user's logon ID to help identify the file. Save the file to a suitable location.

5. Click Next. A completion window opens.

6. Click Finish. The wizard informs you when the export has been successfully completed.

7. Close the Certificates console and proceed to the next section for the steps to import the CER certificate into the Encrypted Data Recovery Agents list.

Adding a DRA to the Encrypted Data Recovery Policy

The following steps describe how to import an X.509 File Recovery certificate into the Encrypted Data Recovery policy that is downloaded by domain clients. Use these steps to assign an additional DRA or an alternate DRA. The FR certificate must be in X.509 (CER) format. This format contains only the public key for the FR certificate. This is all the policy requires. If you need to recover files instead of changing the recovery policy, refer to "Importing EFS Certificates." When you are ready to import the X.509 certificate into the data recovery policy, proceed as follows:

Procedure 14.19 **Manually Adding a DRA to the Encrypted Data Recovery Agents Policy**

1. Open the AD Users and Computers console.

2. Open the Properties window for the Domain object.

3. Select the Group Policy tab.

4. Double-click the Default Domain Policy to open the Group Policy console. If you have multiple policies associated with the domain, make sure that Default Domain Policy is on top. If you do have higher priority policies, make sure they do not have conflicting policies.

5. In the Group Policy console, navigate to Computer Configuration | Windows Settings | Security Settings | Public Key Policies | Encrypted Data Recovery Agents.

6. Right-click Encrypted Data Recovery Agents and select ADD from the fly-out menu. The Add Recovery Agent window opens. (The Create option is the shortcut mentioned in the introduction to this section.)

7. Click Next. The Select Recovery Agents window opens. Use this window to locate the X.509 File Recovery certificate you exported.

8. Click Browse Folders. The Open window opens.

9. Navigate to the folder where you saved the certificate when you exported it.

10. Highlight the certificate and click Open. This adds the user to the list of Recovery Agents. The user name displays as USER_UNKNOWN, but it is still valid.

11. Click Next. The completion window opens.

12. Click Finish. The certificate is added to the list associated with Encrypted Data Recovery Agents. Client computers must restart to get the new policy.

Verifying Functionality of an Alternate Data Recovery Agent

It is difficult to verify directly that clients are incorporating the new agent into the Data Recovery Field for encrypted files. You should perform an indirect verification at the computer where you created the File Recovery certificate.

Procedure 14.20   **Verifying That an Alternate DRA Can Recover an Encrypted File**

1. Log on as a second user, one that is not the DRA.

2. Encrypt a file.

3. Log off, then log on using the account of the DRA.

4. Open the encrypted file. This constitutes a "recovery." You can also toggle off the encryption attribute and convert it back to clear text, if you like. If you are unable to open the file, repeat the steps and try again.

Moving Forward

Now that the files and directories are locked down with NTFS permissions and users can protect their sensitive documents with encryption, it's time to toss open the doors. The next chapter covers how to configure shared resources and, just as important, how to make sure users can find those resources easily.

15

Managing Shared Resources

A SERVER IS A MACHINE THAT MAKES ITS LOCAL resources, such as files, printers, and applications available to the network. A client is a machine that makes use of those resources. Servers give. Clients take. It is the ultimate dysfunctional relationship.

For those readers who are new to Windows networking, the first part of this chapter contains a functional overview of classic NT resource sharing and peer networking. The remaining topics give the steps for configuring and managing shared resources.

Three new features in Windows 2000 are covered in detail:

- Publishing and locating shared resources in Active Directory
- Managing client-side caching and offline file synchronization
- The Distributed File System (Dfs)

The final part of the chapter details how to manage printing in Windows 2000, including the following print configurations:

- Printing to a local print device
- Managing print queues
- Printing from DOS
- Printing to network print devices
- Printing to Windows 2000 servers

- Printing to third-party print servers
- Printing over the Internet

Functional Description of NT Resource Sharing

Servers make their local resources accessible to the network. These resources fall into four general categories:

- **File resources.** Clients are given access to files stored on local hard drives and CDs.
- **Printer resources.** Clients are given access to locally connected printers and network print devices.
- **Remote access services.** Dial-up clients are given access to local resources and to the network through the server's network interfaces.
- **Application services.** Clients are given access to client/server applications running on the server.

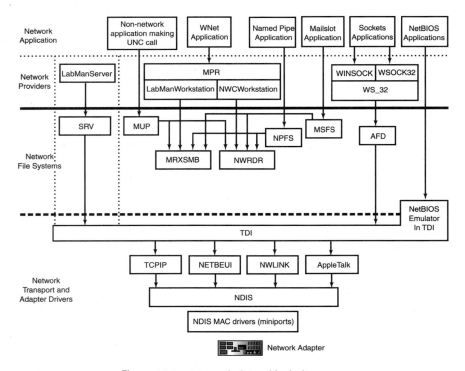

Figure 15.1 Network driver block diagram.

Figure 15.1 shows the general arrangement of network drivers in Windows 2000. The top layer consists of user applications that require network services. These are called applications, but they are generally not "applications" in the sense of spreadsheet applications or word processing applications. They are applications that make active network calls of one form or another. An email package, for example, would have a network module that uses the network to send and receive messages.

The services in Windows 2000 that interact with network applications have two components: one running in user space and one running in kernel space. The user component is called a *provider* because it provides a network interface for the network application. The kernel component is a network file system driver that communicates with a peer service on another computer.

Network providers come in the form of DLLs loaded and managed by the *Service Control Manager*, SERVICES.EXE. Network file system drivers come in the form of SYS drivers that run under the auspices of the I/O Manager in the Windows 2000 Executive. In Figure 15.1, for example, the LanManWorkstation provider is paired with the MRXSMB.SYS network file system driver.

This pairing of user and kernel components takes advantage of the memory- and process-protection schemes in Windows 2000. The network providers run in Ring 3 where they cannot access hardware or memory directly. They get access to network resources by making calls to their complementary kernel components in the Windows 2000 Executive. The Kernel-mode drivers handle network I/O, security, and other system services.

File system drivers communicate with transport drivers using the *Transport Driver Interface* (TDI). Every transport driver (with the exception of DLC, not shown in the diagram) exposes a TDI interface. Thanks to TDI, file system drivers can operate independently of the transport protocols, and vice versa.

Just as the file system drivers do not communicate directly with the transport drivers, the transport drivers do not communicate directly with the network adapter drivers. Instead, the transport drivers communicate with the *Network Driver Interface Specification* driver (NDIS.SYS). The NDIS driver and its helpers communicate with a network adapter using an NDIS MAC driver, where MAC stands for Media Access Control.

The NDIS MAC drivers take the form of miniport drivers written by the adapter manufacturers. NDIS also provides interfaces for asynchronous communications over modem and ISDN lines for use in making dial-up networking connections and accepting inbound dial-up connections via *Routing and Remote Access Services* (RRAS). See Chapter 17, "Managing Remote Access and Internet Routing," for more information on RRAS.

The Windows 2000 Server service works a little differently because it does not interact directly with network applications. It uses the same two-component model but the user component is not a provider, as such. It is a way to communicate operating parameters to the Server service.

To summarize, the network stack in Windows 2000 consists of the following major elements:

- Network applications
- Network providers
- Network client providers
- Redirectors
- Servers

The remaining sections in this chapter contain brief descriptions of each of these networking components and how they interface with each other. This information is useful if you are having difficulties getting network processes to function correctly. You can improve performance, for example, by knowing how the network providers are polled when a network application makes its initial connection attempt to a server.

Network Applications

Most Windows-based network applications use one of three API libraries to access network services. (NetBIOS applications are becoming rare, but are also supported. See the sidebar titled "NetBIOS Support in Windows 2000.")

- **Wnet.** Network applications can use the Wnet API within Win32 to connect and disconnect with Windows servers and get information about the server. For example, the `WnetAddConnection` call connects a network client to a share point on the server.

- **Named pipes.** A pipe is an *Interprocess Connection* (IPC) method where two or more applications share the same memory and communicate with each other by manipulating the contents of that memory. A named pipe is a special form of pipe, in contrast to an anonymous pipe that has no name. Named pipes are commonly used by client/server applications such as database applications.

- **Mailslots.** A mailslot is also an IPC, but one that is unidirectional rather than a connection-oriented IPC like a named pipe. Applications generally use mailslots when sending broadcasts or unicasts. For example, NetBIOS-over-TCP/IP name registration uses mailslots.

- **Winsock.** Winsock stands for Windows Sockets. A socket is a form of IPC first introduced in Berkeley Software Distribution (BSD) UNIX. A socket consists of an IP address, a transport port number, and a flag indicating datagram or stream communications. Winsock is a Windows API that uses sockets. A good starting point for information about Winsock and Winsock–based applications is www.sockaddr.com.

Network applications make their network calls by using function calls in DLLs called *network providers*.

NetBIOS Support in Windows 2000

Unlike the other network providers, there is no client-side component to NetBIOS. NetBIOS applications work by building a data structure called a *network control block* (NCB) in memory, and then making a DOS function call that turns the NCB over to a network driver. This legacy DOS function call is handled directly by TDI using a special NetBIOS emulator.

The NetBIOS emulator converts the NetBIOS function calls into *Transport Device Interface* (TDI) calls. This permits NetBIOS applications to use any of the transports provided by Windows 2000.

Network Providers

Most network applications require an interface to convert their API calls into function calls that can be understood by the network file systems.

- Named pipe and mailslot applications do not require special providers. Win32 handles these API calls and establishes connection to the proper network file system, either the *Named Pipe File System* (NPFS) or the *Mailslot File System* (MSFS).

- NetBIOS applications are handled by the NetBIOS emulator in TDI. It is also possible for an application to communicate directly to the TDI or to the transport drivers themselves.

- Winsock applications use the Winsock provider. Windows 2000 provides both 16-bit (WINSOCK.DLL) and 32-bit (WSOCK32.DLL) libraries that act as interfaces to the main 32-bit Winsock library, WS_32.DLL. This library supports both Winsock 1.1 and Winsock 2.0.

- Wnet applications use client providers designed to interoperate with specific network servers. A Wnet connection to a Windows server, for example, would use the LanManWorkstation provider.

Windows 2000 includes two network providers:

- **Windows provider.** For historical reasons, the Windows client is called LanManWorkstation. The client code is contained in NTLANMAN.DLL.

- **NetWare client.** The NetWare client is called NWCWorkstation. The client code is contained in NWWKS.DLL.

Most third-party NOS vendors have Windows 2000 network clients for their systems. Examples include Novell's own NetWare Core Protocol client, Transarc's *Andrew File System* (AFS) client, and Sun's *Network File System* (NFS) client.

Each provider is paired with a network file system driver running in the Windows 2000 Executive. These file systems are sometimes called *redirectors* based on their historical function of snatching DOS and Windows function calls and "redirecting" them to a server.

Rather than require each client provider to expose the Wnet API, network applications make their Wnet function calls using the *Multiple Provider Router* (MPR). The client providers interface with the MPR. This relieves vendors from the responsibility for creating interfaces for every type of Wnet application.

Another function of the MPR is to choose the correct provider when a Wnet application attempts to connect to a server. In this case, the MPR polls the providers to determine which one has the proper client to talk to that server. It polls based on the network provider order stored in these Registry entries:

```
Key:    HKLM | System | CurrentControlSet | Control | NetworkProvider | Order
Value:  ProviderOrder
Data:   NWCWorkstation | LanManWorkstation

Key:    HKLM | System | CurrentControlSet || Control | Print | Providers
Value:  Order
Data:   NetWare or Compatible Network | LanMan Print Services | Internet Print Provider
```

Setting Network Provider Order

If you have both a NetWare and Microsoft client loaded, you should always put the NetWare client at the top of the provider order. This is true even if the majority of your servers are Windows 2000 and classic NT. NetWare servers take very little time to report back a failed connection. Microsoft servers, on the other hand, take their own sweet time thanks to all the browsing and name resolution that goes on in the background. You'll experience far fewer polling delays by putting the NetWare client first. See the section "Changing the Network Provider Order" later in this chapter.

In addition to specific network client providers, Windows 2000 has a general-purpose provider for applications that do not make active network calls but need access to network resources. This access typically involves a *Universal Naming Convention* (UNC) path, so the general-purpose provider is called the *Multiple UNC Provider* (MUP).

Multiple UNC Provider (MUP)

The MUP is a kernel-level driver that acts as an interface between passive applications and the network file system drivers. If you use Notepad to open a file with the path \\phx-w2ks-32\data\textfile.txt, for example, the I/O Manager recognizes the double backslash as the beginning of a UNC and passes the string to MUP.

MUP parses the line to find the name of the server and the name of the shared folder. It then polls the network file systems, similar to the way MPR polled the network providers, to find the driver that can contact the specified server. When a file system driver reports that it contacted the server, MUP tests the share name. If the share name is valid, the connection is made.

The first file system polled by MUP is always the *Distributed File System* (Dfs) driver. If Dfs returns a positive response, indicating that the UNC path is in the Dfs volume, MUP tests the junction to the host server. If the junction is valid, MUP associates the UNC with the server that hosts the shared resource. See the section "Functional Description of Dfs" later in this chapter for more information. If there is no Dfs entry for the UNC, or MUP gets no response from the host server, the polling continues down the file system list.

After MUP has established an association between a UNC path and a network provider, it caches that association for use in subsequent transactions. If a particular UNC (this includes mapped drives) gets no traffic for 15 minutes, MUP removes it from the cache. The next request for that UNC causes MUP to poll once again. Keep this behavior in mind when troubleshooting intermittent connection problems.

Windows 2000 Handling of UNC Names

In classic NT, a network drive could only be mapped to the shared folder in a UNC path. If a server named PHX-NT4-01 had a share named USERS with a subdirectory called Tjones, for example, a user could map to \\PHX-NT4-01\USERS, the share point, but not to \\PHX-NT4-01\USERS\Tjones, a folder under the share point.

In Windows 2000, a drive can be mapped to any folder under the share point. This is similar to the Map Root functionality in NetWare.

Redirector File Systems

The network client providers and MUP provide only interfaces to the network. The real work is done by the network file system drivers. If a file system driver is used to communicate with a specific type of server or network operating system, it is generally called a *redirector*. (The network providers are also often called redirectors.)

Windows 2000 has two network file system drivers that act as the client side of client/server file and print sharing services.

- **Windows Redirector (MRXSMB.SYS).** This file system driver communicates with Windows servers using the *Server Message Block* (SMB) command protocol.

- **NetWare Redirector (NWRDR.SYS).** This file system driver communicates with NetWare servers using *NetWare Core Protocol* (NCP).

The NetWare Redirector provided by Microsoft is NDS aware, but does not support advanced NDS features such as *Zero Effort Networking* (Z.E.N.) and *NetWare Application Launcher* (NAL).

In addition to accepting function calls from the Wnet client providers, the redirectors also handle network requests from other file system drivers. Both the NPFS and the MSFS use the MRXSMB redirector, for example, when communicating with Windows peers.

Registry Tip

Parameters associated with the file system drivers and providers are located in the Registry under HKLM | SYSTEM | CurrentControlSet | Services. The file system keys have the same name as the drivers.

For example, the HKLM | SYSTEM | CurrentControlSet | Services | MRXSMB key contains parameters and settings for the Windows file system driver.

Server File Systems

The Server service on a Windows 2000 computer also takes the form of a file system driver, SRV.SYS. Like the MRXSMB redirector file system driver, SRV.SYS lives in the Windows 2000 Executive.

An SMB server service, such as SRV.SYS, exposes network resources in the form of *share points*. A share point can be a folder or a printer. A shared folder is often just called a *share*, as in "I need to create a share for that."

The Service Control Manager has a small User-mode service, LanManServer, that is used for creating shares and communicating management information to the server file system. This interface also helps support the Browser service. There is no separate DLL for LanManServer.

Registry Tip
The list of shared folders is stored in the Registry under HKLM | System | CurrentControlSet | Services | LanManServer | Shares.

Client applications cannot make function calls directly to the LanManServer provider, so there is no need for an MPR interface. The SRV.SYS driver depends on the MRXSMB.SYS driver to communicate with other servers.

Additional File System Services
Three other server file systems are available from Microsoft. One, the AppleTalk server, is included in Windows 2000. The other two are available as add-on packages with a price tag.

- **Services for Macintosh (SFM).** Windows 2000 includes an AppleTalk server file system driver, SFMSRV.SYS, as part of the Services for Macintosh suite. This service has two User-mode interfaces: a Macintosh file system interface, SFMSVC.EXE; and a Macintosh print services interface, SFMPRINT.EXE. These services enable Macintosh clients to access files and printers on a Windows 2000 server.

- **Services for NetWare (SFN).** This product contains a *NetWare Core Protocol* (NCP) server and interface drivers for emulating a NetWare file system. An SFN server can accept Bindery-mode NCP requests from NETX, VLM, and 32-bit NetWare clients. FPNW does not provide an interface to NDS, nor does it enable a Windows 2000 server to host NDS partitions.

- **Services for UNIX (SFU).** This product contains a *Network File System* (NFS) server and client along with a suite of utilities that emulate UNIX functionality on a Windows 2000 platform.

Default Share Points

All Windows Server services, including Windows 2000, have several default share points. Some of these shares have names that end with a dollar sign ($). Microsoft calls these *administrative shares*, but they are also commonly called dollar sign shares. They provide access to the server's drives by members of the Administrators local group. The dollar sign suffix hides the share from the browsing interfaces such as My Network Places. The other shares support domain activities by defining shared locations for accessing logon scripts and policies.

Here are the default shares and their function:

- **C$.** The system creates a dollar sign share for the root of every mounted volume. This gives administrators quick access to the volumes.

- **ADMIN$.** This share gives access to the system directory, which is \WINNT by default and is represented by the environment variable *%systemroot%*. You can map a drive to the ADMIN$ share without needing to know the drive letter that contains the system files.

- **IPC$.** This share gives access to a symbolic link called Interprocess Connection (IPC). It is used to support Remote Procedure Call (RPC) connections.

- **SYSVOL.** This share is new to Windows 2000. It gives access to the \WINNT\Sysvol\Sysvol directory, a system folder that stores information such as logon scripts and group policies that are to be replicated among domain controllers. The location of the SYSVOL folder is selected when the server is promoted to domain controller.

- **NETLOGON.** This share gives access to the \WINNT\Sysvol\Sysvol\Scripts directory. All Windows clients of any type are hard-coded to look for a NETLOGON share when they authenticate in a domain. The share contains group policies, system policies, and down-level logon scripts. (Windows 2000 logon scripts are part of group policies.)

You can view the list of share points using the Computer Management console under COMPUTER | SYSTEM TOOLS | SHARES. You can also get a list by opening a command prompt and typing NET SHARE.

Overview of the Server Message Block (SMB) Protocol

SMB is a set of commands that control connections to share points and a protocol for communicating those commands to and from network peers. Table 15.1 contains an example SMB transaction generated when a Windows client opens a file on a Windows 2000 server.

If you decide that you don't want to wade through the details in Table 15.1, here are a few of the high points:

- SMB clients from various platforms can communicate by negotiating a common dialect.

- Kerberos clients pre-authenticate using an encrypted time stamp.

- SMB servers create a session for each connected client. This requires a connection-oriented protocol. In a TCP/IP network, SMB uses TCP to guarantee datagram delivery and sequencing. Over NWLink, SMB uses SPX.

- SMB has its roots in NetBIOS, but is not in itself an implementation of NetBIOS; nor does it rely on the *NETBEUI Frame* (NBF) transport protocol. The content and format of an SMB message is completely independent of the transport protocol. You can use SMB on any of the transport protocols in Windows 2000, including TCP/IP and NWLink (IPX/SPX).

If you decide that you want even more detail on SMB than Table 15.1 contains, take a look at the Windows 2000 Platform SDK documentation available through MSDN. Also, just about any of the current crop of books on SAMBA, the UNIX port of SMB, have lots of information about the structure of SMB messages and the nature of SMB transactions.

Table 15.1   **Typical SMB Transaction**

SMB Command	Action Taken
SMB_COM_NEGOTIATE	SMB comes in versions, or *dialects*. Two computers running SMB negotiate a common dialect. The names of the SMB dialects are: <ul><li>PC NETWORK PROGRAM 1.0</li><li>PCLAN1.0</li><li>MICROSOFT NETWORKS 1.03</li><li>MICROSOFT NETWORKS 3.0</li><li>LANMAN1.0</li><li>LM1.2X002</li><li>DOS LM1.2X002</li><li>DOS LANMAN2.1</li><li>LANMAN2.1</li><li>Windows for Workgroups 3.1a</li><li>NT LM 0.12</li></ul> Windows 2000, classic NT, and Windows 95/98 use NT LM 0.12 dialect. This dialect supports special features, such as Unicode characters and calls to the Distributed File System.
SMB_COM_SESSION_SETUP	SMB is a session-oriented protocol. It is possible to exchange SMB commands in the form of unicast datagrams if there is no need for reliable exchange of messages. Windows 2000 uses the MailSlot File System (MSFS) for this purpose.
	When a Windows 2000 client sends a Session Setup SMB, it includes an encrypted time stamp for Kerberos pre-authentication. If the server cannot decrypt the time stamp using the user's password hash from Active Directory, the logon attempt is immediately rejected.
	After the session is has been established, the server sets up a *listen* for the SMB client. It periodically sends out *heartbeat* packets to the client to keep the listen alive.

continues ▶

Table 15.1   **continued**

SMB Command	Action Taken
SMB_COM_TREE_CONNECT	This command is a request on the part of the SMB client to open a share point on the server. The client first connects to a share called IPC$ to establish a secure RPC link, and then it connects to the requested share point.
	Classic NT had a limitation that the Tree_Connect would work only at the share point itself. Windows 2000 caches the entire path so that the root of the shared drive is the final directory in the UNC name. If you issue the command NET USE E: \\Server_Name\Share_Name\Directory\ SubDirectory, for example, the subdirectory becomes the root of the E: drive.
	The server responds to a Tree Connect request with a handle called a *Tree ID,* (Tid). In subsequent messages, the two computers use the Tid to streamline communications.
SMB_COM_OPEN	The client uses this command to open a particular file. If the file is on an NTFS partition, the user account must be on the *access control list* (ACL) for the file or the user must be a member of a group that is on the ACL.
	The server responds with a *file ID, or* (Fid). This is the equivalent of a file handle on a local file access. The two computers refer to this Fid in subsequent transactions for the file.
SMB_COM_READ	The client uses this command to read the file it just opened. The command includes the Fid, a starting point in the file, and the amount of the file to read.
	The server responds with requested data in the form of an SMB response that holds the data along with flags to indicate the data format and number of bytes and the location of the file pointer after the read.
	In a TCP/IP network, if the SMB message size exceeds the allowable TCP datagram size, SMB relies on the TCP/IP driver to divvy the message into discrete datagrams and reassemble them in order at the other end.

SMB Command	Action Taken
SMB_COM_CLOSE	When the client finishes reading the file, it closes the file and relinquishes the Fid.
	The server responds with success code indicating that the file is closed.
SMB_COM_TREE_DISCONNECT	When the user unmaps the drive or leaves the connection unused for 15 minutes, the server tears down the connection and removes the listen.

Managing Multiple Network Clients

The Microsoft Client is installed by default in Windows 2000 and cannot be removed. This topic covers installing additional clients and configuring the provider order for optimum selection performance. The examples use the NetWare client that comes with Windows 2000.

Installing Additional Network Clients

The NetWare client in Windows 2000 comes on the Server and Professional CD. Third-party clients are generally available from the vendor's Web site. Install a client as follows:

Procedure 15.1   **Installing Additional Network Clients**

1. Right-click My Network Places and select PROPERTIES from the fly-out menu. The Network and Dial-up Connections window opens. (You can also open this window from CONTROL PANEL | NETWORK.)

2. Right-click the Local Area Connection icon and select PROPERTIES from the fly-out menu. The Local Area Connection Properties window opens (see Figure 15.2). If you have more than one network adapter, it doesn't matter which one you choose. The client will be installed and linked to both interfaces.

3. Click Install. The Select Network Component Type window opens.

4. Highlight Client and click Add. The Select Network Client window opens. On Windows 2000 Server, the list has Gateway (and Client) Services for NetWare (GSNW) client. On Windows 2000 Professional, the list has Client Services for NetWare (CSNW). If you need to install any other client, click Have Disk and point the system at the location of the drivers.

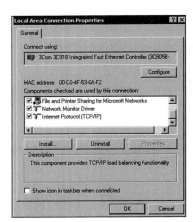

Figure 15.2 `Local Area Connection Properties` window.

5. Click `Add`. The system copies the files from the CD and returns to the `Local Area Connection Properties` window. In the case of the GSNW client, additional windows open to select preferred servers, NDS trees, contexts, and script options.

6. Verify that the client functions by restarting and making connection with a server. In the case of the NetWare client, this involves authenticating either in NDS or a bindery.

Changing the Network Provider Order

If a machine uses multiple network providers, you can improve connection performance by putting the fastest responding provider at the top of the provider list. Both MPR and MUP use this list to poll providers and network file systems. A slow provider can delay resolving a UNC name or making a Wnet connection. Change the provider order as follows:

Procedure 15.2 **Changing the Network Provider Order**

1. Right-click `My Network Places` and select PROPERTIES from the fly-out menu. This opens the `Network and Dial-up Connections` window.

2. From the menu, select ADVANCED | ADVANCED SETTINGS. The `Advanced Settings` window opens.

3. Highlight the provider you want to reposition and click the up or down arrows to position it.

4. Click `OK` to save the changes and close the window.

Sharing Folders

A shared folder represents a path onto the local file system on a server. There are several ways to create a shared folder. You can use the Explorer shell, the `Computer Management` console, or the command line. This section covers all three methods.

Deciding Which Directories to Share

Share points tend to multiply like cockroaches if you aren't careful. When a server sends its resource list to a client, it includes the name of every share, even the hidden shares. If you create thousands of shares, you'll slow network performance.

Windows 2000 permits you to map a drive to a folder underneath a share point. Use this feature to avoid excessive shares. Create a limited number of shares high in the directory, and then map to folders lower down the tree.

Avoid overlapping shares. This confuses users unmercifully. The help desk calls tend to start like this: "I deleted some extra files from my K: drive, but they also disappeared from my L: drive."

Creating a Share Using Explorer

The simplest way to share a folder is to use Explorer. The following steps create a new folder and share it. Proceed as follows:

Procedure 15.3 **Creating and Sharing a Folder**

1. Log on at the console of the server or workstation using an account with administrative privileges.

2. Open Explorer or My Computer.

3. Create a folder. The example in Figure 15.3 shows a folder called Sales.

4. Right-click the folder icon and select SHARING from the fly-out menu. The `Sales Properties` window opens with the Sharing tab selected.

5. Select the `Share This Folder` radio button. The system automatically inserts the folder name as the share name. If you already have a share by this name on the computer, or you want to give it another name, change the entry under `Share Name`.

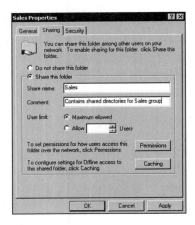

Figure 15.3 Properties window for Sales folder with Sharing tab selected.

Share Name Lengths

Select a share name that meets the allowable name length for the Windows clients in your network:

- Windows 2000 and NT4: 255 characters

- NT 3.51: 15 characters

- Windows 95: 12 characters

- Windows 3.x and DOS: 8 characters

If the share name exceeds the limit, the affected clients cannot see the share in a browse list or map a drive to it.

6. Ordinarily you would leave the Maximum Allowed radio button selected. Set a value under User Limit if you want to limit the maximum number of users who can access the share point. This is a way to meet licensing restrictions for executables inside the share.

7. Click Apply to create the share and leave the Properties window open.

8. Click Permissions. This opens the Permissions window for the share.

9. By default, the Everyone group has Full Control access to a new share. You can delete the Everyone group and select specific groups or users. You can also leave the share open and control access to the files underneath using NTFS permissions. It is nearly always preferable to use NTFS permissions to control access instead of sharing permissions.

10. Click OK to close the window and return to the Properties window. The Caching option is discussed in "Managing Client-Side Caching" later in this chapter.

11. Click OK to save any additional changes you made and close the window. Note that the folder now has a little hand under it indicating that it is shared.

Storing Shared Folders

Shares are stored in the Registry under the following key: HKLM | System | CurrentControlSet | Services | LanManServer | Shares. Each share is represented by a value with several data properties in a Reg_Multi_SZ entry:

- **CSCFlags.** Client-side caching flags: 0 by default, 16 for automatic document caching, 32 for automatic program caching, 48 for caching disabled.

- **Max Uses.** 4294967295 by default (all Fs for a long integer).

- **Path.** Local path to share point. If you change the path so that it does not match this Registry entry, the share no longer functions.

- **Permissions.** This entry supports down-level clients who expect to see share-level security flags in the SMB representing a share point. Windows 2000 and classic NT do not use share-level security.

- **Remark.** Contains the comments for the share.

- **Type.** Always set to 0 in Windows 2000.

Creating Shares on Remote Computers

The Explorer interface has no mechanism for creating shares on remote servers. You can create a share point on a remote computer using the Computer Management console as follows:

Procedure 15.4   Creating Remote Shares Using the *Computer Management* Console

---

1. Open the Computer Management console using START | PROGRAMS | ADMINISTRATIVE TOOLS | COMPUTER MANAGEMENT.

2. Right-click the Computer Management (local) icon and select CONNECT TO ANOTHER COMPUTER from the fly-out menu. The Select Computer window opens.

3. Scroll through the list of servers and workstations until you find the one you want to manage. If you have hundreds or thousands of machines in the directory, you can reduce the search time by selecting a particular domain under the Look In field. You must have Administrator privileges on the computer to make any changes.

4. Click OK to select the machine and return to the main Computer Management console window.

5. Expand the tree under SYSTEM TOOLS | SHARED FOLDERS | SHARES. Figure 15.4 shows an example.

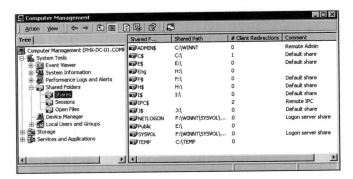

Figure 15.4 Computer Management console showing list of shares on a remote computer.

6. Right–click the Shares icon and select NEW FILE SHARE from the fly-out menu. The Create Shared Folder window opens.

7. Click Browse to locate the folder you want to share. The Browse for Folder window appears (see Figure 15.5). The browse feature requires that you have functioning administrative shares (dollar sign shares) at the root of each volume on the remote computer. If you have deleted the administrative shares, you must enter the local path to the folder manually.

Figure 15.5 Browse for Folder window showing administrative (dollar sign) shares at remote computer.

8. Select the folder you want to share or create a new folder.

9. Click OK to save the selection and return to the Create Shared Folder window.

10. Enter a Share Name and Share Description.

11. Click Next. Select a permissions option. The Custom button opens the Customize Permission window that contains a browse list to select users or groups to add to the list of authorized share users.

12. Click Finish to apply the changes and close the window.

The system responds with a notification that the share was successfully created. If it encountered a problem, you would be notified with an error message. The most common problem associated with creating remote shares is not having sufficient rights. The owner may have set NTFS permissions on the folder you're trying to share, for example, and that would block you from accessing the folder.

Creating Shares Using the Command Line

You can create a share from the command line using the Net Share command with the following syntax:

```
net share share_name=drive:\directory
```

If you want to stop sharing a directory, use the /delete switch as follows:

```
net share home_dir /delete
```

The Net Share command only works at the console of the server containing the directory you want to share. If you want to create a share on a remote directory from the command line, use a Resource Kit utility called RMT-SHARE. The syntax for this command is as follows:

```
rmtshare  \\server\sharename=drive:path [/users:number ¦ /unlimited]
                           [/remark:"text"]
                           [/grant user:perm]
                           [/remove user]
```

If you want to stop sharing a directory on a remote computer, use the /delete switch as follows:

```
rmtshare \\server\sharename /delete
```

Re-Creating Admin Shares

Access to the C$ and ADMIN$ shares (and other shares representing volumes on the server) is restricted to members of the Administrators group. If the shares are accidentally deleted, you can replace them using the *Policy Editor* (POLEDIT). This ensures the proper administrative locks are put on the shares. Proceed as follows:

Procedure 15.5 **Restoring Deleted Administrative Shares with POLEDIT**

1. Launch POLEDIT from the Run window.
2. From the menu, select FILE | OPEN REGISTRY.
3. Double-click the Local Computer icon. This opens the Local Computer Properties window.
4. Expand the tree under Windows NT Network | Sharing.
5. Select Create Hidden Drive Shares (Server).
6. Click OK to save the change and return to the main Policy Editor window.
7. From the menu, select FILE | SAVE. This applies the change to the Registry.

This action places a value called AutoShareServer in the Registry key HKLM | System | CurrentControlSet | Services | LanManServer | Parameters.

Publishing Shares in Active Directory

NT provides two ways to locate shared file resources: *browsing* and *Active Directory publishing*. Browsing has been a feature of Windows networking for years. It is supported in Windows 2000 for backward compatibility, but the preferred method for locating shared folders is by publishing them in the directory where they can be located quickly using LDAP tools. This topic contains a brief overview of browsing for the benefit of readers who are not familiar with it, and then covers how to publish and locate shared folders in Active Directory.

Overview of Browsing

When a user opens My Network Places/Network Neighborhood or views a resource list under Map Network Drive, the server list in the display is the result of a query to a server called a *browser*.

Every network segment has at least one browser, called the master browser. The master browser maintains a database of servers called a *browse list*. Servers register their names with the master browser when they come onto the network so they can be added to the browse list.

The master browser can have backup browsers. It replicates the browse list to the backup browsers and refers client queries to the backup browsers for load sharing

A browser can be any Windows computer with file-and-print sharing enabled. Master browsers are selected on the basis of a *browse election*. There is a hierarchy to Windows servers that is supposed to ensure that only the most capable machine (newest OS, for instance) becomes the browse master. Sometimes this works, other times it is about as effective as a federal election.

The master browser enlists the aid of other Windows servers to act as backup browsers when the number of clients grows to the point that it needs help in handling query traffic. When clients request browse lists, the master browser refers them to one of the backup browsers in round-robin fashion.

When browsing works, it gives users a quick and convenient way to find servers and their shared resources. Browse lists are small and highly portable. They even work for DOS clients using the Net View command. But browsing is one of the most complex parts of classic Windows networking. It frustrates users and causes grief for administrators. Here is a list of its most glaring deficiencies:

- Browse elections and server registrations are done by broadcast, so every network segment has its own master browser.

- Browse elections and server registrations are broadcast on each transport protocol, so there is a high probability that each network segment will have different master browsers for each transport.

- Browser registrations, browse elections, and browse list queries cause a significant amount of broadcast traffic. Every network client in the subnet must process these broadcasts.

- Windows clients query the browse master for the first transport in the binding order. This often results in two machines sitting side by side that display different server lists.

- In a routed TCP/IP environment, master browsers share their browse lists with the primary domain controller, which is also the *domain master browser* (DMB). The DMB distributes its browse list to master browsers in other subnets if they are registered with WINS. DNS cannot be used for this purpose.

- Browse list replication has significant latency. It can take as much as 51 minutes for a downed server to disappear from a browse list. During this time, the dead server continues to appear in Network Neighborhood.

After you have begun migrating to Windows 2000 at the desktop, you can start working on removing browsing from your system. You can do this by publishing shared resources in the directory so that users do not need to browse for them.

Publishing Shares in Active Directory

A shared folder on a domain member server can be represented in the directory by a Shared Folder object. Creating this object is called *publishing* the share. Users can use My Network Places to search the directory for published shares. The LDAP searches are much quicker than relying on browse lists.

Shared Folder objects in the directory are instances of the Volume class. Objects of this class can be placed in any Organizational Unit. The Shared Folder object contains an attribute called UNC-Name that contains the UNC path to the share point. An AD client can use a Shared Folder object to map a drive to the share point listed in the UNC-Name attribute.

Proceed as follows to publish a share in the directory:

Procedure 15.6 **Publishing Shared Folders in Active Directory**

---

1. Open the Directory Management console. The example in Figure 15.6 shows a domain called company.com with an Organizational Unit called Phoenix that contains an OU called Shared Folders.

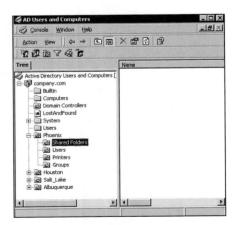

Figure 15.6 AD Users and Computers console showing Shared Folders OU.

2. Right-click the OU in which you want to create the shared folder and select NEW | SHARED FOLDER from the fly-out menu. The New Object - Shared Folder window opens (see Figure 15.7). Give the object the same name as the shared folder. This is not a system requirement, but it minimizes user confusion.

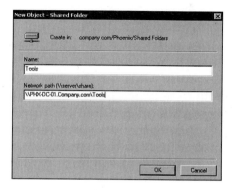

Figure 15.7 New Object - Shared Folder window showing entry named Tools for share named \\PHX-DC-01\Tools.

3. Click OK to save the change and publish the share. The system makes no effort to validate your entry. If you entered the name or path wrong, you will not know it until you test the published share. One common mistake is to forget to use the fully qualified DNS name. If you use the flat NetBIOS name, the share will work for local users but fail when accessed by users in a different domain.

4. Right-click the published share and select EXPLORE from the fly-out menu. The Explore window opens with the shared folder listed under the associated server and domain under My Network Places. Note that the listed name is the share name, not the name you gave the published folder, if they differ. If the Explore window does not open, you entered the path or the share name incorrectly.

At this point, Active Directory–aware clients (Windows 2000 and Windows 9x with the Active Directory add-on) can access the share by navigating through the Directory and double-clicking the Shared Folder object. They can also map to the shared folder object just as they would to a share in a browse list. The next section shows how this works.

Connecting to Published Folders

If your users are familiar with the standard Explorer interface, they'll have no problem mapping drives to published shares. The biggest difficulty is navigating to the Shared Folder icon in the directory. The easiest method is to search the directory using the Find feature in the domain properties. The Search window in the START menu can browse the directory, but does not display shared folder objects.

The following steps show how to locate a published share in the directory and map a network drive to it:

Procedure 15.7 Locating and Mapping a Network Drive to a Published Share

1. Open My Network Places. The default, Web-enabled view shows an Add Network Place icon, an Entire Network icon, and possibly a Network Neighbors icon depending on your browsing configuration.

2. Open Entire Network. A list of search options appears on the left side of the window. The Find Computer option will locate computers by browsing only.

3. Click Entire Contents. Each network provider gets an icon and there is an icon for the Directory. If the Directory icon does not appear, the client is not a member of a domain, has not logged on to the domain, or the member desktop failed to find a domain controller at boot time.

4. Right-click the Directory icon and select FIND from the fly-out menu. The Find Users, Contacts, and Groups window opens.

5. In the Find drop-down box, select Shared Folders. The window title bar name changes to match the selection.

6. In the Named field, enter the first letter of the share or an asterisk to show all published shares.

7. Click Find Now. The list of shares appears in the bottom pane of the window.

8. Right-click the shared folder and select MAP NETWORK DRIVE from the fly-out menu. The Map Network Drive window opens (see Figure 15.8). The Folder field is dimmed to indicate that no additional user entry is permitted. You can click Different User Name to define alternative credentials for opening the connection.

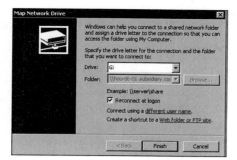

Figure 15.8 `Map Network Drive` window showing mapped selection to shared folder published in the directory.

9. Click `Finish` to map the drive.

Managing Client-Side Caching

Microsoft has been trying for years to find a way to support laptop users who need a way to take their network files with them on the road and then refresh them automatically when they get back on the network. The newest feature in this ongoing saga—and the one that comes closest to actually being useful—is *client-side caching* (CSC), which is displayed in the UI by the friendly name of *Offline Files*. The older Briefcase feature is still supported, but is not nearly as useful.

CSC is primarily designed to support laptop users, but it has a couple of other advantages.

- **Local access to large files.** It can be difficult to work on huge graphics files that are stored a server. Users typically copy big files to their local hard drives to work on them, but they sometimes forget to copy them back at the end of the day to get on the nightly backup. CSC automates this process.

- **File availability during network outages.** Granted, the network should not go down. But users get cynical during periods of instability and often keep their files on the local drive long after the problems have been resolved. If you support end users who are reluctant to save files on servers, CSC can be a way to lure them back to the network again.

Here is what CSC is not good for:

- Don't use it for files accessed by multiple users. This most emphatically includes databases. You especially need to watch out for little user databases that sneak onto a server and become a production environment for dozens of users.

- Don't use it to save local client/server files if the application makes its own provisions for local caching. You can confuse the bejeebers out of your users and possibly corrupt the client/server application.

- Use care when using CSC to cache executable images locally. There is a feature that permits caching local copies of programs, but very often the user is unaware of special support files that are accessed via secondary mappings that do not get cached.

Client-side caching is controlled at the share point and is enabled by default when a folder is shared. You can disable the feature or change the options as follows:

Procedure 15.8 **Disabling Client-Side Caching**

1. Right-click a folder you are currently sharing or one you want to share and select SHARING from the fly-out menu. The Properties window opens with the Sharing tab selected.

2. If the folder has not already been shared, select the Share This Folder radio button.

3. Click Caching. The Caching Settings window opens (see Figure 15.9). The sidebar on the next page titled "Selecting Caching Options" describes each option.

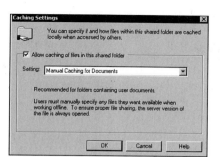

Figure 15.9 Caching Settings window showing default client-side caching settings.

Selecting Caching Options

Three caching options are available for a shared folder:

- **Manual Caching for Documents.** This option provides users with the option to save a single file, a group of files, an entire folder, or the contents of an entire share to their local drives. When set, this option permits local caching of any file type, including executables.

- **Automatic Caching for Documents.** This option does not wait for the user to request a local copy. It downloads a copy automatically. Use this option with care. If you enable caching on a share that has huge documents, you will start filling up local hard drives in a hurry. You also take the chance that a user will inadvertently take a sensitive document off-premise. Because the user did not deliberately choose to cache files offline, the local copies are considered volatile and can be removed without requiring a resync.

- **Automatic Caching for Programs.** This option automatically downloads read-only files and executables. This does not guarantee that the locally cached application will work. There may be DLLs and support files that do not get downloaded. For simple applications, however, this option works as advertised.

4. Click OK to close the window and return to the Properties window. If you made any changes to the caching settings, users who are currently connected with the share retain the old settings. They get the new settings when they next log on and reconnect to the share.

Working with Offline Files

This section describes how the client-side caching options affect operation at the client. From a Windows 2000 client, map a drive to the share you configured in the preceding section, and then proceed as follows:

Procedure 15.9 **Configuring Offline Folders at a Windows 2000 Client**

1. Open My Computer or Explorer.

2. From the menu, select TOOLS | FOLDER OPTIONS. The Folder Options window appears.

3. Select the Offline Files tab (see Figure 15.10).

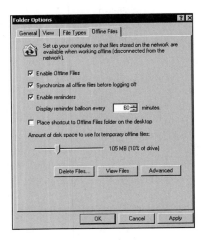

Figure 15.10 Folder options showing Offline Files option.

4. Select the Enable Offline Files option. This enables caching at the client. It does not override the caching settings assigned to the share point at the server.

5. Leave the Synchronize All Offline Files and the Enable Reminders option selected. This ensures that the user does not forget that the files are offline and that the user must stay in sync with the files on the network. This option may cause long logon or logoff delays if many files have changed.

6. I recommend selecting the Place Shortcut ... On Desktop option. This gives the user a handy way to find the local copies of offline folders.

Local Storage Location of Cached Files

Cached files are saved on the local drive under \WINNT\CSC. This can be a problem if the user has very little extra space in the system partition. If the cache gets full, the user is warned that some offline files are not available.

If the user's hard drive crashes while files are cached locally, the network files are unaffected. The user only loses the work that was done offline. Users who go on extended trips may want to refresh the network copies over dial-up lines. This can be slow, but much better than losing the files completely. The system automatically detects slow connections and does not automatically attempt to resynchronize, so the resync must be initiated manually.

7. Click Advanced. The Offline Files - Advanced Settings window opens. The options in this window are useful when selecting different offline behaviors depending on the identity of the server that is unavailable. The user may choose to be notified and begin working offline, for example, if the logon server that holds his or her home directory goes offline, but not if a server across the WAN goes down. Click Add to add specific computers to the list for special options. Otherwise, leave this window at its default settings.

8. Click OK to return to the Folder Options window.

9. The View Files and Delete Files buttons only make sense when there are files in the local cache. Let's add a few files then see how these buttons work.

10. Click OK to save the settings and close the window.

Registry Tip

The Registry entries that are written when CSC is enabled are stored in the following key:

```
Key:     HKLM | Software | Microsoft | Windows | CurrentVersion | NetCache

Values:  DefCacheSize (Dword) - set by the UI

         Enabled (Dword) - flag

         EncrypteEntireCache (Dword) - flag (not exposed in the UI)
```

11. From Explorer or My Computer, open the mapped network drive to view the contents of the share. Any or all of the share contents can be added to the offline files list. For example, right-click a folder and select Make Available Offline. The Offline Files Wizard opens. The wizard gives the same general options as the Offline Files window, but it is specific for a particular user.

Caution Users About Syncing Prior to Logoff

If the user chooses to synchronize at logon and logoff, the Synchronization Manager is added to the list of executables that run when the user logs on. It is important to instruct the user to log off normally or manually sync before removing a laptop from the network.

12. Click Next. The wizard indicates that a file is in the offline database by marking it with a double-headed arrow. The synchronization option Automatically Synchronize is the preferred option and should always be selected unless the user has a reason to not refresh the offline or network files.

Registry Tip

The Synchronization Manager settings are kept under HLKM | Software | Microsoft | Windows | CurrentVersion | SyncMgr. This key has subkeys that identify the users who have locally caches files, their connection type and sync settings. It also identifies the CLSID (Class ID) of the sync handlers, such as the File Sync handler and the WebCheck handler.

The share points associated with a particular share are stored in the following location under a key with the same name as the UNC for the share:

```
Key:     HKCU | Software | Microsoft | Windows | CurrentVersion | NetCache |
         Shares | <UNC>
Value:   ID (binary) and LastSyncTime (binary)
```

The CSC cache is included in the list of files that are not backed up by Backup. This list is controlled by the following Registry entry:

```
Key:     HKLM | System | CurrentControlSet | Control | BackupRestore |
         FilesNotToBackup
Values:  List of MULTI_SZ entries for each directory or file.
The /s switch indicates not to backup subdirectories.
```

Client-side caching requires support of the Windows client redirector, MRXSMB. The flag that enables caching support is located in following Registry entry:

```
Key:     HKLM | System | CurrentControlSet | Services | MRXSMB | Parameters
Value:   CSCEnabled
Data:    1 or 0 (DWORD)
```

13. Click Next. Select Enable Reminders and Create a Shortcut.

14. Click Finish to save the changes and copy the files to the local cache.

Operational Considerations for Offline Files

While the user stays connected to the network, all cached files are accessed through the network. This is true even if the user opens the file from the local Offline Files folder. When the user disconnects from the network, a computer icon appears in the System Tray with a pop up that notifies the user of the broken network connection. If you are testing this feature at a desktop, you can simulate breaking the network connection by pulling the LAN cable or by disabling the logical network connection using START | SETTINGS | NETWORK CONNECTIONS, and then right-clicking the Local Connection and selecting DISCONNECT from the fly-out menu.

While offline, the Explorer shell continues to show the network drive. The connection shows broken with a big red X, but the icon can be opened to show the offline files. Some users may find big red X's disconcerting and they may get flustered when the contents of that icon differ when they are online and offline. These users may be more comfortable accessing the offline files through the Offline Files folder on their desktop.

When the user logs on after reestablishing network connection, the offline files are resynchronized with the network, if you selected that option. The Synchronization Manager icon in the System Tray changes to an informational icon. The user can open the icon to resynchronize.

If the user makes changes to a copy of an offline file and wants to manually synchronize, the easiest way to do this is to right-click the file or directory icon and select SYNCHRONIZE from the fly-out menu.

Disabling Offline File Storage

A user can stop caching files by right-clicking the file or directory icon and deselecting the Make available offline option. The local file copies are not removed automatically. There are a couple of ways to remove them. The simplest way is to use the Offline Folder options window in Explorer. Proceed as follows:

Procedure 15.10 **Deleting Local Copies of Offline Folders**

1. Open My Computer or Explorer.

2. From the menu, select TOOLS | FOLDER OPTIONS.

3. Select the Offline Files tab.

4. Click Delete Files. The Confirm Delete Files window opens.

   The Delete Only Temporary Offline Versions option removes the local files associated with the Automatic Caching options at the server.

   The Delete Both Temporary and Versions Always Available option also removes local copies that were deliberately selected by the user.

   In both cases, only local files are deleted. If the computer is offline and the user is accessing cached files, however, the system does not warn the user that deleting the offline files may cause the network files to be removed when the system resyncs. Users should not do file maintenance while the system is offline.

5. Click OK to close the window.

The second way to delete local file copies is to open the Offline Files folder and selectively delete the files. If you do this, the system prompts to confirm and to tell you that only the local copy is deleted. Once again, if the user has not synchronized prior to deleting the file, all changes are lost.

Key Points for Managing Offline Files

Here are points to remember about managing client-side caching and offline files:

- CSC is enabled at the share point. The default option enables CSC.

- The only limit to the number of files a user can cache is the capacity of the local hard drive.

- Synchronization must be configured to occur during logon and logoff. Otherwise, the user must manually initiate synchronization.

- The Synchronization Manager will inform the user when the system is offline and provides access to the files using the normal drive-letter mappings for convenience.

Resource Sharing Using the Distributed File System (Dfs)

Without a doubt, the most confusing part about a network for the average end user is finding files and directories. To users, saying that a file is "on the network" is like saying "There's a $10 bill waiting for you in Chicago." Server-centric resource sharing also results in situations like that in Figure 15.11 where a user is forced to have many logical drives mapped to several servers to get access to data. Ideally, the user could map to one place and find all the company's information.

Publishing shared folders in the directory helps this situation somewhat, but the user is still faced with knowing that the Phoenix accounting data is in the Phoenix OU and the Albuquerque accounting data is in the Albuquerque OU, perhaps stored in a different container name.

What is needed is a logical structure where all the shared directories in the organization can be displayed and accessed. A user who wants accounting information can go to Accounting folder in this structure to find it.

Nearly three years ago, in NT4, Microsoft introduced a technology called the Distributed File System. This technology promised to eliminate server-centric resource sharing by making it possible to build a Dfs volume consisting of shared folders that users could access instead of hunting for servers.

The NT4 version of Dfs was a little clumsy and could support only local copies of the Dfs volume structure. The Dfs incarnation in Windows 2000 includes new features that enable building a fault-tolerant Dfs system that keeps data at the user's beck and call at all times.

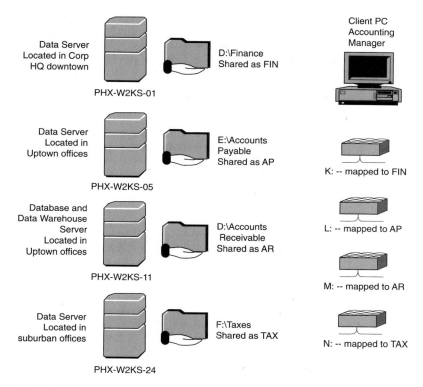

Figure 15.11   Shared directory structure before Dfs. User required to have multiple drives mapped.

Other Distributed File System Technologies

Windows 2000 Distributed File System has similar functionality as other enterprise file systems, such as Transarc's *Distributed File System* (DFS) and IBM's *Enterprise Distributed File System* (EDFS). In this flux of acronyms, Microsoft officially designated its distributed file system as *Dfs*.

These DFS technologies give a nod toward the *Distributed Computing Environment* (DCE) specification promulgated by the *Open Software Foundation* (OSF). In the grand scheme of DCE, any server could have share points (or mount points) in the Dfs volume and users could access those links from any client. None of the DFS vendors, including Microsoft, make products that are totally DCE compliant, so transparent sharing is still a distant dream.

Dfs Organization

Dfs defines a hierarchy of shared folders. The structure mimics a standard directory structure, so you can think of Dfs as being a big volume. Figure 15.12 shows how this volume can be constructed so that the Accounting

users need to know about only one share point to access all their files. This
share point can be published in the directory so that there is no need at all
to know any server names.

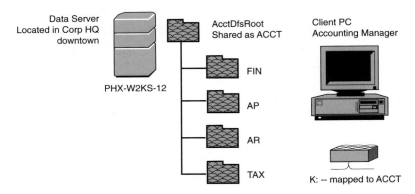

Figure 15.12 Diagram of Dfs structure that replaces server-centric model.

The Dfs volume organizes information in a way that complements the activities of the organization. For instance, a law firm could structure Dfs by liti-
gation type. An oil company could structure Dfs by business
unit—Downstream and Upstream and Midstream and the like.

The "folders" in Dfs are actually pointers, called *junctions*, to shared folders
hosted by servers around the enterprise. When users at a Dfs client map a
drive to a Dfs folder, the client gets a *referral* to the server hosting the shared
resource. This referral takes the form of a standard UNC name.

The Dfs client then goes right to the host server to get access to the
actual shared folder. After this connection has been made, Dfs steps out of
the way and the user communicates directly with the server hosting the
share. The client caches the referral locally, so it does not need to recontact
the Dfs server until the referral expires or the user logs off.

Dfs also addresses another concern, that of continuous data access. This is
increasingly a 7×24 world. Backup windows are tight. Maintenance windows
are nearly gone. Users expect to touch Web sites at any hour of the day or
night, anywhere in the globe, and get a page. Dfs makes it possible to point
the user at mirrored data so that one server can go down for maintenance
while the others are up and taking browser hits. This mirroring does not
work well to support live data, but in the read-only environment of the Web,
or in dishing up static executables in an office, Dfs works very well.

Functional Description of Dfs

Think of Dfs as a special kind of file system. A regular file system is essentially a list of the files and file locations on a hard drive indexed by file name. Dfs is list of shared folders in a forest indexed by share name.

A Dfs volume starts with a *root share* on a server called a *Dfs host*. The volume is built of *junction points* that point at shared directories on other hosts. From a user's perspective, the Dfs volume is no different from any other file system. The fact that the "directories" in a Dfs volume are actually scattered hither and yon does not affect the way users navigate through them. They can launch applications, open data files, and map drives to any of the folders inside the Dfs using the Map Network Drive interface.

Dfs servers manage the Dfs file system using the Dfs service, DFSSVC.EXE. Clients access Dfs volumes via a network file system driver, DFS.SYS.

This section contains details about Dfs volume types, Dfs client versions, and the transactions used by clients to get access to Dfs volumes.

Dfs Types

There are two types of Dfs, depending on the location of the Dfs volume information:

- **Standalone Dfs.** The Dfs volume information is stored in the Registry of the server that hosts the root share. All client requests involving Dfs must go to this server, even if it is in another part of the WAN. The UNC syntax is \\Dfs_host\Dfs_root. If a server named PHX-W2KS-01 were host to a Dfs named ACCT, for example, the UNC name would be \\PHX-W2KS-01\ACCT. If this server were to go down, access to the Dfs is lost until the server is recovered. A standalone Dfs server is recommended only for businesses or departments with limited WAN connections.

- **Fault-tolerant Dfs.** The Dfs volume information is stored in the directory. A fault-tolerant Dfs does not depend on a single server to host the Dfs. If the original host server is lost, users can still connect to the Dfs and locate shared folders inside the Dfs volume. The UNC syntax is \\domain\Dfs_root.

The term *fault tolerant* sometimes gets misused when referring to Dfs operations. This is because Dfs volume replication between domain controllers gets confused with file replication between host servers. File replication is not a feature of Dfs, as such. File replication is used to maintain high availability with Dfs acting as a load-balancing agent.

Dfs Versions

When a network client user touches a Dfs junction, the Dfs service running on the host (or on a domain controller, in the case of fault-tolerant Dfs) returns a *referral* to the server that actually hosts the share. The Dfs client then goes directly to that host server to make the connection.

The SMB dialect NTLM 0.12—used by Windows 2000, NT4, and Windows 9x—supports Dfs. There is no need to load a separate network file system. There are, however, two versions of Dfs.

NT4 and Window 9x clients use Dfs revision 2. Windows 2000 clients use Dfs revision 3. The versions are backward compatible; so a Windows 2000 client can access an NT4 Dfs, and an NT4 client can access a Windows 2000 Dfs.

Dfs Access Transactions

The Dfs version affects how clients initially access the Dfs volume, which can also affect load balancing. Here's how.

When a user accesses a shared folder, the MUP first checks to see whether the resource is associated with Dfs. If so, it passes the request to the Dfs file system driver, DFS.SYS, for processing.

If this is the first time that a shared folder has been accessed, MUP starts down the list of providers. By default, DFS.SYS is the first provider. It is this initial Dfs transaction that differs depending on the client.

- **Windows 2000 initially attempts to get a Dfs referral.** On a Windows 2000 client, MUP first queries for a Dfs referral using an SMB called Transact 2 NT Get DFS Referral. If the UNC does not refer to a Dfs junction, the Dfs volume host (in the case of standalone Dfs) or the directory (in the case of fault-tolerant Dfs) reports back a negative result. MUP continues polling the remaining providers.

- **Classic Windows initially attempts a standard connection.** On an NT4 or Windows 9x client, MUP first queries using a standard SMB asking for attributes of the share from the host identified in the UNC. This query fails in the case of Dfs because Dfs junctions do not have these attributes. MUP then checks the UNC path on the assumption that the user gave the wrong server name. This also fails because a Dfs junction does not expose a standard path to a shared folder. MUP finally queries the Dfs driver with a Dfs referral SMB. This succeeds.

Partition Knowledge Table

Regardless of the client version, after the Dfs host or domain controller has received the Dfs referral request, it sends back a response in the form of a Get DFS Referral Reply. This reply contains a referral to the actual share in UNC format. This referral takes the form of a *partition knowledge table* (PKT). The PKT contains the following information:

- **Dfs revision number.** Version 3 clients get a version 3 reply, and version 2 clients get a version 2 reply. The referrals are the same right now, but they might differ in the future.

- **Dfs filename.** In SMB, share points are treated as files. Clients get handles to these files and open them using standard SMB file commands. This is one of the reasons why classic NT clients cannot map to directories. Windows 2000 clients formulate their request slightly differently.

- **Dfs 8.3 filename.** The short name of the share point.

- **Dfs share name on the host server.** This is the heart of the referral. It tells the client to look for a share point on the server.

- **Time-To-Live.** After the client gets a referral, it caches the location for a given number of seconds. This is 1,800 seconds, or 30 minutes, by default. When the time expires, the client goes back to the Dfs server for another referral. Keep this interval in mind. If the server hosting the actual share goes down, clients could get long response times followed by error messages for up to 30 minutes.

- **Host server type.** Dfs can refer clients to down-level servers such as NetWare servers, OS/2 LAN Manager and WARP, and NFS shares if the server is configured with an NFS redirector. The client can only act on this referral if it has the proper redirector.

Dfs Handling for Multiple Replicas

It is possible more than one junction to be associated with the same share name. From the user's perspective, there is only one share point; in the background, however, the data resides on multiple servers. FRS synchronizes data between servers.

If the Dfs junction includes multiple replicas, the PKT contains referral information about each shared folder. This is another place where Dfs acts differently depending on the version.

- **Classic Dfs servers return unmanaged referral lists.** Version 2 Dfs servers, and version 3 Dfs servers queried by version 2 clients, return referrals in the same order they exist in the Dfs volume list, either in the Registry or the directory. The client is responsible for randomly choosing one to use.

- **Windows 2000 Dfs servers return random referral lists.** Version 3 Dfs servers queried by version 3 clients return a random list of referrals in the PKT. The Dfs client picks the top referral. If it cannot get a reply from that host, it goes to the second referral and so on.

The client also reports back to the Dfs server that it could not find the host referenced in a referral. This `Report Dfs Inconsistency` SMB helps to keep the system free of broken links. Its use is optional, however, so you may encounter situations where the system doesn't realize that a link is broken for quite a while.

Version 3 Reply

The version 3 reply is not completely random. It gives preference to shares that are in the same site as the client. This helps reduce WAN traffic. If a local host of a share that is in Dfs goes down, you can expect quite a bit of complaining if your WAN isn't fast. Keep this in mind when you lay out your fault-tolerant shares.

Multiple Dfs Roots

Figure 15.13 shows the Dfs management console in a Dfs volume that contains 2 directory-enabled Dfs roots. Theoretically, the directory can have up to 12 Dfs roots in the same volume. In a file system, these would be folders at the root directory.

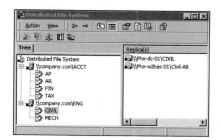

Figure 15.13   Dfs console showing multiple Dfs roots.

Two significant limitations in the Windows 2000 Dfs architecture apply when it comes to handling multiple roots and these restrict your flexibility in designing Dfs volumes:

- **No child links.** You cannot build a child link under another child link in this version of Dfs. Dfs volumes are only one level deep. It's like building a file system where all folders reside at Root.

- **A server can host only one Dfs root.** You can build a hierarchical Dfs structure of sorts by creating a Dfs root for Accounting and one for Sales and one for Engineering, and then linking them together inside a master Dfs, but this requires a separate server to host each Dfs root.

Microsoft has committed to addressing these limitations in future releases of Windows 2000.

Dfs and File Replication

One of the strengths of Dfs is the way it leverages the *File Replication System* (FRS) in Windows 2000. The combination of Dfs and FRS provides continuity of data access in the event of a server outage or a network problem.

FRS is a general-purpose replication engine capable of keeping any given set of directories in sync. FRS can be used to replicate the contents of a shared directory on one host server to the shared directory on another host server. Dfs then acts like a traffic cop, directing clients to either of the two shared directories using the PKT order in the referral response.

The primary share for the Accounts Receivable department might be \\PHX-W2KS-01\AR, for example. An alternative share can be created on \\PHX-W2KS-02\AR that contains the same files as the primary share. When files are added or changed at the primary share, FRS copies the changes to the alternative share. By replicating the shared folders, one server can be taken down for maintenance without losing data availability.

The FRS maintains a Jet database (JDB file) in the \WINNT\Ntfrs directory. This database contains the file locations and their replication precedence: primary or secondary.

When FRS replicates a file, it checks for time stamps and checksums. If the time stamps don't match but the checksums do, it assumes that the files are the same. If the checksums don't match, the file with most current time stamp is replicated to the partner.

FRS is capable of multiple master replication; when used in conjunction with Dfs, however, replication occurs only from a primary to its secondaries. If a replication partner goes down, changes accumulate at the primary in a holding area on disk. When the link is reestablished, the changes are replicated. During this period, FRS informs Dfs that the link is down so that Dfs does not pass out referrals to downed host.

Registry Tip

FRS keys are stored in the following locations:

```
HKLM | System | CurrentControlSet | Services | FileReplicaConn
HKLM | System | CurrentControlSet | Services | FileReplicaSet
HKLM | System | CurrentControlSet | Services | NtFrs
```

A set of objects in the directory under the System container also parallels the Registry entries and makes the FRS fault tolerant. Figure 15.14 shows these objects.

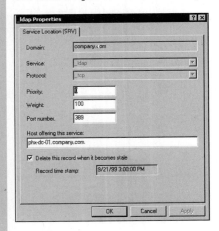

Figure 15.14 AD Users and Computers console showing FRS objects.

Microsoft has tested Directory-based Dfs volumes containing 1,000 shares and standalone Dfs volumes containing 10,000 shares with acceptable performance. A standalone Dfs significantly outperforms a fault-tolerant Dfs because a local lookup in a Jet database and Registry is faster than an LDAP lookup across the network to a domain controller. You sacrifice fault tolerance, however, when building standalone Dfs volumes. Also, a standalone Dfs forces clients to go across the WAN to find the Dfs server to get a referral that might lead them straight back to their own local LAN. In a Directory-based Dfs, the referral comes from the local domain controller.

Some directory limitations also restrict the number of alternative shares that can be serviced by Dfs. FRS has a limitation of 32 replication partners, but a Directory-based Dfs volume is limited to 12 partners because the alternatives are stored in the Directory as a BLOB with a limited size. The BLOB handling in Active Directory is sure to improve in subsequent releases, so look for the Dfs referral limit to go up as well.

Setting Up and Configuring Dfs

Preparing for a Dfs implementation requires a little thought about how you want the Dfs volume structure to appear when users access it. Ideally, the volume structure should match the logical organization of your enterprise so that users can navigate the Dfs as easily as they navigate an organizational chart.

You might want Dfs entries for Accounting, Engineering, and Sales, for example, along with a Common directory to access standard business applications. You may also want functional directories such as Users for home directories and Mail for email files. The challenge when designing Dfs is collecting the hodge-podge of directory names and share names that are scattered around your organization into a consistent structure.

The following outline summarizes the steps involved in setting up Dfs:

1. **Determine which server will host the Dfs.** If you want fault tolerance in case this server goes down, you can directory-enable the Dfs volume. If you think of a Dfs as a file system, directory-enabling it involves copying the critical file system records to special objects in the directory.

2. **Create a shared folder on the Dfs server.** Think of it as the root directory of the Dfs volume. This directory can hold files, but this should be avoided in the same way that you avoid placing files at the root of a file system.

3. **Create a Dfs volume anchored at the shared Dfs folder.** This is the volume that users will see when they browse the network. It looks and acts just like any other shared folder. Information about the Dfs volume is stored in the Registry (standalone Dfs) or in the directory (fault-tolerant Dfs).

4. **Populate the Dfs volume.** The Dfs volume starts out empty. You add links to shared folder on other servers to structure the volume according to your Dfs design plan.

5. **Publish the Dfs root share in the directory.** The Dfs doesn't do users much good if they can't find it easily. By publishing the root share in the directory, you give the users a consistent place to go for location information. Don't confuse the published share with the contents of the Dfs volume that are also stored in the directory. The Dfs root share behaves just like any other share. The other Dfs information is just plumbing.

6. **Replicate critical data referenced by Dfs.** The Dfs volume is just a set of pointers. The data itself resides on the servers that host the shared folder. You can replicate that data to another location and use Dfs as a traffic cop for load balancing and fault tolerance. The Dfs server refers clients in random fashion to equalize load and stops referring clients to a share if the link goes down.

Creating a Dfs Root Directory

Dfs uses a root directory on a host server as the starting point for the Dfs volume. You can use an existing shared directory or create one at the same time that you create the Dfs root. The Dfs root does not need to be empty, but it is best to put files in another location. The volume hosting the root can be any of the Windows 2000 file systems, but NTFS gives the most security.

Procedure 15.11 **Creating a Dfs Root Directory**

---

1. Open the Distributed File System console using START | PROGRAMS | ADMINISTRATIVE TOOLS | DISTRIBUTED FILE SYSTEM.

2. Right-click the Distribute File System icon and select NEW DFS ROOT from the fly-out menu. The New Dfs Root Wizard opens.

3. Click Next. The Select the Dfs Root Type window opens.

4. Select the Create a Domain Dfs Root radio button. This integrates the Dfs into the directory and eliminates the reliance on a single root server.

5. Click Next. The Select the Host Domain for the Dfs Root window opens.

6. Select the domain that will host the Dfs Root. This domain need not be the root domain of the forest. It should be in one of the upper domains if you have a deep forest. This enables the administrators for the upper part of the directory to administer the Dfs.

7. Click Next. The Specify the Host Server for the Dfs Root window opens. Enter the fully qualified DNS name of the server that will host the Dfs root. You can use the Browse button to locate the server. This button searches the directory. It does not use the browser. This makes sense because the server that hosts a directory-enabled Dfs must be a member of the domain. It does not need to be a domain controller.

8. Click Next. The Specify the Dfs Root Share window opens. If you have already created a shared directory for the root, select the Use An Existing Share radio button and pick the share name from the list. Alternatively, you can select the Create a New Share radio button and create the folder and share it as part of the root creation. *You cannot rename the root share name.* Be sure you and all your users agree on the name.

9. Click Next. The Name of the Dfs Root window opens. The default share name for the Dfs root is the same as the name of the host share. You can change this, but my advice is to leave it alone. The users see the root share name when they browse the host server; after they have entered the Dfs, however, they see the share name of the root folder. If the two names differ, it gets very confusing.

10. Click Next. A summary window opens listing the configuration selections you made.

11. Click Finish to create the Dfs root. After the wizard has completed the task, it closes and returns focus to the Dfs console.

At this point, the Dfs is like a freshly formatted disk. It has a root directory but no data. Let's begin adding shares. First, however, you may want to take a look in the AD Users and Computers console to find the Dfs object for the new Dfs root. For example, the Dfs named ACCT would have a distinguished name of cn=ACCT, cn=Dfs-Configuration, cn=System, dc=Company, dc=com.

Populating a Dfs with Shares

A Dfs is built by linking shares from other servers to the tree. A properly constructed Dfs volume has a logical hierarchy of virtual folders that can be intuitively navigated by users. In the example, the Accounting department has data on four servers that they want to access from a single share.

Procedure 15.12 **Populating a Dfs Volume with Shares**

1. Right-click the Dfs root icon and select new dfs link from the fly-out menu. The `Create a New Dfs` Link window opens (see Figure 15.15).

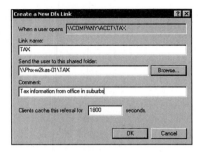

Figure 15.15 `Create a New Dfs Link` window.

2. Under `Link Name`, enter the name that represents the share in the Dfs. This should be the same name as the shared folder. Otherwise, it confuses users.

3. Select the shared folder to associate with the link by either typing in the UNC or browsing to select it. This browse can access both the classic browser and the directory.

4. Click `OK` to save the change and add the shared folder to the Dfs.

5. Repeat the steps to add all desired shared folders into the Dfs.

Users can now browse the contents of the Dfs; because this is Windows 2000, however, it's better to get them accustomed to searching the directory. The next section covers publishing the Dfs volume in the directory.

Publishing Dfs in the Directory

Browsing is a poor way to interact with Dfs because it sends the user to the Dfs root share on the host server rather than to the fault-tolerant root in the directory. This sets the user up for a service interruption should the root server crash.

The Dfs root share point is published in the directory just like any other share point. There is no shortcut in the UI, so you must create the object manually. Do so as follows:

Procedure 15.13 **Publishing a Dfs Root in the Directory**

1. Open the AD Users and Computers console.

2. Expand the tree to show the OU where you want to create the Shared Folder object. As with standard shares, you should put the object for the Dfs root in a location that can be found easily by users. The search tools for finding Shared Folder objects in the directory aren't as intuitive as they could be.

3. Right-click the OU icon and select NEW | SHARED FOLDER from the fly-out menu. New Object - Shared Folder window opens.

   - Name. Enter the name of the Dfs root share. Be sure to use the same name, otherwise users get confused when the underlying share name doesn't match the name they see in the directory.

   - Network Path. Enter the UNC name for the fault-tolerant Dfs. In the example, the Dfs root is named ACCT and the domain is company.com, so the UNC name would be \\company.com\ACCT. Don't unintentionally enter the share name at the host server; otherwise, the users will lose access to Dfs if that server goes down.

4. Click OK to create the object. At this point, the user can browse the directory to find the shared folder.

If the link goes down between the domain controller and the servers hosting the shared folders, the users will eventually be unable to see the Dfs volume. A broken link doesn't cause immediate problems because the Dfs clients have cached a copy of the PKT, so they know where to find the host servers. When the local PKT expires—30 minutes by default—the users remain connected to the host server but cannot remake the connection if it is broken.

One way to avoid the problem of lost data links is to replicate the data. The next section covers how to configure the File Replication Service through Dfs to build redundant shares into the Dfs volume.

Dfs and File Replication

You can create alternative shares for Dfs to use in referrals. When you do this, Dfs works with the *File Replication Service* (FRS) to synchronize the folders.

The initial FRS configuration is much faster if you first copy files from the source folder to the secondary folder or folders. FRS uses time stamps and checksums to control collisions; so by copying the files first, you put the least burden on the service.

FRS Behavior During Initial Volume Replication

If you manually copy files from the primary to the secondary server in preparation for configuring FRS, you may get a surprise the first time you establish file replication between the volumes. The first action taken by FRS is to move all the files in the secondary folder to a folder called NTFrs_PreExisting___See_EventLog. This is a hidden folder, so at first it appears as if FRS deleted all your files.

FRS copies the files to a temp folder so that it can easily distinguish between the files that were initially present when FRS was started and those that are added later. The files in NTFrs_PreExisting___See_EventLog are not staged for deletion, although the Event Log entry makes it appear so.

As users use Dfs referrals to touch files on the secondary server, the time stamps and checksums of the files in the temp folder are validated against the copies on the primary. If the validation passes, the local files are moved back to their original location. If validation fails, the file is copied from the primary and the outdated copy is left in the NTFrs_PreExisting folder.

After the users have touched all the files, you can safely delete the contents of the NTFrs_PreExisting folder. You don't have to wait a year. Even if you delete a file that has yet to be touched, it's not a great calamity. The file will be replicated from the primary as soon as FRS notices it is missing.

Procedure 15.14 **Creating Alternative Shares for Dfs to Use During Referrals**

Create a folder on a separate server to hold the copies of files from the main folder.

1. Copy the files from the main folder to the replica. This saves time by letting the replication engine worry only about updating changes.

2. Share the alternative folder.

3. Open the Dfs console.

4. Highlight the folder you want to replicate and select NEW REPLICA from the fly-out menu. The Add a New Replica window opens.

5. Use Browse to locate and select the alternative folder you just created.

6. Under Replication Policy, select Automatic Replication.

7. Click OK to save the change. The Replication Policy window appears (see Figure 15.16).

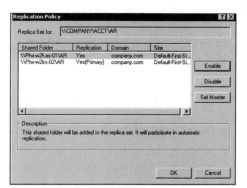

Figure 15.16 Replication Policy window.

8. Select one of the two folders as the Primary using the Set Master button. Use the Enable button to enable replication for the other shares. You can have up to 12 alternative shares in a directory-enabled Dfs and 32 alternative shares in a standalone Dfs.

9. Click OK to save the change. The wizard adds objects into the directory to support the replication and copies any changed files to the alternative share. It also moves all the existing files in the alternative share into a folder called NTFrs_PreExisting___See_EventLog.

10. Open the AD Users and Computers console.

11. Navigate to System | File Replication Service | Dfs Volumes. Figure 15.17 shows an example. Each of the two replicated shares is represented by a Connection object. The object name is a GUID for the connection. These objects are stored under an FRS Member object that also uses a GUID for a name. These are stored under FRS Replica Set objects, ACCT|AR and ACCT, that define the structure of the Dfs. The entire Dfs is stored under an FRS Settings object, DFS Volumes.

12. Test the replica by going to the console of one of the servers, opening the folder that is shared in Dfs, and adding a file. Then go to the console of the server hosting the replica of the file and open the mirrored folder. The replication engine should have already copied the file.

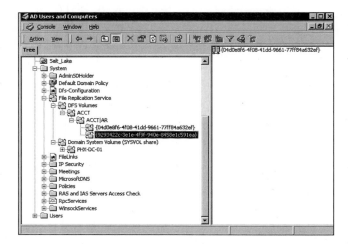

Figure 15.17 AD Users and Computers console showing Dfs volumes.

From a user's perspective, the file updates are transparent so long as the connections are maintained and the changes don't swamp the network line. Watch for errors closely for a few days to make sure the system is stable. Be ready to take action if anything happens to the WAN links, network connections, or host servers involved in file replication.

The best use of replication is for read-only files, but you can use it to store live data as long as the users are aware that network problems might cause their data to get out of sync. Do I see you smiling?

Functional Overview of Printing

There are four P's in system administration that can make or break a user's opinion of the support staff: passwords, printing, performance, and phones. Of all these, it has been my experience that printing is the item that irritates users the most.

A high percentage of help desk calls involve printing problems. You've probably been on the wrong end of "print rage" conversations. I think this is because users think that printing is a trivial thing that any numbskull should be able to get working. They don't realize that network printing is often one of the most complicated set of technologies on the network.

This section examines the Windows 2000 printing architecture and the flow of control during various printing configurations.

When Is a Printer Not a Printer?

If you are unfamiliar with Windows parlance, the term *printer* can trip you up.

In Windows, a printer is a logical object, not a physical one. You create a printer by configuring a set of drivers at a server or workstation.

The physical printer itself is called a *print device*. You would say, for example, "I created a printer on this server using the HPLJ8000 driver, but I can't get a test page out of the print device."

Initial Rendering and GDI

When a user clicks the Print button inside a Windows application, the application uses a set of API calls to communicate the print job to Win32. Native 32-bit Windows applications use Win32 API calls. Older, 16-bit Windows applications use Win16 API calls. DOS applications send out raw print commands using drivers that are provided as part of the application itself. The Win16 calls and DOS print commands are converted to Win32 API calls by the NTVDM driver.

The API calls from the application do not actually touch the printer, of course, or even the Windows 2000 Executive. That would violate the separation of user space and kernel space that is the hallmark of classic NT and Windows 2000. Instead, the API calls are handled by the *Client-Server Runtime Subsystem* (CSRSS), which acts as trusted intermediary between User-mode and Kernel-mode processes.

CSRSS initiates a set of routines inside the Executive that make use of the WIN32K.SYS library, the Kernel-mode side of Win32. More specifically, the routines call on the *Graphic Device Interface* (GDI) portion of WIN32K.SYS. GDI is one of the three key components of the Win32 subsystem. User and Kernel are the other two. As you'd expect from its name, GDI controls all things graphical, both on the screen and for printing.

Print Metafiles and Printer Drivers

When GDI receives a print job, it *renders* the job into a *print metafile*. The metafile does not contain actual print commands. Instead, it consists of a series of native GDI commands that fully describes the printed page. Some printers are built to understand this native GDI language, but most have their own language so that the vendors can add value and differentiate their products. By first building a metafile, the system can quickly return control of the system back to the user.

The print metafile may not contain specific printer commands, but it is not completely independent of the attached printer. GDI needs general information about the printer so that it can design the page to match the printer's capabilities and specifications. For example, it would do no good to build a metafile with 1200dpi color output on an 11×17 page just to feed to a dot-matrix printer. The GDI communicates with a *printer driver* to get specific information about the printer.

Like all Windows 2000 drivers, printer drivers use the *Windows Driver Model* (WDM). This model divides a driver into a class driver, a miniport driver, and one or more filter drivers.

The printer class driver is UNIDRV.DLL. An example of a miniport driver is NEC807.DLL, the miniport driver for the NEC 870 laser printer. Windows 2000 supports legacy NT4 drivers, but you can lose some functionality depending on the way the vendor wrote the legacy driver. And even though the driver itself might be useable, the INF script that loads it might not be compatible with the new INF format in Windows 2000. Visit the vendor's Web site for an updated INF script.

Microsoft provides generic printer minidrivers that come in three parts:

- **Printer graphics driver.** Universal printer minidrivers developed by Microsoft for the three major types of printers:
  - **Adobe Postscript–compatible printers**—PSCRIPT.DLL
  - **Raster image printers such as laser-jets and dot-matrix printers**—RASDD.DLL
  - **HPCL2-compliant plotters**—PLOTTER.DLL
- **Printer interface driver.** User interface drivers. These define what the user sees in the Printer Properties window. Each printer graphics driver has a separate DLL for this function:
  - **Postscript**—PSCRPTUI.DLL
  - **Raster**—RASDDUI.DLL
  - **Plotter**—PLOTUI.DLL
- **Printer characterization file.** Describes specific capabilities and requirements for a particular printer. PCF drivers typically are given a special extension based on their use. Examples include the following:
  - **PPD**—Postscript minidrivers
  - **DLL**—Raster minidrivers
  - **PCD**—Plotter minidrivers

Postscript minidrivers are compatible across both NT platforms. Raster and plotter minidrivers differ for Intel and Alpha platforms. Windows 2000 uses the PRINTER.INF script to install PPD files. Vendors often update this script to accommodate their own PPD file; therefore, if you mix postscript drivers on the same print server, sometimes you can get a conflict.

Spooler

GDI, working with the printer driver, builds the print metafile, and then gives the metafile to the Spooler service to save to disk.

The Spooler service is a client/server system.

- The client part of the Spooler, WINSPOOL.DRV, was the piece that actually took the print job from the application.

- The server part, SPOOLSS.DLL, lives in the Executive and handles further rendering of the job.

The user is the owner of the spooled file. If the user runs out of quota on the volume containing the spool directory or has no rights to the spool directory, the print job fails.

Spool Files

By default, Spooler saves print jobs in the `WINNT\System32\Spool\Printers` directory. Figure 15.18 shows files waiting to print. Spooler saves two files for each print job:

Figure 15.18   Contents of `WINNT\System32\Spool\Printers` directory showing spooled print files.

- **Spool file.** The files with the .SPL extension. These contain the contents of the job itself.

- **Shadow file.** The files with the .SHD extension. These contain information and instructions concerning the job, such as the destination printer, print priority, and originating user.

Changing the Location of the Default Spool Directory

You can change the location of the default spool directory as follows:

Procedure 15.15   Changing the Location of the Default Spool Directory

1. Open the `Printers` window using START | SETTINGS | PRINTERS.

2. From the menu, select FILE | SERVER PROPERTIES.

3. Select the Advanced tab.

4. Under Spool Folder field, enter the local path to the new spool directory. Ensure that proper access rights have been granted to all authorized users so they can print.

5. Click OK to save the change.

6. Stop and start the Spooler service, using `Net Stop Spooler` then `Net Start Spooler`.

Print Processor

The Spooler service consists of several pieces. First is the *print processor*, WIN-PRINT.EXE. This is the foreman of the print team. It makes decisions about where to send the byte stream for further rendering and what to do with potential problems within the byte stream. One of the key functions of WINPRINT is to assign a *data type* to a job. This defines how the job will be handled as it is converted into printer commands. These data types are as follows:

- **Raw.** The print job has already been fully rendered into native printer commands and requires no further processing.

- **Raw (FF appended).** A form-feed command is appended to the end of the rendered print job. This is useful for DOS applications that don't kick out the final page after they have finished printing.

- **Raw (FF auto).** A form feed is appended to the rendered print job if one is not already present. Use this option if you get two blank pages at the end of every job.

- **NT EMF 1.003, 1.006, 1.007, and 1.008 (Enhanced Metafile).** This type indicates that the job came from a Windows 2000, NT4, or Windows 98 client. Older versions of Windows use Journal files, which cannot be sent across the network.

- **Text.** The job must be reworked into pure ANSI-compliant text so that control codes aren't sent to the printer. This is useful for printing Postscript jobs coming from UNIX clients.

WINPRINT assigns data types to the incoming byte stream based on the criteria in Table 15.2.

Table 15.2 **Windows Print Processor Data Type Assignments**

Job Source	Assigned Data Type
Windows 2000, NT4, and Windows 98	Data type NT EMF of the applicable revision.
NT 3.51, Windows 95, and Windows 3.1x	RAW.
DOS applications printing locally or across the network	RAW.
Macintosh clients printing to a Postscript printer on a Windows 2000 server	RAW.
Macintosh clients printing to a non-Postscript printer on a Windows 2000 server	PSCRIPT1. This calls up a second-level print processor to render the Postscript job for a non-Postscript device.
UNIX clients using "l" (as in Lima) parameter	RAW. The "l" parameter indicates job contains printer control codes.
UNIX clients using "f" parameter	TEXT. The "f" parameter indicates non-printing control characters have been filtered out. This includes the ESC character, which will cause incorrect printing by PCL printers.

Print Providers

The Spooler also contains a *router*, SPOOLSS.DLL. This router decides which *print provider* to use for communicating with the printer service that will eventually print the job. Here are the names of the print providers:

- **Local Print Provider** (LOCALSPL.DLL). This provider handles jobs destined for a locally connected printer or a network print server that despools from the local machine. This is another common source of confusion for Windows print terminology. The piece of hardware called "network print server" differs from the server hosting the printer.

- **Windows Network Print Provider** (WIN32SPL.DLL). This provider gets jobs destined for Windows-based servers. If the remote server is running Windows 2000 or NT4, WIN32SPL makes a Remote Procedure Call to Spooler at the remote server, and then sends the EMF file directly.

- **NetWare Network Print Provider** (NWPROVAU.DLL). This provider gets jobs destined for NetWare print servers. The job is sent as RAW print commands.

- **UNIX print jobs.** Jobs intended for UNIX hosts are given to the LPR application for delivery to an LPD server using standard RFC 1179 message protocols. There is no provider.

EMF File Handling and Print Performance

Under normal circumstances, the EMF print file is rendered into printer commands at the host server. This improves print performance in two ways:

- The metafile is typically much smaller than a fully rendered print job, reducing network traffic.

- A server is usually more capable of performing background jobs such as print rendering.

- If the remote server is running some other version of Windows, WIN32SPL renders the job into native printer commands locally and delivers a RAW job to the network redirector.

- The redirector sends the job to the remote server. The Server service at the remote server takes the job and sends it directly to the print device.

Windows 2000 and the NetWare Capture Command

NetWare servers do not manipulate the byte stream. The NetWare client redirector handles the transfer of the spool file to the NetWare server.

DOS applications printing a NetWare print provider cannot take advantage of special features in the Capture command because the print provider does not recognize them.

If you have legacy DOS applications that do gymnastics with graphics that typically require special Capture settings, you should test thoroughly on a Windows 2000 desktop prior to deployment.

Print Monitors

After a job has been rendered into native printer commands, Spooler hands it over to a *print monitor*. This driver is responsible for communicating with the print device itself. Each printer type has its own print monitor. Spooler chooses the right print monitor based on the port associated with the printer.

When Spooler has jobs destined for LPT1, for example, it hands them over to Local Printer Monitor, LOCALMON.DLL. The printer monitors understand the hardware interface such as parallel ports, serial ports, bidirectional parallel ports, and ECP ports. It deals with flow control issues and error handling.

If the job is destined for a remote server, it also generates the necessary network calls. Classic NT had a handful of printer monitors. Windows 2000 has 18 with more possible from third parties. This rapid expansion of printer monitors mostly comes from the Windows 2000 support for Internet printing, online faxing, and a host of new bus interfaces such as infrared and USB.

After the job prints, Spooler deletes the SHL and SPD files from the hard drive unless it is configured to retain them for manual deletion.

During despool, Spooler keeps the SPL file locked. If you kill the print job while it is despooling, the SHD file may get deleted while leaving behind the SPL file. In the UI, it looks as if the file won't go away. It sometimes remains even if Spooler is stopped and restarted.

If this happens, stop the Spooler service, delete the SPL file manually, start Spooler again. You can stop and start Spooler from the `Computer Management` console, but it's much easier just to open a command session and type `Net Stop Spooler` and `Net Start Spooler`. No pending print jobs are lost if you stop the spooler, but jobs that are actively despooling will be interrupted and will restart from the beginning.

Network Printing

The I/O Manager in the Windows 2000 Executive uses NFS drivers to communicate with Server services on remote machines. Remember how Wnet applications needed network providers to interface with the NFS drivers? In the same way, printers need network print providers to interface with the NFS.

The print provider for Windows networking is LanMan Print Services, WIN32SPL.DLL. This driver also acts as the port monitor for communications with a network. The provider for Internet printing is HTTP Print Services, INETPP.DLL. Print jobs destined for third-party printer servers are handed over to the appropriate redirector.

> **Registry Tips**
>
> Registry entries affecting printing are contained in HKLM | `System` | `CurrentControlSet` | `Control` | `Print`. Some of the more important keys are as follows:
>
> - The `Environments` key contains entries for the version of Windows 2000 or NT for the local server and any print drivers loaded to support other environments. The Windows NT x86 entry contains two sets of drivers, version 2 and 3. The version 2 keys are for legacy, non-WDM drivers. The version 3 keys are for WDM drivers from Windows 2000 or Windows 98. This key also contains the `Print Processors` key, which defines the function library for the WINPRINT service, LOCALSPL.DLL.
>
> - There is a `Forms` key that contains the definitions for English and European page sizes, envelope sizes, index cards, standard plotter sizes, and so forth. Application writers are free to update this key; so if you have a form that prints correctly in one place but not another, you might need to install the application to get the form.
>
> - The `Monitors` key contains keys for the various printer monitors. Examples include the LPRMON monitor for using Line Printer, the USBMON for printing to USB devices, and so forth.
>
> - The `Printers` key contains specific parameters and drivers for a particular printer. This information is not generally displayed in the UI, but will be present on the test page.
>
> - The `Providers` key lists the network print providers.

Managing Printing

There are as many different ways to connect computers to printers as there are ways for people to communicate with each other. In general, print topologies fall into five categories:

- **Printing to a local print device.** The print device is connected to the Windows 2000 machine via a parallel port, serial port, USB port, or infrared port.

- **Printing to a network print server device.** The print device has an associated network interface that can understand and respond directly to network print commands. Examples include the HP JetDirect, Castelle LANpress, Intel NetPort, and the x-crowd: Lantronix, Xionics, Emulex, and Extended Systems.

- **Printing to a Windows server.** A Windows 2000 or down-level Windows server that has a printer (logical device) configured as a shared resource. The shared printer accepts print jobs from other computers and despools them to a locally attached print device or a network print server device.

- **Printing to a UNIX server.** Windows 2000 includes a Line Printer (LPR) service for printing to UNIX servers or TCP/IP network print devices. There is also a Line Printer Daemon (LPD) driver that enables UNIX clients to print to Windows 2000 Server or Professional.

- **Printing to a third-party server.** A third-party server that hosts a shared print queue of some sort. A Windows computer prints to this server via the appropriate network client redirector.

- **Printing over the Internet.** A Windows 2000 or third-party server hosts a shared print queue that is exposed via the new *Internet Printing Protocol* (IPP).

- **Printing from mainframe hosts.** This bit of arcanery falls beyond the scope of this book, not because mainframe printing is not a system administrator's problem, but because it involves that most awful of marriages: APPN (Advanced Peer-to-Peer Networking) over SNA to SMB over IP. Just the acronyms themselves are enough to make you want to change professions. For a good reference on this technology, take a look at *Introduction to SNA Networking*, by Jay Ranade. For specifics on mainframe printing in a Windows environment, look at the documentation that comes with SNA Server.

After a printer has been created at a Windows 2000 computer, it can be shared on the network as long as the Server service is operational on the computer. This even applies to a printer that prints to a printer on another server. Users who connect to these shared printers from Windows 2000 computers automatically download drivers and the configuration settings for the shared printer.

Users can find these shared printers either by navigating with a browser or in the directory. As we go through the details of each topology, let's see how this sharing works and get a feel for what the user experiences when finding and using the shared printers.

Printing to a Local Print Device

The topology for a local print device is the simplest of the bunch. A print device is connected to a Windows 2000 server or workstation via a parallel port, serial port, infrared port, or USB port. The physical connection itself makes a difference because the printer setup involves selecting a port.

For the most part, driver installation goes automatically if you use a PnP compatible printer. Connect the printer to its port, turn on the printer, start the computer, and let the PnP enumerator do its job. Have a USB printer, and you don't even have to restart. Insert the USB connector from a live printer in the USB port on the computer and watch as the system finds the new device on the port, finds the driver from the hard drive (or prompts you for a disk), and makes all the peripheral adjustments. When the print device is available and running with the drivers installed, you're ready to make final configuration choices.

Installation Error Using PnP with Terminal Server

If you have Terminal Server services installed, you may get an error when using PnP to install printer drivers. The system does not put itself into Install mode when loading drivers for PnP printers. This should not be a problem because printer drivers are available in every session by definition; if you do experience a problem, however, you must de-install the printer, shift to Install mode using Set User /Change, and then reinstall the printer.

If you are not fortunate enough to have a PnP-compatible printer, proceed with the following installation steps:

Procedure 15.16 **Installing a Non-PnP-Compatible Printer**

1. From the Start button, select SETTINGS | PRINTERS. The Printers window appears with an Add Printer icon.

2. Double-click the Add Printer icon. The Add Printer wizard opens.

3. Click Next. The Local or Network Printer window opens. Select the Local Computer radio button. If you are installing a PnP printer without restarting the machine, try selecting Automatically Detect and Install My Plug and Play Printer. If you had the printer connected when you started the machine and the system didn't see it then, it's not likely to see it now.

4. Click Next. The Select the Printer Port window opens. All available logical ports will be listed under Use the Following Port. Select the port to which the printer is connected.

5. Click Next. The Add Printer Wizard window opens. This should actually be called the Select Printer Driver window. Select your printer from the list of manufacturers and models. If your printer is not on the list, select Have Disk and point the wizard at a floppy disk, CD, or network path that contains the printer driver and its associated INF file.

6. Click Next. The Name Your Printer window opens. If this printer is on a server, give the printer a name that helps your users pick it from a list. Avoid using the default printer name because you may have hundreds of them. The example uses the printer location for the printer name and the share name in the next step. This has the advantage of telling the user where the printer is located, but it means someone has to change the printer name each time the printer is moved (see Figure 15.19).

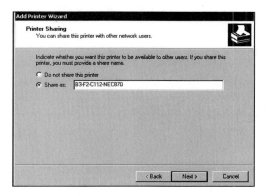

Figure 15.19 Printer Sharing window with Share As button selected and new share name based on location.

7. Click Next. The Printer Sharing window opens. The Share As radio button is selected by default. The wizard truncates long names to 8 characters for the benefit of DOS/Windows clients. The example uses a long name because there are no legacy machines on the network. You may not be so fortunate. Also, even if you use strictly 32-bit desktops, you may have 16-bit Windows applications that cannot print to a long printer name. You can enter a shorter share name, if required.

8. Click Next. The Location and Comment window opens. Enter information that helps the users differentiate between printers. This information is displayed in the Print windows of most 32-bit applications.

9. Click Next. The Print Test Page window opens. It is usually a good idea to print a test page because the information shows what drivers were loaded, their time and data and version, as well as other nice-to-know information about the printer. Keep the sheet in a file for future reference.

10. Click Next. A final completion window shows the selections you made.

11. Click Finish to complete the installation.

After the drivers load, the system prints a test page. The Troubleshoot button opens a Help file for identifying possible problems. This checklist is surprisingly good. It's obvious that someone let the tech support staff have a say in the contents. I recommend it.

If you install a PnP printer without restarting the machine and do not let the PnP enumerator do its job, you may find that the system discovers the device the next time you reboot. At this point, PnP is like a teenager asking for the car keys. It doesn't do any good to ignore it and there's not many ways to argue. You'll probably need to install the printer again. It doesn't take long now that the drivers have been installed.

If the printer is shared, users can access immediately. This brings up issues of managing print queues, managing the printers themselves, managing security, and cost distribution. Unfortunately, Windows 2000 can't help with the last item. Let's take a look at the other three.

Managing Print Queues

You can use the Printer window to check the status of documents in the Print queue and manage both the printer as a whole and individual documents in the print queue. You must have at least Print Operator privileges in the domain or Power User privileges on a standalone machine to manage the queue and its documents. Proceed as follows:

Procedure 15.17 Managing Print Queues

1. Open the Printer window using START | SETTINGS | PRINTERS.

2. Double-click the printer icon. This opens a window with the same name as the printer that displays the jobs in the queue. The example shows the printer paused with one job waiting. (see Figure 15.20).

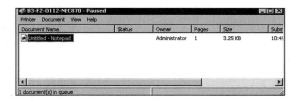

Figure 15.20 Print window showing a paused printer with one job waiting.

3. From the menu, select PRINTER to see the available options. Most of them are self-explanatory. Here are a few items of note:

   Set as Default flags the associated printer as the default for all print jobs sent from applications. This satisfies a standard Win32 API call that many applications make when they launch. Applications that need a printer will fail if there is no default printer configured for the machine.

   Use Printer Offline enables you to send jobs to the queue without getting errors about inability to find a network printer or a locally connected printer to a docking station. Deselecting this option dumps the print jobs to the printer.

   Pause Printing halts all despool activity, but the Spooler will continue to accept new jobs.

4. Click in a neutral area to lift the menu, and then click Document to see the options. These permit the user to exercise fine control over a document in the queue. The user does not have rights to pause the entire queue, but his or her individual jobs can be paused, resumed, or canceled. Canceling the job deletes it from the queue. Resume picks up at the next page, and Restart begins from the first page of the document.

5. Click in a neutral area to lift the menu, and then right-click the document in the queue and select PROPERTIES from the fly-out menu. This opens the Properties window for the individual document.

   The General tab gives information about the job, including the number of pages, assigned data type, name of the print processor (which is always WINPRINT unless the job came from a Macintosh, in which case the system uses SFMPSPRT), time of submittal, and the job's owner.

   The Layout tab control orientation with an Advanced button to show specialized options for the device. These options come from the minidriver coded by the vendor. Examples of printers with a rich feature set include the Xerox DocuCenter printers that have windows that enable you to build folio books with covers.

   The Paper/Quality tab has options for selecting resolution, color matching, paper source, and so forth.

6. Click OK to close the window. Proceed to the next section to see how to set default options for the printer itself rather than individual documents.

Troubleshooting Local Printing Failures

Troubleshooting for printing problems should start with the physical layer. Is the printer turned on? Is it plugged in? Is it connected to the computer? Does the serial printer have the right cable pinouts? I'm sure you know the drill. There are more subtle factors that can affect local printing after you've eliminated the common faults.

- **Bidirectional printing enabled.** Windows 2000 and its classic NT predecessors use bidirectional printing. If you have an older print cable that does not have pinout for two-way communications, the system will either refuse to build the printer or print jobs will hang in the queue periodically. Also, check CMOS for the printer port configuration. Often an EPP/ECP port is set to another configuration that does not support two-way communications.

- **Job in the wrong queue.** If you have a job in the queue that was supposed to be sent to another queue, you cannot drag and drop it to another printer. You must cancel the job and print it again to the correct printer. This is because the print job has already been rendered using the driver associated with the first queue. Moving it to another queue would mean it could possible be incorrectly formatted for the target printer.

- **Jobs print partial pages or odd characters.** If the printed output includes control characters, Postscript code, lacks graphics characters that were in the document, or otherwise does not seem correct based on the screen display, look for a problem with the default data type. Open the Properties window for the printer, select the Advanced tab, click Print Processor, and select a different default data type. If you have UNIX clients who constantly complain that their jobs are getting fouled up in the print queue, for example, create a new printer for them and change the default data type for that printer to TEXT.

- **Slow or erratic print performance.** If you are printing locally from a Windows 2000 Professional desktop and the jobs print very slowly, or the performance at the tube gets erratic, you need more memory or a faster processor or both. If the user demands fast printing but doesn't want to pay thousands for a new machine, one alternative is a network print device. The second-tier pricing on print servers has actually gotten rather reasonable and they all work with Windows 2000 and NT in one way or another. This will not only dramatically improve printing performance, but will make the printer placement more flexible.

- **Inadequate rights to spool directory.** If you set up a printer for a user and it worked fine, but now the user can't get it to work, look for NTFS permissions set on the \WINNT\System32\Spool directory that might be restricting the user's access. You can either change the permissions or change the location of the spool directory.

- **Printer paused or offline.** The printer may be paused or set for offline use, or the document itself may be paused. This one is particularly nasty because no errors are given to the user. The jobs just build up in the queue until the user runs out of patience or disk space or both. A network printer cannot be set for offline. Only Printer Operators and above have the rights to pause a queue. The user can pause a document. Documents from other users will print around it, but no documents from that user will print.

- **PnP error.** If the driver was installed automatically by PnP, check the Device Manager to see whether there is an error. This is especially important if you are using a serial printer. The fastest way to get to the Device Manager is to right-click My Computer and select MANAGE from the fly-out menu. This opens the Computer Management console. Select Device Manager and look for exclamation points. One common error is parallel ports on older machines that lack bidirectional capability, or that use a non-standard IOBase address. You do not ordinarily get IRQ problems with parallel ports, but watch out for add-on devices that either keep the port from working with a printer or demand that IRQ7 be used when Windows 2000 does not enable it by default. If you are using a second parallel port on a legacy machine, make sure that IRQ5 is enabled for legacy devices in BIOS and that it is the IRQ assigned by Device Manager.

- **Verify proper driver.** Windows 2000 drivers changed from NT4. It's not likely that the printer came with WDM drivers for Windows 2000. The Windows 98 drivers would probably work, but the INF script will probably not install them properly, if at all. Check the vendor's Web site. There is no special driver directory on the CD. All drivers are incorporated into PnP.

Managing Printer Properties

You can use the Properties window for the printer to change the default configuration for jobs and to fine-tune the driver options. Details on several of the options are contained in the following section. Proceed as follows:

Procedure 15.18 **Changing Default Print Job Configurations**

1. Right-click the printer icon and select PROPERTIES from the fly-out menu. The `Properties` window for the printer opens with the General tab displayed. This enables you to change the entries you made when you created the printer (see Figure 15.21).

Figure 15.21 `Printer Properties` window showing the `General` tab.

2. Select the `Sharing` tab. Click `Additional Drivers`. The `Additional Drivers` window opens. This window permits you to add more drivers to support other Windows clients that can automatically download drivers (see Figure 15.22).

Figure 15.22 `Additional Drivers` window showing list of clients that can download drivers automatically from Windows 2000 servers. Each client requires a different printer driver.

3. Select one of the options (for example, the Intel environment for Windows 95/98).

4. Click OK. The system downloads the drivers from the Windows 2000 CD. This CD contains printer drivers for all Windows platforms. If you have a third-party driver, select Have Disk and install the proper driver.

5. At the Sharing tab, select List in Directory and click Apply. This creates a Shared Printer object in the Directory. If you create the printer using PnP on a domain controller or member server, this option is selected by default. Figure 15.23 shows an example of the Directory object for the shared printer.

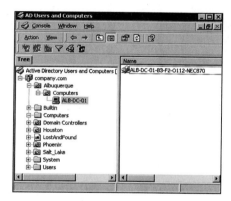

Figure 15.23 Directory object for shared printer placed by Add Printer Wizard shortcut.

6. Select the Ports tab. This lists the available ports on the server with annotations for those with printers attached. The Configure Port button opens windows with options for the port. You can change the transmission timeout for LPT ports and adjust the bit rate, framing, parity and stop settings, and flow control for a serial port (see Figure 15.24).

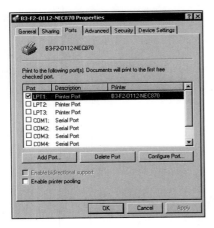

Figure 15.24 Ports tab showing available ports with annotation for ports that are in use.

7. Select the Advanced tab. Table 15.3 in the next section lists details about the options and examples of when they might be useful.

8. Click Print Processor. The Print Processor window opens to show the selected print processor for this printer and its associated data types. Under nearly all circumstances, this option is never used. It is here to permit you to select an alternative print processor provided for special purposes. For example, a vendor might write a special processor tuned for host printing from mainframes.

9. Click Separator Page. The Separator Page window opens prompting you to specify or browse for a file that holds a separator page. Separator pages help users find their jobs in a stack at a network printer. NetWare calls these *banner pages*. They are also called *burst pages* because they are used to separate green-bar paper. Separator page files have an .SEP extension. 10. Select the Device Settings tab. The options in this window are determined by the printer driver and vary for different makes and models of printers. One especially handy feature is the ease with which Postscript font lists can be modified. If a particular printer does not have a certain font, you can use this list to troubleshoot or designate an alternative. If Available Printer Memory (or Postscript Memory) is set too high, a large job with lots of graphics may stall or continually respool. Determine the correct setting by printing a test page using the printer's front panel.

11. Click OK to save any changes.

The next section contains more information about print options.

Additional Print Options

Quite a few features and configuration options are available for printers. The preceding section covered the general options. This section covers the following additional options:

- Setting advanced options in `Printer Properties`
- Configuring printer pooling
- Using the `List in Directory` shortcut
- Creating separator pages

Setting Advanced Options in `Printer Properties`

The `Advanced` print options in `Printer Properties` window contain a variety of selections. See Figure 15.25 for an example of the window. Table 15.3 lists the options, their functions, and gives examples and cautions when selecting the options.

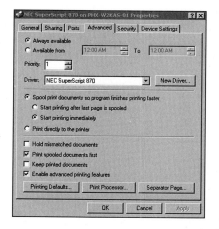

Figure 15.25   Printer Properties – `Advanced` tab.

Table 15.3 **Advanced Print Options**

Option	Function	Examples and Cautions
`Available From`	Assign the hours that the printer will despool to its print device. Print jobs submitted at other times are queued.	If your organization has a color printer that employees can use after hours, you can create a printer and set the `Available From` option so that jobs print at night.
`Priority`	If you have multiple printers that despool to the same print device, Spooler will ordinarily alternate between the two queues. If you want jobs in one queue to print in front of jobs in another queue, set the `Priority` value higher.	You may have a large-format printer owned by the Art department but sometimes used by Technical Documentation. If the graphic designers grouse that they have to wait for the technical writers— I speak from experience on this subject — you can create a separate printer for the graphic designers with a higher priority.
`Driver`	If you get a new driver for a printer, or you change the print device associated with a printer, use this button to load the new driver. If the printer is shared, users who connect to it automatically download the new drivers.	If you change drivers, the installation script may change the name of the printer. If this happens, the connected print clients can no longer use the shared printer even though the share name has not changed. Before installing a driver into an existing printer, copy the printer name to the Clipboard in case you need to reapply it.
`Spool Print Documents … / Start Printing Immediately`	This tells Spooler to accept the incoming print job, render the byte stream as it comes, and despool it to the print device simultaneously.	This option speeds up printing large documents. If the job fails to print for some reason and Spooler is notified of this by the print monitor, the job is permitted to complete spooling, and then it is set to the print device again.

Option	Function	Examples and Cautions
`Print Directly to Printer`	This tells Spooler to bypass local storage of the job. The job is rendered on-the-fly and sent directly to the print device.	If the printer is shared, this option is ignored.
`Hold Mismatched Documents`	This tells Spooler to make sure the printer setup matches the document setup.	If the printer uses a raster driver but the incoming print job is Postscript, this option holds the job. A job cannot be moved to another queue, so the only alternative is to cancel the job and print it again to the correct printer.
`Print Spooled Documents First`	Spooler favors spooled jobs over incoming jobs If two jobs spool at once, Spooler favors the larger job. This option is used in conjunction with the `Start Printing Immediately` option.	Under normal circumstances, Spooler chooses the next job to print based solely on the assigned priority. This means a high-priority, 500-page job that might take an hour to print would get attention while a little 1-page job that has already spooled sits and waits. With this option, the spooled job prints first.
`Keep Printed Documents`	This option holds the spool file after the document prints.	Sometimes it is important that a document print right the first time. For example, accounting packages print reports as part of the end-of-month and end-of-year closings. It is difficult to go back and print the report again if the job fails to complete. You can quickly run out of disk space if you leave it enabled for long.

continues ▸

Table 15.3 **Continued**

Option	Function	Examples and Cautions
`Enable Advanced Features`	With this option deselected, the Advanced options are not available.	If you experience compatibility problems when users take advantage of Advanced features exposed to the UI for their printer, you can deselect this option to disable certain features. The miniport driver must make explicit calls to this flag, however, so it might not resolve your problem.

Configuring Printer Pooling

If you have multiple printers of the same type, or at least that use the same print driver, you can use the `Enable Printer Pooling` option to group the printers into a single *printer pool*.

Print devices in the same printer pool share the same printer name. Assume, for example, that you have three older laser printers that are still serviceable but a bit slow. You can attach print devices to the server or use network print devices as shown in the next section. Then select `Enable Printer Pooling`, and check each printer to add it to the pool.

If a print job arrives and the first print device is busy, Spooler sends the job to the second device and so forth. Print jobs cascade from the first defined port to the last, so put the fastest printers on the first ports.

Using the `List in Directory` Shortcut

The `List in Directory` shortcut in the Add Printer Wizard places the Printer object under its associated server rather than in a designated OU. This prevents users from finding the printer by looking in the directory because Computer objects are not exposed to the UI as containers.

You can move the object later. Or, as shown in the "Printing to a Windows 2000 Server" section, it is easier to use the Search features to locate Printer objects in the directory than to navigate to them directly. This requires a little user training.

The List in Directory shortcut also concatenates the server name to the printer name to arrive at an object name. This appears to torpedo any carefully crafted system of naming shared printers you might have devised, but the server name is stripped off when the object is shown to users.

Creating Separator Pages

When many people use the same network printer, it can be difficult to sort through the jobs in the output tray. Separator pages help by putting a page between jobs that can be easily seen as you rifle through the stack.

Windows 2000 comes with four separator page files in the \WINNT\System32 directory:

- **PSCRIPT.SEP.** Puts a dual-mode printer in Postscript mode but *does not print a separator page.*

- **SYSPRINT.SEP.** Prints a separator page on a Postscript printer.

- **SYSPRTJ.SEP.** Same as SYSPRINT.SEP with the addition of special fonts that support Japanese language modules.

- **PCL.SEP.** Puts a dual-mode printer in PCL mode, and then prints the username, date, and job number of the print job.

The following is a sample separator file:

```
\
\H1B\L%-12345X@PJL ENTER LANGUAGE=PCL
\H1B\L&l1T\0
\M\B\S\N\U
\U\LJob : \I
\U\LDate: \D
\U\LTime: \T
\E
```

Table 15.4 lists the escape codes and their functions. If you want to switch a printer from Postscript to PCL without printing a separator page, for example, use the following separator file:

```
\
\H1B\L%-12345X@PJL ENTER LANGUAGE=PCL\0
```

Table 15.4   **Separator File Escape Codes and Their Functions**

Escape Code	Function
\N	Username of the submitter.
\I	Job number.
\D\T	Date and time.
\Lxxxx	This is an echo option. Prints the characters (xxxx) until another escape code is encountered. Use this to fill a line with characters to make the burst page distinctive.
\Fpathname	Prints contents of the specified file, starting on an empty line, without any processing. Use for printing custom informational messages.
\Hnn	Sets a printer-specific control sequence, where *nn* is a hexadecimal ASCII code. Refer to the printer manual for applicable codes.
\Wnn	Sets the width of the separator page. The default width is 80; the maximum width is 256. Any printable characters beyond this width are truncated.
\B\S	Prints text in single-width block characters.
\E	Page eject. Use to start a new separator page or to end the separator page file. If you get an extra blank separator page when you print, remove this code from your separator page file.
\n	Skips *n* number of lines (from zero through nine).
\B\M	Prints text in double-width block characters.
\U	Turns off block character printing.

Printing from DOS

A DOS application running inside a Virtual DOS Machine is as oblivious to innovations, such as GDI and WDM and font libraries, as a washboard maker is to Maytags. The DOS application expects to push bytes down an LPT port or bits down a COM port and nothing else is going to make it happy. Not only that, because development for DOS applications has dwindled somewhat over the past few years, it's difficult to find drivers for printers more modern than the HPLJII or Epson MX.

One of the functions of the NT Virtual DOS Machine (NTVDM.EXE) driver is to convert hardware function calls to the printer port into Win32 API calls. This works fine for well-behaved DOS applications that play by the ASCII rules and don't try to poke characters directly into the port or into memory to improve performance. Considering that half the coders in the 1980s were working hard at improving performance by breaking the rules, it's little wonder that some legacy applications don't like to print in Windows 2000.

If you have a well-behaved DOS application with drivers that work with modern printers, you should be able to print to a locally attached printer. The most common problems involve the way DOS applications treat a printer port. If the application just slams the file closed without sending an <EOF> byte, WINPRINT thinks the application is still printing. There are several symptoms of this problem:

- Print job doesn't run until the application is closed.

- Last page of a print job stays in the printer, requiring a page feed to clear it.

- DOS jobs get mangled together with pages from different reports and documents mixed up in the same hopper. This is caused by applications that do calculations between pages of the report that are long enough to cause the LPT timer to time out and accept jobs from another source.

If you get these symptoms, try setting the default data type to FF Appended. If you are printing to a NetWare server, don't expect the Capture command to solve the problem. The Capture command is not supported on NT.

If you are trying to print to a nonstandard port, such as a network print device or an IR printer, or you are trying to print from DOS to a printer connected to a network print server, there is no LPT port to keep the DOS application happy. You must give it an LPT port using the Net Use command. This is true even if the machine itself is acting as the despool server for the printer.

Assume, for example, that you have a Windows 2000 server that hosts a printer for a network print device such as an HP JetDirect card. The port for this device does not use LPT1 or LPT2; it uses a special port designed to print to the network device. If you want to print from a DOS application on this server, you must share the printer and redirect a printer port to the shared printer. If you do not want to share the printer, you won't be printing from DOS. The syntax for the printer port redirection is as follows:

```
net use lpt1: \\server_name\printer_share
```

The share name can be longer than eight characters because it is Windows 2000 connecting to the share, not DOS. The DOS application prints to LPT1, just like it would on a DOS machine. You can use any LPT port number between one and nine, but most older DOS applications don't recognize anything above three. You don't need to put the colon on the port number. (I do it just to be consistent.)

Printing to a Network Print Device

As businesses grow, they tend to cross a divide where they start to accept distributed printing technology rather than tethering printers to local machines or stringing cable back to the server room. They usually cross this divide when the person in the corner office signing the checks is inconvenienced enough with getting to the printer to fork over the 350-odd dollars it takes to buy a network print device. It's amazing that these devices still cost that much, but the vendors don't seem to be scurrying to lower their prices.

Printing to a network device means using a communication protocol and command language that the device understands.

- **Protocols.** Virtually all network print devices support the major communication protocols: TCP/IP, IPX/SPX, AppleTalk/EtherTalk, and DLC/LLC. Windows 2000 can use any or all of these communication protocols, although only TCP/IP is loaded by default.

- **Command languages.** Most network print devices run Line Printer Daemon (LPD) to support UNIX printing and NCP to support NetWare (bindery and NDS). Most have Macintosh support for printing Postscript, which requires no special control codes, and a native, proprietary driver for the manufacturer's printer. This last item uses DLC/LLC for a communication protocol.

Windows 2000 treats a network print device as if it were a locally connected printer. Instead of printing to an LPT or COM port, the system prints to an LPR port or a HP port. These special ports and their associated transport protocols must first be installed. Part of the installation includes a port monitor driver, such as LPRMON and HPMON.

This section covers setup and control of DLC-based printing and TPC/IP-based printing. In an IPX-only environment, it is possible to print to a network print device using NWLink at the Windows 2000 server, but that does not enable NetWare clients to use the shared printer. That requires a special product from Microsoft called Services for NetWare.

Network Printing Using DLC

The simplest way to communicate with a network print device is by using DLC/LLC. This stands for Data Link Control/Link Layer Control. In the OSI model, these two drivers sit right above the *Medium Access Control* (MAC) driver. The DLC driver is a pared-down version of IBM's High-Level Data Link Control protocol.

DLC is fast, requires very little overhead at the print device, and is get-down easy to set up. It does have its problems, however:

- **DLC is not routable.** You can use DLC within the same network segment only.

- **DLC can only bind to one network card at a time.** If you have a Windows print server with multiple NICs, only one of them can be used to support DLC printing.

- **DLC has few error-correcting capabilities.** DLC is prone to time-outs and erratic performance under heavy traffic.

The only time DLC is an acceptable option is in small offices that do not have a routed environment and do not want the hassle of working with TCP/IP printing.

Even though simple printing over DLC can be quickly configured at workstations, it is still a good idea to use a central server to act as a despool server. The clients print to the print server rather than directly to the network print device. DLC does not handle multiple clients very well. By letting one server handle the print queue, you'll get better results. It does not need to be a copy of Windows 2000 Server. You are permitted to have up to 10 connections to Windows 2000 Professional. DLC connections count as one of these connections.

Because DLC sits low enough in the networking food chain so that it deals with MAC addresses only, you do not need to do any special configurations at the network print device. By the same token, because the DLC driver sits below the *Transport Driver Interface* (TDI) layer, each high-level application must have its own DLC driver. The DLC driver that comes with Windows 2000 is paired to the HP JetDirect line of network print devices. The only other major line of network print devices that uses DLC is Lexmark, which comes with a LexLink DLC/LLC driver. This driver came with NT4, but you must download the most current driver from www.lexmark.com when you upgrade to Windows 2000.

Install the network print device and make sure it is connected to the network. The DLC client can discover the device as long as you are not in a routed environment. You cannot configure a home user to print using DLC over a RAS connection, for example, because the RAS server acts like a router. The user can print to a Windows print server over the RAS connection, and then the server can despool to the network print device via DLC. Print a test page to get the MAC address for the device. You'll need it to identify the card later on in the installation.

Before you can print to a network device using DLC, you must first install the DLC protocol at the Windows 2000 server or workstation. Do so as follows:

Procedure 15.19 **Installing the DLC Protocol**

1. Right-click My Network Places and select PROPERTIES from the fly-out menu. The Network and Dial-up Connections window opens.

2. Right-click the Local Connections icon and select PROPERTIES from the fly-out menu. The Local Area Connection Properties window opens (see Figure 15.26). If you have multiple network adapters, the protocols and clients you add in this window affects the other interfaces. (You may have noticed by now that Microsoft still has not quite conquered the art of assembling all the necessary tools into one place. There should be a single MMC for the various networking configurations.)

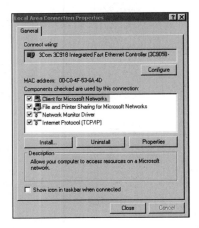

Figure 15.26 Local Area Connection Properties window.

3. Click Install. The Select Network Component Type window opens.

4. Highlight Protocol and click Add. The Select Network Protocol window opens.

5. Select DLC Protocol and click OK. The system prompts for the CD and installs the protocol. There are no configurable properties for the protocol itself.

6. Click Close to close the Properties window.

7. Now it's time to install the printer. Open the Printers window using START | SETTINGS | PRINTERS.

8. Double-click Add Printers. The Add Printer Wizard opens.

9. Click Next. The Local or Network Printer window opens.

10. Select the Local Printer radio button. Windows 2000 considers a network print device to be locally connected.

11. Deselect Automatically Detect and Install My Plug and Play Printer. The PnP enumerator cannot detect the printer because you have not made a network connection to it yet.

12. Click Next. The Select the Printer Port window opens.

13. Select the Create a New Port radio button. Instead of using an existing LPT or COM port, you are going to "create" a port using one of the port drivers in the Type list.

14. Under Type, select Hewlett-Packard Network Port. This is the default DLC port and port monitor. If you have another type of network print device, consult their literature to determine whether they support DLC/LLC, and then get their driver.

15. Click Next. The Add Hewlett-Packard Network Peripheral Port window opens.

16. Click Refresh. The list box fills with MAC addresses. If you have a large, flat network, it might take a while for this to happen.

17. Select the MAC address for the device you want to use. The number is copied automatically to the field above the pick list.

18. Under Name, enter a name for the device. This will become the port name, so keep it short. You should use the same name as that assigned to the device using JetAdmin. This helps future administrators who need to use JetAdmin and the Properties window for troubleshooting.

19. Click `Options`. The `Advanced Options for All HP Network Ports` window opens. You can modify these settings if requested by HP or Microsoft technical support; for the most part, however, they fall into the "fool with at your own risk" category. The one item you really need to be aware of is the `Adapter` entry. If you have multiple network adapters in the server, you must select the adapter that is on the same network segment as the network print device. DLC can only bind to one card.

20. Click `Cancel` to return to the `Add Hewlett-Packard Network Peripheral Port` window. Click `Timers`. The `HP Network Peripheral Port Timers` window opens.

Job-Based DLC Printing

When the DLC port monitor establishes a session with a network print device, a network print device will only accept a DLC connection from one port monitor at a time. The `Connection Based` option under `HP Network Peripheral Port Timers` ensures that a single print server takes control of that DLC connection.

If you have a small office and do not want to use a central print server, configure the workstations to print to the network print device, but change the `Connection` option to `Job Based`. The print monitors will make connection only long enough to send their print jobs.

21. Click `Cancel` to close the window, and then click `OK` to save the changes and close the `Add Hewlett-Packard Network Peripheral Port` window. At this point, the computer has established a connection to the network print device. The `Add Printer Wizard` window opens.

22. Select a manufacturer and model for the printer. If the correct entry is not on the list, click `Have Disk` and supply the driver from the manufacturer.

23. Click `Next`. The system prompts you for the CD, copies the driver files, and updates the Registry. If you already have a printer of the same type configured on the machine, The `Use Existing Driver` window opens to enable you to either keep the current driver or to replace it with a new driver. The existing printer will be affected if you replace the drive, so be sure you have the most current version.

24. Next, assign a `Name` to the printer. Once again, you should give it a name that is unique and easy for users to locate. The name must be less than eight characters for DOS clients.

25. Click `Next`. The `Printer Sharing` window opens. Share the printer with a name that fits your naming scheme.

26. Click `Next`. The `Location and Comment` window opens. Give enough detail about the printer to help users who see the information on the network. This information is copied into the directory to help search for printers.

27. Click Next. The Print Test Page window opens. Leave the Yes radio button selected.

28. Click Next. A final summary window appears.

29. Click Finish to save the changes and create the printer. When the files have been copied, a prompt appears concerning the test page. If you do not get a test page, see the sections that cover troubleshooting later in this chapter.

Printing to a TCP/IP Host

Windows 2000 is an IP product, so it's natural to want to use IP for printing. Most network print device vendors have special tools to configure IP parameters for their products. HP JetDirect comes with JetAdmin, for example, which has a lot of features but can be gruesome to use in a big network. Intel NetPort and LexMark cards are easier to configure because they come with embedded HTTP servers. You can also print to a UNIX host that is running Line Printer Daemon, LPD.

In any case, here are a few considerations when configuring IP printing:

- **Static IP or DHCP.** Any server that prints to the network print device will need to know its IP address. That IP address should never change. You can accomplish this by assigning a static address on the card or by reserving an address in DHCP or BOOTP for the card's MAC address. Reserving the address in DHCP gives you central control and a way to quickly determine whether the card is online. If you change the IP address of the gateway or need to make other changes to core IP services such as DNS or WINS, you can deploy that information to the network print devices quickly and easily. If you ever lose that DHCP or BOOTP database and do not have a record somewhere of the addresses you reserved, however, you are going to be scrambling.

- **Multiple node printing or centralized printing.** Unlike DLC, most top-of-the-line network print devices do a good job of managing print jobs coming from multiple IP clients. If you have a few users and do not want to bother with a central print server, you can configure the users to print directly to the network print device. The lack of centralized queue management limits the usefulness of this option in a good-sized network.

- **WINS or DNS.** Most new adapters have IP stacks capable of registering themselves with WINS and Dynamic DNS. The advantages should be obvious. You can configure workstations to print to the device using its friendly name. You can go down the list of registrations to discover your device status. You can use friendly names in management software. The only downside to having network devices registered in DNS or WINS is that you must make sure the assignment changes if you decide to change the name or move the printer to another segment and change its IP address.

- **SNMP.** Network print devices that support SNMP are becoming more and more common. If you want to spend the extra few dollars, you'll have a device that not only will trap to a management console, it can also be managed from that same console. It's a big win if you have the existing infrastructure. It's not worth the effort if the only thing you're going to manage is printing. You do not need SNMP on the Windows 2000 print server to take advantage of SNMP on the network print device, but it really doesn't make sense to manage one without the other.

After the network print device has been configured with an IP address, you're ready to connect to it from a Windows 2000 server or workstation. First, however, you must install Print Services for UNIX on the Windows 2000 computer. This installs the necessary Line Printer (LPR) client and LPR port monitor along with a Line Printer Daemon driver (LPDSVC) that enables UNIX clients to print to the shared printer on the Windows 2000 server. The LPD service has no settings. It just exposes all shared printers as UNIX print queues.

Registry Tip
The Registry settings that control the LPD service are located in the following keys:

```
Key:     HKLM | System | CurrentControlSet | Services | LPDSVC | Parameters
Values:  AllowJobRemoval | AllowPrinterResume | and MaxConcurrentUsers (set for 64 by
         default)
```

Procedure 15.20 **Configuring TCP/IP Printing**

1. Right-click My Network Places and select PROPERTIES from the fly-out menu. The Network and Dial-up Connections window opens.

2. From the menu, select ADVANCED | OPTIONAL NETWORKING COMPONENTS. The Windows Optional Networking Components Wizard opens.

3. Select `Other Network File and Print Services` and click `Details`. The `Other Network File and Print Services` window opens.

4. Select `Print Services for UNIX` and click `OK` to return to the Optional Networking Components Wizard.

5. Click `Next` to install the drivers. The window closes and returns to the `Network and Dial-up Connections` window. At this point, the LPR and LPD drivers are installed along with the LPRMON port monitor.

Using LPR Without Creating a Printer

You can print a document via LPR without creating a printer by using the LPR command with following syntax:

`lpr -S server_name -Q queue_name file_name`.

6. Now install the printer. Open the `Printers` window using START | SETTINGS | PRINTERS.

7. Double-click `Add Printers`. The Add Printer Wizard opens.

8. Click `Next`. The `Local or Network Printer` window opens.

9. Select the `Local Printer` radio button. Remember that the server considers the network printer to be locally connected.

10. Deselect `Automatically Detect and Install my Plug and Play Printer`.

11. Click `Next`. The `Select the Printer Port` window opens.

12. Select the `Create a New Port` radio button.

13. Under Type, select `LPR Port`. The port monitor for this port, LPRMON, knows how to communicate using Line Printer Protocol to a host running LPD.

14. Click `Next`. The `Add LPR Compatible Printer` window opens.

15. Enter the fully qualified DNS name or IP address of the LPD server. Use a DNS name if possible so that you can change the IP address of the network print device without reconfiguring the Windows 2000 printer. If the network print device or UNIX host has more than one print queue, you must specify the name of the queue. Otherwise, leave the Name of Printer or Printer Queue field blank.

Troubleshooting Queue Name Problems

When the Windows 2000 LPR client first contacts an LPD host, it specifies the name of the queue it wants to use. The host sends back a list of available queues. If the two names do not match exactly, the connection fails. Use Network Monitor to sniff the traffic and see exactly what the LPD server is expecting to see.

16. Click OK to save the changes and return to the wizard. If the wizard cannot connect to an LPD service on the specified device, you will get an error message *Specified Port Cannot Be Added. Operation Could Not Be Completed.*

17. At this point, the computer has established a connection to the network print device. The wizard opens the Add Printer Wizard window.

18. Select a manufacturer and model for the printer. If the correct entry is not on the list, click Have Disk and supply the driver from the manufacturer.

19. Click Next. The system prompts you for the CD, copies the driver files, and updates the Registry. If you already have a printer of the same type configured on the machine, the Use Existing Driver window opens to enable you to either keep the current driver or replace it with a new driver. The existing printer will be affected if you replace the drive, so be sure you have the most current version.

20. Click Next. Assign a Name to the printer. You should give it a name that is unique and easy for users to locate. The name must be fewer than eight characters for DOS clients.

21. Click Next. The Printer Sharing window opens. Share the printer with a name that fits your naming scheme.

22. Click Next. The Location and Comment window opens.

23. Click Next. The Print Test Page window opens. Leave the Yes radio button selected.

24. Click Next. A final summary window appears.

25. Click Finish to save the changes and create the printer. When the files have been copied, a prompt appears concerning the test page. If you do not get a test page, begin troubleshooting.

Printing to a Windows 2000 Server

The printing examples up to this point have been directly to a printer, either locally connected or on the network. In those cases, the metafiles are spooled to the local hard drive and the final print rendering occurs locally. This section covers sending print jobs to a printer on a Windows 2000 server.

Any Windows client—Windows 3.1x, Windows 9x, classic NT, Windows 2000—can print to a shared printer on a Windows 2000 server as long as the user has sufficient access rights. The print jobs run a bit faster between Windows 2000 clients and Windows 2000 servers because the EMF file format is tighter, but you won't see noticeable improvement after upgrading from NT4 unless you print huge documents.

The 32-bit Windows clients—Windows 9x and classic NT—can download drivers automatically when they connect to a shared printer. To use this feature, you must load the correct drivers on the server. The client printer drivers are on the Windows 2000 Server CD.

You must have Print Operator rights or higher to add a printer at a client desktop. When ready, proceed as follows:

Procedure 15.21 **Printing to a Windows 2000 Server**

1. From the Start button, open START | SEARCH | FOR PRINTERS. The Find Printers window opens. The system can do searches based on partial entries in any of the search fields. If the user is in Bldg B, for example, he could enter a *B*" in Location and that would retrieve all the printers starting with *B*. In the examples, I have used building location as the printer name because it helps down-level users who rely on browsing. After you get a purely Windows 2000 network, or at least one where all clients can use the directory, you have more freedom in your naming scheme.

2. Select the Features tab. Enter the desired features, such as paper size, speed, and options.

3. Click Find Now. After searching the directory, a list of printers appears.

4. Locate the printer to which you want to connect.

5. Right-click the printer name and select CONNECT from the fly-out menu.

6. The system locates the server hosting the shared printer, downloads the drivers, and returns to the Find Printers window.

7. Close the window.

8. Open the Printers folder using START | SETTINGS | PRINTERS. The new printer will have an icon on the list.

Troubleshooting Print Clients

Corrupted print drivers at the server will affect any new print clients that download the corrupted drivers. If you suspect you have a problem with corrupted printer drivers, try deleting the drivers at the desktop, and then installing the drivers locally from CD. If this works but a subsequent reconnection to the server still fails, reinstall the printer at the server. You may need to delete the printer connection at the affected clients, remove the old driver files and reconnect to the printer server to download the fresh drivers.

The Windows 2000 client connection to the printer server uses Remote Procedure Calls. If you experience network problems, these RPC connections can break and cause client printing to fail. After a print client has lost RPC, it generally cannot regain it without a restart.

If you have ongoing RPC problems, you may find that you get equally good performance with less hassle by using TCP/IP printing. Configure LPD at the Windows 2000 server and LPR at the desktop. The one disadvantage of this configuration is that users cannot use the directory connect to the printer. They must use the Add Printer option.

Printing to a Third-Party Server

Except for using the directory for locating shared printers, the user takes the same steps for printing to a third-party printer as a Windows 2000 printer.

The network client redirector is responsible for finding servers with shared printers and listing them in the Add Printers display.

The print jobs themselves are rendered locally and sent to the third-party server using the client redirector. This is different from Windows 2000 printing, which creates a quick metafile locally and then ships it off via RPC for the server to render. It generally takes more horsepower at the client desktop to use third-party network printing.

If you are printing to NetWare print servers, you will get a speed advantage by upgrading to NetWare 5 and going to pure IP printing. This is not so much a factor of the increased speed of IP over IPX from the client's perspective, but because you can eliminate NWLink as a transport protocol. Much of the delay in the client redirector comes from inefficiencies in NWLink.

Printing over the Internet

Windows 2000 supports the new *Internet Printing Protocol* (IPP) as outlined in a series of RFCs and Internet Drafts. Visit www.normos.org and search for IPP. There are at least a dozen papers on the subject. In its fundamental form, IPP uses HTTP to frame printer traffic across the Internet. This is relatively slow and clumsy, but has the advantage of convenience and extremely low price.

Placing the print job inside HTTP also enables you to finesse printed documents through firewalls. You can print a drawing or report at a customer's site rather than faxing it. Microsoft also points out in their documentation that vendors such as Kinko's could use IPP to accept print jobs from customers. (Personally, I would not want to be the administrator of a print server that accepts unsolicited jobs from customers all over the world, but that's only one guy's opinion.)

It's only a matter of time before network print device manufacturers build in IPP into their cards. Until then, it is necessary to provide IPP print services from a Web host. Windows 2000 uses Internet Information Server for this purpose. To get IPP, you must load Web services on your print server. The mix is not always a good one. Print servers are one of the most mission-critical servers an organization has. They should never go down. Web servers, on the other hand, tend to need rebooting on a regular basis.

One way to get around this problem is to connect to the production printer queues from the server running Web services. This publishes the secondary printer queues while leaving the main printer queues intact should the Web server need rebooting.

Installing IIS to Support Internet Printing

You must have IIS running on the print server to use Internet Printing. Install IIS as follows:

Procedure 15.22 **Installing IIS**

1. Open CONTROL PANEL | ADD REMOTE PROGRAMS.
2. Click Add/Remove Windows Components. The Windows Component Wizard window opens.
3. Select the Internet Information Services option. Install all components. You may not need FTP or NNTP or SMTP right now, but who knows what small but important piece of functionality you'll need in the future?
4. Click Next. The system loads the drivers. You may be prompted for the CD.
5. After the drivers have finished loading, the Windows Component Wizard closes automatically. You do not need to restart the machine.

Verify that IIS is loaded and functioning by launching Internet Explorer and entering an address of http://localhost. You should get a Site Under Construction window. You do not need to load any default Web pages or do any further work to get IPP functionality.

Configuring a Client for Internet Printing

You can connect to a Windows 2000 shared printer over IPP in two different ways. One is to specify a URL in the Add Printer Wizard. The other is to use a fairly nifty front end in IIS that automates the whole process. First, the dull way: Launch the Add Printer Wizard and proceed as outlined in the "Printing to a Windows 2000 Server" section earlier in this chapter. When you reach the point where you must specify a printer, select the URL option and enter the URL for the printer. Figure 15.27 shows an example. The syntax is as follows:

```
http://server_name/printers/shared_printer_name/.printer
```

Watch out for the dot before the word `printer`. The entry will not work without it.

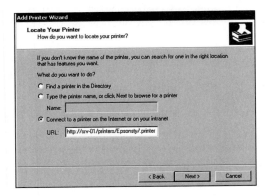

Figure 15.27   Add Printer Wizard showing entry for Internet printing.

When you enter the name, the system prompts you with a warning if the local machine does not have the correct drivers. Acknowledge this warning. IIS will download the drivers to you automatically across the Internet connection. This can take a while because you're transferring files inside HTTP, but they aren't very big and it eventually finishes. At this point, you have a fully functioning printer on the local machine that is configured to print via IPP to the print server. Now for the nifty way to use IPP.

Procedure 15.23   **Configuring a Client for Internet Printing**

1. Open Internet Explorer on a Windows client.
2. Point the browser at the name or IP address of the IIS server you just installed. You should get the `Under Construction` page.
3. Add **/printer** to the end of the address (no dot this time). This opens a `Printer` page that lists the shared printers on the server. Figure 15.28 shows an example. If you are not already logged on to the same domain as the print/Web server, you will be prompted for credentials. The system uses Kerberos as the preferred authenticator, followed by NTLM Challenge/Response, followed by clear text. If you want users from outside your organization to print to your printers, you must give them access. Consider placing the print server outside the firewall in the DMZ.

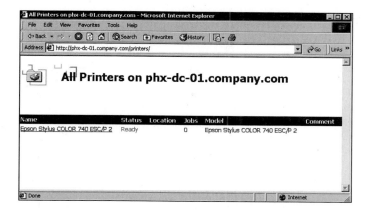

Figure 15.28 Printers page displayed after connection to IIS server hosting printer shares.

4. Click a printer name on the list. The system displays information about that printer.

5. Click Properties in the list of hyperlinks along the left side of the page. The properties of the printer display.

6. Under Printer Actions at the left of the page, click Connect. The printer drivers are copied across the Internet connection and the print is installed and configured on the local computer.

After the local printer connection has been made, the local printer communicates to the print server using the fastest protocol available. If both the client and server are on the same network, they negotiate an RPC connection. If they are connected across the Internet, they use HTTP. This IIS printer selection trick works for IE5 only. No other users will see the Connect option.

Troubleshooting Internet Printing

I'm going to repeat a tip from the body of the topic because it is important and easy to miss. When connecting to a Windows 2000 printer using a URL, the syntax is as follows:

```
http://server_name/printers/shared_printer_name/.printer
```

The dot in the entry /.printer is important.

Authentication is another problem with IPP. An Internet user normally browses an IIS server as IUSER, a special account set up for anonymous access. The IUSER account does not have access to the printers. The user will need an account in the domain or on the print server. Most administrators—myself included—take a dim view of letting outside individuals have accounts, especially an account that is likely to get passed around to friends. Imagine coming in one morning and seeing 50 pages sitting in the output hopper of a four-color plotter that costs $25/page in materials alone.

You can provide Internet printing to your own users and be relatively confident that the Kerberos or NTLM authentication will protect your system. If you want to provide print services to anonymous users, my advice is to put the print server in the DMZ and be prepared for a few denial-of-paper attacks.

If you cannot get a complete list of printers in the Printers page under IIS, you may have configured them to pause or go offline. If that isn't the problem, try stopping and starting the Spooler and then the WWW service. Finally, reinstalling the printer can resolve the problem.

Printer Security and Policies

Printer security is based around controlling management of the printers themselves (logical devices, not physical), the documents in the print queue, and the authorization to print to the device. Three basic rights are associated with printers:

- **Print.** The right to submit a print job to the printer
- **Manage Printers.** The right to create and delete printers, pause and start the queues, and change printer properties
- **Manage Documents.** The right to delete and change the properties of jobs in the queue other than the jobs submitted by that person

Print jobs waiting in the queue have NTFS rights if the spool directory is on an NTFS volume. The owner of the spooled files is the person who submitted the print job. The Manage Documents right essentially gives rights to the files in the SPOOL | PRINTERS directory.

The ACL for printers can be viewed by opening the Printer window, selecting PRINTER | PROPERTIES from the menu, and then selecting the Security tab. The standard rights are as follows:

- **Administrators.** Full Control
- **Creator/Owner.** Manage Documents

- **Everyone.** Print
- **Print Operators** (Power Users on standalone machine). Full Control
- **Server Operators.** Full Control

If you want to restrict access to a printer—for example, you don't want the whole company to print to the $150K IRIS printer—you can assign users and groups to the ACL and give them appropriate rights.

A list of special rights can also be assigned using group policies. Like all policies, they can be assigned to a domain, to a site, to an OU, and to specific groups within these containers. Policies apply to Windows 2000 users only, so you need to take steps to control down-level users during your upgrade deployment. This can be done using Policy Editor for Windows clients and brute-force management edicts for all others. The group policy rights can be accessed from the Group Policy Editor under ADMINISTRATIVE TEMPLATES | PRINTERS. The rights that can be controlled by policy include the following:

- Allow printers to be published
- Automatically publish new printers in the Active Directory
- Allow pruning of published printers
- Printer browsing
- Down-level printer pruning
- Directory pruning interval
- Directory pruning retry
- Directory pruning priority
- Check published state
- Web-based printing
- Custom support URL in the Printers folder's left pane
- Computer location
- Pre-populate printer search location text

The pruning options enable the system to remove printer objects from the directory when they are no longer available. This can cause problems in a WAN if you regularly lose connections to network print devices. Otherwise, without pruning you must go through the directory by hand and delete unused queues. Life has other, more splendid tasks in store.

Moving Forward

If this were a book on home construction, this would be the place to have a house-warming party. Shared resources are in place, so users can store their files and print their documents. The directory is primed and ready with folder objects and printer objects so that the users can find those shared resources. Security systems are functioning to make sure everyone stays honest. By and large, the system is ready for users. The next chapter shows how to configure the users' desktop environment so that the users can take advantage of all these resources that have been prepared for them.

16

Managing the User Operating Environment

Since the advent of Windows 95 and NT4, the standard Windows user interface was been defined by the look and feel of the Explorer shell. No other third-party shell gained even a paltry mindshare, at least in corporate America.

The look and feel, as well as operation, of the Explorer shell is defined by a Registry hive, NTUSER.DAT, a set of folders and files that, taken together, are called the *user profile*. The secret to managing large numbers of users is finding ways to manage the user profiles that reside on their desktops.

At first glance, it looks as though very little changed in the Windows 2000 Explorer shell. The icons are a bit gaudier and a few new menu options are available, but for the most part all the old Desktop components survived. This is not necessarily a bad thing. Users take a long time to get accustomed to an operating environment. Change comes slowly. Even some Linux interfaces are beginning to mimic the Explorer shell to simplify the operating environment for users.

This is not to say that a lot of the plumbing underneath Explorer didn't undergo extensive renovation in Windows 2000. Several of the components changed dramatically, especially in the area of user profiles and profile handling.

In addition to group policies, this chapter covers these aspects of user environment management:

- **Managing User Profiles.** This section covers configuration and control of the files, folders, and Registry hives that govern the Explorer shell.

- **Managing Home Directories.** The user profile in Windows 2000 provides special folders for user data, but nothing is quite so convenient as a good, old-fashioned home directory.

- **Group Policies.** This is the big news in Windows 2000 desktop management. Policies have come a long way from the Registry hacks in Windows 95 and NT4. Windows 2000 Group policies are much more configurable and have quite a few more features. This section covers the nuts and bolts of group policies (quite a few exist), and then steps through configuration, management, and troubleshooting of several example policies.

- **Logon Scripting.** The days of cobbling together batch files and Kix scripts might finally come to an end. This section covers the distributed script management in Windows 2000 and the new script options.

- **Folder Redirection.** Trying to convince users to keep their files on servers where they can be backed up and protected is a never-ending struggle. Folder redirection represents a new approach by taking advantage of the standardized file locations in Windows 2000 logo applications. This section covers the mechanics of folder redirection and shows a few things to watch out for.

- **Legacy DOS and WIN16 Application Support.** Old applications never die, and they don't fade away very quickly, either. Just because a shiny new operating system is running on a machine doesn't mean the applications are new, too. This section gives an overview of the legacy application support in Windows 2000, and then covers the two command consoles in detail to give you a good idea of the standard configuration management tools that are available.

IntelliMirror

If you are following the marketing literature for Windows 2000, you may be wondering why IntelliMirror is not on the list of sections in this chapter. If you are not familiar with the term, IntelliMirror is a Microsoft term that refers to a set of features designed to simplify user management, something like the Zero Administration Kit in NT4 but fully integrated into the operating system.

IntelliMirror is merely an umbrella term for a set of features that involve the automatic movement of data between desktops and servers: offline folders, folder redirection, software distribution, group policies, and remote installation services. No IntelliMirror service must be loaded or configured. No IntelliMirror icon is in the Control Panel. No IntelliMirror Wizard configures any features. That's why it's not on the list of sections. I have a feeling that the IntelliMirror term will fade away as Windows 2000 matures.

Configuring and Managing User Profiles

Windows 2000, like all Explorer-based Windows systems, has a *shell namespace* that defines how the system folders are displayed to the user. This namespace rearranges the file system hierarchy to simplify the application designer's job.

When you open Explorer and navigate to the top of the tree in the left pane, you're looking at the hierarchy of the shell namespace. The Desktop sits at the root of the namespace with My Documents, My Computer, My Network Places, the Recycle Bin, and Internet Explorer just below.

The Explorer namespace is structured around a set of folders and files that are collectively called the *user profile*. This section covers the structure of that profile and how to manage it.

Profile Structure

A Windows 2000 user profile contains the classic Explorer profile elements, such as Desktop, Start Menu, Cookies, and the various Hoods, along with several new components used to store application data and group policies. For a complete list of the special folders in the user profile, see the Platform SDK or the Microsoft KnowledgeBase under CSIDL Values. This is a quick list of the folders that are discussed in this chapter.

- **Application Data.** This folder contains user-specific configuration files for applications that can roam with the user. For example, cryptographic certificates and ID files for the Encrypting File System are stored in this folder.

- **Local Settings.** This folder contains user-specific configuration files for non-roaming applications. For example, Internet Express puts its files in this folder.

- **My Documents.** This is a new location for a classic folder. In NT4, the My Documents folder is kept outside the profile and positioned just under the root of the system volume. Windows 2000 puts My Documents back in the user profile so that it can be included in Folder Redirection and roaming profiles.

- **NTUSER.DAT.** This is the user's Registry hive, and it's loaded into the Registry when the user logs on and becomes the HKEY_Current_User subtree.

- **USRCLASS.DAT.** This is an additional user Registry hive stored in `\Documents and Settings\<username>\Local Settings\Application Data\Microsoft\Windows`. It holds user Registry entries for applications that do not roam.

- **NTUSER.INI.** This is a new file in Windows 2000. It provides a place to put legacy INI settings for Terminal Services. It also includes a list of folders that are excluded from roaming profiles.

- **NTUSER.POL.** This file acts as a local cache for user-based group policies that are downloaded from a domain controller when the user logs onto the domain.

- **Templates.** This directory holds legacy templates for a variety of applications, such as Amipro, Lotus 1-2-3, and older Microsoft Office applications.

All but a handful of the user profile folders are hidden. This reduces the chances of accidental deletion or unwanted experimentation. To view hidden files and folders, proceed as follows:

Procedure 16.1 **Viewing Hidden Files and Folders**

1. Select TOOLS | FOLDER OPTIONS from a folder menu.
2. Select the View tab.
3. Select Show Hidden Files and Folders.
4. Deselect Hide Protected Operating System Files and acknowledge the warning message.
5. Select and click OK.

Step 4 enables you to view so-called *superhidden files*. This is a new term in Windows 2000. It refers to files that have both the Hidden and System attributes set. A group policy blocks the user's ability to show hidden files and superhidden files. For more information, see "Assigning User and Computer Group Polices."

In addition to hiding all but a few folders in the user profile, many of the classic Start menu items are removed. This includes the Administrative Tools selection on Windows 2000 Professional. You can put these options back on the menu as follows:

Procedure 16.2 **Modifying the Start Menu**

1. Right-click the Task Bar.
2. Select PROPERTIES from the fly-out menu.
3. Select the Advanced tab.
4. Select the START menu items you want to display.
5. Click OK to save your selections.

Profile Names, Locations, and Ownership

When a user logs on to a Windows 2000 computer for the first time, a system process called Userinit creates a new profile for the user by copying the contents of the Default User profile stored in \Documents and Settings. This process differs from the NT4 user initialization in several ways:

Profile Locations

In NT4, user profiles are stored in the \WINNT\Profiles directory. Windows 2000 stores user profiles in the \Documents and Settings folder at the root of the system partition. Figure 16.1 shows the folder locations and layout.

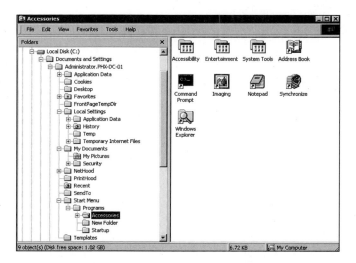

Figure 16.1   Explorer view of a Windows 2000 user profile stored in the \Documents and Settings directory.

If you upgrade to Windows 2000, the profiles are left in their classic \WINNT\Profiles location and all new profiles are put there as well. If you upgrade to Windows 2000 and load Terminal Services as part of the initial upgrade, Setup moves the user profiles to \Documents and Settings. If you do a standard upgrade and then install Terminal Services later, the profiles stay in their classic \WINNT\Profiles location.

You can verify the location of the user profile folders on a desktop by opening a command prompt and entering Set Userprofile. If a user has a roaming profile, the path to the locally cached copy is listed.

Profile Names

In NT4, the top folder in the profile is given the same name as the user logon ID. This basic profile naming method is the same in Windows 2000, but subsequent profiles for the same user are named differently:

- In classic NT, a second profile for the same user is named with the user's logon ID followed by a numerical extension starting with .000, such as JLeno.000. This makes it difficult to determine the origin of multiple profiles on a machine.

- In Windows 2000, the second profile name still starts with the user's logon ID, but the extension specifies the user's domain, such as JLeno.TonightShow. If the user logs on to the local machine rather than the domain, the computer name is used as the extension.

- If a user logs on using the same logon ID and domain as an existing profile, a .000 extension is added to the entire profile name, such as JLeno.TonightShow.000.

Profile Ownership

Userinit assigns Full Control ACL rights for the entire profile, both to the user and to the local Administrators group. This is a change from NT4, where only the user is placed on the ACL. Giving access to Administrators makes handling user profiles simpler without compromising security.

If you create a roaming profile, the server-based profile has only the user's account on the ACL. The same applies to the Registry keys in the NTUSER.DAT file. The user and the Administrators group are given Full Control on a local machine. Only the user has Full Control on the server copy.

Ownership of the profile folders and Registry keys is given to the Administrators group.

Registry Tip: Userinit
Userinit stores the profile name and the SID of the user in the Registry under HKLM | Software | Microsoft | WindowsNT | CurrentVersion | ProfileList.

Using the All Users Profile

The All Users profile under \Documents and Settings contains folders that parallel the regular user profile. Files in the All Users profile are combined with those in the user's profile when displayed in the shell. To view the contents of the All Users folder, right-click the Start button and select ALL USERS from the fly-out menu. (This works only if you have administrator privileges.)

Application programmers have the option of installing START menu shortcuts and Desktop shortcuts to either the user's profile or the All Users profile. This decision generally revolves around where the Registry entries for the application are stored. If the application puts the Registry entries in the HKEY_Current_User hive, the shortcuts will probably go in the user's profile. Some applications are a little smarter and put the shortcuts in All Users and then build interfaces for new users with an installer.

NT4 differentiates between START menu entries in the user's profile and the All Users profile by putting a beveled line in the menu pop-up. In Windows 2000, this is not done. Items from both profiles are mixed together to form a single list. For example, if you create a folder called Company Info in the Desktop folder in both the user profile and the All Users profile, only one Company Info folder appears on the desktop, and it displays the contents of the separate folders in the two profiles.

You can use a Folder Redirection policy to point users at a single All Users profile. This simplifies putting elements on desktops and START menus. See the section "Managing Folder Redirections" later in this chapter for details.

Registry Tip: User Profile locations

User profile locations are stored in the Registry under HKLM | Software | Microsoft | Windows NT | CurrentVersion | ProfileList.

This key contains subkeys with names that match the SID of the user associated with the profile. A ProfileImagePath value in the user's profile key points at the location of the profile.

The ProfileList key contains values that point at the location of the All Users profile and the Default Users profile.

.DEFAULT Profile

Don't confuse the Default User profile with the Registry key called .DEFAULT. This key represents the DEFAULT hive that contains the User parameters for the Local System account. The DEFAULT hive is stored along with the rest of the Registry hives in \WINNT\System32\Config.

Modifying the Default User Profile

By adding folders and files to the Default User profile, you can configure a standard profile and make it part of the desktop files that you deploy throughout your organization. For example, you can add shortcuts to your corporate Web site or standard applications, such as a time card system. The additions to the Default User profile are incorporated into any new profiles created when users log on for the first time.

You can also change the settings in the Default User Registry hive, NTUSER.DAT, if you want to modify the standard Explorer environment for new users. For example, you may want to replace the default desktop background with your organizational bitmap. You can copy the bitmap into the local \WINNT directory, load the NTUSER.DAT hive into the Registry Editor, and then change the wallpaper value for the Desktop as follows:

Procedure 16.3   Changing the Default User Registry Entries

1. Launch Regedt32 from the Run command or the command line.
2. Focus the Registry Editor on the HKEY_USERS window and highlight the HKEY_USERS icon.
3. From the menu, select REGISTRY | LOAD HIVE.
4. Navigate to the location of the Default User profile—either in \Documents and Settings or \WINNT\Profiles. Double-click the Ntuser.dat icon.
5. The Registry Editor prompts you for a name to apply to the key that represents this hive. This is a placeholder name and has no permanent significance in the Registry. You can call it Fred if you want, or Default_User_Hive if you want to be more formal. Click OK when you enter a name. The hive appears as a top-level key in the HKEY_USERS subtree.
6. Drill down to the CONTROL PANEL | DESKTOP key.
7. Find the Wallpaper value. The default entry is None.
8. Double-click Wallpaper to open the String Editor window. You get this window because the data type for the value is Reg_SZ.
9. Enter the name and path of the alternate bitmap file and click OK.
10. The update is applied immediately to the NTUSER.DAT file. No confirmation exists.

11. Now unload the hive. Highlight the top of the Default_User_Hive key and select REGISTRY | UNLOAD HIVE from the menu. The editor prompts for confirmation. Click OK to acknowledge. If you forget to do this step, the hive remains locked and new users get their Registry profile from the system profile, .DEFAULT.

12. Close Registry Editor.

13. Log off and then log on with a user ID that never logged on at this computer. The user gets the new desktop bitmap.

Preserving Local Profile Settings

If you reinstall Windows 2000 on a user's desktop, the user loses desktop configurations and application settings unless you preserve the local profile before performing the reinstallation.

One way to do this is to copy the user's profile to a server along with the rest of the user data you're preserving, format the hard drive, reinstall Windows 2000, and then copy the profile back to the same location. If you use this method, you need to perform a couple of additional steps to give the user access to the profile. First, you must make a quick Registry change. This is required because the HKLM | Software | Microsoft | Windows NT | CurrentVersion | ProfileList key that points to local profiles no longer contains a subkey for the user's profile.

These are the steps for preserving the user profile prior to a reinstallation of Windows 2000 and restoring access to the profile after the reinstallation is complete. The steps assume that the user logs on to a domain.

Procedure 16.4 **Preserving and Restoring Local Profile Settings**

1. Log on using an account with local Administrator rights.

2. Copy the user's profile to a server.

3. Format the drive and reinstall Windows 2000.

4. Copy the user's profile back from the server to the \Documents and Settings folder.

5. Have the user log on. This creates a new profile that uses the contents of Default User. The new profile has a .000 ending.

6. Have the user log off.

7. Log on using an administrative account.

8. Load Registry Editor.

9. Expand the tree to `HKLM` | `Software` | `Microsoft` | `Windows NT` | `CurrentVersion` | `ProfileList` | `<user_SID>`. You can find the right SID for the user by checking the `ProfileImagePath` value under the key.

10. Change the ProfileImagePath value to point at the old profile.

11. Close Registry Editor.

12. Have the user log on. The user gets the original profile settings.

Copying Profiles from One User to Another

Sometimes you may want to give one user access to another user's local profile. For instance, Ted is a department manager, and his computer is set up with the necessary tools to do his job. He leaves the company and Nancy takes his place. Nancy wants to keep Ted's applications and settings rather than reinstalling and reconfiguring them. This requires copying Ted's profile so that Nancy can use it.

Another common situation that requires copying a profile is cloning a master profile that you created for use as a mandatory profile. For more information, see the "Managing User Environments with Mandatory Profiles" section later in this chapter.

You cannot simply point the user's Registry entry at the second profile as was done in the previous section. The files, folders, and Registry keys in the profile have only the original user and the Administrators group on the ACLs. You can modify these ACLs in one whack using the SYSTEM PROPERTIES | USER PROFILES feature in the Control Panel as follows:

Procedure 16.5 **Copying a User Profile and Changing Access Rights**

1. Open Control Panel using START | SETTINGS | CONTROL PANEL.

2. Open the System applet.

3. Select the `User Profiles` tab. The list of `Profiles Stored On This Computer` includes the names of every user who logged on to the machine and got a profile. Figure 16.2 shows an example list.

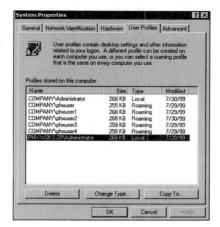

Figure 16.2   System Properties on a local workstation
showing the list of profiles stored on the computer.

4. Select the user profile you want to copy and click `Copy To`. The `Copy To` window opens. See Figure 16.3.

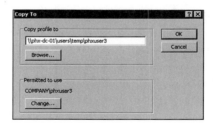

Figure 16.3   `Copy To` window showing the copy options for a user profile.

5. In the `Copy Profile To` field, enter the path and filename for the new profile. If you enter a path that does not exist, the system creates it for you. In this example, the path is the local `\Documents and Settings` folder.

6. You also need to change the access rights for the profile. Click `Change` and select the new user or group from the `Select User or Group` window.

7. At the `Copy To` window, click `OK`. The new profile is created.

8. Load Registry Editor.

9. Expand the tree to `HKLM | Software | Microsoft | Windows NT | CurrentVersion | ProfileList | <user_SID>`. You can find the right SID entry by looking at the `ProfileImagePath` value under the key.

10. Change the ProfileImagePath value to point at the new profile.

11. Close Registry Editor.

12. Have the user log on. The user gets the new profile settings.

Another way of retaining a user profile when reinstalling a machine is to temporarily configure a roaming profile. See the next section for details.

Managing Roaming User Profiles

Users spend inordinate amounts of their time—and your time, too, if you are in desktop support—configuring their desktops to fit their work habits. A user who moves from desktop to desktop does not want to repeat those configuration changes at each move, and you don't want to do it, either. An option for supporting these *roaming users* is to store their user profiles on a server. When the users log onto the domain, the profiles are downloaded to the desktop automatically. These server-based profiles are called *roaming profiles*.

These are the general steps for configuring roaming profiles and the events that occur when the roaming user logs on:

Procedure 16.6 **General Steps for Configuring Roaming Profiles**

1. Select a server to host the roaming profiles. Call this the *profile server*.

2. Create a folder on the profile server where the profiles are stored. Share this folder.

3. Configure the Profile option in the user account to point at the shared folder.

4. The user logs on at any Windows 2000 workstation in the domain.

5. WINLOGON sees that the user is configured to have a roaming profile and tells Userinit.

6. Userinit uses a helper, USERENV.DLL, to copy the user's profile from the profile server to the local hard drive.

7. During the workday, the user makes changes to the profile and they are saved locally. This improves performance and reduces network traffic.

8. When the user logs off, Userinit copies the profile back to the profile server.

Sounds simple, right? In a way, it is. But roaming profiles can become like the first paragraph of *A Tale of Two Cities*—they can be the best of solutions and the worst of solutions. They can be the best because users take their working environment with them wherever they go in the domain. This makes them comfortable and improves efficiency. You are the hero. They can be the worst because a good deal of integration work goes into creating the proper roaming environment. Sometimes that work goes awry and leaves users unable to find their files. If this happens to you, try not to think about the ending of *A Tale of Two Cities*.

Registry Size Limits and Roaming Profiles

One reasonably common problem with roaming profiles under NT4 is an "Insufficient Resource" error that occurs when a roaming user initially tries to log on to a new desktop.

This error occurs because the NTUSER.DAT file in the user's profile is too big to fit in memory based on the default Registry Size Limit (RSL) for the desktop.

In NT4, the workaround for this problem is to log on as an administrator and increase the RSL using System Properties in the Control Panel.

In Windows 2000, the RSL is automatically increased if it is too small to accommodate the user profile.

Planning for Roaming Profile Deployment

Many questions need to be answered as you formulate a plan for supporting roaming profiles.

- **Do your users log on both at Windows 2000/NT and Windows 9x desktops?** You need to create parallel profiles for both worlds. The Windows 9x profile can be stored on the same profile server, but it's a good idea to use a different directory.

- **Do users save tons of files in their local profiles?** You need to take steps to control the profile size and to warn users when profiles get too large. One way to do this is with quotas.

- **Do your users log on to multiple machines simultaneously?** Prepare to deal with lost or overwritten files, although Windows 2000 is much better about managing multiple profiles than NT4.

- **Do you have network and storage bottlenecks at the profile server?** Plan on upgrading your servers before an extensive deployment of roaming profiles. Imagine 100 users downloading thousands of files from the server every morning at 7:30. Build it accordingly.

- **Do some of your users log on with Terminal Services?** Watch out for multiple user sessions caused by users disconnecting rather than doing a clean logoff. The profile is not copied back to the profile server if the user disconnects. If the profile folder gets locked, the user might get a Default User profile on another machine or Terminal Session, and it could overwrite the correct profile.

■ **Do your users dial in from desktops or laptops and expect to get their latest office profile?** You need to set their expectations a little differently.

Configuring a Roaming Profile Server

Use the following list as a guide when selecting and configuring a profile server:

■ **Reliability.** The profile server should be as reliable as possible. You may want to consider using Advanced Server to build a cluster. Or, you can install some other form of reliable server solution such as Vinca Standby Server or Octopus Software, both of which are owned by Legato Software, www.legato.com.

■ **Storage.** Be sure to leave lots of elbow room on the volume. You don't need me to tell you how quickly users go through storage. The volume is likely to need defragmenting on a regular basis, to make sure the disk defragmenter gets 20–30% free space so that it can work effectively. For the same reason, don't compress the home directory volume. This limits defragmentation effectiveness.

■ **Quotas.** You should set aside an entire volume for profiles so that you can use quotas to control data storage. A group policy called Limit Profile Size warns users if their local profiles exceed a certain limit. For details, see "Assigning User and Computer Group Polices" later in this chapter.

■ **NTFS Volumes.** You need NTFS to make sure you can control security for the user's data. NTFS is also required if you use quotas.

■ **Home Directories.** If you use home directories as well as central profiles, you can put both on the same profile server. This simplifies administration by putting all the users' information in one place. Home directories are discussed in "Creating and Managing Home Directories" later in this chapter.

Configuring a Roaming Profile

This section describes how to set up a roaming profile for a user. The shared folder in the steps is called Users and is shared with the same name. The share name is not important because users don't see it. But be sure to limit the name to 8 characters or fewer so that all versions of Windows can access it, just in case you want to use the shared volume to store profiles for downlevel clients and home directories as well as Windows 2000 profiles.

The example steps set the path for the user profiles to `\\server-name\share-name\%username%\%username%`. The `%username%` environment variable maps to the user's logon ID when you save the entry. For example, when applied to a user with the logon ID of JSpringer, the path created on the profile server is: `\\phx-dc-01\users\jspringer\jspringer`.

I use two instances of `%username%` to create two folders identified by the user's logon ID. The top folder becomes the user's home directory and provides a place to store redirected folders. The second instance creates a sub-folder that contains the user's profile.

Procedure 16.7 **Configuring a Roaming User Profile**

1. Open the AD Users and Computers console.

2. Expand the tree to the container where the user objects are stored, or use the Find feature to locate the user you want to configure.

3. Right-click the user object and select PROPERTIES from the fly-out menu. The Properties window for the user opens.

4. Select the Profile tab. This tab is used to set profiles, personal logon scripts, and home directories.

5. Under User Profile, enter a Profile Path that corresponds to the shared folder on the profile server. Figure 16.4 shows an example. The path is `\\server-name\share-name\%username%\%username%`.

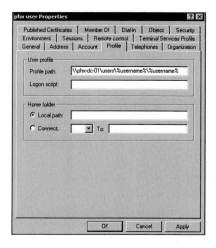

Figure 16.4 User Properties window showing Profile tab with path to user's central profile.

6. Click OK to save the change. The path is created on the profile server the next time the user logs on.

Testing a Roaming Profile

After you configure a user to have a roaming profile, you need to initialize the profile and ensure that it travels with the user.

You can proceed in a couple of ways at this point, depending on whether the user already has a local profile.

- If the user has a local profile and wants to preserve it, have the user log on at her local machine as soon as you configure her account to use a roaming profile. When she logs off, the local profile is copied to the profile server.

- If the user does not have a local profile, she can log on at any Windows 2000 workstation to get a copy of the Default User profile. When she logs off, the new profile is copied to the profile server.

These are the steps for initializing the user profile. The steps assume that the user does not have a pre-existing profile. Proceed as follows:

Procedure 16.8 Initializing a Roaming Profile with a New User Profile

1. From a Windows 2000 desktop, have the user log on to the domain (or log on yourself as the user).

2. Configure the default profile to your organizational standard.

3. Log off. The local profile is copied to the user's folder on the profile server. Depending on network traffic, server load, and the profile size, a delay of several seconds occurs before the logoff is complete.

4. At the profile server, verify that the user's profile is in the shared folder. If you used the double %username% entries to create a home directory as well as a profile folder, the home directory inherits its ACL rights from the parent folder and the profile has the user as the only entry on the ACL.

5. Log on again at a different Windows 2000 desktop using the same roaming account and verify that the operating environment is replicated to the second computer.

6. Open Explorer and navigate to \Documents and Settings to verify that the central profile is copied to the local computer. When you log off, the profile is copied back to the profile server.

Precautions When Using Roaming Profiles

Watch out for these glitches when implementing roaming profiles.

- **Simultaneous logons at multiple computers.** If a user logs on at more than one computer and makes changes to the profile at each computer, some changes may be overwritten when the user logs off and the profiles collide at the profile server. For more information, see the sidebar titled "Roaming Profile Collisions" later in this chapter.

- **Profiles replicate up at logoff only if they are replicated down at logon.** If the user does not make contact with the profile server at logon, Userinit displays an error and then logs the user on, using the cached local profile. If no cached profile exists, a new profile is created with the Default User profile. When the user logs off, the local profile is not replicated, even if the profile server is now available. This protects the files on the server from corruption. At the next logon, the server checks the time stamps on the local files and does not overwrite them. This is different from the behavior of classic NT. For information on merged profiles, see the sidebar titled "Roaming Profile Collisions" later in this chapter.

- **No encrypted files in roaming profiles.** Encrypted files cannot be stored in the user's roaming profile. The keys to encrypt and decrypt files are stored in the user's profile, and the system needs these keys to replicate the files. If a user encrypts a file in his roaming profile and then logs off, Userinit displays an error message, "*Windows cannot copy your profile because it contains encrypted files or directories. Please decrypt the files and try again.*" The user must log back on, decrypt the file, log off, and then log back on and off one more time to restore proper replication. If you want to put encrypted files on a server, use folder redirection. For more information, see the "Managing Folder Redirections" section later in this chapter. Also, see Chapter 15, "Managing Shared Resources," for cautions about storing encrypted files on servers.

- **Attribute changes not replicated unless file changes.** If you change a file's attributes (read-only, hidden, system, archive), its security descriptor, or its compression setting without making changes to the file's data, the changes are not written to the file on the profile server.

- **Terminal Services Profiles.** Roaming users get their roaming profiles when they log on to a Terminal Services console, just as though they were logging onto a regular PC. The local copy of the profile does not replicate back to the profile server until the user completely logs off the Terminal

Services session. If the user simply disconnects, the profile stays active at the Terminal Services server and is not replicated. See the sidebar titled "Roaming User Profile Collisions" later in this chapter for what happens if the user then logs on from another PC or another Terminal Services session.

- **Renaming files.** If a user renames a file in a profile, the original file remains on the server and is downloaded the next time the user logs on. At that point, if the user deletes the file, it is deleted from the central profile at logoff. This problem is resolved in a maintenance update of Windows 2000.

- **Classic NT compatibility.** Windows 2000 profiles are compatible with NT4. A roaming user can log on at Windows 2000 desktops and NT workstations. Any Windows 2000-specific Registry entries are ignored when logging on to NT4. Windows 2000 profiles are not compatible with NT3.51.

- **User ID changes.** If you delete a user account and then re-create it using the same name, a different SID is assigned. Because the new SID does not match the SID associated with the user's roaming profile, the roaming profile cannot be used. Userinit gives the user an *access denied* warning and a new local profile is created using Default User. You can avoid this by changing the user on the profile. For the steps, see "Copying a Profile from One User to Another" earlier in this chapter.

- **Profiles can grow very large.** A profile can grow very large because applications save their configuration files and data to the My Documents folder. Imagine hundreds of roaming users with megabytes upon megabytes of files in their profiles, all logging on and off at the same time. Rather than putting the My Documents folder in the standard profile, you can use folder redirection to put the My Documents folder at a separate place on the network. A group policy warns users if their profiles exceed a preset limit. See the "Administrative Templates" section later in this chapter for a description of this policy.

- **Slow connections.** If a user logs on over a RAS connection, it takes a significant amount of time to transfer the profile over the modem line, especially if the profile includes My Documents and other large folders. To prevent this delay, the system detects a slow link (500Kbps or less) and logs the user on with a locally cached profile. If you set up laptops in a lab environment, be sure you log on as the user at least once to get a copy of your standard profile onto the local drive.

- **Local profile remains on drive.** Roaming users who log on at multiple computers leave behind copies of their profile at every machine. This can be a security problem even if the local drives are formatted with NTFS. If users have local admin privileges, they can take ownership of the local copy of a roaming profile and then set the ACL to gain access. A Registry entry called `HKLM | Software | Microsoft | Windows NT | CurrentVersion | WINLOGON | DeleteRoamingCache` removes the local copy when the user logs off. You can set this directly in the Registry or use a Group policy to control it. The policy is called `Computer Configuration | Administrative Templates | System | Logon | Delete Cached Copies of Roaming Profiles`.

Roaming Profile Collisions

NT4 is not very sophisticated in the way it handles file replication in roaming profiles. In NT4, when a user logs on, the profile is simply copied to the local desktop. At logoff, it is copied back to the server. Any changed files are overwritten. Any files deleted at the desktop are removed from the server, as well, no questions asked.

This replication method is fine for a single logon instance, but it causes real problems for roaming users who log on to multiple machines at the same time. The user might add, modify, and delete different files at different locations and then log off in a different order than logon. The file modifications that result at the server are unpredictable but just about guaranteed to cause pain.

Windows 2000 handles file replication a little more elegantly by *merging* files rather than overwriting them. It does this by comparing time stamps between the source files and the target files.

When a roaming user logs on, the profile server saves a copy of the time stamps on the files in the profile. When the user logs off and the client begins replicating the files back to the server, the server compares the time stamps on the incoming documents with those in the saved list.

- If the time stamp indicates that a modified file is newer than the one on the server, the server file is overwritten.

- If the time stamp indicates that the file on the server is newer, suggesting that it was changed at another desktop and then replicated back to the server, the file on the server is not overwritten.

- If the server has a file that is not among the files replicated back from the desktop that has a time stamp that is newer than the original time stamp on the files, suggesting that it was added from another desktop, the file is retained.

- If the server has a file that is not among the files replicated back from the desktop and the time stamp on the file matches the saved time stamps for that replication session, the file is deleted.

Managing User Environments with Mandatory Profiles

Rather than give each individual user a roaming profile, you may want to define a standard profile for a community of users. This *mandatory profile* is not configurable by users, so it usually takes a while to get the right mix of shortcuts, Start menu items, applications, and so forth to meet everyone's expectations.

A mandatory profile is nothing more than a standard server-based profile with a .man extension on the root folder. The .man extension stands for *mandatory*. For example, if you create a profile for the Sales group, to make it a mandatory profile you simply need to rename the top folder to Sales.man. You can also designate a profile as mandatory by renaming Ntuser.dat to Ntuser.man, but renaming the entire profile is preferable because it gives a clear visual cue.

Worth repeating is the fact that users cannot modify the contents of a mandatory profile. This means that they cannot save files in the My Documents folder. Before you implement a mandatory profile, you must redirect the My Documents folder to a server. See "Managing Folder Redirections" later in this chapter for details.

These are the steps for configuring a mandatory profile for a group of users:

Procedure 16.9   Configuring and Assigning Mandatory Profiles

1. Create a test user.

2. Log on at a desktop with that user's account.

3. Configure the desktop environment to meet your user's specifications.

4. Log out to save the local profile to the local computer.

5. Log on as an administrator.

6. Use the Copy Profile procedure outlined in "Copying Profiles from One User to Another" earlier in this chapter to copy the profile to the profile server. Don't forget to change the access rights to include the group you are going to associate with the profile.

7. Rename the profile to match the group name. This is not required, but it helps to identify the profile in a list on the server. Give the name a .man extension.

8. Configure the user accounts in the Sales group to point at the new profile.

9. Log on as a member of the Sales group to verify that you get the new profile.

Creating and Managing Home Directories

I'm sure you agree that, by and large, the average user has no clear idea where his data actually resides. Anyone who has done a desktop deployment knows the challenge of locating all those data files that users tucked away. This is like finding crumbs in a cookie factory.

This data scatter isn't necessarily the user's fault. Application designers are to blame for a lot of it. Most applications either save their files in the same folder as the executable or have their own configuration method for selecting a default location. Default file locations are not standardized in any meaningful way. Microsoft hopes to change that with Windows 2000.

The Windows 2000 user profile provides standard folders for application data and configuration files. The specific locations are:

- `%userprofile%\My Documents` for data.

- `%userprofile%\Application Data` for application configuration files that roam with the user.

- `%userprofile%\Local Settings` for application configuration files that do not roam. The contents of Local Settings are not replicated to the profile server when saving a roaming profile. They are created on-the-fly in the local profile on disk.

The Windows 2000 Platform SDK urges application developers to save data to these folders. The use of these folders is a requirement to get the Ready for Windows 2000 logo. After the next wave of product releases that comply with the new logo requirements comes out, we might find ourselves in a world where all data goes to predictable locations. It may not be Oz, but it's sure a long way up the yellow brick road.

Still, it's going to take a while for vendors to get their applications up to Windows 2000 logo standards, not to mention the years it will take to actually buy and deploy them. In the meantime, you must still support data storage for legacy applications. For that, nothing is better than a home directory. See the next section for details.

Flexible Folder Locations

The SDK warns against hard-coding an application to use the standard profile folder locations. Instead, it requires the use of API calls to find the profile folder locations. This enables the use of folder redirections and enables future configuration changes should the profile folders need to change location.

Functional Overview of Home Directories

A home directory provides a convenient place to store data on a server. "Put it in your U: drive." Short. Succinct. Easy to grasp.

Preparing home directories for users is a two-step process.

- Set aside a server with a shared folder to hold the directories.
- Configure the user's account to point at the home directory.

Home directory information is stored in the User object in the Directory. Two attributes exist: Home-Directory and Home-Drive. When a Windows 2000 or classic NT user logs on to the domain, the Home-Drive letter is mapped to the path in the Home-Directory attribute. For more information, see "Assigning Logon Scripts to Downlevel Clients" later in this chapter. This is a checklist for preparing user home directories:

- **Home Directory Server.** Any Windows 2000 or NT server can host user home directories. It does not need to be a domain controller. If you use roaming profiles, the natural choice is to use the profile server. If you use a different server, be sure to set aside an entire volume for home directories so that you can take advantage of quotas.

- **Create and share a home directory folder.** An individual home directory takes the form of a folder with the same name as the user's logon ID. These folders are usually stored under a common share point for ease of maintenance.

- **Create user accounts first.** You cannot assign a home directory in New User windows. This may be added in subsequent updates to Windows 2000. Until then, you must first create the user and then assign the home directory.

- **Use a UNC path that includes the %username% variable.** When you specify the path to the user's home directory, use a UNC path name ending with the %username% environment variable. This ensures you don't mistype the user's name. For example, \\phx-dc-01.company.com\users\%username%.

- **Make allowances for downlevel clients.** Users may log on from Windows 9x or Windows 3.1x/DOS machines. If you want them to get a home directory, limit the share name to 8 characters or fewer. Downlevel clients might not understand a fully qualified domain name in the path, so you might need to put a flat name in the path and then take steps to ensure that Windows 2000 clients can find the server. Also, downlevel clients cannot map to a subdirectory, so be sure to put the home directories on an NTFS volume because the home drive contains all the user directories.

You can create home directories in two ways. You can use the graphical user management tools in the AD Users and Computers console, or you can use the command line. Let's start with the console.

Assigning a Home Directory Using *AD Users and Computers* Console

After the shared folder that contains the home directories is in place and the user accounts are created, assign a home directory to an account as follows:

Procedure 16.10   **Assigning a User Home Directory with the *AD Users and Computers* Console**

1. Open the AD Users and Computers console and expand the tree to where the user objects are stored.
2. Double-click the user object to open the Properties window.
3. Select the Profile tab. See Figure 16.5.

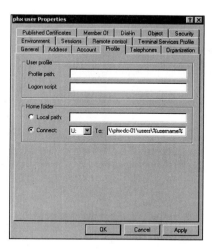

Figure 16.5   User Properties from AD Users and Computers console showing home directory setting under Profile tab.

4. Under Home Folder, select the Connect radio button.

5. Enter the drive letter you want to use for the home drive and the UNC path to the home directory.

6. Click OK to save the changes and close the Properties window. The system automatically creates a home directory at the specified shared directory. The ACLs are set to give the user and the Administrators group Full Control rights.

Creating Home Directories from the Command Line

These are general actions for assigning user home directories from the command line.

Procedure 16.11 General Actions for Assigning User Home Directories Using the Command Line

1. Designate a server to host the home directories.

2. Create and share a folder on an NTFS volume.

3. Create the user accounts.

4. Create the home directories.

5. Assign the home directory to the user account.

6. Set access rights on the directories.

Most of the tools for doing this work come as standard utilities in Windows 2000. A few tools come from the Resource Kit.

The following steps show how to use the command line to create an account, assign a home directory, and set permissions on the directory so that only the user can access it.

Procedure 16.12 Assigning a Home Directory Using the Command Line

1. Open a command prompt and enter the following command to create the user account:

```
net user rmanuel * /add /fullname:"Rita Manuel" /comment:"Help Desk Admin" /domain
```

The * forces Net to prompt for a password and confirmation rather than entering the password on the command line.

The /domain switch adds the user to the Active Directory. Otherwise, if you are at a member server or workstation instead of a domain controller, the net user /add command creates the account in the local SAM.

2. Create a home directory for Rita. This can be done at the console of the server or across the network.

```
MD e:\users\rmanuel
```

or

```
MD \\phx-dc-01\users\rmanuel
```

3. If you choose to create individual shares for home directories, create a share point at the console of the server using the Net Share command as follows:

```
net share rmanuel=c:\users\rmanuel
```

To create a share across the network, use a tool in the Resource Kit called Rmtshare. You must be logged on to the domain with administrator privileges to use Rmtshare. The syntax for this utility is:

```
rmtshare \\phx-dc-01\rmanuel=c:\users\rmanuel
```

4. Now set Rita's user account to point at the home directory. This is also done with the Net User command. The default home drive letter is z:. No command-line option exists for setting a different drive letter. The syntax is:

```
net user rmanuel /homedir:\\phx-dc-01\rmanuel
```

5. When Rita's home directory was created, it inherited access rights that might include the default Everyone group. Now set the ACLs on the directory so that only Rita can get access. The command-line utility for applying NTFS file permissions is CACLS.EXE. You can use CACLS locally or across the network. This is the syntax for giving Rita full control rights and removing everyone else from the ACL:

```
cacls \\phx-dc-01\users\rmanuel /t /g rmanuel:f
```

The /t option applies the change to the directory and all child directories and files.

The /g option grants the specified permissions to the user.

The rmanuel:f option grants Full Control access to Rita's account.

6. When you enter this command, CACLS prompts for confirmation. Enter Y for Yes and the change is applied. You may receive an *Access Denied* error after the processing completes. This is because Rita is now the only authorized user.

7. Finally, if you intend on using quotas, you need to set ownership of Rita's home directory to Rita. This cannot be done using tools from Microsoft. I recommend the chown utility from MKS Software, www.mks.com. This also comes as part of the demonstration utilities in Services for UNIX from Microsoft.

Armed with these Net commands, you can build a script to automate a user addition. The following example shows a simple batch script that accepts the user's login ID, full name, and title as command-line arguments.

```
md \\phx-dc-01\users\%1
net share %1=c:\users\%1 (or rmtshare \\phx-dc-01\%1=c:\users\%1)
net user %1 * /add /domain /homedir:\\phx-dc-01\users\%1   /fullname:%2 /comment:%3
cacls \\phx-dc-01\users\%1 /t /g %1:f
chown -R rmanuel \\phx-dc-01\users\rmanuel
```

You can use VBScript, Jscript, or Perl to make more elaborate user management scripts. The person using the script must have sufficient administrative rights to add user accounts and modify ACLs. The Resource Kit has a utility called Addusers that can add hundreds or thousands of users at once using a comma-delimited file. You can also transfer accounts and build new accounts using LDIFE. See Chapter 9, "Deploying Windows 2000 Domains," for details.

Mapping Home Directories for Downlevel Clients

When you assign a home directory to a Windows 2000 or classic NT user account, the home drive is mapped automatically when the user logs on.

This is not true for downlevel clients such as Windows 3.1x and Windows 9x. Downlevel clients require that the home directory be mapped in a logon script. The most common way of doing this mapping is with the Net Use command and the /home switch. This is the syntax:

```
net use u: \\phx-dc-01\users /home
```

As explained in the sidebar titled "Sharing Home Directories" later in this section, downlevel clients—including classic NT—cannot map to a directory under a share. The Net Use command in the logon script needs to include only the share point unless you are building a script that is also applicable to Windows 2000 clients. You may find that the Group policy options are a better way to distribute Windows 2000 scripts. See "Using Logon Scripts" Later in this chapter.

One way to work around the mapping limitation is to use the Subst command rather than Net Use in the logon script. The drive letter substitutions done with Subst are not limited to share points and work with UNC names. For example, to designate a home drive with Subst, put the following command in the logon script:

```
subst h: \\phx-dc-01\users\%username%
```

This solution works with Windows 2000 clients, as well, so you can use the same logon script for all clients.

Sharing Home Directories

A limitation in classic Windows restricts a drive mapping strictly to a share point.

For example, if you map the U: drive for a downlevel client to \\phx-dc-01\users\dletterman, the client maps only to the users share, so the U: drive contains all the home directories, not just the files for dletterman.

This has been an NT administration headache for years. In small networks, you can get around this limitation by creating a separate share point for each user's home directory and then mapping the home drives to that share point. This is not a good idea in a big network because a large number of shares degrades performance and causes system instabilities. Exceeding 500 shares on a single server is not recommended, although some administrators have put 2000 shares on a server and reported no problems.

You can hide the shares from the browser by giving them a dollar-sign ($) ending. For example, if the physical directory holding home directories is on the E: drive of the server with the path E:\Users\DLetterman, the share point is Dletterman$ and the UNC path is \\phx-dc-01\dletterman$.

The dollar sign does not prevent the share from being sent across the network, so don't use it in place of tight NTFS security on the home directories.

Terminal Services and Home Directories

Some of the changes to user profiles in Windows 2000 were made to accommodate Terminal Services, which now comes in the shrink-wrapped product rather than as an add-on.

A community of Terminal Services users treats the TS server as though it is their own private workstation. Some legacy applications that save configuration information to common folders are not well suited for that kind of multiuser environment. For example, Office 97 applications save user templates to C:\Program Files\Office97\Templates. If this is done in a Terminal Services environment, users will overwrite each other's templates.

The workaround recommended by Microsoft is to replace the application's default common folders with folders that are unique for each user. Instead of user JSpringer saving his templates to C:\Program Files\Office97\ Templates, for example, he saves his templates to C:\JSpringer\Program Files\ Office97\Templates.

Windows 2000 automates the process of creating personalized application configuration folders. It does so by using a set of scripts stored in \WINNT\Application Compatibility Scripts. These scripts run regardless of whether the user logs onto a TS console or does a regular console logon.

The TS logon scripts make use of a special environment variable called %rootdrive% that is inserted at the front of the default data locations. If the user account in the Directory has a home directory assigned, %rootdrive% is set to that path. If a user is not assigned a home directory, one of the TS configuration scripts uses the drive letter substitution command Subst to map a drive letter to a local folder in lieu of a home directory.

The end result of this maneuvering is that data that is normally placed in a common storage area is placed in the user's home directory.

The scripts that make all this happen run even if you do not use a TS Server, so it's worth having at least a quick idea of their operation. If you are a TS server administrator who is troubleshooting problems with legacy applications in a TS environment, you need to know these scripts in detail. What follows is the sequence of events that take place when application compatibility scripts run in a TS environment.

Chkroot.cmd Script

When an application compatibility script is called during initial logon, the first script that runs is Chkroot.cmd.

The first part of the script sets an environment variable in case the user is running more than one script at the same time and then changes directories to where the compatibility scripts are stored.

```
Set _CHKROOT=PASS
cd "%SystemRoot%\Application Compatibility Scripts"
```

The Rootdrv.cmd script now checks to see whether a home directory already exists. If it does, the rest of the script is skipped and the directory is changed to %SystemRoot%\Application Compatibility Scripts\Install to prepare for any subsequent scripts.

```
Call RootDrv.Cmd
If Not "A%ROOTDRIVE%A" == "AA" Goto Cont2
```

The next section creates a script called Rootdrv2.cmd that sets the %rootdrive% letter. The Rootdrv2.cmd script is called each time the user logs on. The user must define a drive letter to use for %rootdrive% if a home directory does not exist. The script does this by echoing remarks into a file and then opening the file in Notepad. The user enters a drive and then saves the script.

```
Echo REM > RootDrv2.Cmd
Echo REM    Before running this application compatibility script, you must >> RootDrv2.Cmd
Echo REM    designate a drive letter, that is not already in use for    >> RootDrv2.Cmd
Echo REM    Terminal Server, to be mapped to each user's home directory. >> RootDrv2.Cmd
Echo REM    Update the "Set RootDrive" statement at the end of >> RootDrv2.Cmd
```

```
Echo REM    this file to indicate the desired drive letter.  If you have >> RootDrv2.Cmd
Echo REM    no preference, the drive W: is suggested.  For example: >> RootDrv2.Cmd
Echo REM >> RootDrv2.Cmd
Echo REM             Set RootDrive=W: >> RootDrv2.Cmd
Echo REM >> RootDrv2.Cmd
Echo REM    Note:  Make sure there are no spaces after the drive letter and colon. >>
RootDrv2.Cmd
Echo REM >> RootDrv2.Cmd
Echo REM    When you have completed this task, save this file and exit >> RootDrv2.Cmd
Echo REM    NotePad to continue running the application compatibility script. >> RootDrv2.Cmd
Echo REM >> RootDrv2.Cmd
Echo. >> RootDrv2.Cmd
Echo Set RootDrive=>> RootDrv2.Cmd
Echo. >> RootDrv2.Cmd
```

RootDrv2.cmd Script

The Chkroot.cmd script opens the Rootdrv2.cmd file created above in
Notepad.

```
NotePad RootDrv2.Cmd
```

The user is supposed to read the paragraph and enter a drive letter. More
likely, the user reads the paragraph and calls the Help Desk. The default drive
letter for %rootdrive% is W:. If you already use the W: drive in your standard
mappings, you should modify the ChkRoot script at the Terminal Services
server to suggest the correct drive letter. That shortens the Help Desk call.

Rootdrv.cmd Script

When the user saves the ROOTDRV.CMD file and closes Notepad, the
script calls the Rootdrv.cmd script that was built. If the user neglected to
enter a drive letter in Rootdrv.cmd, no value is assigned to %rootdrive% and
the script complains and exits.

```
Call RootDrv.Cmd
If Not "A%ROOTDRIVE%A" == "AA" Goto Cont1
Echo.
Echo     Before running this application compatibility script, you must
Echo     designate a drive letter to be mapped to each user's home
Echo     directory.
Echo.
Echo     Script terminated.
Echo.
Pause
Set _CHKROOT=FAIL
Goto Cont2
```

The script comes directly to this label if the user has a home directory or was assigned one using Rootdrv2.cmd. This section creates a file called CHKROOT.KEY.

```
:Cont1
echo HKEY_LOCAL_MACHINE\Software\Microsoft\Windows NT\CurrentVersion\Terminal Server >
➥chkroot.key
echo     RootDrive = REG_SZ %ROOTDRIVE%>> chkroot.key
```

The CHKROOT.KEY file is now used as an argument for Regini to create the associated key in the Registry.

```
regini chkroot.key > Nul:
```

The contents of the UsrLogon script are detailed a little later in this section.

```
Call "%SystemRoot%\System32\UsrLogon.Cmd
```

The exit point for the script leaves the user in a directory containing application compatibility scripts.

```
:Cont2
Cd "%SystemRoot%\Application Compatibility Scripts\Install"
```

Function of Usrlogon.cmd Script

The Usrlogon.cmd script sets up the %rootdrive% environment varlable at each logon. The script is located in the \WINNT\System32_directory, and it is run automatically during WINLOGON regardless of whether the client is logging on using Terminal Services or simply doing a regular console logon.

This is the Registry entry for WINLOGON that runs the Usrlogon.cmd script:

```
Key:    HKLM | Software | Microsoft | Windows NT | CurrentVersion | Winlogon
Value:  AppSetup
Data:   UsrLogon.Cmd (REG_SZ)
```

The UsrLogon.cmd script performs a variety of tasks to set the user environment with Terminal Services. This is an example of the script.

```
@Echo Off
```

The Setpaths script instantiates a series of environment variables that support multiuser Windows.

```
Call "%SystemRoot%\Application Compatibility Scripts\SetPaths.Cmd"
If "%_SETPATHS%" == "FAIL" Goto Done
```

The next section of the script calls a script named Usrlogn1.cmd. This script does not exist by default. Application Compatibility Scripts create this file when they require special procedures but no %rootdrive%. An example is PeachTree, which must load Btrieve to work but does not save data to a default data directory.

```
If Not Exist "%SystemRoot%\System32\Usrlogn1.cmd" Goto cont0
Cd /d "%SystemRoot%\Application Compatibility Scripts\Logon"
Call "%SystemRoot%\System32\Usrlogn1.cmd"
```

The only job that Rootdrv.cmd performs is calling Rootdrv2.cmd. Rootdrv2.cmd sets the %rootdrive%.

```
:cont0
Cd /d %SystemRoot%\"Application Compatibility Scripts"
Call RootDrv.Cmd
If "A%RootDrive%A" == "AA" End.Cmd
```

At this point, the user is verified to have a true home directory drive letter, not an in-lieu drive letter from Rootdrv2.cmd. The next few lines delete any existing uses of the drive letter and then assign it using Subst rather than Net Use. This makes it look like a local drive letter to the system.

```
Net Use %RootDrive% /D >NUL: 2>&1
Subst %RootDrive% "%HomeDrive%%HomePath%"
if ERRORLEVEL 0 goto AfterSubst
Subst %RootDrive% /d >NUL: 2>&1
Subst %RootDrive% "%HomeDrive%%HomePath%"
```

Some Application Compatibility Scripts need to set additional parameters after creating the %rootdrive%. These are stored in Usrlogn2.cmd, which now runs if it is present.

```
:AfterSubst
If Not Exist %SystemRoot%\System32\UsrLogn2.Cmd Goto Cont1
Cd Logon
Call %SystemRoot%\System32\UsrLogn2.Cmd
```

The exit point performs no additional processing.

```
:Cont1
:Done
```

Setpaths.cmd Script

The Setpaths.cmd script called by Userlogon.cmd sets a series of environment variables that point at the new folder locations. It does this using a volatile script called Getpath.cmd that is created at logon based on Registry entries. This is an example of the Getpath.cmd script for a user logging on as phxadmin:

```
SET COMMON_START_MENU=C:\Documents and Settings\All Users\Start Menu
SET COMMON_STARTUP=C:\Documents and Settings\All Users\Start Menu\Programs\Startup
SET COMMON_PROGRAMS=C:\Documents and Settings\All Users\Start Menu\Programs
SET USER_START_MENU=C:\Documents and Settings\phxadmin\Start Menu
SET USER_STARTUP=C:\Documents and Settings\phxadmin\Start Menu\Programs\Startup
SET USER_PROGRAMS=C:\Documents and Settings\phxadmin\Start Menu\Programs
SET MY_DOCUMENTS=My Documents
SET TEMPLATES=Templates
SET APP_DATA=Application Data
```

These scripts are run on any Windows 2000 machine, not just at a Terminal Services logon. They do not have an operational impact for non-TS users, but you need to keep their existence in mind for troubleshooting purposes.

Now that the users' profiles and home directories are in place, it's time to figure out how to control them with as little work as possible. Because a profile consists of Registry entries and INI files distributed in a distinct folder, the control methodology must provide a way to modify all those elements. That's the job of group policies.

Managing User Environments with Group Policies

The concept of using policies to manage the desktop environment was introduced in Windows 95 and has been a hallmark of managing the Explorer shell environment ever since.

Windows 9x and NT4 use classic system policies to perform rudimentary desktop configuration changes. These system policies have several limitations.

- The policy files are binary, fairly large, and make unnecessary changes. This severely limits the scope of the available policies.

- What few policies are available in system policies have a nasty habit of staying around after the policy is removed from the server. Microsoft calls this "tattooing" the Registry. Any administrator who inadvertently changes the system configuration for 5000 users while fooling around with Policy Editor knows how difficult it is to remove a tattoo.

- System Policies do Registry updates only. If a particular environment change falls outside the scope of a Registry change, the administrator must create special scripts to do the work.
- System policies can be distributed in one file only. This hampers the ability of administrators to create policies tailored to specific user communities. System policies can be targeted at groups, but this creates a very large CONFIG.POL or NTCONFIG.POL file that is cumbersome to maintain.

Windows 2000 overcomes these weaknesses by introducing a new policy distribution method called *group policies*. Group policies also control Registry entries, but the changes overlay the Registry settings in memory and do not make permanent changes to the Registry files other than to cache the policies. If a group policy is removed, the original Registry entry takes effect once again.

The functions provided by group policies include a lot more than simple Registry updates. Group policies fall into several categories depending on the configurations they influence. The policy categories are:

- Disk Quota policies
- Encrypting File System Recovery policies
- Security policies
- User and Computer policies (Registry updates)
- Folder Redirection policies
- Logon/Logoff scripts
- Software installation

The first three categories are covered in previous chapters. Software installation falls outside the scope of this book. User and Computer policies are covered in this section. Folder Redirection and Logon/Logoff scripts are covered in subsequent sections in this chapter.

Comparison of System Policies and Group Policies

Support for Legacy System Policies in Windows 2000

Windows 2000 continues to support downlevel clients who use system policies in CONFIG.POL (Windows 9x) and NTCONFIG.POL (NT4) files.

- Classic domain controllers store system policy files in the `\WINNT\System32\Repl\Import\Scripts` directory, which is shared as NETLOGON.

- Windows 2000 domain controllers also use the NETLOGON share, but the underlying folder is `\WINNT\Sysvol\Sysvol\<domain_name>\Scripts`.

The classic tool for creating system policies is the System Policy Editor, Poledit. This tool uses a suite of ADM template files that contain the Registry updates for individual policies. Windows 2000 includes a copy of Poledit and the full set of templates for use in managing downlevel clients.

Functional Description of User and Computer Group Policies

User and Computer Group policies consist of Registry updates distributed to domain clients at logon. These updates are stored in special files called REGISTRY.POL files. Every policy has two REGISTRY.POL files, one to hold User configuration settings and one to hold Computer configuration settings.

The Registry updates in the REGISTRY.POL files are downloaded by clients and applied to local Registry entries in memory. No permanent changes are made to the local Registries other than to cache the settings. If a group policy is removed, the original Registry entry takes control once again.

Refer to Figure 16.6. Group policies are stored on domain controllers in a folder called `\WINNT\Sysvol<domain>`. The contents of this folder are replicated throughout the domain. Local machines also have policies that affect local Registry entries. These policies are stored in `\WINNT\System32\GroupPolicy`.

Each group policy in `\WINNT\Sysvol` consists of a set of folders stored under a folder with a name that matches the Globally Unique Identifier (GUID) assigned to the policy. This is called a Group Policy Object (GPO).

A *Group Policy Container* (GPC) represents in the Directory each Group Policy Object in `\WINNT\Sysvol`. Group Policy Containers are then linked to Directory containers. When a Group policy is linked to a container, the policy elements—Registry updates, logon/logoff scripts, folder redirections, and so forth—are downloaded by the users and computers that are represented by objects in that container.

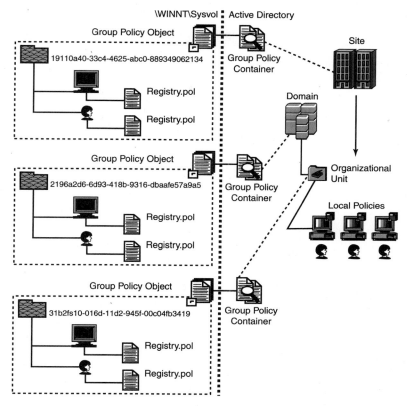

Figure 16.6 Diagram showing relationship of Group Policy
Objects, Group Policy Containers, and Directory Containers.

Using Figure 16.6 as an example, if a user in the Phoenix OU logs on to the
domain, the group policies from the Site, Domain, and Local OU are downloaded. The Registry updates in the REGISTRY.POL files in these policies
are combined with those in the local policy and applied to the Registry settings in HKEY_Current_User that are stored in memory. The hierarchy that
determines the precedence of these updates is described in the "Group
Policy Hierarchy" section later in this chapter.

Group policies are configured and managed using a `Group Policy` console.
Figure 16.7 shows an example console window.

Figure 16.7 Group Policy console showing group policies affecting users.

Unlike most other Windows 2000 administration tools, no general-purpose Group Policy console can be launched from Administrative Tools. A Local Security Policy console is available, but it uses a subset of group policies specifically tailored for security. See Chapter 6, "Understanding Network Access Security and Kerberos," for details.

You can open a group policy snap-in from the Properties window of the Directory container that is linked to the policy. Site policies are accessed via the AD Sites and Services console. Domain and OU policies are accessed via the AD Users and Computers console. Local policies are accessed using a Group Policy Editor (GPE) console, Gpedit.msc, which is opened from the Run window or from a command prompt. This console is not included in the Administrative Tools menu for the same reason that the two Registry Editors are not listed. They can cause problems in the wrong hands.

The Group Policy Editor relies on templates for building the REGISTRY.POL entries associated with each policy. These templates are similar to classic System Policy templates but contain a wider variety of options. The templates are stored in ADM files in the \WINNT\INF directory. (In this case, \WINNT is %systemroot%.)

When clients download policies, the entries in the policy files are applied to local configuration files using client-side extensions. These take the form of DLLs. For example, the client-side extension that handles applying Registry updates from group policies is USERENV.DLL.

Finally, a series of local Registry keys store group policy management information and a local cache of policy updates for use if the domain is unavailable.

As a summary, these are the elements of a User and Computer group policies:

- **\WINNT\Sysvol** folders that are replicated between domain controllers
- **Group Policy Objects** under Sysvol that contain the policy files
- **Group Policy Container** objects in the Directory that point at the GPOs
- **OU, Domain, and Site containers** that have group policies linked to them
- **REGISTRY.POL files** that contain the Registry updates that are applied to the local Registry entries in memory at the clients
- **Group policy snap-in** that is used to configure and manage group policies
- **Administrative templates (ADM files)** that contain the REGISTRY.POL entries associated with each policy
- **Client-side extensions** that process policies locally and apply them to the appropriate configuration files
- **Local Registry files** that contain parameters that control the way group policies are applied and stored.

The remaining sections in the overview cover details of these elements and how they interact with each other.

Use Caution When Modifying Policies on Production Systems

If you experiment with group policies on a production system, you need to be aware that the policy entries you make in the Group Policy Editor are written to the REGISTRY.POL files immediately when you click OK. No "save settings" option, such as that in the Policy Editor, exists. After the entry is written, a client might get a copy of it seconds later during a periodic refresh.

Sysvol Structure

Domain controllers store group policy objects under \WINNT\Sysvol\. Figure 16.8 shows the folder structure.

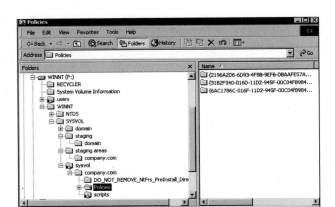

Figure 16.8 Directory and file structure of the \WINNT\Sysvol directory.

These structural elements affect group policy replication and client downloads:

- The \WINNT folder is not necessarily the same as %*systemroot*%. During domain controller promotion, the administrator selects a location for Sysvol. The folder must be on an NTFS5 volume.

- The \WINNT\Sysvol\Domain folder is replicated among all domain controllers in a domain.

- The two Company.com folders are not actually folders. They are reparse points that mount back to folders in \WINNT\Sysvol\Domain.

  \WINNT\Sysvol\Sysvol\Company.com mounts to \WINNT\Sysvol\Domain.

  \WINNT\Sysvol\Staging Areas\Company.com mounts to \WINNT\Sysvol\Staging\Domain.

  These reparse points are the reason that \WINNT\Sysvol must be on an NTFS5 volume.

- The \WINNT\Sysvol\Sysvol directory is shared as SYSVOL. Windows 2000 clients obtain access to the group policy folders through this share.

- Clients access the SYSVOL share on the server that authenticates them. That is the reason the folders must be replicated to all domain controllers.

- Each group policy object is given a separate folder with a name that matches the GUID assigned to the policy. The structure of this GPO is covered in the next section.

Group Policy Object Structure

Figure 16.9 shows the folder structure for an example group policy object. Systems track the location of GPOs based on the GUID of the top folder, so do not rename the folder.

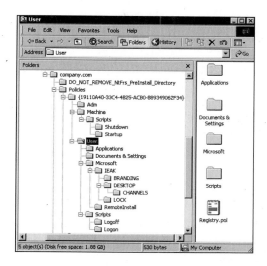

Figure 16.9 Folder structure for group policy stored in \WINNT\Sysvol\Domain.

Most policy folders don't have as extensive a subfolder distribution as the one pictured in Figure 16.9. If you have only a couple of policies assigned to local users and none to computers, the policy folder contains one active element, the REGISTRY.POL file with the user's Registry updates.

Each group policy folder has these basic elements:

- **REGISTRY.POL file.** This file contains the Registry updates that are downloaded by the client and applied to the local Registry entries in memory. If policies are assigned to both Users and Computers, each set of policies is stored in its own REGISTRY.POL file.

- **ADM folder.** This folder contains a copy of the Administrative templates (ADM file) used to generate the entries in the REGISTRY.POL files. These templates are copied from master templates in the \WINNT\INF folder on the domain controller where the policy is updated.

- **User folder.** This folder contains the policies that are applied to the HKEY_Current_User Registry entries when a user logs on.

- **Machine folder.** This folder contains the policies that are applied to the HKEY_Local_Machine Registry entries when a computer logs on.

Group Policy Container Structure

The Directory stores location and configuration information about group policy objects in a series of *Group Policy Container* (GPC) objects under `cn=Policies,cn=System,cn=Configuration,dc=domain,dc=root`.

Each GPC represents a policy. The common name (CN) of the GPC is the GUID that matches the GUID of its associated group policy object in `\WINNT\SYSVOL\Domain`. Figure 16.10 shows the GPC locations in the Directory.

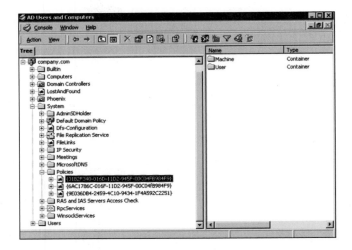

Figure 16.10   `AD Users and Computers` console
showing the locations of Policy objects.

A GPC object contains four attributes used for policy handling. You can view these attributes using the ADSI Editor from the Resource Kit. The attributes are:

- **GPC-File-Sys-Path.** This attribute contains the UNC path of the policy using the domain as the root of the path. This is called a *fault-tolerant path*. For example, the fault-tolerant path to a policy in the `Company.com` domain is:

`\\company.com\sysvol\company.com\policies\{policy-GUID}`

- **GPCFunctionalityVersion.** This attribute contains an integer value that represents the version of the Group Policy Editor that created the policy.

- **GPC-Machine-Extension-Names** and **GPC-User-Extension-Names.** These two attributes contain the GUID of the client-side extensions that support the User and Machine policies. See "Client-Side Extensions" later in this chapter for details.

OU, Domain, and Site Links

GPC objects represent one-half of the link between the OU, Domain, and Site containers to the GPOs on disk. The other half of the link is a GPLink attribute in the OU, Domain, and Site objects. The GPLink attribute contains the distinguished name of the GPC object that is linked to the Directory container. The CN component of that distinguished name is the GUID of the policy.

A GPC can be linked to more than one container. For example, you might have a group policy called Standard User that administrators in various offices can choose to link to their OU, if they want.

By the same token, a Directory container can be linked to more than one GPC. For example, you might have one policy for folder redirections, one for logon/logoff scripts, one for User and Computer configuration, and one for security settings.

Policy Replication

Before continuing with the enumeration of the group policy elements, it's time to pause and look at policy replication.

The GPC objects in the Directory are replicated between domain controllers by the Directory Replication Agent (DRA). The `\WINNT\Sysvol\Domain` folder is replicated between domain controllers by the File Replication Service (FRS).

The FRS does not work in conjunction with the DRA, so it is possible that GPCs and GPOs can be out of sync for a period of time, especially when replicating between sites. When you update policies, if you notice that it takes a particularly long time to get the GPCs and GPOs lined up, you may want to use the Replication Monitor tool to force replication. See Chapter 11, "Managing Active Directory Replication and Directory Maintenance," for details.

Another replication difference between DRA and FRS might cause you problems. The DRA can use SMTP (Simple Mail Transport Protocol) as a transport for sending Directory updates to remote sites over asynchronous connections (dial-up or ISDN lines). FRS does not support SMTP replication. If you have a remote dial-up site that uses SMTP for Directory updates, the domain controller at that site does not get group policies replicated from other domain controllers. If you want to use group policies at that location, you can create a policy at that domain controller (you can do this across the network) and then link the policy to the local site.

If policy replication fails, a File Replication Log in the Event Viewer reports on the problem and possible causes. The FRS Log entries tend to be a little on the obscure side, but at least they give you a starting point for troubleshooting.

REGISTRY.POL Files

Let's get back to the policy elements once again. User and Computer policies consist of Registry updates distributed in the form of REGISTRY.POL files. Each GPO has two REGISTRY.POL files, one for User Configuration Settings and one for Computer Configuration Settings. The REGISTRY.POL files are located in their respective policy folders in Sysvol.

Each User and Computer policy selection made using the Group Policy Editor affects at least one Registry entry. For example, the Enable Classic Shell policy modifies the value for `HKCU | Software | Microsoft | Windows | CurrentVersion | Policies | Explorer | ClassicShell`.

When setting a policy, the Group Policy Editor presents these alternatives.

- **Enabled.** This means the value associated with the policy is applied to the Registry setting. If the Enable Classic Shell policy is set to Enabled, the REGISTRY.POL entry sets `HKCU | Software | Microsoft | Windows | CurrentVersion | Policies | Explorer | ClassicShell` to 1. The user gets only a Classic shell and cannot select a Web-enabled shell.

- **Disabled.** This means the value associated with the policy is removed from the Registry. If the Enable Classic Shell policy is set to Disabled, the REGISTRY.POL entry either sets the `HKCU | Software | Microsoft | Windows | CurrentVersion | Policies | Explorer | ClassicShell` value to 0, or removes the setting completely, depending on how the template defines the action. Either way, the lack of a negative action is a positive action, so this restores the ability of the user to select a Web-enabled desktop.

- **Not Configured.** No external policy is applied. If the Enable Classic Shell policy is set to Not Configured, the REGISTRY.POL entry does not contain any entries for the `HKCU | Software | Microsoft | Windows | CurrentVersion | Policies | Explorer | ClassicShell` value.

REGISTRY.POL File Structure

A REGISTRY.POL file is a Unicode text file with a header and a body.

- The header contains a Registry file signature and the version number of the Group Policy Editor that created it.
- The body contains a series of semicolon-delimited entries containing Registry updates in this form: `[Key; Value; Type; Size; Data]`.

This method of storing Registry updates packs a lot of entries in a small file. It also gives the system a great deal of flexibility in applying updates, because REGISTRY.POL entries from different sources can be easily combined.

Registry updates contained in REGISTRY.POL files overlay existing Registry entries. They do not overwrite them permanently. For example, consider the Registry value `HKCU | Software | Microsoft | Windows | CurrentVersion | Explorer | Policies | NoDesktop` that controls whether icons on the Desktop are shown to the user. A group policy called `Hide All Icons On Desktop` writes to this Registry value. This is the REGISTRY.POL entry that enables the NoDesktop feature:

```
PReg
[Software\Microsoft\Windows\CurrentVersion\Policies\Explorer ;NoDesktop; 4 ; 4 ; 1 ]
```

When the REGISTRY.POL file containing this entry is downloaded, a special process called Userenv applies the update to the Registry keys in memory but does not overwrite the Registry hive stored on disk.

If the `Hide All Icons On Desktop` policy is later set to disable the NoDesktop feature, the REGISTRY.POL entry looks like this:

```
PReg
[Software\Microsoft\Windows\CurrentVersion\Policies\Explorer ;**del NoDesktop; 1 ; 4 ; 20 ]
<<The ** is an action flag. Actions include **DeleteKeys and **SecureKey, among
others.>>
```

For the most part, you do not need to be concerned with the structure of the REGISTRY.POL files. You can make your selections in the Group Policy Editor with the confidence that whatever you select, for better or worse, is propagated to the selected clients in your network.

If you modify a template or create a new template to implement a policy that is not part of the prepackaged list, it's a good idea to check your work by examining the REGISTRY.POL entry that your new policy sends out, just as a final check that it is doing what you intend it to do. See "Modifying ADM Templates" later in this chapter for more information.

Group Policy Hierarchy

Policies can be linked to a variety of containers that affect the same clients. When a client downloads a set of policies from different sources, it merges the REGISTRY.POL files from each policy type (User and Computer) into a single POL file for that type.

- The REGISTRY.POL files for User settings are combined into one NTUSER.POL file stored at the root of the user's profile in `\Documents and Settings`.

- The REGISTRY.POL files for Computer settings are combined into a REGISTRY.POL file stored along with the local policy settings in `\WINNT\System32\GroupPolicy\Machine`.

The Registry updates contained in these REGISTRY.POL files are additive unless a collision occurs. That is to say, if a client downloads several policies with updates that affect different Registry updates, all updates are applied. If two or more REGISTRY.POL files have updates that affect the same Registry entry, the system uses a hierarchy to determine which policy takes precedence.

If a user or computer downloads policies from more than one source, they are put in order based on a hierarchy and applied sequentially. These are the sources of policy-based Registry updates and their hierarchy:

- **Classic NT System Policy.** For backward compatibility, Windows 2000 clients check for an NTCONFIG.POL file at the NETLOGON share on their domain controller. These system policies tattoo the local Registry, so this check can be disabled using the Group Policy `Administrative Templates | System | Group Policy | Disable System Policy`.

- **Local.** A local Windows 2000 computer can have one set of local User and Computer policies.

- **Site.** Site boundaries are set according to WAN topology, not domain topology, so associating a group policy with a Site can be a tricky business because it has the potential of crossing administrative boundaries. The best use for Site policies is distributing networking configurations that are unique to a local network, such as RAS policies.

- **Domain.** A Domain policy is applied to every user and computer in the domain, regardless of site location. Enterprises with a strong, central IT department like Domain policies, but enterprises with a more diffuse management structure may prefer avoiding them in favor of OU policies.

- **OU.** Group Policies associated with Organizational Units have the highest precedence. This gives local administrators the most control over local desktops. For example, let's say the Company.com domain administrators set a policy to remove the Run command from the START menu. The Phoenix administrators get complaints from their users who like the Run command. The Phoenix administrators can set an OU policy that specifically enables the Run command. This takes precedence and gives the Phoenix users the Run command.

In addition to the hierarchy of policy sources, group policies can be applied selectively to particular security groups. For example, a telemarketing organization might have three policies.

- A highly restrictive policy is configured to apply to the Outbound_Sales group.
- A slightly looser policy is configured to apply to the Customer_Support group.
- The least restrictive policy is configured to apply to the Sales_Manager group.

Alternatively, you could put the user objects into three separate OUs and link the policies to the OUs. Unless you have some other administrative reason for dividing the user community by OU, it is easier to manage users in a single container and apply policies by group. No architectural or performance difference exists.

Blocking Policy Inheritance

Local administrators of a particular OU can choose to block policies inherited from OUs higher in the Directory or lower in precedence. This includes Site and Domain policies as well those inherited from parent OUs.

Inherited group policies are blocked by a Block Policy Inheritance option set at the MMC console. Figure 16.11 shows the Properties window for an OU where the Block Policy Inheritance option is checked.

The Standard User policy in Figure 16.11 is applied at the OU level, and the policy block prevents Domain and Site policies from overriding it.

Policy blocks can be overcome with a No Override option set at the Domain or Site policy. Figure 16.12 shows the Group Policy Options window where the No Override option is set under Link Options.

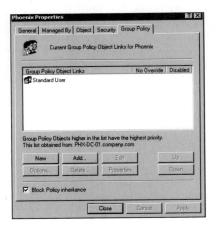

Figure 16.11 OU `Properties` window showing
`Group Policy` tab and list of group policy links.

Figure 16.12 Group policy `Options`
window showing the No Override option.

This method of handling policy inheritance parallels the way administrative
rights are assigned in the Directory. Local administrators in an OU are not
given admin rights at the Domain level. Department administrators in a child
OU are not given admin rights at the Site level. Using the No Override
option might not be a good idea in a big domain with multiple OUs.

Policy Download Mechanisms

When a Windows 2000 client logs on to the domain, it checks the Domain,
Site, and OU objects for links to GPC objects. It then uses the fault-tolerant
path information from the GPC objects to find the policy folders in the
SYSVOL share. Finally, it downloads the policy files and applies the contents
to the local Registry image in memory.

After the client completes logon, he or she polls the authenticating domain controller every 90 minutes for updates to Group Policies. This interval can be changed with a group policy, and the group policy refresh interval can be changed with a group policy. See "Managing Group Policy Policies" later in this chapter.

When the client logs off, it checks again for group policy updates based on the assumption that a policy might be triggered by a logoff event.

Many policies require the computer to restart before they take effect. By distributing policies throughout the workday, you can get a head start on the next day's logon.

While the system is operating, you can refresh a client manually using the Secedit utility with the following syntax:

```
secedit /refreshpolicy machine_policy (or user_policy)
```

The Secedit utility has other features that are intended for use with security-related group policies. See Chapter 6 for more details.

Administrative Templates

The REGISTRY.POL entries that define User and Computer policies are taken from administrative templates. These ADM templates have the same format as their classic System Policy counterparts.

Windows 2000 comes with a prepackaged set of ADM templates stored in the \WINNT\INF directory. This is a list:

- **Winnt.adm.** User interface system policies for NT4
- **Windows.adm.** User interface system policies for Windows 9x
- **Common.adm.** User interface system policies common to both platforms
- **Shell.adm.** Limited number of Explorer Shell restrictions used to control Active Desktop
- **Inetres.adm (loaded by default).** Internet Explorer policies affecting Windows components such as Internet Explorer, Control Panel, Offline Pages, Browser Menus, Persistence Behavior, and Administrator Approved Controls
- **System.adm (loaded by default).** Comprehensive set of system restrictions including Start Menu and taskbar settings; Desktop Settings, Control Panel settings; Network settings; System settings, such as logon/logoff settings and group policy settings; and policies for Windows components, such as Explorer, MMC, Task Scheduler, and Windows Installer

- **Inetset.adm.** Additional Internet Explorer settings, including AutoComplete, default Toolbar buttons, Display settings, Advanced Tab settings, and URL Encoding
- **Inetcorp.adm.** Specialized controls for Internet Explorer languages, dialup restrictions, and caching
- **Conf.adm.** NetMeeting policies
- **Wmp.adm.** Windows Media Player policies, including settings for customizing the WMP navigation bar and network settings

The first four ADM files are included for backward compatibility with NT4. Windows 2000 includes a copy of System Policy Editor, Poledit, for use in constructing NTCONFIG.POL files for managing downlevel clients.

Client-Side Extensions

The Group Policy snap-in has several extensions that define its functionality. For User and Computer policies, the snap-ins take the form of the ADM templates listed in the previous section. Other policy extensions include security entries, folder redirections, scripts, and software installation.

Each of these server-side extensions is paired with a client-side extension that interprets and implements the policy. These client-side extensions come in the form of DLLs. Table 16.1 lists the extensions and their DLLs.

Table 16.1   **Group Policy Extensions and Client-Side DLLs**

Server-Side Extension	Implementing DLL
Registry Administrative Templates (Computers and Users)	USERENV.DLL
Folder Redirection Editor	FDEPLOY.DLL
Scripts (Computers and Users)	GPTEXT.DLL
Security Settings	SCECLI.DLL
Software Installation (Computers and Users)	APPMGMTS.DLL
Disk Quota	DSKQUOTA.DLL
Encrypting File System Recovery	SCECLI.DLL
Internet Explorer Branding	IEDKCS32.DLL
IP Security (IPSEC)	GPTEXT.DLL

Read the following for more information about how these client-side extensions operate:

- Userenv.dll takes responsibility for handling Registry-based properties. It also handles loading the NTUSER.DAT file into the Registry when the user logs on. You may see USERENV.DLL entries in the Event Log from time to time if it has problems handling policies or if the Registry gets too large. See "Group Policy Troubleshooting" later in this chapter for information about troubleshooting Userenv.dll problems.

- GPTEXT.DLL acts as a front end for the Windows Script Host (WSH). It also handles batch files. See "Using Logon Scripts" later in this chapter for more information.

- FDEPLOY.DLL is used to manage file replication between a client and a central file repository. See "Managing Folder Redirections" later in this chapter for more information.

- DSKQUOTA.DLL is covered in Chapter 13, "Managing File Systems."

- SCECLI.DLL is covered in Chapter 15.

- Internet Explorer branding and software distribution are outside the scope of this book.

Registry Tip: Client-Side Extension List
The client-side extension list can be found at HKLM | Software | Microsoft | Windows NT | CurrentVersion | WINLOGON | GPExtensions.

ADM Handling

The Group Policy Editor uses two ADM templates by default. These are System.adm and Inetres.adm. Others can be added by right-clicking the Administrative Templates icon and selecting ADD/REMOVE TEMPLATES. Figure 16.13 shows the list of available templates.

Figure 16.13 List of administrative templates available for loading into the Group Policy Editor.

When the Group Policy Editor loads, it copies the selected templates from the \WINNT\INF folder to an Adm folder, its associated policy folder. The server-side policy extensions use this template when creating their REGISTRY.POL entries in response to selections in the Group Policy Editor.

When you create a policy, you do not alter the template. The entries in the template are copied to the REGISTRY.POL file for the policy.

Two group policies are installed by default:

1. Default Domain Policy, linked to the Domain container

2. Default Domain Controller Policy, linked to the Domain Controller OU

You can either Enable and Disable entries in these policies, or create new policies with different selections.

You can modify an ADM template with your own entries but a catch exists. Each time the Group Policy Editor opens a policy, it refreshes its local copies of the ADM templates with the master templates in \WINNT\INF. If you change a local policy template, you could lose your changes. The system checks time stamps, so the local ADM is not overwritten immediately, but if someone updates the master \WINNT\INF template, all local changes are overwritten the next time the Group Policy Editor is opened. The system does not warn you that this is happening. The next section describes how to modify an ADM template.

Registry Parameters that Control Group Policies

Registry keys and values that control group policy implementation are stored under HKLM | Software | Microsoft | Windows | CurrentVersion | Group Policy. Figure 16.14 shows the arrangement of the subkeys.

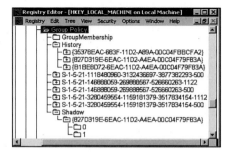

Figure 16.14 Registry Editor showing hierarchy of group policy keys.

The following subkeys are particularly important in controlling the way policies are applied to a machine:

- **History.** This key contains the GUID for each user-side extension called by a group policy. An example of a policy extension is the USERENV.DLL extension that handles REGISTRY.POL file entries. Underneath each extension is a list of sequentially numbered keys that contain details for each policy that makes use of that extension. The keys are assigned in the order that the policies are assigned. Most of the values assigned to the policy are self-explanatory. The GPOLink number starts with 0 for no link; 1=Local Machine, 2=Site, 3=Domain, and 4=OU.

- **SIDs.** This series of keys represents users who logged on to the machine. A GroupMembership key under this entry lists the user's group memberships by SID. If you ever wonder which SIDs constitute a user's access token, this key can tell you.

- **Shadow.** This key lists the security policies that are currently in force on the machine and the order they were applied. The security extension, SCECLI.DLL, uses this key. Its use is covered in Chapter 6.

Modifying ADM Templates

Let's take one final break before ending the discussion of group policy elements. You may find it necessary at one time or another to apply a policy that does not have an entry in one of the prepackaged templates. When this happens, you must either modify an existing template or create a new one.

ADM templates are standard ASCII text files that can be modified using a text editor or Notepad. This is an excerpt from Inetres.adm showing examples of each required component:

```
; shell.adm

CLASS USER

CATEGORY !!Shell
KEYNAME Software\Microsoft\Windows\CurrentVersion\Policies\Explorer
    POLICY !!Shell
        EXPLAIN  !!ClassicShellExplain
        PART !!ClassicShell CHECKBOX
            VALUENAME ClassicShell
        END PART
    END POLICY
END CATEGORY


[strings]
ClassicShell="Enable Classic Shell"
ClassicShellExplain="Changes from Web-based shell to standard Explorer shell."
Shell="Shell"
```

This is a description of the components in this ADM entry:

- **CLASS.** Tells the system which Registry subtree to edit. The USER class modifies HKCU. The MACHINE class modifies HKLM.
- **CATEGORY.** Defines a heading in the Group Policy Editor. Has no effect on the Registry.
- **KEYNAME.** Defines the Registry key that is modified by this policy.
- **POLICY/END POLICY.** Defines the entry that is made to the Registry key.
- **PART/ENDPART**. Defines several types of interfaces in the Group Policy Editor that can be used to collect information for applying to the Registry entry.
- **[strings].** This section defines text to use in place of the string entries in the body of the template. The double-bang (!!) tells the system to search for a string. If you prefer, you can enter the text directly on the line with double-quotes, but string entries are preferred for maintainability.

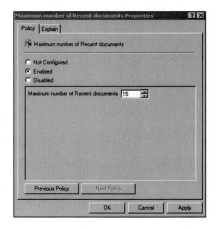

Figure 16.15 Example policy window showing NUMERIC display for PART type.

The PART section, which is optional, is used to create the user input window in the GPE. If a PART is not specified, the GPE displays a standard window. If a PART is specified, the PART TYPE must also be specified. Figure 16.15 shows the GPE display for a NUMERIC type. These are the PART TYPES and their functions:

- **EDITTEXT.** Displays a field for entering text.
- **NUMERIC.** Displays a field for entering numbers. An optional spinner control is available.
- **CHECKBOX.** Tells the GPE to display a check box. When the check box is checked, the value for the policy is set to 1. If it is unchecked, the value is set to 0.
- **COMBOBOX.** Tells GPE to display a combo box.
- **DROPDOWNLIST.** Displays a combo box with a drop-down list. Use this when you want to specify a set of options.
- **LISTBOX.** Displays a list box with *Add* and *Remove* buttons. Use this for applying multiple values to a single key.
- **TEXT.** Displays label text.

After you modify or create an ADM file, be sure to open the Group Policy Editor and load the template. This forces the editor to do a validation check on your entry. The most common mistake is to forget to put the required entries under [strings].

If the GPE rejects an entry, it does not load the template. If you are working on a master template in \WINNT\INF, make sure your change passes muster because it overwrites the local ADM files and can cause no end of grief if the entry is incorrect.

Creating and Distributing User and Computer Group Policies

Like most administrative chores, the complicated part of managing group policies is deciding exactly what you want to do. When you have a plan, creating and distributing the policies to implement that plan takes only a few minutes.

These are the steps for creating a new Group Policy Object and setting a policy with it. The example creates a policy linked to an OU named Phoenix:

Procedure 16.13   Creating and Configuring a Group Policy Object

1. Open the AD Users and Computers console.
2. Right-click an OU containing user objects you want to manage and select PROPERTIES from the fly-out menu. The Properties window opens for that container. Figure 16.16 shows the Properties window after a new policy is created.

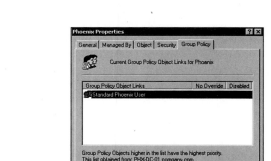

Figure 16.16 `Properties` window for Phoenix OU
after creating a new policy.

3. Click `New`. A new policy entry appears in the list under Group Policy
   Object Links.

4. Give the new policy a short name that describes its function and association, such as `Standard Phoenix User`. You are free to change this name at
   any time. The actual contents of the group policy are defined by a GUID
   that does not change. The policy folder is created in the `\WINNT\Sysvol\`
   `Sysvol\<domain_name>` folder.

5. Click `Options`. The `Options` window opens. Two `Link Options` exist.

   `No Override`--This option blocks Registry entries inherited from policies
   higher in the Directory from overwriting the Registry entries made by
   this policy.

   `Disabled`--This option stops this policy from being distributed. It does not
   return the local Registries to their pre–GPO configuration.

6. Click `Cancel` to return to the `Properties` window.

7. Click `Edit` to modify the contents of the group policy. The Group Policy
   snap-in opens with the new group policy name at the top of the tree.

8. Expand the tree to USER CONFIGURATION | ADMINISTRATIVE TEMPLATES |
   DESKTOP. Figure 16.17 shows the list of Desktop policy options.

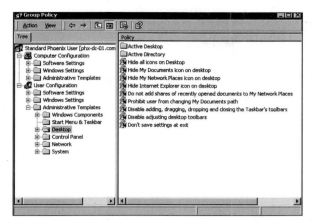

Figure 16.17   Group Policy snap-in showing Desktop policy options.

9. Double-click `Hide All Icons On Desktop`. The `Properties` window appears for this option.

10. Click `Enabled` and then click `OK` to save the change and return to the main `Group Policy` console. The `Setting` entry for the option now shows `Enabled`. The REGISTRY.POL file in the USER folder associated with this policy is updated as soon as you click `OK`.

11. Close the `Group Policy` console and return to the `Properties` window for the OU.

12. Close the `Properties` window to return to the `AD Users and Computers` console.

13. Close the console.

Now verify the policy by logging on at a desktop using an account that is in the OU linked to the group policy you just created. The user does not get any desktop icons.

Locating Registry Entries in ADM Templates

One of the challenges in trying to alter a particular Registry setting with a group policy is figuring out which template, if any, holds the entry that controls that Registry setting.

The Group Policy Editor lists string entries that are supposed to describe the function of the policy, but it can be difficult to be certain of the exact Registry entry that a given policy changes.

No search function exists to look for a particular Registry entry. This is what you have to do.

First, determine the Registry entry you need to change. You can search the Registry for clues to the entry or use Microsoft KnowledgeBase, but I often use the following technique. If I know what triggers a particular Registry entry, I load the Ntregmon utility from www.sysinternals.com and use it to determine which keys are being updated when the Registry change is triggered.

When you know the Registry setting you need to change, search for the Registry key or value in the ADM files in \WINNT\INF using the Search utility in the START menu.

If you can't find the Registry entry you want to change in an existing ADM template, you can modify an existing ADM template or create a new template of your own that contains the changes.

Applying Policies to Groups

The scope of a policy can be narrowed to include only a particular group or groups selected out of the OU, Domain, or Site to which the policy is linked. Using this feature, you can tailor a set of policies to meet the demands of select user populations. Policy selection by group is done using the Security settings for the policy as follows:

Procedure 16.14   **Applying Group Policies to Specific Groups**

1. Open the MMC console containing the object you want to manage. This set of steps uses the AD Users and Computers console.

2. Right-click the Domain icon or an OU icon and select PROPERTIES from the fly-out menu to open the Properties window.

3. Double-click an existing policy to open the Group Policy console.

4. Right-click the Policy icon at the top of the tree and select PROPERTIES from the fly-out menu to open the Properties window.

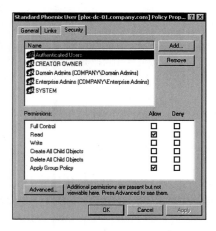

Figure 16.18   Example Group Policy Properties showing Security options.

5. Select the `Security` tab. See Figure 16.18. The `Apply Group Policy` option under `Permissions` determines whether the policy is applied to the highlighted `Name`. The example shows that the policy applies to `Authenticated Users`.

6. Click `OK` to close the `Properties` window and return to the `AD Users and Computers` console.

7. Close the console.

Applying this policy to the Authenticated Users group means that the Registry updates are downloaded and applied by any user who authenticates in the domain who is represented in the Directory by a User object in the linked OU. You can create groups if you want to apply the policy in a more discriminating fashion.

You can also deny access to certain group if this is more efficient. For example, you can set a policy that affects users in one large group—Authenticated Users, for instance—and then deny access to a subset of that population, such as IT_Admins.

Group Policy Creator Owners Group

Windows 2000 comes with several predefined groups to use for delegation. The Group Policy Creator Owners group falls into this category. The group is on the ACL for the `cn=Policies,cn=System,dc=domain,dc=root` container with Create All Child Objects permissions.

Group Policy Troubleshooting

If you set a group policy but it doesn't seem to work, check these items.

- **Event Viewer.** Look in the Application log for entries from the Userenv service. Warnings from this service are your first indication that something went wrong with group policy downloads.

- **Access Rights.** One common problem with group policies is security access rights. Always make sure that the user has rights to the policy you're trying to apply. The easiest way to check this is to use the appropriate AD console to open the group policy properties for the associated container and then select the `Security` tab. The user should be a member of a group with `Allow` privileges.

- **Incorrect Policy Links.** Another common problem when configuring group policies is "losing the map," as they say in fighter pilot training. You may have linked the policy to one container but are testing it with a user account from another container. Or someone may have put another policy in place higher in the policy hierarchy than yours and is either overwriting your entry or blocking it completely. This is an especially frustrating problem in Windows 2000, because no tool is suitable for tracing all the policies that can be or should be applied to a particular user. Microsoft promises such a tool in the next maintenance release.

- **Debug Userenv.** As a last-ditch effort to find the problem, you can enable group policy logging. In NT4, this requires installing the checked version of USERENV.DLL, the client-side extension in charge of Registry updates, to get the required debug symbols. This is not necessary in Windows 2000. The debug symbols are included in the free build of USERENV.DLL. You must add a Registry value to the WINLOGON key to enable logging.

```
Key:     HKLM | Software | Microsoft | Windows NT | CurrentVersion | Winlogon
Value:   UserEnvDebugLevel
Data:    0x10002 (Hex) of type Reg_Dword
```

Restart the computer after adding the value. The log file is located in \WINNT\Debug\Userenv.log. Be prepared with a cup of coffee and some patience. The log contains a *lot* of information.

Creating a Custom Group Policy Editor Console

Rather than use the AD consoles to open group policies, you can create custom MMC consoles to launch the Group Policy snap-in. Single snap-in consoles take less time to load. You can also tailor the console with different snap-in extensions. For example, you can create a console for Operations that loads the User and Computer Policies extension and another console for LAN Security that loads the Security extensions. Create and configure custom group policy consoles as follows:

Procedure 16.15 **Creating a Custom *Group Policy Editor* Console**

1. Open a Run window using START | RUN, enter MMC, and click OK. This opens an empty MMC console.

2. From the console menu, select CONSOLE | ADD/REMOVE SNAP-IN. The Add/Remove Snap-in window opens.

3. Click Add. The Add Standalone Snap-in window opens.

4. Double-click Group Policy. The Select Group Policy Object window opens.

5. Under Group Policy Object, verify that Local Computer is listed.

6. Click `Finish` to add the GPO to the list of standalone snap-ins and return to the `Add Standalone Snap-in` window.

7. Click `Close` to return to the `Add/Remove Snap-in` window.

8. Select the `Extensions` tab. Note that the `Add All Extensions` option is selected by default. You can deselect this option and then select those extensions suited for the task at hand.

9. Click OK to save the configuration and return to the MMC console.

10. From the console menu, select CONSOLE | SAVE AS. The `Save As` window opens.

11. Give the console a name, such as GPE. The console is saved in My Documents unless you choose otherwise.

12. If you are configuring this console for other administrators, take the console out of Author mode. From the console menu, select CONSOLE | OPTIONS. The `Options` window opens.

13. Under `Console Mode`, select `User Mode - Full Access`.

14. Click OK to save the change and return to the main console window.

Using Group Policies to Manage Group Policies

The policies that manage group policies are managed using—you guessed it—group policies. These "policies on policies" are located in the Group Policy Editor under `Computer Configuration (User Configuration)` | `Administrative Templates` | `System` | `Group Policies`. This is a description of the group policy policies and when you may want to use them:

- **Disable System Policy.** This policy tells Windows 2000 computers to ignore classic NT policies distributed via NTCONFIG.POL. Use this policy to avoid getting the permanent Registry updates inflicted by system policies.

- **Group Policy Slow Link Detection.** The system normally uses 500Kbps as the threshold for deciding whether a link is slow or fast. Using this policy, you can change the threshold. The policy changes the Registry key `HKLM` | `Software` | `Policies` | `Microsoft` | `Windows` | `System` | `GroupPolicyMinTransferRate`.

Measuring Link Performance

Unlike classic NT, Windows 2000 actually measures link performance to determine whether a slow or fast link exists. The calculation goes like this:

- Ping a server with 0 bytes of data and time the round trip. If the time is less than 10 ms, it's a fast link.

- Ping the same server with 4KB of data and time the round trip.

- Calculate the delta between the 4KB round trip and the 0KB round trip. This results in the time necessary to move 4KB of data.

- Repeat three times and get an average 4KB transfer time.

- Convert to bits-per-second and compare to benchmark. The default benchmark is 500Kbps.

- **Policy Processing.** This series of policies controls how each client-side extension handles background processing for its policy type. The policies with processing options are Registry policies, Disk Quota policies, Scripts policies, Security policies, EFS Recovery policies, Software Installation policies, and IPSec policies. Most of the policies consist of three parts:

  - A Do Not Apply During Periodic Background Processing option prevents updating the associated policies during the 90-minute polling for updates.

  - A Do Not Apply Over Slow Link policy blocks periodic updates if the user is connected with a link that is slower than the slow link threshold.

  - A Process Even If the Group Policy Objects Have Not Changed option reapplies the policies even if they are updated. This is an expensive option in terms of downloads from the logon server and network traffic.

- **Disable Background Refresh.** Under normal circumstances, user and computer clients first check for group policies during logon, and then about every 90 minutes throughout the workday. Use this policy if you want to disable the periodic refresh. If you disable refreshes, you may have problems distributing policy updates to users who never log off.

- **Group Policy Refresh Interval for Computers (Users).** This policy sets two keys under HKLM | Software | Policies | Microsoft | Windows | System that determine the refresh interval. The first key, GroupPolicyRefreshTime, sets the interval itself. This is 90 minutes by default. The second key, GroupPolicyOffsetTime, randomizes the update intervals so that clients don't inundate the logon server with update requests at the same time throughout the day.

- **Apply Group Policy for Computers Synchronously During Startup** and **Apply Group Policy for Users Synchronously During Startup.** Under normal circumstances, policies must be downloaded and applied before WINLOGON displays the logon prompt. This can delay the appearance of the prompt and cause users to wonder whether the machine has hung. By selecting synchronous options, WINLOGON displays the prompt before policies finish downloading. This mollifies anxious users but does not speed up the overall logon process.

- **Run Logon Scripts Synchronously.** This policy enables the Explorer shell to initialize while a script is running. Don't use this option if you have logon scripts that change the shell.

- **Run Logon Scripts Visible.** Under most circumstances, you do not want to bother users with strange messages during logon. They see enough that they don't understand. By default, logon scripts run in the background. Enable this policy if you want to display scripts for troubleshooting.

- **Exclude Directories in Roaming Profile.** Uncontrolled growth of roaming profiles means headaches for the administrators responsible for maintaining profile servers. The extra data fills up expensive spinning storage and causes additional traffic during morning and evening logon/logoffs. This policy enables you to exclude folders, such as the Temp folder, Temporary Internet Files folder, and so forth. You can also exclude My Documents and Favorites, but it's better to redirect these folders rather than take the chance of losing data.

- **Limit Profile Size (available under System ¦ Logon\Logoff).** This is another policy that helps to control profile-related storage and traffic. Because users can plunk just about anything into their profile, the profile folders get very large. If you try to control profile bloat by using quotas, you could get a user into a position in which the local profile exceeds the quota. If you set the quota so that it cannot be exceeded, when the user logs off, the profile only partially replicates. The Limit Profile Size option uses a utility called Proquota.exe to monitor profile size and warn the user if it exceeds the allowable limit. Set the profile size limit to something less than the user's quota on the profile server.

- **Group Policy Domain Controller Selection.** Ordinarily, clients download their group policies from their Authenticating domain controller. You can use this policy to specify a particular domain controller from which to obtain policies. For example, you might have several domain controllers in a large site but only one or two with the horsepower to handle hundreds or thousands of policy downloads.

- **User Group Policy Loopback Processing Mode.** Because users log on after their computers log on, user policies are applied last and take precedence. You may encounter circumstances when computer policies need to take precedence. This could be a lab computer or a kiosk computer, or simply a computer that you do not want to be affected by user settings. Loopback processing has two options for this: *Merge* and *Replace*. With Merge, user policies are applied and then the computer settings are reapplied. Using Replace, the user settings are ignored.

Using Logon Scripts

Not all environment management involves Registry updates. Sometimes what is called for is a plain old logon script.

Microsoft only grudgingly admits that logon scripts are a necessary and useful way to manage users. Classic NT has such poor support for scripting that an entire industry sprang up to provide scripting capabilities. Some of those third-party tools are included in the Windows 2000 Resource Kit.

But like a reformed substance abuser turned zealot, Microsoft changed its ways dramatically. So many scripting options are stuffed into Windows 2000 that now the problem is deciding which one to spend time learning. All the popular scripting languages are supported, but the star of the show, at least from Microsoft's perspective, is the new on-board scripting engine, *Windows Script Host.*

Windows Script Host, first introduced in the NT4 Option Pack as Windows Script*ing* Host until Microsoft developed a scripting engine called Windows Script and had to change the name of the host, is a full procedural language with all the bells and whistles you would expect. A full command language reference for VBScript, JScript, and Windows Script is included in the Platform SDK, available at www.microsoft.com.

One of the advantages to Windows Script is its capability to support VBScript and Jscript functions as well as extensions for third-party script engines such as Perl, Rexx, Kix, and so forth.

Regardless of the script alternative you choose, the script handling in Windows 2000 is the same. You create the script and put it on a domain controller in the \WINNT\Sysvol\Domain\Scripts folder. From there, it is replicated to all other domain controllers.

You do not need to put the script in a policy folder. The group policy that controls logon/logoff scripts can point at any location in the \WINNT\Sysvol\Domain directory. Recall that the underlying folders referenced by the SYSVOL share are actually reparse points that are mounted back to

`\WINNT\Sysvol\Domain`. By putting your script in the
`\WINNT\Sysvol\Domain\Scripts` folder, it automatically appears under the
SYSVOL share.

Two more advantages to storing your scripts in
`\WINNT\Sysvol\Domain\Scripts` are as follows:

- **Fault-tolerant share names.** Because every domain controller has a
  SYSVOL share, you can reference the share in a UNC with a domain
  name rather than a server name. Microsoft terms this a *fault-tolerant share*
  name. When you specify the UNC path, put the FQDN of the domain
  instead of a server. For example, in the `Company.com` domain, the fault-
  tolerant UNC path to SYSVOL is

  `\\company.com\SYSVOL\Scripts\<script_name>`.

- **Script support for downlevel clients.** Classic Windows clients do not
  download group policies. They must be configured for a specific script,
  and that script must be in the NETLOGON share. Windows 2000 provides support for downlevel clients by sharing `\WINNT\Sysvol\Domain\`
  `Scripts` as NETLOGON. See the sidebar titled "Classic Logon Script
  Replication" for more information.

Classic Logon Script Replication

Classic Windows is hard-coded to look for an assigned logon script in the NETLOGON share of the authenticating server.

The NETLOGON share on a classic NT domain controller points at a directory called `WINNT\System32\Repl\Import\Scripts`, where the `Repl` stands for Replication. A complementary directory, `WINNT\System32\Repl\Export\Scripts`, provides a staging point for script replication.

The classic Primary Domain Controller (PDC) has to be configured to replicate the contents of the `Export` direc-tory to the `Import` directory both to itself and to all Backup Domain Controllers. This ensures that clients authen-ticating to any domain controller get the logon script from the NETLOGON share.

Classic replication uses a service called Lmrepl, or LanManReplicator. Script replication using this service is—I want to put this as professionally as possible—a little ornery.

Lmrepl is not supported on Windows 2000. If you want to continue to provide logon scripting to downlevel clients and you still have classic BDCs, you must configure the Task Scheduler with a batch file to XCOPY the script to the `\Export\Scripts` directory on a BDC. Then, you must configure replication outward from that BDC to the remaining BDCs. Microsoft terms this an Lmrepl bridge.

Assigning Logon/Logoff Scripts to Windows 2000 Clients

This example distributes a small logon script to the users in the Phoenix OU
of the `Company.com` domain. The logon script, Logon.vbs, is a small VB script

that just says "Hello, Administrator. Welcome to the Company.com domain." The script looks like this:

```
Set localnet = Wscript.CreateObject( "Wscript.Network" )
Wscript.Echo "Hello, " & localnet.Username & ". Welcome to the " & localnet.UserDomain
➥& " domain."
```

The actions to load the script and configure the group policy to distribute it are as follows:

Procedure 16.16 **Assigning Logon/Logoff Scripts to Windows 2000 Clients**

---

1. Copy the script to the \WINNT\Sysvol\Domain\Scripts folder. From here it is automatically replicated to the other domain controllers.

2. Open the Group Policy console for the policy you want to associate with the script. For example, if you want users in the Phoenix OU to get a specific logon script, edit the group policy for the Phoenix OU.

3. Expand the tree to User Configuration | Windows Settings | Scripts (Logon/Logoff). Two icons, Logon and Logoff, appear in the right pane.

4. Double-click the Logon icon to open its Properties window. Figure 16.19 shows an example with one script already loaded.

Figure 16.19 Logon Properties window showing existing logon script.

5. Click Add. The Add A Script window opens. See Figure 16.20.

Figure 16.20 `Add A Script` window showing the fault-tolerant UNC path to a script.

6. Use the Browse button to navigate to the `\WINNT\Sysvol\Sysvol\` `<domain_name>\Scripts` folder. Be sure not to go any higher because you'll be out of the reparse area and onto the local drive.

7. Select the script and click `Open` to add the script name and path to the `Script Name` field in the `Add A Script` window. Be sure the UNC path uses a fault-tolerant syntax.

8. Click `OK` to add the script to the list in `Logon Properties`.

9. Click `OK` to save the changes and close the `Properties` window.

Log on using an account that is in the OU or domain linked to the Group Policy containing the script to verify that it works.

Assigning Logon Scripts to Downlevel Clients

Users at downlevel Windows clients must be assigned a logon script in their user object in the Directory. Classic Windows clients are hard-coded to look for their assigned logon script in the NETLOGON share of their authenticating domain controller. See the sidebar titled "Classic Logon Script Replication" earlier in this chapter for more information.

Assign a logon script to a downlevel Windows user as follows:

Procedure 16.17 Assigning Logon Scripts to Downlevel Clients

1. Open the `AD Users and Groups` console.

2. Expand the tree to show the user object you want to configure.

3. Double-click the object to open the `Properties` window.

4. Select the `Profile` tab. Figure 16.21 shows a sample entry for a logon script. Enter the name of the script, not the path. The script must be located in the NETLOGON share, `\WINNT\Sysvol\Domain\Scripts`.

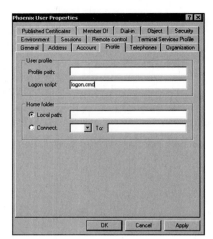

Figure 16.21   User Properties window showing Profile tab and logon script entry.

5. Click OK to save the settings and close the window.

6. Close the console.

7. Test the script by logging on. You should use a downlevel client. Legacy scripts work with Windows 2000, but they do not display by default.

Batch Files and Useful Environment Variables

If coding a logon script using a complex language seems like overkill to you, you can always fall back on batch files. You can build fairly sophisticated batch files using the CMD command interpreter. (I know a few DOS mavens who could probably code an entire operating system in a batch file.) The batch interpreter lacks a sophisticated looping and programming structure, but if all you want to do is set an environment variable or map a few drives, a batch file is more suitable than a VB script.

Running Legacy Scripts on Windows 2000

Windows 2000 automatically runs scripts with a BAT or a CMD extension in the background at the client. This is true even if you put breaks in the script to try to keep it on the screen.

If you want a batch or command file to display on the screen, enable the following group policy:

User Configuration | Administrative Templates | System | Logon/Logoff | Run Logon Scripts Visible

Several environment variables are useful when scripting for user account management. They are:

- **USERPROFILE.** The path to the user's local profile, typically `C:\Documents and Settings\<username>`

- **ALLUSERSPROFILE.** The path to the All Users profile, typically `C:\Documents and Settings\All Users`

- **COMPUTERNAME.** The NetBIOS name of the computer where the user logged on

- **HOMEDRIVE.** The drive letter used to map to the home directory

- **HOMEPATH.** The full UNC path to the home directory

- **LOGONSERVER.** The NetBIOS name of the server that authenticated the user

- **OS.** The operating system running on the user's computer

- **USERDOMAIN.** The domain that authenticated the user

- **USERNAME.** The NetBIOS name of the user

This is a batch file that uses these variables:

```
@echo off
echo Hello, %USERNAME%. Welcome to the %USERDOMAIN% domain.
Echo You have logged on to %LOGONSERVER% from %COMPUTERNAME%.
Echo You are running %OS% from the %SYSTEMROOT% directory.
Echo Your home directory is on %homedrive%%homepath%.
Echo The path to this directory is %homeshare%%homepath%.
Echo Your local settings are located in %USERPROFILE%.
Echo Additional settings are located in %ALLUSERSPROFILE%.
```

The output of this batch file looks like this:

```
Hello, Rmanuel. Welcome to the Company.com domain.
You have logged onto PHX-DC-01 from PHX-W2KP-032.
You are running Windows_NT from the \WINNT directory.
Your home directory is Z:\RMANUEL.
The path to this directory is \\phx-dc-01\users.
Your local settings are stored in C:\Documents and Settings\Administrator [PHX-W2KP-001].
Additional settings are located in C:\Documents and Settings\All Users.
```

Managing Folder Redirections

Applications written to the Windows 2000 logo standards are required to store all user data and configuration files in the user profile. When prompting a user to save a file, application developers can either look for the *%userprofile%* variable, which points at the My Documents directory in Windows 2000, or preferably they make calls to the *SHGetFolderPath* function, which returns location information for all the profile folders.

As Windows 2000 logo applications begin to filter into the market, much of the data scatter involved with desktop support should gradually disappear. One problem is not resolved by saving user data to the My Documents folder, though. The default location of the folder is on the local hard drive. This leads to conversations such as this:

User: You have to do something quickly. My computer made a loud, grinding noise, and now when I turn it on, I get a message saying 'Unable to load command interpreter. System halted.'

Administrator: We'll have someone up there in an hour to replace your hard drive.

User: What about payroll?

Administrator: I'll bite. What about payroll?

User: Today is Thursday. I need my spreadsheets so that I can calculate payroll.

Administrator: What server are they on?

User: I'm not sure. I think it's the *My Documents* server.

You can imagine the rest of the conversation. The Windows 2000 solution to this problem is *Folder Redirection*. This is a set of policies that enable you to substitute server-based storage for critical profile folders. The profile folders that can be redirected are:

- Application Data
- Desktop
- My Documents (and My Pictures)
- START menu

The Application Data and My Documents folders are important to redirect to preserve the users' data. The Desktop and START menu redirections are less critical, but they can help you build a common user interface by pointing an entire community of users at the same location. Rather than use mandatory policies, an easier solution is to build a common operating environment using folder redirections. If you decide to go this route, be careful to lock down permissions on the central files.

Folder redirection settings are stored in an INI file called FDEPLOY.INI located in the profile folder under USER. This is a sample FDEPLOY.INI file showing where the My Documents folder is redirected:

```
[FolderStatus]
My Documents=11
My Pictures=2
[My Documents]
s-1-1-0=\\phx-dc-01\users\%username%\My Documents
[My Pictures]
```

You can use the same server volume to hold redirected profile folders, roaming profiles, and user home directories. This simplifies management, but it also makes the server very valuable. If it crashes or otherwise becomes unavailable, users lose access to all their data and may not be able to run applications because the configuration files are also stored on a server.

The following steps use folder redirection to put the My Documents folders on a central server. The same steps apply to other folder redirections. Proceed as follows:

Procedure 16.18 **Configuring Folder Redirection for the My Documents Folder**

1. Open the AD console containing the Site, Domain, or OU container associated with the policy you want to modify.
2. Navigate to the container, right-click, and select PROPERTIES from the fly-out menu.
3. Select the `Group Properties` tab.
4. Select an existing policy and click `Edit`. If you want to create a new policy, click `New`. The `Group Policy` console opens.
5. Expand the tree to `User Configuration | Windows Settings | Folder Redirection`.
6. Right-click `My Documents` and select PROPERTIES from the fly-out menu. The `My Document Properties` window opens with the focus set to the `Target` tab.

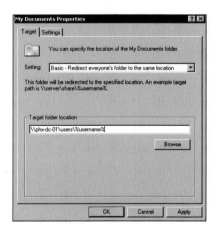

Figure 16.22 `My Documents Properties` window showing Basic settings for profile location.

Two `Settings` options exist for redirecting a folder:

`Basic`: The `Basic` option specifies one location for all users associated with this policy. This is the option shown in Figure 16.22. You can use the `%username%` variable to create unique file locations. For example, under `Target File Location`, you can enter `\\server_name\share_name\location_folder\%username%`.

`Advanced`: This option is shown in Figure 16.23. Using the `Advanced` option, you can specify different locations for users based on their group membership. You can also specify unique folders under those locations using `%username%`.

7. Select the `Settings` tab. This contains handling options for the files in the My Documents folder. Figure 16.23 shows an example.

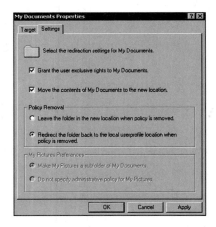

Figure 16.23 `My Documents Properties` window showing `Settings` tab with options set for exclusive use.

Folder Redirection Handling Options

The `Settings` tab shown in Figure 16.23 has several handling options that determine who can access the folder on the server, whether the folder is moved or copied to the server, and where the folder is put when the policy is cancelled.

`Grant the user exclusive rights to My Documents` sets the ACL on the remote My Documents folder so that only the user has full control access rights. This is similar to the way roaming profiles are handled. Do not use this option when configuring a common file repository for groups of users.

Move the contents of my documents to the new location takes the entire My Documents folder off the local hard drive and moves it to the redirected folder server. This gives continuity of service to the user, who may not even realize that the files are now on the server. It also ensures that the user doesn't have copies of the files in two places, which is a good thing. It has its down side, though, if you are one of those administrators who doesn't trust *Move* options. If the user has no backups for the local documents, you might be better off copying the files manually.

The two **Policy Removal** options determine how the user's system reacts when the policy is canceled.

Redirect the Folder Back … makes the most sense for situations in which the user needs immediate access to the files.

Leave the Folder … makes sense if you want to cancel the policy but retain server-based document control.

The **My Pictures Preferences** options stay dimmed unless you select that folder. You may not want users to store large bitmaps on the server.

8. Select the **Target** tab again.

9. Select the **Advanced** option under **Setting**. The window changes to display a **Security Group Membership** field as shown in Figure 16.24.

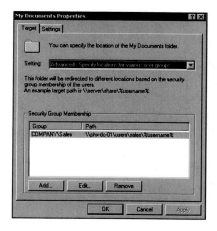

Figure 16.24 **My Documents Properties** window showing Advanced settings for profile location and the Security Group Membership field.

10. Click **Add**. The **Specify Group and Location** window opens. See Figure 16.25.

Figure 16.25 `Specify Group and Location` window showing group membership and target folder location.

11. Under `Security Group Membership`, click `Browse` to open a `Select Group` window, select a group, and click `OK` to return to the `Specify Group and Location` window.

12. Under `Target Folder Location`, enter a path for the location in which you want this group's data to be stored. You can navigate to the target location using Browse. If you want each user to have a unique folder at this location, append `%username%` to the end of the path.

13. Click `OK` to save the change and return to the `My Documents Properties` window.

14. Click `OK` to save the folder redirection policy and close the window.

15. Log on at a workstation using the account of a user in the targeted group. Verify that the My Documents folder now points at the new location.

16. If the user has files in an existing My Documents folder, either on the local drive or in a roaming profile, and you did not elect to move them to the new location, copy them manually at this time. Don't forget to delete the old files so that the user doesn't accidentally save changes to the wrong file.

Laptops and Folder Redirections

Laptops present a problem for a folder redirection policy. Central storage of the data folders makes them unavailable when the user is on the road.

Two solutions to this problem exist. One is to exclude laptop users from folder redirection. This is clumsy because it requires you to know in advance who is using a laptop.

Another solution is to configure laptops to use offline folders. The user can synchronize the contents of the server-based My Documents folder with a folder on the local hard drive before going on the road.

The next section covers running old, 20th–century applications on Windows 2000. This might be the last version of Windows that runs a wide variety of legacy applications. Microsoft has not committed to supporting 16-bit code on 64-bit Windows, and the Millennium project is developing a legacy-free version of Windows 98. You might finally be able to convince management to let go of that Clipper '87 application that runs their accounting software.

Using and Managing DOS and 16-Bit Windows Applications

Support for legacy applications in Windows 2000 is not much different from classic NT. DOS and 16-bit Windows applications are given a special operating environment using a feature in the X86 architecture called the Virtual DOS Machine (VDM).

A VDM emulates DOS function calls, BIOS interfaces, and the segmented memory architecture that DOS applications expect to see. Because 16-bit Windows is simply an extension of DOS, older Windows applications also run inside a VDM.

The job of building a VDM falls to a special 32-bit process, NTVDM.EXE. This process starts up whenever a DOS or 16-bit Windows application is launched. You can see this by launching a 16-bit application—the version of Edit.exe that comes with Windows 2000 is an example—and checking the process list in Task Manager. You see Ntvdm running, not Edit.exe.

Running 16-bit Windows applications on Windows 2000 presents a different sort of problem. First of all, 16-bit Windows is really just a DOS extension with a gunnysack of API calls and some tricks to enable applications to run in protected mode. This involves a good deal of acrobatics when it comes to memory and I/O. Windows 2000 must deal with these acrobatics and turn them into standard Win32 API calls. Second, the old Windows applications are coded to work in a Program Manager shell with its scramble of INI files. Windows 2000 must convince the application to work inside the Explorer shell and somehow store its state information in the Registry.

Some of the basic Windows functions are handled by NTVDM, just as DOS handles them in regular Windows. Dealing with 16-bit API and memory tricks falls to a special process called the Windows-on-Windows subsystem, or WOW. The name of the driver is Wowexec.exe.

Win.com and Windows 2000

Wowexec simulates 16-bit Windows to the point that it is loaded using the Windows loader, Win.com. A copy of Win.com is included in WINNT\System32 for that purpose.

You can verify the operation of Win.com at the command line. Open Task Manager. From a command prompt, enter win wowexec. Return back to the command prompt. Check the Process tab in Task Manager. Notice that Ntvdm is running with Wowexec as a subtask.

Some legacy programs search for the Windows directory by looking for the Win.com file. These programs may put their share files in the incorrect subdirectory because Win.com is in the \WINNT\System32 and not the root of the \Windows directory. No workaround is available.

Registry Tip: WOW Parameters

The WOW parameters are contained in two Registry keys:

- **HKLM | Software | Microsoft | Windows NT | CurrentVersion | WOW.** This set of parameters defines keyboard, mouse, video, network, sound, serial, and shell drivers along with an extensive list of compatibility options for legacy programs.

- **HKLM | System | CurrentControlSet | Control | WOW.** This set of parameters defines the operating limits of the VDM such as memory parameters, timeout parameters, whether to use separate memory by default, and others.

Overview of Unsupported Legacy Applications

Unlike Windows 9x, which is perfectly happy to move aside to enable 16-bit Windows and DOS applications to take over the machine, Windows 2000 and its NT predecessors never provide a true 16-bit environment. If an application refuses to run in a VDM, it does not work on Windows 2000. Windows 2000 contains no "MSDOS Mode."

Most DOS and Windows applications work just fine in Windows 2000/NT. Applications that don't work fall into these general categories:

- **Applications that talk directly to hardware.** NTVDM works very hard to fool DOS applications into thinking they own the machine, but if an application insists on getting behind the curtain and running the show, it is given the bum's rush to the gate. Talking to hardware is the exclusive province of the Kernel, and it guards that province as diligently as a labor union steward does.

Common Unsupported Applications

- Games and amusements that punch information directly to the video buffer instead of using OpenGL or DirectX API calls

- Old communication applications that try to directly control the RS232 registers

- Parallel-port gizmos such as security dongles and CD-ROM boxcars

- Disk utilities that write directly to the drive rather than making supported BIOS calls

- Outdated Btrieve clients, which can be very unstable in a VDM (usese the most current version of Btrieve, if at all possible

- Legacy terminal emulation programs that make their own network calls that do not use supported interfaces

- **TSRs.** DOS applications generally do not share the same memory space. You must configure the batch file that loads the TSRs to use the same VDM. A surprising number of 1980-era TSRs load if you set the configuration files correctly. See the "Config.nt and Autoexec.nt" section later in this chapter.

- **Windows Applications that use VxDs.** These are protected-mode drivers that do their own memory and register management. Windows 2000 and NT do not support VxDs in any fashion. Applications that use them are not enabled to carry the Ready for Windows NT or Ready for Windows 2000 logo.

- **Applications that do not use the Win16 API correctly.** You sometimes find old Windows applications that either play tricks with the Win16 API or avoid it entirely to make direct DOS function calls. This is not necessarily a showstopper, because Microsoft was one of the worst offenders in this regard and nearly all legacy Microsoft code works in the WOW environment. If a Windows application loads, initializes, and immediately blows up in one fashion or another, though, you might have an insurmountable problem.

- **Applications that use unsupported memory functions.** The extended/expanded memory management inside NTVDM supports nearly all flavors of expanded and extended memory and standard DMA. It doesn't support VCPI because it requires direct access to the CPU registers. Applications coded in Assembler that play with memory tags or locations directly do not work.

- **Applications that consume excessive resources.** These applications are not generally a problem for Windows 2000 as much as for Terminal Services. Applications that insist on polling the keyboard 60 times per second or that issue commands in critical loops or refuse to play in a shared memory environment can cause Terminal Services to get unstable. No hard-and-fast rule exists for handling these types of applications. Your best bet is to check the Microsoft KnowledgeBase and to work with a vendor.

After you eliminate the unsupported applications, the work involved with configuring and running the remaining apps falls primarily in three areas:

- Working with the Windows 2000 command interpreters, Cmd.exe and Command.com
- Configuring and managing the Console interface—sometimes misnamed the DOS Box—to support character-based applications, including TSRs and networking applications
- Configuring the WOW subsystem to work with 16-bit Windows applications, including extended and expanded memory support and Win16 network access

Configuring the Command Interpreters

No matter how functional and convenient you might find the graphical user interface in Windows 2000, the inevitable time comes when you need the command line to get real work done. NT provides two console windows, a 32-bit console using CMD.EXE as the command interpreter and a 16-bit console using COMMAND.COM as an interpreter. The COMMAND.COM console provides a DOS 5.0 command environment for running executables and TSRs that require a true DOS environment.

Alternative Consoles

Windows 2000 features two rarely used consoles. One is for POSIX and the other for OS/2. The POSIX support in NT meets government requirements, but third-party products, such as the MKS Toolkit or Reflections, generally provide more comprehensive UNIX support. The OS/2 console supports version 1.1 text-mode applications only and, as such, is hopelessly outdated. OS/2 support in Windows 2000 is like an old wedding snapshot that hangs around in a scrapbook long after the divorce. Microsoft can't seem to throw it away, but it only serves to bring back unfortunate memories.

The CMD and COMMAND consoles do not provide a "DOS Box" in the OS/2 sense of the word. CMD is 32-bit code and provides a true 32-bit environment. COMMAND runs in a VDM but provides a seamless window to the 32-bit CMD interpreter, when required. For example, if you run DIR from a COMMAND console, you see long filenames instead of short names.

When you open a command session using START | PROGRAMS | COMMAND PROMPT, you get the 32-bit CMD console. You can verify this by opening Task Manager and selecting the Processes tab. CMD.EXE is on the list of running images. If you have the Resource Kit loaded, you can also use TLIST /t to check the process list. When you launch a 16-bit application, Windows 2000 first starts NTVDM.EXE and then loads the application into the VDM. If you launch the 16-bit application from a CMD console session, NTVDM.EXE is a thread of CMD.

This capability of COMMAND to run CMD in the background also gives it the capability to launch graphical 32-bit applications. For example, open COMMAND, launch SOL, and then check the process list using TLIST -t. This is a sample:

```
Explorer.exe (130)
  ntvdm.exe (179) C:\command.com
    cmd.exe (168)
      sol.exe (177) Solitaire
```

Note that the 32-bit executable, NTVDM, hosts the 16-bit COMMAND session, which spawned off CMD that, in turn, has a thread to the Solitaire executable. Although TLIST shows these and child processes, if you kill NTVDM, the CMD session and its SOL thread survive.

If you are a Windows 9x user in the habit of launching COMMAND from the RUN window, you should launch CMD instead. COMMAND.COM is *very* slow compared to CMD. You should not run COMMAND to get a console session unless you absolutely need a true DOS emulator.

DOS Versions of COMMAND.COM Unsupported

If you have a dual-boot machine, you may get an error when opening a COMMAND.COM console. This is because you have an older Windows COMMAND.COM in the search path. Remove or rename the older version.

Microsoft enhanced the CMD interpreter to include more command-line functionality than DOS 6.2 or Windows 9x DOS. The CMD interpreter supports a batch language similar to the DOS batch language but richer and capable of calling native 32-bit applications. When building batch files in Windows 2000, give the files a CMD extension to ensure that they run in a 32-bit environment.

Registry Tip: Search priority
The search priority when running applications without specifying an extension is: EXE, COM, BAT, PIF, CMD. You can change this search order, if desired, by using this Registry Key:

Key: HKCU | Software | Microsoft | Windows NT | CurrentVersion | Windows

CMD recognizes registered file extensions, so you can type the name of a data file with its extension to launch the associated application. For example, the registered MMC extension is `.msc`. If you type `dnsmgmt.msc`, the command interpreter opens the DNS Management console. This is also true of running scripts with extensions that are registered with Windows Script Host or other script applications, such as Perl, Rexx, or Kix.

You can also specify CMD in shortcuts that launch character-based applications. This lets you take advantage of the CMD switches that modify the behavior of the session. These are the switches:

- **/C.** This switch closes the session window when the associated application closes. For example, you can use CMD /C to kick off a remote mail client when you want the window to close after the client collects the mail and shuts down.

- **/K.** This switch leaves the session window open after the application closes. For example, you can use CMD /K in the Scheduler to kick off a batch file at night and leave its window open so that you can see any error messages the next day.

- **/D.** This switch disables the AutoRun feature in the CMD processor. The AutoRun feature enables you to kick off an executable or a batch file each time you open a console session. AutoRun is not normally enabled. You can enable it with the following Registry values: HKLM | Software | Microsoft | Command Processor | AutoRun or HKCU | Software | Microsoft | Command Processor | AutoRun.

- **/V:ON.** This switch enables delayed environment variable expansion. Under normal circumstances, environment variables are expanded as soon as they are interpreted. With delayed variable expansion, the variable is not expanded until the command is executed. Ordinary environment variables are delimited with percent signs: %...%. Delayed expansion variables are delimited with exclamation points: (!..!). This is a quick example of how delayed expansion works. Consider a script called TEST.CMD with these two lines:

```
echo %username%
echo !username!
```

This is the way the script executes:

```
C:\>test
C:\>echo admin
admin
C:\>echo !username!
admin
```

Variable expansion is disabled by default. If you want to enable it for all CMD session, add the following Registry value with a data type Reg_Dword and to the Command Processor R:

```
Key:     HKLM | Software | Microsoft | Command Processor
Value:   DelayedExpansion
Data:    1 (type Reg_Dword)
```

- **/Q.** This switch turns off echoes from the associated application.

- **/A or /U.** These switches convert the byte stream sent to a pipe or file redirection into ANSI (/A) or Unicode (/U). The default is /U.

- **/T:fg.** This switch sets the foreground/background colors for a session.

- **/F:OFF.** This switch disables file and directory name completion. Name completion saves typing at the command line by automatically completing an entry based on the first few characters. It works like the old DBase prompt on steroids.

Automatic Path Completion

Windows 2000 and NT both can be set to recognize a special character at the command line to complete a path or filename. By default, the completion character is Ctrl-I. Instead of entering CD \Documents and Settings, you can enter CD \Doc and then press the completion character, Ctrl-I, to expand the rest of the line.

If more than one file or subdirectory has the same starting letters, repeatedly pressing Ctrl-I cycles through the list.

Name completion is controlled by the Registry value HKLM | Software | Microsoft | Command Processor | CompletionChar, which is set to 0x9h (Ctrl-I) by default.

If you enter CMD /F:ON, the completion character is changed to Ctrl-D (0x4h) for directory names and Ctrl-F (0x6h) for filenames. In this configuration, pressing Ctrl-D cycles through directory names only, while Ctrl-I recognizes both file and directory names.

You can change the default CompletionChar character in the Registry.

- **/Y.** CMD includes many enhancements to the standard internal commands. Some of these may interfere with the operation of legacy batch
  files. Use this switch to turn off the enhancements for an entire session
  or in a batch file just before issuing the problem command. Rather
  than using the /Y switch, you can disable CMD extensions for all sessions
  using the following Registry entry:

```
Key:      HKCU | Software | Microsoft |Command Processor
Value:    EnableExtensions
Data:     0
```

- **/X.** This switch enables the CMD extensions after they are disabled.

- **&&.** The CMD interpreter enables entering multiple commands on the
  same command line by separating each command with &&. For example,
  if you need to hone that keen eye/hand coordination that is so vital to
  good system administration, you can launch Minesweeper, Pinball, and
  Solitaire at the same time as follows:

```
winmine && sol && pinball
```

- **/S.** This switch provides special handling for quotes. Under normal circumstances, if the interpreter sees a quote at the beginning of a string, it
  strips the quote from the end of the string, if one exists, and then launches
  the program. For example, enter the two-word name of a bitmap file at
  the command prompt, such as: `c:\>prairie wind.bmp`. CMD responds with
  a *'prairie' is not a recognized command* error. If you enter `c:\>"prairie
  wind.bmp"`, CMD sees the entry as a single string, launches Paintbrush, and
  loads the bitmap. If you enter `c:\>"prairie wind.bmp` (no end quote),
  CMD still sees the entry as a single string. The /S switch demands proper
  syntax. If you enter `c:\>"prairie wind.bmp /s`, CMD responds with an
  error. You can use the /S switch in a batch file to validate user input so
  that you don't take inappropriate actions based on improper input.

CMD Internal Command Extensions

CMD has the usual set of DOS internal commands, but several are modified
or extended to simplify working at the command line and to improve batch
files. This is a list of the most commonly used internal CMD extensions:

- **DEL.** In DOS, DEL /S deletes a file anywhere it appears on a drive, but
  it insists on telling you everywhere it searched. The CMD version of DEL
  /S lists only where the file is found and deleted.

- **CD.** CD /D enables changing directories directly to other drives, including network drives. For example, if the session is currently focused on the C:\ drive, by entering `cd /d e:\anydir`, you move directly to the \anydir directory on the E: drive. CD also has another, more subtle extension. The parser assumes that spaces are part of the directory path, so you can issue this command without quotes: `cd c:\Daily Sales Totals`.

- **SET.** You can search for environment variables using SET followed by the first few letters of the variable. For example, to find all the variables starting with S, issue the command SET S. A more significant extension to SET is the capability to use arithmetic and logical operators with the SET /A switch. For example, let's say you have two existing numeric environment variables, VAR1 and VAR2, and you want to instantiate a new variable VAR3 with the sum of the two other variables. You can do so with this command:

```
set /A var3=var1+var2
```

Notice that when you use the /A switch, the parser does not force you to enter %VAR1% or %VAR2%.

- **IF.** The IF function in DOS is typically used for error handling, such as `IF errorlevel 1 GOTO error_label` or to test for file availability, such as `IF EXIST file_name GOTO action_label`. Using the CMD extensions, you can use `IF /I` to check for Boolean relationships, such as `IF /I %var1% LSS %var2% GOTO action_label`.

- **CALL.** The CALL extensions in Windows 2000 are a spaghetti-coder's dream. They enable using labels as the argument to the CALL statement, such as `call :label_argument`. If you use this feature, keep in mind that the CALL statement shells out to another CMD session. You lose any environment variables you established in the first session. After the called session closes, it exits back to the calling file at the line just after the call statement.

- **SHIFT.** This function takes a list of arguments and shifts them over by one, such as the children's song where the little rabbit jumps into bed and yells "Roll over!" and they all roll over and one falls out. The CMD extensions add an /N switch to select where to start shifting. For example, if you have four arguments and you issue the command, `shift /3`, the final order is `%1, %2, %4`.

- **GOTO.** This extension recognizes a special label, `:EOF`, which sends the action to the End of File regardless of the branch it's in. This is a quick way of exiting a batch file without defining an EOF label.

- **MD or MKDIR.** You can use these extensions to build an entire directory structure at once. For example, this command, MD \MiddleEarth\Shire\ Hobbiton\BagEnd, creates all the directories in the path. You can also do this trick on another drive. For example, you can be on the C: drive and issue the command C:\>MD E:\Elves\Men\Halflings to create the directory structure on the E: drive.

   What the MD extensions *do not* do is change the parsing of the command line if the directory names have spaces. For example, if you issue the command md C:\First Quarter Results and forget to use quotes, the result is three directories at the root of the C drive:

```
C:\First
C:\Quarter
C:\Results.
```

- **FOR /D.** The FOR command is used for looping. The basic syntax is FOR batch_variable IN some_namespace DO some_command. The FOR extensions provide several handy switches. The FOR /D command enables you to specify wildcards for the IN statement. For example, if you want a batch file to perform a directory listing that excludes files, you can issue the following command: FOR /D %1 IN (*) DO @echo %1.

- **FOR /R.** The action in the DO statement is applied to the directory specified in the FOR statement. If subdirectories exist, the DO statement walks the directory tree to each subdirectory. For example, if you want to list all files ending in TXT in a directory called MY_FILES and include all subdirectories, you issue the following command: FOR /R c:\my_files %1 IN (*.TXT) DO @echo %1.

- **FOR /L.** This command performs an action a given number of times. The syntax is: FOR /L %variable IN (start, step, end) DO command %variable. One of my favorite uses of FOR /L is to add lots of user accounts for testing. This is an example. The command FOR /L %1 IN (100,1,10000) DO Net User /add User%1 adds 9,900 users with the names User100, User101, User 102, and so forth.

- **FOR /F.** This switch divvies a file into lines, parses each line into tokens, and displays the selected tokens. The syntax is: FOR /F "parse options" %variable IN (files) DO command %variable. The "parse options" section must be in quotes and contain any or all the following options:

   eol= Enter a special end-of-line marker. If you are reading a standard ASCII file with DOS EOL markers, you can skip this entry.

skip= Enter the number of initial lines to skip. For example, if you are reading a file that has a four–line header before the meat of the file begins, you can use "skip=4" to start reading the file from line 5.

delims= Enter a character that tells the parser how to break the lines up into tokens. For example, if you are reading a comma–delimited file, you enter delims=, to break each token into a data field.

token= The tokens to pass to the FOR statement. If each line has five elements, and you want to see only the second and fourth element, you enter "token=2,4".

This is an example of how to use FOR /F. Let's say you have a file called TESTFOR.TXT with these lines:

```
One, two, three, four
Four, five, six, seven, eight, nine
```

If you enter this command:

```
FOR /F "tokens=1,3-4 delims=," %1 IN (testfor.txt) DO @echo %1 %j %k
```

you get the following result:

```
One three four
Five seven eight
```

If you enter this command:

```
FOR /F "tokens=1,3* delims=," %1 IN (testfor.txt) DO @echo %1 %j %k
```

you get the following result:

```
one three four
five seven eight, nine
```

The second example shows that the extra variables can receive multiple tokens.

- **Special Batch Variable Expansion Options.** Given a batch file, such as test.cmd, that contains a command that uses a batch file variable such as %1, %2, and so forth, CMD enables special modifiers that work as follows:

  %1—Standard variable handling.

  %~f1—Gives the full path name of %1.

  %~d1—Gives the drive letter of %1.

  %~p1—Gives the path of %1.

  %~n1—Gives the filename of %1.

  %~x1—Gives the file extension of %1.

  %~s1—Changes the n and x options to show the 8.3 name vice the long filename.

%~$PATH:1—Searches the directories in the PATH until it finds the entry for %1. Then it uses the PATH entry for the path to %1. This is handy if you want to run the batch file in a different directory than the argument. If the file is not found by searching the path, this modifier gives an empty string.

CMD External Command Extensions

Most of the external commands in Windows 2000 are similar to their DOS counterparts. These miscellaneous commands are not covered elsewhere; you might find them useful.

- **PUSHD** and **POPD.** These two commands come straight from UNIX. Use PUSHD in place of CD to change directories. When you move to the new directory, CMD leaves a pointer to the old directory. Later, you can return to the original directory using POPD. For example, let's say you are in the `C:\Presidents\20thCentury\Democrats` directory and you want to make a quick visit to the `C:\Presidents\18thCentury\Whigs` directory and then come right back. You can enter the following command:

```
PUSHD C:\Presidents\18thCentury\Whigs    : Changes directories.
POPD                                     : Returns to original directory.
```

  You can place several directories in the stack by issuing several PUSHD commands in a row. Each subsequent POPD command moves down one place in the stack until you arrive back to where you began.

- **PROMPT.** CMD has several additional characters you can include in a PROMPT statement to help navigate using PUSHD/POPD. A `$+` entry adds a + to the prompt each time you use PUSHD and removes it when you return with POPD. For example, entering `prompt $p$+$g` displays the following prompt after three uses of the PUSHD command:

  `C:\New_Directory+++>`.

- **ASSOC** and **FTYPE.** One of the special features of the CMD interpreter is its capability to open a data file using its associated application. The association is based on the data file's extension. For example, if you make this entry at a command prompt: `C:\>"furry dog.bmp"`, CMD opens the bitmap file using Paintbrush. See the following sidebar for more information.

File Associations

You can build associations for file extensions at the command line using ASSOC and FTYPE.

- The FTYPE command builds the key that associates a file type with a particular executable. For example, the TXTFILE type is associated with NOTEPAD.EXE.

- The ASSOC command builds the key that associates an extension with a particular file type. For example, the .TXT extension is associated with the TXTFILE file type.

This is how to use the two commands. Let's say you want to automate unzipping files after browsing the Internet by launching PKUNZIP.EXE when you double-click a file with a ZIP extension. To make this association from the command line, issue the following commands:

```
ftype zipfile=c:\zip\pkunzip.exe
assoc .zip=zipfile
```

- **COLOR.** This command changes the foreground and text color of the current command session window. You can use the COLOR command to differentiate between command sessions launched by different applications by building a batch file that runs COLOR and then launches the application.

Text-Mode Color

Some character-based applications shift the video into graphics mode, in which case the COLOR command settings have no effect. The COLOR command accepts a single byte argument that determines color scheme. The byte is divided into two hex digits. The first digit sets the background color and the second digit sets the foreground color. For example, COLOR 47 yields a red background with white text. Table 16.2 lists the available color palette:

Table 16.2 **Hex Designators for Color Command**

Color	Hex Designator
Black	0
Blue	1
Green	2
Aqua	3
Red	4
Purple	5
Yellow	6
White	7
Gray	8
Light Blue	9
Light Green	A

continues ▶

Table 16.2   **Continued**

Color	Hex Designator
Light Aqua	B
Light Red	C
Light Purple	D
Light Yellow	E
Bright White	F

START Command

The START command is one of the most useful of all the external commands and warrants special attention. START can configure shared memory,
the priority assigned to an application, and other tricks. It works with any
executable. These are the START switches and their uses:

- **/I.** The environment passed on to the newly launched application is the
  original environment of the host CMD window. Any environment variables added during the CMD session are not passed.

- **/MIN.** Minimizes the window for the newly launched application to the
  Task Bar. This applies to all applications, Windows and character-based,
  32-bit or 16-bit.

- **/MAX.** Maximizes the window for the newly launched application.
  Character-based applications are windowed, not full screen, and the window has no scrollbars.

- **/SEPARATE.** Launches a 16-bit Windows programs into a separate
  memory space with a new NTVDM and WOWEXEC thread. The benefit
  of running 16-bit apps in separate memory spaces is that it provides stability when running several apps that have a poor track record for uptime. It
  also enables you to run 16-bit applications on separate threads, which
  enables multithreaded performance, instead of having all 16-bit apps share
  the same processing thread, which is the default behavior in both
  Windows 2000 and NT.

- **/SHARED.** Launches a 16-bit Windows program into a shared memory
  space. If no existing shared NTVDM and WOWEXEC thread exists, one
  is created. This is the default behavior.

- **/IDLE, /NORMAL, /HIGH, /REALTIME.** These switches assign a
  priority class to the application. Windows 2000 uses thread priority to
  control software interrupts. A total of 32 priorities exist, numbered 0-31.
  When a thread running at a certain priority issues a software interrupt,
  the system masks all interrupts from threads running at lower priorities.

This ensures that lower-priority applications, such as user apps, do not wrest control from higher-priority threads, such as operating system components. Threads spawned by a process are given priorities relative to the priority class of the parent process. Four classes exist: Idle, Normal, High, and Realtime. If you set a priority class inappropriate to the use of the application, system performance may suffer. This is a nice way of saying, "Don't use `start /realtime excel` to make your spreadsheet calculate faster."

- **/WAIT.** The default action of START is to open a new session and return control of the old session back to the CMD thread that owned it. The /WAIT switch suspends the original CMD session until the application launched by START terminates. This is useful when you start several applications in a batch file and you want each one to wait until the previous one completes.

- **/B.** This switch starts a new application in the existing session window instead of creating a new window. This is the same as launching the application without START, so the switch really isn't useful. It can cause problems for applications that shift the video to graphics mode, even if they seem to be character-based. Also, it turns off Ctrl-C handling, so the only way to break out of a loop is Ctrl-Break.

Extensions to the START command enable you to specify a directory name instead of a program file or executable. For example, if you enter `start ..`, you get a My Computer window showing the contents of the parent directory.

Configuring the Console Interface

All users like to work differently with DOS applications. A user like myself with failing eyesight might have a 21-inch screen and want a big console window with large type. Another user might want a cyan background with green letters. The list goes on and on.

If you right-click the icon at the upper left corner of a CMD session window and select PROPERTIES from the fly-out menu, a `Cmd.exe` Properties window opens. If you do the same to a COMMAND session, an NTVDM PROPERTIES window opens. Figure 16.26 shows an example of an NTVDM Properties window. If you compare the two, you see that you can use them to control fonts, colors, and buffer sizes. You also see that the NTVDM properties include many switches to support the virtual DOS environment. All the clumsy memory, video, and shortcut handling in DOS is supported in the VDM and is configurable by the NTVDM properties.

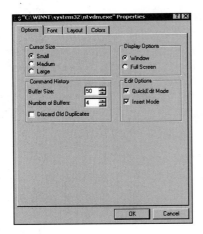

Figure 16.26   NTVDM Properties opened from
a COMMAND.COM console window.

If you make changes to a session window, you are prompted either to save
them to all windows of the same name or only to the current window.
Changes to CMD session windows work as follows:

- If you change the default properties while a CMD session window is
  open, the changes are stored in HKCU | Console and affect all CMD ses-
  sions.

- If you change the properties of a CMD session while a specific application
  is open, the changes are saved to HKCU | Console | PATH_ExecutableName.
  The changes are effective only when running that particular executable
  from that particular directory. (The Registry does not enable spaces in
  directory paths. The Registry Editor inserts underscores automatically.)

Changes to COMMAND session windows affect all 16-bit session windows
because they all use NTVDM. The affected Registry key is HKCU | Console |
C:_WINNT_System32_ntvdm.exe. If you choose to save only to the current window, the system builds a PIF file for the application.

PIF Files

The console settings you make for COMMAND affect every DOS program.
If you have specific settings you want to make for a particular program, you
must put those in a Program Information File (PIF) for that program. Older
versions of NT and Windows 3.x have a PIF editor. NT4 and Windows 2000
create PIF files on-the-fly when you create a shortcut to a 16-bit DOS or
Windows application. You can see how this works as follows:

Procedure 16.19   **Creating a PIF**

1. Open Explorer and drill down until you find a 16-bit application.

2. Right-click the icon and select CREATE SHORTCUT from the fly-out menu. A new icon is created with a default MSDOS icon and the name Shortcut to <filename>.

3. Open the Properties window associated with this new icon. The memory and display settings you make in the PIF are used by NTVDM in place of the default console settings you configured in the Control Panel. A few exceptions exist. Font settings in the default NTVDM properties always take priority. Batch files included in the PIF are ignored. And the Display Toolbar option is ignored. COMMAND windows in NT do not have toolbars.

4. Select the Program tab. Click Windows NT. This opens the Windows PIF Settings window. This window contains pointers to two files, AUTOEXEC.NT and CONFIG.NT. The files themselves are located in the \WINNT\System32 directory. These two files are used in place of AUTOEXEC.BAT and CONFIG.SYS to configure the VDM. We'll take a closer look at these files in the next section.

5. Click OK to close the Windows PIF Settings window.

Config.nt and Autoexec.nt

Windows 2000 uses Config.nt and Autoexec.nt to build the environment within the VDM that DOS builds with Config.sys and Autoexec.bat. The standard Config.nt file has three lines:

```
dos=high, umb
device=%SystemRoot%\system32\himem.sys
files=20
```

The version of Himem.sys is a special A20 handler designed to run in a VDM. It sets up a High Memory Area (HMA) and expanded memory within the flat Windows 2000 address space. CONFIG.NT also supports most of the standard CONFIG.SYS entries:

- **DEVICE.** Can be used in conjunction with special versions of HIMEM.SYS, ANSI.SYS, and COUNTRY.SYS.

- **EMM.** If an application needs a specific amount of expanded memory (an example is WordPerfect 5.1), you can set the RAM switch on EMM386 just as you do using regular EMM386.EXE. Be sure to set the expanded memory PIF setting to the same size.

- **FCBS.** Supports very old DOS applications that use File Control Blocks. You know whether you need this setting because the application errors out with an "Insufficient Control Blocks" message.

- **FILES.** You can use 100 or 200 for this setting. Memory is not ordinarily an issue in a VDM.

- **INSTALL.** Config.nt supports loading TSRs in advance of Autoexec.nt. Block drivers and drivers that access hardware directly are not supported.

- **LOADHIGH.** Use as you would in Config.sys.

- **SHELL.** Use to set environment size. This can also be done in a PIF.

- **STACKS.** Use as you would in Config.sys.

Three additional commands, exclusive to Windows 2000 and NT, affect how programs behave inside a VDM:

- **ECHOCONFIG.** By default, actions in Config.sys and Autoexec.bat are not echoed to the screen to prevent confusion when the VDM loads. Use this switch to enable echoing for troubleshooting.

- **NTCMDPROMPT.** When you launch a COMMAND console session, you get the 16-bit command interpreter. Include this setting if you want to get the 32-bit CMD interpreter in addition to COMMAND.

- **DOSONLY.** This prevents a DOS console session from shelling out to CMD. Use this setting if you have TSRs, environment variables, or network drive mappings that need to stay in memory for a particular COMMAND session. This switch is important if you call batch files that make environment changes. Without DOSONLY, you lose the DOS configuration settings when the called batch file exits.

Use Autoexec.nt just as you do use Autoexec.bat. You can set environment variables, launch TSRs, and call additional batch files. Special real-mode drivers in Windows 2000 configure the VDM to see various protected-mode system components, such as the CD-ROM drive (MSCDEXNT), the Windows network (REDIR), the NetWare network (NW16 and VWIPXSPX), and DOS Protected-Mode Interface memory (DOSX). This is an example that shows how the VDM loads real-mode NetWare drivers:

```
lh %SystemRoot%\System32\mscdexnt.exe
lh %SystemRoot%\System32\redir
lh %SystemRoot%\System32\dosx
lh %SystemRoot%\System32\nw16
lh %SystemRoot%\System32\vwipxspx
```

When running TSRs and calling batch files, the session shells out to CMD by default, even if you launch COMMAND. This can cause TSRs to fail. Set the DOSONLY command in Config.nt to keep the session focused on COMMAND.COM.

You can make copies of Config.nt and Autoexec.nt and modify them for a particular application. For example, if you want to run WordPerfect 5.1 with expanded memory, you can copy Config.nt to Config.wp and make the necessary memory settings. Make sure you retain the existing settings to ensure proper operation of memory and network drivers.

Configuring and Managing 16-Bit Windows Sessions

If you upgrade an existing Windows 3.x machine to Windows 2000, Setup uses the existing INI files to build the necessary Registry entries. This includes entries for any applications loaded on the machine as well as configuration information such as background bitmaps, program manager groups, and the like. Windows 2000 maps the legacy INI files to the Registry under `HKLM\Software\Microsoft\Windows NT\CurrentVersion\IniFileMapping`. This key and its subkeys also act as pointers to update other portions of the Registry. For example, if an application makes an update to `IniFileMapping\Win.ini\Colors`, that same update is sent to `HKCU\Control Panel\Colors`.

When you do a fresh install of Windows 2000, Setup installs a rudimentary WIN.INI and SYSTEM.INI file in the \WINNT directory. The system sets the environment variable `%windir%` to point at this directory so that legacy Win16 applications can write their entries to these files. If you have a dual-boot machine and you make configuration changes while in Windows 3.x, Windows 2000 notes and incorporates the changes into the NT Registry the next time you boot into Windows 2000.

By the same token, if Windows 2000 makes changes that affect the Windows 3.x installation, it attempts to keep the configurations in sync by writing to the WIN.INI and SYSTEM.INI files. This also means configuration errors made in either environment can affect the other, so sometimes you can't dual-boot your way out of a problem.

Registry Tip: Automatic Migration

You can turn off the automatic migration of changes to the INI files with the following Registry keys:

```
HKCU | Windows 3.1 Migration Status
HKLM | SOFTWARE | Windows 3.1 Migration Status
```

You can also force another migration by deleting these keys and restarting.

When you mix WIN16 and WIN32 applications on the same machine, you may encounter DLL incompatibilities. Version control for shared DLLs gets very messy if a vendor overwrites a key DLL without asking permission, or, worse, retains the same name for its own DLLs when it ports its applications from 16-bit to 32-bit.

The reason this causes problems is that Windows 2000 and Windows 3.x treat DLLs differently. To conserve memory, 16-bit Windows loads one instance of a DLL, and all Windows programs running on the machine share it. WIN32 applications cannot share a DLL directly because each process runs in a separate memory space. Windows 2000 loads and registers a DLL image and then uses Virtual Memory Manager to copy pages from the image into the address space of the processes that call the DLL.

Windows 2000 also provides support for 16-bit applications that access function calls in 32-bit DLL images. This is called "thunking." Windows 2000 and NT use a superior thunking method than Windows 9x.

WIN32s applications are also supported. WIN32s is 32-bit code designed to run on 16-bit Windows. Win32s applications expect to find shared DLLs, but they run in separate memory space. Symptoms of mixed or missing DLLs include *Cannot find filename.dll* errors and *Call to Undefined Dynalink* errors. You may see failure of programs that call Mail API (MAPI) and Telephony API (TAPI) interfaces.

The Windows 2000 Resource Kit includes several tools that can help sniff out rogue DLLs. One is Tlist, which gives a snapshot of running processes and their hierarchy.

```
C:\>tlist -t
System Process (0)
System (2)
  smss.exe (20)
    csrss.exe (24)
    winlogon.exe (34)
      services.exe (40)
        spoolss.exe (72)
        RpcSs.exe (80)
        tcpsvcs.exe (83)
        tapisrv.exe (88)
        rasman.exe (104)
        pstores.exe (116)
      lsass.exe (43)
      nddeagnt.exe (57)
Explorer.exe (130) Program Manager
  SysTray.Exe (141)
  loadwc.exe (131)
  Deskmenu.exe (119)
  Winword.exe (59) Microsoft Word - TEST.DOC
```

```
cmd.exe (66) C:\cmd.exe - tlist -t
  sol.exe (75) Solitaire
  TLIST.EXE (46)
```

Tlist is useful for DLL troubleshooting because it can load a program and list the DLLs it uses:

```
C:\>tlist sol
 75 sol.exe          Solitaire
  CWD:      C:\
  CmdLine: sol
  VirtualSize:     17364 KB   PeakVirtualSize:     21524 KB
  WorkingSetSize:    820 KB   PeakWorkingSetSize:    888 KB
  NumberOfThreads: 1
    163 Win32StartAddr:0x02415f00 LastErr:0x00000002 State:Waiting
    4.0.1371.1 shp  0x02410000   sol.exe
    4.0.1381.4 shp  0x77f60000   ntdll.dll
    4.0.1381.4 shp  0x77e70000   USER32.dll
    4.0.1381.4 shp  0x77f00000   KERNEL32.dll
    4.0.1381.4 shp  0x77ed0000   GDI32.dll
    4.0.1381.4 shp  0x77dc0000   ADVAPI32.dll
    4.0.1381.4 shp  0x77e10000   RPCRT4.dll
    4.0.1371.1 shp  0x77370000   CARDS.dll
    4.0.1381.4 shp  0x77c40000   SHELL32.dll
    4.71.1008.3 shp 0x70c70000   COMCTL32.dll
    4.20.0.6201 shp 0x779f0000   MSVCRT.dll
    4.71.1008.3 shp 0x77780000   msidle.dll
```

The Resource Kit also includes a tool called Dependency Walker that loads an executable and displays its DLLs. The advantage to Dependency Walker to a troubleshooter is that it displays the source directory for the DLL. The disadvantage to this tool is that it works with 32-bit applications only.

Also available is a tool for listing the source directory of DLLs and their internal version numbers, called LISTDLLS. You can access it at www.sysinternals.com. This is an example:

```
E:\ntinternals>listdlls -p sol

ListDLLs V2.0
Copyright (C) 1997 Mark Russinovich
http://www.ntinternals.com


- - - - - - - - - - - - - - - - - - - - - - - - - - - - - - - - - - - - - - -
sol.exe pid: 4b
  Base        Size      Version          Path
  0x02410000  0xc000    4.00.1371.0001   C:\WINNT\system32\sol.exe
  0x77f60000  0x5c000   4.00.1381.0004   C:\WINNT\System32\ntdll.dll
  0x77e70000  0x54000   4.00.1381.0004   C:\WINNT\system32\USER32.dll
  0x77f00000  0x5e000   4.00.1381.0004   C:\WINNT\system32\KERNEL32.dll
  0x77ed0000  0x2c000   4.00.1381.0004   C:\WINNT\system32\GDI32.dll
  0x77dc0000  0x3e000   4.00.1381.0004   C:\WINNT\system32\ADVAPI32.dll
```

```
0x77e10000  0x52000   4.00.1381.0004  C:\WINNT\system32\RPCRT4.dll
0x77370000  0x29000   4.00.1371.0001  C:\WINNT\system32\CARDS.dll
0x77c40000  0x13c000  4.00.1381.0004  C:\WINNT\system32\SHELL32.dll
0x70c70000  0x7b000   4.71.1008.0003  C:\WINNT\system32\COMCTL32.dll
0x779f0000  0x46000   4.20.0000.6201  C:\WINNT\system32\MSVCRT.dll
0x77780000  0x6000    4.71.1008.0003  C:\WINNT\System32\msidle.dll
```

None of these tools can trace the actions of 16-bit code inside NTVDM. The virtual space hides the operation of the code within. About the only way to trace actions for WIN16 applications within VDMs is to observe how they act on a Windows system.

Moving Forward

Now that the users have a stable and approachable operating environment in the local network, the Windows 2000 deployment is getting close to its final stages. Now it's time to extend that operating environment to travelers and home workers. Remote offices that don't have full-time network connections also need support. And everyone wants to get on the Internet. The next chapter covers remote access, demand–dial routing, and Internet connectivity.

17

Managing Remote Access and Internet Routing

Now that the Windows 2000 deployment is well underway, it's time to take a break from desktops and servers and think about how to support the gypsies of the Information Age, traveling users and home workers. These users need a way to connect to the network that is reliable, secure, and hopefully doesn't require a graduate degree in computer science to configure.

Microsoft has included remote access features in Windows ever since the release of Windows NT Advanced Server and Windows for Workgroups. For a long time, these features were known collectively as RAS, short for Remote Access Services. In NT4 and Windows 95, Microsoft coined a new term for the client side of RAS, Dial-Up Networking, that was supposed to be more user friendly. Maybe it was, but it sure made for an unfortunate acronym.

About the middle of the NT4 product cycle, Microsoft released a package of extensions to RAS developed under the code name Steelhead. These extensions came in the form of an add-on pack called *Routing and Remote Access Services* (RRAS). The RRAS extensions were a patch on a patch on a patch, but they provided the framework for integrating all network services into a single core function.

The remote access and routing features in Windows 2000 represent the next stage of maturity for RRAS. Here are a few of the high points:

- **Fully integrated.** Rather than being an add-on, the code has been incorporated into the SVCHOST suite along with other network services. The RRAS service is installed by default, so there is no need find the CD when you want to configure the server.

- **Consistent interface.** All network connections, both local and dial-up, use a common interface, the `Network and Dial-up Interface Connection` window. Each connection is represented by an icon with properties to configure and manage the interface.

- **Increased uptime.** The connections in the `Network and Dial-up Interface Connection` window are handled by a new service, the Network Connections Manager, or NETMAN. This service permits disabling, enabling, and modifying most of the connection parameters on the fly. There is seldom a need to restart the system when changing network parameters.

- **Expanded authentication mechanisms.** There is a new form of Microsoft CHAP with enhanced security along with support for *Remote Authentication Dial-In User Service* (RADIUS) and the *Extensible Authentication Protocol* (EAP). The EAP support includes the use of certificates and smart cards via *Transport Layer Security* (TLS) along with hooks for third parties to add other features.

- **Simplified VPN management.** The two *Virtual Private Networking* (VPN) interfaces, PPTP and L2TP, are now installed by default and require no additional configuration. There is also an IpSec provider for enhanced data protection over Internet connections.

- **Network Address Translation (NAT).** RRAS incorporates NAT for making quick and secure Internet connections as well as handling private inbound connections. There is also a simplified method for installing and configuring NAT called *Internet Connection Sharing* (ICS) that Windows 2000 has in common with Windows 98 SE.

Microsoft even tried extra hard to be consistent with their terminology. In Windows 2000, the term *dial-up* is now the general term to describe any asynchronous data connection over a circuit-switched network. The term RRAS refers only to the Routing and Remote Access service itself. A user who is connecting to a server over a dial-up connection is called a *dial-in* user. Using this nomenclature, a *dial-in client* connects to a *dial-up server* over a *dial-up* connection.

A Windows 2000 server that makes a demand-dial connection over a circuit-switched network is called a *demand-dial* server. When a demand-dial server also acts as a router, it is called a *demand-dial router*. If a demand-dial router uses network address translation, it is called a *NAT router*.

The first item of business in this chapter is a quick overview of circuit-switched data communication and how to install and configure modems, including troubleshooting hints in the event that a modem doesn't work (as incredible as that might sound). The overview also covers a functional description of RRAS and how the network handles asynchronous connections, including *Point-to-Point Protocol* (PPP) user authentications.

With the theory out of the way, the rest of the chapter contains step-by-step instructions for deploying the remote access and routing features in RRAS. Here are the configuration topics covered in this chapter:

- Configuring a Windows 2000 Professional desktop as a dial-up server
- Configuring a Windows 2000 Server as a dial-up server
- Configuring a Windows 2000 Professional desktop or server as a dial-up client
- Connecting a Windows 2000 dial-up client to a Windows 2000 dial-up server
- Connecting a Windows 2000 dial-up client to a remote access server at an Internet service provider
- Connecting a Windows 2000 demand-dial server to an Internet service provider as a router
- Sharing an Internet connection using Network Address Translation (NAT)
- Sharing an Internet connection using Internet Connection Sharing (ICS)
- Configuring a Virtual Private Network (VPN) connection between a Windows 2000 dial-up client and a Windows 2000 demand-dial server

Functional Description of Windows 2000 Data Communications

Network communications over a circuit-switched connection is a little like dancing under a strobe light. A whole lot goes on between flashes, but you still get the impression of continuity. Windows 2000 treats a circuit-switched connection just like any other network interface—a very slow interface, to be sure, and not all that reliable, but the same trusty OSI model layers apply (see Figure 17.1).

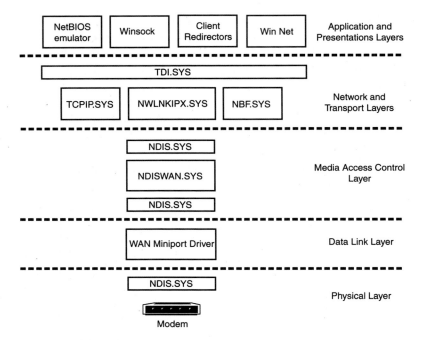

Figure 17.1 Windows 2000 data communications
layers and their corresponding to OSI layers.

- Physical layer connections are handled by protocols in the circuit–switched
  devices themselves and are managed by *Telephony API* (TAPI) drivers.

- Data link and medium access control is managed by *Network Device
  Interface Specification* (NDIS) drivers.

- The data link connections themselves are established, authenticated, and
  verified by the *Point-to-Point Protocol* (PPP).

- Network and transport connections during PPP connections are handled
  by special IP, IPX, and NetBEUI control protocols. After the links are
  established, network and transport communications are turned over to
  network drivers that communicate with NDIS below and the *Transport
  Driver Interface* (TDI) above.

- Application layer protocols such as network file systems and WINSOCK
  sit high enough in the stack to be oblivious to the commotion below.
  They communicate with each other as they normally would over
  Ethernet or Token Ring, only much more slowly.

Physical Layer Connections and TAPI

If you're a follower of cosmological physics—and what self-respecting system administrator isn't—you probably know that one of the chief goals of this branch of science is to arrive at a single, unified description of all the forces in nature. This so-called Grand Unification Theory (GUT) might not result in peace in our time, but it sure would liven up a few *Nova* episodes.

Data communications technology has its own grand unification goal—only slightly less ambitious than the GUT—of developing a single, cohesive methodology for managing and combining circuit-switched telephone networks and packet-switched data networks. The buzzword for this unification is *convergence*. The technology moving it forward exists on several fronts, but the key player is *telephony*.

Microsoft set out many years ago to make NT a major telephony player. They developed a proprietary Telephony API, TAPI, and fought in typical Microsoft style to make it the sole industry standard. They incorporated improved telephony support into every service release. They aggressively prowled among the leaders in the industry for ways to incorporate NT into the switching technology, if not to become the switch itself.

Nowadays, it's difficult to find a major switch vendor that doesn't include an NT interface with its equipment. Smaller PBX units are rapidly disappearing in favor of ruggedized NT servers configured as dedicated telephone switches. Classic TAPI is now at version 2.1 and for all intents and purposes it defines the core architecture in Windows 2000 for communicating with circuit-switched hardware.

Telephony Example

For an elementary example of telephony at work, install and configure a modem using the procedure in the "Installing and Configuring Modem" section. Then take a look at the Phone Dialer accessory in START | PROGRAMS | ACCESSORIES | COMMUNICATION | PHONE DIALER. Figure 17.2 shows the main window. As you can see, this little applet has become a full-fledged conferencing center with the capability to communicate over dial-up lines, Internet phones, and H.323 connections.

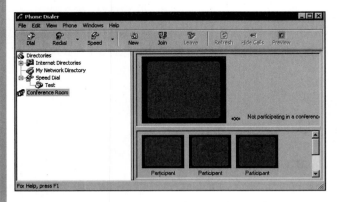

Figure 17.2 Phone Dialer applet showing new telephony features.

Over the past few years, the Internet has changed the communication landscape considerably. *Voice-over-IP* (VoIP) has matured from a hobbyist's curiosity to a full-fledged industry. Streaming media and other IP-enabled communication technologies have fundamentally altered the way people do business together, not to mention the way they lead their personal lives. This is not so much convergence as cataclysm. The days of circuit-switched data communications are coming to a close. The telephone handset as we know it today will soon disappear, as archaic in an IP world as Elliot Ness clacking a hook switch to get the attention of an operator.

In the face of all this change, Microsoft chose to keep TAPI as the interface to their new communication technology but expanded the API by exposing new media services as *Common Object Model* (COM) objects. This enables programmers to use any COM programming language, such as C++ or Visual Basic or Microsoft's Java, to write telephony applications. Classic TAPI is strictly a C API. This COM-based TAPI has a version number of 3.0, but it is all new code. It forms the basis for a variety of telephony and telephony-related technologies, including call center control, *Interactive Voice Response* (IVR), IP multicast conferencing, and voice mail. Over the next few years, look for telephony features in Windows 2000 to become as pervasive as Web technology.

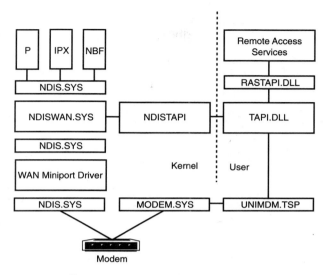

Figure 17.3   WAN driver diagram.

The full range of telephony subsystems in Windows 2000 lies beyond the scope of this book, but it is impossible to discuss remote access without taking a brief look at the way the remote access network drivers use TAPI. Refer to Figure 17.3. When a user initiates a dial-up connection, RRAS calls on the classic TAPI server service, TAPISRV.DLL, to set up the communication link between the modems or ISDN equipment at each end of the connection. Like RRAS, TAPISRV is one of the services provided by SVCHOST.

TAPISRV runs in user memory space. It communicates with underlying Kernel-mode drivers such as MODEM.SYS through a set of *Telephony service providers* (TSPs). For example, the TSP for a modem is the Unimodem TSP driver, UNIMDM.TSP. COM-based TAPI 3.0 does not need a server service. TAPI 3.0 applications talk directly to *Media service providers* (MSPs) that run in user space. They can also talk to the TAPISRV server via an RPC connection.

Registry Tip: Modem Configuration

Modem configuration information is stored in the Registry under the Class ID (CLSID) for modems, 4D36E96D-E325-11CE-BFC1-08002BE10318. The configuration entries are kept in the following Registry entry:

HKLM, System, CurrentControlSet, Control, Class, {4D36E96D-E325-11CE-BFC1-08002BE10318}

Each modem is given a separate key that is a sequential number starting at 0000. Figure 17.4 shows the entries for a typical modem.

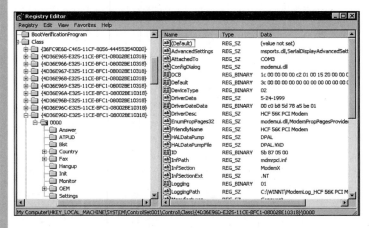

Figure 17.4 Modem parameters stored under the Modem class in the Registry.

If you encounter a modem setup problem that is resolved with a Registry change, make the corresponding change to the INF file in case you install the same modem again.

After TAPISRV has done its work for RRAS by configuring a modem, it falls out of the picture as far as remote access is concerned. RRAS relies on a special NDIS driver, NDISWAN.SYS, to communicate with the modem.

MAC Layer Connections and NDIS

NDIS 5.0 has been rewritten as a *Windows Driver Model* (WDM) interface with overall responsibility for communicating with hardware miniport drivers associated with network communications. NDIS treats a modem just like any other network adapter. For standard adapters, the NDIS.SYS driver talks directly to the adapter miniport driver. In modem communications, NDIS uses an intermediate driver, NDISWAN.SYS, to talk to the modem miniport driver. NDISWAN.SYS performs PPP framing, compression, and encryption.

NSIDWAN also works with TAPISRV to create and remove modem interfaces. This particular interplay has been improved considerably in Windows 2000. You can add and remove modems and associate them with different dial-up connections at your whim without restarting the computer or reconfiguring RRAS. Dial-up interface configurations are covered in "Configuring Dial-Up Clients."

The generic miniport for WAN communications is the RAS Async Adapter driver, ASYNCMAC.SYS. The INF file NETRASA.INF in `\WINNT\INF` contains the setup information for this and other virtual WAN miniport drivers, such as the *Layer 2 Tunneling Protocol* (L2TP) interface, *Point-to-Point Tunneling Protocol* (PPTP) interface, and the direct parallel interface (PTI). The miniport driver talks to the serial port driver, SERIAL.SYS, and the modem driver, MODEM.SYS.

The job assigned to NDIS is to construct a communications frame for data packets so that they can be transmitted over the physical layer devices. For Ethernet and Token Ring and FDDI interfaces, NDIS works with the adapter minidriver to build a frame that conforms to the appropriate IEEE 802 specification. For example, the Ethernet frame conforms to IEEE 802.2.

When communicating over a serial-line connection, NDIS uses an intermediate driver, NDISWAN.SYS, that works with ASYNCMAC.SYS to frame packets using a form of the *High-Level Data Link Control* (HDLC) protocol. The HDLC used by NDIS is the same as that used by PPP. The format is defined in RFC 1662, "PPP in HDLC-like Framing."

HDLC Flavors

HDLC has long been a standard for serial-line data communications. Echoes of HDLC in the LAPB protocol are used for X.25 connections, the LAPD and LAPX protocols used for ISDN, and the SDLC protocol used for SNA.

Point-to-Point Protocol (PPP)

Windows 2000 supports two data link control protocols: *Serial Line Internet Protocol* (SLIP) and *Point-to-Point Protocol* (PPP). SLIP is the older of the two. It is the data communications equivalent of a Dixie cup and a string. Windows 2000 supports SLIP for outbound dial-up only.

PPP, on the other hand, can automatically establish and reestablish connections, has error-correcting protocols, supports multiple network and transport protocols, and can monitor for line condition to keep the link alive. The PPP implementation in Windows 2000 conforms to the requirements of RFC 1661, "Point-to-Point Protocol."

A Windows 2000 dial-up client can connect to any RFC-compliant remote access server. By the same token, a Windows 2000 dial-up server can respond to connection requests from any RFC-compliant PPP client as long as it can deliver proper authentication credentials. This includes Trumpet WINSOCK, Linux PPP, Shiva PPP, and so forth.

It is the multiple protocol support in PPP that makes it especially useful for Windows data communications. A special field in the PPP frame identifies the transport protocol. Examples include `0021`—`Internet Protocol`, `0029`—`AppleTalk`, and `002b`—`Novell IPX`. A variety of control protocols, compression protocols, and authentication protocols can also be loaded into a PPP frame. These protocols are identified and negotiated by the dial-up client and dial-up server when the PPP link is established.

Two computers making a PPP connection resemble a couple meeting for the first time. There is a long, searching moment where the two of them exchange names, make chitchat, and size up each other up. If the encounter goes smoothly, there's a Hollywood moment. If the encounter fails, well, tomorrow is another day. PPP connections are established in three steps:

- **Link establishment.** The two physical devices establish a data link connection.

- **Authentication.** The user is authenticated as an authorized dial-up user. In Windows 2000, dial-up permissions are either granted on a user-by-user basis or as part of a group policy. Dial-in authentication is performed within PPP as a separate process that is independent from network authentication. A variety of authentication mechanisms are provided, including provisions for third-party authenticators.

- **Network layer establishment.** Special control protocol drivers are configured for the transport protocols used by the client and a dial-up session is established.

Link Establishment

A dial-up server waits for a connection by placing its modem in Auto Answer mode and listening for the ring indicator (RI) line to go high. A dial-up client begins the connection by initializing its modem and placing a call to the dial-up server. After the modems establish a physical layer connection using whatever communications protocols they negotiate between themselves, PPP takes over and uses the *Link Control Protocol* (LCP) to establish a data link connection. These parameters include the following:

- **Maximum receive unit (MRU).** The maximum frame size that will be transmitted over the connection. The MRU is set to 1500 bytes by default.

- **Asynchronous-Control-Character-Map (ACCM).** The first 32 ASCII characters can act as control characters in an asynchronous serial connection. They are also potentially part of the data stream if that stream contains binary files. The ACCM option represents control characters as discrete bits in a 32-bit sequence. For example, Ctrl+L (^L) would be represented by bit 12. If the mask is set to all zeros, this indicates that no mapping is required.

- **Authentication type.** This option determines the authentication method that will be used in the next phase of the connection. The method depends on the configuration of the client and server. There are five options for Windows 2000 and Microsoft RAS: EAP (0xC2-27), MS-CHAPv1 (0xC2-23-80), MS-CHAPv2 (0xC2-23-81), MD5-CHAP (0xC2-23-05), SPAP (0xC0-27), and PAP (0xC0-23). The following section details each of these authentication options.

- **Magic number.** A magic number is a random number that validates the packet source. If a host sees its own magic number in a packet, it knows there has been a loopback. It discards the packet and reestablishes the link.

- **Protocol field compression.** This option permits compression of the protocol field in the PPP frame. Both parties must agree to set this option before it can be used. The option is set on by default.

- **Address and Control field compression.** This option permits compression of the 1-byte Address field and the 1-byte Control field in the PPP header. This option is set on by the default.

Authentication

PPP requires that a user present a set of credentials that prove the user's identity and to validate the user's authorization to make the connection. The authentication method is determined during the link establishment phase. PPP itself has no preferred authentication protocol. Windows 2000 supports a variety of protocols. The following list offers a short summary. See the "PPP Authentication Protocols" section later in this chapter for details about each protocol.

- **Password Authentication Protocol (PAP).** Uses clear text passwords transmitted over the wire. This method is unsuitable for all but the most trivial dial-up transactions.

- **Shiva PAP (SPAP).** Proprietary form of PAP used in Shiva LANRovers and other products. This method uses reversibly encrypted passwords transmitted over the wire. Unsuitable for any transaction where there is a potential for authentication impersonation.

- **Challenge-Handshake Protocol (CHAP).** An industry standard authentication method used in nearly all Internet dial-up transactions. This method uses encrypted passwords that are not passed over the wire. Instead, a random value called a *challenge* is sent to the dialer, who encrypts it using the user's password as an encryption key. If the authenticating server can decrypt the challenge using its copy of the user's password, the user is authenticated. For CHAP to work, passwords must be stored at the server in a form that can be rendered into clear text.

- **Microsoft CHAP v1 (MS-CHAP).** Microsoft proprietary version of CHAP that uses the hashed version of user's password to encrypt the challenge rather than the user's clear password. Used by down-level Windows clients such as classic NT, Windows 3.1x, and Windows 95.

- **Microsoft CHAP v2 (MS-CHAP v2).** Extended version of MS-CHAP that includes a peer challenge to the dial-up server. This mutual authentication is meant to foil servers that impersonate standard Windows RAS servers.

- **Extensible Authentication Protocol (EAP).** This is not an authentication protocol, as such, but a mechanism for using alternative authentication methods after the standard authentication phase. Windows 2000 includes several EAP authentication methods, including smart cards, certificates, and a version of CHAP to use for testing. Vendors can add additional methods.

Network Layer Establishment

After the user has been authenticated, PPP gives the helm to the *Network Control Protocol* (NCP). This protocol is responsible for establishing the network link now that the user has been authenticated. NCP has several duties and uses additional protocols to perform them. These include the following:

- Callback Control
- Compression Control
- Encryption Control
- Transport Control

Callback Control

NCP determines the callback options, if any, that have been set for the user by using the *Callback Control Protocol* (CBCP). In Windows 2000, the user's callback options are contained in one of two places. For standalone dial-up servers, the information is stored in the user's SAM account. For domains, the information is stored in the user's Directory object under the MSRADIUS-Callback-Number attribute.

CBCP has three options for setting callback functions:

- **No Callback.** If this option is set, CBCP immediately returns control to the NCP.

- **Callback Set by Caller.** If this option is set, CBCP tells the dial-in client that a callback is required and requests a callback number. The dial-up client prompts the user to enter a phone number. After the user enters a phone number, CBCP acknowledges the dial-up client, terminates the connection, and waits for a callback from the server. CBCP dials the number and lets PPP reestablish the link. The number entered by the user is recorded in the Event Log. This callback option is commonly used to support overseas callers because an outbound call from the States is often much cheaper.

- **Call Back Preset To.** If this option is set, CBCP tells the dial-up client that a preset callback number has been defined. The client acknowledges and then terminates the call and waits for a callback from the server. The server dials the preset number, reestablishes the link, and turns control back to NCP.

Compression Control

The next action by the NCP is to negotiate a compression mechanism, if any. In a stock PPP implementation, this is done using the *Configuration Control Protocol* (CCP). Microsoft uses a variation of CCP called *Microsoft Point-to-Point Compression* (MPPC).

MPPC is a proprietary protocol that negotiates additional features with Windows clients while still supporting standard CCP for non–Windows clients. MPPC uses options set by the dial-up client and server to determine the compression setting.

Windows 2000 dial-up clients and dial-up servers default to having compression enabled. TAPI also has a compression feature that enables hardware compression. You should not use both simultaneously. It wastes cycles trying to compress frames that have already been compressed. Software compression is usually faster. If you want to disable hardware compression, the option is available at CONTROL PANEL | PHONE AND MODEM | MODEM CONFIGURATION PROPERTIES.

Encryption Control

Standard PPP assumes that higher-level application protocols will encrypt the data stream. Microsoft added encryption negotiation in the network establishment phase to simplify setup. This is done with the *Microsoft Point-to-Point Encryption* protocol, or MPPE. The data encryption method is determined by the authentication option negotiated during the authentication phase. Both MPPC and MPPE are negotiated simultaneously.

Control Protocols

After compression and encryption protocols have been defined, NCP turns its attention to the control protocols that configure the interface to the networking protocols used by the system. Each network transport supported by Windows 2000 has a corresponding control protocol. They are as follows:

- **IPCP (IP Control Protocol).** This protocol is defined in RFC 1332, "The PPP Internet Protocol Control Protocol (IPCP)." IPCP sets parameters such as the client's IP address, primary and secondary DNS servers, primary and secondary WINS servers, and the option to use Van Jacobson compression for the IP header. This option is selected by default in PPP Settings.

- **IPXCP (IPX Control Protocol).** This protocol is defined in RFC 1552, "The PPP Internetwork Packet Exchange Control Protocol (IPXCP)." IPXCP sets parameters such as the IPX Network Number, the IPX Node Number, the IPX Compression Protocol, the IPX Routing Protocol, and the IPX Router Name.

- **NBFCP (NetBIOS Frame Control Protocol).** This protocol is defined in RFC 2097, "The PPP NetBIOS Frames Control Protocol (NBFCP)". NBFCP sets parameters such as NetBIOS Name Projection that lists the names of the servers to add to the NetBIOS Name table at the client and Peer Information that declares whether the client is an endpoint or a gateway. There is also an IEEE MAC Address Required option to specify whether transmitted frames include MAC addresses to facilitate communication on the other side of a gateway and a Multicast Filtering option to control NetBIOS broadcasts through the gateway.

After PPP has established the communications link, NDIS can communicate over it just as if the link were a network line. If you view the traffic with Network Monitor or some other packet sniffer, you may see a few sporadic PPP packets. The system uses these to check data link quality, network control link quality, and to periodically reauthenticate the user.

PPP Authentication Protocols

This section contains a detailed look at each of the authentication protocols used by PPP. This information helps you to decide which protocol to use and to troubleshoot connections if the authentication protocols are misconfigured. It also helps to understand how the stock protocols interrelate when attempting a Windows 2000 dial-up server with other dial-up products or authentication packages.

Password Authentication Protocol (PAP)

PAP authenticates a user by collecting the logon credentials and sending them to the server in clear text. The server checks the password and, if it is correct, gives the user access.

PAP is acceptable only when connecting to a trusted server over a trusted phone line. Windows 2000 does not normally store a clear text version of a user's password, so if you enable PAP, you must also enable reversible passwords. See the sidebar titled "Reversible Passwords" for more information.

Shiva Password Authentication Protocol (SPAP)

SPAP is used by Shiva's LANRover products and Shiva-compatible remote access servers. SPAP is supported by RAS both to permit a Shiva client to dial in to a Windows RAS server and to permit a Windows client to dial in to a LANRover device.

Unlike PAP, SPAP uses encrypted passwords, but it is still not completely secure because the encrypted passwords are transmitted over the wire where they can be shanghaied and used for impersonation. SPAP passwords are also reversible, making them susceptible to cracking. See the sidebar titled "Reversible Passwords" for more information.

SPAP should not be enabled as a dial-up authentication protocol. It should only be used by dial-up clients if necessary to connect to a LANRover remote access server.

Challenge Handshake Authentication Protocol (CHAP)

Standard CHAP is defined by RFC 1994, "PPP Challenge Handshake Authentication Protocol (CHAP)." Windows 2000 dial-up servers use CHAP to support non-Windows clients. Windows 2000 dial-up clients use CHAP to connect with non-Windows remote access servers. Here is an outline of a CHAP authentication transaction:

1. The user enters credentials (name, password, and a home domain, if connecting to a Windows dial-up server) an initiates the dial-up connection.

2. At the start of the Authentication phase, the remote access server sends a challenge to the client in the form of a random number and a session number.

3. The dial-in client combines the challenge, the user's password, and the session number and encrypts them using the user's clear text password as the secret key.

4. The dial-in client returns the encrypted challenge to the remote access server along with the user's dial-up login ID in clear text.

5. The remote access server obtains a copy of the user's password from a database and uses it to encrypt the same elements as the client. If the results match, the server sends the client a success message.

6. CHAP also reauthenticates the user periodically, limiting the time that an impersonator could do damage.

CHAP uses MD5 encryption technology. MD stands for *message digest*. The message digest encryption algorithm was developed by Ronald Rivest, one of the founders of RSA Data Security, an independent corporation specializing in encryption and security products. Get more information on MD5 and message digest encryption technologies at www.rsa.com.

An outline of the workings of MD5 is contained in RFC 1321, "The MD5 Message-Digest Algorithm." In brief, MD5 encryption creates a 128-bit message digest, also called a *hash*, that can include up to 512 bytes of original data. The MD5 hash is non-reversible and considered unbreakable by brute force methods.

Every authentication scheme has a weak point. One weakness of CHAP is that the dial-up server must have a copy of the user's clear text password. Without this, the server cannot build an MD5 hash that matches the hash built by the client. See the following sidebar for more information.

CHAP also does not protect against a counterfeit server that pretends to accept the users' credentials but then routes them to an unsecured location.

Reversible Passwords

Neither classic NT nor Windows 2000 store clear text passwords. Instead, if support for CHAP, PAP, or SPAP is required, a second form of the user's password is stored using reversible encryption. This is called the LANMan password because it has its roots in the OS/2 LAN Manager days.

The LANMan password is limited to 14 bytes of uppercase ASCII characters or standard numerals. It is encrypted using reversible, 40-bit DES encryption. When a Windows dial-up server needs a user's clear text password, it obtains the LANMan password from the local SAM or the Directory and extracts the clear text password.

The LANMan password has come under heavy attack during the past three years and has been the source of many serious security breaches. Several utilities are freely available on the Internet for cracking LANMan passwords. For this reason, Windows 2000 does not create nor store a LANMan password unless reversible password storage is required. See the "Supporting Down-Level and Non-Windows Dial-Up Clients" section for details on enabling reversible password storage.

Microsoft Challenge Handshake Authentication Protocol (MS-CHAP v1)

Windows dial–up clients authenticating against Windows dial–up servers have an advantage because they share the same parent company: They can use the same encryption algorithms and keys. Microsoft uses this common technology to provide a proprietary alternative to CHAP called *MS-CHAP*.

MS-CHAP uses a similar set of transactions as standard CHAP with one or two key differences:

1. The user presents credentials at the start of the dial-up transaction, but the user's password is encrypted immediately using the same one-way MD4 encryption used to create a user's Windows password. (MD4 is an earlier version of MD5 that is faster but still resistant to brute force attack.)

2. At the start of the Authentication phase, the Windows dial-up server sends a *challenge* to the dial-in client in the form of a random number and a session number.

3. The dial-in client combines the challenge, the session ID, and its hashed password and encrypts them using the MD4 hash of the user's password as the secret key.

4. The dial-in client returns the encrypted challenge to the dial-up server along with the user's PPP login ID in clear text.

5. If the Windows dial-up server is a standalone server or a domain controller, it obtains the user's MD4 hashed password from its local SAM to encrypt its copy of the challenge, session ID and user's hashed password. If the server is a domain member, it uses pass-through authentication to a domain controller to validate the user's identity.

6. In either case, if the user is authenticated, the server sends the client a success message.

7. MS-CHAP also reauthenticates the user at intervals during a dial-up session to limit exposure to impersonators.

Unlike standard CHAP, MS-CHAP does not require the storage of reversible passwords. It does share the disadvantage of exposure to counterfeit servers. That security threat is handled by an improvement to MS-CHAP, covered next.

MS-CHAP, now known as MS-CHAP v1 because of the new version covered in the next section, is used by down-level Windows clients such as Windows 3.x, Windows 95, and NT4 SP3 or lower. Windows 9x clients are restricted to passwords of 14 characters or fewer owing to a limitation of the 40-bit encryption used in non-domestic Windows.

Microsoft Challenge Handshake Authentication Protocol version 2 (MS-CHAP v2)

Windows 2000, NT4 SP4 and higher, and Windows 98 use a new version of MS-CHAP called MS-CHAP v2. This new version adds an additional peer challenge that is sent by the dial-up client to the Windows dial-up server to authenticate the server. This mutual authentication guards against counterfeit servers. Here are the additional steps:

1. When the peer client responds to the Windows dial-up server with the encrypted form of the challenge, it includes a random number sent as a challenge to the server.

2. After the dial-up server successfully authenticates the user, it creates an MD4 hash that combines its original challenge, the peer challenge it received from the client, the encrypted challenge returned by the client and the user's password hash. It uses the user's password hash as the secret key.

3. If the dial-in client can decrypt the encrypted peer challenge response, it continues with the transaction. Otherwise, it terminates the transaction.

Extensible Authentication Protocol (EAP)

EAP is not an authentication protocol in and of itself. It provides a way to use alternative authentication methods that are not directly supported by PPP. EAP essentially permits the dial-up server to take a rain check during the authentication phase then, when the network transports have been initialized and the session is established, the server completes the authentication using the alternative method.

Windows 2000 comes with two EAP packages: MD5-CHAP and TLS, short for *transport layer security*. Here are details about how they work:

- **MD5-CHAP.** This method uses the same transactions as standard CHAP but initiates them after the network setup phase. It is included to provide a simple way to test your EAP setup because it does not require any additional services such as a certificate server or a smart card repository. See the "Configuring Dial-Up Authentication Options" section for details on configuring EAP.

- **TLS.** This provides the enabling technology for certificate authentication, including smart cards and certificates. TLS is based on Secure Socket Layer 3.0. It is described in standards-track RFC 2246, "The TLS Protocol Version 1.0."

Installing and Configuring Modems

Okay, enough theory, at least for a while. It's time to install a communications device. Plug and Play (PnP) takes a lot of the pain out of this process. Ideally, you should only need to install the modem, boot the machine, and watch PnP do its thing. If you have a laptop, you can install a PC Card modem while the computer is running, and the PnP Manager will find it and install the drivers. USB modems are even easier to install.

The PnP Manager uses a driver called SERENUM.SYS to enumerate serial devices. This includes legacy and PnP devices that are connected to RS-232 ports or attached to the PCI bus.

In the Windows Driver Model (WDM), SERENUM is considered both a bus driver because it enumerates components on the bus, and a filter driver because it builds a virtual device that represents the modem. See Chapter 3, "Adding Additional Hardware," for details on WDM drivers.

When SERENUM finds a modem, it calls on a modem class installer to locate the correct driver. The class installer queries the modem for its make and model, and then it searches for a corresponding INF file in the \WINNT\INF folder.

There are more than 150 modem-related INFs in \WINNT\INF, and each INF contains configuration instructions for multiple modems, so it's rare to come across a modem that doesn't have a driver. Each INF is paired with a PNF file, which is a precompiled version of the INF that can be read more easily by the PnP class installer.

If the class installer cannot find an INF for a modem but the modem responds correctly to a standard Hayes command set, the installer uses a generic INF, MDMGEN.INF. This usually is enough to get basic functionality, but certain features may not be available, and the modem may fail to operate satisfactorily. This is especially true if the init string does not contain key entries required by the vendor.

If PnP succeeded in configuring your modem automatically, you can skip down to "Configuring Windows 2000 Dial-Up Servers." If you have an external PnP modem, and you don't want to restart your computer to initiate a bus scan, see the next section for a way to manually start the scan. If you have a legacy modem that requires manual installation, proceed to "Installing Legacy Modems."

Installing External PnP Modems

If you connect up an external PnP modem and you don't want to restart the computer to initiate the bus enumeration, use the following steps to initiate a PnP bus scan:

Procedure 17.1   **Manually Initiating a PnP Bus Scan**

1. Connect the serial cable between the modem and a COM port on the computer and energize the modem.

2. Open the Computer Management console by right-clicking the My Computer icon on the desktop and selecting MANAGE from the fly-out menu.

3. Highlight Device Manager, and wait a moment for the system to display the list of devices it has already found.

4. Right-click the computer icon at the top of the tree, and select SCAN FOR HARDWARE CHANGES from the fly-out menu. After a few moments of discovery, the system installs the modem drivers for you.

5. Expand the device tree under Modems, and verify that the modem has been installed.

External Modems and PnP

If you have an external modem, make sure that it is turned on any time you start the computer. If you turn on the modem after the system is running and if PnP detects the modem, it will install a second modem thinking that a new one has been added. Microsoft will correct this problem in a maintenance release.

Troubleshooting Modem Installations

Normally troubleshooting sections come at the end, but with modems, it's always good to be prepared in advance. Here is list of things to try if the modem refuses to work.

- Save yourself hours of teeth gnashing by checking the Windows 2000 Hardware Compatibility List first. Just because your modem is not listed does not mean that it won't work, but if the modem vendor has no entries at all on the list, you know you have a problem.
- Check Device Manager to see whether there is a resource conflict.
- Check CMOS to make sure that the COM port is enabled.
- For internal modems, make sure that the ISA slot is set to recognize PnP devices. Some internal modems have dual personalities, one for ISA and one for PnP.
- Check the vendor manual for configuration instructions. This is especially true for legacy modems with jumpers.
- For external modems, check to make sure that the associated COM port is enabled and uses a standard I/O Base address and IRQ. Older laptops are notorious for having non-standard configurations. Table 17.1 shows the standard COM port configurations.

Table 17.1   **Standard COM Port I/O Base and IRQ Settings**

COM Port	I/O Base	IRQ
COM1	3F8	4
COM2	2F8	3
COM3	3E8	4
COM4	2E8	3

- If you are installing an external modem, you can verify that is connected to a functional serial port by opening a command session and entering atdt > com#:. Look for lights on the modem to flicker. If they do not, the serial cable may have the wrong pinouts. Table 17.2 shows the correct pinouts.

Table 17.2 **Serial Cable Pinouts for Connection to Modems**

25-PIN STRAIGHT-THROUGH

Male	Female	Function
1	1	Chassis Ground
2	2	Transmit Data
3	3	Receive Data
4	4	Request to Send
5	5	Clear to Send
6	6	Data Set Ready
7	7	Signal Ground
8	8	Carrier Detect
20	20	Data Terminal Ready

25-PIN TO 9-PIN

Male	Female	Function
8	1	Carrier Detect
3	2	Receive Data
2	3	Transmit Data
20	4	Data Terminal Ready
7	5	Signal Ground
6	6	Data Set Ready
4	7	Request to Send
5	8	Clear to Send
22	9	Ring Indicator (optional)

- For PC Card modems, verify that the card does not require legacy card and socket drivers. Windows 2000 does not support these. Only APM- and ACPI-compatible PC Cards are likely to work correctly if at all.

- Check the Microsoft KnowledgeBase for known issues with the modem.

- Some modems do their processing using the computer's CPU. These include Windows modems and parallel port modems. Windows modems come in a variety of disguises, including IBM MWAVE modems, Compaq Speedpaq modems with a Lucent chipset, and Intel Teladdin modems. These types of modems can be clumsy to configure and require special attention to resources. They are not recommended for dial-up servers.

- Some modems come as part of a multifunction card such as a PC Card combo Ethernet/modem or a combo adapter for MIDI/modem. The card itself may be PnP compatible, but the laptop may use a flavor of APM or PnP BIOS or an older version of ACPI so that the modem component is not recognized. You may need to configure resources manually.

- See the "Troubleshooting Using Modem Logs" section for additional tools for troubleshooting with modem logs and PPP traces.

Even if the modem seems to work, your job may not be finished. Many seemingly unrelated problems can arise when using an incompatible modem. If a system becomes erratic soon after installing a new modem, expect the worst. Some devices are—how should I put this—somewhat under-engineered. NDIS treats a serial device just like a network connection. This exposes design inadequacies.

Even if a modem behaves just fine in a standard terminal connection, it can fail miserably when used for dial-up communications. This is especially true for modems used in dial-up servers, where the devices must accept connections from a variety of clients over a variety of line conditions.

Support for Legacy NT Drivers

Theoretically, you can use legacy NT drivers in Windows 2000, but the INF file used by the Windows 2000 class loader to install the modem drivers has a different format from the INF scripts used by classic NT. If the class loader cannot read the INF, you will get errors such as *The script does not contain information for your hardware*.

Also, there is no support at all in Windows 2000 for legacy modems that use monolithic, pre-TAPI drivers. For this reason, there is no MODEM.INF file in Windows 2000.

You may be able to use Windows 98 drivers because they are written to WDM specifications. You don't know whether the vendor has regression-tested the Windows 98 drivers in a Windows 2000 environment, however, so proceed with caution.

Installing Legacy Modems

If a modem does not use PnP, you must install it manually. The manual installation is handled a generic installation program, RUNDLL32, and a special modem class installer, MDMINST.DLL. The following steps install an external modem.

Procedure 17.2 **Installing a Non-PnP Modem**

1. Connect the modem to a serial port using the correct cable. Energize the modem.

2. Open the Control Panel, and then open the Phone and Modem Options applet. (You can also use the Add/Remove Hardware applet, but for modems this way is faster.) The Location Information window opens.

3. Enter an Area Code. If you dial a Prefix to get an outside line, enter that number.

4. Click OK. The Phone and Modem Options window opens.

5. Select the Modem tab.

6. Click Add. The Add/Remove Hardware Wizard opens with the focus set to Modems. This same wizard is started if you use the Add/Remove Hardware applet in Control Panel, but it takes longer to get to this window.

7. Click Next. The wizard queries each COM port looking for a modem. When it finds one, it queries the modem looking for clues about the make and model. It compares these to a set of INF files in \WINNT\INF. When it finds the appropriate modem INF script, the Install New Modem window opens with a list of the detected modems.

8. It sometimes happens that the wizard selects the wrong modem. If this happens, click Change to open an alternative Install New Modem window where you can install the vendor's drivers or select the correct modem from a list.

9. Click Next. The wizard uses the installer to read the INF file and makes the necessary Registry changes to install the modem. When the wizard finishes, it opens a Successful Completion window.

10. Click Finish to close the wizard and return to the Phone and Modem Options window. The modem now appears on the Modem list.

11. Double-click the modem listing to open its Properties window.

12. The Maximum Port Speed value is normally set to the limit of the port, which is 115200bps for a standard RS-232 port. The modem will negotiate a lower bit rate when it makes a connection. If autonegotiation fails, you can set the Maximum Port Speed to the actual modem speed.

13. Select the Diagnostics tab (see Figure 17.5).

Figure 17.5   Modem Properties window, Diagnostics tab showing Query Modem results.

14. The Query Modem button sends a set of information and diagnostic commands to the modem. Scroll down the list of responses to see whether there are any errors.

15. The Record a Log File option outputs all transactions between the modem driver and the modem to a log stored in the \WINNT directory. The log filename starts with MODEMLOG_ and includes the name of the modem as it is displayed in the title bar of the Properties window. See "Troubleshooting Using Modem Logs" for a description of this log and how to use it.

16. Select the Advanced tab. Use the Extra Initializations Commands field to add any additional entries to the init string. The installed init string is stored in the Registry under the CLSID for modems. Look under HKLM, System, CurrentControlSet, Control, Class, {4D36E96D-E325-11CE-BFC1-08002BE10318}, <sequence#>, Init.

Any entries you make take precedence over the same entry in the default init string. Use this field when you are forced to use the generic modem INF but need to make changes to satisfy a specific peculiarity in a vendor's modem.

17. The Advanced Port Settings button provides a way to set the FIFO buffers and reassign the COM port. By default, the FIFO buffers are set to the maximum of the interface.

18. Click **Change Default Preferences**. The **Default Preferences** window opens (see Figure 17.6). Use this window to change the **Data Connection Preferences** for the modem. Here you would disable hardware compression, for instance, if you use software compression in PPP.

    Leave the **Flow Control** value set to **Hardware**, which corresponds to standard CTS/RTS flow control. Do not use XON/XOFF for dial-up connections.

    Use the **Advanced** tab if you need to use Hardware Settings other than the standard 8N1.

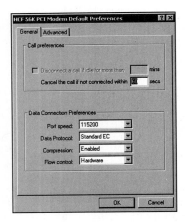

Figure 17.6 **Default Preferences** window for example modem showing standard data connection preferences.

19. Click **OK** to close the window, and return to the **Properties** window.

20. Click **OK** to save any changes, and return to the **Phone and Modem Options** window.

21. Install any additional modems, and then close the window.

22. Test the modem to make sure that it functions with the configuration you selected. The simplest way to do this is to make a quick connection using HyperTerminal, available at START | PROGRAMS | ACCESSORIES | COMMUNICATIONS | HYPERTERMINAL.

23. When HyperTerminal launches, it prompts for a session name. Use any name. Bullwinkle will do, but Test_Session is a bit more professional.

24. If you have a BBS, ISP over SLIP, or other terminal service number handy, call it. Otherwise, you can set up two Windows computers with HyperTerminal, put one of them in Auto Answer mode by selecting CALL | WAIT FOR CALL from the menu, and then dial it from the other. If you can get a connection and echo characters into each terminal window, you have resolved nearly all the potential problems.

Verifying Modem Properties Using Device Manager

If the modem does not work properly after installation, check the device properties to make sure that you do not have a resource conflict or an improper driver. In the following example steps, the properties for an internal PCI PnP modem are examined using Device Manager.

Procedure 17.3 **Using Device Manager to Verify Modem Properties**

1. Open the Device Manager console by right-clicking My Computer and selecting PROPERTIES from the fly-out menu. Select the Hardware tab, and click Device Manager. (You can also use the Add/Remove Hardware applet or the System applet in Control Panel, but this is faster. It's even faster to launch the Device Management console, DEVMGMT.MSC, from the Run command.)

2. Expand the tree under modems to show the modem icon. Figure 17.7 shows an example. Verify that the modem icon does not have a big yellow question mark next to it. If it does, you likely have a resource conflict of some sort.

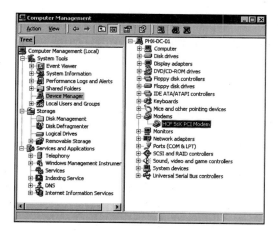

Figure 17.7 Computer Management console showing Device Manager list with focus set on installed modems.

3. If the system disabled the modem for some reason, the Device Manager icon for that modem will be covered with a red X. Right-click the icon, and select ENABLE DEVICE from the fly-out menu. This will either enable the device or start the `Device Problems Troubleshooting Wizard`. If the system can re-enable the device, it displays a success message, and you can close the wizard. If it cannot re-enable the device, the wizard gives more detailed errors and suggested actions.

4. Right-click the modem icon, and select `Properties` from the fly-out menu. The `Modem Properties` window opens.

5. The `General` tab displays the modem's make and model and its current status under `Device Status`. If there is a problem, the window lists the error and possible causes.

6. The `Device Usage` drop-down box gives you the option of disabling the modem for troubleshooting.

7. Return to the `Modem Properties` window.

8. Select the `Modem and Diagnostics` tab. It gives the same information as the `Properties` window options when you first installed the modem.

9. Select the `Driver` tab. If you think a new driver is available, click `Update Driver` to launch the `Upgrade Device Driver Wizard`. See Chapter 3, "Adding Additional Hardware," for more information on device driver upgrades.

10. Click `Driver Details`. The `Driver File Details` window opens. Figure 17.8 shows an example. This modem uses two drivers: `MODEM.SYS` and a Rockwell driver called `WINACPCI.SYS`. You can check the driver provider and file version by highlighting the driver.

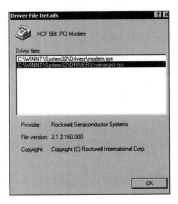

Figure 17.8 `Driver File Details` window showing list of drivers that were loaded to support the modem.

11. Click OK to close the window, and return to the Modem Properties window.

12. Select the Resources tab. Figure 17.9 shows an example.

Figure 17.9 Modem Properties window showing Resources tab with the resource settings for a PCI modem.

13. If you have a PnP modem, all resource settings are dimmed. If it shows specific resource settings that can be changed, the system detected the modem as a legacy device. You may need to move a jumper or change the software configuration for the device.

14. If the Conflicting Device List field shows conflicts, find the conflicting device, and see whether you can set one or the other differently so that they can coexist. You have the option of assigning different IRQs, I/O Base addresses, and DMA channels to a device, but do this only as a last resort. It's usually best to start by uninstalling the devices and letting PnP Manager add them back for you. If the conflict still exists, troubleshoot by changing the resource settings.

15. Click OK to close the window, and close the Computer Management console.

Troubleshooting Using Modem Logs

When a modem goes into trauma, the fix is usually simple, but it can be frustrating trying to figure out the exact nature of the problem. I've often thought that veterinarians would make great data communications technicians because they are good at diagnosing patients who can't talk.

Windows 2000 has two places to get information about a modem: the Modem Detection Log, MODEMDET.TXT; and the Modem Log, MODEMLOG_<*MODEM-NAME*>.TXT.

MODEMDET.TXT

The MODEMDET.TXT log records the interrogations (ATI commands) sent to the modem by the class installer when the modem is installed. The log is only written during PnP detection. Here is an example listing for an external non–PnP modem:

```
A modem was found on COM1:
ATI0<cr> = <cr><lf>3362
ATI0<cr> = <cr><lf>3362
ATI1<cr> = <cr><lf>221C
ATI1<cr> = <cr><lf>
ATI2<cr> = <cr><lf>OK
ATI2<cr> = <cr><lf>OK
ATI3<cr> = <cr><lf>Sportster 33600/Fax V2.31
ATI3<cr> = <cr><lf>Sportster33600/Fax
ATI4<cr> = <cr><lf>USRobotics Sportster 33600 Fax Settings...
ATI4<cr> = <cr><lf>USRoboticsSportster33600FaxSettings
ATI5<cr> = <cr><lf>USRobotics Sportster 33600 Fax NVRAM Settings...
ATI5<cr> = <cr><lf>USRoboticsSportster33600FaxNVRAMSettings
ATI6<cr> = <cr><lf>USRobotics Sportster 33600 Fax Link Diagnostics...
ATI6<cr> = <cr><lf>USRoboticsSportster33600FaxLinkDiagnostics
ATI7<cr> = <cr><lf>Configuration Profile...
ATI7<cr> = <cr><lf>ConfigurationProfile
ATI8<cr> = <cr><lf>OK
ATI8<cr> = <cr><lf>OK
ATI9<cr> = <cr><lf>(1.0USR0003\\Modem\PNPC107\Sportster 33.6 FAX EXT)FF
ATI9<cr> = <cr><lf>(USR\\Modem\PNPC\Sportster33.6FAXEXT)
ATI10<cr> = <cr><lf>ERROR
ATI10<cr> = <cr><lf>ERROR
AT%V<cr> = <cr><lf>ERROR
AT%V<cr> = <cr><lf>ERROR
Modem ID = UNIMODEM7ABE8C8F.
A modem was not found on COM2.
```

The responses to these queries tell the class installer what to look for in the INF files. When the installer finds the right file, it assigns an applicable UNIMODEM ID number to the device (in the preceding example, UNIMODEM7ABE8C8F) as an identifier for the TAPI driver, and then it uses the INF file to install the modem.

MODEMLOG_ Files

The Properties window for the modem has an option called Record A Log File. This option records all commands sent to a modem after it is installed. The file is saved to the \WINNT directory in a file that starts with the word MODEMLOG_ followed by the name of the modem as recorded in the Registry. Here is an example listing for an external, non-PnP modem. The log records a short connection using HyperTerminal to another Windows 2000 computer:

```
21:34:20.140 - File: C:\WINNT\System32\unimdm.tsp, Version 5.0.2053 - Retail
21:34:20.140 - File: C:\WINNT\System32\unimdmat.dll, Version 5.0.2051 - Retail
21:34:20.155 - File: C:\WINNT\System32\uniplat.dll, Version 5.0.2051 - Retail
21:34:20.155 - File: C:\WINNT\System32\drivers\modem.sys, Version 5.0.2066 - Retail
21:34:20.155 - File: C:\WINNT\System32\modemui.dll, Version 5.0.2051 - Retail
21:34:20.155 - Modem type: Sportster 28800-33600 External
21:34:20.155 - Modem inf path: mdmusrsp.inf
21:34:20.155 - Modem inf section: Modem26
21:34:20.218 - Opening Modem
21:34:20.218 - 115200,8,N,1, ctsfl=1, rtsctl=2
21:34:20.234 - Initializing modem.
21:34:20.249 - Send: ATE0Q0V1<cr>
21:34:20.374 - Recv: <cr><lf>OK<cr><lf>
21:34:20.374 - Interpreted response: OK
21:34:20.390 - Send: AT &F1 E0 V1 &C1 &D2 Q0 S0=0 &B1 &A3<cr>
```

This log contains invaluable clues about the modem's operation. You don't want to leave logging enabled for an extended period of time. The file can get very large. The example is only a fraction of the total output for the transaction.

Configuring Windows 2000 Dial-Up Servers

Now that we have modems installed, you can start configuring dial-up connections. Start with dial-up servers.

- Both Windows 2000 Server and Professional can accept inbound dial-up connections, but there is a difference in the features.

- Server supports up to 256 simultaneous connections. Professional supports one.

- Server uses a special Routing and Remote Access console that exposes lots of features for controlling inbound connections. Professional uses a simple Incoming Connection object that exposes very few options.

- Server supports Extensible Authentication Protocol and RADIUS. Professional does not.

All in all, if you need a full-featured dial-up solution, pay the extra few hundred dollars to get the server license.

Even if you are running Windows 2000 Server, you will have a bottleneck if you try to get 256 lines fed into a single box. If you have the budget, you can install multiple T-1 adapters or ISDN PRI adapters. These give you 24 lines apiece. If you prefer to use modem racks, you can install multiport serial cards with octopus connections to the modem rack.

Most of this equipment does not yet have WDM drivers, and it is not PnP. You install the adapters as if they were network adapters. The INF scripts may not be compatible with Windows 2000. If you have an existing classic NT RAS server, check with your vendor for compatibility before upgrading to Windows 2000.

Hardware RAS Options

If you need lots of dial-up connections, you may want to consider a hardware-based remote access solution rather than Windows 2000. Hardware solutions offer more in the way of circuits, performance, stability, and security than a standard Windows 2000 dial-up server.

Another alternative is to buy a turnkey Windows 2000 system that has been built from the ground up as a high-density remote access server. A quick search through the *Data Communications Magazine* Web site, www.data.com, will give you an idea of the options available in this area.

It is not necessary to install any additional services or drivers to configure a Windows 2000 Server or Professional desktop as a dial-up server. The RRAS service is installed by default during system setup and starts automatically each time the system starts. The only prerequisite is to have a circuit-switched device like a modem or ISDN adapter installed and cabled to the proper jack. Let's start with configuring a Windows 2000 Professional desktop.

Using Windows 2000 Professional as a Dial-Up Server

Windows 2000 Professional runs the same RRAS service as Windows 2000 Server. It is artificially limited to hosting a maximum of one inbound dial-up connection, but it can perform encrypted authentications, accept VPN connections, and route dial-in clients to the attached network. This makes it flexible enough to handle inbound data services for small offices.

Security Considerations for Desktop Dial-Up Services

The capability of Windows 2000 Professional to be both a dial-up server as well as a dial-up client can result in serious security breaches. Desktops equipped with modems that can be reached from the outside are often targets for attack.

A large assortment of group policies are available to control dial-up connections at the desktop. See Chapter 16, "Managing the User Operating Environment," for information about group policies or go directly to the group policy editor and look for User Configuration | Administrative Templates | Network | Network and Dial-up Connections.

An inbound dial-up connection on a Windows 2000 Professional desktop is represented as an *Incoming Connection* icon in the Network and Dial-up Connections window. The properties of this icon are used to control the connection. There is no RRAS management console.

The Inbound Connection icon is linked to a modem or ISDN adapter connected to the computer. The same modem can also be associated with an outbound dial-up connection. Obviously, the modem can't do both functions simultaneously, but if you have two modems or ISDN bearer channels, you can use one to accept an incoming connection while the other makes an outbound connection.

Avoid Using Incoming Connection Interface on Servers

The steps in this section can also be used to build an Incoming Connection interface on a standalone Windows 2000 server, but you should avoid doing this. Use the Routing and Remote Access console on the server to handle all incoming connections. The RRAS console has much more flexibility and exposes more features. A domain controller will not permit you to create an incoming connection using the steps in this section.

When you have installed and tested a modem or ISDN adapter on the computer, configure an incoming connection as follows. You must be logged on using an account with administrator rights for the local machine.

Procedure 17.4 **Configuring an Incoming Connection for a Windows 2000 Professional Desktop**

1. From the Start menu, open START | SETTINGS | NETWORK AND DIAL-UP CONNECTIONS. The Network and Dial-up Connection window opens.

2. Double-click Make New Connection. The Network Connection Wizard starts.

3. Click Next. The Network Connection Type window opens (see Figure 17.10).

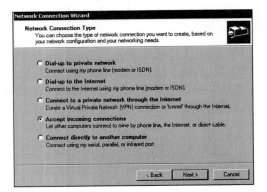

Figure 17.10 `Network Connection Wizard`, `Network Connection Type` window.

4. Select the `Accept Incoming Connections` radio button. This stops the RRAS service; so if you have an existing dial-up connection, it will be broken. The system warns you before doing this.

5. Click `Next`. The `Devices for incoming connections` window opens. Select the modem or ISDN adapters you want to use for in-bound connections. Windows 2000 Profession does not support multilink for incoming connections, so don't bother selecting more than one device.

6. Click `Next`. The `Incoming Virtual Private Connection` window opens. Handling encryption over VPN connections takes a good deal of memory and local processing. Select the `Allow virtual private connections` option only if you plan on letting users connect to desktop over the Internet or some other open networking environment.

7. Click `Next`. The `Allowed Users` window opens. Users are not given dial-up permission by default. Select those users to whom you want to give dial-up permission.

8. Click `Next`. The `Networking Components` window opens. Select the transport protocol to enable for inbound connections. Normally you would select TCP/IP. Deselecting a protocol in this window does not de-install it. It only disables it for use over this inbound connection.

9. Click `Next`. A summary window opens. The default name for the connection is `Incoming Connections` and cannot be modified. The system builds only one incoming connection for all inbound calls.

10. Click `Finish` to build the new connection, and return to the `Network and Dial-up Connections` window. A new icon called Incoming Connections is added to the connection list.

11. Right-click the Incoming Connections icon, and select PROPERTIES from the fly-out menu. The Incoming Connections Properties window opens (see Figure 17.11). The user list shows a few users who were granted access during initial installation. See the following sidebar titled

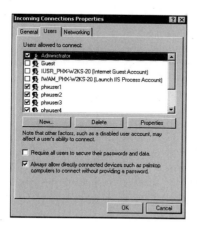

Figure 17.11   Incoming Connections Properties window showing Users tab.

Inbound Connection Authentication

The Inbound Connection properties has two special connection options.

The Require all users to secure their passwords and data option forces dial-up clients to select a secure logon method and to encrypt their files.

The Allow directly connected users ... to connect without providing a password makes it easier for users with IR devices to get access to their computer. Because direct connections involve physical proximity, it should be safe to allow this option. It is selected by default.

13. Select the Networking tab, and then double-click the Internet Protocol (TCP/IP) option to open its Properties window. The Allow Callers to Access… option configures RRAS to permit users to route through the Professional desktop to the network. The preferred method is to distribute addresses from DHCP. Windows 2000 Profession is only capable of handling a single inbound connection; so if you use static addresses, don't carve out more than you need.

14. Click OK to save any changes, and close the window.

At this point, the desktop is ready to accept inbound calls from users who have been granted dial-up permission. There are no additional tools in Professional for controlling calls. You can use the Group Policy editor, GPEDIT.MSC, to access local policies affecting remote access, but these are designed for controlling the user interface, not the connection itself, and they are not of much use on a Professional desktop because inbound dialers cannot inherit them.

Using Windows 2000 Server as a Dial-Up Server

A Windows 2000 dial-up server has several different possible configurations:

- **Standalone server in a classic NT4 or Windows 2000 domain.** The dial-up server authenticates users in its local SAM or in a separate store using EAP. Users can be routed to the domain but may be prompted for credentials if their RRAS authentication credentials do not match their domain credentials.

- **Domain member server in a classic NT4 or Mixed-mode Windows 2000 domain.** The dial-up server authenticates domain users with pass-through NTLM authentication to a classic NT4 domain controller. Users in trusted domains cannot be authenticated.

- **Domain member server in a Native-mode Windows 2000 domain.** The dial-up server authenticates domain users using Kerberos to a Windows 2000 domain controller. Users in trusted domains can be authenticated if the RAS server is a member of the RAS and IAS Users group.

- **Domain controller in either a Mixed-mode or Native-mode domain.** Because the domain controller has a local copy of every user account in the forest, it can authenticate any user.

RAS Limitations Using Standalone Servers

As you can see from the list in the preceding section, using a standalone Windows 2000 server as a dial-up server severely limits your options for authenticating dial-up users.

You can expand the functionality of a standalone server by using one of the EAP authentication methods and configuring a remote authenticator with Internet Authentication Services (IAS), smart card services, or certificates services. See "Configuring Internet Authentication Services (IAS)" at the end of the chapter.

If a dial-up server is inside a firewall and you don't already have a RADIUS implementation, your simplest option is to make the Windows 2000 dial-up server a member of the domain.

RAS Limitations in Mixed-Mode Domains

The presence of classic NT BDCs inhibits full RAS functionality. As long as there is a possibility that the dial-up server could authenticate to a classic BDC, features that rely on user configurations that reside in the Directory cannot be implemented.

One feature that is disabled in a mixed-mode domain is remote access group policies. These are disabled because they modify attributes that are not available in a standard SAM account. The same is true for special configuration options such as assigning static IP addresses and IP routes to specific users.

The second limitation of using RAS in a mixed-mode domain is the inability to do transitive Kerberos authentications to validate users in trusted domains. If a user who is a member of Domain B dials in to a RAS server in Domain A, for example, the RAS server needs a way to validate the user's credentials in Domain B. In a native-mode domain, the domain controller in Domain A checks the user's credentials in Domain B on behalf of the RAS server. That is the "transitive" part of transitive authentication. This transitive authentication check is not available in mixed-mode domains.

In addition to being in Native mode, a couple of other requirements must be met for transitive authentication to work. They are as follows:

- **The dial-up server must be a Windows 2000 server.** This is required because the server must be able to do Kerberos authentications.

- **The dial-up server must be a member of the *RAS and IAS Servers* group in each domain.** This group is new in Windows 2000. It is stored in the Users container in the Directory, but it works like one of the legacy Builtin groups such as Account Operator and Print Operator. See the following sidebar titled for more information.

RAS and IAS Servers Group

The RAS and IAS Servers group is installed by default during Windows 2000 setup. It is on the ACL for the Domain-DNS object at the top of the domain tree with delegated permissions to four extended attributes associated with User class objects. These attributes are as follows:

- Read Logon Information
- Read Group Membership
- Read Account Restrictions
- Read Remote Access Information

In addition, the group has Read/Write and Create Child/Delete Child permissions for the RAS and IAS Servers Access Check object under cn=System,dc=<domain>. This permits RAS and IAS servers to check for the presence of this object. It acts as a flag to verify that group members have access to the Directory.

The net effect of these permissions is to permit members of the RAS and IAS Servers group to do Directory lookups for verifying user access permissions.

Overview of Dial-Up Connection Alternatives

Refer to the diagram in Figure 17.12. The dial-up user is a member of the Subsidiary.com domain. The user has a choice of connecting to a variety of dial-up servers. None of these servers are members of Subsidiary.com. Two of them are members of Company.com, which is a trusted domain in the same forest as Subsidiary.com. The third dial-up server is a standalone server that is a member of WORKGROUP.

The objective is to authenticate the dial-up user without creating dual accounts in the two domains. Here are the alternatives:

- If the user dials in to the Windows 2000 dial-up server, the user's access permissions can be validated using the transitive Kerberos trust.

- If the user dials in to the standalone server, the user's access permissions can be validated using Remote Authentication Dial-In User Services (RADIUS) and Internet Authentication Services (IAS). The IAS server uses the Kerberos trust to authenticate the user in Subsidiary.com. See "Configuring IAS" at the end of this chapter for details on this configuration.

- If the user dials in to the NT4 RAS server, transitive authentication is not possible. NT4 RAS is limited to using NTLM authentication. It is possible to get transitive authentication by loading classic RRAS and configuring the server to use RADIUS for authenticating to the IAS server.

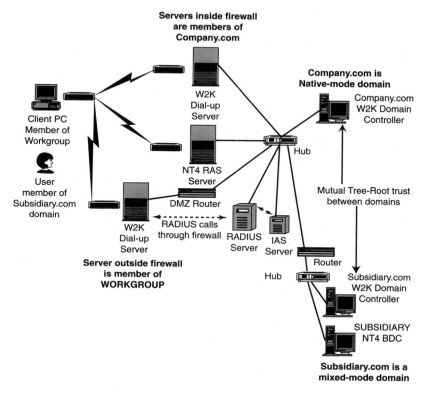

Figure 17.12 Dial-up connection diagram
showing alternatives for authenticating dial-up users.

The next three sections cover each of the dial-up configurations shown in Figure 17.9 except for IAS, which is covered in another section. These are the major actions required:

- Initially configure the RRAS service on the dial-up server.
- Configure the server to accept incoming connections.
- Define the client authentication options that the server is willing to support.

Initializing the RRAS

The RRAS service is installed as part of a standard Windows 2000 setup, but the service is kept in a disabled mode until needed. The RRAS console options are not preconfigured. The service is started the first time you configure an interface.

Registry Tip: Enabling a Modem for RAS or Routing

Enabling a modem for RAS or Routing is controlled by values in HKLM | System | CurrentControlSet | {Modem CLSID} | 0000 | Clients | Ras. You will also find these values for each WAN interface under the CLSID for Network Adapters.

Procedure 17.5   Initializing the Remote Access Service

1. Open the Routing and Remote Access console using START | PROGRAMS | ADMINISTRATIVE TOOLS | ROUTING AND REMOTE ACCESS. A server icon in the left pane represents the Local Server. The icon has a red down arrow, indicating that RRAS has not yet been configured. (If the arrow is green and pointed up, someone has configured RRAS already. This does not change the following steps except that you might change someone else's work.)

2. Right-click the local server icon, and select CONFIGURE AND ENABLE ROUTING AND REMOTE ACCESS from the fly-out menu. An informational message appears notifying you that the RRAS must be shut down before installing. Click Yes to continue.

3. The system stops the RRAS service, and then starts the Routing and Remote Access Configuration Wizard.

4. Click Next. The Routing and Remote Access window opens. Only enable Remote Access. RRAS will route dial-up connections without enabling routing services. Only enable routing when configuring a demand-dial router or a LAN-based router. See the "Configuring Demand-Dial Routing" topic for details on enabling routing after remote access is running.

5. Click Next. The Dial-in or Demand Dial Interfaces window opens. If the server has multiple WAN adapters, you can select which of them to use for inbound connections, or you can leave the radio button set at Enable All Devices for Remote Access. There is no performance penalty for enabling remote access on every circuit-switched interface.

6. Click Next. The Authentication and Encryption window opens. Leave the Only Methods Which Secure the User's Password option selected. This forces the user to select a secure login method. Do not select the All Methods option unless you want dial-up users to give clear text passwords. If you use clear text passwords, you must configure the Directory to store reversibly encrypted passwords. See the "Supporting Down-Level and Non-Windows Dial-Up Clients" section.

7. Click Next. The Routing and Remote Access window appears again; this time prompting you to stipulate access rights. The Access This Server Only option disables the routing features in a remote access connection and

restricts the user to local resources on the dial-up server. The `Access Entire Network` option opens a route to the network through the dial-up server.

8. Click `Next`. The `TCP/IP Settings` window opens (see Figure 17.13). This is where you configure the server to assign IP addresses to inbound dial-up clients. These clients need an IP address so they can access resources on the local network. See the following sidebar for more information.

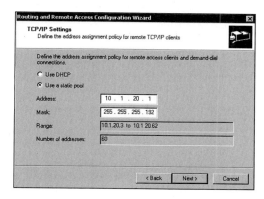

Figure 17.13 Routing and Remote Access Configuration Wizard, TCP/IP Settings showing the use of the `Static Pool` option with a block of addresses available for dial-up users.

Configuring Dial-Up Address Pools

When assigning IP addresses to dial-up users, the `Use  DHCP` option is preferred. This permits the RAS server to lease addresses from DHCP and pass them out to dial-up clients on an as-needed basis. The DHCP server shows special icons for addresses that have been leased by dial-up servers so that you can track their use. You can also configure logging so that you know the identity of each user who gets an IP address for auditing.

If you do not want to use DHCP, select the `Use  a  static  pool` option. You need to define a pool of addresses for use by dial-up users. Figure 17.24 shows an example of the TCP/IP Settings window with the `Use  a  Static Pool` option selected and a block of addresses assigned.

The `Address` and `Mask` values define a range of addresses. The system calculates the `Range` and `Number  of Addresses` values. There are no provisions for assigning non-contiguous addresses or bitwise masks. You cannot assign masks containing anything other than standard subnet boundaries. That is to say, you can only enter 128, 192, 224, 240, or 252.

When you select the base address, make sure that it starts at the initial address of the range defined by your mask. If you select a mask of 255.255.255.192, for example, the last octet of the base address should start at 0, 64, 128, or 192.

You'll notice when you enter ranges and masks that the Number of Addresses field has three fewer addresses than you might otherwise expect. The first two addresses in the range and the last address in the range are set aside. The first address in the range is assumed to correspond to the network address. The second address in the range is set aside for the WAN interface on the dial-up server. The final address is set aside to avoid all ones in the octet, which indicates a subnet broadcast.

The mask you choose for the static address pool becomes the subnet mask assigned to the dial-up client. If you choose an address range that lies within the address space of the dial-up server, RRAS will aggregate the client addresses, and you do not need local a routing table entry.

If you choose an address range outside of the server's address space, you must either put a static route in the local routing table and all adjacent routers or load RIP or OSPF at the RRAS server and integrate it into your existing router infrastructure.

In either case, the dial-up clients do not need a local static route. The default gateway for a dial-up client is the same as the IP address assigned to the dial-up interface. See the "Client Dial-Up Connections and Routing" section for more information.

9. Click Next. A summary window opens detailing the options you selected.

10. Click Finish. The wizard makes the necessary configuration updates, and then offers to start RRAS. Click Yes to acknowledge and start the service.

11. Leave the windows open, and proceed to the next section.

Configuring a Dial-Up Server

Now that the dial-up configurations have been set and the RRAS service has restarted, it's time to configure the dial-up server to accept inbound calls.

Procedure 17.6 Configuring a Dial-Up Server

1. At the Routing and Remote Access console window, highlight the Ports icon under the local server name. The right pane of the console window lists the interfaces that can be used for inbound connections (see Figure 17.14). Notice the Virtual Private Networks interfaces. The system creates five PPTP and five L2TP interfaces by default.

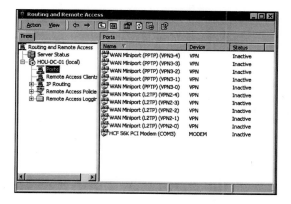

Figure 17.14 `Routing and Remote Access` window showing available interfaces for inbound connections.

2. Highlight the Remote Access Logging icon. The location of the Remote Access Log is displayed in the right pane. The standard log location is `\WINNT\System32\Logfiles`. You can change this location if you want.

3. Double-click the log file icon to open the `Local File Properties` window. Figure 17.15 shows an example. See the sidebar titled "RAS Logging."

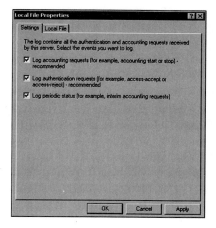

Figure 17.15 `Local File Properties` window for Remote Access logging with all options selected. By default, no logging options are selected.

RAS Logging

The RAS logging options shown in Figure 17.15 give you a way to keep track of activity at the dial-up interfaces. It is an invaluable security analysis tool, but it takes a little patience to interpret.

The attributes and constraints come from RFC 2138, "Remote Authentication Dial In User Service (RADIUS)," with Microsoft extensions documented in RFC 2548, "Microsoft Vendor-Specific RADIUS Attributes." The log is a comma-delimited file with each line representing one record. The first fields are a header that contain information about the dial-in user who accessed the server:

```
10.4.1.1 - IP address
houuser - logon name
08/04/1999 - access date
22:24:5 - access time
RAS - access method
HOU-DC-01 - target domain
```

The next fields are number pairs. The first number is the attribute designator, and the second number is the value for the attribute. Here is a brief example for a user who was denied access:

```
4121,0x00453D36343920523D3020563D33 - CHAP error
4127,4 - authentication type
4130,SUBSIDIARY\houuser2 - Fully qualified user name
4136,3 - packet type (accept-reject)
4142,48 - rejection reason (incomplete accounting-request packet received.)
```

The online help has an exhaustive list of the attribute types and meanings. Search for "Interpreting IAS-formatted Log Files."

The vendor attributes associated with each interface in Windows 2000 is also stored in the Directory in an object called Identity-Dictionary. This object is located in cn=RRAS,cn=Services,cn=Configuration,dc=Company,dc=com. You can view the contents with the ADSI Editor from the Resource Kit.

4. A busy RAS server can build a big log file. The Local File tab has options for handling them (see Figure 17.16).

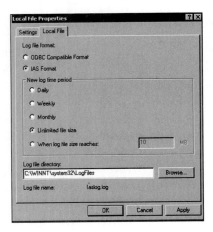

Figure 17.16   Local File Properties window, Local File tab.

5. Click OK to save any changes, and return to the Routing and Remote Access console.

6. Expand the tree under the IP Routing icon, and highlight the General icon. The right pane shows the standard interfaces for a server with a single network adapter. Figure 17.17 shows an example.

The IGMP icon is used to configure Internet Group Management Protocol options for the server. IGMP is a way of notifying members of a multicast group when a member has joined or left the group. IGMP is typically used to support streaming media applications. IGMP is described in RFC 1112, "Internet Group Management Protocol (IGMP)."

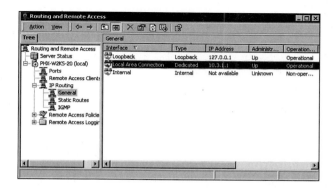

Figure 17.17 Routing and Remote Access window showing routing interfaces under General.

7. Right-click the Local Area Connection icon to see the Show options available on the fly-out menu. If the computer were configured with NWLink (IPX/SPX), those routing options would also appear on the list. Each option opens a separate window to list the designated information. For example, Figure 17.18 shows the static routes assigned to the interface. This information is also available at a command prompt by running route print.

PHX-W2KS-20 - IP Routing Table

Destination	Network mask	Gateway	Interface	Metric	Protocol
0.0.0.0	0.0.0.0	10.3.1.254	Local Area Connection	1	Network management
10.3.0.0	255.255.0.0	10.3.1.1	Local Area Connection	1	Local
10.3.1.1	255.255.255.255	127.0.0.1	Loopback	1	Local
10.255.255.255	255.255.255.255	10.3.1.1	Local Area Connection	1	Local
127.0.0.0	255.0.0.0	127.0.0.1	Loopback	1	Local
127.0.0.1	255.255.255.255	127.0.0.1	Loopback	1	Local
224.0.0.0	240.0.0.0	10.3.1.1	Local Area Connection	1	Local
255.255.255.255	255.255.255.255	10.3.1.1	Local Area Connection	1	Local

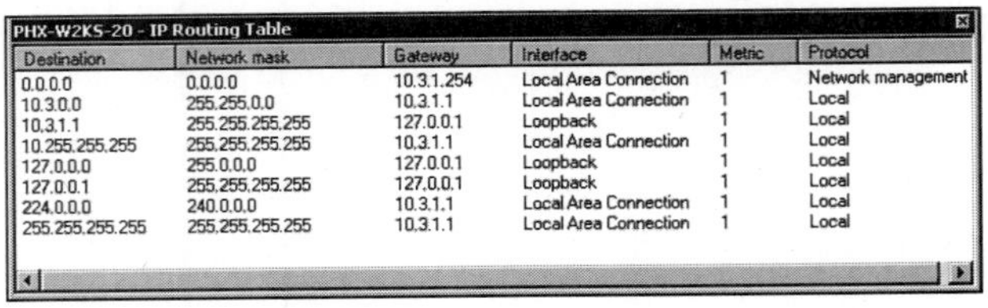

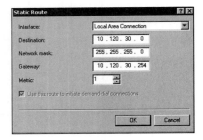

Figure 17.18 `IP Routing Table` window for Local Connection interface.

8. You can add a static route by right-clicking the Static Routes icon and selecting NEW STATIC ROUTE from the fly-out menu. Figure 17.19 shows an example. There is no need to use static routes unless this server must be integrated into an existing router infrastructure. In that case, you can right-click the `General` icon and select `New Routing Protocol` from the fly-out menu. This gives you the option of installing RIP or OSPF, depending on the routing protocol you currently use.

Figure 17.19 `Static Route` window showing entries for a new static route.

The system is just about ready to start accepting dial-in customers. First, let's take a look at how to set the available authentication options. Leave the `Routing and Remote Access` console open, and proceed to the next section.

Configuring Dial-Up Authentication Options

In a perfect world, selecting a suitable PPP authentication mechanism would be as simple as putting a check mark in a menu. It is not a perfect world. In RRAS, authentication options can be selected in four different places:

- **Dial-Up Server Properties.** Individual dial-up servers can be configured to have certain acceptable authentication methods that can be used by a dial-up client. These options are configured using the `RRAS` console. The selected options are stored in the Registry. Configuring these properties is covered in this topic.

- **Dial-In Profiles.** Specific policies can be configured for a particular group, tunnel type, IP address, or other attribute. A profile can be associated with each policy that defines the authentication method. For a local server, these options are configured using the RRAS console under Remote Access Policies. For RADIUS servers, they are configured using the Internet Authentication Service (IAS) console. The selected options are stored in the Internet Authentication Service (IAS) database, IAS.MDB.

- **Incoming Connection Properties.** This interface is used to manage inbound users on Windows 2000 Professional. It has one option, Require All Users to Secure Their Passwords and Data. The selected option is stored in the Registry. Configuring this option is covered in the "Using Windows 2000 Professional as a Dial-Up Server" section.

- **Dial-Up Connection Properties.** A dial-up client requests one or more authentication methods and the server replies with a preference. The client options are configured in the Properties window of the Connection object in the Network and Dial-up Connections window. The selected options are stored in the Remote Access Phonebook, RASPHONE.PBK, at the dial-up client.

- **Demand-Dial Interface Properties.** A Windows 2000 server with RRAS configured as a demand-dial router can request one or more authentication methods from its partner server. The selections are configured using the RRAS console. The selected options are stored in the Router phonebook, ROUTER.PBK. Configuring these options is covered in the "Configuring Demand-Dial Routing" section.

The next steps configure the authentication options at a dial-up server. These options define the authentication methods a server is willing to offer to a client.

Procedure 17.7 **Configuring Dial-Up Server Authentication Options**

1. In the Routing and Remote Access console, right-click the local server icon, and select PROPERTIES from the fly-out menu. The Local Properties window opens.

2. Select the Security tab. Windows 2000 dial-up security uses two primary authentication providers, the Windows Authentication provider, RASAUTH.DLL, and the RADIUS Authentication provider, RASRAD.DLL. These same DLLs also act as accounting providers for logging transactions.

Registry Tip: Authentication and Accounting

The Authentication and Accounting providers are defined by the Registry key HKLM | System | CurrentControlSet | Services | RemoteAccess | Authentication and Accounting.

3. Click Authentication Methods. The Authentication Methods window opens (see Figure 17.20). "PPP Authentication Protocols" has information about the available authentication options. The key things to remember about the selections in this window is that only encrypted authentications are enabled by default and that standard CHAP is not included in the list. CHAP requires that the domain controller or local dial-up server store reversibly encrypted passwords.

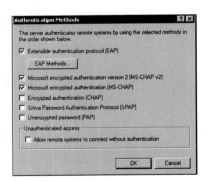

Figure 17.20 Authentication Methods window showing default authentication methods.

4. Click EAP Methods. Two extended authentication methods are included in Windows 2000: MD5-CHAP (RASCHAP.DLL) and Smart Cards and other Certificates (RASTLS.DLL). TLS stands for Transport Layer Security. If you do not use any of these methods, you can uncheck the EAP option; but leaving it checked does not impact performance or security.

Registry Tip: RAS EAP methods

The EAP methods available in RAS are defined in HKLM | System | CurrentControlSet | Services | RasMan | PPP | EAP.

5. Click OK to save the changes, and close the window.

6. Click OK to return to the Properties window.

7. Click OK to apply changes, and return to the RRAS console.

Managing RRAS Servers from a Single Console

You can manage Windows 2000 dial-up servers from single RRAS console. You must have administrator rights on the remote server or the server's domain to manage it. You cannot manage a Windows 2000 Professional desktop from the RRAS console. Add servers to the RRAS console as follows:

Procedure 17.8 **Loading Additional RRAS Servers into the** *Routing and Remote Access* **Console**

1. Right-click the Routing and Remote Access icon, and select ADD SERVER from the fly-out menu.

2. Point the Add Server window at the IP address or DNS name of the server.

You can also choose to search the Active Directory and load all the dial-up servers it finds.

You can also manage NT4 RRAS servers in a Windows 2000 RRAS console, but several of the router options are not available. Your best option in this case is to copy the classic RRAS MMC console to your Windows 2000 desktop and run it from there.

You can indirectly manage a standard NT4 RAS server using the Windows 2000 RRAS management console. When you add the server to the console and click the icon, the RRAS console automatically launches RASADMIN.EXE, the classic NT RAS administration tool.

Managing RAS Servers from the Command Line

Keeping track of dial-up servers can be a challenge, especially if you have quite a few of them in your organization. Windows 2000 includes a general-purpose command-line tool for managing RRAS. The tool is called the *Network Shell,* or NETSH.

NETSH works something like a command prompt at a standard router, but don't expect the commands to follow Cisco IOS, or any other router operating system for that matter. Still, if you want to use shell scripts to manage your RRAS servers, then NETSH is invaluable.

Open the Network Shell interface by typing `netsh` at a command prompt. The system responds by opening the prompt: `netsh>` . The prompt puts you in a namespace like that shown in Figure 17.21.

Each folder in the namespace represents a context. Each context has special commands associated with it. There is a list of standard commands that work in any context. To see the available commands, type `?` at the console prompt. The online help in Windows 2000 has a comprehensive list of the NETSH commands.

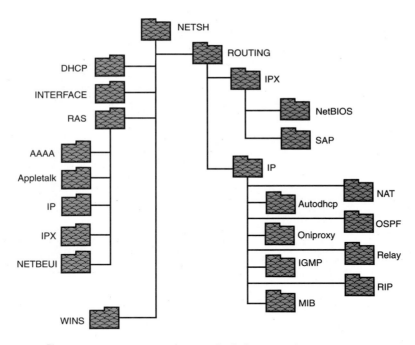

Figure 17.21   Diagram of Network Shell (NETSH) namespace.

Context Availability

The diagram in Figure 17.21 shows all possible NETSH contexts. You will not see a context unless the associated service is loaded. Also, if you're curious, the RAS, AAAA context refers to RADIUS commands.

To go to a particular context, enter the name of the context at the shell prompt. For example, enter ras to go to the ras> context.

You can move from context to context without navigating up and down the namespace. From the ras> context, for example, you can enter interface to go directly to the interface> context.

You can navigate up to the parent context using a double dot (..) like the parent in a directory tree. Type bye, exit, or quit to exit the shell.

To see the commands available at each context, type a question mark at the prompt. Some commands have additional parameters. Enter the command followed by a question mark to see them. For example, the show command lists the current parameter in a context. To change any parameter, use the word set rather than show.

```
ras>show ?
show tracing              - Shows whether extended tracing is enabled for components.
show user                 - Displays RAS properties for a user(s).
show authmode      - Shows the authentication mode.
show authtype      - Displays the authentication types currently enabled.
show link                 - Shows the link properties PPP will negotiate
show multilink            - Shows the multilink types PPP will negotiate
show registeredserver     - Displays whether a computer is registered as a
                                    RAS server in the Active Directory of the given
                                    domain.
show domainaccess         - Displays whether NT4 RAS servers or Windows 2000
                              RAS servers in trusted NT4 domains have been enabled
                                  in the Active Directory of the given domain.
show activeservers        - Listens for RAS server advertisements.
show client               - Shows RAS clients connected to this machine.
show alias                - Lists all defined aliases.
show mode          - Shows the current mode.
```

If you enter a command and get no results, enter it again with a trailing question mark. For example,

```
ras>show registeredserver ?

show registeredserver [ [domain = ] domain [server = ] server ]

    Displays whether the given computer is registered as a RAS
    server in the given domain.

    server - the computer name of the computer in question.
             If no server is specified the computer from which the
             command is issued is assumed.

    domain - the domain.  If no domain is provided, the primary
             domain of the computer from which the command is
              issued is assumed.
```

When you enter the command with the correct syntax, the results appear in the console:

```
ras>show registeredserver domain=company.com

The following RAS server is registered:
        RAS Server:        PHX-DC-01
        Domain:            company.com
```

The Network Shell has two modes, online and offline. In the online mode, any changes you make are implemented immediately. In the offline mode, changes are saved but not implemented. You can implement them using the commit command or discard them using the abort command.

One of the most useful Network Shell features is its capability to dump the current configuration to a script so that you can replay the script and get back your original configuration. The command to show the running configuration is dump.

You can type dump at the shell prompt to see the results on the screen; to save the output to file, however, you must run it from a command prompt and redirect the output to a file. For example, enter c:\>netsh dump > netsh.scr.

If you want to limit the dump to a particular context, put the context on the command line. Here is an example:

```
c:\>netsh ras ip dump > netshrasip.scr


# -----------------------------------------
# RAS IP Configuration
# -----------------------------------------

pushd ras ip

set negotiation mode = allow
set access mode = all
set addrreq mode = deny
set pool addr = 10.1.2.0  mask = 255.255.255.240
set addrassign method = auto

popd

# End of RAS IP configuration.
```

To run the script, enter netsh -f <filename>. For example:

```
c:\>netsh -f netshrasip.scr.
```

You can use NETSH to control other servers either by executing the script remotely using a remote shell or by putting the script in the Windows Scheduler at the remote server for execution at a later time.

Supporting NT4 RAS Servers in a Windows 2000 Domain

You can use classic NT4 RAS servers to give dial-up users access to a Windows 2000 domain, but there are limitations because the NT4 server cannot use Kerberos to get an authenticated connection to a Windows 2000 domain controller to do Directory lookups. Here's why that makes a difference:

- During the initial PPP link establishment phase, the user's credentials must be validated against the user's account in the domain.
- If the NT4 RAS server is a BDC in a mixed-mode Windows 2000 domain, it can do this validation using its local copy of the SAM database.
- If the NT4 RAS server is a member server in a mixed-mode or Native-mode domain Windows 2000 domain, it must query a domain controller to get this information. (Here's where you have to keep your eye on the ball.)
- The RAS service on the NT4 RAS server runs in the Local System security context. This Local System account has no security standing at the domain controller. In other words, the RAS service cannot just do a quick lookup in the Directory and check the permissions.
- This was not possible in classic NT, either, but the RAS server could handle the authentication by doing an NTLM pass-through authentication with the user's credentials. In other words, it would do a network authentication by impersonating the user. When the authentication succeeded, the RAS server could check the user's dial-up permissions via the user's own credentials.
- Windows 2000 RAS servers do a similar impersonation, but they do it with Kerberos delegation. Using Kerberos, they obtain a ticket to the domain controller on behalf of the user, and they use that ticket to check the user's Directory object and verify the user's dial-up permissions.

An NT4 RAS server cannot get a Kerberos ticket and, therefore, cannot check the user's permissions unless some accommodation is made for it to access the user's Directory object. This accommodation comes in the form of special permissions delegated to the Pre-Windows 2000 Compatible Access group.

The Pre-Windows 2000 Compatible Access group has been delegated these permissions for User objects in the domain:

- Read Remote Access Information
- Read General Information
- Read Group Membership
- Read Account Restrictions
- Read Logon Information

The Pre-Windows 2000 Compatible Access group also has these delegated permissions for Group objects:

- Read All Properties
- List Contents
- Read Permissions

The net result is that members of the Pre-Windows 2000 Compatible Access (PW2KCA) group can read user properties and group properties and use them verify remote access credentials.

You cannot add the Local System account of the RAS server to the PW2KCA group because that account does not exist in the Directory. If you have an NT4 RAS server to access user account information, you must add the *Everyone* group to the PW2KCA group.

Here are the actions to take if you have NT4 RAS servers in a Windows 2000 domain. You must take these same actions if you have a Windows 2000 RAS server in an NT4 domain that is trusted by a Windows 2000 domain where the user accounts reside.

- Load Service Pack 4 or higher on the NT4 RAS server to get the NTLM enhancements necessary to read individual attributes exposed by the Directory.
- Make the NT4 server a member of a Windows 2000 domain and add its computer account as a member of the RAS and IAS Servers group.
- Add the Everyone group to the Pre-Windows 2000 Compatible Access group.

Managing Remote Access Policies and Profiles

Windows 2000 uses policies in three ways to control remote access:

- **Local IAS policies.** Each Windows 2000 dial-up server has a set of local policies that are derived from RADIUS. These policies are stored in an Internet Authentication Services (IAS) database, IAS.MDB, located in \WINNT\System32\IAS. These policies define access constraints based on a wide range of dial-up client attributes.

- **Central IAS policies.** Rather than use the local IAS databases that must be individually modified if you want to change an access policy, a dial-up server can be configured to access RADIUS policies from a central server. This server can be a Windows 2000 server running IAS or a third-party RADIUS server. See "Configuring Internet Authentication Services (IAS)" for instructions on setting up an IAS server.

- **Group policies.** Like just about any other local configuration, user settings involving remote access can be controlled using group policies. Group policies are enabled in a native-mode Windows 2000 domain only, however. This is because in a mixed-mode domain a dial-up server might attempt to authenticate users on a classic BDC, and the BDC has no facility for storing or distributing Windows 2000 group policies. Group policies affecting remote access are stored along with the other group policies in the \WINNT\Sysvol\Sysvol\<domainname> directory on all domain controllers. See Chapter 16, "Managing the User Operating Environment," for more information on using group policies.

Configuring Local IAS Policies

All Windows 2000 versions, including Server and Professional, come with a set of RADIUS policies stored in an IAS database. The database is not enabled until RRAS is initialized. This happens automatically when the Routing and Remote Access console is loaded and configured the first time. Initializing the policies requires stopping the RRAS service. Refer to the previous section, "Initializing the RAS," for instructions on loading the RRAS console for the first time. After you have initialized RRAS, configure remote access policies as follows:

Procedure 17.9 **Configuring Local IAS Policies**

1. Open the `Routing and Remote Access` console.

2. Highlight the `Remote Access Policies` icon (see Figure 17.22). The right pane of the console window lists the current policies. On a newly installed system, there will be only one policy in place, the `Allow Access If Dial-in Permission Is Enabled` policy with a `Deny All` setting. This policy blocks all access to the system by default.

Figure 17.22 `Remote Access` console showing default remote access policy.

3. Double-click the default policy to open its `Properties` window (see Figure 17.23). The entries under `Specify the conditions to match` list the constraints associated with this policy. A policy can have several constraints, but policy itself can have only one of two options, either `Grant Remote access permission` or `deny remote access permission`. All constraints must be met before policy is applied.

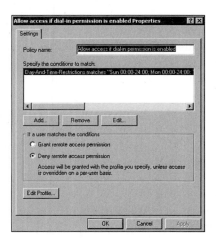

Figure 17.23 `Properties` window showing default assignment.

4. Double-click `Day and Time Restrictions` to edit the entry. The `Time Of Day Constraints` window opens (see Figure 17.24). This standard constraint denies access to all users at all times of the day and night. By changing this option to `Grant Remote Access`, you give 24×7 access to all users with individual dial-in permission set in the local SAM or in the Directory. You can delete this default policy and put others in its place that are better tailored to your operations; be aware, however, that if you remove all policies, access is denied to everyone.

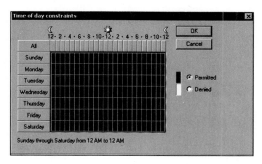

Figure 17.24 `Time of Day Constraints` window showing default 24×7 access restriction.

5. Click `OK` to return to the `Properties` window.

6. Click `Add`. The `Select Attribute` window opens (see Figure 17.25). The attribute types originate from RFC-standard RADIUS and proprietary Microsoft additions. Use this list to select attributes and define constraints associated with those attributes. For example, you can limit access to certain IP Addresses, certain Services, certain Windows-Groups, and so forth. Each attribute has its unique set of constraints.

Figure 17.25 `Select Attributes` window showing list of attribute types that can be selected for controlling remote access.

7. Double-click the Windows-Groups attribute to open the Groups window.

8. Click Add to open a Select Groups window. Select one or more security groups to associate with the policy. If you want to restrict access to members of a group called Dial-Up Users, for example, create that group and then add it to the group list.

9. Click OK to add the selected groups to the group list and return to the Groups window.

10. Click OK to save the changes, and return to the Properties window for the policy. The new attribute and its constraints are added to the Specify Conditions to Match list.

11. Verify that the Grant Remote Access Permission radio button is selected, and then click OK to save the changes and close the window.

With this configuration, the only users who will get dial-up access are members of the Dial-Up Users group in the domain. You can add further attributes to this policy or create additional policies. Policies only affect users who have been given dial-in access permission in the SAM or Directory.

Adding a New IAS Policy

Instead of adding multiple attributes with various constraints to the same policy, you can create multiple policies, each with their own attributes and constraints. A dial-in client must successfully meet the constraints in each policy before gaining access (or being denied access, if it is a Deny Access policy.)

Policies are applied in the order they appear in the Remote Access console. If you have one policy with a time constraint that limits access times to working hours but another policy further down the list has a more liberal time constraint, for example, the more liberal policy wins, all other things being equal.

With the RRAS console open to the Remote Access Policies icon, create a new policy as follows:

Procedure 17.10 **Adding a New IAS Policy**

1. Right-click the Remote Access Policies icon, and select NEW REMOTE ACCESS POLICY from the fly-out menu. The Add Remote Access Policy window opens.

2. Under Policy Friendly Name, enter a name that describes the use of the policy (for example, General Dial-in User Access).

3. Click Next. The Conditions window opens.

4. Click Add. The Select Attribute List window opens.

5. Select the attribute that you want to associate with the policy, and click Add. An additional window appears for entering the constraint values associated with the attribute.

6. Enter the required information, and click OK to return to the Add Remote Access Policy window.

7. Click Next. The Permissions window opens. Grant or deny permission, depending on the policy you want to enforce.

8. Click Next. The User Profile window opens. These user profiles are not the same as Explorer shell profiles. They contain specific dial-up settings only and are stored in the IAS database. User profiles are covered in the next section, so skip it for now.

9. Click Finish to save the changes, and return to the RRAS console. The friendly name of the policy appears in the Remote Access Policies list.

See the next section for details on associating a user profile (dial-up profile) with a policy.

Configuring Dial-Up User Profiles

Dial-in user profiles (also called user profiles in the UI) contain options specific to Windows 2000 remote access. These user profiles can be used to set special authentication and encryption options for a group of users. Configure a profile as follows:

Procedure 17.11 **Configuring a Dial-In User Profile**

1. In the RRAS Admin console, highlight Remote Access Policies. Double-click an existing policy or create a new one, and leave the Policy window open.

2. Click Edit Profile to open the Edit Dial-In Profile window. The Dial-in Constraints tab has options that further limit access beyond the main RADIUS attributes. For example, you can limit access solely to ISDN Async V.120 clients, if you want.

3. Select the Encryption tab. This tab has options to determine the type of encryption that will be negotiated with the client. See the following sidebar.

Selecting Encryption Policies

The policy options under the Encryption tab for a dial-up user profile determine the encryption requirements for dial-up users. There are four options:

- `Basic` uses either 40-bit MPPE RC4 encryption or DES56 encryption, depending on the connection type.

- `Stronger` uses 56-bit MPPE RC4 or DES56.

- `Strongest` (only available in U.S. domestic versions) uses 128-bit MPPE RC4 or Triple DES56.

- `No Encryption` can be included in the mix of available options if you want to provide that type of service.

Selecting `No Encryption` with no other options prevents all forms of encryption.

The remaining tabs define policies that refine and control the configuration of the dial-in clients that are permitted to access the system. Many of these options are redundant to options that can be configured at the Windows clients and at the server's remote access settings. This is because IAS can be used to control any dial-in client, not just Windows 2000 clients.

4. Click OK to save the changes, and return to the Properties window for the policy.

5. Click OK to apply the changes and return to the RRAS console.

Setting policies and their associated dial-up user profiles locally at a single dial-up server is adequate for a small organization with one or two servers, but it can get very cumbersome to manage individual dial-up server policies and profiles in a large organization. Storing these profiles on a central IAS server makes more sense. See the "Configuring Internet Authentication Services (IAS)" section for details.

Dial-up users who are members of a Native-mode Windows 2000 domain can be managed with group policies. Let's see how that works.

Managing Remote Access with Group Policies

Dial-up access permissions and options for users in Native-mode Windows 2000 domains can be managed with group policies. The requirement to be in Native mode comes from the way classic NT stores dial-up restrictions in the SAM. The binary SAM entry for a user does not contain all the possible options for setting group policies. Because some dial-up users might authenticate on a classic BDC in a mixed-mode domain and others on a Windows 2000 domain controller, the policies would be distributed haphazardly.

For this reason, the policies are disabled until you have shifted to Native mode. If you open the `Properties` window for a user account in the `AD Users and Computers` console in a mixed-mode domain, you'll see that the `Control Access Through Remote Access Policy` option is dimmed, as other several other policies that are not supported by classic NT. These options become available as soon as you shift the domain to Native mode.

Precautions When Shifting Domains to Native Mode

Shifting a domain to Native mode requires decommissioning all classic NT domain controllers and has wide-ranging implications on security and group management. You don't necessarily want to make the shift just to get fancier dial-up management. See Chapter 9, "Deploying Windows 2000 Domains," for a discussion of mixed-mode and Native-mode domains.

Local policies at the RAS server take precedence over group policies. You must have at least one local policy in place to give users access. The default local policy called `Allow Access If Dial-in Permission Is Enabled` is suitable after you shift the permission from Deny Access to Grant Access. This only gives access to authorized users.

Most of the remote access options available under group policies restrict the way users create and modify connections. They do not actually stop the user from logging on to a domain. You may find that focusing your attention on creating useful IAS policies is a better use of your time. Still, there are some useful options on the group policy list, so let's see how to set them.

Procedure 17.12   **Setting Remote Access Group Policies**

1. In a Native-mode Windows 2000 domain, open the `AD Users and Computers` console.

2. Expand the tree to an OU where you have user objects. You can also set a Domain policy or a Site policy. Site policies are a convenient place to grant remote access if you have central modem banks and dial-up servers that are shared by users in different domains on a local network.

3. Open the `Properties` window for the OU, Domain, or Site object and select the `Group Policy` tab.

4. Either modify an existing group policy using `Edit` or click `New` to create a new policy. The `Group Policy` console window opens.

5. Expand the tree to highlight the `User Configuration`, `Administrative Templates`, `Network`, `Network and Dial-up Connections` icon (see Figure 17.26). The right pane shows the list of available `Remote Access` policies. See the following sidebar for more information.

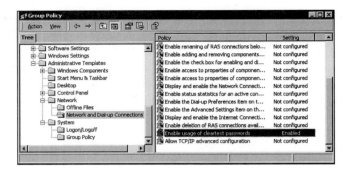

Figure 17.26 `Group Policy` console window showing list of available remote access group policies.

Making Dial-Up Group Policy Selections

When deciding which group policies to apply to a user community, the policy descriptions in the Group Policy Editor give you an idea of the effect of the policy. Figure 17.39 shows an example. These policies are not access constraints like IAS policies. They just make changes to the Registry at the clients.

If you disable the `Enable Connecting and Disconnecting a RAS Connection` policy in the Group Policy Editor, the `Connect` option for the connection icons in the `Network and Dial-up Connections` window disappears. It does not cause the dial-up server to reject connection attempts by the user.

6. Enable or disable any settings you want to apply to the users affected by the policy, and then close the `Group Policy` console. You can assign groups to the ACL of the policy if you want to further target the restrictions. The selected policy options are downloaded by users the next time they log on. They do not take effect until the user logs off and back on again.

You now have dial-up servers that can be managed from anywhere in the network and a set of access restrictions to protect your data and group policies to protect the users from themselves. You're ready to accept inbound dial-up connections. Let's see how to configure the clients to take advantage of all your hard work.

Configuring Dial-Up Clients

The only prerequisite for using a Windows 2000 Professional desktop or Windows 2000 Server as a dial-up client is installing a modem or ISDN adapter. The only configurations you need to make are to decide where to dial, what network protocols to use, and how to authenticate.

A Windows 2000 dial-up client can connect to a variety of remote access servers:

- Windows dial-up servers, either Windows 2000 or classic NT
- Third-party servers such as those used by Internet service providers
- Directly to another computer using a serial line, parallel line, or infrared port
- VPN connection over a dial-up connection or fixed connection such as broadband cable or xDSL

Each of these options involves a somewhat different set of configurations. Rather than try to combine them into a confusing mess, I cover each option separately.

One area of commonality is the way connection information is stored. Both classic NT and Windows 2000 use a phonebook to store dial-up information. Classic NT used a `Phonebook` window with a drop-down box to show the phonebook entries. Windows 2000 exposes them as Connection icons in the `Network and Dial-up Connections` window. In either case, the same underlying executable keeps track of the connection information, the *RAS Phonebook*, or RASPHONE.EXE.

The phonebook used by RASPHONE comes in the form of a file called RASPHONE.PBK. The RASPHONE utility can manage multiple phonebooks.

- The phonebook for a specific user is stored in the user's profile under `\Documents and Settings\<username>\Application Data\Microsoft\Network\ Connections\Pbk`.
- A phonebook with connection information available to anyone who logs on to the computer is stored in the All Users profile under `\Documents and Settings\All Users\Application Data\Microsoft\Network\Connections\Pbk`.
- Classic NT puts the phonebook in the `\WINNT\System32\Ras` directory. If you upgrade an existing computer, you will also get connection information from that phonebook.

The phonebook format did not change from NT4 to Windows 2000. You can copy an existing NT4 RASPHONE.PBK file to the user's profile or to the All Users profile. The entries will appear in the `Network and Dial-Up Connections` window as soon as you refresh the window.

> **Registry Tip: Phonebook Parameters**
>
> Phonebook parameters, including values for alternative phonebook locations, are stored under HKCU, Software, Microsoft, RAS Phonebook. Entries in this key only change the current user's profile. You may find that you are better off creating a standard phonebook and putting it in a central All User's profile using folder redirection. See Chapter 16, "Managing the User Operating Environment," for more information.

Configuring a Dial-In Client

Connecting a Windows 2000 client to a Windows dial-up server involves making a standard PPP connection that is authenticated either by MS-CHAP for connections to legacy Windows RAS servers or MS-CHAP v2 when connecting to Windows 2000 servers. Unless you have created a more restrictive group policy, any user can create a dial-up connection.

Procedure 17.13 Configuring a Dial-In Client

1. From the START menu, open SETTINGS | NETWORK AND DIAL-UP CONNECTIONS. The Network and Dial-up Connection window opens. Alternatively, you can right-click the My Network Places icon on the desktop and select Properties from the fly-out menu.

2. Double-click Make New Connection. The Network Connection Wizard starts.

3. Click Next. The Network Connection Type window opens.

4. Select the Dial-up to Private Network radio button.

5. Click Next. The Phone Number to Dial window opens. Enter the number of the dial-up server with which you want to connect. The Use Dialing Rules option exposes the TAPI settings selected during the modem installation. If you change the TAPI settings later, they will change automatically in any connections you have already created.

6. Click Next. The Connection Availability window opens. See the following sidebar.

> **Selecting Phonebook Options**
>
> The phonebook options in the Connection Availability window affect the way users see dial-up connections by determining which RASPHONE.PBK phonebook to use for storing connection information.
>
> - The For All Users option stores the entry in the phonebook under the All Users profile.
>
> - The Only For Myself option stores the entry in the user's personal RASPHONE.PBK under the current user profile.
>
> If you are setting up a connection for a user while logged on using your account, be sure to select For All Users option. Alternatively, if you want the entry to be used only by this user, you can copy the RASPHONE.PBK file out of your profile and into the user's profile.

7. Click Next. The Internet Connection Sharing window appears. The Enable Internet Connection Sharing option starts a new service called Internet Connection Sharing (ICS) to permit using this connection for routing other users onto the Internet. See the "Configuring Internet Connection Sharing (ICS)" section for details.

8. Click Next. A summary window appears with a Name field for the connection. You can enter any name. It is not used to identify the user or the computer. The examples will show the name Phoenix, meaning that the connection is to the Phoenix office in the Company.com domain.

   Select Add a Shortcut To My Desktop if you want a quick link to the connection. If you do not select this option but later want a shortcut, you can use the standard Explorer shortcut techniques to create a shortcut to the icon in the Network and Dial-up Connections window.

9. Click Finish. The Connect window appears. The account name of the current user is placed in the User Name field and the phone number you configured for the connection is placed in the Dial field.

10. Click Properties. A Properties window for the connection opens. The General tab shows options that were configured by the installation wizard.

11. Select the Options tab (see Figure 17.27). The selections are self-explanatory. Note that Include Windows logon domain is normally not checked. If the user is connecting to a dial-up server in a domain other than the user's home domain, you must check this option so that the user can specify his or her home domain.

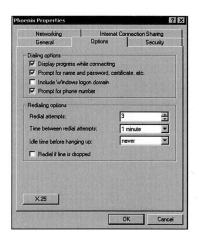

Figure 17.27   Dial-Up Connection Properties window showing Options tab.

12. Select the Security tab (see Figure 17.28). Refer to the following sidebar.

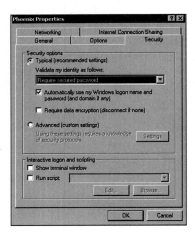

Figure 17.28 Dial-up Connection Properties window showing the Security tab.

Selecting Dial-Up Security Options

Several options are available in the Security tab of a dial-up connection.

The standard option for Validate my identity as follows is Allow unsecured password. You can leave this configuration in place if the dial-up server is configured to require authenticated password.

You may want to change the option to Require secured password, just in case the user dials other access servers and leaves behind a password that matches the user's standard network password.

If the user connects to a dial-up server that is in the same domain as the user's home domain, check Automatically use my windows logon name to simplify logon.

13. Select the Advanced (Custom Settings) radio button, and then click Settings (see Figure 17.29).

With the exception of standard CHAP, the default protocols are the same as the defaults on a Windows 2000 dial-up server. CHAP permits the client to dial a third-party server without making configuration changes.

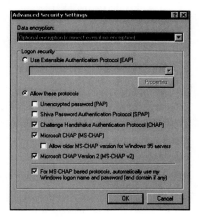

Figure 17.29 `Advanced Security Settings` window showing standard authentication protocol selections.

14. Click `Cancel` to close the window, and return to the `Properties` window.

15. Click `OK` to save any changes, and return to the `connection` icon.

Verifying a New Dial-Up Connection

It's a good idea to make sure that the connection works before turning the machine back over to the user. Do so as follows:

Procedure 17.14 **Verifying a Dial-Up Connection**

1. Double-click the connection icon. The `Connect` window opens with the user's name and the target phone number. Verify that the account has been granted dial-in permission in the SAM of the dial-up server or the Directory.

2. Enter a password for the user. The user can select the `Save Password` option, which caches the password in the local RAS phonebook. See the sidebar for cautions concerning this option.

Registry Tip: Local Password Caching and Laptop Security

Local caching of user passwords presents a security risk on laptops because the machines are not physically secure. The password itself is encrypted using one-way encryption, so that is not a problem, but if the laptop were to fall into unauthorized hands, the intruder could get access directly to your network without entering any credentials.

Prevent local password caching by adding the following Registry entry:

```
Key:        HKLM, SYSTEM, CurrentControlSet, Services, RasMan, Parameters
Value:      DisableSavePassword
Data type:      REG_DWORD
Data:    1
```

This Registry entry is not included as a standard group policy entry. If you want to distribute this as a group policy, you can add it to an existing ADM template or create a new ADM template. See Chapter 16 for details on creating custom policy templates.

3. Enter a password, and click Dial. The system initializes the modem, makes contact with the target server, authenticates the user, and completes the connection. A Connection Complete window opens to notify the user of the successful connection. A connection icon is added to the System Tray.

4. Double-click the connection icon in the System Tray to open the Dial-up Connection Status window (see Figure 17.30).

Figure 17.30 Dial-up Connection Status window.

5. Select the Details option. This is a quick way to determine connection statistics such as the authentication method used and the IP address it assigned (see Figure 17.31).

Figure 17.31   `Dial-up Connection Status` window showing the `Details` tab.

6. Close all windows.

7. Open a command session, and check that you can Ping hosts on the remote network.

8. Close the command session.

9. Now verify that the user can get authenticated in the remote domain. Right-click the `My Network Places` icon on the desktop, and select the MAP NETWORK DRIVE option.

10. Map a drive to a server in the remote network. You may get prompted for credentials depending on whether your local name and password at the dial-up client match those in the remote domain. See the next section for an explanation of domain server authentication over dial-up connections.

Overview of Domain Authentication over Dial-Up Connections

There are two stages to getting authenticated on a remote network. The preceding section tested the first stage by verifying that the machine has connectivity. The second stage verifies that the account is able to contact a domain controller and receive network authentication. That was done by the drive mapping.

The user may be prompted for credentials if the dial-up server is not a domain member. In this case, their dial-up password is not the same as their domain account password. The first time the user touches a domain member server, it rejects the user and prompts for alternate credentials.

Users get irritable at this difference in access credentials. They aren't particularly happy about fussing with modems in the first place and now they have to face another inscrutable network event involving passwords. I usually explain this by saying that the dial-in connection is no different from just plugging their laptop into a hot LAN drop at the office. If they did that, they wouldn't expect to get access to the network until they logged on to the domain. The same is true of that modem connection. This explanation seldom does the trick. The only solution is to keep the passwords on the local desktop and the domain in sync.

There is an option in the `Graphical Identification and Authentication` (GINA) window used by WINLOGON to collect user credentials that permits a user to log on to a remote domain by first initiating a PPP connection to a dial-up server. This option uses a check block on the logon window labeled `Log On Using Dial-up Connection`. This option has a great advantage in that it keeps a traveling user in a consistent logon pattern that is most likely to maintain passwords in sync.

> **Registry Tip: Maintaining Dial-Up Connection**
>
> You can keep a dial-up connection alive when logging out by making the following Registry change:
>
> | | |
> |---|---|
> | Key: | HKLM, SOFTWARE, Microsoft, Windows Windows 2000, CurrentVersion, WINLOGON |
> | Value: | KeepRASConnections |
> | Data Type: | REG_SZ (That is not a misprint. It is a string data type) |
> | Data: | 1 |

Managing Connections at the Dial-Up Server

You can view and manage the connections to the dial-up server using the `Routing and Remote Access` console as follows:

Procedure 17.15 **Managing Dial-Up Connections**

1. At the dial-up server where the client is connected, open the `Routing and Remote Access` console if it is not already open. Highlight the `Remote Access Clients` icon. The client's dial-up connection is shown in the right pane along with the duration of the connection and the number of ports used.

2. Double-click the user's connection icon to open a `Status` window. This should show the same statistics and errors as the `Connection Status` window at the client. Unfortunately, it does not show the name of the modem on which the client made connection. This can be a struggle to determine on a server with multiple lines.

3. Highlight the `Ports` icon. The port to which the user is connected shows `Active` in the right pane. Double-click the user's port icon to open a `Status` window. This window shows the same statistics as the others along with the name of the user and the IP address assigned to the user. This is the only way you can find a troublesome port if a user reports problems with the connection. Maybe this will improve in a maintenance release.

Client Dial-Up Connections and Routing

When you connect a dial-up client to remote network via PPP, it becomes a node on that remote network. If the client is also on a LAN, the dial-up connection creates a miniature router between the WAN interface represented by the modem and the LAN interface represented by the network adapter. Because the system assumes that you had a good reason for making the dial-up connection, the metrics assigned to the WAN connection are set lower than the LAN connection, giving the WAN connection priority for gateway settings, DNS settings, and WINS settings if they are included in the configuration packet passed to the dial-up client.

To see how this looks from the point of view of the interface, open a command session and enter `ipconfig /all`. This lists the IP parameters assigned to each interface. Here is an example listing for a laptop that has a dial-up connection to a server in the `Company.com` domain, IP network 10.1.0.0, and a local connection to the `Subsidiary.com` domain, IP network 10.3.0.0.

```
C:\>ipconfig /all

Windows 2000 IP Configuration

        Host Name . . . . . . . . . . . . : PHX-W2KS-20
        Primary DNS Suffix  . . . . . . . : subsidiary.com
        Node Type . . . . . . . . . . . . : Broadcast
        IP Routing Enabled. . . . . . . . : No
        WINS Proxy Enabled. . . . . . . . : No
        DNS Suffix Search List. . . . . . : subsidiary.com

Ethernet adapter Local Area Connection:

        Connection-specific DNS Suffix  . :
        Description . . . . . . . . . . . : HP (J2585A) PCI LAN  Adapter
        Physical Address. . . . . . . . . : 08-00-09-AA-AA-AA
        DHCP Enabled. . . . . . . . . . . : No
        IP Address. . . . . . . . . . . . : 10.3.1.200
        Subnet Mask . . . . . . . . . . . : 255.255.0.0
```

```
          Default Gateway . . . . . . . . . : 10.3.1.254
          DNS Servers . . . . . . . . . . . : 10.3.1.32

PPP adapter Dial-Up Connection:

          Connection-specific DNS Suffix  . :
          Description . . . . . . . . . . . : WAN (PPP/SLIP) Interface
          Physical Address. . . . . . . . . : 00-53-45-00-00-00
          DHCP Enabled. . . . . . . . . . . : No
          IP Address. . . . . . . . . . . . : 10.1.2.4
          Subnet Mask . . . . . . . . . . . : 255.255.255.255
          Default Gateway . . . . . . . . . : 10.1.2.4
          DNS Servers . . . . . . . . . . . : 10.1.1.100
```

See where the PPP adapter for the dial-up connection has the same IP address for the interface and the default gateway? This is the result of selecting Use Default Gateway on the Remote Network option in the dial-up connection Properties window under Networking | TCP/IP Properties | Advanced.

This option is enabled by default. It configures the machine to send all non-local IP traffic to the remote network over the dial-up connection. It makes this decision based on an internal routing table. You can see the contents of this routing table from the command line by entering route print. Here is an example:

```
C:\>route print
===========================================================================
Interface List
0x1 ........................ MS TCP Loopback interface
0x1b000002 ...08 00 09 aa aa aa ...... HP (J2585A) PCI LAN  Adapter
0x20000004 ...00 53 45 00 00 00 ...... WAN (PPP/SLIP) Interface
===========================================================================
===========================================================================
Active Routes:
Network Destination        Netmask          Gateway       Interface  Metric
          0.0.0.0          0.0.0.0         10.1.2.4        10.1.2.4      1
          0.0.0.0          0.0.0.0       10.3.1.254        10.3.1.1      2
         10.3.0.0      255.255.0.0        10.3.1.1        10.3.1.1      1
         10.3.1.1  255.255.255.255       127.0.0.1       127.0.0.1      1
         10.1.2.4  255.255.255.255        10.1.2.4        10.1.2.4      1
         10.1.2.4  255.255.255.255       127.0.0.1       127.0.0.1      1
   10.255.255.255  255.255.255.255        10.3.1.1        10.3.1.1      1
   10.255.255.255  255.255.255.255        10.1.2.4        10.1.2.4      1
        127.0.0.0        255.0.0.0       127.0.0.1       127.0.0.1      1
        224.0.0.0        224.0.0.0        10.3.1.1        10.3.1.1      1
        224.0.0.0        224.0.0.0        10.1.2.4        10.1.2.4      1
  255.255.255.255  255.255.255.255       127.0.0.1       127.0.0.1      1
Default Gateway:         10.1.2.4
===========================================================================
Persistent Routes:
  None
```

An entry in the routing table with a network destination of 0.0.0.0 indicates a route of last resort, which is the same as a gateway. Two interfaces are configured as the gateway, so the entry with the lowest metric (hop count) is given the honors of being "the" default gateway (that is, the WAN interface).

The LAN interface is automatically assigned a higher metric, meaning that the dial-up interface will be preferred in all routed events. The dial-up client does this because it assumes that the user wants to get off the network or she would not have made the dial-up connection in the first place.

This change in the routing table has interesting consequences. For the most part, it means local network connections stop working. If a user dials from the office to another network, all connections to the local network fail.

This can cause data loss if the user has open documents. And if the user has configured the workstation as a peer-to-peer server, maybe to share a CD-ROM drive, other users will suddenly not be able to connect to the shared resource because the local route table at the workstation will send their responses to the wrong network.

There are endless possibilities for problems caused by the change in the local routing table. What if your network uses a private IP address space and the user dials another network with the same private address space—not an impossible occurrence by any means. The user's local network traffic now goes down the low metric route and starts timing out looking for a host that isn't there. Or worse yet, it finds a host in the remote network with the same IP address as a host in the local network.

There is no good workaround for this problem. As soon as you make a routed connection to another network via dial-up, then any solution that tries to support simultaneous operations is problematic.

If you choose not to enable the `Use default gateway on remote network` option for the connection, the user cannot get a routed connection beyond the interface. This stymies the user, who is probably trying to get onto the Internet.

You can try reconfiguring the local routing table using `route delete` and `route add` commands to give a lower metric to the local LAN interface. This is not a complete solution because now the connection to the remote network may fail.

If the user is dialing an Internet service provider (ISP) and you set the local routing table to prefer the local LAN, for example, DNS queries will go to the local DNS server rather than the DNS server at the ISP.

Still, modifying the routing table is worth a try in specific cases if it can get the user the desired connectivity and functionality. For example, here are the commands that will reverse the metrics for the `route print` listing shown previously:

```
Route delete   0.0.0.0   mask 0.0.0.0   10.4.2.4
Route delete   0.0.0.0   mask 0.0.0.0   10.3.1.254
Route add      0.0.0.0   mask 0.0.0.0   10.4.2.4  metric 2
Route add      0.0.0.0   mask 0.0.0.0   10.3.1.254 metric 1
```

You can add these commands to a batch file that the user runs after making the connection, or add it to a post-connection script.

Using Dial-Up from the Command Line

You do not need to use the graphical user interface to initiate a dial-up session. The executable that handles the connection, RASDIAL.EXE, can be called from the command line or a batch file.

Using RASDIAL, you can configure an unattended workstation to use the Task Scheduler to make dial-up connections to transfer files, pick up email, or to do other periodic chores.

You can configure the batch file to give RASDIAL the name of a phonebook entry from the phonebook. The name of the entry is the same as the name assigned to the `Connection` icon in the `Networking and Dial-up Connections` window.

When RASDIAL makes the dial-up connection, it will use the credentials that are stored with the phonebook entry if you elected to cache them locally. If you have a connection named Home Office, for example, the syntax would be:

```
rasdial "home office"
```

During the time that the system is making the connection, the console displays the same status information that you would see from the graphical interface if you were making the connection manually. When you are ready to hang up, enter the following:

```
rasdial /disconnect
```

If you do not cache your passwords when you use dial-up connections, or you want to provide a different set of credentials than those stored in the phonebook, you can provide this information on the command line. (The parameters are not case sensitive.) Here's the syntax:

```
rasdial "home office" username * /DOMAIN:domain /PHONE:phonenumber /CALLBACK:callbacknumber
/PREFIXSUFFIX
```

The asterisk (★) causes RASDIAL to prompt for a password. You can enter the password on the command line, if you prefer. The /PREFIXSUFFIX switch tells RASDIAL to use the TAPI settings for the modem interface.

You can also modify the phonebook from the command line by entering rasphone on the command line. This opens the standard graphical interface, but at least it's faster than going through all the mouse clicks to get to the Connection icons. If you enter rasphone −a, you are taken directly to the Network Connection Wizard.

Connecting a Dial-In Client to an ISP

At this point, the Windows 2000 dial-up client has only connected to a private Windows 2000 dial-up server and a Windows 2000 network. Let's now configure it to make a connection to a non-Microsoft remote access service, such as an ISP.

Most ISPs use some form of CHAP to authenticate the user's PPP connection. The user's credentials are authenticated by a RADIUS box using a database that can be just about anything, from a massive Oracle database to a small, proprietary DB running on a Linux box or even a DOS engine. (Wildcat will never, ever die.)

So, the user needs to have CHAP enabled at the dial-up client. This is done automatically during the connection setup, so there should not be much to do other than supplying connection information. Proceed as follows:

Procedure 17.16   **Connecting a Dial-In Client to an ISP**

1. Start the Network Connection Wizard using START | SETTINGS | NETWORK AND DIAL-UP CONNECTIONS | MAKE NEW CONNECTION.

2. Click Next. The Network Connection Type window opens. Select the Dial-up to the Internet radio button.

3. Click Next. The scene shifts to the Internet Connection Wizard. You may be familiar with this wizard from Windows 9x and NT4. It has two purposes. One is to configure an Internet connection. The other is to snag the user for MSN. Avoid that route, and select the I Want To Set Up My Internet Connection Manually radio button.

4. Click Next. The Setting Up Your Internet Connection window opens.

5. Select the I Connect Through a Phone Line and a Modem radio button.

6. Click Next. The Step 1 of 3: Internet Account Connection Information window opens. The area code and location come from the TAPI information for the modem. Enter a telephone number for the ISP. See the following sidebar for information about the Advanced button.

Advanced Dial-Up Options

The Advanced button in the Internet Account Connection Information window enables you to specify the following items.

- Connection Type, which is PPP by default and should be left with that setting.

- IP Address, although this is usually not allowed by ISPs.

- DNS Server Address, for use if the ISP does not pass one to the client after the PPP transaction.

- Logon Procedure, explained more fully in the next paragraphs.

Classic NT required the use of a logon script when connecting to an ISP or any other terminal server that prompted for login and password credentials. Windows 2000 handles this interaction without the need for a special script.

If an ISP has a special menu that is sent to PPP users, however, you must configure a login script to handle that menu. It is becoming increasingly rare for ISPs to do this now that they cater to Windows and Macintosh users instead of handling Text-mode connections.

Still, PPP menus still exist, and Windows 2000 comes with a prepackaged set of scripts for handling them. It's usually easier to hack one of the prepared scripts rather than writing one of your own. Use the Terminal Window option to see what information is passed to the client during logon, and then modify the script accordingly.

7. Click Next. The Step 2 of 3: Internet Account Logon Information window opens. Enter the user name and password for the Internet account. Some ISPs require a capital *P* at the front of the user name to signify a PPP connection to the RADIUS server. Others use a realm name for routing, such as ELN/jjjingleheimerschmidt.

8. Click Next. The Step 3 of 3: Configuring Your Computer window opens. This is something of a misnomer because what the name entered in this window is the connection name, not the computer name. Give the connection a name that is descriptive of the ISP, such as MyISP-IdahoPOP.

9. Click Next. The Set Up Your Internet Mail Account window opens. This and the next few windows are designed to configure mail information for the user. Let's select the No radio button. Mail can be configured later.

10. Click Next. A completion window opens. Leave To Connect to the Internet Immediately checked.

11. Click Finish. The settings are saved to the Registry and a Dial-up Connection window opens.

12. Click Connect. The modem dials and makes connection.

After the connection is made, open a command session and run IPCONFIG to check the IP address and DNS information you got from the ISP. Ping the name of a common Web presence, such as www.internic.com. You can also open a browser and check out a Web site; if you can Ping, however, you should probably be able to get HTTP traffic unless you are working through a firewall.

Troubleshooting Dial-Up Connections to the Internet

If any part of the ISP connection process fails, start with verifying that the modem works correctly using HyperTerminal. Then start all over again with a fresh connection. If the ISP connection still doesn't work, try a dial-up connection to a RAS server.

If the modem works fine in HyperTerm, but you can get a solid dial-up connection, you may have a problem with the init string or the modem just might not make the grade for dial-up connections. Check the vendor's Web site for drivers, and look for tales of woe on the Usenet newsgroups. A quick search of www.dejanews.com can save you many hours of toiling over a bad modem.

If the modem connects but the ISP access server responds with an *Access Denied* error of one sort or another, check for proper credentials and be sure to check for case. Most ISPs use UNIX terminals.

If you get a *Loopback* error of some sort, you may need to provide a special prefix or realm name in front of the user's logon name.

If the modem makes connection and the transaction hangs at the authentication, you may have a problem with VJ Header compression. Disable it as follows:

Procedure 17.17   **Disabling VJ Header Compression**

1. Open the Properties window for the connection.

2. Navigate through Networking, Properties, Advanced to open the Advanced TCP/IP Settings window.

3. Deselect the Use IP Header Compression option

4. Click OK to save the change.

5. Close the rest of the windows, and try again.

If it still hangs, call the ISP. Their technical support folks can probably tell you in two seconds what settings work best for their system—if you can manage to get through to them.

You might be encountering a terminal server with a non-standard login sequence. Use a terminal window at login to see what is being passed to the client. Configure the connection to use a terminal window as follows:

1. Open the Properties window for the connection.

2. Select the Security tab.

3. Check the Show Terminal Window option.

4. Click OK to save the change.

Try the connection again, and give your standard credentials when prompted in the terminal window. Look for rejected credentials, unusual menus, or other problems.

Configuring a Dial-Up Client to Use a Direct Connection

If you want to build a little two-node network to test dial-up, you cannot use modems. Modems require ringback and special signalling from a phone switch.

You can buy a modem eliminator, but they are relatively pricey and highly specific in their functions. A more flexible solution is to contact any small phone installer in your area and ask whether they have old PBX units for sale. These can be had for a couple of hundred dollars or so plus another hundred for the programming phone and are invaluable in the lab.

You can also make a direct connection between two Windows 2000 computers using serial cables, parallel cables, or infrared connections. This section shows how to configure that connection. The example uses a serial line, but you can use a parallel cable or an infrared connection, too. There are also USB solutions coming on the market, but they load their own network drivers.

The most critical element when using serial connections is getting the correct pin-outs on the null-modem cable. You cannot use LapLink cable. Tables 17.3 through 17.5 show the pinouts for the cables. For parallel connections, you can use any straight-through 25-pin cable. For an infrared connection, consult the vendor's documentation.

Table 17.3   **Pinouts for 9-Pin Null Modem Cable**

Signal	Remote	Local
Transmit Data (TD)	3	2
Receive Data (RD)	2	3
Request to Send (RTS)	7	8
Clear to Send	8	7
Data Set Ready and Carrier Detect (DSR and CD)	6, 1	4
Signal Ground	5	5
Data Terminal Ready (DTR)	4	6, 1

Table 17.4   **Pinouts for 25-Pin Null Modem Cable**

Signal	Remote	Local
Transmit Data (TD)	2	3
Receive Data (RD)	3	2
Request to Send (RTS)	4	5
Clear to Send	5	4
Data Set Ready and Carrier Detect (DSR and CD)	6, 8	20
Signal Ground	7	7
Data Terminal Ready (DTR)	20	6, 8

Table 17.5   **Pinouts for 25-Pin to 9-pin Null Modem Cable**

Signal	25-Pin	9-Pin
Transmit Data (TD)	2	2
Receive Data (RD)	3	3
Request to Send (RTS)	4	9
Clear to Send	5	7
Data Set Ready and Carrier Detect (DSR and CD)	6, 8	4
Signal Ground	7	5
Data Terminal Ready (DTR)	20	6, 1

After you obtain correctly wired cable, connect the two computers between the COM ports, and then proceed as follows:

Procedure 17.18 **Installing a Direct Serial-Line Connection**

1. Open Control Panel, and then open the Phone and Modem Options applet.
2. Select the Modems tab.
3. Click Add. The Add/Remove Hardware Wizard starts with the focus set to modems.
4. Select Don't detect my modem and click Next.
5. The system pauses for a while to build a list of modems using the INF\PNF files in \WINNT\INF, and then the Install New Modem window opens.
6. Select Manufacturers: (Standard Modem Types) and Models: Communication Cable Between Two Computers.
7. Click Next. The Install New Modem window now prompts to select a port.
8. The modem drivers for the serial line connection are installed, and then a final summary window opens.
9. Click Finish to close the wizard.
10. At the dial-in client computer, open the Network and Dial-up Communications window.
11. Double-click New Connection. The Network Connection window opens.
12. Select the Connect directly to another computer radio button.
13. Click Next. The Host or Guest window opens. Select the Guest radio button.
14. Click Next. The Select a Device window opens. Select the Communications Cable option from the drop-down list.
15. Click Next. The Connection Availability window opens. Select the option that fits your needs, either For All users or Only for myself.
16. Click Next. A final window opens to name the connection. Give it a unique name, although the default Direct Connection name is fairly good.

At this point, you can use the cable connection as you would any modem.

Supporting Down-Level and Non-Windows Dial-Up Clients

Down-level Windows clients can make a dial-up connection to a Windows 2000 dial-up server and access the network just as they would through an NT4 RAS server.

The Windows 2000 server must be configured to accept MS-CHAP authentication unless the clients are running Windows 98 or NT4 SP4 or higher, in which case you can limit authentication to MS-CHAP v2.

Non-windows clients cannot use MS-CHAP because they do not have the Microsoft encryption algorithm for the user password. Instead, they can use standard CHAP or one of the authentication methods provided under Extensible Authentication Protocol (EAP).

Windows 2000 comes with two EAP packages, MD5-CHAP and certificate-based authentications using Transport Layer Security (TLS). Unless you have the infrastructure to handle certificate generation and distribution, you'll find that CHAP or EAP/MD5-CHAP is easier to administer.

Both CHAP and EAP/MD5-CHAP requires the Directory to store reversibly encrypted passwords because the security provider must be able to extract the user's clear text password. See the "PPP Authentication Protocols" section for details.

There are several ways to enable reversible password storage. After setting any of these options, the users must change their existing passwords to generate reversible passwords.

- **Individual users in a Windows 2000 domain.** Enable the `Save Password as Encrypted Clear Text` option in the user's Directory account. Access this option by opening the user's Property window in the `AD Users and Computers` console and then navigating to the `Account` tab, `Account Options` field. Figure 17.32 shows an example.

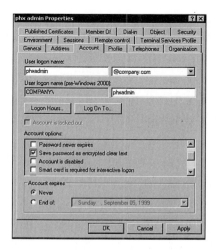

Figure 17.32   Individual user account properties window showing `Save Password As Encrypted Clear Text` option.

- **All domain computers associated with a group policy.** Use the Group Policy Editor to create or open a group policy for a Site, Domain, or OU. Expand the tree to the `Computer Configuration | Windows Settings | Security Settings | Account Policies | Password Policy` icon. Change the status of the `Store Passwords Using Reversible Encryption for All Users` option to `Enabled`. Figure 17.33 shows an example.

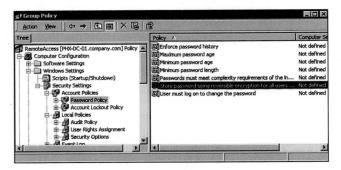

Figure 17.33   Group Policy Editor with focus set to an OU group policy showing Password Policy list with `Store Passwords Using Reversible Encryption for All Users` enabled.

- **All domain users associated with a group policy.** Use the Group Policy editor to create or modify a group policy for a Site, Domain, or OU. Expand the tree to the `User Configuration | Administrative Templates | Network | Network and Dial-up Connections` icon. Change the status of the `Enable Usage of Cleartext Passwords` option to `Enabled`.

- **All users who access a standalone dial-up server.** Use the local Group Policy Editor (GPEDIT.MSC) to modify the local policies for the dial-up server. Expand the tree to `Computer Configuration | Windows Settings | Security Settings | Account Policies | Password Policy`. Change the status of the `Store Passwords Using Reversible Encryption for All Users` option to `Enabled`.

Monitoring Dial-Up Sessions Using Protocol Tracing

Remote Access has an extensive tracing capability that permits monitoring any of the protocols involved in establishing a link. Each trace must be configured manually in the Registry using `HKLM | SOFTWARE | Microsoft | Tracing`.

There is a long list of traceable protocols under this key. Although each protocol has two tracing possibilities, log tracing and console tracing, only log tracing is functional. Changes made to the way services interact with the user space in Windows 2000 rendered console tracing inoperable.

You can enable log tracing on as many protocols as you want. The logs are saved in \WINNT\Tracing under discrete names. Here is a list of the traceable protocols and what their acronyms mean:

- **BAP.** Bandwidth Allocation Protocol
- **H323MSP.** Internet conferencing protocol H.323 media services provider
- **CONFMSP.** NetMeeting media service provider
- **RCAMSP.** Streaming video media services provider
- **IASHLPR.** Internet Authentication Services helper
- **IASPIPE.** IAS Named Pipe interface
- **IASRAD.** IAS Radius interface
- **IASSAM.** IAS Security Account Manager interface
- **IPBOOTTP.** IP Bootstrap Transfer Protocol also used for DHCP
- **IPRIP2.** IP Routing Information Protocol, release 2
- **IPRouterManager.** IP component of the RAS multiprotocol router
- **IPXAutonet.** IPX frame detection
- **IPX Traffic Filter Logging.** IPX traffic filter log
- **IPXCP.** PPP control protocol for IPX
- **IPXRIP.** IPX Routing Information Protocol
- **IPXRouterManager.** IPX component of the RAS multiprotocol router
- **IPXSAP.** IPX Service Advertising Protocol
- **IPXWAN.** IPX Wide Area Network control component
- **NTAUTH.** NT LanMan Challenge/Response user authentication
- **OSPF.** Open Shortest Path First
- **OSPFMIB.** OSPF Management Information Block information used for SNMP (Simple Network Management Protocol)
- **PPP.** Point-to-Point Protocol
- **RASADHLP.** RAS Automatic Dialer helper
- **RASAPI32.** RAS 32-bit Application Programming Interface
- **RASAUTO.** RAS Automatic Dialer service trace
- **RASBACP.** Bandwidth Allocation Control Protocol

- **RASCHAP.** RAS Challenge-Handshake Protocol authentication protocol
- **RASCPL.** RAS Control Panel applet trace—not applicable to Windows 2000.
- **RASDLG.** RAS helper DLL trace
- **RASEAP.** Extensible Authentication Protocol for RAS.
- **RASIPCP.** Internet Protocol Control Protocol
- **RASIPHLP.** RAS Internet Protocol helper DLL trace
- **RASMAN.** RAS Management service, RASADMIN.EXE.
- **RASMON.** RAS Monitor service
- **RASNBFCP.** NetBIOS Frame Control Protocol
- **RASPAP.** RAS Password Authentication Protocol authentication service
- **RASPHONE.** RAS Phonebook service
- **RASSCRIPT.** RAS script service
- **RASSPAP.** RAS Shiva Password Authentication Protocol
- **RASTAPI.** RAS Telephony API driver
- **RASTLS.** RAS Transport Layer Security, used for monitor smart card, RADIUS, and MD5-CHAP
- **RASTLSUI.** RAS TLS User Interface
- **Router.** Traces activity of the multiprotocol router service
- **RTM.** Response Time Monitor, used in SNA
- **TermMgr.** Terminal services manager
- **WaveMsp.** Wave audio media services provider

You can view the contents of a log by double-clicking on the log file to launch Notepad. This does not block updates to the file, but you must close and reopen Notepad to view any changes. Also, the captured data is flushed to the file infrequently to improve performance, so the file sizes displayed for the log files may be smaller than the actual file size. If you refresh Explorer, the file size will update.

Increasing Bandwidth Using Multilink

Bandwidth and stability are priorities when providing remote access service. Users always want bigger pipes, but it isn't easy to supply them at a reasonable cost.

One inexpensive way to get more bandwidth is to use more pipes, in this case more modems, and bundle them together using *PPP multilink*. When modems (or ISDN channels) are bundled, the system balances the load between the shared connections. Two multilinked 56K modems running over clean copper can be nearly as fast as an ISDN line at a fraction of the cost.

The requirements for PPP multilink are defined in RFC 1990, "The PPP Multilink Protocol (MP)." You can multilink any combination of circuit-switched connections: two or more modems, a modem and an ISDN connection, two ISDN "B" channels, or multiple "B" channels from several ISDN adapters or a PRI.

Whether you use modems or ISDN lines or both, you must define a phone number for the incoming lines that makes the multiple connections available to users. The decision of which to use depends on your budget and PBX features. Here are a few common configurations:

- The lines connect directly to your local telephone company's central office and are configured into one or more *hunt groups* associated with a main number. The users call the main number, and if it is busy, the calls cascade through the rest of the numbers in the hunt group until a free line is found.

- The incoming lines come directly from the local telephone company's with no hunt group. In this case, the user must know each number and configure each modem in the multilink to use a separate number. If one a line is busy, the client can be configured with roll-down numbers, but this requires a lot of effort if you have dozens or hundreds of dial-in users.

- The lines are connected to your company's PBX. In this configuration, the PBX divvies up the incoming lines into *zones* with a single phone number associated with each zone. Make sure that the modems or ISDN lines are fed from the same zone. If one modem or ISDN channel is busy, the PBX rolls to the next free line.

After you have two or more circuit-switched interfaces on a dial-up server and a dial-up client, proceed as follows:

Procedure 17.19 **Configuring Multilink and BAP**

1. Open the Routing and Remote Access console.

2. Right-click the local server icon, and select PROPERTIES from the fly-out menu. The Local Properties window opens.

3. Select the PPP tab (see Figure 17.34).

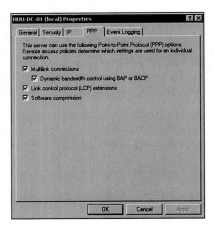

Figure 17.34   Local RAS Server Properties window with PPP tab selected.

4. Select the Multilink Connections option. Figure 17.35 shows an example. You can elect to use Dynamic Bandwidth Control, which makes use of the Bandwidth Allocation Protocol (BAP), along with its associated control protocol, BAPC. See the folowing sidebar for more information.

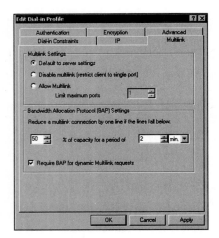

Figure 17.35   Edit Dial-in Profile window showing Multilink tab with BAP Settings.

BAP Settings

BAP monitors traffic over a multilink connection and shuts down one or more lines if traffic falls below 50 percent of rated capacity for two minutes.

You can change the default BAP threshold and interval shown in Figure 17.35 using the Dial-In User Profile associated with the IAS policy that is applied to the user. The BAP settings are located in the dial-in profile under the multilink tab.

For multilink modem lines, the reconnect time is so long that it's really not worth using BAP. The most common use is with ISDN lines, especially if you are in a tariff zone where line charges zoom as soon as the second bearer channel goes up.

5. Click OK to save the change, and close the window.

6. At the dial-in client, open the Networking and Dial-up Connection window.

7. Open the Properties window for a connection. At the General tab you can see that all modems and/or ISDN devices on the machine are listed under Connect Using. Figure 17.36 shows an example.

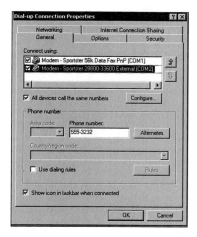

Figure 17.36 Dial-up Connection Properties window showing General tab with multiple interfaces.

8. If the inbound lines to the RAS server are configured to use a hunt group or a single PBX zone, leave the All Devices Call The Same Numbers option checked.

9. If the incoming lines have different numbers, uncheck the option. When you do this, the Phone Number field changes to show the phone number for the highlighted modem. Enter a number for each modem. Click Alternates if you want to configure additional lines for each modem to dial.

10. Click OK to save the changes, and close the window.

11. Double-click the connection icon to make the connection. Only one phone number is listed, but the system dials both. *The PPP connections are negotiated individually for each line.* If you use BAP (Bandwidth Allocation Protocol) to add and drop lines as traffic changes, each call to the dial-up server results in a new authentication.

10. If one of the lines connects and another doesn't, a `Line Bundling Errors` window opens.

11. If you are bundling two ISDN "B" channels and you elected to use BAP, let the connection sit idle for a while to see whether the second channel drops. If it doesn't, look for activity on the line, either using the `Status` window for the connection or by lights on the adapter, if it is external.

Configuring Demand-Dial Routing

The only routing done so far has been a byproduct of a standard dial-up connection between a client and a dial-up server. A dial-up server can also make connections, however; and if that server is also configured to route across that connection and recognize routers on the other side, it can function as a tolerably good point-to-point router either between a branch office and the home network or from an office to the Internet.

A simple dial-up connection can also route, but as far as Windows 2000 and RRAS is concerned, the only true router is one that has been configured with a routing interface. This is where demand-dial routing comes into play. Instead of configuring a modem or ISDN adapter as a standard dial-up interface, it can be configured as a demand-dial router interface so that RRAS treats it just like any other router.

Demand-Dial Routing Versus Full-Time Connections

There is no difference, at least conceptually, between routing over a circuit-switched connection via a modem or ISDN adapter and routing over a leased line via a CSU/DSU. The advantage of demand-dial routing is cost. If a circuit-switched connection that goes up and down based on traffic demands meets your needs, why pay for a full-time leased line?

In the Navy, surface sailors and submariners have the same conversation. Surface sailors say, "I'd never get into a ship designed to sink." Submariners counter by saying, "You've got it all wrong. All ships are designed to sink. Submarines are designed to come back up again."

In most areas where ISDN is available, you can get both bearer channels for a base subscription cost of $20–$50 a month and a line charge of anywhere from 3 to 10 cents per minute, depending on local tariffs. If a branch office keeps the line hot for only 20 or 30 hours a month, you save lots of money compared to a leased line. Demand-dial routing is most useful in conjunction with ISDN lines because of their speed and their quick reaction time when traffic is waiting.

Most ISDN routers have demand-dial routing built in; if you are purchasing new ISDN equipment, however, you can get an attractive price for a simple ISDN terminal adapter that does not do "B" channel bonding or demand-dial routing and let Windows 2000 do those chores.

Demand-dial routing over modems is less expensive than ISDN but the reaction times are so slow that you may want to just leave the lines up all the time. In many areas, the cost of maintaining a routed link using two or three analog lines with 56K modems at each end is far less than a single ISDN line.

At some point, it may make sense to shift from using demand-dial routing to a point-to-point solution using fractional T-1 or a minimal CIR to a frame relay provider. You can still use the Windows 2000 server as a router. Granted that Windows 2000 isn't a replacement for a high-end boundary router, either in terms of power or features, but it is more than capable of handling one or two T1 lines or a broadband or xDSL connection, even with encrypted traffic. This is enough to meet the needs of many small and medium-sized businesses.

Broadband/xDSL Connections Versus Demand-Dial Connections

The advent of affordable high-speed broadband and xDSL has lessened the attractiveness of demand-dial circuit switched solutions and leased lines. These high-speed solutions have their disadvantages, however.

- They are not widely available, especially outside of major metropolitan centers, so you may find that some of your branch offices don't have access to xDSL or broadband cable.

- They are not point to point, making it necessary to use a VPN if you want to connect offices together.

- They are asymmetrical with upstream speeds often not much faster than ISDN.

- They often have tariffs that dramatically increase their cost when used in conjunction with business-based LANs.

The following three configurations are the most attractive for demand-dial routing:

- **Routing between two offices in a private network.** This option involves configuring mutual demand-dial interfaces that can pick up the circuit when traffic is waiting at either end.

- **Routing an office (including a home office) to the Internet.** This option involves configuring a demand-dial interface as an Internet router. This means working with an ISP to get public IP addresses for your LAN and having your network placed on their routing tables.

- **Sharing connections using Network Address Translation (NAT).** This option is most often used to access the Internet, although it can be used for one-way interoffice routing. Connection sharing involves configuring a demand-dial interface, and then using NAT to translate the clients' internal IP addresses into a single public IP address for transmission to the remote network. This option requires that the local LAN be in a private address space such as 10.0.0.0 or 192.168.0.0. The NAT option is attractive because it does not require special configurations or additional services from the ISP.

Registry Tip: Router Control Parameters

Router control parameters are stored in HKLM | Software | Microsoft | Router | This key includes a RouterManager subkey that stores keys containing control parameters for IP and IPX Router Managers. The IP Router Managers include IPRIP, OSPF, IGMP, and IPBOOTP.

Initializing Routing Services

Up to this point, the examples in the chapter have used only the Remote Access features in RRAS. To use any of the demand-dial alternatives, it is necessary to enable the routing features.

You can just as easily enable routing at the same time you enable Remote Access—the feature does not require additional memory unless it is used—but I'm not a fan of indiscriminately deploying routers. All it takes is one curious person fooling around with a software-based router on a slow evening to bring an entire network to its knees.

Enabling routing in RRAS requires disabling then re-enabling any existing RRAS configurations. You will not lose any settings, but the router will come down for a while. Proceed as follows:

Procedure 17.20 **Initial Configuration of Routing Services**

1. Open the `Routing and Remote Access` console.

2. Select the `Remote Access Clients` icon, and verify that no users are connected to the server.

3. Right-click the local server name, and select DISABLE ROUTING AND REMOTE ACCESS from the fly-out menu. A warning appears informing you that disabling the service requires reconfiguration when it is re-enabled. Click `Yes` to acknowledge the warning, and disable the service.

4. After the service stops—and this might take a while—the icon associated with the server changes to a red down arrow. You may need to restart the computer if it takes longer than three or four minutes for the service to stop. After the service has stopped, reinitialize RRAS using the instructions in "Initializing the Remote Access Service" with the following additional steps:

5. At the `Routing and Remote Access` window, select `Enable Server as a Router` and select the `Local and Remote Routing (LAN and WAN)` radio button. Figure 17.59 shows an example.

6. At the `Dial-in or Demand Dial Interfaces` window, select the `Enable All Devices For Both Routing and Remote Access` radio button.

7. The remaining steps are the same. When the RRAS service restarts, the `Routing and Remote Access` console contains an additional icon called `Routing Interfaces`.

After you have enabled routing, proceed to the section that details the demand-dial configuration you want: interoffice router, Internet router, or Internet NAT router.

Configuring a Demand-Dial Interoffice Router

The diagram in Figure 17.37 shows a typical demand-dial routing connection between a small remote network—the example shows a retail store—and the main office. The retail store has its own server. The users only need to access the main office to send email, update accounting files, and file time cards. Oh, and the branch manager needs to browse the Internet on "Very Important Business."

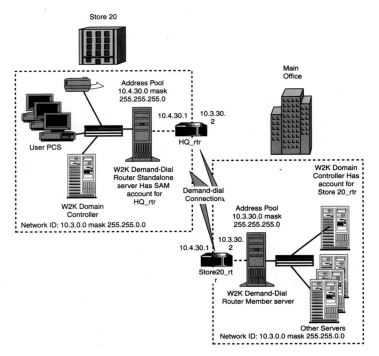

Figure 17.37 Diagram of demand-dial routing between retail outlet and the main office.

Here are the requirements to make a demand-dial connection between two offices:

- A Windows 2000 server equipped with an ISDN adapter or a modem in each office. If you have multiple modems or bearer channels, you can use multilink to bundle them together after the demand-dial interface has been created. Windows 2000 Professional does not support demand-dial routing.

- Routing must be enabled on both servers as detailed in the preceding section.

- Each circuit-switched device must have its own phone number. You cannot use hunt groups.

- You must have administrator rights in the domain, if there is one, or at the standalone servers. The servers can be members of the same domain, different domains, or different workgroups.

- The remote access policies at each server must be set to allow full access by both servers to each other's networks. You may need to create special a special Windows group for the demand-dial accounts. Give the group 24×7 access. You can also use the profile associated with this remote access policy to specify a particular authentication method and to set IP and IPX filters. See "Managing Remote Access Policies and Profiles."

- You must have separate IP networks or subnets in each location. You can use separate public Class C addresses if you have enough clout to get them or you can subnet a private IP address space such as 192.168.0.0 or 10.0.0.0.

- You should have a suitable naming scheme for the demand-dial routers. This is important because each demand-dial router must have a user account in the SAM or Directory at the opposite side so it can dial in and get authenticated. *This is the most confusing part of creating mutual demand-dial interfaces*, so give the naming convention some thought. The demand-dial interface should be given a name that refers to its paired location.

  For example, the demand-dial interface in the retail outlet in Figure 17.37 is named HQ_rtr because it routes to company headquarters. There must be an account in the SAM of the demand-dial server at headquarters, or in its domain, with the name HQ_rtr and that account must have dial-in privileges. This is a change from NT4 RRAS.

Because interface names and account names are so critical to the functioning of mutual demand-dial routing, it's usually easiest to start by creating the user accounts for the demand-dial interfaces.

If you have standalone demand-dial servers, create the accounts in the local SAM using the Computer Management console. If the servers are members of a domain, or are domain controllers in their own right, create the accounts using the AD Users and Computers console. You can put the accounts in any OU, but be sure there are no group policies associated with the container that would prevent the accounts from using dial-up.

Avoid Using Domain Controller as Demand-Dial Routers

If you want to make sure that the demand-dial connection is only picked up when absolutely necessary, you should not use a domain controller as a demand-dial router. The services on a domain controller stay very busy, and they tend to keep the line up unnecessarily.

If the remote location has no domain controller, you should remove the demand-dial server from the domain and use a local SAM to configure the account for the other demand-dial router. This avoids a race condition where the demand-dial server must contact a domain controller to authenticate the other demand-dial server, but it can't access a domain controller until the demand-dial router connection is made.

The local computers and users in the remote network can be domain members. They will authenticate through the demand–dial connection. At each location, create an account that represents the demand–dial interface in the opposite location. RRAS uses the account name of the inbound demand–dial interface to select the correct local demand–dial interface to pair against it.

For example, the retail store in Figure 17.37 has a demand–dial interface that points at headquarters. This interface has the name HQ_rtr. The associated demand–dial interface at headquarters is named Store20_rtr because it points at the Store 20 demand–dial router.

- When HQ_rtr dials Headquarters, it uses a phone number that connects it with the modem or ISDN line of its associated demand–dial interface, Store20_rtr.

- After the physical layer connection is made, HQ_rtr makes a PPP connection using the account name Store20_rtr.

- The paired demand–dial server sees that the inbound account name matches the name of the demand–dial interface and pairs them together.

- At this point, traffic can flow freely back and forth between the two interfaces.

The opposite occurs when Headquarters calls Store 20, as follows:

- Store20_rtr at Headquarters calls its associated demand–dial interface at the store, HQ_rtr.

- After the physical connection is made, Store20_rtr makes a PPP connection using the account name HQ_rtr.

- The demand–dial server in the store sees that the account name matches the interface name and pairs them together.

Again, traffic flows freely back and forth. If this sounds too much like an Abbott and Costello routine, here is a summary:

- The demand–dial interface at the store is named HQ_rtr. It uses the account name Store20_rtr to log on to the remote router.

- The interface at Headquarters is named Store20_rtr. It uses the account name HQ_rtr to log on to the remote router.

- An account named Store20_rtr must exist in the domain at the main office.

- An account named HQ_rtr must exist in the demand–dial router's SAM at the store.

- The accounts must have dial–up privileges.

After you have your hardware, IP addresses, and naming scheme in place, you're ready to begin. Start with creating the user accounts for the demand-dial routers.

Create Demand-Dial User Accounts

It is easiest to create the demand-dial user accounts first. This enables you to test the interfaces as soon as you create them.

Procedure 17.21 **Creating a Demand-Dial User Account**

---

1. At the remote location—the retail store, in the example—open the Computer Management console at the demand-dial server or the AD Users and Computers console for a local domain controller, depending on the domain configuration.

2. Add an account with the same name as the demand-dial interface at the central location. In the example, that would be Store20_rtr.

   Give the account a complex password and select the Password Never Expires option. Make sure that you deselect User Must Change Password at Next Logon. Demand-dial interfaces do not have the necessary RPC functionality to manage their own passwords.

3. In the Properties window for the newly created account, select the Dial-in tab.

4. Give the account Allow Access permissions. Do this even if you have group policies that control dial-up. You do not want your routers to be affected by policy changes intended solely to manage users.

5. Save the changes you made to the account at the remote location.

6. At the central location, add an account with the same name as the demand-dial interface at the remote location. In the example, that would be HQ_rtr. Use the same account parameters as the account in the remote location.

Create Demand-Dial Interfaces

With the accounts in place, create the interfaces as follows:

Procedure 17.22 **Creating a Demand-Dial Interface**

---

1. At the remote office, open the Routing and Remote Access console. (You can start with the central office, if you prefer.)

2. Each communications device must be configured for demand-dial routing. Right-click the Ports icon, and select PROPERTIES from the fly-out menu. The Port Properties window opens.

3. Double-click a device that will be used for the demand-dial interface to open its `Configure Device` window.

4. Select the `Demand-Dial Routing Connections` option, and click `OK`.

5. Repeat for each device that will be used for demand-dial routing, and then close the `Ports Properties` window.

6. Right-click the Routing Interfaces icon, and select NEW DEMAND-DIAL INTERFACE from the fly-out menu. The Demand-Dial Interface Wizard starts.

7. Click `Next`. The `Interface Name` window opens. Enter a name that describes the destination of the router. (In the example, that would be `HQ_rtr`.)

8. Click `Next`. The `Connection Type` window opens. Select the `Connect Using a Modem, ISDN Adapter` unless you are using a VPN. If you select the VPN option, the wizard presents an additional window for `VPN Type` (set to `Automatic` by default) and the IP address or host name of the VPN server.

9. Click `Next`. If you have multiple circuit-switched devices, the Select A Device list appears. Select the device you want to associate with the demand-dial interface.

   If you want to use more than one interface and multilink them together, you must do that after creating the demand-dial interface.

   If the device you want to use does not appear on the list but it is listed under `Ports`, make sure that you configured it for demand-dial routing.

10. Click `Next`. The `Phone Number` window opens. Enter the phone number of the modem or ISDN line at the remote location. The `Alternate` option permits adding additional numbers to call if the first is busy, but this is not appropriate for mutual demand-dial routing.

Location of the Demand-Dial Router Phonebook

Demand-dial interfaces use a standard RAS phonebook named ROUTER.PBK to store connection information. This phonebook is located in `\WINNT\System32\RAS`.

The entries in ROUTER.PBK are not exposed as connections in the `Networking and Dial-up Connections` window. The Registry entry for the phonebook is HKLM | `Software` | `Microsoft` | `Router Phonebook`.

11. Click `Next`. The `Protocols and Security` window opens. Leave the `Route IP Packets on This Interface` selected. If you also need to route IPX traffic, select that option.

Do not use the Add a User Account option. This option is supposed to create a dial-in account for the other interface automatically, but you are much more likely to achieve a successful configuration if you create the account yourself. This ensures that it created in the correct location—the Directory or local SAM—and has the correct dial-in permissions.

12. Click Next. The Dial Out Credentials window opens. Enter the Name, Domain, and Password for the account that will make the dial-up connection. If this is a connection to an ISP, you should not need a domain. In the example network, the account name would be Store20_rtr.

13. Click Next. The final wizard window opens. Click Finish to add the interface and return to the Routing and Remote Access console.

14. Highlight the Routing Interfaces icon. The new demand-dial interface is listed in the right pane with a status of Enabled.

15. Right-click the demand-dial interface icon, and select Properties from the fly-out menu to open a Properties window. See the following sidebar for more information.

Demand-Dial Connection Properties

The Demand-Dial Properties window shows several options that determine how the interfaces connect to each other.

Use the Connection Type option to set an inactivity time for the interface or to make it a Persistent Connection if you do not want the line to hang up.

The Never option under Idle Time accomplishes the same thing as setting a Persistent Connection, but not as elegantly.

The default Redial Attempts is set to zero. This should be acceptable because the target device is, or should be, dedicated to the demand-dial interface. You may want to set the redial value to make a few attempts, just in case the modem doesn't react correctly the first time.

16. At the central location, perform the same actions to create a demand-dial interface. In the example, the interface name would be Store20_rtr and its account name would be HQ_rtr.

Test the Demand-Dial Connection

Before getting much further into the routing configuration, take a couple of minutes to test the connections to make sure that you get a good manual dial-up.

Procedure 17.23 **Testing a Demand–Dial Connection**

1. At one of the RRAS consoles, right-click demand–dial interface icon under `Routing Interfaces`, and select CONNECT from the fly-out menu. The associated modem goes off-hook and dials the interface at the other location. After the interfaces have finished negotiating a connection, the `Connection Status` goes to `Connected`.

2. At the other RRAS console, refresh the window and verify that the `Connection Status` shows `Connected`. If the status stays `Disconnected` but the other connection worked, make sure that you configured the account names correctly. RRAS will not associate a demand–dial interface to a connection unless the names match exactly. (They are not case sensitive.)

If the connection refuses to come up at all or gives an *Improper user name or password* error, make sure that the account names are correctly configured and have been created in the correct location.

You cannot use a SAM account, for example, if the demand–dial server is a domain member (that is, the server is not a domain controller) unless there is a domain controller in the remote location.

Also, if you have different domains, make sure that the credentials for the two demand–dial interfaces specify the correct domain. Check interface credentials at the RRAS console under Routing Interfaces by right-clicking the interface and selecting SET CREDENTIALS from the fly-out menu.

If everything looks right but the connection still refuses to work, try creating a standard dial–up connection under Network and Dial-Up Connections with the same credentials and target phone number. You cannot use this for demand–dial connections, but you'll be able to see whether the user account successfully connects.

If the connection refuses to work, you may have a problem with the authentication selections, although this should not be the case because you are connecting two Windows 2000 servers that are set to use MS-CHAP v2 by default. You can also set a PPP trace to see what happens during the connection phase. See "Monitoring Dial-Up Sessions Using Protocol Tracing" for details.

Configure Static Routes

Now that the "dial" part of the demand–dial connection is functioning, its time to configure the "demand" part. This is done by associating a static route with the demand–dial interface.

Procedure 17.24   **Configuring Static Routes**

1. From the RRAS console at the central location, expand the tree under the `Local Server` icon to show the `IP Routing | Static Routes`.

2. Right-click the `Static Routes` icon, and select CREATE A NEW STATIC ROUTE from the fly-out menu. The `Static Route` window opens (see Figure 17.38). See the following sidebar for more information.

Figure 17.38   `Static Route` window showing route from central location to remote office.

Setting Demand-Dial Routing Values

The `Static Route` window for a demand-dial interface has options that affect how the router reacts when clients send traffic to the interface.

Next to the `Interface` option, select the new demand-dial interface from the drop-down list.

Under `Destination` and `Network Mask`, enter the IP address and mask of the remote network. In the example, this is network 10.4.30.0 and mask 255.255.255.0.

If this RRAS router has multiple routes to the same destination, select a hop-count value under `Metric` that places this interface in correct relationship with the other interfaces.

If you have both an ISDN demand-dial interface and a modem demand-dial interface, for example, give the ISDN link a metric of 1 and the modem interface a metric of 2.

3. Select `Use This Route to Initiate Demand-Dial Connections`. This tells RRAS to pick up the circuit when traffic arrives for this network.

4. Click `OK` to save the changes, and return to the RRAS console.

5. At the remote location, use the same steps to configure a static route for that demand-dial interface, but use the network address and netmask of the central network. In the example, this is 10.4.29.0 with a mask of 255.255.255.0.

After the static routes are configured, test the demand dial function from one location by starting a continuous Ping to an address at the opposite location.

From the remote location, for example, run ping -t `10.4.30.3` (the IP address of a host in the other network) and wait for the lines to pick up. You should see a string of *Destination Host Unreachable* errors until the connection is made; then you should see a series of successful Pings.

Configuring a Demand-Dial Internet Router

Configuring a demand-dial connection to an ISP is much less complex than configuring mutual demand-dial connections between private networks because there are fewer steps involved. You can avoid a routed connection in favor of a NAT connection as described in the next section, but if a fully routed interface is what you want, then here. are the prerequisites for configuring a demand-dial Internet connection:

- A Windows 2000 server equipped with a modem or ISDN adapter. If you have multiple modems or bearer channels, you can use multilink to bundle them together after the interface has been created. Windows 2000 Professional does not support demand-dial routing.

- Routing must be enabled on the server. See "Initializing Routing Services."

- Assign the LAN interface on the demand-dial server a static address and do not assign a gateway. Configure the clients on the network to use the demand-dial server as their default gateway.

- You must have a valid PPP account at the ISP. The ISP must agree to let you connect to their network using a router. This generally involves an agreement to filter all unacceptable traffic. This includes NetBEUI, IPX, and any other transport protocols other than IP. You must also block broadcasts, although ISPs are good about doing that for you at their boundary routers.

- The ISP must also agree to add your network to the routing tables on their routers. This usually comes as part of the fee for the IP addresses. If you provide your own addresses, an extra fee is added. ISP's generally charge fees at the top of the market for this service because they know that without their routers, you cannot connect to the Internet. The routing fee often comes bundled with a service package that includes DNS and email. You may or may not want this package.

- Your network must use an IP subnet with sufficient public addresses to support all the IP devices, including devices that might never access the Internet. Most small and medium-sized ISPs will lease you a class C subnet for a fee, sometimes a hefty fee. Big service providers refuse to bother and insist that you use a private network and NAT.

Installing the Demand-Dial Interface

With the prerequisites in place, you're ready to install the demand-dial inter-face, configure it to route to the Internet, and configure automatic connec-tion pickup. Start with installing the interface. Proceed as follows:

Procedure 17.25   **Installing a Demand-Dial Interface**

1. Open the Routing and Remote Access console.

2. Each communications device must be configured for demand-dial routing. Right-click the Ports icon, and select PROPERTIES from the fly-out menu. The Port Properties window opens.

3. Double-click a device that will be used for the demand-dial interface to open its Configure Device window.

4. Select the Demand-Dial Routing Connections option, and click OK.

5. Repeat for each device that will be used for demand-dial routing, and then close the Ports Properties window.

6. At the RRAS console window, right-click the Routing Interfaces icon, and select NEW DEMAND-DIAL INTERFACE from the fly-out menu. The Demand Dial Interface Wizard starts.

7. Click Next. The Interface Name window opens. Enter a name that describes the destination of the router. For example, use a name like ISP_rtr.

8. Click Next. The Connection Type window opens. Select the Connect Using a Modem | ISDN Adapter unless you are using a VPN. If you select the VPN option, the wizard presents an additional window for VPN Type (set to Automatic by default) and the IP address or host name of the VPN server.

9. Click Next. If you have multiple circuit-switched devices, the Select A Device list appears. Select the device you want to associate with the demand-dial interface. If you want to use more than one device and multilink them together, you can do that after creating the demand-dial interface.

   If the device you want to use does not appear on the list but it does appear on the Port list, make sure that you configured it for demand-dial routing.

10. Click Next. The Phone Number window opens. Enter the phone number of the modem or ISDN line at the remote location. The Alternate option permits adding additional numbers to call if the first is busy.

11. Click `Next`. The `Protocols and Security` window opens. Leave the `Route IP Packets On This Interface` selected. If you normally need to use login scripts when connecting to the ISP, select the `Use Scripting…` option. The wizard presents you with a `Router Scripting` window to select a script.

12. Click `Next`. The `Dial-Out Credentials` window opens. Enter the `Name` and `Password` for the account that will make the dial-up connection. Because this is a connection to the Internet, you should not need a domain unless your ISP uses NT or Windows 2000 to perform authentications.

13. Click `Next`. The final wizard window opens. Click `Finish` to add the interface, and return to the `Routing and Remote Access` console.

Configuring the Demand-Dial Router

Now that the interface is in place, it must be configured to connect to the ISP's access server.

Procedure 17.26 **Configuring a Demand-Dial Router**

1. Highlight the `Routing Interfaces` icon. The new demand-dial interface is listed in the right pane with a status of `Enabled`.

2. Right-click the demand-dial icon, and select PROPERTIES from the fly-out menu to open a `Properties` window. At the General tab, under Connect Using, you can select additional modems or ISDN adapters if your ISP supports multilink.

3. Select the `Options` tab. Use the `Connection Type` option to set an inactivity time for the interface. You can choose to make this a `Persistent Connection`, but this generally violates the ISPs fair use agreement unless you have contracted for a full-time connection.

   The default value for `Redial Attempts` is set to zero. The value you set depends on how often you need to retry the ISP line during the busiest time of the day.

4. Select the `Networking` tab, and then open the `Properties` window for `Internet Protocol`.

   You must obtain a fixed IP address for the WAN interface from the ISP. This is the address that the ISP will put in their routing tables to get to your network. Some ISPs assign a fixed address automatically based your logon ID. In this case, you can leave the `Obtain An Address Automatically` radio button selected. See "DNS and Demand-Dial Routing" for information on configuring local DNS servers.

5. Click `OK` to save the changes, and return to the RRAS console.

Test the connection by right-clicking the demand-dial interface icon and selecting CONNECT from the fly-out menu. When the connection is made and the interface status changes to Connected, Ping a few Internet addresses and names to make sure that you have connectivity and proper DNS operation.

If the connection does not work, test using a standard dial-up connection. If that works, check the name and password you're using by right-clicking the demand-dial interface icon under Routing Interfaces and selecting CREDENTIALS from the fly-out menu.

Configuring Automatic Connection Pickup

Now that the ISP connection is made, you must add a routing table entry so that traffic from clients in the local LAN is routed to the Internet interface. It is impossible to define a routing table that contains all the different IP addresses on the Internet, so the alternative is to configure a gateway that routes all non-local traffic to the demand-dial interface.

The default gateway is defined by a single routing table entry consisting of zeros for network destination and subnet mask. Default gateways are configured automatically for dial-up clients, but you must enter the route manually for demand-dial interfaces. Proceed as follows:

Procedure 17.27 **Configuring Automatic Connection Pickup**

1. You should have already removed the default gateway from the LAN interface as part of the prerequisites. Before configuring a default gateway, verify that one does not already exist. Run route print from the command line. There should be no 0.0.0.0 entries, meaning that there is no default gateway for the router. Here is an example routing table before adding a gateway entry:

```
C:\>route print
===========================================================================
Interface List
0x1 ........................ MS TCP Loopback interface
0xe000004 ...00 53 45 00 00 00 ...... WAN (PPP/SLIP) Interface
0x11000002 ...00 c0 4f 53 6a f2 ......3Com 3C918
===========================================================================
===========================================================================
Active Routes:
Network Destination        Netmask          Gateway       Interface  Metric
        10.1.0.0        255.255.0.0        10.1.1.1        10.1.1.1       1
        10.1.1.1  255.255.255.255        127.0.0.1       127.0.0.1       1
  10.255.255.255  255.255.255.255        10.1.1.1        10.1.1.1       1
```

```
        127.0.0.0        255.0.0.0      127.0.0.1      127.0.0.1      1
        127.0.0.1  255.255.255.255      127.0.0.1      127.0.0.1      1
    206.132.49.94  255.255.255.255      127.0.0.1      127.0.0.1      1
   206.132.49.255  255.255.255.255  206.132.49.94  206.132.49.94      1
        224.0.0.0        240.0.0.0       10.1.1.1       10.1.1.1      1
        224.0.0.0        240.0.0.0  206.132.49.94  206.132.49.94      1
  255.255.255.255  255.255.255.255       10.1.1.1       10.1.1.1      1
  255.255.255.255  255.255.255.255  206.132.49.94  206.132.49.94      1
===========================================================================
Persistent Routes:
  None
```

Addresses with host octets of 255 represent subnet broadcasts. 255.255.255.255 addresses represent general broadcasts. 224.0.0.0 addresses represent multicasts.

2. From the RRAS console, expand the tree under the Local Server icon to show the IP Routing icon.

3. Right-click Static Routes, and select CREATE A NEW STATIC ROUTE from the fly-out menu. The Static Route window opens (see Figure 17.39).

Figure 17.39 Static Route window showing default gateway route.

4. Under Interface, select the new ISP demand-dial interface you just created.

5. Under Destination and Network Mask, enter all zeros (0). This designates the demand-dial interface as the default gateway for the router. The Gateway entry itself is dimmed because demand-dial connections have no gateways.

6. Leave Metric set for one.

7. Verify that Use This Route to Initiate Demand-Dial Connections is selected. This tells RRAS to pick up the demand-dial circuit when any traffic arrives that is not bound for an address on the local subnet.

8. Click OK to save the changes, and return to the RRAS console. The new static route appears in the right pane.

Now test the connection. From a client that is configured to use the demand-dial router as a gateway, Ping the WAN interface on the server. When that Ping succeeds, start a continuous Ping to an Internet address, such as `ping -t 192.80.3.105`. Wait for the demand-dial connection to the ISP to pick up.

At that point, the Ping succeeds. If either Ping fails, use TRACERT to see where the connection is failing. If you get an ICMP echo from the demand-dial router but not from the Internet, check that you correctly configured the routing table at the ISP router. Make sure to keep that connection up while you troubleshoot.

Unless you select the `Persistent Connection` option, the demand-dial connection will eventually time out and disconnect. If you are using a modem, you will need to educate your users to wait for a few seconds after they fire off their browsers while the modem picks up. For ISDN links, you have the opposite problem. You do not want the ISDN line to stay hot continuously. Ask anyone who has gotten a $2000 phone bill the month after installing a spanking new ISDN line. Stay aware of the traffic patterns at the demand-dial router until you're sure that you won't get any surprises.

One note of caution: In this demand-dial router configuration, your network is bare to the Internet. This is not generally considered a safe thing to do, although many businesses are content to take their chances. Hackers are few compared to the number of Internet connections, and it's easy to get complacent. Still, it's good to remember that a 10-year-old with glowing, midnight eyes can do a lot of damage to your network. Rather than wait to get burned, you may want to install firewall software and take other security measures. At the very least, you can keep out the casual hacks.

Connecting to the Internet Using NAT

Have you ever been to a contest of Elvis impersonators? It's a sight to behold. Imagine hundreds and hundreds of dudes decked out strutting, and singing more or less like the King. Eventually these Elvises become nearly anonymous because everyone around them looks, struts, and sings the same way. This is the philosophy behind network address translation. NAT gives every packet leaving your network the same IP address. This enables you to configure your network clients with private IP addresses and maintain their anonymity while they browse the Internet.

NAT in Windows 2000 comes in two flavors. One is suitable for networks with full-time administrators who understand their systems and how they interconnect. The other is one suitable for small office/home office (SOHO) networks that are managed by the business owner, office manager, or a visiting consultant. Think of these as "manual" and "automated" forms of NAT deployment.

The manual method involves installing the NAT protocol in conjunction with a demand–dial connection using the `Routing` and `Remote Access` console. This method requires an administrator because the NAT router must integrate into the existing IP deployment and interoperate with other routers as well as integrate into the existing DNS and DHCP structure. The manual NAT method requires the RRAS console and is only available on Windows 2000 server.

The automatic method uses a new service called *Internet Connection Sharing* (ICS). The ICS suite of services automates the entire demand–dial Internet connection setup, including configuring NAT, distributing private addresses using DHCP, and arranging for DNS resolution using a proxy service to the DNS server at the ISP. ICS is suitable only for small offices that do not use a domain and do not have existing DHCP or DNS services. ICS is available on both Windows 2000 Server and Professional as well as Windows 98 SE.

The two methods, manual NAT deployment and automated ICS deployment, are quite distinct in terms of function and target users. Confusion arises because the documentation uses the term "connection sharing" to describe both deployment methods. In this book, I use the term "connection sharing" only when referring to ICS. Otherwise, I stick with the term "NAT deployment" to mean a manual NAT setup requiring intervention by an administrator.

NAT Features Implemented Only in ICS

A few features are implemented only in ICS. These features may be included in the standard NAT feature set during a maintenance release:

- **H.323 Proxy.** Permits making and receiving NetMeeting calls.

- **LDAP Proxy.** Permits registering with ILS for NetMeeting.

- **Directplay Proxy.** Play Directplay games from behind the NAT router.

The next section contains an overview of the NAT protocol. It is followed by the procedure for NAT deployment, and then one for ICS deployment.

Functional Description of the NAT Protocol

Refer to the diagram in Figure 17.40. This shows a network with several clients that access the Internet through a Windows 2000 router. With standard routing to the Internet, each of these clients would need a public IP address. This public address represents a security problem, because it announces the presence of the client out on the Internet, and an administrative burden because the supply of available IP addresses is dwindling and IPv6 is still years away from widespread deployment.

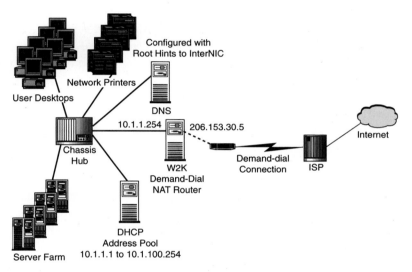

Figure 17.40 Diagram of simple NAT installation showing demand-dial router to ISP and clients in private address space.

This problem of limited IP network addresses was foreseen back in the mid–1990s and work began then on an expanded version of the IP network address scheme. At the same time, a partial solution was suggested in RFC 1597, "Address Allocation for Private Internets," and RFC 1631, "Network Address Translation (NAT)." In these RFCs, certain address ranges were set aside for private use and barred from routing over the Internet. At the same time, a method was put in place to translate the private addresses into public addresses so that users could access the Internet through the translating device. RFC 1597 set aside the following address ranges spaces for private use:

Class A — 10.0.0.0 to 10.255.255.255

Class B — 172.16.0.0 to 172.31.255.255

Class C — 192.168.0.0 to 192.168.255.255

Internet boundary routers and internal routers are configured to block traffic from these private network addresses. Private networks use NAT to substitute a public address for private addresses.

IP Address and Port Mapping

NAT has two ways of handling outbound translations. If it has only one public IP address available, it puts that address in the IP header of the packet and then maps the source TCP or UDP port to a random port number.

When a client on the private side of the NAT router makes an HTTP connection to an external Web site, for example, it sends the traffic to TCP port 80 and picks a random TCP port locally to listen for a reply.

The NAT router substitutes its own IP address into the source address field of the packet then selects another TCP port at random and substitutes that port number for the client's port.

NAT then creates an entry in a mapping table that says, "Send inbound traffic bound for TCP port `<substitute NAT port>` to host `<client's IP address>` at TCP port `<client's source port>`."

If the NAT router has been configured with more than one public IP address, it does not bother with port translations. It performs a one-to-one matching between a private address and a public address until all but one public address has been exhausted. At that point, NAT falls back on port translation. Figure 17.41 shows an example translation table from a Windows 2000 NAT router.

Protocol	Direction	Private address	Private port	Public Address	Public Port	Remote Address	Remote Port
UDP	Outbound	10.1.30.1	137	206.132.49.211	1,025	207.31.71.34	137
UDP	Outbound	10.2.2.1	137	206.132.49.211	1,025	10.2.2.63	137
UDP	Outbound	10.2.2.1	137	206.132.49.211	1,026	207.31.71.34	137
UDP	Outbound	10.1.30.1	1,451	206.132.49.211	1,451	206.165.5.10	53
TCP	Outbound	10.1.1.1	3,004	206.132.49.211	1,025	192.168.0.80	139
TCP	Outbound	10.1.1.1	3,009	206.132.49.211	1,025	10.3.10.2	139
TCP	Outbound	10.1.1.1	3,031	206.132.49.211	1,026	192.168.0.80	139
TCP	Outbound	10.1.1.1	3,099	206.132.49.211	1,027	192.168.0.80	139
TCP	Outbound	10.1.1.1	3,137	206.132.49.211	1,028	192.168.0.80	139
TCP	Outbound	10.1.1.1	3,163	206.132.49.211	1,029	192.168.0.80	139
TCP	Outbound	10.1.30.1	1,450	206.132.49.211	1,450	207.46.133.140	21
TCP	Outbound	10.1.30.1	1,452	206.132.49.211	1,452	206.165.6.209	23
TCP	Outbound	10.1.1.1	3,258	206.132.49.211	1,030	192.168.0.80	139

Figure 17.41 NAT Mapping table showing several connections using HTTP, FTP, and Telnet.

Inbound NAT Routing

Bringing inbound traffic backward through the NAT router is like taking a guest to a State Department dinner. Admittance is strictly by invitation only.

Under normal circumstances, the only inbound traffic the NAT router will acknowledge are responses sent from hosts that received packets from clients inside the NAT router. All other traffic is discarded. This is termed *dynamic* translation.

There may be occasions when you want to allow inbound access through NAT to a particular host. For example, you may have an FTP server or a Web site that you want to maintain inside the NAT boundary but give outside access to. In this case, you can configure a *static* translation by associating a TCP or UDP port on the NAT router with a particular host in the private address space. In this way, traffic sent to `<NAT IP address>` `<static Port #>` is routed to `<host IP address>` at the same port number.

Registry Tip: ICS Control Parameters

Windows 2000 implements NAT as a kernel-side protocol driver, IPNAT.SYS, and a user-side service driver, IPNATHLP.DLL. ICS is implemented as one of the SVCHOST suite of services.

ICS control parameters are stored in the Registry under HKLM | System | CurrentControlSet | Services | SharedAccess.

NAT Editors

In addition to just translating IP header addresses, NAT may need to peer inside the TCP or UDP packet itself to find source IP addresses put there by an application.

When you Ping a host, for example, the ICMP packet contains the IP addresses of the source and destination hosts. The same is true for the FTP Port command and other applications. In addition, there are instances when source addressing is used outside of the TCP or UDP payload. This occurs in PPTP, where the GRE protocol handles IP communication with the TCP and UDP datagrams and their port number tunneled inside the packet. (The embedded IP addresses in L2TP over IPSec are encrypted, making them impervious to NAT translation.)

Windows 2000 NAT uses information stored in special *NAT Editors* to determine the location of IP address information in an application packet. Each application requires its own NAT Editor. Windows 2000 has NAT Editors for FTP, ICMP, and PPTP. NAT. Editors are not included for SNMP, LDAP, Microsoft COM, and RPC.

Here are the key points to remember about NAT before starting to deploy it in your network:

- NAT requires a separate IP network for the local LAN that either uses a private IP address space (preferred) or public addresses that are unique in your organization.

- NAT maintains a volatile mapping of TCP/UDP ports and private IP addresses. If you down the server, this map is lost and clients must reconnect.

- NAT can use multiple public IP addresses. It uses these addresses in a one-to-one mapping until there are no more available, and then it falls back on port mapping.

- If an application inserts IP addresses into the payload of a TCP or UDP packet, or puts IP address information into another protocol, a special NAT Editor must be used to translate the addresses properly.

- Windows 2000 NAT requires a demand-dial connection between the local network and the Internet (or other target network.)

- Network clients must be configured to use the NAT router as a gateway. This is most easily done using DHCP, but you can manually configure clients if you prefer.

The next two sections cover manually configuring a NAT router and using automatic configuration with ICS.

Manually Configuring a Demand-Dial NAT Router

Setting up NAT on a demand-dial interface to the Internet is much simpler than configuring a standard routed demand-dial connection. Using NAT, there is no need to get additional services from your ISP. You simply set up the demand-dial connection, load the NAT protocol, associate NAT with the local and Internet interfaces, and sit back to watch the traffic flow.

There is additional work you have to do at the clients, however, and it may not be trivial depending on the extent of your network. You need to deploy a private IP address space throughout the local subnet and make provisions for handling DNS root searches because the InterNIC root servers cannot communicate with a local DNS server in a private address space.

Here are the other prerequisites for configuring a demand-dial NAT router:

- A Windows 2000 server equipped with at least one network interface adapter and a modem or ISDN device. You cannot configure NAT using two IP addresses bound to the same interface. Do not use a Windows 2000 domain controller as a NAT router. You can get erratic results, especially with DNS and LDAP.

- RRAS must be configured to support routing. See "Initializing Routing Services."

- Each communications device must be configured for demand-dial routing. This is done from the RRAS console by opening the Port Properties window, double-clicking the device to open the Configure Device window, and then selecting the Demand-Dial Routing Connections option.

- You must have a PPP account at an ISP. You may need the ISP's agreement to let you connect a NAT router to their network. Some ISPs have fair use policies barring this practice. NAT routing does a good job of blocking improper traffic, so that isn't the issue. You aren't paying for those additional connections. After you come to a monetary agreement, just about any ISP will let you set up a NAT router.

With these prerequisites in place, you're ready to configure and test the demand-dial interface, configure the NAT protocol, and test Internet access through NAT.

Configuring the Demand-Dial Interface

These steps are nearly identical to the steps for configuring a routed demand-dial interface. Proceed as follows:

Procedure 17.28   Configuring a Demand-Dial Interface to an ISP

---

1. Right-click the Routing Interfaces icon, and select NEW DEMAND-DIAL INTERFACE from the fly-out menu. The Demand Dial Interface Wizard starts.

2. Click Next. The Interface Name window opens. Enter a name that describes the destination of the NAT router. For example, use a name such as ISP_NAT_rtr.

3. Click Next. The Connection Type window opens. Select the Connect Using a Modem, ISDN Adapter… unless you are using a VPN. If you select the VPN option, the wizard presents an additional window for VPN Type (set to Automatic by default) and the IP address or host name of the VPN server.

4. Click Next. If you have multiple circuit-switched devices, the Select A Device list appears. If not, skip this step. Select the device you want to associate with the demand-dial interface. If you want to use more than one interface and multilink them together, you can do that after creating the demand-dial interface.

   If the device you want to use does not appear on the list but it appears on the Port list, make sure that you configured it for demand-dial routing.

5. Click Next. The Phone Number window opens. Enter the phone number of the modem or ISDN line at the remote location. The Alternate option permits adding additional numbers to call if the first is busy.

6. Click Next. The Protocols and Security window opens. Leave the Route IP Packets On This Interface selected. If you normally need to use login scripts when connecting to the ISP, select the Use Scripting… option. The wizard will present you with a Router Scripting window to select a script.

7. Click Next. The Dial-Out Credentials window opens. Enter the Name and Password for the account that will make the dial-up connection. Because this is a connection to the Internet, you should not need a domain unless your ISP uses NT or Windows 2000 to perform authentications.

8. Click Next. The final wizard window opens. Click Finish to add the interface and return to the Routing and Remote Access console.

9. Highlight the Routing Interfaces icon. The new demand-dial interface is listed in the right pane with a status of Enabled.

10. Right-click the demand-dial interface icon, and select PROPERTIES from the fly-out menu to open a properties window. At the General tab, under Connect Using, you can select additional modems or ISDN adapters if your ISP supports multilink.

11. Select the Options tab. Use the Connection Type option to set an inactivity time for the interface. You can choose to make this a Persistent Connection, but this generally violates the ISPs fair use agreement unless you have contracted for a full-time connection.

    The default Redial Attempts is set to zero. The value you set depends on how often you need to retry during the busiest time of the day.

12. Select the Networking tab, and then open the Properties window for Internet Protocol.

You do not necessarily need a fixed IP address at the WAN interface to make a NAT connection work; if you are going to configure static NAT ports for inbound routing, however, you will need a static public address from the ISP. Some ISPs assign a fixed address automatically based on a logon ID. In this case, you can leave the `Obtain an Address Automatically` radio button selected. See "DNS and Demand-Dial Routing" for recommendations on configuring DNS.

13. Click `OK` to save the changes, and return to the RRAS console.

Test the connection by right-clicking the demand-dial interface icon and selecting CONNECT from the fly-out menu. When the connection is made and the interface status changes to `Connected`, Ping a few Internet addresses and names to make sure that you have connectivity and proper DNS operation.

If the connection does not work, test using a standard dial-up connection. If that works, check the name and password you're using by right-clicking the demand-dial interface icon and selecting CREDENTIALS from the fly-out menu.

Configuring the NAT Protocol

After you have verified that the connection works, load the NAT protocol and configure the LAN and WAN interfaces to use it as follows:

Procedure 17.29   **Configuring NAT**

1. Open the `Routing and Remote Access` console.

2. Expand the tree under the `Local Server` icon to show the General icon.

3. Right-click the General icon, and select NEW ROUTING PROTOCOL from the fly-out menu. The `New Routing Protocol` window opens.

4. Select the `Connection Sharing (NAT)` protocol, click `OK` to save the change, and return to the `RRAS` console.

5. Highlight the `IP Protocol` icon. The NAT icon is listed in the right pane.

6. Now load interfaces into the NAT protocol. Under `IP Routing`, right-click the NAT icon, and select NEW INTERFACE from the fly-out menu. The `New Interface For Connection Sharing (NAT)` window opens (see Figure 17.42).

Figure 17.42 New Interface For Connection Sharing (NAT) window showing two available interfaces, the demand-dial interface and the Local Area Connection interface representing the network adapter.

7. Select the demand-dial interface you just created, and click OK. The Network Address Translation Properties window for the interface opens (see Figure 17.43). The default selections of Public Interface and Translate TCP/UDP Headers ensures that clients can send data through the NAT interface to the Internet and receive responses in return. Use the Address Pool tab if you have a pool of public addresses that you want to use for translation.

Figure 17.43 Properties window for NAT direct-dial interface.

8. Close all windows.

Proceed to the next section to set up static ports to represent inbound clients.

Configuring Static Inbound Ports

At this point, you can configure static ports to represent hosts in the private network. For example, you can configure a port to route incoming traffic to a Web server that would not otherwise be visible from the public network.

If you choose not to configure a static port at this time, you can skip this section and return later. If you are returning to this section, open an RRAS console, expand the tree to `Local Server | IP Routing | Network Address Translation`, and open the `Properties` window for the WAN interface icon.

Procedure 17.30 **Configuring Static Inbound NAT Ports**

1. Select the `Special Ports` tab. Use this tab to statically map a TCP or UDP port to a host on the private network. Inbound clients can address traffic to the IP address of the NAT router and this port number to get access to the internal host.

2. Click `Add`. The `Add Special Port` window opens. Figure 17.44 shows an example. See the following sidebar for more information.

Figure 17.44 `Add Special Port` window showing example settings for an internal Web server.

Selecting an Inbound NAT Port

The Add Special Port window pictured in Figure 17.44 has several options that affect how inbound traffic is routed through a NAT router. Configure the options as follows:

- **Incoming Port.** Enter the port number that public clients will use when sending traffic to the NAT router. If you do not use a well-known port number, the DNS entry for the internal host must include the non-standard port ID.

- **Private Address.** Enter the IP address of the internal host that is the target of the outside clients.

- **Outgoing Port.** Enter the port number on the internal host. In the example, the host is a Web server, so the outgoing port would be port 80, unless the Web server has been configured for a non-standard port.

3. Click OK to save the changes, and return to the Properties window. The static mapping is added to the list.

4. Click OK to close the window.

5. Right-click the Network Address Translation icon once again, and select NEW INTERFACE from the fly-out menu. The New Interface For Connection Sharing (NAT) window opens.

6. This time select the Local Area Connection interface, and click OK. The Network Address Translation Properties window for the local interface opens. In this case, the Private Interface Connected to Private Network radio button is selected.

7. Click OK to close the window.

Test the connection from a client on the same subnet as the NAT router that has been configured to use the router as a gateway. Open a command prompt and Ping an Internet address. If the NAT router interface is not a persistent connection, use ping -t to keep retrying until the connection is made. The Ping succeeds as soon as the connection is made.

At this point, the demand-dial interface is configured to pick up the Internet connection whenever a client on the local subnet has traffic destined outside the local network. If you have additional routers for other locations on your private network, and you want those clients to access the Internet through this NAT connection, you must configure the other routers to use the NAT router as a gateway of last resort.

You must also configure static routes for the private routers at the demand-dial server or load and configure RIP or OSPF to integrate the router with the rest of your router infrastructure.

Configuring ICS

The preceding section covered manual NAT deployment on a network managed by administrators who understand how their systems are put together and how to integrate the NAT routing services with those systems.

At the other end of the spectrum is the small business owner who has one or two Windows 2000 servers—or maybe just a handful of Windows 2000 Professional desktops—and needs to share a connection to the Internet.

SOHO businesses are always on the lookout for ways to leverage their computer investment, and they tend to be frugal. They also tend to be strapped for time and impatient with anything that requires too much technical intervention. To meet the needs of this market, Microsoft packaged the core services of NAT, DNS, and DHCP into a single service called ICS.

Here is what happens automatically when ICS is installed:

- The IP address of the LAN interface on the ICS computer is automatically changed to 192.168.0.1, a private address. This is always done and cannot be changed, bypassed, or overridden. If the network already has a different private address, it will have to be changed.

- The WAN interface is converted to a demand-dial router targeted at the ISP.

- A small AUTODHCP service is initialized and prepped to pass out addresses in the 192.168.0.0 network. This service is controlled by the IPNATHLPR.DLL. It is not a full-blown installation of DHCP.

- A small DNS proxy service is installed, also controlled by IPNATHLPR.DLL. This proxy passes client DNS queries to the DNS server that the ICS gets in its BOOTP/DHCP configuration packet from the ISP.

As you can see, this set of automatic operations is not at all suitable for a network with existing IP services. The AUTODHCP service can be especially painful because it will pass out addresses to DHCP clients on your network. One of the first group policies you should consider imposing in your Windows 2000 domain is disabling the ICS service on all clients.

Refer to Figure 17.45. The diagram shows a small professional services agency with five employees. A consultant installed a Windows 2000 network for this business and set up network file and print services on one of the Windows 2000 Professional desktops that doubles as a workstation.

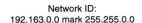

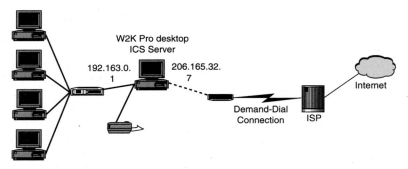

Figure 17.45   Diagram of Internet Connection Sharing for SOHO office.

Each user has a modem and a phone line to the outside that they use to connect to their ISP. The owner has tired of paying for these modem lines and has decided to bring back the consultant for a half day to configure a shared Internet connection.

Here are the prerequisites the consultant needs to meet for deploying ICS using a Windows 2000 Professional desktop:

- The business must have a PPP account with an ISP. The ISP should have a fair use agreement that permits making a NAT connection or one should be negotiated.

- The Windows 2000 Pro desktop must have at least one network adapter and at least one circuit-switched device, either a modem or an ISDN adapter. In place of the circuit-switched device, it could have a second network adapter connected to a broadband or xDSL interface device.

- If the desktop uses a circuit-switched device, it must be configured as a dial-up client to an ISP. The interface must be configured to accept an IP address and IP configuration information from the ISP. There is no need for a static address.

- When the consultant installed the network, she left the TCP/IP settings in their default configuration, which is to use DHCP if a server is available or to fall back on a random address in the 169.254.0.0 address space if DHCP is unavailable. This is acceptable on a small network with no router. The only computer with a fixed network address is the workstation that is doubling as a file and print server. It, too, has an address in the 169.254.0.0 network.

With these prerequisites in place, the consultant is ready to configure ICS. There are two major stages: setting up the ICS service itself, and then configuring it to accept inbound traffic if that is required.

Initial ICS Setup

After verifying that the modem works satisfactorily when connected to the ISP, the consultant proceeds as follows to set up ICS:

Procedure 17.31   **Performing an Initial ICS Setup**

1. At the Windows 2000 Pro desktop with the modem or ISDN adapter installed, open the `Network and Dial-up Connections` window.

2. Verify that users have closed any files that they may have open on the dial-up computer. This is necessary because next few steps result in a change of IP address on the dial-up server.

3. Right-click the dial-up connection icon in Network and Dial-up Connections window—if you have a network adapter connected to a broadband/xDSL device, right-click the icon that represents that connection—and select PROPERTIES from the fly-out menu. The `Properties` window opens for the connection.

4. Select the `Internet Connection Sharing` tab.

   Under `Shared Access`, select `Enable Internet Connection Sharing For This Connection`. When you do so, the `Enable On-Demand Dialing` option becomes available. Make sure that it is selected also.

5. Click `OK` to save the changes. The system presents a warning that the IP address of the local area connection will be changed to 192.168.0.1 and that this may cause loss of connection to the local network. Click `Yes` to acknowledge the warning, and proceed with the ICS installation. The loss of network connection is temporary until the clients acquire a new network address using DHCP.

6. It takes only a few seconds for the updates to take effect. Use IPCONFIG to verify that the IP address of the LAN interface has changed to 192.168.0.1.

7. At each DHCP client, renew the DHCP lease to get the new IP address and configuration information. You can do this in one of two ways.

   At Windows 2000 and NT4 computers, open a command session and enter `ipconfig /renew`.

At Windows 9x computers, open the WINIPCFG utility from the Run command, and click the Renew All button.

In either case, the client obtains a new address from the ICS server. Verify using IPCONFIG or WINIPCFG that the address is in the 192.168.0.0 network and the gateway is 192.168.0.1, which is the address of the ICS server.

8. At a client, Ping an IP address or host name on the Internet. The ICS interface picks up automatically, dials, and makes connection. If you are using a broadband or xDSL interface, the connection is already made. If you are using a modem, it will take a few seconds to get the connection. Run ping -t until the connection succeeds.

If you are using an ISDN line, keep an eye on usage for a while. The DNS proxy should not keep the line hot, but you never know what might happen. Use the Network Monitor to check for traffic if the line does not go down.

Inbound Connection Sharing

You can configure a static inbound connection through ICS to permit access to servers in the private network. For example, you may have a Web server inside the private network that you want customers or the public to see. They can't point a browser at it because it has a private address.

By statically mapping a port number and host address at the shared connection, you can publish the IP address of the computer hosting the shared connection in DNS and the incoming traffic will be routed to the address of the server in the private network. Configure this as follows:

Procedure 17.32   **Configuring Inbound Connection Sharing**

1. Open the Properties window for the shared connection, and select the Internet Connection Sharing tab.

2. Click Settings. The Internet Connection Sharing Settings window opens. This window permits you to define a port to access a service or application inbound through the shared connection.

3. Select the Service tab.

4. Click Add to open the Shared Access Service window (see Figure 17.46).

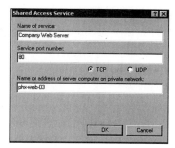

Figure 17.46 Shared Access Service window showing example settings for statically mapping a port to an internal Web server.

5. Give the service a friendly name, and enter the information for the static port and host name or IP address. The example shows settings for a company Web server named PHX-WEB-03 that can be contacted using TCP port 80.

6. Click OK to save the static map. It is listed under Services with a check block that you can de-select if you want to block access to the host.

7. Click OK to close the window. From a client in the public address space, point a browser at the IP address of the NAT router. The NAT router sends the traffic to the designated port on the designated server. Because this is TCP port 80, the HTTP services port, the client gets the home page of the Web server.

DNS and Demand-Dial Routing

If your clients are configured to use an internal DNS server to resolve addresses on your private network and you configure a demand-dial router to connect to the Internet, you must configure your DNS server to pass queries to an InterNIC root server either directly or through NAT. Do this as follows:

Procedure 17.33 **Configuring DNS to Support NAT**

1. First, do a quick check to see whether the DNS server has already been configured to use InterNIC root servers. Open the DNS Management console using START | PROGRAMS | ADMINISTRATIVE TOOLS | DNS. The DNS Management console opens.

If there is a dotted zone (the folder name is .) at the top of the zone list, the server has been configured as a root server and will not pass queries to InterNIC root servers. Figure 17.47 shows an example.

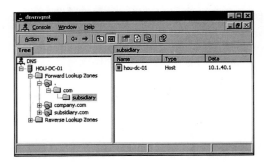

Figure 17.47 DNS Management console showing a root zone.

2. Right–click the server icon, and open the Properties window.

3. Select the Root Hints tab. The window is dimmed with nothing on the Root Server list. For a server to function as an Internet DNS server, it cannot be a root server. To make the Root Hints window available, you must delete the root zone.

4. Close the Properties window.

5. In the zone tree on the right pane of the DNS console window, highlight the root zone, and delete it using the Delete key or by right-clicking and selecting DELETE from the fly-out menu.

6. Right-click the DNS server icon again, and open the Properties window.

7. Select the Root Hints tab. This time the window shows the thirteen InterNIC root servers. Figure 17.48 shows an example. This list of root servers comes from the CACHE.DNS file in \WINNT\System32\DNS. If the list does not appear, try reinstalling DNS or copy the CACHE.DNS file from another Windows 2000 or NT4 DNS server. Start and restart the service to load the root hints.

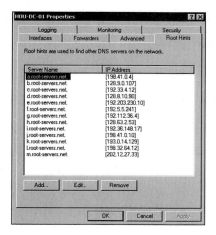

Figure 17.48 Properties window of DNS server showing root servers from CACHE.DNS.

With the root hints in place, Ping an Internet host from a network client that is configured to use the demand-dial router as a gateway. The name resolves to an IP address and the Ping succeeds.

If this does not work, try stopping and restarting the RRAS service. If name resolution still does not work, make sure that you can Ping the root servers from the demand-dial router. At the DNS server, verify that you are not using forwarders. It is not necessary to use forwarding to resolve Internet host names. If nothing seems to work, refer to Chapter 5, "Managing Domain Name System (DNS) Services and Dynamic Host Configuration (DHCP) Services," for DNS troubleshooting hints.

Configuring VPN Connections

In the novel *Dune*, Frank Herbert paints a future where all electronic communications are highly suspect, computers have been banned outright, and technologists were long ago slaughtered in a series of bloody jihads. (I'm not sure about the time frame for *Dune*, but you may want to consider a career change in the next a few years.)

The characters in *Dune* were able to maintain secrecy in their long-distance communications without computers or telephones by implanting special devices—I suppose they were non-technical devices—in the brains of animals and humans that would imprint encrypted material into the brain of the carrier.

Once loaded, the carriers were free to wander about the galaxy. No one could possibly know that deep secrets lurked in their altered brains. When the carriers arrived at their final destination, the device would be tapped and disgorge its contents using the vocal chords and mouth of the carrier, the science-fiction equivalent of a doctoral dissertation.

Secure Internet communications works the same way. Messages are encrypted and then encapsulated into otherwise innocuous transport packets for transmittal. When these packets arrive at their destination, the encapsulation is stripped away, and the data inside is decrypted. The process of encapsulating one protocol as the payload of a different protocol is called *tunneling*. When two hosts use a tunnel to communicate, they form a VPN.

A Windows 2000 VPN consists of three parts:

- A point-to-point connection between a dial-up client and an ISP.

- A point-to-point connection between a demand-dial router and an ISP.

- A method for tunneling (encapsulating and encrypting) traffic between the client and the router.

The data sent through a VPN tunnel must be encrypted, or else why bother. Encryption occurs automatically when a VPN session is established. Any encryption method is permitted. The decision of which to use is a compromise between speed and safety. NT4 uses RC4 streaming cipher encryption, which uses the same MD4 algorithm used by MS-CHAP.

Windows 2000 also supports RC4 and adds Extensible Authentication Protocol-Transport Level Security (EAP-TLS) to support certificates. In both cases, a 128-bit encryption key is used in North America and a 40-bit key overseas. Windows 2000 employs two tunneling protocols: *Point-to-Point Tunneling Protocol* (PPTP) and *Level 2 Tunneling Protocol* (L2TP).

- **PPTP.** This protocol encapsulates the encrypted messages into a standard PPP frame using a special protocol called *Generic Routing Encapsulation* (GRE). The GRE packet transmitted across the Internet using IP. PPTP requires two data streams: a *control channel* negotiated over TCP port 1723 for setting up and tearing down the VPN connection and a *tunnel channel* negotiated over IP using protocol 47, which is the GRE protocol, for actually transmitting the encrypted data.

- **L2TP over IPSec.** This protocol extracts the HDLC portion of the PPP frame, the portion that includes the encrypted message, and puts it directly into the data portion of a standard UDP datagram. The datagram is transmitted over IP to a well-known UDP port, port 1701, at the receiving end of the tunnel. When the packet is received, the UDP portion of the datagram is stripped away, and the encrypted message is extracted from the HDLC frame, decrypted, and routed to the target host. L2TP requires only one channel, which makes it attractive to service providers who want to multiplex VPNs. Control information is transmitted using special L2TP packets within the channel.

These tunneling protocols are a standard component of RRAS, and so there is no need to install any special protocols. A demand-dial router has PPTP and L2TP interfaces pre-built so that they are available immediately once the demand-dial router has connected to the Internet. The only required configuration is to set up a dial-up client to first make a PPP connection to the Internet and then establish a VPN connection over that pipe to the demand-dial server that you want to host the VPN connection. Users in fixed locations such as branch offices can tunnel through the office routers so that the only pipe leaving the office is an Internet connection. This eliminates the need for a private Frame Relay or ATM network.

Commercial VPN Service

VPN services are also available from ISPs and Network service providers (NSPs). The advantage of using a service provider is transparency and performance. Dial-up clients make standard PPP connections to the service provider, and the provider handles the VPN. The tunneling protocols and encryption methods used by the provider are transparent to the subscribers.

The service contract spells out the requirements for bandwidth, throughput, and latency. The disadvantage of using a service provider is that the provider must be informed about changes to the subscriber's user base. If user Fherbert is added to the subscriber's network, for example, the service provider must be informed so that they can modify their user list to recognize a dial-up session initiated by user Fherbert and build the proper VPN tunnel after authenticating him.

This book covers configuring a PPTP connection over the Internet between a Windows 2000 client and a Windows 2000 demand-dial router. L2TP over IPSec lies beyond the scope of this book.

After the client has a reliable dial-up connection to the Internet and can

Ping the server, you're ready to configure a VPN client. (If the server is behind a firewall, it may not respond to ICMP. If the firewall is configured to only pass GRE and control traffic over TCP port 1723, you won't know that you can talk to the server until the VPN is ready to test.) Proceed as follows:

Procedure 17.34 **Setting Up a VPN Client**

1. Start the Network Connection Wizard by selecting START | SETTINGS | NETWORK AND DIAL-UP CONNECTIONS | MAKE A NEW CONNECTION.

2. Click Next. The Network Connection Type window opens. Select the Connect to a Private Network Through The Internet radio button. Use this option even if you are using a VPN through your private WAN.

3. Click Next. The Public Network window opens.

4. Under most circumstances, you want the VPN client to establish the dial-up connection automatically. Therefore, you should select Automatically Dial This Initial Connection. If the client already has an existing connection, such as a cable modem or xDSL line, select the Do Not Dial... option.

5. Click Next. The Destination Address window opens. Enter the fully qualified DNS name or IP address of the demand-dial server that is hosting the VPN.

6. Click Next. The Connection Availability window opens. Select a suitable availability option, either For All Users or Only For Myself.

7. Click Next. The Internet Connection Sharing window opens. A VPN connection can be shared by clients on the local network. Any traffic from those clients is encrypted and tunneled by the ICS server. This can put a significant load on the machine, so equip it accordingly.. For now, do not select the option.

8. Click Next. A final screen opens and prompts for a connection name. Enter a descriptive title, such as VPN to the Home Office.

9. Click Finish. The wizard creates the VPN connection, and then the dial-up service makes the connection. A notification window informs you that the VPN connection first requires making a standard connection. Click Yes to acknowledge and continue.

10. The Connect window for the initial PPP connection opens.

11. Click Dial to make the PPP connection. After it is made, a second Connect window opens for the VPN. If you take a look at the properties for this connection, under the Security tab you'll notice that the Require Data Encryption (Disconnect if None) option is selected. This ensures that the data going through the VPN is encrypted.

Avoid the Negotiate Multilink for Single Link Connections **Option**

At the time of this writing, there is a bug that prevents a VPN connection from working if the Negotiate Multilink for Single Link Connections option is enabled. This option is enabled by default. It is located in the Properties window for the connection. Disable it as follows:

1. Select the Networking tab.

2. Click Settings to open the PPP Settings window.

3. De-select Negotiate Multilink for Single Link Connections.

12. Click Dial. The VPN connection is made, and the icons for both the PPP connection and the VPN connections change to full color in the Network and Dial-up Connections window. Two icons appear in the System Tray, one for the PPP connection and one for the VPN connection.

13. At the RAS server, open the Routing and Remote Access console and expand the tree to show Ports. Both the modem interface and one of the PPTP interfaces show active. You can double-click on an interface to check the status.

That's all there is to it. If you use Network Monitor to examine the traffic between the two computers, you will see GRE packets containing control information and TCP packets containing encrypted data.

Configuring IAS

Most ISPs and organizations that handle large numbers of dial-up users use RADIUS to handle user authentication and to distribute policies. By configuring all boundary hardware to talk to RADIUS servers, it is possible to distribute a consistent set of remote access policies to every point-of-presence.

RADIUS originated with Livingston Systems. A description of the RADIUS protocol is contained in RFC 2138, "Remote Authentication Dial In User Service (RADIUS)," and RFC 2139, "RADIUS Accounting." Microsoft has published extensions to the standard RADIUS attributes in RFC 2548, "Microsoft Vendor-Specific RADIUS Attributes."

Microsoft's implementation of RADIUS was first introduced in the ICS for RAS suite of services in the NT4 option pack. The specific service supporting RADIUS was the IAS.

Windows 2000 bundles the next generation of IAS server in the shrink-wrap. IAS forms a key part of Windows 2000 remote access management even if an IAS server is not installed. All Windows 2000 dial-up server, both Server and Professional, have an IAS database where RADIUS policies are stored and distributed. An IAS server merely provides a central point to collect the policies. This simplifies management.

Multiple IAS servers can be used for fault tolerance. A Windows 2000 IAS server can handle RADIUS requests from any RFC-compliant RADIUS device, not just Windows 2000 dial-up servers. This includes most remote access concentrators, terminal servers, and boundary routers sold by major vendors.

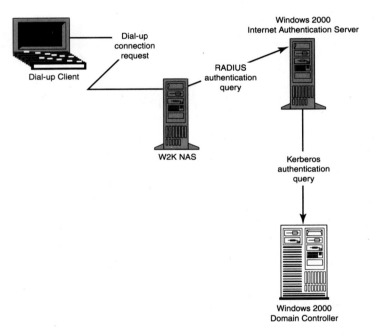

Figure 17.49 Diagram of RADIUS implementation
using an IAS server and Windows 2000 NAS.

Figure 17.49 shows an example of a typical Windows 2000 RADIUS configuration. This configuration uses a Windows 2000 server running IAS as the RADIUS server and a Windows 2000 domain controller as the authenticator.

In RADIUS terminology, the dial-up server is called a NAS. In the example configuration, a standalone Windows 2000 dial-up server acts as the NAS. It accepts PPP connections from users and sends their authentication requests to the IAS server using RADIUS protocols. The IAS server obtains authentication from the domain controller using Kerberos.

Integrating IAS and Existing RADIUS

If you have an existing RADIUS implementation, you need to check the UDP ports used by the NAS servers and the RADIUS servers. (RADIUS uses UDP rather than TCP because it does not require session-oriented transactions.) RADIUS uses two UDP ports, one for authentication and one for accounting.

The current RADIUS standard uses UDP port 1812 for authentication and UDP port 1813 for accounting. This is a change from the superceded RFC 2058 port numbers. Here is an excerpt from RFC 2138:

> There has been some confusion in the assignment of port numbers for this protocol. The early deployment of RADIUS was done using the erroneously chosen port number 1645, which conflicts with the 'Datametrics' service. The officially assigned port number for RADIUS is 1812.

The same kind of confusion forced a change to the default accounting port. The old port, 1646, conflicted with the `sa-msg-port` service. The new port is 1813.

If you have existing RADIUS servers or network access servers, they may use the old port number. You can configure IAS to use the old port number if the port conflict does not impact your current operations.

When you're ready to install IAS, proceed as follows. You'll need the Windows 2000 Server CD.

Procedure 17.35   **Installing IAS**

1. From Control Panel, open the `Add/Remove Software` applet.

2. Click the `Add/Remove Windows Components` to start the Windows Component Wizard.

3. Select `Networking Services`, and click `Details`. This opens the `Networking Services` window.

4. Select `Internet Authentication Service` from the list of available components, and click `OK` to return to the `Windows Components` window.

5. Click `Next`. After the components have finished loading, close the windows.

6. From the Start menu, select START | PROGRAMS | ADMINISTRATIVE TOOLS | INTERNET AUTHENTICATION SERVICE. This opens the `Internet Authentication Service` console, IAS.MSC. Figure 17.50 shows an example. This console includes the IAS snap-in and two extensions: `IAS Logging` and `Remote Access Policies`. These are the same policies listed in the RRAS console.

Figure 17.50 Internet Authentication Service console.

7. Right-click the IAS icon and select PROPERTIES from the fly-out menu. The Internet Authentication Service (Local) Properties window opens (see Figure 17.51).

Enter a name that describes the server. If you have only one IAS server, the default name of IAS is suitable. If you have more than one server, consider identifying them by location or function (Primary IAS, Backup IAS, and so forth). The Logging features should be left on. The log is kept in \WINNT\System32\Logfiles.

Figure 17.51 Internet Authentication Service (Local) Properties window.

8. Select the RADIUS tab. This is where you select the UDP ports to use for authentication and accounting. If you do not have an existing RADIUS implementation, delete the 1645 and 1646 entries. If you have an existing RADIUS server, find out which ports it uses and then delete the other two from this server.

9. Select the Realms tab. If you have an existing RADIUS implementation where users access your network from an ISP or other service provider, their incoming user names may have a prefix or suffix called a *realm name*. These realm names are used for routing through RADIUS. The IAS server must delete the realm name before validating the user's credentials with a domain controller. Click Add to open a Replace Realms window where you can enter the incoming realm name, and replace it with a blank.

10. Click OK to save any changes. You will be prompted to stop and start the IAS service. You can do so by right-clicking the IAS icon and selecting STOP and then START from the fly-out menu.

11. At the IAS console, highlight the Remote Access Logging icon. The Local File log appears in the right pane.

12. Double-click the Local File icon under Logging Method to open the Properties window.

13. Under the Settings tab, select all logging options. Leave these selected for a while until you are familiar with the entries. The online help has an exhaustive list of the attribute types and meanings listed in the IAS log. Search for "Interpreting IAS-formatted Log Files."

14. Click OK to save the settings, close the window, and return to the IAS console. Leave the console window open and proceed to the next section.

Register the IAS Server with the Active Directory

The IAS server cannot use the Directory on a Windows 2000 domain controller to authenticate users until the service has been registered. This registration adds the server's computer account to the RAS and IAS Servers group. See the sidebar titled "RAS and IAS Servers Group Permissions" for more information.

RAS and IAS Servers Group Permissions

The RAS and IAS Servers Group is automatically added to the ACL of the Domain-DNS object with delegated permissions over several extended attributes affecting User object. These attributes allow computers that are members of the RAS and IAS Servers Group to read user access permissions.

The following extended attributes are delegated to the RAS and IAS Servers group:

- Read Logon Information
- Read Group Membership
- Read Account Restrictions
- Read Remote Access Information

The RAS and IAS Servers group has delegated rights only in a particular domain. If you have dial-up or IAS servers in several domains and users cross-authenticate, all dial-up and IAS servers in a forest must be members of the RAS and IAS Servers group in every domain.

You can add the computer account for a domain controller to the RAS and IAS Servers manually, but you may find it more convenient to use the server registration feature in the IAS console. Use it as follows:

Procedure 17.36   **Registering an IAS Server with Active Directory**

1. At the IAS console, right-click the IAS icon and select REGISTER SERVICE IN ACTIVE DIRECTORY from the fly-out menu.

2. A message appears notifying you that the computers that are running IAS must be authorized to read users' dial-in properties and prompting you to confirm that you want to do this. Click OK to confirm.

3. A notice appears informing you that the server has been registered. You are also reminded that it must be added to the RAS and IAS Servers Group in any trusted domains to authenticate users from those domains.

At this point, the IAS server is ready to process authentications. Each NAS must be registered with the IAS server before the IAS server will accept authentication requests.

Configuring an IAS Server to Accept NAS Queries

Before a remote access server can make RADIUS calls to an IAS server, it must share a common *secret* (a fancy term for password) with the IAS server so that the two of them communicate in a secure fashion. If you already have an existing RADIUS implementation, use the existing secret for the Windows 2000 remote access servers and IAS servers. Proceed as follows:

Procedure 17.37   **Configuring an IAS Server to Accept NAS Queries**

1. Right-click the Clients icon, and select NEW CLIENT from the fly-out menu. The Add Client window opens and prompts for Name and Protocol (see Figure 17.52).

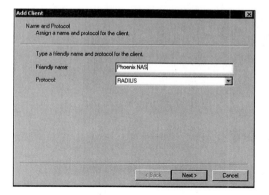

Figure 17.52 `Add Client - Name and Protocol` window showing friendly name for NAS and the access protocol, RADIUS.

2. Enter a descriptive name for the NAS, such as `Phoenix NAS`. The name is only a placeholder. Leave the Protocol entry as RADIUS.

3. Click `Next`. The `Add RADIUS Client` window opens. Figure 17.53 shows an example. See the following sidebar for more information.

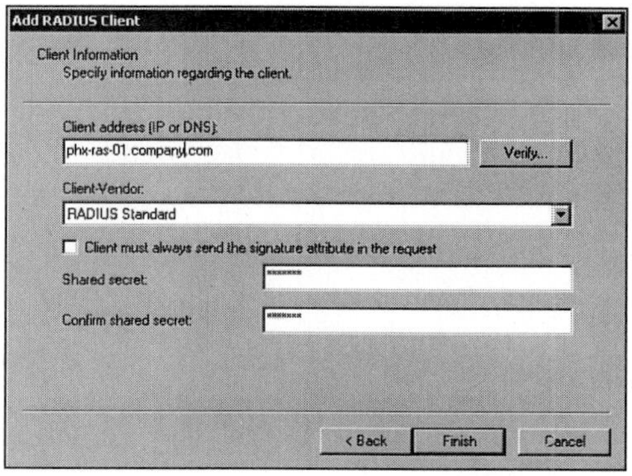

Figure 17.53 `Add RADIUS Client` window.

Configuring New RADIUS Clients

The Add RADIUS Client window in Figure 17.83 has several options that affect how clients connect to a RADIUS server. Configure them as follows:

- Under Client Address, enter the IP address or fully qualified DNS name for the NAS or its IP address. You can use the Verify button to open a Resolve DNS Name window to check that the name you entered resolves to the correct IP address.

- In the Client-Vendor drop-down box, leave the selection at RADIUS Standard. You can change it toMicrosoft, but there is no improvement in performance or security.

- In the Shared Secret field, enter a password that all the RADIUS boxes and NAS servers share. If you have an existing RADIUS installation, use the existing shared secret. Don't forget to confirm.

  4. Click Finish to close the window, and save the settings.

  Proceed to the next section to configure a NAS (dial-up server) to communicate with the IAS server.

Configure the NAS

Now that the IAS server is willing to hear from a NAS, configure the NAS to talk to the IAS server as follows:

Procedure 17.38   **Configuring a NAS**

  1. At the Windows 2000 dial-up server, open the Routing and Remote Access console.

  2. Right-click the local server icon, and select PROPERTIES from the fly-out menu. The Properties window opens for the local server.

  3. Select the Security tab (see Figure 17.54).

Figure 17.54   Local Properties window for dial-up server showing Security tab.

4. For Authentication Provider and Accounting Provider, select RADIUS
   Authentication. Click Configure next to Authentication. The RADIUS
   Authentication window opens.

5. Enter the IP address of the RADIUS server, and then click Add. The Add
   RADIUS Server window opens (see Figure 17.55).

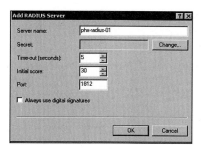

Figure 17.55   Add RADIUS Server window showing example entries for an IAS server.

6. Under Server Name, enter the IP address or fully qualified DNS name of
   the IAS server.

7. Under Port, verify that the port matches the port you configured at the
   IAS server. This is 1812 by default.

8. Next to Secret, click Change. The Change Secret window opens.

9. Enter the same secret you entered at the IAS server. Confirm it, and then
   click OK to return to the Add RADIUS Server window.

10. Click OK to save the changes, and return to the RADIUS Authentication window. The IAS server name is added to the list of RADIUS servers. If you
   have additional IAS or RADIUS servers, enter their names, too. If the
   remote access server cannot contact one, it will work its way down the list
   trying one after another.

11. Click OK. A warning appears that you must restart the RRAS service
   because you changed RADIUS parameters. Click OK to acknowledge, and
   return to the Local Properties window.

12. Repeat the configuration steps to point the Accounting option at the IAS
   server. Once again, you will be prompted to restart the service. Click OK to
   acknowledge and return to the Local Properties window.

13. Click OK to close the Local Properties window.

Test the connection by stopping and starting the RRAS service by opening a command window, entering net stop remoteaccess, and then net start remoteaccess. If you get an error when starting the service, more than likely you did not enter the proper IAS server name, IP address, or you didn't type the secret correctly. Repeat the steps and try again.

Test the Authentication Path

Let's recap the configuration at this point.

- In one corner, you have a standalone Windows 2000 dial-up server that is configured to use RADIUS for authentication. The dial-up server is configured to send PPP authentication requests via RADIUS to the IAS server.

- In the other corner, you have a domain member server running IAS. The server's account is a member of the RAS and IAS Servers group so that it can do lookups in the Directory. The IAS server validates users by making Kerberos calls to the domain controller.

- As a referee (that even Mike Tyson would respect), you have a Windows 2000 domain controller.

All you need now is a dial-up client to see whether this all works. But what authentication protocol should the client use?

The answer is, whatever method the client would ordinarily use. The client does not need to know about RADIUS. Windows 2000 and Windows 98 dial-in clients can still negotiate using MS-CHAP v2 by default. Older Windows clients can still use MS-CHAP. Non-Windows clients still require reversible passwords at the domain controller to support CHAP and EAP/MD5-CHAP. The fact that the dial-up server is passing off the authentication chores to another server is a private matter that only the Information Technology professionals need to worry about.

Test the configuration by making a dial-up connection just as you normally would with the dial-up client. When the client gets authenticated and completes the connection, check the IAS log to see what the transaction looks like. If the user is not able to get authenticated but the connection worked fine with standard authentication, review the steps for the IAS configuration.

Moving Forward

It was a long—you might even say grueling—struggle to get a full range of dial-up services configured for your user community.. Even so, I'm sure they'll be very happy now that they can dial the office from home and do three or four hours of extra work at night.

With the completion of the dial-up services deployment, the enterprise migration to Windows 2000 is just about finished. You should now be able to relax, take that long-delayed vacation, catch up with reading that pile of magazines on your desk (Is that a 1997 issue of *PC Week* I see in that stack?) and generally mind the store. After all, this is modern, soon-to-be-21st century technology you've just deployed. What could go wrong? What could possibly go wrong?

18

Recovering from System Failures

AT SOME POINT OR ANOTHER, NO MATTER HOW MANY layers of fault-tolerant components you build into a system, you experience a loss of service. It doesn't matter what operating system you use or what hardware you run it on. Someday it's going to crash.

I'm not saying those thousands of dollars you spent on high-end RAID controllers with hot-swappable drives and dual power supplies and battery-backup cache were a waste of money. No, sir. Neither were those banks of expensive ECC memory SIMMs or the fault-tolerant fail-over NICs or the on-board management systems or the UPS that does everything but come knock on your door when it senses a line fault. None of that was a waste of money.

But Chaos is King in this universe, as any systems administrator knows, and the voice of Chaos sounds something like this on the phone: "Sorry to bother you. I know you're just about to leave on vacation. But none of our PCs seems to work up here in Finance. Joey in the server room says some kind of blue-screen glitch is on the SAP server. We have to run financials tonight so that we can give the reports to the SEC for the IPO filing. Can you come right over?"

At that moment, you can forget about that certificate on your wall commemorating your years of meritorious service. You can forget about the way your manager pledged his undying gratitude for all your great work. You can forget about the way your friends and colleagues admire your skills and computer knowledge. Forget all that. When that server went down and took all its data and services along with it, it put you all alone in front of Chaos. And Chaos has just one more little question to ask:

"Are you sure about that last backup?"

With that question in mind, this chapter examines in grimy detail all the backup options available in Windows 2000, paying special attention to *getting the data back*.

Some specialized backup and restore operations are covered in earlier chapters. Backing up and restoring Active Directory and SYSVOL files is covered in Chapter 11, "Managing Active Directory Replication and Directory Maintenance." Backing up and restoring Removable Storage Service database files and cloning offline tape libraries is covered in Chapter 12, "Configuring Data Storage." Recovering encrypted files is covered in Chapter 14, "Managing File Systems Security." This chapter covers general backup and restore methods using the Windows 2000 Backup program, Ntbackup, along with details of how Ntbackup interacts with the Removable Storage Management system (RSM).

Restoring system functionality involves more than bringing files back from tape, though. Sometimes more subtle surgery is called for, so this chapter also covers:

- Recovering from blue-screen stops
- Using Safe Mode to restore stable operations
- Creating and using an Emergency Repair Disk
- Booting with the Last Known Good Configuration
- Restoring Functionality with the Recovery Console

Functional Description of Windows 2000 Backup

All Windows products starting with NT 3.51 and extending through Windows 95, NT4, Windows 98, and Windows 2000 come with a stripped-down version of Backup Exec, first from Arcada Software, and then Seagate Software, and now Veritas Software, www.veritas.com.

Over the years, as the commercial versions of Backup Exec improved, the "lite" versions in Windows steadily got more and more useful. The version of Backup Exec in Windows 2000 is good enough to be a strong contender for your primary backup method if you don't need to centralize your backups onto one server.

The backup product in Windows 2000 continues to be called Ntbackup, just as it is in classic NT. If you are upgrading from NT4 or NT3.51 and you are using classic Ntbackup, your tape library and on-disk catalogs are fully compatible with the new version of Ntbackup. If you are using a third-party backup product, you may need to upgrade to the Windows 2000 version to get the package to run.

Windows 2000 Backup is inextricably tied to the RSM. The RSM is a new feature in Windows 2000. Its primary function is to handle robotic tape libraries and CD jukeboxes, but it also serves as a clearing house for any media associated with removable storage devices, such as CD-ROM, CD-R, CD-RW, Zip, Jaz, and Orb drives along with tape devices.

Registry Tip: Ntbackup Parameters

The parameters controlling Windows 2000 Backup are stored in the user's profile hive under the following Registry key: HKCU | Software | Microsoft | Ntbackup.

Ntbackup is managed by the executable itself, not an MMC console. It also has a command-line interface used for running backup jobs in the background and scheduling them using the Task Scheduler. Launch the Ntbackup application using START | PROGRAMS | ACCESSORIES | BACKUP.

Figure 18.1 shows an example of the Backup window with the Backup tab selected.

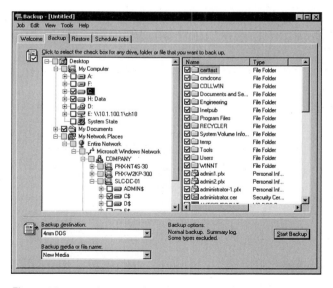

Figure 18.1 Backup window showing files in drives C and H selected along with a shared drive on a server using My Network Places.

The directory tree in the left pane is arranged in the standard Explorer namespace, which is rooted at Desktop and descends through My Computer, My Documents, and My Network Places. Drill down through any of these options to find drives, folders, and files you might want to back up.

When selecting items to back up, you have the option of selecting an entire drive or individual folders or files. A blue checkmark indicates that you selected all the files and folders under that point. If you select an individual item, the folders above it get gray checkmarks indicating a partial backup.

You can back up network files either by selecting a mapped drive or by expanding the tree under My Network Neighborhood and selecting a share from the server's resource list. This is equivalent to using a UNC path and is a better way to structure network backups if you are going to schedule them to run in the background. You don't want the backup to inexplicably fail if you rearrange the persistent drive mappings.

The Backup Destination in the window can be a file or tape backup media. If you back up to a file, the file can be placed on any mountable volume, NTFS or FAT/FAT32, on a local drive or on the network. The filename can be a long filename. If the destination is a tape, the tape name you specify must match the name of a tape that is mounted in the tape device. See "Preparing Tapes for Backup" later in this chapter for more details on tape naming.

You must have Backup Operator privileges or higher on the server you are backing up. A quick check is to try expanding the resource tree under a server icon in the Backup window. If you see the dollar-sign ($) administrative shares, you know you have sufficient rights to do the backup.

Agent-Based Network Backups

Network backups using Ntbackup are limited to files you can reach using a network client redirector. When Ntbackup runs, it works in conjunction with the Local System account to access locked system files. Locked system files cannot be backed up via a network client redirector. It requires an agent running on the server.

An agent provides the link between the local system and a central server where the backup application is running. The agent runs in a privileged security context so that it can access locked system files. It then sends copies of the system files to the backup server, where they are put on tape.

Windows 2000 Backup does not use agents. If you want to back up system files and other locked files such as SQL Server and Oracle databases, try one of the commercial products listed in "Overview of Third-Party Backup Packages" later in this chapter. All those packages have agent-based solutions.

Backup Options

Ntbackup provides five different types of backups classified by the way they handle the archive bit. To view these options, launch Backup and select TOOLS | OPTIONS from the menu. The Options window opens with the focus set to the Backup Type tab.

- **Normal.** This option backs up the selected files and clears the archive bit.
- **Copy.** This option backs up the selected files and does not clear the archive bit.
- **Differential.** This option backs up only those selected files that have their archive bit set and does not clear the archive bit.
- **Incremental.** This option backs up only those selected files that have their archive bit set and clears the archive bit.
- **Daily.** This option backs up only those files with a Modified time stamp that matches the backup date.

The Copy option is primarily used for transferring files to another system and not for scheduled backups. Following are details about the other options, along with criteria to use when choosing one over the other.

Normal Backups

Running a Normal backup every night makes restoration easy. All the files you need to restore a system are right there on the tape (or tapes). Normal backups are time consuming, though, so you have to measure their usefulness against the size of your backup window.

If you are backing up across the network, include network transfer times into your time calculations. The fastest transfer time you can reasonably expect to achieve from a single NIC on a PCI bus is 20 or 30Mbps. This is just barely enough to keep a DLT or AIT tape moving at streaming speeds. If the tape stops and starts, you slow down the backup even more. Many shops build a separate network with a second NIC in the servers to handle backups.

Differential Backups

Differential backups shorten the backup duration while retaining a fairly simple recovery process. Start by running a Normal backup on the weekend. Then, run differential backups on weeknights. The differential backup gets longer and longer as the week progresses, but never as long as a normal backup.

If you need to restore a volume, first restore the last normal backup and then restore the last differential backup. This gives you two tape sets to manage, a big time-saver if the disk crash took your tape catalog and you have to recatalog each tape.

If you need to restore an individual file, first search the catalog for the differential tape. If you don't find it there, go to the tape from the normal backup.

Be sure to design your tape rotations so that the full and differential backup tapes are stored together. It can be embarrassing to overlay the normal restore with the contents of the wrong differential tape.

Incremental Backups

Incremental backups shorten the nightly backup even further, but they can dramatically complicate recovery.

Incremental backups also start with a normal backup on the weekend, but instead of accumulating changed files each subsequent night, the incremental backup captures only the files that changed since the last backup.

If you need to restore a volume, first restore the last normal backup and then restore each of the incremental backups in sequence. If a particular tape fails to restore, the subsequent tapes may include a few of the files. This can cause problems, though, by mixing older and newer versions of files that rely on each other (macro libraries, for instance).

If you need to restore an individual file, search the catalog for each day starting with last night's backup. If the user is a little fuzzy about the date the file was lost, you have a chore in front of you.

Daily Backups

Both differential and incremental backups assume that the archive bit is not being manipulated by any other application. If you run file copy utilities that change the archive bit, files may be skipped. You can avoid this problem by running a Daily backup. A Daily backup ignores the archive bit and backs up files that were modified on the day of the backup.

The same caveats apply to Daily backups that apply to Incremental backups. You must keep them in order and apply them in order along with the full backup to restore a volume.

Backup Logs

The `Backup Options` window has a tab called `Backup Log`. Logging is a critical element of a backup strategy. Without a log, you could be unaware of a problem that puts your data at risk. For example, if you back up files across the network, a problem with the network connection can cause the files to be skipped. Without checking the log regularly, you won't know this happened.

Two logging options exist, `Detailed` and `Summary`.

- `Detailed` logs include the name and path of every file in the backup.
- `Summary` logs include a file count and tell you whether any files were skipped.

Selecting a Backup Log Option

Summary logs are the better choice for standard daily backups because you stand less of a chance of missing a problem buried in a long, detailed report. This is an example of a summary log:

```
Backup Status
Operation: Backup
Active backup destination: File
Media name: "Test Backup File"

Backup of "C: "
Backup set #1 on media #1
Backup description: "Set created 9/28/99 at 12:19 PM"
Backup Type: Normal

Backup started on 10/28/99 at 12:19 PM.
Warning: The file \WINNT\system32\dns\dns.log in use - skipped.
Warning: The file \WINNT\system32\LogFiles\W3SVC1\ex990928.log in use - skipped.
Backup completed on 10/28/99 at 12:25 PM.
Directories: 105
Files: 3623
Skipped: 2
Bytes: 385,732,514
Time:  5 minutes and  20 seconds
```

The summary log reports skipped files. If you are troubleshooting a backup problem involving missed files, enable the `Detailed` option and scan the report for clues on why they were missed. See "File Exclusions" for a possible reason why a file is not included in the backup job.

Backup Log Locations

Backup logs are saved to the local profile of the user who runs the backup. The path is `\Documents and Settings\<logonID>\Local Settings\Application Data\Microsoft\Windows NT\NTBackup\Data`.

The path for the log file is fixed. No Registry parameter can be set to change it. If you want the log file sent to another location, you must include a copy command in the Task Scheduler job that runs the backup.

Each backup job creates a new backup log. The logs are numbered sequentially and renumbered automatically after reaching 10, so the oldest log is overwritten.

File Exclusions

The Backup `Options` window has an `Exclude Files` tab. Figure 18.2 shows an example.

Figure 18.2 `Options` window showing Exclude Files.
The `Add New` button can be used to exclude other file types.

The `Files excluded for all users` field lists file extensions and individual files that are deliberately left out of all backup jobs.

The standard list of excluded files includes the paging file, temp files, the client-side cache for offline files, contents of the debug folder, and the File Replication System database. It also includes any FRS cache folders on volumes containing replicated files (such as `\WINNT\Sysvol`), the Windows 2000 registration files, the Distributed Transaction Coordinator log, and the local cryptographic certificate database.

Adding File Exclusions

You can add file classifications to the exclusion list and narrow the focus to individual folders. You can do this for all backup jobs or jobs run by the current user. Add a new exclusion as follows:

Procedure 18.1 Classifications to the Exclusion List

---

1. Click Add New under the All Users field or the Current User field. The Add Excluded Files window opens.
2. Select the class of file you want to exclude. Use the Applies To Path field to narrow the scope to a particular folder.
3. Click OK to save the selection and return to the Options window.
4. Click OK to save the setting and close the window.

Registering File Types for Exclusion

If you are backing up a volume across the network and you have a file type that you want to exclude but it is not on the extension list, you must register the file locally. The easiest way to do this is as follows:

Procedure 18.2 Registering File Types for Backup Exclusions

---

1. Open the network drive in Explorer.
2. Right-click one of the files of the type you want to exclude and select OPEN WITH from the fly-out menu.
3. Double-click the executable you want to associate with the file type. This closes the window and adds the application to the list in the Open With window.
4. Select the Always use this program to open these files option.
5. Click OK to save the change and make the association in the Registry.

Now that the file type is registered, you can exclude it using the steps in Procedure 18.1.

General Options

In the Backup Options window, select the General tab. Figure 18.3 shows an example. Most of the options are self-explanatory and are selected by default.

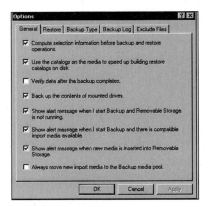

Figure 18.3   Options window showing General options.

Verify data after the backup is complete adds an extra measure of assurance to your backup but significantly increases backup time. With modern equipment and a tape rotation schedule that removes old tapes from service before they fail, you should not need to verify backups.

Back up the contents of mounted drives is a default option. A mounted drive (mounted volume, really) consists of an NTFS reparse point that redirects a process to a remote file system such as another volume, folder, or CD-ROM. If the target volume of the reparse point also has a drive letter that you are backing up, you get two identical backups. No performance penalty exists for backing up via a mount point. If you mounted a CD-ROM that you do not want to include in the backup, de-select this option.

Always move new import media to the Backup media pool is selected by default if you run Ntbackup before running the Removable Storage Manager. In that instance, Ntbackup prompts you with a window that contains the option Always use free media for Backup. This option is appropriate when you use the tape drive only for backup and not for Remote Storage Services or other purposes. By selecting this option, you eliminate the need to use the Removable Storage console to allocate free tape media.

Backup Catalogs

I suppose you've heard the corny old story about the squirrel that works all summer saving nuts, only to die of starvation in the winter when he can't remember where he put them. You face a similar situation if the backup program you're using doesn't enable you to find a file in those racks of backup tapes on your shelf.

Windows 2000 Backup stores the filenames and directory structures for each backup job in a catalog under the local profile of the user who submits the job. For example, if the local Administrator account submits a job, the catalog is stored under `\Documents and Settings\<logonID>\Local Settings\Application Data\Microsoft\Windows NT\NTBackup\Catalog`. The catalogs are assigned hexadecimal sequence numbers with a `V01` extension. An index file with an `SM` extension defines the members of the catalog.

When you restore a file, the `Restore` window shows the contents of the catalogs stored on the disk. For example, Figure 18.4 shows an example of the Restore options with the directory structure and files listed for a particular media item.

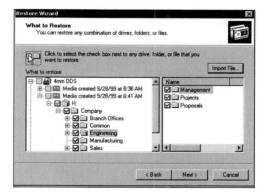

Figure 18.4   `Backup` window showing
`Restore` tab with media listed from catalog.

A copy of the catalog entry for a backup job is saved on the tape, along with the backup job. If you ever need to recover from tape on a system that lost the on-disk catalogs, you can recover the catalog from tape and then use the catalog to recover the rest of the files. This can also be done with tapes created under NT4.

Locked Files

Backup runs in the Local System security context so that it is able to back up system files, such as the Registry and Active Directory, as well as the other databases that support system operations, such as DHCP, WINS, and so forth.

Backup cannot override a lock from a user process, though. If Backup encounters a locked file or a locked data stream within a file, it keeps trying to get access for 30 seconds. Backup does not take any action to free the file or clear the process that locks it. If you are running the backup job interactively, you get a warning message on the console. No notice is given if the job is running in the background. If the file remains locked after 30 seconds, Backup skips the file and makes a notation in the backup log.

Registry Tip: Locked File Parameters

You can change the interval during which Backup keeps trying a locked file with the following Registry entry:

Key: HKCU | Software | Microsoft | Ntbackup | User Interface

Value: Wait Time

Data: 30 (default)

If you run a 7x24 shop, you need to work out strategies for backing up locked files. Take a look at Open File Manager (OFM) from St. Bernard Software, www.stbernard.com. This is a utility that sneaks in below the backup API, nabs individual sectors from the file, and builds a copy in a scratch area. After it assembles the file from pieces, it backs up the copy as though it is the original file. Any changes made by the user during the snatch-and-go phase of this process are lost.

Another way to avoid locked file problems is to run an image backup. Ntbackup does not have this option, but it is available from several third parties. Image backups take a snapshot of the physical volume rather than making file system calls. File restoration can be a problem with image backups, but they are getting much more sophisticated at it. Check out UltraBac from BEI Corporation, www.ultrabac.com, and Replica from Legato Software, www.legato.com.

Security Considerations

When you place an account in the Backup Operators group, or otherwise assign SeBackupPermission and SeRestorePermission to an account, this gives the user permission to back up any file on the machine regardless of its security descriptor or encryption status. Backup operators can also strip security permissions from files during restoration. In short, it's hard to imagine a more serious security breach than giving people backup and restore privileges in an unrestricted manner.

A similar problem exists for third-party backup applications that use client-based backup agents. These agents run in the security context of an account with Backup Operator permissions. These agent accounts are often used for other purposes, so virtually everyone in the back room knows the password. When configuring commercial packages, look for ways to secure the agent password and to make it as strong as possible.

Physical control of backup tapes is also important. You commonly find shops where unauthorized users aren't allowed within 100 yards of a production server, but backup tapes are routinely put in the custody of unbonded couriers and temporary contractors. You need secure, offsite storage with a known and licensed chain of custody for the tapes.

Finally, don't forget about the possibility of data loss due to theft. This is emphatically true for small businesses in strip malls and office parks with lots of glass and easy access from the street. It takes only a few seconds to toss a rock through a window and snatch a computer. Servers look impressive, so thieves often spend a few minutes looking for them. Don't multiply your loss by leaving the backup tapes where they can be scooped up, too.

Backing Up System State Files

Ntbackup groups a long list of files together under the umbrella term *System State* files. It backs up and restores System State files as a unit to maintain consistency between the various data stores. The System State files include:

- The Active Directory database, NTDS.DIT, and its associated log and checkpoint files in the \WINNT\NTDS directory
- Selected files from the Program Files directory
- All Registry hives from the \WINNT\System32\Config directory
- The COM+ class registration database
- All files in the \WINNT directory (%systemroot%)
- System files from the root of the boot drive: NTDETECT.COM, NTLDR, BOOT.INI, BOOTSECT.DOS, AND NTBOOTDD.SYS
- Certificate Services files
- The contents of the \WINNT\Sysvol directory (used to store group policies and other client support files)

You cannot back up System State files across the network. Many of the files are locked, so you cannot simply point Backup at the ADMIN$ share on another server and get a system backup. If you want to centrally back up System State information, you must invest in a commercial package with backup agents.

The procedure for backing up and restoring System State files on a standard server or desktop is no different from selecting any other file or folder. See Chapter 11 for the steps to back up and restore System State files on a domain controller.

Backing Up to a File

One of the nicer features of the new Windows 2000 Backup is its capability to send a backup job to a file rather than to tape. This makes it possible to do quick backups on local desktops and save them to removable media such as Zip, Jaz, or Orb drives. Field technicians like the ability to do a backup of user data across the network to a scratch area on a server prior to changing out a machine.

File backups are also an essential component of encrypted file management. Unless you have specifically configured servers to be trusted for Kerberos delegation, encrypted files cannot be copied across the network. That leaves Backup as the only viable method for transferring encrypted files. See Chapter 14 for more information.

You aren't necessarily limited to magnetic media as the target for file-based backup. For example, DirectCD from Adaptec, part of the EZ CD Creator 4.0 suite of products, can turn a CD-RW drive into a slow but big disk drive. With DirectCD loaded, you can do backups to CD-RW media. This is a great way to take snapshots of projects prior to removing them from a spindle.

File-based backups have their downside. Users with local backup operator privileges might use Backup to back up their local desktops to a file on a server. Consider establishing a group policy limiting access to Ntbackup. See Chapter 16, "Managing the User Operating Environment," for details.

Functional Description of Windows 2000 Removable Storage Management

Windows 2000 includes a service called Removable Storage Management (RSM). This service is responsible for handling all removable media in a system. RSM is primarily intended to handle CD-ROM jukeboxes and robotic tape libraries, but it also controls single-media devices, such as a manually loaded tape drive or a CD-ROM drive.

Ntbackup works with RSM to obtain access to backup tapes. This is done even if you have only one tape drive with no robotic capability. This may seem like overkill, and for small systems it probably is, but the backup needs of the next few years might make RSM more attractive. Moderately priced servers now ship with 70–200GB of RAID storage. Desktops come standard with 18GB drives, and 30GB drives are coming soon. The days of doing full backups using QIC or Travan units connected to a floppy cable are rapidly coming to an end.

Storage densities on tape did not keep pace with disks, so a reasonable backup solution for a server with triple-digit gigabytes of spinning storage includes a tape library of one form or another. A tape library capable of handling a full backup for 200GB of storage might cost as much as the server. Adding another $1,000 onto that price to get backup software that understands a robotic tape handler injures the wallet even further. Including a robotic tape handler such as RSM in the core OS helps ease the pain.

The RSM service was designed and licensed to Microsoft by Highground Systems, `www.highground.com`, the same company that designed the hierarchical storage management technologies in the Remote Storage Services. See Chapter 13, "Managing File Systems," for more information.

RSM Drivers and Databases

RSM is managed with an MMC snap-in called *Removable Storage*. The snap-in is part of the Computer Management console, but it can also be loaded into a custom console for convenience. Figure 18.5 shows a custom Removable Storage console with a CD-ROM, a Jaz drive, and a single 4mm DAT tape backup unit connected to the system.

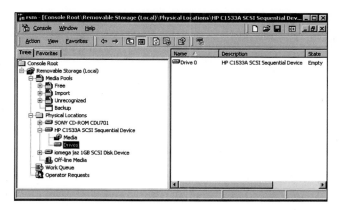

Figure 18.5 Custom MMC console with RSM snap-in showing removable media devices and media pools.

Information about the removable media devices recognized by the system is stored in the RSM database, called Ntmsdata for NT Mass Storage. The Ntmsdata database and other RSM files are stored under \WINNT\System32\ Ntmsdata. An Export folder under Ntmsdata holds dump files of the database files that can be backed up while the system is live.

The RSM driver is NTMSSVC.DLL, one of the SvcHost suite of services. This driver also exposes an RSM API that enables developers to make use of library handling functions, such as:

- Mounting/Dismounting media
- Managing library hardware and media
- Reading and writing to the NTMS database
- Inventorying libraries

The RSM API forms the basis for all Windows 2000 backup systems. This means that much of what is covered in this chapter concerning the relationship of Ntbackup and RSM is applicable to commercial products, as well. Check the HCL prior to installing removable media devices on a Windows 2000 machine (or vice versa) to be sure they are recognized by RSM.

RSM includes a command-line tool, Rsm.exe, which can be used to perform many of the functions in the MMC console, such as mounting and unmounting media and allocating media to a specific service. The Windows 2000 online help contains the command syntax for the RSM utility.

Small CD Changers and Removable Storage Management

In addition to handling tape libraries, RSM also handles CD-ROM changers and jukeboxes. If you have an existing NT system with a CD-ROM changer, you'll find that RSM uses a different method for interfacing with the drive.

Under NT4, each CD in a CD-ROM jukebox or disk changer got a separate drive letter. This was convenient for small changers. For example, drive H: might be the third disk in the changer. This drive could be shared so that network users wouldhave a consistent mapping to that CD.

Life was not so rosy for owners of big CD-ROM jukeboxes, though. The alphabet does not have enough letters to handle a 100-disk CD-ROM jukebox. A lot of proprietary solutions emerged. RSM solves the problem of big libraries by defining one interface to represent the jukebox. The vendor writes the driver using the RSM API to access disks in the jukebox.

Although RSM solved a problem with big CD libraries, it made life difficult for small changers. Now, when a user wants to see the CD in slot 3, the user must issue an RSM Mount command and specify the ID of the disk. You can automate this process using batch files, but it is still awkward.

Media Pools

Each removable storage device is associated with a *media pool*. Three standard pools, along with specialty pools, represent services, such as Backup and Remote Storage. The standard pools are:

- **Free.** This pool contains media that is marked with a Free Media Label and is available for allocation to a suitable device. In this context, *suitable* means that the media type the Ntmsdata database matches the media type associated with the device. For example, a CD-ROM player has one associated media type, the CD-ROM type. You cannot associate CD-RW media with a CD-ROM device.

- **Import.** This pool contains tape media formatted using Microsoft Tape Format (MTF). The media have a recognizable tape label but are not allocated to a particular device. This includes backup tapes created by classic NT.

- **Unrecognized.** This pool contains tape media that are blank or formatted in a foreign format.

RSM allocates media to a particular service, but it does not keep track of the data placed on the media by that service. For example, Ntbackup is responsible for knowing that a file named SomeStuff.txt is stored on media labeled Media Created 9/29/99 at 10:45 PM. RSM is responsible for knowing that the tape labeled Media Created 9/29/99 at 10:45 PM was poked into Slot 5 in the tape library. When Ntbackup calls for the tape, RSM uses the tape library driver to communicate with the robot in the library to have the tape mounted in the drive.

Registry Tip: RSM Parameters

Registry parameters for the service are stored in HKLM | System | CurrentControlSet | Services | NtmsSvc. Registry parameters for the NTMS database are stored in HKLM | System | CurrentControlSet | Control | NTMS. This key holds keys for the three Media Label Libraries in NTMS: HP, MTF, and QIC. These media label libraries understand how to interpret the label at the start of the media. For example, the Mll_mtf.dll label library knows how to read a Microsoft Tape Format label.

Additional RSM Icons

The other top-level icons in the RSM interface are:

- **Physical Locations.** This identifies the devices that are recognized as removable media devices. Each icon represents a device in the Object Namespace, a data structure within the Windows 2000 Executive that contains symbolic links representing physical devices. Each device under Physical Locations has a Drives icon representing the individual drives within the device, and a Media icon representing the media that is currently loaded in the device. In the case of a single tape library, one entry is under Drive and one entry is under Media at any one time.

- **Work Queue.** This contains the operations performed by RSM and stored in the Ntmsdata database. Figure 18.6 shows an example of the work items recorded under Work Queue. Notice that this list does not have items such as "Backup Performed on 10/1/99." The RSM does not know or care about the use of the media, only that the media is used in accordance with the rules. Work Queue entries are cleared after 72 hours by default. You can change that value using the Properties window for the Work Queue icon.

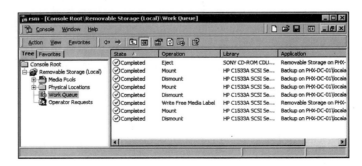

Figure 18.6 RSM console showing the contents of the Work Queue.

- **Operator Requests.** These messages are issued by RSM to the system operator. An example message is "Close a door to the library." Operator Requests are displayed as pop-ups and an icon is put in the System Tray. You can change this behavior with the Properties window for the RSM service itself. Figure 18.7 shows an example.

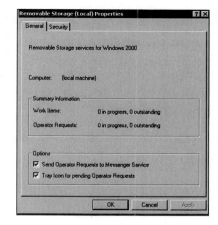

Figure 18.7 `Removable Storage Properties` window showing default handling options for Operator Requests.

RSM Security

The RSM exposes the contents of the NTMS database as Windows 2000 security objects. You can view the permissions assigned to an object by opening its Properties window and selecting `Security`. Three possible permissions can be applied to an RSM object:

- **Use.** Enables a user to open an NTMS session and mount/dismount media.

- **Modify.** Enables a user to create and delete media pools and to allocate and deallocate media to and from those pools.

- **Control.** Enables a user to send commands to the library that control its physical operation.

The RSM service has more responsibilities than just handling backup tapes, but because Backup is the focus of this chapter, let's concentrate on backup tape handling. The next section has steps for configuring RSM to interface with Backup.

Creating a Custom Removable Storage Console

You can use the Removable Storage snap-in inside the `Computer Management` console to configure RSM, but it is much easier and faster to create a custom console that you can launch separately. Create the custom console as follows:

Procedure 18.3 **Creating a Custom RSM Management Console**

1. Open an empty MMC console via START | RUN, and then enter MMC and click OK.

2. From the console menu, select CONSOLE | ADD/REMOVE SNAP-IN. The `Add/Remove Snap-in` window opens.

3. Click `Add`. The `Add Standalone Snap-in` window opens.

4. Select `Removable Storage Management` from the list of `Available Standalone Snap-ins` and click `Add`. The `Select Computer` window opens.

5. Leave the `Local Computer` radio button selected. If you want to be able to select a computer by adding it to the command line when you launch the console (for example, `c:\>rsm.msc hou-dc-01.subsidiary.com`), select the `Allow Selected Computer To Be Changed…` option.

6. Click `Finish` to save the settings and return to the `Add Standalone Snap-in` window.

7. Click `Close` to return to the `Add/Remove Snap-in` window.

8. Click OK to close the window and return to the main console window. The `Removable Storage` tree appears in the left pane.

9. From the console menu, select CONSOLE | SAVE AS. Give the console a short name, such as RSM. Save it in the `\WINNT\System32` folder with the rest of the prepackaged MMC consoles. You can open this custom console from the Run command by entering `rsm.msc`. The file extension is registered to MMC.

The RSM examples used in the rest of this chapter show the custom RSM console rather than the RSM snap-in in the `Computer Management` console.

Tape Names and Ntbackup

Windows 2000 requires that you use the RSM service for handling backup tapes, even if you have only a single tape unit. The benefits of this include improved tape handling, specific tape identification, and a more sophisticated library service for locating tapes. The drawback is that you must assign a unique tape identification label to each tape and manage your backups using those labels. RSM does not write to a tape unless Ntbackup specifies the exact name of a tape that is in the library.

Ntbackup uses tape names in two ways:

- Before Ntbackup writes to a tape, it checks to make sure that the name on the tape matches the name specified by the backup job.

- When Ntbackup overwrites a tape, it applies a new name based on the Media Label value specified in the job.

Keep those two items in mind when you devise a tape rotation schedule. (This is a simplified example to explain tape rotation. Tower-of-Hanoi fans are welcome to get more sophisticated.)

Let's say you rack up seven tapes for a backup rotation. You do Normal backup (full backup) on Sunday and differentials for Monday through Saturday. You save the Sunday tapes for a month and save the last Sunday of the month for a year. The tapes are named for the day of the week.

To establish this rotation, you must configure and schedule a different job for each day of the week. The Monday job, for example, is configured to look for a tape labeled Monday in the Backup media pool. It also writes a media label of Monday when it overwrites the tape.

The Sunday tape requires special handling because of the monthly rotation. Name the tapes Sunday-1, Sunday-2, and Sunday-3. You now configure four different jobs. The first job looks for a tape named Sunday-1 and writes a media label of Sunday-1. Use the same naming scheme for Sunday-2 and Sunday-3.

The fourth Sunday job, the one that writes the full backup you keep for a year, is configured to pull from the Free media pool and to write a label identifying the date and time of the backup so that it stands out in the catalog.

All this reliance on tape naming puts you in a bit of a predicament because at first, the tapes do not have the right labels. To get the ball rolling, configure the first week's jobs to pull from the Free media pool and write their respective media labels. For example, the initial Monday job looks for `New Media` and writes `Monday` to the `Media Label`.

Then, after you go through all seven days of the rotation, change the jobs to look for the actual media label. The backup operator needs to know only the day of the week for the differential jobs and the rotation number for the Sunday jobs.

If you are an NT consultant with an active small-business practice, plan on including a few hours of billable time in reconfiguring your tape backup schemes and re-educating your local backup operators when you upgrade to Windows 2000.

An alternative to this requirement to specify tape names does exist. It revolves around the use of an undocumented Ntbackup switch, called /um, for Unmanaged. If you include the /um switch along with the /p (pool) switch and do not specify a pool, Ntbackup ignores any tape names specified on the command line and writes to whatever tape is in the drive.

Using this option requires manually editing the job in Task Scheduler. See the last steps of "Manually Scheduling a Backup Job" later in this chapter for an example.

The workaround is not appropriate if you have a tape library. You do not want the library to randomly select a tape and overwrite it. Always use specific tape naming when configuring backup jobs sent to a tape library.

Preparing Removable Storage for Backup

This is a quick overview of the actions you need to take to prepare a system to do tape backups:

- Install a tape backup device, if one is not already installed.
- Create a custom console for Removable Storage management. This avoids loading the entire Computer Management console each time you need to change an RSM setting.
- Verify that the tape backup device is correctly configured in RSM.
- Add new tapes and configure them to be available for Backup.
- Configure backup jobs using Windows 2000 Backup.
- Schedule backup jobs to run automatically using the Windows 2000 Task Scheduler.

Installing a Tape Backup Device

As with all hardware, you have the best chance for trouble-free operation if you choose devices that are on the Windows 2000 Hardware Compatibility List. You cannot count on support from the vendor or from Microsoft if you do not use HCL components.

If you are upgrading from legacy NT and your existing tape device did not yet make it to the HCL, it still may work. For example, a standard 4mm DAT or 8mm Exabyte SCSI tape unit that works under NT should probably work under Windows 2000, as well, if the system can find a driver for it on the Windows 2000 CD. But QIC and Travan drives are not supported, and neither are optical drives. Exabyte 8200 units are not recommended. Only a few parallel-port drives are on the HCL.

QIC and Travan Backup Units

Although Microsoft officially removed support for QIC and Travan tape drives from Windows 2000, you may be able to get legacy backup software to work with QIC and Travan devices. Administrators have reported luck using the specialized QIC version of Ultrabac from BEI Corporation, www.ultrabac.com.

Installing a SCSI tape device requires no special configuration as long as the driver is on the Windows 2000 CD. If it is a SCSI device, make sure the SCSI ID does not conflict with another device on the bus. Also verify that the bus terminations are correct.

Note

If you are installing a tape library with multiple drives, place all drives on the same SCSI bus as the associated media changer. This ensures that the drive element addressing used by RSM works properly.

If you are adding additional devices to an IDE or EIDE bus, make sure the master/slave designations and jumper settings are correct. If you are adding a device to the secondary IDE port, make sure the port is enabled in CMOS. Also check to make sure that the device is properly identified in CMOS.

When you start the computer after installing the tape device, the Plug-and-Play (PnP) manager discovers the device during bus enumeration and installs the drivers for it automatically. If the drivers are not on the CD, PnP displays an Unknown Device window and prompts you for the location of the drivers. Obtain the Windows 2000 drivers from the vendor. NT4 drivers probably don't work even though the old *.sys driver is probably still valid. The INF file format changed in Windows 2000, so the class installer cannot read an NT4 INF script.

Verifying Proper Tape Backup Device Configuration in RSM

After the tape device is installed, verify that it is correctly initialized by the RSM service as follows:

Procedure 18.4 **Verifying Tape Backup Device Configuration in RSM**

1. Open the custom Removable Storage console and expand the tree to Physical Location | <device_interface>. An example of a device interface name is HP C1533A SCSI Sequential Device.

2. Right-click the device icon and select PROPERTIES from the fly-out menu to open its Properties window. Figure 18.8 shows an example.

Figure 18.8 Backup device interface Properties window showing General tab.

Inventory Method determines how the device keeps track of its associated media when the library configuration is changed. Ordinarily, the inventory is performed when the library door is opened. A Fast inventory checks any slots that changed since the last inventory. A Full inventory scans bar codes, if they are available, or mounts the media and checks the on-media identifier. The Perform full inventory on mount failure option, selected by default, ensures that a full inventory is performed if the library management system is unable to mount a piece of media.

Enable library, selected by default, enables media in the library to be mounted and used. De-selecting this option prevents the system from using the library. The associate backup device icon gets a red down-arrow, and any backup operations attempted using this library are aborted.

3. Select the Media tab. Figure 18.9 shows an example for the DAT tape drive used in the other examples.

For another example, a CD-RW unit shows Media Types of CD-R, CD-RW, and CD-ROM. Any of those three media types can be placed under the icon for the CD-RW device. If a direct-write driver is loaded, such as Adaptec's DirectCD driver, the CD-RW media can act as backup media for a file-based backup.

The Cleaning Cartridge option is displayed only for robotic libraries. Single-media libraries must be cleaned manually.

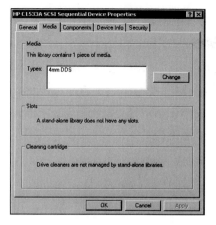

Figure 18.9   Backup media `Properties` window showing `Media` tab.

4. Select the `Components` tab. Figure 18.10 shows an example.

Figure 18.10   Backup device `Properties` window showing `Components` tab.

The `Doors` option is dimmed for a single-media library. For robotic libraries, it defines an allowable time interval for keeping the door open. After this interval, the library is disabled and a warning message is sent to the console.

The `Ports` option defines an allowable time interval for keeping a port open waiting for the robotic assembly to insert the media. After this interval, the port is closed and a warning message is sent to the console.

The `Drives` value lists the number of drives in the library. The `Barcode Reader` field shows whether the library can automatically scan and report barcodes on the media. These barcodes are stored in the Ntmsdata database and are used for sending mount instructions to the library.

5. Select the `Device Info` tab. This is an informational window showing the make/model of the tape drive and its SCSI addressing information

6. Close the `Properties` window.

Now that RSM correctly identified and categorized the tape backup device, the next section covers how to use RSM to prepare a tape for backup.

Preparing Tapes for Backup

The single most significant difference between classic Ntbackup and Windows 2000 Backup is the need to properly name your tapes. If you do not do this—if you simply take your existing Ntbackup tape rotation strategy and try to use it under Windows 2000 Backup—you will get very frustrated.

Windows 2000 Ntbackup writes to a tape under three circumstances only:

- The backup job is configured to use tapes from the Free media pool that are prepared by having a label called `New Media Label` written to the tape. If no free media is in the Free media pool, the backup job aborts.

- The backup job is configured to use a specific tape from the Backup media pool. In this case, the tape name designated by the backup job must match the tape name of an available tape in the Backup pool. If you create a backup job and designate a tape label of `Media Created 10/27/99 at 8:00 PM`, a tape must be available in the tape library with the label `Media Created 10/27/99 at 8:00 PM`. If the tape is not available, the backup job aborts.

- The backup job is configured with the undocumented `/um` switch along with the `/p` switch on the Ntbackup command line. This instructs RSM to use any media currently inserted in the tape device. See "Tape Names and Ntbackup" earlier in this chapter for more information on when to use these switches.

Handling Tape Allocation Errors

If you experimented with Ntbackup before trying to configure RSM, you may get an error when trying to prepare media for the Free media pool. The error is *The requested resource is in use.* This means that the particular media you inserted in the drive was added to the RSM database and allocated to a process. Before you can prepare the tape as free media, you must first de-allocate it. Do so as follows:

Procedure 18.5 **De-allocating Tape Media**

1. Open the custom `Removable Storage` console.
2. Expand the tree to `Backup | <media_type>`.
3. Right-click the media icon and select ALL TASKS | DEALLOCATE from the fly-out menu. The system warns you that deallocating can result in data loss.
4. Click `Yes` to acknowledge and proceed. When the media is deallocated, you are free to move it to the `Free` media pool.

Following are the steps required to prepare a tape for use by Backup. You need at least one blank tape or a tape that you don't mind overwriting. Don't insert the tape yet. Decision points in the steps below affect how the tape is used and recognized.

Procedure 18.6 **Preparing a Tape for the Free Media Pool**

1. Open the custom `Removable Storage` console.
2. Expand the tree to `Removable Storage | Media Pools | Unrecognized`.
3. Highlight the icon representing the backup device. There should be no icons in the right pane because no new tapes were introduced. If you have icons in this pane, tapes were loaded and not properly allocated. Leave the cursor on the tape device icon.
4. Insert the new or recycled tape into the drive. Enable the drive to load the tape and wait for the activity light to stop flashing. If Ntbackup is running and recognizes the format on the tape, an `Import Media Present` window appears with a message prompting to allocate import media.

   If you select `Allocate all compatible import media to Backup`, the media is automatically moved from the `Import` media pool to the `Backup` media pool. Skip this option for now to see how RSM handles imported media. For subsequent imports, you can use this option as a shortcut to allocate classic NT backup tapes automatically.

5. Press F5 to refresh the Removable Storage console. The tape media appears as a numbered icon in the right pane. When RSM sees an item of unrecognized media, it assigns the media the next sequential number from the NTMS database. Figure 18.11 shows an example. The icon also appears under Physical Locations | <tape_device_name> | Media.

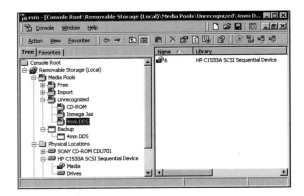

Figure 18.11 Removable Storage console showing new tape media in the Unrecognized media pool.

6. Double-click the icon representing the media to open its Properties window. Figure 18.12 shows an example. See the sidebar titled "Setting Tape Media Options" for more information.

Figure 18.12 Properties window for new tape media.

Setting Tape Media Options

The `Properties` window for a tape shown in Figure 18.16 has several options for configuring a tape. They are:

- **Name.** This is the name assigned to the tape in the NTMS database. You can change this name, but the default sequence number from the Ntmsdata database is usually sufficient.

- **State.** This is the status of the tape. The status is `Idle` unless the tape is in use.

- **Identification.** This field shows the sequence number of the tape and the barcode on the tape as scanned by the library robot, if one is available.

- **Location | Media Pool.** This shows the name of the media pool where this tape currently resides and the drive number if the library has multiple drives.

Deselecting the `Enable Media` option prevents RSM from making this particular tape available for any services, including Backup.

7. Select the `Side` tab. At this point, the media is not assigned an Identification label.

If Ntbackup is waiting for a new tape, you may see another window, such as that in Figure 18.13 appear on your screen. If you see this pop-up while you are in the RSM console, click `Cancel` and proceed with the remaining steps in this section.

If you see this pop-up at any other time, select `Move this media to free now`. This writes `Free Media Label` to the tape and moves it to the `Free` media pool where it is available for backup jobs that are configured to use new media.

Do not select `Allocate this media to Backup now`. This option writes a name of `Free Media Label` to the tape and puts it in the Backup pool where it can be used only by backup jobs that are configured to write to that specific tape name.

Figure 18.13 `New Import Media` window from Backup after new media is inserted.

8. Back at the Removable Storage console, click OK to save the changes and close the Properties window.

9. Right-click the media icon and select PREPARE from the fly-out menu. The system responds with a warning that this action will destroy the data.

10. Click Yes to acknowledge the warning. The system responds with one more request for confirmation.

11. Click Yes to confirm again and proceed with the action. This writes a tape name of Free Media Label - # to the tape, where # is the next sequence number out of the RSM database. It also flags the media as Free in the Ntsmdata database, which moves the icon to the Free pool under the tape device. Figure 18.14 shows an example with several tapes in the Free media pool. Only one tape is currently inserted. The remaining tapes show an Off-Line Media status.

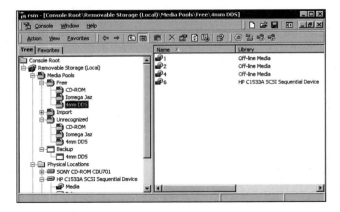

Figure 18.14 Removable Media console showing several media assignments in the Free media pool. The tape currently inserted in the drive is the one with a value other than offline in the Library column.

12. Re-open the Properties window for the newly moved media and select the Side tab. The Identification Label changed to show a Type of Removable Storage Service and Info of Free Media Label #. This label is written to the tape itself. If you remove the tape from the tape device and then reinsert it at a later time, RSM reads the label from the tape and finds the corresponding entry in its database. At the Removable Storage console, the media status indicates that it is available.

13. Close all windows.

With media in the Free media pool, RSM is ready to allocate media to any service that requests it. This includes Ntbackup, Remote Storage Services, or any third-party products. Now, it's time to use the tape to do a backup. Proceed to the next section.

Alternative Media Assignment Method

Instead of using Prepare to write a Free Media label to a tape and move it to the Free media pool, you can drag-and-drop the media icon to the tape device icon under Free. The same warnings and confirmations apply.

You can use drag-and-drop only to move media icons to interfaces that accept that particular media type. For instance, if you drop a tape media icon onto a CD-ROM device, the system responds with an error: *Cannot move <media_item>: media can only be moved to a media pool with the same media type.*

Performing a Backup

You can configure and schedule a backup job in two ways. The fastest way is to make entries directly in the Ntbackup interface and schedule them manually using the scheduling tool in Ntbackup. The second is to use the Backup Wizard, which walks you step-by-step through the configuration. This section covers both methods, starting with the manual method. The examples assume that you are sending the backup job to a tape device. If you are backing up to a file, enter a filename and path instead of identifying a tape backup unit and media. The rest of the steps are the same.

The steps in this section assume that you prepared at least one tape using RSM and placed it in the Free media pool. If you specify free media in the job configuration and you do not have free media in the library when the job runs interactively, the system responds with this error: *There is no unused media available with the selected type.* At that point, you can either insert prepared media or abort the backup job and prepare media in the Free media pool. If the job runs in the background, it aborts if no free media is available.

Manually Configuring a Backup Job

If you are not a fan of Windows 2000 wizards, you can configure a backup job directly by using Ntbackup and then either run it interactively from the Ntbackup window or schedule it to run later using the Task Scheduler. The steps to schedule a job are listed later in this section.

Procedure 18.7 **Configuring a Backup Job Using Ntbackup Window**

1. Start Ntbackup using START | PROGRAMS | ACCESSORIES | SYSTEM TOOLS | BACKUP.

2. Select the Backup tab. Select the drives and/or folders you want to include in the Backup job. You can use My Network Places to select servers and share points, as well.

3. From the Ntbackup menu, select TOOLS | OPTIONS. The Options window opens. Select a Default Backup Type for the job. The example uses a Normal backup. Refer to the "Backup Options" section earlier in this chapter for details determining the correct option.

4. Select the Backup Log tab. Under Information, select either Detailed or Summary. The Summary option is selected by default. A Summary log lists all skipped files and any errors.

5. Click OK to save your configuration and return to the main Backup window.

6. Under Backup Destination, select the tape backup unit.

7. Under Backup Media or File Name, two options exist for specifying the name of the tape media. You must designate the name of the media that RSM will select for the backup job. If you have a manual tape unit, an operator must insert the tape prior to the start of the job. See "Tape Names and Ntbackup" earlier in this chapter for information about what to name the tapes.

8. Run the backup job interactively to make sure it works before scheduling it to run in the background at night. Click Start Backup. The Backup Job Information window opens.

   The field labeled If the media is overwritten, use this label to identify the media is very important if you use a tape library. See "Tape Names and Ntbackup" earlier in this chapter for details on making this selection.

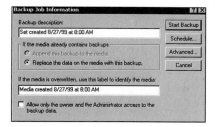

Figure 18.15 `Backup Job Information` window showing default entries for Backup description and media labeling.

9. Click `Advanced`. The `Advanced Backup Options` window opens.

   If you elected to use new media, the `Append this backup to the media` option is dimmed. The assumption is that the free media has no useful data. If the `Append` and `Replace` options are available, select the one that best suits the circumstances.

   If you select `Back up data in remote storage`, you will recall every offline file in the remote storage library. See Chapter 12 for reasons why you might not want to do this and alternatives for backing up remote files.

10. Click `OK` to save the settings and return to the `Backup Job Information` window.

11. Click `Start Backup`. If media exists in the Free pool but it was not prepared with a `Free Media Label` name, RSM gives you an informational message stating, *There is no unused media available with the selected type, but media named: <media_name> is available. Do you want to use this media for this backup?* If you click `Yes`, the media is transferred from the Free pool to the Backup pool and the backup begins. If you click `No`, the system prompts you to add unused media or cancel. This occurs only in an interactive session. A background session run by Task Scheduler aborts if this happens.

12. If recognizable content is on the media and you select the `Replace` option, Backup prompts you to confirm the overwrite. Click `Yes` to confirm. This happens only in an interactive session. A scheduled job overwrites when told to do so.

13. After the backup job commences, the `Backup Progress` window opens and the files begin to flow to the tape.

14. If you cancel out of the job, Backup prompts you to complete backing up the current file. You have the option of bypassing this and canceling the job immediately.

15. When the backup is complete, the `Backup Progress` window informs you of the status. Click `Report` to open Notepad and view the backup log. This is an example log for a job that backed up one file:

```
Backup Status
Operation: Backup
Active backup destination: 4mm DDS
Media name: "Media created 10/27/99 at 8:39 AM"

Backup of "C: "
Backup set #1 on media #1
Backup description: "Set created 10/27/99 at 8:39 AM"
Backup Type: Normal

Backup started on 10/27/99 at 8:46 AM.
Folder C:\
Test.txt                              303370      10/24/99      4:57 AM
Backup completed on 10/27/99 at 8:46 AM.
Directories: 1
Files: 1
Bytes: 307,718
Time:  5 seconds
```

16. Close the `Backup Progress` window.

17. From the BACKUP menu, select JOB | SAVE SELECTIONS. The `Save Selections` window opens. Give the backup job a short, descriptive name, such as `Daily-Differential` or `Weekly-Full`.

    The file is saved with a *.bks extension in your local profile under `\Documents & Settings\<userID\Local Settings\Application Data\Microsoft\Windows NT\NTBackup\Data`. The backup file consists of a few lines of text that define the path to each directory tree included in the backup. The file is only a few bytes.

18. Leave Backup open and proceed to the next section to schedule the job to run in the background.

If you check the Removable Storage console at this point, you'll see that the media icon representing the tape you inserted was moved under the `Backup | <tape_device>` icon. If you open the `Properties` window for this media item and select the `Side` tab, you'll see that the State value changed to Allocated and that the Identification Label information changed to a `Type` of Microsoft Windows NT Backup (Ntbackup.exe). You'll also see that Info changed to the date and that time stamp was applied to the backup job or to the name you assigned in the `Backup Information` window.

You can now either manually eject the tape from the tape backup device or right-click the media icon and select EJECT from the fly-out menu. This starts the Eject Media Wizard, which walks you through returning the tape to its proper place in the robotic library. For single tape drives, it's easier just to press the Eject button on the drive.

Now that you tested the job interactively, use the steps in the next section to schedule the job for execution at a later time.

Manually Scheduling a Backup Job

Regardless of the value you and your users place on your data, you probably don't want to drive out to work at 11:00 each night to configure and run a backup job. You need a way to configure a job and then schedule it to run on its own. In classic NT, this is done by building an Ntbackup batch file and then submitting it to the Scheduler service using the at command. Windows 2000 simplifies this somewhat:

- Ntbackup has a custom interface to build a batch job that has all (or at least most) of the necessary commands to run a job as a background task. The job is saved under \WINNT\Tasks as a *.job file.

- Backup jobs are run by Task Scheduler, Mtask.exe, which is a more sophisticated version of the old Scheduler service. Task Scheduler has a new interface that eliminates the need for running at.

Let's schedule the backup job created in the last section. A job can be scheduled by someone other than the administrator who created it. Proceed as follows:

Procedure 18.8 **Scheduling a Backup Job**

1. In the Backup window, click Start Backup. The Backup Job Information window opens.

2. Click Schedule. The Scheduled Job Options window opens.

3. Enter a name for the scheduled job. This name becomes the filename for the *.job file submitted to Task Scheduler.

4. Click Properties. The Schedule Job window opens.

5. Enter scheduling information for the backup job. If you want to run the job on more than one schedule (for example, running a Normal job every Sunday as well as once a month), click Show Multiple Schedules to change the window so that several schedules can be configured.

6. Select the Settings tab.

   The Scheduled Task Completed option automatically aborts the backup job if it did not complete in 72 hours. This prevents the job from hanging the queue and blocking other jobs. The time interval can be shortened to 12 hours for backups that run every night.

   The Idle Time option is suitable for Professional desktops or SOHO servers where the user works late and does not want the backup to slow down the system.

   The Power Management option is for laptops and prevents a backup job from kicking off if the unit is on battery.

7. Click OK to save the changes and return to the Scheduled Job Options window.

8. Select the Backup Details window. This gives a summary of your selections.

9. Click OK to save the backup job as a ★.job file and place it in the Task Scheduler folder, \WINNT\Tasks.

10. Open the Task Scheduler folder using CONTROL PANEL | SCHEDULED TASKS. The new job appears in the job list.

11. Double-click the job name to open its Properties window.

    If you delete a scheduled job from Backup, it is removed from the Task Scheduler job list. If you remove a job using Task Scheduler, it is removed from the Scheduled Jobs calendar in Backup. You must close and reopen Backup to refresh the window.

12. Close the Properties window.

13. Close the Task Scheduler.

All you need to do now is make sure you have the right tapes in the drive, depending on how you configured the job. The next section covers performing this same task using the Backup Wizard.

Backup Job Structure

A scheduled backup job launches Ntbackup in the background with command-line switches that configure the backup parameters. This is an example of a backup task. The entry is long because the path to the backup file is buried deep in the user profile.

```
C:\WINNT\system32\ntbackup.exe backup "@C:\Documents and Settings\Administrator\Local
➥Settings\Application Data\Microsoft\Windows NT\NTBackup\data\Full_Backup.bks" /n
➥"Monday-1" /d "Monday-1" /v:no /r:no /rs:no /hc:yes
```

These are the switches and their functions:

- **/n.** The name of the tape specified for the job. A tape by that name *must* be in the drive or the job aborts.

- **/d.** The name applied to the tape when it is overwritten. This should be the same name specified in /d so that the same tape can be used the next time.

- **/v.** This sets the Verify option.

- **/r.** This sets the Restriction option. If set, only members of the Administrators group can access the tape.

- **/rs.** This sets the Remote Storage backup option.

- **/hc.** This sets the Hardware Compression option.

If you have a single tape drive and don't want to fool with tape names, add a /um and /p switch at the end of the command line. The designated tape name is then ignored and the job is sent to whichever tape is in the drive. Don't use this option if you have a tape library.

For details on other command-line options, type ntbackup /? at a command prompt.

Configuring and Scheduling Backup Jobs Using the Backup Wizard

If you would rather take a step-by-step approach for configuring and scheduling a backup job, use the Backup Wizard as follows:

Procedure 18.9 Configuring and Scheduling a Backup Job Using the Backup Wizard

1. Open Backup.
2. Select the Schedule Jobs tab.
3. Double-click the date you want the scheduled backups to start running. The Backup and Recovery Tools Wizard starts.
4. Click Next. The What to Back Up window opens.

   The Back up everything on my computer option does exactly what it says. If you have network drives pointed at the root of seven network volumes, Backup dutifully backs up the content of those volumes to your local tape unit. This option is appropriate only for standalone computers or Professional desktops that map only to the user's data files.

The `Only back up the system state data` option limits the backup System State files. See the "Backing Up System State Files" section earlier in this chapter for details.

5. Select `Back up Selected Files, Drives, or Network Data`. This gives you the most flexibility in determining the contents of the backup job.

6. Click `Next`. The `Items To Back Up` window opens.

7. Select the drives, folders, or files you want to include in the backup job. If you select network drives, you need to make sure that the mappings stay in place. A better strategy is to use My Network Places to navigate to the shared folder so that a UNC path is used rather than a hard mapping.

8. Click `Next`. The `Where To Store The Backup` window opens. The Backup Media Type field displays the tape backup unit. See the "Tape Names and Ntbackup" section for details about what to select for `Backup Media or File Name`.

9. Click `Next`. The `Type Of Backup` window opens.

10. Select the backup type that fits your backup strategy. Refer to the "Backup Options" section earlier in this chapter for details.

11. Click `Next`. The `How To Back Up` window opens.

    `Verify data after backup` is necessary only if you want to make absolutely certain that files were correctly stored on tape prior to deleting a volume.

    `Use hardware compression, if available` configures Backup to send the appropriate command to the tape unit driver to enable compression. If you can comfortably fit your files on a single tape or tape library, you should not select this option. It slows down the backup job unnecessarily.

12. Click `Next`. The `Media Options` window opens. Select Replace or Append depending on your backup strategy. If you selected `New Media` as the media type, the `Append` option is dimmed.

13. Click Next. The Backup Label window opens. See Figure 18.16. See "Tape Names and Ntbackup" for information about what to enter in this field.

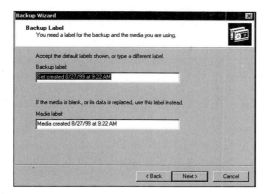

Figure 18.16 Backup Wizard - Backup Label window.

14. Click Next. The When To Back Up window opens.

15. Select the Later radio button. The Set Account Information window opens.

16. In the Run As field, enter the domain name and the account name for the account that Ntbackup uses to run the backup job. This account must have Backup Operator privileges or higher. The password for the account should be configured not to expire.

17. The system assigns the credentials to the job and then releases the Schedule Entry area of the window for entering a Job Name. This name becomes the filename for the job that is given to the Windows Scheduler.

18. Click Set Schedule. The Schedule Job window opens. Select a start time and interval based on your backup strategy. The Advanced button enables you to schedule special-purpose jobs to run for a limited period of time.

19. Select the Settings tab.

    The Scheduled Task Completed option automatically aborts the backup job if it is not complete in 72 hours (the default setting). This prevents the job from hanging the queue and blocking other jobs.

    The Idle Time option is suitable for Professional desktops or SOHO servers where the user works late and does not want the backup to slow down the system.

The Power Management option is for laptops and prevents a backup job from kicking off if the unit is on battery.

20. Click OK to save the settings and return to the Backup Wizard.

21. Click Next. A completion window opens, summarizing your entries.

22. Click Finish to schedule the job and return to the Backup window, Schedule Jobs tab. The window shows an icon for every day that the job is scheduled to run.

23. Click one of the icons. The Scheduled Job Options window opens. Using this window, you can change most, but not all, of the job settings. If you want to change a setting that is not in the Options window, you must delete the job and start over. See the sidebar titled "Backup Job Structure" at the end of "Manually Scheduling a Backup Job" earlier in this chapter for a description of the job structure.

You can now implement your backup plan. Remember that failing to insert the right tape for the right job aborts the backup, so label your tapes carefully.

Restoring Files

The best backup in the world won't help you if you can't get the files off the tape and back onto a disk. This section describes individual file restores because that's why the majority of restores are done. Full restores of a crashed volume or lost system is covered in "Restoring a System Volume" later in this chapter.

Two options are available for file restoration. You can use the Restore Wizard to walk through the process step-by-step, or configure the restore job manually. Both the wizard and the manual method assume that you have an existing catalog of the tape you need to recover. If you do not have a catalog, see "Cataloging a Tape" later in this chapter.

Choosing Restore Locations and Advanced Options

Two windows appear during file restoration that offer special options. Let's review these options before starting the restore so that you know what to expect.

The Restore wizard gives three location options in the Where To Restore window shown in Figures 18.18 and 18.19. They are:

- Original Location. If you select this option, Restore puts the files back where they came from. If the directory structure is no longer present, it is re-created. This option is most appropriate for restoring entire volumes.

Under normal circumstances, you do not want to restore individual user files to their original location because you may overwrite the existing files and lose critical data added since the last backup.

- `Alternate Location`. This option opens up a path field and `Browse` button. Use these to find a folder to hold the restored files. This option writes the original directory structure to the target folder. This is most appropriate for restoring an entire subtree rather than an individual file.

- `Single Folder`. This option also opens up a path and `Browse` button. Use these to find a folder to hold the restored files. This option does not preserve the original directory structure. This is most appropriate when restoring individual files. If you elect to restore an entire directory using the `Single Folder` option, the files are plucked out of the directory and put at the root of the specified folder.

The Restore wizard gives these options in the `Advanced Restore Options` window shown in Figure 18.20. They are:

- `Restore security`. This option applies the original security descriptors to the files. This is the default selection and the one most appropriate for the majority of file restores. If you have a situation where the original security descriptors are no longer valid—you may be restoring data after reinstalling the operating system—or you want to scrub the old descriptors and replace them with the defaults in the restoration folder, deselect this option.

- `Restore Removable Storage database`. This option includes the special shadow copies of the RSS engine database, EngDB, which keeps track of the file locations in the tape system and the File System Agent database, FsaDB, which keeps track of the remote files on disk. These RSS databases are restored to their parent folder, `WINNT\System32\RemoteStorage`. Use this option in conjunction with a restore of the RSS library. See Chapter 13 for details.

- `Restore junction points, not the folders and file data they reference`. This option enables you to restore one volume without reaching through a mount point to the files in another file system. If you are not sure whether a particular volume has mount points, select this option just to be on the safe side. You can restore the mounted volume separately, if necessary.

- When restoring replicated data sets…. This option is used when restoring files to a volume that is replicated using the File Replication System. This option is available only when restoring System State files. By selecting this option, the time and date stamps on the replicated files are made current, so that they become the files that propagate outward to other servers holding a replica of the volume.

Restoring Files Using the Restore Wizard

The following steps assume you are restoring from tape. If you are restoring from a file, select the location and name of the backup file rather than the tape device. The remaining steps are the same.

Procedure 18.10   **Restoring a File Using the Restore Wizard**

1. Insert the tape containing the file you want to restore.
2. Open Backup.
3. Select the Welcome tab.
4. Click Restore Wizard. This starts the Restore Wizard.
5. Click Next. The What To Restore window opens. See Figure 18.17. The information in this window comes from the backup catalog stored in the user profile under \Documents and Settings\<userid>\Local Settings\Application Data\Microsoft\Windows NT\Ntbackup\Catalogs. If you did not perform the backup, log on using that account so that you can see the catalog.

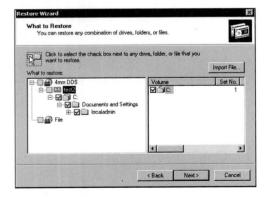

Figure 18.17   Restore Wizard - What To Restore window showing files that were selected for restoration.

6. Drill down through the catalog tree until you find the right date, and then locate the file you want to restore.

7. Click Next. The Completing the Restore Wizard window opens. This window has an Advanced tab for setting additional parameters.

8. Click Advanced. The wizard remains in operation and the Where To Restore window opens. See "Choosing Restore Locations and Advanced Options" at the start of this section for information on making this selection. See Figure 18.18.

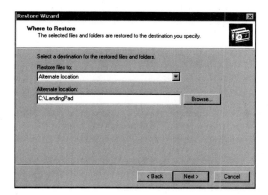

Figure 18.18 Restore Wizard - Where To Restore window showing alternate location for restored files.

9. Click Next. The How To Restore window opens.

   Do not replace the file on my disk skips restoring any files that exist in the destination location. This is most appropriate when you are restoring to an existing location and you want to make absolutely sure no existing data is lost.

   The Replace the file on my disk only if it is older than the backup copy option is appropriate when restoring a file or files to the original location and you're sure that any older files are expendable. My personal preference is never to use this option. "You mean the changes I did this morning that I didn't tell you about are really lost? Lost forever?"

   The Always replace the file on disk option overwrites the files if the names and locations match.

10. Click Next. The Advanced Restore Options window opens. See "Choosing Restore Locations and Advanced Options" at the start of this section for information on making this selection.

11. Click Next. A final completion window opens.

12. Click Finish to submit the restore job. The Restore Progress window keeps you apprised of the job status and tells you when it is complete.

After the files are restored to the alternate location, copy them to their ultimate destination. If you are denied access, you may need to take ownership and change the ACL permissions. If the files are encrypted, see Chapter 13 for your options.

Restoring Manually

If you do not want to use the Restore wizard, you can configure a Restore job manually as follows:

Procedure 18.11 **Restoring a File Manually Using Ntbackup**

1. Open Backup.

2. Insert the tape that contains the files you want to restore.

3. Select the Restore tab and expand the tree in the catalog under the job that contains the file or folder you want to restore. See Figure 18.19.

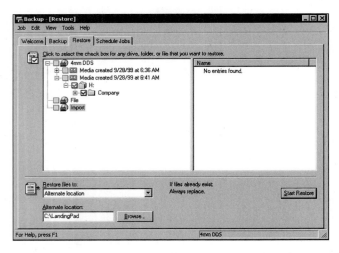

Figure 18.19   Backup window showing Restore tab with settings for a restore job.

4. Select the files or folder you want to restore.

5. Under Restore files to, select one of the three location options. See "Choosing Restore Locations and Advanced Options" at the start of this section for information on making this selection.

6. Click Start Restore. The Confirm Restore window opens, providing you with an opportunity to set Advanced Options.

7. Click Advanced. The Advanced Restore Options window opens. See Figure 18.20. See "Choosing Restore Locations and Advanced Options" at the start of this section for information on making this selection.

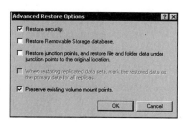

Figure 18.20 Advanced Restore Options window showing default options.

8. Click OK to return to the Confirm Restore window.

9. Click Start Restore. The Restore Progress window keeps you apprised of the job status and tells you when it is complete.

10. When the restore is complete, close the Restore Progress window.

Cataloging a Tape

When Ntbackup writes a backup file to tape, it includes a copy of the catalog entry for that job. If you have a tape that contains backup files but either you have lost the on-disk catalog, the catalog was lost in the same disk crash that took the server, or you are restoring to a different server and you do not have access to the original catalog, you can restore the catalog and then restore the files on the tape. Proceed as follows:

Procedure 18.12 **Cataloging a Tape**

1. Open the custom Remote Storage console.

2. Insert the tape in the tape drive and wait for the tape to be mounted and read.

3. If recognizable content is on the tape, RSM places it in Media Pools | Import. If RSM places the tape in the Unrecognized pool, and you're sure this is the right tape, you have a problem. Either the tape is corrupt, making it unreadable, or the tape heads are slightly different from those in the original device, if two tape backup units are involved. Try using the original tape device to see whether you can read the tape.

4. Open Backup.

5. Select the Restore tab. The imported media appears under an Import icon in the display. The example in Figure 18.21 shows a tape named PHX-DC-01.

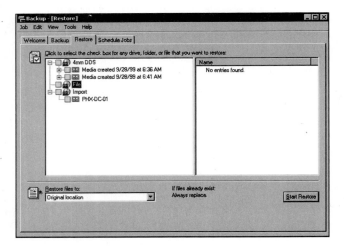

Figure 18.21 Backup window showing the Restore tab with an Import icon holding a recognized tape that does not have a catalog.

6. Right-click the media icon and select ADD TO BACKUP MEDIA from the fly-out menu. This moves the icon to the list of media under the associated tape device icon and makes it available for cataloging.

The other options include Re-tensioning, Formatting, and Erasing. These options are rarely used. Modern tape backup systems format and tension automatically as jobs are run. You really have no reason to erase a tape that you are going to reuse. The contents are overwritten anyway. Don't bother erasing a tape as a security measure. A tape scanner can read ghost data from several overwrites.

7. Right-click the media icon again and select CATALOG from the fly-out menu. When the process finishes, the window closes.

The catalog restore can take a while. Backup accesses the tape, reads the tape header, and then writes the contents to the catalog associated with the user who is currently logged on. A tape could contain several backup jobs, so rather than waste time cataloging them all, Backup shows the top of the list of jobs. As you expand the tree, Backup accesses the tape again and writes the catalog contents to disk.

After a tape is cataloged, you can restore the files by either using the Restore Wizard or by manually configuring the restore job.

Restoring a System Volume

So far, the recovery operations have been for individual files and subdirectories. But what if the system partition goes to the Great Spindle in the Sky?

Ideally, you protected yourself against a loss of the system partition by mirroring the drives, either in software or hardware, and if you're using hardware RAID, you should even have a hot standby that syncs up if one of the mirrored drives crashes. But if all these defensive measures fail, and you get a blue-screen stop followed by an *Unable to Locate Operating System* on the next restart and nothing you do can resuscitate the victim, recovery from tape is really your only alternative.

The general actions required to restore a system volume are:

Procedure 18.13 **Restoring a System Volume**

1. Reinstall Windows 2000. You don't need to install any more than the bare essentials, just enough to get the system up so that you can access Ntbackup.

2. After you have a working system, initialize RSM to see the tape backup device, and then insert the tape containing the system partition files and system state files in the tape unit.

3. Catalog the tape using the steps in "Cataloging a Tape" earlier in this chapter.

4. After you have a visual display of the tape contents, select the C drive (if that is your system partition) and the System State files. If this is a domain controller, see Chapter 11 for the steps to recover the Active Directory.

5. Start the restore. It may take a while to finish. After restoration is complete, restart the machine. It should be back to its old self again.

As you can see, this is a long and somewhat tedious process. The major commercial packages have a disaster recovery option that enables you to boot from the Windows 2000 setup disks, use a fourth disk to load the tape driver, and use a script to automate finding the on-tape catalog and restoring the files. All you need is a formatted disk, and some the products even format the disk for you.

Some shops take the precaution of using Ghost or some other disk duplicating utility (or a replica backup) to take a snapshot of the system partition. Recovery using Ghost or a tape image is about as painless as it gets, but you need a place to put a big image file if you have a 2- or 3GB system partition.

Overview of Third-Party Backup Packages

Five major players are in the Windows NT/Windows 2000 backup game. Table 18.1 shows their names and products. The feature sets change constantly, but you can expect to get these additional features not provided by Windows 2000 Backup:

- Enterprise backup for all operating platforms, including NetWare, UNIX, and VMS
- Single disk disaster recovery
- Fast, flexible file recovery database operations
- Simultaneous backup streams to multiple drives
- Tape striping to improve performance and reliability
- Integrated encryption
- High-end reporting

Table 18.1 **Third-Party Backup Packages**

Product	Company	Web address
ArcServe	Computer Associates	www.cai.com or
		www.cheyenne.com
Backup Exec	Veritas	www.veritas.com
Networker	Legato	www.legato.com
ADSM	IBM	www.pc.ibm.com
Novastor	Novastor	www.novastor.com
Ultrabac	BEI Corporation	www.ultrabac.com

Recovering Deleted Files Without Tape Backups

Nearly all tape restores involve individual files rather than entire volumes. Users are always overwriting files or accidentally deleting files. Their first reaction when they realize their mistake is to request a file restore. NetWare administrators have come to appreciate the Salvage area on a NetWare volume that stores deleted files where they can be quickly recovered with a client-based Filer utility. Windows 2000 does not have a similar feature.

Executive Software, the same company that licensed Diskeeper to Microsoft for Windows 2000, has a utility called Undelete for Windows NT. The Windows 2000 version of this product is slated for concurrent release. Undelete for Windows 2000 has a server component and a client component. The server component stores deleted files and enables them to be undeleted by the user who deleted them. Full product specifications, pricing, and a trial download are available at `www.execsoft.com`.

For local file recovery on a Professional workstation, File Rescue by Software Shelf is a great tool that is very simple to use, a big plus in the undelete racket. Get more information from `www.softwareshelf.com` and at `www.sunbelt-software.com/Filerescue.htm`.

Recovering from Blue-Screen Stops

Windows 2000, like its predecessors, has a long list of core functions that are critical to system operation. A failure in any of these core functions brings the system to a stop rather than risking widespread memory and file corruption. This *kernel-mode stop* is more commonly called the *Blue Screen Of Death* (BSOD).

If you are not familiar with NT, the kernel-mode stop got this name because it kills all processes and calls a kernel-mode routing called KeBugCheckEx. This routine displays a blue screen containing diagnostic information.

Bugcheck Codes

The top lines of the stop screen contain *bugcheck codes* that identify the source of the stop, information about the stop that differs depending on the stop code, and oftentimes the name of the culprit. The information looks like this:

```
*** STOP: 0x0000001E (0xC0000005, 0x8041E9FB, 0x00000000, 0x00000030)
KMODE_EXCEPTION_NOT_HANDLED
*** Address 8041E9FB base at 80400000, DateStamp 377509d0 - ntoskrnl.exe
```

The bugcheck codes are your best bet for finding the problem quickly. The rest of the stop screen usually (but not always) contains stack dump information listing the processes that were in memory at the time of the crash and what they were doing. If you have to expand your investigation to search through that crowd, you need a lot of patience and a copy of *Murder on the Orient Express* as a guide.

This is a brief explanation of the bugcheck information. The first entry after STOP is the hex ID of the stop code. This corresponds to the name on the second line. If no name exists, the exception is so severe that the system cannot refer to the lookup table to generate the name.

The next four entries are parameters that were passed to KeBugCheckEx when the STOP error was issued. The meaning and origin of these parameters vary depending on the type of error. For the 0x1E error displayed in the example, the meanings and origins are as follows:

- **0xC0000005.** Exception code. This particular code is an access violation. The driver attempted to touch an area of memory where it did not have permission to go.
- **0x8041E9FB.** Address where the exception occurred.
- **0x00000000.** Special parameter. The developer of a driver or module can pass a debug value to KeBugCheckEx to display here.
- **0x00000030.** Special parameter. A second place for special diagnostic values.

The line following the bugcheck code specifies the base address of the image that caused the exception, a hex representation of the date stamp on the image, and its name. In this case, the exception was thrown by the Windows 2000 kernel driver, Ntoskrnl.exe.

The fact that a particular executable is implicated by the bugcheck code does not necessarily mean that image was the perpetrator. It might have been the dupe used by the real murderer. For example, the stop error shown in the example was generated by trying to load an old ASPI driver that is not compatible with Windows 2000. The incompatible driver stabbed the system. Poor old Ntoskrnl just happened to come by later and pick up the knife.

The Microsoft KnowledgeBase is the Hercule Poirot of most kernel mode stop mysteries. Start by searching for Q103059, which lists the stop codes and their names. Then check out Q192463 for ways to collect information without doing full-blown kernel debugging. For a full list of stop codes, download the Windows 2000 DDK from msdn.microsoft.com and take a look at the include file, bugcodes.h.

Common Stop Errors

Of the more than 200 kernel-mode stops in Windows 2000, only a few are especially common. The KMODE_EXCEPTION_NOT_HANDLED error in the example is one of them. These are some others:

- **IRQL_NOT_LESS_OR_EQUAL (0x0000000A).** This occurs when a device driver running at one IRQL (IRQ Level) tries to access memory that is owned by a process at a higher IRQL. A total of 32 IRQ priority levels are in Windows 2000. When a thread issues a software interrupt, it does so at a particular IRQL. If it subsequently tries to reach higher, it triggers this stop error.

- **UNEXPECTED_KERNEL_MODE_TRAP (0x0000007F).** This is generally a hardware problem. Refer to KnowledgeBase article Q137539 for a list of common culprits.

- **NTFS_FILE_SYSTEM (0x00000024).** This is commonly caused by a virus, or sometimes an overly aggressive virus checker. This is also commonly caused by file system utilities that attempt to reach around the APIs to access the file system directly. It can also be caused by file system corruption.

- **PAGE_FAULT_IN_NONPAGED_AREA (0x00000050).** This is also commonly caused by virus checkers. It is also tied to many TCP/IP problems, as well. Some fairly notorious denial-of-service attacks result in a 0x50 stop error, so if you start getting this on your DMZ machines, you might start by enabling auditing and applying a packet sniffer to see whether you can capture the source of the problem.

- **INACCESSIBLE_BOOT_DEVICE (0x0000007B).** If this occurs when starting a system that was in operation for a while, it almost always indicates a failed drive, a failed drive controller, or a boot sector virus. If it occurs on a new installation, you may have drive sector translation problems or an improper host adapter driver. This error also occurs if you restart a system following a failure of the primary drive in a mirrored set.

Memory Dumps

If you get a stop error after installing a new piece of hardware, a driver upgrade, or a new application, your first step should be to restart and select the *Last Known Good Configuration* option. See "Restoring Functionality with the Last Known Good Configuration" later in this chapter for details. If that doesn't work, boot to a Recovery Console and delete or rename the offending driver. See "Recovery Console" later in this chapter.

If you are unable to restore normal operation, you can capture the contents of memory at the time of the stop and send it off to Microsoft technical support for them to analyze. They charge a few hundred dollars per incident for this service, but when you compare that against the losses incurred from server downtime, it's probably worth the expense.

By default, the memory contents are dumped to the paging file when the system stops. After restart, the paging file is copied to a file called MEMORY.DMP under \WINNT. For this to work, the paging file must be at least as big as memory, plus 1MB. The paging file must also be in the system partition if you are going to dump memory. You can have paging files on other volumes, but the paging file in the system partition must be RAM + 1MB.

If you have a fire-breathing server with 10 or 20 gigabytes of RAM, you probably don't want to give up the real estate in your system partition for an 11- or 21GB paging file. It wouldn't give much useful information anyway, unless the application is known to leave a clear footprint when it misbehaves. An option does exist to write only kernel information on a stop error. This is usually sufficient.

Configuring Memory Dumps

Memory dump options are controlled by System properties in the Control Panel. Open this window as follows:

Procedure 18.14   **Opening System Properties**

1. Right-click the My Computer icon on the desktop and select PROPERTIES from the fly-out menu. This opens the System Properties window.

2. Selecting the Advanced tab.

3. Click Startup and Recovery. This opens the Startup and Recovery window. Figure 18.22 shows an example.

Figure 18.22 Startup and Recovery window showing default Recovery settings for handling system stop errors.

This is a list of the debugging options:

- `Send an administrative alert` uses the Alerter service, if it is still functioning after the crash, to put out a network broadcast to members of the `Administrators` domain local group to notify them of the stop error. If you have a trap management console of some sort (HP Openview, for example), you should also load an SNMP agent on the server so that it can trap when the failure occurs.

- `Write debugging information to` specifies the name of a file that holds the memory contents after the system reboots. The dump stays in the paging file until the system restarts successfully.

- `Write kernel information only` saves hard-drive space that goes to waste if you have lots of RAM in a server. You can size the paging file by opening Task Manager, selecting the `Performance` tab, and looking at the total memory value under Kernel Memory.

- `Automatically reboot` restarts the system after the memory dump is complete. It has the potential of causing a continuous loop if the cause of the blue-screen stop doesn't go away after restart. For this reason, it is a good idea to monitor your servers with some sort of SNMP tool that notifies you when the server crashes.

Before you burn a 512MB dump file onto a CD for overnight delivery to Microsoft, make sure that useful information is in the file. The Windows 2000 Resource Kit comes with a utility called Dumpchk that verifies the dump file.

Analyzing a dump file requires a practiced eye. If you want to try your hand, the Windows 2000 CD contains a utility called Dumpexam that you can use to examine the contents of a dump file. This utility requires a *symbol tree*, which is a file that contains the debug symbols used to interpret the file contents. The symbol tree file also comes on the CD. The dump file is only a snapshot and may not contain enough information to find the true culprit. You may need to set up an interactive kernel-mode debug trace. The Windows 2000 KnowledgeBase contains details on kernel-mode debugging.

Registry Tip: Recovery Options

The recovery options selected in this window update Registry values in the following key: HKLM | System | CurrentControlSet | CrashControl.

Using Safe Mode

When calamities occur that make the system unstable or cause it to stop, getting the system booted to a stable configuration is the first priority. Windows 2000, like its PnP partners, has a set of special diagnostic operating configurations collectively called *Safe Mode*. When a system is running in Safe Mode, some or most of the services and drivers are disabled. A system that refuses to boot to Safe Mode is a very sick system.

You get access to the SAFE MODE menu options by pressing F8 at the boot menu. This is a list of the options and their functions. Not everything on this list is a Safe Mode option, but they all can help you define and correct a problem in one circumstance or another.

- **Safe Mode.** This mode avoids PnP nearly entirely. It loads a bare set of peripheral drivers, including only mouse and keyboard, 16-color VGA video, SCSI and IDE interfaces and drives, floppy interface and drives, and a few system services. Safe Mode does not load network services. This mode sets an environment variable called SAFEBOOT_OPTION=MINIMAL to indicate that it is running.

- **Safe Mode with Networking.** This option works the same as Safe Mode with the addition of network drivers, including the Workstation and Server service along with server-based services, such as DNS, DHCP, and WINS. This mode is useful when you want to test network connections on a workstation without loading a cacophony of peripheral drivers, or if PnP hangs the machine and you want to download drivers from a network server. If you use this mode on a domain controller, be prepared to wait a long time for it to enable you to log on. This mode sets SAFEBOOT_OPTION=NETWORK.

- **Safe Mode with Command Prompt.** This is the same as Safe Mode, except that the Explorer shell does not start. Use this mode if corruption in the Explorer files or abnormal Registry entries are causing the machine to blue screen or behave abnormally. In this mode, the system boots to a standard CMD window. When there, you can run programs. Avoid running graphical programs, because they automatically launch Explorer. This mode sets SAFEBOOT_OPTION=MINIMAL.

- **Enable Boot Logging.** This is not a Safe Mode option. Use this option if you want to write a log of the kernel service drivers as they load. The output goes to a file called NTBTLOG.TXT in the \WINNT directory. The system boots with its normal compliment of drivers and services.

- **Enable VGA Mode.** This is not a Safe Mode option. It only replaces the currently loaded video drivers with standard 16-color VGA drivers. This is useful for troubleshooting video problems, although it can be a pain, because you must manually reload the correct drivers after selecting this option. If you aren't sure of the correct drivers, you might find yourself searching around for the driver disk or downloading them again from the vendor's Web site.

- **Last Known Good Configuration.** A troubleshooting option designed to return the System hive to a previously stable condition. See the "Restoring Functionality with the Last Known Good Configuration" section a little later in this chapter for more information.

- **Debugging Mode.** This option sets up the system for kernel mode debugging. This requires a serial line connection and a checked version of the operating system. See the Microsoft KnowledgeBase for a description of kernel mode debugging.

- **Directory Service Restore Mode (Windows 2000 domain controllers only).** This is a special version of Safe Mode used to correct Active Directory database problems and to recover the System State files on a domain controller. See Chapter 11 for details about AD recovery. This mode sets SAFEBOOT_OPTION=DSREPAIR.

Special Logon Considerations in DS Restore Mode

When booting to DS Restore Mode, the Active Directory database is not started, so the Kerberos security provider is not available. The MSV1_0 security provider is the only source of authentication for local logon. This provider uses accounts in the SAM database to validate user credentials.

When a server is promoted to the domain controller, the entire contents of the SAM are moved to the Directory and a new Administrator account is created. The Promotion Wizard collects a password for this new Administrator account.

When you boot to DS Repair Mode, you must log on using the recovery account. I recommend writing down the password on a slip of paper and keeping it in a secure place near the server.

While in Safe Mode, you can replace a problem driver or disable a service or install a different driver to correct a problem. You can run Jet repair utilities against any of the support databases. If you think your problem is more fundamental, you can use Chkntfs to schedule a full disk scan at boot time. See Chapter 13 for details.

Windows 2000 (Free) in Safe Mode

Notice, while you are operating in Safe Mode, that a note is on the Desktop listing the Windows 2000 version and build number along with the term *free*. This indicates that you're running a build that is free of debug symbols. A *checked* build consists of system files that contain the debug symbols used for kernel-mode debugging. A checked build runs more slowly and takes more memory.

Using an Emergency Repair Disk

The System File Protection (SFP) service is constantly on guard against unauthorized replacement of system files. Accidents do happen, though, and a critical file might become corrupted or an application might sneak in under SFP's radar and replace a file that should not be touched. More likely, a driver that wasn't quite ready for the big leagues is installed along with a piece of hardware and causes the system to become unstable.

Also, critical disk structures are not protected by SFP. This includes the Master Boot Record, the boot sector, the system files at the root of the boot partition, the Registry, and the special Jet databases that support so many of the special services in Windows 2000.

You have two options when the system refuses to start because of a problem with these files: doing an *Emergency Repair* and using the *Recovery Console*. Both options involve booting with the Windows 2000 Setup disks or the CD.

The Emergency Repair option is best suited for repairing corrupted system files and building a dual-boot startup configuration. The Recovery Console can handle the rest. The Recovery Console is covered in "Recovery Console" later in this chapter. Let's talk about Emergency Repair first.

Functions of the Emergency Repair Disk

The classic Emergency Repair Disk (ERD) changed character considerably in Windows 2000. The classic ERD contains a compressed copy of all the files in the Registry, if you configured it correctly. The Windows 2000 ERD contains a mere three files, and is really good in the following situations.

- **Repairing a multiple-boot startup environment.** This repair option can recover a standard Windows 2000 boot sequence following an overwrite of the partition boot sector by another operating system, such as Windows 9x. This repair option copies the partition boot sector to a file called BOOTSECT.DOS, writes a new boot sector that loads Ntldr, and changes the BOOT.INI file to include the alternate operating system as an option.

- **Repair a damaged Master Boot Record and Partition Boot Sector.** This repair option writes a standard MBR without overwriting the partition table and a standard Windows 2000 boot sector. The MBR repair is similar to running FDISK /MBR.
- **Replace missing or incorrect Windows 2000 system files.** This repair option uses the SETUP.LOG file on the ERD to check the version stamp on the Windows 2000 system files and replace any files that do not match from the Windows 2000 CD.

Of these repair items, the first two are accomplished much more easily from the Recovery Console. That leaves repairing system files as the only real reason for having an ERD, and SFP should make that unnecessary. Still, it's worth looking at how to do an emergency repair just in case you need to do one.

In classic NT, the utility for creating an ERD is Rdisk.exe. This utility is no longer used in Windows 2000. In its place is an option in Backup for creating an ERD. This option can also be configured to make a copy of the Registry files, but the copies are not placed on the ERD, and the emergency repair process does not use them.

Managing Registry Copies

If you are accustomed to running `RDISK /S-` to make backups of the Registry files in classic NT, you can get the effect in Windows 2000 by using a utility from the Resource Kit called Regback. This utility copies all Registry hives from the `%systemroot%\System32\Config` directory to a directory of your choice.

You can build a script or batch file that runs Regback and either make it part of your logon scripting or run it periodically using the Task Scheduler. This is an example of a highly simplified batch file. Regback does not overwrite any existing files, so you must either delete the old files or move them to an archive:

```
rem ***Registry Hive Backup***

del \WINNT\Repair\RegBack\*.* /q
regback \WINNT\Repair\RegBack
copy "c:\Documents and Settings\Default User\Ntuser.dat" c:\WINNT\Repair\RegBack
```

The ERD is not bootable. This is used in conjunction with the Repair option on the Windows 2000 Setup floppies or the Windows 2000 CD. The ERD contains only three files:

- **AUTOEXEC.NT** and **CONFIG.NT.** Used to initialize Virtual DOS Machine (VDM) sessions.
- **SETUP.LOG.** The list of files copied from the CD during setup, along with an identifier used to determine whether the file was changed.

The remaining emergency repair files are stored in the \WINNT\Repair folder. The folder holds copies of the following files:

- **AUTOEXEC.NT** and **CONFIG.NT.** Used to initialize Virtual DOS Machine (VDM) sessions. Copied from \WINNT\System32.
- **DEFAULT.** The user profile hive used by Local System. Copied from \WINNT\System32\Config.
- **NTUSER.DAT.** The default user profile hive. Copied from \Documents and Settings\Default User.
- **SECSETUP.INF.** The security template used to originally configure SECEDIT.SDB, the local security configuration database, and to set the access permissions on the system files. Exists in no other location.
- **SETUP.LOG.** The list of files copied from the CD during setup, along with an identifier used to determine if the file was changed. Exists in no other location.
- **SAM.** The Security Account Manager hive, represented in the Registry as HKLM_SAM.
- **Security.** The Local Security Authority (LSA) hive, represented in the Registry as HKLM_SECURITY.
- **Software.** The Software hive, represented in the Registry as HKLM_SOFTWARE.
- **System.** The System hive, represented in the Registry as HKLM_SYSTEM.
- **USRCLASS.DAT.** The non-roaming HKCR keys copied from the Administrator's local profile.

It bears repeating that these files are not involved in an emergency repair, per se. If you need to use them to replace a damaged Registry hive, you must boot to the Repair Console and copy them to the \WINNT\System32\Config folder manually.

To do an emergency repair, you need the Windows 2000 Server or Professional CD, depending on the system you are repairing. The two cannot be interchanged. If the computer can boot from a CD (El Torito specification), you're all set. If not, you need Windows 2000 Server or Professional setup floppies. If the computer does not have a CD and you installed Windows 2000 across the network, you cannot do an emergency repair. Your only alternative is the Repair Console.

These are the key actions in preparing for and running an emergency repair:

- Create an ERD using Backup.
- Boot from floppy or CD and use the `Repair` option.
- Do a fast or manual repair.
- Restart and verify successful logon.

Creating an ERD

The Windows 2000 Backup program is used to create an ERD. Proceed as follows:

Procedure 18.15 **Creating an ERD**

1. Open Backup using START | PROGRAMS | ACCESSORIES | SYSTEM TOOLS | BACKUP.

2. From the menu, select TOOLS | CREATE EMERGENCY REPAIR DISK. The `Emergency Repair Diskette` window opens.

3. Select the `Also backup the registry to the repair directory` option and click `OK` to continue. This option is not checked by default, but it should be. No Registry files are copied to the ERD. Without current copies of the Registry files, you cannot recover a system following Registry loss or corruption.

4. When the Registry files are copied to `\WINNT\Repair\RegBack` and the three configuration files are copied to the ERD, the `Emergency Repair Diskette` window reports a successful save. Remove the ERD and save it for future use.

Performing an Emergency Repair

One potential scenario can be resolved with an ERD. The Help Desk gets a call early on a Monday morning and the user says, "I installed Windows 98 on my computer over the weekend because I needed to run a mission-critical application that would not work on Windows 2000." The Help Desk operator refrains from asking what particular game the user was trying to install. "Now when I boot my machine, I can only get to Windows 98, not to Windows 2000 where all my other applications are installed. Can you help me?"

This capability to install a different operating system would not be an option if the system partition were formatted as NTFS, but this particular organization prefers to leave the system partition as FAT. Many do. By installing Windows 98, the user overwrote the Partition Boot Sector with one that loads the bootstrap loader for Windows 98, IO.SYS. Without NTLDR in the boot sector, Windows 2000 cannot load. This is how to resolve this situation using ERD:

Procedure 18.16 **Using the ERD to Repair a Boot Sector**

1. Insert the Windows 2000 CD in the drive. You cannot perform an emergency repair without the CD, even if you do not need to check system files.

2. Boot from the Windows 2000 Setup disks or the Windows 2000 CD, if your hardware supports it.

3. At the `Welcome to Setup` screen, select `R` to `Repair a Windows 2000 Installation`.

4. At the `Windows 2000 Repair Options` screen, select `R` to select the `Emergency Repair` option.

5. The next screen prompts to `Select one of the following repair options`. Two options exist, `Manual Repair` and `Fast Repair`. The manual repair isn't very manual and the fast repair isn't very fast. These are their functions:

   `Manual Repair` gives a list of the three repair options and enables you to select which you want to perform.

   `Fast Repair` assumes you want them all and plows ahead.

6. Press `M` to select `Manual Repair`. The next screen displays three options:

```
[X]  Inspect startup environment.
[X] Verify Windows 2000 System Files.
[X]  Inspect Boot Sector.
```

The `Inspect startup environment` option copies the existing Partition Boot Sector to a file called BOOTSECT.DOS and overwrites the boot sector with a standard Windows 2000 boot sector that is coded to execute the standard NT bootstrap loader, NTLDR. It then makes an additional entry to the BOOT.INI file that points at the drive letter containing Windows (Windows 95 or 98) or DOS, as the case may be.

The `Verify Windows 2000 System Files` option opens the SYSTEM.LOG file on the ERD and uses it to verify each Windows 2000 system file on the drive by doing a CRC check. Any files that fail CRC are replaced from CD. If you installed a service pack or did a Windows Update, *do not select this option*.

The `Inspect Boot Sector` option copies a standard Windows 2000 boot sector but does not copy the existing boot sector to a BOOTSECT.DOS file or configure the machine with a second boot option.

7. To de-select an option, highlight it and press `Enter`. In the example scenario, you could de-select all options except for `Inspect startup environment`.

8. Highlight `Continue` and press `Enter`.

9. The next screen prompts for the ERD. Insert the disk and press `Enter`. If you do not have an ERD, press `L` and the system attempts to locate the `\WINNT\Repair` directory in the Windows 2000 boot partition. If Setup can locate the folder, it presents the option to use it. If it cannot locate the folder, you must have an ERD to proceed.

10. Press `Enter` to proceed. A yellow progress bar gives an indication that Setup is doing something. In this instance, no system files need to be checked, so the repair takes only a few moments. The system restarts automatically.

11. Let the system restart and verify that the Windows 2000 boot menu displays and that Windows 2000 loads normally. Because Windows 98 changed the FAT, which leaves a dirty flag in the boot sector, `Autochk` runs to verify file system consistency.

The machine is now configured for dual-boot. If the user selects the Windows option in the boot menu, NTLDR places the BOOTSECT.DOS image at memory location 0x700h, shifts the processor back to real mode, and turns the system over to the executable code in the boot sector image.

This section covered recovering from damage to the system files, which happens only rarely. The next section covers recovering from damage to the Registry, which is far more likely and happens much more frequently.

Restoring Functionality with the Last Known Good Configuration

This happened to me. If you are an NT administrator or user, it probably happened to you, too. You pop in a CD to install the driver for a snazzy new piece of hardware or a fancy system application that is supposed to save you hours and hours of time by streamlining your administrative chores.

You watch as the installation churns along for a while. Everything seems to be going smoothly when BLAM. The system comes to a grinding halt and the infamous blue screen appears. After a few minutes, the system restarts automatically. You watch as the bars across the bottom of the screen tell you that Ntldr is doing its job and loading the system drivers. The screen shifts to graphics mode and Ntoskrnl takes over and BLAM. Blue screen once again.

It doesn't take a diagnostics genius to figure out that the driver or application you installed made a change somewhere in the deep recesses of the machine that is giving Mr. Computer indigestion. The problem becomes how to restore the system back to functionality.

The most obvious step is to keep that driver from loading. Drivers are loaded by Registry entries, so if you can get back the old Registry that doesn't have the updates for the new driver, life should be good again. Windows 2000 anticipates this need and maintains a backup copy of a portion of the System hive called the Control Set. The backup of the Control Set is called the *Last Known Good Configuration*.

Structure of Control Sets

Refer to Figure 18.23, which shows the Registry Editor, Regedt32, with the focus set to the HKEY_Local_Machine subtree and the upper keys in the System hive expanded.

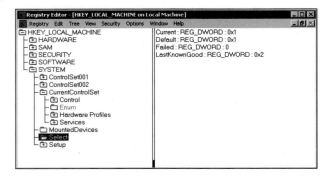

Figure 18.23   Regedt32 showing HKLM | System keys.

Three Control Sets exist. A Control Set holds four high-level keys that are used to set system operational parameters:

- **Control.** This key contains the parameters that the system needs to boot, including critical information concerning software classes, device classes, load sequencing for drivers, and security settings. It also contains parameters used by the Configuration Manager to access the Registry. This leads to a Catch-22 situation. The Configuration Manager needs parameters in the Control key to tell it how to read transaction tracking logs. If an update to the Control key is in the transaction log, the system might fail to start. For this reason, a complete backup copy of the System hive, System.alt, is stored in case the primary hive is corrupted or missing.

- **Enum.** This key is also called the Enum Tree. This is a volatile key that contains the results of the PnP enumeration. When you open the Device Management console and see the list of devices and their associated parameters and resources, you are looking at a graphical representation of the Enum Tree.

- **Hardware Profiles.** This key is like a miniature control set that is used to control special parameters that affect system operation in a Docked or Undocked condition. Hardware profiles are rarely needed for Windows 2000 thanks to PnP, but if you define profiles, the special configuration settings associated with that profile are saved here. If multiple hardware profiles exist, Ntldr presents a selection menu right after the standard boot menu.

- **Services.** This key contains the parameters for all services and drivers.

If you encounter a blue-screen stop or other system instability following the installation of an application, often a setting in one of the Control Set keys is the source of the problem. This is the reason for storing three copies of the Control Sets. Highlight the Select key, which sits outside the control sets. Select has three values:

- **Current.** This points to the control set used to boot the machine. Normally, Control Set 1.

- **Default.** This points to the control set that used to boot the machine if the user does not intervene by selecting the Last Known Good Configuration option. Normally, Control Set 1.

- **Failed.** This points to a control set marked as failed following the selection of a new default control set. The normal entry is 0, meaning that no control sets are marked as failed.
- **LastKnownGood.** This points at the control set that last successfully booted the machine before booting from the Current control set. Normally, `Control Set 2`.

Recovering the Last Known Good Configuration

Procedure 18.17 **Recovering the Last Known Good Configuration**

With this information in mind, this is the sequence of events when a machine boots and the user selects the `Last Known Good Configuration` option.

1. The machine POSTs and then loads the boot sector image. This loads the NT bootstrap loader, Ntldr.

2. One of Ntldr's duties is to check HKLM | SYSTEM | SELECT to find the identity of the Default control set. It passes the number of this control set to the NT Kernel driver, Ntoskrnl.

3. If the user interrupts the standard boot process by pressing F8 at the boot menu, Ntldr displays the `Windows 2000 Advanced Options Menu`. One of the options is `Last Known Good Configuration`.

4. Highlight the `Last Known Good Configuration` option and press Enter. The system returns to the boot menu with a red message across the bottom of the screen saying `Last Known Good Configuration`.

   At this point, two things happen in the Select key. The original Default control set, which was Control Set 1, is now marked as Failed. Also, the `LastKnownGood` control set, Control Set 2, is set as Default.

5. Select the standard boot menu item, which should say Microsoft Windows 2000 Server (or Professional), and press Enter. NTLDR starts loading drivers, and then displays the `Hardware Profile/Configuration Recovery Menu`.

6. The RECOVERY Menu is a combination of the hardware profile selection menu and a control set selection window. This window is a holdover from classic NT. No action should be taken.

7. Press Enter to continue or enable the counter to do it for you. The Windows 2000 Executive loads, shifts to graphics mode, and then initializes the system based on the contents of the Default control set, which at this time is Control Set 2. In other words, Control Set 2 becomes the Current control set.

8. If the system boots successfully, defined as all services starting, all drivers loading, and a user logging on successfully at the console, a value of 1 is set in the ReportBootOK value under the Winlogon key in HKLM | Software | Microsoft | Windows NT | CurrentVersion.

9. A ReportBootOK of 1 indicates that the current control set successfully booted the system. The contents of the current control set, which is now Control Set 2, is copied to a new control set, Control Set 3, which becomes the LastKnownGood control set.

The resulting control set assignments in the Select key are:

- **Current.** Control Set 2
- **Default.** Control Set 2
- **Failed.** Control Set 1
- **LastKnownGood.** Control Set 3

This game of musical chairs among the control sets works only if the original source of the system instability is an entry in one of the Control Set keys. If it is caused by an entry in some other hive, such as Software, the system continues to be unstable.

If you want to change the criteria for a successful boot, you can design a little executable code that checks for your particular parameter, and then writes a 0 or a 1 to the ReportBootOK value in the Winlogon key.

Recovery Console

The Recovery Console is a new feature in Windows 2000 that enables booting a system to a bare command prompt suitable for replacing drivers, setting partitions, and doing a few file system checks. The Repair Console can be loaded in one of three ways.

- Boot from the Windows 2000 setup floppies and select the Repair option.
- Boot from the Windows 2000 CD (if supported by hardware) and select the Repair option.
- Install the console files on the local drive and make the Recovery Console part of the boot menu.

This last alternative gives the most flexibility. The console option is not installed by default. Let's install it and then see how the Recovery Console works.

> **Dynamic Volumes and the Recovery Console**
> Because the Recovery Console does not load a full-fledged copy of the Logical Disk Manager, it is unable to determine the content of dynamic volumes that are soft-linked to the LDM database. See Microsoft Knowledgebase article Q227364 for more information.

Installing a Bootable Copy of the Recovery Console

The following steps copy the boot files from the Setup CD to the boot drive and configure a new boot option that loads the Recovery Console. You need the Windows 2000 Server or Professional CD, depending on the platform you're using.

Procedure 18.18 **Installing the Recovery Console**

1. Insert the Windows 2000 Server or Professional CD in the CD-ROM drive.
2. Open a command session and navigate to the \I386 directory on the CD.
3. Run winnt32 /cmdcons. After a fairly long pause, the Windows 2000 Setup window opens with a Recovery Console warning.
4. Click Yes to acknowledge the warning and install the console.
5. After Setup installs the Recovery Console files, it displays a Successful Completion message and then exits.

The Recovery Console installation makes the following changes to the drive:

- Creates a hidden folder, \Cmdcons, directly under Root. This folder contains the same files that are on the installation floppies. Essentially, the \cmdcons is one big Windows 2000 installation floppy.
- Copies the Partition Boot Sector from the Windows 2000 system volume to the \Cmdcons folder in a BOOTSECT.DAT file.
- Puts an alternative bootstrap loader, Cmldr, at the root of the boot partition.
- Modifies the BOOT.INI file to include the alternative for booting to the Recovery Console.

The BOOTSECT.DAT file is a standard Windows 2000/NT method for launching an alternative operating system. When Ntldr displays the boot menu, if the alternate operating system represented by the contents of the Bootsect file is selected, Ntldr shifts the computer back to real mode. It then loads the contents of the Bootsect file at memory location 0x700h just as though it was loaded by a standard Int13 call, and turns control over to the executable code in the boot sector image.

In the case of the Recovery Console, the executable code in the BOOTSECT.DAT file points at an alternative bootstrap loader called Cmldr. This bootstrap loader opens up an alternate command interpreter that has just enough versatility to do file checks, copy drivers, and diagnose a few errors.

The BOOT.INI file is modified to load the BOOTSECT.DAT file as follows (the new line is in bold):

```
[boot loader]
timeout=30
default=multi(0)disk(0)rdisk(0)partition(1)\WINNT
[operating systems]
multi(0)disk(0)rdisk(0)partition(1)\WINNT="Microsoft Windows 2000 Server" /fastdetect
C:\CMDCONS\BOOTSECT.DAT="Microsoft Windows 2000 Recovery Console" /cmdcons
```

To boot to the Recovery Console following this installation, restart the machine. When the boot menu appears, select `Microsoft Windows 2000 Recovery Console`. Proceed to "Recovery Console Options."

Booting to the Recovery Console from Floppy or CD

If you do not want to install the Recovery Console files on the local drive, you can load the console by booting from the setup disks or the Windows 2000 CD.

Procedure 18.19 **Booting to the Recovery Console**

1. At the Welcome to Setup screen, select R to Repair a Windows 2000 Installation.
2. At the Windows 2000 Repair Options screen, select C to use the Recovery Console.
3. Let the remaining drivers load.

Recovery Console Options

Whether you boot from the on-disk files, the Setup disks, or the CD, you eventually get to the same point, a text-based screen called the `Microsoft Windows 2000`™ `Recovery Console`. The console screen lists all the Windows 2000 installations it found on the disk and presents them as a menu. Select the number of the drive\path that points to the installation you want to use for logon. (Don't press `Enter`. That restarts the system.)

When you select a number, the Recovery Console completes loading, and then prompts you for the Administrator password. For standard servers and Professional desktops, this is the Administrator password in the local SAM. For domain controllers, this is the Administrator password you entered when you promoted the server to domain controller. That password was written to a special Administrator account in the SAM of the domain controller. You do not have the option of choosing an alternative account. You must know this password.

Administrator Name Changes and the Recovery Console

Changing the name of the Administrator account in the local SAM of a standalone server or workstation does not impair your ability to log on at the Recovery Console. You could change the local Administrator account name to Harvey, for example, with a password of Rabbit. The underlying SID for the account remains the same. When you boot to the Recovery Console, the prompt asks for the Administrator password, but you can enter Rabbit and the logon will succeed.

The Recovery Console leaves you at a console prompt in the `\WINNT` directory (or whatever the `%systemroot%` folder is on your machine). The console command interpreter supports a small list of commands. Most have standard DOS functions. Others are specific to the Recovery Console. This is a list of the commands with special functionality for the Recovery Console:

- **`Dir`.** Displays creation time stamp, long name, and attributes (Directory, Archive, Hidden, System, Read-only, Compressed, Encrypted, Reparse point). No special extensions available.

- **`Attrib`.** Changes the attributes of a file but does not display them. Use `Dir` to see attributes.

- **`Batch`.** Runs the contents of a designated text file as a batch file. For example, `batch script1.txt`. Only commands that are part of the Recovery Console command interpreter can be part of the script.

- **`Enable/Disable`.** This pair of commands can turn off a service that is the source of your troubles. By disabling a service, you can then restart and try to fight your way to the Explorer shell.

- **Diskpart.** This opens up a partition manager very similar to that used in the text-based portion of Setup. You can use this utility to create the partition and then the Format command to install a file system.

- **Fixboot.** This copies the contents of the BOOTSECT.DAT file onto the partition boot sector. This option is not useful when booting from the hard drive, of course, but when booting from floppy or CD, it provides a way to repair the boot sector.

- **Fixmbr.** This writes a new Master Boot Record while leaving the Partition Table intact. This is similar to using FDISK /MBR and has the same potential for making the machine unbootable if the Master Boot Record is nonstandard.

- **Listsvc.** This command lists the services that are in the Registry, along with their status setting. Use this command in conjunction with `enable/disable`. This is a handy way to look up the short name for the service.

- **Logon.** This initiates the same logon routine that you encountered when the Recovery Console first loaded. You can use it to logon to another instance of Windows 2000 on the local system. You cannot use it to logon to the network because no network services are loaded.

- **Map.** This lists the symbolic links under `\Device` in the Object Namespace that represent partitions.

- **Systemroot.** This takes you to the system root for the Windows 2000 instance that you logged on to.

- **Exit.** This exits the console and restarts the machine.

The Recovery Console comes in handy in any scenario where you need to get access to a partition to replace files. This is just as secure as a standard Windows 2000 console because the local SAM is used for authentication.

This is an example of how you might use the Recovery Console. Let's say that the Registry entry causing the kernel-mode stop error is not in the Control Set keys but is in the Software hive where it is not eliminated by booting to the Last Known Good Configuration. In that case, you can boot to the Recovery Console and copy the backup Software hive file from `\WINNT\Repair\RegBack` to `\WINNT\System32\Config`. This requires that you have a current copy of the Registry hive in the `RegBack` directory. If not, you can use another system to restore the file from tape, put it on a floppy, and copy it to the `\WINNT\System32\Config` directory. The system should restart normally with the replaced hive in place.

If you are unable to resolve the system instability using Last Known Good Configuration or the Recovery Console, you probably need to reinstall Windows 2000 and recover from tape. Before taking drastic measures, be sure to contact Microsoft Technical Support and explain the problem to them. There might be a fix that has not made its way into the KnowledgeBase. The money you spend on that support call is much cheaper in the long run than reinstalling Windows 2000 and reconfiguring the applications. You might even get your money back if Microsoft can't solve the problem.

Moving Forward

This is the last chapter of this book, but certainly not the last episode of your experiences with Windows 2000. Only a few real satisfactions are in the IT game. Mastering a technology to the point where you can provide stable and reliable service to users is one of them. I hope you were able to find some help in this book toward achieving that goal.

Procedures Index

Chapter 18 Procedures

Index

Symbols

A

E

G

H

Q-R

X-Z

Windows 2000 Answers

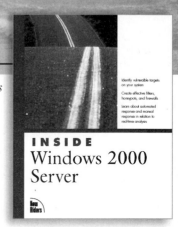

Updated edition of New Riders' best-selling *Inside Windows NT 4 Server*. Taking the author-driven, no-nonsense approach we pioneered with our Windows NT *Landmark* books, New Riders proudly offers something unique for Windows 2000 administrators—an interesting and discriminating book on Windows 2000 Server, written by someone in the trenches who can anticipate your situation and provide answers you can trust.

ISBN: 1-56205-929-7

Architected to be the most navigable, useful, and value-packed reference for Windows 2000, this book uses a creative "telescoping" design that you can adapt to your style of learning. Written by Steven Tate, key Windows 2000 partner and developer of Microsoft's W2K Training Program, it's a concise, focused quick reference for Windows 2000.

ISBN: 0-7357-0869-X

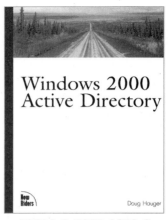

Windows 2000 Active Directory is just one of several new Windows 2000 titles from New Riders' acclaimed *Landmark* series. Focused advice on planning, implementing, and managing the Active Directory in your business.

ISBN: 0-7357-0870-3

Advanced Information on Networking Technologies

New Riders Books Offer Advice and Experience

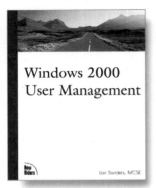

LANDMARK

Rethinking Computer Books

We know how important it is to have access to detailed, solutions-oriented information on core technologies. *Landmark* books contain the essential information you need to solve technical problems. Written by experts and subjected to rigorous peer and technical reviews, our *Landmark* books are hard-core resources for practitioners like you.

ESSENTIAL REFERENCE

Smart, Like You

The *Essential Reference* series from New Riders provides answers when you know what you want to do but need to know how to do it. Each title skips extraneous material and assumes a strong base of knowledge. These are indispensable books for the practitioner who wants to find specific features of a technology quickly and efficiently. Avoiding fluff and basic material, these books present solutions in an innovative, clean format—and at a great value.

MCSE CERTIFICATION

Engineered for Test Success

New Riders offers a complete line of test preparation materials to help you achieve your certification. With books like the *MCSE Training Guide*, *TestPrep*, and *Fast Track*, and software like the acclaimed *MCSE Complete* and the revolutionary *ExamGear*, New Riders offers comprehensive products built by experienced professionals who have passed the exams and instructed hundreds of candidates.

Windows NT Performance
Monitoring Benchmarking and Tuning
By Mark Edmead and Paul Hinsberg
1st Edition
288 pages, $29.99
ISBN: 1-56205-942-4

Performance monitoring is a little like pre-ventive medicine for the administrator: No one enjoys a checkup, but it's a good thing to do on a regular basis. This book helps you focus on the critical aspects of improving the performance of your NT system, showing you how to monitor the system, implement benchmarking, and tune your network. The book is organized by resource components, which makes it easy to use as a reference tool.

Windows NT Terminal Server and Citrix MetaFrame
By Ted Harwood
1st Edition
416 pages, $29.99
ISBN: 1-56205-944-0

It's no surprise that most administration headaches revolve around integration with other networks and clients. This book addresses these types of real-world issues on a case-by-case basis, giving tools and advice on solving each problem. The author also offers the real nuts and bolts of thin client administration on multiple systems, covering relevant issues such as installation, configuration, network connection, management, and application distribution.

Windows NT Power Toolkit
By Stu Sjouwerman and Ed Tittel
1st Edition
900 pages, $49.99
ISBN: 0-7357-0922-X

This book covers the analysis, tuning, optimization, automation, enhancement, maintenance, and troubleshooting of Windows NT Server 4.0 and Windows NT Workstation 4.0. In most cases, the two operating systems overlap completely and will be discussed together; in other cases, where the two systems diverge, each platform will be covered separately. This advanced title comprises a task-oriented treatment of the Windows NT 4 environ-ment, including both Windows NT Server 4.0 and Windows NT Workstation 4.0. Thus, this book is aimed squarely at power users, to guide them to painless, effective use of Windows NT both inside and outside the workplace. By concentrat-ing on the use of operating system tools and utilities, Resource Kit elements, and selected third-party tuning, analysis, opti-mization, and productivity tools, this book will show its readers how to carry out everyday and advanced tasks.

Windows NT Network Management: Reducing Total Cost of Ownership
By Anil Desai
1st Edition
400 pages, $34.99
ISBN: 1-56205-946-7

Administering a Windows NT network is kind of like trying to herd cats—an impossible task characterized by constant motion, exhausting labor, and lots of hairballs. Author Anil Desai knows all about it; he's a consulting engineer for Sprint Paranet who specializes in

Windows NT implementation, integration, and management. So we asked him to put together a concise manual of the best practices, a book of tools and ideas that other administrators can turn to again and again in managing their own NT networks.

Planning for Windows 2000
By Eric K. Cone, Jon Boggs, and Sergio Perez
1st Edition
400 pages, $29.99
ISBN: 0-73570-048-6

Windows 2000 is poised to be one of the largest and most important software releases of the next decade, and you are charged with planning, testing, and deploying it in your enterprise. Are you ready? With this book, you will be. *Planning for Windows 2000* lets you know what the upgrade hurdles will be, informs you how to clear them, guides you through effective Active Directory design, and presents you with detailed rollout procedures. Eric K. Cone, Jon Boggs, and Sergio Perez give you the benefit of their extensive experiences as Windows 2000 Rapid Deployment Program members, sharing problems and solutions they've encountered on the job.

MCSE Core NT Exams Essential Reference
By Matthew Shepker
1st Edition
256 pages, $19.99
ISBN: 0-7357-0006-0

You're sitting in the first session of your Networking Essentials class, the instructor starts talking about RAS, and you have no idea what that means. You think about raising your hand to ask, but you reconsider—you'd feel foolish asking a question in front of all these people. You turn to your handy *MCSE Core NT Exams Essential Reference* and find a quick summary on Remote Access Services. Question answered. It's a couple months later, and you're taking your Networking Essentials exam the next day. You're reviewing practice tests and keep forgetting the maximum lengths for the various commonly used cable types. Once again, you turn to the *MCSE Core NT Exams Essential Reference* and find a table on cables, including all the characteristics you need to memorize in order to pass the test.

BackOffice Titles

Implementing Exchange Server
By Doug Hauger, Marywynne Leon, and William C. Wade III
1st Edition
400 pages, $29.99
ISBN: 1-56205-931-9

If you're interested in connectivity and maintenance issues for Exchange Server, this book is for you. Exchange's power lies in its capability to be connected to multiple email subsystems to create a "universal email backbone." It's not unusual to have several different and complex systems all connected via email gateways, including Lotus Notes or cc:Mail, Microsoft Mail, legacy mainframe systems, and Internet mail. This book covers all of the problems and issues associated with getting an integrated system running smoothly and addresses troubleshooting and diagnosis of email problems with an eye toward prevention and best practices.

Exchange System Administration

By Janice K. Howd
1st Edition
400 pages, $34.99
ISBN: 0-7357-0081-8

Okay, you've got your Exchange Server installed and connected; now what? Email administration is one of the most critical networking jobs, and Exchange can be particularly troublesome in large, heterogeneous environments. Janice Howd, a noted consultant and teacher with over a decade of email administration experience, has put together this advanced, concise handbook for daily, periodic, and emergency administration. With in-depth coverage of topics like managing disk resources, replication, and disaster recovery, this is the one reference book every Exchange administrator needs.

SQL Server System Administration

By Sean Baird, Chris Miller, et al.
1st Edition
352 pages, $29.99
ISBN: 1-56205-955-6

How often does your SQL Server go down during the day when everyone wants to access the data? Do you spend most of your time being a "report monkey" for your coworkers and bosses? *SQL Server System Administration* helps you keep data consistently available to your users. This book omits introductory information. The authors don't spend time explaining queries and how they work. Instead, they focus on the information you can't get anywhere else, like how to choose the correct replication topology and achieve high availability of information.

Internet Information Services Administration

By Kelli Adam, et. al.
1st Edition Winter 2000
300 pages, $29.99
ISBN: 0-7357-0022-2

Are the new Internet technologies in Internet Information Server giving you headaches? Does protecting security on the Web take up all of your time? Then this is the book for you. With hands-on configuration training, advanced study of the new protocols in IIS, and detailed instructions on authenticating users with the new Certificate Server and implementing and managing the new e-commerce features, *Internet Information Server Administration* gives you the real-life solutions you need. This definitive resource also prepares you for the release of Windows 2000 by giving you detailed advice on working with Microsoft Management Console, which was first used by IIS.

SMS 2.0 Administration

By Darshan Doshi and Michael Lubanski
1st Edition Winter 2000
350 pages, $39.99
ISBN: 0-7357-0082-6

Microsoft's new version of its Systems Management Server (SMS) is starting to turn heads. Although complex, it allows administrators to lower their total cost of ownership and more efficiently manage clients, applications, and support operations. So if your organization is using or implementing SMS, you'll need some expert advice. Darshan Doshi and Michael Lubanski can help you get the most bang for your buck, with insight, expert tips, and real-world examples. Darshan and

Michael are consultants specializing in SMS, having worked with Microsoft on one of the most complex SMS rollouts in the world, involving 32 countries, 15 languages, and thousands of clients.

UNIX/Linux Titles

Solaris Essential Reference
By John Mulligan
1st Edition Spring 1999
350 pages, $19.99
ISBN: 0-7357-0023-0

Looking for the fastest, easiest way to find the Solaris command you need? Need a few pointers on shell scripting? How about advanced administration tips and sound, practical expertise on security issues? Are you looking for trustworthy information about available third-party software packages that will enhance your operating system? Author John Mulligan— creator of the popular Unofficial Guide to Solaris Web site (sun.icsnet.com)— delivers all that and more in one attractive, easy-to-use reference book. With clear and concise instructions on how to perform important administration and management tasks and key information on powerful commands and advanced topics, *Solaris Essential Reference* is the book you need when you know what you want to do and only need to know how.

Linux System Administration
By M Carling, et. al.
1st Edition Summer 1999
450 pages, $29.99
ISBN: 1-56205-934-3

As an administrator, you probably feel that most of your time and energy is spent in endless firefighting. If your network has become a fragile quilt of temporary patches and work-arounds, this book is for you. For example, have you had trouble sending or receiving email lately? Are you looking for a way to keep your network running smoothly with enhanced performance? Are your users always hankering for more storage, more services, and more speed? *Linux System Administration* advises you on the many intricacies of maintaining a secure, stable system. In this definitive work, the author addresses all the issues related to system administration, from adding users and managing file permissions, to Internet services and Web hosting, to recovery planning and security. This book fulfills the need for expert advice that will ensure a trouble-free Linux environment.

GTK+/Gnome Application Development
By Havoc Pennington
1st Edition
492 pages, $39.99
ISBN: 0-7357-0078-8

This title is for the reader who is conversant with the C programming language and UNIX/Linux development. It provides detailed and solution-oriented information designed to meet the needs of programmers and application developers using the GTK+/Gnome libraries. Coverage complements existing GTK+/Gnome documentation, going into more depth on pivotal issues such as uncovering the GTK+ object system, working with the event loop, managing the Gdk substrate, writing custom widgets, and mastering GnomeCanvas.

Developing Linux Applications with GTK+ and GDK
By Eric Harlow
1st Edition
400 pages, $34.99
ISBN: 0-7357-0214-7

We all know that Linux is one of the most powerful and solid operating systems in existence. And as the success of Linux grows, there is an increasing interest in developing applications with graphical user interfaces that take advantage of the power of Linux. In this book, software developer Eric Harlow gives you an indispensable development handbook focusing on the GTK+ toolkit. More than an overview of the elements of application or GUI design, this is a hands-on book that delves deeply into the technology. With in-depth material on the various GUI programming tools and loads of examples, this book's unique focus will give you the information you need to design and launch professional-quality applications.

Linux Essential Reference
By Ed Petron
1st Edition Winter 2000
400 pages, $24.95
ISBN: 0-7357-0852-5

This book is all about getting things done as quickly and efficiently as possible by providing a structured organization to the plethora of available Linux information. We can sum it up in one word—value. This book has it all: concise instructions

on how to perform key administration tasks, advanced information on configuration, shell scripting; hardware management, systems management, data tasks, automation, and tons of other useful information. All of this coupled with an unique navigational structure and a great price. This book truly provides groundbreaking information for the growing community of advanced Linux professionals.

Lotus Notes and Domino Titles

Domino System Administration
By Rob Kirkland
1st Edition
880 pages, $49.99
ISBN: 1-56205-948-3

Your boss has just announced that you will be upgrading to the newest version of Notes and Domino when it ships. As a Premium Lotus Business Partner, Lotus has offered a substantial price break to keep your company away from Microsoft's Exchange Server. How are you supposed to get this new system installed, configured, and rolled out to all your end users? You understand how Lotus Notes works—you've been administering it for years. What you need is a concise, practical explanation of the new features and how to make some of the advanced stuff work smoothly. You need answers and solutions from someone like you, who has worked with the product for years and understands what you need to know. *Domino System Administration* is the answer—the first book on Domino that attacks the technology at the professional level, with practical, hands-on assistance to get Domino running in your organization.

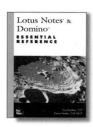

Lotus Notes and Domino Essential Reference

By Dave Hatter
and Tim Bankes
1st Edition
500 pages, $45.00
ISBN: 0-7357-0007-9

You're in a bind because you've been asked to design and program a new database in Notes for an important client that will keep track of and itemize a myriad of inventory and shipping data. The client wants a user-friendly interface without sacrificing speed or functionality. You are experienced (and could develop this application in your sleep) but feel that you need to take your talents to the next level. You need something to facilitate your creative and technical abilities, something to perfect your programming skills. The answer is waiting for you: *Lotus Notes and Domino Essential Reference*. It's compact and simply designed. It's loaded with information. All of the objects, classes, functions, and methods are listed. It shows you the object hierarchy and the relationship between each one. It's perfect for you. Problem solved.

Networking Titles

Cisco Router Configuration & Troubleshooting

By Mark Tripod
1st Edition
300 pages, $34.99
ISBN: 0-7357-0024-9

Want the real story on making your Cisco routers run like a dream? Why not pick up a copy of *Cisco Router Configuration & Troubleshooting* and see what Pablo Espinosa and Mark Tripod have to say? They're the folks responsible for making some of the largest sites on the Net scream, like Amazon.com, Hotmail, USAToday, Geocities, and Sony. In this book, they provide advanced configuration issues, sprinkled with advice and preferred practices. You won't see a general overview on TCP/IP. They talk about more meaty issues, like security, monitoring, traffic management, and more. In the troubleshooting section, the authors provide a unique methodology and lots of sample problems to illustrate. By providing real-world insight and examples instead of rehashing Cisco's documentation, Pablo and Mark give network administrators information they can start using today.

Network Intrusion Detection: An Analyst's Handbook

By Stephen Northcutt
1st Edition
360 pages, $39.99
ISBN: 0-7357-0868-1

Get answers and solutions from someone who has been in the trenches. Author Stephen Northcutt, original developer of the Shadow intrusion detection system and former Director of the United States Navy's Information System Security Office at the Naval Security Warfare Center, gives his expertise to intrusion detection specialists, security analysts, and consultants responsible for setting up and maintaining an effective defense against network security attacks.

Understanding Data Communications, Sixth Edition
By Gilbert Held
6th Edition
500 pages, $39.99
ISBN: 0-7357-0036-2

Updated from the highly successful Fifth Edition, this book explains how data communications systems and their various hardware and software components work. Not an entry-level book, it approaches the material in textbook format, addressing the complex issues involved in internetworking today. A great reference book for the experienced networking professional, this offering was written by the noted networking authority Gilbert Held.

Other Books By New Riders

Windows Technologies

Planning for Windows
2000 0-7357-0048-6
Windows NT Network Management:
Reducing Total Cost of Ownership
1-56205-946-7
Windows NT DNS
1-56205-943-2
Windows NT Performance Moni-
toring, Benchmarking, and Tuning
1-56205-942-4
Windows NT Power Toolkit
0-7357-0922-X
Windows NT Registry: A Settings
Reference
1-56205-941-6
Windows NT TCP/IP
1-56205-887-8
Windows NT Terminal Server and
Citrix MetaFrame
1-56205-944-0
Implementing Exchange Server
1-56205-931-9
Exchange Server Admninistration
0-7357-0081-8
SQL Server System Administration
1-56205-955-6

Networking

Cisco Router Configuration and
Troubleshooting
0-7357-0024-9
Understanding Data Communications, Sixth Edition
0-7357-0036-2

Certification

A+ Certification TestPrep
1-56205-892-4
A+ Certification Top Score Software
0-7357-0017-6
A+ Certification Training Guide, 2E
0-7357-0907-6
A+ Complete v1.1
0-7357-0045-1
A+ Fast Track
0-7357-0028-1
MCSE Essential Reference: Core
NT Exams
0-7357-0006-0
MCSD Fast Track: Visual Basic 6,
Exam 70-176
0-7357-0019-2
MCSE Fast Track: 6-in-1 Bundle
1-56205-909-2
MCSE Fast Track: Internet
Information Server 4
1-56205-936-X

MCSE Fast Track: Networking
Essentials
1-56205-939-4
MCSE Fast Track: TCP/IP
1-56205-937-8
MCSD Fast Track: Visual Basic 6,
Exam 70-175
0-7357-0018-4
MCSE Fast Track: Windows 98
0-7357-0016-8
MCSE Fast Track: Windows NT
Server 4
1-56205-935-1
MCSE Fast Track: Windows NT
Server 4 Enterprise
1-56205-940-8
MCSE Fast Track: Windows NT
Workstation 4
1-56205-938-6
MCSE Simulation Guide: Windows
NT Server 4 Enterprise
1-56205-914-9
MCSE Simulation Guide: Windows
NT Workstation 4
1-56205-925-4
MCSE TestPrep: Core Exam Bundle,
Second Edition
0-7357-0030-3
MCSE TestPrep: Networking
Essentials, Second Edition
0-7357-0010-9
MCSE TestPrep: TCP/IP, Second
Edition
0-7357-0025-7
MCSE TestPrep: Windows 95,
Second Edition
0-7357-0011-7
MCSE TestPrep: Windows 98
1-56205-922-X
MCSE TestPrep: Windows NT
Server 4 Enterprise, Second Edition
0-7357-0009-5
MCSE TestPrep: Windows NT
Server 4, Second Edition
0-7357-0012-5
MCSE TestPrep: Windows NT
Workstation 4, Second Edition
0-7357-0008-7
MCSD TestPrep: Visual Basic 6
Exams
0-7357-0032-X
MCSE Training Guide: Core Exams
Bundle, Second Edition
1-56205-926-2
MCSE Training Guide: Networking
Essentials, Second Edition
1-56205-919-X
MCSE Training Guide: TCP/IP,
Second Edition
1-56205-920-3

MCSE Training Guide: Windows 98
1-56205-890-8
MCSE Training Guide: Windows
NT Server 4, Second Edition
1-56205-916-5
MCSE Training Guide: Windows
NT Server Enterprise, Second
Edition
1-56205-917-3
MCSE Training Guide: Windows
NT Workstation 4, Second Edition
1-56205-918-1
MCSD Training Guide: Visual Basic
6 Exams
0-7357-0002-8
MCSE Top Score Software: Core
Exams
0-7357-0033-8
MCSE + Complete, v1.1
0-7897-1564-3
MCSE + Internet Complete, v1.2
0-7357-0072-9

Graphics

Inside 3D Studio MAX 2, Volume I
1-56205-857-6
Inside 3D Studio MAX 2, Volume
II: Modeling and Materials
1-56205-864-9
Inside 3D Studio MAX 2, Volume
III: Animation
1-56205-865-7
Inside 3D Studio MAX 2 Resource
Kit
1-56205-953-X
Inside AutoCAD 14, Limited
Edition
1-56205-898-3
Inside Softimage 3D
1-56205-885-1
HTML Web Magic, Second Edition
1-56830-475-7
Dynamic HTML Web Magic
1-56830-421-8
Designing Web Graphics.3
1-56205-949-1
Illustrator 8 Magic
1-56205-952-1
Inside trueSpace 4
1-56205-957-2
Inside Adobe Photoshop 5
1-56205-884-3
Inside Adobe Photoshop 5, Limited
Edition
1-56205-951-3
Photoshop 5 Artistry
1-56205-895-9
Photoshop 5 Type Magic
1-56830-465-X
Photoshop 5 Web Magic
1-56205-913-0

We Want to Know What You Think

To better serve you, we would like your opinion on the content and quality of this book. Please complete this card and mail it to us or fax it to 317-581-4663.

Name _____

Address _____

City_____State_____Zip _____

Phone _____

Email Address _____

Occupation _____

Operating system(s) that you use _____

What influenced your purchase of this book?
- ❏ Recommendation
- ❏ Cover Design
- ❏ Table of Contents
- ❏ Index
- ❏ Magazine Review
- ❏ Advertisement
- ❏ New Riders' Reputation
- ❏ Author Name

How would you rate the contents of this book?
- ❏ Excellent
- ❏ Very Good
- ❏ Good
- ❏ Fair
- ❏ Below Average
- ❏ Poor

How do you plan to use this book?
- ❏ Quick Reference
- ❏ Self-Training
- ❏ Classroom
- ❏ Other

What do you like most about this book?
Check all that apply.
- ❏ Content
- ❏ Writing Style
- ❏ Accuracy
- ❏ Examples
- ❏ Listings
- ❏ Design
- ❏ Index
- ❏ Page Count
- ❏ Price
- ❏ Illustrations

What do you like least about this book?
Check all that apply.
- ❏ Content
- ❏ Writing Style
- ❏ Accuracy
- ❏ Examples
- ❏ Listings
- ❏ Design
- ❏ Index
- ❏ Page Count
- ❏ Price
- ❏ Illustrations

What would be a useful follow-up book to this one for you?_____

Where did you purchase this book? _____

Can you name a similar book that you like better than this one, or one that is as good? Why?

_____

_____

How many New Riders books do you own? _____

What are your favorite computer books?_____

_____

What other titles would you like to see us develop? _____

_____

Any comments for us? _____

_____

_____

_____

Inside Windows 2000 Server 1-56205-929-7

www.newriders.com • Fax 317-581-4663

Fold here and tape to mail

New Riders Publishing
201 W. 103rd St.
Indianapolis, IN 46290

New Riders How to Contact Us

Visit Our Web Site

www.newriders.com

On our Web site you'll find information about our other books, authors, tables of contents, indexes, and book errata.

Email Us

Contact us at this address:

newriders@mcp.com

- If you have comments or questions about this book
- To report errors that you have found in this book
- If you have a book proposal to submit or are interested in writing for New Riders
- If you would like to have an author kit sent to you
- If you are an expert in a computer topic or technology and are interested in being a technical editor who reviews manuscripts for technical accuracy

newriders@mcp.com

- To find a distributor in your area, please contact our international department at this address.

nrmedia@mcp.com

- For instructors from educational institutions who wish to preview New Riders books for classroom use. Email should include your name, title, school, department, address, phone number, office days/hours, text in use, and enrollment in the body of your text, along with your request for desk/examination copies and/or additional information.

Write to Us

New Riders Publishing

201 W. 103rd St.

Indianapolis, IN 46290-1097

Call Us

Toll-free (800) 571-5840 + 9 +4511

If outside U.S. (317) 581-3500. Ask for New Riders.

Fax Us

(317) 581-4663